THE
Great
Movie Stars

1

The Golden Years

THE
Great
Movie Stars

The Golden Years

1

DAVID SHIPMAN

Macdonald

A Macdonald Book

Copyright © David Shipman 1970, 1979, 1989

First published in Great Britain in 1970 by
The Hamlyn Group, London
Reprinted in 1971, 1972, 1974
Revised edition published in 1979 by
Angus & Robertson (UK)
Second revised edition published in 1989 by
Macdonald & Co (Publishers) Ltd
London & Sydney

British Library Cataloguing in Publication
Data
Shipman, David
   The great movie stars 1: the golden years.
   – Rev. and updated ed.
   1. Cinema films. Actors & actresses –
   Biographies
   I. Title
   791.43′028′0922

   ISBN 0 356 18146 4 (Hardback)
   ISBN 0 7088 4397 2 (Paperback)

Printed and bound in Great Britain by
Richard Clay Ltd, Bungay, Suffolk
Set in Times & Avant Garde by Tek Art
Limited, Croydon, Surrey

Macdonald & Co (Publishers) Ltd
66–73 Shoe Lane
London EC4P 4AB

A member of Maxwell Pergamon Publishing
Corporation plc

For picture research, grateful
acknowledgment is made to The Odhams
Periodicals Library, The Kobal Collection,
The British Film Institute, and Tracy Lee;
and to MGM, Warner Bros., 20th Century-
Fox, Paramount, RKO, Universal,
Republic, Columbia, United Artists, UFA,
The Rank Organization, London Films,
British Lion, Ealing Studios, Woodfall,
Cinema Center and Walt Disney.

The Stars of The Golden Years . . .

The stories of other stars, from the post-war period to the present day, are contained in the companion to this volume:
THE GREAT MOVIE STARS — THE INTERNATIONAL YEARS

Abbott and Costello
Don Ameche
Fatty Arbuckle
George Arliss
Jean Arthur
Fred Astaire
Mary Astor
Lew Ayres
Lucille Ball
Tallulah Bankhead
Theda Bara
John Barrymore
Richard Barthelmess
Freddie Bartholomew
Warner Baxter
Wallace Beery
Constance Bennett
Joan Bennett
Jack Benny
Ingrid Bergman
Elizabeth Bergner
Joan Blondell
Humphrey Bogart
Clara Bow
Charles Boyer
Louise Brooks
Jack Buchanan
Billie Burke
James Cagney
Eddie Cantor
Madeleine Carroll
Lon Chaney
Charlie Chaplin
Ruth Chatterton
Maurice Chevalier
Claudette Colbert
Ronald Colman
Gary Cooper
Cicely Courtneidge
Joan Crawford
Laird Cregar
Bing Crosby
Bebe Daniels
Marion Davies
Bette Davis
Olivia de Havilland

Dolores del Rio
Marlene Dietrich
Richard Dix
Robert Donat
Melvyn Douglas
Marie Dressler
Irene Dunne
Deanna Durbin
Nelson Eddy
Douglas Fairbanks
Douglas Fairbanks Jr
Frances Farmer
Alice Faye
Gracie Fields
W.C. Fields
Errol Flynn
Henry Fonda
Joan Fontaine
George Formby
Kay Francis
Clark Gable
Greta Garbo
John Garfield
Judy Garland
Greer Garson
Janet Gaynor
John Gilbert
Lillian Gish
Paulette Goddard
Betty Grable
Cary Grant
Ann Harding
Cedric Hardwicke
Jean Harlow
Will Hay
Helen Hayes
Rita Hayworth
Sonja Henie
Katharine Hepburn
Wendy Hiller
Valerie Hobson
Bob Hope
Miriam Hopkins
Leslie Howard
Walter Huston
Betty Hutton

Emil Jannings
Al Jolson
Boris Karloff
Buster Keaton
Ruby Keeler
Alan Ladd
Veronica Lake
Hedy Lamarr
Dorothy Lamour
Elissa Landi
Harry Langdon
Charles Laughton
Laurel and Hardy
Vivien Leigh
Harold Lloyd
Margaret Lockwood
Carole Lombard
Myrna Loy
Paul Lukas
Ida Lupino
Jeanette MacDonald
Aline MacMahon
Fred MacMurray
Fredric March
Herbert Marshall
Mary Martin
The Marx Brothers
James Mason
Jessie Matthews
Joel McCrea
Victor McLaglen
Ray Milland
Carmen Miranda
Maria Montez
Robert Montgomery
Grace Moore
Frank Morgan
Paul Muni
Anna Neagle
Pola Negri
Ramon Novarro
Merle Oberon
Margaret O'Brien
Laurence Olivier
Lilli Palmer
Mary Pickford

Walter Pidgeon
Dick Powell
Eleanor Powell
William Powell
Tyrone Power
George Raft
Luise Rainer
Claude Rains
Basil Rathbone
Michael Redgrave
Ralph Richardson
Paul Robeson
Edward G. Robinson
Flora Robson
Ginger Rogers
Will Rogers
Mickey Rooney
Rosalind Russell
George Sanders
Norma Shearer
Ann Sheridan
Sylvia Sidney
Ann Sothern
Barbara Stanwyck
Anna Sten
James Stewart
Margaret Sullavan
Gloria Swanson
Robert Taylor
Shirley Temple
Franchot Tone
Spencer Tracy
Claire Trevor
Lana Turner
Rudolph Valentino
Conrad Veidt
Erich Von Stroheim
Anton Walbrook
John Wayne
Johnny Weissmuller
Orson Welles
Mae West
Diana Wynyard
Loretta Young
Robert Young
Roland Young

Introduction

The stars and the system

The first film players worked on both sides of the camera and were uncredited; but as some of them became familiar to audiences there was a buzz of recognition. Since most nickelodeons and variety halls hired their films from the same film-exchanges which relied in turn on the same film suppliers, it was not long before the entrepreneurs began to appreciate that a familiar face could be an asset.

Already there were film studios – in sheds or properties that had been warehouses – turning out sometimes several films a week. In 1908 Edison was in The Bronx and Vitagraph in Flatbush: Biograph, probably the oldest company, was on 14th Street in New York; Selig and Essanay were in Chicago. These five companies and five others formed, in 1909, the Motion Picture Patents Co., claiming the exclusive right to photograph, print and develop motion pictures. Edison himself was involved and the patent was quite legal. But when they attempted to control the exchanges and nickelodeons they came up against opposition from those who were making huge fortunes from distribution, like Carl Laemmle of the Laemmle Film Service. He fought the monopoly in court and out – by ridicule in the trade press and by producing his own movies (the first was a one-reel *Hiawatha*). For his Independent Motion Picture Co. (IMP) he was determined to get one of the best-known personalities in pictures, 'The Biograph Girl'.

This lady had already been identified as Florence Lawrence. She and her husband Harry Salter had started with Vitagraph and had moved on to Biograph when she was offered a further $10 a week – making $25. By 1910 she was sufficiently popular for Laemmle to offer her the violently excessive sum of $1,000 a week. Then she vanished. Laemmle planted a story in the press to the effect that she had been run down and killed by a trolley car in St Louis, and then asserted in an advert in the trade press that the story was an invention of his enemies. Miss Lawrence appeared in St Louis to prove that she was alive – and was mobbed. All of this focused much attention on her and on IMP, proving not only the vast popularity of film-players but underlining their value as commercial properties.

The following year she went to the Lubin Co., one of the patents group, where she teamed with Arthur Johnson for some pop-ular comedies. Fame did not last. In the 20s she was in Britain working in minor parts when Marion Davies heard of her plight and sent her the fare to come to Hollywood, plus the offer of a small part in a movie. She became an extra and committed suicide in 1938, completely forgotten. Her rival, Florence Turner 'The Vitagraph Girl', fared little better. When her career began to wane around 1912 she went to Britain with her Vitagraph co-star Larry Trimble and they formed their own company, in conjunction with Cecil M. Hepworth, and were successful for a while. By 1924 her parts were few and small; she returned to the US and played a few more brief roles, such as Buster Keaton's mother in *College* (27).

Mary Pickford was on the scene by 1909, and there were other melting heroines like Blanche Sweet, Clara Kimball Young and Norma Talmadge: romantic heroes like Francis X. Bushman, Earle Williams and Maurice Costello: cowboy stars Tom Mix, Bronco Billy Anderson and William S. Hart; and the comedy team of Flora Finch and John Bunny. It occurred to Adolph Zukor, another exhibitor, that if the public would turn up to see these people, they might be curious to see the great stars on the stage.

The idea was not entirely his. In France Sarah Bernhardt had been persuaded to commit her Camille to two reels of celluloid for the sake of posterity, and as a reprise she was a four-reel *Queen Elizabeth*. Zukor had invested some money in the latter when it got into difficulties during production and therefore held the American rights. He discovered that Bernhardt gave cinemas not only respectability but huge receipts. He conceived the idea of 'Famous Players in Famous Plays' and many Broadway names were cajoled into movies. Few of them stayed because Zukor's prestige pictures were dreary (if worthy): those who did had lucrative careers.

Artists were coming in from vaudeville. Mack Sennett directed his first film for Biograph in 1910 and not long afterward the variety halls began to be raided for comics and for acrobats. Pearl White, who became the queen of the serials in *The Perils of Pauline* (14), had been an aerialist. It was essential for all these film players to have, if not striking good looks, some great *physical* characteristic such as agility or a funny walk or funny expressions or a dimple. (In the Talkies an actor with a strongly individual voice would find this an asset above and beyond looks or physical presence.)

During the First World War Mary Pickford and Chaplin knew an undreamed-of world-wide popularity and by 1920 the studios were fashioning most of their pictures around one individual personality – a personality considered to be, commercially, that film's major attraction. Under no circumstances was there more than one star to a film. No matter who in the public's estimation was a star, the billing required only one name above the title – that of the 'official' star: much publicity accrued when contract players were hoisted to 'official' stardom. The contract lists were a huge source of pride, even if the players were like caged animals – to be petted and pampered and exhibited before admiring multitudes, but starved of space in which to fly and move: unable to move artistically. In the early 30s the rules were changed. Said Picturegoer with some awe in 1932: 'It looks as though the two-star film is here to stay – at least for the time being.' Very soon MGM set the fan-magazines buzzing when they announced that *Grand Hotel* would have *six* stars – but it did not often make sense, economically, to put several stars in one film, when the public would turn up just as eagerly to see one or two.

So much effort went into making and then maintaining a star. In the star-vehicles which constituted the major output of all the studios, infinite care and skill went into costumes and lighting so that the star appeared to best advantage; great care was taken over the first entrance, over the choice of leading man or leading woman: and when the star was undis-guisedly ageing, even that fact was turned to advantage.

But if the Hollywood factories were adept at packaging these enticing products called stars, an examination of the 183 stars in this book proves that few careers had much in common. Getting to the top seems to have been a question of chance, with hazards not unlike those encountered on the 'Monopoly' board. For every vital and intelligent talent that makes it several others fail; the history of films is strewn with the names of people who seemed to have the requisite looks, personality and talent but yet who somehow fell down a hole. At the same time there are artists deficient in all three who became world-wide favourites. Ambition must be considered a factor: Laurence Olivier once said that to be a star 'you have to be a bit of a bastard', and we know of artists who devoted every waking minute to being a star. Joan Crawford, not blessed with the talent of Olivier, was one – at the sacrifice, apparently, of her happiness (Cary Grant once said that

he never met a happy actress, and, for instance, one of John Wayne's associates observed that he had sacrificed happiness to his career). Youth can be an asset, and so can familiarity – when audiences become conditioned to certain looks and mannerisms; and you can even be taken in by the aura. It has been frequently claimed that the relation-ship between star and public is like a love-affair – but it is an affair with an element of harlotry: the public will only pay out its money for stars with sufficient skill and personality to sustain the relationship.

Actual acting ability can be minimal, though no screen actor survived who didn't quickly acquire at least a technical profi-ciency. Considering the elements involved in creating a star performance and the frag-mented way a film is made, it is surprising how consistent most artists were/are – variously good from film to film but seldom variable within a film. John Gielgud was once asked to define the basic requirements of an actor. He replied: 'Imagination, self-discipline, indus-try, a sense of humour if possible. And certain basic qualities of appearance, of authority, of originality. Sort of commonplace prettiness is not very interesting, you know. Just good looks aren't interesting; but interesting looks can be used – a malleable, flexible body and face, and voice. Voice, of course, I think is very important.' Gielgud was not asked to differentiate between screen and stage acting, but it might be noted that very few stage-trained actors have failed in films (the reverse is not the case). A stage-trained actor is equipped with certain advantages such as the ability to play to other actors, to build a scene to a climax, and even – on an elementary level – to handle dialogue. His effectiveness – on stage or screen can depend on physical condi-tions like co-stars and climate, and in films it can depend largely on what happens in the cutting-room.

Which is just as well. Film actors in the past had more to cope with than mere acting. Just being a star was at times overwhelming. They were well-paid and were protected from scandal (in most instances) but photographic sessions, interviews, costume fittings and per-sonal appearances usually took precedence over acting. The amount of publicity that they once had to cope with is staggering. And something else was required – and it was akin to ambition: the will to survive.

Many stars had to fight – every step of the way. They fought for better parts, better movies, better terms. If there were signs of public apathy the firing-squad were on stand-by in the morning. The studios protected their interests by the contract with options, but the star had no recourse if he thought the studio was sabotaging his standing with poor films. Talent was his sole ally. Some artists did triumph over every adversary placed in their way by the studios. It is not a coincidence that most of the female stars who had long careers also had strong masculine qualities, but even a Bette Davis can, after years of fighting, become, in Robert Aldrich's words 'a strange lady. She has been misled so many times, and placed her confidence so many times in situations and/or people that didn't pay off, that she's naturally terribly hesitant to trust anybody.' (He added: 'Once she trusts you, she's marvellous.')

The system was firmly rigged against the individual in favour of the machine, and it is hardly surprising that it destroyed talents which did not know how to come to terms with it, like Marilyn Monroe and Judy Garland. Some artists returned to the stage, always a much saner operating ground – and those artists who were equally stage stars usually found it easier to weather the cinematic storms than the others. It was and is a hazardous business: even Charlton Heston – in a TV interview – once confessed that he was insecure 'like all actors' (though as at that time he was being paid $750,000 per film it was difficult to sympathize). Actors, not unreasonably, tend to be extrovert, vain and emotional, and the enclosed self-centred and fantasy world of Hollywood exaggerated these qualities without being beneficial to them either as artists or individuals.

Fame via the casting-office couch is always a possibility (there are good reasons why this object is not so mythical) but an examination of the way most people got to the top in this particular field proves it to have been rather by industry, chance and intelligence. Perhaps some later stars did it more by wheeling and dealing, but most of the pre-war stars were of a different breed. This Hollywood generation was extraordinarily blessed with talent, and from all that was written about them there emerges much to admire and little to dislike. In interviews most of them appear to have been realistic and frank (it is only the second-raters who brag of minor successes and gloss over failures – the same tactics that are used by politicians). But what matters of course is what was up there on that screen, and when you see it – the best of it – you are in no doubt as to why movie-stars are the twentieth century's contribution to mythology.

The question of what constitutes star quality must detain us briefly. David Lean said once that he preferred to direct stars because two of them together accept each other as a challenge. They strike sparks. As long as films depended on the theatre (or novels) those with a genuine star player started with an advantage. It's in the nature of that particular beast. The performing arts generally have always been dependent on star performers: in larger than life-size roles you must have performers to fit. You simply cannot do 'King Lear' or 'Macbeth' without stars, or 'Tosca' or 'Private Lives'; but you can do 'The Three Sisters' or 'The Importance of being Earnest' or 'Look Back in Anger'. (In the theatre the rapport between star and audience or the current charging between them is, of course, much more palpable than anything comparable in the cinema.) In film terms, despite the overall skill of, say, Hitchcock, his movies were always more effective when he had strong leading players. It is the way of the Hollywood system: virtually no Hollywood director is at his best with unknowns or mere actors. The habit is too ingrained; and Hollywood takes much of its material from plays and books which in turn were influenced by Hollywood. Elsewhere there have been films where you could not have had any sort of star – Ray's *Apu* trilogy, Olmi's *Il Posto*, Ichikawa's *Alone on the Pacific* and, even, his *An Actor's Revenge*. Ichikawa's *Tokyo Olympiad* did not even have actors. To this writer these films are masterpieces, but as I've found it extremely unlikely to encounter a masterpiece every time I go to the cinema I'll settle for something else – like Garbo, if I'm lucky. Her performances are the sole justification of the films in which she appeared. In *Camille*, labouring under every disadvantage that any player ever faced – except direction and perhaps dialogue – she provides an experience as potent as, if different from, that of *Tokyo Olympiad*. The nature of that experience has been analysed by virtually every writer on films – and it remains unfathomable. Of lesser artists one can be more certain: beauty, magnetism, personality, ability – one of these or a combination of these to a degree that is not ordinarily encountered in one's friends or in other actors. The great stars were all originals and any description more precise founders on their individuality. James Mason tried in *A Star Is Born* with the aid of Moss Hart's script: 'It's that little something extra that Ellen Terry talked about.' It must remain undefined; but you know it when you see it.

A note on the films

It was clear from the outset that motion pictures of ordinary life were not going to be enough, and the film pioneers looked primarily to the stage for inspiration. It was the first mistake they made, for the stage, in the early years of this century, was not a subject for emulation, inundated as it was with barnstorming melodramas (melodrama:

'a variety of drama, commonly romantic and sentimental' – Webster). True, these plays, transcribed, proved ideal for cinema audiences, but thus the pall of melodrama was to settle on films for more than 50 years. Technical inadequacy – including of course the lack of speech – caused further strait-jacketing, and it was some time before it was revealed that movies could be told *technically* – not only via images but by the arrangement of same, by cutting and the rhythm of cutting, by the camera's own motivation. D.W. Griffith claimed, falsely, to be the greatest of the innovators – but he was certainly the most admired film-maker of his day. His taste in stories was unsophisticated, however, with all characters and situations polarized into black and white. His very success may have daunted any spirit who saw life in more sober terms – though certainly his taste in screen fiction was in key with both his audiences and the moguls, whose attitudes were likely to have been moulded by the same factors. In Europe the plots were equally melodramatic, but there were compensations of atmosphere or feeling: and when Hollywood seduced the best continental directors most of them were forced to conform with patterns already established. A few overcame the handicap of Silence, but if the essence of all drama is conflict – the clash of opinion, motives, personalities – there were few who could portray it in other than simplistic terms. In Russia, Eisenstein, with the prerogative of genius, solved the problem when dealing with the greatest conflict of the age: the motives and behaviour of his protagonists (*October, Strike*, etc.) are told wholly and satisfactorily in moving picture terms.

A few film-makers – Keaton, Lloyd – turned the lack of Sound to their advantage (and not only that, but the primitive cameras, filmstock, etc.). Their films dealt in conflict, and *The General* indeed is about opposing factions in the War between the States: there is not a single facet of the struggle (Keaton on his train and the enemy on theirs) which Keaton couldn't handle with visual wit: the two great comics rival Eisenstein as a visual writer. They knew instinctively that you could not do drama with only a camera and a splicer – at least not the sort of 'drama' that the Silents wanted to show.

Few other Silent films yield much except to buffs (in which respect of course they are like pre-Elizabethan drama). The so-called classics were lauded for what they attempted rather than achieved – both because this was a medium which, for the first time in history, could communicate to millions and because it was denied the privilege of Sound. There was a further drawback due to the fact that at the start all films were of one-reel or less: although they increased in length it was not until the late 20s that many directors were able to sustain a mood or impose any consistency. Plots were often a series of episodes built round a central theme, and in a film like the 1920 *Mark of Zorro* the scenes could have been shifted without any loss to logic. Everything – not only the sets – seemed made of cardboard and if there was any character development it was in the crudest terms.

Many of the early Talkies were no better: they spoke but did not say anything. Titles still abounded, and as late as 1935 *Clive of India* was little more than a series of conversations with the plot developments explained by lengthy titles. Films were still constructed with little regard for logicality, though some adaptations of plays and novels were impressive, such as John Ford's *Arrowsmith* (31), where the dialogue and situations of Sinclair Lewis's novel were handled by a director with both a feeling for these and a sense of the medium's potentialities. In France René Clair used music and dialogue to enhance his fond and witty view of the (Parisian) universe: he, rather than Hollywood, ushered in the inconsequence – the ordered chaos – which was to mark the films of the next decade. In Hollywood and Britain also the introduction of Sound brought in music, and in American films the dialogue was often sharp, fast and slangy. The writers and directors, if left to themselves, went untrammelled by convention. Sound was the *modus vivendi* and inexperience in itself a virtue. They had no failures behind them. It was an era of great confidence. These were to be the golden years – in directing, in screenwriting and in performing. Certainly, at least in comedy.

In the 30s films had an incredible gaiety. Consider this lot: *Duck Soup, The Awful Truth, Nothing Sacred, A Slight Case of Murder, True Confession, A Hundred Men and a Girl, Ninotchka, Sing Baby Sing, Star of Midnight, The Adventures of Robin Hood, She Done Him Wrong, Bringing Up Baby, Mr Deeds Goes to Town, Swing Time, It's a Gift, Snow-White and the Seven Dwarfs.* Mainly comedies: most of them knowing, some of them innocent, all of them insouciant, elegant, confident, captivating. In the world of the dictators, in the shadow of war, Hollywood knew how to make the world forget its troubles.

The vast film factories were churning out entertainments like these as from an assembly line. All studios aimed at diversity: musicals, Westerns, gangster thrillers, detective thrillers, smart comedies, folksy comedies, historical dramas, women's dramas, etc. The films had a different surface gloss, but the products of individual studios were otherwise inter-changeable. Certain predilections are discernible – Warners, for instance, liked anything that smacked of a social conscience while the more conservative MGM definitely did not: but a pattern only emerges in that all the studios were willing to repeat a success and therefore seemed to specialise in a certain genre. The overall product did reflect, if not the taste of the front office, the level of its brow and its insatiable quest for conformity.

Whatever the genre, the films were much of a muchness: they fed on each other and not on life. It did not matter if in comedy the mirror held up to life was distorted – it had its own validity – but in drama it was stifling: stock characters in stock situations. And the star vehicles were hardly conducive to originality, even though there is, clearly, a magic about the best of them: and, because these were the important films, you can often discern a lot of good ideas and themes trying to get loose.

The big budgets were saved for these – the prestige pictures, adaptations of worthy best-sellers and Broadway hits: when they do not work today it is usually because of their Olympian view of the human race. They were supposed to educate the public – the lowest common denominator of it, and Thalberg, for instance, for all his insistence on the best stories and the best writers, demanded absolute conformity in the denouements. In the 40s Jean Renoir brought some of his humanity to Hollywood, but his films still seemed to end with a Selznick sunset; and Fritz Lang, later, said that he resigned his Hollywood sinecure because the battles were not worth the ulcers.

Few stars, in any case, wanted to be associated with anything that might be termed 'experimental'. The studios did not care to have the reputations of their players jeopardized, and the stars hesitated because they knew they were held personally responsible for the success or failure of their films. After the system had broken down, in the 50s, certain stars were willing to back new talent and new ideas – but by this time it was no longer accepted that any individual performer decisively affected a film's performance at the box-office.

The changes of the 50s to the 80s are outside the province of this book, but there should be noted (1) the end of the long-term contract (2) the rise of the actor-impresario (3) the growth of internationalism and, not with sorrow (4) the passing of the B-picture or second feature. These in the early 30s supplanted the shorts and two-reelers which had preceded the feature movie – though by the end of the decade shorts, newsreels and cartoons were filling in time between features.

In this book all B-features are designated as such, and these can be taken to mean films of low-budget, with a running time of about one hour and destined for the lower half of the programme. The expression 'programmer' – or programme-filler – refers to those films without pretence to art or huge grosses made merely to keep cinemas busy, and a 'dualler' was the same thing, only in this case it was not considered strong enough to play with a B-picture but needed another film like itself. Few duallers were made as such – they just turned out that way.

Some more trade jargon which should prove useful: a 'sleeper' is a low-budget picture which does unexpectedly well; an 'indie' is an independent production made away from one of the big studios – though sometimes released by one of their distribution companies; a 'sudser' is a species of 'soap-opera' – sometimes a 'weepie' – aimed primarily at the distaff half of the audience; a 'biopic' is a film biography (an invariably depressing species); a 'melo' is obviously a melodrama; and a 'road show' or 'block-buster' a film of huge budget designed to play separate performances at legitimate theatre prices. I must say that I do not like the slang, but in a text as long as this an abbreviation becomes necessary; thus, when dealing with television credits, I have only attempted to differentiate between a one-off film and a mini-series. In the case of the latter it refers to a work spread over two evenings or more. It is simply too complicated to indicate whether this was three hours or in some cases twenty. These titles are italicized, in the sense that, like movies for the cinema, they may be frequently re-shown. Other work for television, including weekly series, appears in Roman type.

The fan-magazines

The fan-magazines were originally house-magazines, like the British 'Pictures', founded in 1912 and later evolving into 'Picturegoer'. In the US the Vitagraph Co. started a magazine to publicize its own stars and films, and both at first were not unlike the trade-journals, with their news of showmen's campaigns and advice to the pianist in the pit. It was soon realized that there was a vast public interest in the off-set activities of its favourites, who were then pictured at home by log-fires or welcoming European royalty to the set. The pose of being infinitely glamorous had to be maintained, and the more prosaic information about current and forthcoming films was interspersed with articles on the romances of their leading players. The fan-magazines of the 20s believed, probably rightly, that their chief readers were women and they bolstered their contents with items such as beauty hints and fashion notes. The (American) 'Photoplay' of the 20s had a concerned and critical attitude towards films, but its articles on personalities were devoid of any real matter; and by the end of the 30s its film reviews, also, had succumbed to the requirements of the studios. The 'Picturegoer' of the 20s was without character but when it went from monthly to weekly in 1931 it became both informative and responsible. (Both magazines have been drawn upon for much of the material of this book, plus certain trade journals, notably the indispensable 'Variety'.)

By the beginning of the Talkie period the fan-magazines were forces to reckon with. In the US they were monthly; and though the number fluctuated there were seldom less than half-a-dozen. In Britain in the 30s there were four weeklies – 'Picturegoer' and 'Film Weekly', 'Picture Show' and 'Film Pictorial'. They combined into two at the outbreak of war and continued as a duo till the late 50s, when each folded after a brief attempt at jazzing-up. 'Film Weekly' and later 'Picturegoer' had the finest writer ever to make a living from studying Hollywood, W.H. Mooring, a liberal and kindly man who was more interested in films than in personalities and scandals.

The American magazines only appeared to have the same freedom. They and the studios were mutually dependent: the magazines wanted information – exclusive if possible – and the studios wanted favourable mention of their films and stars. So the magazines were content to reprint the 'copy' turned out by the studio pubmills and by the mid-40s were depicting a never-never (even neverer) land which was later to degenerate into a morass of make-believe scandal. They seemed to be about only plastic people in a plastic world. Nor must one overlook the immense power of the syndicated and broadcasting gossip-columnists, who at their worst were vicious and at their best patronizing: and, with the exception of Hedda Hopper, singularly lacking in humour – if not without their insights. Most stars viewed the columnists as parasites, and the uneasy relationship between them has elements of pathos, with some stars desperately anxious for publicity and the columnists forever fending off a series of imagined snubs. But the columnist always won: it was too simple to write a piece repeating every unfavourable rumour and opinion, finishing with a sop like 'But we believe none of it: we believe he can do it.'

Such pieces were, however, uncommon until the post-war years when a harsher light was cast and stars were deglamorized. Until then, too, perhaps only Garbo and Chaplin

were remarked by the more serious sections of the press, and it was not till the 50s, with the advent of Brando and Monroe, that star-gazing was accepted as a worthwhile occupation for the higher brow. It was not till then that the serious movie magazines were much interested in stars.

Elsewhere the cinema has not been lucky in its commentators. The majority of books on movies are riddled with errors and that includes all but a few listed at the back as sources. The best non-academic textbook on the American film is still Griffith and Mayer's 'The Movies'. The magazine and newspaper critics most often quoted in this book are those whom I feel were and are the masters of their craft. All references in the text to 'the critics' and to 'the press' means the majority unless specifically stated: quotes are used solely to evoke critical response to a particular star – but there were some fine artists who had long careers without kindling any great critical fires.

The industry has never cared for critics, which it sees as sourpusses determined to prevent the public from turning out for the latest million-dollar masterpiece: but the two sides have lived together so long that it is rather like the Trojan War, with moments of bitterness and fury but a general feeling of something to be lived with. The enthusiasm by the best critics for the medium has been underrated by the industry, though it has been quick to use their good opinions in its advertisements. The critics never made a star, but, like the fan-magazines, they could create a setting where a new personality or a particular performance became a landmark to be seen; and there have been artists of little commercial value who have been utilized by producers because they could be relied upon to bring in favourable notices.

The box-office

Public acceptance has been the surest and perhaps most satisfying barometer of success, and the box-office lists were always carefully studied by studio chiefs. They had other ways of telling, but an appearance in the annual list of top money-makers in the 'Motion Picture Herald' considerably increased that actor's power and/or earning capacity: to head the list was commercially on a par with winning an Oscar.

The statistics can be deceptive. Exhibitors are asked to vote for those artists who bring most money into their tills during one calendar year, so that someone with three successful films to his credit appears more advantageously than another with only one; and many exhibitors are unable to assess the actual appeal of any film so that they credit –

or blame – the star at whim. British exhibitors have been wont to vote for any star appearing in a hit, so the British lists have contained a freakish proportion of artists who otherwise did not mean a thing to patrons. All references in this book to box-office popularity refer to the lists as printed in the 'Motion Picture Herald'. Popularity polls – such as that conducted by Sydney Bernstein for the patrons of his Granada circuit – are all clearly designated as such.

As far as the films are concerned, the figures of box-office takings have been culled from both the 'Motion Picture Herald' and 'Variety'. 'Variety' annually lists the all-time grossers, i.e. all films that took over $4 million, but as very, very few in the 20s and 30s took as much as this, the earlier figures are taken from the 'Motion Picture Herald'. Rising seat prices should be kept in mind when considering all details of finance, including salaries: for instance, in 1930 a film with a take of $1 million was a giant hit, while in 1978 a film will expect to take $10 million before beginning to recover its costs. (It might be generally accepted that before the Second World War, £1 sterling equalled $4, and after it $3.)

A word of caution on salaries: these are reprinted in good faith from 'Variety', 'Picturegoer', etc., and are included as guide-lines, failing more complete statistics – but like dates of birth, details of wages (and contracts) were not something about which either studios or agents were scrupulously honest.

The awards

The Academy of Motion Picture Arts and Sciences was founded by Louis B. Mayer in 1927 in an attempt to prevent unionisation of actors and artisans. It has an elected membership of some 3,000 film-workers considered to have reached the top in the industry or in their own particular branch of it. Of these, specialists in 13 sections determine the award nominations, normally five in each category. The winners receive their awards, a gold statuette known as Oscar, in an annual ceremony in Los Angeles.

The first ceremony in 1929 was a private affair, but the publicity value of the awards was soon apparent. Televised live today, the Oscar ceremony traditionally draws the largest audience of the American viewing year. Both to audiences and within the industry an Oscar is the supreme award. To receive one is to enter a golden hall of fame. Books have been written about it. It has been reviled and admired and fought for. Both James Mason and Spencer Tracy are on record as saying that it is invidious to pick *one* performance from the year's best and that to be nominated is sufficient honour. But to receive one is considered the peak of a film actor's career: his fee goes up, and the major awards (Best Film, Best Actor and Best Actress) are reckoned to add as much as $1 million to the film's gross.

However, both in terms of the award itself and its effect on any career, the Oscar is a dazzling enigma. Some have not benefited from it and to some it has merely been a crystallization of the high regard in which they are held by their fellow-artists. Just when you despair as to how some films and players even got nominated something perfectly right happens like the awards to Simone Signoret and Rod Steiger. Who on earth voted for *The Greatest Show on Earth* as Best Film of 1952? – over *High Noon* and *The Quiet Man*, not to mention *Moulin Rouge* and *Ivanhoe* (or *The River* and *Singin' in the Rain*, which weren't even nominated). But then John Ford won the Best Director award that year for *The Quiet Man*, his fourth Oscar. At a time when Luise Rainer won two, neither Garbo nor Margaret Sullavan (among many others) won one; neither *Paths of Glory* nor *2001 A Space Odyssey* were even nominated when the winners were, respectively, *The Bridge on the River Kwai* and *Oliver!* – but *Midnight Cowboy* won and *Anne of the Thousand Days* did not.

There is no doubt that voters are influenced by fine reviews *plus* big business. Sentiment plays a part; and so does publicity – that is just a fact of the Hollywood way of life and the intense campaigning on the part of certain artists should not reflect on their talent or popularity. Also, certain rules are observed: it is easier to win in drama than in comedy, and still easier if the character portrayed is (1) living in sin or penury (2) neurotically afflicted or (3) noble and uplifting. Even with fine critical notices it is difficult to get nominated for a performance in a flop movie. The nominations in themselves are interesting, but because of the waywardness of the system and because of their uncertain value to the nominee's career they have not as a general rule been noted in this book.

Other awards since the 50s have proliferated to the point of idiocy. Some are given merely to ensure a personal appearance, supposing that everyone benefits from the mutual publicity: these often have names like 'Middletown Women's Guild Star Mother of the Year Award'. Clearly the law of diminishing returns becomes relevant, and while the Golden Globe awards (decided by the Hollywood correspondents of the foreign press) have been growing in prestige only one other award has major prominence – the New York critics award, given annually since 1935.

Its winners generally become the favourites in the Oscar sweepstakes.

In Britain for years the only award of consequence was the 'Picturegoer' Gold Medal, voted by its readers: so often it was won by major talents that it had considerable prestige for most of the life of the journal. The British Film Academy began giving acting awards in 1952, and so that Hollywood would not sweep the board the four awards were divided into Best British and Best Foreign. The growing internationalism within the British film industry finally made the distinction untenable and it was dropped in 1969. But the acting awards remained four in number, with the adoption of two Best Supporting awards, after the Hollywood pattern. These British awards have sometimes been more pleasing than their Hollywood counterparts but are knee-high to a grasshopper in prestige, a situation unlikely to change until the ceremony has more weight.

About the book

This book does not, could not, tell the whole story of the stars of the golden years and you might well look for all those fine players who supported the stars and contributed so much to that era. We have managed to include some who achieved star-billing and for the rest, their presence is felt. The choice has been guided by the box-office figures, by popularity polls and by the reputation that remains. There are some box-office stars who do not appear (Charles Farrell, Joe E. Brown, Jane Withers, Gene Autry and Roy Rogers) mainly because their entire careers do not seem to justify inclusion, nor have we included stars from radio and the stage who made only occasional forays into films.

For similar reasons the Silent stars included are only those who are remembered today. There is enough to be written on the stars of the Silent screen to make a book twice this length – enough heartbreak and triumph – but for the most part they remain unseen, their films gathering dust in the corners of warehouses, or disintegrating. And some of them, when seen, are very dubious contenders for a pantheon of great stars. The continental stars of the period, unless they worked in Hollywood, have been left to a later volume, on the understanding that from the introduction of Talkies until well after the Second World War even the best of these players were known outside their own countries only to film societies or to the patrons of 'specialized' cinemas.

This survey therefore includes those artists who achieved stardom before and in some cases during World War II. I deeply regret the exclusion of Max Linder, Asta Nielsen and William S. Hart, for instance, but do not believe that they belong within the province I have set myself to cover 'The Golden Years'. The selection has had to be arbitrary: John Wayne was not a major star until after the war and yet he seems to belong to this period; while Rex Harrison, David Niven and a few others who were in starring roles before the war seem to belong to the post-war period – and are featured in 'The Great Movie Stars: the International Years'. Care has been taken to examine the stars and their films in the light of their own era, and to balance contemporary opinion against recent showings of the same films. Because of institutions like New York's Museum of Modern Art and London's National Film Theatre, and old movies on television, it is possible to re-examine and discover the films of the part – but one should note, in passing, that this was not always so. Until the 50s the majority of movies were dead and forgotten the day after by all but the public: neither fan-magazines nor critics nor the producers nor the stars themselves ever expected cinemagoers to remember more than six months back.

Each individual entry lists all feature films made by that particular star – i.e. all films of four reels and over. In the case of Silent stars who made one- and two-reelers a selection only has been included, and shorts made by Talkie actors have not normally been included. For space reasons we have neither attempted a separate filmography nor tried to list the co-star and producing company of each film. All films are set down in release order except where otherwise stated (in these cases it seemed that readers sufficiently interested as to which film followed which by a month or two would know where to research such facts). The dates given in parentheses are for the first film *reviewed* in any calendar year per the 'Film Daily Yearbook' – i.e. January to December, and all films following that date were reviewed the same year. (Films are sometimes dated by year of copyright and sometimes by the year of release; because the records of the 'Film Daily' are complete it seems to me best to take their review date, i.e. the date when the film was complete and shown to exhibitors.) It should be borne in mind that many films are not premièred till some months after the star has finished filming, by which time he or she might well have made several stage appearances, etc.

All film titles are given as in the country of origin and an appendix lists the titles of American films that were re-named for the British market and vice-versa. The appendix also lists a few continental films which were re-titled for the British or American market. In the text, the title is always given in the language of its country of origin, and I think it is clear when any subsequent titles for the same film are given that they refer either to an English-language version, a co-production, or an attempt to convey to the reader the English version of the original title.

In the first edition of this book I made a clear indication between movies and television programmes, and while I have still indicated those films which were made for TV, I have italicized the titles when it seems likely that they will be around as long as most films made for theatres.

I am extremely grateful to the following, all of whom read the manuscript, or most of it, and offered invaluable help and comment: Felix Brenner, David Holland, Michael Stapleton, James Tinline and André Vannier. My especial gratitude is due to James Tinline who, when he was supposed to be teaching me English literature in the tropical heat of Singapore preferred to talk about this golden age of movies. It was he who first fired me with enthusiasm for artists I had not then seen, like Garbo and the Marx Brothers. My thanks are also due to the following for help above and beyond the call of duty: Honor Blair, Richard Chatten, Bruce Goldstein, Lyn Lasko, James Morton, Van Phillips, Lita Torgersen-Sherman, Barbara and Jay Williams, Ann Wilson, Brian Wood and Fred Zentner. I am also deeply indebted to the staff of the British Film Institute Library and Information Section, who were unfailingly courteous even in answering what must have seemed to them many footling questions.

Note to the Third Edition

In the first edition of this book, in the above paragraph, I indicated that between us my colleagues and I had seen most of the films mentioned: since it was published almost 20 years ago, I have managed to see most of the films listed, and have accordingly been able to make extensive revisions. I have taken advantage of old films emerging from the archives, and of new material written on the subject of the stars, in biographies, memoirs and books about the studios themselves; I have also managed to make a number of corrections, and would like to thank the many people who have kindly written to me about this book.

ABBOTT AND COSTELLO

Bud Abbott was the straight man. Lou Costello was the funny one, a roly-poly little man liable to mishap and misunderstanding. They were a comedy team of the 40s and astonishingly popular. Their humour was mainly verbal but when they did get involved in slapstick they hardly seemed to contribute. Their films are as revivable as those of Wheeler and Woolsey, a team which had served RKO 10 years earlier.

Abbott was born in Asbury Park, New Jersey, in 1895; Costello in Paterson in the same state in 1908. Costello started out as a salesman in a hat shop, became a prize-fighter and saved enough to try his luck in Hollywood. The only job he could get at first was labouring at MGM but later he was a stunt man: he once doubled for Dolores del Rio. Then he tried vaudeville. Abbott came from a show business milieu – his parents were part of a circus troupe. He became a sailor at 15, then worked as a box-office clerk in a burlesque theatre: he was selling tickets and Costello was on the bill, and Costello's straight man didn't turn up . . . thus the art was formed. This was in Brooklyn in 1930. They formed a team and played on the bump-and-grind circuit without success for seven years, until a New York booking in 1938 led to them replacing Red Skelton (Hollywood-bound) on Kate Smith's radio show. The following year, along with Carmen Miranda, they supported Bobby Clark and Jean Sablon in a Broadway revue, 'The Streets of Paris'. They were probably the only major comics to emerge from the generally despised medium of burlesque.

This was the great era of guest appearances and MGM offered them $17,500 to do some of their routines in their musicals. While they were considering this, Universal offered $35,000 to provide comic relief in a musical destined to push the careers of Allan Jones and Robert Cummings, whose stars were not shining too brightly. *One Night in the Tropics* (40) also had songs by Jerome Kern. Abbott and Costello's cross-talk was of secondary importance to the romantic-farcical goings-on, but audience response was enthusiastic, causing Universal to offer the standard long-term contract at $50,000 per film plus – which was rare then – a 10 per cent share of the profits, the money to be split (as throughout their career) on a 60/40 basis, with Costello getting the higher sum. Their fee envisaged a series of B movies and they started off officially in support of two semi-demi stars, Lee Bowman and Alan Curtis, in *Buck Privates* (41), a low budget effort which took in so much money that the studio rushed out

Bud Abbott (left) and Lou Costello as they were when they met the Invisible Man *(50) – one of their series of unhistoric meetings.*

In the Navy, where they were supporting Dick Powell. Meanwhile, the studio dickered with *Hold That Ghost*, made before that, and achieved a rather schizophrenic thriller-musical, but at least it seemed worthy of these new favourites – who were top-billed for the first time. After the army and the navy, *Keep 'em Flying*, with Martha Raye as contrasting twins, and at the end of 1941 our heroes trailed only Mickey Rooney and Clark Gable as box-office kings.

Costello now demanded that they be renamed Costello and Abbott, but Universal protested that they had bought Abbott and Costello. However, a new contract was negotiated, at $150,000 per film plus 20 per cent of the profits, together with a commitment to loan them to MGM for one film a year. Louis B. Mayer at MGM, still smarting at having lost Deanna Durbin to Universal, had not taken kindly to what he considered a second deprivation – and the studio had so little star power of its own that it might want to borrow some of MGM's players. MGM would also pay Abbott and Costello $150,000, but they would also enrich Universal's coffers to the same amount. So after *Ride 'em Cowboy* (42) they reported to that studio to take on Wheeler and Woolsey's old roles in a topical (i.e. war) revamp of *Rio Rita*. An apology, *Pardon My Sarong*, and a question, *Who Done It?*, plus the pay-off dates of most of all these movies brought them to Number One at the box office. The formula was already established. The two of them were put into a specific setting (an army installation, a department store, a radio station) where they could wreak havoc, to be relieved now and then by some studio juveniles and some songs by popular recording artists, e.g. Ella Fitzgerald, the Ink Spots, the Andrews Sisters.

Universal sensibly limited them to two films a year: *It Ain't Hay* and *Hit the Ice* (43); *Lost in a Harem*, at MGM, and *In Society* (44). Their box-office rating slipped to 3rd and 8th in those years, and it was not to be raised by either *Here Come the Co-Eds* or *The Naughty Nineties* (45). Indeed, after the failure of *Bud Abbott and Lou Costello in Hollywood* they would not again be found at MGM, for the studio cancelled their contract. Universal persevered but split them up for plot purposes: *Little Giant* (46), in which Abbott had a double role, and *The Time of Their Lives*, a ghost story. When in doubt, remind the public of their biggest hit: so *Buck Pirates Come Home* (47), but it was now double-bill time – *The Wistful Widow of Wagon Gap* (who was Marjorie Main) and *The Noose Hangs High* (48), produced independently and released by J. Arthur Rank's Eagle-Lion. Universal, though it had shares in some of Rank's British companies, was not best pleased and hurt the films' already slim chances by reissuing several old A and C opuses.

It did, however, confirm that Costello dithered effectively if confronted by a villain or another evil force – he was nothing if not a coward (and nothing near as funny as Bob Hope in the same situation). Thus it was devised that *Abbott and Costello Meet Frankenstein*. That put them back into the Top Ten, so Costello demanded that Universal pay them another $25,000 per film; they were suspended instead, but under the new management almost all the studio's films were losing money and they gave in. Also, a popular new formula seemed to have been found, so after *Mexican Hayride* (based on a Cole Porter musical, with the score now thoughtfully withheld) it was agreed that *Abbott and Costello Meet the Killer, Boris Karloff* – that gentleman being honoured in the title after relenting, for he had refused to be in the earlier film. *Africa Screams* and *Abbott and Costello in the Foreign Legion* (50) returned to the old formula, but *Abbott and Costello Meet the Invisible Man* played safe and used the new one. *Comin' Round the Mountain* had them caught in a Kentucky feud, but Variety declared that their 'fun-making routines have become decidedly wearing'.

By now, *Lost in Alaska* (52), the pictures had become poverty-row efforts and the two tired comedians were entoured by some of the tiredest talents in Hollywood. They turned to Alex Gottlieb, who had signed a lucrative contract at Warners after producing their early hits. He recalled that Laurel and Hardy had once found a new audience with some musicals aimed at younger audiences, so thus:

Jack and the Beanstalk and *Abbott and Costello Meet Captain Kidd*, both filmed in SuperCinecolor, so called because it was not as awful as ordinary Cinecolor. They did not get the children, or anybody, effectively ending their (and Gottleib's) commitment to Warners. In 1953 they played the London Palladium and there began what would be a series of battles with the IRS over unpaid taxes. They were reckoned to be earning $1,750,000 a year, but claimed heavy expenses ($100,000 for material, $175,000 in agents' commission, $40,000 legal fees, $75,000 accountants' fees, $30,000 for travel, $50,000 on entertaining and $10,000 for clothes).

They in turn brought a suit against Universal, alleging unfair practices in the studio's distribution, but they withdrew it when they were offered a new contract – on the theory that their new weekly TV series would bring them a new audience. The critics certainly doubted it and when they made *Abbott and Costello Go to Mars* (53) the 'New York Times' observed (if on a later occasion), 'And about time'. After *Abbott and Costello Meet Dr Jekyll and Mr Hyde* there was talk of a serious film about Mayor La Guardia, *The Fighting Flower*. A mystery surrounds *Fireman Spare My Child*, from which they officially withdrew because Costello was pronounced ill from overwork. They can, however, be recognized in longshot and it has been suggested that his sickness was a ploy to get Universal to help them out of their horrendous financial difficulties. They were, in the event, replaced by Hugh O'Brien and Buddy Hackett – who would play Costello in the 1979 telemovie, *Bud and Lou*. That, based on the biography by Bob Thomas, is one of the better show business movies and perhaps too kind to Abbott, who was an alcoholic (and an epileptic); it certainly did no favours to Costello, pictured as a vicious little bully and the most unedifying individual to star in movies between Charles Ray and Mario Lanza.

Their fee for *Abbott and Costello Meet the Keystone Cops* (55) and *Abbott and Costello Meet the Mummy* was a reported $200,000, plus 50 per cent of the profits – but since these were elusive Universal terminated the agreement. They formed a production company and UA agreed to release *Dance With Me Henry* (56), which added sentimentality (orphaned kids) to their old formula, but there was hardly a trickle to the box-office. Their difficulties with the IRS forced them into a gruelling time on the nightclub/casino circuit, till Abbott turned up drunk once too often and the team split. Costello continued as a single and tried a screen come-back, in *The Thirty-Foot Bride of Candy Rock* (59), but died of a heart attack before it was shown – which was hardly anywhere.

At the time of his death Abbott was suing him for over $222,000 which he claimed was owing him from their TV series; the IRS continued to hound him and he sold his rights to the profits from his films for $100,000. He had a mild stroke in 1964 and died in 1974 without seeing any revival of interest in his work with Costello. Their certified draw at the box-office 1941–44 and 1948–51 is one of the curiosities of movie history.

DON AMECHE

If Don Ameche's early screen work was not highly regarded, it is probably because he appeared in so few first-class films – and because 20th Century-Fox wasted him in vehicles for their singing-and-dancing blondes. Further, his reputation had been dogged by his once inventing the telephone. He was always a cheery fellow and when offered the chance – in *Heaven Can Wait*, in *Midnight* – he was as accomplished a light comedian as movies have known.

He was born (Dominic Amici) in Kenosha, Wisconsin, in 1908, of Italian-German-Irish parentage, and read law at the University of Wisconsin. He made a name in college dramatics and was persuaded by a friend to substitute for one of the leads in a stock company production of 'Excess Baggage' when the actor concerned didn't show up – and that decided him to abandon law. He worked in stock and got the juvenile lead in 'Jerry for Short' in New York; he did a vaudeville tour with Texas Guinan, then was in radio for five years. He married in 1932 Honor Prendergast, whom he met in a church choir; they had five children. In 1935 MGM tested him and were unimpressed, but a year later 20th did so and signed him to a seven-year contract. They gave him *two* important roles in *The Sins of Man* (36) as the sons of Austrian sexton Jean Hersholt, and he impressed the critics.

There followed a series of romantic leads, first in the big-budgeted *Ramona*, which was the fourth feature made in Technicolor – a remake of the old tale about a brave (Ameche) and his half-breed squaw. In *Ladies in Love* Janet Gaynor got him and he was 'brilliant' said 'Picturegoer'; then there was *One in a Million* with Sonja Henie; *Love Is News* (37) – only he lost the girl (as he was to do frequently), Loretta Young, to Tyrone Power (whom he had known since his radio days); *Fifty Roads to Town*, snowbound with Ann Sothern; *You Can't Have Everything*, as a top Broadway figure enamoured of Alice

Alice Faye and Don Ameche were teamed in several films in the late 30s and early 40s. This one is Hollywood Cavalcade (39).

Faye; and *Love Under Fire*, in which Miss Young was a suspected jewel thief and he a Scotland Yard inspector, a crazy comedy set against the Spanish Civil War (top marks for that one). His roles varied, but not the breezy Ameche image: *In Old Chicago* (38) with Faye and Power, as a politician; *Happy Landing* with Henie, as a pilot; and *Alexander's Ragtime Band* where he sang, and actually married Faye before surrendering her to Power – a very good performance in a difficult role.

In *Josette* he vied with Robert Young for Simone Simon, then on her way out as a star at 20th. In *Gateway* Arleen Whelan was on her way in, via Ellis Island, as an Irish

Don Ameche, Paris taxi-driver, and Claudette Colbert, gold-digger, just before she realizes that she loves him, in the immortal Midnight *(39). Made at a time when the world had more on its mind and quickly forgotten, it wasn't till the 60s that it was rediscovered and acknowledged to be one of the most sparkling of Hollywood's comedies, as directed by Mitchell Leisen from a Wilder-Brackett script.*

immigrant; Ameche was a war correspondent. In *The Three Musketeers* (39) he was a dashing D'Artagnan and the Ritz Brothers were the three lackeys, and they all sang. In *Midnight*, at Paramount, he was a Paris taxi-driver who poses as Claudette Colbert's husband – and it's a performance to rank with William Powell and Melvyn Douglas at their best – suave, arrogant, not given to tolerating the heroine's tantrums. Then came the telephone film, with Young and Henry Fonda, *The Story of Alexander Graham Bell*, by no means the least of the Hollywood biopics of that era; and *Hollywood Cavalcade*, where he was an old-time movie director too busy to notice – till the last reel – that Alice Faye loved him. Ameche's next movie combined elements of all his successful pictures – music, nostalgia (as interpreted at that time) and Americana: *Swanee River* (40), a biopic of Stephen Foster, slowly dying of drink. Alice Faye was, however, the focal point of another biopic, *Lillian Russell*, in which he had a smallish role as the pianist who marries her and dies before he can make her the toast of London.

These were the peak years of Ameche's screen career. He was suspended for refusing a loan-out to Paramount for *The Night of January 16*, but he was normally amenable. Thus he got clobbered with *Four Sons*, the remake of John Ford's success, now about a Czech family torn apart by war, updated and anti-Nazi, with Mary Beth Hughes and Eugenie Leontovich; and even less interestingly, the 'nothing' romantic lead of a musical, *Down Argentine Way* with Betty Grable. *That Night in Rio* (41), with Faye, gave him a double role – it was a remake of *Folies-Bergère*, but another remake (of *Three Blind Mice*), *Moon over Miami*, with Grable, completely wasted him. His brisk, urbane approach to his silly lines only emphasized the waste. But a couple of pictures on loan-out restored a flagging reputation: *Kiss the Boys Goodbye*, at Paramount, a musical based on Clare Boothe Luce's witty play sending up the search for Scarlett O'Hara, with him and Oscar Levant trying *not* to discover Mary Martin; *The Feminine Touch* at MGM was a better-than-average marital comedy with Rosalind Russell and Kay Francis. In *Confirm or Deny* he and Joan Bennett were Americans falling in love in the blitz, and in *The Magnificent Dope* (42) he and Fonda were contrasted as city slicker and country cousin. Joan Bennett was his *Girl Trouble*, and *Something To Shout About* (43) at Columbia wasn't, but he sang 'You'd Be So Nice To Come Home To' and other Cole Porter ditties to Janet Blair.

Then came *Heaven Can Wait*, the supreme example of the later Lubitsch touch, from a Broadway play called 'Birthday'. Ameche got his best notices, playing, as Dilys Powell put it, 'with unexpected range of mood'. The piece was fantasy, about a dead man (Ameche) who tries to explain to the devil (Laird Cregar) why he should be sent to hell, but is sent back to earth for a bit. This was a theme in common with the next one, *Happy Land*, about a ghost (Harry Carey) returning to say why he died and why we should go on fighting. It seemed like a good idea at the time. Ameche played the ghost's son, a druggist, and was then a composer in an indifferent musical, *Greenwich Village* (44), knowing no success till his concerto is turned into 'Whispering'. He had little to do as a pilot in *Wing and A Prayer*, a (true) story set on an aircraft carrier, and so can hardly be blamed when he refused 20th's offer to renew his contract.

Freelancing, he distinguished himself by asking for a guest spot in Fred Allen's *It's in the Bag* (45), but most of his subsequent films were weak: *Guest Wife*, a comedy with Claudette Colbert; *So Goes My Love* (46), another, in period dress, with Myrna Loy, in which he was again an inventor. He had a financial interest in both of these, but a third announced along the same lines was never made. Instead he did *That's My Man* (47), a soggy drama about a gambler who's a wow in the stables but a drop-out in the boudoir. Catherine McLeod played the long-suffering wife, one of two expensive efforts by Republic to make her into a big star (the other was *Concerto* with Philip Dorn). After that, not unexpectedly, Ameche turned to murder in a lower-case thriller, *Sleep My Love* (48): wife Colbert was the intended victim and he was very suave about it. His last film in a long while was the minor – but good – *Slightly French* (49), as an impresario promoting Dorothy Lamour. Then, as he said later, 'I was through'; it had been a 'terrible mistake' to turn down that contract, though he added that in any given subsequent year he earned more than he needed to live on.

In 1951 he turned to TV, and he later signed with an independent company, Princess Pictures, to do a couple of Bs, *Phantom Caravan* (54), as a detective, and *Fire One* (55). In 1955 he had a big hit in New York with Cole Porter's 'Silk Stockings': audiences found him in person a master of the light comedy/songs business. He was even better in 'Goldilocks' (58), a delightful spoof on Silent movies with Elaine Stritch. For a long time he ran a TV programme on international circuses, and he appeared in a documentary about them called *Rings Around the World* (66). Meanwhile, looking very distinguished, he played a senator in *A Fever in the Blood* (61), which starred Efrem Zimbalist Jr, and he graced a silly B chiller, *Picture Mommy Dead* (66), as the father of a girl who has a strange effect on her new stepmother (Martha Hyer). He had a supporting role again in a tele-movie, *Shadow Over Elveron* (68), in which a doctor (James Franciscus) fought local corruption. More welcome were appearances in *Suppose They Gave a War and Nobody Came* (70) and Disney's *The Boatnicks*, in both as a commanding officer. Another tele-movie, and another outing for the movies' one-time teenage moppet, found him married to Joan Bennett: *Gidget Gets Married* (72).

His only notable work in a while was a tour of the musical 'Good News' (75) reunited with Faye, who had been starring in it on Broadway; but Hollywood again beckoned – for *Trading Places* (83), when Ray Milland was unable to do it (because of his terminal illness). Ameche was partnered by Ralph Bellamy, as the old codgers who replace smart yuppie Dan Ackroyd with street hobo Eddie Murphy. The film was not only immensely popular but from Ameche's point of view drew attention to his practised comedic skills. His career was revitalized and he was topbilled (if for alphabetical reasons) in another box-office success, *Cocoon* (85), with Gwen Verdon as his wife and Hume Cronyn, Wilford Bramley and Jack Gilford as other Florida 'oldies' rejuvenated by sci-fi means. The Best Supporting Oscar he received was not only for sentimental reasons. He co-starred with Bob Hope in a tele-movie, *A Masterpiece of Murder* (86) and then with John Lithgow in *Harry and the Hendersons* (87), playing a doctor in this weak E.T. clone made by the *E.T.* producers, Amblin.

His new career suffered a setback when the money ran out on *Single Room*, where he and Shelley Winters were two of the occupants, but then he and George C. Scott were *Pals*, a telemovie about two ex-army buddies who find a small fortune – and he was offered another of these in David Mamet's *Things Change* (88), playing an elderly Sicilian shoe-shine who agrees to go to jail for a gangster lookalike: the film was basically about a weekend spent in Lake Tahoe with his minder (Joe Mantegna) and it brought him a Best Actor award at the Venice Festival, as well as superb notices. On either side of that he reprised two recent roles: in *Coming to America* he and Bellamy reprised their double-act, as guest stars, for the benefit of Mr Murphy; and he was in *Cocoon: The Return*, despite his distaste for the script, but he felt it ungracious to turn it down after receiving the Oscar. He said in the same interview: 'The camera was kind to me. But I was never a screen personality like Gable or

Flynn. The camera did something with their faces that was special . . . I'd listen; that was what it was all about. Listen as hard as you can and be totally honest in trying to be that individual, trying to *think* like that individual.' In 1989 he returned to Broadway, taking over the role of the stage manager in a revival of 'Our Town'.

FATTY ARBUCKLE

Roscoe 'Fatty' Arbuckle was the victim of the first major scandal involving cinema stars. Had he been tall, dark and handsome, it is just conceivable that he might eventually have weathered it, but he was round and clumsy and rather foolish on the screen. He was not unlovable, and his fun, if not subtle, was inventive, but whereas Fatty on the screen chasing a girl was coy and endearingly vulgar, Fatty in real life at the same game – in admittedly more lurid circumstances – was quite unforgivable. Thus the moon-faced, gentle loon faded away.

Fatty usually chased the girl, in this case Harriet Hammond, until she became interested – and then he wasn't quite sure what to do. The film is Leap Year, *released in Europe in 1922, but due to the Arbuckle 'scandal' not publicly seen in the US.*

Arbuckle was born in 1887 in Smith Center, Kansas; the family moved to Santa Ana, California, and the boy Arbuckle sang at local socials. Stage-struck, he worked with a touring company in nearby San José. He would have done anything to stay in show business, and he did; he collected tickets, sang ballads in a nickelodeon, did a black-face act in vaudeville; he had a double-act with Leon Errol for a year and when it broke up, he struggled on solo and turned to other things when he could not get bookings. About 1907 he appeared in some one-and two-reelers for the Selíg Co., and little is known of this time except that in his first film he supported Tom Santschi. He returned to vaudeville and in 1913 applied to Mack Sennett for a job in his Keystone comedies, just then in their first flush of fame. Sennett was not impressed; Arbuckle danced a bit and did some back flips, but Sennett had an odd fancy that the public might find a fat policeman funny, so he made him a Keystone Cop at $3 a day: *In the Clutches of the Gang*. After that, Sennett liked him enough to feature him in a funny bucolic comedy, *Passions He Had Three*.

The company Arbuckle joined consisted of popular comics such as Mabel Normand, Fred Mace, Ford Sterling, Al St John and Minta Durfee (to whom Arbuckle was later married); among the later arrivals was Chaplin, who quickly went to the fore. Arbuckle can be seen in several Chaplin shorts, e.g. *Tango Tangles*, *His Favourite Pastime* and *The Rounders* (14). When Chaplin left the studio, Sennett decided to promote the team of Arbuckle and Normand as a replacement, and they quickly became popular. Here are some of the many titles: *Fatty and Mabel's Simple Life* (15), *Mabel and Fatty's Wash Day*, *Mabel and Fatty's Married Life*, *The Little Teacher*, *Fatty's Flirtation*, *Fatty and Mabel Adrift* (16) and *Fickle Fatty's Fall*. The last film they did together was *The Bright Lights*.

In 1917 Joseph Schenck lured Arbuckle away by promising him his own company, and in the two-reelers he now made Arbuckle went on to a greater popularity. Buster Keaton, who joined him during this time, found him 'conscientious, hard-working, intelligent and eager to please . . . He would invent priceless routines and also had a well-developed directorial sense.' Most of these Arbuckle produced and directed: *A Reckless Romeo*, *Rough House* (17), *His Wedding Night*, *Oh Doctor!*, *Out West*, *The Bell Boy* (18), *A Desert Hero* and *The Garage* (19). There are others: many are primitive, and the quality varies.

Famous Players-Lasky distributed, and they now made a bid for Arbuckle's services, offering the same creative freedom. The matter was resolved by him remaining with Schenck, who guaranteed him $1,500 a week, with an additional $3,000 a week from the studio and 25 per cent of the profits of the company jointly owned, Comique. Like the other clowns, he was moving gingerly into features. The first (not full-length) was *The Round-Up* (20) and it was followed by *The Life of the Party* (cruelly ironic title), *Brewster's Millions* (21), *Dollar a Year Man*, *A Travelling Salesman* and *Gasoline Gus*.

Then, in September 1921, Arbuckle went to a party in a San Francisco hotel and a girl died, a bit-player and girl-around-Hollywood called Virginia Rappe. Arbuckle was accused of rape and worse, on the evidence of something the girl said while dying in hospital ('He hurt me, Roscoe hurt me'). Arbuckle claimed that he had merely placed some ice on her thigh after she was taken sick. His friends believed him. And so did the juries: he was tried three times for manslaughter and eventually acquitted. The press victimized him and the public wrote abusive letters to his studio. Exhibitors boycotted his films in the US and Britain; feeling was so strong that his studio – although it had $500,000 bound up in unshown Arbuckle films – was powerless. Friends stood by him, like Lew Cody; Schenck paid his legal fees and invited him to rejoin Comique, now renamed Buster Keaton Productions, guaranteeing him 35 per cent of all profits of all films made. Nothing came of this, but in 1923 Schenck formed a new company for him, Reel Comedies Inc, capitalized at $200,000 and financed equally by Keaton, Metro, Paramount, Goldwyn, Universal and Educational, with the last-named also distributing. Again, no more was heard of this venture – perhaps because, as Keaton sadly noted in his memoir, Arbuckle was not funny any more.

Keaton was one of many friends who stood by him, and in 1924 he engaged him to direct *Sherlock Jr*, but he found the changed Arbuckle so difficult that he got him off the lot by persuading Marion Davies to take him on to direct *The Red Mill*. Arbuckle's name was still such anathema to the public that the film (and a couple of others he did) was credited to William B. Goodrich – a corruption of the punning Will B. Good. His wife, who had remained with him through his troubles, divorced him in 1925; he returned to vaudeville, but attracted only curiosity-seekers. In 1927 he toured in a farce, 'Baby Mine', and in 1928 was booed in Paris. He remarried, and in 1932 contracted with Warner Bros to make 12 short comedies. Some were made and shown without opposition in the US but British exhibitors had longer memories and banned the first to arrive, *Hey*

Pop! The series might have been abandoned had Arbuckle not died in 1933, but those that survive (*Buzzin' Around, In the Dough, How've You Been?* etc.) suggest that contemporary thumbs-down was based on prejudice.

GEORGE ARLISS

George Arliss had two screen careers. The second began triumphantly with *Disraeli* and Mordaunt Hall of the 'New York Times' enthusing about 'an artistry and vigor that is a joy to behold'. Five years later and Mr Hall finds that in *The House of Rothschild* he 'outshines any performance he has contributed to the screen'. It was not only the 'New York Times': everyone thought he was the cat's whiskers. He was generally referred to as 'The First Gentleman of the Screen' and not merely because of the condescending manner and the monocle he sported. Of course, it was classy – playing a series of historical characters, even if the plots of the films required him to do little more than play Cupid to the juveniles. If in fact his artistry and vigour are undeniable, they are used monotonously and with a smugness which exceeds even that of Meryl Streep. Arliss too – still today – has his admirers, but most modern commentators find him hammy, not so much (perhaps) in the tradition of Irving as of some saloon-bar declaimer; that he should have been accepted above virtual contemporaries such as Edmund Gwenn and H.B. Warner must remain among the miracles of the movies.

Arliss was born in London in 1868, the son of a printer-publisher. He worked for his father for a while, but was so keen on the stage that he started his own amateur company; he turned pro as a super in a production at the Elephant and Castle of 'Saved From the Sea'. His first West End appearance was in 'Across Her Path' (90); he worked in musical comedy for a while and was later engaged by Mrs Patrick Campbell for her company. He made his first West End success in 'Mr and Mrs Daventry' in 1900, but the following year accompanied Mrs Pat to the US, and stayed there. He had success in 'The Second Mrs Tanqueray' and 'The Notorious Mrs Ebbsworth', and worked for David Belasco in 'The Darling of the Gods' and with Mrs Fiske's company in 'Becky Sharp' (as Steyne) and 'Hedda Gabler' (as Brack), among other plays. His first starring role – he was upped from feature-billing after the first night – was in Ferenc Molnar's 'The Devil' in New York in 1908; and he had other great hits: 'Disraeli' (11), 'Paganini', 'Alexander Hamilton' (17), and 'The Green Goddess' (21), which he played in both London and New York.

He was persuaded to immortalize some of these performances: *The Devil* and *Disraeli* (21). He also made *The Ruling Passion* (22), a lesson that work is more beneficial to millionaires than medicine, and *The Man Who Played God*, about a musician who becomes embittered with deafness but finds comfort in philanthropy. He reprised his role in *The Green Goddess* (23), and in *Twenty Dollars a Week* (24) he was a man who disguises himself as a clerk in order to make a man of his son. But in all these films his presence was more prestigious than effective. In 1924, he scored again in 'Old English' and a few years later was an admired Shylock. It was his last stage appearance.

Among the slew of photographed plays thrown up by Sound, Warner Bros came up with *Disraeli* (29), with Arliss recreating his famous part and his wife, Florence Montgomery (or Arliss), also cast. As with his other historical films he spent less time politicking than playing cupid to the juveniles. The film was a great artistic and financial success (it ran a record 10 weeks in London) and was awarded the 'Photoplay' Gold Medal as the year's outstanding film; it also brought Arliss an Oscar for the year's Best Actor. Because of the way the Oscar voting was then done, he also got some votes for *The Green Goddess* (30), as the wily potentate into whose hands

George Arliss in Disraeli *(29), the film that established him as the Finest Actor of the Talking Screen and as a top box-office draw.*

fall a party saved from an air-crash – both film and performance ludicrous, but such was the thrall of the 'Theatre' that this ageing trouper was accepted as 'The Finest Actor on the Screen' by the readers of 'Movie Fan' magazine, who voted him such. Readers of 'John Bull' magazine voted him Second Most Popular Cinema Artist, after Chaplin (and before, in descending order, Ronald Colman, Marie Dressler, Janet Gaynor, Norma Shearer, Clive Brook and Garbo). Warners paid him a salary of $10,000 a week, a figure only equalled elsewhere by Marion Davies, and enthusiastically rushed him into: *Old English*, as Galsworthy's hedonist; *The Millionaire* (31), a remake of *The Ruling Passion*, with his wife; *Alexander Hamilton*, though too old for the role; and, another remake, *The Man Who Played God* (32), at his most restrained. There followed: a comedy, *A Successful Calamity*; *The King's Vacation* (33), a Ruritanian story with his wife; *The Working Man*, about a tycoon who anonymously gets a job in his rival's factory and straightens things out; and *Voltaire*. At this point Warners announced that they were releasing Arliss from his contract due to the difficulties of finding subjects, but that they hoped he would work for them again.

When Darryl F. Zanuck left Warners to found his own company, 20th, he took Arliss with him for three films and, as if to prove that you can't have too much of a good thing, cast him as two members of *The House of Rothschild*, which had a last sequence in colour and was one of the top hits of 1934. But critics were now carping. Lionel Collier: '. . . . he is apt to be mannerized and, in every characterization he gives, presents a good deal of Arliss.' Still, he was *The Last Gentleman* for 20th, a comedy about an old man's revenge on his greedy family – to be exacted after his death. He went to Britain to make a film for Gaumont-British, *The Iron Duke* (35), and as Wellington he was, it was generally agreed, 'miscast'. After a trip to Hollywood for *Cardinal Richelieu*, he returned to Britain to take up his career there, on a two-year GB contract.

Sir Michael Balcon, then head of GB, stated in 'A Lifetime of Films' that this was against his wishes. 'Bluntly, he [Arliss] had that exaggerated self-importance which is just pomposity . . . and he certainly tried to convey the idea that he was conferring a great favour on us to be working at all. His contract called for very substantial payments, in fact, more than we had ever paid to an artist, yet by the time he came to us the Arliss novelty was beginning to wear off. . . .' Balcon admitted he resented the favourable conditions of the Arliss contract and also that the GB films

were not good: *The Guv'nor* (Arliss was unconvincing as a tramp), *The Tunnel* (special 'courtesy artist', playing the British prime minister) and *East Meets West* (36), a virtual repeat of his performance in *The Green Goddess*, right up to the jewel in the turban. He started on a historical film called *The Nelson Touch*, but it was abandoned – just before 'Picturegoer' said: 'The Arliss historical portrait gallery has become an international joke.' A plan to play Shylock was abandoned when the other Shakespeare films failed. Instead, he did the minor *The Man of Affairs, His Lordship* (in a dual role) and *Dr Syn* (37), a picturization of Russell Thorndike's novel with a parson-by-day/smuggler-by-night hero. Few of these were widely distributed in the US (as GB had hoped, when agreeing to Arliss's terms) and as his star had set in Britain, too, the contract was not renewed. He refused further offers as his wife was going blind and he preferred to stay with her. He died in 1946, monocled to the last. His nephew, Leslie Arliss, was a British director of the 40s.

JEAN ARTHUR

The coming of the Talkies brought into Hollywood an influx of stage-trained actors and actresses, more 'real' not only because they spoke. That they wise-cracked inevitably made them seem more in touch with modern life; and the mood of the Depression required stars who were tough, resilient and supremely capable. This new breed of stars was a remarkable event in the history of Hollywood – indeed, today it looks miraculous. Yet, amidst the brightest new names imported from Broadway were three girls who had been in films for years without getting anywhere specific. They were Myrna Loy, Carole Lombard and Jean Arthur. They were not at all alike – except in skill – and it would be impossible to confuse them. The thing about the great stars is that they were/are all highly individual; at the same time these three shared attributes with each other and with the other fine comediennes of the time. They were warm and loyal to their leading men but never taken in; were more at ease in restaurants and honking city streets than in nightclubs or boudoirs; they moved quickly to keep up with their men and spoke to them crisply and incisively; they were men's equals, but regarded the world with less illusion.

Loy never lost her cool – Lombard did. Lombard delighted in outraging people – Loy never. Jean Arthur didn't abide by such rules. She was Miss Average American, usually a shop girl or secretary, with blonde good looks and a ready smile; and above all, perhaps, a fetching husky voice, childishly querulous at one moment, deeply reassuring the next. It never left you in doubt and was curiously touching when she was sentimental or wistful; and very cheering when she was in high spirits.

She was born in New York in 1905. Her father was a professional photographer and while still at school she began modelling for photographers. Inevitably, one advert came to the attention of a Fox talent scout, and she was screen-tested. A year's contract followed – and 10 years of small parts. At Fox, initially, she was the heroine's best friend in John Ford's *Cameo Kirby* (23), but was sufficiently unimpressive to be demoted from a leading role to a mere apparition as a bathing beauty in the next, *The Temple of Venus*. She finished the contract on the receiving end of a series of custard pies, uncertain whether to stay in Hollywood – but she found work easily in slapstick shorts and in B Westerns produced by minor companies like Artclass and FBO: *Fast and Fearless* (24), *The Drugstore Cowboy* (25), *Tearin' Loose, A Man of Nerve, Thundering Through* (26), *The Hurricane Horseman, The Fighting Cheat, The Cowboy Cop* and *Twisted Triggers*. She was also in *The College Boob* and *The Block Signal*. 1927 saw a certain amelioration, with leading parts in two films for Tiffany – *Husband Hunters* and *Broken Gates* – and three for Pathé – *Horse Shoes* and *Flying Luck*, in both as Monty Banks's girl, and *Born to Battle*. And in *The Poor Nut* that year, cast as a co-ed, she was spotted by Paramount and placed under contract. Before arriving there she was in *The Masked Menace* a serial, and *Wallflowers* (28).

Stills of her at this time show her as a squirrel-like creature, with a timid expression and dark bobbed hair. She was certain she could not act, and her early parts at Paramount were of little consequence, starting with *Warming Up* as Richard Dix's love interest; as ditto for George K. Arthur in MGM's *Brotherly Love*; as Jannings's daughter in *Sins of the Fathers* (29); *The Canary Murder Case*, made in Silent and Talkie versions; and *Stairs of Sand*, a Western. Through *The Mysterious Dr Fu Manchu* (with Warner Oland in the title role), *The Greene Murder Case* (as a murderess – a part intended for Ruth Chatterton) and Clara Bow's *The Saturday Night Kid* (a good comedy about salesgirls, in which she was the bad sister). She accustomed herself to filming with Sound. She went on marking time through *Half-Way to Heaven*, where she and Charles 'Buddy' Rogers were partners on a tightrope: a melo-

drama called *Street of Chance* (30) in a subsidiary role; William A. Wellman's *Young Eagles*; *Paramount on Parade* and *The Return of Dr Fu Manchu*. She was not good. In most of her parts she was at best insipid, and films like *The Silver Horde* were no help: she was the priggish ingénue who loses Joel McCrea to Evelyn Brent at her most worldly and Barbara-Stanwyckish in this fishing drama. Also at RKO she was in *Danger Lights*; then she returned to Paramount for two last films, a comedy with Jack Oakie, *The Gang Buster* (31) and a melodrama with Clive Brook, *The Lawyer's Secret*. There was an offer to do two comedies at Universal, *The Virtuous Husband* ('Jean Arthur has all the requisite "It" as a disappointed wife' said 'Picturegoer') and *Ex-Bad Boy*. The latter was based on the silent *The Whole Town's Talking*, about a blameless man (Robert Armstrong) who invents a past to impress his fiancée; Lola Lane played a movie star called Letta Larbo.

Arthur thought it essential to learn to act if she wanted to stay in the business, and went back to New York to do stage work, announcing that she was quitting films. She later said that these years were the happiest of her life. She also married a Broadway producer, Frank J. Ross Jr, who later became a Hollywood producer (they were divorced in 1949). She also did stock. Among these East Coast plays were 'Foreign Affairs', 'The Man Who Reclaimed His Head' with Claude Rains, and 'The Curtain Rises', and she received nice notices for all of them. Hence, perhaps, she returned to the screen with greater assurance, but *Get That Venus* (33) gave very few patrons a chance to find out: a cheap (in every sense) comedy, made by a company called Regent, it got almost no bookings. At RKO she played an actress, a supporting role, in *The Past of Mary Holmes*, a remake of *The Goose Woman*, and at Columbia she was Jack Holt's daughter in a melodrama, *Whirlpool* (34). The latter won her a long-term contract with Columbia.

The first two for her new studio sank without trace: *The Defense Rests* as the assistant of lawyer Holt; and *The Most Precious Thing in Life*, a drama of mother-love (she is a cleaning woman at a boys' school and guess who is in one of the dormitories). But *The Whole Town's Talking* (35) was one of the year's funniest comedies. John Ford directed, with Edward G. Robinson in the dual role of mild little clerk and ruthless mobster. Arthur was the clerk's self-reliant co-worker, who starts by pitying him, then encourages him and finally falls in love with him. It was the sort of part she was to make her own – and this was the first occasion she showed her mature comedy style. Columbia found her less

The face of Jean Arthur in the 20s . . .

and in the 30s.

9

Bored society wife Jean Arthur falls in love with headwaiter Charles Boyer in Frank Borzage's History Is Made at Night *(37).*

easy to handle thereafter; she had script and director approval, and exercising this privilege led to tears and tantrums, fights and suspensions. There can be no doubt that she was right: her early Columbia films were not a patch on those she elected to do for other studios and the later ones, when she was Queen of the Lot, are classics of the period. *Public Hero No. 1* (MGM) was an exciting G-man thriller, with Arthur as a gangster's sister who falls for the cop, Chester Morris; *Party Wife* was a bland small-town picture, co-starring Victor Jory; *Diamond Jim* was a Universal biopic, with Edward Arnold as Jim Brady and Arthur in a dual role as two of the women in his life; *The Public Menace* was a

programmer – gangsters and George Murphy; and *If You Could Only Cook* a mild Depression comedy about a penniless girl and a sad tycoon (Herbert Marshall) who masquerade as domestic servants.

Her notices were consistently good, but Columbia were surprised when their prize director, Frank Capra, insisted on her for his next film: to play the cynical sob-sister out to 'get' country cousin Gary Cooper on his first visit to New York. Charmed by his naïvety, sickened by the opportunism of his opponents, she changed sides. The result was amusing and in every way memorable: *Mr Deeds Goes to Town* (36). Capra always referred to her, along with Barbara Stanwyck,

Only Angels Have Wings (39). Jean Arthur listens, with Thomas Mitchell and Allyn Joslyn, as airline operator Cary Grant radios instructions to a pilot in difficulty.

as his favourite actress. She was *The Ex-Mrs Bradford* (RKO), a comedy-mystery, matched with William Powell, and she was very hot property, but the best Columbia could do for her was *Adventure in Manhattan*, a crook comedy with Joel McCrea. She was Calamity Jane at Paramount in *The Plainsman*, with Cooper as Wild Bill Hickok, but Columbia then lumbered her with *More Than a Secretary*, with George Brent. At UA, she was a bored wife in love with head-waiter Charles Boyer in a delicious ship-board comedy, *History Is Made at Night* (37) – but the history made was a shipwreck which changed the farce to tragedy. *Easy Living* (Paramount) was 100 per cent farce, a witty concoction by Preston Sturges about a penniless stenographer who is installed in a penniless hotel because the hotel management think she is wealthy Edward Arnold's mistress.

Then she quarrelled bitterly with Columbia and was off the screen for almost a year: the matter was resolved with a new three-year contract, two films a year. Her comeback film was outstanding: *You Can't Take It With You* (38), a Broadway comedy about a crazy family, bought for a record sum by Columbia and entrusted to Frank Capra. Around this time, she told an interviewer that though she loved acting, she hated being a star. Stars, she said, owed a duty to the public: 'It's a strenuous job to have to live up to the way you look on the screen every day of your life.' *Only Angels Have Wings* (39) was another big success, an aviation drama directed by Howard Hawks at his most adroit, with Arthur as a stranded showgirl at first indifferent towards Cary Grant and later yearning – she was at her most independent, tender and entrancing. Capra again directed her in *Mr Smith Goes to Washington* and this time she rooted for hick politician James Stewart the way she had rooted for Gary Cooper. *Too Many Husbands* (40) was a beguiling version of Somerset Maugham's farce, 'Home and Beauty', with Melvyn Douglas and Fred MacMurray, and *Arizona*, obviously, was a Western. *The Devil and Miss Jones* (41) was yet another good comedy, about a salesgirl who reforms crotchety boss Charles Coburn (not, of course, knowing who he is). She made two comedies for George Stevens, *The Talk of the Town* (42) caught between Cary Grant and Ronald Colman and the better *The More the Merrier* (43), about overcrowded Washington, with Joel McCrea – for which she received her sole Oscar nomination; director Stevens later described her as 'one of the greatest comediennes the screen has ever seen'. Her husband was now at RKO and he borrowed her for *A Lady Takes a Chance*, a funny comedy with John Wayne. Then she did

The Impatient Years (44) with Lee Bowman, the one about the wartime couple who marry and are strangers when reunited. She was 'rather tiresome' said 'Picturegoer', and who wouldn't have been?

That completed her contract and, according to Bob Thomas in his biography of Columbia boss Harry Cohn, the day her contract finished she ran around the set whooping with joy. Thomas also said of her: 'Miss Arthur's was an evanescent personality, shining with brilliance before the cameras and fading into timidity in her private life.' It had been known for some time that she was considering retiring; she had been uncooperative with the press and difficult about personal appearances. It would appear that, at the height of her career, shyness did overcome all other considerations. During the remainder of the 40s, she studied philosophy, anthropology and sociology – and did one film and one play. The play was 'Born Yesterday' (45) and she turned down *Anna and the King of Siam* to do it; but during the out-of-town tour her nerves failed and the part went to Judy Holliday. The film was Wilder's fine *A Foreign Affair* (48), the first of a three-picture deal at Paramount. She played a prim Congresswoman investigating GI morale in Berlin, and especially John Lund's – and quite outclassed Dietrich as her rival.

In 1950 she had a great success on Broadway in 'Peter Pan', in which she invested; there was an Equity dispute when she insisted on a holiday after a bout of voice trouble. In 1952 Paramount despaired of satisfying her and dissolved the contract, paying her $200,000 in compensation rather than the $300,000 due for the two other pictures. Then, at Paramount, George Stevens insisted upon her to play the homesteading wife of Van Heflin in *Shane* (53). In 1954 she was on a pre-Broadway tour of 'Saint Joan', but it never got there because she became ill: she said later she thought this due to differences with the director, Harold Clurman. 'Picturegoer', earlier, at the time of her come-back in *Shane*, had observed that she was an actress continually needing reassurance and that she was subject to crying bouts – one once lasted three days. After years of silence, she did an episode in TV's 'Gunsmoke' and apparently liked it so much that she agreed to do a TV series. She played a lawyer in 'The Jean Arthur Show' in 1966 but it did not run. The following year she invested and was about to star in 'The Freaking out of Stephanie Blake', but a few days before the Broadway opening, the project was cancelled after some previews: Arthur herself said the play was rewritten for the worst, and her confidence sapped.

Later she taught drama at Vassar; in a rare

interview in 1972 she disclosed that she still received Hollywood offers: two she had recently turned down were the Ida Lupino role in *Junior Bonner* and the lady missionary in *Lost Horizon*.

In 1975 she co-starred with Henry Fonda in 'The First Monday in October' – in Cleveland. By the time the play reached Washington her role was being played by Jane Alexander.

FRED ASTAIRE

Within a couple of years of making his first movie, Fred Astaire had acquired legendary status. Gene Kelly called him 'one of the blessed' and on another occasion prophesied that '50 years from now, the only one of today's dancers who will be remembered is Fred Astaire'; and while Kelly's own contribution to the screen musical has been superlative, Astaire was usually just that much in front. He was a pleasing light comedian and a convincing actor; all his work was informed by charm, elegance, precision and grace, but nothing so much as his dancing – once described by André Sennwald in the 'New York Times' (discussing *Roberta*) as 'not only an aesthetic excitement but comedy of a unique and lofty order'. He sang in a thin, reedy voice, but to some observers, like Oscar Levant, 'he is the best singer of songs the movie world ever knew'; certainly, no one, except Ethel Merman, had as many classic popular songs written expressly for him.

His name has also found its way into dozens of songs, usually as a synonym for lightness and ease – 'the nimble treat of the feet of Fred Astaire' (Cole Porter's 'You're the Top'), but a different approach was made by Lorenz Hart ('Do It the Hard Way' from 'Pal Joey') – 'Fred Astaire just works so hard. . . .' Astaire's rehearsing was famous: probably no Hollywood actor worked so hard. 'Puttin' on the Ritz', for instance, in *Blue Skies*, demanded five weeks of back-breaking physical work. He was a lifelong professional.

His father, an ex-Viennese called Austerlitz, was in the beer business in Omaha, Nebraska, when Fred was born in 1899. Fred began dancing lessons at five, along with his sister Adele, and they acquired a renown in local church halls. Two years later, their mother took them to New York and enrolled them in a bigger dancing school; via school recitals, the two Astaires were offered their first pro engagement, in Keyport, NJ. Over the next few years, they toured in vaudeville (their mother schooled them) and appeared in James Kirkwood's short, *Fanchon the Cricket* (15). They were eventually offered a spot in a Broadway musical, 'Over the Top' (16), followed by others in 'The Passing Show of 1918', 'Apple Blossoms' (19) and 'The Love Letter' (21). Their first big success was in a show written for them, 'For Goodness Sake' (22), which they took to London under the title 'Stop Flirting'. Gershwin wrote 'Lady Be Good' and then 'Funny Face' (27) for them, and both shows had happy seasons in both cities. After a so-so effort, 'Smiles' (30), they had another hit, 'The Band Wagon' (31), but Adele was preparing to marry into the British aristocracy and planned to retire. Fred alone – and not without qualms – went into Cole Porter's 'The Gay Divorce', and then asked his agent to negotiate for a film contract. (Paramount at one time had been mulling over 'Funny Face' as a film, with the Astaires; and they had done a Vitagraph short in 1931.)

Goldwyn signed Astaire but released him after a few months. RKO jumped at the chance of getting the illustrious Astaire; they were planning a spectacular musical, *Flying Down to Rio*, and a Broadway song-and-dance man seemed a good choice for lead Gene Raymond's sidekick. However, it was not ready and he was loaned to MGM to appear as himself in *Dancing Lady* (33), in a guest spot with Joan Crawford. He then did the musical at RKO, *Flying Down to Rio*, fifth-billed, and did a dance with the fourth-billed Ginger Rogers – whom he had known as a showgirl in New York. Both of them seemed to be in the film as an afterthought, but their dance – 'The Carioca' – brought them great notices. Astaire was not happy with the way he looked and thought he had no future in films, but his notices for *Rio* and its success (a record-breaking three weeks at Radio City Music Hall) persuaded him to sign a long-term contract with RKO. They recalled him from London where he was doing 'The Gay Divorce', and they filmed that as *The Gay Divorcée* (34). Diana Wynyard was originally announced as his partner and Astaire was appalled when she was replaced by Rogers, whom he thought miscast as an upper-crust English divorcée. The reception, however, brought about a third teaming, supporting the studio's biggest star, Irene Dunne, in Jerome Kern's *Roberta* (35), he as a bandleader and she as a girl he had known back when, but now posing as a Polish countess. And that led to a revamp of the marital misunderstandings of *The Gay Divorcée*, called *Top Hat*, with music by Irving Berlin. C.A. Lejeune wrote: 'The tonic appearances of young Mr Fred Astaire in dancing comedy – top hat, white tie, tails, and all the rest of it – are, to me, amongst the greatest joys of the modern cinema. It doesn't much matter where, why, or in what story he

*Fred Astaire and Ginger
Rogers in* Roberta *(35),
dancing to one of Jerome
Kern's most beautiful
melodies, 'Smoke Gets in
Your Eyes', though it is
sung in the film by Irene
Dunne.*

*Bottom left, Astaire and
Judy Garland in* Easter
Parade *(48), which he
regards as one of the 'high
spots of enjoyment' in his
career. Bottom right,
Leslie Caron was ballet-
trained, and one of
Astaire's favourite
partners:* Daddy Longlegs
(55).

happens along . . . the engaging thing about Mr Astaire's dancing is the effect of spontaneity. No one, of course, can round off a formal dance number like "Top Hat" or "Isn't This a Lovely Day?" with more neatness and style. . . . Fred Astaire may not be in the leading ranks of the screen's great lovers, its foremost thespians, or even its golden-voiced singers. He is, however, one of the most talented and tonic personalities with a genius for making people happy, and the cinema would be poorer without him by a very long way'.

The public concurred with the critics: *The Gay Divorcée* was one of the top money-makers in 1934, and *Top Hat* and *Roberta* were second and third respectively the following year, when the Astaire-Rogers team were voted the fourth biggest draw. As a team, they balanced each other: he was debonair, an unassuming and somewhat innocent man-about-town, bent on winning her chivalrously if possible, but if not, not. She was a bright, sassy and suspicious, her chorine background somewhat shaded by his interest. He gave her class and she gave him sex-appeal (as a studio executive admitted). Both seemed delightful people, humorous, intelligent and charming; but what made the films so popular with contemporary audiences was their gaiety and the dance routines (it has been suggested that the cinema screen was invented expressly for Astaire to gambol on it). When he whisked her into a dance, it was in a natural way: they did not need a back-stage excuse or a hundred grand pianos whirling in the background. Their artistry was considerable, and so were the songs. None of this has dated. The plots creak today, with their mistaken identities and disguises, but aided or hindered by the likes of Helen Broderick, Eric Blore and Edward Everett Horton, they pass the time between the dances.

Astaire worked horribly hard on the dances, with choreographer Hermes Pan till Rogers took over towards the end of the rehearsal period; he knew that the best Broadway composers wrote the songs, but he did not care for some of the scripts and he did not think his salary commensurate with the money his films were making, for it was a modest $1,500 a week plus another $500 when he was actually working. A new contract was negotiated, with details not announced. Later it was said that he and Rogers were earning $150,000 per film (though she made two more a year than he did) and one source speculated that he was getting a huge $400,000 per picture, in compensation for being shackled in the partnership that now did *Follow the Fleet* (36), with music again by Berlin, and *Swing Time*, with the music this time by Kern. In the former he was a sailor involved in an off-again on-again affair with showgirl Rogers; in the latter he was a dancer and she a dancing instructress. It was directed by George Stevens, who insisted on a visual elegance to match that which Astaire naturally had. It is easily the best of their films, and so went contemporary opinion, though Astaire, according to his 1959 memoir, 'Steps in Time', did not agree. He balked again at a further reteaming and was mollified by the offer of 10 per cent of the films' profit, but only agreed to do *Shall We Dance?* (37) provided *A Damsel in Distress* was not Ginger. The Gershwins wrote the scores for both, immensely helping frail little stories, respectively about a Russian ballet dancer pursuing a musical comedy queen and an American chasing an English heiress: she was played by a non-dancer, Joan Fontaine, to avoid comparisons, and Burns and Allen were joyfully included to bolster the box-office. P.G. Wodehouse had written the story, Stevens again directed – and of its kind, it was masterly. The score of the first of these contains the only song Astaire and Rogers sang to each other, 'They All Laughed' (apart from the duet, 'A Fine Romance', in *Swing Time*); the loveliest song in the score, 'They Can't Take That Away From Me' he sings to Rogers, but he *dances* it, later, with Harriet Hoctor, perhaps as a deliberate snub to Rogers.

Although in 1936 and 1937 Rogers and Astaire as a team were again among the top 10 draws, there had been a falling-off, but RKO had no choice but to reunite them, for the studio was floundering in the red throughout this period – and it no longer had any other major star under exclusive contract. The budget restrictions are evident in *Carefree* (38), which was originally to have been made either wholly or partly Technicolor; and it is less prodigal with its songs – Irving Berlin's – than others in the series. Since Astaire's contract would be up after the next, *The Story of Vernon and Irene Castle* (39), RKO were safe in announcing that it would be the last. It differed from the others in that it utilized a true story, old songs and a backstage plot; also it ended sombrely, with Astaire killed – something the 'New York Times' found 'practically as disconcerting as it would be if Walt Disney were to throw Mickey Mouse to the lions'. The film confirmed Gene Kelly's later observation that 'When Ginger Rogers danced with Astaire, it was the only time in the movies when you looked at the man, not the woman', but RKO did not feel the same way: the studio was happy to help her realize her wish to be a serious actress and let him go off to other fields to seek fresh partners. It would not be easy, because he was, in Rogers's own words, 'a hard taskmaster, a perfectionist. He always got a little cross with me because my concentration was not as dedicated to the projects as his was.' Their producer Pandro S. Berman described their years together as 'six years of mutual agression' and dance director Hermes Pan later observed: 'Except for the times Fred worked with real professional dancers like Cyd Charisse, it was a 25-year war.'

Astaire's name had figured on that list of exhibitors' box-office poison, but MGM thought he might team well with their dancer, Eleanor Powell, who was not shining as brightly as they hoped. Besides, the very title, *Broadway Melody of 1940* (40), had popular appeal. Cole Porter wrote the score and the film did well enough for an independent producer to sign Astaire for *Second Chorus*, which Paramount were to release; the girl was Paulette Goddard and they had only one brief dance together. Hollywood remained unsure that Astaire was a draw without Rogers, but Columbia had under contract a trained dancer who was their new star and she had not yet demonstrated on screen her abilities in that respect: Rita Hayworth and he did team marvellously on *You'll Never Get Rich* (41), a slight tale of a Broadway star who joins the army, with a score by Porter.

At Paramount he and Bing Crosby were rivals in *Holiday Inn* (42), for two ladies without stellar rank, Marjorie Reynolds and Virginia Dale, because the war was on and the studio could not afford four large salaries. But the film, with Berlin's music, was a big success and Columbia reteamed him with Hayworth, this time to Kern's music, in *You Were Never Lovelier*, playing a dancer down on his luck who is employed to 'melt' a frigid South American heiress. It confirmed Astaire's box-office standing and RKO invited him back for *The Sky's the Limit*. Harold Arlen wrote the score, Joan Leslie was the girl and Astaire was a pilot on furlough. James Agee took the occasion to write: '. . . Fred Astaire has a lot, besides his Mozartian abilities as a tap-dancer, which is as great, in its own way, as the best of Chaplin. It is in the walk, the stance, the face, the voice, the cool, bright yet shadowless temper and it would require the invention of a new character, the crystallization of a new cinematic form, to be adequately realized.'

In his memoir Astaire said there were no further offers, ignoring Columbia's overtures for *Cover Girl* with Hayworth, because he did not want to be linked again to any one performer; and at MGM Arthur Freed – responsible for more fine musicals than any other producer – had long cherished a desire to have Astaire under contract there. So

Astaire became one of many star names in *Ziegfeld Follies* (44, released 46), a series of 'turns', of which Astaire had four, one with Gene Kelly and another to the tune of 'Limehouse Blues', which was a big leap forward towards screen ballet (at MGM, Astaire's style moved considerably nearer the balletic): his partner this time, Lucille Bremer, danced with him again in *Yolanda and the Thief* (45). Vincente Minnelli directed both. It was released before the *Follies* and though much of it was imaginative, the whole concept was too whimsical for wide appeal. Also, he looked his age – somewhat older than was expected of a leading man. Paramount needed him for a reunion with Crosby when Broadway's Paul Draper wasn't making out: but *Blue Skies* (46), found him dispirited. It was only too easy to see why Joan Caulfield preferred Bing to him. The bulk of the sons went to Crosby and Astaire may well have decided that if he was going to have to go back to playing the leading-man's sidekick, he might as well give up. MGM were having script trouble with a vehicle for him and Judy Garland, *The Belle of New York*, and, thinking that the Crosby film would be a big one to finish on (it was), he announced his retirement. MGM released him on condition that if he ever decided to return, he would fulfil his commitment to them.

In fact, MGM needed him when Kelly broke an ankle during rehearsals for *Easter Parade* (48); it had a Berlin score and Astaire jumped at the chance of working with Judy Garland. They played a dance team which almost splits up because he works her too hard and does not notice that she is in love with him. The picture was a smash hit, so they were cast in *The Barkleys of Broadway* (49), as a song and dance team threatened with a split because the lady wants to go dramatic: the autobiographical element increased when Garland fell ill and Miss Rogers came in as replacement. The MGM publicity department was delighted and so was Charles Walters, who directed both films: but the atmosphere on the set of this one, he recalled, was anything but cordial: Rogers had only taken the role because no others were being offered and Astaire considered it a step backwards. Nevertheless, the reunion was box-office dynamite as expected. There was no question of him returning to idleness. In 1949 he was given a special Oscar for 'raising the standard' of screen musicals, and he made *Three Little Words* (50), ostensibly the story of songwriters Kalmar and Ruby (Red Skelton was the other), with Vera-Ellen as his partner. At Paramount he did *Let's Dance* which, said Lejeune, 'effectively cancels out Betty Hutton's natural ebullience by teaming her with

Astaire in Ghost Story *(81)*

Irresponsible' was one of the best songs written for Astaire that he never sang – as he recognized when it was auditioned for him (others would be in the score of 'On Your Toes', which Rodgers and Hart had written for him, in the hope of luring him back to Broadway). In 1954 he became a widower (his wife was Phyllis Potter, whom he had married in 1933). 20th planned *Daddy Long Legs* (55) especially for him; but though he liked working with Leslie Caron, they did not jell, they were both too elfin; and the film was meagre with its undoubted charms though the biggest financial success of all his films. The May-September romance was tried again with *Funny Face* (57) fulfilling his commitment to Paramount. The girl was Audrey Hepburn, the tunes were the Gershwins', the settings the Paris fashion world – and as directed by Stanley Donen it was all very *chic*. It was received with rapture and so, to a lesser extent, was *Silk Stockings*, directed by Rouben Mamoulian from a Broadway show (Cole Porter's), based on *Ninotchka* – with Cyd Charisse in that role. It did not do very well and, with musicals supposedly out of fashion, Astaire turned to TV and did a series of spectaculars which, despite a touch of coyness, won every award in the TV book.

He accepted a (dramatic) supporting part in *On the Beach* (59), which starred Gregory Peck, and he did a comedy at Paramount, *The Pleasure of His Company* (61), appropriately titled, but when he danced a few steps, you knew they were mad not to give him a whole number. He supported Jack Lemmon in a comedy, *The Notorious Landlady* (62), and then he went into semi-retirement, emerging for an occasional TV show and for Francis Ford Coppola's invigorating version of an old Broadway musical, *Finian's Rainbow* (68); the role was suited to his years, the old magic worked, but he danced little. He had a part in another straight film, *The Midas Run/A Run on Gold* (69), starring Anne Heywood, but no one involved emerged with any credit.

He continued to make spasmodic appearances: in a TV series, 'It takes a Thief', in 1969; a TV film, *The Over-the-Hill Gang Rides Again* (70), as a drunken ex-law officer; in *The Towering Inferno* (74), as a con-man; in the linking episodes of *That's Entertainment Part II* (76), dancing a little with Gene Kelly in this lesser celebration of MGM's musicals (and he had been one of the comperes in the earlier one); in *The Amazing Dobermans* (76), again as a con-man; in *Le Taxi Mauve/ The Purple Taxi* (77), a French-Irish whimsy with an international cast and himself as the local cabbie/doctor; and a telemovie with Helen Hayes as his wife, *A Family Upside Down* (78), as a retired house painter who

Fred Astaire, and just as effectively cancels out Fred Astaire's natural elegance by teaming him with Betty Hutton'.

In 1951 he signed with MGM for two more films. Jane Powell was his partner in *Royal Wedding* (51) and Vera-Ellen again in *The Belle of New York* (52) – reactivated; Astaire said he enjoyed making it, but that it was a disaster with press and public – due to its fantasy and thin plot (curiously, its very inconsequence today is one of its charms and at times – particularly when the stars are dancing – it looks suspiciously like his most enchanting work). The next one, however, *The Band Wagon* (53), was by general consent one of the best musicals made till then, a modest, Minnelli-directed backstage musical, with Cyd Charisse, and the Astaire role based very loosely on himself. This was the first of a new three-picture deal at MGM, at $100,000 each. But there was difficulty in finding the right material and he considered retiring again (he only made one more film for Metro).

Eventually he signed for two at Paramount on the strength of there being one with Crosby; but he sensibly refused the script of *White Christmas*. The other, *Papa's Delicate Condition*, was eventually made with Jackie Gleason, in 1962, and its hit song, 'Call Me

suffers a heart attack – a performance which brought him a Best Actor Emmy. He remarried in 1980 – Robyn Smith, a jockey much younger than he, who shared his passion for race-horses. His last telemovie was a fantasy in which he played seven different roles, *The Man in the Santa Claus Suit* (79), and his last work for the cinema a horror film, hopefully with class, *Ghost Story* (81), in which he, Douglas Fairbanks Jr, John Houseman and Melvyn Douglas were four old boys with a guilty secret. He died of pneumonia in 1987, claiming till the end gratitude for the 'legend' and his past, but no interest in either ('We worked hard to make it good,' and then harder to make it better'). But the obituary writers had no doubt: his films will be watched 100 years from now.

MARY ASTOR

Among buffs at least, Mary Astor's reputation today stands second to none. During a very long career she made many films that have been much-revived and her acting, incisive, but delicate, is not the least factor in their reappearance. Inevitably, in over 100 pictures, she played the same part countless times, with a neat line in bitches at one end of the scale and syrupy moms at the other. The only consistent elements in her portrayals were her beauty, intelligence and a brittleness; she was never less than competent and frequently more. She chose to be a featured player, which meant that her parts were often small and non-sustaining: she had to make the maximum effect in a few minutes. It is known that she cared little for her craft, but much thought and sensibility went into her best interpretations. Given a big – and sometimes difficult – role, as in *Dodsworth* or *The Maltese Falcon*, she achieved greatness.

She was born (Lucille Langehanke) in Quincy, Illinois, in 1906 of a German immigrant father and an American mother who both, at various times, were teachers. Her father set his mind on her becoming a movie star and left no stone unturned in pursuit of this aim. She was still at school, but father was fired by the success of young artists like Mary Pickford and Mae Marsh. The family moved to Chicago and then New York in attempts to get the child nearer the studios. In New York father became friendly with Charles Albin, a photographer who knew Lillian Gish (as he was well aware): Albin thought the child had a Madonna quality (which she retained at least till Talkies) and a screen test was arranged with Griffith, who turned her down; but father got her tested again while ostens-

ibly arranging with Famous Players to translate texts of German imports. She was signed to a six-month contract and dropped at the end of it, having had only three bits: in *Sentimental Tommy* (21) with Gareth Hughes; a propaganda short, *Bullets or Ballots*, and *Bought and Paid For* (22) with Agnes Ayres.

Albin then got her the title part in a two-reeler, *The Beggar Maid* (21), with Reginald Denny, based on 'King Cophetua and the Beggar Maid', and she made some more shorts for the same company, Tri-Art (*The Young Painter, Hope,* etc.), and then some features: *John Smith* (22) for Lewis Selznick; *The Man Who Played God* with George Arliss; *Second Fiddle* (23), a Glenn Hunter vehicle, as the girl he yearns for; *Success*, at Metro, with Brandon Tynan; *The Bright Shawl*, with Richard Barthelmess; and a couple for Hodkinson, *The Rapids* and *Puritan Passions*, the latter a historical tale with Glenn Hunter. Her work in these attracted the attention of Famous Players (Paramount) again, and she signed with them again – for one year at $500 a week. Accompanied by her mother, she went out to Hollywood, to star in *To the Ladies*. But Paramount changed their minds and instead she did *The Marriage Maker* with Charles de Roche and Agnes Ayres. She supported Thomas Meighan in *Woman Proof* and was the heroine of *The Fighting Coward* (24), directed by James Cruze, a Mississippi love story taken from Booth Tarkington's 'Magnolia'.

Among those impressed by her beauty was John Barrymore and he asked Warners to cast her as his leading lady in *Beau Brummel*, for which (to her father's delight) she was paid $1,100 a week. In the film she was an English milady: off-set, he became her lover (according to her memoirs). She was loaned to Universal for *The Fighting American*; back at Paramount she won Richard Dix from Bebe Daniels in *Unguarded Women*.

After an independent picture, *Price of a Party* with Hope Hampton, she signed a long-term contract with First National, who put her into *Inez from Hollywood*, which had Anna Q. Nilsson in the title role. She was Reginald Denny's leading lady in *Oh Doctor*, one of his Universal comedies, and back at First National she appeared in two movies with another British-born actor, Clive Brook: *Enticement* (25), as a bobbed-hair jazz baby who shocks his English family; and *Playing With Souls*, standing by William Collier Jr in time of trouble. Douglas Fairbanks borrowed her to play a Spanish grandee's daughter in *Don Q Son of Zorro* – and she was easily the most fetching of his leading ladies. She was the rich but steady girlfriend of speed-mad Ben Lyon in *The Pace That Thrills* and the girlfriend of

Lloyd Hughes in *The Scarlet Saint*, causing him no end of bother. At the end of the year she was one of the chosen Wampas Baby Stars (i.e. a star of the future – girls only – chosen by the Western Association of Motion Picture Advertisers; other 1926 names on the list were Joan Crawford, Dolores del Rio and Janet Gaynor).

After *The Wise Guy* (26), with Betty Compson and James Kirkwood, Warners borrowed her again to be Barrymore's beloved, in *Don Juan*. She was co-starred with Lloyd Hughes again in the next two ('They thought we'd make a great team and teams were "in" at that time. We didn't. We were the most unsexy pair ever to appear on the silver screen' – Mary Astor in 'A Life on Film'): *Forever After*, based on a play about small-town life – rich girl loves poor boy, who becomes a war hero; and *High Steppers*, a study of the 'new generation' in Britain. At Paramount, Charles Farrell and Charles Emmett Mack fought over her before going to fight in Cuba: *The Rough Riders* (27). Back on her home lot, she was a Spanish peasant girl in *The Sea Tiger*, with Milton Sills, and the girlfriend of William Collier Jr in *Sunset Derby*. Most of these films she considered 'drivel'; in her first memoir (1959), she says she begged for good roles, 'instead of perpetually playing the insipid ingénue in third-rate pictures', but in her later book (1971), she says that her father – her manager – 'was never interested in the quality of a script or the kind of part I had. And so, neither was I'; but she did like *Rose of the Golden West*, playing a California senorita wooed by caballero Gilbert Roland. And she very much liked *Two Arabian Knights*, as an exotic beauty involved with war buddies William Boyd and Louis Wolheim – a raucous and funny comedy directed by Lewis Milestone for United Artists. Also, she was quite happy with a comedy with Hughes, *No Place To Go* – a desert island where she taught the cannibals to charleston.

She did another with Hughes, *Sailors' Wives* (28), a title which bore no relation to the plot, and was then loaned to Fox for *Dressed to Kill*, playing 'a sultry but angel-faced girl who actually packed a gun'. Her performance pleased her and the critics and Fox, who offered a contract. She worked out her First National days in two films with Hughes, *Heart to Heart*, an endearing comedy about an impoverished princess (by marriage) returning to her home town in Ohio; and *Three-Ring Marriage* – they were Wild West riders in a circus.

Her Fox contract paid her $3,750 weekly for 40 weeks, a top salary, she said, 'for anyone below full star rating'; but she was the top-featured name in *Dry Martini*, a bright comedy set in Paris with Matt Moore. And in *Romance of the Underworld* (29) with Ben Bard; *New Year's Eve* with Earle Fox; and, in a blonde wig, *Woman from Hell*, with Robert Armstrong. At that point she expected Fox to pick up her option, advancing her to $4,000 per week for 52 weeks. But she flunked the test for Talkies and the studio lost interest, though it did offer to keep her on at half her usual salary (a better deal than many of the newly imported stage-trained actors were getting – sometimes a mere $500 per week). Astor turned down the offer.

No other studio was interested. She spent some months being refused jobs, till Florence Eldridge helped to get her a part in a local production of Victor Lawrence's 'Among the Married' with Edward Everett Horton. She scored a success with the Los Angeles critics and soon had five movie offers. She accepted *Ladies Love Brutes* (30) at Paramount, with George Bancroft and Fredric March, from a play by Zoë Akins. During its making, her husband, director Kenneth Hawks, was killed in a plane accident while on location; along with the other widows, Astor sued, but she lost her case when it was revealed she had remarried. He was a doctor, Franklyn Thorpe, and the marriage endured 1931–35. Later, Miss Astor was married to Manuel del Campo 1936–41 and Thomas Wheelock 1945–55.

RKO-Pathé reunited her with Lloyd Hughes for a comedy, *The Runaway Bride*,

Mary Astor and Ann Harding in the first film version of Philip Barry's Broadway comedy Holiday *(30), reckoned to contain 'the best dialogue yet heard from the screen'.*

and kept her on to play Ann Harding's materialistic sister in *Holiday*. She returned to First National (now owned by Warner Bros) to star opposite Richard Barthelmess in *The Lash* (31) and then signed a year's contract with RKO: *The Royal Bed*, an enjoyable Ruritanian satire directed by the co-starring Lowell Sherman; *Behind Office Doors* with Robert Ames; *The Sin Ship*, with Louis Wolheim, who also directed, not very successfully, as a gangster's moll pretending to be a vicar's wife; *Other Men's Women* at Warners, extraordinarily convincing as a suburban wife who falls in love with the best friend (Grant Withers) of her husband (Regis Toomey); *White Shoulders*, with Ricardo Cortez; and *Smart Woman*, again with Ames (who had drunk himself to death before it was released). She had another good part at Warners, in *Misbehaving Ladies*, as one of them with Louise Fazenda, and then had two fairish roles at RKO. In *Men of Chance* (32) she portrayed the perils of being a gambler's wife, again with Cortez, and in *The Lost Squadron* she was an actress called Follette Marsh, who had betrayed Richard Dix while he was at the front and was now unhappily married to a vicious film director played by Erich Von Stroheim.

She says in her memoirs: 'RKO wanted to give me a starring contract, but I made the right decision and turned it down. Once your names *goes above* the title of a picture, it must never come down or your prestige is gone.' Instead, Astor decided to freelance. She had proved beyond doubt to have a clear voice for Talkies and she had established herself: now she determined to keep the bidding high by signing only for two or three pictures at a time. She continued to make about half a dozen a year, playing parts big and small. She became regarded as a not quite run-of-the-mill feature player. What set her apart was the fact that she was too chic, too worldly, to get lost among the supporting players and that she never allowed herself to be type-cast.

She was off the screen for the birth of a daughter, returning with three pictures in a row: *A Successful Calamity*, at Warners, as George Arliss's wife; *Those We Love*, at World Wide, as the Other Woman in this triangle tale with Kenneth MacKenna and Lilyan Tashman; and *Red Dust*, at MGM, as the puritan wife – of Gene Raymond – tempted to yield to the lust of Clark Gable. It was at this point that her parents decided to sue her for maintenance; and she signed a three-year deal with Warners. She was the society gal who befriends ex-gangster Edward G. Robinson in *Little Giant* (33); was a pal of Sylvia Sidney in *Jennie Gerhardt*; aged from 20 to 65 in *The World Changes*, as Paul Muni's

neurotic wife; and was the beloved of William Powell – and a suspect – when he solved *The Kennel Murder Case*. She went to *Convention City* with Adolphe Menjou, as a breezy wisecracker, and then found him *Easy To Love* (34); and allowed husband Warren William to philander with Ginger Rogers in *Upperworld*. The next four were thrillers: *Return of the Terror*, with Lyle Talbot, set in a madhouse; *The Man With Two Faces*, with Edward G. Robinson, as the sister for whom he commits murder; *The Case of the Howling Dog*, with Warren William as Perry Mason; and *I Am a Thief* (35), travelling on a train with Ricardo Cortez because she is after the diamonds he is carrying. She said later: 'All as good as some paperback whodunit. All enjoyable for me in a sort of social way: congenial people, no problems – set it up and shoot it. Lunch and jokes in the commissary. No sweat. No *nothing*.'

Most of her next pictures were Bs in which she starred: *Red Hot Tires*, as Talbot's loyal girlfriend; *Straight From the Heart* at Universal, as nurse to Baby Jane Quigley, that studio's answer to Shirley Temple; *Dinky*, as Jackie Cooper's imprisoned mother; *Page Miss Glory*, as Frank McHugh's girlfriend, jealous when he flirts with Marion Davies; *Man of Iron*, who was Barton MacLane; and *The Murder of Dr Harrigan* (36) with Cortez. She moved over to Columbia on a two-year deal: *And So They Were Married*, opposite Melvyn Douglas, and *Trapped by Television* with Lyle Talbot. In William Wyler's *Dodsworth* at Goldwyn she was tender and glowing as the widow Walter Huston turns to when wife Ruth Chatterton becomes unbearable.

During its filming her career was threatened when her diary became the most famous object in America. She had not contested her second husband's divorce case but she did fight when custody of the child arose. Since her diary had been mentioned her lawyer thought it best to admit it in evidence – whereupon some forged pornographic excerpts were released to the press by someone who knew that he featured in it (not, presumably George S. Kaufman, the dramatist, with whom she admitted having an affair, since his wife had long disregarded his infidelities). The industry's leading figures called her to a meeting in Goldwyn's office, where her lawyer convinced them that the real diary contained only minor indiscretions. Goldwyn could have exercised the morality clause in her contract with him, but decided that better publicity might be mined from the situation of a mother fighting for her child: but – perhaps significantly – the diary was found mutilated when produced, and therefore inadmissible. Whether or not the industry had rallied

Mary Astor and Humphrey Bogart in John Huston's The Maltese Falcon (*41*): *one of the screen's classic teamings. He was tough and cynical; she was cool and treacherous.*

around Astor for its own sake, the public supported her; but she made only one other film for Columbia, *Lady From Nowhere*, with Charles Quigley. One thing the diary did reveal: 'I don't like the work and I hate Hollywood'.

Selznick brought her back in a good role – the pathetic Antoinette de Maubin in *The Prisoner of Zenda* (37) – and she had another imposing second lead in another big one, John Ford's *The Hurricane* at Goldwyn, playing the disillusioned wife of Raymond Massey. Three important performances should have made her a hot property again, but instead she was in, at MGM, *Paradise for Three* (38) with Frank Morgan and Robert Young; at Columbia, *No Time to Marry*, a good funny B, with Richard Arlen, in which she was a sob-sister, and *There's Always a Woman*, in support of Douglas and Joan Blondell; at MGM again, *Woman Against Woman*, as Herbert Marshall's bitchy wife; and *Listen Darling*. as a widow matched by daughter Judy Garland to Walter Pidgeon. Concurrently, she had been getting good notices for a second stage attempt, in the West Coast production of 'Tonight at 8.30'; and in 1939 she toured in 'The Male Animal', but decided not to accompany it to New York because of her child. Instead, she did *Midnight* (39) with Claudette Colbert, a comedy in which she was an evil-tongued society bitch; *Turnabout* (40) from Thorne Smith's novel, supporting Carole Landis and John Hubbard as the couple who

do just that, sexually, but married to the top-billed Adolphe Menjou (in a sane world, they would have had the leads); and *Brigham Young Frontiersman*, as an amalgamation of the wives of that character.

Despite (most recently) her marvellous work in *Midnight*, Warners insisted that she test for *The Great Lie* (41) – to play another bitch, contrasting with the Bette Davis character. It was Davis who wanted Astor – ironically, for it was the only time in her career that any player stole a film from her. Astor wrote later: 'Davis handed it to me on a silver platter. Bette has always had the wisdom, rare in this business, to know that a star cannot stand alone; she appears to much better advantage if the supporting actors are good.' Astor, venomous in a shingle, got a Best Supporting Oscar and another plum part at WB, when Geraldine Fitzgerald turned it down, in *The Maltese Falcon*, directed by John Huston. She was the lovely, frightened Brigid O'Shaughnessy, the prototype of all frail ladies who turn out to be two-faced and lethal. She, Bogart and Huston followed it with *Across the Pacific* (42), where she was equally enigmatic. At Paramount she gave another brilliant comic portrayal as the feckless, garrulous heiress of *Palm Beach Story* – at which point she signed an advantageous contract with MGM, who announced that they would launch Astor as a fully fledged star. They didn't; nor did they appear to have seen her last four films – for she was to be

While George Brent was lost in the Amazon Bette Davis and Mary Astor fabricated The Great Lie *(41): one bore his son, the other brought him up as her own. Before George knew what was happening the girls had fought it out: Bette won the baby and Mary the show.*

wasted in roles she referred to as 'Mothers for Metro': *Young Ideas* (43) – that of Susan Peters; *Thousands Cheer* – Kathryn Grayson's; and *Meet Me in St Louis* (44) – Judy Garland's. She did do a triangle story with Philip Dorn and Gloria Grahame, *Blonde Fever*, and she was allowed leave to do a Broadway play, 'Many Happy Returns'. They did not let her go to Britain to play the second wife in *Blithe Spirit* and she was idle apart from an Esther Williams picture (released a while later). She enjoyed *Claudia and David* (46), on loan to 20th, playing a Connecticut neighbour of Dorothy McGuire, and then mothered again – Elizabeth Taylor in *Cynthia* (47) and Miss Williams in *Fiesta*. She was Lizabeth Scott's mother in *Desert Fury* at Paramount, and this was the sort of role for which she was now clamouring – a gambling town queen, vicious woman, obsessed by her daughter: the film wasn't good, but she was. Said Miss Scott: 'What a special woman! She is compassionate, gifted, charming. A marvellous actress. I somehow always felt that in the depths of her, her assessment of life was in proper perspective.'

Her role in *Cass Timberlane* was small – the wife of Albert Dekker, a colleague of Spencer Tracy's. But she had a fine chance – and was harrowingly good – in Fred Zinnemann's *Act of Violence* (48), as a middle-aged trollope who befriends Van Heflin. But – predictably as Marmie – *Little Women* (49) broke her spirit: 'My bitterness grew, my resentment

built higher and higher. The hot lights, the long waits, the heavy woollen costumes, trying to be patient with the silliness of Mlles Allyson, Leigh, Taylor and O'Brien – it wore me down.' She asked for her release – and after a small role in *Any Number Can Play* MGM let her go.

The 50s were unkind professionally. Her autobiography speaks candidly of a drinking problem (it had begun in the days of *Zenda*), but she says that it did not impair her work – besides, drinking problems were and are a Hollywood commonplace. The rare film work she did was as polished as ever; she turned to TV ('The Women', 'Sunset Boulevard', 'The Ninth Day' and 'The Lonely Stage' among many) and to the stage – 'Biography' in stock, tours of 'The Time of the Cuckoo' and 'Don Juan in Hell', and a brief Broadway venture with Eva Le Gallienne, 'The Starcross Story'. But, incredible as it now seems, Hollywood did not want to know. In 1953 an agent got her a small role in *So This Is Love* at Warners, but she had an accident and could not do it; two years later the same company turned her down for the role of Jane Wyman's mother in *Miracle in the Rain*.

Later: 'a week's work in a picture . . . a trashy story, and no part at all, but the $300 looked wonderful'. This was *A Kiss Before Dying* (56), at United Artists, as Robert Wagner's doting mother. There were other offers for cameo-roles: *The Power and the Prize* with Robert Taylor, as the wife of tycoon Burl Ives; *The Devil's Hairpin* (57), as Cornell Wilde's mother; *This Happy Feeling* (58), as John Saxon's mother; and *A Stranger in My Arms* (59), as another obsessed mother – antagonistic to June Allyson. When 20th had trouble casting *Return to Peyton Place* (61), Miss Astor suddenly landed a plum role – as jealous mother and town busybody. She stole the notices: 'Sight & Sound' found it watchable for her 'exemplary job of scene-stealing, and some fanciful notions about how best-sellers get written', a summary which equally fits *Youngblood Hawke* (64), an inept version of Herman Wouk's novel about a budding writer. Miss Astor, in another fat role, was his benefactress; and she was effective, if seemingly aged, in *Hush Hush Sweet Charlotte*, with Bette Davis. In her two sequences – as the lady with the key to the mystery – she glittered as brightly as she ever did. 'Turn her loose,' said Davis to the director, 'you might learn something.'

After that, she retired, though she published an occasional novel. She began to write after the success of her first volume of memoirs, and produced several, including 'Image of Kate' and, in 1969, 'A Place Called Saturday'. She died in 1987.

LEW AYRES

Because he starred in one of the most famous films ever made, *All Quiet on the Western Front*, the name of Lew Ayres has been well-known for almost 60 years. His career has been disappointing, however, and consisted mainly of B pictures. When better things were offered, he proved with comfort that he was worthy of them.

He was born in Minneapolis in 1908 and

Lew Ayres as the young German soldier in All Quiet on the Western Front (*30*): *one of the most impressive starts to any film career.*

studied medicine at the University of Arizona. He played the banjo, guitar and piano, and joined Henry Halstead's orchestra; later he was with Ray West's orchestra at the Cocoanut Grove, LA, and there was spotted by Pathé executive Paul Bern, which resulted in a six-month contract with that company – and one part, a bit in a silent called *The Sophomore* (29). He was dropped, but when Bern moved over to MGM he thought of Ayres for *The Kiss*, as the boy who demands just that from Garbo while her lover was away; there were good notices and Bern recommended him for Universal's *All Quiet . . .* (30) and a Universal contract. The film was directed by Lewis Milestone from Erich Maria Remarque's novel; it was (and remained) unique among US films in that it saw the war from the German side and from the point of view of a group of boy soldiers whose enthusiasm and patriotism gradually change into resignation (towards death) and disillusionment (about military glory). Its impact was tremendous and in 1930 it was among the top five box-office pictures; a worldwide reissue in 1950 and recent TV showings have again proved its validity.

Ayres had the principal part and it got his career off to a terrific start. Hollywood immediately saw him as a great new actor, and Warners borrowed him to play a desperate gangster in *Doorway to Hell*, but he was much too young and boyish to be believable; he was more convincing at Fox as Constance Bennett's seducer in *Common Clay* and, back on his home lot, as a society boy involved with Chinatown Charlie (Edward G. Robinson) and Ming Toy (Lupe Velez) in *East Is West*, a version of the old melodrama. *Many a Slip* (31) was well named, a tasteless comedy about whether Joan Bennett was or was not pregnant: neither she nor Ayres were at ease with the wise-cracks and they both slipped. He sank lower with *The Iron Man, Up for Murder* and *Heaven on Earth*, a romance of the Mississippi, but James Whale's *The Impatient Maiden* (32) was a slight improvement – Mae Clarke had the title role, intended for Clara Bow before her disgrace, and Ayres was a doctor. His salary was now $1,750 a week and he was battling for better pictures than *The Spirit of Notre Dame* and *Night World*, the latter a nightclub drama with Clarke again. Critics commented that if Ayres made more like that, he would soon be through. But he did one even worse: *Okay America*. Fox borrowed him for *State Fair* (33) to play the big city reporter who falls for Janet Gaynor, and he had another good chance there opposite Lillian Harvey in her first Hollywood film, *My Weakness* (though she failed to duplicate in the US her European success and was soon

Young Dr Kildare (39):
*Lew Ayres in the title role
in the first of that series,
with Lionel Barrymore as
Dr Gillespie, permanent
representative of the Old
Guard.*

winging her coy way back to home ground).
Ayres returned to Universal for *Cross Country Cruise* and *Let's Be Ritzy* (34), a poverty-stricken comedy about a ditto-couple who try to live above themselves; Fox then took over his contract and put him with Alice Faye in *She Learned About Sailors*, as a sailor, and Gaynor again in *Servants Entrance*, as the chauffeur she falls for.

In *Lottery Lover* (35) with Pat Patterson he was a shy cadet trying to return a garter to a famous actress; it was a B and the new management at Fox – now 20th Century-Fox – kept him in B pictures: *Spring Tonic* with Claire Trevor and *Silk Hat Kid* with Mae Clarke. In the latter he played a killer – and made the 'New York Times' nostalgic because he and Miss Clarke had not been seen together for some time. He left Fox and could see little future as an actor; he wanted to change to directing and Republic agreed to let him direct a couple of films provided he would act in one: *The Leathernecks Have Landed* (36). He directed *Hearts in Bondage* with Clarke and James Dunn, but Republic reneged on the second one and Ayres returned to second features – a couple at Columbia, *Panic on the Air* with Florence Rice and *Shakedown* with Joan Perry; and a bevy at Paramount: *Lady Be Careful*, as a shy sailor with Mary Carlisle; *Murder With Pictures* and Gail Patrick; *The Crime Nobody Saw* (37) with Ruth Coleman; *The Last Train From Madrid*, as a breezy newspaper man helping local girl Olympe Bradna to escape; *Hold 'em Navy* with Mary Carlisle; and *Scandal Street* (38) with Louise Campbell. He made *King of the Newsboys* at Republic, but he was virtually forgotten until he was allotted the part of Katharine Hepburn's brother, a

casual, hard-drinking layabout, in *Holiday*.

Interest was rekindled and Ayres told an interviewer: 'Hollywood, quick to acclaim, soon washed its hands of me. And let me tell you, the snubs you get sliding down aren't nearly as pleasant as the smiles going up.' He thought he was in some measure to blame for his fall by thinking he could coast along on a personality performance. He now was signed to a contract by MGM, who cast him in *Rich Man Poor Girl*, supporting Ruth Hussey and Robert Young, as Cousin Henry. This was a B and so was *Young Doctor Kildare*, with Ayres in the title-role as an idealistic medico opposed by a crotchety old one, Lionel Barrymore. Ayres played with an eager, simple sincerity and the girl was Laraine Day. The film was popular and spawned a series – as MGM had hoped. Meanwhile, Ayres was in: *Spring Madness*, opposite Maureen O'Sullivan, as the victim of a sorority house plot; *Ice Follies of 1939* (39), dallying with Joan Crawford; and *Broadway Serenade*, as the composer husband whose career clashes with Jeanette MacDonald. There was the second of the series, *Calling Dr Kildare*, and then *These Glamour Girls*, as a wealthy college boy who falls for taxi-dancer Lana Turner. Then: *The Secret of Dr Kildare*; *Remember?*, as the guy Greer Garson jilts for Robert Taylor; *Dr Kildare's Strange Case* (40); *Dr Kildare Goes Home*; *The Golden Fleecing*, as an insurance agent trying to protect the life of a mobster client – a comedy part-written by S.J. Perelman; *Dr Kildare's Crisis*; *Maisie Was a Lady* (41), joining Ann Sothern in her series, as a wealthy scion; *The People vs Dr Kildare*; *Dr Kildare's Wedding Day* – which was tragic, for Laraine Day gets killed on the eve (it was a way of writing her out of the series); *Dr*

*Joan Crawford was known
to look back on* Ice Follies
of 1939 *with much
despondency: it would be
strange if James Stewart
and Lew Ayres didn't feel
the same way.*

Kildare's Victory; and *Fingers at the Window* (42), as an actor trying to prevent a mass-murderer getting at Laraine Day.

The fact that there was no mention of Dr Kildare in the title of the next showed that the series was faltering: the one *Born to be Bad* was Phil Brown who, like Ayres, was a Quaker. Both had registered as conscientious objectors, but Brown changed his mind and went to serve Uncle Sam. Ayres did not, with the result that Brown was recalled to re-shoot much of his footage with Philip Dorn, who replaced Ayres as a new doctor: and a title change to *Calling Dr Gillespie* indicated that emphasis had been changed to the Barrymore character. Ayres left films and went to work in a lumber camp, but the public was not appeased. Exhibitors boycotted his films and they were withdrawn from circulation. He volunteered for non-combatant duties and served as a medic and later a chaplain's aide. He returned from his experiences thinner, lined and moustached: an altogether more interesting actor. With *The Dark Mirror* (46), starring Olivia de Havilland, he finally bounded to the front of Hollywood leading men, but the offers were few. Hollywood seldom forgives or forgets and Ayres had not returned as a war hero like Gable or Taylor. Warners did give him a long-term contract, but he did only two parts for them, both sympathetic: with Ann Sheridan in *The Unfaithful* (47) and the kindly doctor in *Johnny Belinda* (48), both of which he played quite beautifully.

He made *The Capture* (49) with Teresa Wright and *New Mexico* (50) with Marilyn Maxwell, followed by two even lesser ones, *No Escape* (53) with Sonny Tufts and *Donovan's Brain*. He told interviewers that he was semi-retiring from the screen and studying world religions: in 1955 he presented a film he had made about them, called *Altars of the East* after a book he had published of the same name. For a long time his only work in front of the cameras was in occasional TV shows, but he made a welcome come-back among the many old stars in *Advise and Consent* (61), playing the Vice-President. In 1964 he made *The Carpetbaggers* – and that year he married again, after a bachelorhood of 24 years; he had previously been wed to Lola Lane (1931–33) and Ginger Rogers (1933–40). He appeared frequently in tele-movies: *Hawaii Five-0* (68), a pilot for the series, as the Governor; *Marcus Welby M.D.* (69), supporting an old colleague from MGM, Robert Young, as a doctor; *Earth II* (71), as the President in this sci-fier, shown in cinemas abroad; *She Waits* (72), a thriller starring Patty Duke, again as a doctor; *The Stranger* (73), more sci-fi, as a professor; *The Questor*

Tapes (74), ditto; *Heatwave!*, more doctoring; *Francis Gary Powers, the True Story of the U2 Spy Incident*, as Allen Dulles; *Suddenly, Love* (78) married to Joan Bennett, but they were not starring; *Letters From Frank* (79) with Art Carney, who was; *Reunion* (80), about a high school get-together; and *Of Mice and Men* (81), in the best role after the leads (Robert Blake, Randy Quaid), that of Candy.

Ayres's cinema films of this period were: *The Biscuit Eater* (72) for Disney, as the young hero's father's boss; *The Man*, made for television, but diverted to cinemas; and *Battle for the Planet of the Apes* (73), as an ape. There was, later, a cameo in *End of the World* (78) and a larger role in *Damien – The Omen II*.

Salem's Lot (80) was a TV mini-series, cut down to size for cinemas abroad and cassette, a Stephen King tale much improved thereby. *Don Camillo* (83) starred Terence Hill, an ill-advised remake, with Ayres as the village doctor. He was Robert Wagner's father in a series, 'Lime Street' (85); and his last work to date is a tele-movie, *Under Siege*.

LUCILLE BALL

Lucille Ball is far better known for her TV work than for films, though she was in more than 50. Her sensational success in that other medium has always been considered as some sort of judgment on Hollywood, who failed to develop her, failed to give her adequate vehicles or failed to utilize her rich comic talent; in reality, her success in TV illustrates rather the different standard operating around CBS, NBC, ABC, etc. For Lucy, though she *was* wasted for years, did have some great chances in films; but the cinema public never really took to her in a big way. She was always one of Hollywood's better comediennes, always professional, always predictable, always welcome, and always pretty; more accomplished than, say, Marilyn Monroe, but much less extraordinary; never quite as funny as Judy Holliday and much less subtle.

She was born in 1910 in Jamestown, New York, where her father was a telephone linesman. She did some amateur performing as a child and at 15 entered the John Murray Anderson Dramatic School; she knew she was not good and left after a year for a job in a tour of 'Rio Rita'. It lasted five weeks (she was sacked). She next worked at a soda fountain in New York, but persevered with her showbiz ambitions and eventually became a model for Hattie Carnegie. With several other Carnegie models she went to Hollywood to appear in Goldwyn's *Roman Scandals* (33) and, unlike them, she stayed. Goldwyn put her under contract and she appeared for him and 20th Century (one of his partners in United Artists). Her first released films were *Broadway Through a Keyhole* and *Blood Money*, and she was unbilled. After *Roman Scandals* she could be briefly glimpsed in *Moulin Rouge* (34); *Nana*, as a chorus girl; *Bottoms Up* and *Hold That Girl*, both at Fox; *Bulldog Drummond Strikes Back*; *The Affairs of Cellini*; and *Kid Millions*. Goldwyn dropped her and Columbia offered a contract (at $75 a week). She made some more appearances, still uncredited, in *Broadway Bill*; *Jealousy*; *Men of the Night*; and *Fugitive Lady*. Her first credit was as 'nurse' in *Carnival* (35), starring Lee Tracy and others. Columbia dropped her and she had a bit as a model in RKO's *Roberta*, which resulted in a contract at that studio (at $50 a week). She remained unbilled: *Old Man Rhythm*, a college musical with Charles 'Buddy' Rogers; *Top Hat*, one line with her back to the camera; and *The Three Musketeers*, with Walter Abel and Paul Lukas. Thereafter she was credited and her parts slowly began to get bigger: *I Dream Too Much*, as the youngest of a family of tourists; *Chatterbox* (36), starring Ann Shirley as a stage-struck country girl; *Follow the Fleet*, with about five lines, as a showgirl; *The Farmer in the Dell*; *Bunker Bean*, a B farce starring Owen Davies Jr that had been filmed twice as a Silent, with the prefix *His Majesty*; *That Girl From Paris*, starring Lily Pons; and *Don't Tell the Wife* (37) with Guy Kibbee and Una Merkel. There was a stage offer, 'Hi Diddle Diddle', and though it did not make Broadway she got good reviews. RKO were still not much interested. It was Ginger Rogers (her mother, Leila, was Ball's dramatic coach) who recommended her for a leading part in *Stage Door*: she was conspicuous among the aspirants in that film. It led to better parts: in *The Joy of Living* (38) as Irene Dunne's sister; a B, *Go Chase Yourself*, co-starring with Joe Penner; and *Having Wonderful Time* – second lead to Rogers as an affable girl called 'Screwball', and partnered with Red Skelton.

Now RKO rushed her from film to film, but real stardom was still a couple of years off: *The Affairs of Annabel*, a B comedy, as a temperamental star whose PR – Jack Oakie – gets her into stunts; *Room Service*, as the actress who will star in Groucho Marx's play; *Next Time I Marry* with Lee Bowman – she 'played in a delightfully provocative spirit' – 'Picturegoer'; *Annabel Takes a Tour*, a sequel to her earlier film; *Beauty for the Asking* (39) with Patric Knowles; *Twelve Crowded Hours* as Richard Dix's girlfriend; *Panama Lady* – she starred as a showgirl in this B melo with

Allen Lane, a remake of *Panama Flo*, who had been Helen Twelvetrees; *Five Came Back with* Chester Morris, as a girl with a past; and *That's Right – You're Wrong*, a Kay Kyser musical. In *The Marines Fly High* (40) she was leading lady to Richard Dix and Chester Morris. There followed *You Can't Fool Your Wife* (in a dual role) and then *Dance Girl Dance*, where she and Maureen O'Hara fought over Louis Hayward. She was top-billed, as a spoiled heiress, in *Too Many Girls*, a campus musical with Ann Miller, Richard Carlson, Eddie Bracken and Desi Arnaz (whom she married). Though Harold Lloyd produced it, *A Girl, a Guy and a Gob* (41) was poor stuff; *Look Who's Laughing* threw her in with Edgar Bergen and Charley McCarthy and Fibber McGee and Molly, as Bergen's secretary; *Valley of the Sun* (42) was a Western with James Craig and Dean Jagger; and *Seven Days' Leave* a minor musical with Victor Mature. The only one with pretensions above double bills was called *The Big Street*, with Henry Fonda, a Damon Runyon story about a temperamental crippled actress and the bellhop who adores her – and she was given the role on Runyon's recommendation. It is the only one of her films that she liked. Said James Agee in 'Time': 'Pretty Lucille Ball, who was born for the parts Ginger Rogers sweats over, tackles her "emotional" role as if it were sirloin and she didn't care who was looking.'

The performance brought Ball to the attention of MGM, who were having difficulty finding a star for the role Ethel Merman had played on Broadway in *DuBarry Was a Lady* (43): Hollywood had long considered Merman unphotogenic and indeed this studio had already cast Ann Sothern in her role in *Panama Hattie*. MGM considered that Lucy, like Sothern, had not had either the right breaks or the star treatment only they knew how to give. It was unusual for studios to bother about those who had not quite made it and they were only rarely successful, as in the case of Betty Grable at Paramount – but she, neither more nor less talented than she ever was, was now the biggest female star in Hollywood. In Miss Ball's case, with her gleaming red hair, she looked a dream in Technicolor, as was proved for the second time when she took over from a pregnant Lana Turner in the film of another Broadway musical, *Best Foot Forward*, playing a movie star on campus – in fact, herself, her singing voice dubbed and, prophetically (for MGM), not too sympathetically portrayed. She was in a sketch in the all-star revue *Thousands Cheer* and then played another star, from Broadway this time, who is challenged by Dick Powell to become a riveter in a shipyard, in *Meet the*

People (44). 'Picturegoer' remarked that she 'supplies glamour and little else', a review confirming MGM's own view that their attempts to build her had been in vain. In this case the film was terrible, as the public quickly discerned, but MGM blamed her and she was off the screen for over a year before being forced into featured billing on *Without Love* (45); the stars were after all Tracy and Hepburn (she played Hepburn's agent) and a compromise was reached whereby Ball's name was in bigger letters than that of Keenan Wynn, regarded as the studio's lead supporting player. Then she sat out her contract in an office at MGM (with Buster Keaton) – except for her turn in *Ziegfeld Follies*, not shown until 1946. She was better served by *Easy to Wed* (46), an unsurprisingly poor remake with music of *Libeled Lady* – and stole the notices cleanly from Esther Williams and Van Johnson. She was loaned to 20th for *The Dark Corner*, a straight heroine part in a not-very-straight thriller, and then, with John Hodiak, made *Two Smart People*, a light-hearted drama which Jules Dassin directed. With that one, MGM and she called it quits.

She freelanced. At Universal she sparkled in a weak marital comedy with George Brent, *Lover Come Back*, but she had more difficulty trying to carry *Lured* (47) at UA, a whodunit with George Sanders. At Columbia she did *Her Husband's Affairs* with Franchot Tone and at Paramount *Sorrowful Jones* (49), opposite Bob Hope, a second excursion into Damon Runyon country. But though she traded quips well with him, this was a standard leading lady performance. She was at her considerable best, however, in *Easy Living* at RKO, playing another secretary, the ever-loving girlfriend of ball-player Victor Mature. Columbia then offered her a three-picture deal, at $85,000 each – and the first was *Miss Grant Takes Richmond*, a comedy with William Holden. Hope had liked her work with him and asked for her for *Fancy Pants* (50). This time her comedy as a gun-totin' Western heiress was less inhibited.

Meanwhile, she toured with her husband in a sketch, 'Cuban Pete', and in Elmer Rice's 'Dream Girl'. She did another at Columbia, *The Fuller Brush Girl*, with Eddie Albert, but that studio wanted to get out of the last of their deal and offered a Sam Katzman cheapie, *The Magic Carpet* (51), thinking she would turn it down. She knew the reason and did not – a woeful experience and in her own opinion her worst movie. Paramount again offered resurrection: De Mille wanted her for

Lucille Ball with two clowns: Red Skelton in DuBarry Was a Lady *(43) and Bob Hope in* The Facts of Life *(60). Although she has often been teamed with comedians, her dominant style is more effective when supported by a straight man – as her TV partners have been. However, in* The Facts of Life *both she and Hope played relatively straight, and it was a peak in both their careers.*

The Greatest Show on Earth, but at the last minute she became pregnant and the part went to Gloria Grahame.

Realistically, her thoughts had already turned to TV and in 1951 she began 'I Love Lucy' with Arnaz. Discussing once why she had made it where other girls had failed, she said: 'Maybe because they turned down more working jobs or social opportunities and I did just the opposite. As a result, I've never been out of work in this town except for two hours once between contracts.' TV was just such a move. It brought her undreamed of popularity, and more – in 1952, Universal offered her 50 per cent of the takings for a film called *Sing Your Way Out*. She chose not to do it but later she and Arnaz accepted an offer from MGM – for a joint $250,000 (when last at MGM she was getting $3,500 a week and Arnaz $650): *The Long Long Trailer* (54), a comedy with gorgeous moments directed by Vincente Minnelli, and a big success. However, a second for MGM, *Forever Darling* (56), was a soggy thing about a couple whose marriage is saved by an angel. A little later, Arnaz retired from the TV series – but not before they had both become very, very wealthy. They had bought the old RKO studio and founded their own corporation, Desilu. TV continued for her solo – often because whenever she spoke of retiring, the networks came up with bigger and bigger offers. Everyone really did love Lucy, even in a flop Broadway musical, 'Wildcat' (61). In 1960 she and Arnaz were divorced and the following year she married a producer, Gary Morton.

In more than a decade, Madame Executive-Impresario Ball took time off from her TV programmes to do only three films: two hits and a miss. *The Facts of Life* (60) was an agreeable comedy with Bob Hope, but a reunion three years later, in the film of Ira Levin's play, *Critics Choice* (63), was suitable for neither of them. They were, respectively, a couple in quest of an adulterous affair and a Broadway critic whose wife writes a play. After a guest spot in *A Guide for the Married Man* (67) came *Yours Mine and Ours* (68), where she and Henry Fonda, widow and widower, had almost a score of kids between them. She was never better, never funnier, and the film went on to make a small fortune for her (needless to say, she produced). Its production was a change from the various TV series built around scatterbrained 'Lucy' – a lady increasingly given to mugging. Though no artist was technically more adept at getting a laugh, this one had always tended towards the mechanical – which was why, when she returned to the big screen to play Angela Lansbury's stage role in *Mame* (74), no one went to see it after the word-of-mouth was out

(it had broken records the first week at Radio City Music Hall). Overdressed, over-made-up and seemingly photographed through gauze, she croaked out the songs and reportedly quarrelled on set with Robert Preston, who almost singlehandedly tried a rescue job. Its failure doomed ABC Pictures, who produced. She herself had tired of weekly TV and, with hundreds of Lucy shows remaining in syndication, she elected around this time to restrict her appearances to specials.

A tele-movie finally tempted her, *Stone Pillow* (85), playing a Manhattan bag lady, and then she was back, no kidding, for yet another series, 'Life With Lucy' (86). The new generation of viewers was not interested and it limped away after two months – 'the worst flop of the season' according to 'Variety'. She died in 1989 after massive open-heart surgery.

TALLULAH BANKHEAD

'Miss Bankhead's personal life had such flair that in her last years, when she did so little stage work, there was a tendency to underestimate her talent by a generation that had never seen her as the eternal prostitute, Sabrina, in Thornton Wilder's "The Skin of Our Teeth", or as the mercenary Regina in Lillian Hellman's "The Little Foxes"': so wrote Murray Schumach in the 'New York Times' on the occasion of her death. And just as her reputation as a *bonne vivante* overshadowed her stage work, so both eclipsed her film career. As a star of the silver screen she did not, as the saying goes, make it: but for a brief while she was a name to conjure with and her film performances do convey something of the vibrancy of her personality.

She was born in 1902 in Huntsville, Alabama, into a wealthy family (her father was a Congressman); as a child her tantrums were famous and she moved from school to school. She herself decided that the theatre was the best outlet for her temperament and chance seemed to favour her when she won a beauty contest organized by 'Picture-Play' magazine: the prize was a trip to New York and a film contract at $50 a week. The contest was merely a circulation-builder, but the Bankhead connections insisted that the result was honoured. Tallulah went to New York and she did indeed get some bit parts in three unimportant (and unrecorded) movies. She got a walk-on in a play called 'The Squab Farm', through family influence; and for the same reason she was taken on for a film called *When Men Betray* (18). A month or so later, Goldwyn signed her to appear with Tom Moore in *Thirty a Week*, as an heiress who runs off with the chauffeur. Later Universal gave her a role in *The Trap* (19), as the sister of the traduced heroine, Olive Tell, and First National put her into *The Virtuous Vamp*, supporting Constance Talmadge. In the theatre, she was in 'Footloose', '39 East' and other plays, and she had collected a small following by the time of 'The Exciters' (22), but it was not enough, she thought, and she jumped at an offer by C.B. Cochran to play London. She caused a sensation on her first night – 'The Dancers' (23) – and became one of the brightest lights on Shaftesbury Avenue. Among the plays: 'Conchita' (24), 'Fallen Angels', 'The Green Hat' (25), 'They Knew What They Wanted' and 'Let Us be Gay' (30). She appeared in a sketch at the London Palladium ('The Snob') and as Nina in a film version of Pinero's *His House in Order* (28) with Ian Hunter. Her salary was £500 a week, said to be the largest sum yet paid to a film-player in England. She also scaled the heights of the international celebrity set – gossip columnists wrote her up, women aped her hairdos, her clothes and the husky inflexions of her voice.

When Talkies came, Paramount tested her in a scene from her current London play, 'The Lady of the Camellias', and signed her for five films at a salary of $50,000 each. This was Dietrich's studio and she was seen as a home-grown rival to that lady – with more than a dash of Norma Shearer. She went to Hollywood to play the same sort of parts she had done on the stage – sophisticated, jaded and very glamorous. She was publicized as the first *American* sex-star. The titles are indicative: *Tarnished Lady* (31), deserting husband Clive Brook for a no-good lover, under Cukor's direction; *My Sin* (drugs and murder); and the remake of Paramount's old war-horse, *The Cheat*. The notices were so dreadful that she

lost *Rain* to Joan Crawford. She was inclined to pose, but otherwise the failure of these films was hardly her fault. It was thought that one of the troubles was that at Paramount, Dietrich was on the inside track. But there was public resistance: uncertain whether her appeal should be more to men than to women, the studio despoiled her of white-walled penthouses and dumped her – twice – in a Man's World. Charles Bickford and Paul Lukas fought over her in *Thunder Below* (32). Said 'Picturegoer': '. . . no better and no worse than her other three starring vehicles . . . hopelessly artificial triangle plot.' Charles Laughton and Gary Cooper fought over her in *The Devil and the Deep*. It did not work. While Paramount hesitated over a new contract she went to MGM to make *Faithless* with Robert Montgomery, running 'the gamut of sex and degradation' ('Picturegoer') in her quest for luxury. Despite her failure, Paramount eventually asked her to re-sign and MGM wanted her to sign a contract at a greatly reduced salary – $2,500 a week against the $6,000 she had been getting at Paramount – but with the promise of some of Jean Harlow's parts (Louis B. Mayer felt that Harlow's husband's suicide might hurt her box-office): but Bankhead did not care to be trapped in any more such parts and turned it down. Or so the story went. In fact, Mayer asked her about her rumoured lesbianism and instead of denying it she said 'You mean like so-and-so?' naming one of the studio's biggest stars. In 1933 she returned to the stage in 'Forsaking All Others'.

She soon achieved in New York the eminence she had known in London, though some of the things she did flopped: 'Dark Victory', 'The Circle' and a particularly despised Cleopatra in Shakespeare's play. She had a small success in a revival of 'Rain' and in

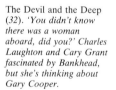

The Devil and the Deep (32). 'You didn't know there was a woman aboard, did you?' Charles Laughton and Cary Grant fascinated by Bankhead, but she's thinking about Gary Cooper.

1939 gave one of the great performances of the American theatre, in 'The Little Foxes'. She was married 1937–41 to the actor John Emery, but before and after (and probably during) was indiscriminate in picking lovers of both sexes. Selznick wanted her to play Belle Watling in *Gone With the Wind*, but since the role was small (if telling) her agent may have withheld the offer, for her rages could be spectacular. After a guest appearance as herself in *Stage Door Canteen* (43), helpfully assuring some GIs, 'Remember, if you do your job well, we'll do our job well', Alfred Hitchcock asked her to play the journalist in *Lifeboat* (44), a cunning thriller which took place entirely on same: it was a commanding performance and in the end affecting, and it brought her the New York critics' citation as the year's Best Actress. 20th, who produced, were so pleased that they invited her back, raising her fee from $75,000 to $125,000. The film concerned was *A Royal Scandal* (45), a Lubitsch comedy (Preminger directed) about Catherine the Great which had once been *Forbidden Paradise* with Pola Negri. Where Negri had smouldered, Bankhead was capricious, all style and no heart as she seduced – he had no choice in the matter – a young officer (William Eythe). The subject was not one that interested postwar audiences and the film died. She was one of several actresses who turned down the role of Lady Macbeth in Orson Welles's *Macbeth* and later she was one of many who tested to play the role of the mother in *The Glass Menagerie*, but Warners had enough trouble with one drunk (i.e. Errol Flynn) and were not prepared to tolerate another – although the director, Irving Rapper, thought her the best possible choice for the role, when not interfering in the tests of other actors.

Meanwhile, her theatre work varied – in quality and content: among several were 'The Eagle Has Two Heads' (47) and an attempt to revive the 'Ziegfeld Follies' (56). She appeared in cabaret and became a familiar figure guesting on TV; earlier (in the late 40s) she had acquired her greatest fame, on radio as the hostess of 'The Big Show': she insulted her guests and her catch-phrase, 'Hello Daaahlings', became nationally famous. That she was a genuinely witty woman was revealed by a best-selling autobiography, 'Tallulah', and that most of the revelations in it were likely to be true was confirmed by a court case which followed publication (her secretary was accused of blackmail). The programme meant that she was the only legit actress people in the sticks had ever heard of, so when MGM put together an odd little package called *Main Street to Broadway* (52) it was obligatory that she was invited to play herself. In 1964 she

appeared in New York in 'The Milk Train Doesn't Stop Here Anymore' and that summer she toured in 'Glad Tidings'. In 1965 she returned to Britain for a minor Hammer horror, at a fee of $50,000, as a religious *Fanatic* and murderess; it revealed that her once great beauty had completely gone. She was reported as saying: 'They used to shoot Shirley Temple through gauze. They should shoot me through linoleum.'

She died of pneumonia in New York in 1968.

THEDA BARA

There was a film which went like this: (1) A happily married young diplomat learns that he is being sent on a special mission to Europe (scenes of felicity, tinged with sadness). (2) On the voyage over, he meets the Vamp, not entirely by chance on her part (scenes of wiles and resistance). (3) He succumbs (scenes of seduction). (4) The family learns of his Fall (scenes of grief). (5) The diplomat and the Vamp disport themselves in Europe (scenes of debauchery). (6) They return to New York (scenes of ostracism). (7) The Vamp leaves him (scenes of finding solace with the Bottle) for other men and pastures new (more scenes of debauchery). (8) His wife attempts to reclaim him (scenes of heart-rending pathos). (9) She is about to win when the Vamp returns: 'Kiss me, my fool,' she cries and he, drunken, drug-addicted, dying, cannot resist (scenes of Nemesis).

Such was (or is) *A Fool There Was*, made in 1914, virtually the only one of Theda Bara's films to survive – which, on this evidence, is no deprivation. The scenes of debauchery consist of little more than couples dancing or lolling about in over-stuffed salons, with a few bottles and packs of cards around; the scenes of seduction consist of a bit of arm-flinging and back-arching on Miss Bara's part, and much hard staring – unrecognizable today as any sort of come-hither look. Yet she was the first glamour-girl, sex-queen, whatever: *A Fool There Was* gave the word 'vamp' to the language ('the only permanent contribution of the Fox-Theda barrage to the world', accurately predicted Terry Ramsaye).

The barrage consisted of some 40 films and publicity which is still remembered. Her name was supposedly an anagram of 'Arab Death', but was in fact a contraction of her Christian name, Theodosia (Goodman) plus a bit of her grandfather's middle name (Baranger). She was supposedly born in the shadow of the Sphinx (actually in Cincinnati, Ohio, in 1890), the offspring of either an Italian or French artist and an Arabian princess (or a sheik and a European princess). She was weaned on serpents' blood, was 'a crystal-gazing seeress of profoundly occult powers', came to films via stardom on the Paris stage and spent her spare time driving men mad with love. She was frequently photographed with skeletons and always with strings of pearls and jewels, peering intensely at the camera, eyes rimmed with eye-shadow and looking years older than she was. 'The motion-picture public went to the theater to see about all this promisingly snaky stuff and found that the effect on the screen was up to the advance notices. Theda Bara of the screen, working her willowy way with men, became the vicarious and shadowy realization of several million variously suppressed desires' (Terry Ramsaye). Audiences believed they were sharing a way of life they knew nothing about. How deliciously sinful it was! But as far as can be judged her acting is as incredible as the roles she played.

She had, however, been a stage actress (as Theodosia de Coppet); little is known of her beginnings, though Hedda Hopper records having met her while she was appearing in a tour of 'The Quaker Girl', and she appeared in New York in 1908 in 'The Devil' by Ferenc Molnar. By 1914 she had not got as far as she wanted to and began to haunt movie studios (whether she was or was not an extra is debatable; she herself said not). Though 'circumspect and demure', she immediately struck director Frank Powell as a likely candidate for a film he was planning and she was signed at $75 a week. It was to be a version of a 1910 London and New York success, in turn inspired by Rudyard Kipling's poem, 'The Vampire' ('A fool there was and he made his prayer/Even as you and I/To a rag and a bone and a hank of hair/We called her the woman who did not care'): *A Fool There Was* (14). Bara became famous overnight and the film the box-office rage; the publicity boys got busy and Bara proceeded to make a fortune for the film's producer, William Fox (it is also estimated that he made her – that she was the first star created by publicity). He formed his own company on the profits from *Fool* and signed her to a contract which, among other things, forbade her to marry or to enter a Turkish bath and insisted that she went heavily veiled in public. To cash in on public interest, she was rushed into a Nance O'Neil vehicle, *The Kreutzer Sonata* (based on the Tolstoy story) as the sister who steals her husband.

Her third film was *The Clemenceau Case*, based on a play by the younger Dumas, in which she was an unfaithful wife stabbed by her husband before her lover. She was a vengeful vampire in *The Devil's Daughter*,

adapted from 'La Giaconda', which D'Annunzio had written for Duse. She was a murderess in *Lady Audley's Secret*, an old Victorian melodrama, and in *Sin* she played something the adverts referred to as 'Destiny's Dark Angel'. She played a sympathetic part in another old (French) melodrama, *The Two Orphans*, but it flopped. After that – and an average of one Bara film per month was released over the next three years – she seldom played anything but a vamp. Roles widely different (such as Shakespeare's Juliet) were angled in that direction – partly because some tentative touches of goodness were found to be unacceptable to the public and partly because, in a sympathetic role, her style of playing and the public's disposition to find her evil combined to make it seem not so. In time there were copy-vamps (Valeska Suratt, Virginia Pearson, Louise Glaum, and later Barbara La Marr) – some of them at the Fox studios itself, kept as threats. She competed with opera diva Geraldine Farrar as *Carmen* – the Farrar version directed by De Mille, and much superior, was released at the same time. Her 1915 schedule finished with *The Galley Slave* (the adverts this time said 'Destiny's Dark Archangel') and *Destruction*, trying to seduce her stepson.

And more of same: *The Serpent* (16), as a Russian peasant out for vengeance on the Count who had wronged her; *Gold and the Woman*, as a Mexican adventuress; *The Eternal Sappho* – only she wrecked the lives of four men; *East Lynne*, as Lady Isobel; *Under Two Flags*, as Cigarette, the legion's 'mascot'; *Her Double Life*, as a pretender in high society; *Romeo and Juliet*, with Harry Hilliard (released at the same time as the Metro version with Beverley Baine and Francis X. Bushman); and *The Vixen*, in, obviously, the title-role. There were fewer the following year: *The Darling of Paris* (17), reputedly based on some of 'The Hunchback of Notre Dame'; *The Tiger Woman* – 'The Champion Vampire of the Season' ran the slogan; *Her Greatest Love*, from a novel by Ouida, 'Moths'; *Heart and Soul*, from a novel by Rider Haggard, 'Jess'; *Camille*, with Albert Roscoe as her Armand; and *Cleopatra*. The latter was road-shown and a symphony orchestra accompanied prints to the more important bookings: it was one of Bara's biggest hits. (In the cast was Art Acord, who subsequently starred as Buffalo Bill in B Westerns till Talkies revealed his high-pitched voice; he subsequently and briefly became a miner before committing suicide in a Mexican flophouse). In *Rose of the Blood* (18), she was, very topically, a Russian revolutionary; then she was *Madame Dubarry*; she was an artist's model on *The Forbidden Path*, posing

'The barge she sat in. . . .'
Theda Bara in Cleopatra,
*a super-production of
1917. Gazing up in
adoration is Antony – Art
Acord.*

Theda Bara in When a
Woman Sins (*18*). *She was
Poppaea, a trained nurse
who becomes a notorious
wanton, but reforms when
she falls for a young
divinity student.*

for the Madonna before she had taken it, and Mary Magdalene afterwards. She begged to be allowed to widen her range, but when Fox permitted her to film a story she had written herself it turned out to be the same old thing – Javanese priestess renounces her vows to lure a Scotsman to death and destruction: *The Soul of Buddha*. Other films she made that year: *Under the Yoke*, advertised as 'A Volcanic drama of the Philippines – She Scorched her Soul to Save an American Cavalry Officer'; *When a Woman Sins* – 'The Greatest Woman's Story Ever Filmed – The Regeneration of a Modern Vampire'; inevitably *Salome*; and *The She-Devil*, set among the flesh-pots of Paris.

And still more: *The Light* (19) – only hers was fading; *When Men Desire*, a war story; *The Siren's Song*, as an opera singer; and *A Woman There Was*, as a South Seas maiden in love with a missionary. These were all directed by J. Gordon Edwards, who had in fact been her exclusive director since *Under Two Flags*. Fox now appointed a new director, Charles J. Brabin, who succumbed and let her play a new kind of role – partly in the hope that it might boost her sagging popularity: a pure young Irish colleen in *Kathleen Mavourneen*, from a play by Boucicault. It did the reverse: she was hopelessly miscast and

Hibernian societies caused chaos at many theatres because an Irish girl was being played by a Jewish girl. Earlier that year, she had demanded and got a salary rise from $1,500 to $4,000 a week. Her three-year contract was up and Fox waited for the results of two unreleased films before renegotiating: *La Belle Russe*, directed by Brabin, in which she had a dual role; and *The Lure of Ambition*, in which she again played a vamp. Fox did offer a new contract, on his terms, but she did not want to continue to play vamps.

There were no other takers. She waited more than a year and then decided that the theatre might restore her to glory – not a bad move, considering that she demanded and got $6,000 a week. She toured with 'The Blue Flame' to SRO business but New York quickly let it die out. In 1921 she married Brabin and became a noted Hollywood hostess. Some plans were announced by her in the early 20s but came to nothing – indeed, in 1922 Lewis Selznick signed her for one film but could not find the right scenario. Then a small outfit called Chadwick signed her to appear in *The Unchastened Woman* (25), as a neglected wife who goes a-vamping to win back her husband. Hal Roach proposed that she guy her old image in a short, *Madame Mystery* (26), directed by Richard Wallace and Stan Laurel (Hardy was in the cast). Neither did much business. The days of the vamp were over. A remake of *A Fool There Was* (with Estelle Taylor) in 1922 was a complete flop; Bara's place had been usurped by more sophisticated – and more believable – sirens like Gloria Swanson. Still, she was not entirely forgotten: when in 1932 US critics were polled to find the greatest all-time female star, she was third (Garbo was first, Pickford second, Constance Bennett fourth, Swanson fifth and Marion Davies sixth).

She did a few plays without success; and burlesqued herself in more shorts. But her marriage was happy and enduring. All the same, as Griffith and Mayer note, 'almost to her death she advertised that she was "at liberty" in the Hollywood casting directory'. She was reported as losing her sight in 1954; and died of cancer the following year.

JOHN BARRYMORE

The legacy of the Barrymores, John, Lionel and Ethel, is, as it is available to us today, for the most part singularly unimpressive. They have a golden name. Surviving colleagues still speak of them with awe and the glowing notices they had in their lifetimes are some-

times called into play. Their work in the theatre may have been magnificent, but on the evidence of their screen work, there is little to be said for any of them. True, they were past their prime: all we know of Ethel and Lionel is a series of cantankerous old people with hearts of gold. Lionel was adept at grandfathers, uncles, old bankers, doctors, any aged but authoritative man. Ethel was the matriarch par excellence, dispensing wisdom with a trowel. But their performances are invariable: from Ethel – *None But the Lonely Heart, Pinky, That Midnight Kiss* and *Young at Heart*, etc.; and Lionel – *Grand Hotel, Dinner at Eight, David Copperfield, Camille, Three Wise Fools, Key Largo* and others. To get the measure of Ethel as a film actress one need only compare her with Helen Westley, say, or Florence Bates. Lionel, often excellent in the early Sound Period, became an old bore – compare him with Guy Kibbee, Albert Basserman, Reginald Owen. . . .

John is a different matter. Throughout his lifetime he was regarded, quite simply, as a great actor. He was reputedly a great Hamlet and a front-rank light comedian. As a film star, unlike his brother and sister, he was a big draw – a name that really meant something. His performances were much more varied than those of the others and he carried a lot of films. Some of his work is impressive, giving credit to the reputation, but some of it, like his Mercutio in *Romeo and Juliet*, is overcooked, thickly cut ham. At the time there was controversy about this performance: there were those who claimed that he was the only one in the film who knew what his character was about – and there were and are apologists who insist that he was performing in the old Shakespearian tradition. But another 'traditional' actor, Laurence Olivier, was around the same time playing Orlando in *As You Like It* and his performance in that film has in no way the bilious colours of Barrymore's Mercutio. However, among his Talkie work are some good, naturalistic, comedy performances: he was an actor who could do most with least.

He was born in Philadelphia in 1882, a few years after Lionel (1878) and Ethel (1879). They came from theatre parents (on both sides). Ethel began acting while young, as did Lionel, but the latter gave it up for a while and went to study with John at the Beaux Arts in Paris. They both intended to become journalists, painters or commercial artists. John succumbed first, in 1903 (Lionel did not return to the theatre till 1907). He was not making a success of journalism and Ethel got him a part in a play in which she was appearing, 'Captain Jinks of the Horse Marines'. Later that year, he made his Broadway debut in 'Glad of It' at the Savoy. His biographer, Gene Fowler ('Goodnight, Sweet Prince', 1944), says that he was already drinking heavily. The play that established him was 'The Fortune Hunter' in 1909: thenceforward, he was considered the leading light comedian of the New York stage – in plays like 'Princess Zim-Zim', 'Half a Husband,' 'The Affairs of Anatole' and 'Believe Me, Xantippe'. His fame took him into vaudeville in 1913, in a sketch called 'His Wedding Morn'.

Daniel Frohman approached him to make a film for Famous Players and he agreed to take the lead in *An American Citizen* (13), adapted from a stage success. He said: 'The film determines an actor's ability, absolutely, conclusively. It is the surest test of an actor's qualities. Mental impressions can be conveyed by the screen more quickly than vocally. The moving picture is not a business, it is an art.' The following year, he signed a contract with Famous Players–Lasky to make a series of comedies: *The Dictator* (14), from a play in which he had toured, including Britain and Australia; *The Man From Mexico; Are You a Mason?* (15); *The Incorrigible Dukane*, about a New York reprobate who proves his manhood out West; *Nearly a King* (16); and *The Lost Bridegroom*, who is knocked out by a thug and joins a gang burgling his fiancée's home. They were much like the Fairbanks films: this was the time of over-age male stars, so the plots required misdirected high spirits – both these players had such ebullience that they were most effective clowning: but whereas Fairbanks was charming, Barrymore seemed only dissipated. He himself looked upon these films as fun, but the next, he declared seriously, was 'the worst picture ever made'. It was *The Red Widow* and he was an American corset manufacturer in Russia, involved with same. His serious energies were saved for the stage: 'Kick In', Galsworthy's 'Justice', Tolstoy's 'Redemption' and 'The Jest' (19), with Lionel, reckoned to be the biggest non-musical hit the New York theatre had yet known.

While appearing in 'Peter Ibbetson', he made a film for an independent company, *Raffles the Amateur Cracksman* (17), in the title-role of this confusing version of E.W. Hornung's crime stories. Seen today, it reveals him as somewhat more accomplished than his contemporaries – because more alive: but the quizzical stare, the jaunty self-confidence and the flamboyant aura of a failed Don Juan – his stocks in trade – are no more interesting here than later. He signed again with Famous: *On the Quiet* (18), another of his stage-roles; *Here Comes the Bride* (19); *Test of Honor*; and *Dr Jekyll and Mr Hyde* (20), which brought him world acclaim:

Agate, eight years later, commented that the Talkies could not improve on 'this masterpiece of acting'. Meanwhile his Broadway career was reaching a zenith – in 1920, after a flop play, 'Claire de Lune', by his second wife, Michael Strange, he had essayed a much admired 'Richard III'. *The Lotus Eater* (21) was a desert-island drama about a playboy who rejects (at first) the advances of a native girl because he loves the unfaithful wife he left behind. The filming was extremely slow, due to the drinking bouts that Barrymore shared with Marshall Neilan, the director, but Colleen Moore, who played the girl, remembered Barrymore as 'charming and witty and ever so debonair, and I adored him'.

In 1922 he was *Sherlock Holmes* – it was made in Britain with Roland Young as his Watson. And this year he first did his 'Hamlet', which broke records. He also toured with it, taking it to London with success in 1924. The only film that he did was *Beau Brummell* (24) at Warners. Overall it is a poor, even ludicrous performance, especially in the culminating mad scene: but he does brilliantly as the proud, poverty-stricken Brummel in Calais. The film was so successful that Warner Bros signed him to a contract, at the huge fee of $76,250 per picture, plus $7,625 per week if it was not completed within seven weeks; *plus* all expenses paid (film-making had now moved almost completely from New York to Hollywood, but as Barrymore, officially, had not, that meant house, servants, car, chauffeur, etc., each time he was in Hollywood). His billing, furthermore, read: 'Mr John Barrymore'. He consented to Don Juan provided that he could play Ahab in a film of 'Moby Dick'. The result was called *The Sea Beast* (26) and Barrymore's initial objection to the introduction of a love interest was much assuaged when it turned out to be Dolores Costello. They later married and he wanted her cast in *Don Juan* instead of Mary Astor, for whom his love had grown cold (according to her memoirs). He did not get his way. The film was billed 'The World's Greatest Actor as the Greatest Lover of all Ages'; and his next picture would be advertised with the tag 'The Greatest Lover of the Screen'. The latter designation he took particularly seriously in life, when he was not drinking.

Don Juan did spectacularly well because it was the first feature to be released with Sound (music only, synchronized on disc). But the reviews were unfavourable: 'Artistically, the only thing we could say about Mr Barrymore's performances is that he brings to them remnants of his tricks and mannerisms that stiffen them slightly and perhaps convey the sense of acting to a public that has seen but little of it' (Stark Young in 'New Republic'), and 'Mr

Don Juan (26), was the first film released with a soundtrack (music and sound-effects). The desired one is Mary Astor, and although this still suggests evil intent, the Don was really a regular joe at heart.

Barrymore himself is almost as bad, at times, as he was in *The Sea Beast* . . . the movie Barrymore, with a few flashes of brilliance and a great many glints of supreme silliness' (Robert E. Sherwood in 'Life' magazine). Part of the trouble was that his Fairbanks-like bravado was totally artificial (he was much better playing Don Juan's father in the prologue). Nor was there a kinder reception for *When a Man Loves* (27), which was 'Manon Lescaut' re-titled: Costello was Manon and Barrymore played des Grieux. This was the last of his three pictures for Warner Bros, and he decided to move over to United Artists for $100,000 per film plus a share of the profits; after two films the sum was upped to $150,000 to offset the fact that there had not been any profits till then, plus the loss of living expenses. Still, it looked like a good investment, for Barrymore had just come top of one of the first US box-office surveys (the others, in descending order: Harold Lloyd, Colleen Moore, Gloria Swanson, Richard Dix, Thomas Meighan, Tom Mix, Lon Chaney, Buster Keaton and Rin-Tin-Tin). The three films he made for UA were: *The Beloved Rogue*, the Francois Villon saga (*If I Were King/The Vagabond King*) all over again, with the swashbuckling hero – Barrymore – appallingly unattractive in every possible way; *The Tempest* (28), as a Von Stroheim-influenced Russian officer, lascivious and self-indulgent; and

Eternal Love (29), directed by Lubitsch, which cast him and Camilla Horn as ill-fated lovers killed in an avalanche.

Don Juan had paved the way for Talkies and now Barrymore returned to WB for his first Sound feature. His contract was for five films at $30,000 per week, plus a percentage of the profits, a sum owing much to the current studio infatuation for stage actors. *General Crack* required of him no more than to wear a white-powdered wig as an officer of the Austrian Emperor; in the all-star *The Show of Shows* he did the Richard III 'ambition' soliloquy from *Henry VI Pt III*; *The Man From Blankleys* (30) was a mild comedy which cast him as a Scottish lord; *Moby Dick* found him as Ahab again, with Joan Bennett as the girl; *Svengali* (31) had him hypnotizing Marian Marsh; and *The Mad Genius* was practically a reprise of the Svengali idea; the role was based on Diaghilev and Donald Cook played the Nijinsky role: but there was no hint of impropriety. Warners did not care to renew.

MGM, ever certain that they could show-case a classy talent where others had failed, signed him to a non-exclusive contract at $150,000 a film. Lionel was one of their more prestigious players, if hardly a pulling power, but a teaming of the two of them might prove a box-office novelty. So Sûreté cop Lionel pursued arch-criminal *Arsène Lupin* (32), which did something to re-establish him, if not enough to justify the huge fee. *Grand Hotel* did the trick, however, because for the first time there was an all-star cast and he was the crooked baron who romanced Garbo; it was also one of the year's top money-makers. (Garbo permitted herself to be photographed on the set with him during the making, a rare gesture.) He moved over to RKO for a thriller with Helen Twelvetrees, *State's Attorney*, and there he was Hepburn's father in *A Bill of Divorcement*, returning to MGM for a film with his brother and sister, *Rasputin and the Empress*. Lionel was the mad monk, Ethel the Tsarina and John played a character clearly based on Prince Felix Youssoupoff: Diana Wynyard was his wife and in the film was raped by Rasputin. The Youssoupoffs sued for libel in the English courts in 1934 and were awarded £25,000 plus huge costs. In Britain the film was withdrawn from circulation, which was no loss to historical studies or the art of the cinema – it was much inferior to the still current Conrad Veidt *Rasputin*.

He did *Topaze* (33) at RKO: 'As a non-admirer of John Barrymore, I was all the more agreeably surprised to find myself completely won over by his charmingly subdued (for him) performance as Pagnol's French schoolteacher, bluffed and bewildered by big business, who himself becomes a business tycoon' (Peter John Dyer in 1967). He was

The first screen teaming of the Barrymores was reckoned to be one of the cinematic events of 1932: Rasputin and the Empress. *Lionel (left) and Ethel had the title roles, and John was the slightly fictitious Prince Paul. The boy in Rasputin's arms is the Tsarevitch; the man at the back a member of the Imperial Guard.*

type-cast as the egocentric Grand Duke who returns for a *Reunion in Vienna* with one-time mistress Miss Wynyard, but this version of Robert E. Sherwood's play was not a success. The Barrymore brothers had their own reunion in both *Dinner at Eight* and *Night Flight*, the two MGM 'all-star' films which (more than *Grand Hotel*) destroyed the old one-star-to-a-film policy. In the former he was the fading matinee idol hooked on drink, 'an extraordinary performance as an untalented, fourth-rate actor', said George Cukor, who directed; in the latter he was Clark Gable's ruthless boss, the owner of an airline. In life, drink had begun seriously to affect his work: his memory began to falter and cue cards had to be held up round the set. For the moment, however, his name was big enough for the studios to tolerate the delays which his drinking caused.

He was again excellent in *Counsellor-at-Law*, from Elmer Rice's play, at Universal, restrained by William Wyler, who also brought from him one of the best-rounded characters in movies at that time; and was good again as a reprobate nightclub manager in *Long Lost Father* (34) – Helen Chandler's – at RKO. He should have then made *Hat, Coat and Glove* at the same studio, but had trouble with his lines and was taken off the film (Ricardo Cortez took over his role). Of the next, Gene Fowler wrote that Barrymore's talent 'flared brilliantly'. The film was *Twentieth Century*, from the play by Ben Hecht and Charles MacArthur, at Columbia; Barrymore played the egomaniac producer trying to lure temperamental actress Carole Lombard into signing a contract.

John Barrymore demonstrating why he was known both as 'The Great Lover' and 'The Great Profile'. The lady receiving his favours is Garbo, in Grand Hotel *(32).*

Caricature by Otis Shepard.

Around this time there were two plans to film Barrymore's *Hamlet*. Selznick wanted to do it in Technicolor, financed by John Hay Whitney, but the tests made in 1935 were not sufficiently encouraging for the project to go ahead. A year later in London, Barrymore signed with Korda to do it, but decided that he was too old and too portly. But he did make his Hollywood return in a Shakespeare film, the Shearer-Howard *Romeo and Juliet* (36) as Mercutio, and when his drinking brought his brief participation to a stop the role was offered to William Powell (who refused because Barrymore had given him his start in films). He finally completed it and MGM, ever ready to help, announced that he would appear in *Camille* (in the role that Henry Daniell eventually – and superbly – played); instead, he entered a clinic for alcoholics. When he came out, he played a similar part, that of Jeanette MacDonald's protector in *Maytime* (37). It was a supporting role, as was the part Selznick engaged him to play in *A Star Is Born*, that of the movie executive. But when it was discovered that he could neither remember his lines nor read them from a blackboard, he was replaced by Adolphe Menjou (who had already parodied Barrymore in *Sing Baby Sing* and would do so again in *A Letter of Introduction*). Some months later, Paramount signed him for a B picture, *Bulldog Drummond Comes Back*, as Inspector Neilson of Scotland Yard, boss to John Howard's Drummond. He replaced Sir Guy Standing, who had died since the first of the series, and was top-billed. Paramount kept him on for another B, *Night Club Scandal*, with Lynne Overman, and, still at

One of the several pathetic self-parodies Barrymore did towards the end of his life – Playmates *(42) with Patsy Kelly, one of the screen's funniest supporting players.*

Paramount, he supported Carole Lombard in *True Confession*. He was given the role at her insistence and the press made much of the fact that the great Barrymore had been demoted to feature billing. He played the Inspector again in *Bulldog Drummond's Revenge* and stayed at Paramount for *Romance in the Dark* (38), supporting Gladys Swarthout and John Boles, and *Bulldog Drummond's Peril*, overplaying so atrociously – in what had become a nothing role – that it was no surprise when H.B. Warner took over for the rest of the series. Barrymore went over to MGM to play Louis XV in *Marie Antoinette* and, still seesawing, was very good indeed; then he returned to Paramount to take a supporting role (billed under Akim Tamiroff), a drunken newspaper editor in *Spawn of the North*, starring Henry Fonda. In his only lead that year, *Hold That Coed* at 20th, he was a corrupt political boss on campus.

At RKO he played a drunk who reforms for the sake of his children: *The Great Man Votes* (39), a superior B, directed by Garson Kanin. At Paramount he was quite brilliant in *Midnight*, much a matter of quizzical glances as he persuades Claudette Colbert to lure away his wife's lover. He spent the rest of the year in a dreadful play, 'My Dear Children', with his fourth wife, Elaine Barrie. It toured, notably in Chicago where it ran 34 weeks, and finally opened in New York in January 1940: its success was widely believed to be due to audiences flocking to see Barrymore making a spectacle of himself (forgetting his lines, sometimes falling over). He was fully aware of this; and when he abandoned the play, at the behest of 20th, it was to appear in a thinly disguised parody of his own decline – and a B at that – *The Great Profile* (40). It was, in fact, based on some well-publicized events in his own life. He had a similar role – that of a broken-down old ham, usually drunk – in Rudy Vallee's radio show throughout 1941. His films were negligible: *The Invisible Woman* (41), at Universal, a screwball comedy, as a professor with magic powers; *Premiere* with Frances Farmer, as an eccentric film producer; and *Playmates*, also a B, with a plot about press agents cooking up a scheme whereby an old has-been ham teaches bandleader Kay Kyser to play Shakespeare. Both play themselves, but Kyser is the solo-billed star. Warner Bros tested him for *The Man Who Came to Dinner*, but he was unusable. He died in 1942, penniless.

His daughter (by Michael Strange), Diana Barrymore, had a brief film career – notably *Between Us Girls* (43) – and later became an alcoholic. Her biography was filmed in 1958, two years before she died (aged 38); in the film – *Too Much Too Soon* – Errol Flynn played John Barrymore. His son, John Drew Barrymore, had a mild career in Hollywood, mostly in B actioners.

Alpert's book on the Barrymores has these words by Ethel as a foreword: 'We who play, who entertain for a few years, what can we leave that will last?'

RICHARD BARTHELMESS

It is improbable that many people, looking at a photograph of him, would agree that Richard Barthelmess 'had the most beautiful face of any man who ever went before the camera', as Lillian Gish asserts in her memoirs. His face is round, pasty and undistinguished, though he had large, sombre eyes and good blunt features . . . at least, he was and is unprepossessing in stills. But the motion-picture camera caught the beauty, an inner beauty, spiritual; not always, but certainly in *Tol'able David* and *Broken Blossoms*, Barthelmess gave startlingly beautiful performances: he was *pure*. His character in some of his later films has affinities with Scott Fitzgerald's Anson Hunter ('The Rich Boy'). In Talkies he was usually too glum to be taken for Galahad or Prince Charming, though he played variations of both parts. Normally, he was the champion of the oppressed, almost a Dickens hero: realistic, involved in a recognizable world, but elusive. His was a remarkable talent on a minor scale.

He was born in New York City in 1895 and educated at Hudson River Military Academy at Nyack and Trinity College, Hartford, Connecticut. His father had died when he was a baby and his mother earned her living on the stage, so from his early days he worked in theatres between schooling – ASM or walk-ons. He graduated in 1913, acted that year in 'Mrs Wiggs of the Cabbage Patch' and began in films as an extra. He was in the Kleine serial, *Gloria's Romance* (16), which starred Billie Burke, and he had his first important role later that year in *War Brides* with Nazimova, based on her vaudeville sketch – it being no coincidence that his mother was Nazimova's coach. As a result of that, J. Searle Dawley at Famous Players chose him to be leading man to Marguerite Clark in a version of Grimm, *Snow White* (17) and he had another good role opposite Anna Q. Nilsson at Erbograph, in *The Moral Code*, as her unhappily married editor-boss. At Metro he supported Olga Petrova, who had the *Soul of a Magdalen*, and at Selznick he was disconcerted to discover, in *The Eternal Sin*, that his mother was Lucrezia Borgia; at Pathé he was Gladys Hulette's army-deserter

brother in *The Streets of Illusion* (they were New York's) and then he smiled at *The Valentine Girl*, who was Miss Clark. She and Dawley found Barthelmess the ideal leading man and he played opposite her again in *Bab's Diary* and *Bab's Burglar*, in which she was a mischievous schoolgirl; the more serious side of him was seen again at Triangle, in *For Valor*, as a Canadian conchie, after which he returned to Miss Clark for an adaptation of Hans Andersen, *The Seven Swans* (18). Famous Players parted them, to pair him with *Sunshine Nan*, a warm-hearted colleen – who was their equally popular Ann Pennington; and they were teamed yet again in *Rich Man Poor Man*, in which she was a slavey who impersonates an heiress. As a change of pace he supported George M. Cohen in a comedy about Billy Sunday and Prohibition, *Hit-the-Trail Holiday* for Artcraft, and for that company (like Famous Players, part of the Paramount set-up) he returned to leading man status: *The Hope Chest* (19), a comedy about an engaged couple whose parents oppose their match. The star was Dorothy Gish.

In *Boots* he was a Secret Service man and Dorothy a London waif – and thus began a rewarding association with both Gish sisters and with their mentor D.W. Griffith. Griffith at this time was looking for a successor to his usual leading man, Robert Harron. He wanted someone more robust – but equally sensitive – and he tried out Barthelmess in *The Girl Who Stayed at Home*, as the grave young (and impeccably tailored) American who falls in love with a French girl, Carol Dempster. Harron was in it, as his brother, 'The Oily Peril', and he and Clarine Seymour, as Cutie Beautiful, had more footage than the romantic leads: but the role was comic relief. (Harron shot himself in New York the following year.) Griffith signed Barthelmess to a personal contract for three years, going from $300 to $450 a week; and when he was not working for him, he was with Paramount, who released the Griffith films. In *Three Men and a Girl*, with Clark, he was a misogynist; he was a doctor in *Peppy Polly* and a reporter in *I'll Get Him Yet*, both with Dorothy. Griffith then co-starred him with Lillian in *Broken Blossoms*, the story of a tragic Limehouse friendship between a Chinese and a slavey ill-treated by stepfather Donald Crisp. Karel Reisz wrote years later: 'Richard Barthelmess plays The Yellow Man with a restraint and tenderness rare in the silent cinema.' The film's success firmly established him. He played a good-bad bandit (based on Joaquin Murietta) in *Scarlet Days*, with Dempster and Seymour as the two women in his life, Easterner and Mexican respectively; and he was a beachcomber in *The Idol Dancer* (20),

Richard Barthelmess in Tol'able David *(21), directed by Henry King, and probably the least crude, the most fresh and moving, of any silent melodrama.*

involved with South Seas beauty Seymour (her last film before her death a few months later). This was the first of two movies Griffith made at the same time on exotic locations. The second was *The Love Flower*, which had yachtsman Barthelmess discovering Miss Dempster on a desert island. It was not a success, but Griffith had by now turned his attention to United Artists (of which he was one of the founders) and his first film for that company: *Way Down East*, with Lillian Gish, who declared that he 'transformed a crude melodrama into a compelling masterpiece'. She was the country girl seduced and abandoned, and Barthelmess was the farmer's son who stands by her when her past is discovered. The film was enormously popular and is still shown.

Barthelmess then made *Experience* (21) with Nita Naldi and was invited by Charles H. Duell to form his own company in partnership, Inspiration, on a five-year agreement. Its end coincided with a lawsuit involving Lillian which completely discredited Duell, but those years produced one masterpiece and several other remarkable films, most of them directed by Henry King. The masterpiece is the first, *Tol'able David*, Joseph Hergesheimer's story of a Southern boy called upon to take on a man's responsibilities, defending the US Mail. There followed *The Seventh Day* (22); *Just a Song at Twilight*, an outside studio

attempt to dramatize a popular song; the excellent *Sonny*, with Barthelmess in a dual role and his wife, Mary Hay, in the cast; *The Bond Boy*, resisting the advances of his stepmother; *The Bright Shawl*, another Hergesheimer story, with D. Gish, and as background, the Cuban Revolution; and *Fury* (23). Like *Sonny*, this has affinities with *Tol'able David*: Barthelmess is the gentle son of a stern sea captain (Tyrone Power Sr), who avenges his mother's ruin and ends up with his faithful Limehouse waif (Dorothy Gish). In *The Fighting Blade* he was a member of Cromwell's army: the leading lady in this, and in *Twenty-One*, was Dorothy Mackaill. And it was May McAvoy in the next, *The Enchanted Cottage* (24), from Pinero's romantic play. Then he did *Classmates*, as a West Point cadet; *New Toys* (25), a poor comedy; *Soul-Fire*, as a musician who finds fulfilment in the South Seas with Bessie Love; *Shore Leave*, a version of the musical, 'Hit the Deck'; *The Beautiful City*, as an Italian in love with Irish Dorothy on New York's East Side; *Just Suppose*, as an English prince visiting the US and meeting Lois Moran (in Britain the intertitles changed him to Ruritanian prince, but the new title, *Golden Youth*, still managed to suggest the Prince of Wales). *Ranson's Folly* was an unconvincing period piece about American army life with Mackaill and *The Amateur Gentleman* was more period stuff, from Jeffrey Farnol's novel. *The White Black Sheep* with Patsy Ruth Miller found Barthelmess as an English gentleman ranker at a desert outpost, and in *The Dropkick* (27) he was at college.

Since *Shore Leave*, the Inspiration product had been released through First National and, with the disgrace of Duell, Barthelmess decided to sign a contract with that company, at the reputed (but improbable) figure of $375,000 per film. The first film of the association was *The Patent Leather Kid*, the stock tale of a cocky prize-fighter unwilling to go to war; it was so highly regarded that it was road-shown when first released: it ran 16 weeks in New York and, following this run of mediocre films, re-established Barthelmess as one of the screen's leading actors. In *The Noose* (28) he was in prison for a murder he did not commit; in *The Little Shepherd of Kingdom Come* (the famous old bestseller) in the title role; in *The Wheels of Chance* Russian twins separated in childhood; in *Out of the Ruins* a French officer; and in *Scarlet Seas* in love with Betty Compson.

With the coming of the Talkies, he was made to sing – in *Weary River* (29), as a bootlegger who got framed. It was afterwards admitted that he was dubbed, but the important thing was that he talked well – though a certain withdrawal was revealed which called for more careful casting. But his popularity held at least for a couple of years (he appears sixth on one of the box-office polls for 1931). He made *Drag* at MGM, a newspaper story; *Young Nowheres*, a 'modern' story; *The Show of Shows*, introducing a turn; *Son of the Gods* (30), in which he, Constance Bennett and the

audience all discovered at the end that he was not Chinese, as they thought; and *The Dawn Patrol*, as an English pilot, a much-admired and popular war movie – and probably the most famous of his Sound films. Forgotten now are *The Lash* (31), a Spanish-American romance with Mary Astor, and *The Finger Points*, in which he was a crusading journalist out to get racketeer Clark Gable, among others. But rescued from oblivion nearly 40 years later was *The Last Flight*, a study of a group of ex-flyers in postwar Paris and the girl (Helen Chandler) they briefly pick up. Directed by William Dieterle, written by John Monk Saunders, it outclasses Hemingway's portrait of the Lost Generation at every point: except technically, it is invincibly modern (non-sequential, flip, witty, pessimistic), the rare example of a film years in advance of its time (one can only speculate on the consequences had it been successful). Barthelmess is rightly dour as the leader of the group.

Nor were his subsequent pictures at First National (now Warners) very popular: *Alias the Doctor* (32), a confused hospital melodrama with Marian Marsh; *Cabin in the Cotton*, very glum as a cotton-picker who betters himself and becomes involved with the boss's trampy daughter (Bette Davis); *Central Airport* (33), as a pilot, directed by William A. Wellman; and *Heroes for Sale*, again as a disillusioned war veteran, curing himself of drugs but losing wife Loretta Young in an accident, also directed by Wellman. The courage of this film is almost equalled by *Massacre* (34), in which Barthelmess is an Indian rodeo performer championing his race against exploitation – and he deserves credit

Richard Barthelmess in 1931.

Helen Chandler, Walter Byron and Richard Barthelmess in The Last Flight *(31), a remarkable film that lay forgotten until 'rescued' by London's National Film Theatre in 1968.*

for making a third serious contemporary subject in a row, *A Modern Hero*, directed by G.W. Pabst. In the title-role, via various ladies, he climbs from the circus to the world of high finance: miscast in a rare unsympathetic role, he stayed that way for *Midnight Alibi*, a Damon Runyon story, as a tough young gambler who becomes New York's leading racketeer. The toll of the Talkies took him at last. His salary was one of the highest in Hollywood – reported in 1933 to be $8,500 a week – and when his contrct expired, Warners did not renew it (he left at the same time as William Powell and Ruth Chatterton).

Freelancing for the first time in his 16 years as a star, Barthelmess stayed mean for *Four Hours to Kill* (35), at Paramount, as a crook handcuffed to a cop: it did not resuscitate his Hollywood career. He went to Britain to play a French aristocrat in *A Spy of Napoleon* (36), with Dolly Haas, and appeared on Broadway in 'The Postman Always Rings Twice'. He retired, but a couple of years later mentioned to an interviewer that he would like to make a film and was offered a featured role in *Only Angels Have Wings* (39), as Rita Hayworth's failed, cowardly husband. It was reported that he would sign with 20th, but he made only three more pictures: *The Man Who Talked Too Much* (40) at WB, as a gangster, with George Brent; *The Mayor of 44th Street* (42) at RKO, as a racketeer, with George Murphy; and *The Spoilers* (42) at Universal as the sad-eyed, limping barman. He joined the Naval Reserve, and after the war did not return to acting. He lived on Long Island with his second wife and died of cancer, after a long illness, in 1963. He left over a million dollars.

FREDDIE BARTHOLOMEW

Only in the great age of the child star could Freddie Bartholomew have made it: bless him, for he did no harm to anyone, but he was not very talented. To Hollywood, he represented a very young scion of the British aristocracy, but in fact he came from a fairly humble (London) home. Born in 1924, he was brought up by his grandparents in Wiltshire, where he made a local name for himself reciting at socials and church bazaars. With his parents' consent, his Aunt Cissie 'managed' him, getting him amateur jobs as well as bits in films locationing locally: *Fascination* (30) and *Lily Christine* (32). He was taken to London to study under Italia Conti, who recommended him to George Cukor and David O. Selznick, in Britain looking for a David Copperfield. They liked him, but due to British government restrictions on child actors, he was reluctantly let go. Auntie and Freddie then (1934) travelled to the US, ostensibly to visit relatives, but they wound up in Hollywood – fortuitously, as Cukor and Selznick, having examined more than 10,000 applicants, were again fighting Louis B. Mayer's choice of Jackie Cooper for the part. Thus Bartholomew became the young hero of the first part of *David Copperfield* (35), under a seven-year contract starting at $175 and going to $500 a week: but after playing Garbo's son in *Anna Karenina* the contract was revised to stand at $1,000 a week. It is now difficult to see why either Garbo or MGM loved him so much.

He was borrowed by 20th for *Professional Soldier* (36), where Victor McLaglen had the

Greta Garbo as Anna Karenina (35) *and Freddie Bartholomew as her son.*

title role as a retired colonel plotting to kidnap a European king (Freddie); and by Selznick (who had now left MGM; in exchange for the services of George Cukor) for *Little Lord Fauntleroy*, the first of several films in which Mickey Rooney was to appear somewhere in order to point up Freddie's gentility and bearing; and he was in *The Devil is a Sissy* with both Rooney and Cooper. They resented him, but it turned out – of course – that he was no squealer. When 20th wanted to borrow him again MGM agreed provided he got top billing – though in *Lloyds of London* he was only in the first part (he grew up to be Tyrone Power). He surprised the critics by giving a good performance in *Captains Courageous* (37): as the spoilt little hero his prissiness and petulance were apt and his change under the tutelage of Spencer Tracy was well done. MGM fashioned *Thoroughbreds Don't Cry* for him, as an English boy in the US with his horse: this would bring him up against Rooney again – but Aunt Cissie refused to let him play it. MGM discovered Ronald Sinclair, who was so similar that Auntie thereafter cooperated with Metro. Bartholomew was borrowed by 20th again for the juvenile lead in Robert Louis Stevenson's *Kidnapped* (38) and was then *Lord Jeff*, an orphan boy exploited by grown-ups conniving with Rooney. He had his first teenage role in *Listen Darling*, a programmer with Judy Garland, helping that young lady to marry off her mother (Mary Astor).

His popularity had distinctly declined. MGM had no plans for him and loaned him to Universal, then on a teenage kick because of the success of Deanna Durbin: *The Spirit of Culver* (39), a remake of *Tom Brown of Culver*, and *Two Bright Boys*, a B, in both of which Cooper (who was also not fulfilling the studio's hopes for him) discovered that Freddie was at heart just a doggone, down-home real boy at heart. It was announced that Bartholomew would do 'The Boy David' on Broadway, but it did not materialize. To make things worse, life was troubled by legal battles between his Aunt Cissie and his parents over custody and salary: the case went to court 27 times in all and, whoever was legally or morally right, Bartholomew sided with his aunt – and lost, in lawyers' fees, altogether, almost every penny he had. He was loaned to RKO for two weak versions of English classics, *The Swiss Family Robinson* (40), with Thomas Mitchell and Edna Best, and *Tom Brown's Schooldays*, and then to Columbia for a B, *Naval Academy* (41). He supported Rooney, now a very big star, in *A Yank at Eton* (42) – indeed he was billed fourth, after Ian Hunter and Edmund Gwenn. One of the troubles was, as 'Picturegoer' pointed out,

that 'Hollywood had developed with vigour the qualities of lordliness and preciousness always inherent' in his character. After another B for Columbia, *Junior Army* (43), and an independent production, *The Town Went Wild* (44), a farce about two feuding families, he joined the USAAF. He was 18. When he returned there was little work for him: only *Sepia Cinderella* (47), a Billy Daniels vehicle for RKO, and *St Benny the Dip* (51), as a priest, involved with crooks and losing his pants. When movies would not have him, he went into TV in 1949, hosting an afternoon show about films; from there he passed on to directing TV shows, to TV commercials and finally to Madison Avenue, definitely retired from acting. Whether he regrets the past is not known, but he is one of the few child stars to have married happily and is settled with his second wife in New Jersey.

WARNER BAXTER

'He is the beau ideal, a Valentino without a horse and the costume of a sheik. He is the fellow the girls meet around the corner, that is, if the fellow were Warner Baxter. He is the chap the lonely woman on the prairie sees when she looks at the men's ready-to-wear pages in the latest mail order catalogue': this appraisal by Jim Tully appeared in 'Picturegoer' in 1936. Baxter was certainly the inspiration for artwork in mail-order catalogues and adverts for pipes, the prototype for men modelling cardigans or pullovers or tweeds. During the early Sound Period he was one of Hollywood's leading actors. There was no éclat with him: no scandals, no Hollywood careering. Women liked him because he was mature and reliable. He was a good workhorse of an actor, often at the mercy of his material. When it was good, he gave positive, likeable performances. It was a long career but he is hardly remembered today.

He was born in Columbus, Ohio, in 1892; his father died when he was five months old. In 1905 his mother moved to San Francisco and they lost all their possessions in the great earthquake the following year; he went to the Polytechnic High School in that city and in 1908 returned to Columbus where he started work as an office boy. He sold typewriters, cars and agricultural implements, then began his stage career in Louisville, Kentucky, when a friend recommended him to Dorothy Shoemaker when her vaudeville partner fell ill. The engagement did not last long. He later trained as an insurance salesman, then invested all his money in his brother-in-law's garage in Tulsa – but it went broke. At that point, 1914, he determined to fulfil his acting ambition and got a job with a touring company: his first part was as the juvenile in 'Brewster's Millions'. In 1918 he married his second wife, Winifred Bryson. He joined Morosco's stock company in Los Angeles, alternating leads with Richard Dix and Edmund Lowe. There was also a film part in *All Woman* (18), starring Mae Marsh. Morosco sent him to New York in the hit 'Lombardi Ltd' and afterwards Baxter toured in it for two years. Returning to Los Angeles, he found that his stage fame now brought movie offers: *Sheltered Daughters* (21) at Realart; *Cheated Hearts* at Universal, opposite Marjorie Daw; and three at Paramount – *The Love Charm; First Love*, in the title-role, a flashy operator who deceives Constance Binney, leaving her older and wiser; and *Her Own Money* (22). He was already established as the slightly older leading man – in the manner of the medium's first male stars, and Vitagraph chose him to play opposite Alice Calhoun in two of her vehicles, *The Girl in His Room* (which meant nothing more sinister than the fact that she lodged in his home in his absence) and *A Girl's Desire*, in which he was a philanderer. Morosco was reclaiming his services, but Baxter preferred to be in pictures and falsely claimed the studio lights had affected his sight – enough to keep him off the stage, for the moment. He said in an interview in 'Picturegoer' in 1935 that at this moment he had an offer to appear with Wanda Hawley, and was thus free to take it: but he never made a film with this lady and may have been referring to Ethel Clayton, who had liked him so much when they made *Her Own Money* that she insisted upon him for a Ruritanian romance at FBO, *If I Were Queen*.

Vitagraph offered an excellent role in a Colleen Moore vehicle, *The Ninety and Nine*, a small town tale, as a man suspected of murder, and he had another at FBO, in *Blow Your Own Horn* (23), as a destitute war veteran. At Fox he featured in a once-popular old tale, *St Elmo*; and after going *In Search of a Thrill* at Metro with Viola Dana, he was involved with the *Alimony* (24) problems of Grace Darmond, at FBO. He should have been part of Lubitsch's *The Marriage Circle* at Warners along with Florence Vidor, but after some days' shooting was replaced by Monte Blue. However, he managed to get into a couple at First National, *Those Who Dance* and *Christine of the Hungry Heart*, with Florence Vidor as its much-married heroine. And he was in *Her Market Value* with the fading Agnes Ayres, which got some bookings two years later.

Paramount liked him enough to offer a contract: *The Female*, a South African romance, and *The Garden of Weeds*, both with Betty Compson. De Mille chose him to play Lillian Rich's playboy lover in *The Golden Bed* (25) – he ungratefully deserts her and she has to seek forgiveness from husband Henry B. Walthall. He got leading roles but not star billing: *The Air Mail* with Billie Dove; *Welcome Home*, a fairly tedious comedy from a play by Ferber and Kaufman about a couple (Lois Wilson was the wife) saddled with the husband's appalling father; *Rugged Water*; the remake of *A Son of His Father*; *The Best People* with Margaret Livingstone; *Mannequin* (26) from Fannie Hurst's story, playing with Alice Joyce the parents of the title character, Dolores Costello; *Miss Brewster's Millions* starring Bebe Daniels; and *The Runaway*. His best chance came when chosen to play opposite Gilda Gray in *Aloma of the South Seas*, as the educated native chieftain who falls for his pagan bride – but the film was silly, being mainly a vehicle for Miss Gray, who could not do much but shimmy. He was loaned to First National for *Mismates*, then had the title-role in a version of a recent bestseller, F. Scott Fitzgerald's *The Great Gatsby*. After *The Telephone Girl* (27) from an old William De Mille play, *The Woman* – already filmed in 1915, now with Madge Bellamy in the title-role – he was loaned to Fox for *Singed* with Blanche Sweet; then did his last for Paramount, *Drums of the Desert*. He freelanced: *The Coward* at Radio, *A Woman's Way* at Columbia, *Tragedy of Youth* (28) at Tiffany and *Three Sinners* at Paramount. Then he got the part which made him for virtually the first time seem like star material: the noble Indian, Alessandro, in the third of the four screen versions of *Ramona*, opposite Dolores del Rio. He played the long-suffering husband in the first of three screen versions of *Craig's Wife*, with Irene Rich in the title-role. He then did *Danger Street* at FBO and supported Lon Chaney in *West of Zanzibar* at MGM. He is the hero, certainly, a drunken doctor – but the role is so unprepossessing as to suggest he took any work going.

His great opportunity came by chance. Raoul Walsh had been set by Fox to direct and star in the first 'outdoor all-Talkie', *In Old Arizona* (29), based on O. Henry's 'The Caballero's Way', but he was involved in an (eye) accident after some weeks' shooting and replacements were needed. Irving Cummings took over direction and some dozen actors were tested for the role of the Cisco Kid. Baxter got it, starring alongside Edmund Lowe, and he later won an Oscar for the year's best male performance. Fox hastened to sign him. He had meanwhile done a production for an independent company, *Linda*, directed by Mrs Wallace Reid; but now in a series of Fox pictures he at last obtained screen fame and popularity: *Through Different Eyes*, with Lowe and Mary Duncan; *Behind That Curtain*, with Lois Moran, a Charlie Chan mystery (E.A. Park was Chan); *Far Call*, made as a Silent and released with a music track; *Romance of the Rio Grande* with Mary Duncan and Antonio Moreno – whose star was fading now – as the villainous don who tries to cheat him of his heritage; *Happy Days* (30), Fox's all-star revue; and *Such Men Are Dangerous*. He returned to the part of the Cisco Kid in *The Arizona Kid* and then did a Foreign Legion story, *Renegades*.

He made *Doctors' Wives* (31) with Joan Bennett and then co-starred with the studio's top star, Janet Gaynor, in *Daddy Long Legs*, giving a performance as her 'elderly' benefactor which melted every female heart in the audience. Then he was loaned to MGM to play the role undertaken by Dustin Farnum in 1914 and Eliott Dexter in 1918. *The Squaw Man* – directed by De Mille for the third time (one of the two films he made for MGM in his period away from Paramount): in support were Lupe Velez and Eleanor Boardman, and Baxter did very well as the aristocratic Englishman who flees to the American West when his honour is besmirched.

He returned to Fox for *Their Mad Moment*; *Surrender*, a well-meant but silly film about a French prisoner of war (Baxter) who falls for the daughter (Leila Hyams) of one of his captors; and *The Cisco Kid*, another sequel. Then followed: *Amateur Daddy* (32) with Marian Nixon, a sentimental piece about a man who mothers a brood of orphans; *Man About Town* with Karen Morley, as a secret service agent; *Six Hours to Live*, as a man brought back from the dead to serve his country; *42nd Street* (33), on loan to Warners, as the tired but tyrannical stage director; *Dangerously Yours*, as a Raffles-like burglar, with Miriam Jordan; *I Loved You Wednesday*; and *Paddy the Next Best Thing*, which reunited him with Gaynor. Most of his Fox pictures were mediocre and he got into a good one again on a second loan-out that year: *Penthouse*, with Myrna Loy, W.S. Van Dyke's superb sophisticated thriller, as a society lawyer.

The next was poor: *As Husbands Go* (34), wisely saving wife Helen Vinson from the clutches of a European admirer. This was the sort of film Fox fashioned for him. So was *Such Women Are Dangerous*, about a young girl (Rochelle Hudson) whose infatuation for an older man leads to her suicide. Then he did another musical, *Stand Up and Cheer*, playing a State Secretary of Amusement who diverts the nation with a show including John Boles, Aunt Jemima and Stepin Fetchit. The ads offered '1,001 surprises!' plus '1,000 Dazzling

Warner Baxter was normally a sobersides executive-type actor, but from time to time in the 30s he played a romantic Mexican bandit, the Cisco Kid – here in the film of that name, with Conchita Montenegro.

Girls! 5 Bands of Music! Vocal Chorus of 500! 4,891 Costumes! 1,200 Wild Animals! 1,000 Players! 335 Scenes! 2,370 Technical Workers!' He was ideally cast as a doctor in *Grand Canary*, from a novel by A.J. Cronin, with Madge Evans.

He was loaned to Columbia for Capra's delightful *Broadway Bill* with Loy – though miscast as an executive who gives up his job because he loves horses too much; and then did a feeble war picture about flying: *Hell in the Heavens*. He was with Gaynor again in *One More Spring* (35), as a victim of the Depression, living with her and Walter King in a shed in Central Park, a film 'fairly dripping with sweetness and light' ('Photoplay'). There followed: *Under the Pampas Moon*. again in gaucho garb, romancing Ketti Gallian; and *King of Burlesque*, in the title-role, a musical with Alice Faye. The next is probably his best picture, John Ford's *The Prisoner of Shark Island* (36), as the unfortunate Doctor Mudd who set the broken leg of John Wilkes Booth as he was fleeing from the scene of the crime and who was, despite his innocence, imprisoned for life: an unbearably tense picture, beautifully told and beautifully acted by Baxter. It was his first film under the new regime at Fox (now 20th Century-Fox) and they loaned him out for another good one, at MGM, *Robin Hood of Eldorado*, one of several films about Joaquin Murieta, who was more factual than the other Robin. Murieta was one of several Mexicans dispossessed when Spain ceded California to the US, and William Wellman's film remains a strong study of injustice. Baxter, with his Cisco Kid accent, was good as Murieta; and he had two more good movies: *The Road to Glory*, a war picture with Fredric March, and *To Mary With Love*, a romantic drama with Loy. However, *White Hunter* with June Lang was no great shakes. He was the captain of *Slave Ship* (37), when MGM refused to release Clark Gable, involved with the African slave trade of 1850 till a last reel reformation, and then a couturier in Wanger's *Vogues of 1938*, again married to Helen Vinson. Loretta Young and Virginia Bruce were the other title-rolers of *Wife Doctor and Nurse*, and it was Freddie Bartholomew who was *Kidnapped* (38), with Baxter as Alan Breck (for which he was some years too old). *I'll Give a Million* was formula Baxter stuff, as a millionaire who disguises himself as a hobo because he wants to be loved for himself: the girl was Marjorie Weaver. It did poorly and Baxter's days as a top star were drawing to a close. Like the later Barthelmess, his sober, three-piece-suited personality seems an anachronism in the age of Cagney and Gable, but in that lay his appeal to family audiences

– and when they finally lost interest it was less because of the wrinkles than the blandness.

Wife Husband and Friend (39) co-starred him with Young again, as a woman who wants a singing career, and he as the husband who achieves success at same, encouraged by prima donna/vamp Binnie Barnes. It was a funny film, but these did not help: *Return of the Cisco Kid*, yet another in that series, with Cesar Romero in a small role (he later played the title role in a B series based on the same character): *Barricade* with Alice Faye; and *Earthbound* (40), an appropriately named whimsy about a man who returns from the dead (again!) to put things right on earth. It was his last film for his old studio. His salary was enormous. Variety estimated that he was the second highest paid show business personality in the US in 1940 – at $279,907. (Claudette Colbert was first; Bing Crosby was third). He moved over to Columbia for *Adam Had Four Sons* (41), playing a widower whose love for governess Ingrid Bergman is almost thwarted by daughter-in-law Susan Hayward.

He was off the screen two years and returned in the first two of a B series for Columbia, in the title-role, *Crime Doctor* (43) and *Crime Doctor's Strangest Case*. Both of these he ignored in a later interview, explaining his absence as due to a nervous breakdown (he blamed years of intensive work) and expressing an anxiousness to return as a character actor. His part in *Lady in the Dark* (44) was hardly a character one – he was Ginger Rogers's elderly admirer – but it was certainly small. He spent the rest of his career in Bs for Columbia: *Shadows in the Night, The Crime Doctor's Courage* (45), *Just Before Dawn* (46), *Crime Doctor's Manhunt, The Millerson Case* (47), *The Crime Doctor's Gamble, A Gentleman From Nowhere* (48), *Prison Warder* (49), *The Devil's Henchman, The Crime Doctor's Diary* and *State Penitentiary* (50).

During these latter years he had been active in civic affairs in Malibu, where he lived; and had suffered from chronic arthritis. He died of bronchial pneumonia in 1951.

WALLACE BEERY

Wallace Beery started in films in low comedy; became typed as a villain and was given a new lease of life as such by the Talkies, whereupon he did an about-turn and specialized in bluff, lovable rogues with, as one writer put it, 'a heart of gold functioning on all six cylinders' (the reverse, apparently, of his character in real life). Physically, if he was not going to be the baddie, this was the only solution. 'Like

Warner Baxter in 1941.

my dear old friend, Marie Dressler,' he said once, 'my mug has been my fortune.' For a long while he was extremely popular and occasioned such comments as this in 'Picturegoer' by Frank Shaw in 1931: 'He is of the salt of the earth, and is a son of the earth.' He could be *cabotin* or he could coast along in formula Wallace Beery films as befitted the veteran he was; and he could, when he felt like it, act.

The facts concerning his early life are difficult to sort out, if only because most later studio biographies give his birth date as 1889. But taking an earlier source giving 1886, the following seems the most likely. He was born in Kansas City, Missouri, half-brother to Noah Beery (1884–1946) who went into films not long after he did and had a more or less parallel career, but without the same fame. Their father was a policeman and the family, which was numerous, was not well-off. Wallace ran away from home when he was 16 and joined the Ringling Bros. Circus, assisting the man who looked after the elephants. He is supposed to have quit after two years, but he was certainly in New York in 1903 as a chorus boy in the shows of Henry W. Savage – in, among others, 'The Prince of Pilsen'. He had a big role in 'A Yankee Tourist' (07). For the next few years he did stock in the summer and sang for Savage in the winter; eventually he garnered a small renown playing 'grotesque old woman' parts. His first film appearance was in the split-reel *His Athletic Wife* (13), but he first became known for his role of the dumb Swedish housemaid in the 'Sweedie' series, at Essanay, which he continued to play over the next year. He moved with Essanay from Chicago to Hollywood, where he wrote and directed for Universal before moving over to Keystone, where he renewed acquaintance with Gloria Swanson – and they were briefly married. He appeared with her in a couple of two-reelers, and his colleague from his 'Sweedie' days, Ben Turpin; then made his mark as a villain in *Patria* (17), a serial with Mrs Irene Castle. With clipped hair, he could pass as a wicked Hun and was thus employed by Mary Pickford in *The Little American* and *Johanna Enlists* (18). He went to Japan to direct a film there and imprinted himself on the filmgoing consciousness for the first time as the Hun who tried to rape Blanche Sweet in *The Unpardonable Sin* (19). At Paramount he got another break when he replaced his brother in *The Love Burglar*, which starred Wallace Reid and Anna Q. Nilsson. The following list includes only the features in which he appeared: *Life Line* with Jack Holt; *Soldiers of Fortune* with Norman Kerry; *Victory*, from Conrad's novel, with Jack Holt as Schomberg; *Behind the Door* (20) with

Hobart Bosworth, as the commander of a German submarine; Tod Browning's *The Virgin of Stamboul*, as a wicked Turk, and *The Mollycoddle*, starring Douglas Fairbanks.

He did *The Round-Up* with Fatty Arbuckle; *The Last of the Mohicans*, directed by Maurice Tourneur, from the novel by J. Fenimore Cooper, with Beery as the wicked Magua; and *The Rookies Return* (21). In *813* he had a dual role; in *The Four Horsemen of the Apocalypse* he was seen briefly as a German; in *A Tale of Two Worlds* he was a Chinatown boss; and he was wicked in three Westerns, *The Northern Trail*, *The Golden Snare* and *The Last Trail*, the latter from a story by Zane Grey. In *The Rosary* (22) he was involved with pirates, and in *Wild Honey* with politics. *The Man from Hell's River* featured Rin-Tin-Tin and *I Am the Law* Alice Lake: Beery was again a Chinaman. There followed: *Trouble*; *Hurricane's Gal*; the Fairbanks *Robin Hood*, as Coeur de Lion; *The Sagebush Trail*; and *Only a Shopgirl*. He later claimed that Fairbanks gave him his real start, but at all events he did not lack work: *The Flame of Life* (23); *Stormswept* with brother Noah; *Patsy*; and *Bava*, with Estelle Taylor, as a Russian revolutionary. Erich Von Stroheim chose him to play in *The Merry-Go-Round*, but when Von Stroheim was sacked, Beery left and his footage was re-shot. After an interval Frank Lloyd put him into *Ashes of Vengeance* with Norma Talmadge. Then he was in: Tod Browning's *Drifting*; Buster Keaton's *The Three Ages*, as his rival; *The Eternal Struggle* with Barbara La Marr; *The Spanish Dancer*, starring Pola Negri and Antonio Moreno; *Richard the Lion-Hearted*, in the title-role (made partly from footage left over from *Robin Hood*); and *The White Tiger*.

He made: *Drums of Jeopardy* (24); Clarence Brown's *The Signal Tower*, starring Virginia Valli; *Unseen Hands*, a study of a total villain, played by himself; *Another Man's Wife* with Lila Lee; Rafael Sabatini's novel *The Sea Hawk*, as a free-booter, starring Milton Sills, the top box-office picture of the year; *The Red Lily*, starring Enid Bennett and Ramon Novarro; *Dynamite Smith* with Charles Ray; *Madonna of the Streets*; *Let Women Alone* (25), with Wanda Hawley, and *So Big*, as the illiterate farmer poor Colleen Moore marries, in this version of Edna Ferber's bestseller. In February, three Beery films were released and he had reached an eminence where he was top-billed in the first two: Victor Fleming's *The Devil's Cargo*, at Paramount, with William Collier Jr – and turns out to be the devil; and *The Lost World*, as Prof Challenger in this adaptation of Conan Doyle, with its unconvincing monsters. He was the heavy in the other film, *The Great Divide*, a Metro Western with Conway Tearle and Alice Terry. These were his last as a freelance: he signed a featured contract with Paramount and appeared in the following: *Coming Through* with Thomas Meighan ('Picturegoer' said Beery made 'a glorious ruffian'); *Adventure*; *The Night Club*, starring comedian Raymond Griffith; *In the Name of Love* with Ricardo Cortez; *Rugged Water*, as a cowardly captain; *The Wanderer*, at First National; and *The Pony Express* with Cortez. Then Paramount teamed him with another actor mainly associated with villainy, Raymond Hatton, for an army comedy, *Behind the Front* (26). It was a wild success and Beery's activity decreased under the stress of new-found stardom: *Volcano* with Bebe Daniels; James Cruze's masterly *Old Ironsides* with Charles Farrell, Esther Ralston and George Bancroft, from a story by Laurence Stallings based on an actual incident in the British–American war of 1812; and *Casey at the Bat* (27) in the title-role, with Zazu Pitts. Paramount, meanwhile, were preparing a series of comedies for him and Hatton: *We're in the Navy Now*, probably the best of the series; *Fireman Save My Child*; *Now We're in the Air*; *Wife Savers* (28); *Partners in Crime*; and *The Big Killing*, a satire on Western feuds. But a big killing was not made at the box-office: Beery and Hatton suffered both from overexposure and from the cheapness of the later ones – they did disastrously at the box-office. Paramount lost interest, but William A. Wellman gave him a good part – a return to villainy – in *Beggars of Life* with Louise Brooks and used him again in *Chinatown Nights* (29), a story of a Tong War with Florence Vidor, made in Silent and Talkie versions. He was in *The Stairs of Sand*, a Zane Grey Western with Phillips Holmes and Jean Arthur, and, way down the cast list, in *River of Romance*.

Paramount were convinced that Beery was not going places with Talkies and dropped him. MGM were, however, interested: they considered teaming him with Buster Keaton in *Free and Easy*, but instead used him in a part intended for Lon Chaney before he died: *Big House* (30), as the thug who leads the prison revolt, a thug without a single redeeming feature. Beery's ferocious performance brought raves and a long-term MGM contract; all the same, MGM could not have guessed at this point that this ugly character actor would become one of their biggest money-makers over the next 20 years. Real stardom was only a step away. He was P.T. Barnum in *A Lady's Morals* (they were Grace Moore's, as Jenny Lind) and Pat Garret, the implacable foe of *Billy the Kid* (Johnny Mack

Wallace Beery and kids: in The Champ *(31), his Oscar-winning performance with Jackie Cooper.*

Brown). Then the studio had the good sense (and good luck for all concerned) to cast him and Marie Dressler as sparring partners, *Min and Bill*: in the era of the Depression, these two old soaks making do and making up were a tonic, and the film hit the astonishing gross of $2 million.

He was put into *Way for a Sailor* in order to bolster John Gilbert at the wickets; he did a strong gangster melodrama, *The Secret Six* (31), and then *The Champ*, playing his usual role, a dirty rogue: but nothing could shake the devotion to him of boy star Jackie Cooper, and this time Beery had a heart of gold. Under King Vidor's direction he was more lovable than he had been with Dressler. Audiences cried buckets: enough of them to put this one, too, among the year's top grossers. Beery won the year's Best Actor Oscar (along with Fredric March for *Dr Jekyll and Mr Hyde* – Beery was in fact just a few votes behind) and at the end of 1932, when the film played off, found himself for the first time among the year's top 10 box-office draws. There were some more big ones in the immediate future: a submarine drama, *Hell Divers*; *Grand Hotel* (32), a fine performance as the nasty little financier; and *Flesh*, as a German champion wrestler, with Karen Morley and Ricardo Cortez – which was a flop.

Tugboat Annie (33) was the second – and last – picture he did with Dressler: more sentiment and laughs (his resource in getting liquor, hers in managing the tug), and more good film-making and big box-office. MGM signed Beery to a new starring contract. Dressler was also in *Dinner at Eight*, but this time Beery as the tough, uncouth tycoon was

In Bad Bascomb *(46) he appeared with another MGM tot, Margaret O'Brien. The lady singing hymns is Marjorie Main, who partnered Beery in a dozen films at the end of his career.*

concerned only with the carrying-on of his tarty wife, Jean Harlow. He was then loaned to 20th Century Pictures, the new production company formed by Darryl F. Zanuck and Joseph M. Schenck, releasing through United Artists, for their first film, *The Bowery* (Schenck's brother, Nicholas, was the president of Loew's Inc., which owned MGM – and indeed he was one of the financial backers of Twentieth Century: this meant that that company could draw on MGM for talent, which it did for some years, despite Louis B. Mayer's objections). The cast of *The Bowery* included George Raft to quarrel and fight with, and Jackie Cooper, for sentiment. Then Beery had what was probably his best part – and he gave a superb performance – Pancho Villa in *Viva Villa!* (34), a good account of the Mexican Revolution. He was Long John Silver in *Treasure Island*, with Jackie Cooper as his Jim Hawkins in this adaptation of Stevenson, and then he played P.T. Barnum again in 20th's *The Mighty Barnum*. 1935 was his last consecutive year in the top 10 box-office list: *West Point of the Air*, as a sergeant, with Robert Young; *China Seas* with Clark Gable and Harlow, as a sadistic villain; *O'Shaughnessy's Boy*, again with young Cooper; and *Ah Wilderness!*, as the Uncle.

He was loaned to 20th again for another Mexican subject, *A Message to Garcia* (36) with Barbara Stanwyck top-billed, as a local renegade, and was officially 'demoted' from the roster of top MGM stars. He increasingly made programmers – 'mush and muscle' pictures as they were called: *Old Hutch*, as an incorrigible loafer; *The Good Old Soak* (37); 20th's good, stark melodrama, *Slave Ship*, co-

starring Warner Baxter; *Bad Man of Brimstone* (38) with Virginia Bruce; *Port of Seven Seas* with Frank Morgan as Panisse and Beery poor in Raimu's old role (César). After co-starring with Mickey Rooney in the well-named *Stablemates* he starred with Robert Taylor in *Stand Up and Fight* (39), as a lovable old rogue who goes in for slave-running – an activity which this (silly) script tried to gloss over. He followed with *Sergeant Madden*, directed by Josef von Sternberg, as an Irish cop, and *Thunder Afloat*, which the 'Daily Mail' (London) thought 'the best performance Wallace Beery has given since *Min and Bill*'. But it was formula Beery stuff: captain of a tug-boat who joins the Navy to get revenge on the Germans who sank his boat, resisting discipline under former rival Chester Morris and becoming a hero after chasing the German subs.

Beery made a surprise reappearance in the top money-making stars in 1940: *The Man From Dakota*, a Western; *Twenty-Mule Team*, paired with Marjorie Rambeau in an attempt to find a partner that might have the same sort of lure as Marie Dressler; and *Wyoming*, where a small-part actress, Marjorie Main, was effectively cast as a blacksmith. It was Main who seemed most to fit Dressler's boots; Beery and MGM were delighted and she was signed to a long-term contract. After he had done *The Bad Man* (41) with Ronald Reagan, they were teamed several times: *Barnacle Bill*, *The Bugle Sounds* (42) and *Jackass Mail*. He was off the screen for a while, returned in *Salute to the Marines* (43), with Fay Bainter as his wife, and then suffered *Rationing* (44) with Main. They were not as popular as Beery and Dressler; Main, a fine character actress, lacked some of Dressler's 'heart' – she was altogether more predictable; but then the scripts were never as good. Main recalled later that she did not find it easy working with Beery, because he would not rehearse and kept changing his dialogue and business.

He did *Barbary Coast Gent*; *This Man's Navy* (45) with Tom Drake – it was in fact about airships; *Bad Bascomb* (46) with Main and Margaret O'Brien; *The Mighty McGurk*, a remake of *The Champ*, with Dean Stockwell; and, after a long interval, *Alias a Gentleman* (48). He got out of the dualler slot and into tails for a musical with Jane Powell and Carmen Miranda, *A Date With Judy*. His last picture, *Big Jack* (49), was released posthumously; he died of a heart attack in 1949, just as he was about to start what would have been his first non-MGM film in more than a decade, *Johnny Holiday* (William Bendix replaced him). He married Areta Gilman in 1924 and they separated in 1939.

CONSTANCE BENNETT

Although Constance Bennett specialized at one time in sob-and-sex dramas where she was morally somewhat soiled – usually an unmarried mother – she is remembered best as a glamorous light comedienne. She is in fact remembered extremely well considering that she was a top star only during the early part of a long career. But then she was special in comedy – one of the specialists – with a subtle, worldly wise approach, never ruffled, always one step ahead. Said 'Picturegoer' of her in 1931, when she was returning to films after an absence: 'Fans raved over her elegance, her perfect manners, her personality. Her voice was intriguing to a degree. It was the last word in sophistication.'

She was born in 1905 in New York City, into a theatrical family; her father was Richard Bennett, a well-known stage actor and later a supporting player in movies (he appeared in Connie's *Bought*). There were two younger sisters, Barbara, who had a short career in movies starting as a child, and Joan, who became as famous as Constance. Constance married in 1921, a student, Chester Moorehead, but it did not last. To keep her occupied, father Bennett got her small roles in two movies for Lewis Selznick, *Reckless Youth* (22) and *Evidence*. In *What's Wrong with Women?* she played a flapper, but her career lapsed until she met Sam Goldwyn socially. As a result, he gave her a large role in what was his third independent production, *Cytherea* (24), from the novel by Joseph Hergesheimer. Lewis Stone was the star and Bennett was a movie-star in this melodrama noted more for its two two-colour sequences

Constance Bennett had established herself as a comedienne in the Silent era, but her early Talkies were maudlin melodramas, often with Joel McCrea. Like Born to Love *(31).*

than for the coherence of its plot. Then she played a society girl kidnapped by a gang of crooks, in *Into the Net*, released by Pathé as both a serial and a feature; and a wild flapper succumbing to a calm Owen Moore in *Married?*, a quickie that got few bookings.

It was *The Goose Hangs High* (25), directed by James Cruze – a funny small-town piece about a flapper daughter (Bennett) – which first attracted attention to her, and the next made her a star: *Code of the West*, as a flirtatious flapper being tamed again by cowboy Owen Moore. There followed *My Son* (from Martha Stanley's hit play) and the son was Nazimova's – Jack Pickford, being tempted by Bennett. In *My Wife and I* she stole Irene Rich's husband and in Clarence Brown's *The Goose Woman* was again the sweetie of Pickford, son of a has-been diva (Louise Dresser) who finds fame again as witness to a murder. MGM cast her, Joan Crawford and Sally O'Neill as *Sally Irene and Mary*, and liked her well enough to offer a long-term contract; but first she had to honour two commitments: *Wandering Fires* and *The Pinch Hitter* (26). Instead of reporting to Metro, she asked for an annulment of the contract. As a contemporary report put it: 'About this time she eloped with a young millionaire, Philip Plant, and gave up film work. She lived mostly abroad. Obtained a divorce and subsequently returned to the screen.'

But she did not return to MGM, who had first call on her services; she signed with Pathé, doubtless due to the influence of one of their executives, the Marquis de la Falaise, soon to be Gloria Swanson's ex- and Bennett's next husband (1932–40). The contract stipulated three months' vacation: said she, 'Hollywood is pretty painful even in small quantities.' Her come-back film was a hit comedy with Edmund Lowe, *This Thing Called Love* (29), a Talkie. She was borrowed by Warner Bros. for *Son of the Gods* (30) and promptly stole it from co-star Richard Barthelmess; she was in *Rich People* with Regis Toomey, discovering that wealth was a bar to happiness; and in *Common Clay* at Fox as the housemaid seduced by the son of the house (Lew Ayres) and battling in the courts for their bastard. This, one of the year's most popular films, led to a run of similar parts – though thereafter she was more ambitious: her sinning was done strictly in the cause of luxury. First there was an oft-filmed thriller, *Three Faces East*, as a spy pretending to be a nurse in an English mansion with Erich Von Stroheim as the butler; a comedy with Kenneth MacKenna, *Sin Takes a Holiday* – he paid her a salary to marry him and thus avoided being named in a divorce scandal; then *The Easiest Way* (31) – she took it; and

Born to Love – Joel McCrea, the father of her son in this artificial war romance. Pathé liked this teaming – his boyish character vis-à-vis her sophistication – and reunited them for *The Common Law*, where she was a kept woman, encountered in Paris, in confrontation with his family. In *Bought* she was illegitimate herself. Ben Lyon was in it and they were re-teamed for a comedy in which she is said to be too 'soiled' to be married to anyone in the smart set, *Lady With a Past* (32) – called *Reputation* in Britain, and very good for hers, too ('Connie Bennett as a real person this time,' said 'Photoplay'). *What Price Hollywood?* was a comedy-melodrama about a Brown Derby waitress who becomes a big star and marries another (Neil Hamilton): *A Star is Born* later borrowed much of this, though here the drunk was a director (Lowell Sherman) and it was her understanding of his problem which provided the climax – break-up of marriage and flight from stardom. A brilliant film by any standards, directed by George Cukor, and possibly Bennett's best performance.

These were her peak years. In 1931 she was second only to Garbo in a poll of US exhibitors and in 1932 she was second to Norma Shearer in a poll of British cinema-goers (the Bernstein questionnaire). Her salary reflected this: agent Myron Selznick had got $30,000 a week for her for *Bought* at Warner Bros. – the highest salary paid up to that time – in what was ostensibly her vacation. When she returned to Warners for *Two Against the World* (Hamilton was an attorney in love with her despite her unsavoury past) her salary again broke records: $150,000 for four and a half weeks' work, as opposed to

$8,000 weekly at Pathé. The money was some consolation for not getting Jo in *Little Women*, which went to Pathé–RKO's new star, Katharine Hepburn. The studio did let her have her way over *Rockabye*, a project they were not keen on. She played a stage-star, again in love with McCrea. Cukor directed it and the next, *Our Betters* (33), a static version of the Maugham play. Both were conspicuous flops. In *Bed of Roses* (with McCrea) she was a hooker working the Mississippi and in *After Tonight*, as the ads said 'A Beautiful Russian Spy . . . A gay Viennese Officer': he was Gilbert Roland, upped from a minor role in *Our Betters* (as a kept man) and later in life her husband (1941–45).

Her contract expired and Pathé were not anxious to renew. Bennett signed a two-film deal with 20th: *Moulin Rouge* (34) with Franchot Tone, a remake of *Her Sister in Paris*, which had starred Constance Talmadge (Miss Bennett would play in another version, *Two-Faced Woman*, but the leading role – twins – would be played by Garbo); and *The Affairs of Cellini*, a factitious costume drama, stolen from her and Fredric March by Frank Morgan. She moved on to MGM on a three-year contract, but only two films emerged: *Outcast Lady*, another – poor – version of 'The Green Hat', originally intended for Norma Shearer, and *After Office Hours* (35), a comedy with Clark Gable. Publicity still referred to her as 'the highest paid actress in the world', but after three years of mainly conveyor-belt films her popularity had gone and Hollywood was unwilling to pay. After a year of inactivity she made *Everything is*

Constance Bennett and millionaire Wilfred Lawson in Ladies in Love (36), *the first flowering of 20th Century-Fox's perennial about three girls in search of wealthy husbands.*

Thunder (36) for Gaumont-British, in Britain, playing a Berlin whore 'on a note of concentrated sweetness and light' ('Picturegoer') who aids an escaped p.o.w. (Douglas Montgomery). It was an unhappy experience, and she later sued G-B for breach of contract and won. She returned to Hollywood no longer a major-league star.

20th asked her to play in the multi-star *Ladies in Love*, but alas she lost millionaire Paul Lukas to precocious Simone Simon. Hal Roach offered a contract and with it went the two films for which she is best remembered: *Topper* (37), in which she and Cary Grant were ghosts; and, even funnier, *Merrily We Live* (38), with Brian Aherne, a variation on *My Man Godfrey*. At Universal she played a husband-hunting dame in *Service de Luxe*, a weak comedy, and then she did her last for Roach, *Topper Takes a Trip* (39), a fair sequel to the earlier film. At 20th, she was billed below Alice Faye in *Tailspin*, a silly film about women flyers. *Escape to Glory* (40), with Pat O'Brien, and *Law of the Tropics* (41) were mere programme fodder; the latter was a remake of *Oil for the Lamps of China* and Warners paid her $10,000 for her services.

She accepted below-the-title billing for *Two-Faced Woman* because Garbo was in it; she played her rival for Melvyn Douglas and there were critics who thought Miss Bennett outshone her. Still, she knew her star had slipped when she agreed to do these: *Wild Bill Hickock Rides* with Bruce Cabot; *Sin Town* (42) with Broderick Crawford, in a role turned down by Mae West; and *Madame Spy*. In 1940 she had toured in Noël Coward's 'Easy Virtue'; she returned to the stage, touring, in 'Without Love'. Since the beginning of the war in Europe she had worked tirelessly for refugees; when not acting she went into cosmetics and fashion, and did a radio show. In 1946 she married Colonel John Coulter and she was, wrote her sister Joan later, very happy for the last 20 years of her life.

Under the auspices of United Artists, she produced herself and Gracie Fields in *Paris Underground* (46), but the public had long tired of Resistance dramas. At 20th she played Jeanne Crain's glamorous aunt in *Centennial Summer* and at Warners she was Claude Rains's girl-Friday in *The Unsuspected* (47). The next were Bs: *Smart Woman* (48), produced by herself at Monogram, with Brian Aherne, who said later, 'it died unseen'; and *Angel on the Amazon* (49) at Republic, as a psychiatrist, with George Brent. She headed the supporting cast in *As Young As You Feel* (51), as the wife of executive Albert Dekker, falling under the spell of Monty Woolley. In the 50s she appeared on TV, did a brief bit as

herself in *It Should Happen to You* (54), had a nightclub act for a while and toured in 'Auntie Mame' (58). She toured briefly in 'Toys in the Attic' (61) and did a good featured part in *Madame X* (65) as Lana Turner's mother. Not long before, a fan magazine had written: 'Temperament plus a rather hectic personal life were responsible for hampering her professional success', but the truth was rather that she was too intelligent and independent to play the game except her way – and she never cared much whether she worked or not. Not long afterwards (1965) she died of a cerebral haemorrhage.

JOAN BENNETT

Joan Bennett was always glamorous and capable, the epitome of the film star. It has been a standard Hollywood story: fresh blonde newcomer and then star – with jet-black hair ('Let's talk of Lamarr, that Hedy so fair/Is it true that Joan Bennett wears all her old hair?' ran a lyric in Cole Porter's 'Let's Face It'), impecable professional reputation as she aged and the inevitable decline set in; three marriages, one scandal. In Bennett's case, there were no apparent pretensions: she was workmanlike – from her days as a demure and distinctly dewy-eyed heroine, a more virginal edition of her elder sister Constance, to her emergence, especially under the direction of Fritz Lang, as one of the more memorable of the species *femme fatale*.

She was born in Palisades, NJ, in 1910 and expensively educated – there was a finishing school in Versailles. At 16 she ran away with the son of a millionaire and at 17 was a mother (later, of course, she became 'Hollywood's youngest and most beautiful grandmother'). The marriage did not last and she was briefly a Hollywood extra in *The Divine Lady* (28), before getting a small part in *Power*; then her father, actor Richard Bennett, engaged her to support him at the Longacre, New York, in 'Jarnegan' by Jim Tully. They were an acting family and he wanted her to have the same screen success as Connie. She was tested by both Fox and Paramount, who turned her down; but Goldwyn tested her and signed her on behalf of United Artists. He put her into his *Bulldog Drummond* (29), with Ronald Colman, but after *Three Live Ghosts* she was dropped. She had no difficulty getting work: *Disraeli*, as the ingénue; *The Mississippi Gambler* at Universal, with Joseph Schildkraut more or less reprising his role in *Show Boat*; *Puttin' on the Ritz* (30), at United Artists, a backstage drama with Harry Richman; *Crazy That Way*, at Fox, as a girl with three suitors, including Kenneth MacKenna; *Moby Dick* with John Barrymore, where, clearly, she was an interpolation; and *Maybe It's Love* with Joe E. Brown and the All-American Football Team. She played leads and being Connie's sister was not detrimental.

United Artists planned to star her in a new version of *Smilin' Through*, but MGM had their eyes on that property for Norma Shearer. Bennett instead signed a two-year contract with Fox which would bring her (July 1931) $2,000 a week – a pittance compared to her sister's salary. She appeared in: *Scotland Yard* with Edmund Lowe; *Doctors' Wives* (31), as one of them, neglected by Warner Baxter; *Hush Money*, as mistress of racketeer Owen Moore; *Many a Slip* at Universal with Lew Ayres – 'another of the "unwanted baby" type of picture' said 'Picturegoer'; *She Wanted a Millionaire* (32) – which she got, wishing she had stuck with Spencer Tracy; *Careless Lady*, as a small-town girl who gets sophistication, with John Boles; *The Trial of Vivienne Ware* with Donald Cook; and *Weekends Only* with Ben Lyon. She was off the screen for several months due to a riding accident and this year married screenwriter Gene Markey. She returned to films in the usual mixed bag: *Wild Girl*, a pioneer drama with Charles Farrell and Ralph Bellamy; and *Me and My Gal*, wise-cracking with Tracy. The film had been meant for Sally Eilers and James Dunn, but Tracy had asked for it for himself and Bennett. The 'Motion Picture Herald' thought her 'a sheer delight', but she was hardly at home as a hash-slinger. She made one with Dunn, *Arizona to Broadway*, a gangster burlesque.

At this point Fox dropped her because – they now decided – she was not yet ready for stardom. She announced that she was going to freelance and after some months got a smaller part than she was used to, but in a good film for once, *Little Women* (34), as Amy. This brought her to the attention of independent producer Walter Wanger, who signed her, which meant that he loaned her around, usually to his distributing company, Paramount, for whom she did an engaging comedy about the American Revolution, called appropriately *The Pursuit of Happiness*. She was in *The Man Who Reclaimed His Head* (35) at Universal with Claude Rains and had a rare good role supporting Claudette Colbert and Charles Boyer in *Private Worlds*, as Joel McCrea's fluffy wife. She was not very good; but after being crooned to twice by Bing Crosby, in *Mississippi* and *Two for Tonight*, she was excellent in a comedy with George Raft, *She Couldn't Take it*, at Columbia, as a daffy spoilt beauty. At 20th, Ronald Colman asked for her: *The Man Who Broke the Bank*

Joan Bennett as a blonde: the winsome heroine of The Pursuit of Happiness *(34) with Francis Lederer.*

at Monte Carlo, playing casino-bait.

Four Bennett films were released the following year: *Thirteen Hours by Air* (36), as a passenger in Fred MacMurray's plane; *Big Brown Eyes*, produced by Wanger, as a manicurist-cum-sobsister, involved with detective Cary Grant; *Two in a Crowd*, a race-track comedy with Joel McCrea; and *Wedding Present*, again with Grant, as reporters falling in and out of love. Wanger had moved over to United Artists and he put Miss Bennett into two of his own films: *Vogues of 1938* (37), which had Warner Baxter, colour, lots of fashion parades and very little else; and *I Met My Love* (38), a poor romantic drama with Henry Fonda. She divorced Markey and toured in 'Stage Door'; at Paramount she did *The Texans* (38) with Randolph Scott ('They faced a thousand frontier terrors for love'); and *Artists and Models Abroad*, with Jack Benny, as an heiress who gets involved with some down-and-out mummers.

Wanger produced *Trade Winds* (39), where detective Fredric March chased her round the world: 'with eyes at half-mast and voice lowered an octave, I positively smouldered all over the South Seas,' she said later. She wore a black wig, at the suggestion of Tay Garnett, who directed: as a joke, to imitate Hedy Lamarr. The effect was sensational and she decided to stay dark: it was the start of a new, more interesting Bennett. She marked time: *The Man in the Iron Mask* for Edward Small-UA, with, in the title role, Louis Hayward, thought at that time to be going places; *The Housekeeper's Daughter* for Hal Roach, in the title-role, a gangster's decoy who hides out in the mansion where her mother works, in this strange comedy with Adolphe Menjou; and *Green Hell* (40) at Universal with Douglas Fairbanks Jr, in high heels in the jungle.

In 1940 she married Wanger and he celebrated the event by putting her in a good thriller, *The House Across the Bay*, caught between convict husband George Raft and new boyfriend Walter Pidgeon. It was her last film under her deal with him and she signed with both Columbia and 20th, the latter for two pictures a year. These were mainly medium-budgeters and the first of the batch was the most interesting: *The Man I Married*, who was Francis Lederer, a German-American whom she watches fall under the spell of Nazism: good anti-Nazi propaganda. There was a brief return to escapism with *Son of Monte Cristo*, with Louis Hayward; then *She Knew All the Answers* (41) and Franchot Tone asked the questions. In another anti-Nazi piece, Fritz Lang's *Man Hunt*, she played a Cockney tart (at least, she wore the regulation mac and beret) who helped Walter Pidgeon: it could not be said that she was remotely convincing, but it was a gallant try. The others: *Wild Geese Calling*, loving a wander-lusting Henry Fonda; *Confirm or Deny*, in a wartime romance with Don Ameche: *Twin Beds* (42), sharing them with George Brent in this antique farce for Small at United Artists: *The Wife Takes a Flyer*, with Franchot Tone: and *Girl Trouble*, letting her apartment to a playboy (Ameche) and posing as her own maid. *Margin for Error* (43), based on a play by Clare Boothe Luce, was a pre-TV attempt to make a star out of

Joan Bennett as a brunette: the tramp known as Lazy-Legs in Scarlet Street (46) *with Dan Duryea.*

Milton Berle – playing a New York Jewish detective involved with German consul Otto Preminger (who also directed). Bennett was the consul's wife.

She was off the screen, twice pregnant, for almost two years; then Fritz Lang cast her as *The Woman in the Window* (44), the hooker (?) with whom professor Edward G. Robinson gets involved. This was a version of the treacherous Mary Astor character of *The Maltese Falcon* and a staple of the films of the decade. Bennett, tantalizingly sexy, was one of the best. She moved up in the social scale, to *Nob Hill* (45), enticing George Raft from saloon singer Vivian Blaine. *Colonel Effingham's Raid* (46), with Charles Coburn, was a B, but she had formed a production company with Fritz Lang. He directed her and Robinson again, and Dan Duryea, in *Scarlet Street*; her floozie this time was much less equivocal. She was satanic again in *The Macomber Affair* (47), cuckolding Robert Preston with Gregory Peck, and was up to the same tricks in Jean Renoir's *Woman on the Beach*, deceiving Charles Bickford with Robert Ryan. The film, however, was preposterous, and so was Lang's *The Secret Beyond the Door* (48) as Michael Redgrave's frightened bride. After *The Scar* she worked under a third distinguished European director coincidentally below his best, Max Ophuls: *The Reckless Moment* (49) with James Mason, as a housewife coming to terms with blackmail. But all three films were more interesting than most she made – certainly more than *The Scar*, a silly film with Paul Henried as a gangster at Eagle-Lion (the company part-owned by the British Rank Organization).

In 1948 (and 1951) Bennett toured in 'Susan and God': in films she suddenly became middle-aged, married to Robert Cummings in a dire whimsical comedy, *For Heaven's Sake* (50), and better, but older, married to Spencer Tracy for *Father of the Bride* and *Father's Little Dividend* (51). She made *The Guy Who Came Back* with Paul Douglas; and began working extensively in radio and TV to pay off debts incurred by her husband's film, *Joan of Arc*, with Ingrid Bergman. Also in 1951 her husband, Wanger, took a pot-shot at her agent, Jennings Lang, when he was talking to her in a parking lot. Wanger admitted jealousy, but no allegations were made other than that Bennett preferred Lang's professional advice to Wanger's. Wanger was convicted and served a short jail sentence; he and Bennett were reconciled in 1953 and remained married till she finally divorced him in 1965.

In 1953 she toured in 'Bell, Book and Candle'. Her subsequent films do not indicate much good advice on the part of any agent, beginning with *Highway Dragnet* (54), with Richard Conte at Allied Artists. She said later that the scandal killed Hollywood interest in her, but almost all the female stars of her generation began to feel the draught in the early 50s. Humphrey Bogart helped her by insisting on her for *We're No Angels* (55), but she had featured billing and only a smallish role as the shopkeeper's wife. A soon-forgotten soap, *There's Always Tomorrow* (56) co-starred two other artists who had also seen better days: Fred MacMurray, who played her husband, and Barbara Stanwyck, as the old flame who tempts him. Miss Bennett's film career virtually ended with *Navy Wife*, produced by Wanger, with Gary Merrill; and *Desire in the Dust* (60), a well-named Southern drama co-starring Raymond Burr. She did some TV and worked in the theatre; apart from 'Love Me Little' in 1958, in New York, she was content to tour: 'Best Foot Forward', 'Anniversary Waltz', 'Janus' (56), 'Once More With Feeling', 'The Pleasure of His Company' (59) and 'Never Too Late'. In the latter she made her London stage debut (63), but the play got dreadful notices. In 1968 she began in a TV series, 'Dark Shadows', and she made a film of it, *House of Dark Shadows* (70).

She has filmed intermittently since: *Gidget Gets Married* (72), which reunited her with Ameche; *The Eyes of Charles Sand*, as an aunt; *Suspiria* (76), a German-Italian co-production and the only one of this batch not made for TV, as the head of a ballet school; *Suddenly Love* (78), produced by that old star-lover Ross Hunter, married to Lew Ayres; *This House Possessed* (81), as a bag lady; and *Divorce Wars* (82), which starred Tom Selleck.

JACK BENNY

It was part of Jack Benny's routine that he was a flop in pictures: which is not the case. He was not an outstanding success, either, certainly not in the same class as his friend and rival Bob Hope. Their screen personas were much alike. Benny was cowardly, inept, boastful and, of course, mean. In one thing Benny is/was right: *The Horn Blows at Midnight* was a horrendous film and certified box-office loser: for once the perfection of his timing was wasted.

Benny (Benny Kubelsky) was born in 1894 in Waukegan, Illinois. On leaving school he worked in his father's haberdashery and played the violin in the local theatre band. In 1912 he was part of a double-act called Salisbury and Benny; later that year he was

billed as 'Ben Benny, the Fiddlin' Kid'. He served four years with the navy during World War I and returned to vaudeville (and flopped on his first two dates in New York City). In 1928 he was emcee at New York's Little Club and appearing at Loew's. His act was caught by Harry Rapf of MGM and he was signed to a long-term contract, two pictures a year at $1,500 a week. Talkies had just come in and Benny was basically a stand-up (talk) comedian. They put him into *The Hollywood Revue of 1929* (29), as an emcee, and *Chasing Rainbows* (30), as the stage manager. Due to his film success he was a smash hit at the London Palladium and he also had a success in 'The Earl Carroll Vanities' (30) in New York. MGM, on the other hand, had no plans for him and Benny asked for his release. His film career thereafter was distinctly chequered. He was *The Medicine Man* with Betty Bronson for Tiffany; there was a Vitaphone short, *Bright Moments*, and another called *The Song-Writers Revue*, released by Metro-Movietone; and *Mr Broadway* (33), released by the Broadway-Hollywood Co. But his great success and fame came with radio: on CBS in the 30s with his wife Mary Livingstone and stalwarts such as Eddie 'Rochester' Anderson.

Encouraged by his national following, UA (Edward Small) put him in *Transatlantic Merry-Go-Round* (35), murder on the high seas, as a broadcaster, with music, Nancy Carroll and Mitzi Green. MGM signed him again: *Broadway Melody of 1936* (35), playing almost straight as a trouble-making columnist; and *It's in the Air*, with Una Merkel, in which he is seeking to find a way to avoid paying taxes. Then Metro let him go again. Paramount tried and had more success: *The Big Broadcast of 1937* (36), as the manager of a radio station bothered by Gracie Allen – while George Burns looked on. They made a blissful duo, joined again by George – and Mary Boland and Martha Raye – in the delightfully daft *College Holiday* (37). *Artists and Models* and *Artists and Models Abroad* (38) are not, despite their titles, related: in the first, Benny is an advertising man, in the second the manager of a show troupe stranded in Paris. The latter was the first of a new Paramount contract, calling for two films a year at $100,000 each. *Man About Town* (39) was a moderate success, but both *Buck Benny Rides Again* (40) and *Love Thy Neighbour* were big hits, and Benny was riding high as a screen star, in Britain as well as the US.

He made no more pictures for Paramount, whose top banana was now Bob Hope; but the fact that Benny's film career was marked by so many scrapped contracts in curious. He was popular and he was not temperamental, but

Jack Benny and all-star co-stars. The line-up is from Chasing Rainbows (30) *and includes Benny (third from left),* Bessie Love, Eddie Phillips, George K. Arthur, Marie Dressler *and* Polly Moran. *One of the musicals MGM made to cash in on the success of* Broadway Melody.

the camera did have difficulty hiding the effeminacy of his walk. He was much too old for *Charley's Aunt* (41), at 20th, but was ingratiating and thus believable as an undergraduate (just as, for his sake, when he protests against his reputation for meanness, one tries – hard – to believe him). The film anyway was great fun and included some unusual examples of Benny doing visual gags. As a result of its success, 20th announced that Benny was contracted to to three pictures over the next four years.

At UA he co-starred with Carole Lombard in *To Be or Not To Be* (42), easily his best film: – and he was superb as a 'great' Polish classical actor, much in love with himself and involved with the Nazis – from which it was a climb-down to a comedy about a dilapidated farmhouse, at Warners, *George Washington Slept Here*, with Ann Sheridan. But the only other film he made for 20th was a 57-minute effort with Priscilla Lane and Rochester, *The Meanest Man in the World* (43) – and considering this script, also the most unfortunate.

But that was nothing: *The Horn Blows at Midnight* (45) was next, a whimsy that began in heaven but was hellish in every respect. Warners had let him fiddle a bit and give some indication of his vaude act, as himself in *Hollywood Canteen* (44), but it was too slight a bit to compensate. Benny had also guest-starred in one marvellous sequence in *It's in the Bag* (45), starring a comedian even more rarely in films (and another friend and radio favourite), the great Fred Allen. Benny's subsequent film appearances were merely in guest spots unbilled, such as *Somebody Loves Me* (53) and *The Seven Little Foys* (55). Instead of worrying about films, he went on to conquer TV. His last guest appearance was *A Guide for the Married Man* (67). He died in 1974, just before he was due to start his first starring role in a film in three decades, *The Sunshine Boys*: his friend George Burns replaced him.

INGRID BERGMAN

'Say,' went a joke in New York in 1945, 'today I saw a picture without Ingrid Bergman in it.' *Saratoga Trunk*, *The Bells of St Mary's* and *Spellbound* were playing simultaneously and the point is that *everyone* was going to see them. She was the uncrowned Queen of Hollywood, on a tide of popularity that looked like rolling on forever. A gallup poll that year in the United States found her the most popular female star (followed by Bette Davis, Judy Garland, Greer Garson and Betty Grable, in that order). Then came the most unexpected scandal in Hollywood's history, and banishment.

Few stars had evoked such praise and fervent admiration: since she had arrived from Sweden in 1939 Bergman represented ideal womanhood to millions of Americans: she was so much more attainable than her great compatriot, Garbo, that comparisons were rarely made. Like Garbo, she was born in Stockholm, in 1915. Her mother died when she was two; her father when she was 12, and the spinster aunt who had raised her died a few months later. She went to live with an uncle and with her inheritance, later, studied at the Royal Dramatic Theatre in Stockholm. In 1934 she went into films, with the encouragement of Dr Peter Lindstrom, who became her husband in 1937. She was in fact visiting a friend at a film studio when spotted: Svenskfilmindustri signed her to a contract. In her first film, *Munkbrogreven* (34), she had a small part as a hotel maid, making her first entrance with a smile, which would be entirely appropriate to her film career. She was given the lead in *Bränninger* (35), as a fisherman's daughter who is raped by a priest. In Gustav Molander's family drama *Swedenhielms*, she was the prospective daughter-in-law of the old patriarch (Gosta Ekman). Then she did another first-rate melodrama, *Valborgsmässoaften* (36), the daughter of Victor Sjöstrom, in love with her unhappily married boss, Lars Hanson. She was now a star in Sweden; and might have made a Hollywood star if producers read the 'New York Times', which spoke of her 'natural charm . . . [she] dominates the picture throughout'. The picture concerned was *Pa Solidan*, again with Hanson, in which she was an orphan who almost succumbs to temptation at a picnic. *Intermezzo* followed, a romantic drama directed by Gustav Molander about a famous violinist (Gosta Ekman) and his adulterous affair with a young pianist (Bergman). Molander directed her again in *Dollar* (38), a marital comedy with George Rydeberg; in *En Kvinnas Ansikte*, remade by MGM as *A Woman's Face*; and *En Enda Natt* (39) in which she resisted the advances of her guardian's bastard son. The latter was shown in the US in

Ingrid Bergman and Leslie Howard in Intermezzo: A Love Story (*39*), *re-titled in Britain* Escape to Happiness, *suggesting somewhat its seven-year-itch theme – on which it was a very romantic variation.*

1942 and Archer Winsten observed in the 'New York Post': 'Whoever in Hollywood discovered Miss Bergman doesn't deserve much credit, no one could have missed her talent.' Meanwhile, she went to Germany for *Die Vier Gesellen* (38), a story of four young girl graduates.

A print of *Intermezzo* found its way to New York and was seen by Kay Brown, Selznick's story editor. She recommended this one, along with Bergman, but Selznick was not impressed – he would have preferred Loretta Young – and took her only because Brown insisted that her qualities were essential to the film. She was able to accept his offer only when a UFA film about Charlotte Corday was cancelled in Germany. Later she claimed that she signed for only one film with an option on both sides, for she had no desire to be yet another European actress who had not succeeded in Hollywood; but in fact the contract was for two films a year for five years with the right to do outside pictures in a language other than English. Selznick would pay $20,000 (i.e. $2,500 a week) for the first, increasing to $40,000. Leslie Howard played the violinist in the new version, *Intermezzo: a Love Story* (39), which conclusively demonstrated that a new star had arrived. Hollywood had never seen anything like her and much publicity – directed by Selznick – accrued from her naturalness, her lack of both sophistication and make-up (Joan Fontaine has recalled that she and Vivien Leigh were then chastised by Selznick for using lipstick). 'Picturegoer' said: 'She is intelligent, natural and wholly charming without being beautiful' – the reservation being one which no one else shared. Bergman *was* different from the standard Hollywood star: there was about her a curious, unique freshness. Possibly it was specifically Nordic – a combination of directness/gentleness/good health/sex (it made plausible and even palatable *Intermezzo*'s thesis on marital infidelity). In her third Hollywood film Robert Montgomery says of her: 'If she had her way she'd make the whole world happy,' and it is as good a description of Miss Bergman's artistry as you're likely to get.

She was not surprised to find herself a Hollywood star, for she had much self-confidence, and her colleagues in Sweden had always regarded her as abnormally ambitious. Returning amongst them her Hollywood grooming showed, for she was much less lacquered than in most of her other Swedish films: *Juninatten* (40), a melodrama about a Stockholm chemist whose past catches up with her in the shape of a former lover, an unstable sailor (Gunnar Sjoberg). Leslie Howard now wanted her for a film in Britain, but Selznick would not permit it; he could not have

prevented her from accepting an offer from Germany, but knew that if she did she could no longer expect (because of the war) acceptance by audiences elsewhere. So he recalled her with the promise of a film on Joan of Arc: in fact, he had nothing for her and with trepidation – because of her inexperience on the stage – allowed her to do 'Liliom' on Broadway with Burgess Meredith. Paramount wanted her for *Victory*, but Selznick's asking price was $75,000 and they would not go higher than $50,000 – which is twice what he would have paid her. She was not resentful of this, nor that she would exist on loan-outs since he had virtually ceased production: but she did want to work. So he sent her to Columbia and then MGM (who paid him $34,000 for her services): *Adam Had Four Sons* (41), as a governess in love with her charge's father, and *Rage in Heaven*, as the unfortunate wife of paranoic Robert Montgomery. MGM asked her to stay on to play the ingénue in *Dr Jekyll and Mr Hyde*, but she begged to play the floozie, swopping parts with Lana Turner. Both co-star Spencer Tracy and director Victor Fleming fell in love with her, understandably (and as Sheilah Graham once said, it was easier to list the directors and leading men with whom she didn't have affairs than otherwise). Her performance in the film was only partially successful, but the 'New York Times' (Theodore Strauss) said it proved again that 'a shining talent' could make something of a poor part – in contrast to Turner and the rest of the supporting cast, who moved 'like well-behaved puppets'. She sought the role of Maria in *For Whom the Bell Tolls*, but even with Hemingway's blessing Paramount turned her down – in favour of Vera Zorina. She consoled herself by playing Anna Christie in Santa Barbara and San Francisco. Warner Bros. meanwhile were desperate for a continental heroine for *Casablanca* (42). This had originally been planned for Dennis Morgan and Michèle Morgan; Humphrey Bogart had now taken on the male lead and the Morgan role had been offered to Hedy Lamarr, who had turned it down: the role was one she might have played well – the conventional woman of mystery, part *femme fatale*, part true love. Bergman's acting in the role is not acting of a high order, or indeed of any order, but she is superbly right and completely magical. No other actress is conceivable in the role. She and Bogart were memorable together and the film was a solid-gold hit. After Selznick saw it, he observed that it confirmed his view that she would become 'one of the great stars of the world'; and it made her a sure box-office draw.

That fact, coupled with the rushes of Zorina non-emoting in *For Whom the Bell Tolls* (43)

Bergman as a saint and sinner: as saint in The Bells of St Mary's *(45) and* Joan of Arc *(48) and as sinner in* Arch of Triumph *(48) and* Saratoga Trunk *(43). There is no question that audiences preferred her as a good woman.*

caused Paramount to beg Bergman to take over the part. Her love scenes with Gary Cooper seemed remarkable at the time, but she was an unlikely Spanish peasant. Still, as James Agee wrote: 'Miss Bergman not only bears a starting resemblance to an imaginable human being; she really knows how to act, in a blend of poetic grace with quiet realism which almost never appears in American pictures.'

The Bergman fervour was on, and all studios scrambled to employ her; and, although it was not foreseen at the time, this was the beginning of the end for the star-contract system. She was a better box-office proposition than any female star except perhaps Greer Garson and Bette Davis, both tied to their own studios. Selznick had got $25,000 for her services in *Casablanca*, plus the promise of Olivia de Havilland on loan and Bergman playing the lead in *Saratoga Trunk* (though Warners had bought it for either Bette Davis or Vivien Leigh). Paramount paid him $90,666.55, of which $31,770.38 was passed on to her; now that *Saratoga Trunk* came up, Warners paid $253,802.08 – of which she got $69,562.30 – plus the services of Miss de Havilland for a mere $30,000. Bergman then went to MGM for $235,750, but picking up only $75,156.25 for herself, despite Selznick's contention that 'Ingrid's devotion to me reminds me of Ronald Colman's friendship – both apparently give me the privilege of costing myself money.' Throughout this time he tried to get her to tear up her old contract and replace it with the standard seven-year agreement, threatening to restrict her to one film a year if she did not.

Saratoga Trunk played service installations, but release was delayed until 1946, both because Warners had more timely items and because postwar conditions would probably mean longer runs for the bigger films. Reunited with Gary Cooper, Bergman was a Creole adventuress chasing him – less convincingly than either Davis or Leigh would have been. Neither was *Gaslight* (44) originally intended for her: Columbia had bought it for Irene Dunne and then sold it to MGM, who wanted it for Hedy Lamarr. Either again might have done as well as the frightened wife of Charles Boyer: Bergman was just not frightened or frail enough, but nothing could prevent her from getting the 1944 Best Actress Oscar for her performance. Selznick himself produced *Spellbound* (45). Hitchcock directed and Gregory Peck co-starred: Bergman was a psychiatrist and the New York critics thought hers the year's Best Female Performance. The other was at RKO as a nun opposite Bing Crosby's priest: *The Bells of St Mary's*, adding

her tact to his to dampen the stickiness. She did it against Selznick's wishes; he got $175,000 for her services plus the rights to two properties – *Little Women* and *A Bill of Divorcement* – and the services of Gregory Peck. The package was deemed to be worth about $425,000 and he was miserable because he had to pay her $25,000 when the film started after the day stipulated in her contract.

Selznick and Hitchcock were responsible for *Notorious* (46) with Cary Grant. She was once more unconvincingly cast, as a lady prone to alcohol and casual affairs. Selznick, in fact, sold the film to RKO for $800,000 and half the profits. It was her fourth consecutive box-office smash and in 1946 she was the biggest female attraction in the US (she was also in the top 10 in 1947 and 1948). No one could have guessed that *Notorious* would be her last successful movie for 10 years.

Her contract was up and Selznick still hoped to sign her for another seven years with favourable terms (it carried with it *The Farmer's Daughter* and *To Each His Own*, both of which earned Oscars for their eventual stars). Bergman's husband vetoed the idea and she freelanced. As a change of pace she played a prostitute in Milestone's version of Erich Maria Remarque's *Arch of Triumph* (48), with Boyer and Charles Laughton, but the public did not want to see their beloved Bergman in such a part (its failure doomed Enterprise Productions, the new studio which had produced it – she had got $175,000 for her role, and was to have received 25 per cent of the profits: but in fact the film lost $2 millon). She went back to being good for the same fee, in *Joan of Arc*, a heroine on whom she was fixated – indeed, she had played the part on Broadway the previous year and had been voted the year's Best Actress by theatre critics. The film was based on the play ('Joan of Lorraine' by Maxwell Anderson), but this time there were no laurels flying about; the press loathed it and, although it did not do badly at the box-office, it failed to recover its costs (and also perhaps hastened the death of its director, Victor Fleming). *Under Capricorn* (49) found Bergman in the Australia of 100 years ago, an Irish dipsomaniac; neither she nor director Hitchcock seemed happy with their material and no one flocked to see it. It lost money. Hitchcock observed later that he only made it because Bergman was involved – and she was the biggest star in Hollywood. They didn't always agree – 'she only wanted to appear in masterpieces,' he said.

The truth was – and it was just beginning to dawn on people – that Bergman's ambitions outweighed her talent. She was beautiful and bewitching and patently sincere in everything she did, she had a radiance which was special to her; but time and again her resources failed her and she was forced back on the same old gestures. There were hundreds of Hollywood actresses more limited, but they did not try to play *everything*. She was unbelievable as a bad woman, but that was a role that she was about to be cast in, by the press and vast sections of the public because of her private life.

The furore now seems incredible – the acres of newsprint used, the amount of indignation (mostly on the part of the American women's clubs) expended (c.f. the relatively minor fuss made over Vanessa Redgrave or Mia Farrow, in similar circumstances, but 20 years later). What happened was that Bergman fell in love with Roberto Rossellini: she was one of the many admirers of his *Roma Città Aperta* and, seeking refuge from the standardized Hollywood product after two expensive disasters (*Under Capricorn*, not yet released, would make a third), wanted to work with him. Howard Hughes of RKO agreed to her usual fee – $175,000 – but offered 40 per cent of the profits. As she and Rossellini began locations on *Stromboli* (50) he began to woo her; when the film was over, she gave birth to his baby. As Jean Renoir said, she was 'so honest that she will always prefer a scandal to a lie'. Facing a barrage of worldwide criticism, she claimed that her marriage had been over for years and as soon as it was possible, she and Rossellini were married; but the public – particularly the American public – were not about to forgive her. *Stromboli* was banned or ostracized and although its news value did attract some spectators it soon faded into semi-oblivion. That did not matter, since it had few merits of its own; it fudged a simple plot about the hostility felt towards a foreign woman who has married one of the island's fishermen. Around the same time an enterprising New York distributor bought her second movie, *Bränninger*, and rechristened it *The Surf*. In it, she played an unmarried mother. Curiously, as the storm was breaking, 'Daily Variety' polled Hollywood for its own opinion of movie greats: Bergman was second to Garbo in the overall period, first when the Silent era was subtracted.

In 1952 Rossellini directed her in *Europa '51* with Alexander Knox, an ambitious allegory in which she takes the troubles of the world on her shoulders. Seen today, it is far from negligible, but at the time it got few bookings outside Italy. The next four marked a serious decline: an episode in *Siamo Donne* with a quarrelsome chicken; *Viaggio in Italia* (53), a muddled marital drama with George Sanders; *Jeanne au Bucher*, a static film version of the Honegger concert-piece that she and Rossellini had carted round European capitals; and *Angst* (54), a melodrama made in Germany. None of them was at all successful and it was also clear to Bergman that her marriage was working out as badly as their professional collaboration.

They were bankrupt and her confidence as an artist had completely gone. Luckily,

Bergman with one of her favourite co-stars, Cary Grant, in Stanley Donen's Indiscreet (57), *based on Norman Krasna's Broadway comedy, 'Kind Sir'. She played an actress, he an American diplomat and the film delightfully detailed their bumpy romance.*

Renoir had something planned for her; he felt that no film had quite captured her gaiety and designed *Elena et les Hommes* (56) to showcase it. In the event, it did little else and was too slight and wayward to do much on its few US showings (as *Paris Does Strange Things*).

Kay Brown, now an agent, was looking for something to reintroduce Bergman to American audiences and she came up with the title-role of *Anastasia* (57), from a successful play about the pretender to the Tsarist fortune. 20th polled theatre owners and made it known that the sales force would have preferred Jennifer Jones; but Darryl F. Zanuck and director Anatole Litvak insisted on Bergman, offering the considerable sum of $200,000. She made it in Britain and returned to Paris, to do 'Tea and Sympathy' on the stage. *Anastasia* opened and she was welcomed back with great enthusiasm everywhere. She won a second Oscar and a second New York Critics Award, tokens of appreciation for herself rather than for her performance.

In Britain, she made two more films for American companies: *Indiscreet*, for $75,000 plus 10 per cent of the gross above $4 million, with Cary Grant, one of the friends who had loyally stood by her in bad times; and *The Inn of the Sixth Happiness* (58), a touching story of a Chinese missionary. Once again as a lady with a mission, her sincerity was awesomely clear: but even in a role she cared for, she sometimes gave a brisk impression of not caring for the make-believe world of acting.

After that, none of the announced projects worked out and she settled down to domestic life with her third husband (1958–78), Lars Schmidt, a Swedish impresario living in Paris. She was off the screen until she starred in the film of Françoise Sagan's *Aimez-vous Brahms?* (61) – 'Brahms, oui' went the text of one French review. Again she was unsuitably cast, as a 40-year-old woman afraid of losing looks, husband and lover. Said 'Playboy': '[She] walks away with honours for The Old Bag We'd Most Like to Be Saddled With.' A nebulous English title – *Goodbye Again* – and draggy playing by Yves Montand and Anthony Perkins served the piece ill. It did well in Europe but failed in the US. *The Visit* (64) attracted fewer audiences everywhere and after a disastrous reception 20th gave it a severely limited release. From a play by Dürrenmatt which the Lunts had done in London and on Broadway, it became an international co-production with staff literally from all countries and the result partially dubbed. As the vengeful, vicious millionairess, Bergman was again unconvincing in an unsympathetic part; and she was miscast for most of her episode of *The Yellow Rolls Royce* (65), as a bad-tempered American tourist converted to love and charity by Yugoslav peasant Omar Sharif. It was a dire film but presumably because of its 10 stars (she got one of the bigger salaries: $275,000) a big hit. She did another episode film, *Stimulantia* (67), hers directed by Molander (and the others by Ingmar Bergman, Jörn Donner and Vilgot Sjöman). It does not seem to have been shown outside Sweden.

It is likely that her further absence from the screen was involuntary: in interviews she said that she was as ambitious as she ever was and several projects were announced only to fizzle out. She did a certain amount of prestige TV work – 'Hedda Gabler', 'The Human Voice', etc.; and appeared on the stage: as Hedda, in Paris in 1963; in Britain in 'A Month in the Country' (65) and in the US in Eugene O'Neill's 'More Stately Mansions'. In that she scored a gigantic personal success, underlining her position as one of the lode-stars of the business; as a result Columbia signed her to a two-picture deal: a film version of a stage success, *Cactus Flower* (69), with Walter Matthau (billed over her except on the Continent) and Goldie Hawn, and *A Walk in the Spring Rain* (70), a *Brief Encounter*-type story with Anthony Quinn. The former was another personal success for her and became a hit everywhere, but the other was not and did not. It was more than 20 years since she had filmed in Hollywood.

She returned to the stage, in 'Captain Brassbound's Conversion', which she did in

Ingmar and Ingrid: the Bergmans finally film together: his eloquent An Autumn Sonata (78) *where she is the concert pianist mother of Liv Ullman (right). It is entirely typical of her to look her age – probably the only Hollywood star of her generation willing to do so.*

London (71) and the US (72). When she was in Washington with the play, Senator Percy, in her own words, 'stood on the same floor of the United States Senate where 23 years ago I was more or less thrown out of the country as a corrupting influence on American womanhood, and apologized. An apology he said was long overdue!'

In New York she appeared in an independent production, *From the Mixed-Up Files of Mrs Basil E. Frankweiler* (73), a tale of two children who decide to live in the Metropolitan Museum; as the millionairess of the title, she does not appear till late in the film – which after flopping badly was rechristened *The Hideaways*. In a dull all-star Agatha Christie tale, *Murder on the Orient Express* (74), she was a bright spot as a shy spinster, her best claim yet for consideration as a character actress; it won her a Best Supporting Oscar – in her acceptance speech she named another performance she considered superior. She played in London and in the US in Maugham's 'The Constant Wife' and had another film failure with *A Matter of Time* (76) as an elderly woman indulging the fantasies of Liza Minnelli. She appeared with Liv Ullmann, as her mother, in *An Autumn Sonata* (78) directed by her namesake, Ingmar, and she described the experience as one of the happiest of her career; speaking Swedish again rounded out her career, she said, predicting that there would be no more films. There were not the roles for her years, she explained, before playing 'Waters of the Moon' in the UK, where she had lived for some years. In truth, she had known for a long time that she had cancer; but even ill, and aged, they had to work hard to make her look like Israeli premier Golda Meir in a TV miniseries, *A Woman Called Golda* (82). Her death a few months later brought forth, unsurprisingly, a huge display of posthumous affection.

ELISABETH BERGNER

'St John Ervine and James Agate [the most respected critics of their time] have recently been playing pitch and toss in the Sunday newspapers over the degree of greatness of Elisabeth Berner's acting, judging from the evidence of the stage version of "Escape Me Never". For once I find myself in agreement with the former who states that the critic who could not instantly tell that Bergner is a great actress after seeing her in Margaret Kennedy's play is incapable of pronouncing an opinion on acting,' said 'Cinema Quarterly' of the film of that play – which admittedly is not to

modern tastes, with its lovable waif of a heroine gurgling infectious laughter in the face of adversity. She and her director husband obviously gave careful thought to every gesture and expression, and by jiminy every gesture and expression are perfect: but you can see the work that went into them. In films, like other middle-European actresses, she is pure dirndl; and if her stage performances were as unvaried as those on the screen she must have turned some of the heroines of Ibsen, Shakespeare and Shaw into gurgling lovable waifs.

She was born in Vienna in 1900 and studied at the Conservatoire from 1915 to 1919. She made her stage début in Zurich and there played Ophelia and Rosalind, a part she soon was playing in Vienna. She acted in Munich and Berlin, achieving a mighty reputation in the German-speaking countries, especially in classic plays. Among her parts: Viola, Katherine ('The Shrew'), Nora in 'A Doll's House', Marguerite Gautier, Hannele, St Joan (Shaw's), Miss Julie, Portia – and 'The Last of Mrs Cheyney', Tessa in 'The Constant Nymph' and Nina in 'Strange Interlude'. She made her first film: *Der Evangeliman* (23) and loathed it. But Paul Czinner persuaded her that she would be effective under his direction: *Nju* (24), married to Emil Jannings but swept away by Conrad Veidt; *Der Geiger von Florenz* (26), masquerading as a boy; *Liebe*, based on 'La Duchesse de Langeais'; *Donna Juana* (27); *Königin Luise*, in this case with Czinner handing over to Karl Grune; and *Fraulein Else* (29), as a silly little goose preferring death to dishonour (and her dad's chum seemed such a sweet middle-aged man!). In 1928, recognized everywhere as a great actress, she toured the Netherlands, Scandinavia and Germany in a variety of plays; in 1930 she was Juliet to Franz Lederer's Romeo for Max Reinhardt; and the following year she was notably successful in 'Amphytrion 38'.

Ariane (31), the tale of a student in love with an elderly roué (Rudolf Forster), is infinitely the best film either she or Czinner made. It was shot in Paris with two simultaneous other versions, *The Loves of Ariane*, with Percy Marmont, and *Ariane Jeune Fille Russe* – but Bergner ceded her role in the French version to Gaby Morlay. As with *Nju*, there was trouble with the British censor. (It was remade as *Love in the Afternoon*.) Forster also co-starred in *Der Träumende Mund* (32), a tragic triangle drama – and once again in the French version Mlle Morlay replaced Bergner. Bergner's French was clearly not as good as her English and with the advent of the Nazis she and Czinner settled in London. They married about the same time.

There was considerable interest in the showbiz world when it was announced that Korda had signed Bergner to a long-term contract: he later tried to flog it to Paramount in a deal which required them to finance the uncompleted *The Private Life of Henry VIII* – the money had run out – but Paramount was interested in neither *Henry* nor Elisabeth. In the event, Bergner made only one film for Korda, *Catherine the Great* (33), and she was, if anything, even less convincing than Dietrich in her concurrent version (and the film itself inferior). She made her stage bow in London in Margaret Kennedy's 'Escape Me Never' (33), a trite and artificial tale about a waif's devotion to a heel: it ran almost a year and in 1935 duplicated its success in New York. Her husband directed her in a British film version for which it was reported she got a fee of £20,000. She won the 'Picturegoer' Gold Medal, and in the US 'Photoplay' described the film as 'lighted by the magic of Elisabeth Bergner's divine acting'. Flushed with this triumph, Bergner and Czinner got 20th to back their pretty-pretty version of *As You Like It* (36), usually referred to as 'Elisabeth and Her German Arden'. One of the kindest reviews of her Rosalind was Sydney W. Carroll's in the 'Sunday Express' (London): 'It is too nervous, too restless . . . . There is too much Barrie in the conception and too little Shakespeare.' Barrie, as it happened, admired Bergner inordinately, and wrote a

play for her – and the title-role, 'The Boy David'. It was religious. And a fiasco. And his last play.

Bergner signed a five-year contract with United Artists – the films to be made in Britain; the first was to have been a version of Jack London's 'The Little Lady of the Big House', but instead she did a version of her last German film, now called *Dreaming Lips* (37), with Raymond Massey as the lover. 'Picturegoer' thought it 'inferior' to the earlier manifestation and noted that 'Bergner's mannerisms are apt to become irritating' in her usual part of 'the little, lovable, clinging young woman'. She played St Joan at the 1938 Malvern Festival and then did a film that her old friend Margaret Kennedy wrote for her, *A Stolen Life* (39), with Michael Redgrave. She played twins, one of whom loses him to the other, whom she impersonates after she has drowned. 'Picturegoer' this time thought '. . . the fact is that Bergner is Bergner in both parts'. Paramount, not UA, released it.

In 1940 she contracted to make *49th Parallel* (with Olivier, Leslie Howard, etc.) but after doing the locations in Canada did not return to Britain for interiors and went to the USA. The film was restarted with Glynis Johns. Bergner's action was interpreted in Britain as, at best, ingratitude, and only a few calm minds pointed out that, had Hitler invaded, Bergner would have been one of the first to be marched off to a concentration camp – but then, so might the people who had sheltered her and given her work. In Hollywood she did the truly appalling *Paris Calling* (42), as a patriotic society girl, 'Little Wipers' – the name bestowed on her by Nazi protector Basil Rathbone. Then she went to New York and played in 'The Two Mrs Carrolls'; she confined her US work to the stage thereafter, though in the late 40s she did some TV. In 1950 she toured Australia in 'The Two Mrs Carrolls' and reappeared in Britain, in Manchester and London, in a version of 'Le Malade Imaginaire': but amidst a furore both reviews and business indicated that the British had no intention of forgiving her. Nevertheless, she and Czinner settled quietly in Britain again, though she did not attempt to restart her career there for almost 20 years. She worked intermittently in Germany and Austria during that time and Czinner occasionally directed films of stage performances using a TV technique. In 1962 she was in a German film of J.B. Priestley's play, 'Time and the Conways': *Die Glücklichen Jahre der Thorwalds*. In 1968 she did a play in Oxford and a TV play; then accepted a role in a British Vincent Price vehicle, *Cry of the Banshee* (70). She was widowed in 1972 and later accepted a role in *Der Fussganger/The*

Elisabeth Bergner in As You Like It (36), *directed by her husband, Paul Czinner, in Britain.*

Pedestrian (74), directed by Maximilian Schell in Munich, with Françoise Rosay, Peggy Ashcroft, Lil Dagover and Peter Hall in the cast.

She had become, as you can imagine, the cutest little old lady imaginable. And as such, there was employment to be found: *Der Pfingstausflug* (79), with Martin Held, as old-age pensioners having adventures; *Kurier des Zaren* (80), an Italian-German remake of *Michael Strogoff* with John Philip Law, as his mother; *Feine Gesellschaft – beschränkte Haftung* (82), a farce masquerading as a satirical comedy, with Lilli Palmer as her very different sister; and *Angelo und Luzy*, as a charitable old lady whom that couple are trying to cheat. She died in 1986.

JOAN BLONDELL

Joan Blondell had an expressive face with slightly pop eyes and a snappy way with a line. She was loyal, cynical and cuddlesome – in her own words, 'the happy-go-lucky chorus girl, saucy secretary, flip reporter, dumb-blonde waitress, I'll stick-by-you broad'. It was a type very common in the 30s, essayed by, among others, Thelma Todd, Lucille Ball, Gladys George, Ginger Rogers, Ann Sheridan and Glenda Farrell. Some of them were sometimes teamed, a conglomeration of gold diggers – Americans striking back at the Depression, dames after money first and men second. The type went out of fashion at the end of the decade; during the War heroines became anaemic and blondes became cheaper (and more venal). Later attempts to revive it – even with the talent of a Gloria Grahame – never quite caught on, though most of the 30s' blondes were still in there pitching (of course), if blowsy now, like Ann Sothern and Blondell herself. None of them was a great star in the accepted sense, but Blondell combined reliability and versatility with an overall attractive personality: to anyone believing that professionalism is the greatest of showbiz virtues, it is difficult to overpraise her.

She came from a professional background: her parents were vaude troopers. She was born in New York City in 1909 and was with her parents' act from child to soubrette, sometimes billed as the original Katzenjammer Kid. The act toured not only in the US, but throughout Europe, in China and Australia. In the latter country Blondell launched out on her own, then returned to the States and worked in stock in Dallas. She was a Miss Dallas and with that achievement tried her luck in New York – partly to help the family,

now that movies were killing vaudeville. Eventually she got a part in 'The Trial of Mary Dugan' (27), starring Ann Harding; was also in 'Tarnish' and did a season in the 'Follies'. She was in two plays with James Cagney, 'Maggie the Magnificent' (29) and 'Penny Arcade', and when Warners bought the second of them for filming, they took the two stars along with the rights. The film was called *Sinners' Holiday* (30) and immediately Warners saw the first rushes with Blondell and Cagney, they took up their option on her services and signed her to a five-year contract – $200 a week to go to $500, but unusual in that it was for 52 weeks a year instead of the customary 40. Released first was Blondell's second picture, *The Office Wife*, a drama starring Lewis Stone and Dorothy Mackaill. She had already begun to churn them out. She supported Barbara Stanwyck in *Illicit* (31); Helen Twelvetrees and Lilyan Tashman in *Millie* at RKO, all of them gold-diggers; Bebe Daniels in *My Past*, as her friend; and Frank Fay, who had the title-role in *God's Gift to Women*. A month later she was featured in *Other Men's Women* (also known as *The Steel Highway*) as a hash-slinger with a yen for Grant Withers.

She also supported Cagney in *Public Enemy*, as a gangster's moll, and was, as Tynan once observed, 'a perfect punch-bag for his clenched, explosive talent'. One of the reasons she was perfect was that she was never

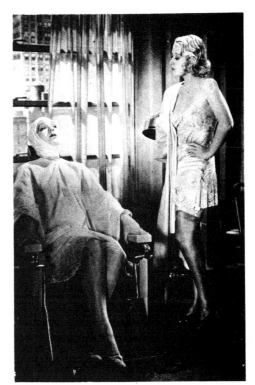

Ina Claire and Joan Blondell in The Greeks Had a Word for Them (*32*).

taken in by him. For the moment she continued in second-leads: *Big Business Girl*, with Loretta Young, as a divorce case co-respondent; *Night Nurse*, as Stanwyck's side-kick; and *The Reckless Hour*, as Dorothy Mackaill's sister. Press and public had liked the Cagney-Blondell combination and she got her first lead opposite him, in *Blonde Crazy*. In her 10 1932 pictures she had the lead or top-billing in most of them, starting with *Union Depot* with Douglas Fairbanks Jr, as a chorus girl. She went to Goldwyn to replace Carole Lombard (taken ill after filming began) for *The Greeks Had a Word for It*, a title which horrified the censor and became *The Greeks Had a Word For Them*, though the 'it' was the way in which gold-digger Ina Claire managed to pinch the admirers of Madge Evans and Blondell – a very funny film. Blondell also snaffled the cameraman, George Barnes, in real life and they married later (1933–35). Then: Howard Hawks's *The Crowd Roars*, as Eric Linden's wife; *The Famous Ferguson Case*, with Leslie Fenton, as a reporter; *Make Me a Star* at Paramount, befriending Stuart Erwin in this remake of *Merton of the Movies*; *Miss Pinkerton*, a cooler role – an amateur sleuth – than usual in this conventional thriller with George Brent; and *Big City Blues*, this time befriending small town boy Eric Linden during his three disillusioning days in New York. The *Three on a Match* were her, Ann Dvorak and Bette Davis, in that order, and then she was a hick in New York's *Central Park* with Wallace Ford. *Lawyer Man* was a William Powell vehicle and she was his loving secretary.

Then she was *Blondie Johnson* (33) at Fox, victim of a heartless landlord who decides virtue does not pay – and becomes a fully fledged gun-moll, with Chester Morris. It was she and Ginger Rogers who were *Broadway Bad*, fighting Ricardo Cortez for the custody of her child. She was one of the *Gold Diggers of 1933*, memorably singing of her Forgotten Man, and then Warren William said *Goodbye Again* to her. And in a second of the year's big musicals, *Footlight Parade*, she was more than merely decorative, she was nuts for Cagney – only he did not know it. She did not show it – because she had his number. Slang-bang, bang-slang it went when they met, but it ended in a clinch. She and Glenda Farrell were *Havana Widows*, gold-diggers; and then she went to *Convention City* to tempt Adol-phe Menjou; Dick Powell was also there – he and Blondell were later married (1936) and the film, a comedy, was a big success.

Warners did not consider her one of their top stars despite reviews invariably referring to her versatility and phrases such as 'worth watching' and 'as good as ever'. She was a brunette hello girl in *I've Got Your Number* (34), the first of several with Pat O'Brien; also in the cast were Allen Jenkins and Glenda Farrell – and she and Farrell once again made a great team. Warren William and Edward Everett Horton fought over her in *Smarty*; *He Was Her Man* was Cagney; and she was one of the *Dames*, giving that musical 'the snap it needs' ('Photoplay'). Finally Warners raised her to official stardom in *The Kansas City Princess*, with Farrell. The studio teamed them again in *Travelling Saleslady* (35) and she was in the title-role, in defiance of her toothpaste-manufacturing father. Powell was the *Broadway Gondolier*, a New York taxi-driver in Venice, an enjoyable comedy with music; it was Farrell with Blondell proclaiming *We're in the Money* and acclaiming her *Miss Pacific Fleet*. Lionel Collier commented that the teaming of the two of them 'was something of a stroke of genius, and the pictures they have made together always reach a level of infectious mirth that it is impossible to resist'. Ruby Keeler was *Colleen* (36) and Powell was in it, an overlong drama where gold-digger Blondell's cracks were doubly welcome. Joe E. Brown was one of the *Sons o' Guns* and she was a French mamzelle; she was a moll once more, a good-hearted one, in *Bullets or Ballots*. *Stage Struck* has one of her most brilliant performances, as an affected and dumb leading lady losing her place to newcomer Jeanne Madden, perhaps the wettest ingénue of all time. The plot had Powell loathing her and loving Madden, underlining WB's inability to see them as a romantic team, which could hardly have pleased her. She was also pretty terrific in the fine film version of the hit farce, *Three Men on a Horse*, teamed with Sam Levene and Frank McHugh, as the stripper; and in *Gold Diggers of 1937* – which did team her with Powell. She was not gold-digging for long – he gets her a job as a stenographer (and in other ways the series had declined).

The King and the Chorus Girl (37) – Fernand Gravet was the king – started life as *A Royal Romance*, a tale by Groucho Marx and Norman Krasna about a king who marries a commoner: one of the movies' oldest themes. But this was 1937 and Warners got cold feet; it did not turn up in Britain until 1939, further retitled *Romance Is Sacred*. She was *Back in Circulation* with Pat O'Brien, clearly a newspaper story, and she was a reporter again in *The Perfect Specimen*, who was Errol Flynn in this funny version of *It Happened One Night* in reverse. She got a big fillip when Leslie Howard asked for her to co-star in *Stand-In* at Wanger-UA. It was her usual part, the knowing blonde, in this case a stand-in who guides innocent Howard through the Hollywood jungle, but she invested it with more depth than even her most devoted fans expected. She got raves, mostly of the what-have-Warners-been-hiding variety. She said later: 'I wasn't such a tremendous star I could afford to revolt', but from this point on she was more than ever discontented with the Warner lot. A good comedy at Columbia with Melvyn Douglas, *There's Always a Woman* (38), as his scatty wife, was followed by a programmer that she particularly loathed making: *Off the Record* with O'Brien, in which they were reporters. She was determined to leave Warners. She told reporters that she had read a book called 'May Flavin' and wanted to play the title-role: 'I'd like to show that I can do things besides girl reporters and girl detectives.' She was permitted to go to Universal for *East Side of Heaven* (39), but was then in *The Kid From Kokomo*, an unbelievable melodrama with Wayne Morris, as a bubble-dancer. Her contract and Powell's expired at the same time: they tried for increased salaries, director-approval, etc., and were not surprised to find that Warners turned them down.

Columbia had liked her teaming with Melvyn Douglas: both were expert light comedians and there seemed to be an infinite number of plots to be extracted from his stuffiness and her sassiness, the one of course detracting from the other. She had been scheduled for *There's That Woman Again*, but was at Universal so they borrowed Virginia Bruce. Now the studio signed her to a three-picture deal, the first two of which were with Douglas, *Good Girls Go to Paris* and *The Amazing Mr Williams*, respectively as professor and waitress, as detective and his fiancée. She freelanced with success: *Two Girls on Broadway* (40) – Lana Turner was the other; *I Want a Divorce* with Powell, a very serious film – and a very poor one; *Topper Returns* (41), as a sexy ghost (Constance Bennett's old part) in one of the creepie comedies popular at that time; *Model Wife* with Powell, a comedy; *Three Girls About Town* at Columbia, with Binnie Barnes and Janet Blair; and *Lady for a Night* (42), a corny costumer, top-billed over John Wayne. When the US entered the war she entertained the troops without waiting for the formation of organized tours and her film activity was cut considerably. *Cry Havoc* (43) was a war melodrama superbly acted by her as an ex-burlesque queen, Ann Sothern and Margaret Sullavan. That year she went to New York to play a stripper-novelist in a play by Gypsy Rose Lee, 'The Naked Genius', presented by Mike Todd, whom she married in 1947 after her divorce from Powell (1945).

The part of Aunt Cissy in *A Tree Grows in Brooklyn* (45) had originally been intended for Alice Faye as a 'straight' venture; Blondell played it as a character part and there was

A Tree Grows in Brooklyn (45), *Elia Kazan's version of a bestseller by Betty Smith which was a good deal more honest than most of that species. Lloyd Nolan, Joan Blondell with the family at the centre of the story, Dorothy McGuire, James Dunn with Ted Donaldson and Peggy Ann Garner. When pa dies of drink the upright Nolan becomes ma's new suitor.*

much talk of a come-back, which it was not, but she did steal the notices. 20th offered her a contract and put her in a programmer with William Bendix, *Don Juan Quilligan*; and lent her to MGM for *Adventure*, billed below the title for the first time in 12 years – but the stars were Gable and Garson so it did not seem too face-losing, especially as she again stole the notices. But when 20th wanted to put her into more supporting roles she was suspended – and did not film for over a year. She starred with George Brent in *The Corpse Came COD* (47), destined for double bills; and had a good part – which she played superbly – as Tyrone Power's first patroness, a much-lived carny queen, in *Nightmare Alley*. *Christmas Eve* was an independent production effort with several (by then) doubtful box-office names.

She was out of the news for three years, except for a back-stage fracas involving Todd at the Princeton Drama Festival – cause unknown; but it was known that Todd, still a minor theatre impresario, resented reporters paying more attention to her than to him. They were divorced in the early 50s. As a come-back picture, she could have done better than *For Heaven's Sake* (50), with Joan Bennett and Clifton Webb. The notices were dire, but 'Variety' said she had 'been absent from the screen far too long: she's that good'. She had an excellent part as a fading vaudeville star in *The Blue Veil* (51) and got a Best Supporting nomination for it. It was not enough. During the 50s she toured in a variety of roles – those of Shirley Booth in 'Come Back Little Sheba' and the musical version of 'A Tree Grows in Brooklyn' (as Aunt Cissy); in Helen Hayes's part in 'Happy Birthday' and

Merman's in 'Call Me Madam'; in 'The Dark at the Top of the Stairs' and, in 1961, 'Bye Bye Birdie'. There was a Broadway appearance: 'The Rope Dancers' (57).

She returned to Hollywood to three outstanding feature roles for MGM: *The Opposite Sex* (56) in Phyllis Povah's old role in this remake of *The Women*; *Lizzie* (57), as Eleanor Parker's tippling aunt; and *This Could Be the Night*, as the hustling mother of a dancer. There were two for 20th, back where she started as the heroine's sidekick: *The Desk Set* (58) with Katharine Hepburn and *Will Success Spoil Rock Hunter?* with Jayne Mansfield, in a role originally intended for Thelma Ritter. In 1961 she had a good part in *Angel Baby*, where George Hamilton and Mercedes McCambridge were revivalists; but with the exception of *The Cincinnati Kid* (65), where she had a few striking scenes with another Warner alumnus, Edward G. Robinson, her other films were undistinguished: *Advance to the Rear* (64) as a madam; *Paradise Road* (66); *Ride Beyond Vengeance*; *The Spy With the Green Hat*, a 'Man From Uncle' effort; *Winchester '73* (67), a remake for television with Tom Tryon and Dan Duryea, as a saloon-keeper; *Waterhole No 3* with James Coburn, again as a madam; *Kona Coast* (68), with Richard Boone, originally a pilot for a TV series; *Stay Away Joe* with Elvis Presley; and *The Phynx* (70), a comedy about rockstars and kidnapping, with several other one-time names (Louis Hayward, Johnny Weismuller, Patsy Kelly, Butterfly McQueen, Pat O'Brien, Joe Louis, Martha Raye, etc.): it was so bad that Warners only released it in a couple of spots. In 1968–70 there was a successful TV series, 'Here Come the Brides', based very loosely on *Seven Brides for Seven Brothers*. In 1971 she appeared in New York – off Broadway – in 'The Effect of Gamma Rays on Man-in-the-Moon Marigolds' and was seen as a saloon-keeper supporting James Garner in *Support Your Local Gunfighter* (71). In 1972 she published an autobiographical novel, 'Center Door Fancy', with a most unflattering portrait of Dick Powell.

After three tele-movies, *The Dead Don't Die*, with Ray Milland, *Winner Take All* (75), and *Death at Love House* (76) with Dorothy Lamour and Sylvia Sidney, there was another stint with many old stars in bit roles, *Won Ton Ton the Dog who Saved Hollywood*. Her glittering performance as the playwright made bearable some scenes of Cassavetes's *Opening Night* (77), but she had little to do in her guest spot in *Grease* (78), as a friendly soda-jerker. TV claimed her for *Battered*, playing Howard Duff's wife, and *The Rebels* (79), a four-hour mini-series, one of several names in this tale of the American Revolution. She had a good

Blondell scene-stealing towards the end of her career – though it was something she had effortlessly always done – in The Champ *(79).*

role as a society matron in Zeffirelli's remake of *The Champ* with Jon Voight, but was only one of several veterans (Aldo Ray, Keenan Wynn) doing comic 'turns' between the horrors of *The Glove*, starring John Saxon. Made a year earlier, it did not surface till two years after Blondell's death in 1979.

HUMPHREY BOGART

Humphrey Bogart's place in the legends of Hollywood is assured; every two-bit reporter who ever got near him has a fund of stories and several of them have written books about him. No Hollywood figure has been more biographed and few (Garbo, Chaplin and Monroe) have been so extensively analysed and studied. Everyone has pronounced, from John Crosby ('Off screen, Bogart didn't diminish, which is more than you can say for most movie stars') to Stanley Kramer ('He had the damnedest façade of any man I ever met in my life. He was playing Bogart all the time, but he was really a big, sloppy bowl of mush'). Other stars have been the subject of cults (Garbo again, W.C. Fields, the Marx Bros.), but no cult has been bigger than the Bogart one – and considering the qualities which the screen Bogart exemplified, this particular cult can only be a very healthy thing.

He was much acclaimed while he was alive, but his intrinsic appeal seems to be stronger now: interest centres not on his ability or even on the overall Bogart, but on the screen character he played in his middle years. Still, even after he had remarkably extended his range, he was always Bogart: he took all sorts of characteristics and varying situations, and made them fit the Bogart persona. That persona gave him a head-start as an actor, because it was a compound of opposing qualities, mixed sometimes ambiguously. He was wiry and not handsome, but women found him attractive; he behaved towards them courteously and at the same time contemptuously. He was both cavalier and dependent. His voice was something between a rasp and a lisp, and he seldom beamed at people or smiled except with reluctance (he went through some films with a single expression of thundering pessimism), but he had an odd, private and mirthless chuckle which he used mostly for scoffing at authority. He looked out for phonies; any opposition roused the cynic in him (it was easily roused). He could be avaricious and mean but stubbornly heroic – when he was on the right side of the law he went after his man with dogged determination. He was true to himself and, in his

sympathetic parts, to his friends.

Yet the object of all this interest almost never made it. When stardom came, virtually by chance, he had been in films 12 years: he was always good, though almost alone the Warner Bros. did not know it. He became a star despite them.

Accounts differ as to his date of birth, but it was around 1900, in New York City. His parents were wealthy – his father was a doctor, who was disappointed when Bogart failed to get the sort of marks which would have got him to Yale. Bogart served briefly in the US Navy at the end of World War I; and began acting in 1920, via knowing Alice Brady's brother Bill: Miss Brady offered him a job as a company manager for 'Experience' and he had two lines in it. He had a small part in 'Drifting' with Miss Brady, and Alexander Woollcott wrote: 'The young man who plays the sprig is what is usually and mercifully described as inadequate.' All the same, Bogart began to work non-stop, usually as the romantic juvenile: 'Meet the Wife' (23), 'Cradle Snatchers' (25), 'Saturday's Children' and others. He made a short film in 1930, *Broadway's Like That*, around the time he was spotted in 'It's a Wise Child' by a Fox talent scout. He was signed at $750 a week, made five pictures for Fox and one on loan-out to Universal: *A Devil With Women* (30), in the sort of role he had done on Broadway; *Up the River*, starring Spencer Tracy, both playing prisoners; *Body and Soul* (31), a war story; *Bad Sister* at Universal, as a city slicker who marries and deserts Sidney Fox; *Women of All Nations* with Victor McLaglen; and *A Holy Terror*, with George O'Brien.

Fox then dropped him, so he went back to New York and appeared in John Van Druten's 'After All'; he returned to the Coast to make a film for Columbia, *Love Affair* (32) co-starring Dorothy Mackaill; and did two featured parts for Warners, *Big City Blues*, as a New York partygoer, and *Three on a Match*, as a hoodlum, his looks and presence so striking that it is a wonder Hollywood could not 'see' him. But it did not, so he returned to New York for good and did a play called 'I Loved You Wednesday' with Henry Fonda also in the cast. He worked regularly; he made a film in New York for Universal: *Midnight* (34), starring Sidney Fox. In 1935 Bogart auditioned for a part in Robert E. Sherwood's 'The Petrified Forest' and to his surprise was cast as a gangster, a small-time hoodlum who holes up in a lonely Arizona inn, his gun at the ready. The play's star, Leslie Howard, promised Bogart that if the play was filmed, he would do his utmost to see that he reprised his Duke Mantee. Warner Bros. bought the play but were unimpressed by Bogart's New

The Petrified Forest (36). Humphrey Bogart as Duke Mantee, a vicious gangster who holes up in a gas station-café in the Arizona desert. Bette Davis, Leslie Howard and Dick Foran are his prisoners.

York success: did they not have Edward G. Robinson under contract for such parts? Howard fought for Bogart and Warners tested him 15 times before reluctantly signing him, at $400 a week.

If WB were aware of critical and public reaction to Bogart's performance in *The Petrified Forest* (36), they did not show it. Apart from Robinson, they also had Cagney under contract and the best they could do was to put Bogart in support of them, either as one of their gang or one of their enemies or (with a midway switch) both. WB's billing policy was erratic, but no matter how big his part, Bogart was mostly below the title: *Bullets or Ballots*, opposing Robinson as a cop; *Two Against the World*, starring in this B remake of *Five Star Final*; *China Clipper* as one of Pat O'Brien's pilots; *Isle of Fury*; *The Great O'Malley* (37), who was O'Brien, a cop – Bogart was a waspish petty crook; and *Black Legion*, starring in an A that failed, playing a small-minded factory worker who joins the Klan. Now deep in crime, he was a rat-faced crook in *San Quentin*, his first Warner film in the pen; he plotted against Robinson in both *Marked Woman* and *Kid Galahad*, in the former a polished and driving performance as a determined D.A., and in the latter a mean-minded boxing promoter. 'In the first 34 pictures,' Bogart told George Frazier (quoted in Richard Gehman's monograph, 1965), 'I was shot in 12, electrocuted or hanged in eight, and was a jailbird in nine. I was the Little Lord Fauntleroy of the lot.' Gehman adds that Bogart told him: 'I played more scenes writhing around on the floor than I did standing up.'

Cagney was the original choice for *Dead End*, but Goldwyn was advised not to get caught up in his current battles with Warners; and George Raft turned it down. Bogart was excellent as the local hood made good, as he was again on another loan-out, in *Stand-In* with Howard, as the disgruntled, hard-drinking movie director. Neither performance cut any ice with Warners, who put him into *Swing Your Lady* (38), which he thought the worst film he ever made and in his opinion there was plenty of competition. A hillbilly farce, it was considered too American for foreign tastes and got only a limited distribution. *Men Are Such Fools* was the first after a battle over salary and was perhaps the Brothers' revenge. *Crime School* starred Bogey, but was a B; he was its principal – but was back toting a gun in *The Amazing Dr Clitherhouse*. Of *Racket Busters* he said: 'I made so many pictures like that, I used to get the titles mixed up. People would ask me what I was working on, and I'd have to think about what it was called.' But with *Angels With Dirty Faces* both title and film were memorable: Bogart, as a crooked lawyer, got his from fellow-gangster James Cagney. He was *King of the Underworld* (39), a B, and turncoat pal to *The Oklahoma Kid*, both he and Cagney improbable in stetsons. Despite constant beefing about his material, and suspensions, he seemed to work non-stop: *Dark Victory*, unconvincing as Bette Davis's Irish groom; *You Can't Get Away With Murder*, as a crook who is a bad influence on Billy Halop; *The Roaring Twenties*, as a big-time bootlegger who double-crosses his partner, James Cagney; and *The Return of Dr X* as Dr X, a B, and referred to by its star as 'this stinking movie'. Incorrigibly villainous, apparently, he supported the studio's new acquisition, George Raft, in *Invisible Stripes* (40), as his mobster pal; and Errol Flynn (an actor he particularly despised) in a second Western, *Virginia City*, cutting little ice as a half-breed bandit; and in *It All Came True*, hiding out in a boarding house of eccentrics, he forced Ann Sheridan to choose between him and nice Jeffrey Lynn. In *Brother Orchid* he supported Robinson, again playing a double-crossing gang boss, and in *They Drive by Night* Raft again, as his fellow truck-driver.

The turning point came when Paul Muni, Raft, Cagney and Robinson all turned down *High Sierra* (41): Raoul Walsh directed from a novel by W.R. Burnett and Bogart gave one of his best performances, as a tired, ageing gangster wanting to retire. Ida Lupino got top-billing, but in the next, *The Wagons Roll At Night*, a circus story, he was top-billed. He was put on suspension for refusing another Western, *Bad Men of Missouri* (which Dennis

Morgan did), but that was lifted when Raft turned down *The Maltese Falcon* because it was 'not an important picture'. True, the studio had little confidence in it and with former scriptwriter John Huston directing for the first time it was assigned a budget somewhere between an A and a B feature: but it became a triumph for all concerned, including Bogart as Sam Spade, sardonic private eye. He said: 'I had a lot going for me in that one. First, there was Huston. He made the Dashiell Hammett novel into something you don't come across too often. It was practically a masterpiece. I don't have many things I'm proud of . . . but that's one.' He did *All Through the Night* (42), again turned down by Raft, as a Broadway gambler pitted against a Nazi spy ring; and *The Big Shot*, as a one-time gangster trying to go straight. The *Maltese Falcon* team (Huston, Bogart, Mary Astor, Sidney Greenstreet) was reassembled for *Across the Pacific* and that was a pretty good one, at its best in the flip dialogue exchanges between Bogart and Astor, at its worst with Bogart single-handedly gunning down the Jap spies. James Agate summed up at this point: 'Bogart is always the same, but he always delights me. He had charm and he doesn't waste energy by pretending to act. He has a sinister-rueful countenance which acts for him. He has an exciting personality and lets it do the work. His expression never changes, whether he is looking on his mistress, the dead body of a man he has murdered, or a blackbeetle. He acts even less than Leslie Howard. And I like him.'

The hoodlum parts were now behind him, and he was the man who had been biffedabout, conceivably the best hero the American cinema ever produced. A new seven-year contract was drawn up at $3,500 a week, without options. And Warners at last planned a film for him, ignoring Raft when he campaigned for the role: *Casablanca* (in which Bogart did not say 'Play it again, Sam') found him the proprietor of a bar there, still in love with ex-flame Ingrid Bergman, now married to Paul Henried: certifiably the best bad film ever made. It won a Best Picture Oscar and made a mint, and Bogart was king of the Warner lot. From then on, he only made what he wanted to and got a hike in salary. At the end of 1943 he entered the top 10 list and stayed there until 1949 (and was thereafter never far out of it). There were a couple of war films, *Action in the North Atlantic* and *Sahara*, at Columbia, a remake of a Russian film, *The Thirteen*, with the action transferred from Central Asia; and a guest appearance in *Thank Your Lucky Stars*; then a couple of imitations of *Casablanca*. *Passage to Marseilles* (44), was hokey, but the other, *To Have and*

Bogart with Ingrid Bergman in Casablanca *(42), at one of the rare moments when he's not saying 'Here's looking at you, kid' or one or the other of them isn't asking Sam to play 'As Time Goes by'. A sensation in its time, the film was relegated to oblivion with other wartime kitsch to be rediscovered a generation later and recognized as one of the most heartbreakingly romantic of all movies.*

Bogart and Lauren Bacall in To Have and Have Not *(44): they were the right chemistry on screen, and off it she became his fourth wife.*

Maybe she wasn't quite in the same class as Lauren Bacall, but Lizabeth Scott did very well as the devious dame in Dead Reckoning *(47). As for Bogey, this is one of those films in which he was so splendidly himself that it is pure gold from start to finish. They both gave the impression of having been around a long, long time.*

Have Not, was superb, a distortion of Hemingway's novel, but well directed by Howard Hawks. A new girl, Lauren Bacall, said to Bogart: 'If you want anything, just whistle.' He did and she became his fourth wife. After reluctantly playing a wife-killer in *Conflict* (45), he was with Bacall again in Hawks's *The Big Sleep* (46), a masterpiece of the *film noir*, after Chandler, who considered him 'so much better than any other tough-guy actor'; and he signed an unprecedented 15-year agreement with Warners, which permitted him to do what he liked provided he made one a year for them, at $200,000 per film, plus $1,000 a week expenses for location work.

Dead Reckoning (47) at Columbia was ideal Bogart – fast-moving stuff, with Lizabeth Scott as the lethal dame – and he formed his own unit, Santana, to release through that company. Warners, having failed with him once as a wife-murderer, had him at it again in *The Two Mrs Carrolls* – and it is a shame, for this was the only time he was teamed with Barbara Stanwyck. Teamed again with Bacall, he was in the dim *Dark Passage*, hidden by bandages for most of the footage: but Warners made restitution with *The Treasure of Sierra Madre* (48), filmed in Mexico. Away from the studio, Bogart encouraged Huston to make it the way he wanted – much to the

consternation of WB, viewing the rushes. It turned out to be one of Warners' biggest prize-winners, a gripping tale of gold-lust, an 'artistic' triumph, but a no-no at the US box-office. 'Bogart is excellent; already realistically dishevelled and depraved at the start, he grows more insanely selfish and suspicious as the film develops, until he becomes frighteningly inhuman at the end.' (Peter Ericsson in 'Sequence'.) Bogart himself was very fond of the film. Huston also directed *Key Largo*, from Maxwell Anderson's play, with Bogart as a war veteran pitted against a gangster (Edward G. Robinson): Bacall was in it, and it was entirely worthy of all three performers. We may not, however, think similarly of Santana's first two contributions to his career: *Knock on Any Door* (49), as an attorney from the backstreets defending a youngster (John Derek) from the same milieu; and *Tokyo Joe*, as a test pilot up to his neck in Nippon mayhem. He was a pilot again in *Chain Lightning* (50), at Warners, and a screenwriter suspected of murder in *In A Lonely Place*, for Santana. The good film he needed at this point – though he himself had been on peak form throughout these otherwise thankless movies – was *The Enforcer* (51) and he played a dedicated D.A. determined to break 'Murder Inc.'. It was his last film for Warners,

though the contract was not terminated – over choice of material – till two years later. For Santana he did *Sirocco*, which had echoes of *Casablanca* and one of his cynical best performances, casually sharing the joke with the audience, up to his neck gun-running in Damascus.

Huston then put him in *The African Queen*, from C.S. Forester's novel about a gin-sodden old boatman and the prissy spinster (Katharine Hepburn) who falls reluctantly in love with him: it was a huge success all round, and Bogart's salary and percentage fee was said to be worth $750,000 within six months. His performance surprised even his most fervent admirers. He pinched a Best Actor Oscar from under Marlon Brando's nose and the British readers of 'Picturegoer' voted him the year's best actor. From then till his death, he flexed his acting muscles as never before, most notably in a startling performance as the psychopathic captain in *The Caine Mutiny* (54). Despite a propensity for alcohol and a not unfounded reputation for living it up, Bogart took his profession very seriously indeed; he once said, 'The only thing you owe the public is a good performance', and he took pains to ensure it, with the maximum of professionalism.

His last films, however, were a mixed bunch: Richard Brook's *Deadline USA* (52) and a cliché-ridden newspaper story, with Kim Hunter; *Battle Circus* (53) was just that; and *Beat the Devil* was a crime spoof, written by Truman Capote and directed by Huston, with Jennifer Jones, Robert Morley, Gina Lollobrigida and all. It just broke even, and was considered a mess by Bogart (though it had – and has – a cult appeal). He followed with *The Caine Mutiny* (54), a big hit from Herman Wouk's bestseller; and was a last-minute replacement for Cary Grant in *Sabrina*, from Samuel Taylor's play – not improved under Billy Wilder's direction, with William Holden (whom Bogart loathed) and Audrey Hepburn. He was in Mankiewicz's *The Barefoot Contessa*, as a film director for the second time in his career; *We're No Angels* (55), from another play, as a convict – but a fairly amusing one; *The Left Hand of God*, a heavily panned effort, as a priest; and *The Desperate Hours*, from yet another play (by Joseph Hayes) and directed by William Wyler, as a really evil hoodlum menacing Fredric March and family. In his last movie, *The Harder They Fall* (56), Bogart returned to a more typical part, as a broken-down journalist, a bit on the wrong side of the law, who gets integrity in the last reel.

He became somewhat obstreperous during

In some ways Bogart's best-ever partner was Katharine Hepburn, a personality as trenchant as he but – unlike Bacall – a completely contrasting one. The African Queen (51) was, among other things, one of the screen's great love stories. On the left is Robert Morley, who played her brother.

his last years, a period well covered by reporters (the accounts of his happiness with Bacall are touching to read). He died of throat cancer in January 1957. Huston spoke at the funeral: 'He is quite irreplaceable. There will never be anybody like him.' But he left a fine legacy, four or five films which are classics and a score which can be watched over and over. And are.

CLARA BOW

The 20s would have been quite different without Clara Bow: she was totally representative of the era, but to what extent she created the flapper and how much derived from her could probably never be calculated. With her bob, her cupid's-bow lips, her saucer eyes, her beads and bangles and her jiggle, she shook up cinema audiences everywhere: she was the bee's knees, she was the cat's pyjamas. She was gay and vivacious, as befitted the new, emancipated woman, and entirely self-confident. She dimpled her cheeks and primped her hair whenever a man hove into view; she winked roguishly at any male who showed more than a passing interest, and indeed had a battery of expressions and stances with only one meaning, come-hither. She liked to touch her men, to flick their lapels or fix their ties, and she moved like a butterfly – as her husband observes in *Mantrap*, nervously contemplating their future together. When she is repulsed, she pouts – but she is never depressed for long: she radiates a huge enjoyment of life, as long as there is a man to enjoy. She was not subtle. 'Miss Van Cortland seems rather lacking in reserve' says someone in *It*, which is one of the great, classic understatements. All this presumably sprang from her off-screen character, restless, jazzy and nimble; it is recorded that she was seldom still. To the extent that the age was vulgar, she was vulgar, and was dismissed as such by Anita Loos, who considered that she 'succeeded in being at one and the same time innocuous and flashy'.

This was hardly the opinion of another eminent literary lady, Elinor Glyn, who discovered in Clara Bow the epitome of 'It' (how typical of the period that having or not having 'It' was almost a *cause célèbre*!). Among Madam Glyn's endless definitions of 'It' was this: 'a strange magnetism which attracts both sexes . . . there must be a physical attraction but beauty is unnecessary.' Probably the nomination of Bow as the 'It' Girl was a studio scheme with which Elinor Glyn was happy to comply, but in the founding of the whole silly syndrome, Bow was an entirely worthy cen-

trepiece. Even if the whole thing, including what she did on the screen, was evolved from the sort of girl she was, her life and career still seem to have been dreamed up by one of her scriptwriters.

She was born in Brooklyn in 1905, into extreme poverty. Her father was an occasional waiter, her mother a semi-invalid with neurotic tendencies. Her first job was as a telephone receptionist for a doctor, but it did not last long because she won a beauty contest run by 'Motion Picture Classic'. The prize included – provided that the magazine would plug the film – a small role in *Beyond the Rainbow* (22). That got left on the cutting-room floor (though after her success the scenes were restored and the film reissued). None of the other New York studios was interested, until director Elmer Clifton chanced upon Bow's picture in one of the fan magazines when he was looking for cut-price talent for *Down to the Sea in Ships* (23); it was a secondary role and required her to masquerade as a boy, but the press noticed her – and the film was good. A New York agent took her on and got her a small role at Goldwyn, in *Enemies of Women*, starring Lionel Barrymore. But B.P. Schulberg had seen *Down to the Sea in Ships* and he signed her at $50 a week plus her fare to Hollywood.

Schulberg was at that time turning out programme-fillers under the name 'Preferred' (which they were not) and much of his profit came from lending his contractees to other studios. Miss Bow progressed slowly – though she soon lost her virginal appearance, due perhaps to the rate at which she worked: 14 Bow pictures were released in 1925. Schulberg gave her a brief role in *Maytime* and loaned her for another in *Daring Years*; but she had a star role in *Grit* (24), an underworld tale – and an unimportant one (even if it was specially written by Scott Fitzgerald). She had a featured role in *Black Oxen* which starred Corinne Griffith and concerned glandular rejuvenation – but it was the first of her flapper roles. *The Poisoned Paradise* was Monte Carlo, with an attempt to break the bank there, and the *Daughters of Pleasure* were Bow and Marie Prevost, with Prevost's dad (Wilfred Lucas) offering jewels to her chum (Bow). *Wine* was a topical bootlegging tale and the year finished with *Empty Hearts*; *This Woman*, a melodrama with Irene Rich and Ricardo Cortez; and *Black Lightning*, which starred Thunder, the dog.

The 14 Bow films of 1925 were: *Capital Punishment*, some premature propaganda against; *Helen's Babies*, a vehicle for Baby Peggy; *The Adventurous Sex*; *My Lady's Lips*; *Parisian Love*, as an apache, with Donald Keith; *Eve's Lover*, as a bright relief from the

Clara Bow, the 'It' girl: how she got it and what she did with it. As My Lady of Whims (26), top left, with Francis Macdonald, before she had it, but easily outflapping all the other flappers. Knowing she has it, for this is It (27) itself, using it to ensnare her boss, Antonio Moreno, top right. But it isn't doing her much good in this publicity still from Wings (27), bottom, the first film to win an Academy Award; she looks particularly doleful as Charles 'Buddy' Rogers congratulates fellow-flyer Richard Arlen. She was the girl next door who followed Arlen to the front.

sombre doings of Irene Rich; Lubitsch's *Kiss Me Again*, a good French farce with Marie Prevost and Monte Blue; *The Scarlet West*, a mediocre Western; *The Primrose Path*, as a nightclub dancer; *The Plastic Age*, which gave her her best chance to date – and she was billed as 'The Hottest Jazz Baby in Films', a 'moral' tale showing how jazz parties and other vices almost ruin the academic career of Donald Keith; *Keeper of the Bees*, miscast in a shoddy version of the Gene Stratton Porter novel; *Free to Love*, as a wrongly convicted prisoner; *The Best Bad Man*, a Tom Mix Western; and *Lawful Cheaters*, posing as a boy again. By this time Bow had achieved her first popularity and was liked, whether in the poor Schulberg films or the secondary parts she did on loan-out. She was in *The Ancient*

Mariner (26), purportedly based on the Coleridge poem, and then was *My Lady of Whims*, flouting her family by living in Greenwich Village with a very masculine sculptress and going for rides in old men's yachts – but finally succumbing (unconvincingly) to Donald Keith, who has been employed to spy on her. *Shadow of the Law* and *Two Can Play* were both quickies made before moving on to the Paramount lot.

Schulberg was (re)joining that company and Paramount, as part of the agreement, took on some of his contract-artists (Bow was, in fact, the lure). Her first, in a supporting role (as Kittens Westcourt), was *Dancing Mothers*, starring Alice Joyce and Conway Tearle; she starred in her next, *The Runaway*, in the title-role, as a film star in the Kentucky mountains, meeting Warner Baxter and William Powell; and the next one, *Mantrap*, was her first big hit. Directed by Victor Fleming from a story by Sinclair Lewis, it was one about the old man (Ernest Torrence), the young wife and the stranger (Percy Marmont) from out of town: the whole thing came up quite fresh and Bow put more depth into her characterization than was usual. Paramount were so pleased that after a stint bolstering Eddie Cantor in his first film, *Kid Boots*, a film was built around her: *It* (27). Madam Glyn even appeared in it, to explain to Antonio Moreno what 'It' was. Naturally Bow had buckets of it, as a lingerie salesgirl who sets her cap at the boss and gets him all in a tizzy. The film was a big success and millions of girls began to ape her make-up and fashions.

Identification was easier in that Bow's screen occupations were resolutely humdrum – and they were also roles which gave her plenty of opportunities to wear a swimsuit or strip to her drawers (so that the appeal was not only to the distaff side). The 'It' girl tag now replaced the earlier one of 'The Brooklyn Bonfire' and more than ever Bow was the honeypot round which the bees clustered. Schulberg now sold her contract to Paramount, having made a considerable profit from renting her services. In *Children of Divorce* with Gary Cooper, however, sex did not bring happiness and she committed suicide; in *Rough House Rosie* she was a girl from the East Side trying to make it in the Park Avenue Set and not in the most orthodox way. She was in *Wings* rather to bolster the box-office than for any other reason, but *Hula* was all her, plus a bit of Clive Brook. Fleming directed, in a Hawaii setting. *Get Your Man* – Charles 'Buddy' Rogers was a French aristocrat – and she did; and was an equally unabashed gold-digger in *Red Hair* (28) – though she reformed when she fell in love, with the ward of her two best beaux.

'Picturegoer' felt there was no need to describe to readers 'the way she struts her stuff' – in different ways as seen by her three admirers. Glyn wrote it and the opening sequence was in colour to justify the title. (Bow had a famous limousine to match her hair; and she drove down the street in an open car with two red chows, dyed to match.) She was one of the *Ladies of the Mob* (with Richard Arlen) and, as a Frisco dance hostess, delighted to learn that *The Fleet's In!* (with James Hall). Glyn again provided the scenario of *Three Weekends*, with Bow as a showgirl pursuing married Neil Hamilton.

It could not be said that Bow was everywhere popular: one of the most persistent arguments (especially in Britain) against Talking pictures was the thought of vulgar, gum-chewing, little Clara talking. Her nasal tones were anticipated, but, in fact, she made the transition easily (though her penchant for darting about the set had to be curbed because microphones at first could not follow her). *The Wild Party* (29) found her as the school's bad girl in pursuit of Professor Fredric March (it was shown in Britain only as a Silent – perhaps to placate 'Picturegoer'); in *Dangerous Curves* she was in a circus with Arlen; and in *The Saturday Night Kid* again in a department store – it was a remake of *Love 'Em and Leave 'Em*, and if both titles might refer to the Bow philosophy, her toughness was all on the outside. Everyone thinks she is fast and loose, but the real cute one is her sister (Jean Arthur). In *Paramount on Parade* (30) she sang 'I'm True to the Navy Now' and that provided the title for the next, *True to the Navy* – only she was only true to March (the plot had him trying to believe it). *Love Among the Millionaires* was perhaps a more agreeable idea to her (but the brightest spot was Mitzi Green) and *Her Wedding Night* was fun: she shared it – as a movie star trying to get away from it all – with Ralph Forbes. At this point she was getting $5,000 a week – considerably less than she was worth (but more than the $2,800 of a year earlier) and less than rivals like Alice White and Colleen Moore were getting (and a national US poll in 1929 found she was the most popular female star and Colleen Moore was second). But suddenly she was no longer worth even a tenth of that amount.

Already in 1930 there had been two scandals. The first was when she admitted paying off the wife of a Dallas physician who was suing her for alienation of affection; and the other when she refused to settle some gambling debts (with Will Rogers at a casino in Nevada she signed blank cheques until she realized the amount was in the thousands and stopped the cheques). And it was widely believed her engagement to stage star Harry Richman was a stunt to get him known outside New York. Early in 1931 she sued her former secretary, Daisy de Voe, for embezzling $16,000. The sacked de Voe had attempted to blackmail Bow and the latter in retaliation sued her. De Voe was convicted on only one of the 37 larceny charges and went to jail for a year; and hers was the victory: her revelations in court (drink, gigolos and drugs) brought down on Bow's head a barrage of criticism from newspapers and magazines. The two Bow pictures which followed the trial, *No Limit* (31), as an usherette put in charge of a gambling saloon with Dixie Lee, and *Kick In*, with Regis Toomey, did no business. The latter was her first attempt at drama in many years and 'Picturegoer' described it as a 'valiant' one; but, it went on, 'the public decided to have none of her'. Bow suffered a nervous breakdown and was replaced in *The Secret Call* by Peggy Shannon and in *City Streets* by Sylvia Sidney. She returned to work in *Manhandled*, but work was stopped and her contract was dissolved with less than a year to run (reports vary on this: she said that she suddenly decided to quit moviemaking, but it was suggested that Paramount dropped her due to the complete lack of public support). It was announced that she had retired through ill-health.

She married Rex Bell, who had had a bit in *True to the Navy* and who was to become a successful cowboy star in B pictures; and they retired to his ranch in Nevada. A year later, in 1932, it was announced that she was going to become a director and there were rumours that she would play in *Red-Headed Woman* at MGM – but the part went to Jean Harlow. Mary Pickford wanted her for a role in *Secrets* and impressed Hollywood when she issued a statement defending Bow: 'She is a very great actress and her only trouble has been that she hasn't known enough about life to live it the way she wanted to live it.' Instead, she made two films for Fox, at a reported $125,000 each: *Call Her Savage* (32), as a spoilt brat whose odyssey includes whoredom, booze and countless men – including Gilbert Roland as Moonglow; and *Hoopla* (33, not released till 35) as a carnival dancer in this adaptation of Kenyon Nicholson's 'The Barker'. Both were lurid but fascinating and both indicated that she was having a weight problem. In 1934 she said that she planned to make a film in Britain, but nothing came of it and early in 1937 it was announced that she had been approached to take over Simone Simon's part in *Under Two Flags* when the latter's English proved not up to it: but presumably she could not diet in time (in 1939 she was reputed to be 200 lb).

Bow and Bell left Nevada in 1937 to open a cabaret – called 'It' – in Hollywood, but it did not last long. She was out of the news until 1947 when she appeared on TV as Mrs Hush, the mystery guest in 'Truth and Consequences'; and in 1960 she made news when she told Hedda Hopper: 'I slip my old crown of "It" Girl not to Taylor or Bardot but to Monroe.' Bell died in 1962; they had been separated – though not divorced – for several years. Bow was a chronic insomniac and seems to have spent several sessions in rest homes. She became a recluse in her later years, painting and reading. In 1965 she died of a heart attack. Ann Pacey commented in the 'Sun' (London): 'Hollywood is ruthless with its victims, but it owes much to personalities like Clara Bow, who helped to create the glamour it has never entirely lost.'

CHARLES BOYER

The French do not usually transplant. Hollywood has looked worldwide in its search for talent, but somehow the French never make it. Germans and Austrians have thrived there but the French wither and die. Danielle Darrieux took one look, made one film and returned; Hollywood has never managed to harness the huge resources of talent at large in the French film industry. Renoir, Clair, Duvivier and so on right down to Henri Verneuil did not manage to come to terms with the Hollywood system for more than a film or two; Michèle Morgan, Jean Gabin and Jeanne Moreau have done their least interesting work in US movies; Belmondo and Bardot held out. The shining exception (Chevalier perhaps apart) is Charles Boyer, and he only made it in Hollywood after a bitter struggle.

He was born in Figeac (Lot) in south-west France in 1899; he wanted to be an actor from childhood and after a course at the Sorbonne studied drama at the Paris Conservatoire. While still there Marcel L'Herbier engaged him to play the hero's friend, a callow and curly-haired ne'er-do-well, in his free adaptation of a Balzac story, the Swedish-influenced sea tale, *L'Homme du Large* (20); and Boyer was then on the stage in 'Les Jardins de Murcie'. The director Georges Monca gave him supporting roles in *Chantelouve* (21) and *L'Esclave* (22), and he was featured in Manoussi's *Le Grillon de Foyer*; on the stage he had a success in 'Le Voyageur', which made him an idol of the *théâtre de boulevard* for as long as he cared to remain there. He returned to films in the title-role of *Le Capitaine Fracasse* (27), a historical romance; *La Ronde Infernale* (28) was another big hit for him and on stage he was in the long-running 'Mélo', which first brought Hollywood attention to him. But he had already signed with UFA to make French versions of German movies in Berlin: after only one, *Barcarolle d'Amour* (30), a version of *Brand in der Oper*, MGM approached UFA to buy his contract – for they wanted him for French editions of their movies. In Hollywood he did a French *Big House* entitled *Révolte dans la Prison*, in the Chester Morris role, and *Le Procès de Mary Dugan*; when it was decided to abandon separate foreign versions he hung around doing nothing till loaned to Paramount for a French subject, *The Magnificent Lie*, with Ruth Chatterton. He returned to UFA for *Tumultes*, the French version of *Sturm der Leidenschaft*; and then had an excellent role in another Paramount film, the Enoch Arden-themed *The Man From Yesterday*, as Claudette Colbert's second husband – Clive Brook was the first.

This led to his own studio, MGM, casting him in *Red-Headed Woman*, but the role – Jean Harlow's chauffeur-lover – was small; they promised to delete the role if the film was shown in France, but he was bitter and sought release from his contract. Hollywood, he decided, liked him no more than he liked it and he returned to France to do *Sous d'Autres Cieux* with Marie Bell, directed by Augusto Genina. For UFA he did some more French versions: *F.P.I. Ne Répond Pas*, in the Paul Hartmann role, and *Moi et L'Impératrice* (33), with Lilian Harvey, a musical about a duke who thinks a girl's singing has cured his injuries; he was also in the English version of the latter, *The Only Girl* (*Heart Song* in the US), and then returned to Paris, where he was an undisputed star. He made *L'Epervier*, as a Hungarian count whose wife (Natalie Paley) helps him cheat at cards (it was shown in the US in 1940 as *Les Amoureux*); and, in a role he had just done on the stage, *Le Bonheur*, with Gaby Morlay replacing Yvonne Printemps, she as an actress whom he, as an anarchist, is supposed to murder – but they fall in love. He had also done *La Bataille* (34) on the stage, in a small role, in 1921: now he was in the lead, the Japanese naval commander, that Sessue Hakayawa had played in the Silent version; Annabella co-starred and there was an English version, *The Battle* (*Thunder in the East* in the US). Fox saw it and invited him back to the US; encouraged by Ruth Chatterton, he took the plunge after making *Liliom* for that company – Molnar's play, directed in French by Fritz Lang (filmed in English in 1930 with Charles Farrell), as the big-headed show barker.

Fox announced that they had signed Boyer for a series of 'romantic yarns of the Valentino type': they thought, he said later, 'they might make capital of a man whose eyes could look as though they mirrored all the sorrow in the world' – and he cooperated, seldom showing the particular vitality or versatility of his selfish loafer in *Liliom*. He became a Hungarian violinist caught between countess Loretta Young and fellow gypsy Jean Parker in *Caravan* (or between Annabella and Conchita Montenegro in the French version, also directed by Erik Charrell): it was a well-deserved flop and he bought up his contract. Despite this setback, Walter Wanger offered him a role opposite Miss Colbert in *Private Worlds* (35), as the head of a mental hospital who falls in love with her, a doctor (during its making he met and married an English actress, Pat Paterson): for the first time American audiences were impressed and Wanger signed him to a personal contract, with permission to do one film a year in France. He then played opposite Katharine Hepburn in *Break of Hearts* when Francis Lederer walked out during the first week's shooting; and did another film with Miss Young, *Shanghai*, as a Eurasian. In Paris he was the Crown Prince Rudolph in *Mayerling* (36) for Anatole Litvak, with Darrieux, which was probably the peak of his popularity in his native land – and which was much adored on its showings elsewhere. More than anything that had gone before, this established Boyer in the eyes of Anglo-Saxons as the great 'lovair'.

He was dark and handsome, and it had already been proved that when he spoke English he had a fascinating accent: where Chevalier had been cute he was sombre. He was something of a rogue, something of a dilettante; his eyes were dreamy, but they could spark *or* melt when a woman was near, which she invariably was. In *The Garden of Allah* it was Dietrich. By virtue of its being in Technicolor and much publicized it was talked about if not a big success; and his moody monk, though romancing on the sands of Sahara, typed him as a sheik of the boudoir. He did not act other than to look pained, but as on other of these lesser occasions, he got by on a compelling sincerity. That he could act and had a sense of humour was established ably by *History is Made at Night* (37), playing a head-waiter fleeing a murder-rap (he is innocent) and falling in love with Jean Arthur. Indeed he was proficient at whatever he turned his hand to: his Napoleon to Garbo's Marie Walewska in *Conquest* provided, said the 'New Yorker', 'the first time she has had a leading man who contributes more to the interest and vitality of the film than she does'. British readers of 'Picturegoer' voted him the year's Best Actor.

Conquest (*38*). *Charles Boyer as Napoleon and Garbo as his Polish mistress Marie Walewska. With no guidance from the script he managed to suggest the ambition, the greatness and the pettiness of the Emperor without abandoning the romantic allure that audiences expected.*

Charles Boyer and Hedy Lamarr in Algiers (*38*). *He didn't actually say 'Comm wiz me to the Casbah', but that was the general idea.*

From an emperor he became a servant, a Russian one, in a comedy for Litvak, with Claudette Colbert, *Tovarich*. It was set in Paris, and in Paris Boyer did a French film, *Orage* (38), adulterously in love with Michèle Morgan; and it was the remake of a French film that made him the most famous (and parodied) screen lover of his era: *Algiers*, about the fatal attraction a society beauty has for underworld chief Pépé Le Moko (which was the title of the Jean Gabin version, bought up by Wanger for this remake). Despite Boyer's following, exhibitors warned Wanger that they would not book foreign players and Wanger was forced to drop him; the matter apparently infuriated Wanger for some years – and it had no discernible effect on the demand for Boyer's services. At RKO he did a movie with Irene Dunne which was so successful that Universal retained them for another: the superb *Love Affair* (39), in which they meet, fall in love and part; and the much less enjoyable *When Tomorrow Comes*, in which they meet, fall in love – and she discovers he is unhappily married.

He returned to France to make *Le Corsair*, from a play by Marcel Achard which Louis Jouvet had done, but it was abandoned at the outbreak of war. Boyer joined the French army, but his government thought he would be more useful as a propagandist in the US.

He did notable work for the Free French; and became an American citizen in 1942.

His films of this period were all superior novelettes: *All This and Heaven Too* (40), again for Litvak, as a French count secretly in love with governess Bette Davis; *Back Street* (41), as a tycoon secretly in love with Margaret Sullavan; and *Hold Back the Dawn*, as a gigolo who discovers that he loves the woman he has married in order to get a US passport – Olivia de Havilland. The *Appointment for Love* was also with Miss Sullavan, and was also superior. He was effective in Duvivier's *Tales of Manhattan* (42), in the episode with Rita Hayworth; and in *The Constant Nymph* (43), as the egotistical musician loved by Joan Fontaine, who later called him her favourite leading man, for he was the only one, with the exception of Fred Astaire, who cared more for the film than himself. He joined up with Duvivier again, to co-produce with him, and to star in, another episode film, *Flesh and Fantasy*; in fact, it was the first of a new actor-producer pact that he had signed with Universal – but its failure presumably caused that studio to annul the deal.

Boyer wanted, above all, to be taken seriously as an actor and he had managed, among his lovers and romantic heroes, to instil a good many human faults and failings; but it was not until *Gaslight* (44) that he played his first real villain – as the sinister husband trying to drive Ingrid Bergman to insanity. Briefly he and Irene Dunne were *Together Again* – a film not up to the occasion – and then he played the title-role in *Confidential Agent* (45), the experienced Spanish loyalist who becomes, among other things, mixed up with English heiress Lauren Bacall. It was taken from Graham Greene's novel and Greene liked Boyer's performance (he also thought the film the best of the poor Hollywood attempts to film his stories). His nationality changed again: he was a Czech refugee involved with plumber's niece Jennifer Jones in the Lubitsch *Cluny Brown* (46), and was then off the screen till *A Woman's Vengeance* (47). It was Aldous Huxley who might have felt vengeful about this version of his play 'The Gioconda Smile'. Boyer played a 45-ish man who marries a much younger woman (Ann Blyth) after his first wife had died in mysterious circumstances, and it did not help his career. Nor did *Arch of Triumph* (48), again with Bergman, he as a refugee from Nazi Germany, a surgeon, and she as a Paris *poule*. As a freelance Boyer could hardly afford such flops; and in 1948 he left Hollywood to do 'Red Gloves' (Sartre's 'Les Mains Sales') in New York.

When he returned to the screen it was as a character actor, perhaps as bored by some of

Sometimes in the 40s it seemed that you couldn't go to the movies without finding a malevolent male trying to drive his wife insane: Charles Boyer and Ingrid Bergman in Gaslight *(44), which was the first of the species. Only it wasn't, quite, for it was a remake of a British film made four years earlier.*

his later performances as audiences had been, seemingly having learned his words by rote with little else to offer now that his youthful soulfulness had gone. At any rate, he abandoned his toupee and gleefully attacked any elderly part which came his way. *The Thirteenth Letter* (51), a remake of Clouzot's *Le Corbeau*, also found him bearded – and some of the magic had undoubtedly fled; he remained a persuasive actor, but seldom a memorable one. *The First Legion*, as a priest, *Thunder in the East* (52), as an Indian politician, with Alan Ladd, and *The Happy Time* were not, in any case, remotely distinguished and Boyer was much better served by Ophuls's *Madame de . . .* (53) in France, an elegant triangle tale with Darrieux and Vittorio de Sica. He filmed mainly in France over the next 10 years, but appeared notably in the US on TV: he was one of the originators of 'Four Star Playhouse', was in a series called 'The Rogues' and did 'There shall Be No Night' with Katharine Cornell. On Broadway he was in 'Kind Sir' (53) filmed as *Indiscreet*, with Mary Martin, 'The Marriage-Go-Round' (58) with Claudette Colbert and 'Lord Pengo' (63). His pictures were not too hot: *Nana* (54) with Martine Carol, as the aristocrat who murders her; *La Fortuna di Essere Donna* (55) with Sophia Loren, as a theatrical agent; in Hollywood, Minnelli's *The Cobweb*, a reprise of his role in *Private Worlds*, and *Around the World in 80 Days* (56), a cameo appearance; in *Paris Palace Hotel* he fell for Françoise Arnoul; and in *Une Parisienne* (57) for Brigitte Bardot. Then he was Charlton Heston's assistant in *The Buccaneer*. Back in Europe, he was an impoverished aristocrat in *Maxime* (58) with Michèle Morgan, after which he did: the Hollywood *Fanny* (60) in Raimu's old role; *Les Démons de Minuit* (61) with Pascale Audret; and *Adorable Julia/Julia du bist Zauberhaft* with Lilli Palmer, a dire Franco-Austrian emasculation of Somerset Maugham's 'Theatre'.

In 1964 Boyer made his London stage début in Rattigan's 'Man and Boy'. In films he continued to play character parts, sometimes billed below the title, and usually in Hollywood made-in-Europe products: *The Four Horsemen of the Apocalypse* (61); *Love Is a Ball* (62) when director David Swift spoke in awe of his 'professionalism'; *A Very Special Favor* (64) as Leslie Caron's father; *How To Steal a Million* (65) and *Paris Brûle-t-il?/Is Paris Burning?*; *Casino Royale* in Britain and *Barefoot in the Park* (67), in Hollywood; *Rublo de las dos Caras/The Day the Hot Line Got Hot* (68); *The Madwoman of Chaillot* (69); and *The April Fools*. After some years' absence, he returned in the dim remake of *Lost Horizon* (73) as the head lama, subse-quently appearing in Resnais's fine *Stavisky* (74), supporting Jean-Paul Belmondo, and Minnelli's *A Matter of Time* (76), with Liza Minnelli.

He died in 1978 on his ranch in Arizona, from an overdose of drugs, only a few days after the death of his wife.

LOUISE BROOKS

In 1957 Ado Kyrou wrote in 'Amour-Eroticisme et Cinéma' that Louise Brooks was 'the only woman who had the ability to transfigure – no matter what the film – into a masterpiece. . . . Her vivid beauty, her absolutely unique acting (I do not know of a greater tragedienne on the screen) predisposed her to the top rank. Not one woman exerted more magic, not one had her genius of interpretation. Nevertheless she disappeared in 1931 in a manner altogether inexplicable, at the age of 24. . . .'

When she disappeared, hardly anyone noticed. She is revered today, but in the 20s neither she nor anyone else thought her a good actress, let alone a goddess. *That* is what is inexplicable. See her in her two films for Pabst, wide-eyed as a child as she journeys into the forbidden world of champagne, diamonds and men, no coquette and not mistress of her fate, but a luminous presence and perhaps a nymphomaniac, unfathomable as she surveys the delicious prospect before her.

She was born in Cherryvale, Kansas, in 1906. From 1921 to 1924 she danced with Ruth St Denis and Ted Shawn and their company; she transferred to George White's 'Scandals' and thence to the 'Ziegfeld Follies' (25). Ziegfeld promised to star her, but her looks had attracted Paramount, who signed her and gave her a bit part in *The Street of Forgotten Men* (25). She preferred to be a star in movies and was a beauty-contest winner in *The American Venus* (26), starring Esther Ralston and Ford Sterling. Most of the time she was a shop girl, in bangs and a beret: *A Social Celebrity* starting Adolphe Menjou as a small-town barber who takes her, his manicurist, to New York; *It's the Old Army Game*, as the assistant in W.C. Fields's store – and in life she wed its director, Eddie Sutherland (it lasted two years); and *The Show-Off*, from George Kelly's Broadway hit, with Ford Sterling in the title-role, as the girl next door. That would be filmed three more times, and *Love 'em or Leave 'Em* would turn up again as *The Saturday Night Kid* with Clara Bow as the girl who sacrifices her job for the sake of her gold-digging sister, Jean Arthur. Their

Louise Brooks is remembered best for the two films she made in Germany for G.W. Pabst: Pandora's Box *and* Diary of a Lost Girl (*both 29*). *Two scenes from* Diary of a Lost Girl, *left with Kurt Gerron.*

roles were played here by Evelyn Brent and Brooks, a delicious little minx. She and William Collier Jr went to First National (he stayed) for *Just Another Blonde* and around this time 'Picturegoer' noted her subtle vamping: 'She is extraordinary vital and alive. The sheer, sharp grace of face and figure, the very chic of her bob, combine to draw struggling heroes into her net'. There followed: *Evening Clothes* (27), and it was Adolphe Menjou wearing them while falling for her, as a Paris cabaret girl; *Rolled Stockings*, and these were hers, driving wild the college boys who included Richard Arlen; *The City Gone Wild*, directed by James Cruze, an underworld story with Thomas Meighan; and *Now We're in the Air*, a Beery-Hatton comedy, in a dual role.

She was loaned to Fox to play a circus high diver in Hawks's *A Girl in Every Port* (28), being fought over by Victor McLaglen and Robert Armstrong, and is magical – as she is in William A. Wellman's moving *Beggars of Life*, dressed as a boy and riding the freight trains with Arlen.

G.W. Pabst, at any rate, saw the magic. After he had seen the Hawks film he wanted her at once for his long-planned *Die Büchse von Pandora* (29), adapted from Wedekind's 'Lulu'. Paramount refused. Later there arose the question of their option on Brooks, and because of the arrival of Sound, they gave her the chance of sticking at her old salary or quitting. She quit and immediately advised Pabst that she was free – just as he was about to take the then little-known Dietrich (who said later: 'Imagine Pabst choosing Louise Brooks when he could have had me'). Thus Brooks became the most entrancing nymphomaniac in film history. Said Paul Rotha:

'. . . the performance he [Pabst] extracts from Brooks is one of the phenomena of the cinema.' As a vehicle for her, Pabst decided to remake *Tagebuch einer Verlorenen*, which also concerns a young girl's odyssey into a world of sin and luxury – an innocent who moves instinctively and wholeheartedly into a milieu of sex for money. Then, against Pabst's advice, she returned to her homeland.

Her incredible, incandescent performances were somewhat overlooked outside Germany and certainly in the US, where Silent films were *démodé*. Paramount asked her to dub *The Canary Murder Case* (William Powell as Philo Vance), which she had made before her German trip, so they could release a synchronized version, but she refused (Margaret Livingstone substituted). She also turned down *Bad Girl*, which Paramount offered, and returned to Europe where she was idolized. For Augusto Genina, in France, she made her first Talkie, *Prix de Beauté* (30), a lush, exquisite melodrama about a shop girl who found tragedy when she won a beauty contest and became a star.

She returned to Hollywood with the offer of a $500 a week contract from Columbia: it was never signed, partly because she refused to test for a Buck Jones Western. She got a part in a two-reel comedy, *Windy Riley Goes to Hollywood*, directed by Fatty Arbuckle under his pseudonym; and had supporting parts in *It Pays to Advertise* (31) at Paramount and, at Warners, *God's Gift to Women*. At Wellman's request, Warners wanted to keep her for *Public Enemy*, but she turned it down (Jean Harlow played it) because she wanted to go to New York. She had at this time a wealthy lover who seemed to her more

important than Hollywood. As she said later, the collapse of her film career was mostly her own fault; but matters were not helped when she was sacked from an out of town tour of 'Louder Please'.

She also claimed that she had never behaved like a movie star, but nevertheless or therefore she was declared a bankrupt in 1932. In 1933 she went back to dancing, mostly in nightclubs, and in 1935 was dancing with Dario in the Persian Room in New York. She went to Hollywood to test for Republic – a role in *Dancing Feet* – but did not get it. She stayed on, broke and desperate to work, and finally played opposite Buck Jones in a B Western at Universal, *Empty Saddles* (36). Then Columbia offered her a test for a star part if she would appear in the chorus of Grace Moore's *When You're in Love* (37). She did, and stills were issued with captions thus: 'Louise Brooks, former star, who deserted Hollywood at the height of her career, has come back to resume her work in pictures. But seven years is too long for the public to remember, and Louise courageously begins again at the bottom.' The only results from this were a bit part in *King of Gamblers* and the lead in a B Western with John Wayne, *Overland Stage Raiders* (38). It is such an ordinary role (in a cheap movie) that it is impossible to tell whether she should have stayed in films.

In 1940 she opened a dance studio in Kansas; in 1943 she returned to New York and worked intermittently in radio, in publicity offices and finally as a salesgirl, until in 1948 she became a recluse. In 1955, two years before Kyrou's tribute was written, James Card, the Curator of Motion Pictures at Eastman House in Rochester, NY, sought her out and found her oblivious to the fact that she had been rediscovered by film buffs: after 25 years in limbo she found, like Buster Keaton, that she was not forgotten. Remembrance was limited to film societies, but it was intense. The Paris Cinémathèque had this programme note: 'Those who have seen her can never forget her. She is the modern actress *par excellence* because, like the statues of antiquity, she is outside time. . . . It is sufficient to see her to believe in beauty, in life, in the reality of human beings. . . .' Brooks herself began taking an interest in films and wrote superbly on screen acting and other subjects. She died in 1985. James Card wrote in 1958: '. . . from the day the preservation of great films began, the petty plotting of small and selfish men to wipe out the record of beauty and truth that has sometimes been achieved in spite of them was forever frustrated. The return of Louise Brooks to the screens of the world is a portent: the art of the film has its own immortality.'

Louise Brooks: in homage to her Jean-Luc Godard made Anna Karina wear her hair in the Brooks bob in Vivre Sa Vie *in 1962.*

JACK BUCHANAN

Jack Buchanan was no Fred Astaire, but his strictly limited song-and-dance talent found a large number of admirers. He sang, or rather crooned, with an attractive, nearly nasal casualness; and danced, or rather tapped, with an easy elegance. He was the epitome of that 20s/30s hero, the debonair man-about-Mayfair, adept at a silly ass line, and, as such, was often satirized and imitated: what the others lacked was his disarming sense of modesty. The British theatre has seldom seen anyone as good in that particular line (not high praise) and the British cinema no one else at all. His films are probably remembered less by his contemporaries than his stage appearances, but many of them are rather charming in an awful sort of way.

He was born in Helensburgh, near Glasgow, in 1891, the son of an auctioneer. Stagestruck, he had no training, but in 1912 made an unsuccessful début in a small part at the Grand, Glasgow. Later that year he had a walk-on in London at the Apollo in 'The Grass Widow'; got a good job understudying Vernon Watson in a revue, 'All the Winners', and had his first taste of success touring (15–17) in 'Tonight's the Night'. That proved his forte was light comedy. He attracted attention in London in 'Bubbly'; and was really established by Charlot's 'A to Z' revue in 1921, along with Beatrice Lillie and Gertrude Lawrence. The three of them went to New York for 'The Charlot Revue of 1924' and became the rage of the Great White Way. Other successes of the 20s included 'Battling Butler' in 1923, 'Toni' in 1924, 'Sunny' in 1927 and 'That's a Good Girl' in 1928.

He started in films with *Auld Lang Syne* (17); with *Her Heritage* (19), he began leading roles in some very bad films: *The Audacious Mr Squire* (23); *The Happy Ending* (25) and a triangle drama, *Settled Out of Court* (26), both with Fay Compton; and *Bulldog Drummond's Third Round*. The first successful one was *Confetti* (27) – at least he was good in a serious part, in love with an older woman. When he brought *Toni* (27) to the screen, playing again the millionaire who poses as his detective lookalike to help a girl, he seemed forced and the film was unfunny. When Talkies came in Hollywood called him for a musical (with colour sequences) in which he played Irene Bordoni's *Paris* (29) stage partner, helping her when an American matron (Louise Closser Hale) accuses her of stealing her son. While at Warners he filmed a spot for the all-star *The Show of Shows*, but it did not make it to the final print. He went to New York for 'Wake Up and Dream' with Jessie Matthews and then returned to Hollywood for

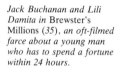

Jack Buchanan and Lili Damita in Brewster's Millions *(35), an oft-filmed farce about a young man who has to spend a fortune within 24 hours.*

Monte Carlo (30), a Lubitsch frolic in which he was a count posing as a hairdresser for the sake of Jeanette MacDonald. The part, intended for Maurice Chevalier, must have been re-written, since the nimble and ascetic Buchanan was unable to suggest that ripe eroticism that Chevalier suggested in his films with that lady. Indeed, the film goes downhill once Buchanan appears and it did nothing to ingratiate him with American audiences; accordingly, his plans to produce his own films in Hollywood came to nothing. Instead, he became involved in stage production and real estate. In Britain, he built the Leicester Square Theatre, originally to house his own musicals. It opened in 1931, but that year he starred at the London Hippodrome in 'Stand Up and Sing'. Paramount gave him a second chance when its British arm produced *Man of Mayfair* (31) – who was him posing as a milord to win over his beloved: but they too quietly dropped him when local audiences proved unappreciative.

Herbert Wilcox, however, felt that his genial, gracious image had not been well-used by films – and as far as he was concerned he was a 'name' in the US. He put him into *Goodnight Vienna* (32), based on a radio musical, as a playboy officer who falls for a shop girl (Anna Neagle), and they co-directed *Yes Mr Brown* (33), also set in Vienna (it was based on the German *Ein Bisschen Liebe*) about a secretary who poses as an absent wife to impress Buchanan's American boss. The role was played by Elsie Randolph, his favourite leading lady, and they were reunited on *That's a Good Girl*, which successfully opened out a stage show which he had done (as star and producer) – a knockabout farce about a rich ne'er-do-well and his even richer aunts, set on the Riviera. It also contains one of the most evocative 30s numbers, 'Fancy Our Meeting'.

After starring in the West End in 'Mr Whittingham' Buchanan returned to his ambition of becoming an international movie star. In the Silent era he had been scathing about the local film industry, but much had been learned since then. And indeed, since his last film for Wilcox that gentleman had signed an agreement with United Artists, now looking to them for the sort of product which the American public would buy. So his next three films were based on old farces popular on both sides of the Atlantic: *Brewster's Millions* (35), about a young man who has to spend a small fortune in order to inherit a larger one; *Come Out of the Pantry*, about a milord in New York forced to work as a footman; and *When Knights Were Bold* (37), about a young officer from India who hopes to win over his stuffy family by learning the art of chivalry.

Buchanan gathered around him Americans living in London: for the first, Thornton Freeland, who had directed *Flying Down to Rio*; for the other two as leading lady Fay Wray (whose husband, John Monk Saunders, was working for Korda); as his chief writer, Ralph Spence, author of *The Gorilla* and an experienced Hollywood hand; and Van Phillips, his musical director. All the same, seeing these films today, it is easy to understand why UA made only tentative attempts to release them in the US.

Later Phillips would say: 'No one was as much loved – for his position – as Johnny B, as we all called him. He was meticulous, but nothing and no one were too unimportant for him to give time and trouble to.' Whether Wilcox loved him at this time is uncertain, since Buchanan broke away before the last of that trio – though to show there was no ill-feeling he agreed to do a guest role in Wilcox's *Limelight* – and he invited Wilcox to produce and direct his second film for Rank's new distributor, GFD. *This'll Make You Whistle* (37) was yet again set on the Riviera and yet again had our hero as a millionaire posing as A.N. Other to unmask a criminal: but it began Buchanan's new regime on a high note, since the film and the original show were running in London at the same time. After a trip to Broadway for 'Between the Devil' with Evelyn Laye, he returned to Britain with film plans dimmed: *Smash and Grab*, a thriller hopefully in the mould of *The Thin Man*, directed by the American Tim Whelan; *The Sky's the Limit*, obviously about aeroplanes, which he co-directed with American cinematographer Lee Garmes; and *Sweet Devil* (38) with Bobby Howes, which he produced only. He made a last bid for the big time: *Break the News*, a remake of *La Morte en Fuite* directed by René Clair, with a Cole Porter song, and Maurice Chevalier (who was billed after him) and he as chorus boys involved in a publicity stunt – partly to win June Knight (who replaced Adele Astaire during filming). The film is good, especially in the context of Clair's oeuvre, but no one then wanted to know – including American audiences in 1941, when Monogram released it. Dispirited, Buchanan tried producing for the last time, again playing the debonair insurance investigator hero of *Smash and Grab*, but with Googie Withers replacing Randolph as his wife: *The Gang's All Here* (39) with Freeland directing and fellow Americans Otto Kruger and Jack La Rue in the cast. Despite them, it was not shown in the US till 1945, released by PRC, and it must have looked horribly old hat. Associated British released in Britain and he stayed with them for a final couple: *The Middle Watch*, frankly middle-aged as the ship's captain from whom a couple of girls must be hidden in this version of a stage farce; and *Bulldog Sees It Through* (40), a thriller but the Bulldog was not Drummond.

In 1940 he had a setback when a big show on tour, 'Top Hat and Tails', collapsed – at the same time as France, and the two events were not simply coincidental. Britain, during the first year of the war, had no time for top hats and tails, and Buchanan became merely a memory, along with 'Stop Me and Buy One' and street-lighting. He entertained the troops and continued to act on the stage under his own management, notably in a revival of 'The Last of Mrs Cheyney' and in 'Canaries Sometimes Sing'.

It was Hollywood which restored him to public favour. Minnelli co-starred him with Fred Astaire in *The Band Wagon* (53): the character was unsympathetic – a temperamental and egotistical producer, reputedly based on Minnelli himself – but Buchanan played with some tongue-in-cheek and had several fine numbers with Astaire and Nanette Fabray. He will be remembered for these – ironically, for he was petrified with nerves at the prospect of working with Astaire. In London he played a respectable businessman whose household is disrupted by a pop singer – a feeble farce and a disaster on the first night till Buchanan impersonated Johnny Ray singing 'Cry'; it ran long enough for him to be invited to repeat the role on film – *As Long As They're Happy* (55). In a last flurry of filming he was Glynis Johns's uncle, relating the exploits of *Josephine and Men*, and a typical Englishman living among the bewildering French with luscious Martine Carol as his wife, in *Les Carnets de Major Thompson*. Pierre Daninos's book had been a bestseller and the combination of Buchanan and director Preston Sturges made it a *succès fou* in France: but whether in the original or the botched export version it is dire. Buchanan returned to TV, in a cheapjack series unworthy of him, on the new independent network; and died in 1957 after a long battle with cancer.

BILLIE BURKE

Ginger Rogers, among others, refers to the 30s as Hollywood's Golden Years. It is not just looking back through rose-coloured glasses, though to artists like Rogers there must have been in herself and around the studios an atmosphere of self-confidence, of success and all's-right-with-the-world. The big studios pampered and protected their stars; and they churned out film after film without a consideration of losing money. They were the Golden Years because there were so many really funny comedies and because there was, behind them, a glittering assembly of supporting players whom the public knew and loved almost as much. In the Astaire-Rogers pictures, there were stalwarts like Edward Everett Horton, Eric Blore, Helen Broderick and the great Alice Brady.

Billie Burke, like Alice Brady, was a considerable stage actress doomed to playing the same part in pictures; that of the fluttery, irresponsible older lady whose lack of logic induced despair in the rest of the cast and hilarity in the audience. Burke wrote in her memoirs ('With a Feather on My Nose', 1949): 'These characters, these bird-witted ladies whom I have characterized so often that I presume you know them – how could you escape? – derive from my part in "The Vinegar Tree". I am neatly typed today, of course, possibly irrevocably typed, although I sincerely hope not, for I should like better parts.' She did not get them and audiences perhaps should be grateful: Billie Burke's bird-witted lady was one of the perfect things in an imperfect world. In real life, she must have been different, for she once said: 'To survive in Hollywood, you need the ambition of a Latin American revolutionary, the ego of a grand opera tenor and the physical stamina of a cow pony.'

Prior to taking on this part, she had been a great beauty and a great stage favourite on both sides of the Atlantic. She was born in Washington in 1885, into a family of entertainers. Her father brought his company to Europe and Burke toured in Russia, France, Germany, etc.; they arrived in Britain where she sang 'coon songs' at Birkenhead and appeared in panto at Glasgow and Sheffield. Her first major legit role was in 1903 at the London Pavilion, in 'The School Girl', singing 'Mamie, I Have a Little Canoe', after which she had important roles, at one point taking over the lead in 'The Belle of New York'. One of the great impresarios of the period, Charles Frohman, took her back to New York to co-star with John Drew in 'My Wife', in 1907, and she worked with him for a number of years – in plays such as 'Love Watches', Maugham's 'Mrs Dot' and 'The Land of Promise', and Pinero's 'The Mind-the-Paint Girl' and 'The Amazon'. It was Maugham who introduced her to Florenz Ziegfeld, recently divorced from Anna Held, and she married him.

Thomas H. Ince made picture overtures for Triangle and in what was already Hollywood she made *Peggy* (16), playing a Scots maid, with William Desmond as her leading man. She got $10,000 a week, the highest sum yet paid to a movie artist. Ince offered her a five-year contract, but she realized the difficulty of being a movie star and remaining Mrs Ziegfeld, and declined; however, she agreed to do a serial for an independent company in Florida, *Gloria's Romance*, with David Powell, as a young hoyden getting into mix-ups. The film companies remained insistent and she finally signed with Famous Players-Lasky (Paramount) because they had a New York studio and she need not be separated from her (philandering) husband. She made: *The Mysterious Miss Terry* (17), with Thomas Meighan; *Arms and the Girl*; *The Land of Promise*, from Maugham's play, with Meighan; *Eve's Daughter* (18); *Let's Get a Divorce*, from another play – Sardou's 'Divorçons'; *In Pursuit of Polly*, with Meighan, a comedy in which she was mistaken for a German spy; *The Make-Believe Wife*, a poor farce; and *Good Gracious Annabelle!* (19), one of her biggest successes. *The Misleading Widow* was a wartime comedy of some skill, but the rest were poor: *Sadie Love*; *Wanted a Husband*; *Away Goes Prudence* (20); *The Frisky Mrs Johnson* (21); and *The Education of Elizabeth*. She lost interest and returned to Broadway – Booth Tarkington's 'Intimate Strangers', Noël Coward's 'The Marquise' (27) among others – but was mainly Mrs Ziegfeld. Ziegfeld, by 1930, was penniless – partly due to some flops, partly via poor speculation and partly because of the circumstances caused by the Depression; and Burke returned to the stage, in her first character role, in Ivor Novello's 'The Truth Game'; that led to an offer to appear in the Los Angeles production of 'The Vinegar Tree' (31) by Paul Osborne, which in turn brought a Hollywood offer. But in 1930, according to some sources, Goldwyn – who considered himself Hollywood's Ziegfeld – put her under contract as a favour to Ziegfeld (who needed the money) when they were partnered on *Whoopee*. She did eventually make one film for him and once she had started in Talkies was in such demand as a supporting player that she could take assignments as she pleased: but only in 1936 did she appear in the exhaustive contract lists ('Where to Write to the Stars') published most months in 'Photoplay'. She was then with the other Goldwyn stars under 'United Artists' – while filming chiefly at MGM.

In 1930 she appeared in some Pathé-Rodeo (short) comedies; but *A Bill of Divorcement* (32) is usually listed as her Talkie début. The invitation came from director George Cukor and she played the pretty but thoughtless wife of mentally ill John Barrymore. Originally she was co-starred with Barrymore, but as it became apparent that the film belonged to the débuting Katharine Hepburn, the billing was changed and Hepburn's name added: Burke then went below the title to keep her company. She followed with another with Hepburn, *Christopher Strong* (33), as the wife of her lover (Colin Clive); and then at MGM was Lionel Barrymore's wife, the vapid hostess giving the *Dinner at Eight* (in New York revivals her outburst when things finally get too much for her is greeted with applause). She was already typecast: *Only Yesterday* (34) at Universal; at RKO *Finishing School* starring Frances Dee and Bruce Cabot, as a society mother; *Where Sinners Meet* with Diana Wynyard, as the wife of a particularly obtuse Reginald Owen; and *We're Rich Again*, co-starring with Edna May Oliver, a comedy involving much match-making; and at MGM, two Clark Gable vehicles, *Forsaking All Others*, as Joan Crawford's aunt, and *After Office Hours* (35) as Constance Bennett's mother; and *Society Doctor* with Chester Morris.

It was announced that MGM had offered her a contract – mainly as the result of her cooperation over *The Great Ziegfeld* which they were preparing (Myrna Loy played her) but she turned it down. She co-starred with Will Rogers, then Fox's – and the US's – top box-office star, in *Doubting Thomas*, an ingratiating comedy about a plain man whose silly wife has stage aspirations; and then went on to gurgle but briefly as a Duchess at the ball on the Eve of Waterloo in *Becky Sharp*. She made: *A Feather in Her Hat*, starring Pauline Lord and Basil Rathbone; *She Couldn't Take It*, as Joan Bennett's mother, the two of them – and father Walter Connolly – made saner by ex-gangster George Raft; *Splendor*, as one of New York's society set, her only film for Goldwyn; *My American Wife* (36), as Ann Sothern's doting mother; *Piccadilly Jim*, as one of a family (Madge Evans, Frank Morgan) mocked by cartoonist Robert Montgomery; *Craig's Wife*, as Rosalind Russell's kindly neighbour; and *Parnell* (37). Then Hal Roach was inspired to cast her as Mrs Topper in *Topper*. Roland Young was Topper and they were an irresistible combination: both well-meaning and both vague, but where he bumbled, she dithered.

Then: *The Bride Wore Red*, as the Countess who sees through Miss Crawford; *Navy Blue and Gold* with Lionel Barrymore and Robert Young; *Everybody Sing* (38), as Judy Garland's mother; and again for Roach, *Merrily We Live*. This had the classic virtues of the period: a crazy comedy about a crazy family. Burke was the daffy mother who insisted on adopting a fake tramp (Brian Aherne) and making him the chauffeur. Said the 'New Statesman': 'Billie Burke's mother attains (like Parsifal) to a foolishness so pure that it

Billie Burke with Thomas Meighan in The Land of Promise *(17), directed by Joseph Kaufman from Somerset Maugham's play about settlers in Canada and one of Miss Burke's rare serious pictures.*

verges on beauty.' Clarence Kolb was the father, but Burke was back with Roland Young in the equally delightful *The Young in Heart*, with Douglas Fairbanks Jr and Janet Gaynor, and in *Topper Takes a Trip*. The 'New Statesman' again enthused: 'Here I must pay tribute to Billie Burke who . . . excels all her previous studies in good-natured imbecility, her every word proceeding from a wonderfully complete inner vacuum.' Also for Roach she was Oliver Hardy's wife in *Zenobia* (39), after which she was Robert Young's flighty mother in *Bridal Suite* and Glinda the Good Fairy in *The Wizard of Oz*, her favourite film part she said, and the nearest to her stage roles. She was in *Remember?* as Greer Garson's mother; *Eternally Yours* as Loretta Young's aunt; *The Ghost Comes Home* (40) with Frank Morgan; and *And One Was Beautiful*, as Laraine Day's mother. She starred with several fine contemporaries (Charles Coburn, Beulah Bondi, Helen Broderick, Helen Westley, Marjorie Main), in *The Captain Is a Lady*. *Dulcy* was an Ann Sothern vehicle in which Burke was married to Roland Young again, and she was married

The Young in Heart (*38*): *Janet Gaynor and Billie Burke, right, playing cards with Minnie Dupree, and fleecing her. They were two of a family of con-artists, and the film amusingly told of their regeneration because of their kindness.*

Spencer Tracy, as the Father of the Bride (*50*), *drinks to the groom's father, Moroni Olsen. Billie Burke was the groom's mother and Joan Bennett the bride's.*

to Morgan again in *Hullabaloo*. She and Young were *not* married in *Irene* and as a Long Island matron she had only a couple of scenes with him; she spent *One Night in Lisbon* (41) with Fred MacMurray and Madeleine Carroll, as a British dowager; and was back starring with Young in *Topper Returns* and with Frank Morgan in *The Wild Man of Borneo*, the last under her MGM contract. She was ideally cast as the mother of the

house in *The Man Who Came to Dinner* with Bette Davis and after *What's Cookin'* at Universal, a musical starring the Andrews Sisters, was Davis's bedridden mother, in *In This Our Life* (42). The Joan Crawford-Melvyn Douglas *They All Kissed the Bride* was the last she did with Roland Young (he was an attorney and she was Crawford's mother). She supported Don Ameche and Joan Bennett in *Girl Trouble* and then went to Broadway for 'This Rock'; after playing Martha Scott's mother in *Hi Diddle Diddle* (43), she starred in a clutch of Bs: *Gildersleeve on Broadway*, one of a series that starred Harold Peary; *So's Your Uncle*, with Donald Woods, and *You're a Lucky Fellow, Mr Smith*, with Allan Jones, two Universal musicals. Another not-too-successful Broadway venture, Zoë Akins's 'Mrs January and Mr X', kept her from films for a year, except for *Laramie Trail* (44), a Republic Western with Smiley Burnette; after which there was another Universal B, *Swing Out Sister* (45), with Rod Cameron as a classics composer with a secret passion for swing.

The Cheaters was a Republic programmer which reprised threads from other, better Burke pictures: how ham actor Joseph Schildkraut reforms a well-to-do and somewhat crooked New York family. Burke, of course, was the mother, selfish, spoilt and unthinking; it was a straight performance but audiences wanted to laugh at her. She was unacceptable now except in comedy, partly because, as she grew older, her voice more than ever was – so appropriately – like the twittering of birds. Alas, her activity decreased: *Breakfast in Hollywood* (46), built around Fred Breneman's radio programme of the same name, as the wife of philandering Raymond Walburn; *The Bachelor's Daughters* (47), in which four store clerks pretend to be society and employ Adolphe Menjou and Miss Burke as their parents; *The Barkleys of Broadway* (48), again as a Long Island hostess; and *And Baby Makes Three* (49) with Robert Young and Barbara Hale. She was groom Don Taylor's mother in *Father of the Bride* (50) and in the sequel, *Father's Little Dividend* (51), and in between was one of several talents wasted in *Three Husbands* (50) and *Blaze of Glory*, which starred Lo McCallister. After that she did varied TV work, had a small part in *Small Town Girl* (53) and then retired. She was induced out of retirement for a couple of plays in stock (including 'The Solid Gold Cadillac') and for very small parts in *The Young Philadelphians* (59), *Sergeant Rutledge* (60) and *Pepe*, playing fluttery old ladies. She died in 1970.

JAMES CAGNEY

Cagney the actor has been, perhaps inevitably, overshadowed by Cagney the gangster. He was the best gangster there was. He came from the back streets, with a square trilby clapped on his grinning head. The clothes marked his new affluence; he was dapper, assured, smug. Like someone's pet terrier:

bouncing, eager. He moved on the balls of his feet, the fists ready. Otherwise, only the eyes betrayed the necessary wariness – a quick glance, a quick frown; then the snarling and the yelping. But not pitiful, rather defiant. Come the three corners of the world in arms and he would, still, shock them. He was convinced of his own invincibility. They would never get him. That was his charm. He never asked – he commanded, but in a voice that itself was a wheedler, skitting breathlessly, high-pitched, on its sentences, like the butter-covered knife he jabbed in the air, accompanying the words between mouthfuls. Women kept their place around him. He was convinced of his appeal: so what they didn't like it, there was another broad someplace. Said Kenneth Tynan in 1952: '. . . but he possessed, possibly in greater abundance than any other name star of his time, irresistible charm. . . . Even the most ascetic cinéaste will admit that it is impossible to forget how he looked and talked at the height of his popularity.'

But C.A. Lejeune earlier (in 1946, reviewing *Blood on the Sun*) admired the talent: 'James Cagney is one of the best screen actors of our time, with gifts of pathos and an impish humour second to none. . . . With no hint of a four-dimensional character to work from, little material to suggest the hero's past and background, or even his tastes and way of living, Mr Cagney is content to convey all the immediate reactions of a man who is exuberantly alive today and expects to be terribly dead tomorrow. It is a lesson to all young film actors to study how he does this. . . . Few heroes of melodrama can claim that so much skill of such a high order has been spent in bringing their poor bones to life.'

The persona, of course, was tremendously strong. Cagney was *always* dynamic, alert, tough and fast-moving, as if some ferocious inner energy was carrying him along. He could have played few of the roles that someone like Burt Lancaster regards as 'acting' but his versatility was much admired. The key lies in his own words: 'There's not much to tell you about acting but this: never settle back on your heels. Never relax. If you relax, the audience relaxes. And always mean everything you say.'

He was born in 1899, on New York's lower East Side and, although he studied briefly at Columbia, family circumstances compelled him initially to such jobs as a department-store wrapper, a waiter and a racker in a pool room. To earn more he applied for a job in vaudeville and was in 'Every Sailor', which seems to have been a 1914–18 equivalent of 'Soldiers in Skirts'; he was one of the chorus girls, and then he moved over – in a double sense – to the chorus of 'Pitter-Patter' (20); later in its run he was given a speciality dance. He toured in vaudeville with his wife, June Vernon (always known as 'Bill' or 'Willie'), occasionally getting a break in short-lived Broadway musicals. He made his mark in 'Outside Looking In' (25) and the following year did a cabaret act with his wife, called 'A Broadway Romeo'. In 1927 Jed Harris engaged him to play the lead in the London production of 'Broadway', but changed his mind and had him understudy Lee Tracy in the New York presentation. Cagney had a small role in a Mary Boland vehicle, 'Women Go On Forever', and another in 'Grand Street Follies'. A big part in 'Maggie the Magnificent' (29) with Joan Blondell led to another co-starring assignment, in 'Penny Arcade'; he was a weak little murderer prepared to let someone else take the rap.

Al Jolson bought the rights and then sold them to Warner Bros., who brought the two players to Hollywood to film it, rechristened *Sinners' Holiday* (30); the billed stars were Grant Withers and Evalyn Knapp and it was a mild success. Cagney got $500 a week for three weeks' work with an option on his services – which Warners took up – reducing his fee to $400 a week. He was billed fifth on *Doorway to Hell*, as one of Lew Ayres's (double-crossing) hoodlums, and had just two minutes as a fast-talking insurance man in *The Millionaire* (31), with George Arliss. There was another supporting role in *Other Men's Women*, as a railroad man – but he had a moment as magical as any in movies (and it was improvised), when he peels off his oil-skins and dances impatiently over to the dance-floor and his girl. William A. Wellman directed and he gave Cagney the second lead in *Public Enemy*, as the buddy of star Edward Woods. After three days' shooting Wellman had them swop roles. They played thugs with a taste for luxury and Cagney in particular had a complete disregard for any honest means of achieving it: till he ended up dead, riddled with bullets, on his mother's doorstep. He also, memorably, pushed a grapefruit into Mae Clarke's physog. The film was good and much praised for its realistic view of vice; and audiences went wild over Cagney. Wellman said, years later: 'The thing that made it successful was one word – Cagney.'

Cagney, meanwhile, was playing henchman to Warners' established Number One gangster, Edward G. Robinson, in *Smart Money*, and the Brothers smartly upped him to co-star billing. Robinson and he would not again appear as rivals or colleagues: there was no advantage to studio finances to put them both in the same film. A series of Cagney vehicles was inaugurated with *Blonde Crazy* – the blonde was Joan Blondell, but the title, in any case, was incidental: he was a bellboy supplying broads and booze who works himself up into big-time con-rackets and finally into prison. 'Honest men are scarcer than feathers on a frog,' he said, a philosophy he would stick to through the next dozen films. In *Taxi* (32) he was a cab-driver fighting the rackets, 'an outstanding performance', said 'Picture-goer', 'he gets under the skin of his role as a tough of the goodhearted but hot-to-anger type'. In Hawks's *The Crowd Roars* he was a track-driver and *Winner Take All* a prize-fighter.

These pictures were not high cinematic art. They were made quickly and cheaply, and were not considered important – though the deliberately implied social criticism was recognized. Today they are still entertaining: paced by Cagney's own dynamic energy, they move jump-jump-jump through the clichés, at least emotionally honest.

Cagney himself did not like being restricted to roles generally referred to as 'dese, dem and dose'; he was already engaged in a series of battles over salary. *After Blonde Crazy* he had walked out, till Warners raised his salary from $450 to $1,400 a week. Now he wanted a rise from $1,600 to $4,000 – still considerably less than some Warner stars. (Before they took salary cuts because of the Depression, Ruth Chatterton and William Powell got $6,000, Robinson, Fairbanks Jr and Kay Francis $4,000, and Loretta Young $1,000). At the onset of shooting *Blessed Event* Cagney walked out (Lee Tracey took over), claiming he was doing too many pictures for too little. He offered to do three for nothing, provided that at the end of the year he was given his real due. He told an interviewer: 'My stand is based on the fact that my pictures, for the time being, are big money-makers – and that there are only so many successful pictures in a personality. And don't forget that when you are washed up in pictures you are really through. You can't get a bit, let alone a decent part. . . . I don't care if I never act again. If I never had to do another scene, it would be all right with me. I have no trace of that ham-like theatrical yen to act all the time no matter what. I shan't miss trouping.' After arbitration, the Warners offered $1,750, but with a guarantee of periodic hikes.

His return picture was the appropriately titled *Hard to Handle* (33), as a press agent who cons his way up from dance marathons to the big-time, loving or losing Mary Brian as his fortunes wax and wane – at the instigation of her mother, a very funny Ruth Donnelly. In *Picture Snatcher* he was an ex-con turned photographer; in *Mayor of Hell* a prison

Angels with Dirty Faces
(*38*) *had the same plot idea
as* San Francisco *two years
earlier. That it all seemed
fresh was due partly to
Cagney's effervescent
personality and a cast that
included henchman
Bogart.*

governor; in *Footlight Parade* a theatre producer. As such, he sang and danced ('Lookin
for My Shanghai Lil') and hustled the cast like
a whirlwind – a performance which would be
exhausting were it not so captivating. Large
audiences were captivated: the film grossed
the then outstanding sum of $1¾ million. In
Lady Killer he was a hood turned film star,
dragging Mae Clarke across the floor by her
hair; and then he was *Jimmy the Gent* (34).
Said Mordaunt Hall in the 'New York Times':
'a swift-paced comedy in which he gives
another of his vigorous, incisive portrayals';
but *He Was Her Man* was soggy. The her was
Blondell again, as a hooker, and he was an ex-
con. *Here Comes the Navy* was the first of
several in which Pat O'Brien was his rival or
sparring partner; after Cagney had played a
truck-driver in *The St Louis Kid* they went
virtually through the same story – in the
Marine Corps – in *Devil Dogs of the Air* (35).
He was on the right side of the law in *G-Men*
(which Robinson had turned down), a terrific
anti-gangster piece in which he said, 'I seen
too many back alleys as a kid to want to go
back to them.' O'Brien was a cop and Cagney
his wastrel brother in *The Irish in Us*, the most
tedious of their teamings.

There followed the film that Warners

claimed was 'Three Centuries in the Making',
A Midsummer Night's Dream, and Cagney
was Bottom. John Marks found him 'so
sensitive, so dramatic, and so sure of his
rendering . . . that it is worth sitting through
the whole ordeal once for the sake of his scene
with Titania and the sweet fooling of his
fellows'. Robert Forsythe lamented the collapse of the comedy: 'Since I would rather die
than admit that Mr Cagney is not a great
actor, I must blame it on Shakespeare or
Reinhardt. Something is wrong and it isn't me
and it isn't Cagney.' What was wrong was that
Reinhardt's basic conception was vulgar, but
the damp reviews were offset by a gigantic
publicity campaign and the 'Motion Picture
Herald' listed its gross as a surprising $1½
million.

Frisco Kid was more – indeed, very –
conventional, with Cagney as a dock-rat:
'Picturegoer' thought it 'rather much to ask
one's sympathy' for a murderer, but that he
'has a magnetism' which let him get away with
it. *Ceiling Zero* had Cagney and O'Brien
doing their Flagg and Quirt act again, as
commercial airline pilots, Cagney as a fast-
talking Don Juan: Howard Hawks directed
and it was great fun. But not to Cagney: it was
his fifth film within a year, despite the

Cagney with the magnificent Gladys George in an exciting recreation of The Roaring Twenties *(39). It is she who speaks his epitaph: 'He was a big shot.'*

contracted four. His salary was now $4,500 a week but he looked for a technical point to break his contract and found it when a cinema bannered O'Brien's name above his for *Devil Dogs of the Air* – a film which, he added gratuitously, 'had no reason for being filmed under any circumstances'. The case went to court, but pending the outcome he signed a contract with a minor studio, Grand National, reputedly for a down-payment of $100,000 plus story approval (the other majors were backing Warners with that solidarity always shown to recalcitrant employees). Two films resulted: *Great Guy* (36), on the side of the law – as a meat inspector; and *Something to Sing About* (37), a musical. Neither was outstanding and he could not have been sorry when Warners made overtures – the case still not settled – to him to finish out his contract at $150,000 per film plus 10 per cent of the gross after returns of $1½ million and a 'happiness clause'.

The studio had learnt something and so had he. That they needed each other is shown by the record of the top 10 draws: he had crept into the list in 1935, at tenth, returned in 1939 at ninth, and was solidly entrenched again 1940–43 inclusive, until he left the studio. His first film was good: *Boy Meets Girl* (38), from the Spewacks' Broadway hit about Hollywood, with O'Brien and Marie Wilson (and for some reason not shown in Britain till 1940). And the second, which he had planned to do at Grand National, was even better, *Angels With Dirty Faces*: the one about the boys who grow up together and part – Cagney a hood and O'Brien a priest. A fine cast included Humphrey Bogart and Ann Sheridan, and the New York critics voted Cagney the year's Best Actor. He and Bogart were

pitted against each other in *The Oklahoma Kid* (39), mainly memorable because they both felt inconguous in chaps and sent the whole thing up; *Each Dawn I Die* was a superior pen epic, with George Raft as a fellow con; and *The Roaring Twenties*, almost the last major gangster film Warners made, ended the series with a bang. Said Graham Greene: 'Mr Cagney, of the bull-calf brow, is as always a superb and witty actor. Mr Bogart is, of course, magnificent.'

Cagney's contract finished in 1940 and he wanted to start his own company, but because of the world situation he signed on for two years more with Warners, on condition that his brother William was associate producer on his films. The next two were to have been *Knut Rockne All American* and *John Paul Jones*, but Notre Dame (where Rockne had been coach) insisted on O'Brien, to Warners' consternation, because he could not carry a film; and the world situation meant the cancellation of the other project. Instead, Cagney did a story about World War I, *The Fighting 69th* (40), playing the cocky recruit who finds God in the last role; and the infinitely preferable (though he thought it formula stuff and fought against doing it) *Torrid Zone*. These were his last two films with O'Brien and in the second one they are on a banana plantation squabbling over the usual stranded showgirl, Ann Sheridan. *City for Conquest* was New York; Cagney was a boxer and Arthur Kennedy his composer kid brother. This was a melodrama directed by Anatole Litvak with a much admired poetic touch – the very quality which has dated it more then most in the Cagney canon. Almost undated is *Strawberry Blonde* (41), a small-town romance with Olivia de Havilland. *The Bride Came C.O.D.* was a fairly unhappy excursion into comedy for him and Bette Davis, and *Captains of the Clouds* (42) a banal tribute to the Royal Canadian Air Force: both contributed to Cagney's being the second highest paid US citizen in 1941 (Louis B. Mayer was first). Earlier, another citizen had officially accused him of Communism. The charge was dismissed, but Cagney was determined to show publicly where his feelings lay and chose to do a biography of the all-American Broadway showman, George M. Cohan, *Yankee Doodle Dandy*. It took the vast sum of $4 million in the US and was equally popular in Britain, so clearly for 1942 the ingredients were perfect: sentiment, nostalgia, patriotism and music plus the salt-and-pepper of Cagney's performance, which brought him another New York Critics award and a much applauded Oscar. It is his own favourite film and one of the few in which he took 'a real pride'.

*Cagney's own sister,
Jeanne, made one of her
rare appearances as his
screen sister in* Yankee
Doodle Dandy (42), *a
tribute to George M.
Cohan – for which Cagney
won the Oscar.*

*Cagney's early fans loved
the caveman way he treated
his women. Here's an
example from a later film,*
Blood on the Sun (46).
*The stoic lady is Sylvia
Sidney.*

He formed his own company with his brother William to make five films for UA release, with his salary of $150,000 deferred as part of the financing. The first was *Johnny Come Lately* (43), in which he helps an honest small-town paper to survive against its corrupt and more powerful rival. It was the sort of subject liberal-minded actors like and the crusading role was the kind they tend to take when they become their own employees. But the piece was only moderately successful, so he did a more typical vehicle, *Blood on the Sun* (45), again playing a reporter, but an all-American one pitched against the entire might of Imperial Japan. Then 20th invited him to play a role turned down by Rex Harrison, that of an Intelligence instructor in *13 Rue Madeleine* (46), a far-fetched entry in the new 'documentary' thrillers. When the brothers decided to do William Saroyan's sentimental bar-room slice-of-life, *The Time of Your Life* (48), they signed with Warners because they disliked the Pickford-Chaplin management at UA. UA wanted to sue, but as the Cagneys had not asked them for completion money as called for under their agreement, they offered it on this occasion – to secure the film: but it did only modestly and they lost their investment.

Cagney's years as an independent had been neither prolific nor profitable, so he accepted an offer from Warners worth $250,000 per film, one a year for 10 years. He, Hollywood and the studio had changed – for one thing, *White Heat* (49) was bloodier and more brutal than the gangster films of yore: but it was a brilliant reunion for him and director Raoul Walsh, and he was on top form as a gangster with a mother (Margaret Wycherly) fixation. The films that followed were of lesser quality, though 'Variety' found him 'a delight' in *The West Point Story* (50), 'particularly his bombastic, temperamental storming, his hoofing and cocky personality whether making love or directing a stage show'. He did another and lesser gangster film, produced by his own company, *Kiss Tomorrow Goodbye*; and a likeable drama about an ex-alcoholic journalist, *Come Fill the Cup* (51). Warners were now paying him $250,000 per film, but after a guest role in *Starlife* he left to freelance. John Ford's remake of *What Price Glory?* (52) found the sentiment badly dated, Cagney and Dan Dailey were badly miscast and the film was an out-and-out flop; plus *A Lion in the Street* (53), which came too soon after *All the King's Men* to claim serious attention – nor was his stab at the Huey Long-type part anything but superficial.

After an absence, Cagney returned in *Run for Cover* (55), but, although a good Nicholas Ray Western, his career really was in low gear. There had been so little critical and public attention during these years that a burst of activity was talked of as a come-back: as the neurotic captain in *Mister Roberts*; The Gimp, Doris Day's racketeer husband, in *Love Me or Leave Me*; and George M. Cohan, an effective guest appearance in Bob Hope's *The Seven Little Foys*. In 1956 he took over from Spencer Tracy the lead in an indifferent Western, *Tribute to a Bad Man*, and again at MGM was involved in a minor domestic drama with Barbara Stanwyck, *These Wilder Years*. He gave a sympathetic performance as Lon Chaney in *The Man of a Thousand Faces* (57), notable otherwise only for the perfect reconstructions of Chaney's make-up; and then directed competently a remake of *This Gun for Hire* called *Short Cut to Hell!* A Universal musical with Shirley Jones, *Never Steal Anything Small* (59), utilized his talents well – he was a crooked labour boss – but in most other departments it was deficient; and he was also well cast in *Shake Hands With the Devil*, a melodrama about the Irish troubles, but the acting generally, like the dialogue, was platitudinous.

He returned to independent production, in conjunction with Robert Montgomery, who directed *The Gallant Hours* (60), a sober tribute to World War II Admiral William F. Halsey Jr; Cagney did his best to give dimension once more to a character written without any, but the film was too sober, too well-intentioned. Billy Wilder directed him in *One Two Three* (61), playing a Coca-Cola executive in Berlin whose boss's daughter falls in

Still tough in his last picture, One Two Three *(61), Cagney berates his personal assistant Hanns Lothar for a scheme that went wrong.*

love with a young Red: he rattled off his lines in his own fashion – a virtuoso display in a well-nigh perfect comedy. But a certain audience coolness indicated that he no longer had his old hold. He retired, and turned down a million dollars to play Dolittle in *My Fair Lady*. Among other rejected projects were *Harry and Tonto* (written for him, and which won Art Carney an Oscar), *The Godfather Part II, Kotch, The Championship Season* and *Once Upon a Time in America*. In his 1976 autobiography he made it clear that performing had never been essential to him, but he returned to work on the instructions of his doctor, as therapy against his diabetes. *Ragtime* (81), in which he played New York's police chief, was directed not coincidentally by Milos Forman, who lived near Cagney's ranch. Cagney's physical infirmities helped increase the budget, though his role was not a major one. He made one more film, for CBS Television, *Terrible Joe Moran* (84), in a role originally written for Katharine Hepburn. It was changed from former tennis pro to ex-prize-fighter – whose granddaughter (Ellen Barkin) hoped to fleece him. Mr Carney was in support, as his faithful friend. Not surprisingly, Cagney's death in 1986 brought acknowledgment that he was one of the very greatest of the great movie stars.

EDDIE CANTOR

There was a generation of performers who seem to have become immortal; they came at that point when American show business was at its most confident: vaudeville had become the most popular art from the world had yet known and, allied to it but slightly higher up the social scale, the musical theatre was in the hands of great showmen and great songwriters. The artists thrown up during these years are legendary: Fanny Brice, W.C. Fields, Helen Morgan, Al Jolson, Sophie Tucker, Eddie Cantor and so on. (Cantor writes warmly and revealingly about many of the others in his two memoirs, 'My Life Is in Your Hands', 1929, and 'Take My Life', 1957.) Movies and records increased their popularity (in most cases) and perpetuated it. Cantor, small, dapper, Jewish, 'Banjo-eyes', was for some years one of the most popular of screen comedians (though the Motion Picture Almanacks of the time do warn that the huge grosses listed for his films were 'supplied by Mr Cantor himself'). Today, many of his effects look forced, but let him skip around (and sing) as he did in his vaudeville act and there is some magic.

He was born in the heart of the ghetto in New York in 1893. His parents died while he was a child and he left school early to become an office boy. He began performing at amateur nights till there wasn't one within miles he had not covered. His first pro job was in a burlesque show, 'Indian Maidens', as a stooge, and in 1912 he was in Gus Edward's 'Kid Kabaret'; he did a double-act with Sammy Kessler, but they split in London in 1914 and Cantor went into Charlot's 'Not Likely'. His first New York show was 'Canary Cottage' (16), after which Ziegfeld put him in the 'Follies' in 1917, 1918 and 1919. They quarrelled and Cantor worked for other managements in 'The Midnight Rounders' and 'Make it Snappy' among others; but they made it up and Ziegfeld had one of his greatest hits with Cantor in 'Kid Boots' (23). The plot concerned an officious (but lovable, of course) golf caddie who bootlegs on the side and cannot be sacked because he knows too much. Paramount decided to film it: *Kid Boots* (26) with Cantor and Clara Bow and a different plot. It was a big success, but a follow-up film he did for that studio was a flop: *Special Delivery* (27). Cantor was also one of the very first radio stars: and it could be said that *Kid Boots* was the first movie plugged in another medium.

His next film appearance was in a musical to which Ziegfeld lent his name for promotion purposes, *Glorifying the American Girl* (29), in a guest spot, in the once famous Jewish tailor sketch. His ethnic origin was never again stressed. Meanwhile, he had given Ziegfeld another giant hit, 'Whoopee' (28): it was taken off (after a year) only because Ziegfeld was broke and needed the money Goldwyn had offered for the screen rights. And Goldwyn had signed Cantor as star and consultant at $100,000 plus 10 per cent of the profits. The film (30) was no more than a photographed (in two-tone Technicolor) stage show – the adventures of a hypochondriac out West; it was a great hit and Goldwyn exercised his option on Cantor's services: *Palmy Days* (31) – a punning title, with the star as a front for, and then a fugitive from, a gang of fake spiritualists. Its success caused Goldwyn to sign Cantor for five pictures, to be spread over five years. They were *The Kid From Spain* (32) – comic bull-fighting with the Goldwyn Girls and Lyda Roberti; *Roman Scandals* (33), going back in time with the GGs and Lyda Roberti; and *Kid Millions* (34) and *Strike Me Pink* (36), both with Ethel Merman, in the former inheriting a fortune and in the latter fighting gangsters in a luna park. According to the figures supplied by Cantor, all but the last two did sensational business. However, 'Variety' named him the biggest US draw in cinemas abroad (followed

Eddie Cantor, full flight, in Strike Me Pink *(36), his last film for Goldwyn.*

by Garbo, Dietrich, Shearer, Janet Gaynor, George Arliss, Muni, Gable, Claudette Colbert and Ronald Colman, in that order). He meanwhile had become a big star on radio in New York – a fact which Goldwyn blandly refused to appreciate; Cantor resented sitting around on the Coast, losing his radio fees, while Goldwyn tinkered with the scripts and made other changes. They also quarrelled when Goldwyn offered only $150,000 for the film rights of 'Three Men on a Horse', which Cantor felt would be ideal for him. The last film of the contract was not made. In 1931 Cantor could command $8,000 a week in vaudeville and on one occasion in 1936 he would get $25,000 for a week's work. (His radio fee would have brought in around another $5,000 a week.) In 1934 he was the highest paid actor in pictures, earning $270,000 (including his percentage).

Cantor moved over to 20th on long-term contract and had another success with *Ali Baba Goes to Town* (37), going back in time

again, this time to the Arabian Nights. There was, however, some dispute between them as to how financially successful it was; there were also disagreements over material, and the contract was dissolved. He tried a change of pace at MGM, a sentimental comedy based on *Le Mioche* called *Forty Little Mothers* (40), playing a professor whose pupils think he is minding a baby – which he is, but it is not his. Support was headed by Judith Anderson, as the headmistress, a strange teaming which cut no ice at the box-office. Given Cantor's eminence and his continued popularity on the radio it is probable that the studio had an option on his services; if so, it was not exercised. He went back to Broadway – 'Banjo-Eyes' (41) – but he returned to films in *Thank Your Lucky Stars* (43) in a dual role, as an acting hopeful and as himself – the star all the other stars are trying to avoid. They were most of those on the Warner lot; and the film's success reawakened Hollywood's interest. RKO signed him to do *Show Busi-*

ness (44), a cosy and not unlikeable collection of all the clichés in the backstage book; aided by Joan Davis, George Murphy and Constance Moore, it did very well – so well that he was asked to do another one with Davis: *If You Knew Susie* (48). He adored working with her and she was an extremely funny lady in her own right – but the script was poor and the film failed. He appeared in only two further films, in both guesting as himself. The first was *The Story of Will Rogers* (52). His popularity had soared again after moving into television, but he went into semi-retirement after a heart attack in 1953 – events covered, among others, in *The Eddie Cantor Story* (53), which was the brainchild of Sidney Skolsky, producer of *The Jolson Story*. On the assumption that Jolson and his songs were forgotten when that came out, but that Cantor and his songs were well-known, Warners (who produced) reputedly guaranteed Cantor $1 million over a 10-year period. But the film was a gigantic flop – due in part to Keefe Braselle's alienating impersonation of the star; Cantor and his wife (since 1914) played themselves in the opening sequences, arriving to see it. In 1956 he was given a special Oscar 'for distinguished service to the film industry' and he died in 1964.

MADELEINE CARROLL

Madeleine Carroll belonged to that unselect band of ladies whose looks were more immediately apparent than her acting ability. In 1937 James Montgomery Flagg said that he considered her the most beautiful woman in the world. However, few of her parts demanded much more of her than to be cool and lovely while embroiled in creakily melodramatic situations: it is not surprising that Hitchcock used her twice in the 30s and her greatest claim to fame may well be as the first of his blondes.

She was born in West Bromwich in 1906, studied at Birmingham University (hence the later publicity which emphasized that she was a beauty with brains), where she acted; began teaching at Hove, but abandoned it to try her luck as a professional actress. For a while she modelled hats but she eventually got a part in a tour of 'Mr What's His Name' starring Seymour Hicks, which led to her West End début, 'The Lash' (27). She applied for the female lead in a war picture, *The Guns of Loos* (28), and was chosen from 150 girls. It gave her few chances, but enabled her to get into another three West End plays (all at the Vaudeville) and brought more film offers: in *The First Born* she was married to a relentless

philanderer, Miles Mander (who also wrote and directed, rather well): 'You unutterable cad!' she calls him, understandably. In *What Money Can Buy* she was persecuted by a merciless philanderer and she was again with Mander in *The Crooked Billet* (29). She went to France to make *L'Instinct*, but because it was Silent it was never seen in Britain or the US. Her first Talkie was *The American Prisoner*, a period piece set on Dartmoor, followed by *Atlantic* and *Young Woodley* (30), the second film version of John Van Druten's play (a Silent had been made a year or so previously but because of the craze for Talkies was never shown). She did *The W Plan*, a stilted thriller about a British officer (Brian Aherne) behind the German lines. As a fraulein, she looked frumpish, with acting to match, but that did not prevent her from getting more leading roles: *Escape*, from the play by Galsworthy, with Gerald du Maurier (who took over from Clive Brook after several weeks' shooting); *French Leave*; and *The School for Scandal*, which premièred simultaneously. The former was a comedy that she had done on the stage (she had also recently been in 'The Constant Nymph' and 'Beau Geste') and the latter a shabby version of Sheridan made by Maurice Elvey; Carroll was Lady Teazle and the cast included the charming Dodo Watts, considered by many to be Carroll's likely successor.

Carroll was by now the biggest female star in British films, though her popularity by no means approached that of the American stars. She was not very much beyond being charming and pretty – in a mousy way – certainly not the sleek creature of the Hollywood years. The first time she was unmistakably blonde was in *Madame Guillotine* with Aherne. In 1931 she made *Kissing Cup's Race*, *Fascination* and *The Written Law*, and then officially retired from the screen – due, she complained, to the quality of these films. She had also married an army officer, but she continued to work on the stage. Gaumont-British finally offered her a generous contract (a reported £650 per week) and starred her in two of the better British films of the period, *Sleeping Car* (33) with Ivor Novello and *I Was a Spy*, a true story about a Belgian woman (Carroll) who spied for the British and sabotaged German communications. 'Film Weekly' readers voted it the Best Film of the Year.

Carroll's performance in it was barely adequate, but she was patently sincere and beautiful. Earlier in the year, she had turned down a Hollywood offer, but as a result of *I Was a Spy* Fox negotiated to borrow her for *The World Moves On* (34), a two-part saga (1824 and World War I) with Franchot Tone as the American cousin who twice loves her,

Madeleine Carroll in two of the films which established her as the perfect story-book heroine – frail but brave and very beautiful: with Tyrone Power (left) in Lloyds of London *(36) and with Ronald Colman in* The Prisoner of Zenda *(37). Both were period dramas.*

his British cousin. It was directed by John Ford and was a well-deserved flop. Back in Britain she was loaned to Toeplitz for *The Dictator* (35), Clive Brook's first British film after years in Hollywood: he played Struensee, the Hamburg doctor who became virtual dictator of Denmark, and Miss Carroll was the queen – an English-born princess – who became his mistress. This also was a deserved failure, not helped by being retitled *Loves of a Dictator* and *The Love Affair of a Dictator*. In 1935 she made her last London stage appearance in 'Duet for Floodlight'. Hitchcock cast her in *The Thirty-Nine Steps* opposite Robert Donat, but despite the film's success, there were no further offers. Korda finally signed her to a contract and loaned her to Gaumont-British for another Hitchcock melodrama, *Secret Agent* (36), with John Gielgud, based on Somerset Maugham's 'Ashenden'. It was reported that she fretted in the British studios because they were less efficient than those in Hollywood: so it was with no surprise that it was learnt that Korda had sold her contract to Hollywood, to be shared by Walter Wanger and 20th Century-Fox.

During her Hollywood years, she became

many a man's dream girl: she seemed to be made of sugar and spice – good enough to eat. And she appeared in some of the more notable films of the period. This was not a phrase, however, which could be applied to the first, *The Case Against Mrs Ames* (36) with George Brent; but *The General Died at Dawn*, with Gary Cooper and Akim Tamiroff (as the General), was a strange and moody adventure story. And two she did at 20th were both popular: a historical saga with Tyrone Power, *Lloyds of London*, and a musical with Dick Powell, *On the Avenue* (37) as an heiress lampooned by him. She was not required to sing or dance: Alice Faye took care of that side of things. Meltingly lovely, she was the Queen – heroine *par excellence* – opposite Ronald Colman in *The Prisoner of Zenda*; but the considerable good done by this trio was undone by a comedy at Columbia with Francis Lederer, *It's All Yours* (38) – which was the way the public responded. Wanger finally put her into one of his own films, *Blockade*, playing a White Russian who joins up with a Spanish peasant, Henry Fonda, to flee the current Civil War: it was intended as propaganda and was negligible as entertainment.

Paramount, having lost Carole Lombard, needed another luscious blonde to co-star with Fred MacMurray, who had not quite made it on his own. So she was a member of *Café Society* brought down to earth by him, a journalist; and *Honeymoon in Bali* had the same general idea. She was not a natural comedienne; and gave probably her best performance in a drama, *My Son My Son!* (40), on loan to UA. Playing the beloved of novelist Brian Aherne – who cannot see that his son (Louis Hayward) is a wastrel – she proved that with the right material she was more than a pretty face. *Safari* was, if not right, not what she or Douglas Fairbanks Jr deserved; nor could she do much with her role opposite Gary Cooper in *Northwest Mounted Police*. She and MacMurray were dramatic as she tried to sell the old homestead in *Virginia* (41), but spending *One Night in Lisbon* they were farcical: it was an updating and revamping of 'There's Always Juliet'. Heading the supporting cast in *Virginia* was Sterling Hayden, whom she married. Paramount had noticed how good they looked in Technicolor, so it embellished them again taking the *Bahama Passage* (42), liking their blonde and tanned near-nakedness: but when it came to making love he replied, 'No, let's fish', which reduced audiences to hysterics. Bob Hope did likewise, if deliberately, when he dubbed her *My Favorite Blonde*, a title which hid a comic parody of *The Thirty-Nine Steps*. Then she asked Paramount to release her in order to devote herself to the war effort: she and Hayden changed their names in order to avoid publicity.

She did much for the Allied Relief Fund and was active in the Red Cross. Her interest in these prompted her return to movies, in the British *White Cradle Inn* (47), a well-meaning melodrama about an unwanted Swiss boy, with the then little-known Michael Rennie as her heel of a husband. It was announced that she had formed a company to make semi-documentaries 'to promote a better understanding between the peoples of the world', but nothing emerged. In 1948 she appeared on Broadway in 'Goodbye My Fancy' and that may have reawakened Hollywood's interest. At all events, she made a couple more films: *Don't Trust Your Husband* (48), with Mac-Murray at UA, and *The Fan* (49) at 20th as Mrs Erlynne in this heavy version of Oscar Wilde, both of which failed with critics and public. Afterwards she kept out of the limelight, working at one time for UNESCO. But that she had not entirely abandoned show business was proved when she accepted a part in the Broadway-bound 'Beekman Place' in 1964: however, she left the cast before it hit town – wisely, as it turned out. Her fourth marriage, to 'Life' magazine publisher Andrew Heiskel, ended after 15 years in 1965. She spent her last years in London, Paris and Marbella; and died in 1987.

LON CHANEY

In the Silent era, audiences loved to be thrilled by Lon Chaney. They sat aghast as he clambered about the screen as one monster or freak after another: 'The Man of a Thousand Faces'. His make-up and disguises were sources of wonder: part of his success was due to audience curiosity as to what weird guise he would materialize in next. He took painstaking hours over preparation and in private suffered for it; the last years of his life were a martyrdom of permanently aching limbs, headaches and eye-strain. It is difficult to say to what extent Chaney, beneath the make-up, was an actor in the technical sense: these were physical creations. But that he was a cathartic figure, there is no doubt. His creatures were vulnerable and sympathetic, immensely powerful and real; though considering the extent to which they were maimed and mutilated – armless, legless, one-eyed, hunchbacked – we might well wonder about his audience.

He was born in Colorado Springs in 1883 of deaf-mute parents. He started on the stage as a boy because his brother owned a theatre, but his father had him taught paper-hanging and carpet-laying. He returned to the stage, however, working as prop man, actor, transportation agent. In 1899 he and his brother produced 'The Little Tycoon'; they did one-night stands. Chaney became second comic in 'The Red Kimono' and a song-and-dance man. In 1905 he married Cleva Creighton, who became a popular singer – and an alcoholic. He divorced her finally in 1914, but had already quit travelling for the sake of their son; like many another travelling actor at this time he sought a job in films.

He began as an extra and small-part player in two-reelers. His first credit was *Poor Jake's Demise* (13), followed by about 70 shorts, mostly Westerns, in which he was usually the villain. Many of them were directed by Tod Browning, who was to be so significant in Chaney's career. Indicative of things to come was one called *The Lion the Lamb and the Man* (15), where Chaney was a grotesque and hairy primitive man. He himself directed some two-reelers that year; he signed a contract with Universal and became a general-utility actor for them: (the list that follows includes only Chaney's features of three reels and over; for most of the information on his early films I am indebted to DeWitt Bodeen's outstanding piece on Chaney in 'Films in Focus', May–August 1970): *The Grind*, as an old man; *Bound on the Wheel*, as a drunken husband; *The Fascination of the Fleur de Lis*, as an aristocrat; *A Mother's Atonement*, as a would-be seducer; *The Millionaire Paupers*, as the villain; *Father and the Boys*, his first five-reeler; *The Grip of Jealousy* (16), as a Southern planter; *Tangled Hearts*, as a society husband; *The Gilded Spider*, as a half-crazed Sicilian; *Bobbie of the Ballet*, as the villain; *Grasp of Greed*, as a castaway; *The Mark of Cain*, as a man who suffers for his father's crime; *If My Country Should Call*, as a doctor; *Place Beyond the Winds*, as a crippled half-breed; *The Price of Silence*, as a blackmailer; and *The Piper's Price* (17), as a suitor for the heroine's hand.

His first really important role is generally considered to be in *Hell Morgan's Girl*, as a Barbary Coast politician; the stars were Dorothy Phillips and William Stowell – as indeed they were for most of the films in which Chaney appeared. Universal released all these pictures, though some were made by various subsidiary companies (Bluebird, Jewel, Gold Seal, etc.): *The Girl in the Checkered Coat*, as the villain; *The Flashlight*, in a dual role – as twins; *A Doll's House*, a version of Ibsen, as Nils; *Fires of Rebellion*, as The City Tempter; *The Rescue*, a domestic drama, in a sympathetic role; *Triumph*, as a drama critic; *Pay Me*, a Western, as a man who accidentally kills a friend's wife; *The Empty Gun*, another Western, in a leading role; *Bondage*, as a seducer; *Anything Once*, as a greedy man; *The Scarlet Car*, as a bank cashier suspected of robbery; *Broadway Love* (18), as a country suitor of the heroine; *The Kaiser the Beast of Berlin*, with Rupert Julian in the title-role, as Admiral von Tirpitz; *Fast Company*, as the snobbish hero in this comedy; *The Grand Passion*, as the heroine's Greek uncle; and *A Broadway Scandal*, as a man about Manhattan. He was loaned out to play the villain in William S. Hart's *Riddle Gawne*, which was his first success. A month later he scored at his home studio as the villain in *The Devil Bateese*, but Universal were unimpressed by this notable double and kept him in poor parts: *The Talk of the Town*, as a playboy; *Danger Go Slow*, as a newspaper editor; and *The Wicked Darling* (19), directed by Browning, as a man enamoured of the heroine. His contract was about to be renewed but only on the old terms – said to be $35 a week. Refused the money and the roles he wanted, he was persuaded by his (second) wife to freelance; *False Faces* with Henry B. Walthall, as a German spy; *A Man's Country* with Alma Rubens, as a gambler. When he heard that Paramount were looking

for a contortionist to play a bogus cripple in *The Miracle Man* he applied; it was a low budgeter – $120,000 – but it grossed world-wide over $3 million and made stars of Chaney and his fellow-players Betty Compson and Thomas Meighan.

Chaney was now much in demand at other studios and for the next few years he free-lanced with great success: *When Bearcat Went Dry*, a backwoods romance with Vangie Valentine, as the heavy; *Paid in Advance*, with Phillips and Stowell, as the heavy; *Victory*, a version of Conrad, as the villainous Ricardo; *Daredevil Jack* (20), as the villain in one episode of this 15-chapter serial; *Treasure Island*, at Paramount, with Shirley Mason as Jim Hawkins and Charles Ogle as Long John Silver, in a dual role as Pew, the blind pirate, and as Merry; *The Gift Supreme*, with Seena Owen, as a dope addict; *Nomads of the North*, with Lewis Stone; and *The Penalty*, as a legless czar of the underworld out to revenge himself on the surgeon responsible. It could not be said that Chaney at this point was a popular artist, but he was respected within the industry and when Tod Browning wanted him for a melodrama at his old studio, Universal, they had to meet his terms. The film was *Outside the Law* and Chaney had a dual role as a gangster and a Chinaman. Then: *For Those We Love*, as a man who champions the heroine (Betty Compson); *Bits of Life*, an episode film, as another Oriental in the final sequence; *Ace of Hearts*, with Leatrice Joy, as the heavy; *The Trap* (22) a snowbound melodrama with Alan Hale; *Voices of the City*, another tale of the Frisco underworld, as a gangster; *Flesh and Blood*, as a deranged and crippled crook; *The Light in the Dark*, with Hope Hampton, as a thief with a heart of gold; *Shadows*, with Marguerite de la Motte, as a Chinese laundryman; *Oliver Twist* at First National, with Jackie Coogan in the title-role, as Fagin – and remembered by the young star as 'a miserable old bastard'; *Quincy Adams Sawyer*, with Blanche Sweet, as the heavy; *A Blind Bargain*, in a dual role – a mad scientist and an ape-like man; *All the Brothers Were Valiant* (23), as one of the brothers – the other (the star) was Malcolm MacGregor; *While Paris Sleeps*, actually made three years earlier, as a mad waxworks guide out to kill John Gilbert; and *The Shock*, as another underworld cripple (the title referred to the San Francisco earthquake).

The latter film was made by Universal, part of a two-picture deal; and it was made while they built the sets for an expensive version of *The Hunchback of Notre Dame*, from Victor Hugo's novel of medieval Paris. Chaney's performance as Quasimodo, the hunchback, was much admired and it is perhaps his most

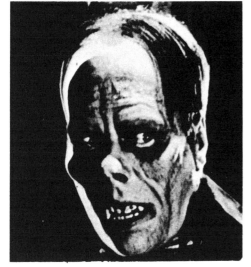

Lon Chaney: four of his thousand faces. All the Brothers Were Valiant (*23*), *top left;* He Who Gets Slapped (*24*), *top right, with Norma Shearer;* The Phantom of the Opera (*25*), *lower left; and* West of Zanzibar (*28*), *lower left, with Mary Nolan.*

famous part: in the US it grossed $1½ million, one of the year's top films. It also concluded his contract, and there were lots of offers. He played a Spanish dandy in *The Next Corner* (24) at Paramount, a marital drama with Dorothy Mackaill and Conway Tearle, and then – at the instigation of Irving Thalberg who had just left Universal for MGM – he signed a lucrative deal with MGM. His first film there was *He Who Gets Slapped*, from Leonid Andreyev's tragic play about a circus clown; Norma Shearer was the object of his Pagliacci passion and it was directed by Victor Sjöström, who said that 'he is without question one of the most marvellous actors in the history of stage or screen'. The second was *The Monster* (25) – yet another demented scientist. 'Picturegoer' commented that Chaney did not need sound: ' . . . he makes such

Lon Chaney and Norma Shearer in The Tower of Lies (25), *directed from Selma Lagerlof's novel by Victor Sjöström. Since Sjöström was the greatest of the Silent directors, the loss of this film is incalculable – and intriguing: for his Swedish versions of Lagerlof are among the cinema's richest treasures, and this was not particularly well-received.*

a palpable, menacing reality out of every shadowy movement that no audible "atmosphere" is necessary to bring gasps of horror from spectators.'

Then Browning came to MGM. For the last two years he had been drinking heavily, but Chaney talked Thalberg into signing him for *The Unholy Three*, a tale of three crooks; Chaney was a ventriloquist who spent much of the movie as a sinister old woman: it was a huge success and the start of the Browning-Chaney partnership (Browning was responsible for roughly half the Chaney films to come). The success of *Hunchback* caused Universal to plan another Paris horror story – but only on condition that they could borrow Chaney. It was a source of much satisfaction to him to return in triumph. The film was *The Phantom of the Opera* (25), from Gaston Leroux's novel about a musician, his face scarred by acid, who haunts the subterranean passages of the Paris Opéra. Mary Philbin was the girl he secretly loved. In the US this was another Chaney triumph, but in Britain it was not seen. As a publicity gimmick, the cans of film were met at Southampton Dock by a brigade of guards and escorted to the railway station. Questions were asked in Parliament; it was never disclosed who had 'loaned' the guards to Universal's publicity outfit, but the

film was banned as a result (the ban was lifted in 1929, when some Sound sequences were added, but it was too late: it was not a success).

MGM then put him into *The Tower of Lies*, with Shearer, Victor Sjöström's study of tragedy in a Swedish village. Browning was responsible for the next two: in *The Blackbird* (26) Chaney was a Limehouse criminal who disguises himself as a crippled bishop; and in *The Road to Mandalay* he was Singapore Joe, an evil saloon-keeper with a cataract eye. He looked like himself for the first time in years as the sergeant in *Tell It to the Marines* (27). There followed *Mr Wu*, in the title-role and as his father; *The Unknown*, as an armless knife-thrower in a Madrid circus, with Joan Crawford; *The Mockery*, as a dim-witted Russian peasant; *London After Midnight* in another dual role – a police inspector and a vampire; *The Big City* (28), as a gangster; and *Laugh Clown Laugh*, where he again eschewed his sinister make-up and gave a 'perfect' characterization and 'his best work since *The Unholy Three* ('Photoplay'). He again looked somthing like his real self playing a detective in *While the City Sleeps*, but he was in 'costume' again in *West of Zanzibar*, as a crippled trader taking revenge on Lionel Barrymore by bringing up his daughter to be a drunken whore (only she turns out to be his own daughter!).

The last one Browning did was *Where East is East* (29), a Malayan story, with Chaney as a man who traps animals for circuses, Lupe Velez as his daughter and Estelle Taylor – outstanding – as his wife. Then there was *Thunder*, with Phyllis Haver, a railroad drama. Early in 1930 he signed a new five-year pact with MGM which stipulated Talkie remakes of most of his old hits. A new, inferior, version of *The Unholy Three* (30) was the first of these. It was followed by *Big House*, but during filming his throat cancer was diagnosed as fatal and he was replaced by Wallace Beery. Browning paid him this tribute: 'He was the hardest working person in the studio.'

His son, Creighton Chaney, just then beginning in films, soon changed his name to Lon Chaney Jr. Apart from a fine performance in *Of Mice and Men* (40) he did little of interest, but he worked consistently till he died in 1973, mainly in horror films. He did not play his father in a biopic, *Man of a Thousand Faces* (57): James Cagney did.

CHARLIE CHAPLIN

Charlie Chaplin lived long enough to see his supremacy challenged by Buster Keaton. Because Keaton's reputation was underprivileged for so long and because Chaplin's appeared unassailable, the rediscovery of Keaton brought the Chaplin-knockers. Jacques Tati, for instance, felt it incumbent upon him to praise Keaton at Chaplin's expense; and it can be said that the taste of the present finds Keaton more palatable: it responds at once to his fantasies rather than to Chaplin's, to his battles with mechanisms, to his lack of sentimentality. Chaplin's art, unlike Keaton's, is rooted in Victorian melodrama and sentiment.

Keaton himself said of Chaplin: 'At his best, and Chaplin remained at his best for a long time, he was the greatest comedian who ever lived.' He mesmerized his own generation: 'I believe . . . that Charles Chaplin is a genius' (Beatrice Lillie). 'Oh well, he's just the greatest artist that ever lived' (Mack Sennett). 'Chaplin will keep you laughing for hours on end without effort; he has a genius for the comic. His fun is simple and spontaneous. And yet all the time you have a feeling that at the back of it all is a profound melancholy' (Somerset Maugham). 'But when Chaplin talked about pictures we all sat still and listened hard. We knew very well what we had among us. The greatest actor of our time, unique, irreplaceable. He stood quite outside the jurisdictions or embroilings of Hollywood. He was beyond jealousy. He was an absolute' (Agnes de Mille). 'The man who has made more people laugh than any other man who ever lived and who may be truly called a genius' (Theodore Huff). 'I think he is the greatest of all film stars' (Ruby M. Ayres). '. . . the greatest clown the world has ever seen, magnificent egotist, trampler on conventions, unique, lonely, loved and unforgettable, the wittiest, most sophisticated, the most graceful, the most moving actor on the screen, and possessed of a unique capacity to confer these gifts on all who work with him' (Michael Powell). 'I don't think there's any greater in the business or ever will be. He's the greatest artist that was ever on the screen' (Stan Laurel). 'Chaplin is not only the greatest theatrical genius of our time, but one of the greatest in history. . . . If I were to recall the three greatest performances I've ever seen on the screen, all of them would be performances by Charlie Chaplin' (Charles Laughton). 'The son of a bitch is a ballet dancer. . . . He's the best ballet dancer that ever lived, and if I get a good chance I'll kill him with my bare hands' (W.C. Fields). 'If people don't sit at Chaplin's feet, he goes out and stands where they're sitting' (Herman J. Mankiewicz). 'One of the worst appreciators of comedy outside himself and his own genius' (James Thurber).

There has been more serious comment on Chaplin than any other screen artist, star or director and, like Proust, he seems to inspire his commentators. But then, there is hardly an adjective that does not apply: Chaplin's Tramp, as James Agee said, was universal. He could be jaunty, malicious, soppy, wistful, cunning, crass, observant, beautiful, painstaking, annoying, mean, innocent. . . .

He was born in 1889 in Lambeth, in South London. His parents were music-hall entertainers, though not particularly successful ones: his father died while he was a child and his mother was committed to an infirmary. Much of his boyhood was spent in poverty. He made his first stage appearance at the age of five, at Croydon, deputizing for his mother: he sang one of her songs. When he was eight, he joined a music-hall act, 'The Eight Lancashire Lads', and from then on worked nonstop, all over Britain as well as in Paris; he was in a play at the London Hippodrome called 'Giddy Ostend' in 1900; he played Billy, the office boy, in 'Sherlock Holmes' and was a wolf in 'Peter Pan'. When he was 17, he joined Fred Karno's company, first of all to play in a sketch called 'The Football Match'. He progressed with the company, until he was one of the leading comedians; and as such he played in 'Mummingbirds' or – its US title – 'A Night at an English Music Hall' on a tour of the US in 1910–11. On a second and longer tour in 1912–13, he was seen by Adam Kessel and Mack Sennett of the Keystone Co. who invited him to replace Ford Sterling, whose popularity was waning. Thus he joined Keystone for $150 per week (twice his Karno salary), to make one- and two-reelers with already established artists like Sterling, Mabel Normand, Chester Conklin, Fatty Arbuckle and Mack Swain.

He arrived in Los Angeles in December 1913 (Keystone was in the vanguard of the studios to location in California) and his first one-reeler, *Making a Living*, was released in February 1914. The studio was not enthusiastic about it. During 1914 he made 35 films: from *Twenty Minutes of Love*, made in one afternoon, to *Dough and Dynamite*, made in nine days at a cost of $1,800 (which was $800 over the budget). Most of them were made in one week. They were crude stuff and only the Chaplin name has kept them from oblivion. Mostly Charlie was the villain or some kind of blundering intruder thinking himself just the thing for Mabel Normand, though she was not prepared to go beyond a mild flirtation. They were full of slapstick among cardboard sets and they all ended with what seemed to be wild drunken chases. In the second one, *Kid Auto Races in Venice*, Chaplin wore his famous costume for the first time on screen,

but in most of them he was made up with the vestiges from his music-hall act – top hat, frock coat, a masher's moustache; similarly, they merely hint at the comic to come, as he worked towards mastery of the medium. Robert Payne, in his 1952 biography, observes of this time: 'Charlie is at home in the empty streets and the crowded doss-houses; most of all he is at home when he has a mop and pail in his hand, and goes about his business. He was born to be a nightwatchman or a janitor . . . erratic as a chauffeur, incompetent as a boxing referee, awkward as a lover, a perverse scene-shifter, he is at full powers as a janitor.'

After four or five films, he was anxious to write and direct his own: he was assigned to one that Mabel Normand was directing – probably *Caught in a Cabaret* (actually, his twelfth film), and there was some altercation; but the next one, *Caught in the Rain*, he directed himself, and he later directed Normand (and himself) in *The Fatal Mallet*, *Mabel's Busy Day*, *Mabel's Married Life*, etc. Others of the Keystone films: *Laughing Gas*, *The Face on the Bar Room Floor*, *The New Janitor*, *His Trysting Place* and *Tillie's Punctured Romance*, the latter a six-reeler with Marie Dressler. It was this one that really made him famous. His last picture for Keystone, *His Prehistoric Past*, was a burlesque of De Mille's *Man's Genesis*, in which he wore his bowler (and a leopard skin). He was now getting $175 a week and, though Keystone were prepared to up this considerably, Chaplin preferred an offer from Essanay at $1,250 weekly, plus bonuses.

Essanay's announcement that they had signed Chaplin pulled no punches: 'The world's greatest comedian,' it said. The first Essanay picture (made in Chicago; the rest were made in San Francisco and then Los Angeles) was *His New Job* (February 1915), which was set in a film studio: it was still Keystonian slapstick, but the setting gave Chaplin some opportunities for satire; he followed it with *A Night Out* – he and Ben Turpin were drunks; it was also the first picture in which appeared Edna Purviance, who was to be his leading lady over the next eight years (and was on salary with the Chaplin studio till she died). Then: *The Champion*, *In the Park*, *The Jitney Elopement* and *The Tramp*, 'generally considered to be Chaplin's first real masterpiece' (Theodore Huff) – and also the first 'in which he injects a note of pathos'. He was now permitted to take more care and trouble, and after *By the Sea* only one Chaplin appeared per month – *Work*, *A Woman*, *The Bank* (perhaps the most popular as well as the most accomplished of the Essanay period), *Shanghaied*, *A Night* in the *Show*, *Carmen* (a burlesque on De Mille's *Carmen*: Chaplin played Darn Hosiery) and *Police* (March 1916). Another Essanay two-reeler, *Triple Trouble*, released in 1918, consisted only of unused bits from these films.

Chaplin's popularity was by now enough to justify several imitators (e.g. Billie West, 'Billie' Richie), though few of them were accepted by the public. There was also a Charlie Chaplin cartoon created by Pat Sullivan, as well as numerous songs about him. Further, no less than Mrs Minnie Madden Fiske wrote an article in 'Harper's Bazaar' entitled 'The Art of Charlie Chaplin', referring to him as an 'extraordinary artist'. He thought his Essanay salary was inadequate, both because he wrote, directed and starred, and because they sold their product in 'blocks' on the strength of his films being among them. He went to Mutual who offered him $10,000 a week, plus a $150,000 bonus. He made 12 films for Mutual (May 1916–October 1917), a remarkable outburst of creativity. He was permitted more preparation; the advance on his Essanay work was considerable (just as the First National films were to be an advance on these) – the slapstick might have been just as beautifully timed, but it was gradually becoming more inventive, less mechanical. Chaplin, in fact, was becoming daring as a comic and he was finding his way towards the emotionalism he was to exploit later in his feature films. Neither of the first two Mutuals, *The Floorwalker* or *The Fireman*, were as good as those to come, but Chaplin noted himself in his memoirs that after the first, 'I was in my stride'. He said that this was the happiest period of his career, because he was unencumbered by financial considerations. *The Floorwalker* broke all records up to that time – its 200 prints were reckoned to be earning $10,000 a day. The third Mutual, *The Vagabond*, was an almost straight film; *One A.M.* has him in pantomime, drunk, a solo performance; *The Count* has him impersonating same in order to win Miss Moneybags – Edna Purviance; and *The Pawnshop* has Charlie getting a gag from everything in sight and foiling a robbery at the end. *Behind the Screen* takes place in a film studio again and has some outrageous camp humour; *The Rink* is Charlie at his most inventively graceful; and *Easy Street* finds him at his most ingratiating – trying to rob the Mission poor-box and then, with ingenuity, foiling the crooks. He arrives for *The Cure* with aplomb and a case of booze, and promptly falls foul of gouty, black-bearded Eric Campbell, the marvellous heavy of many of this series. And as *The Immigrant* he is arriving in the USA, a funny film which veers startlingly into poignancy and is as good

as anything he did; while as *The Adventurer* he was merely back at slapstick, though the level of inventiveness is much higher than in, say, *The Floorwalker*.

Public admiration and esteem – everyone everywhere was singing a song, 'The Moon Shines Bright on Charlie Chaplin' – was tempered by the fact that Chaplin had not gone to war: this was the first of those attacks on him that were to mark his career. Later his first two divorces made screaming and hostile headlines.

Early in 1918, his brother, now his manager, arranged for him to go to First National to make eight two-reel comedies at $150,000 each. The first three, *A Dog's Life* (18), *Shoulder Arms* and *Sunnyside* (19), are, according to Robert Payne, 'more magical than any he composed before or afterwards . . . one dealt with poverty, another with war and the third was paradise'. *Sunnyside*, in fact, was almost a ballet, as befits paradise. There followed *A Day's Pleasure* and then *The Kid* (21), in which the Tramp – or The Little Fellow, as Chaplin himself referred to his character – found the baby Jackie Coogan, a miniature version of his own pathos and artfulness. The film was a six-reeler (there were rows with the studio over

Chaplin in The Kid (*21*): *a much-loved film for the generation before last. Today, for us, it has mediocrity and meanness, but moments of pure gold.*

The Gold Rush (25). *It is New Year's Eve and the heroine (Georgia Hale) has forgotten that Charlie asked her to dinner. He falls asleep waiting and dreams that he is entertaining her with the ballet of the buns. The pit-piano player was instructed to play 'The Oceana Roll'.*

this); it took 18 months to film and cost $500,000 – but it was more profitable than any movie made up to that time, with the exception of *The Birth of a Nation* (an estimated $3½ million against *The Kid's* $2½). First National therefore did not balk when, after *The Idle Class* – the Tramp samples the pleasures of the rich – and *Pay Day* (22) – the Tramp's working day – Chaplin asked to do another feature, i.e. a four-reeler, which would replace the final two shorts contracted for. He was finding the company 'inconsiderate, unsympathetic and short-sighted', despite the fact they gave him a guarantee of $400,000

and an interest in the profits. The film was *The Pilgrim*, in which Charlie, as an escaped convict, is forced to post as a priest. There are, as usual, marvellous gags and the ending – Charlie skipping on the frontier between American Law and Mexican Banditry – is tremendous.

He was now free to join United Artists, which he had formed with Mary Pickford and Douglas Fairbanks: the idea was that they kept the profits from their films (at First National, lesser stars had got higher salaries than Chaplin, clearly paid from the receipts of his films). His first film was a starring vehicle for Edna Purviance, *A Woman of Paris* (23), which he directed only. Much admired and reputedly influential, he refused to let it be re-shown till the last year of his life – when it turned out to be a weak, unsophisticated comedy about a girl caught between true love and money. He took two years to prepare *The Gold Rush* (25), the Tramp in the Frozen North. He said at the time: 'This is the film I want to be remembered by' (he said it about *The Kid* and would say it about *Monsieur Verdoux*) – and in the 'Sight and Sound' 1952 poll of the world's movie critics it was judged the second-best film ever made (*Bicycle Thieves* was first); in the same poll 10 years later it had slipped to tenth. It was an episodic piece, reaching a peak perhaps in the dance of the rolls on New Year's Eve: in 1925 the world laughed and cried at this, and the gross was $2½ million against a probable cost of $650,000. In 1926 he produced *A Woman of the Sea*, for Purviance, directed by Josef von Sternberg, but according to his daughter Geraldine, was 'so consumed by personal and professional jealousy' that he destroyed it without showing it publicly.

In *The Circus* (28) the Tramp is taken on as a clown: the laughter is sparse, even at the high-wire climax, beset by monkeys and falling pants. He did not permit it to be reissued till 1969 and does not mention it at all in his memoirs. He was awarded a special Oscar, however, at the first Oscar ceremony, for 'versatility and genius in writing, acting, directing and producing *The Circus*'.

As he prepared his next film, it became clear that Sound was here to stay: Chaplin's only compromise was to compose a score for the soundtrack (though he did announce *Jew Süss* as a Talkie, starring himself). UA, as distributors, were apprehensive and many predicted failure: but *City Lights* (31) grossed $1 million, the fourth biggest money-maker of the year. It is perhaps his most sentimental film – the Tramp has a crush on a blind girl, pays for her operation and is rejected by her when she is cured – but it has some funny sequences with a millionaire who is friendly with the Tramp when drunk and knows him not when not.

There was one last Silent, though Chaplin did speak a few words of gibberish: *Modern Times* (35), which borrowed freely from *A Nous la Liberté* in its satire on mechanics and machines. It was equally a show case for Paulette Goddard, with whom the Tramp is in love. Press criticism was guarded (for the first time) but the public stayed faithful – it took $1,800,000, being beaten that year only by *San Francisco*.

He had toyed with many ideas since he had begun making features and during the 30s many projects were put into motion, not to get very far; one that did not come to fruition, though some meetings were held, was a Napoleon story, with Chaplin as Bonaparte, Garbo as the female lead and Jean Renoir directing. But his 1940 film, *The Great Dictator*, was ambitious enough: he played a dual role, as a Jewish barber and as a dictator clearly based on Hitler. Jack Oakie was Mussolini and Paulette Goddard was the barber's girl-friend. The film had some mammoth statements to make about tyranny and freedom, and it attempts to be the most adult and most bitter of the anti-Nazi films. The press raved. The New York Critics voted Chaplin the year's Best Actor (he refused to accept the award) and its gross of $2 million made it the top money-spinner of 1941 – and Chaplin's biggest financial success. Pro-German forces in the US were unlikely to forgive Chaplin for this film; and he managed to alienate a good many more American citizens by his championship of Russia's cause during the war. After the war a paternity suit – though he was patently innocent and was finally cleared – sent his stock sinking.

Then, in 1947, he had the effrontery to make a comedy about murder, *Monsieur Verdoux*, based on Landru, the mass-murderer. The thesis of the – very wordy – script was that Landru/Verdoux's crimes were no worse than war; the sets were amateurishly painted and much of the film technically inept. Howard Barnes of the 'New York Herald Tribune' said: 'It has little entertainment weight, either as somber symbolism or sheer nonsense. . . . It is also something of an affront to the intelligence.' The onslaught by the American press determined its future: in places where it was not banned, no one went to see it. Yet there were critics who liked it. Agee wrote: 'It is permanent if any work done during the past 20 years is permanent'; and of

Chaplin and Marilyn Nash, 'one of his discoveries', in Monsieur Verdoux *(47).*

Chaplin's own performance as the fastidious, foppish Verdoux: 'the best piece of playing I have ever seen'. Chaplin himself believed that *Verdoux* was 'the cleverest and most brilliant film I have yet made'. It did better in Britain and Europe than in the US – where it had taken a mere $325,000 by the time Chaplin withdrew it two years later. To add to his public embarrassment, his political views were the subject of a prolonged enquiry by the House of Un-American Activities.

His differences with Miss Pickford over the management of United Artists resulted in the company barely keeping its head above water and he eventually sold off most of his interest in 1951. He still owned 25 per cent by the time they came to release *Limelight* (52) but he did not get the same favourable terms that he had had in the past. The film is a portrait of an ageing clown, old-fashioned and rather maudlin. In Europe, both press and public applauded – for the last time; in the US business was poor; his stock there was even lower, due partly to a refusal to take out American citizenship and to a hostile press which had not forgotten a disastrous press conference at the time of the *Verdoux* showings. The industry was also much aware that his greed and selfishness had contributed to the decline of UA. When he announced his intention of going to Europe with *Limelight* to première it there, he was informed that he might not be permitted a re-entry visa. In the event, he did not apply for one, but settled in Switzerland with his family and his fourth wife, Oona, daughter of Eugene O'Neill. He did not return to the USA and he refused to allow *A King in New York* (57) to be shown there. This film, made in Britain, had some fun at the expense of American advertising and commercialism, but it was a disappoiintment by even journeyman standards and critics were baffled; it seems, however, a gem beside *A Countess From Hong Kong* (66), made in Britain and backed by Universal. Brando and Loren starred, while Chaplin himself did a cameo as a steward. The best thing about it was that it was reminiscent of 30s comedies, a not disagreeable anachronism. Despite massive interest, the reviews killed it at the box-office. In 1970 he planned to make a film with his children and in 1972 he said he wanted to make another film but could not get backing.

In 1942 Chaplin had reissued *The Gold Rush* with an unctuous commentary and a music-track; and he subsequently revived most of his features, plus *A Dog's Life*, *Shoulder Arms* and *The Pilgrim*, in a compilation called *The Chaplin Revue* (60). Between these reissues he rigorously denied showings, even to film societies, but in 1972 he finally sold all his major features to various distributors on a country-by-country basis – both for cinemas and television (earlier, in the 60s, the BBC had paid a record price for *The Gold Rush* – but although then the sole Chaplin feature to go to TV, the viewing figures did not justify the cost). Public reception of these revivals was spotty: in France and Germany, for instance, the audiences were as large as for new products; in other places there appeared to be something not much bigger than a cult following. In Britain and the US his reputation continued to decline, especially when full-scale revivals of Harold Lloyd proved him to be, as with Keaton, Chaplin's superior in the matter of getting laughs – which is ironic in view of his daughter's confession after he died that he was intolerant of all film-work except his own. There was a reconciliation with Hollywood, and a special Oscar in 1972; and he was knighted in 1975. His death in 1977 was marked by some revivals of his films, but the laughter was sparse.

RUTH CHATTERTON

Among the actresses consistently given material unworthy of them, Ruth Chatterton holds a high place. Her films were True Magazine stuff, and she suffered nobly in them, caught – indeed trapped – in the wicked ways of the world. She was put-upon but resigned, sensitive but mature (physically – being in her mid-30s when she started in films, no one tried to keep her young) and usually upper-bracket: she was the sort of woman with whom all women could identify, if not necessarily sympathize. Men liked her because she was a woman of experience, because she had a 'class' rare at that time, and for an intriguing blend of serenity and humour in her eyes. There were no mannerisms or histrionics: she was completely believable and made almost compelling the most dishonest dialogue. She dominated the screen and was in advance of her time, though contemporary appreciation was not lacking. James Agate said once: 'as an actress La Chatterton seems to me to knock La Garbo silly', and in 1931 the readers of 'Movie Fan' voted her the 'Finest Actress on the screen'. She was often referred to as the First Lady of the Screen, but is little remembered today, for her films – with the exception of *Dodsworth* – are seldom revived.

Her spell in Hollywood, however, was but a brief interlude in a long career. She was born in New York City in 1893; her parents separated and to earn money at 14 she got a job as a chorus girl in a play in Washington (Helen Hayes played the same girl, younger, in Act I). From there she went into stock and

Lionel Barrymore and Ruth Chatterton welcome her husband Ralph Forbes to the set of the classic tearjerker Madame X *(29). Barrymore directed.*

in 1911 made her Broadway bow in 'The Great Name'; she had her first success the following year in 'The Rainbow' under Henry Miller's management. Most of her subsequent plays were for him; among them: 'Daddy Long Legs' (as Judy), 'Come Out of the Kitchen', 'Mary Rose' (which she also directed) and 'The Little Minister'. She became one of New York's leading Leading Ladies and the movie people were interested – but she either wanted too much money or script approval. However, she went to Hollywood in 1925, accompanying her husband who had been offered a part in *Beau Geste*. (He was Ralph Forbes, a Britisher and some years her junior, who was successful during the late 20s and early 30s; a sleek, moustached actor with slightly watery eyes. They were divorced in 1932; he died in 1951.)

Chatterton did a couple of plays on the Coast and in one of them, 'The Devil's Plum Tree', whe was seen by Emil Jannings. Although Paramount had already tested her unsuccessfully for *The Docks of New York*, he insisted on their taking her on to play his

second (and worthless) wife in *Sins of the Fathers* (28). She was good and Paramount signed her: her stage training was an asset with the advent of Talkies. She was a faithless wife again in *The Doctor's Secret* (29), with H.B. Warner, but true to Fredric March in *The Dummy*. However, in *Madame X* (29), she ditched her husband again and was paid the wages of sin in various parts of the world, finally standing trial for the murder of a man who planned to blackmail her husband – and defended by a young lawyer who does not know she is his mother (all the same, he concludes: 'She was a good woman, whoever she was'). This old stage weepie was a big one for MGM who produced and Chatterton's performance was, considered 'Picturegoer', 'the most poignant thing the Talkies have given us to date'.

She returned to her home lot as a big attraction and did *Charming Sinners* (from Maugham's 'The Constant Wife') and *The Laughing Lady*, both with Clive Brook, in the latter as a divorcée falling unwillingly in love with her husband's attorney. It was considered notable mainly for her performance, as (even more so) was *Sarah and Son* (30) – as a German immigrant returning disgraced to the Fatherland, becoming a famous diva and going back to the US to reclaim her son. March co-starred and it was to him she sang 'My Marine', as a French tart, in a sketch in *Paramount on Parade*. MGM borrowed her to play Nancy in *Oliver Twist*, but when this was cancelled she was their *Lady of Scandal*; then at Paramount she was *Anybody's Woman*, but Brook's in particular (as a downtown chorus girl reforming him, a lawyer, after he had married her one alcoholic night).

It had become customary to regard Chatterton as one of the few screen actresses able to absorb herself completely in her character and her next role was considered a *tour de force*, playing both Mother and Daughter in *The Right to Love*. The man in question was Paul Lukas and Chatterton then proceeded to be *Unfaithful* (31) with him – but that made three wretched films in a row. She listened to the advances made by Warner Bros. (it was said she was annoyed at the money being spent to publicize Dietrich which – if it worked – would presumably entail her own demotion from queen of the lot). There was another dud, *The Magnificent Lie* (31), about a cabaret singer who deceives a blind doughboy into believing she is the woman he once loved (Françoise Rosay). During the making it was announced that she had signed with Warners – a statement considered unethical as she still had two films to go at Paramount. These were: *Once a Lady*, as a Russian, with Ivor Novello; and *Tomorrow and Tomorrow* (32), as a bored wife who turns to doctor Lukas to get herself a baby. 'Picturegoer' commented that if her films at Warner Bros. were not an improvement her days as a star were numbered.

The Warner contract was for two years, for a total of $750,000; at the end of that time, Warners could exercise an option to extend the contract for two years – for $1 million. She also had a say-so on material; and was advertised with a tag: 'Acting from a contented actress'. The first was a mildly amusing comedy, *The Rich Are Always With Us* (32), co-starring George Brent, who soon became her second husband (too soon: the rapidity of their marriage less than 24 hours after her decree became final created a sensation in the summer of 1932). The studio cast them together again to capitalize on their romance, in *The Crash*, even if the plot had her being unfaithful to him. It was well-named as far as receipts went and Chatterton, all too conscious of being in a rut, wanted to leave Hollywood. She stayed because of Brent, whose career was just beginning, and fought against making *Frisco Jenny* (33), which was

a doing-over of *Madame X* with the Earthquake thrown in. She was miscast in both *Lilly Turner* (as a cooch dancer) and *Female* (as a career woman who sexes herself up in a bid for love). Brent was in both of these, but by the end of 1934 the marriage was over and so was the Warner contract. The last one might hae been better had it been directed by G.W. Pabst, as intended, *Journal of a Crime* (34): the crime was hers, shooting the mistress of husband Adolphe Menjou and letting someone else die for it. The crime was also the Warners', who had given her even worse films than Paramount (she had walked out of one, *Mandalay* – Kay Francis replaced her); she was now dead at the box-office and MGM, who had pursued her eagerly over the years, lost interest.

Chatterton also collided with Hollywood's obsession with youth: outside of star character actors like Marie Dressler, she was the oldest female star of the time. After almost two years' absence from the screen, Columbia starred her in some more mother-love nonsense, *Lady of Secrets* (36), and 20th gave her what was basically a supporting role in the naïve *Girls' Dormitory* (she lost fellow-teacher Herbert Marshall to Simone Simon). Goldwyn cast her as the vapid, self-centred Fran, who finds European culture and men more exciting than husband Walter Huston in *Dodsworth* – considered by many to be the best performance of her career. It was an untypical role and, according to Mary Astor, she loathed playing it – because, like Fran, she was desperately trying to cling to her youth; as a result, she fought throughout with director William Wyler. Goldwyn had announced his intention of starring her in *Stella Dallas*, but he changed his mind in favour of the more popular Barbara Stanwyck.

Instead she went to Britain, to co-star with Anton Walbrook in *The Rat* (38) and with Pierre Blanchar in *The Royal Divorce* – an unconvincing Josephine to his Napoleon. Neither was of a quality to resuscitate her screen career. She told a reporter, explaining why she had left Hollywood: 'But I don't feel inclined to fight against bad parts in plays or films; it isn't worth it; and even if it were, I'm just too lazy.' In London she also appeared in a revival of 'The Constant Wife' and got poor notices; in the US she toured in 'West of Broadway' and got there again in 1940 in 'Leave Her to Heaven'. She married again (Barry Thomson) and did stage work, TV and radio in the 40s and 50s, including tours of 'Pygmalion' (40–41), and 'Private Lives' (42), a City Center revival of 'Idiot's Delight' in New York in 1951 and a TV Gertrude to Maurice Evans's Hamlet. That year she appeared on TV in 'Old Acquaintance' with

George Brent and Ruth Chatterton play husband and wife in The Crash *(32). At this time they were husband and wife in real life as well.*

Chatterton with Paul Lucas in The Right to Love *(31), one of several films they made together. It was a saga of mother-love in which she aged cleverly and ended up playing her own daughter.*

Edna Best. Her last appearance was in St Louis in 1956 in 'The Chalk Garden'. And between 1950 and 1958 she published four novels, notably 'Homeward Borne'. She died in 1961, of a cerebral haemorrhage, in Redding, Connecticut.

MAURICE CHEVALIER

'Every little breeze seems to whisper Louise. . . .' Maurice Chevalier sang it in his first American film and even during the years of eclipse it remained (on disc) one of the most easily identifiable sounds in the world. Maurice: debonair, the eternal boulevardier, with his cane and *canotier*: one of the wonders of show business, even in his latter-day renaissance as a twinkle-eyed French uncle. On the stage he remained one of the best one-man shows (if not *the*). On film, his best work was in his early American Talkies – gems which glitter as brightly now as they did then. Under (mainly) the direction of Lubitsch, Chevalier starred in a series of farces with music which effectively presented him as a ne'er-do-well whose interests seldom wandered far from the bedroom. But, as Lubitsch put it: 'Chevalier can make even the most scabrous situation acceptable.' By less than a wink, less than a grin, he was more suggestive than another actor ripping off a girl's blouse; and he showed a mastery of boudoir comedy which other actors could only try to imitate.

He described his career once thus ('The Times', London, 1968, to Peter Daubeny): 'My career consists of low comedian with red nose; low comedian without red nose, going elegant with straw hat and jacket; music-hall comedies; Hollywood; return with straw hat and jacket to Paris; one-man show; return to America and dramatic actor.' He was born in Menilmontant, a quartier of Paris, in 1888, the ninth of 10 children – of which three survived. His father was a house-painter and a drunk: he died when Maurice was 11. The boy was at one time in an institution; he started work as an electrician and was later apprenticed to a metal engraver, but did not like this and at the age of 12 tried to get up an acrobatic act with his brother. He entertained in the cafés of the quartier for some years, until accepted by the Casino de Tourelles (06); at their café-concerts he imitated famous stars for 12 francs a week. Subsequently he was a *boxe-boy* in vaudeville and about the same time he made his first film, *Trop Crédule* (08), in a bit part, and was Mistinguett's dancing partner at the Folies-Bergère. During this period he made three movies: *Un Marié qui se Fait Attendre* (10),

La Mariée Récalcitrante (11) and *Par Habitude* (12). Just before he joined the army, he and Mistinguett made a film of their popular act at the Folies-Bergère, *La Valse Renversante* (14), directed by Henri Diamant-Berger. He was wounded in the war and captured (he learnt English from a fellow-prisoner). Released, he joined Mistinguett for another movie directed by Diamant-Berger, *Une Soirée Mondaine* (17). When the war was over, he made his first London appearance – in February 1919, succeeding Owen Nares in a revue, 'Hullo America' – the start of a career as '*la plus typiquement* (*et conventionellement*) "*parisienne*" *des vedettes internationales*' (Seghers's 'Dictionnaire du Cinéma', 1962).

He returned to Paris and Mistinguett, but they split soon after it was clear that he could make it as a solo performer: she left him a clear field at the Casino de Paris, where he played for three seasons. Diamant-Berger asked him to put in a guest appearance in his boxing film, *Le Match de Crique-Ledoux* (22) – because the actual fight had lasted just over a minute and needed padding. Chevalier was fascinated by movies. He formed his own company and the five films it made were all directed by Diamant-Berger: *Un Mauvais Garçon*, in which he was involved in his sister's shady love-life; *Gonzague* (23), invited to dinner at the home of his girlfriend; *Par Habitude*, getting involved with the new tenants of his old apartment; *Jim Bourgne, Boxer*, posing as a prize-fighter in order to win over his girl's father; and *L'Affaire de la Rue Lourcine*, from a play by Labiche, about a murder committed one night on the town. He abandoned films temporarily when he was in a big Paris success, 'Dédé', which ran for two years – and which he planned to take to Broadway; but during rehearsals in the US he experienced a breakdown and returned to France. He went back to the Casino de Paris and remained for three seasons. In 1926 he married a dancer he had discovered, Yvonne Vallée (they were divorced in 1935). Together they appeared in London without great success in 'White Bird' (27). Back in Paris, Thalberg of MGM offered Chevalier a screen test: it was negative, but Chevalier kept it and showed it to Lasky of Paramount, who signed him.

Chevalier's first Hollywood movie, *Innocents of Paris* (29), was tawdry and sentimental, but he was an instant world hit: with his second picture, *The Love Parade*, he was a world sensation. Jeanette MacDonald co-starred and Lubitsch directed, with a visual wit and gaiety which made it a model for subsequent musicals; but above all it was a triumph for Chevalier, with his roguish smile and ver' Frainch accent. James Agate, in one of the rare downbeat assessments of Chevalier, offered this significant note: 'Nevertheless this French star has the quality which transcends all others – the quality of being a success.' The same was said of Jolson, with whom he shared several characteristics: both were of mature age when they made a success in movies; they were loathed by their colleagues, who found them financially mean; they only came alive when they were performing; and they were bisexual (Chevalier's last lover, for many years, was his valet).

Chevalier's salary had been tripled after *Innocents*, but Paramount now offered a fabulous $8,000 a week and dumped him in *The Big Pond* (30), pursued across the Atlantic by a determined Claudette Colbert, for a satire on American big business (vs European charm and know-how); concurrently he could be seen in a 'nautee' sketch and some numbers in *Paramount on Parade* (which rated a separate French version, with some French artists replacing the American ones; there was also a separate French version of his film with Colbert, called *La Grande Mare*, and most, but not all, of his other early American films rated a simultaneous French version). At this time he was also to be found in person singing in New York and in London – in the latter city at a reported £4,000 a week, but over-publicity spoiled the occasion and he did a

concert to a virtually empty Albert Hall. In Chicago he was paid $12,000 a week and again failed to draw – but blamed the movie on the same bill (at this time most major cinemas in the US combined movies and vaudeville).

But cinemas were full and Paramount signed him to a new contrct: four films for $1 million. *The Playboy of Paris* (French version: *Le Petit Café*, directed by Diamant-Berger, with Yvonne Vallée replacing Frances Dee as his leading lady). 'Photoplay' observed: 'Maurice Chevalier deserves better than this light farce which is amusing only in spots' – and he got it in spades with the next three. Lubitsch directed *The Smiling Lieutenant* (31) and the concurrent French version, *Le Lieutenant Souriant*, a version of 'The Waltz Dream' with a hapless Chevalier caught between musician Colbert and queen Miriam Hopkins, and he supervised *One Hour With You* (32); Cukor directed, uncredited (and there was again a French version, *Une Heure près de Toi*). This time Chevalier was caught between MacDonald and Genevieve Tobin, in rhyming couplets, and even more enchantingly. He was one of several Paramount stars guesting in *Make Me a Star*. Rouben Mamoulian directed *Love Me Tonight* with the same vivacity: Chevalier was involved in more risqué situations with MacDonald. But off the screen he was unhappy, fighting (well-publicized) battles against his material. He

Maurice Chevalier has Jeanette MacDonald in his bed and sex on his mind in One Hour With You (*32*): and why not? – since they are married. But marital love in his early Hollywood films was made to seem as exciting as any clandestine infidelity.

Chevalier and MacDonald worked winningly together several times under Ernst Lubitsch. But Rouben Mamoulian directed Love Me Tonight (32), *which was almost as risqué and just as delightful.*

lamented years later ('With Love', 1960): 'Paramount and I were still miles apart, too. I was still asking their top people why every picture I made must be in the same mould, why every character I played must be debonair and cute and devoid of emotional depth, and I was still receiving the same answer – that my films were making too much money to risk a change of pattern.'

But there were already signs of a falling box-office and *A Bedtime Story* (33) matched the star and Helen Twelvetrees in a conscious attempt to emulate the maudlin success of the early Jolson pictures; and *The Way to Love* (French version: *L'Amour Guide*), with its synthetic Paris, did even more poorly. Audiences were tired of the cuteness. But at MGM both Lubitsch and Thalberg had faith in Chevalier and he moved over to MGM on long-term contract, starting with a new Lubitsch version of *The Merry Widow* (34) made also in French, *La Veuve Joyeuse*: a sparkling film, great reviews – but business did not meet its astronomical cost. The Widow was MacDonald, against Chevalier's opposition – because he was uncertain as to what extent the success of their Paramount films was due to her. He had wanted Grace Moore, but because she had flopped in two films for Metro, Thalberg refused. Chevalier was loaned to 20th (for $10,000 a week, plus a percentage) to star in *Folies-Bergère* (35), with Ann Sothern and Merle Oberon, a gay dual-identity skit, but receipts were only so-

so. There was a simultaneous French version, *L'Homme des Folies-Bergère*, with Natalie Paley and Sim Viva (it was shown in New York the following year). As a second MGM venture, the studio proposed a Chevalier-Moore teaming, in *The Chocolate Soldier*, and that was because the lady had just had a huge success at Columbia in *One Night of Love*. But she insisted on top-billing. He refused to concede and an exasperated Metro announced that the contract was dissolved by mutual consent. Chevalier left Hollywood declaring that he would rather top the bill at the Montparnasse Casino at 100 francs a day than be second at the Palace, New York, at $1,000 a day.

In London Chevalier did another revue. 'Stop Press', and in Paris played an engagement at his old haunt, the Casino de Paris. He made two films, Duvivier's *L'Homme du Jour* (36), a musical, as an electrician with stage ambitions (in one sequence he meets himself playing himself), and *Avec le Sourire*, as a vagabond who gets a job backstage and rises to be a leading force in the theatre. This is one of the best ideas a musical ever had, since we know him to be a great entertainer and cannot wait for him to take the stage: but the film turns serious and since we know he had a monstrous ego we decide that he was more attractive as a simple entertainer. He tried to retrieve his international reputation when offered the remake of William J. Locke's 1906 bestseller by Toeplitz, as ever emulating Korda by bringing in talent from all over. It was designed for Russ Colombo, who died, and was offered to Cary Grant, then filming in Britain. With Chevalier's acceptance, *The Beloved Vagabond/Le Vagabond Bien-Aimé* was made in two versions and he sported an itty-bitty moustache as an architect who returns to France to wander across half of it without realizing he is in love with the waif (Margaret Lockwood/Hélène Robert). It is a sunny film and his charm is as formidable as ever, but 'Variety' thought it unlikely to cause Hollywood to invite him to return or to ensure American release of any other European venture. Chevalier must have had higher hopes of another British film, *Break the News* (38), since the director was René Clair, who had an international reputation, but there was only a pallid welcome for it as produced by Chevalier's co-star, Jack Buchanan. In France Robert Siodmak directed him in *Pièges* (39), a thriller about a serial killer in which he, as a nightclub singer/owner, was one of the chief suspects.

During the war he sang in the non-occupied zones and was tainted with collaborationist suspicions because he had sung to German troops: later it was proved that he had done this to try to help some Jewish friends. He returned to films in 1947 when Clair cast him in a character part – an old-time movie director – for *Le Silence Est d'Or*: its charm was too quiet. He sang in New York and in London over the next couple of years – the beginning of the hit one-man shows which he was to do all over the world. But only the French cinema offered him movie-work; *Le Roi* (49), as a king on a visit to Paris, a role played in the 1936 version by Victor Françen; *Ma Pomme* (50), as a clochard, and *J'Avais Sept Filles* (54), in which he was a count besieged by seven girls claiming to be his daughters. He went to Italy about this time to appear in an episode film, *Cento Anni d'Amore*, whose cast included Giulietta Masina and Vittorio de Sica; and he appeared as himself in a German musical starring Walter Gille, *Schlagerparade*. Paramount did announce (in 1950) that he would be returning to star in *A New Kind of Love*, but nothing came of this and Mike Todd offered him a guest role in *Around the World in 80 Days*, but he wanted his name at the foot of the cast-list (the guests were in alphabetical order) and Todd would not agree to this. However, he did accept a Hollywood offer from Billy

Wilder, who wanted him to play Audrey Hepburn's father in *Love in the Afternoon* (57), made in Paris, a small part but, in his hands, not a negligible one. However, it was *Gigi* (58), as a charming and dapper old roué, that brought him back with a bang: he had a small triumph.

Hollywood, ever to make amends for neglect (provided the artist has proved again to be commercial), in 1958 presented Chevalier with a special Oscar; and in between stage, nightclubs and TV appearances, he brightened a not inconsiderable number of pictures – most of which were in dire need of same: *Count Your Blessings* (59), as Deborah Kerr's father-in-law; *Can-Can* (60) in a limp replay of his *Gigi* double-act with Louis Jourdan; *Un, Deux, Trois, Quatre*, as himself, compèring this ballet film; *A Breath of Scandal/ Olympia*, as the father of princess Sophia Loren; *Pepe*, as himself; *Fanny* (61) as Panisse, who marries Leslie Caron; *Jessica* (62), as a priest; Disney's *In Search of the Castaways*, as an eccentric professor; *A New Kind of Love* (63), in a guest appearance as himself; *Panic Button* (64), with Eleanor Parker and Jayne Mansfield; *I'd Rather Be Rich*, in the Charles Laughton part – the

Count Your Blessings (59) *was a romantic drama starring Deborah Kerr and Rosanno Brazzi, but was memorable mainly for Chevalier's presence.*

heroine's grandfather – in this remake of *It Started With Eve*; and Disney's *Monkeys Go Home!* (66), again as the village priest. In 1969 he put an advert in 'Variety' saying that his one-man shows were over, but that he was looking for a film or TV part (he had appeared in several TV specials, both in France and in the US).

During his last years, when he could no longer work, he became a recluse and, reputedly, morose. He lived among Chevalier memorabilia and it was rumoured that he wanted his house to become a Chevalier museum. His last public appearances were connected with a ninth volume of memoirs, published in 1970. He died on New Year's Day, 1972, disappointed to the last that the various projects to film his life-story had come to nothing (in 1956 Danny Kaye had been announced to play the part).

CLAUDETTE COLBERT

Claudette of the bangs and apple cheeks, with her saucer eyes and her throaty laugh, once likened to a cat's purr: Claudette with whom half the world was once in love. Throughout the 40s and before, she enjoyed a huge popularity, as the always controlled Miss Above-Average America. Hers was not a spectacular personality – nor was she a lady inclined to make headlines – so the fan-magazines were reduced to writing copy like this: 'In private life Claudette is Mrs Norman Foster, and their marital experiment of living in separate houses is one of the wonders of Hollywood' (it did not work, apparently – they were divorced in 1935; but for more than 35 years, until she was widowed in 1969, she was happily married to Dr Joel Pressman). Dated that sort of gubbins may be, but Colbert's way of playing comedy has not. Like so many of her contemporaries, it remains stunning.

She did not only play comedy; she played serious and dramatic roles with a certain skill, but in the latter today she sometimes seems miscast. She is probably, after Dietrich, the most consistently unreal of all the great stars. She is the perfect wife and mother, the perfect hostess, gracious, well-dressed, considerate: 'Did he beat you?' she asks about a golf game in *Tomorrow Is Forever*, for all the world as though she really cared. In that film, in *Since You Went Away*, she is not remotely like a real person; she appears to be acting behind a perspex screen. Her style was beautifully suited to comedy, to the calculations of *It Happened One Night* and *Midnight*. She once observed that the prime rule of comedy was never to go soft; and privately she remarked

that one of the reasons why the remake of *It Happened One Night* did not work was because its heroine was so anxious to be liked. But even if it is hard to accept her as puritan maid or strumpet, missionary wife or saloon-singer, she was always likeable.

And she ran her career with great acumen. In her autobiography, Gracie Fields records that she was once surprised by Constance Bennett's preparations for a scene (lighting, etc.). Replied Bennett: 'If you think I'm bad, you should see Claudette Colbert. Mind you, that's why she is Claudette Colbert.'

She was born in Paris in 1905, but was educated mainly in New York, whither her parents emigrated when she was six. She became a stenographer, but wanted to be an actress, an ambition realized with 'The Wild Westcotts' (23) after a chance meeting with the play's author. Her notices were not sensational, but they were good enough to ensure that (apart from a later starry production of 'Leah Kleshna') she thereafter appeared only in leading roles. Broadway producer Al Woods put her under contract and over the next few years she appeared in some half-dozen plays, including 'We've Got the Money', 'The Cat Came Back', 'A Kiss in a Taxi' (25), 'The Ghost Train' and 'The Barker' (27), with Walter Huston and Norman Foster. It was her biggest hit and she later did it in London. Meanwhile she signed a three-picture deal with First National and made *For the Love of Mike* (27), a tale of three bachelors – Jewish, Irish, German (George Sidney, Ben Lyon, Ford Sterling) – who adopt a boy and send him to Yale. Capra directed; but Colbert's ingénue part got her nowhere. She did not like herself and broke the contract. She was in Eugene O'Neill's 'Dynamo' when film companies started combing Broadway for new talent for the Talkies: Paramount negotiated to buy her contract from Al Woods.

Her first movies were made in New York: *The Hole in the Wall* (29), as a child kidnapper, and *The Lady Lies*, as a shopgirl involved with Walter Huston (by night she was appearing in 'See Naples and Die', her last play for over 20 years); *L'Enigmatique Mr Parkes* with Adolphe Menjou, the French version of *Slightly Scarlet* (in the roles played by Evelyn Brent and Clive Brook) and one of the few 'foreign' versions to get a US showing; and *The Big Pond* (30), which she got because she was bilingual (it was made in two versions – *La Grande Mare* was the French one). Chevalier was the star and he had admired her on the stage ('She was lovely, brunette, talented and a delicious comedienne, and her English was perfect'). Then she starred in *The Young Man of Manhattan*, as a gossip columnist married to sports writer Foster: they quarrel and he takes to drink. 'Picturegoer', later, found it ironic that he was her weakest leading man: 'he did not seem to get any sincerity into his love scenes'.

Colbert's first really serious film was very stark indeed, a remake of Leatrice Joy's old melodrama, *Manslaughter*, about a girl convicted of same by her fiancé, Fredric March: it was the first of several together. There was *Honor Among Lovers*, as March's secretary, secretly in love with him, but it was the next which really made the customers sit up: as a mousy violinist, she demonstrated that she knew how to hold her man better than Queen Miriam Hopkins. The man was Chevalier, *The Smiling Lieutenant* (French version : *Le Lieutenant Souriant*), and Colbert hands him over to Hopkins with some bizarre sung advice about winning him over: 'You've got to jazz up your lingerie.'

It was another year before she got another prize part, but Paramount kept her busy: *Secrets of a Secretary*, a conventional marital drama with Herbert Marshall; *His Woman* with Gary Cooper; *The Wiser Sex* (32), which concerned politicians and racketeers; *The Misleading Lady*, a comedy with Edmund

Lowe; and *The Man From Yesterday*, a modern version of the Enoch Arden theme, with Clive Brook and Charles Boyer as the two men in her life. She played herself in a brief sequence in *Make Me a Star* and was pretty, vivacious and very taking in *The Phantom President* as the former president's daughter whom both George M. Cohans want to marry – for it was a dual role (nice medicine man substitutes for a presidential aspirant no one is likely to vote for). The big one was De Mille's *The Sign of the Cross*, playing Poppaea and taking her famous bath in asses' milk and, gosh, she was mean and evil. This Roman antique was reissued during the war with a modern prologue, but at the time it was not especially popular (Eddie Cantor's spoof, *Roman Scandals*, did far better). Fredric March played the object of Poppaea's passion, and they were teamed again in *Tonight Is Ours* (33), a Noël Coward frivolity (originally 'The Queen Was in the Parlour').

She was loaned to United Artists for *I Cover the Waterfront*, but she was miscast as a fisherman's daughter suspected of smuggling by the 'I' of the title – who was Ben Lyon, top-billed as a reporter. Then she quarrelled with Paramount over *Disgraced* and faced

De Mille's The Sign of the Cross *(32). Charles Laughton was Nero and Claudette Colbert Poppaea. She had an uncontrollable passion for Captain of the Guard Fredric March, seen here defying Nero for love of Christian girl Elissa Landi.*

Clark Gable, reporter, and Claudette Colbert, spoilt heiress, on a cross-country bus in It Happened One Night (34), *journeying to their happy ending. There was an even happier one later, when they both won Oscars (the only time in over forty years in which the Best Actor and Actress awards went to performers in the same film).*

suspension; but Paramount gave in and gave the role to Helen Twelvetrees. Instead she did *Three-Cornered Moon*, a delicately done Depression comedy, working hard to support the family, including Mary Boland as her mother. *Torch Singer* found her again in murky waters, from maternity home to stardom in cabaret, but finally marrying the father of her baby. De Mille then cast her as a mousy schoolteacher (in the beginning), one of the *Four Frightened People* (34); the others were Herbert Marshall, William Gargan and Miss Boland, stuck in the Malayan jungle. It was one of De Mille's few 'modern' Talkies, and one of his rare flops.

Then came *It Happened One Night*, in the role turned down by Myrna Loy, Margaret Sullavan, Miriam Hopkins and Constance Bennett (though the last-named offered to buy the script to have it rewritten for herself). 'Lovely and feminine as they come, Claudette had a mind as bright as a dollar, and a French appreciation of its lustre,' observed Frank Capra after she agreed to do the film for $50,000, twice her fee at Paramount, for a quick four-week stint during a vacation. She played a runaway heiress and Clark Gable was

the reporter pursuing her for a story. The result was a milestone in the development of screen comedy and Columbia Pictures, delightedly noting extended engagements and eventually a fistful of Oscars, including Best Actress to Colbert, reputedly boarding a train at the time of the ceremony because she thought so little of her chances.

For De Mille again she did *Cleopatra*, in the title-role, a *papier mâché* epic enlivened fitfully by its dialogue ('Poor Calpurnia! – of course, the wife is always the last to know') and the Colbert sense of merriment. Henry Wilcoxon was Anthony and Warren William Caesar. Then she began to alternate between comedy and drama, and in the end the latter lost out: there was a clutch of good comedies in her future. The dramas were tear-jerkers like *Imitation of Life*, from Fannie Hurst's novel of mother-love, on loan to Universal; and the comedies were all rather like *The Gilded Lily* (35), playing a stenographer who becomes the toast of Broadway – aided by newsman Fred MacMurray, the first of several films together. *Private Worlds* was a drama about mental hospitals, with Charles Boyer, and it was 'panned unmercifully' (in the words of its producer, Walter Wanger). At Columbia *She Married Her Boss* – Melvyn Douglas: a comedy directed by Gregory La Cava and deservedly one of the year's top successes; and she stayed light-hearted for *The Bride Comes Home*, with MacMurray.

In 1935, she was the sixth-ranking star at the box-office and she was eighth the following year, despite the fact that she made only one movie – *Under Two Flags* (36), called in by 20th to play Cigarette, the legion mascot, when Simone Simon's English proved inadequate (it was said). As it happened, Miss Colbert's temperament was too mild to play a spitfire vamp. Her Paramount contract expired and her manager (who was her brother) renewed it on exceptional terms – seven pictures over a two-and-a-half-year period (not all of which were made). She succeeded Carole Lombard as the highest-paid star; and although only one Colbert film was released in 1938, she led the list of the best-paid performers, at $426,944 (followed, in order, by Bing Crosby, Irene Dunne, Charles Boyer, Wallace Beery, Cary Grant, Shirley Temple, Joan Crawford, Norma Shearer, Warner Baxter, Clark Gable, Garbo and Fred Astaire).

In the meantime, she came fifth in the Bernstein Popularity Poll and appeared in: *Maid of Salem* (37), in the title-role, a tepid piece about witch-hunting, directed by Frank Lloyd; *I Met Him in Paris*, a comedy with Melvyn Douglas; and *Tovarich* at Warners, with Boyer, from a stage success about White Russians working as domestic servants in Paris. Anatole Litvak directed, and there was trouble when he sacked Colbert's own cameraman. Prevailed upon eventually to accept a replacement, she insisted again on her own after she had seen the rushes, offering to waive her salary if the film went over schedule. (*En passant*, it can be noted that she was seldom seen in left profile, but if the scene absolutely demanded it the settings were reversed, so that her left could pass for right – a fact she has publicly denied: but Sheilah Graham for one remembered watching the scene-shifters at work). After that, there was another good comedy, *Bluebeard's Eighth Wife* (38), in which her tongue-in-cheek was neatly countered by Gary Cooper's blink.

Chance again played a hand and she was summoned to play *Zaza* (39), when Paramount were having their own difficulties with an imported actress, Isa Miranda: it would be Miss Colbert's last 'naughtee-girl' role (singer falls for Herbert Marshall, discovers he is married, revenges herself by becoming the rage of Paris) – perhaps because the film failed with both critics and public. She was, however, a gold-digger in *Midnight*, with Don

Joel McCrea and Claudette Colbert in Preston Sturges's very funny The Palm Beach Story (42).

Ameche, and she made the character scatter-brained but cagey, a characteristic touch – a soft but not mushy centre in a hard (and hilarious) film. At MGM, she did *It's a Wonderful World* with James Stewart, a private-eye comedy in which – as his unwanted assistant – she uncovered the murderer. With the same aplomb, she moved West, as Henry Fonda's pioneer wife in the Technicolored *Drums Along the Mohawk*, directed by John Ford at 20th. She returned to MGM to play Clark Gable's loving wife in *Boom Town* (40) and about the same time turned down a seven-year contract worth $200,000 a year because she could freelance more profitably. 'Variety' estimated her 1940 earnings the highest in the US, at $301,944; for the next few years her fee was $150,000 per film.

Back at Paramount, she did a couple with Ray Milland: *Arise My Move*, a Wilder-Brackett script that begins with a crackle but soon runs into war-angled bathos; and *Skylark* (41), a completely forgettable marital comedy. She moved to 20th to play a spinster schoolteacher in *Remember the Day*: Agate found it sloppily sentimental throughout, 'but once again Claudette Colbert is her clever, witty and typically Parisian self: indeed, there are moments when she reminds one of any French actress and thus gives us that distinc-

Even the superstars posed for fashion stills.

comedy – the one about the career woman (a novelist) chasing the carefree hero (John Wayne) because she wants him to star in the film of her book.

There was another cruddy soap-opera, *The Secret Heart*, with Walter Pidgeon. Richard Winnington wrote: 'There never was a screen heroine who carried so bravely and girlishly and irritatingly such a burden of idiotic sacrifice as does Claudette Colbert through the longueurs. . . . I noticed in her last film that she has developed a maddening flutter, a sort of half-embarrassed dither, doubtless occasioned by the inanities that encircle her. She has let it grow on her in this film, and though the poor girl has every excuse, she is very hard on the nerves.'

In truth, even her comedy playing now seemed mechanical, notably in a truly horrible bucolic piece, *The Egg and I* (47), again with MacMurray; humour consisting mainly of people falling over in the farmyard somehow carried it to huge box-office success – Miss Colbert's last. The next three played double-bills: *Sleep My Love* (48), in which Don Ameche tried to murder her; *Family Honeymoon*, with MacMurray and loads of kids; and *Bride for Sale* (49), with Robert Young and George Brent. In the circumstances, it was unfortunate that she missed out on two good films. She had signed – at a fee of $200,000 – to do *State of the Union* with Gary Cooper, but when Spencer Tracy took over the lead it became impossible to fulfil her contractual requirement of finishing at 5 p.m. instead of 6. The other movie was *All About Eve*, which she lost when she broke her back. However, *Three Came Home* (50) was successful, the story of a woman in a Japanese prison camp.

The Secret Fury was a thriller and so was *Thunder on the Hill* (51): in the latter Miss Colbert was a nun. She returned to comedy, *Let's Make It Legal* with Macdonald Carey and Zachary Scott. Frank Quinn in the 'New York Daily News' said that Colbert was 'a capable farceur . . . but when her co-stars take over the plot labours.' She began *One Minute to Zero*, but was taken ill with pneumonia and replaced by Ann Blyth; later, she travelled to Britain to play *The Planter's Wife* (52), with Jack Hawkins, a phoney drama about the Malayan troubles: it had a success in Britain, but none in the US.

She decided to stay in Europe to take advantage of the new US tax concessions, but two French films were little seen outside that country: *Destinées* (53), with Michèle Morgan as Joan of Arc, Martine Carol as Lysistrata and Colbert as a modern woman coping with the same subject (war); and *Si Versailles m'était Conté* (54), a historical panorama directed by Sacha Guitry, one of an all-star

tion, at once so brittle and so elegant. . . .' Preston Sturges's *The Palm Beach Story* (42) is a strong contender for the most satisfying comedy film ever made and Colbert was captivating as the would-be divorcée (from Joel McCrea). After that, *No Time for Love* (43) with MacMurray was small fry and so was *So Proudly We Hail*, a tribute to the nursing service.

She took top-billing in Selznick's big, big (and synthetic) drama about the women that waited at home, *Since You Went Away* (44). It was helped to success by drum-beating, but no one was fooled that the typical American wife was like Claudette Colbert. Her last for Paramount was *Practically Yours*, with MacMurray. At war's end she was in Sam Wood's irrelevant comedy, *Guest Wife* (45) with Ameche, and then in a banal tale about a woman whose husband (Orson Welles) returns from the dead, *Tomorrow Is Forever* (46). *Without Reservations* was a railroad cast in one of the largest roles, as one of the mistresses of Louis XIV. She played a crusading editor in *Texas Lady* (55), a Technicolored Western at RKO.

In 1956 she returned to Broadway, taking over the lead in 'Janus' from Margaret Sullavan (earlier, in Westport, she had done Noël Coward's 'Island Fling' – later called 'South Sea Bubble'); and two years later, she and Boyer kept 'The Marriage-Go-Round' running for 450 performances. TV appearances included 'The Royal Family of Broadway' (with March and Helen Hayes) and 'Blithe Spirit' (with Lauren Bacall and Coward, whose published diaries contain only uncomplimentary references to Colbert). She continued to do occasional stage work. In 1961 Warners suddenly asked her to play Troy Donahue's mother in *Parrish*: the press was glad to see an old friend, but few cinemagoers knew she was in it; it did poor business and the ads played her down in favour of the teenage 'stars' who, as it turned out, were merely passing through.

When a reporter asked her some years later why she did not make more films, she replied: 'Because there have been no offers.' A report ('Evening News', London, 1968) said there had been offers for TV situation comedies and unsuitable films, and added that Colbert had asked her agent to stop untrue press reports of offers and come-backs. She said they embarrassed her before her friends. The agent said: 'In all my years in this very tough business, it was the closest I ever came to shedding tears, to hear that grand lady say that.' In 1974 she toured in 'A Community of Two', returning more than contentedly to her home in Barbados, but came out of retirement to do 'The Kingfisher' (78) with Rex Harrison on Broadway.

In Washington in 1981 she was in a wheelchair for 'A Talent for Murder' with Louis Jourdan, a poor play which Angela Lansbury and Laurence Olivier elected to do on TV. Colbert, looking incredibly youthful, co-starred with Harrison again in Lonsdale's 'Aren't We All?', successively in London (84), New York (85), Los Angeles (86) and Australia (86/7). And she made a welcome reappearance before the cameras in a TV mini-series based on a true story, *The Two Mrs Grenvilles* (87), as the wealthy matriarch, implacably hostile but gracious on the surface, who opposes her son's marriage to showgirl Ann-Margret. It was an interesting role, made all the more so because Colbert had not appeared before the cameras for almost 30 years: stylish, chic and ever youthful, using all her 60 years' experience by cleverly underplaying, it was a performance to make the armchair viewer want to stand up and cheer.

RONALD COLMAN

In 1927, 1928 and 1932 Ronald Colman was voted the top male star in the Bernstein Questionnaire; in 1932 the readers of a British women's magazine voted him their No. 1 favourite. He was a heart-throb for almost three decades – he was in his 50s when *Random Harvest* was made in 1942 and women everywhere were falling for him all over again. He is almost the only major Silent male star apart from Chaplin who remained a star well into the Talkie era (curiously enough, two others who survived, William Powell and Richard Barthelmess, were intimates of Colman). Colman was the dream lover: calm, debonair but dignified, trustworthy. Although he was a lithe figure in adventure stories, his glamour – which was genuine – came rather from his respectability: he was an aristocratic figure without being aloof. In Talkies, he proved to have a voice not quite classless, not quite transatlantic, but authoritative, gentle . . . the perfect voice for the face. In his great romantic roles it had the ring of an Irving while being completely right in film terms. He might not have that famous quizzical expression, but the voice had immortal longings. And there was a charm, a formidable charm. He was not always an inspired actor, but he was never bad or dull. Like all great stars he left his imprint very firmly on all his films. A Colman performance lingered in the memory.

He was born in 1891 in Richmond, Surrey, the son of a silk importer. His father died when he was 16 and he became an office boy in the British Steamship Company; he was with them five years, during which time he became an enthusiastic amateur actor (and he started out as a professional with a tenth-rate concert party, 'The Mad Medicos'). In 1914 he joined the London Scottish Regiment and served in France until 1916, when he was invalided out, with a fractured ankle. He managed to get a part in a Lena Ashwell sketch at the Coliseum (wearing blackface) and having by now had some experience as a light comedian, he was offered a small part in 'The Misleading Lady' starring Gladys Cooper. He was in a play called 'Partnership' at the Court and in 1918 had the lead in a production of 'Damaged Goods'.

George Dewhurst saw him in it and offered him the lead in a two-reeler, at £1 a day, which included scene-shifting. Dewhurst wrote and directed, but the result, made in a room over a garage, was never publicly shown. Dewhurst gave him a leading role in *The Toilers* (19), as a widow's selfish son, and he had a small role in *A Daughter of Eve*, a high society drama with Stewart Rome, produced by Walter West. Cecil Hepworth gave him an even smaller role in *Sheba* and then West employed him again – in *Snow in the Desert*, an elopement story set in Colombo but filmed in Cornwall. It was West who gave him his first lead, one of several Jewish roles he played about this time: *A Son of David* (20), as a pugilist out to avenge the death of his rabbi father; his co-star was Poppy Wyndham, who was drowned not long afterwards. He went down the cast-list in Hepworth's *Anna the Adventuress*, in which Alma Taylor played twins, and then went to Monte Carlo to film *The Black Spider*, in the title-role – a French nobleman who operates a large-scale burglary business. He also married at this time actress Thelma Raye; they were not divorced till 1935, but the marriage broke down early and the fan-magazines of the 20s considered him single, 'The Man of Mystery'.

His one leading role had led nowhere and there was a slump in the British film industry. He decided to try the US and sailed in 1920. His first American job was a walk-on in 'The Dauntless Three'; there were more small parts, including one in 'The Green Goddess' and another in 'East is West', which starred Fay Bainter. He got a role as a playboy, fifth-billed, in a Selznick (*père*) drama made on the East Coast, *Handcuffs or Kisses* (21), and finally landed a good role in a play starring Ruth Chatterton, 'La Tendresse'. Lillian Gish saw it; her director, Henry King, confirmed the choice of Colman as her next leading man.

The film was *The White Sister* (23) and Colman played Gish's soldier lover (it was his first film with the famous moustache). It made him a name – though the next movie to be released was one he had done earlier, uncredited, for Goldwyn, *The Eternal City*, a drama set in Rome with Barbara La Marr. He got another part in a Selznick film, *Twenty Dollars a Week* (24), as the son of George Arliss, wagered by the old man that he could not live on that amount. Then Gish and King wanted him to partner her again, in *Romola*. While making it, in Italy, Goldwyn announced him for one movie and that led immediately to a starring contract. The film was *Tarnish*, a triangle story with May McAvoy and Marie Prevost; and he was then loaned to First National (at that time Goldwyn's distributing company) for *Her Night of Romance* – Constance Talmadge's, and he was a nobleman disguised as a doctor. Next to be released was *Romola* and with these three films coming along together, Goldwyn was able to sense a more than favourable response. He started to plan a series of Colman vehicles (during Colman's time with him, he presented 30 films, of which 18 starred Colman): *A Thief in Paradise* (25) in

Samoa, with Doris Kenyon, as a derelict who impersonates a dead man in order to inherit his fortune; *His Supreme Moment* and *The Sporting Venus*, both with Blanche Sweet (the latter at MGM). In the former he was a South African mining engineer and in the latter a Scottish medical student. He was loaned again to First National for *Her Sister From Paris*, with Constance Talmadge as twins, one impersonating the other to woo back husband Colman. Then came two of Goldwyn's four-handkerchief efforts and two of his all-time hits – and the success of the first one, Colman later considered, was the turning-point of his life: *The Dark Angel*, in which Colman's love for Vilma Banky is all but destroyed by his being blinded in the war; and *Stella Dallas*, as the bounder who married beneath him and then deserted her – an unforgettable performance by Belle Bennett. From a novel by Olive Higgins Prouty, it was one of 1925's top successes.

Colman went to Warners for Lubitsch's version of Wilde's *Lady Windermere's Fan*, to play Lord Darlington with McAvoy and Irene Rich. At First National, he was Norma Talmadge's leading man in *Kiki* (26) and at Paramount, in the popular and much-liked version of *Beau Geste*, from P.C. Wren's novel about the Foreign Legion. Dashing and determined, Colman was the ideal Beau. Meanwhile, Goldwyn had taken his pictures to UA on a five-year contract, which stipulated six films with Colman or Banky or both – and this most popular of 20s love teams was in *The Winning* of Barbara Worth, a modern Western, he as an engineer from the East, *The Night of Love* (27), a swashbuckler built around the *droit de seigneur* idea with Colman as the gypsy hero; *The Magic Flame*, in a dual role as a pathetic circus clown and an evil monocled prince; and *Two Lovers* (28), more of same – it was based upon a novel by Baroness Orczy set during the Spanish occupation, with Colman as a patriot. But Lily Damita starred with Colman in *The Rescue* (29), from Conrad's story.

Then Goldwyn prepared his prize property for his Talkie début. Richard Griffith has written on this: 'Striking good looks were perhaps the basis of his Silent fame, but from the moment he spoke it was apparent that here was an actor who not only understood his craft but was far ahead of his time. . . . It was also clear from his performance that restraint, underplaying, and the ability to react in pauses between lines of dialogue were to be the essentials of acting in the new medium.' The film was *Bulldog Drummond*, horribly dated today. However, critics then sat up and cheered, and queues for it became a permanent feature of London, New York and other cities for months. It was also soon clear that Colman was the pre-eminent Talkie actor. Said Elinor Glyn: 'Undoubtedly the greatest male personality in present-day pictures'; and Goldwyn satisfied overwhelming public demand for him by rushing him into a series of movies. Banky got left behind in the rush. There was *Condemned*, as a convict in love with governor's wife Ann Harding; *Raffles* (30), E.W. Hornung's novel about an amateur cracksman, with Kay Francis; *The Devil to Pay*, with Loretta Young, a good comedy by Frederick Lonsdale, specially written for Colman, who played a black sheep; and *The Unholy Garden* (31) with Fay Wray, a love story set in the Sahara which Goldwyn made against his better judgment (it was a great flop).

Colman gave a sensitive performance in John Ford's *Arrowsmith* (from Sinclair Lewis's novel), a film that has dated but little, and was even better in *Cynara* (32), as a lawyer who dallies with a girl while the wife (Kay Francis) is away. He had another dual role in *The Masquerader* (33), as a journalist who impersonates his cousin, a drug-addicted politician, at a time of crisis. During its making the publicity department issued a statement, purportedly by Goldwyn himself, to the effect that Colman looked better on screen when mildly dissipated and that he played his love scenes better after several drinks. Colman was furious and reportedly sued for $2 million, with the case being settled out of court: in fact, he used the incident to accept a better offer from Joseph Schenck, who had just set up 20th Century Pictures. Schenck also headed UA, which released the films of both companies, and Goldwyn thought it more politic to settle Colman's contract (which had brought him $6,500 a week in 1932, the tenth highest-paid star in Hollywood).

The new company cautiously put him into *Bulldog Drummond Strikes Back* (34) and *Clive of India* (35), both with Loretta Young. 20th was having some success with historical figures and films extolling the virtues of British colonisalism were a commercial staple of Hollywood at that time. Of its type, *Clive* was okay and Colman was fine – though many sob-sisters used up newsprint in mourning the loss (for the first time) of the famous moustache. But it returned when Colman became *The Man Who Broke the Bank at Monte Carlo*, a pleasant comedy.

At MGM, he was Sidney Carton, holding together the spectacular but meandering *A Tale of Two Cities*. 'The Times' thought his performance 'subtle . . . Dickens created in Carton the most psychologically complicated of all his characters, and Mr Colman, who has never acted so well before, has realised it'. At

Ronald Colman and Vilma Banky in Two Lovers *(28), a drama of the Spanish Netherlands and one of the five movies they made together. They were perhaps the most famous co-starring team of the 20s, but the Hungarian-born Miss Banky did not survive the coming of Talkies.*

Talkies did give a new lease of life to Colman's career, and this one was particularly good: Arrowsmith *(31), directed by John Ford from the novel by Sinclair Lewis. Myrna Loy was the Other Woman.*

There was a laughable
remake, quickly forgotten:
Frank Capra's Lost
Horizon (37) stays in the
memory – not for its
concept of Shangri-La,
revealing its age-old truths,
but for its grace and spirit
of adventure and for
Ronald Colman's
performance as an
international figure of
acknowledged charisma.
With him is Jane Wyatt, as
the Shangri-La lady who
caught his affections.

20th, he did a version of Ouida's silly adventure novel, *Under Two Flags* (36), as a nonchalant British officer with Something in his Past – and it almost catches up with him in Africa, when Rosalind Russell comes to visit.

After that, he freelanced. No studio planned vehicles for him, as MGM did for Clark Gable and Robert Montgomery, for instance, so he reduced his activity and waited for the plum roles. He was still a very big star indeed. MGM had offered *A Tale of Two Cities* to Brian Aherne, but jettisoned him when they learnt that Colman was free. Now Columbia threw Aherne overboard when they found they could get Colman to play the hero who found love and wisdom in Shangri-La: *Lost Horizon* (37), directed by Frank Capra from James Hilton's novel. It cost so much that even a great box-office performance was not enough: but prestige accrued – and the film's lingering charm is due much to his beautiful

performance. Then Selznick cast him in the famous dual role, *The Prisoner of Zenda*, from the novel by Anthony Hope which added Ruritania to the world's maps. Of the four film versions, this is the definitive one.

Selznick announced hopefully that he had signed Colman to a seven-year contract, but in fact the loan-out for *Lost Horizon* was the first of a three-film deal. While Selznick looked for a subject for the third film the actor signed with Paramount for two pictures. The first was an indifferent version of an old swashbuckler, *If I Were King* (38), one of the four movie versions of the François Villon story (two with music as *The Vagabond King*). The Villon of the 1920 version, William Farnum, had a small role. Colman turned down *The Rains Came* (the George Brent character) and returned to Paramount for a film once mooted for Gary Cooper or Ray Milland, *The Light That Failed* (39), from Kipling's story. It was an odd addition to

Hollywood's series of 'Empire' films, and with its tragedy and pessimism badly timed (Britain had just entered the war). Colman was at first glance a good choice to play Helder, the ex-solider who becomes a successful artist; as with Sydney Carton he is or becomes drunken and disillusioned, so the role was not outside his range – but he is not convincing as a man without integrity.

He had had a remarkable run and made the mistake of turning down both *Intermezzo* and *Rebecca* (both offered by Selznick), further weakening his stock by two weakish comedies which he co-produced with Lewis Milestone: *Lucky Partners* (40), as an artist sharing a raffle ticket with Ginger Rogers; and *My Life with Caroline* (41), a marital romp seriously hurt by the inadequacy of Anna Lee as the wife. At Columbia he took third-billing, to Cary Grant and Jean Arthur, in *The Talk of the Town* (42) – but as a law professor had the best role. He returned in force with *Random Harvest*, James Hilton's novel that MGM had bought for Spencer Tracy. As the amnesiac who marries Greer Garson twice without realizing it, Colman's quiet weight and charm made it all seem almost plausible – one of the best examples of that sort of sleight of hand in the history of cinema acting. MGM retained his services for the remake of *Kismet* (44), but his deft spoofing touch was not equalled by other participants in this Arabian Nights extravaganza.

He appeared in a civilized film version of John P. Marquand's *The Late George Apley* (47), silver-haired now; and in *A Double Life* (48), written by Garson Kanin and directed by Cukor, a medium melodrama about a Shakespearian actor who takes to doing 'Othello' offstage – with fatal consequences to waitress Shelley Winters. It brought Colman's fourth Oscar nomination and his first win: but it was hardly his most notable performance and the film is much less well-remembered than *Champagne for Caesar* (49), which played on dual bills. It was a funny film about quiz programmes and his last film role of any importance. The film flopped. His fee was a participation deal of 7 per cent – to go to 10 per cent over a certain amount, with a guaranteed minimum of $100,000. This came to light when he sued in 1952. He had a guest spot in *Around the World in 80 Days* (56), as an Indian railway official and a good role, as the defender of Mankind, in *The Story of Mankind* (57); and he guested on TV, notably with his wife in a Jack Benny show, conceivably the drollest 30 minutes in the history of that medium. They also appeared in a series, 'The Halls of Ivy'. She was his second wife, a charming English actress, Benita Hume, whom he married in 1938. He died in 1958 of pneumonia (the direct result of an old war wound).

GARY COOPER

Agent-turned-producer and old Hollywood hand Arthur P. Jacobs had no doubt: 'He was the greatest film star there has ever been – and that includes Gable.' He, Gary Cooper, was certainly on all counts one of the most successful. His career spanned 35 years and, except at the very beginning and during the last few years, he was one of the biggest attractions in films (during the period 1936–57 he missed the Exhibitors' top 10 list on only three occasions and he was first in 1953, second in 1944 and 1952). He won two Oscars and for the same two films, *Sergeant York* and *High Noon*, the New York critics designated him Actor of the Year. Early in his career John Barrymore said: 'That fellow is the world's greatest actor. He can do, with no effort, what the rest of us spent years trying to learn: to be perfectly natural.' And Charles Laughton admired him: 'I knew in a flash he'd got something I should never have . . . that boy hasn't the least idea how well he acts.' After his death Robert Preston spoke of him: 'Now, Cooper doesn't have the reputation as a great actor except with us who knew him as an actor. But he was great. People used to comment on what they called his idiosyncrasies, his little foibles. But Cooper never made a move that wasn't thoroughly thought out and planned. He is probably the finest motion picture actor I ever worked with.'

The strange thing is that Cooper (as his TV interviews showed) had in life a number of effeminate mannerisms. However, on the screen he was virility personified, all that was required of a hero: honest, courageous and determined – determined to do what must be done at whatever the cost. The image was fixed quite early, though he did, with surprising elasticity, manage from time to time less admirable qualities: mawkishness, craftiness, hesitancy. But he could never be villainous. He himself considered that his consistent popularity stemmed from the fact that he always played 'the part of Mr Average Joe American. Just an average guy from the middle of the USA.'

The middle of the USA was actually Helena, Montana, but Cooper's parents were British immigrants; his father was a judge. Cooper was born in 1901 and was educated in Britain for some years before World War I; at college he became known for his cartoons and caricatures, and intended to make a career from drawing. He proceeded to Los Angeles with his family, but could not get a job. Through friends he got work as an extra in movies, including *The Eagle* (25). Because he could ride, most of these films were Westerns, and he occasionally had a line. His father introduced him to Marilyn Mills, who produced and starred herself in two-reel Westerns. She engaged Cooper to play the heavy in a couple of them, *Tricks* (25) and *Three Pals*, but he did not like being a villain and returned to 'extra' work; he began to mail his photograph to all the studios. He acquired a new agent, Nan Collins, who changed his name from Frank to Gary Cooper and arranged a screen test which she showed around: at Paramount John Waters – director of Zane Grey Westerns – thought he would be right for *Arizona Bound*. Meanwhile, he was taken on for extra work on a Western at Goldwyn at $15 a week; but when the actor cast as Ronald Colman's rival (for Vilma Banky) was held up on another film the director Henry King offered the role to Cooper, whose salary was raised to $65 a week. When Goldwyn eventually saw the rushes (the film was being made away on location) he offered a contract at the same fee, but found to his chagrin that Paramount had just signed the actor to a seven-year contract, starting at $150 per week.

Arizona Bound was not ready, so he filled in with a minuscule part in *It* (27), as a reporter whose story causes Clara Bow a whole heap of trouble. As a result he was promoted to her leading man in *Children of Divorce*. According to Hedda Hopper, who was also in it, he was stiff and gave a 'horrible' performance – but he was learning to relax and the studio had faith in him. He had the lead in *Arizona Bound* and a small but vital part in *Wings*. Mostly, he was in actioners: *Nevada, The Last Outlaw* and *Beau Sabreur* (28); *The Legion of the Condemned*, a war story with Fay Wray ('Paramount's Glorious Young Lovers'); and *Doomsday*, as the simple farmer Florence Vidor discovers she loves after she has married for money. As a fisherman he gave *The First Kiss* to Miss Wray, the richest girl in town, and was then loaned to First National for the cheerless *Lilac Time* with Colleen Moore, an aviation drama adapted from an old (1917) Broadway play. He was shipwrecked on a desert island with *Half a Bride* Esther Ralston, having abducted her. Talkies had arrived: *Lilac Time* had had Sound effects, and the next would be a part-Talkie: *The Shopworn Angel* (29). Cooper was a naïve young solider drawn to kept woman Nancy Carroll; and he played another nice young man drawn to Lupe Velez in *Wolf Song*; he supported Emil Jannings in the unsuccessful *The Betrayal*; and then starred in

his first all-Talkie, *The Virginian*, from Owen Wister's novel. It was a hit and made him a top draw (he remained fond of the film, though in later years was irritated that the laconic dialogue – 'yep' and 'no' – was forever associated with him). During its making he learnt that blocks of films were being sold on his name alone, so he applied for a rise. He was about to go to $1,250, but this was readjusted to $3,750. And he was officially raised to stardom with *Seven Days' Leave* (30), co-starring Beryl Mercer, and called in Britain *Medals*, being a slushy version of Barrie's 'The Old Lady Shows Her Medals'. The other 1930 movies were mostly actioneers: *Only the Brave*, with Mary Brian, a Civil War story; *Paramount on Parade*; O. Henry's *The Texan*, with Fay Wray; *The Man From Wyoming*, an artificial war romance with June Collyer; the first of the three Talkie versions of Rex Beach's *The Spoilers* (there had been two Silent ones), with its famous climactic saloon brawl with William Boyd; and *Morocco*, as a foreign legionnaire who falls for Marlene Dietrich.

There was *Fighting Caravans* (31), a Western with Lily Damita; Mamoulian's fine *City Streets*, as a Westerner unwillingly drawn into the Underworld, with Sylvia Sidney, and one of the year's top money-makers; and *I Take This Woman*, as a cowhand courting Carole Lombard.

In one of her books, Hedda Hopper claims that Cooper's off-screen companions at this time were well-known homosexuals and that she warned him that she would ruin him unless he found more suitable ones (though she did not become a powerful columnist till much later). He certainly took her advice, for much publicity accrued to his romance with the fiery star Lupe Velez and again at this period with the Countess de Frasso. He was living the high life with her in Europe when Paramount recalled him for *His Woman* – she was Claudette Colbert and he was a freighter captain. He also discovered that the studio was in dire straits, needing him badly: so he asked for a new contract starting at $5,000 a week. He returned to Europe; but was back in Hollywood for a guest spot as himself in *Make Me a Star* (32) and to do a triangle drama with Charles Laughton and Tallulah Bankhead, *The Devil and the Deep*. Six months later two of his best-remembered films were released: *If I Had a Million* and *A Farewell to Arms*. Cooper was in one of the poor episodes of the first of these and the film was in fact indifferently received – it played the lower half of double bills (its later reputation was due to two episodes and the cast). He was Hemingway's soldier in *A Farewell to Arms*, with Helen Hayes at his

doomed light o'love. He was another novelist's soldier in *Today We Live* (33) at MGM –
one of William Faulkner's: but this drama of
an American pilot (Cooper) and a British girl
(Joan Crawford) was far-fetched and awash
with 'British' patriotism. He married in 1933
– Veronica Balfe, known as 'Rocky'; it was
one of the few Hollywood unions to endure –
though it would be severely threatened in the
late 40s when Cooper had a long affair with
his co-star Patricia Neal.

He returned to Paramount for *One Sunday
Afternoon* and, if all critics remembered the
1932 *A Farewell to Arms* when reviewing the
1957 remake, one critic remembered this
when faced with the remake (*Strawberry
Blonde*) with James Cagney: 'Mr Cooper,
abandoning for once his role of the laconic
scout, cowboy, or Deadeye Dick, appeared as
a dentist; an honest, insensitive lout, pursued
through life by an adolescent passion for a
beauty who fooled him, and hatred for her
husband; the audience saw him grow from
booby to domestic cynic . . . the natural
deliberation of Mr Cooper's playing gave the
simple story character and truth' (Dilys
Powell).

There were four poor ones. As one of the
two men in Miriam Hopkins's life, *Design for
Living* proved he was not yet ready for
drawing-room comedy. *Alice in Wonderland*
found him unrecognizable as the White
Knight and *Operator 13* (34) back at MGM,
this time in the arms of Marion Davies, as a
reb soldier. And there was the painful discovery in *Now and Forever* that both he and
Carole Lombard were gooey-eyed over Shirley Temple. Thereafter, for many years, he
managed to avoid making any real clinkers.
The public flocked to see him, moustached
and self-sacrificing, in a stirring tale of the
North-West Frontier, *Lives of a Bengal Lancer* (35); under Henry Hathaway's direction it
was his most popular picture to date.

He was coming into his own and at the end
of the year his earnings would be $311,000. At
Paramount he drew $6,000 a week and could
get more on loan-out. Goldwyn offered him
$75,000 for four weeks' work on *Barbary
Coast*, but he put him to bolstering Anna Sten
instead: in *The Wedding Night* – he played the
novelist who falls in love with her after she has
married. The public was not smitten with
either that or *Peter Ibbetson*, directed by
Hathaway, with Cooper and Ann Harding as
the ill-fated lovers who meet in dreams after
their parting: a curious piece, not sufficiently
Victorian-Gothic, filmed because a Broadway
version of the old novel had been a success.
Cooper returned to more congenial circumstances with *Desire* (36), produced by Lubitsch
and directed by Frank Borzage, underplaying

Gary Cooper, an
American serving with the
Italian army, and Helen
Hayes, British nurse, in A
Farewell to Arms (*32*).
Frank Borzage directed,
from Hemingway's novel,
and no movie-maker ever
served this writer better.

to good effect as an innocent American tourist
conned by the worldly Marlene Dietrich. And
he was in his element in Capra's *Mr Deeds
Goes to Town*, as the country boy who is
taken for a ride by, but finally routs, the city
slickers. Graham Greene said his performance was 'subtle and pliable . . . it must be
something of which other directors have only
dreamed.' The film itself won prizes (the
'Picturegoer' Gold Medal for Cooper), made
a mint and is today hardly less funny or
relevant than it was then.

Cooper followed with a spate of adventure
films: Lewis Milestone's tortuous but exciting
The General Died at Dawn with Madeleine
Carroll; *The Plainsman*, as Wild Bill Hickok
to Jean Arthur's Calamity Jane – one of De
Mille's better epics and another giant grosser;
and Hathaway's indifferent *Souls at Sea* (37),
buddy-buddying with George Raft, an actor
to make Cooper seem an even more splendid
fellow than usual. This adventure of slave ship
days was to have been Paramount's answer to
Mutiny on the Bounty and it was initially road-
shown – but then cut for ordinary screenings
because word-of-mouth was so bad.

Cooper was negotiating a new contract
when his agent agreed one with Goldwyn, still
bitter at losing the actor years ago. He would
now be paying him $150,000 each for six
pictures over a six-year period. That still left
Cooper with much free time and since Paramount had put the matter in the hands of their
lawyers the contract specified that he could
not accept any other offer till rejecting one
from them. The new association began badly
with *The Adventures of Marco Polo* (38),
which had begun as a project of Douglas
Fairbanks for himself before selling it to

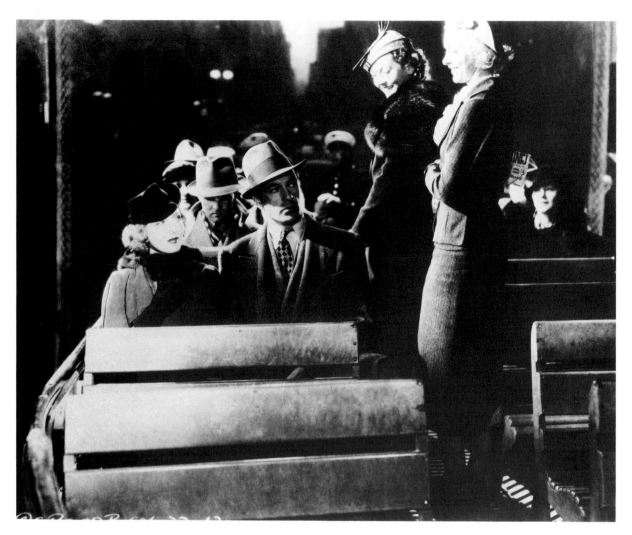

Mr Deeds Goes to Town
(36) – and when he did, he
rode on the top of a Fifth
Avenue bus. Jean Arthur
and Gary Cooper in a film
which tried to say
something trenchant about
the way America was then.
Contemporary critics
thought it succeeded, and
posterity, generally, has
found it wonderfully
funny.

Goldwyn, who had originally intended to star Fredric March. Robert E. Sherwood's light-hearted script was only that in intention, but audiences did roll in the aisle during the scene in which Marco Cooper teaches the Chinese princess (Sigrid Gurie) how to kiss. Lubitsch's *Bluebeard's Eighth Wife* was a happier occasion for all concerned, including Paramount and Claudette Colbert, who co-starred. Cooper's now ample comedic skills were more sorely needed in *The Cowboy and the Lady*, a cynical reworking of 'The Taming of the Shrew' by Leo McCarey (who had no intention of directing, and a further 27 writers – possibly a record – were employed to get his idea into a script); McCarey knew that Goldwyn was desperate to co-star Cooper with Merle Oberon, who was making little impression on American audiences. With *The Wedding March*, this meant that Goldwyn had presented Cooper with the only three real flops of this period of his career. He went back into action: the popular and sympathetic

Beau Geste (39) at Paramount, though you had to shut your ears to believe he was British; and *The Real Glory*, in which he was a doctor in Manila just before the Spanish-American War. This was a conscious effort of Goldwyn to find a role reminiscent of *Lives of a Bengal Lancer* and he wanted to put him in a Western, a genre back in popularity after a decade of neglect – because of *Stagecoach*, which Cooper had turned down. At least *The Westerner* (40) would be directed by Wyler, who had turned down the earlier Goldwyn Coopers after reading the scripts. Cooper plays a horse thief who joins up with the farmers to defeat the evil Judge Roy Bean (Walter Brennan), his first performance for a couple of years that did not rely mainly on mannerisms and his reticent charm; and some forgettable but successful De Mille stuff, *North West Mounted Police*. For this period (1939–40), Cooper was the highest salaried actor, at just under $500,000.

He did another for Capra, *Meet John Doe*

(41): crusading it was and Christ-like he was, as an unemployed baseball-pitcher picked by sob-sister Barbara Stanwyck to be her John Doe. *Mr Deeds* it was not and it did not repeat its success. Warners had borrowed him for that and they were to borrow him again – from Goldwyn in exchange for Bette Davis – to play *Sergeant York*, the Quaker country boy who became a hero in World War I. Cooper refused the part several times, but the producer – Jesse Lasky – held out for him and he won his first Oscar, under the direction of Howard Hawks. Hawks also directed *Ball of Fire* for Goldwyn and Cooper's co-star was again Miss Stanwyck: he as an absent-minded professor and she as a hard-boiled showgirl in this very funny gangster comedy. Cooper played a second real-life hero in *The Pride of the Yankees* (42), Lou Gehrig, the baseball player who had died the previous year – and one of the few successful pictures built around that sport.

It was the last movie due under his Goldwyn contract, though some sources claim that Goldwyn loaned him to Paramount for *For Whom the Bell Tolls* (43). At all events he was another Hemingway hero – at the author's insistence – this time on the side of the Loyalists in the Spanish Civil War. Ingrid Bergman co-starred as the local girl he loves and the film, like most of this batch, was synthetic and a roaring success. He and Bergman went to Warners for *Saratoga Trunk*, a cotton-wool epic from a novel by Edna Ferber: his role as a suave railroad pioneer was somewhat subsidiary to the lady's. Release was delayed for a couple of years. Returning to Paramount he played another all-American hero for De Mille – *The Story of Dr Wassell* (44): only the real Dr W was an elderly man – a truth twisted 'to be regretted beyond all qualifications' (James Agee).

Certainly Cooper was now free of a long-term contract and it was said that he would be involved with a new concern, International; but like the other big names involved in independent production companies in the immediate postwar period, his association was brief: *Casanova Brown*, a pleasant comedy with Teresa Wright, a remake of *Little Accident*; and *Along Came Jones* (45), which he produced himself, a Western about a wayfaring stranger who aids damsel-in-distress Loretta Young. RKO released both (International later amalgamated with Universal). The big one that year was *Saratoga Trunk*, partly because of the stars' popularity: and indeed the Gallup poll of 1945 found that Cooper was America's favourite male star, followed by Bing Crosby, Cary Grant, Bob Hope and Spencer Tracy in that order.

That may be why Warners were happy to pay him $300,000 for Fritz Lang's *Cloak and Dagger* (46) with Lilli Palmer, again as a professor in this wartime espionage tale. De Mille then called him back to Paramount for an epic and during its making he did a guest appearance in *Variety Girl* (47). The De Mille picture was *Unconquered*, an idiotic adventure of pioneering days with Paulette Goddard. For Leo McCarey at RKO, Cooper was *Good Sam* (48), a soft touch who found in return there was no help when he needed it: a sentimental comedy with Ann Sheridan.

Cooper's popularity had diminished but little – but the situation was no longer as favourable as it once was. The studio's priority, more than ever, was to find vehicles for their contract stars – and if they wanted a freelance, well, Gregory Peck was younger and more highly regarded. Cooper signed a new deal with Warners, for a minimum of six pictures and a maximum of 10, with a guarantee of earnings of $3 million, the contract renegotiable in five years' time. Few of the films were good, but his annual salary thereafter was never less than $500,000. He made: *The Fountainhead* (49), a rip-roaring melodrama from an ambitious novel by Ayn Rand, as an idealist architect pursued by socialite Patricia Neal; *It's a Great Feeling*, passing through as himself in this Doris Day musical; *Task Force*, a tribute to aircraft carriers; *Bright Leaf* (50) with Miss Neal and Lauren Bacall, a rambling saga of the tobacco industry which did particularly badly; and *Dallas*, a revenge Western with Ruth Roman. At 20th, he was the captain of the *USS Teakettle* (51), but that proved so unseaworthy that it was withdrawn and put out again – successfully – as *You're in the Navy Now*. He did another spot in a Doris Day musical, *Starlift*, and at MGM was in the Texas episode of the all-star *It's a Big Country*.

The following year he did three Westerns, always safe material for an ageing star: *Distant Drums* (52), *High Noon* and *Springfield Rifle*. The first and third of them were made at Warners and both just got by at the box-office. *High Noon* streaked ahead, the story of a sheriff (Cooper) who finds his territory very lonely when faced with three avenging killers. Under Fred Zinnemann's direction it was taut and intelligent; rave notices and a theme song brought in crowds. Cooper won another Oscar and his reputation soared again. There was a run of acceptable films: *Return to Paradise* (53), based on some James A. Michener stories, as a preacher in Polynesia; *Blowing Wild*, an oil-rig drama with Barbara Stanwyck; *Garden of Evil* (54), a Western with Richard Widmark, as an adventurer; and – best of all – *Vera Cruz*, a Western

Cooper with Audrey Hepburn in Love in the Afternoon (57), *a comedy about a young French girl who spends her afternoons in the Ritz Hotel apartment of an elderly and wealthy American: under Billy Wilder's direction it was an acceptable situation.*

and *The Hanging Tree* (59), and there were two adventure stories, Robert Rossen's *They Came to Cordura* with Rita Hayworth, one of Cooper's rare masochistic performances, and the entertaining *The Wreck of the Mary Deare* (60) with Charlton Heston. He then made *The Naked Edge* (61), in which wife Deborah Kerr spent most of the time wondering whether he was a murderer. The film was implausible in other ways, too, but it did good business. By the time it came out 'Coop' was dead, of cancer, in 1961 and audiences went to see it for a last, sad look at their old favourite. A month before he died he was awarded an honorary Oscar for services to the industry.

CICELY COURTNEIDGE

Cicely Courtneidge is not everyone's cup of tea. The ebullience which was her stock-in-trade a minority find alienating – and some find her vitally enervating. No one could deny her a professionalism of a very high order: in the consistently poor stage roles with which she landed herself in later years her way with a line or a piece of business could be joyous and with first-class material she could be very droll. Her films were modest affairs, sometimes made in tandem with her husband, Jack Hulbert, and not startlingly original, not very witty. But they are (still) fitfully amusing: Hulbert is a likeable if languid leading man and light comedian, and Cis is – well Cis: uninhibited, infectious, a top lady clown. The trouble is that for all their energy and 'versatility' they fail to surprise us.

She ws born in Sydney in 1893, the daughter of Robert Courtneidge, a famous theatrical manager who was touring Australia at the time. She made her stage début in 1901 as Peaseblossom in 'A Midsummer Night's Dream' at Manchester, returned to Australia with her father, reappeared in Britain at the same Manchester theatre in 'Tom Jones' (07), the start of a short and inglorious career as ingénue in musical comedy – some half-dozen shows, including 'The Pearl Girl' (which provided her first meeting with Hulbert; they were married in 1919) and 'The Cinema Star'. Later, when she tried to get work outside her father's management, agents scoffed at her, so she turned to the (music) halls and began singing comic songs. Her success was almost instantaneous; she played panto and became a music-hall topliner (songs and sketches) before venturing back into the West End – 'Ring Up' (21). In 1926 she made her New York début in 'By-the-way', a revue that had been a great success in London; other hit shows of the period included 'Lido Lady',

which pitted him against a grinning Burt Lancaster.

The Court Martial of Billy Mitchell (55), an account of that fractious affair, was a dud. So, more surprisingly, were both William Wyler's *Friendly Persuasion* (56) and Billy Wilder's *Love in the Afternoon* (57). The latter couple were produced by Allied Artists in a bid to move from minor to major status. Cooper apart, both directors were among the most admired in the business, but critical opinion was divided. The Wyler film, a gentle comedy about Quakers and pacifism (from a novel by Jessamyn West), did do good business in certain territories (it won a Grand Prix at Cannes) and finally did well due to a hit theme tune. Wilder's picture concerned an affair between the 50-ish Cooper and teenager Audrey Hepburn: treated with the director's customary wit, delicacy and melancholy, but the public did not want to know. He then blundered into a similar tale, John O'Hara's *10 North Frederick* (58), but the director was no Wilder and Suzy Parker no Hepburn (indeed Spencer Tracy had turned down the role because he refused to act opposite an ex-model).

Two Westerns did better: *Man of the West*

'Clowns in Clover' (27) and 'The House That Jack Built' (29). She and Hulbert were among the top half-dozen draws in the West End.

In 1930 the Hulberts were invited to appear in *Elstree Calling*, a revue styled after the Hollywood film revues of the period but supposedly a series of turns in a television station; they did 'Folly to Be Wise' (31) at the Piccadilly and were two of the stage stars now in demand for Talkies. Gainsborough signed them and they took as enthusiastically to films as to their stage work: the remake of *The Ghost Train* (31) was based on a hit comedy-thriller by Arnold Ridley, with Hulbert as the lead and Courtneidge as a middle-aged spinster; they subsequently did *Jack's the Boy* (32) and *Happy Ever After*, the latter an English version of a UFA vehicle for Lilian Harvey – Courtneidge had only a supporting role. But both Hulberts were, for a few years, box-office attractions in their own right. With Edward Everett Horton she did one of her biggest successes, *Soldiers of the King* (33), as both mother and daughter; then teamed with Hulbert again for *Falling for You*, as rival reporters trying to get an exclusive interview with the heiress with whom he is smitten. It followed a simple plot formula: she got into as many scrapes and disguises as possible, helped out of difficulties by an exasperated Hulbert. She was on her own in *Aunt Sally* (34), as a showgirl who becomes a big success as a Mistinguett-like star – for her boss, an American gangster hiding out in Britain, Sam Hardy. The director was also American, Tim Whelan, and another American 'name', William Gargan, was imported for *Things Are Looking Up* (35), in which she is a circus equestrian rider who impersonates her twin sister, a prim disciplinarian schoolteacher. It may be her best film, and *Me and Marlborough* is perhaps the worst: in drag she joins the army in what may be the only film set in the reign of Queen Anne.

The partnership temporarily disbanded when MGM sent for Courtneidge to co-star with Frank Morgan in *The Perfect Gentleman*. According to her memoirs, 'Cicely' (1953), the part was wrong for her and the first few days' work 'shockingly unfunny'. To her astonishment she found that the film's producer had no knowledge of her previous work, but later he ran through some of her earlier films and as a result built up her part: 'I did not think the result very good. I will go further, I thought it was rubbish. We remade the rubbish, twice with different directors.' The film was a flop on both sides of the Atlantic – in Britain it was rechristened. 'They call it *The Imperfect Woman* and, by gosh, it is,' said C.A. Lejeune, noting that MGM had failed to capture her 'unique brand of bubbly'.

In the US André Sennwald in the 'New York Times' had admitted that he had never liked her: 'Frequently her humour is down around its old level of elephantine burlesque and vaudeville athleticism. But she can be surprisingly effective on occasion'.

The American welcome for her earlier films had been muted. Gainsborough prepared the last two for local audiences only: *Everybody Dance* (36), as a cabaret singer who poses as a social worker; and, reunited with Hulbert, *Take My Tip* (37), as an aristocratic couple down on their luck and up to any number of disguises. This proved them unable or unwilling to adapt their stage techniques for the screen, which may be why audiences lost interest. He was still filming when she was offered a stage show, 'Hide and Seek', and the following year they were together on stage in 'Under Your Hat', a farce with music about a film star couple involved with spies in the South of France. It ran for two years, but when they filmed it for Grand National the war had started and *Under Your Hat* (40) was, rather, Old Hat.

In 1945 came 'Under the Counter' in London, which she subsequently played in New York (where it failed), Australia and on TV; she did 'Her Excellency' (49) and 'Gay's

Cicely Courtneidge's vehicles always required her to wear funny costumes – often disguises – and usually to do a comic dance or so: here's one with Jack Hulbert from Under Your Hat *(40).*

the Word' (51). The British industry was not making comedies of their kind, but she played the title-role in *Miss Tulip Stays the Night* (55), though it was in fact a vehicle for Diana Dors. She had a featured role in a terrible Agatha Christie effort, *Spider's Web* (60), with Glynis Johns, and toured with the original play in the leading role, off and on for many years afterwards. There were few stage successes for a while, but Courtneidge had appeared regularly on TV. In a way, all the failures were compensated for by *The L-Shaped Room* (62): she had a featured role, playing an ageing and lonely lesbian, and by any standards it was an outstanding performance. She subsequently had bits in *Those Magnificent Men in Their Flying Machines* (65), unbilled, which was wise of her; and *The Wrong Box* (66), as a Salvation Army major, one of several eccentrics encountered. In 1967 she, with her husband, got glowing notices in a West End revival of 'Dear Octopus'. She appeared in other plays and with Hulbert had a supporting role in an unnecessary screen transcription of a West End farce, *Not Now Darling* (73). She was made a Dame in 1972; Hulbert died in 1978 and she herself died the following year.

JOAN CRAWFORD

'Movie stars? I don't like the name. . . . The words "movie stars" are so misused they have no meaning. Any little pinhead who does one picture is a star. Gable is a star, Cooper is a star, Joan Crawford, as much as I dislike the lady, is a star. But I don't think the so-called others are. To be a star you have to drag your weight into the box-office, and be recognized wherever you go.' Humphrey Bogart said that once to reporter Ezra Goodman and his grudging admiration for Miss Crawford reflects contemporary opinion – colleagues and critics – over half a century (almost).

The length of Crawford's career is awesome, especially as she was never considered much of an actress – nor did she make a habit of appearing in good films. Yet in the 50s she was the only major female player surviving from the Silent era. She had to be, as she looked, as tough as old boots. Her life, as with many others, might be fashioned after one of her scenarios: struggle, fight, get to the top, stay there. . . . Some accounts reckon that she survived because she changed her style, adapted herself to new fashions: but only in the physical sense did she adapt – new hairstyles, modes. The essential Crawford did not change, whether as dancing daughter, sophisticated heroine or tragic lady. She

played one sort of American woman for 50 years. She admitted that she worked hard at the acting game – but she achieved little beyond the projection of that woman. Her repertory of gestures and expressions was severely limited. Scott Fitzgerald years ago complained in a letter of the difficulties of fashioning a script for her: 'She can't change her motions in the middle of a scene without going through a sort of Jekyll and Hyde contortion of the face, so that when one wants to indicate that she is going from joy to sorrow, one must cut away and then back. Also, you can never give her such a stage direction as "telling a lie" because if you did she would practically give a representation of Benedict Arnold selling West Point to the British.'

Yet Michael Redgrave wrote almost 20 years later (in 1955): 'How splendid that she can still outstare us all!' Perhaps that is the clue: the big eyes, the determination, the conviction she seemed to feel, even in the egregious melodramas in which she played. The worse the film, the more mesmerizing she is, stalking through the jungle of clichés like a tigress, burning brightly: the working girl from the wrong side of the tracks, clawing her way to the top. Depending on the whim of her scriptwriters, she defended her honour or gave it away and generally suffered the vicissitudes of the damned – only to suffer a bit more, when she reached the top, the agony of the guilty and/or the lonely. A pile of men lay at her feet discarded, as she defiantly faced the future, her shoulders flung back – those shoulders, draped by Adrian or Orry-Kelly, that were always so much more eloquent than her face.

'Picturegoer' in 1932 wondered whether, as a Silent star, she could survive much longer. A few months later, it wrote: 'Joan wants to stay in pictures until she is 40 and believes that she has nowhere near reached the peak of her career yet.' Her career started in 1906, in San Antonio, Texas, though she did not arrive in Hollywood till 1925, when she was 19. Betweenwhiles she had been a waitress, a shopgirl in Kansas City and according to some sources, a hooker. Studio publicity always insisted that fame began to come when she won a Charleston contest. Her first professional appearance as a dancer was in what she has described as an 'out-of-the-way' café in Chicago and that led to the chorus-line of a Detroit club, which led to a Shubert revue on Broadway, 'Innocent Eyes'. At some point, she changed her name from the baptized Billie Cassin to Lucille Le Sueur. She had been on the stage three years when MGM executive Harry Rapf discovered her: she was still in the chorus (of 'The Passing Show of 1924'). She was tested and sent out to Hollywood.

Her first job was doubling for Norma Shearer, playing a double role, in *Lady of the Night* (25), in long-shots, and then she was one of the *Pretty Ladies* – in fact a vehicle for Zazu Pitts, playing a star of the Follies (based on Fanny Brice), adored by her audiences but not, because of her face, by men. Crawford was one of the chorus, seen at first only in the distance: but soon she is in every frame when possible and even gets a close-up – which suggests a sugar daddy, in fact Mr Rapf. There was a walk-on in *The Only Thing*, but then the ingénue part in a Jackie Coogan vehicle, *Old Clothes*. This was better: it was very important to succeed, to show the people of Kansas City, who 'had never believed in my talent'. MGM sponsored a contest in a fan-magazine to find a new name and so Lucille Le Sueur became Joan Crawford in time for her first big part, in *Sally Irene and Mary*. MGM took up her option, embarked on a publicity campaign and put her into *The Boob* (26). She was voted a Wampas Baby Star and was not pleased to be loaned out for Harry Langdon's *Tramp Tramp Tramp*, because valuable properties were not loaned. Most of her films were rush jobs; *Paris*, as an apache dancer who falls for an American country bumpkin (Charles Ray); *The Taxi Driver* (27) with Owen Moore – rechristened in Britain *The Taxi Dancer*; *Winners of the Wilderness* with Tim McCoy; *The Understanding Heart*; *The Unknown*, starring Lon Chaney, as a circus girl; *Twelve Miles Out*, starring John Gilbert; and two William Haines vehicles, *Spring Fever* and *West Point* (28). She was a silent *Rose Marie*, singing mutely while the pit piano played from a score provided by MGM (MGM had started a *Rose Marie* two years earlier, with Renée Adorée, but had abandoned it). Also that year: *Across to Singapore* with Ramon Novarro; *The Law of the Range* with Tim McCoy; and *Four Walls* (described by 'Variety' as 'another underworlder') with John Gilbert.

But that one followed *Our Dancing Daughters*: 'I'd read the story. . . . I'd stolen the script, gone to producer Hunt Stromberg, begged for it and was given it.' It was a Clara Bow part (Bland Johaneson in the 'New York Mirror' thought she had 'beauty, charm and more refinement than the trim-legged Bow'): 'I was the flapper, wild on the surface, a girl who shakes her wind-blown bob . . . and dances herself into a frenzy while the saxes shriek and the trombones wail, a girl drunk on her youth and vitality.' This film, more than any of Bow's up to that time, showed the sticks what the jazz babies were all about. It made Crawford. MGM doubled her salary and her name went up on marquees: 'I'd drive

Joan Crawford more or less as audiences first knew her – the jazz-mad flapper of Our Dancing Daughters *(28). Her partner is Johnny Mack Brown and behind to the left are Dorothy Sebastian and Nils Asther.*

around with a small box camera taking pictures of "Joan Crawford" in lights.' She was top-billed in the next, over Nils Asther and Aileen Pringle, *Dream of Love*, based on 'Adrienne Lecouvrier', the play by Scribe and Legouvé about a famous actress (Crawford). There was another film with Haines, *The Duke Steps Out* (29) and then a sequel, *Our Modern Maidens*, with Crawford's fiancé, Douglas Fairbanks Jr, in the cast. It was one of the few Silents that did well in a market avid for Talkies, so Metro did not rush to make Joan speak.

But she did sing (and dance – 'Gotta Feeling for You') in *Hollywood Revue of 1929* and she sang two songs in *Untamed*, in which she was a dusky maiden. There was *Montana Moon* (30) and then another flapper picture, *Our Blushing Brides*. But Crawford had had enough of bright young things: she wanted the big meaty roles that went to Garbo and Norma Shearer. Unwillingly she played the ingénue in a film version of Vincent Youmans' stage musical, *Great Day* – but she thought she was horrible in it and persuaded Louis B. Mayer to close it down (at a loss of $280,000, somewhat more than that earlier abandoned *Rose Marie*). Looking round for something to do, she found the script of *Paid*, intended for

Stills like these poured forth from MGM to herald each new Crawford opus: no matter where the characters came from in reel one they would certainly be in evening dress by the end. With Clark Gable in Possessed *(31).*

Grand Hotel and reputedly delayed filming by playing records of Dietrich (supposedly Garbo's rival) to get herself into the right mood. But she had no scenes with Garbo. However, exposure in it did no harm (the ex-chorine among so many proved talents) and certain critics thought she stole the film (today, only the Garbo scenes stand up). In a way, the laugh was hers: she was voted the third top money-maker at the end of the year and Garbo was fifth (for 1933 Crawford came tenth and Garbo was thirty-first).

Her Sadie Thompson in *Rain* (on loan to United Artists), a fairly hysterical performance, was not much liked – and the film flopped – nor was she better as an English girl in *Today We Live* (33). She confessed later: 'The whole picture missed. I missed most of all.' It flopped, but *Dancing Lady*, re-teamed with Gable, helping her get to the top, was the success she needed. And she was at her best, pleased all right that they like her singing and dancing, but always aware that you're a mug if you don't try for the big time. Married now to Franchot Tone, she played with him in *Sadie McKee* (34), formula stuff, as a servant girl who is married by Edward Arnold while he is drunk. Then there were two triangle stories with Gable, *Chained*, in which the third side was Otto Kruger, and a comedy, *Forsaking All Others* (35), in which it was Robert Montgomery. This one, in particular, was a great success. After *No More Ladies* with Montgomery and Tone, and *I Live My Life* with Brian Aherne, she wanted to break from formula and asked for *The Gorgeous Hussy* (36), her only period Talkie; she was an innkeeper's daughter married to a member (Tone) of Andrew Jackson's administration. Frank S. Nugent ('New York Times') found her 'gorgeous, but never a hussy . . . sweet, demure, trusting. . . . ' The film did well despite studio scepticism; and she had further successes with *Love on the Run*, with Gable and Tone, and *The Last of Mrs Cheyney* (37), with William Powell and Montgomery.

MGM had always backed Crawford with potent male leads and the grosses of her films had justified this; but her tremendous popularity had abated somewhat by now: in 1937, for the first time for years, she did not appear among the top money-making stars. It could be that the novelty had worn off: it is tempting to assume that her popularity had much to do with her cooperation with the press, even her monotonous habit of baring her soul to the fan-magazines. In 1937 she even talked about seeing herself on the screen: 'And then I wish I could crawl away and die. Because it appears to me that I haven't given a thing – that not the faintest spark of emotion has been picked up.' (Earlier, in 1934, when she had spoken

Shearer, who was pregnant, and went after it. It was a role new to her – a tough role, a girl ruined by the law – and her success in it caused comment. Already filmed twice (with Alice Joyce and Norma Talmadge, as *Within the Law*, the original title of Bayard Veiller's old, underworld, play) it was again a success and would lead to more of the same for Joan. In *Dance Fools Dance* (31) she was a socialite who, rendered penniless, becomes a top reporter: Clark Gable was featured and he was her co-star in *Laughing Sinners*, as a Salvation Army worker who befriends her, a (blonde) sort-of streetwalker. The next one, *This Modern Age*, was described by one critic as 'a shopgirl's delight' and rebuked by 'Picturegoer' as 'so obviously a concession to the present vogue of screen sensationalism'. Nor did that magazine care for Crawford in *Possessed*, finding her 'prone to strive for effect to the point of artificiality'. She was a small-town girl out to better herself and Gable was the politician who marries her: a silly film which was one of the year's top grossers. *Letty Lynton* (32) was based on Mrs Belloc Lowndes's novel based on the Madeleine Smith poison trial.

According to contemporary reports, she was not pleased to be *just one of* the stars in

Gable and Crawford again, in Dancing Lady *(33). She's a hoofer aiming for stardom and he's the dance director. Despite the baubles offered by a Park Avenue swell (*Franchot Tone*) they end in a clinch in the last reel. In life, well, she married Tone for a while and had an intermittent affair with Gable which lasted much longer.*

of the new Metro contract to be signed the following year, she had announced that it would give her six months off annually for stage work; thereafter she was able to announce regularly that she had not found the right vehicle.)

Then *The Bride Wore Red*, with Robert Young and Tone, failed at the box-office. If it was neither better nor worse than most of her films, it was still pretty bad with a heavy performance by its star, as a loose lady pretending to class in the Tyrol. 'Your enjoyment of it will depend on how much of Miss Crawford you can take at a stretch,' said Howard Barnes in the 'New York Herald Tribune.' Nor was *Mannequin* (38), with Spencer Tracy, very popular: 'Joan Crawford plot No 1,' said 'Picturegoer', 'with the star as an ambitious factory girl. . . .' However, MGM had just signed her for five more years, at $1½ million and five pictures a year, and they were not immediately alarmed when she appeared on the list of stars declared box-office poison in the famous full-page ad in the 'Hollywood Reporter', placed there by exhibitors 'tired of losing money on the glamour

stars detested by the public'. To counter that, the press department noted that Crawford had just received her 900,000th fan letter – she had kept count of every one. However, when *The Shining Hour* did not do too well – despite a strong cast including Margaret Sullavan – MGM worried. The executives started believing the fan-magazines which persisted in the cry that Crawford was through, which was poetic justice, because she had always ardently believed in them. So they ditched her in *Ice Follies of 1939* (39) which she later described as trash, echoing contemporary opinion.

'At this critical moment I set my sights on the part of Crystal, the hard-boiled perfume clerk who uses every wile to catch another woman's husband in *The Women*.' In this, Crawford did well, a delicious vixen, overplaying with precision. She also did the part off-screen, bitching Shearer and being bawled out by director George Cukor for unprofessionalism. The decline was halted, if temporarily, and Crawford got Gable back as leading man for *Strange Cargo* (40): but if top-billed, her part was much subsidiary to his. It was one

'Do you like music?' asks Conrad Veidt. 'Symphonies? Concertos?' Joan replies, 'Some symphonies, most concertos.' A Woman's Face (41).

of her least typical and best performances, even though hampered by lines like 'As for going any place with you, I still pick my own gutters.' *Susan and God* did poorly (her performance as a socialite whose religious mania causes havoc in those around her was a poor imitation of the one that Gertrude Lawrence had given on the stage), but *A Woman's Face* (41) was a big success, the remake of a melodrama that Ingrid Bergman had done in Sweden. Cukor directed, and Crawford was at her least mannered as a woman whose scarred face has embittered her towards society.

She was a novelist in *When Ladies Meet*, with Robert Taylor, generally considered inferior to the earlier version, and a career woman in another comedy, *They All Kissed the Bride* (42), with Melvyn Douglas at Columbia (it had been planned for Carole Lombard: Crawford gave her salary for it to the Red Cross, who had found Lombard's body). Then she helped the Resistance in mink: *Reunion in France* ('You are France,' says Philip Dorn. 'Whenever I think of France I think of you') and *Above Suspicion* (43). 'Undiluted hokum,' said she. 'If you think I made poor pictures after *A Woman's Face*, you should see the ones I went on suspension not to make!' (One of them was *Cry Havoc*.)

She left MGM. 'The consensus of opinion among the top brass was that I was washed up again,' and, indeed, it had been a long run by the prevailing standards. Warner Bros. signed her at a third of her MGM salary, but did not use her apart from a brief appearance in *Hollywood Canteen* (44) – GI Dane Clark falls down in a dead faint when he realizes he is dancing with *Joan Crawford*! Disturbed by rumours that they wanted to drop her, Crawford got hold of a script which Bette Davis had turned down (she said; Davis says not) and which was to go ahead with Barbara Stanwyck: *Mildred Pierce* (45). She talked producer Jerry Wald into letting her do it and seized her chance: as the waitress turned restaurateur who kills for her cherished but vicious daughter ('I don't know whether it's right or whether it's wrong but that's the way it's gotta be') she won a Best Actress Oscar.

Warners capitalized on the demand for her by making her the tough and bored society dame who takes up humble violinist John Garfield in *Humoresque* (46), though playing second fiddle to him: 'Bad manners,' she says admiringly, 'the infallible sign of talent.' Then they signed her for seven years at $200,000 per film, anxious perhaps to punish Bette Davis, who might have been their glory but was also the biggest thorn in their flesh. 'Variety' said, 'Crawford's back and MGM hasn't got her,' and Warners prepared to let their phoenix fly in the sort of stuff which had been Davis's dramatic beef: *Possessed* (47) – not a remake – with Van Heflin, as a schizophrenic; *Daisy Kenyon*, at 20th Century-Fox, with Henry Fonda, as a fashion designer ('I've got to be going somewhere, somewhere interesting – even if it's to the moon'); *Flamingo Road* (49), with Zachary Scott, as a carnival dancer; *It's a Great Feeling*, in a two-minute guest appearance, as herself; and *The Damned Don't Cry* (50), which took us back to Joan Crawford Plot No. 1, plus, happily, the appendages of Late Period Joan.

At Columbia, she was the overbearing house-proud *Harriet Craig*, somewhat more dislikeable than Rosalind Russell in the earlier version (*Craig's Wife*); back at Warners she was a politician in a dud comedy, *Goodbye My Fancy* (51). *This Woman Is Dangerous* (52) she has described as 'a cheap and corny one', the tale of a gangster's moll who is redeemed by the doctor (Dennis Morgan) who saves her life. Bosley Crowther's review referred to Crawford's 'stony charm' and thought 'the incredibly durable star' had 'a theatrical personality' which had 'now reached the ossified stage'.

Be that as it may, Crawford now asked to be released from her contract and Warners let her go for a fee of $200,000. (It had four more

The years roll by and Crawford is still in jewels and furs; the gun is new, but shows the greater toughness of middle-period Joan. Flamingo Road *(49) with Sydney Greenstreet.*

years to run, one film a year.) She set about becoming a producer and with a partner put together a thriller, *Sudden Fear*, which she took to RKO. It was so successful that it confounded the scoffers.

Amidst a fanfare of trumpets she returned to MGM for *Torch Song* (53), her first in colour and a rather trying effort about a Broadway actress who does not know what she wants and lives in solitary splendour stubbing out cigarettes all over the place. She danced, but her singing was dubbed by India Adams. Charles Walters, who directed, said that she was 'scared stiff. We had to have three vodkas before she would leave the dressing-room – and this was nine in the morning.' She went to Republic – at a fee of $200,000 – for a Freudian Western, *Johnny Guitar* (54), with Mercedes McCambridge, who records that the technicians applauded her at the end of one scene, which made Crawford 'mad – and she *was* the star of the picture. I guess if I were Joan Crawford I'd be mad if some Mamie Glutz horned in on my territory that way.' Said Sterling Hayden, who

co-starred: 'There is not enough money in Hollywood to lure me into making another film with Joan Crawford', and Nicholas Ray, who directed: 'As a human being, Miss Crawford is a very great actress.' Stories that eventually emerged told of Crawford's paranoiac jealousy, culminating in an incident when she was discovered very drunk on the highway where she was depositing McCambridge's wardrobe. She turned up in two more classics, the hysterically grim *Female on the Beach* (55), in which she thinks her lover (Jeff Chandler) is out to murder her; and the more deliberately funny *Queen Bee*, in which writer-director Ranald McDougall brilliantly exploited every aspect of the screen Crawford in her 'bitch' hat (this time *all* the characters wanted to murder her – with some justification).

She did another at Columbia, *Autumn Leaves* (56), as a spinster in love with a younger man, and then was in Britain to make *The Story of Esther Costello* (57), from Nicholas Monsarrat's novel. None of these made much of a splash and though Crawford's

A lesson in indestructibility: Berserk (67) *with Crawford and Diana Dors, of whom a wag once wrote (unjustly), 'Forgotten but not gone.' Crawford made certain it could never be said of her.*

place in the star hierarchy was unassailable, it was not surprising that she was offered nothing worthwhile till *The Best of Everything* (59) at 20th – and that was hardly the biggest part.

Then something unexpected happened: Robert Aldrich cast her and Davis as two ex-movie queens holed up in eccentric isolation: *Whatever Happened to Baby Jane?* (62). It was a box-office triumph, partly because of its 'horror' content. As a result Crawford was offered several similar pieces: *The Caretakers* (63), a melodrama about mental hospitals, as a Senior Nurse who taught her underlings judo (she was billed third, after Robert Stack and Polly Bergen!); *Straitjacket* (64) and *I Saw What You Did* (65), both programmers for William Castle. In the former she played an axe-murderess, in the latter the victim of a grim practical joke. In 1964 she and Davis began a follow-up to *Baby Jane* called *Hush Hush Sweet Charlotte*, but Crawford was taken ill and was replaced by Olivia de Havilland – a genuine illness according to director Aldrich, though he believes it was induced by the realization that hers was a supporting role. Production stills showed the new cast ostentatiously drinking Coca-Cola (Crawford had been a great propagandist for the rival, Pepsi-Cola, since marrying its head in 1956 – her fourth husband; she was widowed, but did much for Pepsi in a PR capacity).

In 1967 Crawford injudiciously appeared in two silly films: in one of the UNCLE films, *The Karate Killers* (a guest spot but wasted) and a British horror film, *Berserk*. She

became annoyed when journalists referred to such work as 'horror' films, but it is a question of definition: the British *Trog* (70) was supposed to be sci-fi. But there is no question: these were all programmers. She last appeared before the cameras when she replaced her adopted daughter Christina (who was ill) in a live afternoon soap opera emanating from New York: it was grotesque, of course, trying to play someone 40 years younger, but Joan bulldozed her way into the studio and would not be gainsaid.

She adored meeting her fans: Spencer Tracy once observed that she liked to have them follow her when she went shopping. In her memoir ('Portrait of Joan', 1962), she says of a visit to England in the 30s that her fans 'tore my evening coat off my back and I basked in their fond affection'. Hedda Hopper once said: 'She's cool, courageous and thinks like a man. She labours 24 hours a day to keep her name in the pupil of the public eye.' In the last years, when there were no offers, she became a recluse, drinking heavily; and died alone, in 1977. Christina Crawford wrote a memoir, 'Mommie Dearest', which became a bestseller and a film (81), with Faye Dunaway as Joan. The world now knew the star as a vicious, uncaring, unsparing mother, motivated only by publicity and selfishness, but the revelations were mild compared with those to come, which showed her possessed of a voracious sexual appetite which was not confined to the opposite sex. She would surely have preferred to be remembered as a bitch than not at all.

LAIRD CREGAR

Laird Cregar was one of the screen's best villains, a burly, stylish actor with a remarkable range; but his girth and height typed him. His studio saw him as a junior Sydney Greenstreet, but he brought compassion and understanding to the hackneyed roles he played. He never played a hero and he was only 28 when he died. He was born in Philadelphia in 1916, one of six brothers (fully grown, at 6 foot 3 inches, he was the smallest of them). He was educated at Winchester College, UK, as well as various US schools; he ran away from home at 13 and later did a variety of jobs – theatre bouncer, book salesman, etc. He won a scholarship to the Pasadena Community Playhouse but when, later, money ran out, he slept in a parked car and depended on friends for food. He got bit parts in Warners' *Granny Get Your Gun* (40) and Universal's *Oh Johnny How You Can Love*. In 1940 he managed to persuade a local

Laird Cregar as The Lodger (*44*). *Note the bag: slowly the family with whom he is staying will begin to realise that it contains the scalpels of Jack the Ripper.*

Linda Darnell and Laird Cregar in Hangover Square (*45*), *a study of a schizophrenic composer compelled to murder every time he hears a wrong note. It was Cregar's last film.*

company to put on 'Oscar Wilde' with himself as Oscar: the Los Angeles press gave him rave notices, 20th signed him and began to build him – it did not need much: from his first entrance in *Hudson's Bay*, as a French fur-trapper, here was clearly an actor of authority. He had a small part in *Blood and Sand* (41), as an aficionado of the bull ring, then demonstrated a fine comedy technique as Sir Francis Chesney in *Charley's Aunt*; but he first came into his own on the screen as the sinister detective in *I Wake Up Screaming*, with his pathetic crush on the murdered girl (Carole Landis). He was loaned to RKO for *Joan of Paris* (42) as the head of the Paris secret police; played a confidence trickster in *Rings on Her Fingers*; was loaned to Paramount for *This Gun for Hire*, as the double-crossing boss-man who hires the gun (Alan Ladd); and was the martinet major in charge of the *Ten Gentlemen From West Point*.

In *The Black Swan* he was Captain Henry Morgan, Tyrone Power's ally, and he brought more accomplishment than it deserved to *Hello Frisco Hello* (43), playing the hero's friend, an adventurer whose sudden fortune at the end brings smiles all round; but he was at home in the elegance of Lubitsch's *Heaven Can Wait*, as the devil, with Don Ameche. He was bearded as a tyrannical art-dealer in *Holy Matrimony*, with Monty Woolley, and was *The Lodger* (44) – otherwise Jack the Ripper – in a creepy adaptation of Mrs Belloc-Lownde's thriller, loping through the gaslit fog-bound streets of a Hollywood Whitechapel in search of his prey. As a follow-up 20th took Patrick Hamilton's novel *Hangover Square* (45), set it back to the turn of the century and cast the top-billed Cregar as a schizophrenic who murders Linda Darnell between composing concerti. In the book the protagonist had been a gentle fellow with a few complexes and because that was what he wanted to play, Cregar had brought the novel to the studio's attention. He reluctantly accepted the changes, but because he did not want to be the new Chaney or Karloff he started dieting with a view to surgery which would make him into leading man material. His heart was fatally weakened and he died in 1944. In a fond tribute in 'Picturegoer', its Hollywood correspondent W.H. Mooring described him as 'somewhat eccentric'.

BING CROSBY

It could be argued that no one in the history of mankind has given so much pleasure to so many people as Bing Crosby, not even Chaplin (who was perhaps the pioneer of popularity when the era of mass communications began). During the 10-year peak of Crosby's film career he was consistently voted the most popular actor and nine of his films remain in 'Variety's' all-time grossers, a record unequalled till more recent years of exorbitant seat prices – and smaller audiences. He was also for 15 years one of the very top attractions of radio and from *circa* 1930 onwards the greatest seller of records of his time: 20 of his discs have sold a million copies or more, and one of them, 'White Christmas', is far and away the biggest seller of the century at 30 million copies – out of a total Crosby sale of over 350 million.

Crosby himself attributed most of his success to good fortune. He was modest about his singing and of his acting he said (in a memoir, 'Call Me Lucky', 1953): 'Once or twice I've been described as a light comedian. I consider this the most accurate description of my abilities I've ever seen. That's just about all I am, a light comedian. I'm not a very funny fellow and I'm not a very serious fellow either. Nor do I give off a terribly romantic aura' – a summing-up of his screen image which is totally in keeping with it: amiable, unassuming, casual, charming. Maybe what attracted people to him was that they wanted to be like that, just as easy. Or maybe, as Ella Fitzgerald once said, there is nothing as relaxing as watching Bing Crosby. James Agee wrote in 1945: 'I would enjoy Crosby . . . probably even if he did nothing more than walk across a shot.'

It was one of the movies' most accomplished acts. Gary Cooper was once asked (by Rock Hudson) why the stars were such 'terrific people' and after a moment's thought he agreed, 'Yes, I suppose we are, the ones who are on top. But watch out for the ones who haven't quite made it, or are past it.' Crosby made it, but you had to watch out for him. He was ruthlessly ambitious and many colleagues of his band days resented all his life his ingratitude. He could be a friendly fellow, but many found him distant, self-seeking and vain. These may be positive qualities in a *star*, but in this case they are at extreme odds with the movie persona.

He was born in Tacoma, Washington, in 1901. He studied at Gonzaga University, but there was nothing he fancied so much for a living as singing and in 1921 he teamed up with Al Rinker, 'Two Boys and a Piano – Singing Songs Their Own Way'. Some years later they were taken up by Paul Whiteman, who added Harry Barris to the act and rechristened it 'Paul Whiteman's Rhythm Boys'. Crosby also did some solo recordings and made a Pathé short, *Two Plus Fours*: on the strength of both factors he was signed by

Mack Sennett to make some shorts built around songs he was making popular ('Please', 'Just One More Chance', 'I Surrender Dear'). Around the same time he made his feature début in *King of Jazz* (30), with the Rhythm Boys (he should have had a big solo number, 'Song of the Dawn', but when it was due to be filmed he was in gaol for drunken driving and it went to John Boles). He appeared as one of the Rhythm Boys in *Check and Double Check* and sang solo, billed eighth, in *Reaching for the Moon*; he became famous overnight when he was given his own radio show (1931). That coupled with a crowd-pulling season at the Paramount, New York, and favourable reviews for the Sennett shorts caused Paramount to offer him a three-year contract at $300,000 for five films. He played himself in *The Big Broadcast* (32) and the 'New York American' said: 'Bing Crosby is the star, make no mistake about it. The "Blue of the Night" boy is a picture personality, as he demonstrated in his two-reelers. He has a camera face and a camera presence. Always at ease, he troupes like a veteran.'

Two years later he was voted for the first time one of the 10 biggest draws in films. Usually playing a singer or a songwriter, he made an average of three films a year during the 30s, mainly distinguishable now by their songs (which were good, but not of the calibre Astaire was getting at RKO) and by first-class supporting talent, something that he insisted upon. Jack Oakie, Burns and Allen, Mary Carlisle and Richard Arlen supported him in *College Humor* (33), fortunately for 'Picture-goer', who thought his 'screen personality and histrionics negligible'. He improved: through *Too Much Harmony* with Oakie; *Going Hollywood*, on loan to MGM and Marion Davies; *We're Not Dressing* (34), with Carole Lombard, Ethel Merman and Burns and Allen, as 'Crichton' in this totally revamped version of the Barrie play; *She Loves Me Not* with Miriam Hopkins; *Here Is My Heart* with Kitty Carlisle; *Mississippi* (35) with W.C. Fields, a new version of Booth Tarkington's 'Magnolia'; *Two for Tonight*; and *The Big Broadcast of 1936*, with Oakie, Charlie Ruggles and Mary Boland. He was one of the roster of guest stars, with just one song. His contract expired again and Paramount were anxious to renew it – but Crosby's business manager, his brother Everett, would only agree to another three-year deal, two pictures a year with the possibility of another – either there or at another studio. The vehicles which Paramount had fashioned for Crosby had all been enjoyable but the next batch were even better, beginning with *Anything Goes* (36), a splendid version of the Cole Porter musical with Merman, directed by Lewis Milestone; and *Rhythm on the Range*. At Columbia he had one of his biggest successes, *Pennies From Heaven*, with Madge Evans and Louis Armstrong; and with *Waikiki Wedding* (37) and *Double or Nothing* he made it to fourth in the box-office 10 that year. *Doctor Rhythm* (38) was a very good one (based on an O. Henry story) with Crosby involved with an heiress and aunt Beatrice Lillie; Louis Armstrong was again in the cast.

In his early films Crosby always serenaded the heroine: here she's Marion Davies in Going Hollywood (33). *The brunette onlooker is Fifi D'Orsay.*

Bing Crosby and Marjorie Reynolds in Holiday Inn *(42), a genial musical with a score of Irving Berlin songs including, for the first time, 'White Christmas', here being reprised for the finale.*

Between songs in *Sing You Sinners* he had some straight acting to do and did it very well. Otherwise he was polishing up his comedy technique: *Paris Honeymoon* (39) with Franciska Gaal and Shirley Ross; or doing a bit of both: in *East Side of Heaven*, a sentimental comedy at Universal with Joan Blondell, and *The Star Maker*, a biography of Gus Edwardes, whose songs were sung though his name was not mentioned. Edwardes apparently produced kiddie-shows and since this was the great age of child-stars, this film has a Durbin imitator (and when Crosby returned to Universal it was to co-star with Gloria Jean, kept as a threat to that young lady).

Crosby needed everything he knew about comedy when he came up against Bob Hope. They had been friends for some time, but their teaming came about by chance, when Fred MacMurray refused a vehicle for him and George Burns: *Road to Singapore* (40). A fairly nondescript script with the two of them in pursuit of Dorothy Lamour, it became funny due to their empathy, a spontaneity and free-wheeling in their playing, and according to the 'Motion Picture Herald', it was the year's most popular film. *If I Had My Way* at Universal and *Rhythm on the River* with Mary Martin did well and Crosby came in again in the Golden 10. He had signed again with Paramount in 1938 and at this point another three-year deal was arranged, for nine films, at $175,000 each, plus again one outside movie if he so wished. In addition he earned annually $7,500 from radio and about $75,000 from records. Paramount reunited him with Hope and Lamour for *Road to Zanzibar* (41)

and this time there were no holds barred, a deliberately silly story that was a spoof of the jungle films that Lamour usually made and a zany, funny film. Bing and Bob ad-libbed much more: and the film gave them a sharp push towards the stratospheric popularity that was to be theirs for more than a decade. *Birth of the Blues* with Mary Martin was one of Crosby's own favourites and then came a real big one, *Holiday Inn* (42), with Fred Astaire and a fine Irving Berlin score, including 'White Christmas', ubiquitous in the autumn of that year and every Christmas since. In between entertaining the troops, he hit the road for the third time, *Road to Morocco* (43); guested with top-billing in *Star Spangled Rhythm*, singing 'Old Glory' at the climax; and played songwriter Dan Emmett in *Dixie* with Lamour, his first in colour.

At the end of the year he was No 4 at the box-office and the following year he reached No 1, a position he held for the next four years in both the US and Britain (except in 1946, there, when James Mason just edged him out). Helping him get there was *Going My Way* (44), though it was only made in the first place because the producer-director was the esteemed Leo McCarey. Perhaps its most popular aspect was the antagonism between the new young (singing) priest and an older one – Barry Fitzgerald at his most cantankerous. Both of them won Oscars and the Academy and the New York critics thought it the year's Best Picture. Said the 'New York Times': 'Old Bing is giving the best show of his career. That's saying a lot for a performer who has been one of the steadiest joys of the screen'; and the 'Spectator' (London): 'Yet the whole production turns about the increasing virtuosity of Mr Crosby. We have watched him develop from an anonymous jazz-band voice to the screen's friendliest actor.' The performance was further endorsed by the year's 'Picturegoer' Gold Medal.

Playing someone like himself he was pursued by two Betty Huttons in a patriotic musical, *Here Come the Waves*, and otherwise the best thing about that is that it inspired no similar tribute to the WACs: He did a sketch and sang one song in an opus based on a radio show, *Duffy's Tavern* (45). 'Variety' gave him one of the rare front-page banner headlines devoted to a performer: 'Bing's Bangup Box Office in '45' and called him 'the hottest guy in showbiz today'. Paramount negotiated a new deal, and it was to run for seven years, with a considerable salary increase (he had got $125,000 for *Going My Way*: most studios used the war to cut actors' salaries). His annual earnings had risen from $260,000 in 1940 ('Variety' estimate) to $868,000 in 1946 ('Fortune' estimate). Paramount was under-

The man usually just called 'Bing' throughout his career. Stills like this helped to sell not only Paramount pictures, but sheet music as well.

standably reluctant to let Crosby do an outside picture, but he went to RKO for the sequel to *Going My Way*, since McCarey had arrived from that studio insisting that only Crosby could play Father O'Malley: and RKO's price for that loan was Crosby in return. His co-star in *The Bells of St Mary's* was Ingrid Bergman, as a nun: 'If you're ever in trouble dial O for O'Malley' he told her. The film did even better than the first one: they wound up at third and fourth among the most successful yet made (beaten only by *This Is the Army* and *Gone With the Wind*). *Road to Utopia*, actually set in Alaska, had been completed almost two years earlier, but had been held up both by the expectation of an Oscar nomination (proving that Crosby was a serious actor) and by a backlog of more topical pictures: its release proved that Paramount had been sitting on a gold mine in both senses. Bonanza-time continued with *Blue Skies* (45), a reunion with Astaire and Irving Berlin which 'Time' called 'a $3 million Technicolored exhibition of Old Masters'; and there was a warm welcome for *Welcome Stranger* (47), formula stuff with Fitzgerald, as opposing doctors. *Variety Girl* was the third and last of the studio's all-star pieces, like the others presenting the place as cheerful and paternal with stars as special beings – and especially nice. 'Nice fellow' says a starlet of Bing, which was the way Paramount wanted everyone to think of him. He did not sing in it, but he did a warm-up with Hope – for *Road to Rio*, which later in the year continued that series in strength. *The Emperor Waltz* (48) was much seen but not much liked, a cynical Billy Wilder concoction – ersatz Lubitsch – with Crosby as an American at the court of Franz Joseph.

Then he was *A Connecticut Yankee in King Arthur's Court* (49), his first really poor film for years. An Irish comedy with Fitzgerald, *Top of the Morning*, was even worse, but there was a return to form with *Riding High* (50), Capra's remake of his own *Broadway Bill* – and an improvement, he thought, since Crosby (unlike Warner Baxter) really liked horses. He also said: 'Bing Crosby is not an easy man to know. In virtually everything he does . . . he is relaxed as a cat stretched out in the sun. But if you let that lazy, old-shoe casualness fool you into thinking the Bingle doesn't know what's going on – you're living in a dream world. His wit can devastate you.' Capra also observed that Crosby had always had a good press, but in Hollywood his reputation was more controversial; that within Paramount, for instance, he was regarded as unreliable because he liked to go off to play golf, or come in late. Crosby certainly began to show up on time for him and must have taken note of the changes in Hollywood over the next few years: Charles Walters, directing him later in *High Society*, said 'Bing is a hell of a worker – if you put in a call for 8.30, he's there at 8.00.' *Mr Music* was another remake – of *Accent on Youth* – and it was witness to the studio's dilemma when confronted with a very big star now facing middle age: Nancy Olsen was the youngster with a crush on him. Crosby disliked the title and so, apparently, did the public, for Crosby had slipped from the top spot. He was reunited with Capra for *Here Comes the Groom* (51) with Jane Wyman, who gave him a career high spot when they duetted 'In the Cool, Cool, Cool of the Evening'. The two stars established such a good offscreen rapport that they were reunited in *Just for You* (52), in which she helped him, a big Broadwayite, solve his problems with his teenage kids. Then the old team had a hit when they hit the *Road to Bali*, for which Hope and Crosby had contributed one-third each of the budget: but more than one critic pointed out that it was rather like two indulgent uncles and an aunt dressed up for a children's party.

To the horror of Marghanita Laski, Crosby was cast in the film of her novel about an American searching for his son in Europe years after the war, *Little Boy Lost* (53), but after she had seen it, she admitted she had been wrong (even though he still sang four songs). After an interval, he sang a lot of songs, and they were Berlin's, in *White Christmas* (54): his sidekick was Danny Kaye and there must have been something right about the teaming, for the public flocked to it and it still gets huge ratings on TV in the US (other countries found the mawkish patriotism considerably embarrassing). Crosby had announced his retirement after this, but the offers were too attractive. For him, the leading role in the film of Odets's *The Country Girl* was changed from has-been actor to broken-down musical star: he acted with considerable emotional depth and got great notices. Grace Kelly was in it, and William Holden, and it was a hit; but his last for Paramount, a remake of *Anything Goes* (56) with Mitzi Gaynor and Donald O'Connor, was weak in every respect. Then came what was to be his last film success – at a fee of $200,000 plus 5 per cent of the gross: *High Society* (56), and his last big record hit, 'True Love' – his twentieth Golden Disc; there was a Cole Porter score and a lot more going for it – Grace Kelly, Sinatra, Celeste Holm. And as with *The Country Girl*, his co-stars were considered bigger factors in its sucesss than he – by exhibitors.

Perhaps he should have capitalized on its success, but instead he did a serious film (he sang only over the credits): *Man on Fire* (57), as a divorced man squabbling with his ex-wife over their son. It was generally disregarded by the press and lit no fires at the box-office, which was a pity for Crosby's 'spontaneous' rendering of 'urgent' dialogue gave a pale tale class. But if 1957 marked a low in his professional life, privately things were better when he married starlet Kathryn Grant. In a later interview he admitted that the previous years had been tough. His wife since 1930, ex-star Dixie Lee, had died, an alcoholic, in 1953; his grown sons had reputations as roisterers; and it was believed he was morose about the course his career had taken. He had, he said, been reading deeply and learning languages; and then his new wife presented him with a family.

His film career, however, never again got moving. He produced and starred in two films for 20th: *Say One for Me* (59), as a priest again, and *High Time* (60), as a middle-aged college freshman; there was nothing to tempt old admirers from fireside TV and the young players in both did not attract young cinemagoers. his marvellous lazy singing style was out of fashion, pushed out by the frenetic phrasing of Sinatra; but it was curious that

Crosby, a millionaire several times over, had not commissioned better material. It must have seemed a good idea to do *The Road to Hong Kong* (62) and indeed the public went to it, but it was a pale shadow of past glories.

There had been guest appearances in 1960 in *Let's Make Love* and *Pepe*; and, though he was working often in TV, he wanted to film again and asked Sinatra for a small role in *Robin and the Seven Hoods* (64), a comedy about Chicago in the Prohibition days. He had three songs, in one of which Sinatra and Dean Martin chided him for not having 'Style': but he showed them, leaving them further back than was intended – right at the starting post. He was also the best thing about the remake of *Stagecoach* (66), as the tippling doctor: but when he was not on screen it was not worth watching and the reviews killed any box-office potential it may have had.

Film offers were not lacking and included the Lee Marvin role in *Paint Your Wagon*, which he refused because he did not want to do location work; he appeared regularly on TV and turned down the lead in the series 'Colombo', which Peter Falk played. He played a kindly doctor in a horror movie for TV, *Dr Crook's Garden* (70), and towards the end of his life began again doing personal appearances, clearly to see whether he still retained his following. SRO houses and glowing press notices proved that he did; and at the London Palladium he proved in better voice than ever – one of the very few exceptions to the rule that all performers should be forcibly retired in middle age. He also played New York and, after a return engagement in London, died, on a golf course in Spain, in 1977. There was to have been another 'Road' picture with Hope and Crosby playing their ages, but it was not perhaps a good idea.

BEBE DANIELS

Bebe Daniels had a long career in Silent pictures and made the transition to Talkies with ease, though Talkies hardly utilized her talent. She was not yet 30, but in the roles they gave her she was usually somewhat passée: a grande dame, an adventuress. Her playing was incisive, but she was able only to hint at the impishness and warmth that had made her such an appealing Silent comedienne.

She was born in Dallas, Texas, in 1901, of a Scottish father and Spanish mother; both were on the stage and at three Bebe was appearing in her father's stock company, as one of the Princes in 'Richard III', billed as

'The World's Youngest Shakespearian Actress'. Two years later she was on the Los Angeles stage in 'The Squaw Man' and then in the film version (06); at seven she was in 'The Common Enemy' and repeated in the film version (08) for Selig-Polyscope. She got into pictures because her mother was casting director for Kalem and other companies: she was considered to have 'kid-appeal'. She also found time to get some education at the Sacred Heart Convent in LA. She left – at 13 – when she heard that Hal Roach at Pathé was looking for a leading lady and she presented herself for an interview. She was taken on at $10 a week – which went to $25, $50 and then $100 – and she made over 200 two-reel comedies with Snub Pollard and Harold Lloyd: she was in most of the 'Lonesome Luke' series with Lloyd, featured as 'the charming little comedienne'. She and Lloyd were often seen together socially and won several dancing contests. Cecil B. De Mille saw them at Santa Monica and offered Daniels a contract, but she refused because her contract with Roach had a year to run. When it expired (her last short with Lloyd was either *Just Neighbors* or *Captain Kidd's Kids*) she approached De Mille, who signed her to a four-year contract starting at $1,000 a week. Most of her films during that period were made for Realart, a subsidiary of Paramount, for whom De Mille worked. When the deal expired, Paramount signed Daniels to a long-term contract: thus, in effect, she worked for that company from 1919 to 1928. Her first picture for De Mille was *Male and Female* (19) and she had only a tiny bit as Thomas Meighan's concubine in the Babylon sequence. She was Vice in *Everywoman*, a modern morality tale, and the Other Woman in *Why Change Your Wife?* (20) with Meighan and Gloria Swanson. Then she achieved star status, or at least was the leading woman: Sam Wood's *Dancin' Fool* and *Sick Abed*, both with Wallace Reid; *The Fourteenth Man*, based on 'The Man From Blankley's; *You Never Can Tell*, which had no connection with the Shaw play; *Oh Lady Lady*, as a small-town girl who makes it on Broadway; *Two Weeks With Pay* (21), in a dual role; *She Couldn't Help It*, a remake of Mary Pickford's *In the Bishop's Carriage*; *Ducks and Drakes*, *The March Hare* and *One Wild Week*, a triology of comedies directed by Maurice Campbell, in which she was a madcap heiress; and De Mille's *The Affairs of Anatol* (21), based on Schnitzler's play, with Reid, and playing a vamp called Satan Synne.

In 1921 she was caught speeding by the county police and spent 10 days in gaol, which occasioned a bonanza of publicity, not all of it unfavourable: it turned out to be a rather

luxurious 10 days and Realart capitalized on the event by rushing her into a movie about a movie queen who goes to gaol, *The Speed Girl*. She was an orphan in *Nancy From Nowhere* (22) and a señorita in *A Game Chicken*. *North of the Rio Grande* was a Western with Jack Holt and *Nice People* a version of a play by Rachel Crothers: ironically, it cast Daniels as a hard-drinking flapper and Reid as the innocent Westerner – one of his last pictures before dying of drug addiction. She did *Pink Gods* with James Kirkwood; *Singed Wings* with Conrad Nagel; and *The World's Applause* (23), whose plot bore more than a passing resemblance to another recent scandal – the murder of William Desmond Taylor, with Daniels as the star who, like Mary Miles Minter, was ruined thereby. She was increasingly cast as a playgirl, a cross between Gloria Swanson of a year or two before and Joan Crawford or Clara Bow to come – not too flippant, not too worldly: *The Glimpses of the Moon*, from Edith Wharton's novel, hunting romance in Europe with Nita Naldi; *The Exciters* with Antonio Moreno; and *His Children's Children*, with Dorothy Mackaill as her equally jazz-mad sister.

She then did a Zane Grey Western, *Heritage of the Desert* (24); was loaned out for *Daring Youth*; and did *Unguarded Women* with Dix, a study of a 'reckless, anchorless girl of today' ('Picturegoer'). She was Valentino's leading lady in *Monsieur Beaucaire* and was stuck on a desert island with Richard Dix in *Sinners in Heaven*. Her first official starring picture was *Dangerous Money* – she inherited it – with Tom Moore. It was a mild box-office success and so were those that followed: *Argentine Love* with Ricardo Cortez, a romance of what the fan-mags called 'tangoland'; *Miss Bluebeard* (25), as a French actress in London with two husbands plus Raymond Griffith; *The Crowded Hour*, from a play about an actress who leaves her career for the man she loves – fighting in France; *The Manicure Girl*, who discovers that wealth is not everything; *Wild Wild Susan* with Rod La Rocque; *Lovers in Quarantine* with Alfred Lunt and Harrison Ford; *The Splendid Crime* with Neil Hamilton; *Miss Brewster's Millions* (26), the old comedy with a sex-change to accommodate her; *Volcano*, a tropical melodrama with Cortez; *The Palm Beach Girl*, a silly comedy about a first visit to the sea; *The Campus Flirt* and *Stranded in Paris*, both with James Hall.

Gloria Swanson and Pola Negri remained Paramount's top two stars; but Daniels made a good third. Like them, she was photographed in all manner of exotica – lace, feathers, jewels. 'Let who will be good but

Bebe will be beautiful' said one caption. But she was warmer, more approachable – almost like middle-period Myrna Loy, but more reckless and often in risqué situations. 'Picturegoer' at one point was worried that she was becoming 'the screen's leading male impersonator'. She was certainly Paramount's principal light comedienne and got the pick of the comic scripts. All of them were directed by Clarence Badger and some were very good; *A Kiss in a Taxi* (27); *Senorita*, at one point as a fiery Spaniard, and *Swim Girl Swim*, both with Hall; *She's a Sheik* (28), kidnapping Foreign Legionnaire Richard Arlen; *The Fifty-Fifty Girl*, sharing ownership of a mine with Hall; and *Hot News*, as a newspaper photographer, with Neil Hamilton and Paul Lukas. Then: Gregory La Cava's *Feel My Pulse* with Arlen, as a pill-bred beauty in a sanatorium used secretly by bootleggers; and *Take Me Home* and *What a Night!*, both with Hamilton. With the coming of Talkies her star at Paramount tottered and fell: other studios wanted to nurture their stars through the Talkie period, but Paramount wanted to drop theirs, whom they considered overpriced, in favour of the stage talent they were importing. They did not put Daniels in a Talkie, nor even test her; after some months of inactivity, she bought up the remaining nine months of her contract.

At RKO erstwhile Paramount producer William Le Baron was in charge of production. He had heard Daniels sing privately at parties and signed her for the lead in a

Bebe Daniels was John Barrymore's secretary in Counsellor at Law *(33), based on Elmer Rice's play about a hectic day in the life of same.*

production that tried to transfer to the screen the lavishness and glamour of a Ziegfeld show – in fact, a Ziegfeld musical, *Rio Rita* (29). Hollywood thought it an impetuous step as Daniels was considered all washed up; but it turned out that she not only spoke effectively, but had a soprano voice of warmth and charm. She had to speak wiz a heavee Spaneesh accent, playing a ranch-owner who falls in love with the head (John Boles) of the Texas Rangers, out on a manhunt. RKO had not been able to afford her salary – $5,000 weekly at Paramount – so asked her to take a percentage: so she did well when the film became one of the year's biggest grossers, at $2 million. As Hollywood hastened to congratulate Daniels and RKO, Paramount executives sat red-faced. 'You didn't tell us you could sing,' they said reprovingly to Daniels. 'You never asked me,' she replied. She began a new career at RKO: *Love Comes Along* (30) with Lloyd Hughes, where she sang; and *Alias French Gertie*, an agreeable crook melodrama where she and Ben Lyon were partners in crime – until they went straight. In life, they were married, and columnists predicted it would not last: he had just reached the top after years as a feature player and she, despite *Rio Rita*, was considered part of the former generation. Also, the very happiness of the marriage conflicted with the public image: stars like Daniels were not (yet) expected to settle for domesticity. Her screen image was one of glamour – as in the remake of *Lawful Larceny*, in which she had to compete with the

vamp who had stolen her husband, in the process outwitting the crooked Lowell Sherman, who also directed. Reunited with some other principals from *Rio Rita*, including Wheeler and Wolsey, she did another lavish musical, *Dixiana*, but the public had had a surfeit of all-singing all-dancing extravaganzas. RKO blamed Daniels for its failure and dropped her.

She did not have to worry since Douglas Fairbanks wanted her to be his leading lady in *Reaching for the Moon* because he fancied doing a musical, but as musicals were now out of favour most of the Irving Berlin songs were cut. Warners then signed Daniels to play the fading beauty who falls in love with young Lyon in *My Past* (31): most of her past consisted of being Lewis Stone's mistress (it was from a bestseller called 'Ex-Mistress') and it was all very unconvincing, despite her alluring appearance. Warners liked her, however, and signed her to a contract: *The Maltese Falcon* with Cortez, in the part later played by Mary Astor; *The Honor of the Family*, said to be a modern version of Balzac, as an old man's seductress whose wiles are exposed by his nephew, Warren William; *Silver Dollar*, as the beauty for whom Edward G. Robinson leaves wife Aline MacMahon; and *42nd Street* (33), as the temperamental has-been actress whose inability to go on brings stardom to chorine Ruby Keeler. She really should have refused the role, for it was soon noted that she was no longer on the Warner contract list; and her last film on the lot was a programmer, *Registered Nurse*. Further, it was shelved for over a year.

In the meantime, like most stars on the decline in those days, she went to Columbia – *Cocktail Hour* with Randolph Scott – and Britain. BIP had invited her to do two musicals, *The Song You Gave Me*, with Victor Varconi, and *A Southern Maid*, Spaneesh again, in a dual role. She returned to Hollywood to play John Barrymore's faithful secretary in *Counsellor at Law*, but her excellence elicited no further offers. Nor did the 1934 release of that last film for Warners. Eventually Fox signed her to play another has-been actress, this time a movie actress touring in vaudeville who is replaced by Alice Faye when she gets the chance of a Hollywood come-back: *Music is Magic* (35). But there was no come-back in real life. She toured in 'Hollywood Holiday' and returned to Britain, ostensibly because the Lyons' nurse was planning to kidnap their baby daughter: but a three-week stint at the London Palladium was successful enough to keep them there. They also accepted a film offer, *Murder in the Stalls*, finally shown in 1939 as *Not Wanted on Voyage* – and not wanted was its eventual fate. Daniels did make another British picture and it was a slight improvement, *The Return of Carol Dean* (39), a mystery story.

By this time she and Lyon were established headliners in British music halls and in 1939 they did a revue at the Holborn Empire called 'Haw Haw!' which took them into the days of the blitz. During this period they began a BBC radio show, 'Hi Gang!' with Vic Oliver, and their snappy American style and their expertise made other comic shows look slow. Their publicity then and subsequently made much of the fact that, as American citizens, they had stayed to entertain the British during the dangerous days of the blitz, but there is no doubt that (*a*) the British became genuinely fond of them and (*b*) they became genuinely fond of their adopted country. They also worked for ENSA, trooped round factories doing a comedy act and singing; and Daniel's work for US servicemen, as organizer and entertainer, brought her in 1946 the US Medal of Freedom. She, Lyon and Oliver made a film based on their radio programme, *Hi Gang!* (41), about the same time as the Lyons were in a West End revue, 'Gangway'. Later Daniels appeared in the British edition of Cole Porter's 'Panama Hattie'.

They returned to Hollywood in 1945 when Lyon took up an executive position with 20th; in 1948 Daniels produced and wrote a low-budget comedy for Hal Roach, *The Fabulous Joe*. But they were homesick for Britain and Lyon negotiated a British job with 20th. In 1949 they began a second series of 'Hi Gang!'

but it did not repeat its earlier success; in 1950 they began a popular series, 'Life With the Lyons', whose cast included daughter Barbara and adopted son Richard. Daniels wrote most of the scripts and it became a TV series as well as spawning a couple of weak pictures, *Life With the Lyons* (53) and *The Lyons in Paris* (55): but it was in any case a dreadful series, unworthy of their work in the past.

In 1963 she had a stroke and was a long time in convalescence; but in the last year or so of her life was occasionally glimpsed at premières. She died in 1971. About a year later her widower, Lyon, married Marion Nixon, who had been a Fox contract-player in the early 30s.

MARION DAVIES

'And Marion never looked lovelier!' The line is reiterated by T.C. Jones in an otherwise unfunny sketch about Hollywood in the 30s. He is taking off Louella Parsons, ace film gossip of the Hearst press, and in that one line he evokes the whole bizarre saga of Parsons, William Randolph Hearst and Marion Davies, who was Hearst's protégée, mistress and lifelong companion. In this campy way – or as the original of the character played by Dorothy Comingore in *Citizen Kane* – is she remembered today. W.A. Swanberg writes in his biography of Hearst: '. . . it was Hearst's considered intention to make Miss Davies the greatest star in the nation'. Hearst lost, it was estimated, over $7 million in the attempt. He loved her with great devotion and would certainly have married her had his wife consented to a divorce; it was his penchant for romance – as well as glory – which prompted him to try to impose Davies on the public. Only a handful of her films made money. And yet in her Silent films she was an actress of considerable charm and a comedienne of some talent. Swanberg writes: 'Her friends, then and now, are unanimous in judging her an incredibly warm and winning personality – fun-loving, joyous, a born comedienne, wildly sentimental and generous.'

The relationship would presumably be accepted today by moviegoers in the same spirit as it was accepted at the time by Hollywood society and by the distinguished guests at their home, San Simeon; but the press of the period – not only Hearst's – never linked their names. The official publicity line on her was that she was Hollywood's leading bachelor girl.

She was born in Brooklyn in either 1897 or 1900 and educated in a convent, from where, apparently, she went straight into the chorus line of 'Chin-Chin'. Her father was a lawyer, but her brother-in-law was a theatrical producer – hence the show business ambitions. She was in the chorus of several shows, including an edition of the Ziegfeld Follies; she was also in a movie, *Runaway Romany* (17), directed by her brother-in-law, George Lederer. She played a gipsy girl adopted by a famous star – who turns out to be her real father at the end. 'Picturegoer' enthused: 'Miss Davies is petite, winsome, and altogether charming, at times a little reminiscent of Mary Pickford.' It is uncertain when the showgirl – a budding movie star and already a kept woman – made the acquaintance of newspaper tycoon Hearst, but by the beginning of 1918 he had decided that she was to become a great movie star – the greatest. He tutored her himself and had her tutored, and 'arranged' for her first starring vehicle, *Cecilia of the Pink Roses* (18), a tale about a slum girl at a posh finishing school. The Hearst press, which till then had evinced only a mild interest in films, was transformed overnight: all of Hearst's papers discovered 'a movie masterpiece' and they hailed a fabulous new star, 'a vision of loveliness', 'a bewitching beauty'. The other papers were markedly less enthusiastic.

He produced a serial for her, *Beatrice Fairfax*, and a few months later *The Burden of Proof* appeared, a silly story based on Sardou's 'Diplomacy' in which she was suspected of spying, and then *The Belle of New York* (19), from the stage success. She was a Salvation Army lass. Tom Milne has written (1967): 'She is the only thing worth watching in a creaky melodrama; her exquisite beauty shines through soulfully, and she acts with a restraint and repose rare at the time.' Next, she was Mary in *Getting Mary Married*, a girl who prefers love to money (an inheritance).

In 1919 Hearst formed an agreement with Adolph Zukor to release Marion Davies pictures through Paramount: the producing company was called Cosmopolitan and, though it was to make other pictures through the years apart from those with Davies, it was around her that the whole operation revolved. Milne's praise is mild compared to that of the Hearst columnists; instructions went out to all Hearst papers that Davies's name was to be mentioned in some way at least once in every issue.

The films that followed: *The Dark Star*, another espionage drama; *The Cinema Murder* (20), where she was a budding star torn between a wealthy old man and a poor young one; *April Folly*, where she outwitted some crooks; *The Restless Sex*, a sophisticated drama in the manner of Gloria Swanson – but the only thing restless was the audience,

Marion Davies as Mary Tudor (the one who married Louis XII of France) with Ruth Shepley in a successful historical film of 1922, When Knighthood Was in Flower.

thought the 'New York Times'; and *Buried Treasure* (21), about a girl who could divine where to find some during trances. Meanwhile, she had made her last stage appearance, in a revue with Ed Wynn. She now signed a new five-year contract with Cosmopolitan and made the following: *Enchantment*, as a silly young vamp 'cured' by a strategy of her father's; *Bride's Play* (22), in which she had a double role – a modern bride and a Norman one; *Beauty's Worth* – in which she learns just that when converted from simple Quaker to socialite; and *The Young Diana*, which was somewhat similar in theme – only it all turned out to be a dream. They all lost money, though one of the reasons was that Hearst insisted on the best for Davies, down to the smallest detail. *When Knighthood Was in Flower* cost the extraordinary sum of $1½ million, and Hearst commissioned Victor Herbert to write two special songs for cinemas that were playing the film: one was called 'The Marion Davies March'. Davies played Mary

Tudor, sister of Henry VIII (Lynn Harding), in a generally lively historical romp. It was good, but not quite as good as the Hearst press maintained: 'Marion Davies soars to new heights', 'Superlative performance by the talented star'. By some fluke it turned a profit, but the next one did not: *Adam and Eva* (23), in which she was a fast-spending girl who learns the value of money when her father's agent (T. Roy Barnes) gets her to work on a farm. The 'Kine Weekly' hesitated to recommend it 'even for halls where Marion Davies and Cosmopolitan Productions generally are popular. It will place a severe strain on the most unquestioning loyalty.'

Hearst and Zukor now split and Cosmopolitan moved over to the Goldwyn Co., where it made *Little Old New York*, in which the star had to dress up as a boy in order to inherit a fortune. Then: *Yolande* (24), a not unsuccessful attempt to repeat the success of *Knighthood* with Harding this time as Charles the Bold; *Janice Meredith*, another historical drama; *Zander the Great* (25), with Mary Pickford curls in this Western melodrama built around an unwanted baby; and a backstage story, *Lights of Old Broadway*. This, too, netted Hearst a profit, though, according to Bosley Crowther in his book on MGM, it was the only one to do so during the Cosmopolitan–MGM tie-up. Goldwyn had amalgamated with M and M to become MGM, whose head, Louis B. Mayer, made a proposal to Hearst, and it was a staggering

one: MGM would finance Cosmopolitan's films *and* pay Davies the unprecedented salary of $10,000 per week. Further, Hearst would get a percentage of the profits. It was tacitly understood that all MGM films would be getting as much publicity in Hearst's 22 papers as Davies (and certainly Hearst was also to contribute financially in some way).

Davies had, in fact, accumulated quite a following and they turned up in reasonable numbers to see her in the Ruritanian – or Graustarkian – *Beverley of Graustark* (26) – where she masqueraded as a boy again – a version of the popular novel, originally filmed in 1916; *The Red Mill* (27), an awful 'Dutch' effort; *Tillie the Toiler*, as a girl torn between love and the lure of wealth – an adaptation of a comic-strip; *The Fair Coed*, a college romance with Johnny Mack Brown; and J.M. Barrie's *Quality Street*, with Conrad Nagel. A propos that one and the Hearst columnists, Swanberg notes 'regardless of how colossal her previous pictures were, the latest ones were always greater'. (In Britain, of course, no one told 'Picturegoer' to describe the Davies performance as 'adorable'.) All the same, not enough people agreed. The trouble was that Davies was not suited to the virginal heroines, the dainty country maidens, the Mary Pickford parts, that Hearst wanted to see her in: her forte was light comedy, as she had demonstrated in *The Fair Coed*. That was sufficiently well received for Hearst to reluctantly agree to three more comedies. *The*

Playing a would-be movie star, Marion Davies mimics the grand manner of a screen queen in Show People *(28), one of the films which exploited her comic ability. Watching her are, left, William Haines (who retired from films and became a successful interior decorator) and Dell Henderson.*

Patsy (28) was also based on a comic-strip, a satire on family life with Davies as a flapper, doing very funny impersonations of Pola Negri, Mae Murray and Lillian Gish. King Vidor directed and the film did more for Davies than her last 10 films put together. She did well again in *The Cardboard Lover* with Nils Asther and even better in Vidor's *Show People*, designed as a burlesque on Gloria Swanson's career from slapstick to dramatic actress: it ended without much pungency, but Davies was amusing, especially with some more facial clowning.

Talkies were going to be a problem, because she stuttered. She half-completed a film version of a Broadway musical, *The Five O'Clock Girl*, but it was abandoned without explanation. Talkie audiences saw and heard her sing in *The Hollywood Revue of 1929* (29), in which she also danced on a drum. Her voice proved to be adequate in *Marianne*, a sentimental romance about a French girl and her two loves – an American soldier and her blind fiancé. She sang a couple of songs, but otherwise had little to do. The project was a favourite one of Hearst's and indeed they had made it as a Silent before redoing most of it with Sound. The next, *Rosalie*, was also from a Broadway musical (it had starred Marilyn Miller), but no completed version ever reached cinema screens. She was ineffectual in most of her Talkies. 'She has too few chances' was a constant plaint of reviewers, or else she was much too old for the roles in which she was cast: *Not So Dumb* (30) with Donald Ogden Stewart, as a 'dumb' blonde who sets out to impress the boss of her fiancé – a version of the Kaufman–Marc Connelly comedy, 'Dulcy'; *The Floradora Girl*, a wallow in nostalgia built around the old musical; *The Bachelor Father* (31), from a big stage hit, with C. Aubrey Smith as the father in question; *It's a Wise Child* with Lester Vail, in which she protected an unmarried friend by pretending her baby was hers; *Five and Ten* with Leslie Howard; and *Polly of the Circus* (32), an updated version of an old Silent favourite, with Clark Gable. She was also *Blondie of the Follies*, a girl from the wrong side of the tracks trying to make it in show business – and insiders gasped as she deserted her elderly sugar daddy for a younger man, Robert Montgomery. Then she was *Peg o' My Heart* (33), a Barriesque piece of whimsy done years before by Laurette Taylor and now updated and musicalized. Once again the public greeted the Davies movies with indifference, so to boost her appeal Paramount was raided for Bing Crosby and Gary Cooper, to co-star in *Going Hollywood* and *Operator 13* (34) respectively. Crosby says in his memoir that filming – only a little every day – was accompanied by dance bands and much drinking and a good deal of fun. Davies's hospitality in her studio bungalow was famous. Raoul Walsh, who directed *Going Hollywood*, said later: 'She was a great girl, she was terrific.'

But the bungalow was now to be dismantled and carted from Culver City to Burbank. The Hearst-Mayer rift began with *The Barretts of Wimpole Street*. Hearst and Davies insisted that it was just the ticket for her, but MGM (Thalberg and Mayer) had earmarked it for Norma Shearer. Davies insisted on testing, in a black wig, but Shearer played it. After the one with Cooper, Davies and Hearst took off for Europe and while they were 'doing' Versailles they decided that Marie Antoinette should be Davies's next role. Coincidentally, Thalberg had the same idea for Shearer. This time the dispute was acrimonious and Mayer decided to settle it by offering the subject to Hearst, providing he would pay the production costs. Hearst considered, and declined. He approached WB with what Jack L. Warner described as 'a multimillion-dollar proposition': Davies, Hearst, Cosmopolitan and bungalow settled on the Burbank lot.

Shearer's name was not mentioned in the Hearst press (nor for some years to come). It was announced that Davies would be making strong dramatic pictures, among them a life of Marie Antoinette and *Twelfth Night*, as Viola – though the failure of the other Shakespeare films put paid to that. Certainly *Page Miss*

This was the sort of part which William Randolph Hearst preferred to see Miss Davies in: Operator 13 *(34) with Gary Cooper. In Britain it was called* Spy 13.

Glory (35) was made to please Hearst. Like Bing Crosby before them, Dick Powell and Pat O'Brien went under the title for the pleasure of working with Davies and to prove what a big star she was; and the cream of Warners' supporting players supported. Moreover, the plot enabled her to do her comic cut-ups before becoming a raging beauty: audiences, like Hearst, were supposed to be impatient for the transformation, as a chambermaid is persuaded into impersonating a fictional beauty – described as an amalgam of Dietrich, Harlow and Kay Francis. In real life Davies fell for Powell, who was told to make himself scarce in case Hearst found out, but she was given him for her leading man in *Hearts Divided* (36), about that Bonaparte who fell for a Baltimore beauty and the only one of this quartet which is not a comedy. To show there were no hard feelings MGM loaned Gable and Robert Montgomery (admittedly in exchange for Paul Muni and Leslie Howard) for *Cain and Mabel* and *Ever Since Eve* (37) respectively. The former was a musical about a Broadway star and a prize–fighter engaged in a publicity romance, and the second about a venus who dons glasses to stop men making passes. Except when clowning, Davies remained ineffectual as a Talkie actress; make-up could no longer disguise the fact that with the years she was no longer passably pretty – and the organdie dresses and bouffant sleeves which Hearst so much liked were less suitable than ever. Still, given the chance to clown (as in *Eve*), she entered with a will and was modestly effective. Said Warner: 'It may surprise the dour prophets to know that they all brought in a solid profit.' However, Davies made no more pictures for WB or anyone else. Hearst in 1937 found himself in considerable financial difficulties and she came to his aid, dipping into her own hefty private fortune. It is not known whether either of them continued to nourish hopes of movie fame – she, probably not, for she had never had much ambition in that direction, but had humoured the old man.

He died in 1951 and within 24 hours the instructions regarding the daily mention of Davies's name were rescinded (it is doubtful whether, by this time, many readers remembered who she was). Four months later, she married: 'For the first time,' said one paper significantly. She died of cancer in 1961.

BETTE DAVIS

Provided you are taking the retrospective view, that old tag 'The First Lady of the Screen' – after examining all the contenders – belongs decisively and firmly to Bette Davis. Speaking of her great years, when she was not only gilt-edged box-office but in a variety of roles a wonder to the critics, Gene Ringgold has written ('The Films of Bette Davis') that her films 'comprise an admirable record, one that may never be equalled by another film actress'. When everything has been said against her, she remains unrivalled as a screen actress. She broke the old mould for female stars: she did not want to get up on that screen and be decorative, to be mysterious like Garbo, to be sympathetic like Janet Gaynor, to pose as an actress like Norma Shearer: she wanted to *act*, to illuminate for audiences all the women she found within her – waitresses, dowagers, spinsters, harridans, drunks. She fought to play them. All subsequent screen stars owe her a debt, in that she proved that an actress could be an excellent judge of material, and her dedication destroyed a lingering belief that stage acting was 'superior' to film acting. She once told a reporter that one of the reasons she worked so hard was because there were so few real actresses in films.

She never disappeared inside a part: she was too intense, too electric, too mannered (increasingly, as time went on), but she shaped her roles to herself, burying as much of herself as she could. The end result then – this 'admirable record' – is a bewildering gallery of screen portraits, a total of 10 Oscar nominations (beaten only by Katharine Hepburn), a reputation that a mostly latent tendency to ham cannot tarnish and an undiminishing army of admirers.

It has been a long career and she has written a ferociously intelligent book about it ('The Lonely Life', 1962). It all began in Lowell, Massachusetts, in 1908. She decided at school that she wanted to be an actress and studied at the John Murray Anderson school; from there she was employed with a stock company in Rochester, until its director, George Cukor, fired her. She got a job with the Provincetown Players, 'The Earth Between' (28), and then did a tour alternating 'The Wild Duck' (as Hedwig) and 'The Lady From the Sea' (as Boletta). After a spell in rep, her agent got her a leading role in 'Broken Dishes', a mild domestic comedy and a success; then she had another good part in 'Solid South'. During the first play she failed a Goldwyn screen test, but then she passed one for Universal, whose boss, Carl Laemmle, thought she might be right for the daughter in *Strictly Dishonorable*. He had not met her; when he did, he observed that she had 'as much sex-appeal as Slim Summerville'. This confirmed her fears that she would not fit into a Hollywood deeply committed to glamour and beauty. Still, she was getting $300 a week and did her best in the film they did put her into, *Bad Sister* (31), as the good sister. The response to this mousy little girl did not surprise Universal: there wasn't any. They gave her roles in *Seed* and *Waterloo Bridge*, loaned her out for a truly horrendous bucolic comedy, *Way Back Home* (32), and a routine Edgar Wallace melodrama, *The Menace*.

But she was getting wised up: she dyed her hair blonde for *The Menace*. According to most versions, a friend of George Arliss saw her in this and recommended her for the lead opposite him in *The Man Who Played God*; but Jack L. Warner insisted that she was recommended to him by a Warner talent scout when Universal dropped her. At all events, after a B for Capital, *Hell's House*, she was cast in the Arliss film and signed by Warners. Being Arliss's leading lady gave her status, but beyond that she clearly was talented. She supported Barbara Stanwyck in *So Big* and Ruth Chatterton in *The Rich Are Always With Us*, as 'the pest of Park Avenue'; was Warren William's chic leading lady in *The Dark Horse* and Richard Barthelmess's in *Cabin in the Cotton*, as a teenage tramp: Warner said there first appeared 'the magic quality that transformed this bland and not beautiful little girl into a great artist when she was playing bitchy roles'. She was a stenographer in *Three on a Match*, with showier roles for Joan Blondell and Ann Dvorak, but *20,000 Years in Sing Sing* (33) show-cased her as Spencer Tracy's moll; *Parachute Jumper* was a Fairbanks Jr programmer about the Depression; and in *The Working Man* she was a spoilt heiress reformed by Arliss.

She worked – very hard: much later she observed that the MGM stars were treated like queens and the Warner players like factory workers. She must have thrived on it. In each picture there was a little more confidence, a little more mastery. However, in what was to have been her first official starring picture, blonded-up again, most critics found her inadequate: *Ex-Lady*, 'a piece of junk', she said, 'my shame was only exceeded by my fury'. Nor did the public like it (having seen it two years earlier as *Illicit*). Studio publicity started to play her down again; but they kept her churning out programmers: *Bureau of Missing Persons*, a fast-

Bette Davis with Leslie Howard in Of Human Bondage (*34*), *the film that established her as one of the cinema's outstanding actresses: there was considerable surprise when she wasn't even nominated for an Oscar for it.*

paced thriller with Pat O'Brien, whose mistress she becomes while looking for her husband; *Fashions of 1934* (34), as a designer of them, a musical in which neither she nor William Powell sang; *The Big Shakedown*, a poor racketeer drama with Ricardo Cortez and Charles Farrell; *Jimmy the Gent*, a small role but she liked working with Cagney; and *Fog Over Frisco*, one of her best early performances, as a reckless society girl.

Director John Cromwell at RKO wanted to borrow her for *Of Human Bondage*, but Warners refused. She fought; she was desperate to do it. And did. As the vicious, grasping waitress who enslaves Leslie Howard, she gave 'probably the best performance ever recorded on screen by a US actress' ('Life'). Warners were delighted with the general acclaim and cast her in *The Case of the Howling Dog*. She flatly refused to do it and her hand was strengthened by the two films she had in the can (the second of them was in fact made before *Bondage*). Her performance as the *Housewife* (Ann Dvorak was her rival) was admired, but she got raves again for her work in *Bordertown* (35), as the two-timing wife who goes to pieces under the stress of having murdered (with dialogue like 'I thought I told you to stay out of my life' and 'We're riff-raff you and I. We belong together'); her mad scene in court, done more realistically than was usual, was particularly appreciated.

She petitioned John Ford for the role of Elizabeth in the *Mary of Scotland* he was preparing, but he refused. She and Warners made it up and they 'officially' starred her for the first time again: *The Girl From Tenth Avenue*. Like *Front Page Woman* (she was a reporter) and *Special Agent* (a quickie with Farrell) it did nothing for her, but then came *Dangerous*, a tenuous tale about a dipsomaniac ex-actress who throws a jinx on anyone who comes near her. She says she found the script maudlin and mawkish, but went to work on it: the performance today is both powerful and subtle, suggesting she would have been a great Hedda. The Oscar she got for it she (and others) thought was a consolation prize for not getting one the previous year (she thinks it should have gone to Hepburn for *Alice Adams*), but when both films are seen today, her performance in *Bondage* is revealed as conventional, despite the same attention to detail.

Surprisingly, the next was also first-rate: *The Petrified Forest* (36), as the girl in the sticks with a yen for France and poetry. Frank S. Nugent thought it 'demonstrates that she does not have to be hysterical to be credited with a grand portrayal', and it was also a landmark for Bogart and Leslie Howard.

After that, the critics thought she made much out of little with *Golden Arrow*, a comedy with George Brent, but she could do little with *Satan Met a Lady*, the second and worst of the three filmizations of 'The Maltese Falcon'. Her dissatisfaction with her material increased when the studio refused her a part in *Anthony Adverse* and instead cast her in *God's Country and the Woman*. God's country, she decided, could do without this particular woman. She was suspended and taken off salary, at which point Ludovic Toeplitz, one of the money-men in British films, approached her with an offer: a movie to be made in Italy with Douglass Montgomery and one in France with Chevalier – plus script approval.

She sailed to England to begin work, but Warners issued an injunction. She filed suit and the moguls in Hollywood waited anxiously for the verdict: She lost: her contract bound her to Warner Bros. and only Warner Bros. until 1942. They, generously, paid her share of the damages – and had also, in her absence, prepared some better scripts. *Marked Woman* (37) marked a turning point in more ways than one, even if her performance in this underworld melodrama was over-illustrious; she had a similar role in *Kid Galahad* as Edward G. Robinson's moll, not caring to look back on her past or daring to look to the future. In *It's Love I'm After* she and Leslie Howard were a squabbling thespian couple and *That Certain Woman* was a gangster's widow starting afresh: 'Photoplay' found her 'exerting every ounce of her undeniable ability to turn sheer melodrama into legitimate melodrama', which must have pleased Edmund Goulding, who directed this version of his earlier *The Trespasser* after suggesting it as a vehicle to display her range. She had welcomed the film with Howard for the same reason, but when Warners suggested another comedy, *Hollywood Hotel* (in a dual role: sisters Rosemary and Lola Lane substituted), she reasonably declined on the ground that one slapstick role was enough for the time being.

Then, with *Jezebel* (38), began the great series of Davis vehicles, as smooth as limousines, elegantly crafted, designed to display every facet of her talents. Whether or not she chose *Jezebel* in order to urge herself to the forefront in the Scarlett O'Hara sweepstakes, the two parts have much in common: this was another beguiling novelette about a wilful Southern belle, directed for considerably more than it was worth by William Wyler. To him and Fay Bainter (suberb as an aunt) Davis gave credit for her performance. Said Freda Bruce Lockhart: 'By the pure power of imaginative acting she gives a performance as

vivid and inspiring as any star display of personality – and an infinitely deeper level of truth.' James Shelley Hamilton commented that Davis was 'growing into an artistic maturity that is one of the wonders of Hollywood'. She won a second Oscar and so, coincidentally, did Spencer Tracy, which prompted the 'New York Times' to refer to them as the King and Queen of American films. Her salary at this time, she has said, was $640 per week: but this is unlikely in view of the fact that her 1938 earnings were listed as $143,458 – still low for a star of her standing.

She was still battling for material; she was suspended again for refusing two scripts, but was satisfied with *The Sisters*, a period piece with Errol Flynn, bought originally for Kay Francis; and she loved *Dark Victory* (39), a hollow but likeable story about a spoiled society girl going blind and a 'Picturegoer' Gold Medal winner for her. She did not care for *Juarez* after Paul Muni had cut down her part and Brian Aherne's, as Maximilian, and beefed up his own. Still, she was impressive as Carlotta. Then she did the title-role in Edith Wharton's *The Old maid*, with Miriam Hopkins. Graham Greene wrote: 'Great actresses choose old mediums and perhaps Miss Davis is a great actress. Her performance . . . is of extraordinary virtuosity – as the young girl, as the secret mother, and the harsh prim middle-aged woman'. The film was one

of the year's top money-makers. She was with Flynn again in her first (and only, till the 50s) colour picture, *The Private Lives of Elizabeth and Essex*. It has odd conceits (the Queen visiting Essex in the Tower), but with entirely the wrong-shaped face Davis managed an uncanny resemblance to the Queen and she dominated the film as Elizabeth had her court. Peter John Dyer observed that by this time her 'mannered emotionalism had acquired an added dimension of more disciplined restraint. She had become the mistress of the dry, disillusioned inflection and telling, angular gesture, and it is these qualities, together with a ribald wit, that makes this story of Elizabeth and Essex so compulsively viewable.'

'Fortune' magazine's popularity poll noted that Davis had supplanted Shirley Temple as America's favourite star and the exhibitors' poll confirmed it; in 1940 she was voted the Queen of Hollywood (Mickey Rooney was King). These triumphs made it easier to get her own way and what she got was pretty good: an outstanding film version of Rachel Field's bestselling sob-story, *All This and Heaven Too* (40), about a governess in love with the Master (Charles Boyer); *The Letter*, also improved from book to film, a superb melodrama from Maugham's pot-boiler, with Wyler getting from Davis what has been described as 'very likely the best study of

The Private Lives of
Elizabeth and Essex (39):
Bette Davis presides at the
conference table. Left to
right, Henry Daniell,
Henry Stephenson, Ralph
Forbes, Errol Flynn, Leo
G. Carroll.

female sexual hypocrisy in film history'; and *The Great Lie* (41), more women's magazine stuff, but put over superlatively well with the aid of Mary Astor. Davis then did a footling comedy with Cagney, *The Bride Came C.O.D.*, as a spoiled heiress tamed by him.

Goldwyn borrowed her – at a fee of $385,000 – for *The Little Foxes*, with Wyler directing. Later he told the 'New York World Telegram': 'I am not knocking Bette for she is a great actress but I am relieved the picture is done. May be she is just as relieved.' They fought over interpretation, he wanting something warmer than Tallulah Bankhead's stage performance, she insisting that *that* was the only way to play it. Dilys Powell (ignoring this?) thought he was 'enormously helped by his chief player: Bette Davis has never given a finer performance than as the cold murderess. . . .' It was one of the year's top grossers and remains today the classic example of its kind (passions in Southern mansions) and type (photographed plays – in this case Lillian Hellman's). She did another filmed play, *The Man Who Came to Dinner* (Monty Woolley), and showed herself a surer mistress of comedy than the year before; then played another bitch – quite unlike all the others – wreaking

havoc all around her in *In This Our Life* (42), quite justifying the ad-line: 'No one is as good as Bette when she's bad.' *Now Voyager*, one of her best-loved films, was first offered to three outside talents, Norma Shearer, Irene Dunne and Ginger Rogers. It is basically more sob-stuff ('Oh Gerry don't let's ask for the moon – we have the stars'), but somewhat compelling, due to the transformation of put-upon frump to soignée woman of the world – but even Davis could not sustain the second half, cosseting the weird child of lover Paul Henried. The 'Manchester Guardian' observed that 'Bette Davis has no superior in the matter of emotional film acting' and 'Picturegoer' readers voted her another Gold Medal.

These were the confident years too: there was a directness of emotion seldom equalled in films and, as Laurence Olivier once commented, at climactic moments she never failed you; and, throughout, you could never be sure how she would react. Her luck held: she amused everyone by croaking her way through 'They're Either Too Young or Too Old' in *Thank Your Lucky Stars* (43); and gave a self-effacing portrayal in Hellman's *Watch on the Rhine* with Paul Lukas. And she was fine again with Hopkins as her rival in the film of John Van Druten's *Old Acquaintance*. C.A. Lejeune called it bosh, but thought Davis almost saved it: 'With her intimate command of detail in gesture and expression, her sensible way with lines, and her positive genius for being in the right place on the set at the right moment, she does manage to keep you consistently interested. . . . There is no actress in Hollywood more expert at giving an intelligent reading of a part that need never have been written in the first place.' She then did some hugely enjoyable hokum about a selfish woman whose beauty is fading, *Mr Skeffington* (44), with Claude Rains, and turned up in *Hollywood Canteen*, a servicemen's rendezvous which in life she had been instrumental in founding, which excuses her appearance in the embarrassing circumstances.

It is considerably more viewable now than *The Corn is Green* (45) from Emlyn Williams's play about a village schoolmistress, a serious subject (the education of the industrial poor at the turn of the century) betrayed by novelettish writing and Hollywood earnestness. James Agee wrote of Davis's performance: 'It seems to me that she is quite limited, which may be no sin but is a pity, and that she is limiting herself beyond her rights by becoming more and more set, official and first-ladyish in mannerism and spirit, which is perhaps a sin as well as a pity. . . . I have a feeling that Miss Davis must have a great deal of trouble finding films that seem appropriate, feasible and worth doing. . . . For very few people in her position in films mean, or could do, so well.' She chose the next subject (and produced it) but it was hardly appropriate, feasible, or worth doing: the remake of *A Stolen Life* (46) – though it gave her a chance for virtuosity as twins. Later that year she was involved in *Deception*, again with Rains and Henried, the one as a jealous lover and the other the naif husband, acting out their kitsch emotions in the luxurious penthouses inhabited by New York's music set. Cecelia Ager's comment was: 'It's like grand opera, only the people are thinner. . . . I wouldn't have missed it for the world.' She was still either just in or just out of the box-office lists, but the decline had begun. She took a year's vacation (and had a baby), but returned with *Winter Meeting* (48), an underrated talkie-talkie piece about a poetess and a naval officer. *June Bride*, a comedy with Robert Montgomery, did well, but *Beyond the Forest* (49) was sneaked into flea-pits some months later: a ludicrous small-town drama directed by King Vidor. She wore a Dracula-like wig and was described as 'a twelve o'clock girl in a nine o'clock town'. She fought against making it and during filming asked for release from her contract. Warner granted it and his version is that he could no longer take the entourage from MCA (her agents) so 'I told Bette I was through'. In 1948 she had been the highest-paid star, at $365,000.

RKO offered her a choice role in a conventional divorce drama with Barry Sullivan, *Payment on Demand*, but withheld release pending the one that she was doing at 20th, *All About Eve* (50). The script had been turned down by Gertrude Lawrence and was scheduled for Claudette Colbert, who became ill (it was based on an incident that happened to Elisabeth Bergner and not Tallulah Bankhead, as was generally supposed). Director-writer Joseph L. Mankiewicz offered it to Davis – and probably never did a wiser thing.

The protagonists of Old Acquaintance *(43): Bette Davis and Miriam Hopkins. Davis wrote 'literary' books and Hopkins trashy best-sellers, but loses both husband and daughter to the former: at the end, they drink a toast to the prospect of middle-age. There were no toasts in real life: they loathed each other, but it was Hopkins's lack of professionalism (*not *Davis's) which was commented on.*

Another of the pure gold Davis vehicles of her great years: Mr Skeffington (*44*) *with Walter Abel. She is a society beauty who can't retard ageing and isn't too pleased about it.*

vivid, overwhelming force she possesses.' Some critics felt this saga of a Broadway star and her would-be usurper (Anne Baxter) too talky, but it has the highest quotient of (verbal) wit of any film made before or since. It won a Best Picture Oscar, was a triumph for Mankiewicz and a box-office smash. Davis won the New York Critics award, but the Oscar went to Judy Holliday.

She was back on top with a vengeance and might have stayed there had she not elected to go to Britain for *Another Man's Poison* (51). Frank Hauser wrote in the 'New Statesman': 'It is fascinating watching Bette Davis, a superb screen actress if ever there was one, play everything in a blaze of breath-taking absurdity. From beginning to end, there is not a lifelike inflection, a plausible reaction . . . it is like reading Ethel M. Dell by flashes of lightning.' Her co-star was fourth husband Gary Merrill and he was also in *Phone Call From a Stranger*, an episoder: her part was short, but showy. Still at 20th, she was again an ageing actress, this time in movies, *The Star* (52), a role based on Joan Crawford (according to Davis, it was written by one of Crawford's ex-secretaries). This time Claudette Colbert had declined the part; Davis was paid $75,000 on completion and $75,000 a year later – plus 25 per cent of the profits. Winnington wrote: 'The career of Bette Davis has been a 20 years battle to protect her talent from the effects of Hollywood processing. As the result of travelling the hard way her status as a film actress is unique and unassailable. But with the long battle won the two-edged nature of victory is manifest. Miss Davis with more say than most stars as to what films she makes seems to have lapsed into egoism. The criterion for her

James Monahan wrote: 'Bette Davis as an ageing star who has heart, mind and temper has perhaps never had so richly human a part to play: she plays it magnificently', while Richard Winnington observed that she 'is always in command of a very great talent'. In the US, Alton Cook: 'Bette Davis, for nearly two decades one of the greatest actresses and worst performers, finally is shaken out of her tear-jerking formula and demonstrates what a

All About Eve (*50*). *The moment when Margo Channing (Davis) realizes that she will miss Monday's performance, leaving the stage clear for her understudy, Eve. Celeste Holm and Hugh Marlowe have arranged for the car to run out of gas, as a favour to Eve.*

choice would appear to be that nothing in the film must compete with the full display of each polished facet of the Davis art. Only bad films are good enough for her.'

Later, hearing that 20th were to make a film about Sir Walter Raleigh, Davis asked to play Elizabeth. The part was built up and the film renamed *The Virgin Queen* (55). Her dialogue was a brilliant pastiche of Elizabeth's letters and speeches, and she was even better than she had been in 1939. However, whenever the Raleighs appeared (Richard Todd and Joan Collins), the film delved into insipidity; and failed at the box-office. Nor was there much popular welcome for *Storm Center* (56), a modest drama about a small-town librarian, or *The Catered Affair* (56), a Paddy Chayevsky piece where she was merely overblown as an Irish-Bronx mother. In 1959 she did a cameo (Catherine the Great) in a produced-in-Spain biopic, *John Paul Jones* (Robert Stack): but she did not come on till the end and wise spectators had left long before. She was no luckier with *The Scapegoat*, made in Britain from a dreary Daphne du Maurier suspense story: she quarrelled with co-star Alec Guinness during filming and her part later was cut to ribbons (it also wasted Irene Worth and Pamela Brown).

During the 50s she had done some stage work: 'Two's Company' (52), a revue; 'An Evening With Carl Sandburg', readings with Merrill, starting in 1954; and in 1961, 'The Night of the Iguana': it was not the leading role but she did it to please author Tennessee Williams, who had created many of his heroines with her in mind. She returned to films with *A Pocketful of Miracles* (61), at the behest of Capra who directed from an old film of his, and it was a misguided venture: Davis was conscientiously tearful as 'Apple Annie', the lady for a day; and she and co-star Glenn Ford quarrelled when he told the press he had given her this chance of a come-back. Then the film failed at the box-office.

No other offers were forthcoming, so she took full-page adverts in the trade press asking for work, adding that she had 'had' Broadway. Newspapers picked up the story, but offers were forthcoming: Aldrich's *Whatever Happened to Baby Jane?* (62), a chiller about two grotesque old dears living in crumbly isolation. Joan Crawford was the other. Each was paid $50,000, far less than they used to command, but they were offered a share of the profits and eventually made over a million each. The director later referred to her as 'easily the most knowledgeable and talented person I ever worked with'. She followed with a minor but expert thriller, playing twins again, *Dead Ringer* (64), directed by Henried. 'Time' said: 'And her

acting, as always, isn't really acting; it's shameless showing-off. But just try to look away.' In Italy she did *The Empty Canvas*, directed by Damiani from a novel by Moravia; making it was, she said, a nightmare: just so for audiences – acres of boredom (Horst Buchholz and Catherine Spaak) punctuated by her. The same could be said of *Where Love Has Gone*, where her authority and verve were in greater supply. There was a dispute about interpretation: ' . . . so I said to them, if she has to be shown as a monster at least give me one scene being really monstrous to the daughter so that people will really believe it. Unfortunately Miss what's-her-name didn't see it that way, and she did get top billing, so . . . ' (interview in 'Sight and Sound'). Her fee was $125,000.

Hush Hush Sweet Charlotte (65) was a follow-up, and superior, to *Baby Jane*. Kenneth Tynan wrote: 'An accomplished piece of Grand Guignol is yanked to the level of art by Miss Davis's performance as the raging, ageing Southern belle: this wasted Bernhardt with her screen-filling eyes and electrifying vocal attack, squeezes genuine pathos from a role conceived in cardboard. She has done nothing better since *The Little Foxes*, 24 years ago.' Her next two movies were made in Britain, for Hammer, which specialized in pallid horror films. *The Nanny* (65) was better than most of their products, thanks to Davis's equivocal performance in the title-role, but *The Anniversary* (67) ranks as one of the most squalid films ever made: a monster-mother's birthday party, with no cohesion (the original director was replaced during the first week's shooting) and Davis at her most baroque. She had done nothing worse since *Another Man's Poison*. She later said she felt like a 'Boris Karloff in skirts': but she still was grateful to the first of these films (*Baby Jane*).

She told an interviewer, Rex Reed, in 1968: 'You want to know what's ruined this business? Actors. They'll walk across the screen for anything, but I'm the only one of those dames who kept her price. My price for putting my name on that marquee is $200,000 and 10 per cent of the gross and I won't even talk to anybody for less because when they see me on screen they're seeing 37 years of sweat. They pay for my experience and if that loses its importance I might as well get lost.' She added that the greatest recent disappointments of her career were not getting her stage part in the film of *The Night of the Iguana* and the lead in *Who's Afraid of Virginia Woolf?* which author Albee had wanted her to play. Later that year she was further disappointed in not getting *The Killing of Sister George*.

Unfortunately, the films she did make were much less distinguished than those three –

Bette Davis in Connecting Rooms *(70), made in Britain. With her is Alexis Kanner.*

colleague), *Lo Scopone Scientifico*, playing a card-mad millionairess: it was little seen in the US or Britain, but it enjoyed a belated success in France. She sued for breach of contract when *And Presumed Dead* – to have been made in Mexico and Switzerland – was cancelled; and there were further travails when a musical version of 'The Corn is Green', called 'Miss Moffat', failed to reach Broadway. She emerged with credit from two horror stories, *Scream Pretty Peggy* (73), made for TV, and *Burnt Offerings* (76), in both as a more-or-less innocent bystander. For TV, she stood by and watched Faye Dunaway, as her daughter, play Aimee Semple McPherson, in *The Disappearance of Aimee*, and all viewers knew how much better she might have been in that role had she been young enough for it.

In 1977 there was talk of a co-starring film with Katharine Hepburn; but she did a film for Disney, *Return from Witch Mountain* (78), *The Dark Secret of Harvest Home*, for TV, as a nice old crone, who later turns out to be a witch, and one of the roles – a bitchy dowager – in the all-star *Death on the Nile*. During these years she did a number of personal appearances in the US, Australia and Britain, discussing her career over the footlights – to be greeted by an affection and esteem rare in this business.

She won a Best Actress Emmy for *Strangers: the Story of a Mother and a Daughter* (79), a superior telefilm about a widow who resented the return of her long-absent daughter (Gena Rowlands). Her only movie for cinemas in a while was another for Disney, *A Watcher in the Woods* (80), playing the old crone who had rented her house to the family subsequently troubled by strange happenings. After initial engagements it was withdrawn, written off at a $6 million loss, but reshown – to little better results. Davis made *White Mama* (80), for CBS, concerning a New York woman who befriends a teenage black boy, and *Skyward* for NBC, as a former stunt woman teaching a paraplegic youngster to fly. Also for NBC there was a four-hour mini-series, *Family Reunion* (81), in which she was a stubborn, self-willed old lady – a teacher – who discovers that the family wish to redevelop her land. Considerably better were *A Piano for Mrs Cimino* (82), the tale of an unwanted woman, diagnosed as senile, who finds happiness with an old friend (Keenan Wynn), and a mini-series, *Little Gloria . . . Happy at Last*, as that young lady's imperious grandmother – they both being Vanderbilts, for this was based on the famous court cases of the 1930s; it also boasted participation of Angela Lansbury and Maureen Stapleton. Prompted by the success of Fonda and Hepburn in *On Golden Pond*, someone decided to

perhaps because, as she said, she refused guest-star or below-the-title billing; and there were not as she admitted, many big roles for ladies of her age. Once she could not go above the title, she said, she would retire. But billing seemed an insufficient reason for doing *Connecting Rooms* in Britain with Michael Redgrave, a stale boarding-house drama in which her lonely spinster turns out to be a busker. Made in 1970, it had a few isolated showings in Britain two years later and, even later, a few US TV bookings. For AIP she did *Bunny O'Hare* (71) with Ernest Borgnine, as a middle-aged couple who disguise themselves as hippies and rob banks; after a few showings she sued for $5 million damages alleging it contravened her contract in being 'a tastelessly and inartistically assembled slapstick production' – in which, however, she could be seen to be giving her best performance in years, touching as an unwanted mother. Again in Britain, she played *Madame Sin* (72), a master criminal in a dim little thriller with Robert Wagner – destined for TV in the US, but unaccountably offered in its country of origin in cinemas. *The Judge and Jake Wade* was a TV pilot, with footage added to make a TV film, and she was the judge, engaged on detection. In Italy she made a comedy-thriller with Joseph Cotten and Alberto Sordi (whom she found a difficult

In Lo Scopone Scientifico (72).

unite Davis with another veteran, James Stewart: but *Right of Way* (83) was not depressing because its subject was euthanasia. It was simply unworthy of either player. Davis had chosen these vehicles wisely, with regard to her age, and true to her art she tried to give each new character a fresh shading. All the same, most of them concern indomitable old women fighting the system – and in this particular case, not about old age at all but about aged stars playing old people.

She brought her considerable presence to the role of the hotel's proprietress in *Arthur Hailey's Hotel*, less a remake of the 1967 film

than telepilot for a series. She explained her wish to make a series as preferable to retirement, but in the event was replaced by Anne Baxter, since she had a stroke which prevented her from going ahead. The effects of her illness were apparent in the telemovie *Murder with Mirrors* (85), a vehicle for Helen Hayes, playing Agatha Christie's Miss Marples; but as a British milady she was still the one you watched, despite a cast including Dorothy Tutin and Frances de la Tour. *The Whales of August* (87) was a belated return to cinemas and a fine one, sharing warm reviews with Lillian Gish, whose blind sister she played. There was little welcome for *Wicked Stepmother* (89), in which as Lionel Stander's new wife she is suspected of witchcraft by his children: she disappears halfway through, 'Variety' suspected because of differences with producer-director Larry Cohen. If she had studied his credits she should not have made the film in the first place. Still, it is good to have her around again, but it does not make much difference. The revivals of her best films always reconfirm her as the Screen's First Lady.

OLIVIA DE HAVILLAND

The appeal of Olivia de Havilland was never better expressed than by James Agee in his review of *The Dark Mirror* in 1946: 'She has for a long time been one of the prettiest women in movies; lately she has not only become prettier than ever but has started to act, as well. I don't see any evidence of any remarkable talent, but her playing is thoughtful, quiet, detailed, and well-sustained, and since it is founded, as some more talented playing is not, in an unusually healthful-seeming and likeable temperament, it is an undivided pleasure to see.' At that time she had just won a long struggle, the basis of which was to prove that she was not just a pretty face, and was getting, at last, parts worthy of her abilities. She went on to win a couple of Oscars and to a reputation as one of the most prestigious of film actresses; but one thinks of her less as a tragedienne than as a player whose delicacy and daintiness were very winning.

She was born in Tokyo in 1916 of British parents. They separated when she was five and Mother took the two daughters to live in California (the other became Joan Fontaine). De Havilland's entrée into films was fortuitous and simple. While still at college she was in a local (Saratoga) production of 'A Midsummer Night's Dream', as Puck, and was seen by a talent scout who recommended her to Max Reinhardt, then preparing both a production of the play for the Hollywood Bowl and a film of it for Warners. Without great enthusiasm de Havilland became first an understudy and on the first night Hermia in the play; and was cast in that role in the film. She showed inexperience but was the best of the quartet of lovers (a poor compliment). Warners had signed her to a seven-year contract and made her Joe E. Brown's stooge in *Alibi Ike* (35) and James Cagney's adored-one in *The Irish in US*, both released before the *Dream*.

She was to become accustomed to standing on the sidelines looking pretty, mostly to gaze adoringly at Errol Flynn (though their first film together had been turned down by Marion Davies, and Anita Louise was the rejected first choice for the next two). It was a combination that was to bring a lot of money into the Warner coffers (though he was to overtake her in popularity and for a while was billed solo above the title, with her featured below). They first co-starred in *Captain Blood*, a Caribbean sea story: the dashing Flynn and the demure de Havilland complemented each other in a fairy-tale way. His lack of experience may have inspired her to an assured performance, and she is surprisingly effective in *Anthony Adverse* (36), as a cook's daughter, Fredric March's love-light and later a prima donna, Napoleon's concubine. She was with Flynn again in the mammoth *The Charge of the Light Brigade*, courted equally by Patric Knowles; the ingénue in *Call It a Day* (37), an English family piece by Dodie Smith with Ian Hunter; in *The Great Garrick* with Brian Aherne as the actor, a movie which flopped at the box-office; supporting Bette Davis and Leslie Howard in *It's Love I'm After*, very funny as a dithery debutante; and involved with George Brent in a Technicolor adventure story, *Gold Is Where You Find It* (38). None of them did much for her, but at the very least she must have melted the hearts of a million schoolboys when she was Maid Marian to Flynn's Robin in *The Adventures of Robin Hood*. Years later she saw it again and said she 'was enchanted with the gaiety and charm of it and its excellence on its own terms' – which was the way it was then. She was a spoiled heiress in a couple of comedies, the witty and sophisticated *Four's a Crowd* with Flynn and the routine *Hard to Get* with Dick Powell; but was given little to do in *Wings of the Navy* (39), a dim aviation drama with Brent and John Payne. She was effective as a crusading newspaper woman in *Dodge City*, with Flynn. Bette Davis was her rival for same in *The Private Lives of Elizabeth and Essex*, and though a Queen, lost out to maid-of-honour de Havilland (not that it mattered in the end).

When casting *Gone With the Wind* Selznick interviewed Joan Fontaine with a view to playing Melanie – this was before *Rebecca* – but decided that she was too chic: not too kindly, she suggested he see her sister. The role was quickly de Havilland's, but Jack L. Warner was adamant that she should not play it – partly because he suspected that when she returned she would want more than the $1,000 a week Warners were paying her; so she enlisted the help of his wife. The role is impossible, butter-wouldn't-melt-in-her-mouth (Amelia to Vivien Leigh's Becky), and

Olivia de Havilland as Melanie in Gone With the Wind *(39). An object-lesson in how to play a very good woman and yet be quite captivating.*

audiences can only sympathize with Scarlett's contempt. That de Havilland, honey-tongued, made this ninny not only real but enormously moving was proof that she was 'a born actress', as Mervyn Le Roy called her later. Warner had been right in prophesying that she would no longer be content on her home lot and she joined the distinguished battle line who fought him for better roles – and working conditions: for while struggling in and out of her period costumes for the last two listed films she was also working on loan for Goldwyn in *Raffles* (40) – and that was a challenging role as the fiancée of that gentle-man, David Niven. Nor did she care for *My Love Came Back*, a breezy comedy with Jeffrey Lynn. She did her penultimate film with Flynn, *Santa Fe Trail*, as the tomboyish heroine fought over by him and Ronald Reagan. Years later she said of Flynn: 'He wanted success, I wanted respect.' She did not realize that he was genuinely in love with her as she resisted him – and as he lost interest, she developed a crush on him. She was glad it turned out that way, 'I'm not going to regret that – it could have ruined my life.' She did like her next two movies: *The Strawberry Blonde* (41), as the gentle wife who keeps on losing Cagney to Rita Hayworth; and at Paramount, an impressive soap opera written by Brackett and Wilder, *Hold Back the Dawn*, as a shy schoolteacher wooed and married by suave refugee Charles Boyer in order to get a US visa. She was nominated for an Oscar but lost to her sister.

She was Mrs Custer in her last with Flynn, *They Died with Their Boots On*, which she did reluctantly after her sister had turned it down. She was further annoyed that she was having to work simultaneously on *The Male Animal* (42) with Henry Fonda, game as his wife in this saccharine version of a hit Broadway play. She ceded her roles in *The Bride Came C.O.D.* and *The Man Who Came to Dinner* to Bette Davis, and that in *King's Row* to Betty Field; but she appeared with Davis in *In This Our Life*, a superior melodrama in which Davis, as her sister, bitched her and every other member of the family. Director John Huston had her play in brisk, flippant style so that it was not inconceivable that they could attract the same men (Dennis Morgan, George Brent). In fact, most of the movie was directed uncredited by Raoul Walsh, since Huston, who was in love with de Havilland, tended to favour her and both the studio and Davis objected – though the film led to a long friendship between the two (after Davis had ignored her on *Elizabeth and Essex*).

Davis also admired her for fighting the studio. De Havilland was still horribly over-worked. She rebelled against starting both *The Gay Sisters* and *Saratoga Trunk* for that reason (both were made with other actresses); she turned down *George Washington Slept Here* because she disliked the script. In revenge (?) Warners offered the role she wanted – *The Constant Nymph* – to her sister, with whom relations were less than cordial. In *Thank Your Lucky Stars* (43) she and Ida

Lupino had a guest spot doing a boogie-woogie, shaking their legs; and her Warner contract finished with two medium comedies, *Princess O'Rourke* with Robert Cummings, and on loan to Selznick, who used the deal to loan her to RKO, for *Government Girl* with Sonny Tufts (Sonny Tufts?). Warners asked only $30,000 for her but RKO thought she was worth $130,000 – so Selznick made a $100-grand profit. At least she thought her contract was finished, but Warners had arranged another loan, to Columbia, claiming an extra six months for times she had been on suspension. She filed suit against the studio and was later backed by the Screen Actors Guild; after long legal wrangles (and $13,000 of her money) the case was settled and seven years became the upper limit for any film contract (including suspensions where necessary), an important decision in the history of studio and player relationships. 'Hollywood owes Olivia a great deal,' said her sister admiringly, in a TV interview, going on to unconvincingly pooh-pooh the reputed feud between them.

Jack L. Warner ensured that she did not film for anyone else; he even tried to prevent her from touring the war zones and selling war bonds. Her agent finally fixed a one-picture deal at Paramount in case the public were forgetting her – but, for legal reasons, she could not receive a salary: *The Well-Groomed Bride* (45), a comedy with Ray Milland that had been planned for Paulette Goddard. As shooting finished, the case was settled. She stayed at Paramount for a drama of (unwed) mother love, *To Each His Own*: John Lund played both father and son, fliers in both wars ('I got a glimpse up there – of what it could be like between you and me'). For her performance she won a Best Actress Oscar. Then, Warners released (or let escape) a film she had made three years earlier: *Devotion*. It never made clear who was devoted to whom or what, unless it was curate Paul Henried, an object of passion for Charlotte (de Havilland), Emily (Lupino) and Anne (Nancy Coleman). They all wrote novels and had a drunken brother called Branwell. (*N.B.* this film contains one of the screen's immortal exchanges – as Charlotte is walking with Sydney Greenstreet they meet a man: 'Good morning Mr Thackeray', 'Good morning Mr Dickens'.) At Universal she did an efficient thriller with Lew Ayres, *The Dark Mirror*, as twins, one nice and one nasty (natch). Also in 1946, she married Marcus Goodrich the novelist ('Delilah') and emerged from the sheltered life she had led; she said later that she had until then lived an incredibly quiet life for a movie star.

The peak of her career was approaching. At 20th she was a patient in a mental home, *The Snake Pit* (48), a brave and unusual film, well made by Anatole Litvak. The reviews were almost unanimously favourable and included this by Peter Ericsson in 'Sequence': '*The Snake Pit* will always be remembered for Olivia de Havilland's performance. . . . Looking back over a number of years there is no other performance in a comparably developed part to equal it. One has almost to go back to the Silent period to find acting which combines intelligence and feeling, insight and variations of mood in the same moving way. Olivia de Havilland, one feels, is intuitively aware of the whole complexity of her part at all times. She plays all her scenes with an appreciation and subtlety which counteract the occasional clumsiness in the direction, and overcome the inadequacy of those who play opposite her. . . .' The film was a big box-office success and de Havilland's performance was considered the year's Best on the distaff side by the New York Critics; which august body gave her the palm again the following year, for *The Heiress* (49); and she won a second Oscar as well. There were dissenters – she was said to be too attractive despite the make-up; but in her gaucheness and clumsiness this was an honest attempt at an Ugly Duckling, in some ways an improvement on Wendy Hiller's Broadway performance and Peggy Ashcroft's London one (the play was based on Henry James's 'Washington Square'). William Wyler directed and the film was not a great popular success.

At this point she decided to establish herself as a stage actress and played Juliet and Candida on Broadway: neither performance increased her reputation, though the Candida was the better of the two. She returned to the screen as the enigmatic (innocent or guilty?) *My Cousin Rachel* (52), from one of Daphne du Maurier's lesser bestsellers, and was away again until she played the one-eyed Princess of Eboli in *That Lady* (55), with a silky sweetness that was entirely inappropriate. Gilbert Roland was the hero and Terence Young directed; Young said later that the film would have been better had the leads been Olivier and Ava Gardner, but added, more correctly, 'I made a mess of it.' Concurrently, de Havilland was miscast as a blonde Swedish nurse in *Not As a Stranger* (56).

She had married, in 1955, Pierre Galante, the editor of 'Paris Match', and went to live in France; and she indicated to interviewers that she was no longer very interested in filming – something that was sometimes apparent from her subsequent performances, where her ladylike manner was somewhat disconcerting, though in *The Ambassador's Daughter* – filmed in Paris – she was more like her younger, gayer self, and in *The Proud*

returned to the large screen to play a philandering wife in *The Adventurers* (70, a hunk of Harold Robbins commerce, and was announced for a role in the grandiose *Waterloo* – but it was played by Virginia McKenna. She might well have renounced the role she did in another trounced historical, *Pope Joan* (72), as Liv Ullman's Mother Superior; but there was a superior TV film from a Ray Bradbury story, *The Screaming Woman*.

Plumpish, she was one of the many stars in the third of a series, *Airport 77* (77), a middle-aged woman reunited with old lover Joseph Cotten; in another of the decade's disaster films, *The Swarm* (78), she was being wooed by Fred MacMurray. In both she was one of several names, as she was in an earlier film, *The Fifth Musketeer*, finally released in 1979. That year she appeared in the series *Roots: the*

De Havilland as the plain, awkward Catherine Sloper – The Heiress (49), a film adaptation of a play based on Henry James's 'Washington Square'. She won her second Oscar for it.

Olivia de Havilland as Richard Burton's enigmatic My Cousin Rachel (52), a role originally meant for Garbo. Even she couldn't have brought more class to it than de Havilland, but it never amounted to much. She did look beautiful, however.

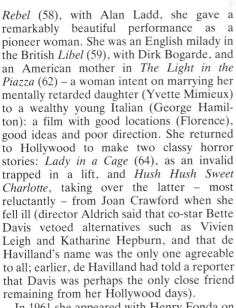

Rebel (58), with Alan Ladd, she gave a remarkably beautiful performance as a pioneer woman. She was an English milady in the British *Libel* (59), with Dirk Bogarde, and an American mother in *The Light in the Piazza* (62) – a woman intent on marrying her mentally retarded daughter (Yvette Mimieux) to a wealthy young Italian (George Hamilton): a film with good locations (Florence), good ideas and poor direction. She returned to Hollywood to make two classy horror stories: *Lady in a Cage* (64), as an invalid trapped in a lift, and *Hush Hush Sweet Charlotte*, taking over the latter – most reluctantly – from Joan Crawford when she fell ill (director Aldrich said that co-star Bette Davis vetoed alternatives such as Vivien Leigh and Katharine Hepburn, and that de Havilland's name was the only one agreeable to all; earlier, de Havilland had told a reporter that Davis was perhaps the only close friend remaining from her Hollywood days).

In 1961 she appeared with Henry Fonda on Broadway in 'A Gift of Time' and in 1963 published a book on her life in Paris (where she lived till 1978, though separated), 'Every Frenchman Has One' (a liver). Appearances on TV included *Noon Wine* (67), from Katherine Ann Porter's story, a performance as good as any of her best on film. She

Olivia de Havilland

Next Generation and her most recent work has also been in TV: *Murder is Easy* (82), an Agatha Christie 'mystery' with Helen Hayes; *The Royal Romance of Charles and Diana*, as the Queen Mother (other queens should be so lucky!); the mini-series *North and South Book II* (86); and *Anastasia: the Mystery of Anna*, as the Dowager Empress, a role which brought her a Golden Globe for Best Supporting Actress.

DOLORES DEL RIO

Dolores del Rio was one of the screen's early exotics, Latin-style, 'the first of the Mexican mamas'. She played the highly emotionally charged young foreign girl, alternately a vamp or a saint. She was exceptionally beautiful – 'orchidaceous' – with dark eyes, an oval face and jet-black hair; but her screen presence was somewhat shadowy. Her career lasted, but her best period was at the beginning, in the late 20s.

She was born in Durango, Mexico, in 1905, in comfortable circumstances (her father was a bank manager) and convent-educated. She was a second cousin of Ramon Novarro. At 16 she married the wealthy Jaime del Rio and she lived the life of a wife appropriate to her station: until they were visited by film director Edwin Carewe and his wife on a visit to Mexico City for the wedding of Claire Windsor and Bert Lytell. Carewe thought Dolores should be in pictures and persuaded her to take a small part in *Joanna* (25) which he was directing, as a rival to its heroine Dorothy Mackaill. Carewe put her under personal

contract and directed her again in *High Steppers* (26), supporting Mary Astor, and *Pals First*; then loaned her to Universal for an Edward Everett Horton vehicle, *The Whole Town's Talking*; then to Fox for *What Price Glory* with Edmund Lowe and Victor McLaglen. Del Rio was a girl of dubious morals called Charmaine (the song called that was written to be played in cinemas at the time) and made an impression with her beauty, if not with her personality. The film was the year's second biggest, with $2 million taken at the domestic box-office. Carewe then directed her in an adaptation by himself and Count Ilya Tolstoy of Count Leo's *Resurrection* (27) with Rod La Rocque as Prince Dimitri: her performance as the childhood friend he later seduces and betrays was for some years considered her best.

She turned down Douglas Fairbanks, who wanted her for *The Gaucho* (Lupe Velez took the role), and played instead another señorita, in *The Loves of Carmen*, directed by Walsh, with Don Alvarado as her Don José and McLaglen as Escamillo. She stayed on the Fox lot, playing a native girl in *The Gateway to the Moon* (28), with Walter Pidgeon, and then moved to MGM to play a demure maiden on *The Trail of '98*, through Alaska, for gold. When Ralph Forbes finds that more alluring, evil Harry Carey moves in and she's a painted dance-hostess when he returns: 'There's not enough gold in the world to make things right again' she tells him. At United Artists, Carewe provided her with one of her most famous roles – and another song hit – *Ramona*, the third film version of Helen Hunt Jackson's novel of old California; Warner Baxter played her Indian lover. Back at Fox

The beautiful Dolores del Rio, at the beginning of her Hollywood career . . . towards the end of her stardom, in Lancer Spy *(37) . . . and as she looked in 1961, for* Flaming Star.

164

she did *No Other Woman*, a melodrama with Alvarado, and one so bad that after previews release was delayed for two years; and *The Red Dance*, a drama about a Russian peasant girl and her Grand Duke (Charles Farrell). Carewe also directed her in *Revenge*, as a proud and tempestuous gypsy girl tamed by James Marcus. In an attempt at another hit song, Carewe commissioned none other than Al Jolson to write the one for *Evangeline* (29), adapted from the poem by Longfellow – only this time del Rio would sing it on the screen (despite a recent pronouncement: 'Nevair, nevair, will I make a Talkie. I zink zey are tairibble'). She serenaded the hero at the end of the film and as she finished, he died – not surprisingly, said the critics. It was a heavy film and not very popular. It marked the end of the artistic association of Carewe and del Rio: his wife divorced him at the same time as del Rio's husband left her. The Carewes later remarried, in 1931 – while Carewe was making *Resurrection* as a Talkie with Lupe Velez and John Boles; Mr del Rio not long after died in Germany and fan-magazines were highly critical of the loving cable that del Rio had sent him on his deathbed. The widowed Dolores soon married MGM art director Cedric Gibbons.

She signed a contract with United Artists (Carewe sued: the matter was settled out of court) at $9,000 a week and made *The Bad One* (30), her first all-Talkie, as the señorita sailor Edmund Lowe breaks ship for. But her contract lapsed when she was taken ill with what was probably a nervous breakdown (at the time it was said to be acute pyelitis); recovered, she signed with RKO, who put her into *The Girl of the Rio* (32), an adaptation of Willard Mack's play 'The Dove', which United Artists had been preparing for her a year earlier. And for this studio she made King Vidor's *The Bird of Paradise*, with Joel McCrea, as the Polynesian girl who sacrifices herself to a volcano: she probably never looked more beautiful. And she looked good in bouffant sleeves in *Flying Down to Rio* (33), as a South American heiress pursued by an American band-leader, Gene Raymond. But she did not act, she posed; and although officially the star of the film, her footage was small. Indeed, she had been off the screen for two years when RKO put her into this musical, surrounded by Fred Astaire and others; after it, they dropped her.

The next studio to try was Warners, who put her into *Wonder Bar* (34) with Al Jolson, as the fiery beauty who stabs her dancing-partner (Ricardo Cortez). But she was pallid and Warners thought it wiser to capitalize on her beauty: in *Madame Du Barry*, directed by William Dieterle, one of his lighter looks at

history; in two more musicals, *In Caliente* (35), as a dancer hotly pursued by Pat O'Brien, and *I Live for Love*; and in *The Widow From Monte Carlo* with Warren William. She went to Britain to appear in Douglas Fairbanks Jr's *Accused* (36); back in Hollywood, Columbia announced that the first picture under a new contract with them would be *Continental*, but the only one she made there was a programmer with Richard Dix, *The Devil's Playground* (37). At 20th there were two more programmers, both with George Sanders; *Lancer Spy*, as a cabaret singer in wartime Berlin, and *International Settlement*, as a dangerous beauty in contemporary Shanghai. She was off the screen for two years, till MGM offered her the part of Wallace Beery's leading lady in *The Man From Dakota* (40). Later she had a much-publicized and stormy affair with Orson Welles and she appeared in his *Journey into Fear* (42), but only in the first two reels. Realizing at last that her Hollywood career was a lost cause, she returned to Mexico, where she signed a deal that gave her a percentage of the profits.

She immediately made four pictures under the direction of Emilio Fernandez, all co-starring her masterly compatriot, Pedro Armendariz (also just returned from Hollywood, after failing to make a go of it as Armen Dariz): *Flor Silvestre* (43), in which they were a young couple banished by his wealthy father and facing revolution (the 1911 one) together; *Maria Candelaria*; *Bugambilia* (44); and *Las Abandonadas*, about a girl who becomes a whore in order to bring up her son – and is desired by an army officer. Only the second, retitled *Portrait of Maria*, was widely seen outside Mexico, when MGM distributed it some years later, a common tale of a girl who loves too much and gets stoned to death by her neighbours. In 1945 she made *La Selva de Fuego* and in 1946 *La Otra* (from the same novel which became Bette Davis's *Dead Ringer*). World cinemagoers saw her again when John Ford made *The Fugitive* (47), mainly filmed in Mexico; she was a magdalen who befriends Henry Fonda, posed and photographed throughout as a madonna. She signed to appear in Abel Gance's *Giselle*, to be made in Spanish, French and English, but it was not made in any of them.

In Argentina she made *Historia de una Mala Mujer* (48), a version of 'Lady Windermere's Fan', and in Mexico she confirmed her position as the country's leading star: *La Malquerida* (49), with Armendariz playing the new husband who falls for her daughter; *La Casa Chica* with Miroslava; *Dona Perfecta* (50), plotting the death of the lover of her daughter (Esther Fernandez); *Deseada* (51), in love with her sister's lover; *Reportaje* (53), with Maria Felix, a musical; and *El Niño y la Niebla*, a lurid tale of heredity insanity. She had also begun to appear on the stage. In 1954, 20th offered her a role in *Broken Lance*, but her visa did not come through in time and Katy Jurado played it; instead she went to Spain to make *Señora Ana* (54).

She returned to the US two years later to do 'Anastasia' in stock; in Mexico, later, she returned to films: *La Cucaracha* (58), another Revolutionary tale, with Armendariz torn between her and the fiery Maria Felix; and *A Donde van Nuestros Hijos*, as a working-class mother. In 1959 she married Lewis J. Riley, an American impresario working south of the Border. They lived in a suburb of Mexico City.

Miss del Rio accepted a Hollywood offer – and later regretted it: *Flaming Star* (60), as Elvis Presley's mother, a Red Indian (Hollywood never forgets). Her next film was *El Pecado de una Madre* (62), some sob-stuff à la *The Old Maid*, as a widow who 'adopts' her husband's mistress and baby. There was another offer from the US: John Ford's *Cheyenne Autumn* (64), in which she was a Mexican peasant. While in the US, she did the first of her occasional appearances on TV in that country; then she went to Spain to make *La Dama del Alba* (66). In Mexico she played a madam in *Casa de Mujeres* and was in another story of revolt, *Rio Blanco* (67). Around the same time she did *C'era una Volta* with Sophia Loren: it was only a small role, but Carlo Ponti was particularly anxious to have her play Omar Sharif's mother – looking as well as she ever did, and acting about as little. In Mexico: *Otro Dia Veremos la Resurrecion de la Mariposas Disecadas* (69) and *Emiliano Zapara*. In Hollywood: *The Phynx* (70), one of many old stars in this odd, missing effort; around the same time she was in an episode of 'Marcus Welby M.D.'. After *Les Motivos del Lobo* she was absent till she did two Mexican films, *Salsa* (77) and, in English, *The Children of Sanchez* (78) with Anthony Quinn. She died in 1983.

MARLENE DIETRICH

Marlene! The name has magic. She is the living legend. She has been much-hymned: by Hemingway ('If she had only her voice, she would break your heart'), by Cocteau ('Your beauty is its own poet, its own praise') and by scores of lesser lights. Curtis Harrington wrote in 1952: 'Like Garbo, she transcends any period, though some of her films do not. Her style throughout remains constant, within little characteristic variations, and as a personification of sexuality her lustre never dims.' From our first glimpse of her in *The Blue Angel* ('I can only say that she makes reason totter on her throne' – James Agate) to her last concert, the world was at her feet. She has fascinated four generations or at least part of them. She is fêted, she is renowned, she is one of the most famous women of the century – perhaps its second goddess, or its third. Age does not wither her, nor custom stale her infinite sameness.

Her witchery would seem to work from a combination of opposites and from qualities which, on examination, offer only a blank. She is as enigmatic (and as graceful) as a cat. Like a cat, she invites love and then disdains it. She is a solitary. She is beautiful but her looks have been rendered by the addition of too much make-up, crazy eyelashes, feathers, furs and male-drag: dolled up, she is the apotheosis of chorus-girl glamour, but beneath is discernible a really glamorous, mysterious woman. She offers a parody, both conscious and unconscious, of sex, suggesting, as she gets her men to commit mighty mayhem for her or as she leads them, steely-hearted, to destruction, that it is all a delusion after all. She is witty about it and then on other things – herself – singularly humourless; she is both androgynous and feminine, practical and scatty. Jacques Feyder once said of her: 'She has great charm. She uses it with stunning virtuosity', and that is what Dietrich the artist is all about: spontaneous and mechanical – sometimes, unbelievably, at the same time, intuitively right and then agreeably ridiculous, calculating and as phoney as a feline.

Her comments on herself are consistent but untrue: she has said that she made no films before *The Blue Angel* and that she was a student when Von Sternberg discovered her, but due to admiring research in recent years her early career is well documented – someone dug up her birth certificate, a compliment clearly not appreciated. The year is given as 1901, the place Berlin: her father was in the Royal Prussian Police. She studied the violin, gravitated towards show business, touring in the chorus and studying at the Deutsche Theaterschule. She was in small roles on the stage and was given a brief one, as a maid, in *Der Kleine Napoleon* (23) aka *So Sind die Männer*. She was seen to more advantage – in feathers and a monocle, in close-up – in the two-part *Tragödie der Liebe*, directed by Joe May, with Emil Jannings as a wrestler finally on trial: she was the judge's mistress. The casting director was Rudolf Sieber, whom she married: they never divorced and later Hollywood publicity made him a doctor who maintained a separate establishment. (Her name was later romantically linked with Von Sternberg, John Gilbert and Jean Gabin; and in Budd Schulberg's memoirs he says that she invited his mother to her stateroom to drink champagne and peruse a book of lesbian pictures because 'in Europe . . . we make love with anyone we find attractive'.)

There were further brief appearances: in *Der Mensch am Weg*, with Alexander Granach and William Dieterle, as a peasant girl; in *Der Sprung ins Leben* (24), a circus tale with Xenia Desni; Pabst's *Die Freudlose Gasse*, with the great Asta Nielsen, in the queue of butcher Werner Krauss when Garbo faints; and then she briefly retired. Returning, she was in *Manon Lescaut* (26), with Lya de Putti in the title-role, as one of the denizens of her world; and had a similar role as a coquette in *Eine Dubarry von Heute* – who was Maria Corda – with three scenes; but for the same director, Alexander Korda, she was merely glimpsed at a party in *Madame Wünscht Keine Kinder*. After another snippet in *Kopf Hoch Charly!*, a romance between a neglected wife and a shipowner, she was in a stage revue, which led to her flirting with *Der Juxbaron* (27), who was Reinhold Schünzel (also directing), a farce about a tramp impersonating a marriageable baron; seemingly typecast, she decorated the Paris and Riviera parties of *Sein Grösster Bluff*, which was about jewels and twins (Harry Piel, who also directed). While touring with Willi Forst in 'Broadway', in Vienna, they were offered roles in Uckicky's *Café Electric*, she as a well-born girl who haunts that den of iniquity: the title in Germany was *Wenn ein Weib den Weg Verliert*. She was a Parisian coquette teaching a prince (Walter Rilla) how to love in *Prinzessin Olala* (28), directed by Robert Land, and after making her name singing Mischa Spoliansky's songs in a revue, and playing in 'Misalliance', that director made her co-star to Harry Liedtke in *Ich Küsse Ihre Hand Madame* (29) – but it was the same old role, a flirtatious Parisian divorcée. And in *Die Frau nach der Man Sich Sehnt* she was a coquette caught betwen her vicious lover (Fritz Kortner) and a husband (Udo Henning) who was not hers. For a change, she was an American aviatrix picked up in the Atlantic by the German-French *Das Schiff der Verloren Menschen/La Navire des Hommes Perdus*, with Kortner as the gloomy captain; and she was an innocent girl on a train in *Gefahren der Brautzeit* aka *Liebesnacht* (and other titles), seduced by a baron (Forst) who discovers she is his best friends's wife.

Von Sternberg claimed to have discovered her in a revue, 'Zwei Kravatten', noting that she was unprepossessing but he could see she

had something: but she was a star with a sexy image – certainly to have been recommended to him and Emil Jannings, coming from Hollywood to make *Der Blaue Engel/The Blue Angel* (30): and in some of her earlier films she had looked much more glamorous than she did here. Von Sternberg needed her

If you've not too well acquainted with both films, you may think this is from The Blue Angel, *but Dietrich was plumper then. It's from her first Hollywood film,* Morocco *(30), after grooming had begun.*

167

because his first choice, Brigitte Helm, was unavailable, and her cheapness was right for Lola-Lola, the good-time girl who insolently enslaved Professor Jannings. The role was older than Theda Bara, but she was new: top-hatted, silk-stockinged, white thighs gashed by black suspenders, she lolled back, sensual, promising, indolent, 'falling in love again' – with Hans Albers, leaving poor old Jannings to the birds. She herself disliked the part and thought it would ruin her, but before the film was premièred von Sternberg had shown a rough-cut to Paramount (his American employers), who signed her for one film: *Morocco*. She was again a cabaret entertainer, the older man this time Adolphe Menjou, the younger one French legionnaire Gary Cooper, for whom in the end she sacrificed everything, trekking after him in the desert in evening dress. It was premièred in New York about the same time as the English-language version of *The Blue Angel* and the furore was such that Paramount wanted her to stay at any price.

This was $125,000 per film, von Sternberg directing, and the right to okay publicity. There are conflicting statements on these Paramount contracts, but it seems that each was for two or three films at a time. According to Arthur Knight, Paramount spent a reputed $5 million on publicity – which, initially, emphasized a rivalry with Garbo. Garbo was making *Mata Hari* and Paramount, not afraid of the comparison, made Dietrich a spy in *Dishonoured* (31). She was also a shady lady ('It took more than one man to change my name to Shanghai Lily') in *Shanghai Express* (32), a slight tale of international intrigue which was her and von Sternberg's biggest American success with a gross of over $3 million. Unlike the Garbo vehicles, Dietrich's films were mainly from original stories concocted especially for her – but they all seemed to have come from the same mould as the Garbo films. *Blood and Sand* was announced for her, unsuitably *A Farewell to Arms* and more appropriately *R.U.R.*, but instead she was the *Blonde Venus*, working in a nightclub

Again in Morocco *(30) she played a cabaret singer and at one point she gets into drag (as she did in at least one other film), with Paul Porcasi. When she gives a female customer a flower in provocative manner, you may wonder again about the movies' age of innocence.*

and being kept by Cary Grant in order to pay for an operation which will save the life of husband Herbert Marshall – who, ungratefully, tells her to choose between them: she runs away and sinks from poverty to prostitution until in the end all is discovered and forgiven. Despite the fact that in a song called 'Hot Voodoo' she emerged from a gorilla skin, the film was far from the anticipated success and Paramount decided to separate star and director: speculation about their artistic association crescendoed when von Sternberg's wife sued for alienation of affection and libel (Dietrich won). On his advice, Dietrich accepted Rouben Mamoulian for *The Song of Songs* (33), replacing Miriam Hopkins announced for the role. This was a remake of *Lily of the Dust*, and described by the 'Sunday Express' (London) as 'a field-day of hokum'. It is liable today to drive audiences into hysteria – there is a climax with a blazing house and the star being chased through the woods by (1) husband Lionel Atwill, (2) true love Brian Aherne and (3) a casual love, a game-keeper on the estate. Replicas of the nude statue used in the film were exhibited in cinema foyers.

Rumours persisted that Dietrich would return to Germany – and indeed Hitler had ordered her to do so (she refused and her films were banned there). Instead, she played Catherine the Great (had not Garbo played Queen Christina? Catherine, after all, had been a German princess) in *The Scarlet Empress* (34). She was considered foolish to compete with Elisabeth Bergner, then making a British film about Catherine, and was roundly trounced: C.A. Lejeune said her performance 'suggests a lady with a good pair of legs and few other resources at all'. The film was a box-office disaster (so was Bergner's) despite an all-pervading eroticism and a triumphant finale with the soundtrack blending 'The Rider of the Valkyries' and the '1812 Overture'. After Russia, Spain: *The Devil Is a Woman* (35), and it is Atwill she ensnares again, with Cesar Romero as the younger competitor (after Joel McCrea sensibly walked out). This is her own favourite film: 'Because I looked more lovely in that film than in any other of my whole career' – certainly she was accoutred in as many feathers and as much lace as possible. Von Sternberg had been increasingly decorating his films beyond a reasonable standard of the exotic and now went too far: more than ever she was simply a prop among the décor. Paramount no more liked seeing their investment reduced to this than they liked von Sternberg's careless expenditure. The film failed and the studio did not protest when the Spanish government, claiming misrepresenta-

tion, asked for it to be withdrawn from circulation. Von Sternberg announced that he had brought Dietrich as far as he could.

Paramount tried to pick up the pieces: her films now might be less visually stunning, but they would be, mostly, less banal. It was decided that Lubitsch should handle her, and he produced and Frank Borzage directed *Desire* (36), a romantic comedy with Gary Cooper: she was a European con-woman and he an American innocent, pursuing each other through most of Spain. It appeared that comedy was her forte and the film succeeded in its attempt in reviving interest in her. However, she began a remake of *Hotel Imperial*, now called *I Loved a Soldier*, with Charles Boyer: but after a few days shooting it was abandoned (reputedly because Dietrich refused to continue after Lubitsch had made changes; it was restarted with Margaret Sullavan, but did not make it to the screens of the world till 1939 with Isa Miranda as the star). Selznick grabbed both stars for the Technicolor remake of *The Garden of Allah*, ditching on the way Merle Oberon, who sued for the $25,000 she was to have been paid – as opposed to Dietrich's $200,000 fee (earlier, Garbo had turned it down). Boyer and Dietrich mooned about the desert and she was never more beautifully photographed; aware of this, perhaps (she always kept a pier-glass on the set), she acted less than ever. Korda then offered her a fee with expenses that worked out at almost $450,000 to make in Britain *Knight Without Armour* (37) with Robert Donat, a story set in the aftermath of the Russian revolution with her as a countess fleeing the plebs and finding at one point a stunning ballgown at a remote military outpost. Lubitsch fashioned *Angel* for her, another cunning, candy-floss comedy, with Melvyn Douglas and Herbert Marshall. She was superb, but it did not turn the tide. Rumours had been emanating from the studio that she had quarrelled with both Borzage and Lubitsch, and 'Picturegoer' reported that Lubitsch and Mitchell Leisen had refused to direct her in *French Without Tears* (like *Midnight*, also bought for her, it went to another actress). At the end of 1937, it was discovered that she rated 126th at the box-office, so Paramount bought up her contract, at a variously reported $200,000 or $250,000 – the price of the one film to come. It was not surprising that she was prominent on the list of stars said to be box-office poison – thus did America repay her for becoming naturalized about this time.

There was immense speculation on her screen future. Critics and fan-magazines liked her, if the public did not. MGM were interested, but in the end she signed deals for

In each succeeding von Sternberg film Dietrich was more outrageously gowned and coiffeured: this costume is one of the lesser efforts in The Devil Is a Woman (35), *which – fortunately perhaps – was their last together. With her is Lionel Atwill, the 'protector' obsessed with her.*

The film that changed the Dietrich image – profitably, for all concerned: Destry Rides Again (39), *with James Stewart as the shy sheriff who tames her, but loses her to a killer's bullet.*

one picture each with Columbia (to play George Sand) and Warners (a remake of *One-Way Passage*). Both were postponed and the studios collected her commitments later on other properties. In 1938 she signed for a French film, to be made the following year – at a fee of $100,000 plus a percentage – in both French and English. Of the several projects announced the most persistent was *Dédée d'Anvers*, with Raimu. Conditions in 1939 were not, however, favourable and the film was postponed until world conditions improved. Thus she had been off the screen more than two years when she was advised to accept – at a fee reputed to be less than $50,000 – the part of the brawling, strident Frenchie in a spoof Western, *Destry Rides Again* (39): it was really a variation of Lola-Lola but a public accustomed to the von Sternberg Dietrich, aloof and slinky, now enjoyed her. Universal signed her to a contract, but, in Arthur Knight's words, 'all her new employers could see was a sleazy sexy hussy for strong men to fight over'. *Seven Sinners* (40) was no more than an attempt to satirize South Seas films in the way that *Destry* had Westerns, but Dietrich did her Sadie Thompson act with aplomb. She was more in command and more compelling than the old

Dietrich. René Clair tried to combine old and new Dietrichs in *The Flame of New Orleans* (41), but it was one of his lesser efforts. Edward G. Robinson and George Raft brawled over her in *Manpower*; she was a musical comedy actress in a weak farce at Columbia, *The Lady Is Willing* (42); and John Wayne and Randolph Scott were the antagonists in both *The Spoilers* and *Pittsburg*. It was said that she was dissatisfied with her roles and considered retiring – but instead she went off on long and valiant tours entertaining the troops.

She let Orson Welles saw her in half in a guest spot in *Follow the Boys* (44) and she was painted gold all over for a dance sequence in MGM's *Kismet*, an agreeable send-up of that old play, with Ronald Colman. Then it was announced that she would take up her French commitment at a fee now of $30,000, plus all expenses plus 5 per cent of the net. With her offscreen friend Jean Gabin, she would make *Les Portes de la Nuit*, to be directed by Marcel Carné, at that time the most prestigious director in French films. At the last minute Dietrich withdrew because she disliked her role, and Gabin with her. There was an outcry in the French press and the film they subsequently did together, *Martin Roumagnac* (46), was a boom neither in France nor anywhere

Seven Sinners (*40*), *a title that referred not to any of the cast, but to the sailors' rendezvous where Dietrich sang, among other things. The British title was* Café of Seven Sinners. *With her are John Wayne and Broderick Crawford.*

else (other French projects included, still, the *Dédée d'Anvers* that Signoret eventually played, and Death in Cocteau's *Orphée*). Dietrich returned to Paramount, unconvincing as a gypsy in the silly *Golden Earrings* (47), but ideal as a Berlin cabaret entertainer in Billy Wilder's brilliant *A Foreign Affair* (48), though her role was subordinate to Jean Arthur's. A grandson was born around this time and she became tagged as 'the world's most glamorous grandmother'.

The rest of her movie career indicates mutual wariness: she wanted to make films because films meant the big money and prestige, but she was exacting about parts, co-stars, billing, etc. (two she turned down were *Gigi* and *Pal Joey*). Hollywood needed her only because she was one of its legendary names; her value at the box-office continued to be, at the most, doubtful. She played a stage-star in *Stage Fright* (50), a flashy if minor role in a minor-league Hitchcock, and she was a famous movie star in *No Highway* (51) with James Stewart, which was a big success. Her last good part was out West again as a saloon singer in Fritz Lang's masterly *Rancho Notorious* (52). Lang's comments are revealing: he says that they could only get a small budget for the film, that Dietrich resented moving into the category of more mature parts and that on the set she was a trouble-maker and increasingly difficult. Her fee was $40,000 plus $70,000 deferred plus 25 per cent of the profits (as against Arthur Kennedy, her co-star, who got $25,000 plus $35,000 deferred). A few months earlier MGM had balked at her $150,000 fee and she had lost the part (in *The Man with the Cloak*) to Barbara Stanwyck. Her salary demand for a film called *The Widow* went down to $75,000 – and the producers preferred her to Hedy Lamarr, who was asking $125,000. However, the film was postponed (and was later made with Patricia Roc). In 1952, instead, she toured what 'Picturegoer' called 'the lesser US' doing 'songs and monologues' for a fee of $500 per week. In *The Monte Carlo Story* (57), an Italo–American effort with Vittorio de Sica, she was a confidence trickster – shades of *Desire* (shades indeed!). She wasted her time even more grievously with an unconvincing guest appearance in Welles's *Touch of Evil* (58), as a Mexican madam, but she liked it: 'I think I've never been as good as I was in that teensy part,' and also *Witness for the Prosecution*, where her Cockney impersonation gave the whole game away. Further, she looked gaunt and seemed to be afraid to smile; but in her spot in the coloured *Around the World in 80 Days* (57) she had vaulted time with years to spare. Her last film in more than a decade was *Judgment at Nuremberg*

(61), where she was 'a stagy Junker widow' (Dwight Macdonald).

In the early 50s she had a radio series. 'Café Istanbul' (espionage tales), but she evinced little interest in TV. She told one reporter that she always thought of herself as 'a very bad actress' and to another she said her real work began during the war when she sang to the troops; she aimed ever since to become a *chanteuse* like Piaf – telling a story in song. In 1954 she appeared in cabaret in London, at a reported $6,000 a week, and for equally fabulous sums, in equally stunning gowns, she appeared regularly in Las Vegas. She also appeared in clubs or in concerts in most countries in the world from Russia to Australia, notably in Germany where, because of her noted anti-Nazi stand, she was not expected to be entirely welcome; but she played to the same packed houses, at the same high prices as elsewhere, and her German recording of 'Where Have All the Flowers Gone?' became one of the all-time best-selling records in Europe. She did not make her New York début till 1967. Among other quoted remarks are that she worked only for money and that she loathed being a film-star. She told Rex Reed: 'It's so boring, all that talk about the legendary Marlene and the legendary films of von Sternberg. . . . I do not like to be interviewed any more by pansy film-fan writers, because all they want to know about is *Blonde Venus* and *Shanghai Express*.' It is a curious remark since most of her act – which altered by hardly a syllable or even an intonation over the years – consisted of songs from her Hollywood years. She abandoned cabaret after reportedly falling on stage – and it was a wise decision in view of a cruel TV showing of same. She finally agreed to make another film – *Schoener Gigolo Armer Gigolo/ Just a Gigolo* (78), in Germany with an odd cast (David Bowie, Kim Novak, etc.); and then it was announced that she was returning to cabaret. She was paid $250,000 for two days' work and recording the title song. Jack Tinker of the 'Daily Mail', watching her perform, wondered 'Can this be the lame old lady who was helped so painfully on to the set the day before?' Well yes, photographed through gauze and a veil from a distant camera, she croaked her song and a couple of lines in a pathetic reminder of past glories. It was announced that she was returning to cabaret, but the little she did showed her no longer at her best; and there was mutual acrimony over a TV appearance featuring her act. The columnist Earl Wilson wrote: 'She's devoid of graciousness; she's rude to everybody. She's hard of hearing. She's got an old lady's stoop. She insults everyone who gets near her. She's a complainer; she's impossible to satisfy. I think she behaves like an idiot.'

When she permitted herself to be interviewed for a full-length documentary, *Marlene* (84) – in fact, she instigated the project – it was with the proviso that she would not be photographed. Maximilian Schell questioned her and is credited with the direction, getting from this irritable and contemptuous old lady, 'a fascinating display' said David Denby in 'New York Magazine', 'of egotism, lying, contentiousness'.

RICHARD DIX

Today only older filmgoers know the name Richard Dix and most of them will remember him as a stalwart of second features in the late 30s and 40s; but before that he had been successful for a good number of years. Indeed, other than Richard Barthelmess and Ronald Colman, he was the only male *star* to survive from the early Silent era well into the Talkie period. He was not an inspired actor, but he was an honest one, projecting a certain degree of masculine charm. Although he played the brother not tempted to break *The Ten Commandments* (Rod La Rocque was the one who did), he had as a young man an oddly dissipated appearance, as if he had spent too many nights on the town: consequently he was often cast as a wild young man – a product of his era – only waiting for the right woman to happen along and reform him. Since he looked very good in an Arrow collar, he was best cast as a city boy of certain means: he was not an ordinary drunkard – he just liked getting high with his chums after a football game and if they went to a nightclub and started breaking it up, well, that was just a boyish prank. The film best presenting this image was *Let's Get Married* and it says much of audience taste that they tolerated such things – until the Depression, when Dix did a turnabout and became a figure of authority.

He was born in St Paul, Minnesota, in 1894; he studied medicine at the University of Minnesota and acted with the university drama group. A travelling troupe one day advertised for a local to play a football player in 'The College Widow' and Dix applied: he had the bug, and thereafter gave up medicine. He worked in stock in Philadelphia, Dallas and Montreal; spent the war years in the army, returned and got his New York break: in 'The Hawk' in 1919. He did some other plays (including 'The Song of Songs', Gorki's 'A Night's Lodging') and was then offered star parts with an LA stock company: which inevitably led to screen tests. On the second, he was offered two star parts in *Not Guilty*

(21) – twins; whereupon Goldwyn offered him a contract: *The Sin Flood*; *Dangerous Curve Ahead*, marital difficulties with Helen Chadwick; *All's Fair in Love*; *Poverty of Riches* with Leatrice Joy; *The Glorious Fool* (22) and *Yellow Men and Gold*, both with Helen Chadwick. Other leading ladies: Colleen Moore in *The Wallflower*; Claire Windsor in *Fools First*; and Betty Compson in *The Bonded Woman*. He was then sent to Britain for the film of Sir Hall Caine's *The Christian* (23), directed by Maurice Tourneur, playing a minister in love with an actress (Mae Busch) but giving her up when he thinks that Doomsday is nigh. *Souls for Sale* was his last for Goldwyn, a story of the movies, with Busch again and Eleanor Boardman, Barbara La Marr, Lew Cody, William Haines and Aileen Pringle.

It was rumoured that he would do *Ben Hur* eventually, but Paramount had just lost Wallace Reid (his death from the too enthusiastic use of drugs was a scandal that shook Hollywood) and they anxiously needed a replacement. Dix, though considerably unlike, would be able to do the same sort of he-man roles, thought Paramount, and they made him an attractive offer. His first films there had been intended for Reid: *Racing Hearts* with Agnes Ayres; *The Woman With Four Faces*, ironically – but topically – about a DA who breaks up a dope ring; and two from Zane Grey novels, *To the Last Man* and *Call of the Canyon*, both with Lois Wilson. Between these two he was in the modern half of De Mille's all-star *The Ten Commandments*, the second biggest grosser of 1923 (at $2½ million, a million behind *The Covered Wagon*). He made *The Stranger* (24) from Galsworthy's 'The First and the Last'; *Icebound*; *Unguarded Women* (Bebe Daniels and Mary Astor); *Sinners in Heaven* with Daniels; *Manhattan*; as a bored society boy who seeks thrills in the underworld with Jacqueline Logan; *A Man Must Live* (25), a newspaper story again with Logan, from I.A.R. Wylie's 'Jungle Law'; *Too Many Kisses* with Frances Howard; *Men and Women*; *The Shock Punch*; *The Lucky Devil*, an uproarious comedy about a car with the voodoo; and Zane Grey's *The Vanishing American*, a notable performance as a Red Indian. There followed *Womanhandled* (26) – Esther Ralston doing the handling; *Let's Get Married*, a comedy with Lois Wilson again, as a wild young man who takes Bible-lady Edna May Oliver – she stole the picture – to a ngithclub; *Say It Again*, a Ruritanian comedy with Alice Mills; *The Quarterback* with Ralston; *Paradise for Two* (27), a comedy about a bachelor who must marry or lose an inheritance, with Betty Bronson; *Knockout Reilly* as a boxer on the come-back trail; and

Esther Ralston and Richard Dix in The Lucky Devil *(25), one of the auto-racing pictures popular at that time. The public liked this teaming so much that they played together on three more occasions. Ralston was one of Paramount's biggest stars of the 20s.*

Man Power as a luckless youth who makes good – and *Shanghai Bond*, both with Mary Brian.

Most of these had been filmed in New York, which Dix preferred to Hollywood, and when Paramount closed its NY studio he complained; he wanted out of his contract and as a further lever complained about Paramount's re-release of an independently produced film he had made in 1923, *Quicksands*. He complained later: 'I made my name in a few good parts, then they gave me a series of walk-throughs in shoddy productions.' Paramount retaliated by upping his salary to $4,500 a week. He went on to make *The Gay Defender* (28), a biopic of the bandit later played by Warner Baxter in *Robin Hood of El Dorado*; *Sporting Goods*, a remake of Fatty Arbuckle's *The Travelling Salesman*; and *Easy Come Easy Go*, 'a fast-moving comedy with Richard Dix as a debonair young bankrupt who is innocently taken in by a gentleman crook' ('Photoplay'). The heroine was Nancy Carroll; in *Warming Up* it was Jean Arthur and Dix was a small-town pitcher who makes it to the top. He had the title-roles in both *Moran of the Marines*, a far-fetched adventure tale, and *Redskin* (29), his troubles

starting because he has been educated as a white (it had some colour sequences). His first Talkie was *Nothing But the Truth*, having to tell just that in this version of an old farce; and since his studio saw him mainly as a comedian, he followed *The Wheel of Life* (moustached as a British officer, in love with Esther Ralston) with *The Love Doctor*, in the title-role prescribing love as a treatment and getting involved himself.

Since he had proved his worth in Talkies, he asked for more money to do another big Western, *The Virginian*, but was refused. The contract was dissolved by mutual consent and he signed a new deal with RKO, whose head of production, William Le Baron, had once been Associated Producer at Paramount and while he had doubts about Dix's worth, the new company needed established players for its contract list. They started him off amidst the confusions he had conquered at Paramount: the oft-filmed Earl Derr Biggers–George M. Cohan mystery-farce, *Seven Keys To Baldpate*, as the writer who cannot get on with the job because the hotel he is in is a maelstrom of chaos; *Lovin' the Ladies* (30), written by Le Baron, as an electrician who accepts a bet that he can fall in love with a designated lady; and *Shooting Straight*, as a racketeer who reforms after impersonating an evangelist. Public enthusiasm was muted, but Dix seemed an ideal choice to play the lawyer-newspaperman hero of *Cimarron* (31), Edna Ferber's epic of the Oklahoma land-rush days, directed by Wesley Ruggles, with Irene Dunne as the faithful, ill-used wife. It was highly praised and popular; and it won a Best Picture Oscar; but due to its high cost it did not make money – which the new company desperately needed – till its reissue five years later. Dix's demands for a salary increase were not appreciated – especially as he was particularly hammy in this film and was having trouble controlling his girth.

It was soon clear that he was a star in gentle decline, but RKO took great trouble in finding the right properties, if by necessity most of them were programmers: *Young Donovan's Kid*, from a Rex Beach story with Jackie Cooper in the title-role; *The Public Defender* (he turned crook to trap some dishonest financiers); *Secret Service*, a Civil War story; *The Lost Squadron* (32) as a disillusioned war hero; and *The Roar of the Dragon* with Gwili Andre. *Hell's Highway* is a short, stark film about convicts: (the framed) Dix attempts to escape. He moved back to A picture status with *The Conquerors*, with Ann Harding, but it did not repeat the success of *Cimarron*, which it deliberately resembled: and he convincingly aged 60 years during its course. After it he made another, similar, period drama, *The Great Jasper* (33), with

Wera Engels; *No Marriage Ties*, as a hard-drinking reporter; *Day of Reckoning*, another marital drama – at MGM, with Madge Evans; *The Ace of Aces*, an aviation drama; *Stingaree* (34), another big one with Irene Dunne but almost incredibly bad; *His Greatest Gamble*, sacrificing all for his daughter's happiness; *West of the Pecos*, a good Western from a novel by Zane Grey; and *The Arizonian* (35) with Margot Grahame and a screenplay by Dudley Nichols.

In 1935 in Britain he was one of the engineers building *The Tunnel*, a drama with an Anglo-American cast handicapped by the poor direction of Maurice Elvey; back in Hollywood he finished his RKO contract with *Yellow Dust* (:36) and *Special Investigator*, both Bs. He did four Bs for Columbia, *Devil's Squadron*, *The Devil's Playground* (37), *The Devil Is Driving* (no connection between them, despite the titles) and *It Happened in Hollywood*, a B about a Western star who fails at first in Talkies, but triumphs later; as a gimmick lots of 'doubles' played stars. He returned to RKO for *Blind Alibi* (38), *Sky Giant* with Joan Fontaine and *Twelve Crowded Hours* (39) with Lucille Ball. At Republic he did one of their bigger ones, *Man of Conquest*, a biopic of Sam Houston, and at 20th *Here I am Stranger*, as alcoholic father to Richard Greene. He went back to RKO, to Paramount, Universal, etc., making a decent living in programmers – most of them, coincidentally, of above-average quality: *Reno* (40) with Gail Patrick; *The Marines Fly High* with

Irene Dunne and Richard Dix in Cimarron *(31), the film that put her on the map and was certainly the most important and successful of the hundred that he made.*

Chester Morris; *Men Against the Sky; Cherokee Strip*; the remake of Fatty Arbuckle's *The Roundup* (41), an A budget picture with Patricia Morison; *Badlands of Dakota* as wild Bill Hickok, billed under Robert Stack and Ann Rutherford; *Tombstone the Town Too Tough to Die* (42); *American Empire; Eyes of the Underworld* (43); and *Buckskin Frontier* and *The Kansan*, both with Jane Wyatt, Albert Dekker and Victor Jory. He had a change as the father of *Top Man* Donald O'Connor, but returned to the action stuff with Val Lewton's *The Ghost Ship* (directed by Mark Robson), as a homicidal captain. Then Columbia signed him to a series of low-budgeters, based on CBS's long-running 'The Whistler' programme: *The Whistler* (44), *The Mark of the Whistler*, *The Power of the Whistler* (45), *The Voice of the Whistler* (46), *The Mysterious Intruder*, *The Secret of the Whistler* and *The Thirteenth Hour* (47).

Dix died, a wealthy man, in 1949 after a series of heart attacks. He was married twice – in 1931 and 1934.

ROBERT DONAT

The story of Robert Donat, though not overly dramatic, is a heart-rending one. He was a highly gifted actor, one of the aristocrats of his craft, notable for a beautiful speaking voice and a quiet and diffident charm. Charles Laughton once referred to him as 'the most graceful actor of our time'. Most of his stage-work was admired and in films he enjoyed a popularity and prestige in the US (at least for a time) on the level of that of Olivier and Leslie Howard: but Donat only ever made one film in Hollywood and few in Britain. His tragedy was that the promise of his early years was never fulfilled and that he was haunted by agonies of doubt and disappointment (which probably were the cause of his chronic asthma). For most of the last years of his life he was unable to work, to function as an actor.

He was the first choice for roles which became milestones (more or less) in the careers of Laurence Olivier, Ronald Colman, Errol Flynn, Leslie Howard, Gary Cooper, Ralph Richardson, Robert Taylor, Fredric March, Spencer Tracy, Robert Montgomery and John Mills, among others.

He was born in Withington, Manchester, in 1905. His father (Polish by birth) loathed the office work which he himself did and planned to send the boy to Canada for an adventurous life (as he had sent the elder sons); but Donat's mother thought he was too shy. To help overcome this, and to cure a stammer, he

was given elocution lessons. His teacher gave recitals with Donat accompanying him, which led to his stage début in Birmingham in 1921 in a small part in 'Julius Caesar'. He became private secretary to his tutor and through him met Sir Frank Benson and was taken on by him. The Benson Company toured the provinces in the classics – the famous business of 'bringing culture to the hicks'. It was not an especially distinguished company, but Donat learned his craft, over a four-year period, and later referred to this as the happiest period of his life. In 1928 he joined Liverpool Rep for a season and moved on to Cambridge, working with Flora Robson and Tyrone Guthrie. (In 1929 he married Ella Annesley; they were divorced in 1946.) Then he decided to try London and was offered a part in 'Knave and Queen' (30). It flopped. So did the next half-dozen plays, but in 1931 he did a good Dunois in 'Saint Joan' and in 1932 made his mark in an adaptation of 'Precious Bane' put on in a peripheral London theatre (the Embassy, Swiss Cottage): he made sufficient mark for Irving Thalberg to approach him about *Smilin' Through*, but he was not interested in Hollywood. As a struggling actor he did several screen tests in Britain and Korda signed him for three years: one of his first discoveries. He put him in a story of Oxford undergraduates, *Men of Tomorrow* (33), directed by Leontine Sagan, on the principle, Korda thought, that she was an expert on adolescents. The next two films were even less significant: *That Night in London*, in which he had the lead, as a bank clerk who goes to town with the money he has embezzled; and *Cash*, a comedy about a nice young man who helps a hard-up inventor (Edmund Gwenn). By an odd stroke (Korda was having distribution difficulties) these films were much more widely shown in the US than in their country of origin. He did a play, 'When Ladies Meet', and in his next film became an international name, though he had only a supporting role: that of Culpeper, the man who cuckolded a king (Charles Laughton) in *The Private Life of Henry VIII*. And by the time it was shown, Donat had scored a great West End success in James Bridie's 'The Sleeping Clergyman' in two different parts.

Hollywood beckoned and Korda loaned him for *The Count of Monte Cristo* (34). Edward Small, the producer, had Donat forced on him by the director, Rowland V. Lee (who had made *That Night in London*), but he liked him well enough later to double the budget. Said the 'Sunday Times' (London): 'a striking performance . . . his part is a long one. It has many difficult scenes, but he handles it with superb assurance, an ease and a certainty that mark him as a finished actor.' Beyond that, the film was a good version of Dumas and very popular. Small later sued Donat, claiming that he had promised to appear in a sequel, and there was later litigation with Warner Bros., who claimed a three-picture agreement signed at this time – two of which were to be *Anthony Adverse* and *Captain Blood*, at a salary of $21,500 for six weeks' shooting.

In London, he did a play with Flora Robson, 'Mary Read', and Korda loaned him to Gaumont-British to play Richard Hannay in Hitchcock's exciting version of Buchan's *The Thirty-Nine Steps* (35), considered then the ultimate in screen thrillers and later accepted as a classic. C.A. Lejeune observed: 'For the first time on our screens we have the British equivalent of a Clark Gable or a Ronald Colman playing in a purely national idiom.' Hitchcock observed later: 'He was as much as anybody responsible for the world-wide success . . . I am sure that his performance really made it so delightful: he was not in any sense a comedian, but he had a beautiful dry quality and that was the great contribution.' There followed another hit, René Clair's *The Ghost Goes West* (36), in a dual role (originally meant for Charles Laughton), as the ghost accompanying the castle being removed brick by brick to the US by millionaire Eugene Pallette, and as his modern descendant. Donat next decided to do another Hitchcock, *Sabotage*, at a salary of £30,000, but Korda balked. He had, he complained, bought several properties for Donat: 'Precious Bane', a piece about Nelson, and was preparing a film *Hamlet*. He had also bought *Knight Without Armour* (37), by

James Hilton, and Donat did that instead, co-starring with Dietrich in a far-fetched tale of the Russian revolution. (During filming his asthma attacks worsened and Laurence Olivier was on standby to replace him if necessary.)

He never arrived in Hollywood to make the films which Warners announced for him – which also included *Robin Hood*. Their case against him was dismissed. Other roles he declined at this stage of his career included Marco Polo, the Squire in *South Riding*, *Peter Ibbetson*, Romeo to Norma Shearer's Juliet, *Beau Geste* and the heroes of *Magnificent Obsession* and *The Four Feathers*. Among plans that came to nothing were a Lawrence of Arabia and The Old Pretender in a version of A.E.W. Mason's *Clementina*.

RKO also had a claim on Donat's services, should he go to Hollywood, so when Donat signed a four-picture contract with MGM it was specified that they should be made in Britain – with the period unspecified because of his health. His fee was to be £25,000 per film and the first was *The Citadel* (38), from A. J. Cronin's bestseller about the local GP who loses his idealism when he becomes a Mayfair specialist. Donat played with candour and enthusiasm, and the director, King Vidor (later, in his memoir) described him as 'the most helpful and cooperative star' he had encountered during his career. The next was an even bigger triumph, *Goodbye Mr Chips* (39), from James Hilton's story of a gentle schoolmaster and his dedication to his pupils; the world cried at this grossly sentimental picture and Donat won a Best Actor Oscar and the 'Picturegoer' Gold Medal. Paul Muni

Robert Donat as the gentle schoolteacher, Mr Chipping, introducing to the school the wife he has met and wooed while away on a walking tour: Goodbye Mr Chips (39) *with Greer Garson.*

Donat as The Young Mr Pitt (42) *– ageing. Carol Reed's study of the man who became Prime Minister at the age of 24.*

was quoted as saying: 'This is the most magnificent performance I've ever seen on any screen. Not a false motion – not a wasted gesture. He is the greatest actor we have today.' (Donat, incidentally, listed Muni as one of the five greatest performers, along with Chaplin, Garbo, Spencer Tracy and Deanna Durbin.)

As a result, Hollywood again clamoured. Small announced his *Son of Monte Cristo*, but Louis Hayward played it. Donat turned down MGM's plans to make him Mr Darcy opposite Greer Garson and some properties bought especially for him, *Waterloo Bridge*, *Rage in Heaven*, *Beau Brummell* and *Dr Jekyll & Mr Hyde*. It was thought, because of the war, he might go to Hollywood; he was turned down for military service. Instead, he planned an Old Vic season – aborted by the war – and in London played Dick Dudgeon in 'The Devil's Disciple' (40). He persuaded MGM to let him do a film for 20th-British, partly because it was a propaganda effort, *The Young Mr Pitt* (42), directed by Carol Reed; and he managed well enough to express that statesman's fervour and single-mindedness. *The Adventures of Tartu* (43) was the only film MGM made in Britain during the war, a special endeavour to hold Donat to his contract: but after a longish period in the Culver City cutting rooms it emerged as nothing special – just another Resistance drama, but with the star on fine form as a British bomb disposal expert pretending to be a dandified Greek merchant in a Czech factory. On the stage he was Shotover in 'Heartbreak House', and he dithered over playing the Chorus in Olivier's *Henry V*, but MGM appear to have frowned on that project. A while later they sought an injunction to prevent him working except for them, but the case never came to court. He did one last film for them, produced by Korda, *Perfect Strangers* (45), with Deborah Kerr, as a couple separated, and changed, by the war. It was also the last of his films – except the final one – to have a wide showing in the US.

He had leased a London theatre and had gone into management, but this was a venture which, in the end, went sour on him. Perfectionist he may have been but he was also finicky and vacillating: for this reason, a film of *Precious Bane* for Rank (who now held the rights) came to nothing. But he was disappointed at being turned down for Sykes in *Oliver Twist* after testing. Later, he pondered a film of 'The Sleeping Clergyman' (filmed, with Richard Todd, as *Flesh and Blood*) which he revived at this time. He also played Benedick in 'Much Ado'.

Thus he was off the screen till *Captain Boycott* (47), a tale of troubles in Ireland, in a cameo role as Parnell. Garson Kanin tried

Deborah Kerr and Robert Donat in Perfect Strangers *(45) – their separation and war service has rendered them somewhat more glamorous to each other.*

to persuade him to do the role Ronald Colman eventually played in *A Double Life*, but Donat thought the strain on his health would be too great. However, for Korda, at a salary of £20,000, he gave a brilliant performance as the Defending Counsel in *The Winslow Boy* (48), from Terence Rattigan's play about a naval cadet accused of stealing a postal order. For Korda again, he starred in *The Cure for Love* (49), a Northern comedy about a soldier and the women who want to marry him. He was much too old for the part and the direction, by himself, provided a double failure. However, the sweet girl who got him, got him in real life, too: Renée Asherson. They were married in 1953 (but separated two years before his death). In 1951 Donat played Friese-Greene, whom the British claim invented the cinema. The film was *The Magic Box* and it was a combined effort by the British film industry to celebrate the Festival of Britain: some 60 stars played bit parts, but it was mostly notable for being a biopic in dramatic rather than chronological order. It was not, to put it mildly, a success.

He had to turn down an offer from 20th to do *No Highway*, but in 1953 he returned to the stage as Becket in Eliot's 'Murder in the Cathedral' for the Old Vic; he was very ill and cylinders of oxygen were kept in the wings. No indication of his difficulties was visible to the audience, but later that year he had to abandon plans to play Mossop in *Hobson's Choice* with Charles Laughton. John Mills took over. However, a year later he did manage to do a leading role, an Anglican parson, in a pleasant rural picture, the aptly named *Lease of Life* (54). 'The Times' (Lon-

don) said: 'It is legitimate to infer that he takes great pains with his parts, and he knows how, scrupulously and decently, to subdue himself to his part, to adapt his personality without abandoning it.' During his last years he was desperately ill. So much money was spent on treatment that he was virtually penniless when 20th signed him for a supporting role to Ingrid Bergman in *The Inn of the Sixth Happiness* (58). As a Chinese mandarin, his last words on the screen were: 'We shall not see each other again, I think.' It was the impeccable performance expected, but he had worked himself into a complete total and physical wreck; while in hospital, his left lung collapsed. He left only his fee for the film, £25,000. C.A. Lejeune saluted him: 'An actor of honour, a man of courage.'

MELVYN DOUGLAS

In the 30s Melvyn Douglas was one of the screen's most accomplished farceurs. Dapper and invariably frivolous, he chased after, or was chased by, all the comediennes of the time. He was a prop for the girls, unlike, say, William Powell, who was a star in his own right. Later, like Powell, he was always married. In 'Picturegoer' Lionel Collier observed that he was cast only in marital comedies: 'The movie moguls seem to have discovered that Melvyn has a suave manner, a way with the ladies and an enigmatical smile which can be used only in a certain kind of production.' Douglas himself said: 'I earned what became an international reputation for

being one of the most debonair and witty farceurs in Hollywood.' With his clipped moustache and three-piece suits he looks to modern eyes a bit of a bounder, and that was the way scripts would have him then – but only in the cause of romance. That he made such pursuits seem both innocent and honourable is due to the inflexions of his voice rather than to his manner. He was, like all but a mere handful of players, typecast and not happy; he returned to the stage and when he came back to films it was as a character actor.

He was born in Macon, Georgia, in 1901, the son of concert pianist Edouard Hesselberg. He got the acting bug in high school and made his stage début in Chicago in 1919; he worked in stock and toured in everything from Shakespeare to Broadway hits, until 1928, when he made his New York bow in 'A Free Soul' with Fay Bainter. There were other plays and in 1930 he was in a big success, 'Tonight or Never', which brought him marriage (to Helen Gahagan, who was in the cast) and a Hollywood offer. Gloria Swanson persuaded Sam Goldwyn in his capacity as production head of United Artists (as he was at that time) to buy the play for her and Goldwyn signed Douglas along with it, at a starting fee of $900 a week. *Tonight or Never* (31), however, did nothing for Douglas – playing the young man adored by temperamental prima donna Swanson (despite the fact that she believes he is being kept by Alison Skipworth, who is really his aunt). Then, of all incredible things, he was chosen to play Garbo's lover in *As You Desire Me* (32), an

Robert Donat in The Winslow Boy *(48) as the fashionable KC hired to clear the name of the naval cadet accused of stealing a postal order.*

Melvyn Douglas was a young actor fresh from Broadway and not established in films when Garbo chose him to be her leading man in As You Desire Me *(32).*

accolade that led nowhere. It was released after: *Prestige*, in which he was an alcoholic in charge of an Indochina penal colony and loved by Ann Harding; *The Wiser Sex*, in which he was a brilliant young lawyer caught up with gangsters and Claudette Colbert; and *The Broken Wing*, in which he was a pilot who crashes in Mexico and is cared for by Lupe Velez. For none of these did he get good notices, but at least he was in fine company in *The Old Dark House*, stranded there with Raymond Massey and Laughton, as the juvenile. All these were on loan-out and Goldwyn sent him to the despised Majestic for *The Vampire Bat* (33), hunting same as a detective in a small German town. That was a B and so was *Nagana*, in which he was a doctor in the African jungle with Tala Birell, a Continental import being tested for stardom by Universal. Douglas understandably asked for release from his contract and returned to Universal to play a small role as an admirer of *Counsellor-at-Law* John Barrymore. Then he returned to New York for a comedy, 'No More Ladies'.

When his wife was offered the lead in *She* – the only film she made – by RKO, that studio put him into three B pictures: *Dangerous Corner* (34), from J.B. Priestley's play, with Conrad Nagel and Virginia Bruce, as the head of a publishing company; *Woman in the Dark*, who was Fay Wray, caught between virtuous ex-con Ralph Bellamy and wicked ex-lover Douglas; and *The People's Enemy* (35), an old-hat melodrama, as an attorney, with Preston Foster as a gangster. He was really a back number when Gregory LaCava at Columbia was having difficulty in getting a big draw to co-star with Claudette Colbert in *She Married Her Boss*: so he became the store-owner who finds out that his perfect secretary does not make a perfect wife. Columbia liked him so much that they signed him to a seven-year contract, but promptly loaned him out to RKO for *Annie Oakley*, playing Buffalo Bill's partner; and Paramount for *Mary Burns Fugitive* (36), who was Sylvia Sidney, with Douglas as her blind chemist friend. Columbia put him into two Bs, *The Lone Wolf Returns* with Gail Patrick and *And So They Were Married* with Mary Astor. The first of these resurrected the jewel thief turned sleuth who had featured in a couple of Columbia Silents and at this series-happy time the studio considered that a likely project for Douglas: but the Lone Wolf would be played by Francis Lederer, Warren William and then other actors. For Douglas received fine notices opposite Irene Dunne, as the artist who designs the jacket for her book and the reason why *Theodora Goes Wild*. In fact, he was billed below the title and he was fifth down the cast-list on loan to MGM for *The*

Gorgeous Hussy, as the true love of that lady, Joan Crawford, the senator from Virginia. The critics thought him the best thing in the film and so, apparently, did MGM, for they negotiated with Columbia to share his contract. According to himself, both contracts had the usual options and he expected to be dropped before they ran their full terms.

And so, he also said, he became 'a run-of-the-mill leading man'. Maybe; but one who was instantly at home, stylish and nimble. With a player of his own class he could bat back dialogue like a champion ping-pong player. He was well-mannered and deferential; his look was quizzical rather than sarcastic (or enigmatic) – not that his skill was much needed in either *Women of Glamour* (37) with Virginia Bruce or *I'll Take Romance* with Grace Moore. But there were two upper-bracket comedies at Paramount, *I Met Him in Paris*, competing with Robert Young for Claudette Colbert, and *Angel*, ditto with Herbert Marshall for Dietrich. He had only a supporting role, as Freddie Bartholomew's father, in *Captains Courageous*.

He was the French gentleman crook who came back in *Arsene Lupin Returns* (38) and an authority on rare books in *Fast Company* with Florence Rice, one of the several *Thin Man* imitations that he made around this time. After competing with Mr Young again – for Luise Rainer, *The Toy Wife*, a Southern melodrama, he did another one, *There's Always a Woman* – and she was Joan Blondell. *The Shining Hour* was Joan Crawford's, and it was Deanna Durbin at *That Certain Age*, with a crush on him. *There's That Woman Again* (39) was a singularly unfortunate title, for while it was a sequel, Blondell had been replaced by Virginia Bruce; after which it was *Tell No Tales* – to Louise Platt, a B at MGM about a newspaper editor who turns amateur detective. Douglas's skill by this time was equally as good as William Powell's, but he had never achieved Powell's eminence at MGM; however, the latter's illness at this time gave Douglas the chance of playing opposite Garbo again in *Ninotchka* – though in fact he plays against her, flippant where she is solemn, cheaply insincere where she has great glooms of feeling. It was a perfect mating. He found working with her 'an extraordinary experience' and he enjoyed working again with Lubitsch, with whom had done *Angel*. 'Of all the movies I made, I liked just two or three, and that was chiefly because of the directors'. (He also liked Richard Boleslawski, who directed *Theodora*.)

After two programmers with Blondell, *Good Girls Go to Paris* and *The Amazing Mr Williams*, he romanced almost half the leading ladies in Hollywood: Jean Arthur in *Too*

She fell hook, line and sinker but then played hard to get in Third Finger Left Hand (40), a comedy whose banalities were offset by the playing of Myrna Loy and Melvyn Douglas.

After a long absence from movies, Douglas returned as a character actor, in Hud (63), and promptly won a Best Supporting Actor Oscar.

Many Husbands (40), as the second of them; Loretta Young in *He Stayed for Breakfast*, a satire on Communism, *Ninotchka* in reverse; Rosalind Russell in the remake of *This Thing Called Love*; Myrna Loy in *Third Finger Left Hand*; Merle Oberon in Lubitsch's *That Uncertain Feeling* (41), as the husband who almost loses her to Burgess Meredith; Joan Crawford in *A Woman's Face*, as her surgeon and lover, his only straight picture in this batch; Ruth Hussey in *Our Wife*; Garbo in *Two-Faced Woman*; Norma Shearer in *We Were Dancing* (42); Crawford again in *They All Kissed the Bride*; and Ann Sothern in *Three Hearts for Julia*.

He combined film-making at this period (41–42) with defence work in Washington; he enlisted in the US Army as a private and was demobbed in 1946 as a major.

He was happier in the army than back in Hollywood: *Sea of Grass* (47) at MGM, supporting Tracy and Hepburn, as the man with whom she is unfaithful; *The Guilt of Janet Ames* at Columbia with Russell, as a drunken reporter. Then, according to his own account, his lawyer found a loophole in his contract and he made only a couple of films before leaving Hollywood. In fact, he was in: *Mr Blandings Builds His Dream House* (48) with Loy and Cary Grant, third-billed as their lawyer and best friend; *My Own True Love*, as a British widower whose son threatens to take his much younger fiancée, Phyllis Calvert; *A Woman's Secret* (49), as a composer

embroiled with socialite Maureen O'Hara; *The Great Sinner*, as Ava Gardner's fiancé, a Casino official; *My Forbidden Past*, as her cousin, scheming against Robert Mitchum; and *On the Loose* with Lynn Bari, in which they were parents of a wild teenager (Joan Evans). But he was back on Broadway in 1949, in 'Two Blind Mice'; and subsequently in such plays as 'Time Out for Ginger' (52), including tours in the US and Australia, 'Inherit the Wind', 'The Waltz of the Toreadors', 'The Gang's All Here' and 'The Best Man' (60), winning a Tony for his performance. He described this time as 'except for my early years, the most productive and most satisfying of my life'. He also worked in TV, including 'Do Not Go Gentle Into That Good Night' (70) with Shirley Booth.

Douglas returned to the screen in *Billy Budd* (62), as the Dansker; and the following year was the grandfather in *Hud* (63), for which he won a Best Supporting Oscar. There followed: *Advance to the Rear* (64), a Civil War comedy, with Glenn Ford, as a colonel; *The Americanization of Emily*, as an eccentric admiral, his comic mastery shining through; *Rapture* (65), a title ill-befitting the film, a soppy romance, as the heroine's father; *Hotel*, as its owner; and *Companions in Nightmare* (68) for TV, with Gig Young. He was Burt Reynolds's foster-father, the town's most important citizen, in a tele-movie, *Hunters are for Killing* (70), and was particularly fine as

Gene Hackman's father in *I Never Sang for My Father* and again as the older man befriending Trish Van Devere in *One is a Lonely Number* (72). There was another TV film, *Death Takes a Holiday*, and a role as Robert Redford's father in *The Candidate*; while *The Going Up of David Lev* (73), made in Israel with Claire Bloom, found an odd US TV date. *The Death Squad* (74) was an undistinguished telemovie starring Robert Forster. Polanski's *The Tenant* (76) was better unmade and Douglas almsot the sole participant to emerge unscathed; *Twilight's Last Gleaming* (77) was also made in Europe and little seen, a disaster movie in which he was Secretary of Defense.

Once again (he had done so in *The Candidate*) he played elder statesmen in both *The Seduction of Joe Tynan* (79) and *Being There*, in the former as a scheming senator on the verge of senility and in the latter as one of America's most powerful *éminences grises*. The first was much the better picture, as directed and scripted by Alan Alda; the second, which starred Peter Sellers, was more talked about. The Los Angeles critics voted him the year's Best Supporting Actor for both, the New York critics dubbed him thus for the second, which also brought him his second Best Supporting Oscar. He was a senator again, albeit retired, in a classy horror film, *The Changeling* (80), and he was the husband of dying Lila Kedrova in *Tell Me a Riddle*, playing heavily Jewish for the first time in his career. His wife died in 1980 and he afterwards gave a moving interview to the 'New York Times', justifiably proud of her political career and her opposition to Nixon. He himself died a year later, leaving three films to be released posthumously: *Ghost Story* (81) with Astaire; *Portrait of Grandpa Doc* (82), a tele-movie and his last performance; and *Hot Touch*, as the mentor of Wayne Rogers, an art-forger. Like *The Changeling*, it had been filmed in Canada two years earlier. It is unlikely that he will be remembered for any of his last films, but there is a richness – and sometimes, when called for, a humour – which is invigorating.

MARIE DRESSLER

In 1933 the 'Motion Picture Herald' and the 'Hollywood Reporter' both named the same lady at the top in their annual polls to discover the biggest draws in films. She was not young or glamorous – a Garbo or a Shearer or a Gaynor – but an ageing, ugly and bulky lady whose speciality was low-life drunks: Marie Dressler. She had been a has-been for most of

the 20s, but had returned to fame with the coming of the Talkies and within a year had achieved a great popularity (in 1931 the first female star in a 'John Bull' poll of favourites; in 1932 third in the Bernstein Questionnaire, top of the 'Motion Picture Herald' list).

At that time the private lives of stars were common property, to a degree far surpassing that of the current PR-angled show business scene, and every cinemagoer knew that Dressler had triumphed over adversity: thus she had a very special meaning during the years of the Depression. It was once said that she was the Heart of America, just as Douglas Fairbanks Sr was the son of America and Mary Pickford its girl next door. But Doug and Mary (apart from the fact that they had been around so long) were out of tune with the times, with their optimism and high spirits, their gracious living and innocence: the public wanted rather to see the pessimistic and worldly wise Dressler.

Her popularity was in no way a freak. She was a considerable actress and a prodigious comedienne. She was required to give her all and she did. There is never any doubt of her feelings. Her normal expression was one of extreme scepticism, since she is the only sane person around. She could seem stern and unforgiving, but her heart is breaking underneath. Greatness in her field has nothing to do with subtlety. Her chins wobble and her eyes dart about, but unlike her famous partner – Wallace Beery – she never chews scenery. She gives us what, say, Celia Johnson does in *Brief Encounter*, someone with whom we are immediately in empathy. Most of the early humour she generated was crude references to her girth. She realized early, she said in her memoirs, 'The Life Story of an Ugly Duckling', that she 'was too homely for a prima donna and too big for a soubrette'.

She was born in Coburg, Ontario, in 1869 and made her first public appearance as a Cupid in a church hall pageant. She never went to school and, at 14, after answering a newspaper ad, joined a roving light opera troupe and worked mostly in the chorus. Her first major appearance was in a minor version of 'Under Two Flags', as Cigarette, out in the wilds, in 1886; by 1892 she had progressed to New York and made her début there in 'Robber on the Rhine', a play by and with Maurice Barrymore. It was Barrymore who realized her potentialities as a comic: in 1896, still in her 20s, she played Mrs Malaprop and then Barrymore persuaded her to go into vaudeville, where she was featured with Weber and Fields. In 1901 Weber (with Ziegfeld) featured her in a revue, 'Higgledy-Piggledy'. She became one of the nation's leading artists and scored also big successes in

London in 1907 and 1909, though on the latter occasion she collapsed from an ulcerated throat, the show closed and she lost all the money that she had put into it. She recouped her losses with 'Tillie's Nightmare' the following year, probably her biggest New York success. In 1912 she was with Weber and Fields again when they were reunited for the opening of Fields' 44th Street theatre. In 1913 came 'Marie Dressler's All Star Gambol' and in 1914 she was in 'A Mix-Up'.

She was in Los Angeles that year when Mack Sennett talked her into making a film version of 'Tillie'. No expense was spared: it was going to run to an unprecedented six reels instead of the usual one or two and have a shooting schedule of 14 weeks; and Dressler was to be supported by two of Sennett's star attractions, Charlie Chaplin and Mabel Normand. Audiences everywhere roared at the antics of these three: the mercenary Chaplin pursuing alternately the pretty Mabel and the formidable – but now suddenly wealthy, his ex-sweetheart – Dressler. The film was called *Tillie's Punctured Romance* (14) and it was reissued countless times (sometimes retitled *For the Love of Tillie* or *Tillie's Millions*) both in Britain and the US, right up to the 60s. But two that Dressler did without her co-stars and for other producers, *Tillie's Tomato Surprise* (15) and *Tillie Wakes Up* (17), had little success. She incorporated her own company and made some two-reelers: *The Scrublady*, *Fired* (18), *The Agonies of Agnes* and *The Cross Red Nurse*, in all of them as a lovable battleaxe.

Her main centre of activity remained vaudeville. However, at the same time as her film career failed to get off the ground, that turned sour on her. In 1917 she was one of the champions of the chorus-girl strike (which led to the founding of Equity) and after it she was *persona non grata* with most important managements. She was in a Broadway show in 1923, 'The Dancing Girl', and did some one-reel comedies in France: but by 1926 she was on the breadline. Allan Dwan gave her a small part in Fox's *The Joy Girl* (27), starring Olive Borden – and it literally saved her life: she got it because he chanced upon her in a hotel – and, she told him later, she was on her way upstairs to commit suicide. Other reports have her considering taking a job as a housekeeper on Long Island but, Dwan says, when the filming was over, he paid for her to get to Hollywood and there MGM scenarist Frances Marion came to the rescue. Dressler had shown great kindness to Marion at the time of *Tillie Wakes Up* and in return Marion now fashioned a screenplay for her and 'sold' the idea to Irving Thalberg. She was signed at $1,500 per week and another comedienne, Polly Moran, co-starred: *The Callahans and the Murphys*. After a few showings, however, various Irish pressure groups worked militantly against it and MGM withdrew it.

Marion persuaded her to stay in Hollywood and she got a part in *Breakfast at Sunrise* which starred Constance Talmadge; then Marion found another part for her – and Moran – in *Bringing Up Father* (28), an adaptation of George McManus's popular

They were the public's favourite screen lovers in the early Talkie period: Wallace Beery and Marie Dressler in Min and Bill *(30). It was one of the year's outstanding successes.*

comic strip; and again at MGM Dressler had a supporting part to Marion Davies in *The Patsy*, as her mother. When there were no more film offers she joined Edward Everett Horton's stock company in LA, but, once again in demand, due to the need for stage-trained performers, she left him flat, much to his indignation. She took to Talkies with ease: *The Divine Lady* (29) at First National – Corine Griffith as Lady Hamilton, as her mother; and *The Vagabond Lover* at RKO, as Rudy Vallee's aunt, shocking Long Island society – the best thing in the film, but not enough to save it or his career as a romantic leading man. At MGM she did a turn in *Hollywood Revue of 1929*, as Venus rising from the sea, and she played a passé actress in *Chasing Rainbows*: Moran was also in it, but it was basically a starring vehicle for Charles King and Bessie Love, who had been in *Broadway Melody*.

Dressler was established as a funny supporting woman. Marion persuaded Thalberg to let Dressler test for the part of Marthy in *Anna Christie* (30) – a serious part: the old harridan who welcomes Garbo when she returns looking for her father. Garbo was reputedly impressed; so were the critics and MGM, who now offered Dressler a contract. She was loaned out for *One Romantic Night*, playing Lillian Gish's mother and a queen – she hardly sounded or behaved like one – and put into *The Girl Said No*, a comedy that starred William Haines. Audiences still talked about her in *Anna Christie* and MGM tried again a teaming with Moran, *Caught Short*, with Dressler as a boarding-house dragon who ends up on Wall Street. The studio had doubts because of the lack of love-interest, but it was a big success.

She was the high spot of *Let Us Be Gay*, as the society matron who persuades Norma Shearer to vamp her ex-husband (to prevent him ruining her granddaughter); and the star, with Wallace Beery, of *Min and Bill*, in which she ran a waterfront tavern and he was her loyal admirer – till he falls for her best friend, when there follows a battle in which the best he can do is fail to get killed. This adroit mixture of slapstick and sentiment was a huge hit in both Britain and the US and brought Dressler a Best Actress Oscar. She became, officially, a star and was paid a salary of $5,000 a week. Dressler and Moran were teamed again: *Reducing* (31) – getting thin – and *Politics* – municipal variety – still and always as bosom pals, incessantly fighting and bickering. Although she clowned, Dressler's was a serious character study: Moran was more robust and much less sensitive. In 1931 she signed a new long-term contract, while making *Emma* (32), in which she was Jean Hersholt's indispensable maidservant and (in the last reel) bride. This was a 'Picturegoer' Gold Medal performance and the film was, again, big box-office. There was a reunion with Moran, *Prosperity* – a Depression comedy with Dressler as the president of a small-town bank – and one with Beery, *Tugboat Annie* (33). 'The Times' (London) reported that the stars played 'with finished technical cunning and an immense communicable energy of joy in the job. She is a game old woman, the captain of a tugboat, who is inordinately proud of her son (the captain of a liner) and has an ineradicable fondness for her husband (the tugboat's chief liability), "who has never struck me except in self-defence" . . . both Miss Dressler and Mr Beery have that exceptional power of making a comic point with complete certainty, of isolating it, and the next moment of making with the same certainty an effect that wins a sympathetic response deeper than laughter. Always – and it is their supreme merit – they have abounding life.'

MGM billed Dressler as 'The World's Greatest Actress' and fan-magazines referred to her as 'that grand old trouper'; it was agreed (probably truthfully) that she was the most beloved star on the lot. She dispensed homely philosophy (but kept quiet about the two broken marriages in her past). In films she brought her fine common touch to the role of the actress down on her luck in *Dinner at Eight* and to that of the housekeeper in *Christopher Bean*. She died in 1934, of cancer, while still topping popularity lists. Said 'Photoplay' in memoriam: 'It is the greatest of all tributes to Marie Dressler to say that her appeal was universal. . . . I do not care what your status in life may be, of one thing I am certain: if you ever saw Marie Dressler on the screen she went straight to your heart. That was because the shining qualities that made her so beloved by everyone that knew her personally, were revealed – every word, gesture and facial expression – in her film interpretations.'

IRENE DUNNE

Irene Dunne's forte was indestructible dignity. In the slushy melodramas she made at the start of her career she suffered with patience: she was noble in *Cimarron*. When she turned to comedy she was invincibly ladylike – it is hardly a coincidence that Deborah Kerr inherited two of her old parts. Kerr is possibly a better actress, but you cannot tell for sure: a different sensitivity was required in the well-oiled Dunne vehicles of the 30s than is needed in the more realistic (supposedly) films that Kerr made. Miss Dunne had more lightness, more humour. It is more than a small achievement to have played the poor blind lady of *Magnificent Obsession* in glittering gown and an artificial Paris and remain more than touching today, but then Miss Dunne's way with such material was to underplay everything and find whatever humour there was going. She is literally superb in *Love Affair*, but that has comedy sewn in among the tears – and few actresses could play comedy as she did: there is a brief sequence in *The Awful Truth* where, her back to the camera, she is contemplating the antics of Cary Grant – her gurgling, smothered laugh more eloquent than many another's close-ups. She had the best timing, he said, of anyone he

ever worked with. She was airy and rather super.

She was born in Louisville, Kentucky, in 1904, the daughter of a government official, and educated there at the Loretta Academy. She graduated from the Chicago College of Music, with a local reputation as a fine singer, and was quickly taken on to play Irene in the touring company of the musical of that name. Her first New York appearance was in 'The Clinging Vine' (23). She also appeared in 'Lollipop' (24), 'Sweetheart Time' (26), 'Yours Truly' (27), 'Luckee Girl', 'She's My Baby' (starring Beatrice Lillie and Clifton Webb), etc.; in 1929 she was chosen to play Magnolia in the road company of 'Show Boat' and that led to Hollywood and a starring contract with RKO.

First she was tucked away in a cheerful army musical (from Broadway's 'Present Arms') with Eddie Foy Jr and a host of comics, *Leathernecking* (30), and might have languished had Richard Dix (who had seen her on the stage) not recommended her for the lead with him in *Cimarron* (31), as wife Sabra Cravat in Edna Ferber's story. She ended up a Congresswoman and an Oscar nominee; the film won a Best Picture Oscar and, at $2 million, was 1931's biggest money-maker (in Britain, too). Dunne was now a big star. RKO put her into *Bachelor Apartment*, a sophisticated comedy with Lowell Sherman directing and co-starring; loaned her to MGM for *The Great Lover*, a backstage romance with Adolphe Menjou finally sacrificing his own happiness for the sake of hers and Neil Hamilton's; involved her with Pat O'Brien, on the rebound, in a *Consolation Marriage*; and made her a crippled schoolteacher in love with fashionable Jewish doctor Ricardo Cortez in *Symphony of Six Million* (32) wanting to bring him to his senses – and back to the ghetto. This was a much-praised movie, directed by Gregory LaCava, from a novel by Fannie Hurst. She was one of the *Thirteen Women*, the only one not bumped off by Myrna Loy; but there was *No Other Woman* (33) for Charles Bickford.

Meanwhile, she lived in *Back Street* (32), another Hurst novel, as the mistress of married man John Boles, one of the weepies by which other weepies are measured. And more handkerchiefs were required for *The Secret of Madame Blanche* (33), a wartime story with Dunne as a Frenchwoman standing trial for a murder committed by a British Tommy – the son she lost to his British father at birth. MGM borrowed her for this, presumably because none of their own stars would do it. She was at least a bit more positive in *The Silver Cord*, opposing a possessive mother-in-law (Laura Hope Crews) in this version of

When a woman loves a man . . . she will live in Back Street *for him, welcoming his mighty visits before he goes home to his wife. Irene Dunne and John Boles in one of the big hits of 1932. There were two later versions.*

Women the world over wept when Irene Dunne, blind, was loved by Robert Taylor in The Magnificent Obsession *(35).*

Sidney Howard's play: Joel McCrea was in the midst of the tug-of-war. And there was more of same: *Ann Vickers* with Walter Huston; *If I Were Free*, a John Van Druten story with Clive Brook and Nils Asther; *This Man is Mine* (34), a triangle drama with Ralph Bellamy and Constance Cummings; *Stingaree*, reunited with Dix, an Australian drama about an outlaw and a singer who finally make it for peace to the outback; and *The Age of Innocence*, with Boles, which contrived to make Edith Wharton's novel as much like *Back Street* as possible.

Reminded by *Stingaree* that Dunne could sing, Warners borrowed her for the film of Jerome Kern's stage hit, *Sweet Adeline* (35), with Donald Woods; and RKO co-starred her – though she was top-billed – in Kern's *Roberta*, with Astaire and Rogers. It was a welcome touch of levity, but Dunne said: 'Heavy dramatic roles are essential for an actress of my type. I know definitely that the status I have achieved has been achieved through tears. So for my career I cry.' Her contract was up and she signed short-term deals with Universal and Columbia. Universal starred her in another sudsy tale, Lloyd C. Douglas's *Magnificent Obsession*, as the woman blinded by playboy Robert Taylor in an accident (he makes amends by – secretly – caring for her); and *Show Boat* (36), done as a straightforward melodrama with songs, with Allan Jones and Dunne superb in her old stage part. Columbia, however, took a risk and put her, against her will, into *Theodora Goes Wild*, a sunny, harum-scarum comedy about a small-town girl who writes a hot bestseller and is humanized by Melvyn Douglas. She got great notices and the film was popular: with that and *Show Boat*, her stock soared.

She continued to freelance, picking her vehicles with care, with an almost rigid alternation between comedy and drama (she was announced for lives of Madame Curie and Mary Baker Eddy, but nothing came of either project). There was another comedy, a remake, the delicious *The Awful Truth* (37) with Cary Grant, a will-she-won't-she-divorce-him; which was sandwiched between two musicals, both with Kern music: *High, Wide and Handsome* with Randolph Scott at Paramount and *Joy of Living* (38) with Douglas Fairbanks Jr at RKO. Wrote Fairbanks: 'One of the more civilized women. She's a dream, an absolute dream, one of the most professional women I've ever known. Nothing is instinctive, everything she does is carefully thought out, she knows every movement, every intonation, every nuance. She's a first-class craftswoman. Her hours are like office hours, she's never late, she never slips, but instead of being dull and perfect, she's absolutely enchanting and perfect.'

In 1939 Dunne had a very successful *Love Affair* with Charles Boyer – her own favourite of her films ('not only because it was so well done, but also because we had such a good time making it') – but *Invitation to Happiness* (society girl marries boxer Fred MacMurray) was hardly that as far as audiences were concerned. *When Tomorrow Comes* was another four-handkerchief effort with Boyer in love with her and keeping from her the fact that he has a wife who is loco. There were two

more with Grant: *My Favorite Wife* (40), about the wife who returns from the grave just after he has remarried; and George Stevens's *Penny Serenade* (41), a series of vignettes of married life – relentlessly sentimental, but exquisitely done. If you could take two Dunne films to your desert island, you would choose this or *Love Affair* – and certainly not *Unfinished Business* or *Lady in a Jam* (42), both directed by Gregory LaCava in decline. She was, respectively, a small-town girl reforming playboy Robert Montgomery and a scatty impoverished heiress 'cured' by Patric Knowles. Moving on to MGM, she did two of the bigger wartime weepies, *A Guy Named Joe* (43), being told by Spencer Tracy that 'this thing is bigger than you and me', and *The White Cliffs of Dover*, loving Alan Marshall. The latter concerned a British family in two world wars inspired by *Mrs Miniver* – and the ads blatantly aimed it at the same public. 'Antiquity and quaintness are the keynotes,' observed Forsyth Hardy, noting that Dunne, as an American learning to understand the British, 'plays with a generous warmth of feeling'.

Then she and Boyer were *Together Again*, she as a prim mayoress and he as a sculptor: the outcome was predictable. *Over 21* (45), with Alexander Knox, was even less agreeable, but she was offered three big ones in a row, the first of which she turned down at first. *Anna and the King of Siam* (46) was a successful and enjoyable version of Anna

Leonowens's book. Richard Winnington commented: 'The indomitable Victorian governess is a smart, witty, resourceful woman, in fact, Miss Irene Dunne, and nobody but.' Rex Harrison, her co-star, later cited her as the most impressive of the actresses he had worked with: 'Extraordinary. A really remarkable woman, as a woman.' The other two were both from Broadway successes, both 'memory' pieces: *I Remember Mama* (47) and *Life With Father* (48). *Mama* was made by Stevens, a tender story of a Norwegian community in the US at the turn of the century, and *Father* (William Powell) was upper-class New York in the 90s: the latter was funnier and one of the year's biggest money-makers.

She then made a mistake: 20th, taken in by the matriarchal image she had now assumed, cast her in *The Mudlark* (50), the tale of a Cockney kid who visits Queen Victoria (Dunne). The British press resented an American actress being imported for this part, which is perhaps why British audiences stayed away – despite the presence of the then-potent Alec Guinness in the cast. American audiences stayed away too – maybe because they did not want to see Dunne padded and in a rubber mask. Two modestly budgeted comedies did nothing to restore her to favour – the inaptly titled *Never a Dull Moment* with MacMurray and *It Grows on Trees* (52) with Dean Jagger, the latter described by her as 'a terrible mistake'. She has not filmed since. Two films she turned down were *We're No Angels* and the 1962 remake of *State Fair*.

In 1956 she appeared in a TV drama and the following year she became an Alternative Delegate at the 12th Session of the UN General Assembly. In 1965 her husband of almost 40 years died. Occasionally her picture appears in the press, taken at some Hollywood function. In 1966, when Leslie Halliwell did a British TV programme on the Oscar Ceremony, he wrote in 'Films and Filming' that of all the celebrities he had met in Hollywood, Dunne was by far the most unaffected and most charming.

Later Miss Dunne was one of the screen's perfect wives: notably in Penny Serenade *(41) with Cary Grant.*

DEANNA DURBIN

In 1942 there was a unique programme playing the Odeon circuit throughout Britain: 'The Durbin Festival – designed to give the public seven Happy Days with Deanna. . . . From the child of our hearts to the woman we love.' Each of the films played for one day only, but it was the same film in all the cinemas; and there were second features. A considerable feat of organization (transport-

Hollywood's Deanna as the world fell in love with her, left, singing, and Hollywood's Deanna, right, after they tried to turn her into the standardised glamour girl – though it's a pity that some of the other child stars didn't grow up to look as smashing as this. Centre, Deanna's Deanna – and her husband's favourite picture of her. When the photographer told her that he wanted to photograph her like an angel she replied that she would rather look like the devil. The picture shows quite clearly why she said later she wished they had offered her the sort of role Tatum O'Neil had in Paper Moon.

ing prints, etc.): but the Festival played to packed cinemas. Durbin's popularity was considerably greater in Britain than the US; in Britain during the four years 1939–42 she was easily the top female box-office draw, but she was liked everywhere and was a critics' pet. The qualities they praised in her – charm, spontaneity, naturalness, her artlessness and her singing voice – were more highly prized then than they are now, but she was probably the most agreeable child who ever starred in movies.

In private life she was extremely self-assured and there are touches of wit and acerbity in her performances which place her easily in the forefront of those girls who have made a career out of playing Cinderella. These qualities were matched, in the almost perfect vehicles of her early period, by the cynicism of some of the supporting cast: 'She's not going to *sing*?' says her cousin in *First Love*, half-contemptuously, half-despairingly.

She was born in Winnipeg, Canada, in 1921 or 1922 (studios lied about the age of child stars), of émigré-Lancashire parents, who moved to Los Angeles soon after. Her remarkable singing voice attracted attention and at one point she auditioned before Disney for the voice of Snow White, but he thought hers too grown-up for the role. It did bring an MGM talent scout to her school to hear her; his studio planned a life of opera singer Eva Schumann-Heink and Durbin was signed with a view to playing her as a child. The film was abandoned and she was put into a short with Judy Garland, *Every Sunday* (36); then, at the end of six months, dropped (legend has it due to a misunderstanding: Louis B. Mayer said 'Drop the fat one', meaning Garland). Uni-

versal producer Joe Pasternak (who was also considering Edith Fellows) ran the short with a view to signing Garland for a movie he was making about three teenage girls who reunite their divorcing parents, but Garland had just been loaned to 20th and Pasternak ran the short again to see whether Durbin could substitute; and Universal signed her. By this time her parents had found an agent to handle her and he got her a job singing on the Eddie Cantor Radio Hour – so that she was nationally famous by the time *Three Smart Girls* (37) was shown. It was a programme picture designed to keep the studio in business after a series of massive flops and a change of management, with a medium budget and five 'name'-players who as a team might attract patrons. Their names on the credits are followed by 'and Universal's new singing discovery' – for Universal knew they had a gold mine when they saw the rushes: apart from the voice, the child had warmth and high spirits; and she seemed to be enjoying herself hugely. Her part was padded and the budget doubled. Public response was immediate and $2 million poured into the studio's empty coffers. Historically she was Universal's first real star since the Silent era: big names had come to the studio to work, but very few under long-term contracts.

Bankruptcy averted, Universal gratefully gave Pasternak what he wanted for their new asset, some 'highbrow' music: the plot of *One Hundred Men and a Girl* had Durbin persuading an unwilling Stokowski to conduct an orchestra of Depression-hit musicians. Said the 'New Statesman' (P. Galway): 'Useless to pretend that I am tough enough to resist the blandishments of Miss Deanna Durbin. The candid eyes, the parted lips, the electric energy, the astonishing voice; if they bowl over 50 million or so, surely a critic may be pardoned for wobbling a little on his professional cynical base. For this is pure fairy tale; but it comes off.' Universal proffered a new contract, going from $1,500 to $3,000 a week, plus a bonus of $10,000 per film, and they got a bargain. Pasternak noted independently at this time that a top star was worth $10 million, adding (significantly) that every bad film caused a $2 million depreciation.

No need to worry: he had an uncanny knack of selecting the right vehicles. In her 1938 films she brought romance in the shape of Herbert Marshall to unhappy mother – *Mad About Music* – and had a schoolgirl crush on Melvyn Douglas in *That Certain Age*. 'The New York Times' called her 'pert and charming' and the 'New York Herald Tribune' 'innocent and captivating'. In Britain, wrote the 'Sunday Express': 'These Deanna Durbin pictures – and this is the fourth – are the miracle films of today. They never put a wrong foot forward. They never overreach themselves. They never for a moment lose that sparkle. They never miss.' And 'Punch' said: '. . . in her other films her ability often struck me as miraculous; now it seems to me instinctively perfect.' Hollywood concurred: she was awarded a special juvenile Oscar. In 1939 her enthusiastic followers watched *Three Smart Girls Grow Up* and then saw, with trepidation, their idol receive her first screen kiss (from Robert Stack), an event covered by the presses of the world without moderation, in *First Love*, an undisguised modern rendering of 'Cinderella' which is probably her best film. Admirably she was being eased into adult roles: in *It's a Date* (40) losing the man (Walter Pidgeon) to whom she and her actress mother (Kay Francis) are both attracted; in *Spring Parade* playing a Viennese pastry cook who falls for a dashing officer (Robert Cummings) and, startlingly, in *Nice Girl?* (41), a youngster so fed up because her boyfriend (Mr Stack) prefers cars to her that she dolls herself up to visit a Manhattan playboy (Franchot Tone). The situation was handled with taste (it could have brought down her,

In It's a Date *(40) Deanna developed a crush on Walter Pidgeon, who then fell in love with her mother, Kay Francis. This is how Universal enabled Deanna to grow up – a much more satisfying way of handling adolescent stars than making them match-makers.*

Universal and even Hollywood had it not been) and proved her ready for her first real adult role, in *It Started With Eve*, as the hat-check girl Cummings gets to impersonate his fiancée, for the sake of his dying father, Charles Laughton – to whom she gives credit for teaching her to relax on set for the first time, though that is not evident from the confidence in her work. In 1940 a new contract had been negotiated, at $400,000 per film.

She married; and the transition to adult star having been successfully accomplished, Pasternak could not agree with Universal on her treatment and moved to MGM. Immediately the lack of guidance began to show and she was suspended for refusing *Boy Meets Baby*: she returned only when given story and director approval. Because Pasternak and Henry Koster, who had directed her most frequently, had been European, Universal looked for guidance to the German-born screenwriter, Felix Jackson, who had worked on most of her films. He became producer of all but the next of the nine films which followed – and, subsequently, her second husband. More puzzlingly, they wanted to put her into 'European'-type films – despite the fact that her vehicles had little in common with art-house movies. A Wilder-Brackett script was not, in the event, used for *The Amazing Mrs Holliday* (43) and Jean Renoir resigned from the direction because, he said, 'the star was unable to escape from the style that made her famous'. In fact, he floundered and at one point persuaded the studio to abandon the project in favour of a modern version of 'The Taming of the Shrew' with Durbin as a gas station attendant. He grew tired of that too and left, so they returned to the original story, which emerged as an unlikeable film about a missionary's daughter who pretends to be the widow of an aged magnate in order to house some Chinese orphans. Edmond O'Brien was another of the less-than-dynamic Durbin leading men. But she herself 'maintains her fetching natural-ness' ('News Chronicle') and 'has never given a more natural or lovelier performance' ('Daily Mail').

Hers to Hold was another – loose – sequel to *Three Smart Girls*, with Joseph Cotten and a patriotic story of a rich, headstrong girl who because of him goes to work in a munitions factory, and as *His Butler's Sister* she per-suaded Pat O'Brien to let her wait at table for a Broadway composer, Franchot Tone. Frank Borzage directed this escapist comedy and she was again, as rarely, given another first-rate director, Robert Siodmak, to guide her in her bid for acceptance as a dramatic actress, in *Christmas Holiday* (44). Although she was

not, as in Maugham's novel, a Russian whore working in Paris but a nightclub singer in New Orleans, the public refused to accept her in the part. The film was a considerable box-office hit, but the outcry was such that Universal refused to consider a similar experi-ment, at which point Durbin lost all interest in films. It is a pity: Graham Greene had observed – half a dozen films earlier – 'There is no doubt any longer of Miss Durbin's immense talents as an actress,' and this performance more than proved him right.

Pasternak had prophesied that Durbin was one of 'those personalities which the world . . . insists on regarding as its personal property', and her public stayed faithful through divorce and remarriage and attempts to publicize her as just another cutie; but they blenched a little at the harsh make-up and the blonde curls of *Can't Help Singing*, even if she was in colour for the first time and had songs by Jerome Kern. It was the last real Durbin hit, though a comedy-thriller, *Lady on a Train* (45), directed by Charles David, allowed her a high old time as an amateur sleuth: but she is over-made-up and overdressed in this film particularly. It is easy to sympathize with her wish to escape the girl-next-door image of her early films, and she had emphatically not been at all like that since becoming an international idol, but the studio looked at the grosses and did not sympathize. The old Deanna returned in *Because of Him* (46), a reunion with Messrs Laughton and Tone, as actor and playwright pestered by a waitress for a role in their play. The idea was good, the film was not.

Deanna had matured into a polished light-comedy player, but where her old co-star Judy Garland (their careers and private lives had run parallel for some time) was being given colour and the best talent MGM could afford, Durbin was not (and it is tempting to wonder what the Freed unit might have done with her). Rescue seemed at hand when Leo Spitz and William Goetz bought Universal, primar-ily to acquire her services – and they believed, because she could look glamorous and had a wide musical range, she could become the biggest star in Hollywood. But *I'll Be Yours* (47), then in production, did little to support that view: it was a lacklustre remake of *The Good Fairy* with the star as a country girl in the Big Apple. Tom Drake was the leading man, and Deanna was then lumbered with John Dall in *Something in the Wind*, but otherwise this is easily the best of the late Durbins, an entertaining musical about a radio announcer who through misunderstand-ings is thought to be an old man's darling. It showed that the new management was really trying and they bought a popular Broadway musical for her, *Up in Central Park* (48), about a colleen caught up with a corrupt Tammany politician (Vincent Price) and the reporter (Dick Haymes, horribly miscast) who wants to expose them. The film cried out for Technicolor, but the studio argued that that – and co-stars of box-office weight – had to be withheld because her salary swallowed most of the budget. She herself said later that each time she asked for stronger material they offered her more money; in 1945 and 1947 she was the highest-paid female star in Hollywood.

If her public had deserted her, it was with justice: this last film must be one of the worst – stodgy, misconceived – star vehicles ever made, though it has competition from *For the Love of Mary* (49), in which Durbin plays a meddling Washington telephonist with three cut-rate admirers, Edmond O'Brien, Don Taylor and Jeffrey Lynn. Although she herself denies this, most sources indicate that it was made before *Up in Central Park* and put on a shelf – which is entirely the best place for it. She also says that the studio instinct was to get every ounce of value from her contract and that therefore she worked it out, but when she was released in 1949, with much publicity, a spokesman said that it was due to 'increasing public apathy', that she had not done any work for them in the last two years and that they were paying her the salary due to her for three more films. It may be true that they had tried to force her out without that payment, for her last two films are not only terrible in themselves but show-case her particular talents with an ineptitude so absolute that it might have been deliberate; but it is equally true – and sad – that Universal seemed incapable of making any film of any merit throughout this period.

There were reports of other offers – Pasternak dreamed for years of getting her to MGM – and she turned down 'My Fair Lady', then in an embryo stage, because she 'had a ticket to Paris in my pocket' at the time. She announced her retirement, postponed from the time of her first marriage when she had been persuaded to stay because it was wartime and she was an entertainer. She herself had been unhappy during these last years, 'in a blue funk' as she puts it herself, partly due to the failure of her first two marriages; and she felt strongly that Hollywood was not the place to bring up her children.

She married Charles David and settled near Paris. Unlike Judy Garland, her money had been invested wisely and she had become a very wealthy woman. With her happy family life this Cinderella ending contrasts with that of most stars. She refuses to see the press, but has emerged from retirement to squash rumours of a come-back. She told Eddie Cantor: 'I don't want to have anything to do with show business ever', and in one announcement she made it clear that she had disliked Hollywood and stardom and, what is more, had loathed 'the concocted Durbin personality' which 'never had any similarity to me, not even coincidentally'. Perhaps; but that personality has continued to generate new legions of admirers. During the last decade or so the BBC in Britain has several times said that they get more requests for her records and her films – followed by Alice Faye – than any other star of Hollywood's great era.

NELSON EDDY

The phenomenal success of the Jeanette MacDonald-Nelson Eddy operettas owed more to her than to him. In commercial terms, he was always some paces behind (she was one of the top 10 draws in Britain 1937–42 inclusive; he trailed behind on three occasions, 1939–41) and although he could sing manfully – in his own way as stolidly good as she in hers – he had not much facility with a line and his presence on the screen was not unlike that of a cold suet pudding at a children's tea-party. Most of what he was given to do was impossible, even within the conventions, but the same is true of her material and she is much less risible today.

He was born in Providence, Rhode Island, in 1901, and as a boy sang soprano in church choirs. He moved to Philadelphia in his teens and worked there as a switchboard operator and shipping clerk. Through a friend, he got a job writing obituaries on a local paper and worked his way up in journalism; but he had the urge to sing and appeared in an amateur musical, 'The Marriage Tax', and in Gilbert and Sullivan; and won a competition to sing with the Philadelphia Civic Opera. His first role was Amonasro in 'Aïda' (24) and he made his New York début, at the Met, when the Civic Opera visited there with 'Pagliacci': he was Tonio. In New York in 1931 he played the Drum Major in Berg's 'Wozzeck', but from 1928 onwards he had concentrated on recitals and concerts. These, and radio work, made him quite well known: MGM, when they got hold of him, tried to render him anonymous again. Ida Koverman had seen him in concert in Los Angeles and had persuaded the studio to sign him, but for a couple of years all he did were guest stints, singing one song in *Broadway to Hollywood* (33), *Dancing Lady* and a terrible Jimmy Durante vehicle, *Student Tour* (34).

He languished, in fact, while MGM searched for a leading man for MacDonald for

We shall not see their like again – the 'Singing Sweethearts' in Rose Marie *(36), perhaps the only one of the MacDonald-Eddy films which can be recommended to non-devotees of operette.*

Naughty Marietta (35). It was a pet project of Mayer's and it was he who finally insisted that Eddy be given his chance. The result was box-office pow and Eddy was assigned to co-star with Grace Moore in *Rose Marie* (36). However, she would not be ready till he had left on a concert tour, so MacDonald replaced her. The box-office this time was pow-wow and when the Moore and Eddy schedules once more conflicted over *Maytime* (37), MGM had no hesitation in once more casting Mac-Donald. He sang, however, to Eleanor Powell in *Rosalie* (37), as a West Point Cadet who falls in love without knowing she is a European princess; but he was back with MacDonald in *Girl of the Golden West* (38) – *most* unlikely as a dashing Mexican bandit – and *Sweethearts*, in which they were a squabbling Broadway couple. That proved conclusively that Eddy could not play comedy, and in other ways he was disappointing to MGM. It did not help that he stood on the set with a stop-watch to ensure that she had no more close-up time than he. They were separated and the studio tried to give him a more masculine image by

making him a two-fisted homesteader in *Let Freedom Ring!* (39), a gird-our-loins drama which fell by the wayside despite Virginia Bruce's rendition of 'The Star-Spangled Banner'. *Balalaika*, based on a West End show, was heard of for a few years hence with Eddy as a Cossak prince pretending to be a student to win Ilona Massey – who had been kept in the wings as a threat to the sometimes recalcitrant Jeanette. This was something akin to adultery to fans, who were delighted to have the Singing Sweethearts together again in *New Moon* (40) and *Bitter Sweet*, even if they were perceptibly ageing.

Metropolitan star Risë Stevens was his co-star in *The Chocolate Soldier* (41), which was not a version of that stage musical, but of 'The Guardsman' – the stars, however, played actors appearing in 'The Chocolate Soldier'. MacDonald and Eddy were back again in *I Married an Angel* (42) – for the last time, just as MGM had announced before it went into production. Some mystery surrounds the break: the receipts of the series had decreased but slightly; the most likely explanation is that

Hunt Stromberg, who had produced most of them, was leaving to set up his own company – plus the fact that the studio felt that the very high production costs had become risky in the changed world situation. MacDonald's contract was almost up and Eddy's was allowed to lapse.

After an interval, he turned up at Universal in *The Phantom of the Opera* (43), with hair dyed black and a pencil-line moustache, supposedly transformed into a Frenchman: the film was a huge success but it took him a year to find another role, in the film version of the Weill-Anderson *Knickerbocker Holiday* (44), with Constance Dowling and Charles Coburn. It broke agreeably from backstage conventions and he was much more animated than hitherto, but it was not what you would call popular. RKO dickered with the idea of a MacDonald-Eddy musical and both were agreeable despite an animosity which had not lessened with the years, but the executive who had favoured it died and the project was shelved. After a longer silence, broken only by his dubbing of Willie the

Whale in Disney's *Make Mine Music* (46), he was reduced to working at Republic, with Massey, in *North West Frontier* (47), which the British distributors prophetically renamed *End of the Rainbow* – and for which they had difficulties getting bookings. Allan Dwan, who directed, said the film sent up the Eddy character. He added that Eddy 'was the ham of hams – a nice guy, but he wanted to play a cowboy above all things'.

Eddy did concerts and records, and then had a rather unexpected success on the night-club circuit, with a girl called Gale Sherwood: most of the act consisted of reprises of songs from his film musicals. While appearing at Miami Beach, in 1967, he collapsed on stage and died of a stroke. He left a widow, Anne Franklin, whom he had married in 1939.

DOUGLAS FAIRBANKS

The elder Fairbanks inspired one of the most moving tributes ever penned by a critic to a star. This is C.A. Lejeune, the week he died: '[His death] has robbed the movies of a bit of themselves – a drop of the life-blood that first made them gay, and great, and indomitable . . . Fairbanks never really knew how good he was. Behind those acrobatic stunts and that schoolboy exuberance, there was real genius. His leaps, and fights, and swift, violent trajectories were thrilling to watch, but they were inventive, too; they had about them the quality of beauty and surprise. He was an unconscious harlequin. Everything he did had poise and rhythm. . . . We may have forgotten the names of the pictures, but that tough, stocky little figure, that friendly grin, and the sense of almost illimitable mastery of space and time stays with us.'

And his friend, Chaplin (in his memoirs): 'It was not for naught that Douglas captured the imagination and love of the public. The spirit of his pictures, their optimism and infallibility, were very much to the American taste, and indeed to the taste of the whole world. He had extraordinary magnetism and charm and a genuine boyish enthusiasm which he conveyed to the public.' The word used by Oscar Levant in an odd moment was 'magical'. He was unique and greatly loved. Fans merely smiled indulgently when learning that his hobby was listed as 'Doug'.

Fairbanks was born (Douglas Ulman) in Denver, Colorado, in 1883, the son of a Jewish lawyer and a Roman Catholic mother (Fairbanks was the name of her first husband, to which she reverted when the boy's father deserted). He was expensively educated and spent some months at Harvard before decid-

When Austrian composer Nelson Eddy can't sell his operas he and his English débutante wife Jeanette MacDonald take to performing in the streets of Vienna: a scene from MGM's distortion of Noël Coward's Bitter Sweet *(40).*

ing to bum around Europe for the sake of experience; at one point he worked in Paris as a labourer, but back in New York he had more suitable ambitions. He toyed with stock-broking and the law, but was most strongly drawn to the theatre. He had acted with Frederick Warde's touring company in 1900; in 1902 he had a small part in a Broadway play, 'Her Lord and Master', and, finally, later that year, he decided to make the stage his career. He was in the chorus of 'Fantana' (03) when producer William A. Brady heard of him from his wife, Grace George, and decided that his exuberance would lead to stardom. He signed Fairbanks for five years and during that time Fairbanks played juveniles in New York and on tour. His first lead was in 'As Ye Sow' and he had a big success in 'The Man of the Hour' before he married Beth Sully in 1907. She persuaded him to join her father's firm, but when it went broke he

Douglas Fairbanks in his early days as a star.

returned to the stage – in 'All for a Girl' in 1908; after that he toured in 'A Gentleman From Mississippi' and did a sketch in vaudeville. He was also in 'Hawthorne of the USA', later filmed with Wallace Reid. By 1914 he had become a popular Broadway actor and as such was sought by Triangle (D.W. Griffith, Thomas H. Ince and Mack Sennett), as represented by Harry E. Aitken, who noted later that Fairbanks was picked 'because of the splendid humanness that fairly oozed out of him'. The film industry's new gambit of signing stage names was chiefly in a bid for respectability (huge grosses had been registered by films starring the likes of Sarah Bernhardt, which the curious went to see). Fairbanks hesitated, but was swayed by the cash ($2,000 a week), by the thought that he was merely another ageing juvenile and, finally, by the concept of a new movie era ushered in by the showing of *The Birth of a Nation* (his own first movie was also to have a swank première with Paderewski as guest of honour and was to play New York at theatre prices – $3 a seat). Typically, he was fascinated by the risk involved in beginning a new career. When the run of 'The Show Shop' was over, he entrained to Hollywood to make *The Lamb* (15), based on 'The New Henrietta', in which he had starred on Broadway (it later became *The Saphead*, with Buster Keaton).

His exuberance on-set alienated many on the unit, including the supervising Griffith, who thought Fairbanks might do better in two-reel comedies with Mabel Normand; but both film and performance were a hit with critics and public. Griffith directed *Double Trouble*, in which Fairbanks had a dual role, and then he was turned over to director John Emerson and scenarist Anita Loos, who are usually credited with harnessing his huge smiling energy; from their creation was to come the eventual Fairbanks persona, though at this point he usually – indeed, to modern eyes, monotonously – played a wealthy ne'er-do-well whose basic decency would be revealed after exposure to true American values. This was a character especially acceptable to American audiences during the uneasy period of neutrality and then war. The films debunked the phoney and pretentious, leavened with some even healthier athleticism: *His Picture in the Papers*; *The Habit of Happiness*, as a black sheep helping some hobos; *The Good Bad Man*, a Western with Bessie Love; *Reggie Mixes In*, as a playboy saving Bessie from gangsters; *Flirting With Fate*; *The Half-Breed*, in which he braved a forest fire; and *The Mystery of the Leaping Fish*, a cod melodrama in which he was a detective.

Of the next one, *Manhattan Madness*, Fairbanks's biographers, Ralph Hancock and

Letitia Fairbanks ('Douglas Fairbanks: The Fourth Musketeer', 1953), note that a contemporary critic commented that it was 'really nothing more than St Vitus' Dance set to ragtime'. And David Robinson (in 'Hollywood in the Twenties', 1968) finds that Fairbanks's back-slapping 'looks nowadays a ludicrous caricature of the extrovert personality'. But the film was a wow at the time; hardly less so were *American Aristocracy* (also with Jewel Carmen), *The Matrimaniac* (with Constance Talmadge) and *The Americano* (down South as 'an all-round chap, just a regular American'). With this one his contract was up; he was now getting $10,000 a week, but considered this chicken-feed compared with what his pictures were earning: thus was set up the Douglas Fairbanks Pictures Corp., with distribution through Artcraft (later Famous Players–Lasky). With him went Emerson and Loos, and director Allan Dwan,

though Fairbanks himself worked increasingly on the creative side of his pictures.

In Again Out Again (17) was the first: 'Doug again, too – sounds like him, doesn't it?' said 'Picturegoer'. It was a modest effort which sent up the pacifist movement. *Wild and Wooly* marked a further refinement of the character: here he was chained to a desk, but hung up on shooting Red Indians out west. Henceforward he was to represent a free spirit, at odds with that Brooks Brothers suit mentality. In *Down to Earth* he sent up hypochondriacs – a scenario he wrote, as he did the next one, *The Man From Painted Post*. *Reaching for the Moon* rounded out his 1917 releases (in all but the first of which Eileen Percy was his leading lady). In 1918 came *A Modern Musketeer* (a young chap inspired by reading about D'Artagnan); *Headin' South*, *Mr Fix-It*, *Say Young Fellow*, *Bound in Morocco*, *He Comes Up Smiling* and, prob-

The Thief of Bagdad (*24*): *Fairbanks was just over 40 when he made it, and still at the height of his athletic powers. The lady being threatened is Anna May Wong.*

ably his worst film, *Arizona* – the only one he directed himself. His leading lady this year (except in *Morocco*) was Marjorie Daw and she was also with him in his last under his contract, *The Knickerbocker Buckaroo* (19).

During much of this time, Fairbanks, with Mary Pickford and with Chaplin (three heroes such as American history had never known), sold millions of dollars worth of war bonds. Now the war was over, the three of them (with Griffith) founded United Artists to produce and distribute their own pictures: *His Majesty the American* and *When the Clouds Roll By*, in the latter as a failed stockbroker whose silly superstitions are swept away after overcoming mad psychiatrists, myriad crooks, pretentious socialites and a flood. Both reflected his postwar optimism, a mood enhanced by his love for Miss Pickford. Both were afraid of the effect of the respective divorces on their popularity, but their marriage (1920) was the most natural thing that could have happened, 'the logical finale of the Fairbanks role as popular philosopher. . . . [They] came to mean more than a couple of married film stars. They were a living proof of America's chronic belief in happy endings' (Alistair Cooke). They honeymooned in Europe and the cities where they stopped were never quite the same again. Simultaneously *The Molly-coddle* was released, a tale of an effete American bred on the Riviera who finds red blood in his veins when he returns to his native west.

A similar idea was employed in the next one, *The Mark of Zorro* (20) – Zorro was an indolent fop by day and a dashing Robin Hood by night, but otherwise it marked an entirely new departure, with the emphasis on swashbuckling rather than on social comedy. It was already clear that the disillusioned, more permissive postwar world found Fairbanks the 'do gooder' somewhat dated and the actor was anxious to break the mould: nor should his eager desire to please the public be underestimated. He did one more like that, in case *Zorro* failed: *The Nut* (21), in and out of scrapes, partially undressed as usual, while trying to help a philanthropic fiancée. Not only was the formula by now exhausted, but it confirmed that he had not found an identity till donning doublet-and-hose and taking sword in hand. As the returns of *Zorro* came in he began to realize a long-cherished dream, to play D'Artagnan in *The Three Musketeers*, a role he had played throughout his life, both on and off the screen – and he kept thereafter the moustache he had grown for the film. The film's success was such that at last his earning power rivalled that of Pickford and Chaplin. *Robin Hood* (22) had the biggest sets and cast assembled in Hollywood up to that time – and

For years fans had been clamouring to see 'Doug' and Mary co-starring. With the coming of Talkies they gave in to their fans and chose – unwisely – The Taming of the Shrew (29).

although it was not evident from his Ariel-like presence on the screen, Fairbanks had become absorbed by producing: these costume spectacles would have been notable without his (very) physical participation. This was one of the most expensive films made up to that time, but it made a profit. These were the golden years: Doug was unrivalled, the uncrowned King of Hollywood.

The Thief of Bagdad (24) was the peak of his career, the most financially successful of his films and the most praised: 'It is an entrancing picture' said the 'New York Times', 'wholesome and beautiful, deliberate but compelling, a feat of motion picture art which has never been equalled and one which will enthral persons time and again.' Today it looks a little fusty, along with its predecessors, but the remaining swashbucklers remain superb, even if the actor himself was losing, slowly, his agility: *Don Q, Son of Zorro* (25) with Mary Astor; *The Black Pirate* (26) – in colour, with Billie Dove; and *The Gaucho* (27), perhaps his best film, a satisfying mixture of swordplay and the sinister. In 1929, a Silent *The Iron Mask* appeared, to do well amidst the more vogueish Talkies (there were music and sound effects; and Fairbanks introduced the film with a speech to the audience): but it was a farewell to the Fairbanks fans knew: playing in this D'Artagnan again, he played him as an old man and died for the first and only time in a film. A few months later he and Pickford, co-starring at last, came out with his first Talkie, *The Taming of the Shrew*: there were theatre prices and separate performances, but the public were not deceived into thinking that it was better than a third-rate rep production. Its failure did not help an already shaky marriage – due, apparently, to some casual infidelity on the part of the husband. There is reason to believe that (in the manner of great romances) they continued to love each other and the melancholia of his last years seems to be due as much to the divorce (in 1935) as to the demise of the career. He once observed that there was nothing as humiliating as being a has-been.

In 1931, tired of producing, but still at United Artists, he accepted a fantastic salary of $300,000 (or $5,000 a day) to do *Reaching for the Moon*, a satire on big business, with Bebe Daniels, which had only a fair success; then *Around the World in 80 Minutes*, which he co-directed with Victor Fleming. It was virtually a travelogue – and like the next, *Mr Robinson Crusoe* (32), was disastrously unworthy of him. He now had shares in Korda's London Films and it was announced that he would make several British films. But the first was a great flop: *The Private Life of Don Juan* (34) – one of Korda's several

attempts to emulate the success of his *Henry VIII*. Fairbanks again proved himself competent as a Talkie actor but his accent grated and the old magic had gone. There were no others.

During his last years, he lived frequently in Europe and after his divorce was married to Sylvia, Lady Ashley (who later briefly nabbed Clark Gable). In 1936 he publicly announced that he had retired from acting. Two years later in London he announced he had formed Fairbanks-International, a new producing company, with capital of £500,000 sterling. He was planning *The Californian* to star his son, Doug Jr, when he died in his sleep of a heart attack in December, 1939. A folk-hero had departed.

DOUGLAS FAIRBANKS JR

Douglas Fairbanks Jr was the first instance of the second generation in movies. He never achieved anything like his father's renown and maybe because he was his father's son he was always underrated. They were hardly comparable, except on those few occasions when Doug Jr turned swashbuckler, when he was equally as athletic as his father and just as debonair. He had even more charm and attempted with ease a wider range of parts; but in a generally unsatisfactory career he was less overshadowed by Senior than by other actors of his own very gentlemanly type. Watching him, one is aware of a host of other actors – Ronald Colman, John Barrymore, Errol Flynn, William Powell, even on occasion Gary Cooper and Cary Grant. He explained once why he never really cared for acting: 'I began to be embarrassed that the interpretation was really someone else's creation . . . realizing my own limitations, I became aware that I could never be a creative actor. I would only be an interpretative one or an imitator' (quoted by his biographer, Brian Connell, 'Knight Errant', 1955). As for following in his father's footsteps, they 'were so light that they left no trace for anyone to follow. My respect for his work is so considerable that I don't believe *anyone* could successfully emulate him.' But if Junior's talent was neither individual nor varied, it was always refreshing.

He was born in New York in 1909, of his father's marriage to Beth Sully. After the divorce, the boy lived with his mother. The first film offer came to them when he was 13, from Jesse Lasky of Paramount, who frankly admitted that his aim was to exploit the Fairbanks name. The film in which he starred the boy, *Stephen Steps Out* (23), was carefully carved from Richard Harding Davis's 'The Grand Cross of the Crescent' and told of Stephen's adventures in the wicked Orient; but despite kind reviews, it was a miserable failure. Senior, whose views on Junior's film career were widely publicized, took some consolation from that fact; later, he accepted that Junior wanted and could have a successful career, and in the early 30s they became at last quite close friends. At the moment, however, a career seemed out of the question: the youngster was petitioning Paramount for work (because the Sully family fortunes were in a bad way and he was the only one likely to make much money) and that studio, because of the film's failure, were not much interested.

Finally he was given a contract at a minute sum, and expected to work as an extra and do any job as well as acting in any parts that might seem suitable: *The Air Mail* (25) with Warner Baxter and *Wild Horse Mesa* with Jack Holt. Goldwyn cast him as the young lover in *Stella Dallas* and he got good notices but nothing much to follow up – only small parts at various studios: in *A Texas Steer*, Rex Beach's *Padlocked* (26) with Lois Moran, *Broken Hearts of Hollywood* starring Patsy Ruth Miller, *Man-bait* (27) starring Marie Prevost, *Women Love Diamonds*, *Is Zat So?* with George O'Brien, *The Brass Band*, *Dead Man's Curves* (28), *Modern Mothers* and *The Toilers*. At the same time he was so hard up that he eked out his pay by writing titles for some Ronald Colman-Vilma Banky pictures as well as for his father's *The Gaucho*. He also acted on the stage – in LA – in 'Young Woodley' and 'Saturday's Children', and this attracted favourable attention to him; but his career did not take a real upward swing until he met Joan Crawford. Egged on by her, he became more ambitious – they were engaged and the darlings of the fan magazines. He got a good part in Capra's *The Power of the Press* at Columbia, and another at Warners in *The Barker*, turning up to remind Milton Sills, in the title-role, of the responsibilities of fatherhood. That was a part-Talkie and in the same manner he and Marceline Day represented *The Jazz Age* (29) at Radio – the sort of movie that Crawford was making. Her studio, MGM, made him Garbo's wastrel brother in the Silent *A Woman of Affairs* and Warners had him married to Loretta Young and accused of murder in *The Fast Life*.

Married now to Crawford (despite the disapproval of Pickfair; the marriage lasted till 1933), MGM cashed in on fan interest by casting them together in *Our Modern Maidens*: 'Must you be told', asked 'Photoplay', 'that it's a sure-fire hit?' Warners, however, saw him as a partner for Miss

Young, and after trying to strangle her in *The Careless Age* – and singing 'A Bicycle Made For Two' with Chester Conklin in their revue, *The Show of Shows* – he was trying to impress her on the field in *The Forward Pass*, another Warner melodrama of little consequence. That studio asked him to be in *Moby Dick*, but changed its mind and put him into *The Dawn Patrol* instead – a chance he leapt at. He was an awkward actor, but he had looks, his name and his connection with Crawford: further, at a time when leading men were popping like flies, he had an excellent speaking voice. Warners finally offered him a long-term contract.

He had already contracted to do *Little Accident* at Universal, from the stage farce, about a professor, an ex-wife (Anita Page) and a baby; he was good in it, and better in a supporting role at Warners, in *Outward Bound* as a card-sharp. Then: *The Way of All Men* with Dorothy Revier, a remake of *The Sin Flood*, literally about a flood and repentance; and *One Night at Susie's* with Billie Dove, and one night, said 'Photoplay', 'is enough of this sort of thing'. With *Little Caesar*, playing a gigolo, he at last emerged as a name in his own right and not as his father's son: Warners rewrote his contract, reducing his output to four films a year and giving him some of the supervisory powers his father had – over script, direction, etc. However, his importance was relative, for he was put into

L'Aviateur (31), the studio's French-language version of *Going Wild*, in the role played in that by Joe E. Brown; and there was no appreciable difference in quality: *Chances*, as a British soldier in France, and *I Like Your Nerve*, falling in love with Miss Young again, saving her from marriage to an older man. *L'Athlète Incomplet* was another Joe E. Brown role – *Local Boy Makes Good* – for showings only in France; *Union Depot* (32) with Joan Blondell was a personal hit, as a hobo who becomes a 'Gentleman for a Day' (which became its British title). *It's Tough to be Famous*, with Mary Brian, was based on national adulation for Lindbergh – coinciding with the kidnapping of the Lindbergh baby and hence withdrawn for a while; *Love Is a Racket* was based on the power of gossip columnists, with Fairbanks miscast as one of them, with and Ann Dvorak and Lee Tracy as his allies. *Scarlet Dawn* was set against the Russian Revolution, with him as a palace guardsman and Nancy Carroll as a serving wench. Around this time he grew his moustache and had a story published in 'Liberty Magazine', 'Gay Love'.

Along with Bette Davis and Frank McHugh he was one of the unemployed in *Parachute Jumper* (33), though he gets work as the title explains; and more fortunate on loan to RKO for *Morning Glory* as a playwright – only he loses Katharine Hepburn to Adolphe Menjou and then fame. He was a boxer accused of

A bench in Central Park during the Depression: Bette Davis and Douglas Fairbanks Jr in Parachute Jumper *(33). At the moment he's a chauffeur, but he'll take to the skies in reel nine.*

The younger Fairbanks made some swashbucklers quite as good as his father's: The Corsican Brothers *(41). Between them/him is J. Carroll Naish as the faithful retainer.*

murder, hiding out with Miss Young and Aline MacMahon in *The Life of Jimmy Dolan*; and then at sea in *The Narrow Corner*, 'freely adapted' – a large understatement – from Maugham's novel, and at the front in *Captured!*, with Leslie Howard. Then he really was unemployed: Warners were unhappy because the veto power he had over his material was not being compensated at the box-office and because he had very cleverly kept the profit they should have made from the loan to RKO – and he refused to re-sign unless his salary was restored to its pre-Depression level; the quarrel was of such bitterness that his name was removed from the credits of his last films. He did some stage work, including 'No More Ladies'.

Paramount offered him *Design for Living*, but he was ill and Fredric March played the part; then with his father he went to Britain, where they both acted for Alexander Korda, who had impressed them as a film-maker of international potential. Fairbanks Jr played the mad Czar in *Catherine the Great* (34) and was fairly good while neither film nor Catherine (Elisabeth Bergner) were. He returned to the US and RKO for *Success at Any Price*,

one of Colleen Moore's last films, throwing her over for the ritzy Genevieve Tobin in his ruthless scramble to the top. But Britain held his attention for the next few years; his name was linked privately with that of Gertrude Lawrence and professionally in two plays, 'The Winding Journey' and 'Moonlight Is Silver', and a film, *Mimi* (35), an unsuccessful version of 'La Bohème'. When he needed money, in 1936, he did a quota quickie for WB-British, *Man of the Moment*, set in Monaco and co-starring Laura La Plante; then, ambitiously, decided to found his own production company. Partnered by Marcel Hellman, he made: *The Amateur Gentleman* (36), from Jeffrey Farnol's Regency romance, with Elissa Landi; *Accused*, a courtroom drama, with Dolores del Rio; *Crime Over London*, with Paul Cavanagh (and in which he himself did not appear); and *Jump for Glory* (37), with Valerie Hobson. They had mainly American directors: and Tay Garnett was to have directed a fifth, a border story – till adverse weather conditions would not permit shooting. There was no money available – only the first of these had been successful – and the partnership was dissolved with bitterness. Fairbanks said that the films 'for what they are, have been disastrously expensive' and he considered his career had been 'devalued beyond recognition'.

He returned to Hollywood and Selznick offered him the part of the laughing villain, Rupert of Hentzau, in *The Prisoner of Zenda*: it was not the leading role, but it firmly re-established him and he signed a contract with Selznick for one film a year. He followed up wisely with a couple of comedies at RKO, playing the maverick scion of a banking family who shows Irene Dunne the *Joy of Living* (38) and *Having Wonderful Time* at a holiday camp with Ginger Rogers. Better was *The Rage of Paris*, which made Danielle Darrieux briefly the rage of the US; despite the title, it was set in New York and concerned a gold-digger and the man who saw through her but got caught all the same. Even better was *Young in Heart*, with Fairbanks as one of the family of cons (his only other picture for Selznick). Then came a bevy of action pictures, most of them – to Fairbanks's satisfaction – incorporating much pro-British propaganda: George Stevens's *Gunga Din* (39); *The Sun Never Sets*, a silly colonial drama; *Rulers of the Sea*, about the first Atlantic steamship; *Green Hell* (40) and *Safari*, both

jungle melodramas. He was in the city jungle with *Angels Over Broadway* (41); then was both of *The Corsican Brothers* (41) in a fairish version of the Dumas swashbuckler. Both of these he co-produced. He joined the US Navy; became a Lt-Commander and perhaps the most honoured of the stars who served.

After four years away, he was greeted by Joan Crawford at a party: 'Darling, of course you're so behind the news, aren't you? I suppose you haven't even heard that I'm no longer with MGM. I'm with Warner Bros. now' (quoted by Connell). Hollywood had not changed; RKO was eager for him to play *Sinbad the Sailor* (47) and he did – it was the most financially successful film of his career. Encouraged, he again formed his own production company, releasing through Universal, and did a couple of similar films, *The Exile*, as Charles II in the Netherlands, and *The Fighting O'Flynn* (49), as a soldier of fortune against Napoleon. Both were in monochrome when rival subjects were in Technicolor and his box-office standing was further devalued by a trip to 20th between the two, to play a dashing Hungarian commander who bewitches Betty Grable, *That Lady in Ermine* (48), a Lubitsch frou-frou that did not please her public.

That Lady in Ermine (*48*) was an unsuccessful attempt to get away from the Betty Grable formula film: but Douglas Fairbanks made a very dashing Prince Charming. It was about a man who falls in love with a portrait and then meets her modern-day descendant.

The British knighted Fairbanks in 1949 (one of some 70-odd Americans to be so honoured) for his work in promoting Anglo-US relations and it was the British who offered him his next film, and one of his best – an exciting political thriller, *State Secret* (50), but it played only unimportant houses in the US. The next was a fantasy about a duck who lays a uranium egg, and so did the film: *Mr Drake's Duck* (51), one of the few films made by director Val Guest to promote his wife, the American Yolande Donlan – an engaging talent, but like the film, too slight. It was Fairbanks's last full-length film for over 20 years. He went back to the US and Connell says, 'made every attempt to pursue his professional career . . . [but] it became clear that film production in Britain provided the only outlet'. (Two of Fairbanks's projects were made by other studios, *Knights of the Round Table* and *Elephant Walk*.)

In the event, his British production company began producing TV films, screened as 'Douglas Fairbanks Presents'. He starred in some; and some were shown as featurettes in cinemas (where they looked even more junky than they had on TV). Living till the early 70s mostly in Britain with his second wife, he became a social lion. His interests diversified; and in the 60s his only active show business work was guesting on TV and some successful stock appearances in the US in 'My Fair Lady'. From 1973 onwards he played in 'The Pleasure of his Company' – in London, Australia and on tour in the US. Among his other – very occasional – work: *The Crooked Hearts* (72), a comic telemovie, as a wealthy bachelor pursued by a widow (Rosalind Russell) via a Lonely Hearts Club; *The Hostage Tower* (80), a telefilm written by Alistair Maclean, as the head of UN Security, trying to prevent some crooks, including Keir Dullea, from taking over the Eiffel Tower; *Ghost Story* (81) with Fred Astaire and some other oldies (the youngsters did not make much impression); and *Strong Medicine* (86), a TV miniseries, as a company president. He 'gives the humdrum affair some class,' said 'Variety'. 'Twas ever thus. Or almost. In 1988 he began *Old Explorers* but left after some days' shooting due to 'artistic differences'.

FRANCES FARMER

Beauty and the Beast: the Beauty was Frances Farmer and the Beast was Alcohol. It was a short and not dazzling career, but what happened to her was a shame because she was talented, intelligent and gorgeous to look upon. She made very few films, and most of them were rotten, but she is unforgettable in the good ones.

She was born in Seattle, Washington, in 1914, the daughter of an attorney. Whether he was a wealthy attorney is not known, but Farmer worked her way through college (the University of Washington) by waiting on tables and ushering in cinemas, a very serious girl with a keen interest in Little Theatre activities. She was consumed with ambition to join the Group Theater in New York and her drama teacher gave her an introduction, when she visited that city en route for the USSR. Although Paramount's publicity claimed that she had won a newspaper contest for 'the most marriageable girl', she had in fact won a subscription contest organized by the local communist paper. Returning, she remained in New York and since the Group did not want to know, a friend of a friend arranged a test with Paramount, who offered a seven-year contract starting at $100 a week. Her first film she described later as 'a dull professionally humiliating experience' and it is clear that she loathed Hollywood and filming from the moment she stepped off the train. That film was *Too Many Parents* (36), a military-school yarn with Colin Tapley, and she followed with another B, *Border Flight* with John Howard. The reaction was strong and she was upped to being Bing Crosby's leading lady, an heiress, in *Rhythm on the Range*. Goldwyn borrowed her for *Come and Get It*, to replace Miriam Hopkins, whom Howard Hawks refused to direct; and the result is jointly credited to William Wyler when Goldwyn replaced him during shooting. Based on a conventional Edna Ferber novel set in lumberjack country, it has Edward Arnold and Joel McCrea sparring over mother and then daughter, both played by Farmer. The daughter is not too interesting, but the mother in the early part of the film, a brassy saloon singer, knocks spots off Dietrich's similar role in *Destry Rides Again*.

Farmer became a sensation, the hottest tip for the next big star. 'Photoplay' reported that 'her studio says she is now too precious to play a mere lead, as planned, opposite Gary Cooper'. But her studio was also finding her a thorn in their flesh, as 'difficult' as Hepburn or Maggie Sullavan, having as little truck with the Hollywood silliness. In the end her parts in her next three films were hardly spectacular: *The Toast of New York* (37) as the actress promoted by Jim Fisk (Edward Arnold) – on loan to RKO, and a chore she particularly loathed; *Exclusive*, a newspaper story with Fred MacMurray; and *Ebb Tide*, with Oscar Homolka and Ray Milland, at sea as a captain's spunky daughter – and very pretty in Technicolor. She was unhappy and she then made Paramount *very* unhappy by insisting on going to New York to do the Group Theater's

'Golden Boy': her lack of stage training showed and her looks singled her out as a Hollywood beauty whether she would or no: but she was happy with the Group.

Paramount considered the momentum had been lost and when she returned put her into a programmer, *Ride a Crooked Mile* (38), a silly prison drama with Akim Tamiroff and Lief Erikson. (Erikson became her husband, in 'a marriage of convenience' – as she described it in her posthumous memoir, 'Will There Really Be a Morning?') She rebelled again, preferring to be in New York and demanding better scripts. To punish her, she was loaned to United Artists to play a saloon girl in a crass jungle film, *South of Pago Pago* (40) with Jon Hall. She insisted on doing *Flowing Gold* at Warner Bros. with the Group's John Garfield, but Paramount threw her into three Bs in a row after that: *Badlands of Dakota* (41) at Universal, as Calamity Jane, with Robert Stack; *World Première* with John Barrymore, in a small role as a haughty film star in an unbecoming black wig; and *Among the Living* with Albert Dekker. Her career might still have been saved by *Son of Fury* (42), because she played one of the two loves of Tyrone Power, a proud English beauty who is the daughter of George Sanders: but she was up on a charge of drunken driving. During these years she had acted again on Broadway and in stock; there had been a traumatic love affair with Clifford Odets, a court case with her 'discoverer' over fees, and family quarrels. On her agent's advice, she began a film in Mexico, but walked out and began a small film for an independent company, which she calls *There Is No Escape* in her memoir: but she left that and early in 1943 broke probation and was ordered to a sanatorium.

'From then on', went a later newspaper report, 'Frances Farmer's epic was one of drinking bouts, nervous breakdowns and mental homes. With a fair amount of clatter she disappeared.' In 1944 it was reported that she had had another breakdown and had entered an institution – and she was in and out of mental homes until 1949. What is certain is that Hollywood turned its back on her and the fan magazines had already forgotten her.

In 1957 she was discovered in a San Francisco hotel working as a receptionist; shortly afterwards she appeared on the Ed Sullivan Show, singing one song. She said that she hoped to restart her career and was fourth-featured in *The Party Crashers* (58), a teenage drama made for Paramount, starring Mark Damon, Connie Stevens and another Hollywood lost one, Bobby Driscoll. It was Grade Z stuff and they did not get around to distributing it in Britain until 1969. Also in 1958, Farmer married her third husband, Leland Mikesell, a San Francisco consultant. From 1960 for six years she did a TV programme in Indianapolis on movies. She died of cancer in 1970. Her story was told, almost simultaneously, in *Frances* (82) with Jessica Lange and *Committed* (83) with Sheila McLaughlin.

ALICE FAYE

Alice Faye belongs absolutely to the 1930s. If the quintessential star of that period was one of those up-and-at-'em dames, Faye, better than anyone, represents the other heroines, the gentle, yielding ones. She was blonde, cuddly, shapely and kind – almost bovine. When men crossed her, she did not start throwing things (as Betty Grable did later) but quietly left the room, her eyes welling with tears. She smiled a lot. Men in particular adored her. She had a warm contralto voice and, invariably leaning against a pillar with palm trees and a moon behind, she was given some remarkably fine songs to sing ('Wake

Up and Live', 'Now It Can Be Told', 'This Year's Kisses', 'You Turned the Tables on Me', 'There's a Lull in My Life', 'You'll Never Know'), all of which she did stylishly. As far as we can tell, for she was given few roles to test her, she was no great actress, but hers is the supreme example of an amiable temperament caught by the camera. She was always a pleasure to see and her position in the constellation cannot be overlooked. It was for years, but TV showings of her movies brought her a new army of fans.

She was born in New York's 'Hell's Kitchen' in 1915 and at 14 joined the Chester Hale Dance Group, touring the Atlantic Coast resorts. She later got a job in the chorus of 'George White's Scandals', starring Rudy Vallee, who heard her sing at a cast party and gave her a weekly song on his radio show. When Fox filmed *George White's Scandals* (35) she was scheduled for one song, but when Vallee's co-star, Lilian Harvey, withdrew (reputedly because her part was too small but in fact because she quarrelled with George White), Vallee persuaded White to give her the lead. Her vivacity impressed and Fox gave her a contract.

A moonlit balcony and the sea beyond: the perfect setting for 30s romance and certainly a constant in Alice Faye's films. It's Tyrone Power here who's just realized he loves her. Alexander's Ragtime Band (38).

She was just another blonde at first. In *Now I'll Tell* she got involved with big-time gambler Spencer Tracy and was killed in a car accident; then *She Learned About Sailors* (a weak effort with Lew Ayres) and spent *365 Nights in Hollywood* (also originally intended for Harvey). After *George White's 1935 Scandals* (35), she reported to Paramount *Every Night at Eight* with George Raft and discovered that *Music Is Magic*. Warner Baxter was the *King of Burlesque* (36), in a plot that was entirely typical of her films. Up to that time she was a sub-Harlow blonde, peroxided, with plucked eyebrows and a brassy front, but Zanuck thought she had something better and decided to groom her. Halfway through the transformation she and Jack Haley as a vaudeville team were nice enough to be around Shirley Temple, the *Poor Little Rich Girl*, and her salary was raised to $2,000 a week. Two Cole Porter musicals were announced for her, including *Nymph Errant*. She was tested, unsuccessfully, for a straight role in *A Message to Garcia*. Instead she was in a funny comedy, *Sing Baby Sing*, as an aspiring actress whose PR man gets her involved with a drunken has-been actor (Adolph Menjou). She supported Miss Temple again in *Stowaway*, travelling as companion to Helen Westleigh, and lost Dick Powell to the more classy Madeleine Carroll in *On the Avenue* (37), winding up with a sugar-daddy.

Faye imposed herself in three pleasant musicals: *Wake Up and Live, You Can't Have Everything* and, on loan to Universal, *You're a Sweetheart*. She had improved out of all recognition. Freda Bruce Lockhart noted in 'Film Weekly' at the end of 1937 that Faye 'has emerged as a personality of rare charm, a singer whose acting touches a deeper level of sincerity than any previous musical comedy artist'. Now she was a fully fledged star, someone you built musicals around. But first she took on a role which had been meant for Jean Harlow. The film was one of two consecutive hits, both with Tyrone Power and Don Ameche: *In Old Chicago* (38), some fiction tagged on to the great conflagration, and *Alexander's Ragtime Band*, some fiction built round the early days of 'jazz' and more than 20 Irving Berlin songs – a peach of a musical, her own favourite film and that of the director, Henry King, who said it worked because the three stars liked each other so much. She also did a musical remake of the Constance Bennett movie about chorus girls, *Sally Irene and Mary* (Joan Davis had Joan Crawford's old part); and she made the top 10 money-makers that year. She stayed there in 1939, with a straight film, *Tailspin* (as an aviatrix), and two musicals trading on nostalgia: *Rose of Washington Square*, with Power, a thinly disguised account of the first marriage of Fanny Brice (who sued and settled out of court for $750,000); and *Hollywood Cavalcade*, with Ameche, her first in colour, a story

of the Silent days. Another straight film, *Barricade*, was filmed over a 16-month period and was inevitably a hodgepodge – about a cabaret singer fleeing a murder rap and a drunken reporter (Warner Baxter) holed up in a mission in China besieged by rebel forces: filmed in one month it would still have been a fiasco.

There were two more 'historical' pieces. In *Little Old New York* (40), a tale of the first steamship, with Richard Greene as Robert Fulton, she was a saloon keeper who settles for Fred MacMurray. Her performance was so spirited as to suggest a different actress: Henry King directed and she seems to have responded better to him than her other directors. As *Lillian Russell*, in the craze for movie biographies, Faye played that toast of Broadway as gracious and level-headed, i.e. like herself and not Miss Russell, with Edward Arnold playing Diamond Jim Brady for the second time. And there was another attempt by 20th to rehash the formula of *Alexander's Ragtime Band*: *Tin Pan Alley*, in which she and Betty Grable were a sister act involved with songwriters Jack Oakie and John Payne at the time of World War I.

20th, as it happened, had a new formula: romance in exotic spots plus Carmen Miranda and Technicolor. Faye had missed the first one (*Down Argentine Way*) through illness and the part had gone to Grable. Now she did

one, *That Night in Rio* (41), and another in the 'nostalgic' groove, *The Great American Broadcast*, a conventional story of the early days of radio, with Payne and Oakie again. She did another with Miranda, *Weekend in Havana*, but Betty Grable did the rest of the series. It is not true that Grable and Faye did not get on, or that Zanuck put Grable's career first. Faye turned down *Sweet Rosie O'Grady* (which Grable did) and missed several movies because of pregnancy – *My Gal Sal* (which went to Rita Hayworth), *Springtime in the Rockies* (Betty Grable) and, later, *Greenwich Village* (Vivian Blaine). She had divorced Tony Martin after three years of marriage in 1940 and the following year had married bandleader Phil Harris. With marriage and motherhood she lost interest in films, especially as she felt doomed to being, as she described it, 'a painted doll-like dummy'. Because she wanted better parts, she was announced for both *Roxie Hart* and Aunt Cissy in *A Tree Grows in Brooklyn*, but both were played by other actresses.

She was absent for more than a year and returned in yet another period musical with Payne and Oakie, *Hello Frisco Hello* (43), singing 'You'll Never Know'. She sang 'No Love No Nothin'' in *The Gang's All Here*, a romance beetween a nightclub singer and a sergeant (James Ellison) – and a lousy film, despite its camp revival in 1971. She was so badly made-up, dressed and in particular photographed as to suggest sabotage.

Then, another absence, punctuated by a guest spot in *Four Jills and a Jeep* (44). There was talk of retirement but she signed a new contract, one picture a year with story approval. She said that she was tired of doing the same plot over and over, and in the event made only one film, a murder mystery, *Fallen Angel* (45), in which she was a wealthy spinster 'taken' by Dana Andrews, who had the more glamorous Linda Darnell on the side. She liked the role and the film, and was furious when Zanuck cut it to build up Darnell because he wanted another *Laura*. 20th begged her to stay on for *The Dolly Sisters*, but had to replace her with June Haver. She refused the Anne Baxter role in *The Razor's Edge* and over the years declined several other attempts to woo her back: *Wabash Avenue*, *A Letter to Three Wives*, *I'll Never Forget You*, *Stars and Stripes Forever* and *There's No Business Like Show Business*. If she remained angry, she also wanted to devote herself to her family.

With Harris she did occasional radio and TV shows, notably 'Hollywood Palace'. She looked back on her Hollywood career as great fun and when she did make a movie comeback, as the mother in the otherwise uncharming remake of *State Fair* (62), she made it quite clear that she was not back permanently. Later, she said that she loathed making it, that there was no direction and she was lit and photographed badly. She told the 'Evening Standard' (London) in 1970 that she would like to make another movie, 'but what in God's name would they want me for now?' The interviewer found her 'natural, relaxed, untroubled by a need to retain the image as it was, completely undisappointing to meet'. And genuinely surprised she should be so affectionately remembered. But such love encouraged her to return to Broadway in a successful revival of 'Good News' (74). She had said in 1973: 'I don't want to say anything bad about anybody, but the only thing I hope is that I live to see Darryl F. Zanuck washed up in this business . . .' She did; and after a guest stint in *Won Ton The Dog Who Saved Hollywood* (76), had guest roles in *The Magic of Lassie* (78) and *Every Girl Should Have One*.

GRACIE FIELDS

In their study of the inter-war years, 'The Long Weekend', Robert Graves and Alan Hodges quote a conservative writer, Major Rawdon Hoare, on the subject of Gracie Fields. He described her in 1934 as the only outstanding personality providing healthy entertainment. 'In her own way she has done a tremendous amount of good. In the cinemas there is an absence of healthy amusement, there is too much sex-appeal: but in the performance of Gracie Fields we get a breath of fresh air and an opportunity for some real laughter. This all helps to keep the right spirit of England together – clean-living, with a total absence of anything bordering on the unnatural.' Graves and Hodges go on to say: 'Indeed, Gracie Fields's Lancashire accent and humorous, long-suffering but optimistic sentiment more truly represented contemporary England than slick Americanistic film comedies or heavily modern problem plays.'

This paragon – as 99 per cent of the population of Britain in the 30s could have told you – was born in Rochdale, Lancashire. In 1898. Over a fish-and-chip shop. She started her career by singing in a local cinema and then joined troupes of various child performers, such as Charburn's Young Stars (at 4s. a week). She later toured the halls as a solo act and made her only pantomime appearance as the Princess in 'Dick Whittington' (14) at the Grand, Oldham, before being booked into a revue at Manchester, 'Yes, I Think So'. One of the cast was Archie Pitt and he later put together another revue, 'Mr Tower of London', and asked Gracie to join it. It toured the provinces, with tremendous success, from 1918 to 1922, when it was finally brought to London: and she conquered London as easily as she had captured the rest of Britain. She was in a straight play with Gerald du Maurier, 'SOS' (28), by which time she was a music hall top-liner. In 1930 she did two weeks at the Palace in New York – and flopped. In the meantime she had married Pitt and he arranged a three-picture contract with the British branch of RKO. The first was a cheap effort adapted from a North Country comedy 'The Likes of 'er', *Sally in Our Alley* (31), with Gracie as the idol of the quarter, a café waitress: it was a thumping big success.

Looking on the Bright Side (32) made her a manicurist who is 'discovered' for show business and the film, co-directed by Basil Dean, borrows badly from René Clair's films. ATP produced for RKO release and the latter's subsidiary, Realart, made *This Week of Grace* (33), in which – for £20,000 – she played an unemployed factory worker who goes into service. Neither film solved the problem of looks – the broad face and sagging jowls; but for the later vehicles they prevented her flashing her dentures when she sang. She did not like filming, but the demand was there – and Dean at ATP was offering £25,000 for five films, starting with *Love, Life and Laughter*

Gracie Fields in The Show Goes On *(37). Here it's going on backstage, with Queenie Leonard, Isobel Scaife and Elsie Wagstaffe.*

(34) in which she was a village pageant Nell Gwynn falling in love with Ruritanian king John Loder. She did not of course, get him. Dean, who directed, saw her less as a heroine than as a clown and she was normally love-lorn, only to lose the man to an ingénue in the end. Most of the humour was broad carica-ture. In *Sing As We Go* she was a factory girl on holiday in Blackpool. Dorothy Hyson got Loder and Fields did not even get comic cop Stanley Holloway. J.B. Priestley wrote it, perhaps his best work for the screen. It was a tremendous success and its title song became a theme song for the Depression years in Britain. A snub, however, was administered by C.A. Lejeune: 'We have an industrial north that is bigger than Gracie Fields running around Blackpool Fun Fair.' She had become the biggest female draw in British cinemas. Priestley also wrote *Look Up and Laugh* (35), which surrounded her with a flock of music-hall comics, and that also packed them in: she was a music hall star who fought the local bigwigs on behalf of street traders.

Dean did not want to direct *Queen of Hearts* (36) and assigned it to Monty Banks, a former Hollywood Silent comic; he gave her something approaching Hollywood glamour and this time, as a seamstress with a crush on a matinee idol, she did get Loder at the end. In British cinemas only Shirley Temple, and Astaire and Rogers were bigger attractions, but the hoped-for American market stayed closed. Dean directed *The Show Goes On* (37), about a North Country girl who via the halls, becomes a famous star, having been 'moulded' by a prominent composer. It was suspiciously autobiographical, especially as she later divorced Pitt and married Banks (though she makes it clear in her memoirs that she was more in awe of Pitt than in love with him).

Her records continued to sell like hot cakes, her stage appearances played to SRO and when she made a rare radio appearance all of Britain stayed home. Parliament was adjourned because she was about to broad-cast. Later, in 1939, when she was seriously ill, multitudes gathered outside the hospital, waiting, and the press gave it as much cover-age as a royal sickness. Everyone knew her simply as 'Our Gracie'.

Hollywood had watched her with interest, but was cautious. In 1936 MGM's British boss, Sam Eckman, compared her to Will Rogers: 'two of the greatest comedians of their time, but their humour is strictly natio-nal'. However, Darryl F. Zanuck of 20th decided to take the plunge. He offered £200,000 for four films, 'the highest salary every paid to a human being', with the option of two more at £60,000 each (some reports speak also of a percentage). Amidst great fanfare, she went to Hollywood, but she did not like it and asked whether her first 20th film could be made in Britain. The studio complied; however, they gave her the beauty treatment, and two US leading men, Brian Donlevy and Victor McLaglen, to fight over her. But *We're Going To Be Rich* (38), set in a South African mining community, had a poor plot. She said: 'I thought we were going to get something fancier like, so that we could show American audiences what I can do. This film won't do it.' Still, Frank S. Nugent wrote in the 'New York Times': 'We insist that hereafter the English include us in the possessive whenever they refer to "Our Gracie". Like W.C., she's one of the grandest Fields under Comedy cultivation.' She returned to Hollywood, but without publicity, and still refused to film there: 'I have always been afraid that if I came to Hollywood to work, they'd make me half an' half, sort of, and they mightn't use the right halves either.'

Gaumont-British had bought *The Show Goes On* to distribute in the States, but it received an even more dusty welcome. 20th lost interest, confident of getting a return on their interest from British takings, and left the handling to Banks, who astutely made her a music-hall star in *Keep Smiling* and *Shipyard Sally* (39), in the first managing a stranded concert party and in the second championing the shipyard workers. This in particular confirmed the impression that she was not interested in what she was doing – understandably, in view of the material given her; these films did nothing to impair her popularity in Britain – or impose it in the USA.

Then came the war. In the autumn of 1939 she went to sing to the BEF in France, with a great morale-booster, a song called 'Wish Me Luck As You Wave Me Goodbye'. In 1940, when Italy entered the war, Banks was declared an alien (born in Italy, he had in fact lived in the US since he was 10) and she decided that her place was with her husband:

he became an American citizen later, but in the meantime, 'the storm broke. Every British newspaper screamed that I had deserted my own country and taken all my money. . . . I was a traitor. . . . I'd run away.' Overnight, the national heroine was a dead duck. True, she had settled in Beverly Hills, but she continued to give concerts in Canada and the US, donating all the proceeds to the British war effort (she estimated that she earned £1½ million), and she toured the world entertaining Commonwealth troops; she came to Britain and sang at munitions factories. Most of the time, when singing in Britain, she met an initial hostility; and eyewitnesses report how, after two songs, she had – movingly – won over her audience. Her war effort went mostly unnoticed in the British press.

There were film offers in Hollywood: she turned down a Laughton picture, *The Man From Down Under*, despite his pleas (Binnie Barnes played it), but fulfilled her commitment to 20th by co-starring with Monty Woolley in *Holy Matrimony* (43), a much-liked adaptation of Arnold Bennett's 'Buried Alive'. 20th looked around for a follow-up and came up with *Molly and Me* (45), a story based on a hypothetical incident in Marie Dressler's life by her friend Frances Marion, once announced by MGM for Sophie Tucker, when they had plans to turn her into a big movie star. Woolley co-starred and Fields was again a housekeeper – this time taking a group of out-of-work actors under her wing. She had had a guest spot in the all-star *Stage Door Canteen* (44), but her version of The Lord's

'Our Gracie' after she had received the 20th Century-Fox glamour treatment. Later, James Agee found her performance in Molly and Me *(45) 'a perfectly beautiful one . . . I think Miss Fields is about as nice a woman over forty as I have ever seen; I have certainly never seen anyone in movies to approach her in that age bracket.'*

Prayer was cut for British showing. She co-starred with Constance Bennett in *Paris Underground* (46) – its British title, *Madame Pimpernel*, explains the plot: it was a poor film, but Gracie's portrait of an ageing but energetic Scottish spinster was first-class.

She did not make another, though in 1945 she was reported as having signed a deal to make six in Australia. In 1947 she won Britain back via a BBC radio series and a hit song, 'Now Is the Hour', and turned down the lead in the London production of 'Annie Get Your Gun'; in 1950, at the London Palladium, to cheers, she showed a new generation what all the fuss was about. She was semi-retired from then on, living on Capri with her third husband. Unlike many American 'light' entertainers she hardly reached legendary status, but she was as good as the best of them. She sang comic songs and sad songs with equal skill, but her magic came mostly from a personality which was 101 per cent natural. She loved her audiences, she loved entertaining, she loved to make people laugh; she was joyously irreverent and if she had any artifice, it never showed. In British show business, there has never been anyone like her: none of the subsequent British girl singers came up to her big toenail. Just as Gertrude Lawrence was way out in front as a star of revues and musicals, so Fields easily outclassed all other stars of the music hall. In 1978 she celebrated her 80th birthday, opened the theatre in Rochdale named after her and headlined the Royal Variety Show at the London Palladium; she was also made a DBE. She died in 1979.

W.C. FIELDS

The world owed a living to W.C. Fields. He was set upon and put upon by friend and foe alike and even by inanimate objects – even things like socks, telephones, dustbins and golf-clubs. His family (usually) despised him, strangers distrusted him, his employers (if any) disregarded him, children kicked him; he was fair game for cops, an American small-town Lear, permanently encouraged by several large whiskies. 'He played,' said Kenneth Tynan, 'straight man to a malevolent universe which had singled him out for destruction.' He proceeded warily, gingerly sidestepping some pitfalls, tumbling into others with the air of resignation which was his habitual mien. He is not, in *The Man on the Flying Trapeze*, remotely astonished that he can commit a motoring offence while parked – indeed several; and he accepts his tickets from the cops with an almost devil-may-care air of obsequiousness. There was no point in protesting

his innocence. On the few occasions he tried, he did it half-heartedly and never got beyond one sentence. If you looked carefully into his puffy little eyes you saw a glimmer there of revolt: the gaze was baleful and there was a dream of revenge. Otherwise his sole defence was to mutter some misanthropic comment out of the side of his mouth. His self-esteem remained unharmed and his confidence unshaken in the belief that he was the sole sane member of the community; and when he found a like-minded crony he did not complain, but invented some implausible tale of which he was the shining hero: in *Mississippi* he boosts his ego with some valorous deed in the struggle against the Indians: muttering continuously of the way he cut his way through a wall of human flesh. There is a famous instance in *My Little Chickadee* where he boasts of knocking down Waterfront Nell to a barman, who angrily wants the credit for that deed. Unfazed, Fields replies, 'Well, I started kicking her first.'

He was as much a coward as he was a braggart; he cheated at cards; he lied; he drank. In *Poppy* he sold a talking dog (he was a ventriloquist) to a barman; in *The Bank Dick* he tried to persuade his son-in-law to steal some money from the bank where he worked for some fake scheme. His philosophy was perhaps best expressed in his well-known remark: 'Any man who hates small dogs and children can't be all bad.'

Yet James Agee thought him not only the toughest but 'the most warmly human of all screen comedians'. His perversity and his low opinion of humanity were appealing and he was consistent, like all great comics, in his approach to adversity. And, like all great comics, his universe is uniquely his own.

It is reckoned that a childhood of exceptional hardship contributed to his comedic beliefs. Certainly, offscreen, he was remarkably like the character he played – if perhaps more aggressive. He was born in Philadelphia in 1879, the son of a British immigrant. When he was 11 he ran away from home after a row with his father and for several years lived rough (his rasping, wheezy voice was said to be the result of the colds he experienced at this time, just as his bulbous nose was the result of fights with other yobs). He did odd jobs and took up juggling, which was a vaudeville feat he much admired. At 14, he got a job juggling in an amusement park near Norristown, Pennsylvania, and for the next few years he lived a hand-to-mouth existence in one seedy vaudeville outfit after another. However, vaudeville was prospering and so was he, and by the time he was 20 he was getting top billing. (He married in 1900.) In 1901 he went to London to appear at the

Palace; later he toured Europe, South Africa and Australia. In 1907 his act was incorporated in a 'book' show, 'The Ham Tree'; in 1913 he appeared at the Palace with Sarah Bernhardt who, because of his reputation waived her contract rule that no juggler appear on the same bill; in 1914 he was in a Dillingham show, 'Watch Your Step', doing his billiard act, but after the first night he was cut. However, one of Ziegfeld's aides had seen him and he joined the 'Ziegfeld Follies', where he stayed until 1921. During the run of his first 'Follies' he made a short, *Pool Sharks* (15), which was mostly his stage act.

In 1923 he had the lead in 'Poppy', a musical about a carnival man and the pretty ward he carts round the country with him. All of his subsequent roles stemmed from this one – a conniving but good-natured juggler. During its run he had a small part – comic relief – in a Marion Davies costume epic, *Janice Meredith* (24). Paramount bought 'Poppy' as a vehicle for Carol Dempster and eventually decided to have Fields in his stage role, now somewhat reduced. Alfred Lunt was the juvenile lead: D.W. Griffith directed (it was not one of his major efforts) and for some reason it was retitled *Sally of the Sawdust* (25). Fields was a great success and Paramount signed him to a contract; he played Dempster's father in another Griffith picture, *That Royle Girl* (26) – he was supposed to be a light relief in what was protracted melodrama. The next one was a star vehicle for him, a series of gags built round him as a village druggist, his mishaps and the unlikely things that happen to him, *It's the Old Army Game*. It set a pattern which almost all subsequent Fields films followed – including its reception by the public, which was cool. Most of them were liked by the critics and he had a healthy following, mostly among men, mostly in urban areas; but there were numerous people who did not see him as a star attraction and for them Paramount kept the running time of his films short enough to constitute a supporting film; and the shorter time also kept costs down.

Fields then made *So's Your Old Man*, *The Potters* (27), *Running Wild*, in all of which he was at odds with his family and/or the local townsfolk; and *Two Flaming Youths* and *Tillie's Punctured Romance* (28), which had carnival and circus backgrounds respectively. Louise Fazenda had the Marie Dressler role in this revised version. Fields tried to con Chester Conklin, as a rich oil man; they made a third consecutive film together, *Fools for Luck*, but were not a notable team. This terminated his contract. He wanted more money and his price was too high – it included the right to insert into his films any material

he thought necessary. Indeed, he was difficult to work with and his celebrity made him impossible. He returned to the stage, in 'Ballyhoo', but continued to think of himself primarily as a screen comic.

His first sound film, *The Gold Specialist* (30), was a two-reel re-enactment of one of his stage routines. He made four more shorts in 1932–33 for Mack Sennett (at an amazing $5,000 a week) – *The Dentist*, *The Fatal Glass of Beer*, *The Pharmacist* and *The Barber Shop*. Paramount distributed and it was with Paramount again that he eventually signed, after casting around Hollywood to see who would pay him most. His first two Talkies for Paramount were on a picture-by-picture basis and it was not until the success of *International House* that they put him under contract. First, at WB he did *Her Majesty Love* (31), as the disreputable father of a Marilyn Miller aiming at high society.

Paramount suffered under him, as Tynan put it, until 1938, but the majority of the films he made were classic. With Sound, Fields had come into his own, and the critics' approval became adoration – but public reception remained as it had been. The series consisted of: *Million Dollar Legs* (32), a delicious comedy set in a mythical European republic, with Jack Oakie and no discernible plot or logicality; *If I Had a Million*, an episode in which he and Alison Skipworth, the perfect femine counterpart in guile, deliberately wrecked the cars of road hogs; *International House* (33), which was just as inconsequential as *Legs*, certainly after Fields literally drops into it; *Tillie and Gus*, with Skipworth, as a card-sharper who takes over a decrepit river boat; and *Alice in Wonderland* found him unrecognizable as Humpty Dumpty. The *Six of a Kind* (34) were Fields, Shipworth, Burns and Allen, Mary Boland and Charlie Ruggles – only they weren't really: Fields and Shipworth were not the sort of crooks the other four innocents ever expected to tangle with, on this trip out west or anywhere else. They do not appear until towards the end of the film, but the other four were marvellous: this might well be the funniest film ever made. *You're Telling Me* was a remake of *So's Your Old Man* and *The Old-Fashioned Way* was from a story by Fields himself, about a bunch of theatrical troupers in the sticks, whose leader, the Great MacGonicle, always needs to keep one step ahead of the sheriff. *Mrs Wiggs of the Cabbage Patch* was a historic soap opera about Mrs Wiggs (Pauline Lord) living in happy squalor, made bearable only by Zazu Pitts as a spinster neighbour and by Fields in a last-minute appearance as her (Pitts's) eye-to-the-main-chance suitor. *It's a Gift* is quintessential Fields, trying to cope

with Baby LeRoy and nagging wife Kathleen Howard. André Sennwald wrote in the 'New York Times': 'Perhaps if the W.C. Fields idolators continue their campaign on his behalf over a period of years his employers may finally invest him in a production befitting his dignity as a great artist. In the meantime such comparatively journeyman pieces as *It's a Gift* will serve very adequately. . . .' It hardly looks journeyman today.

Fields was now reaching the peak of his popularity and idolators must have been happy when Paramount loaned him to MGM for *David Copperfield* (35). Blessed with good direction (Cukor's) and a fine cast (Edna May Oliver, Basil Rathbone, Roland Young, Lewis Stone, Elsa Lanchester, etc.) it was in every way a good reflection of the original and press approval carried it into the 'Motion Picture Herald' list of the year's top money-makers. He played Micawber and was very flattered at being asked; but he did not play the part with an English accent as his contract stipulated and he reputedly tried to insert a sequence where he did some juggling. The result, however, was a true and touching Micawber.

Mississippi came from an old Booth Tarkington story, dusted off the shelf as a vehicle

Cukor's David Copperfield *(35): some who saw the 1970 British version thought longingly of this earlier version and especially of Fields's Micawber. Freddie Bartholomew was David.*

If the expression on the Great Man's face is unusually benign it's because he's looking at his daughter, Mary Brian. Besides, it's easier to get from that to cowed, which is what his wife, Kathleen Howard, expects when she next glares or bellows at him: The Man on the Flying Trapeze *(35), coming up for its 70th anniversary and twice as funny as anything Hollywood has sent us in the last twenty years. Or more.*

One of the greatest comic teamings of all time: Mae West and W.C. Fields (plus Indian) in My Little Chickadee *(40). But the film, alas, wasn't very funny.*

The Bank Dick (40): Fields as Egbert Souse (pronounced Sousé, he insists) held up by bandit Al Hill on his first day as bank guard.

for Bing Crosby, with Fields as a standby. The result was something of a shambles, because Crosby and all concerned let Fields have his way with most of his scenes; but among the magnolia and crinolines, Fields's humour was welcome. 'The Times' (London) thought his Commodore 'a glorious creation, and he can, from the audience's point of view, never tell too often of his deeds against the Indians'. *The Man on the Flying Trapeze* was a meaningless title: Fields was henpecked with a vengeance. It is one of his funniest films. Then *Poppy* (36) was remade, under its rightful name. He was seriously ill during much of the shooting and it was completed with a sometimes clearly visible double. He was off the screen for two years, for a year of which he gave up drinking (which proved to his friends how ill he was); and in *The Big Broadcast of 1938* (38) he looked considerably older. But he was not too ill to fight with Paramount or to seek a new studio which would pay him more money. He went to Universal.

His biographer, Robert Lewis Taylor, states that 'he was at the height of his powers. His illness, his troubles, his suspicions, his worries and frights had only served to sharpen his genius. He was at once at the twilight and at the climax of his career.' At Universal he got $125,000 per film, plus $25,000 for contributing the story, which was usually merely an outline on a scrap of paper. Taylor remarks that Universal, like Paramount, deserve great credit not only for their forbearance with an extremely difficult man, but their courage in permitting him 'to turn out products of his that defied every law of the industry, and sometimes netted a minute financial return'. The Fields cult was by this time quite large and vociferous; and his four films with Universal were greeted hysterically. Truth to tell, only one is very good. *You Can't Cheat an Honest Man* (39) co-starred him with Edgar Bergen, the ventriloquist, and his dummy Charlie McCarthy (Fields did a radio programme with them). Officially directed by George Marshall, Fields's sequences were directed by old friend Edward Cline, because Marshall was incapable of handling Fields – and Cline found it little easier. *My Little Chickadee*, the historic meeting with Mae West, was no better – again due to internal dissensions: they were supposed to have collaborated on the script, but Fields was non-cooperation personified. West said: 'There is no one quite like Bill. And it would be snide of me to add, "Thank God". A great performer. My only doubts about him come in bottles.' However, *The Bank Dick* (40) worked. Fields wrote story and screenplay (under the name Mahatma Kane Jeeves) which was why, perhaps, 'Time' was able to describe it as '74 minutes of almost clear Fields'. James Agee bracketed it later with *It's a Gift*, 'fiendishly funny and incisive white-collar comedies, [which] rank with the best comedies (and best movies) ever made'. At the time William Whitebait wrote: 'Fields is a comedian of almost Shakespearian mould. He is loud-voiced, dauntless, self-sufficient – one of those human balloons no amount of puncturing can deflate.' The title of the next one came from P.T. Barnum's famous dictum, already used to advertise one of Fields's silent pictures, *Never Give a Sucker an Even Break* (41). It has marvellously droll moments and bits of the best of Fields, including a lack of plot (contributed by him). Agee felt that backstage bickering may have marred it.

Certainly there were then no takers in Hollywood. He cast around for new deals without success. Ill with polyneuritis, he also stepped up his drinking. In 1942, 20th put him with Margaret Dumont in one episode of *Tales of Manhattan*, but it was cut from the final print; his other three film performances were as himself in grade B musicals: he did his pool-hall act in *Follow the Boys* (44); reopened his feud with Charlie McCarthy in one short scene of *Song of the Open Road*; and was one of several turns (Cab Calloway, Sophie Tucker, etc.) in *Sensations of 1945*. He died on Christmas Day, 1946 – ironically, for he pretended to loathe Christmas. His friends put an ad in the 'Hollywood Reporter' which described him as 'the most authentic humorist since Mark Twain'.

He did not lack for panegyrists during his lifetime – and has certainly not since his death. Taylor's excellent biography (49) paints a vivid picture of a great artist and impossible man; his films, after a lag in the late 40s and early 50s, have been constantly revived and by the late 60s he had become a cult figure. A record of soundtrack clippings was issued in the US in 1968. His voice is aped by comics as often as those of James Cagney and Peter Lorre. In 1976 Rod Steiger played him in *W.C. Fields and Me*, based on a memoir by Carlotta Monti, his last mistress: it was a box-office failure.

ERROL FLYNN

Errol Flynn's notoriety considerably outstripped his fame even at its height, and his fame way outstripped his talent. He blamed his studio, claiming that the run of stereotyped roles caused him to lose faith in himself as an actor. He might have been a poor actor, but as a personality – in those stereotyped roles – he was unique. More recent actors in tights just are not in the running; and, in the Talkie period, no actor swashed so blithe a buckle as this laughing cavalier. When Flynn stopped fighting and fencing, costume films became much less fun. He was also handsome and his screen work gave just the impression of the real-life peccadilloes for which a big movie star might be forgiven: vanity, impatience, lechery, suavity. Sometimes it seemed he belonged in a scented boudoir rather than in the Warner studio, but there were some memorable occasions on screen. Said Jack L. Warner in his memoirs: 'As a matter of fact, he had mediocre talent, but to the Walter Mittys of the world he was all the heroes in one magnificent, sexy, animal package. . . . Actor or no actor, he showered an audience with sparks when he laughed, when he fought, or when he loved.' He was, he went on, 'one of the most charming and tragic men I have known'.

Flynn was born in 1909 in Hobart, Tasmania, into a family more respectable than he was ever to be (his father was a professor). Before he arrived in films he was a professional and bisexual adventurer: he had worked passage on ships, prospected for gold, managed a plantation, hunted tropical birds, smuggled diamonds and served with the New Guinea Constabulary. He once stood trial for the murder of a native marauder on a jungle

Robin Hood has a midnight tryst with Maid Marian (Olivia de Havilland) in her room at Nottingham Castle – for the most innocent of reasons. But then there is a knock on her door. The Adventures of Robin Hood (*38*).

camp. Or so he claimed in an early memoir, 'Beam Ends'. There was a grain of truth in some of it: but certainly in 1926–27 he was a shipping clerk. Later he accompanied an expedition to New Guinea and his appearance in a film of that trip led to an offer to play Fletcher Christian in a local semi-documentary, *In the Wake of the Bounty* (33). MGM bought it and used bits in their own *Bounty* film. The producer, Charles A. Chauvel, advised him to leave Australia if he wanted to act and in Britain he landed a job with the Northampton Rep. A couple of their productions found their way to London, and he was offered the lead, a reporter, in a Quota quickie, *Murder at Monte Carlo* (35). Warners produced and during shooting he was offered a Hollywood contract starting at $150 a week.

On the transatlantic voyage he met Lili Damita, a fading French-born star, but clearly one bigger than he; and they were subsequently married. In Hollywood he was eleventh-billed playing a corpse in a Perry Mason (Warren William) mystery, *The Case of the Curious Bride*: but since corpses are not usually billed, it is a cinch that he will get at

least a flash-back – scowling. He supported William again in a B comedy, *Don't Bet on Blondes*. Warners had a big one on the stocks, *Captain Blood*, Rafael Sabatini's pirate hero, which was designed for Robert Donat, who did not consider himself definitely committed, and then Leslie Howard turned it down. Warners went after Ronald Colman and Gable, tested both George Brent and Brian Aherne, who came much cheaper; according to some sources Aherne turned the role down, but by this time both Damita and Flynn's new friend, Dolores del Rio, were campaigning for him and they persuaded Mrs Jack Warner that the role could be played by an unknown. The sets were waiting. Much of the early shooting was scrapped because of Flynn's inadequacy (and his Australian acccent is sometimes clear), but he began to acquire authority – and the charm was there (not that acting was required with dialogue like 'Follow me, m'hearties' and all). His contract was revised, to go to $800 immediately, increasing to $2,500 with a bonus of $750. Olivia de Havilland had been his leading lady, most effectively, so they were re-teamed in *The*

Charge of the Light Brigade (36), a stirring tribute to British gallantry set in India (except for the finale – otherwise it was our old friend, the Bengal Lancers picture). The contrast between the prim and pretty de Havilland and the assured, gallant Flynn was a happy one and it made happy box-office; and they liked each other. Says de Havilland's friend, Bette Davis, in her memoirs: 'But it was Olivia de Havilland whom he truly adored and who evaded him successfully in the end. I really believe that he was deeply in love with her.'

He wanted to show his versatility and was cast as a playboy doctor who reforms in *The Green Light* (37), based on a sanctimonious weepie by Lloyd C. Douglas. By this time he knew he was a very big star and demanded more money: so Warners tested contract-players Ian Hunter and Patric Knowles for *The Prince and the Pauper*, but though the character appeared late and briefly, it was felt that only Flynn was dashing enough; the Mauch twins had the title-roles in this version of Mark Twain's story. *Another Dawn* was a triangle melodrama with Hunter and Kay Francis, played out on an army installation of the Raj, and *The Perfect Specimen* was a funny comedy – *It Happened One Night* in reverse, with Joan Blondell as the reporter and Flynn as the wealthy scion. *The Adventures of Robin Hood* (38) had been originally planned for James Cagney, till *Captain Blood* convinced Warners that Flynn was born to play the role – as was de Havilland that of Maid Marian. Perfectly cast throughout, it was a story-book come to life, a 'magnificent entertainment' ('Photoplay') and an enduring one. *Snow-White* apart, it was the first greatly successful Technicolor feature.

The *Four's a Crowd* were the screen's new love team plus Rosalind Russell and Patrick Knowles, and Flynn (after Joel McCrea turned it down) was a fly PR man. He was a newspaperman in *The Sisters*, approved by his co-star Davis, who otherwise did not care for him, 'but handsome, arrogant and utterly enchanting, Errol was something to watch'. The MFB did not approve, opining that his 'superficial and unintelligent acting' did not help the film. He was excellent as the spirited, doomed British officer in the superior remake of *The Dawn Patrol*, but not exactly at ease in *Dodge City* (39), or How Law and Order Came to Dodge City and Guess Who Brought It; he was an Irish adventurer, de Havilland the editor's assistant, and they looked handsome in colour.

This was Flynn's biggest year and he made the box-office 10 (and was in the British list for some years further); his biggest fan was not Davis, 'appalled' at the prospect of him as Rhett Butler when it was proposed that Warners lend them as a package to Selznick for *Gone With the Wind*, and she fought for Laurence Olivier as against Flynn for *The Private Lives of Elizabeth and Essex* (39) – nor was she happy about the title, which was changed from the original *Elizabeth the Queen* because Flynn's contract required there to be a reference to him. Still, if a beardless Flynn made no attempt to look or act the part, he was easily the jewel of the court.

Olivia de Havilland had again played his light-of-love, but because in life she rejected his advances he fought against a re-teaming: and so in *Virginia City* (40), as a Civil War veteran, he romanced Miriam Hopkins; and in another Sabatini swashbuckler, *The Sea*

Flynn made a number of Westerns, which was just as well because he wasn't very convincing except as a man of action: Virginia City *(40), with Randolph Scott and Miriam Hopkins.*

Hawk, as an Elizabethan seaman, the lady was Brenda Marshall playing a Spanish princess. It was back to the Civil War and de Havilland in *Santa Fe Trail*, which had Raymond Massey as John Brown. The studio had bought *The Constant Nymph* for him, but decided the role was not masculine enough for his image; and a film about Captain Hornblower, turned down by Olivier, was postponed because of the world situation. Because of that, too, Warners packed away his sword and tights and even his chaps: he was a detective in *Footsteps in the Dark* (41), with Marshall, and a flyer in *Dive Bomber*. Like most of his big films, it was directed by Michael Curtiz, but they quarrelled and Raoul Walsh took over *They Died with Their Boots On*, which was also the last with de Havilland, her gentle Mrs Custer dominating his reckless, headstrong General: but it is one of his most winning performances. The title of that film proved a boon to jokers later when it was learned in court that Flynn made love with his socks on. Stories of Flynn's amatory escapades now culminated in a trial for the rape of two under-age members of his fan club aboard his yacht. He was acquitted and it would become clear that the revelations had not affected his box-office standing. He also was enjoying several homosexual affairs (one with Tyrone Power), though it is unlikely that Warners knew about these, for a later director – Vincent Sherman – considered him only an 'incipient' homosexual; but most of his later action movies were made by Walsh, known as a man's director and capable of projecting Flynn's image as Warners wanted it presented.

The Aussie accent had long since gone; the Irish charm was to take some years to fade, but after de Havilland departed Flynn was never quite the same. It was coincidental, but the adventure stories he made thereafter were weak. *Desperate Journey* (42) was rightly panned, an absurd thriller about a downed RAF crew wreaking havoc in Germany, with Flynn (playing an Australian) at the end crying: 'Now for Australia and a crack at those Japs!' The outcry was so fierce that Hollywood resolved to be more circumspect in its depiction of war. In *Gentleman Jim* he was a cocky boxer, Jim Corbett; in *Edge of Darkness* (43) the bravest member of the Norwegian underground. He did a Cockney sailor routine in *Thank Your Lucky Stars* and was in some more war melodramas directed by Walsh: *Northern Pursuit*, as a Mountie suspected of being a Nazi; and *Uncertain Glory* (44), as a philanderer who joins the French Resistance. With this film his contract was redrawn, to allow him a say in production, a share in the profits and the right to do a second film annually for an outside studio if he and the studio could not agree on a subject. For whatever reason, *Objective Burma* (45) atones for Flynn's other war movies and it concerns one specific American unit which is parachuted into that country, led by Flynn. The lack of any British participation in the Burma campaign caused it to be withdrawn from British cinemas within days, but the outcry continued across the Atlantic, where critics reinforced the view that Flynn was winning the war single-handed.

He had become an American citizen at the outbreak of the war in Europe, to avoid serving in the British or Australian army; later he was disqualified medically to serve in the US army and David Niven believed that his disintegration began with guilt feelings. Jack L. Warner's book places the start at this time, adding that during the final years of his contract he was drunk more often than not.

A Technicolor Western, *San Antonio*, helped silence the ridicule heaped on Flynn for his celluloid war exploits. Then the studio tried to lower his profile and change his image with: *Never Say Goodbye* (46), a marital comedy with Eleanor Parker; *Cry Wolf* (47), a thriller in which he was sinister to Barbara Stanwyck; and *Escape Me Never*, a weepie not unlike *The Constant Nymph*, in which he was mean to Ida Lupino. They also lowered his box-office standing, so Warner reunited him with Walsh to play an ambitious riverboat gambler in *Silver River*, with Ann Sheridan as the ranch-owner's wife he covets. They then gave him an even bigger budget and Technicolor again for *The Adventures of Don Juan*, directed by Sherman, which restored him to favour. But his drinking was a problem and the studio was relieved when MGM borrowed him to play Soames – efficiently – in *That Forsyte Woman* (49). Uncertain how to handle him, Warners put him into two Westerns, *Montana* (50) and *Rocky Mountain*, in the latter with Patrice Wymore, who became his third wife. There was a brief rehabilitation and an important but smallish role at MGM, the Afghan horse-dealer who works for the British secret service in *Kim*, Kipling's young hero, played by Dean Stockwell.

Partnered with William Marshall, he made *Hello God*, which Marshall wrote, and *The Adventures of Captain Fabian* (51), which he scripted: it was made in France with Marshall's wife, Micheline Presle. The first was never shown and was the subject of litigation two years later; the second caused a row with Warners, since Republic released and Flynn's contract stipulated that any outside project had to be handled by a major distributor. He returned to his home studio very much a back number and with a dull adventure tale, *Mara*

Maru (52), the studio terminated his contract.

Universal was at that time a haven for fading talent and he was welcomed for *Against All Flags*, but his old zest had gone. Like many other stars he took himself to Europe to take advantage of tax concessions and he persuaded Warners to produce *The Master of Ballantrae* (53) in Britain. Swashbucklers remained popular and he was the screen's foremost exponent still: *Don Juan* had been his most successful opus in the last decade, but Warners were not prepared to put up a similar budget – indeed, it could have cost little more than the £80,000 which he was paid. In Italy he assembled *Crossed Swords/Il Maestro di Don Giovanni* with Gina Lollobrigida, but it was not a success; and he lost his last cent trying to finish *William Tell* in Switzerland. The requisite finance was not forthcoming, but Herbert Wilcox offered to pay Flynn's creditors in exchange for a six-picture deal. He believed the combination of roisterer Flynn and demure Anna Neagle would be box-office and put them into two musicals which proved the reverse to be true: Flynn did not sing but he took a few steps in *Lilacs in the Spring* (54) as part of a musical comedy team, husband and father to the lady (who had a multiple role); and he looked even more embarrassed in *King's Rapsody* (55), as the king who renounces his mistress for a wife, Miss Wymore. The failure of both put Wilcox into debt for the rest of his life; he later admitted that Flynn's fans were not Neagle's or vice-versa. He did not mention him in his memoirs, perhaps because Flynn refused to come to his aid when he was again receiving Hollywood offers. For the moment there was one from Britain, for *The Dark Avenger*, which Allied Artists released in the US (as *The Warriors*); and back home, from Universal, for *Istanbul* (56), a routine remake of *Singapore*. Tired of sitting around drunk and bitter he accepted a cheap programmer, *The Big Boodle* (57), which mercifully got few bookings.

20th revived his career by asking him to play one of the drunken wastrels in *The Sun Also Rises*; the director, Henry King – echoing Lewis Milestone's opinion – found him a professional at work and a gentleman in life. His own memoir, 'My Wicked, Wicked Ways', boasted otherwise and it reawakened Warners' interest when they were casting *Too Much Too Soon* (58), based on Diana Barrymore's autobiography. Dorothy Malone played her and Flynn was father John in his last drunken days: 'I wasn't acting, I was just playing myself,' he said. He was also now a registered drug addict and when the notices and business for this particular film proved another career setback he returned to the stage, touring in 'Jane Eyre'; but he left after two weeks because he could not remember his lines and was suspended by Equity. 20th again came to the rescue with another screen drunk, in John Huston's *The Roots of Heaven*, and as before at this studio he was favourably received. However, the only offer was a messy little independent venture, *Cuban Rebel Girls* (59), in which he played himself, helping Fidel Castro to overthrow Battista. It also featured his current flame, the teenaged Beverly Aadland. There were virtually no bookings, despite more sensational revelations unleashed after his death, of a heart attack, in Vancouver, in October 1959. The coroner observed that the body was that of an old, tired man and Jack Warner says that during the making of *Too Much Too Soon* 'he was one of the living dead'. It is a sad epitaph on the man who was the screen's gayest, sprightliest and most disarming Robin Hood.

His son Sean Flynn, by Damita, had a brief career in French and Spanish films, often swashbuckling, in the 60s; he worked as a photographer in the Vietnam conflict, during which he disappeared, presumed killed.

A familiar sight in his later films: Flynn and bottle. This one is The Roots of Heaven *(58).*

HENRY FONDA

Other stars come and go, but Henry Fonda seemed to go on forever, with none of the ups and downs that milestone most long careers. It was a career without éclat, though there was at one time a tendency to regard him as a giant among film actors. The view is hardly tenable, though there are ample reasons why he endured when so many have fallen by the wayside; and it was a relief to find him still with us in those years of the psychotic and/or cocksure leading man. He was Honest Joe, deliberate, intelligent, slow to anger, chary: as a Western hero, brother to Gary Cooper, the antithesis of men of action like Gable or John Wayne. He spoke quietly with a deliberately (although he himself believed it limited him) flat, unaccented, unemotional voice. As a young man he was rather Caspar Milquetoast, a pleasing light comedian, a patient and finally successful rebel. He really was that dependable, likeable actor that so many others have aspired to be.

He was born in Grand Island, Nebraska, in 1905 and started acting as an amateur (with Marlon Brando's mother) with the Omaha Community Playhouse; he became a full-time professional in 1928 and played with the Provincetown Players and later the University Players Guild (Joshua Logan, James Stewart, Margaret Sullavan, Bretaigne Windust, etc.). He married Miss Sullavan one morning before a matinee of 'The Ghost Train'. His first New York appearance was a walk-on in 1929 ('The Game of Life and Death'); he did stock and was for a while a scene designer. He was in New York in 'I Loved You Wednesday' (32) and 'Forsaking All Others' (33); his big chance came as one of the 'New Faces of 1934' and he acquired an agent, Leland Hayward, who married his ex-wife Sullavan and persuaded the independent producer Walter Wanger to sign him to a contract, for two pictures a year starting at $1,000 a week. Wanger was not too interested in him, so Fonda remained in New York to star in 'The Farmer Takes a Wife'. Fox bought the film rights and when neither Gary Cooper nor Joel McCrea was available they contacted Wanger, who asked and got $5,000 per week for Fonda's services; but he generously upped Fonda's weekly fee to $3,000. In *The Farmer Takes a Wife* (35) Janet Gaynor is a bargee's housekeeper who falls unwillingly in love with a nice guy who wants to leave the canals for a farm. She, as it turned out, was almost at the end of her career while he was just starting; but they made a beautiful team, as Fox could see, for they saw him as the natural successor to her old partner, Charles Farrell. They should have been teamed again in *Way Down East*, but she had an accident and Rochelle Hudson replaced her. He then went to RKO to play an American composer who marries French girl Lily Pons when drunk in *I Dream Too Much*, which wags called 'I Scream Too Much'.

Wanger claimed him for three consecutive films: *The Trail of the Lonesome Pine* (36), the third version and the first outdoor Technicolor picture; *The Moon's Our Home*, a comedy with Sullavan, as a bestselling writer; and the trifling *Spendthrift*, in the title-role, with Pat Patterson. In the first of these he played a backwoodsman in danger of losing his loved one, Sylvia Sidney, to a city slicker; he was so intense and humourless that it is no surprise to learn from Al Capp that he inspired L'il Abner. At the same time the role established the Fonda persona as resolute and idealistic. His quiet, insistent approach made him almost unique among *jeune premiers*; seldom very different, he fitted wherever he was slotted: *Wings of the Morning* (37) for 20th, the first British Technicolor feature, as a Canadian in Ireland who falls for Annabella when he discovers she is a girl (she had been in drag); Fritz Lang's *You Only Live Once*, a moving story of an ex-convict who is not given a chance, with Sylvia Sidney as his wife, for Wanger; and *Slim*, a rowdy triangle drama with Pat O'Brien and Margaret Lindsay. That 'was a C picture' he said, 'but there was something good about it'. It was made at Warners and he remained there to be a playboy who reforms for *That Certain Woman*, who was Bette Davis. He aged from adolescence onwards to become a teacher in *I Met My Love Again* (38), a Wanger romance with Joan Bennett, and returned to Warners and Davis for a period piece, *Jezebel*, as the steady but strong-willed beau who will take only so much of her affectations. His last film for Wanger was *Blockade*, a silly story of the Spanish Civil War with Madeleine Carroll.

He went to Paramount for *Spawn of the North*, playing a cannery owner, boyhood chum of George Raft: they replaced Cary Grant and Randolph Scott, when the publicity pictures of their domestic bliss rebounded, but Jules Furthman's dialogue retains more than hints on that matter. At RKO Fonda was a newspaper editor bothered by *The Mad Miss Manton*, a murder mystery which remains one of the best screwball comedies, though he considered it 'trashy', recalling it only because of the pleasure of working with Barbara Stanwyck. At 20th he was brother and partner-in-crime to Tyrone Power, *Jesse James* (39), and at Columbia a cabbie wrongly accused of murder, Maureen O'Sullivan's fiancé, in *Let Us Live*, which was based on fact. It was only a programmer, but was the sort of project he thought worth doing. At 20th again he was Don Ameche's friend and partner in *The Story of Alexander Graham Bell* and he had the title-role in *Young Mr Lincoln*, a leisurely bucolic piece directed by John Ford. Its critical reception firmly established him but it was not a great popular success; however, *Drums Along the Mohawk* was, and he and Claudette Colbert looked fine as pioneers in Technicolor.

Ford directed again for 20th and he wanted Fonda for *The Grapes of Wrath* (40), based on John Steinbeck's novel about Dustbowl migrants who refuse to be depressed by the Depression: 'Can't nobody wipe us out. Can't nobody lick us. We'll go on forever, Pa. We're the people,' said Jane Darwell, whose performance really made the film (she got a Best Supporting Oscar). Many considered it the first honest, non-sentimental film about poverty. Zanuck had wanted the film for his biggest box-office star, Tyrone Power, and had only capitulated when Steinbeck added his voice to Ford's; but he knew the role of Tom Joad was an important one and would only assign it to Fonda if he signed the usual long-term contract. He promised to make him the biggest star on the lot, but that did not happen and the next few years were not professionally happy. Fonda had liked Wanger and at least had not minded the films for which he had been loaned. But he disliked most of his films at 20th: *Lillian Russell*, playing Alice Faye's greatest fan, a newspaperman and a nothing role; Fritz Lang's *The Return of Frank James*, reprising a character he had played a year before; and *Chad Hanna*, as a farm-boy who joins a circus for love of Dorothy Lamour. He did love *The Lady Eve* (41), Preston Sturges's brilliant comedy at Paramount, playing the innocent who turns the tables on Stanwyck; and after experiencing wanderlust in *Wild Geese Calling* he was reunited with her for another comedy, *You Belong to Me* at Columbia, but it was not of the standard of their earlier teamings. He also liked *The Male Animal* (42), the Thurber-Nugent comedy at Warners, playing a professor, and another at RKO, from Damon Runyon this time, *The Big Street*, as a bus-boy smitten with temperamental cabaret star

Henry Fonda as the ultimate home-spun hero: in John Ford's Young Mr Lincoln *(39). With him is Spencer Charters.*

Jane Darwell, Henry Fonda and Russell Simpson in John Ford's version of John Steinbeck's novel; The Grapes of Wrath *(40) was one of the most enduring of Hollywood's wholly serious 'social protest' films.*

Lucille Ball. At least its director, Rouben Mamoulian, disliked *Rings on Her Fingers*, a tinny comedy about con-men, and it would be hard to feel affection for either the Fonda-Ginger Rogers episode in *Tales of Manhattan* or a comedy with Don Ameche, *The Magnificent Dope*, country boy vs city guy again and retitled from *The Magnificent Jerk* just before filming began. Fonda played a cowboy for the first time in William A. Wellman's *The Ox-Bow Incident* (43), which was not a Western but a tale of a small-town lynch mob: and the people who loathed this included the 20th front office, till it began to win prizes and critical plaudits. *The Immortal Sergeant* was Thomas Mitchell and Fonda was a Canadian corporal in the Libyan desert: he objected to this partly because the studio had had him deferred in order to make it.

When he returned from the navy he owed 20th three pictures, of which *My Darling Clementine* (46) was Ford's contribution to the Wyatt Earp mythology, with Victor Mature as Doc Holliday. At RKO he took on Gabin's role, rebel against society, in the remake of *Le Jour se Lève/The Long Night* (47), which was not so inferior to the original, despite critical mauling then. After a Joan Crawford novelette at 20th, *Daisy Kenyon*, Fonda returned to RKO to play the whisky priest in Ford's *The Fugitive*, an attempt to film Graham Greene's 'The Power and the Glory' that was never less than misguided – and not helped by Ford's losing interest when hemmed in by religious and political difficulties during the Mexican location work. Fonda and his old friend James Stewart played musicians in an episode of *On Our Merry Way* (48) and then he returned to Ford for his first unsympathetic role, the martinet commander of *Fort Apache*.

He refused, with some acrimony, the next script from 20th and another long-term contract; he was 43 and felt that he had to re-establish himself on Broadway: 'Mister Roberts', by Thomas Heggen and Joshua Logan, in the title-role, the well-liked lieutenant of a World War II cargo ship; 'Point of No Return' (51); and 'The Caine Mutiny Court Martial', as the defending counsel, the role played by José Ferrer in the film version. The first two of these ran for two years or more and the third for a year. Warners had bought *Mister Roberts* (55) and favoured either William Holden or Marlon Brando (who had accepted) for Fonda's role. He was no longer considered box-office and was thinking of playing the older role of the doctor when Ford, directing, refused to go ahead without him: ironically, they fought over Ford's vulgarization of a text Fonda loved, and even came to blows. Officially Ford became too ill to continue and he was by all

Fonda as the wealthy innocent taken by cardsharp Barbara Stanwyck, with ship's steward, in The Lady Eve *(41), one of Preston Sturges's ageless comedies.*

accounts drinking heavily; Fonda said he would never work with him again and Mervyn LeRoy took over. The finished film was the year's biggest hit (apart from *Cinerama Holiday*, a special case).

That Fonda had been missed was apparent from the flurry of offers: he was Pierre in the US–Italo *War and Peace* (56). There was again disagreement about interpretation – with producer de Laurentiis this time: Fonda fought to play the part as written. The result, said 'Time', was that he seemed to be 'the only cast member who had read the book'. He was still blatantly miscast. Then he had the title-role in Hitchcock's documentary-keyed *The Wrong Man*. It was a box-office dud and so was *Twelve Angry Men* (57), which he set up himself after being impressed by it as a TV play, a drama about jurymen: but it was a critical success and he said that he was prouder of it than anything he had done. His performance won a BFA Best Actor award. Sidney Lumet (his début) directed and he also helmed *Stage Struck* (58): a remake of *Morning Glory* with Fonda in the Menjou role; it was fatally injured by Susan Strasberg's inability to fill Hepburn's old shoes. Fonda then did a couple of Westerns, *The Tin Star* and *Warlock* (59).

He returned to Broadway in 'Two for the Seesaw' (58) and his film appearances subsequently were scattered between some more long runs – 'Silent Night Lonely Night' (59), 'Critic's Choice' (60), 'Gift of Time' (62), etc. He also had a successful TV series, 'The Deputy', in the late 50s. He said that he did films less for love than money and to keep his name before the public. The results were not in later years spectacularly interesting, being almost equally divided between ageing sheriffs and ageing politicians (or public officials

Four of Hollywood's most
likeable actors in one film:
James Cagney, Fonda,
Jack Lemmon and William
Powell in Mister Roberts
(55). The title role had
been a great success for
Fonda on Broadway – he
played it three years.

of some sort). But they were all chock-a-block
with typical Fonda qualities: *The Man Who
Understood Women*, which he connived to do
because he liked Nunnally Johnson's script –
but he thought the result a mess and that
Johnson should not have directed it (it is a
strong contender for the worst film ever
made); *Advise and Consent* (62), from Allen
Drury's novel, as the liberal politician the
president (Franchot Tone) wants to appoint
Secretary of State; *The Longest Day*, one of
its many guest stars, as Brigadier General
Theodore Roosevelt; the Cinerama *How the
West Was Won* (63), ditto, as an Indian scout
got up to look like Buffalo Bill; the folksy
Spencer's Mountain with Maureen O'Hara,
which he disliked (later, adapted, it became
TV's 'The Waltons'); *The Best Man* (64) and
Fail Safe, two more excursions into political

drama. The first was Franklin Shaffner's
version of Gore Vidal's absorbing account of a
convention, with Fonda as the intellectual
contender for the Presidency, pitted against
Cliff Robertson (who in his previous film, *PT
109*, had played the young Jack Kennedy); the
second was Lumet's nightmarish 'hot line'
thriller, with Fonda actually the President, on
the line to Moscow. *Sex and the Single Girl*
was another of Fonda's pet dislikes, mainly
because director Richard Quine reneged on
several promises (including one to build his
and Lauren Bacall's parts till they were as big
as Tony Curtis's and Natalie Wood's).

If he remained as confident and engaging in
most of these as he ever was, he could no
longer carry a movie to success; and after
playing a cameo role as an admiral in *In
Harm's Way* (65), with John Wayne, he saw

The Rounders, a comedy Western with Glenn Ford, go on the lower half of double bills. And although in some markets *The Battle of the Bulge* (he was a high-ranking Intelligence officer; and this was another film he loathed) did well, another 'starry' international piece, *La Guerre Secrète*, got very few bookings in the US (as *The Secret Agents*) or Britain (as *The Dirty Game*). Fonda was a master spy in his sequence, filmed in Britain by Terence Young. In *A Big Hand for the Little Lady* (66) he and Joanne Woodward were innocents caught up with cardsharps in old Laredo and despite good notices it did not do well, while *Welcome to Hard Times* (67), an out-and-out Western, was only too well-named and suffered the fate of *The Rounders*. It was time to turn to television and Universal offered another Western, *Stranger on the Run*, with him in the title-role, Anne Baxter and direction by Don Siegel; but it was also his last tele-movie for some years. He was not at ease as the baddie in *Firecreek* (68), opposing his old pal James Stewart, while Siegel's *Madigan*, an otherwise first-class thriller, with Richard Widmark, was flawed by Fonda, whose police chief had not so much integrity as sanctimoniousness. But he partnered well with Lucile Ball on *Yours Mine and Ours*, a successful comedy, and again as a police chief he was seen to advantage in *The Boston Strangler*, who was Tony Curtis.

He elected to do a Western, Sergio Leone's *C'era una Volta il West/Once Upon a Time in the West* (69), as a double-dyed villain, billed after Claudia Cardinale, a film – and an experience – which he so disliked that he refused thereafter to discuss it; and he got $50,000 for two days' work in Robert Aldrich's *Too Late the Hero* (70). Reunited with Stewart, they played with great professionalism two naïve cowboys landed with a brothel in *The Cheyenne Social Club* and he stayed out West for *There Was a Crooked Man*, as warden of a prison which includes Kirk Douglas. In 1969 he observed of his TV series, 'I'd have to be awful hungry to do [one] again', but in 1971 he did, playing a cop in 'Smith'. In cinemas he was seen as Paul Newman's father in *Sometimes a Great Notion* (71), still extending his range – for the man is a roaring backwoodsman.

He elected to do two tele-movies, a remake of *The Red Pony* (73), with Maureen O'Hara, and *The Alpha Caper*, as a criminal mastermind. The choice then seemed to lie between retirement and Europe. He chose the latter, but to little-seen results: *Le Serpent/The Serpent* with Dirk Bogarde, as the head of the CIA; *Ash Wednesday*, as Elizabeth Taylor's husband; *Mussolini Ultimo Atto/Mussolini Dead or Alive* (74) with Rod Steiger, as a

cardinal; and *Il Mio Nome è Nessuno/My Name is Nobody*, a parody Western starring Terence Hill, as a famed gunfighter. He played Clarence Darrow in a one-man show and made his London début in the same play the following year; and after playing General MacArthur in a tele-movie, *Collision Course* (75), he returned to films as one of the ageing stars playing top brass in *Midway* (76), in fact as Admiral Nimitz. He turned down the role for which Peter Finch won an Oscar in *Network*, for the correct reason – he found the piece hysterical: but he then accepted a role in an Italian rip-off of *Jaws*, called *Tentacoli/Tentacles*, which also ensnared John Huston and Shelley Winters. *Captains and the Kings* was an expensive mini-series with a host of names, from Taylor Caldwell's novel, and he was a senator.

Now back in Hollywood, he played the boss of safety expert George Segal in *Rollercoaster*, the briefest role he may have had since walking on as a young actor; and he was an ageing trucker completing his last haul, with some hookers, in *The Great Smokey Roadblock* (77), but the film itself got nowhere under this or several other titles. *Home to Stay* (78) was made for TV, in Canada, and Fonda was an old boy on a trip with his granddaughter so as to prevent himself being put in an old people's home. He was one of several names in three disaster movies: *The Swarm* (78), as a scientist; *City on Fire* (79), as the fire chief; and *Meteor*, again as the President of the US. Between the first and second he did a guest stint, as himself, in Billy Wilder's story of the film industry, *Fedora* (78), and played in an important mini-series, *Roots: the Next Generation* (79) with Olivia de Havilland as his wife; and he did another film between the second and the third, for his son Peter – directing and starring – in *Wanda Nevada*, playing an old prospector. The three disaster movies were something else, of a quality to devalue his name, and he turned to television: *The Oldest Living Graduate* (80) was a rare 'live' airing and the first he had done in 18 years; *Gideon's Trumpet* and *Summer Solstice* (81) were superior tele-movies. In the former, based on fact, he played a down-and-out Florida convict who changed the legal system and in the latter he co-starred with Myrna Loy.

His acting had taken on a different timbre, even a new confidence, 'a continuing source of wonder' as 'The New York Times' put it reviewing 'Show-down at the Adobe Motel', which he did at Stamford, Connecticut, playing a former rodeo star. There was nothing whatsoever of the old Milquetoast in *On Golden Pond*, as a crusty, querulous, outspoken old man. Both he and Katharine Hepburn, playing his wife, won Oscars – in his case his second, since he had been awarded an honorary Academy Award just a year earlier. Picking it up for him, daughter Jane said there would be no more performances – and it was she who chose this meretricious Broadway piece as a late co-starring vehicle for the two of them. He was then in hospital and he died a few months later (in 1982).

He had married his fifth wife in 1965 and it was reckoned to be his only successful marriage. Jane and Peter are the children of his second wife, Frances Seymour Brokaw, who committed suicide after hearing that he had fallen in love with another woman. It was an awesomely long career. He once said: 'I remember when I first started, working with Fred MacMurray in *The Trail of the Lonesome Pine*. We had both sort of fallen into this, and we were talking about this fantastic money we were making and how, if we could only last two more years and put it in the bank, we could say the hell with 'em. And [Henry] Hathaway [the director] just laughed, saying we'd still be at it in – I don't recall, 20 years or something like that, and we both thought he was absolutely insane. But here we are, both of us. I think it's incredible.'

JOAN FONTAINE

As a young woman, Joan Fontaine was one of the loveliest of stars. She looked – as she still does – so right. In her early movie roles she was angelic and unaffected, and later, when she became sophisticated in a typical moviestar way, she remained fetching. Like her sister, Olivia de Havilland, she was impeccably genteel, without seeming either inhibited or formidable. And her acting was not bad either.

She was born in Tokyo a year after Olivia, in 1917, of parents who were divorced shortly after. The children went with their mother to the US – to Saratoga in California; their mother remarried in 1925 (a man called Fontaine, hence the eventual stage name). In her teens Joan paid a visit to her father in Tokyo and when she returned, Olivia was a successful actress. She started towards the same goal and she says in her autobiography that the resentment her mother and Olivia expressed was to result in the life-long estrangement between the sisters; they later disapproved of her relationship with Conrad Nagel, the matinée idol whose career had been ruined by Louis B. Mayer (for his work in strengthening the Hollywood unions). Under the name Joan Burfield, Fontaine worked first with a little theatre group in San José, then in a production of 'Kind Lady' starring May Robson. MGM tested her and cast her as Joan Crawford's sophisticated rival in *No More Ladies* (35), but it was a minute role and nothing came of it. She returned to the stage (as Fontaine) in Dodie Smith's 'Call it a Day' – the same role her sister played in the film version. This was in LA and producer Jesse Lasky caught a performance: he signed her to a seven-year contract, but almost immediately sold it to RKO.

She had an insignificant role as one of the inhabitants of *Quality Street* (37), starring Katharine Hepburn, who recommended that she be given experience with leads in Bs. Thus she did *You Can't Beat Love* with Preston Foster; and then was leading lady in two musicals, *Music for Madame* with Nino Martini and *A Damsel in Distress* with Fred Astaire. There had been much speculation as to who would succeed Ginger Rogers as his partner and Astaire had turned down Ruby Keeler as being unsuitable to play an English aristocrat: Fontaine was right for that; she was unlike Rogers in many ways – and was given only one dance so that comparisons were not invited. But she caused little comment whatever and returned to Bs: *Maid's Night Out* (38), *Blonde Cheat*, *The Man Who Found Himself* with John Beal and, more importantly, *Sky Giant* with Richard Dix and *The Duke of West Point* with Louis Hayward. She was Fairbanks Jr's love interest in *Gunga Din* (39), directed by George Stevens, and was loaned to Republic to play Dix's first wife in *Man of Conquest*, her first bitchy part. RKO then dropped her, but she was interviewed by George Cukor for Scarlett O'Hara; as a result he cast her as one of the few sympathetic divorcees in *The Women*.

He thought of her when Selznick consulted him – because Alfred Hitchcock, who was to direct, had not yet arrived from Britain – on the casting of *Rebecca* (40), for which they had already considered de Havilland. The publicity story at the time was that she was contemplating giving up her career now that she had married Brian Aherne and had been discussing Daphne du Maurier's novel at a dinner party with Selznick, when he knew she would be ideal in the role. As it happened, she was, but only after testing, along with Margaret Sullavan, Loretta Young, Anne Baxter and others: and also after showing initial inexperience on the set, as well as being goaded by Hitchcock, who kept reminding her that Laurence Olivier had wanted Vivien Leigh to play the role, that of his shy, mousy, uncertain second wife. Her poignancy added immeasurably to the drama and suspense: Hitchcock, said W.H. Mooring, 'has succeeded in transforming Joan Fontaine from an unsatisfying feminine decoration into a great

'It's Rebecca's body lying there on the cabin floor':
Laurence Olivier and Joan
Fontaine in Hitchcock's
Rebecca (*40*), *from*
Daphne du Maurier's
novel.

screen actress'. 'Picturegoer' readers voted her their Gold Medal. Selznick had her under contract, but he found her difficult to handle. She refused to go to Universal for *Back Street*, claiming it was an unworthy follow-up to *Rebecca*; part of the trouble was that he saw her as a defenceless, very feminine heroine, while she considered herself more the Constance Bennett type. George Sanders, who had worked with her on *Rebecca* and who would co-star with her in the 50s, later observed that her on-screen bearing was 'in fine contrast to a private life of considerable vitality and colour'.

For the moment Selznick won: she was another uneasy wife (Cary Grant's) in *Suspicion* (41), loaned with Hitchcock to RKO, for this version of Francis Iles's 'Before the Fact': the performance brought her an Oscar and the New York critics' award, though observers considered these were compensations for not winning with *Rebecca*. In *This Above All* (42) she and Tyrone Power made a very solemn couple, oh-so-British, with her showing him the way to patriotism in the end; the British atmosphere was sillier than most. She was a teenager in the film of Margaret Kennedy's *The Constant Nymph* (43) and Charles Boyer was the composer (a part played by husband Aherne in the British version of 1935). Then she was *Jane Eyre* (44) among studio-bound Yorkshire moors, and much too pretty, but by sheer will she managed to project some of the right innocence before the film rolled downhill. *Frenchman's Creek* found her as another Daphne du Maurier heroine, a Restoration

milady on vacation with pirate Arturo de Cordova: lush and silly. At a cost of $4 million it was the most expensive film yet made in the US (concurrent with MGM's *Ziegfeld Follies*) and not the hoped-for box-office sensation.

Fontaine's appearance in it was extremely glamorous and she now got a chance to play the sort of part for which she yearned: *The Affairs of Susan* (45) – it was also her first film in years not set in Britain. She was a woman seen through the eyes of four different suitors (George Brent, Dennis O'Keefe, Don Defore and Walter Abel) and it was quite funny; but in appearance she had become interchangeable with any other Hollywood female and was, into the bargain, developing a fey quality that had once been incipient. Meanwhile, relations with Selznick had worsened: she resented his getting huge sums for loaning her out (he had paid her $11,500 for *Rebecca*, $17,000 for *Suspicion*) and she refused the role that Ginger Rogers eventually played in *I'll Be Seeing You*. After being suspended for most of the year, they decided to call it quits and she returned to RKO for *From This Day Forward* (46) with Mark Stevens, a story of young marrieds in the Bronx.

She signed another long-term contract with that studio, because her (second) husband, William Dozier, was a producer there: but he promptly went to Universal, which is why she mainly filmed there over the next few years (and when Howard Hughes bought RKO, she found herself under contract to him). She was in Edwardian costume for three films, starting with *Ivy*, originally offered to her sister: the

story of an ambitious lady who did not shrink from using poison as a means to the wealthiest possible husband. The artificial streak in Fontaine's acting sat easily on this character. Later, stronger directors would curb it (and when they did not, she was uninteresting): it was not countenanced by Billy Wilder on *The Emperor Waltz* (48) – but she was merely decorative in this Bing Crosby musical – nor by Max Ophüls on *Letter From an Unknown Woman* (produced by her husband). Of the latter, William Whitebait praised 'the enchantment of the whole piece and especially of Joan Fontaine's performance in it': it is possibly her best work, a beautiful piece of kitsch, young love lost/remembered. Stefan Zweig wrote the original story and Louis Jourdan was the lover who did not remember. Universal disliked it so much they sold it off in Britain to another distributor, who cast it out into the flea-pits, from whence it was rescued by a couple of British critics; but it was never very popular. Fontaine's other Universal pictures were both conventional, *Kiss the Blood Off My Hands*, a phoney domestic drama with Burt Lancaster, and *You*

Louis Jourdan and Joan Fontaine in Max Ophüls's synthesis of old Vienna, Letter From an Unknown Woman *(48). Though you wouldn't know it from the credits of either film, Universal had made it years before as* Only Yesterday.

Gotta Stay Happy, a run-away-heiress comedy with James Stewart.

She hit the wicked-lady trail again in one that had originally been announced for her by Selznick, *Born To Be Bad* (50), and sold in the interim to RKO as a vehicle for Barbara Bell Geddes, whom Hughes did not wish to promote. It lived up to its title and was the only film Fontaine made for Hughes, which left her freedom to sign a three-picture deal with Paramount. *September Affair* was an astute and ingratiating mixture of Kurt Weill's 'September Song', Rachmaninoff, Joseph Cotten and Italian locations: a poor girl's *Brief Encounter*. It was popular, but the other two disappeared on completion: *Darling How Could You!* (51), a predictably feeble adaptation of Barrie's 'Alice-Sit-By-the-Fire', with John Lund; and George Stevens's *Something to Live For* (52). Stevens was a talked-about name because of *A Place in the Sun*, but Paramount threw this away, an intelligent if over-glamorous study of alcoholism. She was a budding actress bent for the skids and Ray Milland an ex-lush from AA sent to help her. She was infinitely touching, proving again that she had no peers when she really tried. With one exception it was her last good film.

Ivanhoe wasted her – she was Rowena; *Decameron Nights* (53), with Jourdan, a four-part film based on Boccaccio, was misbegotten from the start and she was arch in all her roles; *Flight to Tangier* was a programmer and she was an FBI agent; *The Bigamist* a serious but sentimental look at that subject; and in *Casanova's Big Night* (54) she was little more than Bob Hope's feed. She was Mario Lanza's society 'protector' in *Serenade* (56), once offered to Tallulah Bankhead and in the original novel a man, and was in one of the late and lesser Fritz Langs, *Beyond a Reasonable Doubt*; she had the 'daring' role of the woman loved by Harry Belafonte in *Island in the Sun* (57), though most audiences were asleep for the clinch that never came. Still, there were many of them, perhaps influenced by the original novel's bestseller status. Her one good picture was Robert Wise's evocation of wartime New Zealand, *Until They Sail*: she played the eldest sister with much of her old skill and warmth.

A Certain Smile (58) with Rosanno Brazzi and *Voyage to the Bottom of the Sea* (61) with Walter Pidgeon were uneasy versions of popular French novels: in the latter she got an overdose of radiation and was then eaten by a shark. She had a supporting role but star billing in *Tender Is the Night* (61) and her brittle limning of Nicole's sister was the only thing in the film that critics liked. After an absence she appeared in one of the better Hammer horror pictures, *The Witches* (66),

but her own performance was unremarked upon.

In 1954 she replaced Deborah Kerr in the Broadway production of 'Tea and Sympathy', and has done occasional stage work since, mainly in stock. She married for the fourth time in 1964 (it did not last) and lives in New York, a lady of some wealth and considerable social achievement. She did not need to make pictures, she said, and was content to wait until a part came along which she liked: most of the current parts for women of her age were parts she definitely did *not* want to play. She did begin an Italian picture (*A Girl Called Jules*) in 1970, but there was disagreement over the contracted salary terms and she walked out. In 1972 she did 'Dial M for Murder' in stock and in 1978 published a memoir, 'No Bed of Roses'. At the English Theatre in Vienna she appeared in 'The Lion in Winter' (79), but the little work undertaken since has usually been for TV, often guesting. There were more substantial roles in: *The Users* (78), as a society butterfly in this tele-movie with Tony Curtis; *Crossings* (86), as a talkative woman in a mini-series starring Cheryl Ladd, made three years earlier; and *Dark Mansions*, a Gothic melodrama and a pilot for a possible series, co-starring Michael York, as the matriarch – a role meant for Loretta Young till she read the script.

GEORGE FORMBY

The character played by George Formby was not original: the North Country bumpkin tolerated or despised by everyone in the film until the last reel when – more by luck than good judgement – he ousts the baddies and daringly wins the heroine, the girl who all along had been aware of his simple faith and preferred it to his more flashy rivals. At some point he would cause the contents of a shop to fall about its customers, at some point he would unwittingly cross a local dignitary, innocently disclose the secret plans to the villains, or find himself without his trousers; then, realizing, he would scream 'Ooooh Mother' and flee. The films always ended with a chase or a fight.

It was a character assumed in the 50s by another British music-hall comic, Norman Wisdom. Both used certain characteristics: the shy grin, the slapstick, the chirpy self-confidence, the resignation over their lack of sex-appeal. But Formby never played for sympathy and the worst of Wisdom's faults, like the cringe-making attempts at pathos, were never hinted at; and the admittedly rudimentary humour of the Formby vehicles eschewed the sort of unfunny falling over in which Wisdom indulged himself. What made Formby so endearing and ultimately unique was the air with which he carried his naivety. He had a ukelele which he strummed in moments of stress or with which he serenaded the girl and most of his songs had a quota of crude double entendres: his expression, when he came to those lines, was perfect, a combination of 'Look what a naughty boy I am' and 'It's all in your minds'.

Like Wisdom, Formby never broke the American market, but in Europe, in the then British Empire and in Britain both held sway. For 10 years, 1936 to 1945, Formby was one of the top money-makers for British exhibitors. He was top of the British artists from 1938 to 1942 and during that time the only Britisher able to pull his weight with the Tracys, Durbins and Gables. That his appeal was insular – beyond the fact that at that time you could not sell in the US a Lancashire accent – was due less to his abilities than his vehicles, which were simple-minded and somewhat frowsy compared with the Hollywood product (West End audiences never liked them). Everybody else liked him because they thought they knew him.

His expertise undoubtedly came from a solid music-hall background. He was born in Wigan in 1904, the son of a popular North Country comedian. He became a jockey but apparently decided to become a comic after hearing another comedian using his father's material: his first pro appearance was at the Hippodrome, Earlestoun, under the name of George Hoy. Later, he paid a local impresario £300 to learn the pantomime business. It was not until he was topping the bill that he felt able to take on his real name – his father's name. He later dropped the Jr. His career was managed by his wife, known simply as 'Beryl': he was a shy man and almost certainly would not have bothered but for her.

Originally, he toured the North of England, but as he ventured South he discovered that he was equally appreciated there (which was rarely the case: another North Country comedian, Frank Randle, operating in the 40s, used to film at Manchester little comedies for release in the North, where they were widely successful; the South never took to them at all). Formby's first film, *Boots Boots* (34), was set mainly in the kitchen Below Stairs where he was the humblest servant. Beryl co-starred to save costs – they were exactly £3,000 – and it was made in a converted garage in two weeks and looked like it. It was successful enough for the budget to be upped somewhat on the next, *Off the Dole*. Again it did nice business and at the same time he was becoming nationally famous via radio and records.

Ealing Studios, then called ATP, offered him a contract and starred him in *No Limit* (35), an unpretentious story about a young man mad on motor bikes and determined to make his name by winning the Isle of Man TT. The smarties sneer at him and, just as obviously, he overcomes all obstacles (in this case, literally) and wins. There was a girl to encourage him (Florence Desmond), as there was to be in all his films (as in life: but when he was earning £30,000 per film, Beryl allowed him only five shillings a day pocket-money). The Ealing films are rather attractive, with some broad and good-hearted satire at the expense of some easy targets. Like Will Hay at a rival studio, like Wisdom later (and like most American comics), the milieu was clearly defined. He followed a readily recognizable craft – thus in *Keep Your Seats Please* (36) he was a bus conductor. There followed: *Feather Your Nest* (37); *Keep Fit*, a send-up of the then current League of Health and Beauty, with Kay Walsh; *I See Ice* (38), ice-skating; *It's in the Air*, the RAF; *Trouble Brewing* (39), from a comic novel by Joan Butler, with Googie Withers; *Come on George* as a jockey; *Let George Do It* (40) with Phyllis Calvert, cashing spies in Norway; *Spare a Copper*, as a would-be policeman; and

George Formby was hardly a hair-cream ad but he had only to strum his ukelele and sing a saucy song for the heroine to capitulate. This one is Googie Withers, later one of Britain's best actresses. Trouble Brewing *(39).*

Turned Out Nice Again (41), as the salesman in a ladies' underwear factory, obviously the place where his double entendres would be most at home – and indeed the opus was named after one of his best-known catchphrases, normally used after he had innocently offended. His scriptwriters knew how to exploit him – from these same talents came most of the best postwar comedies – but once the war came, circumstances changed and Formby was no longer the cornerstone of Ealing economics: the last two films at least show a marked decline, as though the heart had gone out of the production team (Michael Balcon in his memoir discloses that he cared little for Formby as a person, suggesting he was dumb rather than difficult). Will Hay had left Gainsborough and joined Ealing, and Formby in turn moved on to Columbia, not otherwise noted for taking an interest in British production; he was guaranteed £500,000 for seven films, suggesting that they had been impressed by the grosses of his films for Ealing.

His appeal, however, was fading – not because he worked less hard or tried to change his persona, but the gormlessness which was at the heart of it seemed less attractive as he reached his 40s. His plots became more amorphous, less constraining: *South American George* (42), with frizzled hair and gigolo moustache, the inevitable wartime spy comedy; *Much Too Shy*, as an over-age art student who gets into hot water when someone adds nude bodies – for soap ads – to the faces he has drawn; *Get Cracking* (43), about rival Home Guard units; *Bell Bottom George*, in the Navy; and *He Snoops to Conquer* (44), as an odd-job man elected to the local council. During this time he travelled throughout Africa, and elsewhere, entertaining troops, but his film popularity sank. Both *I Didn't Do It* (45) and *George in Civvy Street* (46) played double bills.

Formby's rejection by the British film industry was complete and it was not due to merely ailing box-office. The industry, during the war, had discovered that it could make more important films than George Formby comedies. It was a portent when James Mason replaced Formby as the biggest British draw and there began a wholesale rejection of the lighter people who had made the country laugh in the tense pre-war days; in the immediate postwar period there was no laughter from the British studios, only turgid, phoney dramas with titles like *When the Bough Breaks* and *Good Time Girl*. It must have come as quite a shock to their perpetrators – so keen on turning out Hollywood imitations and chunks of British 'art' – to find that the homely cut-ups of pre-war comedy stand up much better in later years.

With the collapse of his film career, Formby went back to the halls and the South heard little of him until he appeared at the Palace Theatre, London, in 1951, in a musical, 'Zip Goes a Million' – a belated West End success. He left the cast after a heart attack, but knowing that he had retained the affection of the public. Eighteen months later, in an era dominated by American stars, he topped the bill at the Palladium; and he had another success in London, in panto in 1956, as Idle Jack in 'Dick Whittington'. He did summer seasons and occasional TV and was plagued by ill health. In the winter of 1960-1 he was forced to leave the panto he was doing at Bristol. Simultaneously his wife died and there was much comment in the press when it was announced that Formby planned to marry at once a young schoolteacher. He felt called upon to inform the press that the marriage believed to be ideally happy had been killed years earlier by his wife's drinking. Suddenly the British public became sentimental over him and wished him happiness; but he died of a heart attack in February 1961, not long before the wedding date. Towards the end of his life he said 'I wasn't very good, but I seemed to have something the public wanted.'

KAY FRANCIS

Wavishing Kay Fwancis (she had trouble with her Rs) was not one of the greater talents, but she had beauty and intelligence; and in the early 30s – her heyday – her fashions and make-up were eagerly watched by women the whole world over. She was always on the lists of the best-dressed stars. For the men, a good plus was a suggestion that underneath the chic was a nice warm heart. In *Mandalay* she has an entrance – in a white number, at the top of a flight of stairs – which is as breathtaking as anything of its kind in the whole history of movies, but even then her doll-like features had to be carefully photographed if they were not to look bloated; so when the inevitable decline set in, the studio did everything, as it turned out, to hasten it.

She was born in Oklahoma City in 1905, the daughter of a vaudeville artist, Katherine Clinton, and a drunken father who deserted them; she dabbled in a number of jobs and marriage before aiming her sights on her mother's profession, if a little higher – and the right contacts got her a job as the understudy to Katharine Cornell in 'The Green Hat'; but her first professional acting was as the Player Queen in a modern dress 'Hamlet' (25) starring Basil Sydney. She acted under her own name of Katharine (it did not become Kay till after she was in pictures). Some parts followed, both in stock and in New York, culminating in a feature part in 'Elmer the Great' starring Walter Huston: which led to a good part with that actor in *Gentlemen of the Press* (29), as a vamp, and Paramount liked her enough to offer a contract starting at $500 a week. She had only a small part in *The Cocoanuts*, as a shady lady outwitted by the Marx Bros; and was equally slinky and little more important in: *Dangerous Curves*, a circus tale with Clara Bow; *Illusion*, in which Charles 'Buddy' Rogers and Nancy Carroll had a stage 'magic' act; and *The Marriage Playground*; though it was generally conceded that she stole the first of these from its star. However, after driving William Powell to his doom in *Behind The Makeup* (30) she had her first sympathetic role, with him, in *Street of Chance*. She was loaned to Warners for *A Notorious Affair*, trying to snaffle Basil Rathbone from Billie Dove, and to Goldwyn for *Raffles*; and was offered as a prop for Jeanette MacDonald and Jack Oakie in *Let's Go Native*. Paramount thought her chic the correct accompaniment to Powell's dapper and cast them as lovers in *For The Defense*, he as an attorney and she as an actress who lets another take the rap for her drunken driving.

She took a step towards stardom with *The Virtuous Sin*, the first of a series of pulsating romances where she was either forbidden or forgiving (in that particular one she gave herself to Huston in order to save scientist husband Kenneth MacKenna, who became her husband in life); *Passion Flower* at MGM with Charles Bickford and *Scandal Sheet* (31) with George Bancroft and Clive Brook, both triangle dramas; and *Ladies' Man*, as one of Powell's married mistresses. In the midst of these she signed with Warners: since Paramount was having money troubles, Warners approached agent Myron Selznick with a view to filching two of his big Paramount clients, Ruth Chatterton and Powell, plus Miss Francis. There was a court battle resolved by Warners offering to lend her to Paramount when required. That company rushed her from film to film to get their money's worth before she left: *The Vice Squad* with Paul Lukas; *Transgression* at RKO, as a lonely wife turning to Ricardo Cortez for comfort; *Guilty Hands* at MGM, as a murder suspect (only prosecuting attorney Lionel Barrymore really did it); *24 Hours*, as the bored wife of dipsomaniac Clive Brook, *Girls About Town*, as one of them, gold-digging with Lilyan Tashman; and *The False Madonna* (32) which was she posing as a dead woman in the hope of collecting a fortune. The last under her Paramount contract was *Strangers In Love*,

opposite Fredric March, which confirmed earlier hints that her idea of playing comedy was to raise and quicken her voice and look as cheerful as possible. Warners celebrated their acquisition by offering this as official publicity: 'Has very tender vocal chords and is unable to scream when called upon to do so; to save her throat has somebody else to scream for her.' And by putting her into a couple of stinkers, *Man Wanted* (David Manners as her secretary) and *Street of Women*, whose sole enlivenment was Roland Young.

But then they teamed her with Powell, first in a tricky but gay comedy, *Jewel Robbery*, in which she was a baroness and he a burglar, and *One-Way Passage*, falling in love as they cross the Pacific – he to go to the Chair and she to die. It is so perfectly balanced (with humour) and achieved that it has attained classic status; at the time it was respectfully received, but as with many of Francis's straight films, some spectators had difficulty keeping a straight face. Laughter was appropriate for Lubitsch's *Trouble in Paradise*, for which she returned to Paramount, though resentful that Miriam Hopkins was top-billed over her. It went over schedule and WB refused to delay the start of *42nd Street*, so Bebe Daniels was given the part intended for Francis, to the latter's annoyance. But it meant that she was free to answer an urgent call from Goldwyn when his socialite discovery, Dorothy Hale, did not make it before the

Kay Francis and William Powell in One-Way Passage (32). *The reason it was one way was because she had an incurable disease and he was being escorted home for the Chair.*

cameras; the film was *Cynara* and as Ronald Colman's wife Francis gave one of her most lovely, most typical performances. There were three murky dramas: *The Keyhole* (33), on shipboard (yet again) with George Brent, who has been paid by her elderly, jealous husband to frame her by making her fall for him; *Storm at Daybreak* at MGM, with Huston; *Mary Stevens MD*; and then a good one, *I Loved a Woman,* though it was basically a vehicle for Edward G. Robinson. In both *The House on 56th Street* (34) and *Mandalay* she bumped off Ricardo Cortez: the former was a not unenjoyable period melodrama where she sacrificed herself for her daughter after 20 years in prison and the latter a delirious tropical melodrama in which she was the most notorious cabaret girl in the Orient. Both had been rejected by Chatterton, whose place as Queen of the Lot Francis was slowly usurping.

Wonder Bar – an Al Jolson musical and a big box-office film – was the cause of a well-publicized quarrel with Warners, when her part was chopped down to make way for that of new contract player, Dolores del Rio: it was the beginning of a mutual disenchantment that was to end tragically for her. Meanwhile, *Doctor Monica* gave her a good part and *British Agent*, with Leslie Howard, a daft role as Lenin's secretary. Three consecutive pictures with George Brent, *Living on Velvet* (35), *Stranded* (both directed by Frank Borzage) and *The Goose and the Gander*, indicated that they were not the public's favourite screen team and of her films that year, only the four-handkerchief *I Found Stella Parrish* (with Ian Hunter) found much favour at the box-office. Warners hoped for better results from *The White Angel* (36) – Francis as Florence Nightingale. After all, director William Dieterle had just done wonders with Paul Muni as Louis Pasteur. But the press considered both film and star antiseptic and when they died the death at the box-office, Francis was on her way out. It was, said 'Variety' later, the 'final crusher' when WB decided against putting her into *Tovarich*, which they had bought for her. They borrowed Claudette Colbert for the part and Francis started a lawsuit which she was persuaded to drop. The real trouble was that her huge salary ($227,500 in 1937) was not justified by public response and there were others on the payroll breathing down her neck – like Bette Davis, whose salary was one-fifth of Francis's.

The studio persevered for a while longer: *Give Me Your Heart* with George Brent, from a stage weepie about mother-love, 'Sweet Aloes'; and *Stolen Holiday* (37), set up by financier Claude Rains in her own fashion business. The holiday concerned was with Ian Hunter, the sort of well-turned-out gent – following Powell and Brent – whom Warners saw as Francis's vis-à-vis. Ian Hunter was also in *Another Dawn*, just another triangle drama, with Errol Flynn. *Confession* with Basil Rathbone was a shot-by-shot remake of Pola Negri's recent (German) *Mazurka* – in turn based on Gloria Swanson's *The Coast of Folly*, about a mother who kills her ravisher when she learns he is about to lead her daughter down the same primrose path: but ah, she finishes in Hunter's arms. Filming was marred by battles between Francis and director Joe May. It was too late for Francis to refer to this batch of films as 'real stinkeroos', too late for producer Hal Wallis's gallant statement: 'It is the producer's business to gauge his public; it is the star's business to trust the producer's judgement. Kay Francis is possibly the only star in the entire history of Warners who has realized this fact and who has been ready to meet us more than halfway.' She said: 'Even if it was me the public so kindly want to see, there was a limit to the number of times a certain type of story or motif could be repeated.'

Warners could not be held entirely to blame. There was a point in the career of virtually every star, no matter how popular and talented, when they failed to draw. Some were lucky – a change of formula or a change of studio worked. There was no public anti-

Always in My Heart (42): Kay Francis involved with another convict, Walter Huston. She was his unfaithful wife, here visiting him in prison.

pathy towards Francis; people were simply tired of the sort of films she made and when the formula was changed not enough of them heard about it. Maybe they would have done if she had co-starred with Flynn again, when he became big box-office, or Cagney, or Gable, but the salaries of the mighty men stars, along with her own, could not be fitted into the budgets. There were two comedies: *First Lady*, as a wise-cracking society dame in a part that had been a hit for Jane Cowl on Broadway, and *Women Are Like That* (38), a marital romp with Pat O'Brien as her drunken husband. 'Poor Kay Francis certainly got a dirty deal in this. Unbelievably gauche and tiresome. . . . Maybe we'd better pretend we didn't know about it' ('Photoplay'). A couple of duallers were no better liked: the sentimental *My Bill*, a remake of *Courage*, which had starred Belle Bennett, coping with a horde of kids (her own), and *Secrets of an Actress* – and since the men were Brent and Hunter there were few secrets with which audiences were not familiar. Francis begged for the part of the Empress Carlotta in *Juarez*, but instead WB announced that she would work out her contract in Bs – at $4,000 a week. The trade was shocked and the fact that the move was announced was a professional blow to Francis. She put on a good face and told reporters that she was tired of being a star and looking forward to retiring (now divorced from Kenneth MacKenna, she was expected to marry a German baron), but W.H. Mooring wrote later that Warners almost broke her heart.

Comet Over Broadway, with Hunter, had

been turned down by Davis, who got the important *The Sisters*, bought for Francis. *King of the Underworld* (39) was a remake of *Dr Socrates*, with a sex-change: it had been intended as a big one for Francis, but was made on a B budget and Francis was billed *below* the title, in letters one-half the size of Humphrey Bogart, starred above. After *Women in the Wind* – she was an aviatrix, with William Gargan – she left the Warner lot and Bette Davis took over her bungalow.

Carole Lombard helped her off the skids by getting her into *In Name Only*, as the unhappy wife (emoting heavily) in this triangle drama, and Francis had another good featured part as Deanna Durbin's mother in *It's a Date* (40). She got top-billing again in *Little Men*, as Jo at RKO, but it was a cheap little film. There were more such: *When the Daltons Drove*, a Randolph Scott Western; *Playgirl*, an unsavoury piece about an older woman passing on the tricks of the trade to a young girl now that she is past it; *The Man Who Lost Himself* (41), a comedy with Brian Aherne – and then the title-role in Jack Benny's *Charley's Aunt*. She played with style and spirit, but it was a part easily overlooked. With equal zeal she supported Don Ameche and Rosalind Russell in *The Feminine Touch* and scored a great success: enough for Warners to agree to Huston's wish that she return to co-star with him in *Always in My Heart* (42). At Universal she starred with Diana Barrymore (*her* bid for screen stardom), playing her mother in a comedy, *Between Us Girls*, one romancing Robert Cummings and the other John Boles.

When the US entered the war she joined USO and did a tour with Martha Raye, Carole Landis and Mitzi Mayfair; in 1944 20th decided to star the four of them (as Themselves) in a film about it, *Four Jills in a Jeep*. In 1945 she toured in 'Windy Hill', written by Patsy Ruth Miller and directed by Ruth Chatterton, allowing for a trio of movie-queen egos backstage. Foolishly she allowed herself to be wooed by the most persistent of poverty-row studios, Monogram (audiences groaned when their logo came up on the screen); she co-produced with Jeffrey Bernerd and co-starred in: *Divorce* (45), *Allotment Wives* and *Wife Wanted* (46), as a fading movie star. She found the experience humiliating and presumably the experience was similar for the audiences in the US (they do not appear to have been exported). She went to New York and replaced Ruth Hussey in 'State of the Union' (46) and toured with it. In 1948 in Columbus, Ohio, she was taken to hospital after what was said to be an overdose of pills, caused by the strain of the tour (in fact, she was drinking heavily and had sat down naked on a radiator and got third degree burns). She appeared in stock in the East for four years and then retired.

During her years as a big star she had been uncooperative with the press; had she been otherwise, the columnists might have tried to help her during her decline (as they had for others). In her later years she refused to see journalists or discuss her career, reputedly bitter on the subject. She died of cancer in 1968, leaving a sum little short of $2 million, most of it for guide dogs for the blind.

CLARK GABLE

Clark Gable once said to David O. Selznick: 'The only thing that kept me a big star has been revivals of *Gone With the Wind*. Every time that picture is re-released a whole new crop of young movie-goers gets interested in me.' Each revival of *GWTW* easily reconfirmed Gable's place among the immortals. His reputation, having been unassailable throughout the first phase of his screen career, fluctuated in the postwar years and after his death (unlike the reputations of Cooper or Bogart or Tracy) went into diminuendo. But in 1967 Joan Crawford could write, without fear of contradiction: 'Clark Gable was the King of an empire called Hollywood. The empire is not what it once was – but the King has not been dethroned, even after death.'

Gable was born in Cadiz, Ohio, in 1901 and began working in stock companies in his teens, mostly as a handyman. At one point,

stranded during a tour, he worked as a lumberjack and no one, certainly not his colleagues, took seriously the odd acting chores he did. He was working as a telephone repair man when he met his first wife, Josephine Dillon – he came to repair her phone. She was a drama coach and 14 years older than he. He broke his engagement to another girl to marry her. She trained him and got him 'extra' work in, among other films, *The Merry Widow* (25), *The Plastic Age* and *North Star*. However, no studio evinced the interest they hoped for. He toured in a production of 'Romeo and Juliet' and was the juvenile in 'The Copperhead' with Lionel Barrymore. He went to New York and began to be noticed in small parts in Broadway plays, such as 'Machinal' (28), 'Hawk Island' and 'Love Honor and Obey' (30), which starred Alice Brady. While in the latter he was offered the West Coast lead in 'The Last Mile', Killer Mears, the part that Spencer Tracy was playing on Broadway – reputedly because Rhea Langham, a wealthy Texan divorcee, had arranged it. In Los Angeles an old friend, Barrymore, got him a test at MGM: for some reason he appeared in a Polynesian get-up, with a flower behind his ear. Thalberg said no and he was also thumbsed-down by Darryl F. Zanuck at Warners, who tested him for the lead in *Little Caesar*. His agent, however, got him a part – at $750 a week – in a Pathé Western, *The Painted Desert* (31), as the heavy. Then he went to Warners for a lead in *Night Nurse*, which was not released for some time. MGM took him on to play Constance Bennett's brother-in-law in *The Easiest Way*, eighth on the cast list. When the rushes were shown, MGM changed its collective mind about him and gave him a contract, for two years with six-monthly options, starting at $350 a week; and he was rushed into a supporting role in a Joan Crawford vehicle, *Dance Fools Dance*. She played a society girl who worms her way into his gang – he played a gang leader and murderer. It was in fact the second Gable film shown, the second of the 12 Gable features released that year. Then came *The Easiest Way*; then *The Finger Points* at Warners, with Richard Barthelmess, playing another gang boss; then *The Secret Six*, another gangster story, but he was a reporter this time; and then *A Free Soul*, still in a supporting role – but supporting MGM's goddess, Norma Shearer, as her gangster lover. He was rough and tough and slapped her around, and audiences loved it. It was clear that MGM had a new star. He continued to rush from film to film, to capitalize on the furore – though at one point, interest waned so quickly that MGM were prepared to drop him. It was

Thalberg who insisted on keeping him. For the moment the studio was so impressed with Gable-Crawford sequences in *Dance Fools Dance* that a film she had just made with Johnny Mack Brown was scrapped and Brown's scenes re-shot with Gable: *Laughing Sinners*, in which he, as a Salvation Army worker, redeems her from sin. Then Warners released *Night Nurse*, in which he impressed in a short role, as a sinister chauffeur who is probably his boss's wife's lover, just as MGM were giving him his first starring role, in *Sporting Blood*, with Madge Evans. It still was not much of a role and he did not get the girl at the end, but then he was featured opposite Garbo in *Susan Lennox: Her Fall and Rise* – a part originally destined for John Gilbert, with whom, reputedly, she refused to work. He was back with MGM's other goddess, Crawford, in *Possessed*, as a politician who makes her his mistress. Said James R. Quirk in 'Photoplay': 'He's everybody's big moment': but not in Britain – the censor banned it (because politicians were thought to be above reproach). As the year ended, fans crowded to see him in *Hell Divers*, with Wallace Beery.

Meanwhile, he had divorced his wife and married Mrs Langham (who was 17 years older than he). Miss Dillon told reporters later that he had been frank in admitting that he had wished to marry Mrs Langham 'because she could do more for him financially'. Needless to say MGM always played down Gable's marriages – and other emotional ties. It was also rumoured that he had 'accommodated' at least two of his leading ladies in the days before he was famous – Alice Brady and Pauline Frederick, both, again, somewhat senior ladies.

MGM needed a new male star more than a little. Their two biggest bets, John Gilbert and Ramon Novarro, were, with the coming of the Talkies, very much on the wane (some vehicles designed to refurbish their he-men images were later reassigned to Gable): and ever since Cagney had pushed a grapefruit in Mae Clark's face, a new type of leading man was in fashion. The 20s idols had been suave, slick and attentive towards women. Cagney was not. And Gable was better looking than Cagney and, in a word not current then, more sexy. He had – at first, anyway – little natural instinct for acting, but he was manly and magnetic. He was not courtly. He pushed women around, traded insults with them, pinched their behinds; he pretended to despise them, while secretly adoring. And just as he was every woman's ideal lover (they now realized), he was every man's man, at home in a garage or in a fishing boat; almost a heel, but too considerate; boisterous, unafraid and

casual. However, for the moment, he was labelled the second Valentino.

Thrilled as MGM were by the money he was minting, they (according to a biographer, Charles Samuels) 'kept on insisting that Gable was a freak box-office attraction who would disappear once the public was tired of gangster pictures'. When Gable asked for a rise they offered $50 a week. So he stayed away from the set of *Polly of the Circus* (32), playing a priest with Marion Davies, until the studio was forced (by the volume of fan-mail) to give in. A year later a new seven-year contract was negotiated, starting at $2,500 a week.

He was paired with Shearer again, in the decent film of O'Neill's *Strange Interlude*; and then with Jean Harlow in *Red Dust*. The formula of the latter was not new: he chased prim, newly wed Mary Astor while the tarty Harlow chased him. But the wise-cracks were fresh and the finish classic: while he is recuperating after the now-smitten Astor has tried to kill him, Harlow reads him an especially inane children's story – and his hand creeps up her leg. At the end of 1932 he appeared on the list of the top 10 moneymakers and he was to stay there till the war interrupted his career. Most of the time he was at second position: somehow he was overtaken by Shirley Temple, Mickey Rooney or Abbott and Costello.

After that he was loaned to Paramount for *No Man of Her Own*, with Carole Lombard, and then did the remake of *The White Sister* (33) with Helen Hayes. He made *Hold Your Man* with Harlow ('They're at it again,' said 'Film Daily', 'a sure-fire hit'); *Night Flight* with Hayes and Myrna Loy; *Dancing Lady*, with Crawford, as the dedicated driving director of a Broadway show; and Capra's *It Happened One Night* (34), as the reporter who pursues a runaway heiress for an exclusive. Capra was directing for Columbia (curiously, MGM had once owned the property) and that studio, having failed to get Fredric March, had negotiated with MGM for Robert Montgomery; but on the eve of filming, MGM released *Fugitive Lovers*, also a cross-country tale, also with Montgomery. Columbia indignantly refused him and demanded Gable – and MGM complied (to punish Gable, who had just baulked at another gigolo-type role opposite Crawford). Both Gable and co-star Claudette Colbert were gloomy about the script and resentful at being farmed out to this minor studio; Capra coaxed them until they finally enjoyed making it, but neither suspected that it would bring them an Oscar apiece and win another as 'Best Film' – as well as bring in enough cash for Columbia to consider itself a major studio.

Clark Gable as Fletcher Christian, the unwilling leader of the mutineers (all rebels in Hollywood films started by being unwilling): Mutiny on the Bounty *(35), with Charles Laughton.*

Gable's whimsical, good-natured performance revitalized his career and brought him the 'Picturegoer' Best Actor Gold Medal. MGM scrapped his contract and offered a new seven-year one at $4,000 a week. Another sidelight: because he was seen to be wearing no undershirt it was acknowledged that sales of said garment fell almost to zero in the US (till the exigencies of World War II brought in the T-shirt).

Myrna Loy was now Gable's leading lady in *Men in White* (doctors) and *Manhattan Melodrama* (gangsters): she became the third of his three staple co-stars of the period; then he was: with Crawford in *Chained*, which she was – to Otto Kruger, while falling in love with Gable on a cruise, and in *Forsaking All Others*, waiting patiently by while she prepares to marry Robert Montgomery; with Constance Bennett in another comedy, *After Office Hours* (35), and never more ingratiating; and with Loretta Young at 20th for Jack London's *Call of the Wild*. In *China Seas* he is the brawling but disciplinarian captain, torn between aristocratic Rosalind Russell and tarty Harlow, and we all know whom he will choose in the end. He was demoted to First Mate for another expensive sea story, and only a whit less enjoyable: *Mutiny on the Bounty*, opposing the wicked Captain Bligh. As a hustling publisher, he was torn between two ladies in *Wife Versus Secretary* (36), Loy and Harlow. His box-office rating justified all these ladies and all this expenditure: and *San Francisco*, ending with the earthquake, was

even bigger – with Gable at his strongest as a no-good saloon owner who finds heroism. This and *Mutiny* were the most popular of his early films and he had resisted doing both: that one because he expected to be ridiculous in silk breeches and this because he thought he would be second fiddle to prima-donna Jeanette MacDonald. Spencer Tracy supported them both, a player Gable admired with caution, for he recognized him as a much superior actor.

He was loaned to Warners to play a boxer, for the last time without his moustache, in *Cain and Mabel*; and he was a newspaperman in another comedy, *Love on the Run*, with Crawford. He and Loy were voted King and Queen of Hollywood – the title stuck to him – and were rewarded by MGM with *Parnell* (37), a supposed biography of the Irish statesman. The two leads, said the 'New Yorker', 'give not the slightest indication of trying to understand anything' – which was one of the kinder reviews: this was the only pre-war Gable film to lose money. He was a book-maker in *Saratoga*, Harlow's last film, after which, his activity decreasing, he was reunited with Loy and Tracy for *Test Pilot*, one of the year's big pictures. She was with him again in *Too Hot to Handle*, a preposterous but enjoyable tale to the Gable formula, concerning rival news cameramen. He could clearly be seen enjoying himself as a song and dance man in *Idiot's Delight* (39), with Shearer.

Then came *Gone With the Wind*. When

Hollywood Gable had had an affair with the Silent star, William Haines. However, public opinion had been right; the casting of Gable as Rhett Butler was one of the most right things in the history of films and it contributed then, and still does, more than somewhat to the success of that film. In 1942 MGM acquired Selznick's interest in the picture and have made huge sums on periodic reissues: during Gable's lifetime it was (by far) the most financially successful film ever made and one of his many grudges against MGM when he left was that they had never offered him even a token gift for bringing the film their way in the first place. However, now his $4,500 a week salary was upped to $7,000, on a new five-year contract.

After *GWTW*, it was back to running-the-mill at his own studio, but he carried at least the first two into the year's biggest money-grabbers. The *Strange Cargo* (40) was Ian Hunter as Christ (perhaps) in an allegorical but otherwise routine effort abut escaping cons, with Crawford; and *Boom Town* was an overlong epic drama about oil-wells, bolstered by Tracy and Colbert. But MGM at last

Before the earthquake: San Francisco (36). Gable ran a gambling saloon, much to the mocking disapproval of diva Jeanette MacDonald. He mocked her too, but he loved her really.

'Those famous lovers we'll make them forget/From Adam and Eve to Scarlett and Rhett': so ran a song Judy Garland once sang. Gable and Vivien Leigh in Gone With the Wind (40).

Selznick first bought the book for filming he announced briefly that the leads would be taken by Tallulah Bankhead and Ronald Colman; but as Margaret Mitchell's novel became the decade's bestseller, the casting of the movie became, apparently, a major concern to all literate Americans. Bosley Crowther writes in his history of MGM: 'On the casting of Rhett, there was no question. Although there was some mention of Gary Cooper, the overwhelming sentiment was that Gable *must* play the role.' There were two snags: Selznick released through UA and MGM would not loan Gable unless they had distribution rights; and Gable did not want to play Rhett. He said later that he only read the book to find out why everyone clamoured for him to play the role – and he still did not want to. However, the decision was not up to him and Selznick, to get him, postponed production until his agreement with UA expired, in order to make a deal with Metro (the delay was providential because of the difficulty of casting Scarlett). Two years after buying the book, a year after signing Gable, production commenced, with George Cukor directing. He was soon fired and it was later admitted that Gable had had him removed because of his preferential treatment of the female stars (Vivien Leigh, Olivia de Havilland); the crunch came when Cukor insisted that Gable cry (on hearing of his daughter's death): Gable felt this would hurt his screen image, though Cukor believed the real reason was that he knew that as a young actor in

conceded the right to top-billing, contractually, so it was finis to Crawford-Gable and Shearer-Gable and when Tracy in turn insisted on top-billing, the Gable-Tracy team was no longer possible. Gable got some new leading ladies: Hedy Lamarr in *Comrade X*, a *Ninotchka*-like comedy in which he was a journalist; Rosalind Russell in *They Met in Bombay* (41), a spectacularly silly piece of pro-British propaganda – he was a con-man who joins the British army to escape justice and becomes a hero; and Lana Turner in both *Honky Tonk* and *Somewhere I'll Find You* (42). In the former he was a saloon-keeper insistent that she would appeal to him more in black lace and feathers, and in the latter a reporter following her out to the Pacific war zone. It was, as everyone knew, his last film before he joined the army and to many moviegoers that was a deprivation on a level with rationing.

Gable himself suffered a loss when his third wife, Carole Lombard, was killed in a wartime air-crash. Later he married, briefly, Sylvia, Lady Ashley, who had been married to the elder Fairbanks, and finally a non-professional, Kay Spreckles, who bore him his only child, a son, after his death – John Clark Gable, who made his film début in 1989.

He returned to a salary of $7,000 per week plus temporarily, a percentage of the profits. His first postwar film, *Adventure* (45), had originally been planned as a vehicle for Freddie Bartholomew. His co-star was Greer Garson, who had risen to Queen of the Lot in his absence. He did not like her (he distrusted clever women) and loathed the slogan 'Gable's Back and Garson's Got Him' (even less did he like one critic's jibe, 'and they deserve each other'). He told the press that he thought the film 'lousy' (and the critics agreed with him). Joan Blondell was in the film and she spoke later of the off-set Gable: 'It was the joy of your life to know Clark Gable. He was everything good you could think of. He had delicious humour; he had great compassion; he was always a fine old teddy bear. . . . In no way was he conscious of his good looks, as were most of the other men in pictures at that time. Clark was very un-actory.' And he also disliked *The Hucksters* (47), a goodish drama of the advertising world. (Indeed, he stalled so long that at one point Errol Flynn was about to start it, borrowed from Warners in exchange for William Powell.) His presence in both ensured them places in the top grossers of their years, but thereafter his appeal began to falter. MGM tried hard, but the formula was never quite right: *Homecoming* (48), a wartime romance with Turner (with whom, said Anne Baxter, who was also in it, he was having an affair. Other sources claim that their romantic liaison began when they had worked together earlier and certainly in the case of Joan Crawford their affair had lasted intermittently over the years); *Command Decision*, an excellent if static war drama where he was over-grim as a general; *Any Number Can Play* (49), with Alexis Smith, a confused gambling story; *Key to the City* (50), a comedy about a mayors' convention with Loretta Young in which he gamely trotted about in a Fauntleroy suit and socks and garters; and *To Please a Lady* – Barbara Stanwyck – an on-again-off-again romance between a racing driver and a lady editor. Like garters for a sagging box-office, MGM tried two Westerns, *Across the Wide Missouri* (51) and *Lone Star* (52), with Ava Gardner, and they held up. But Gable was not happy. He refused a movie to be called *Sometimes I Love You* and was suspended by Dore Schary, the new head of the studio – much to his indignation. He turned down the role Kirk Douglas eventually played in *The Bad and the Beautiful*, but agreed to do a minor Iron Curtain romance, *Never Let Me Go* (53), as an American journalist in love with Russian ballerina Gene Tierney. The film was cruelly titled, for MGM were not too eager to renew his contract. With Cooper and Cagney, he was one of the highest Hollywood earners, at $275,000 per film; James Stewart and Tyrone Power were getting more, because they were on a percentage, and during his next picture Gable asked again for that, plus an increase. MGM rejected the request, offering only a two-year extension of his contract.

The film concerned was *Mogambo*, a remake of *Red Dust*, shot in Africa, with John Ford directing and Ava Gardner and Grace Kelly as the ladies competing for him. Hugely enjoyable, it proved that in the right film Gable was still the King; and, as the returns rolled in, MGM changed their mind. He was offered his own company and 50 per cent of the gross, with a guarantee of $200,000 per film. He was not staying, however: he had made more money for them than any other individual and was bitter. Over the years he had petititioned for a percentage from *Gone With the Wind*, claiming that he would have asked for one at the time had he not been so concerned with his divorce settlement in order to marry Lombard; and although MGM had given him a copy of all his films from 1930 onwards, they demanded $3,200 for this one. Further, under the studio's pension plan, he was due only $400,000 if he retired, or $31,000 per annum. The actual parting film, *Betrayed* (54), another war drama with Turner, found him dispirited. It did not do well.

He signed with 20th for two, for $100,000 each against a percentage of the profits, and these were originally announced as *Heaven Knows Mr Allison* and one with Marilyn Monroe. Instead, he did *Soldier of Fortune* (55), looking for Susan Hayward's husband in Hong Kong: it did fair business, but a Western, *The Tall Men* with Jane Russell, 'the Gable picture the women have been waiting for during the past 10 years' ('Hollywood Reporter'), copped a huge $6 million. Gable came in at 10th on the list of top money-makers. Edward Dmytryk, who directed *Soldier of Fortune*, found Gable 'a wonderful guy to work with, like most of the oldtimers. The one noticeable thing about the older actors . . . is that they were so very well disciplined. Actors like Gable, Spencer Tracy, Bogart, Van Johnson, all of them were always on time, and very rarely did any of them complain about anything. Gable was never late on the set. He had only one rule. He always quit at five – I think so he could start drinking. Gable was quite a drinker. In fact, most of the older actors were. . . . Never, of course, on the set. He always came to work ready and clear. But in the evening he was a heavy drinker. As a matter of fact, he told me once that if he couldn't drink he'd just as soon die.' Dmytryk went on to observe that at this stage you could not do long takes of Gable in close-up because he started to shake after a while; he put this down to tension rather than the night-before's alcohol.

MGM had begun to allow reporters to interview him again, after 20 years during which he was pictured as mysterious as Garbo: but the press found him in the flesh more enigmatic than in his absence. There is no hint of this from his colleagues and among his other co-stars to speak warmly of him are Ava Gardner ('A true gentleman . . . not like some I could name') and Doris Day ('He was anything but macho. He was the gentlest, dearest man').

He had formed a production company with Miss Russell and her husband, but only one film emerged, *The King and Four Queens* (56), a Western which performed indifferently. He went to Warners, to do a replay of Rhett Butler in *Band of Angels* (57) with Yvonne de Carlo, and then the tide began to turn again: *Run Silent Run Deep* (58), in a submarine with Burt Lancaster, as its martinet commander; and three comedies for Paramount: *Teacher's Pet*, as a newspaper editor who wants a come-uppance for a teacher of journalism, Doris Day (who later recalled him as the nicest and 'most humble' man she had ever met); *But Not for Me* (59), a flat remake of *Accent on Youth*, as a Broadway impresario tempted by young protégée Carroll Baker; and *It Started in Naples* (60), as a lawyer – a role originally conceived for Gracie Fields –

trying to wrest his nephew from a cabaret singer, Sophia Loren. Business was nice on all three, and if he was looking his age, he was still the King (concluded the fan magazines, having examined some odd contenders, such as Richard Egan) – even if he was regarded less as an actor than an institution. His playing could still be incisive, but he was more tolerant and the old *désinvolture* had a hint of sadness.

His last film was *The Misfits* (61), written by Arthur Miller for Marilyn Monroe, who played a defenceless divorcee taken up by him, a rootless old cowpoke. Gable neither liked nor understood the role and could not see himself in it, but he took it because he could not see anyone else in it either. 'But,' said producer Frank Taylor, 'we felt there was only one actor in the world who expressed the essence of complete masculinity and virility that we needed for the leading role – and that was Gable.' He was paid $750,000 for it, plus $48,750 for each week after the 14-week schedule (and it went over schedule). He died a few weeks after completion of shooting (in

Most of Gable's post-war pictures were more serious than those before, as befitted 'The King', who had both served and suffered in the war; but none of them quite hit the public fancy till Mogambo *(53) with Grace Kelly. It is a remake of* Red Dust, *not as raunchy or as funny, but still mightily entertaining.*

November 1960), due possibly to the strenuous location work. Hedda Hopper suggested unkindly that his desire for the fee overcame health considerations and it is probable that he would have liked to have gone out on what looked like a hit. But it is sad that he could not have seen his reviews – overwhelmingly the best of his career: a beautiful and indeed moving performance. Said 'The New York Times' obituary: 'Gable was as certain as the sunrise. He was consistently and stubbornly all man.'

GRETA GARBO

She is, ultimately, the standard against which all other screen actresses are measured. Since the time of her second, if not her first, Hollywood film she has not been surpassed. For over 50 years the mystery, the enigma of Garbo has been a statutory feature of magazine journalism, her ability a source of wonder to critics: 'After much brooding and re-appraisal I still cannot make up my mind whether Garbo was a remarkable actress or simply a person so extraordinary that she made everything she did, even acting, seem remarkable' (Isabel Quigley in the 'Spectator'). Writers have speculated, eulogized, have written rhapsodies to her; just as Hollywood itself has never got over her, neither have critics. Here are three more, taken at random over the years. Tully Marshall in 'Vanity Fair', 1927: 'This affectedly sad, languid, indifferent girl is vibrant with inner life. She has the power to charm men and women. Thousands have called her the Sarah Bernhardt of the films, but Garbo is one of the few who deserve to be mentioned in the same breath.' 'Life' magazine in 1928: 'She is the dream princess of eternity – the knockout of the ages.' André Sennwald in 'The New York Times' in 1934: 'She is the most miraculous blend of personality that the screen has ever seen': and in 1936 Alistair Cooke despaired: 'When you start to write about Garbo, you are reminded more forcibly than ever that practically all the criticism of emotional acting we have reads like a fourth form essay on the character of Napoleon.'

'La Divine' the French call her. When she was sad there was all the sadness in the world; when she was happy, never such self-indulgence. Fatalistic, enslaving, tough but never bitter, wary but never unpassionate. . . . Art? Instinct? No one has solved the mystery, not least, it is said, the lady herself. She stands apart from every other star.

She was born in 1905 in Stockholm, the daughter of a labourer. Her first job was soaping men's faces in a barber's shop and later she worked in the PUB department store. She was chosen for a PUB advertising short (21), which led to her doing another, for the Co-op Society's Bakery department, and that led, indirectly, to a comic short called *Luffar-Peter*, made by and with Erik A. Petschler. She cavorted in a bathing suit, but was encouraged to try for a scholarship to the Royal Stockholm Theatre School; while there, she was recommended to Mauritz Stiller, who was looking for an ingénue for *The Atonement of Gosta Berling* (24), an Italian countess who had married into the Berling family. Thus began an association considered for years to be akin to that of Trilby and Svengali.

The film was not a great success, nor was Garbo noticed: but it did well enough in Germany for its distributor there, Trianon, to offer to Stiller and Garbo a four-year joint contract and they went to Istanbul to make *The Odalisque from Smyrna* (or *Smolna*), a tale of White Slavery during the Crimean conflict. Trianon, however, went bankrupt before filming began and Stiller and Garbo returned to Berlin to look for work. Through the intervention of fellow-Scandinavian Asta Nielsen, Garbo was signed for the film that she was making for Pabst, *Die Freudlose Gasse* (25), a gloomy portrait of postwar Vienna. Garbo again was the ingénue (if tempted to swop poverty for a life of easy virtue). At the same time Louis B. Mayer was in Europe looking for talent: he had seen *Gosta Berling* and wanted Stiller, but Stiller would not go without his protégée. Mayer thought her too fat but finally agreed to sign her to get Stiller; she was given a three-year contract starting at $350 a week.

Garbo arrived in Hollywood frizzy-haired and dopey-eyed to an MGM which did not know what to do with her. They photographed her with automobiles and animals and hopefully labelled her 'The Norma Shearer of Sweden'. It was Stiller who arranged a striking photo of her in 'Vanity Fair' and that prompted the studio to use her. Stiller got her salary upped to $500 and if Thalberg remained unimpressed by Garbo, there was a part available which he did not consider good enough for Shearer, that of a Spanish peasant who loses childhood sweetheart Ricardo Cortez but wins him back after becoming (in the twinkling of an eye) a famous Paris prima donna. Garbo thought the part silly. The film was *Ibanez' Torrent* (26), aka *The Torrent*, and when it opened, she was acclaimed: 'This girl has everything, with looks, acting ability and personalty' ('Variety').

MGM had realized what they had after the

first few rushes and Stiller, still smarting from not being assigned to her first film, began preparing *The Temptress*; but the studio removed him during shooting (he later made three films for Paramount, returned to Sweden in 1928 and died there not long afterwards). This time Garbo was a Paris hostess who pursues lover Antonio Moreno to South America, destroying him and a lot of other men en route (she ends, appropriately enough, back in Paris as a hooker – at least in Europe: in the version shown in the US she and Moreno were miraculously reunited). She balked at playing another unfaithful wife in *Flesh and the Devil* (27), but enjoyed filming with director Clarence Brown and co-star John Gilbert. Audiences were thrilled by the way Garbo loved Gilbert: no screen actress had ever loved as she did, hungrily, passionately. . . . This was an even bigger success than the first two and, unlike them, was liked in Europe.

But she refused a fourth such part, in *Women Love Diamonds*; and encouraged by Stiller, she stayed at home until her salary was increased from $600 per week to $5,000. It took MGM seven months to capitulate and then, to placate her, they made her Anna Karenina in *Love*. Tolstoy had been modernized and Garbo thought her character had been distorted by the script as well, but she played it – with Gilbert as Vronsky. MGM then decided that she should play Sarah Bernhardt, but after the script had been rewritten eight times it bore little resemblance to the play about Sarah that they had bought – indeed, *The Divine Woman* (28), with Lars Hanson, was the *n*th Hollywood variation on the 'Nana' theme. In *The Mysterious Lady* Garbo was a Russian spy who shoots her chief after she has fallen for an enemy officer (Conrad Nagel). The returns were not as good as expected, so Garbo was co-starred again with Gilbert (much was being written about a reputed offscreen romance): *A Woman of Affairs* (29), allegedly based on Michael Arlen's bestseller 'The Green Hat'. It was a popular film which can now be seen to contain some of her most magical work. In *Wild Orchids* Javanese prince Nils Asther challenged husband Lewis Stone for her favours; and in *The Single Standard* she found redemption in the arms of Johnny Mack Brown after a fling with Asther. *The Kiss* re-hashed similar themes, but was given some distinction by Jacques Feyder's direction.

These last four films had been rushed through before the public completely rejected Silents and it was clear that Garbo would eventually have to 'talk'. MGM delayed as long as possible and interest in her Talkie début continued to mount: by the time it

Garbo as MGM saw her till they – reluctantly – allowed her to try her powers as a tragedienne: The Single Standard (29), as a free spirit, a woman who loved not wisely but too well. The man enslaved is John(ny) Mack Brown, and it was a high point in his career (he was to spend most of the next decade in B Westerns).

finally appeared, Talkies had been in for over two years and virtually every star of Continental origin had gone or was going. MGM advertised *Anna Christie* (30) with the slogan 'Garbo talks!', a phrase that lives on today. After 34 minutes of screen-time, she did: 'Gimme a visky with chincher aile on the saide – and don't be stingy, baby.' The world breathed again and the film's reception 'proved that Garbo talking was an even more magical figure than Garbo mute' (John Bainbridge in 'Garbo', 1955). A German version was made at the same time, by Feyder, and Garbo reputedly much preferred that version (it could not have been difficult; the US version is a literal transcription of the O'Neill play). MGM and Garbo relaxed: the studio began to cater to what were regarded as her whims: her distaste for publicity, her insistence on 'closed' sets. The stories of her aloofness were legion, but she was liked and respected by her co-workers.

Romance cast her again as an opera singer, and again with Stone (this time, her protector), and Stone was also with her in *Inspira-*

It would be impossible now for movies to re-create the anticipation the world experienced as it waited for Garbo to talk – and indeed she made several Silents while the public clamoured for Talkies. As so many players of Continental origin had fallen by the wayside, the world was able to breathe again when they saw and heard her in Anna Christie (30), *Eugene O'Neill's lady with a lurid past who returns to her father, George F. Marion, in an attempt to find either peace or redemption, or both.*

tion (31), which critics found neither inspired nor inspiring. Lionel Collier thought Garbo's temperament in it 'so consistently unhappy that it is apt to exhaust the average person's patience'. Anyway, they had seen it all before: she in her familiar role of the tarnished lady who finds true love and suffers when he (Robert Montgomery this time) deserts her 'on hearing of her lurid past'. The presence of new heart-throb Clark Gable did give a lift to the formula in *Susan Lennox: Her Fall and Rise* and helped to make it one of her biggest successes – an absurd thing about a wood sprite who, spurned by him after a misunderstanding, rises to being one of New York's leading courtesans (seen today, it is not only believable but moving – a remarkable demonstration of her powers). 'Nobody', said 'Photoplay' at this time, 'has had such a place in the film firmament. Nobody has ever had such a hold on the imagination of the public.'

She had a hankering to play Shaw's St Joan, she told reporters, but MGM cast her instead as that other great lady of war, *Mata Hari* (32), with Ramon Novarro. The 'Hollywood Reporter' found her 'so ravishing, so glamorous and so radiant that her previous performances fade by comparison'. Garbo herself said in a delightful interview in 'Picturegoer': 'Screen vamps make me laugh tremendously. The fact that I am considered one makes me

laugh even more.' (Presumably an authentic interview, though a later issue of this magazine says she gave her last interview in 1928, i.e. four years earlier.)

The formula was shattered when she played the ballerina in *Grand Hotel*, notable also because it broke with a vengeance the rule of one star = one film. There were five stars! One of them, John Barrymore, issued this statement: 'Greta is simple and that is her greatest quality. She's also extraordinarily dexterous. She has a very powerful personality which gives her command of everything she does, but she never depends on it, never considers it an asset. What she does consider is that acting is her job, and she keeps everlastingly at it. It is because she is so completely simple that Garbo bears the unmistakable mark of greatness. Modjeska had it, that same simplicity, so that when she came on stage you expected to see the theatre catch fire. Ellen Terry was another who made it felt, a sudden arrestation, a strange power that held you. Garbo has only to flash on the screen to seize our attention. Her brilliance dispels our dullness. She takes us out of ourselves by the mere accident of her presence. It isn't acting; it has nothing to do with acting; it is something which holds us in its spell – a kind of magic. This magic is Garbo.' *Grand Hotel's* author, Vicki Baum, on Gar-

bo's performance, thought it better than expected, 'and I expected the utmost'. The author of the next one, *As You Desire Me*, Pirandello, thought Garbo 'at the highest peak of her art' – though he disliked the film of his play. Still, although cast as 'an amnesiac Budapest cabaret artist', Garbo's embroilments were less puerile than usual and she was able to give her most polished performance yet.

1932 was certainly Garbo's peak as a commercial property: for the last two or three years she had been appearing near the top of popularity polls and box-office lists, but would not again (in the US, at any rate). Her contract had expired and there were rumours

of retirement. MGM was offering $7,000 a week and Garbo was sticking out for $10,000. She went to Europe on vacation and would only return on her own terms. They were agreed: a two-picture deal, one of MGM's choice and one of Garbo's – and that one a picture about Christina of Sweden. *Queen Christina* (33) was extravagantly admired for itself (Rouben Mamoulian directed) and brought Garbo the best personal notices that she had yet had. Said C.A. Lejeune: 'Under the most fearsome battery of close-ups ever given to a star, she remains aloof. Every inch of the Garbo countenance is exposed to the scrutiny of the audience, every eyelash and

Garbo in the first role she played that was at all worthy of her: Queen Christina *(33).*

'Garbo Loves Taylor in Camille,' said the posters and ads in 1936. It is impossible to believe in her as a demi-mondaine; and impossible not to be moved by her.

Garbo as Marie Walewska in Conquest (37).

pore of the skin presented for our consideration. There is a bedroom scene which would
have stripped any other actress spiritually
naked. But Garbo is still her own mistress at
the end of it.' In Britain, the readers of
'Picturegoer' voted this the year's best female
performance with a huge 42 per cent of the
poll.

Despite the praise, *Christina* was only a
modified success in the US and so was MGM's
choice, *The Painted Veil* (34), a chunk of
Hollywood-oriented Oriental hokum (only in
her performance does some of the quality of
Maugham's original novel come through;
MGM, incidentally, announced that
Maugham had been commissioned to write
stories especially for Garbo, but nothing ever
came of this). The credits refer to the star
simply as 'Garbo' and the word is held in
white under the other credits. Despite this,
MGM executives in Hollywood had decided
to drop her. Those in New York were for
keeping her: if her name was weak in the US,
she was still the biggest draw everywhere in
Europe and her prestige was needed often
enough to sell an otherwise indifferent package of films. 'Variety' acknowledged that she
was a goodwill asset and MGM finally agreed
to increase her salary to $250,000 per film, but
on a one-film-at-a-time basis.

The first under the new arrangement was a
serviceable version of *Anna Karenina* (35) –
done at her insistence instead of *Dark Victory*,
the studio's choice. Her performance won the
New York critics' Best Actress award. She
rejected an offer to appear on Broadway at a
fee of $10,000 a night, holidayed in Europe
and returned to Hollywood to play *Camille*
(36), generally considered to be her finest
performance (under Cukor's direction): again
the New York critics thought her the year's
Best Actress (but in Hollywood, the Oscar
voters thought Luise Rainer was: *Camille*

provided Garbo with her *first* nomination).
Garbo's next part was Marie Walewska in
Conquest (37), opposite Charles Boyer's
Napoleon and under Clarence Brown's direction (he directed her several times; in 1939 he
said, 'Garbo to me is a never-ending source of
wonder'). MGM were more generously lavish
than ever: the film cost over $2 million, almost
an unprecedented amount, but it did not get
back its cost in the US as was normal
(European takings were 'profit'). During its
making Garbo was awarded Sweden's highest
honour, the medal 'Litterie & Artibus', and
named by theatre owners of the US as one of
the 'box-office poison' stars.

Again, her career was in peril. She threatened again to retire and few voices were raised
at MGM to gainsay her. The solution was
found: comedy. She had begged the studio to
buy *Tovarich* for her, without success; and
now in 1939 MGM did buy *Idiot's Delight* –
but Shearer did it. Yet plans went ahead to
make Garbo gayer. It had long been clear that
whereas Shearer and the others had to end in
a clinch, audiences did not mind Garbo dying:
but those that stayed away from her gloom
might find her attractive in comedy. As the
world darkened, it was informed that 'Garbo
laughs!'. The film was Lubitsch's *Ninotchka*
(39) and, as Kenneth Tynan pointed out, she
pleaded the world's cause: 'Bombs will fall,
civilizations will crumble – but not yet – give
us our moment!' The mood generally was
witty and gay (a Communist converted to
Western ways by Melvyn Douglas and Paris)
and the world queued to see it. Garbo got
another Oscar nomination.

Reassured that the home public wanted to
see Garbo in comedy, MGM postponed
Madam Curie (a pet project of studio and star,
though Garbo worried whether it was not too
'intellectual' for her) and began to prepare
another 'light' subject. There are several

versions of the salary negotiations which preceded filming, but the most likely story seems to be that Metro asked her whether she would do *two* pictures for her normal fee. After some thought, Garbo agreed to do one for $150,000; MGM came back and asked whether she would do two for twice that sum, but she would not. The result, anyway, was *Two-Faced Woman* (41) and under Cukor's direction, Garbo enjoyed making it: but she disliked the material, suspecting that it was a studio plot to kill her off. MGM was merely misguided. As *Ninotchka* demonstrated, she had no comedy technique, but she had an instinct for funny situations and a sense of humour that had nothing to with tongue-in-cheek: Myrna Loy or Carole Lombard she was not. This was frivolous, heartless stuff, posing as her twin sister to win back philandering husband Melvyn Douglas. She appeared (briefly) in a swimsuit and danced the Chica-Choca. Critics and public, yelping for their idol, hurled abuse at MGM; to make things worse, it was condemned by the Legion of Decency and banned in Australia. It was withdrawn 'for tidying up' (a line was inserted to suggest that Douglas knew of the impersonation) but, even so, did indifferent business.

Its failure caused Garbo to reject MGM's next offer and she decided to withdraw until the European market was open again, until she could play the sort of parts she felt were suitable. Her popularity actually declined in the US after *Two-Faced Woman* because she was not seen to take part in wartime fund-raising schemes like other stars: the American public failed to understand that she could not muck in like other stars and columnists made the situation worse by tut-tutting over her refusal to 'entertain' by filming, adding that her salary demands were excessive in these 'difficult' times. One biographer, Fritiof Bill-quist, suggests that, at the war's end, she considered herself too old to return to film-making: but of all the speculation over her retirement the only definite fact is that she at first regarded it as temporary. In 1944 it was announced that she would make *Woman of the Sea* for producer Lester Cowan at United Artists and then she was supposed to do *Arch of Triumph* and a film with Bing Crosby. In 1945-6 she seriously considered a remake of *Flesh and the Devil* and a Selznick-produced life of Bernhardt and a year later a life of George Sand, involving Cukor and Laurence Olivier (but in this case backing fell through). In 1947, Jean Renoir was to have directed her in *Woman of 100 Faces*; she certainly turned down the role Irene Dunne played in *I Remember Mama*. In 1949 she signed a contract and accepted a salary advance for a US-Italian version of *La Duchesse de Langeais*, to be directed by Max Ophüls, but according to projected co-star James Mason, backing was withdrawn when she refused to meet the backers except in a darkened room. In 1951 Dore Schary of MGM interested her in John Gunther's 'Death Be Not Proud' and was sufficiently encouraged to ask Gunther to prepare a treatment; and a year later Cukor persuaded her to do *My Cousin Rachel*, but she changed her mind the next day: 'I can't go through with it. I have not the courage to make another picture.' In 1952, television made an offer – to repeat her role in 'Anna Christie'. In 1953, Vittorio De Sica asked her to make a film called *Duo*; someone else had the bright idea of teaming her with Chaplin in *The Madwoman of Chaillot*. The following year she was offered *The Country Girl* when Jennifer Jones became pregnant. Later she flirted with the idea of doing *The Deep Blue Sea*.

She had ever been a timorous actress. Lubitsch had described her as 'the most inhibited person I've ever worked with' and Melvyn Douglas said that she worried at not being a trained actress (her failure in her last film might seem to have confirmed her limitations).

In the first years of her withdrawal the press hounded her as they had always done, producing unflattering pictures of her hurrying, in big hats, across airport tarmacs. She still is not left entirely alone by a curious world, but little is known of her personal life; and people who claim to have glimpsed her in the flesh can dine out on it for weeks. It is news when she is said to be considering a film offer, but we have given up hoping she would not withhold herself from us; we ask nothing more of her. MGM are the guardians of the legacy.

For over a decade she was away from us: to the postwar generation she was a name and a catchphrase ('I vant to be alone', originally 'I t'ank I go home now'). In London there was only a week of *Ninotchka* in 1949 and brief showings of that and two others at the NFT in the winter of 1953-4. It was not till 1955 that MGM obliged and showed *Camille*. In the 'New Statesman' John Freeman wrote: 'In a series of mostly trivial films – unlike Chaplin she never seems to have *bothered* to insist on the setting which could have heightened her lustre – we fell in love with her, until suddenly . . . she disappeared. . . . Was it possible that the light could shine as we remembered it through a 25-year-old melodrama? But we needn't have worried. From the corny melodramatics of the re-issued *Camille* she distils more femininity, more passion, more humanity, more sheer beauty than the post-war generation has ever seen. Emerging again from eclipse, she is a more refulgent star by comparison with the evanescent galaxy of hellcats and cuties who succeeded her. She died, the other afternoon, in a fierce and tearful silence, broken only by the sobbing of two very young women. . . . My generation was vindicated. At least we knew how to jerk a tear.' And Derek Prouse wrote in 'Sight and Sound': 'One leaves the cinema after *Camille* uncertain for the moment where familiar bus routes pass, unwilling to dissipate the awed and uplifted certainty that one has been in the presence of greatness.'

Since then, MGM have sneaked out occasional revivals in the world's great cities, but they have been niggardly. The films were shown on TV in the US, but were later withdrawn; when they were shown on Italian TV in 1962-3 cinema attendances fell by 75 per cent. In London in 1963 a Garbo festival created the longest cinema queues seen there for years and the five-week season was repeated twice. Clarence Brown said that year: 'Today, without having made a film since 1940, she is still the greatest. She is the prototype of all stars.' In 1968 the first complete Garbo retrospective in New York was sold out before it opened. The films are not, as films, much to be proud of, but even the MGM of today, changed beyond measure, must feel proud of having been once associated with her. The old MGM was: their London flagship, the Empire, was on occasion hung with English and American flags – and one Swedish flag.

JOHN GARFIELD

John Garfield was a strong, sympathetic actor too often trapped in run-of-the-mill films. The titles of two of his early films give an indication of the sort of character he was usually called upon to play – *They Made Me a Criminal* and *Dust Be My Destiny*: it was he of course who was made a criminal, he who was searching for destiny. Chronologically, he came after the Henry Fonda of *You Only Live Once* and before the Brando of *On the Waterfront*. He was invariably the boy from the other side of the tracks, the boy with the chip on his shoulder – but idealistic, you know: he often ended up killed or a killer. When he left WB, which had nurtured him, it was clear that a real talent had been obscured: with all his vigour and pugnaciousness there was a real sensitivity.

Clifford Odets once described his rise from the slums of New York to Hollywood fame as illustrating 'one of the most cherished folkways of our people'. Odets was a personal friend and it was his play 'Golden Boy', in a

supporting role, which brought Garfield to the attention of Hollywood. He was born (Jules Garfinkle) in New York City in 1913. He won a scholarship to the Ouspenskaya Drama School and served his apprenticeship with Eva La Gallienne's company. He tried Hollywood and was an extra in the 'Shanghai Lil' number in *Footlight Parade* (33); his New York career went better when he became connected with the Group Theater, where he met and worked with Luther and Stella Adler, Odets, Elia Kazan, etc. He was with them in the Weill musical, 'Johnny Johnson', and had his first Broadway lead in 'Having Wonderful Time' (37).

Warners signed him to a seven-year contract which allowed him time off for the theatre; they changed his name and put him into *Four Daughters* (38), a Fannie Hurst story about four motherless daughters (the Lane Sisters and Gale Paige): he was the poor boy who got mixed up with one of them (Priscilla Lane). He was a boxer on the lam in *They Made Me a Criminal* (39), a remake of *The Life of Jimmy Dolan*; and a reporter in a B gangster comedy, *Blackwell's Island*. After a small role, as a Mexican general, in

Priscilla Lane and John Garfield in Dust Be My Destiny *(39); said the original caption: 'The story of a boy who went to reform school to forget what environment had taught him . . . he couldn't forget the school-warden's daughter though!'*

Juarez, he was reunited with Miss Lane. Warners liked this team, but as he had been killed off in *Four Daughters* an exact sequel was not possible: but *Daughters Courageous* was near enough, with him as a rootless young bum with whom she becomes infatuated. In *Dust Be My Destiny* they were married – and on the run, in the post-Depression era. *Four Wives* was a sequel to *Four Daughters* and he was in it by virtue of a flashback.

The subjects he was given to do were quite predictable, in these declining years of Warners' tough social-conscience melodramas: *Castle on the Hudson* (40), in Spencer Tracy's old role in this remake of *20,000 Years in Sing Sing*, with Ann Sheridan and Pat O'Brien; *Saturday's Children*, another remake, Maxwell Anderson's dated piece about hardworking New Yorkers, with Garfield as one who dreams of escape to exotic climes; *Flowing Gold*, a tale of the oil-wells; *East of the River*, another programmer, the perennial about guys growing up on different sides of the law, with William Lundigan on the right side; and *The Sea Wolf* (41), getting out of the rut in this good version of London's novel – except that he was again a rebel. *Out of the Fog* was Group Theater stuff – Irwin Shaw's 'The Gentle People', about a Brooklyn family terrorized by a gangster; *Dangerously They Live* was more formula – Nancy Coleman was a spy in Nazi hands and he rescues her.

He got away from type-casting and into a better film when MGM borrowed him for *Tortilla Flat* (42), as Spencer Tracy's fisherman chum; but he was even more deprived, back as underdog, in *Air Force* (43) – bitter because he flunked pilot training, but bringing down the wounded plane unaided. His gutsy determination made him the ideal war hero: in *The Fallen Sparrow* at RKO, another espionage tale, and *Destination Tokyo*, as one of the submarine crew. Prior to this he sang 'Blues in the Night' in one of Warners' two wartime revues, *Thank Your Lucky Stars*, and after playing the card-sharp in *Between Two Worlds*, another remake (of *Outward Bound*) he washed up in *Hollywood Canteen*, the other one. The studio, meanwhile, had refused to lend him to Columbia for *The Adventures of Martin Eden* or to UA for *Jack London*.

He was *The Pride of the Marines* (45), an ex-soldier adjusting himself to blindness; and Lana Turner's lover in *The Postman Always Rings Twice* (46) at MGM, making good chemistry in this version of James M. Cain's diabolical thriller. Then it was back to more standard fare in *Nobody Lives Forever*, setting out to swindle Geraldine Fitzgerald and falling in love with her; and as a back-street violinist he tolerated dipso patroness Joan Crawford in *Humoresque*, the last under his contract. Warners wanted him to re-sign, but he considered that he had been badly treated: he had either been given the Cagney and Bogart rejects, or stuck behind the eight-ball in the same old propaganderish story. Instead he formed his own production company and did one of the two films generally considered his best – *Body and Soul* (47), playing a boxer with dumb eloquence. Robert Rossen directed, from a screenplay by Abraham Polonsky – and the film was a big success. At 20th he was the Jewish soldier in *Gentleman's Agreement*, at a fee of $150,000, with Gregory Peck; and then he did his other good film, directed by Polonsky at his suggestion, *Force of Evil* (48), a crime story which did poor business at the time it was released. Dilys Powell wrote: 'John Garfield, who for years has been allowed to re-play himself, is returning to solid interpretation; and his quick, cursive delivery of difficult dialogue is worth attention.' Huston's *We Were Strangers* (49) at Columbia, a tale of revolutionary intrigue in Latin America, did little better at the wickets; nor did *Under My Skin* (50) at 20th, from a Hemingway story about racing. Garfield then returned to Warners for another Hemingway subject, 'To Have and Have Not': when WB had originally filmed it, with Bogart, they kept little but the title, so now, when they re-filmed it straight, they dreamed up a new title, *The Breaking Point*. It ranks as one of the best screen versions of Hemingway; Garfield's own performance ('A man alone ain't got no chance') was exceptionally true. For his old production partner, Bob Roberts, *He Ran All The Way* (51): well, as a hood he ran for a bit before hiding out with Shelley Winters's parents.

Because of suspected left-wing sympathies, he was finding it increasingly difficult in this McCarthy era to find work in Hollywood. He returned to the stage during those years: 'Skipper Next to God' (48) and Odets's 'The Big Knife' (49), having turned down the lead in 'A Streetcar Named Desire'. Years later a Reuter's article quoted 'a writer friend' as saying: '. . . the tragedy was that Garfield wasn't accused of anything. He was a street boy with a street boy's sense of honour, and when they asked him to give the names of friends at parties he refused. They blacklisted him for that. When he wasn't able to work he ran around in a violent, stupid kind of way. In the end he died of a heart attack. The blacklist killed him.' He was in New York for a revival of 'Golden Boy', in the lead this time, when he died in 1952.

JUDY GARLAND

There was a tribute to her on Australian
television after she died: not, said the narrator, 'a blow by blow description of the
prolonged finale when press agents were
doing dreadful things to the human soul, but
the way it was for us in the golden Hollywood
years when all was tinsel, glitter, bluebirds
and rainbows, when the whole apparatus of
illusion was the dream factory in full blast
producing its masterpiece – Judy.'

Judy Garland was born of vaudeville
parents (like her old sidekick, Mickey
Rooney) in Grand Rapids, Minnesota, in
1922. She made her stage début at three,
singing 'Jingle Bells' in the theatre her father
managed, and was later teamed with two
older sisters as 'The Gumm Sisters' (they were
born Gumms). As a kiddie act, it was not very
successful and broke up when one of the
sisters married; but Judy had already established herself as the outstanding talent of the
three and, encouraged by her mother, continued solo. Songwriter Lew Brown caught
her act and had her screen-tested at Columbia
where he worked; Columbia was not buying,
but Mother Gumm had acquired an agent who
got a test at MGM, who signed her for seven
years, starting at $100 a week to go to $1,000
in the final year. Her pianist for the test was
Roger Edens, who, 20 years later, described
her advent as 'the biggest thing to happen to
the MGM musical'. She was 13 and her father
had just died.

She made a short with Deanna Durbin,
Every Sunday (36), but nothing else. Edens
got her on to the Jack Oakie Radio Hour,
where a 20th scout heard her and arranged for
her to be borrowed for *Pigskin Parade*, a rah-
rah college musical of no particular merit; and
Garland, ninth on the cast list, was just
another puppy-fat kid. Edens would not give
up and wrote a special version of 'You Made
Me Love You' for the child to sing to Clark
Gable at his birthday party on the lot: Metro,
at last enthusiastic, rushed her and song into
Broadway Melody of 1938 (37). Her notices
were warm and she was featured in *Thoroughbreds Don't Cry* with Mickey Rooney; *Everybody Sing* (38) with Allan Jones and Fanny
Brice; *Listen Darling* with Freddie Batholo-
mew and Mary Astor; and *Love Finds Andy
Hardy* with Rooney. She had the lead in most
of them – invariably playing a stage-struck
youngster – but there was front-office opposition when producer Arthur Freed wanted to
cast her as Dorothy in the big-budgeted *The
Wizard of Oz* (39): however, when 20th
refused to loan Shirley Temple for it ('thank
God' said Freed later), Garland it was. It was
a miracle film: from L. Frank Baum's story

*Two little girls who became
among the most loved of
all stars: Deanna Durbin
and Judy Garland in an
MGM short subject,* Every
Sunday *(36) – when, on a
park bandstand, one sang
sweet and the other hot.*

*A detour on the yellow
brick road to the Land of
Oz: Ray Bolger and Judy
Garland in* The Wizard of
Oz *(39). Disney apart, it is
the screen's most
enchanting fairy-tale.*

Judy in her first solo starring role with her two leading men, George Murphy and Gene Kelly: For Me and My Gal *(42). It was one of the year's most popular films, and the record she made with Kelly of the title song is still much played.*

about the Kansas schoolgirl who journeys to the magical land of Oz with the Scarecrow (Ray Bolger), the Tin Man (Jack Haley) and the Cowardly Lion (Bert Lahr). Frank Morgan was the Wizard. A big hit at the time, it has seldom been out of circulation and nowadays nets MGM a cool million annually when it is telecast in the US. It made Garland world-famous, won her a special Oscar and gave her a hit record and identification song ('Over the Rainbow', which was at one point deleted from the finished film).

Babes in Arms, with Rooney, consolidated her success and they were re-teamed in *Andy Hardy Meets Debutante* (40) and *Strike Up the Band*: the first and third of these were to a

new formula which MGM happily exploited, of a bunch of kids putting on a show. Contemporary critics thought he overshadowed her, but there is something winning about her work – a directness of emotion in her usually unspoken crush on him and her sad little songs, and the unforced precocity of her handling of the more typical peppy songs. MGM revised her contract, her $750 a week to go to $2,000 at once, rising to $3,000 a week for the last two of the seven years; and she rewarded them by coming in at 10th that year in the top 10 list. Meanwhile her burgeoning talent got a good chance in *Little Nellie Kelly* with George Murphy, where she played both mother and daughter and as the former had a

command of her form of make-believe.' '. . . and how good *she* is!' said Agate. 'She is no Venus, let us admit it – but how delightful is her smile, how genuine her emotion, how sure her timing, and how brilliantly she brings off her effects. . . .' Kelly himself said later, 'The finest all-round performer we ever had in America was Judy Garland. There was no limit to her talent. She was the quickest, brightest person I ever worked with.' *Presenting Lily Mars* (43), from a Booth Tarkington story, found her as another stage-struck girl and *Girl Crazy*, an old Gershwin musical, again with Rooney. She toured with USO and in MGM's starry support for troop morale, *Thousands Cheer*, sang 'The Joint Is Really Jumpin' Down at Carnegie Hall', accompanied by José Iturbi. She looked thin and edgy. To compensate, MGM (Arthur Freed; and against her will) put her into *Meet Me in St Louis* (44), the second miracle film of her career. It was the first screen musical in years not to use some sort of 'backstage' technique to introduce its songs, a slight, gay, utterly enchanting portrait of a well-to-do St Louis family (Leon Ames, Mary Astor, Margaret O'Brien, and Tom Drake as the boy next door) at the time of the World's Fair. It is as fresh today as the year it was made – when it was the highest grossing film musical up to that time and MGM's biggest grosser apart from *Gone With the Wind*.

The director was Vincente Minnelli, who replaced Fred Zinnemann on her next (she and Zinnemann did not get on) and later became her second husband. *The Clock* (45) was a straight film, a New York weekend with a CI on furlough (Robert Walker) and the girl he meets. James Agee said it proved 'beyond anybody's doubt that Judy Garland is a very sensitive actress. She can handle any emotion in sight, in any shape or size, and the audience along with it.' At the end of 1945 she was one of the top 10 money-makers again, but mostly on the strength of *St Louis*. MGM therefore revised her contract again (five years at just under $6,000 a week, for two films a year, top-billing) and refashioned *The Harvey Girls* (46) as a musical for her – it was originally planned straight for Turner – and it was almost as good: 'nice' waitresses vs saloon girls in the Old West. John Hodiak was the man. Also that year Garland sang 'The Great Lady Grants an Interview' in the revue-format *Ziegfeld Follies* and she had two songs, guesting as Marilyn Miller, in the otherwise dreary *Till the Clouds Roll By* (47).

Kelly partnered her in Minnelli's crazy musical spoof of swashbucklers, *The Pirate* (48), a neat money-maker but otherwise probably the least successful of her MGM films; and she was with Fred Astaire in Irving

Judy Garland looking wistfully at 'The Boy Next Door': a scene from Minnelli's enchanting Meet Me in St Louis (44).

death scene; and in *Ziegfeld Girl* (41), where she, Lana Turner and Hedy Lamarr were aspirants to stardom – and only she made it, which gave the film a conviction it lacked elsewhere.

She followed with *Life Begins for Andy Hardy* and *Babes on Broadway*, both with Rooney, and married bandleader David Rose. *For Me and My Gal* (42) marked her first solo billing, supported by Murphy and Gene Kelly, a pleasant vaudeville musical with a patriotic finale. Said Howard Barnes in the 'New York Herald Tribune': 'Miss Garland is someone to reckon with. Of all the youngsters who have graduated into mature roles in recent years, she has the surest

Berlin's joyous *Easter Parade*, one of the top half-dozen grossers of 1948. A successor with Astaire was planned, but before shooting began she was replaced by Ginger Rogers. This was the first time that her health troubles were publicized and the beginning of the reputation for unreliability. The reason given then (and afterwards) was 'nervous exhaustion' and it became common to blame MGM for all Garland's subsequent troubles. She herself claimed that her mother vilely ill-treated her in her pre-Hollywood days, for professional reasons; and it would seem that from those days began a pattern of adoration and reversal, as, for instance, audiences applauding and the family admiring, but till her second year with Metro much indifference within the business to her talent. There is no question that as a youngster she was on a treadmill, regimented in matters of diet, routine, etc., and by the time she made *The Wizard of Oz* she had become hooked on sleeping pills and pep pills: after her death it was disclosed that for years she had relied on pills not only to prepare her for entertaining but for living. Mr Harry Ansliger, former Narcotics Commissioner of New York, 'said that he had attempted to help the singer give up morphine'. His recommendation that she be given a year's rest was rejected by a film studio executive on the ground that 'we have $14 million tied up in her'. But whatever caused her to crack then was presumably the cause of all the later difficulties. Witnesses have said that at one point during these years she first suffered from a lack of confidence and never again recovered it. In later years she believed she had a God-given talent and reviews and audiences testified to it: but she never overcame her fear of performing. Though it was seldom evident in her work, she suffered from anxiety to an acute degree. She had a neurotic fear of loneliness – and indeed she lived the rest of her life on the prolonged verge of a nervous breakdown – when, that is, she was not actually in a sanatorium. From the late 40s onwards a nervousness is evident in her work and it is probable that part of her genius sprang from that – the wistfulness, the fleeting smile, the quirky way with a comic line, the warmth poised on the brink of sadness. She had a reputation as Hollywood's wittiest woman. James Mason at her funeral said that she was like the little girl with the curl: 'and when she was good, she was not only very, very good, she was the most sympathetic, the funniest, the sharpest and the most stimulating woman I ever knew'.

In 1948 she seemed edgy again in her segment (two songs, one with Rooney) of *Words and Music*, another 'composer' biopic (Rodgers and Hart). But she was more her old self with Van Johnson *In the Good Old Summertime* (49), replacing a pregnant June Allyson. This was *The Shop Around the Corner*, now selling sheet music and transferred to the Chicago of 1904, but in many ways identical. Halfway through filming *Annie Get Your Gun* she walked off the set and did not return. The property had been bought for her at the then unprecedented price of $700,000 and the film's costs were then $500,000. She was suspended and Betty Hutton replaced her. After hospitalization, she returned for *Summer Stock* (50) with Kelly. As shooting dragged along he was reported as saying (echoing Van Johnson's comments the previous year): 'I don't care how long I wait for that girl – I'd wait forever for that magic.' Producer Joe Pasternak said: 'It took six months to make . . . but never once did I hear a cross word, a tart comment, a bitter crack . . . they all understood.' When shown, the film turned out to be a gay 'putting-on-a-show' musical. 'Life' magazine said: 'The great song-and-dance actress makes this movie a personal triumph.'

Garland later said that she was insufficiently rested (and her marriage was breaking up) when recalled, to replace Allyson again, in *Royal Wedding*: one day she did not show and was suspended. The papers reported a suicide attempt (the news is said to have prompted Max Ophüls to conceive his *Lola Montès*) and she was again hospitalized. Plans to star her in the new *Show Boat* were suspended and in June 1950 MGM quietly and reluctantly scrapped her contract. She was 28.

Apart from singing on radio with Bing Crosby – who later described her as the most talented woman ever to work in Hollywood – the only offer of work came from Britain, to appear in person at the London Palladium. The season (51) was a modified triumph – she lacked assurance; but by the time she had finished a record-breaking run at New York's Palace Theater later that year she had begun to acquire that authority and command which were to make her the most potent stage performer of her generation. Indeed, if it can be measured by the pitch of excitement in the auditorium, Garland was the greatest artist of the century: no one who was ever at one of her concerts could ever forget the tiny stocky figure on stage, the huge, warm, dramatic voice and the hysteria invoked in the audience. Because of this latter and because she so absurdly embodied so many show business myths, commentators later passed her up; but at the times when she was 'fashionable' she probably got better notices than any of her contemporaries.

Hollywood now wanted her back and Sid Luft (her third husband) arranged a three-

The third miracle film of her career: Judy Garland and James Mason in A Star Is Born (54).

picture deal at Warners, starting with a remake of *A Star Is Born* (54). Shooting went over-schedule and over-budget – though director Cukor publicly insisted that this was not Garland's fault; early shooting was scrapped and redone in CinemaScope. It would seem that the original budget of $4 million – already very high – went to $7 million, for several reasons, including Luft's inexperience as a producer and Cukor's quest for perfection: a friend and admirer of Garland for years, he was at first appreciative of her contractual agreement to work only when she felt at her best, but towards the end of the protracted shoot he found her behaviour as capricious and unreasonable as it had ever been in her MGM days. The result was, said 'Time', 'just about the finest one-woman show in modern movie history'. Penelope Houston in 'Sight and Sound': 'Since Judy Garland temporarily deserted the screen . . . some of us have been grudging about even the best musicals. Whatever they had, they hadn't got Judy Garland, and although Hollywood may have found singers or dancers more expert, no one has been able to match the high-strung vitality, the tensely gay personality that made Miss Garland such a uniquely stimulating performer. . . . Her comeback picture proves the sort of personal triumph that helps to explain, and justify, the star system. . . . If we are to believe that Vickie Lester has that elusive, indefinable attribute of star quality, then the actress playing her must positively dazzle us with it. But the special fascination of Judy Garland's playing is the way it somehow contrives to bypass technique: the control seems a little less than complete and the emotion comes through as it were, neat. In this incandescent performance, the actress seems to be playing on her nerves: she cannot but strike at ours.' The 'New Statesman':

'Miss Judy Garland is a world in herself. A new world . . . [she] really is one of those feminine wonders that scriptwriters are always trying to conjure up out of the relentless tedium of Hollywood's self-intoxication. The film has got something, too, if not quite as much as Miss Garland. . . .' The 'Spectator': 'In the end, however, it is for Judy Garland to withstand the full torrent of my admiration. She has lost a little in looks but gained enormously in talent. Warm, sensitive, touching, she always was, but now her pathos has a poignancy and her singing a passion. After hearing her sing "The Man That Got Away" and "Born in a Trunk" I felt she had seized the torch I carry for her from my hand and scorched my soul with it!' This performance did not win an Oscar – Groucho Marx described it as the biggest robbery since Brink's – and the omission remains the film city's greatest injustice. In Britain, she won the 'Picturegoer' Gold Medal 'by an astounding margin' – 30 per cent more votes than her nearest competitor. The film itself got raves (and so did co-star James Mason) and restored in 1983 to its three-hour version it stands as one of the most enduring films ever to come from Hollywood; but back then Warners cut 30 minutes after a few initial showings and only got it into the top 10 box-office movies of the year by juggling with the figures, claiming $6 million instead of the $4,355,000 (domestic) that it actually took. That would still bring it into the top 20, but Warners concluded that they had 'over-relied on our star', whose popularity with the trade was not shared by the public at large, and they reneged on the other two pictures. (One of them was *The Helen Morgan Story*, which Ann Blyth did.)

Garland spent the next six years in cabaret and concerts, and in the early 60s was

Her last film: I Could Go on Singing (*63*).

accidental overdose of sleeping pills, shortly after her fifth marriage, hard-boiled journalists were amazed at the huge demonstrations of public affection. Said Ray Bolger: 'Judy didn't die of anything, except wearing out. She just plain wore out.' She had earned during her career $8 million, but left debts of $1 million.

She had said recently: 'What do I do when I'm down? I put on my lipstick, see my stockings are straight and go out there and sing "Over the Rainbow".' Daughter Liza Minnelli spoke of 'the legend', writers spoke of the gaiety of the young Judy, but finally it is tragic. Just how tragic is witnessed by these British reviews of *I Could Go On Singing*: 'Watching Judy Garland, I have a surge of affection. . . . It is for something beyond acting that one cherishes this vivid, elated little creature. . . . It is for the true star's quality. The quality of being' (Dilys Powell); 'One of show-business's all-time magical greats' (Dick Richards); 'She is a harrowingly good actress' (Penelope Gilliatt); 'A few great players are alchemists, who can turn corn golden, and Judy Garland is one of the few' (Paul Dehn); 'She is personally as superb as ever, as enchantingly vulnerable, as thrillingly strident. . . . Always fascinating to watch, she sometimes makes much out of little' (David Robinson); 'She is a star; the genuine outsize article. . . . She is an actress of power and subtlety; a singer whose way with a song is nothing short of marvellous. . She is a great artist. She is Judy. She is the very best there is' (Philip Oakes).

commanding $5,000 nightly. In 1960 at the London Palladium she hit the peak of her form in a concert, which was repeated the following year at Carnegie Hall and described as the greatest night in show business history. A two-record recording of it sold an unparalleled two million copies. Various film projects had come to nothing (*Carousel, South Pacific*) and Garland had had weight problems. In the wake of this new wave of adulation, Hollywood tried again. In *Judgment at Nuremberg* (61), she had an effective nine-minute spot as a blowsy German hausfrau defending her marriage to a Jew: she got raves ('tremendously moving' – Dwight Macdonald) and an Oscar nomination. But the two she carried were hardly successful. *A Child Is Waiting* was a box-office disaster: Burt Lancaster co-starred and he could not save it, a quiet, controlled piece, about mongoloid children. Garland was a teacher. She sang, obviously, in *I Could Go On Singing* (63), made in Britain with Dirk Bogarde, but it offered little to non-devotees: the press loved her but trounced the film, a 30s-type sob story about mother-love. It was announced, however, that she was considering three more films; but she returned to personal appearances, records and a series for CBS TV. In 1965 she was announced as the mother in the Electronic *Harlow*, but did not play it, and in 1967 20th proudly stated that they had captured 'the legendary Judy' for *Valley of the Dolls*, but she could not be persuaded to leave her dressing-room for the set and was sacked. There were débâcles at concerts when she appeared late, as at her last engagement in cabaret in London in 1969: but she was still breaking house records and, more curiously, was deeply loved backstage. She never lost the great love she had within show business and when she died in 1969 from an

GREER GARSON

Greer Garson arrived at the time when MGM and cinema audiences really needed her. Garbo and Norma Shearer were on the verge of retiring and Hollywood needed a big suffering lady (emphasis on the word lady). Irene Dunne, Joan Crawford and others were all very well, but no one was as right as Greer for the matriarch in the mansion. To millions of war-weary women she represented an ideal of nobility and matronhood, clear-browed, capable and unruffled: you really felt she could do her own marketing if called upon to do so. Men cared for her less, but when she was not being comfy-wifely, she had a bewitching Irish charm. As an actress she is a puzzle, as up and down as they come: in any given scene in, say, *Random Harvest*, she is as wily, as actressy and as self-consciously charming as it is possible to be and the next minute she will take your breath away – effortless, sincere and dead right.

She was born in County Down, Ulster, in 1914. The family moved to London and she studied at its university, intending to become a teacher; instead, she went into advertising and spent her evenings at amateur dramatic clubs. A friend gave her an intro to Birmingham rep and she bowed there in 'Street Scene'. She was there for two seasons, then made her London début in the 1934 season in Regent's Park Open Air Theatre, after which she was engaged by Olivier to understudy in 'Golden Arrow' (35): but when he could not get Carol Goodner for the lead he promoted her. It was her first break and she became a successful West End ingénue – in 'Twelfth Night' and 'The School for Scandal' among others. On TV she was Juliet to Olivier's Romeo. She had the lead in 'Old Music' (38) and Louis B. Mayer was in the audience, under the misapprehension that it was a musical: she impressed him so much that he signed her to a contract starting at $500 a week. In Hollywood she collected her pay check and nothing else, though illness prevented her from taking a supporting role in *Dramatic School*, which went to Paulette Goddard, and since it is that of a gold-digger it would seem that MGM could only see Garson in the mould of an earlier import, Binnie Barnes. She was about to return to London when director Sam Wood saw a test she had done and requested her for *Goodbye Mr Chips* (39) with Robert Donat; so she returned to London anyway, for the filming. She did not want to play Mrs Chips because the part was too small (she died after 20 minutes): but the film was a great success and made her famous.

She returned to Hollywood to be much less suitably cast in *Remember?*, a comedy with Robert Taylor that she referred to later as 'Forgive and Forget'; but was appropriate enough as Elizabeth Bennett in *Pride and Prejudice* (40), a part originally intended for Norma Shearer: Clark Gable had long ago refused to play Darcy, so Olivier and she found themselves playing together again. He said later: 'Darling Greer seemed to me all wrong as Elizabeth . . . she was the only down-to-earth sister but Greer played her as the most affected and silly of the lot.' She then played Mrs Edna Gladney, a real-life lady who crusaded on behalf of bastards, clearly the *Blossoms in the Dust* (41), an over-sickly piece with Walter Pidgeon, directed by Mervyn LeRoy. With Crawford she did *When Ladies Meet*: the French called it *Duel de Femmes* and Garson was a runaway victor. Crawford in fact had been hoping to inherit Shearer's queenly place at the studio and was now disconcerted to see it going to Garson. Shearer turned down *Mrs Miniver* (42)

because she did not want to play a mother and it was assigned to Garson who, more reasonably, did not want to play a mother either. After a fight she gave in (and fell in love with the actor playing her son, Richard Ney; at the studio's request the marriage – her second – was delayed till the film had gone the rounds). Pidgeon was her film husband, William Wyler directed and the film, a stiff-upper-lip drama about the British Home Front, was an enormous success. It is said to have done more for the British cause (the US entered the war while it was in production) than any other single factor; more surprisingly – because, though well-meant, it is phoney – it was a hit in Britain. Garson won a Best Actress Oscar for a performance which included rounding up a Nazi parachutist (Helmut Dantine) in the garden.

But if *Miniver* was a success, *Random Harvest* was hardly less so, another big money-maker, directed by LeRoy: from James Hilton's novel, with Ronald Colman as an amnesiac and Garson as the faithful wife he marries twice. She did a song and dance in it, in tights, which made news and doubtless helped it break records at the Radio City Music Hall and the Empire, Leicester Square. And she won the 'Picturegoer' Gold Medal for the third consecutive year (the first was for *Blossoms*). MGM negotiated a new contract, a remarkable seven-year one *without options*, and one peak followed another, handsomely mounted square vehicles like *Madame Curie* (43), directed by LeRoy, which James Agate did not think had much merit, but 'I am

Garson in Random Harvest *(42), with Ronald Colman: as an amnesiac she marries twice. The cherry-blossom was much in evidence in the film.*

inclined to think the time has come to recognize Greer Garson as the next best film actress to Bette Davis'. Mr Miniver was Monsieur Curie. There followed: *Mrs Parkington* (44), a family saga, again with Pidgeon; *The Valley of Decision* (45), more family saga, with Gregory Peck; and when Gable returned after war service, it was to her arms and *Adventure* (46). It was a hit but critically knocked – and her fans did not care for her much as a sailor's pick-up. Significantly, she disappeared from the top 10 the following year, but the film concerned, *Desire Me* (47), was a disaster, going out without director credit. Her co-star, Robert Mitchum, later said that he stopped taking Hollywood seriously when she took 125 takes to say 'No'. A while earlier she had been about to do a parody-great-lady number in *Ziegfeld Follies*, but had withdrawn because she thought it undignified (Judy Garland did it): now, in an effort to renew box-office interest, she took pratfalls with Pidgeon in *Julia Misbehaves* (48), an unfunny version of Margery Sharpe's comic novel, 'The Nutmeg Tree'. More suitably, she was Irene, *That Forsyte Woman* (49), a stagey version of part of Galsworthy's saga: but the complex emotions of the marriage were beyond her and Errol Flynn. It did well but *The Miniver Story* (50) was a mistaken resurrection.

MGM tried another comedy, a remake of *The Last of Mrs Cheyney* called *The Law and the Lady* (51) with Michael Wilding, but it was longwinded and Garson's attempts at vamping in a black wig were disheartening. Apart from what was a cameo role – Calpurnia – in *Julius*

Caesar (53) audiences were encouraged to forget her: both *Scandal at Scourie* with Pidgeon and *Her Twelve Men* (54) with Robert Ryan were shop-soiled sentiment. In June, 1953, just before the former was released, MGM (according to 'Picturegoer') informed Garson that she would have to take much less than her $5,000 a week or leave: she agreed, on condition that she could make outside films. MGM did take conscience that her last two films at least were unworthy and made some revitalizing plans - *Remembrance Rock*, an American epic written by Carl Sandburg, and a life of opera singer Marjorie Lawrence. But Garson, in March 1954, asked for release from her contract and was given it. (The Sandburg film was never made and the other went to Eleanor Parker.)

Mervyn LeRoy had also left MGM and had returned to Warners, where he had worked in the 30s. He persuaded Warners to take Garson on for a Western, *Strange Lady in Town* (55), but it failed to draw. She was one of the first big stars to do television, 'Reunion in Vienna' (55), with Brian Aherne, and 'The Little Foxes' (56). She then went to New York to replace Rosalind Russell in 'Aunti Mame'. Warners called again for Garson to play Eleanor Roosevelt in the film of Dore Schary's play *Sunrise at Campobello* (60): Ralph Bellamy was Franklin. Her make-up was remarkably like and she received her seventh Oscar nomination, but the film did only faint business in the US and was yanked off a West End screen after a week – and has not been heard of since. The same year she did a guest appearance in *Pepe*. She had married a wealthy Texan, her third husband, in 1949 and did not need to work; and she certainly did not need to make *The Singing Nun* (66), a small part as the all-wise Mother Superior. She played with all the old mischievous twinkle, alas. Better was *The Happiest Millionaire* (67), but it was not one of Disney's happier efforts and the press hardly bothered to mention that she was in it. In 1968 she played in 'Captain Brassbound's Conversion' in Los Angeles; she turned down the role of Queen Mary in the Broadway production of 'Crown Matrimonial', but played it on TV (74). Also in that medium she was in a four-hour TV pilot, 'Little Women' (78), in which Dorothy McGuire was Marmee. She was Aunt March. She has also guested in the 'Love Boat' series.

JANET GAYNOR

Janet Gaynor was the first woman to win an Oscar – in 1927-8, for three films (the awards were given thus, originally): *Seventh Heaven*, *Sunrise* and *Street Angel*. She was also, and for some subsequent years, one of the biggest stars in the firmament, in 1931-3 trailing only Marie Dressler in popularity polls and in 1934 the Box-Office Queen. She took over Mary Pickford's role as Leading Waif and her title, 'America's Sweetheart'; and, as befitted the sobriquet, she was winsome and wistful. 'Because she is of Quaker origin she knows how to be demure,' wrote Marjorie Collier in 'Picturegoer'. Sex was merely a potential – despite the fact that the gamins she played were very often ladies of the pavement. She was, of course, more sinned against than sinning. The wholesomeness of her heroines was due to her charm and large eyes, not to mention her naivety: thespian ability hardly entered into it.

She was born (Laura Gainor) in Philadelphia in 1906. The family moved to Chicago to Florida to San Francisco to Los Angeles, where Gaynor decided she would be happier doing extra work in films (she had worked as a theatre usherette and as a bookkeeper in a shoe store). She did extra work for four years, gradually rising to small parts in two-reelers at the Roach studios; at Universal she was given the lead in a two-reel Western and then Herb Moulton, a newspaper executive, arranged for a test at Fox (she and Moulton later eloped, but did not marry). Fox liked her and gave her the second lead in a fictional account of a 19th-century tragedy, *The Johnstown Flood* (26), which she promptly stole from stars George O'Brien and Florence Gilbert. She was offered a five-year contract at $100 a week and starred in *The Shamrock Handicap*, a horse tale set in Ireland and the US, directed by John Ford; *The Midnight Kiss*; Ford's *The Blue Eagle*, being fought over by O'Brien and William Russell; and *The Return of Peter Grimm* (from the dead: David Belasco's very serious ghost whimsy).

Her work in *Peter Grimm* impressed Fox sufficiently to raise her pay to $300 a week, even though she was still little known; and pressure was brought on two studio directors to use her in their new films. F.W. Murnau had wanted Lois Moran for *Sunrise* (27), but Gaynor was good in it, as the little wife whose husband abandons her for a city vamp. Until they are reconciled, the film is, in Arthur Knight's words, 'at least one-half of a masterpiece': then it goes off in wild, melodramatic whirls. It was released after Frank Borzage's version of a Broadway play, *Seventh Heaven*, which made her a star, a sordid little love story about a Paris streetwalker redeemed by and redeeming sewer-rat Charles Farrell: the direction gave it a fairy-tale quality. She then made a comedy, *Two Girls Wanted*, but the

Charles Farrell and Janet Gaynor when they were the world's favourite sweethearts. Farrell's films without Gaynor were much less popular than those they did together and he retired from films while still comparatively young. He was never so effective in Talkies.

returns from *Heaven* were now coming in (it was the second biggest grosser of 1927, behind *The Jazz Singer*) and Fox hastened to re-team Gaynor and Farrell in as similar a story as could be found, *Street Angel* (28). Again business was fantastic and whenever Fox were in doubt, over the next few years, they co-starred them, 'America's Favorite Lovebirds'. Farrell's popularity never reached the heights of Gaynor's. Her career was personally guided by the production chief of Fox, Winfield Sheehan. She was, said 'Picturegoer' once, 'not only a Winfield Sheehan star, but *the* Winfield Sheehan star'.

Christina (29), *Four Devils* (as a trapeze artist, Murnau again directing) and *Lucky Star* (with Farrell; a sentimental rural drama) were all part-talking; *Sunny Side Up* was Gaynor's first real Talkie, a musical – or 'talkie-singie' – which smashed at the box-office (it took over $3 million). Her voice was not too hot, but she enjoyed singing and dancing – for the moment. She was an East Side girl and Farrell a Long Island boy. After a duet with him in Fox's contribution to the all-star revue cycle, *Happy Days* (30), she was with him again in one concocted to cash in on the success of *Sunny Side Up: High Society Blues*, a little-girl-makes-good tale. She fought against doing it (she liked the saccharine parts but not the skittish ones) and begged Fox not to put her in any more musicals. Fox would not promise, so she walked out and the part that they had promised her in *Liliom* went to Rose Hobart. Also, she was fed up with the Fox publicity, which depicted her as a little darling. The little darling took herself off to Hawaii and waited for Fox to capitulate. She was off salary for seven months (losing her $1,500 weekly) when she gave in.

As a peace offering, Fox put her in a starkly dramatic piece, in which she was a cabaret queen turned junkie and Farrell was a wealthy scion turned dipso, *The Man Who Came Back* (31). It was a success, but Gaynor said later, 'It was positively the worst picture I made', and she was more amenable thereafter. And the next one was a big one, *Daddy Long Legs*, from Jean Webster's bestseller about the orphan girl and the wealthy guardian (Warner Baxter) who falls in love with her. Like *Tess of the Storm Country* (32) with Farrell, it was a remake of an old Mary Pickford vehicle, though Gaynor did refuse to do Pickford's *Rebecca of Sunnybrook Farm* around the same time. Marion Nixon played it, an artist whom Fox hoped might supplant Gaynor in popularity (to this end, she was teamed with Farrell a couple of times). Before *Tess*, Gaynor and Farrell were also teamed in three pictures; *Merely Mary Ann* (31) as a cockney waif; *Delicious*, another big hit, the story of a fey Scots lassie in a glengarry in the US; and *The First Year* (32), laughter-and-tears among the newly weds.

But the team was doomed. In 1933 Gaynor signed a new contract with Fox and thereafter she appeared only once with Farrell. She had,

however, another big grosser – though she fought against doing it – *State Fair* (33), sharing starring honours with Fox's No. 1 male star, Will Rogers (as her father). Her co-star in *Adorable* was Henri Garat and she was a princess in this remake of a German film, with music by the Gershwins. Her leading man in *Paddy the Next Best Thing* was Warner Baxter. In this load of old Irish whimsy 'she displays more acting ability than usual', said 'Screenplay', while 'Picturegoer' thought the next, *Carolina* (34), contained her best performance: 'Her simpering affectations are non-existent and she brings real character to the part.' It was also a good film, about a broken-down family in the South, with Robert Young. *Change of Heart* teamed her with James Dunn and Farrell with Ginger Rogers – at the outset of the film: but it was their twelfth and last together, and much more modern than most of the other ones. There followed *Servants Entrance* with Lew Ayres; *One More Spring* (35), as a waif in this Depression romance with Baxter, a film she particularly liked; and *The Farmer Takes a Wife*, with Henry Fonda.

But there were now no longer any queues at the box-office. Fox had amalgamated with 20th Century and the new boss, Darryl F. Zanuck, was not interested in promoting Gaynor's career. *Banjo on My Knee*, intended for her, was given to Barbara Stanwyck and,

Janet Gaynor and Henry Fonda in The Farmer Takes a Wife (35). *She was a canal-boat girl who ran away from home and he was the boy who befriended her. It was his first film and one of her last.*

perhaps in retaliation, she refused to do the remake of *Seventh Heaven*; nor were strained relations at 20th alleviated when she had an accident and had to leave the remake of *Way Down East* (with Fonda; Rochelle Hudson replaced her). Recovered, she was loaned to MGM (in exchange for Robert Taylor) for *Small Town Girl* (36), married by city slicker Taylor while he was drunk. It was a comedy.

On her home lot, she learned that it was proposed to star her with Constance Bennett, Loretta Young and newcomer Simone Simon (tipped to take her place) in *Ladies in Love*. She had no wish to share either title or billing with other luminaries and wanted to sue (she had been, after all, an official 'star' longer than any queen except Garbo); further, her salary for it was to be reduced from her customary $150,000 per film to $115,000 (still one of the best fees in Hollywood). Eventually, she did the film and then looked around for a new home.

She signed with Selznick for two and MGM for one. Both Selznick movies are fondly remembered. The first was the first version of *A Star Is Born* (37), a moving, literate Hollywood saga (with Fredric March as the star on the wane whose wife, Gaynor, waxes): Gaynor has said she thought it superior to the remake, but despite a good moment impersonating Garbo, Hepburn and Mae West her own work is (inevitably) light years behind Judy Garland's. The film was the first to stay *three* weeks at the Radio City Music Hall. The MGM film was *Three Loves Has Nancy* (38), a dull antic about a small-town housekeeper and her New York novelist boss Robert Montgomery. The other Selznick picture was *The Young in Heart*, an endearingly funny tale by I.A.R. Wylie about a family of confidence tricksters (Gaynor, Douglas Fairbanks Jr, Roland Young and Billie Burke) and the old lady (Minnie Dupree) for whom they reform.

On this high note Gaynor announced her retirement and her second marriage at the same time – to Adrian, MGM's top dress designer (the first was to a lawyer, Lydell Peck). She said later that she might not have stayed away if the marriage had not been so happy. (It was announced in 1940 that she had bought a property, *Forever*, for herself, but nothing came of it.) In 1957 20th persuaded her to play Richard Savage's mother in *Bernadine*, which starred Pat Boone, but the occasion garnered little publicity. After her husband's death in 1959 she toured in 'The Midnight Sun', but it did not reach Broadway. Throughout the decade she made occasional appearances in TV dramas. In 1964 she married stage producer Paul Gregory. In 1980 she appeared in the short-lived Broadway 'Harold and Maude' (based on the film) and

observed that since she did not need to work she was only interested in doing so in 'something that gave me a real outlet'. She appeared in an episode of TV's 'The Love Boat' with Lew Ayres and in 1981 she was in the Chicago presentation of 'On Golden Pond'. She died in 1984.

About her reasons for quitting, she told reporter Roy Newquist: 'I really felt that I had had it all. I had all the pleasure and excitement of being at the top and I wanted to know about other things in life. I felt I didn't want to spend my whole life being an actress.' And she added: 'I think I had a wonderful career; I enjoyed it all, and have no sad tales to tell you.'

JOHN GILBERT

'In the time of Hollywood's most glittering days, he glittered the most', wrote Ben Hecht. 'He needed no greatness around him to make him feel distinguished. He drank with carpenters, danced with waitresses and made love to whores and movie queens alike. He swaggered and posed but it was never to impress anyone. He was being John Gilbert, prince, butterfly, Japanese lantern, and the spirit of romance.'

Alas, Gilbert is remembered as the classic case of the Silent star ruined by the coming of Sound. There is an element of myth in it, but he was the leading male actor of the late 20s and absolutely finished within months of the arrival of the Talkies. Much has been written about his fall from grace: Griffith and Mayer quote an unnamed critic who found it 'embarrassing' to review a John Gilbert Talkie: 'It isn't that Mr Gilbert's voice is insufficient; it's that his use of it robs him of magnetism, individuality, and strangest of all, skill. He becomes an uninteresting and inexperienced performer whose work could be bettered by hundreds of lesser-known players.' That contemporary opinion is substantiated by the only one of Gilbert's performances that most modern audiences have seen, playing opposite Garbo in *Queen Christina*. Like the head of the village drama group who has cast himself as Hamlet, Gilbert is inadequate for the part: he is weedy and prissy, ill at ease in his costumes and his voice, of course, is light and inexpressive. But in his Silent pictures, he had superb dash and authority. For what it is worth, Elinor Glyn thought him 'greater than Valentino', and he was indeed: alone, his unforced and unaffected use of his intense eyes makes him one of the best Silent actors.

He was born in 1897 in Logan, Utah, into a family of strolling players. He was educated as they went along and sent to a military school in California for a while. His mother died when he was 14 and his stepfather told him that he was on his own from then on: he was supposed to have enough experience of the theatre to get a job in one and indeed after two years of menial work (scrubbing floors, washing dishes) he became stage manager for a stock company in Spokane. After seeing one of his mother's old associates on the screen he approached his stepfather for work as an actor; he was refused because he had no experience, but his stepfather did contact an old friend, Walter Edwards, who was directing with the Thomas H. Ince company. Ince-Triangle offered the boy $15 a week to do extra roles, the first of which was in *Matrimony* (15). There were another six, in the last of which, *Hell's Hinges* (16) starring William S. Hart, he is clearly visible. He was billed for the first time – as Jack Gilbert – on *Bullets and Brown Eyes* and then Hart cast him as his younger brother in *The Apostle of Vengeance*. There were featured roles in *The Phantom*, *The Eye of the Night*, *Shell 43!*, *The Sin Ye Do* and *The Weaker Sex* (17). His first lead was in *Princess of the Dark* – who was a blind Enid Bennett, who did not know that her prime admirer was a hunchbacked cripple. He was more himself in *The Dark Road* and mostly cast as the Other Man or in unsympathetic parts for which, Ince thought, his looks qualified him: as in *Happiness*, in which he was a rich boy trying to woo Bennett away from her poor sweetheart. There followed: *The Millionaire Vagrant* starring Charles Ray, *Hater of Men*, *The Mother Instinct*; *Golden Rule Kate*, a Western with Louise Glaum, with Gilbert as an outlaw who reforms at the end; *The Devil Dodger*; *Doing Her Bit*, which was never released; and *Up or Down*.

Triangle dropped him when that company changed hands and he joined other Triangle alumni at Paralta: *One Dollar Bid* (18), playing a gambler vamped by Glaum and then reformed by her sweet little sister, Leatrice Joy – who later became his second wife (1923–4). Paralta itself was soon to go under and Gilbert moved about quite a lot, usually to the lesser studios: *Nancy Comes Home*, a belated Triangle release; *Shackled* and *Wedlock*, both with Glaum; *More Trouble*, as the son of star Frank Keenan; *The Mask of Riches*; and *Three X Gordon* and *Sons of Men*, both Westerns starring J. Warren Kerrigan. Vitagraph took him on to play opposite Bessie Love in her first film for the company, but that led to no further offers. He was called up for military service the day the Armistice was signed, so did not serve for long. He had petitioned Ince for a role (because he had no money), so was cast in *The Busher* (19), a baseball comedy, as a shallow rich cad who loses Colleen Moore to Charles Ray. The director, Maurice Tourneur, cast him opposite Mabel Ballin in *The White Heather* and offered him a contract, but then decided that he could not afford to pay him the half-salary agreed when not actually working. So Gilbert returned to supporting roles: *The Man Beneath* with Sessue Hayakawa; *The Red Viper* with Ruth Stonehouse; *Widow by Proxy* with Marguerite Clark; *The Heart o' the Hills* with Mary Pickford; and *Should a Woman Tell?* with Alice Lake.

Tourneur then sent for him again, to star in: *The White Circle* (20), based on Robert Louis Stevenson's 'The Pavilion in the Links'; and *The Great Redeemer*, directed by Clarence Brown under Tourneur's supervision, about a convict who paints a Crucifixion on the walls of his cell and its effect on the other inmates. Gilbert was also the assistant director on both and he co-wrote the scripts with Jules Furthman; he was sole scenarist on both *Deep Waters*, an undersea adventure in which he also starred, and *The Bait* (20), in which he did not (or even appear), a starring vehicle for Hope Hampton, the protégée of one of Tourneur's backers, Jules Brelatour. It was interference from this source which brought the break-up of Tourneur's company and *The Glory of Love*, made at this time for Paramount, did not turn up till three years later, distributed by Hodkinson and retitled *While Paris Sleeps:* Gilbert was a tourist who steals Mildred Manning from Lon Chaney. *The Servant in the House* (21), which now turned up, was something Gilbert had made two years earlier.

Brelatour invited Gilbert to write and direct *Love's Penalty*, a vehicle for Hampton, and the experience he found so discouraging, and the result so bad, that he did not expect to work again. But he did, as an actor, for Fox, in *Shame* – something he experienced on learning that his mother was Chinese, so he went off to Alaska. He was billed John Gilbert for the first time and reaction to the film, though irredeemably silly, was such that Fox offered a three-year contract. In the meantime he did a supporting role for Mayflower-Paramount in *Ladies Must Live* with Betty Compson. Fox put him into *Gleam o'Dawn* (22), a tale of Hudson Bay adventurers with Barbara Bedford as his leading lady. This was, said 'Photoplay', a chance to examine the much-touted new star, but it offered no report while relegating the film to its back pages, which was comment in itself. Fox persisted: *Arabian Love*, one of the many attempts to capitalize on the 'Sheik' craze started by Valentino; *The Yellow Stain*; *Honor First*, the first of several teamings with

Renée Adorée; *Monte Cristo*, after Dumas; *Calvert's Valley*; *The Love Gambler* with Carmel Myers; *A California Romance* with Estelle Taylor; *Truxton King* (23); *The Madness of Youth* with Billie Dove; *St Elmo* with Barbara La Marr and Bessie Love; *The Exiles*; *Cameo Kirby*, directed by John Ford from the popular play by Booth Tarkington and Harry Leon Wilson, with Gilbert as a Mississippi riverboat gambler who is really a good egg with a bad reputation; *Just Off Broadway* (24) with Marion Nixon, as an amateur detective; *The Wolf Man*, as a milord who flees to Canada because he thinks (wrongly) that he is a murderer and who is forgiven for attempted rape by Norma Shearer after he has risked his life to save her from drowning; and *The Lone Chance*. The only two of these films to survive are *Monte Cristo* and *Cameo Kirby*.

It was in the Ford picture that Irving Thalberg first saw Gilbert and observed. 'Fox doesn't know what they have in Gilbert. He could be a star.' He signed him for MGM

immediately his contract was up, convinced he could become a very big star with the right material; also, he was dark and Latin-looking, and that was a positive asset in an industry dazzled by the success of Valentino. Accordingly, he was given parts – often in uniform – in which he could cut a dash. Like Valentino, he was encouraged to use his eyes – and, in fact, he used them better: they were big, dark eyes and he became adept at two expressions in particular – fiery passion and deep compassion. He needed all the former quality chasing Aileen Pringle round the boudoirs in *His Hour*, which King Vidor directed and Elinor Glyn adapted from one of her own steaming novels; and he used the compassion in *He Who Gets Slapped* with Lon Chaney and Norma Shearer, as the equestrian partner she loves and is not supposed to have. Between the two he put in a guest appearance in *Married Flirts*, a sophisticated comedy with two of the studio's biggest stars, Pauline Frederick and Conrad Nagel. Thalberg had launched him spectacularly, but Gilbert

Neither producers nor audiences approved of John Gilbert without his moustache, but he didn't sport it in his biggest success, The Big Parade *(25).* King Vidor directed, and his leading lady was Renée Adorée. Here Adorée is introducing him to her family.

loathed the Glyn film and derided his image as a screen lover. To show his range he requested the title-role in *The Snob*, a professor whose ambitions wreck his marriage to Shearer and also ruin her life, a situation that would have been prevented if she had only told him she was an heiress. 'Picturegoer' commented that 'the screen has never given us a more sustained character portrait of an utter rotter', but Louis B. Mayer was incensed by Gilbert's preference for the one role over the other and by the timing of his divorce; his vindictiveness would grow and eventually prove fatal.

For the instant he was silenced as Gilbert became the studio's biggest male star. Gilbert was reunited with Vidor and Pringle for *The Wife of the Centaur*, with Eleanor Boardman in the title-role, faced with losing him, a novelist, to Pringle and debauchery – though that was as nothing compared to that to be slobbered over in *The Merry Widow* (25), with Mae Murray in that role and he as a profligate Prince Danilo. Erich von Stroheim directed and there are touches which set it apart from the other Ruritanian romances that Gilbert made (and it was also the only enjoyable musical filmed without music): the public presumably were titillated, because the film was one of the year's biggest grossers, at an estimated $1½ million. But this was less than half what Gilbert's next clocked up – *The Big Parade*, 1925's most popular film and certainly the most highly regarded. It ran for two years at the Astor in New York and grossed an estimated $15 million worldwide. This was so far the best of the films inspired by the war, neither pro- nor anti-, but a wry look from the point of view of the average doughboy. King Vidor's direction was masterly and Gilbert was excellent. He started on a new – and his highest – phase of popularity.

Vidor also directed his next two, *La Bohème* (26) – he was Rudolph and Lillian Gish was Mimi – and *Bardelys the Magnificent*, a swashbuckler based on a novel by Rafael Sabatini and an attempt to establish him as a Fairbanks-type hero. In his next, there were love scenes which 'Photoplay' described as 'smolderingly fervent': the lady was Greta Garbo and the film *Flesh and the Devil* (27): he kills her husband in a duel after he had found them making love and they start *that* all over again after she has married his best friend (Lars Hanson). An offscreen affair, though publicly denied by Garbo, gave the film an aura for the fans: in fact, they shared a house off and on and planned to marry at a double wedding with Vidor and Boardman. Garbo changed her mind and did not turn up, causing Mayer to accost Gilbert, 'What do you have to marry her for? Why

don't you just fuck her and forget about it?' Gilbert attacked him, beating his head against the wall till they were separated. Mayer said, 'You're finished, Gilbert. I'll destroy you if it costs me a million dollars.'

Not yet, however: indeed, the studio hastened to find a suitable vehicle for the two stars. In the meantime Gilbert did *The Show* with Adorée, a melodrama set in Budapest where he was an apache of sorts, and *Twelve Miles Out*, as a rum runner with Joan Crawford. When Garbo was ready he was Vronsky to her Anna Karenina in a modern version called *Love*, another fine credit for him except for their reunion in the end (in the American version, but not in the one released in Europe). Also of first-class quality is *Man Woman and Sin*, in which he is a young journalist who kills in self-defence his rival for society editor Jeanne Eagels – and finds she will not speak up for him. *The Cossacks* (28) was based on another Tolstoy story, with Gilbert as a weakling who redeems himself after preferring the company of Adorée to killing Turks. He was so popular that MGM happily paid him $10,000 a week – currently the highest paid star in movies. The public queued to see: *Four Walls* with Crawford, as a Jewish gangster who tries to go straight after leaving the pen; *Show People*, glimpsed with other stars; Sjöström's now lost *The Masks of the Devil*, as a philanderer, a performance which stamped him as 'one of the greatest dramatic actors of the screen', said the 'New York Telegram'; *A Woman of Affairs* (29) with Garbo, as her true love, but his father refuses to let them marry; *Desert Nights*, a melodrama combining a diamond mine, a sandstorm and eroticism; and *A Man's Man*, a William Haines vehicle in which both Gilbert and Garbo made guest appearances. These all came out while the craze for Sound was sweeping the studios and cinemas, and it was clear that Gilbert could not be silent much longer.

MGM were not certain whether Gilbert's voice would record well, but as far as Gilbert was concerned they would not have a chance to find out: he wanted to get as far away from Mayer as possible. Douglas Fairbanks thought he would be an asset to United Artists and on their behalf Joseph Schenck offered him $125,000 per picture, to a maximum budget of $750,000, with the option of directing himself or choosing his director. At the same time Schenck's brother, Nicholas, was discussing the possibility of merging MGM with William Fox's studio and Fox was insisting on Gilbert as part of the deal. Since UA might also be part of the merger, the Schenck brothers discussed the Gilbert situation and it was decided that Nicholas Schenck would offer

Garbo and Gilbert in a modern version of 'Anna Karenina', called simply Love (27). Earlier in the year 'Photoplay' had called their love scenes in Flesh and the Devil 'smolderingly fervent' and the same seems to be true here. The fact that they were reputed to be in love in real life did not hurt either film at the box-office. Note the still MGM preferred for the ads, and how the advert overcomes the then rule of one star to one film: Garbo's fame and popularity had been so sudden and so huge that she couldn't go under the title, as Gilbert's contract would have specified.

him $250,000 per film for two a year for the next four years, with the right to select his own material. Gilbert pointed out that the deal with UA gave him more freedom, but his agent said that he had often erred in predicting which of his vehicles would be successful. Nicholas Schenck allowed a clause into the contract permitting Gilbert to break it at any time and, most importantly, Gilbert would be under personal contract to him – with the assurance that the hated Mayer would, in any case, soon be leaving MGM. When the merger talks failed, Mayer was in a stronger position than before and even more in command of Gilbert's destiny.

Meanwhile, Gilbert made his talkie début in *The Hollywood Revue of 1929*, in a Technicolor sequence, doing the balcony scenes from 'Romeo and Juliet' with Shearer and then a burlesque of it in modern argot: as 'Liberty Magazine' said at the time, it was difficult to know which was the more embar-

rassing. But the crunch came with *His Glorious Night*, adapted from Molnar's 'Olympia', with Catherine Dale Owen: they coped with dreadful dialogue and while some audiences sniggered, others fell about. The fate of Silent stars in Talkies was big news and the fan magazines were quick to pounce: 'Is Jack Gilbert through?' Their writers knew that *Redemption*, made prior to this, had been shelved and when it did appear it made the Gilbert situation even more perilous. A version of Tolstoy's 'The Living Corpse', with Gilbert as a ne'er-do-well who deserts his new wife (Boardman) to return to his gypsy love (Adorée), it was – into the bargain – ineptly directed by Lionel Barrymore. In Britain it was shown first and 'Picturegoer' stoutly assured its readers that as a Talkie actor, 'his success seems assured'. It has been suggested that MGM tried to ruin Gilbert by recording him badly – to punish him for his 'greed' at the time of the Fox negotiations – but it is

261

more probable that Mayer simply sat back and let the box-office figures do the undoing he wanted done. At all events, MGM offered Gilbert $500,000 to 'go away some place' as 'Photoplay' put it: he angrily refused. In an attempt to make audiences forget the contentious voice, he was cast as a tough gob in *Way for a Sailor* (30), but instead they ignored the film. Like *Redemption*, it lost a lot of money (but unlike *His Glorious Night*, which made a handsome profit). He was asked, unsuccessfully, to take a salary cut and his misery was not helped by the fact that Ina Claire, his current wife (1929–32), was a Broadway actress and therefore doing relatively well in Hollywood.

Mayer was publicly criticized by other Hollywood executives and by the press for his treatment of Gilbert, but the public still did not want to know about: *Gentleman's Fate* (31), in which he discovered that his family were gangsters, and 'Photoplay' was 'happy' to see him back on form; *The Phantom of Paris*, based on Gaston Leroux's 'Cheri-Bibi', one of the many films of that time about Houdini-like con-men who are essentially noble at heart; and *West of Broadway*, in which he was a drunkard who inherits a ranch. Seen today, these films prove that Gilbert's voice was acceptable and that he was still supreme in all those qualities he had so exemplified – romance, arrogance, nonchalance – but his lack of confidence was also apparent, for in the overheated moments he was horribly hammy, which he had never been in his Silent days. That the old majesty had gone was confirmed by *Downstairs* (32), an amoral tale which he had written, playing a chauffeur who seduces every woman in sight – including Virginia Bruce, who became his fourth wife (1932–34). The trailer showed a 'sophisticated Hollywood audience' rising to its feet in approval, reminding it of Gilbert's Silent triumphs, but: 'taint so. He may be admired again for tackling an unsympathetic role, but both that and the story were anathema to Mayer: and could *he* have ordered Gilbert's clothes to be made several sizes too big so that this once-glorious screen personality was just another wimp/wanker you hardly noticed?

Gilbert had already lost co-starring roles in *A Free Soul* with Shearer and *Susan Lennox: Her Fall and Rise* with Garbo to Clark Gable and now *Red Dust*, bought for him, went also in that direction. MGM tried for the last time and, on the principle that it was Gable's treat-em-rough virility which made him so appealing, they made Gilbert a tough construction worker in *Fast Workers* (33): 'He drinks freely, punches men he does not like, mistreats his women, deceives his friends and

shows himself to be an intolerable braggart', said 'The New York Times'. 'In real life [he] would have been pitched from a convenient skyscraper by his fellow workers for one tenth the things he does in the picture.' Few, other than critics, bothered to see it. And that was that, or almost: some months later MGM sent for him to replace Laurence Olivier as Garbo's leading man, at her insistence, in *Queen Christina*, but it did nothing to re-establish him.

To get the role Gilbert had signed the standard seven-year MGM contract, at one-tenth of his old salary, and there was talk of putting him into the remake of *The Merry Widow* and *Chained*, opposite Joan Crawford, but these roles went to Maurice Chevalier and Gable respectively. A typically impetuous ad appeared in the trade press: 'Metro-Goldwyn-Mayer will neither offer me work nor release me from my contract, Jack Gilbert.' MGM released him. Director Lewis Milestone, an old friend, was able to get him to Columbia, since Harry Cohn loathed Mayer and liked cut-price names, but only if Gilbert tested. The result was a quite decent picture, *The Captain Hates the Sea* (34), with Gilbert, fourth-billed, as a drunken writer. It was not a hard role to assume, but after a week on the wagon he was an alcoholic mess and difficult to handle, partly because the contract called for 'star treatment'. In 1935 he was due to make a personal appearance tour, starting in Baltimore, when his offscreen companion, Marlene Dietrich, secured a test for him, for *Desire*, which she was to make with Gary Cooper: he got the role, but suffered a mild heart attack while swimming with her and was replaced by John Halliday. She was also negotiating with Korda to have Gilbert co-star with her in the British film she was planning to make; she also managed to make him cut down on his drinking, but there had been too many years of that and he died in 1936, after a series of heart attacks. Watching Gilbert blaze away in his great Silents, it is easy to think of him as a tragic figure: unquestionably he came up against the considerable might of the despicable Mayer, but there was in this actor, for all his intelligence, an element of self-destruction.

LILLIAN GISH

'I think the things that are necessary in my profession are these: Taste, Talent and Tenacity. I think I have had a little of all three,' Lillian Gish told 'Sight and Sound' in 1957. Most observers seem to think that there was more than a 'little' talent. In her time she was considered to hold in films the sort of place that Bernhardt or Duse had in the theatre and today she repays close examination. To most modern (i.e. film society) audiences she is at first resistible: a wraith-like heroine in raggedy-Ann clothes gazing passively and innocently at the world which is wronging her so cruelly. But she can be seen admirably enacting everything that was required of her by her directors and her plots – and the demands were heavy. Given the strong Victorian sentiment which inspired D.W. Griffith and some others among her directors, she reacted with a spirituality and charm which not only harmonized with it, but sometimes infected it with a sense of urgency; and while her frail body cowed under the blows inflicted on it in the cause of melodrama, the camera recorded a peculiar and very personal intensity.

Gish was born in 1896 in Springfield, Ohio. Her father was a drifter and drifted away altogether not long after the family (which now included a younger sister, Dorothy) had settled in New York. To pay the rent, Mother Gish sought a job as an actress, but found that it was simpler to let the children act: there were good parts for juveniles in the dramas of the day, if they were not caught up with by one of the societies which wanted to ban child performers. Thus Lillian made her stage bow at the age of five back in Ohio, in a town called Rising Sun, in a play called 'In Convict's Stripes'. In time Mother and both daughters were acting in touring companies and among their colleagues was the child who became Mary Pickford. They visited Pickford on the Griffith lot after she had gone into movies and Pickford persuaded Griffith to give the two girls contracts. They débuted together in *An Unseen Enemy* (12). The films they made were one- and two-reelers and some of them were made in two days or less: like the others (Pickford, Lionel Barrymore, Robert Harron, etc.) in Griffith's company, the Gish sisters played parts of all sizes. Lillian's films are: *Two Daughters of Eve*, in a bit part; *In the Aisles of the Wild; The Musketeers of Pig Alley*, a gangster story; *My Baby*, in a bit; *Gold and Glitter*, about lumberjacks; *The New York Hat; The Burglar's Dilemma; A Cry for Help; Oil and Water; The Unwelcome Guest; A Misunderstood Boy* (13), as his (Harron's) sweetheart; *The Left-Handed Man; The Lady and the Mouse*, with Dorothy, as girls who discover a hobo is a millionaire; *The House of Darkness*, curing Barrymore of insanity; *Just Gold; A Timely Interception*, as a farmer's daughter helping to best a crooked oil company; *The Mothering Heart*, almost losing her husband to a vamp; *During the Round-Up*, as a flirt redeemed by

her true love; *An Indian's Loyalty; A Woman in the Ultimate*, defying her stepfather; *A Modest Hero*, menaced by a robber; *The Madonna of the Storm*; and *The Battle of Elderbush Gulch*, menaced by Indians. *Judith of Bethulia* (14) was Griffith's first feature-length film and she played a young mother. She returned to the stage, but collapsed from lack of food; when she returned to Griffith he upped her salary from $5 a day to $50 a week.

When he left Biograph for Mutual, the Gish sisters went with him; after *The Green-Eyed Devil*, he directed her in another feature, *The Battle of the Sexes*, in which she pretended to go astray to save her father from a vamp. Then: *Lord Chumley; The Hunchback*, as an orphan raised by same; *The Quicksands; Man's Enemy*, which was an anti-drink tract; *Home Sweet Home*, an episode film built round that song; *The Rebellion of Kitty Belle*, as a neglected wife; *The Angel of Contention*, saving her husband from hanging; *The Tear that Burned*, as an innocent girl forced into crime; *The Folly of Anne*, as a reckless writer; and *The Sisters*, a love-tangle with Dorothy. The last of these were made in Hollywood, whither Griffith had moved and where he planned *The Birth of a Nation* (15), his grandiose response to the European epics which were now showing in America's big cities and changing the whole concept of cinema-going. His backers were wary and when it went over its $25,000 budget, money was raked in from other sources (the total cost was $91,000 which included $30,000 for exploitation, etc.). It ran an unprecedented 12 reels and opened in New York at $2 a ticket. The movies had become Art – and Big Business: its gross is uncalculable, but 'Variety' puts it around $5 million, which includes numerous reissues. Even in the 40s it could play commercially, but its apparent approval of the institution of the Ku-Klux-Klan (regardless of anything else) makes it unwatchable today. Gish was considered important enough to be its chief heroine – though Blanche Sweet was the original choice – the Northern girl who falls in love with the Southern colonel and is saved by him, like many another Griffith heroine, from a last-reel rape, in this case by the drunken mulatto governor.

While Griffith prepared his next epic, Gish went on working – but only in features from now on, all of them until 1922 for the Griffith company or under his auspices or direction (several producing companies were involved). She was in: *The Lost House*, as a captive heiress; *Captain Macklin*, rescued by the Foreign Legion; *Enoch Arden*, as the unfortunate wife; *The Lily and the Rose*, comforted by an old lover when her husband goes off

Henry King directed this version of George Eliot's Romola *in 1924. Lillian Gish was the sweet young heroine and William Powell her wicked husband.*

vamp; *The Children Pay*, as the daughter of divorced parents: *The House Built Upon Sand* (17), as a spoilt girl recognizing her husband's worth; and *Souls Triumphant*, another domestic drama. *Hearts of the World* (18) was shot in Britain and France, with the cooperation of the British Government; it was the story of a boy (Robert Harron) and a girl in an idyllic village, torn asunder by the war and reunited in the midst of conflict. Today: crude, obvious and melodramatic, like all Griffith's work, but Gish is splendid in the second half when she can act instead of merely moon.

He directed all the films she made for the next few years: *The Great Love* and *The Greatest Thing in Life* (19), two more war stories, and *A Romance of Happy Valley*, all reuniting her with Harron. In *Broken Blossoms* she played opposite Richard Barthelmess: the quintessential Limehouse story and her own favourite among the Griffith films. James Agate, re-seeing it some years later, wrote that Gish's performance 'still seems to me surpassingly true and moving. She puts into her scenes of terror as much power and pathos as Sarah ever put into Tosca, and I think that, if I were to hear her cries, she would move me more. As it is, the film scene is the more nearly unbearable. I do not say that this little girl is as great an actress as Sarah. For all I know she may not be able to speak the President's American. What I do know is that in this one picture she ranks with the world's great artists.'

Gish was *True-Heart Susie*, another hit – and Griffith's only durable film – and in *The Greatest Question*, both with Harron, in the latter as the servant of a murderous farm couple; and then in *Way Down East* (20), with Barthelmess, and *Orphans of the Storm* (21), with her sister. Both were taken from hoary old plays and both are awash with reversals and sentiment: *Orphans*, set during the French Revolution, works the better of the two, with Gish, kindly and heroic, tending sister Dorothy. During this period she signed with a new company which went broke during what should have been her first film for them, *World Shadows*, and she also directed her sister in *Remodelling Her Husband* (20). Her parting with Griffith came when *Orphans* went over budget and he would not pay her the salary to which she felt entitled; good offers were being made by other companies: Tiffany offered $3,500 a week, but she went to Inspiration at $1,250 plus a percentage of the profits, because they gave her story approval.

For them she made two films in Italy, both directed by Henry King, both with Ronald Colman. *The White Sister* (23) was from Marion Crawford's novel about a girl who

with a vamp; *Daphne and the Pirate* (16), a historical tale; *Sold for Marriage* – which she is, as a Russian immigrant; and *An Innocent Magdalene*, as a Southern belle who marries a gambler, directed by Allan Dwan, who said later: 'She was a queen – very fine, very gentle. And her sister, Dorothy, was a clown, a little hoyden. They were both great – on different ends of the scale.' In Griffith's *Intolerance* she was the cradle-rocker who bound the four parts together, a simultaneous telling of stories set in old Babylon, in Christian times, in Huguenot France and in the present day. It ran longer than *Nation*, cost more and was a financial disaster. She did *Diane of the Follies*, in the title-role, scorned by her husband's friends; *Pathways of Life*, her married life once more threatened by a

Lillian Gish as Hester Prynne in The Scarlet Letter (26), *the third of the three film versions of Nathaniel Hawthorne's novel.*

takes the veil when she thinks – wrongly – that her lover has been killed in battle. The women's clubs of America were outraged at the prospect of this 'sensational' novel being filmed but, because of Lillian's respectability, proposed to lift the ban if she would hold herself 'personally responsible'. The second film was an adaptation of George Eliot's novel about medieval Italy, *Romola* (24). Inspiration then sued her for breach of contract: she had refused to work further when she realized that the president of the company, Charles H. Duell, had been via professed friendship whittling away her contractual rights and because she thought the profits of *Sister* had been wrongly accounted; amidst the bitterness, Duell alleged that she had promised to marry him. On these matters he was later convicted of perjury.

Metro had released the two Inspiration films and it was to MGM she now moved, with a contract worth $800,000 for six films and creative approval. She did not do *Romeo and Juliet* as she had hoped, but with John Gilbert made two other famous lovers, Mimi and Rudolph: *La Bohème* (26). On the strength of *The Big Parade* she had chosen King Vidor to direct. He said of her later: 'She is the most dedicated actress I have ever known. . . . She makes you believe [a scene] is actually happening.' Fresh from this triumph she insisted on doing Nathaniel Hawthorne's *The Scarlet Letter* against studio and censor opposition: she chose Victor Sjöström to direct and Lars

Hanson to co-star, thinking that Swedes could get closer to the Puritan New England setting. Her Hester Prynne is one of the screen's great performances, with a directness of emotion and an ability to project thought and feeling that does not need intertitles, let alone speech. Once again it did well, but *Annie Laurie* (27) – a tale built round the massacre of Glencoe – did so badly after poor reviews that the studio retitled it *Ladies From Hell*. Neither of the next two did well, despite glowing reviews: the pacifist *The Enemy* (28) and *The Wind*. She was reunited with Sjöström and Hanson for the latter, about a Virginia girl in the Texas prairies, a film amazingly vivid and alive. MGM insisted on a happy ending.

Before it was released, the studio wanted to take her off salary, as they had nothing ready for her – but she considered that their fault and not hers. Commercially she had been a disappointment and to buck up her box-office Thalberg suggested that the studio invent a scandal for her. She refused. They decided to let her go without making the last film of her contract – for one thing, her fame as a serious actress was now overshadowed by Garbo's. She signed a contract with UA, at $50,000 per film plus 50 per cent of the profits, and the first was to be directed in Germany by Reinhardt, about a German peasant girl (then living) with a stigmata: but with the advent of Sound, UA decided that her Talkie début should be made in Hollywood. So, instead, she did *One Romantic Night* (30) from Molnar's 'The Swan' with Rod la Rocque; it was not a success, even though she had mastered the microphone with ease. ('The Miracle Girl with the Miracle Voice' said the adverts.) Next, she considered a remake of *The White Sister* as well as *Strange Interlude* with Colman – but a plagiarism suit was brought against Eugene O'Neill and that was postponed. In the end, she asked to be let out of her contract.

Thus, as Louise Brooks put it, 'stigmatized as a grasping, silly, sexless antique, at the age of 31, the great Lillian Gish left Hollywood for ever, without a head turned to mark her departure'. In fact, the screen was overrun with actresses very different from Gish and her sort of film was now old-fashioned. Her talent was undeniable, but continued public acceptance was something else again. She turned to the stage and did three plays, including 'Uncle Vanya' (30) and 'Camille', both on Broadway, and did make another film, *His Double Life* (33), with Roland Young, an adaptation of Arnold Bennett's play, 'The Great Adventure'. Paramount released; Gish made no pictures for RKO, who announced at this time that they had signed her. She did two more plays on Broadway and in 1936 toured in Britain in 'The Old Maid', but the play did not make London; later that year she played Ophelia to Gielgud's Hamlet in New York. In 1937 she did Maxwell Anderson's 'The Star Wagon' and in 1938 'Dear Octopus', both in New York; later she toured in 'Life With Father'. She was asked to play Belle Watling in *Gone With the Wind*, and she did return to the movies in a supporting role in *The Comman-*

After almost 10 years away from films, Miss Gish returned in the early 40s and was soon being driven to drink by Lionel Barrymore in David O. Selznick's expensive Duel in the Sun *(46). With her is Jennifer Jones as the half-breed girl her sons were fighting over.*

dos Strike at Dawn (42); then she and Richard Dix played Donald O'Connor's parents in *Top Man* (43). She was a spinster running a boarding house in *Miss Susie Slagle's* (46) and the consumptive wife of former co-star Lionel Barrymore in *Duel in the Sun* – her only Oscar nomination. She found filming 'much less exciting. . . . Before, I had been responsible for my films; I had involved myself in various facets of production. Now acting in films was largely a matter of doing as you were told and collecting your salary.'

Since 1948 she had kept three careers going: in TV as well as on the stage and in films, invariably playing genteel spinster ladies. TV plays include 'The Trip to Bountiful', 'Morning's at Seven', 'Ladies in Retirement' and in 1969, with Helen Hayes, 'Arsenic and Old Lace'. On the stage she was in 'Crime and Punishment' (47), 'The Trip to Bountiful' (53), 'The Chalk Garden' (56) on tour with her sister; 'The Family Reunion' (58) and 'All the Way Home' (60), both in New York; 'A Passage to India' (62) in Chicago; Mrs Mopply in 'Too True to Be Good' (63) in New York; the Nurse in 'Romeo and Juliet' (65); 'Anya', a flop version of 'Anastasia'; and 'I Never Sang for My Father' (67), among other plays. Her rare screen appearances did not belie her reputation as a magnificent film actress: in supporting roles in *Portrait of Jennie* (48), as a Mother Superior; and *The Cobweb* (55), as the almoner of a mental home, kindly beneath a brisk exterior. In a leading role in Charles Laughton's *The Night of the Hunter*, a philanthropic spinster who looks after the beleaguered children, she played sharply, against convention; and she had another goodish role, as the hero's mother, in the British anti-war *Orders to Kill* (58), made by Anthony Asquith. She was the mother of Burt Lancaster iin *The Unforgiven* (60); and was in Disney's *Follow Me Boys* (66), *Warning Shot* and *The Comedians* (67), with Paul Ford making some scenes bearable of that disaster.

In 1932 she published 'Life and Lillian Gish' and in 1969 'The Movies, Mr Griffith and Me'. She was awarded a special Oscar in 1971; and she made her dramatic television début in *Twin Detectives* (76), who were Jon and Jim Haber, who had hoped that it might lead to a series. She returned to films in Altman's *The Wedding* (78), dying upstairs as the bride's grandmother, and she was a grandmother again, for television, in *Thin Ice* (81); also in that medium she headed the supporting cast of *Hobson's Choice* (83), which starred Richard Thomas and moved the action to New Orleans. She was engaged to play a role in *The Bostonians*, but ceded to Jessica Tandy when offered a larger one in *Hambone and Hillie* (84), the story of a little dog looking for his missing mistress. She was Mrs Loftus in *Adventures of Huckleberry Finn* (85), a TV mini-series which became a tele-movie the following year. She had a telling couple of scenes as Alan Alda's senile mother in *Sweet Liberty* (86), but then had a large role as Bette Davis's caring sister in *The Whales of August* (87). Survivors both. In the case of Gish it is extraordinary. Movies practically began with her and she is still, fortunately, active.

She has never married. She and her sister Dorothy were very close until the latter died in 1968. Dorothy also had a successful career, parallel to her sister's in many ways, including the fading from films when Sound came; and she was an agreeable actress in her own right.

PAULETTE GODDARD

When Charles Chaplin Jr published his memoir of his father, Paulette Goddard found herself the heroine. The author wrote that he and his brother 'looked into that friendly face with its mischievous, conspiratorial smile and we lost our hearts at once'; later he added, 'She wasn't just pretty. She was warm and enthusiastic about everything.' Thus did wartime audiences also fall for her. She had no outstanding ability as a dramatic actress and she played comedy with verve rather than finesse: indeed, Ray Milland, who acted with her several times, observed that she could not play comedy, since she had no sense of timing. But she worked hard, he went on – and they did wonders in the editing. She was also vivacious, pert and *very* pretty. She would probably have made it to the top even without Chaplin.

She was born in Great Neck, Long Island, in 1911; the home broke up and she became a breadwinner at an early age. At 14 she was a Ziegfeld girl and she had some lines in 'No Foolin'; she had a small role in 'Rio Rita' and then married – Edgar James, a timber magnate – and retired. When her marriage broke up she and Mother headed for Hollywood and she got bit parts in *The Girl Habit* (31), *The Mouthpiece* (32) and *The Kid From Spain*. She was a Goldwyn Girl in the latter and that got her a job at Roach. When Chaplin met her – on Joseph Schenck's yacht – she was just another blonde about Hollywood. She was about to invest her $500,000 alimony in a phoney film venture and he prevented that; he also bought her contract from Roach and persuaded her to let her hair grow back to its original brunette. *Modern Times* was conceived as a vehicle for them both: he began the script in 1932 and the film was not premièred until 1936 (in which year they were

supposedly married at sea). He coached her unceasingly in the part of the gamine, but in the finished film it appears to be a performance of complete spontaneity – and is quite delightful.

Among Chaplin's projects over the next few years were several for his wife (including one with Gary Cooper – a script that eventually saw the light as *A Countess From Hong Kong*), but he worked so slowly that she began to get restless in case the public forgot her. Eventually it was agreed that she might test for the part of Scarlett O'Hara. Selznick liked her enough to sign her and for a long time she was a favourite for the part. In the meantime he put her in a comedy, *The Young in Heart* (38), with Janet Gaynor, and loaned her to MGM for the undramatic *Dramatic School* with Luise Rainer and then to be one of *The Women* (39). Her first star part was opposite Bob Hope in *The Cat and the Canary* at Paramount. That studio wanted her for another film with Hope and Selznick did not want her for Scarlett, so he sold her contract to Paramount. Thus she was again a frightened heroine in *The Ghost Breakers* (40). She had a smallish role, as a gypsy, in *North West Mounted Police*, but then was Fred Astaire's co-star in *Second Chorus*: she had one dance with him and the chance to get to know Burgess Meredith, whom she later married. Intermittently she was working with Chaplin on *The Great Dictator* – now much less harmoniously: she was established and experienced and he was exacting. In his autobiography he says that he was angered by her agent's demands over billing. At all events, they separated in 1942 without, apparently, bitterness on either side.

Meanwhile Paramount loaned her to UA for a dim 'swing' musical with James Stewart, *Pot o' Gold* (41), which was produced by one of Roosevelt's sons; and gave her second lead in *Hold Back the Dawn*, where her brittle gaiety contrasted with the spinster schoolteacher, Olivia de Havilland. But back with Bob Hope in *Nothing But the Truth*, one of the year's top grossers, she was the star; and the studio began to give her more important vehicles. *The Lady Has Plans* (42) with Ray Milland, was a witless spy film, followed by another with Milland, marginally more enjoyable, De Mille's *Reap the Wild Wind*: her role was clearly designed to compensate her for not getting Scarlett O'Hara, even if it had been offered first to Katharine Hepburn. *The Forest Rangers* was more spectacle – a forest fire – with Fred MacMurray. She did a number with Dorothy Lamour and Veronica Lake in *Star Spangled Rhythm*; was in a poor comedy with Milland, *The Crystal Ball* (43), which Paramount cleverly sold to United

Paulette Goddard and Ray Milland made four films together, of which the first was this one, The Lady Has Plans (*42*). *It was also one of the year's silliest films.*

Artists; then a war drama, *So Proudly We Hail* (nurses), with Claudette Colbert and Lake. With MacMurray there was *Standing Room Only* (44) in overcrowded Washington and with Sonny Tufts *I Love a Soldier* – only the trouble was she appeared to love them all.

She was now among the top two or three women stars at Paramount and was re-signed to a new seven-year pact. She had a whole-some quality that set her apart from the other wartime pin-ups, but now that she or the studio were bent on making her a dramatic actress, it began to disappear. *Kitty* (45) was from a novel by Rosamund Marshall and it had a plot almost identical to *Forever Amber*, only this guttersnipe got started by a liaison with a painter, Gainsborough (Cecil Kell-away); then it veered towards Pygmalion, with Milland as the Professor. It was reasonably free of anachronism, handsome to look at, less dull than *Amber* and a big success. She

guested in *Duffy's Tavern* and then gave probably her best performance, in Renoir's *Diary of a Chambermaid* (46), produced by him and husband Meredith, who also acted in it: indeed she is as good as (though different from) Jeanne Moreau in the later Buñuel version of Octave Mirbeau's novel (just as the films are different and excellent: gay-black and grey-grim respectively). There was a weak comedy with MacMurray, *Suddenly It's Spring* (47), a guest spot in *Variety Girl* and then more costume pictures: De Mille's mam-moth and boring *Unconquered*, with Gary Cooper, where she was a slave girl lusted after by Howard Da Silva in the New World – probably her worst performance.

She was allowed one outside film a year and she signed a deal with Korda. At first he announced a *Carmen* for her, but instead she did his version of Wilde's *An Ideal Husband* with Michael Wilding: she was Mrs Chevely

Paulette Goddard didn't make many good films, but Diary of a Chambermaid *(46) was certainly one of them. With her here, in a character role, is her husband at the time, Burgess Meredith, playing the neighbour who, like every other male in the film, was mad for her.*

and one of the few lively things about that film. It did not do well in the States and was indeed one of the turkeys which virtually finished her career. The others were *Hazard* (48), a so-called comedy with Macdonald Carey; *On Our Merry Way*, an episode comedy with Goddard and Meredith as the link, and a weak link it was; and *Bride of Vengeance* (49) in which she played Lucrezia Borgia. Ray Milland said that it was the only film he refused to do during his 21 years at Paramount. He added: 'Richard Maibaum was the producer, Mitchell Leisen was the director, John Lund replaced me, Paulette Goddard, John Sutton, Albert Decker. Every one of them was fired after the film was previewed.' This is presumably an oversimplification, but Goddard did not work for Paramount again, despite an astonishing new contract running to 1959, for only five films. In 1952, Paramount paid her $100,000 for *not*

making two of these five movies and presumably did not back her when she campaigned for the role of the Elephant Girl in De Mille's *The Greatest Show on Earth*. The studio said that they had recalled her to make the remaining three films: in 1954 they announced that Goddard had fulfilled the contract.

She made a version of *Anna Lucasta* in which the original Negro community became white, but despite the notoriety which the play had had (Anna was a whore), the film did poor business (the producers had wanted Susan Hayward, but Goddard had had a prior claim on the material); and her next job was in a Mexican film with Pedro Armendariz, *The Torch* (50), where 'both [her] appearance and talent [are] out of place' ('Variety'). He, Armendariz, played a bandit and she was a Mexican aristocrat. Her Hollywood career trailed off in a seris of B films with pretensions – *Babes in Baghdad* (52), an Arabian Nights lark with Gypsy Rose Lee, produced by the Danziger brothers before they favoured British audiences with their B pictures; *Vice Squad* (53) with Edward G. Robinson; *Paris Model* with Marilyn Maxwell, a four-part film – she was in only one of the episodes; *The Sins of Jezebel*, in which she was a Biblical queen; and *The Charge of the Lancers* (54) with Jean-Pierre Aumont, in which she was a gypsy girl. She returned to Britain for *The Stranger Came Home*, one of the dreadful second features of the 50s with passé Hollywood names made in an effort to get bookings in the US market (in this case by the people who later became Hammer Films). In 1958 she married Erich Maria Remarque and gave up any serious thought of working; later, she said, 'I never took my career seriously like some actresses.' Some years later she did do an Italian movie, from a Moravia novel, *Gli Indifferenti* (64). Despite a distinguished cast – it includes Rod Steiger – it was not much seen. A rare TV appearance was in *The Snoop Sisters* (72), as an ageing movie queen. Whether Goddard will film again is debatable. She would not do it for the money. She does not need it: her jewellery collection is famous.

BETTY GRABLE

'Her special forte was the backstage musical in which her famous legs were put on display on the most absurd of pretexts. Miss Grable's beauty – if that is the word for it – was of the common sort. Nor did she offer much in the way of character or maturity. She was, at best, a sort of great American floozie, and her appeal to lonely GIs was surely that of every hash-house waitress with whom they ever flirted': such is Richard Schickel's judgment on Betty Grable in his book 'The Stars'. She herself, looking back, was hardly kinder: 'As a dancer I couldn't outdance Ginger Rogers or Eleanor Powell. As a singer I'm no rival to Doris Day. As an actress I don't take myself seriously. I had a little bit of looks yet without being in the big beauty league. Maybe I had sincerity. And warmth. Those qualities are essential. I don't think I've ever had a good review. My films didn't get them either. Yet they did well at the box-office' (to interviewer James Green of the London 'Evening News'). Had she wanted to, Grable might have boasted more of that box-office glow: she really had her contemporaries beaten. She was one of the exhibitors' Golden 10 in the US for 10 consecutive years – for four of them the top female draw, with Greer Garson the runner-up. The British preferred Garson and nowhere outside the US was Grable's home

popularity equalled. She was very American, she *was* like a hash-house waitress – but in a nicer way than Schickel intended: she was bright, friendly, brash and comfortable. She was one of the crowd.

Certainly it took Hollywood long enough to distinguish her among the ranks of starlets. She was born in St Louis in 1916 and when she was 12 she went with her mother to Los Angeles to study dancing – and in no time was in the chorus line, blacked-up with 63 other girls, in a film musical called *Let's Go Places* (30), at Fox; they signed her to a year's contract as a chorus girl and she could be glimpsed briefly in *New Movietone Follies of 1930*. She was dropped as the All-Singing All-Dancing phase abated and was one of 1,500 girls who applied to Golden to appear in *Whoopee*: she became a Goldwyn Girl with a five-year contract, a new name – Frances Dean – and bits in *Kiki* (31), also reputedly teaching Mary Pickford her dance-steps in that, *Palmy Days*, *The Greeks Had a Word for Them* (32) and *The Kid from Spain*, with a huge close-up as she sings the opening song. Dropped by him, she got some parts in some Educational shorts and a role in *Probation* at Chesterfield, a love story with Sally Blane. RKO signed her and made her the romantic interest – along with Edna May Oliver – in a Wheeler and Woolsey comedy, *Hold 'em Jail*. Plans were made to make her a star, but once again she was footloose and in bit parts: *Cavalcade* (33) and *Child of Manhattan*, as Nancy Carroll's fellow dance-hostess. The latter was made at Columbia, who gave her a similar role, Jean Parker's pal, in *What Price Innocence?*, a tale of juvenile delinquents; she was a stewardess in *Melody Cruise* at RKO and then on tour with 'Tattle Tales', with Barbara Stanwyck, which was followed by eight months' singing with Ted Fiorito and his band – with whom she appeared in *Sweetheart of Sigma Chi*. That led to a role in an MGM musical with Jimmy Durante, *Student Tour* (34), and a duet with Edward Everett Horton in *The Gay Divorcée*, 'Let's Knock Knees'. On the basis of that RKO signed her again and put her into *By Your Leave*, a Frank Morgan vehicle. She toured with the studio's comedy team, Wheeler and Woolsey, and was a murder suspect in their *The Nitwits* (35), which George Stevens directed; she played a coed in both *Old Man Rhythm*, with Charles 'Buddy' Rogers, and *Collegiate* (36) at Paramount, with Joe Penner and Jack Oakie. She was hardly to be glimpsed in *Follow the Fleet* and then, after an appearance in a thriller, *Don't Turn 'Em Loose*, that was exactly what RKO did with her. She had a biggish role as a coed in *Pigskin Parade* at 20th, but that studio was not interested.

Betty Grable made almost 30 films before becoming a star. Here she is, left, in one of them, Man About Town (*39*) *with Binnie Barnes, Jack Benny, Dorothy Lamour and, behind, Edward Arnold and Phil Harris.*

At that time the former child star, Jackie Coogan, was limbering up for the later court case for the possession of his earnings; on a wave of publicity he embarked on a vaudeville tour and Grable was part of the entourage; they were married in 1937, simultaneously with a crisis at Paramount, over an unimportant movie called *This Way Please* (37), starring Charles 'Buddy' Rogers (his last for the studio) and Shirley Ross. Also in the cast was Jack Benny's wife, Mary Livingstone, and as Benny beefed up her part Ross walked out. Grable replaced her, as the usherette who falls in love with a Hollywood idol, and she was put into a B opposite Leif Erickson, *Thrill of a Lifetime*, as the secretary he realizes he loves when she takes off her glasses. Paramount was thrilled, signing her to a contract and planning a publicity campaign to push her into major stardom. Her sunny personality certainly suited the cheerful comedies the studio turned out: *College Swing* (38), in which Burns and Allen inherit a school and employ some vaudevillians, including Martha Raye; *Give Me a Sailor*, as Raye's sister;

Campus Confessions, a B with William Henry; and *Man About Town* (39) with Jack Benny and just one song – which she had filmed before she became ill: the rest of the role was taken over by Dorothy Lamour. Paramount, like Goldwyn, decided that she was not ready for stardom and after decorating *Million Dollar Legs* (not hers, the football team's) she was dropped.

She returned to Vaudeville until RKO offered a role in a B, *The Day Bookies Wept*, as Joe Penner's girlfriend. She went to New York for the second lead in 'Du Barry Was a Lady' – not very enthusiastically, for she had no illusions about her singing voice: but the show was a hit and so was she. Columnists stopped referring to her as 'Coogan's Ex'. More importantly, 20th now wanted her to sign a contract, feeling they could promote her where the others had failed. She was on tour with 'Du Barry' when Alice Faye went down with appendicitis and 20th needed her at once for *Down Argentine Way* (40), replacing Faye opposite Don Ameche. It was in colour, which greatly enhanced Grable's appeal. The studio was pleased and cast her as Faye's sister in *Tin Pan Alley*, then as one of three girls seeking millionaire husbands in *Moon Over Miami* (41).

That one was a favourite plot at 20th (she later played in one of its remakes) and it established Grable as a fairly mercenary charmer, on-the-make career-wise if nothing else. She was seldom on the level and the plots had to do with the leading man discovering this the hard way and getting reconciled to it in time for the final fade-out. It was always the same plot – backstage romancing – with almost identical routines. The dialogue was witless, the direction featureless, most of the supporting cast talentless. The same dearth of imagination hit the ads: *Pin Up Girl* was labelled 'The Zenith of Musicals', not capitalizing on Grable's popularity with the troops. First off were two straight movies: *A Yank in the RAF*, as Tyrone Power's snappy sweetheart, and *I Wake Up Screaming* (42), uncovering the murderer of her sister, Carole Landis. She looked fetching in Technicolor in a grass skirt in *Song of the Islands*, scrapping with Victor Mature, and she did her third in a row with him, *Footlight Serenade*, he as a boxer, she as a showgirl, but John Payne was her romantic interest. It was her last in black and white: she had entered the Top 10 (at No. 8) and in 1943 she would be No. 1. A grateful studio promised Technicolor for all Grable vehicles as long as she was under contract. They also insured her legs with Lloyds of London for £250,000 (cf. Fred Astaire's at £200,000, Dietrich's at £175,000).

While the armies of the Allies drooled over those legs, on clippings pinned above their beds, she cheered them in escapist nonsense: *Springtime in the Rockies* with Payne and bandleader Harry James, who became her second husband and the most envied man in the world; *Coney Island* (43) with George Montgomery and *Sweet Rosie O'Grady* with Robert Young, both period pieces to allow her to strut in a bustle; *Four Jills in a Jeep*, back to monochrome for a guest appearance; *Pin Up Girl* with John Harvey; and *Billy Rose's Diamond Horseshoe* (45) with Dick Haymes. These generally innocuous leading men were chosen, like the material, to disguise her limitations. As the troops came home, Grable and June Haver were *The Dolly Sisters* (46), one of the year's top money-makers, even if turned a true story into the same tired concoction. But 20th seemed to be mindful at last of the poor reviews and cast Grable in a period piece with rediscovered Gershwin songs, *The Shocking Miss Pilgrim* (47) – shocking because she was a typist. Her character was softened and there was another untypical vehicle, *Mother Wore Tights*, with

'Welcome to the Diamond Horseshoe' sang Betty Grable in a musical set in and around the nightclub of that name. The film was called that too (45).

her as Mother ('Are you being quite fair, Mikie? Do you think your friends would stop liking you because your parents are on the stage?'). Dan Dailey was Father and the film was liked by press and public (though its charm is singularly elusive today). A third attempt to get her out of the rut, *That Lady in Ermine* (48), was liked by neither; Douglas Fairbanks Jr co-starred in this mock-Ruritanian piece directed by Lubitsch for a week before his death (it was finished – off – by Otto Preminger).

She was re-teamed with Dailey in *When My Baby Smiles at Me*, a re-run of 'Burlesque', and then turned over to Preston Sturges for a further attempt at classy material: *The Beautiful Blonde From Bashful Bend* (49), playing a saloon singer masquerading as a schoolmarm, but this misjudged tramp round Li'l Abner territory played double bills. Having failed yet again to interest the carriage trade, the studio gave up and sent her to *Wabash Avenue* (50) with Mature, which was simple *Coney Island* revisited. *My Blue Heaven*, some sentiment about old troupers wanting kids, and *Call Me Mister* (51), from a Broadway show about troop entertainers, showed merely that there was a diminishing audience for the Grable-Dailey team. She was still a big draw according to exhibitors (No. 3 in 1951), but 20th accountants knew differently: besides, a young girl called Mitzi Gaynor had stolen the

notices of *My Blue Heaven* and was having a vehicle called *Golden Girl* built for her. And the 20th musical was a dead duck, killed by what was happening in this field at MGM. In 1952, Grable was suspended for refusing *The Girl Next Door* – which June Haver did. 20th announced some ambitious plans, including remakes, with music, of *Heaven Can Wait* and *Bad Girl*. They also planned *Gentlemen Prefer Blondes* for her. None of these she did and a year later she was suspended for refusing *Pick-Up on South Street*, which Jean Peters did. 20th did finally take a leaf from Metro's book and gave Grable a good (Harold Arlen) score, lovely (Lake Erie) locations and *no* backstage plot for *The Farmer Takes a Wife* (53), a remake of the Janet Gaynor film, but the Metro magic was missing and it was released as the lower half of double bills.

The golden girl at 20th was not, in the end, Gaynor, but Marilyn Monroe and she usurped Grable's position as surely as Grable had earlier usurped Faye's; and it was the still-new Monroe who got top-billing on the ads for *How to Marry a Millionaire*, though Grable was first on the screen credits. Grable said she was delighted to do it, as she had had one line in the original (*The Greeks Had a Word for Them*). Her gold-digger was one of her most endearing performances, but it came third to those of Monroe and Lauren Bacall. Monroe's biographer Zolotow reports that Grable told Monroe: 'Honey, I've had it. Go get yours. It's your turn now.' Later, Monroe took over her dressing-room.

20th loaned her to Columbia – at a fee of $150,000 – for a musical remake of Jean Arthur's *Too Many Husbands* called *Three for the Show* (55), but reviews and business were poor. 20th tried once more with Grable, cast again as a wise-cracking showgirl, but the film, a campus comedy, *How to Be Very Very Popular* (55), was a damp squib; and its publicity ignored Grable to focus on co-star Sheree North and how 20th had *her* ready to take Monroe's place should the latter become very, very difficult. Most of the publicity that Grable got was about her now being out in the cold. She signed with United Artists to produce her own movies. Nothing came of this and she joined husband Harry James in Las Vegas.

After sitting around there for a year or two (the marriage ended after 20 years in 1965), she accepted leads in café-musicals, most notably 'Guys and Dolls'; she also did 'Born Yesterday' and was one of the Broadway Dollies ('Hello Dolly'). In 1969 in London she starred in the disastrous 'Belle Starr' and got warm personal notices (though less for what she did than what she was). As she also said to James Green: 'All I want to do is please the public. I'm a professional and always set out to do the best I can.' In 1972 she was announced as being off to tour Australia in 'No No Nanette', but was prevented by illness. She died of cancer a year later.

CARY GRANT

In 1935 (he had made more than 20 films and was officially a star) Cary Grant received less than one per cent of the votes cast in the 'Motion Picture Herald' poll to find the year's top attractions. Within two years he had become one of the most sought-after leading men and in the mid-40s he edged into the list of the top 10 draws. He was in there twice more in that decade and then, after a break, came in at second in 1959 – and stayed there through eight consecutive years. When he and the century entered their 60s, much was made of his continuing popularity, looks and youthfulness. He was everyone's favourite uncle, brother, best friend and ideal lover: more than most stars he belonged to the public. When his fourth wife divorced him and in court did a thorough character-assassination job on him, no one cared, no one was interested – they looked the other way. He really was charismatic. He stayed young. We loved Gable, Crosby, Cooper as much, but they aged. The appeal of many of them lay in familiarity: unlike us and the world, Grant was changeless.

It was his elegance, his casualness, his unaccented charm; he was, as Tom Wolfe put it, 'consummately romantic and consummately genteel'. It certainly was not from acting ability: his range must be the most limited of all the great matinée idols. His gift for light comedy has been much touted, but it has been a mite heavy at times and one can think of half a dozen names who were sometimes better. Katharine Hepburn (interviewed by Roy Newquist) once summed him up: 'Cary Grant, I think, is a personality functioning. A delicious personality who has learnt to do certain things marvellously well. He can't play a serious part or, let me say, the public isn't interested in him that way, not interested in him at all, which I'm sure has been a big bugaboo to him. But he has a lovely sense of timing, an amusing face and a lovely voice.'

Grant was born in Bristol in 1904, into what is known as a 'broken home'. There was a theatrical tradition (one of his grandfathers had been an actor) and he became callboy at Bristol Hippodrome, joining, without parental permission, a company who were appearing there, Bob Pender's troupe of acrobats. With them he sang, danced and juggled, and with them he travelled to the US in 1920. He liked it there and decided to stay; after the

troupe had returned home, he did odd jobs (he sold painted neck-ties, did a vaudeville stint with a mind-reading act). In 1923, he went back to Britain and managed to get some small parts in musical comedies. Arthur Hammerstein saw him and took him back to New York to play the juvenile in 'Golden Dawn', a musical written by Oscar Hammerstein II; then Grant was in 'Polly' with Fred Allen and 'Boom-Boom' with Jeanette MacDonald (they were both screen-tested, but nothing came of it). He did some operettas in St Louis and then returned to New York to appear in 'Nikki' (based on the same novel as the movie *The Last Flight*), playing Cary Lockwood (hence the first half of his screen name; his own name was Archie Leach). When it folded he went to Hollywood and was hired by Paramount to feed lines to an actress being tested: he got a contract and she did not. He started at $450 a week, in a good part in *This Is the Night* (32), a musical about the European luxury set starring Charles Ruggles, Lily Damita and Roland Young.

He had supporting roles in *Sinners in the Sun*, *Merrily We Go to Hell* and *The Devil and the Deep*, then was spotlighted as the cause of Dietrich's ruination in *Blonde Venus*. Paramount were excited by Grant: they announced a *Blood and Sand* for him and Tallulah Bankhead, seeing him as a successor to Gary Cooper. Instead he did a couple that Cooper had turned down: *Hot Saturday*, topbilled in this tale about teenagers (playing 'the dour he-man lover somewhat woodenly' – 'Picturegoer') and *Madame Butterfly*, as Pinkerton to Sylvia Sidney's Madame. Mae West's story that Grant was an extra when she picked him for *She Done Him Wrong* (33) is clearly untrue, but exposure with her did not harm him any; however, he was not helped by *The Woman Accused* starring Nancy Carroll, which was religiously based on a 10-part magazine serial by 10 different writers (including Zane Grey and Vickie Baum). In *The Eagle and the Hawk* he was an aviator; in *Gambling Ship* a gangster; in *I'm No Angel* another of Mae West's victims; in *Alice in Wonderland* the Mock Turtle; in *30-Day Princess* (34) a publisher; in *Born to Be Bad* (at 20th-UA) a millionaire; and in *Kiss and Make Up*, with Genevieve Tobin, a beauty specialist. From time to time he struck a spark, but he was exceptionally heavy-handed in *Ladies Should Listen*, involved with several of said ladies; then there was *Enter Madame* (35), Elissa Landi; *Wings in the Dark* as a blind man; and *The Last Outpost*, moustached.

RKO borrowed him to play a Cockney con-man in *Sylvia Scarlett* (36) opposite Katharine Hepburn, with Cukor directing. Cukor found

Again Puccini without the music: Sylvia Sidney as Cio-Cio-San and Cary Grant as the unfaithful Pinkerton in a rather foolish film made by Paramount in 1932.

him 'rather wooden . . . inexperienced, too' but noted that for the first time since he had been an actor 'he felt all his talents coming into being . . . he suddenly burst into bloom'. It was a part in which Grant felt at home. MGM borrowed him for Jean Harlow's *Suzy*, sandwiched between two on his home lot with Joan Bennett, *Big Brown Eyes*, one of the better imitations of *The Thin Man*, and *Wedding Present*. That concluded his contract. He asked for control over his parts before re-signing, but Paramount would not grant it, so he did not.

He took himself off to his homeland to do the Sound remake of E. Phillips Oppenheim's *The Amazing Quest of Ernest Bliss*, which flopped. In Britain it was retitled *A Rich Young Man* and in the US it turned up as *Romance and Riches*. Grant hurried back to Hollywood, where he was surprised to find himself much in demand – mostly as a result of the Hepburn and Harlow movies. He signed joint contracts with RKO and Columbia, with script approval – and few stars ever made a wiser move: from the doldrums of *Ernest Bliss* he went into some of the best films of the period. True, luck played a good part in it, for though both studios were rich in talent, little of it was in the male-star category (Paramount, MGM and Warners had the big

actors of the period).

Not that it started auspiciously: Grace Moore's leading man in *When You're in Love* (37) and a conventional part of the friend of hero (or anti-hero) Edward Arnold in *The Toast of New York*. But at the Roach studios he was one of the ghosts in *Topper*, with Constance Bennett, giving the first real proof that he had been polishing and indeed burnishing his comic style. Back and forth between his two studios he went, getting better and better: *The Awful Truth*, brilliantly flippant with Irene Dunne; and a couple with Hepburn, the hilarious, slapstick *Bringing Up Baby* (38) – baby was a leopard – and the quieter *Holiday*. *Baby* had been turned down by Ray Milland, Robert Montgomery and Ronald Colman; and Grant was able to do it when *The Pioneers* with Jean Arthur was cancelled. It was a triumph for him. Said Basil Wright: 'Cary Grant, adept by now at knockabout, adds real wit and acting ability.' There were two super and popular adventure films, *Gunga Din* (39), directed by George Stevens, 'inspired' by Kipling's poem ('Cary Grant makes a perfect Cockney soldier – goodnatured, pugnacious, optimistic' – 'Film Weekly'), and Howard Hawks's *Only Angels Have Wings*, batting insults marvellously with Jean Arthur; but the year finished lamely with

To judge from the many movies set on outposts of the British Empire, that was something which amazed and fascinated the Hollywood moguls. Most of them are rousing adventure yarns, still exciting to see, and none is better than Gunga Din (39), which used Kipling's poem for a tale of three fearless brothers-in-arms – Victor McLaglen, Cary Grant and, not seen here, Douglas Fairbanks Jr.

years. There was a long grim war film at Warners, *Destination Tokyo*, and a further comic deterioration, *Once Upon a Time* (44), about a boy with a dancing caterpillar, with Janet Blair (intended for Bogart and Rita Hayworth, till she turned it down). But *Arsenic and Old Lace* was a pippin, as adapted from Howard Lindsay and Russell Crouse's black farce and Broadway hit, with Jean Adair and Josephine Hull as the dear old killers and Grant as their understandably manic nephew. The ladies had filmed it during their vacation from the New York production, in fact in December 1941, for Frank Capra had produced and directed it speedily before leaving for the army. Because of the quick shoot and the war, Grant asked only $100,000 for his services, which he gave to War Relief charities. The contracts specified that it could not be released till the Broadway run finished.

Grant was anxious to play the Cockney tramp hero of Richard Llewellyn's bestseller *None But the Lonely Heart*, directed and screen-played by Clifford Odets, and he was Oscar-nominated: but the film did not click. And Cole Porter was anxious to have Grant play him in his biopic, *Night and Day* (46) – or so he pretended: in fact, he made the suggestion facetiously to WB, but they took him at his word. Grant got $150,000 for a film with almost no relation to fact, some good tunes and indifferent acting. Monty Woolley played Porter's friend instead of his lover and the film has an added piquancy with the revelations about Grant after his death. It did well in a year of big musicals, but not as well as Hitchcock's *Notorious*, with government agent Grant, among the plotters of Rio, trying to get Ingrid Bergman on 'our' side. Even more popular was *The Bachelor and the Bobby Soxer* (47), one of the year's top hits. Three more comedies – the mushy *The Bishop's Wife* with Loretta Young, the agreeable *Mr Blanding Builds His Dream House* (48) with Myrna Loy and *Every Girl Should Be Married*, with Betsy Drake – did not quite make it into the golden money-makers, but Hawks's *I Was a Male War Bride* (49), with Ann Sheridan, stands on the 'Variety' list as a huge earner. Grant was the bride and the plot's convolutions caused him at one point to appear in drag: one instance where he skated easily on perilously thin ice.

He was no longer tied to any studio and his price went up to $200,000 per film, but it is doubtful whether MGM found it worthwhile for Richard Brooks's gloomy if gripping tale of South American politicking, *Crisis* (50); or 20th for Mankiewicz's *People Will Talk* (51) and how they did! Nor were there any flags out for *Room for One More* (52) with Drake, a comedy about kids. Drake was a discovery

a conveyor-belt drama, *In Name Only* (Kay Francis was the wife and Carole Lombard the Other Woman).

More comedy: *His Girl Friday* (40) with Rosalind Russell; *My Favorite Wife* with Dunne; a break for *The Howards of Virginia* with Martha Scott, a hopeless family saga set at the time of the American Revolution and one of Grant's worst late performances; *The Philadelphia Story* with Hepburn at MGM; and the tender *Penny Serenade* (41) with Dunne. His salary at this time was $150,000 per film. Another break for a serious film, Hitchcock's *Suspicion*, silly but successful (you knew damned well he was not going to murder Joan Fontaine, whatever *she* thought); then, Stevens's *The Talk of the Town* (42) with Jean Arthur and Ronald Colman, followed by two even thinner comedies, *Once Upon a Honeymoon*, running round Nazi Europe with Ginger Rogers, and *Mr Lucky* (43). Because the latter gave him a basically serious role – his first for years, he considered – he was particularly fond of the film, believing it prolonged his career by 20 of his, a delightful actress and the longest lasting (1949–59) of his wives. The others: Virginia Cherill (1933–35), who had been in *City Lights*; Woolworth heiress Barbara Hutton (1942–45); actress Dyan Cannon (1965–68), the mother of his daughter; and secretary Barbara Harris (1981 and his widow). Revelations of homosexuality after his death surprised few, especially those who had seen the publicity stills of Grant and Randolph Scott keeping house in the 30s, issued innocently till Paramount became alarmed that people were reading the real implications of the situation. Since both stars behaved blatantly over the relationship, they may have been testing the morals clause in their contracts. Late in life Grant sued for libel when Robin Williams referred to him on television as gay: he won the case and gave the proceeds to homosexual charities.

Monkey Business was another Hawks comedy, about rejuvenation, notable only for Marilyn Monroe's cameo; and *Dream Wife* (53) an engaging enough trifle with Deborah Kerr which suffered a fate common to films at that time with waning stars – going out without benefit of press-showings, showcasing and ballyhoo. It was MGM that did that to Grant. The fan magazines decided he was through (though it was not known at the time, he had changed his mind at the last minute about doing both *Sabrina* – the Bogart role – and *A Star Is Born*, two of 1954's biggest hits; earlier a one-picture deal with Korda had fallen through and Grant had thus missed *The Third Man*).

It was Hitchcock who brought him back, making nice music with Grace Kelly in *To Catch a Thief* (55), proving that two years' absence and *Dream Wife* had not impaired his appeal. He was absent again for a bit, filming *The Pride and the Passion* (57) in Spain – 'It's just a big circus' was Grant's own comment. Stanley Kramer directed from a C.S. Forester novel about the Peninsular War. Grant was disastrously miscast and the film dreary, but it did finally make back its enormous cost. He made up for lost time by immediately making *An Affair to Remember* with Kerr, Leo McCarey's poor but popular remake of his own 1939 *Love Affair*, and *Kiss Them For Me*, a wartime comedy that was the first film of Grandon, the production company set up by Grant and Stanley Donen. It was a bad start: reviews were fair, but antipathy to co-star Jayne Mansfield severely limited bokings.

The next one atoned: *Indiscreet* (58), not a better film, but Bergman was in it and audiences responded warmly; and *Houseboat* (59) was pleasant, though, like most comedies of this time, elongated. Sophia Loren was the girl and she said that she learnt more from playing with Grant than any other actor. Another big one followed, *North by Northwest*, a classic 'running man' concoction of Hitchcock's – he said he wanted Grant because audiences could identify with him. *Operation Petticoat* (60) was the beginning of Grant's association with Universal and probably the biggest financial hit of his career; as with the majority of his subsequent films, most of the profits went to him: Universal was in a slump and generously permitted him 75 per cent of the profits – and he made about

Cary Grant in two of the most fondly-remembered of his late films, both thrillers: left, To Catch a Thief *(55) with Grace Kelly, directed by Alfred Hitchcock, who regarded him as one of his favourite leading men; and right* Charade *(63), with Audrey Hepburn, directed by Stanley Donen. Incidentally, Grant didn't do badly where his co-stars were concerned, moving from Jean Arthur and Irene Dunne to the classiest ladies of the next generation.*

$3 million from this. The last production of Grandon, *The Grass is Greener* – he was an English earl with Deborah Kerr as his wife – just broke even. Then he made another $3 million with another smash comedy, *That Touch of Mink* (62), with Doris Day. Grant was unique among Hollywood stars in handling his own business activities: and he had full control over every aspect of the films he made. *Charade* (63) was a tongue-in-cheek thriller with Audrey Hepburn. Less successful were *Father Goose* (64), though sustaining brilliantly a noteworthy performance as a grouchy beach bum who is tamed by prim schoolmistress Leslie Caron; and *Walk Don't Run* (66) with Samantha Eggar – *The More the Merrier* remade with Grant in the Charles Coburn part, set against the Tokyo Olympics.

The general opinion was that these films were not worthy of everyone's favourite (old) film star. Well, he chose them. No one else of his generation, except John Wayne, looked so good to the money-men, but he refused all film offers and became a director of Rayett-Fabergé, engrossed, apparently, in big business. Queried about his future in 1969 he said: 'I'm not really making pictures and I don't know whether I'll ever make any – or whether I'll make one or 10.' He did not need the money and he probably did not expect an Oscar – though in 1970 he was given a special one for sheer 'brilliance' in the acting business. Among the roles he turned down was one in *Heaven Can Wait* (78). He died of a stroke in 1986 in Iowa, on his way to one of his Q & A sessions, 'A Conversation with Cary Grant'. He holds one record unlikely to be broken: 28 of his movies played the Radio City Music Hall, said to have had the pick of all films scheduled to play New York, for a total playing time of 113 weeks (runners-up are Katharine Hepburn: 22 pictures and 64 weeks; Fred Astaire: 16 pictures and 60 weeks).

ANN HARDING

Ann Harding: once a name to conjure with, now a lingering memory of serene loveliness and dignity. She was one of the screen's aristocrats and sometimes she seemed aware of it; but she brought wit and sympathy to a series of heavy-breathing melodramas and in so doing brought them a reality they did not deserve. Her method was partly to break her sentences in a way that is entirely modern: hours after seeing her in a film, the sheer humanity of her reading remains to haunt the spectator – and indeed the warmth of the whole interpretation. It is a shame that she is

not better known.

She was born in 1902 at Fort Sam Houston, Texas, the daughter of an army officer, and educated at Bryn Mawr, whence she went to work for an insurance company. She also worked in Paramount's reading department and friends there persuaded her to join the Provincetown Players for recreation: she made her first appearance with them in 'The Inheritors' (21). Her 'recreation' that summer led to a New York offer – 'Like a King' – and she embarked on an acting career, despite parental disapproval. In Philadelphia she appeared in Ibsen and Shaw, and had her first big New York success in 'Tarnish' (23); at one point she returned to stock in Detroit, but was a New York favourite – culminating in a long run in 'The Trial of Mary Dugan' (27). During that run, she was offered the role of Lena in 'Strange Interlude', but her producer refused to release her; she did tour with it, in 1929, with Harry Bannister, whom she had married in 1926. When he was offered film work he went with him to Hollywood, to find herself receive five immediate offers.

She chose to do *Paris Bound* (29), Philip Barry's domestic comedy, with Fredric March, on a one-picture deal at Pathé, who subsequently signed her to a seven-year contract. In a dramatic role in *Her Private Affair* she was unforgettable, conscience-stricken after committing a *crime passionel*, with John Loder; in *Condemned*, she was married to cruel warden Louis Wolheim and in love with prisoner Ronald Colman – with alternate endings (happy and unhappy) for Europe and the US. That was made on loan to Goldwyn, who paid $5,000 a week for her services – as opposed to the $3,500 she was getting: she made protestations to Pathé, who raised her salary accordingly and extended her contract by two years.

Thus, after three films, was her popularity confirmed: and when the studio first bought Barry's play, *Holiday* (30), Ina Claire was announced for the lead – but she was paid $55,000 not to do it (according to 'Photoplay') and the lead was given to Harding, ideally cast as a rich girl in love with a poor man (Robert Ames). She was loaned to Warners to do Belasco's *The Girl of the Golden West* and then to Fox for some more hoary old goulash, *East Lynne* (31), with Clive Brook and Conrad Nagel – but not too sickly an experience in the hands of Frank Lloyd and certainly better than a modernized version going the rounds some months later, *Ex-Flame*. During her absence Pathé was merged with RKO by their joint owner, RCA, and David O. Selznick was brought in as production head. He announced for Harding a *Jane Eyre* and *Rebound*, from Donald Ogden Stewart's play,

Ann Harding's unfilmstar-like appearance made her a critic's pet; and she could act as well.

but the former was cancelled and the latter given to Miss Claire (who had done it on stage). Instead, Harding posed as a Cockney governess to be near the man she loved, Leslie Howard, in *Devotion*; and out East in *Prestige* (32) was tempted by her husband's superior officer, Adolphe Menjou, because he, Melvyn Douglas, drinks too much.

Her own prestige took a severe knock when she divorced her husband – an almost unprecedented action for a Hollywood star of this type: and RKO quickly abandoned one project because this was an inappropriate time to change the image – so the role of the hooker in *Bed of Roses* was played by Constance Bennett. Harding did play a divorcée in *Westward Passage*, but an innocent and still-loving one, badly treated by her writer husband – a tyro Laurence Olivier, who remembered for years her kindness, her consideration and help with his part. Then she did *The Conquerors* with Richard Dix, a big epic about an American family during the latter part of the last century and a bit of this. 'Picturegoer' wrote at this time: 'Although she does not share the glare of the big lights to the same extent as Garbo, Dietrich and Tallulah, she is certainly their equal in acting talent. In fact, I personally put her with Chatterton and Genevieve Tobin, ahead of her perhaps more glamorous rivals.'

Another Barry stage hit, *The Animal King-dom*, cast her as the woman Howard preferred to his wife, Myrna Loy: but it was a comedy and another triumph for Harding. The rivalry of Harding and Loy had gone down so well that MGM borrowed Harding for *When Ladies Meet* (33), the first and best of the two versions of Rachel Crothers's play. This time Harding was the wife – of publisher Frank Morgan, whom aspiring writer Loy thinks she wants (till Robert Montgomery dissuades her). It was the first of the 'bitchy' films, so it was perhaps appropriate that it was stolen from both ladies by another, Alice Brady. Harding was now getting $9,000 a week, for 40 weeks work per year, but in view of a number of suspensions the figure may have come to something less. There was constant disagreement with RKO; she had particularly disliked *Prestige* and had been furious at their refusal to allow her to do 'Mourning Becomes Electra' on the stage. There were reports that she planned to retire when suddenly she was in *Double Harness* with William Powell (vamping him) and had *The Right to Romance* Nils Asther, a 'Drama that lays bare a woman's heart' (said the ads).

Her contract expired, but she signed on again for two years (three films a year, one of them at an outside studio). *Gallant Lady* at 20th-UA was her own choice, a creditable mother-love piece with Brook, directed by Gregory La Cava; but *The Life of Vergie*

Ann Harding and William Powell in Double Harness *(33), one of the few films where she was allowed to look glamorous. Said the 'Kine Weekly': 'This delightful marital drama is intelligent stuff.'*

Some of the cast of the sparkling first version of When Ladies Meet (*33*): *Myrna Loy, Alice Brady, Robert Montgomery, Ann Harding, Martin Burton.*

Winters (34) with John Boles was merely a rehash of *Back Street*. *The Fountain* was a version of Charles Morgan's novel, a triangle story with a wartime background, with Brian Aherne as the British lover and Paul Lukas as the German husband. The notice in 'Photoplay' gives an idea why Harding's movies were now faltering at the box-office. 'A beautiful, contemplative novel is made into a film exquisite to look at, but moving with measured tread. . . . Fine restrained acting. . . .' MGM liked her and tried to revive interest: *Biography of a Bachelor Girl* (35), a version of S.N. Behrman's 'Biography', with Robert Montgomery; and *The Flame Within* with Herbert Marshall. She was a psychiatrist, but it was Harding-formula stuff and poor at that. *The Enchanted April* was another superior bestseller (by 'Elizabeth') adapted for Harding, and Frank Morgan, and business was again disappointing. She went to Paramount for *Peter Ibbetson*, playing the childhood love of Gary Cooper who meets him clandestinely after marriage and goes on meeting him in dreams as he lives out his life incarcerated in prison; she was ideal as the real lady and suitably ethereal as the dream one. After that high point RKO could come up with nothing better than Harding-formula, *The Lady Consents* (36), in which she loses husband Herbert Marshall in reel one and waits lovingly and patiently for him to return at the end. Audiences had seen it several times too often. RKO wound up her contract by shoving her

into *The Witness Chair*, a B, again as a sorrowing woman, with Walter Abel.

Harding was 'dead' in Hollywood. Like Chatterton earlier and Kay Francis later, she was killed by formula material. Some stars survived by battling for better material, like Bette Davis, or prolonged their careers by turning to comedy, like Claudette Colbert and Irene Dunne (apart from the fact that they were more entertaining, the values and standards in the comedies reflected more accurately real life than the dramas of the period); only MGM had the knack of keeping interest alive in its Dramatic ladies. Failing Hollywood offers, Harding went to Britain, where she sat around while a long search was made for the right material: presumably she felt that a thriller would open up the wider audience the weepies had closed for her and she chose *Love From a Stranger* (37), a popular stage play by Frank Vosper as adapted from a short story by Agatha Christie. You may wonder what a great actress is going to do to a one-dimensional character. Pulverize it, that's what. As the frightened lady, the intended victim of sinister husband Basil Rathbone, she is breathtakingly good. She played 'Candida' in London, the play's first West End production, and married Werner Janssen, the orchestra conductor.

She returned to the US and it was reported that due to her British success her Hollywood terms had risen. She did not make films, but made headlines in several court battles over the custody of her daughter. She toured the Pacific Coast in 'Candida' in 1938; and had a breakdown. She disappeared from view and reappeared with the minimum of fuss, as an old friend of blind detective Edward Arnold in a B directed by Fred Zinnemann, *Eyes in the Night* (42). It was a brief role and perhaps just a way of announcing that she was back. She was Walter Huston's wife on that *Mission to Moscow* (43) and with him again in the USSR to see *The North Star*, but briefly, as a peasant woman tortured by the Nazis. She top-billed in a B at Columbia, *Nine Girls* (44), a comedy mystery set in a sorority house, and then had two or three feature roles playing mothers: *Janie* to Joyce Reynolds, with Mr Arnold as father; *Those Endearing Young Charms* (45) to Laraine Day; and *Janie Gets Married*. She remained as charming as ever, but the individuality of her earlier playing was suppressed – even when she had star roles again in *It Happened on 5th Avenue* (47) with Victor Moore and Don Defore, one of Monogram's more ambitious efforts, and in *Christmas Eve*, playing an ageing spinster in this sentimental comedy with the Georges Raft and Brent.

She returned to the theatre: toured in 1949 in 'Yes My Darling Daughter' and took over Ruth Hussey's part in 'Goodbye My Fancy'; then made three films for MGM: *Two Weeks Without Love* (50), in the back seat as Jane Powell's mother; *The Magnificent Yankee* (51), as the wife of Oliver Wendell Holmes (Louis Calhern) in a biopic that was beautifully done but too placid for popular taste; and *The Unknown Man* (51), a confused crime melodrama with Walter Pidgeon. She did not film again until 1956 when she did three films: *The Man in the Grey Flannel Suit* as Fredric March's wife; *I've Lived Before* starring Jock Mahoney; and *Strange Intruder* starring Edmund Purdom and Ida Lupino. Theatregoers were luckier: in 1958 she took over two of the leading parts in Tennessee Williams's one-acters, 'Garden District', and she toured in 'September Tide' and 'The Corn Is Green'. Her last Broadway performance was in 'Abraham Cochrane' in 1964. She appeared frequently on TV; in 1962 she divorced Janssen, who had returned to Germany, giving her no option other than to go with him. She died in her Connecticut home in 1981.

CEDRIC HARDWICKE

He was one of the very few actor-knights ever to use his title professionally and 'Sir Cedric Hardwicke' on a cast-list was an indication of two aspects of him: he did sell out to the Hollywood vineyards and he was a remote, aristocratic actor. He never deserted the stage completely and rather despised films, but he is remembered best for his movie work and his capacity as a good supporting player, middle-aged and usually gruff. He always looked somewhat sad, which meant that he seemed understanding when he played kindly old men and embittered or sardonic when he was villainous. He was not a very sympathetic actor, but he was a fine craftsman and most of the films in which he appeared were the richer for his presence.

He was born in 1893 in Lye, Stourbridge, Worcestershire. He trained for the stage at RADA and made his first appearance as a walk-on, in 'The Monk and the Woman' in London in 1912. In need of money, he agreed to do a movie (two reels), in which he played six different parts, *Riches and Rogues* (13), for the sum of 10 guineas. As a result, the Vitagraph Company offered him $60 a week in the US, but he preferred to stick to the stage. After serving in World War I he joined the Birmingham Rep and began to make a name for himself, mostly in Shaw: Shaw himself liked his Captain Shotover, but what established Hardwicke with the public were two plays by Eden Phillpots, 'The Farmer's Wife' (24) and 'Yellow Sands' (28). In films, he played the title-role in *Nelson* (26). His career went upwards: he played Captain Andy in 'Show Boat' at Drury Lane (28) and originated the part of Magnus in 'The Apple Cart' (29); Shaw wrote a part into 'Too True to Be Good' for him. In 1930 he had a big West End success in 'The Barretts of Wimpole Street', which interested MGM, who had the movie rights – but he was not interested in MGM.

He did, however, make some British films: *Dreyfus* (31), an indifferent view of that affair, in the title-role; *Rome Express* (32), as the falsely philanthropic millionaire; *Orders is Orders* (33), as a peppery brigadier faced with a film company in the barracks; and *The Ghoul*, with Boris Karloff, as a shady lawyer. He was knighted in 1934, while appearing in 'The Late Christopher Bean', presented by Gilbert Miller, who put him under personal contract. Miller directed him in *The Lady is Willing* (34), a comedy with Leslie Howard, as the villain of the piece, a swindling businessman. But when MGM wanted him for *Vanessa* and *David Copperfield*, Miller kept him, much to his annoyance, to a tour of the play. He made some British films instead: *Bella Donna*, a triangle drama from Robert Hitchens's old novel, with Conrad Veidt and Mary Ellis, as the husband she wants to poison; *Nell Gwynn*, Charles II to Anna

Not the wittiest of Nells nor the merriest of monarchs: Anna Neagle and Cedric Hardwicke in Nell Gwynn (34).

Neagle's pert Nell; *Jew Süss*, as the rabbi; and *The King of Paris*, in the title-role of this tale of theatrical life. Miller then did arrange for him to take up a Hollywood offer, the flinty Marquess of Steyne in *Becky Sharp* (35) – a performance which is by far the best thing in the film. While waiting for production to resume (when the original director died), he went to 20th to play the Bishop in *Les Miserables*; then returned to London to do 'Tovarich' – his last London stage appearance iin 10 years. On film he was reunited with Neagle, as David Garrick to her *Peg of Old Drury*. He then did *Things to Come* (36) for Korda; *Tudor Rose*, a very popular picture about Lady Jane Grey (Nova Pilbeam), as the Earl of Warwick, who schemed to have Jane succeed Edward VI and was thus the instigator of her doom; and, amusingly, the spongeing brother-in-law in the film of J.B. Priestley's *Laburnum Grove*.

Warners sent for him to play another Bishop, in the nonsensical *The Green Light* (37), and he made his New York stage début in 'The Promise', under Miller's management. MGM signed him for *Kim* in Hollywood and he was leaving when they telephoned him on the 'Queen Mary' to ask him to play in *A Yank at Oxford*: he refused and in Hollywood found that *Kim* was not even about to start. Apart from a trip to Britain to play Allan Quartermain in *King Solomon's Mines* he was for the next few years on Broadway, notably in 'Shadow and Substance'; but he settled in

Hollywood in 1939, while out there to play Mr Brink (his favourite film part) in MGM's *On Borrowed Time*, a goodish piece of whimsy with Lionel Barrymore and Beulah Bondi. He was excellent again as Livingstone in *Stanley and Livingstone*, with Spencer Tracy at 20th, and as Frollo in *The Hunchback of Notre Dame* with Charles Laughton at RKO. RKO signed him to a contract, four films a year. Most of them were made on loan-out: *The Invisible Man Returns* (40) at Universal, as the villain; *Tom Brown's Schooldays*, as Dr Arnold; *The Howards of Virginia* at Columbia, as a crippled reactionary; and *Victory* at Paramount, from Conrad's book. Said Howard Barnes: 'The Hardwicke characterization of the evil, woman-hating Mr Jones is the only one that comes through with the impact it had in the book. It is superb. Terror stalks the screen from the moment Mr Jones appears and builds into an irresistible crescendo. . . .'

He was established as one of the leading supporting actors in Hollywood and he no longer aspired to star billing. He took brief bits in both *Suspicion* (41) and *Sundown*, and better parts in several poor programmers: *The Ghost of Frankenstein* (42); *Valley of the Sun*, a Western; *Invisible Agent* with Jon Hall; and *The Commandos Strike at Dawn* (43) with Paul Muni, as a British admiral. Then came *Forever and a Day*, the story of a London house through several generations, of which he was the begetter. In 1940 he had suggested to RKO an all-star charity film to aid British War Relief, the idea being that British artists in Hollywood should give their services free and RKO provide facilities and distribution. They liked the idea and asked him to undertake the project as producer. It eventually began filming in 1941; and the several episodes were only completed finally due to the persistence of Hardwicke and directors Frank Lloyd and Herbert Wilcox. Other directors involved were René Clair and Victor Saville, and the cast, if not as starry as at first announced, still had some strong box-office names. Hardwicke himself did slapstick with Buster Keaton. The picture was shown finally in 1943, when its profits were split with American War Relief – but they were not huge. For Hardwicke it had been a miserable experience. His contract was up and 20th wanted him to play the Nazi commander in Steinbeck's *The Moon Is Down*, the leading role in an important film; to make Hardwicke worthy of it and vice versa - to ensure he did not do bit roles with other companies – they signed him to a three-year contract. He went to MGM for *The Cross of Lorraine* to play a priest and then did three for 20th: *The Lodger* (44), as the householder; *Wing and a Prayer*, as an admiral; *Wilson*, as Henry Cabot Lodge; and *The Keys of the Kingdom*, as another high-ranking cleric. He did not consider himself fully employed and petitioned the studio for release from his contract: it took them a year to grant it (June 1944).

He did not film in 1945, but was in a flop play in London and in New York directed Gertrude Lawrence in 'Pygmalion'. His work over the next few years alternated between the two countries and while his parts in American films became smaller, his British work propped up his career. He returned to 20th for *Sentimental Journey* (46), as a doctor who befriends John Payne. He was good as a doctor in the British *Beware of Pity* and good again in one of his studies of bleak, implacable villainy, Ralph Nickleby in *Nicholas Nickleby* (47), an attempt by Cavalcanti at Ealing to film Dickens: there were some other good eccentrics (Sybil Thorndike, Athene Seyler, Stanley Holloway), but weak leads (Derek Bond, Sally Ann Howes). He returned to Hollywood: *The Imperfect Lady*; *Ivy*, as a Scotland Yard inspector; *Lured*; *Song of My Heart*, a Monogram biopic of Tchaikovsky (Frank Sundstrom); *Tycoon*, in the title-role, with John Wayne; *A Woman's Vengeance*; and *I Remember Mama* (48). He returned to Britain to play father Winslow in *The Winslow Boy*, then in Hollywood was another father, more tragically, in *Rope* (it is his murdered son in the trunk) and the king in *A Connecticut Yankee in King Arthur's Court* (49).

In London he joined the Old Vic Company for the 1948–9 season and played the warden in a prison drama, *Now Barabbas . . .*, which starred Richard Greene and never reached the US. In New York a revival of 'Caesar and Cleopatra' with Lilli Palmer boosted him, but in films his parts were either routine or prestigious five-minute bits: *The White Tower* (50), as a British scientist; *Mr Imperium* (51); *The Desert Fox*, as an anti-Hitlerite; *The Green Glove* (52), as the village priest; *Caribbean*, a coloured B pirate picture with John Payne and Arlene Dahl, unconvincing as a pirate chief; *Salome* (53), excellent as Tiberius, with about three minutes' screen time and one deathless line, 'What is it the illustrious Julius Caesar said: "I came, I saw, I conquered"?'; *Botany Bay*, as a colonial governor; and *Bait* (54) directed by and starring Hugo Haas, in the prologue as the Devil. He was recalled to Britain by Olivier to play Edward IV in *Richard III* (55), which renewed his prestige and resulted in a series of cameo parts: *Helen of Troy*, as Priam; *Diane*, as Catherine de Medici's astrologer; *Gaby* (56), as the hero's uncle; *The Vagabond King*, as adviser to Louis XI; *The Power and the Prize*, as a British businessman; *The Ten Command-

Cedric Hardwicke in what was virtually his only leading role in Hollywood. The Moon Is Down (43), a drama about the Nazi occupation of Norway.

ments*, as another ruler, the Pharaoh; *Around The World in 80 Days*, as an Indian army officer; *The Story of Mankind* (57), as the heavenly judge of man; and *Baby Face Nelson*, as a broken-down and drunken doctor. He said around this time that he would work in anything for the money – and then had economic security for a while on Broadway in a big hit, 'A Majority of One'.

In the 60s he did TV as well as stage work, and wrote an autobiography, 'A Victorian in Orbit'; none of these ventures was wildly successful. He was in the film version of *Five Weeks in a Balloon* (62) and had a tiny but effective part in *The Pumpkin Eater* (64). He died later that year in virtual poverty – he had been married twice and it was believed that he was crippled by alimony. His first wife was actress Helena Pickard and their son Edward Hardwicke has been one of the company at Britain's National Theatre.

JEAN HARLOW

To those unacquainted with Jean Harlow the oft-made comparisons with Marilyn Monroe must have seemed impertinent. Their personal lives had many similarities, including early deaths, but why should the genuinely attractive Monroe have been constantly compared with Harlow, platinum blonde, cross-legged in her hideous shapeless body-revealing sateen dresses, her smile the genuine toothpaste advert? Monroe was often rumoured to be on the verge of playing Harlow in a film lifestory, it is true; but Monroe was like a marshmallow and Harlow was as hard as rock candy. Harlow was coarse, tarty – much more Iris Adrian or Marian Martin; when she wanted something, like Mae West she asked for it straight out. (At one point Metro approached West to write Harlow's dialogue.) She moved with unfettered ease, swaggering before her men, not appraising them but demanding them to appraise her. She vamped, with humour, and when men were indifferent she did not shrug like West or melt like Monroe, but shouted and glared. She was never innocent, like Monroe, though the situations that screenwriters got both girls into were frequently similar; audiences were titillated that both girls used sex blatantly, openly enjoying it (cf. *Red Dust* and *Clash by Night*), an attitude in the 30s assumed to be extraordinary.

Where the comparison freely stands is that both were outstanding comediennes and both survived early critical hostility, emerging with solid reputations. Here is a skeleton of Harlow's notices: 1931: André Sennwald in 'The New York Times': '. . . it is unfortunate that Jean Harlow, whose virtues as an actress are limited to her blonde beauty, has to carry her share of the picture' (*The Iron Man*); and Mordaunt Hall, in the same paper: 'The acting throughout is interesting, with the exception of Jean Harlow' (*Public Enemy*). Irene Thirer in the 'New York Daily News': 'She is a decorative person but lacks the spark needed to make her shine as a personality' (*Goldie*). 1932: 'Variety': '. . . does better than might be expected, but she fails to be convincing' (*Three Wise Girls*). Later that year, Richard Wtts Jr in the 'New York Herald Tribune': 'The flagrantly blonde Miss Harlow, who hitherto has attracted but intermittent enthusiasm from this captious department, immediately becomes one of its favourites by her performance in *Red Dust*. . . . She proves herself a really deft comedienne.' 1933: Watts again: 'For those of us who are enthusiastic for the increasing talents of the distinguished Miss Harlow, *Bombshell* is chiefly important for the fact that it provides the first full-length portrait of this amazing young woman's increasingly impressive acting talent.' Sennwald again: 'Miss Harlow, who simply must be accepted as a fine comedienne in her particular sphere, plays her laughs too

shrewdly to warrant the frequently heard opinion that not all her humor is intentional' (*The Girl From Missouri*). 1936: Howard Barnes in the 'New York Herald Tribune': '. . . she vitalizes the material throughout. She proves anew that she is a really fine comedienne' (*Libeled Lady*).

Jean Harlow was born in Kansas City, Missouri, in 1911; when she was 16, and still at school, she eloped with a wealthy Chicago boy, but it did not last. With her mother and stepfather, she found herself in Los Angeles, where she began to work as an extra in films: in *Moran of the Marines* (28), in *The Love Parade* (29) and *City Lights*. She appeared in some Christie comedies in 1929–30 and earlier had been quite conspicuous in a couple of Laurel-and-Hardys at Roach, including *Double Whoopee!* She had a fairish-sized part in *The Saturday Night Kid*, as a salesgirl in the store where Clara Bow and Jean Arthur worked, but was back on the Roach lot afterwards, waiting to be discovered. She was.

Howard Hughes had begun *Hell's Angels* in 1927, a tale of the Royal Flying Corps in World War I; after two years of filming much of the film was scrapped, in order to add sound, and with the salvage went Greta Nissen, whose accent little qualified her to play a British girl. Hughes saw Harlow at the Roach studios and signed her to replace Nissen. It cannot be said that Harlow's own accent sounded even remotely British, nor did those of Ben Lyon and James Hall resemble Oxford undergraduates – not that it matters today, because the film is now extremely dull. In its time, however, it was impressive and it was one of the top 10 money-makers of 1931. Hughes put Harlow under contract at $250 a week.

Because of her low-cut gowns and equivocal role – she takes on both Lyon and Hall and has an affair with a third man – Harlow became instantly famous. She was loaned out quickly: to MGM to play a gangster's moll in *The Secret Six* (31), to Universal to play the loose-living wife of boxer Lew Ayres, *The Iron Man*, and to Warners for another moll in *Public Enemy*. In Fox's *Goldie*, a remake of *A Girl in Every Port*, the word 'tramp' was used for the first time on screen to describe a woman – but nevertheless, or therefore, Spencer Tracy and Warren Hymer still pursued her. She came into her own at last as Capra's *Platinum Blonde* at Columbia, miscast though she was as a society girl who woos and wins reporter Robert Williams, but loses him to Loretta Young because, *inter alia*, she insists he wears garters: an extremely funny film. Still at Columbia (who were paying Hughes $1,750 a week for her services), she was a country girl in New York, and Mae

Jean Harlow, Louise Beavers and Lee Tracy, as Harlow's press agent, in Bombshell (*33*), a hilarious satire about a poor little rich movie star longing to live a 'normal' life. When, in this scene, Harlow asks Beavers about some lingerie she gave her, Beavers has to admit that it 'got all torn up day before yesterday': 'Your day off sure is brutal on your lingerie,' observes Harlow.

Clarke and Marie Prevost were the others of the *Three Wise Girls* (32).

Her agent then stepped in. Hughes had no further movie plans and she would exist indefinitely on loan-outs. The agent wanted her at a studio who would build her and he wanted her at MGM; furthermore, MGM wanted her. They bought her for $60,000 plus the right for Hughes to use her for two pictures within five years at her normal salary: which would be $1,250 weekly up to a ceiling of $5,000 over a seven-year period (though for 52 weeks annually instead of the customary 40 only). She was thrown away, as a gangster's moll again, in *The Beast of the City*, but the second role at Metro was one that Crawford and Shearer had turned down: *Red-Headed Woman* from Katherine Bush's bestseller. She was an unscrupulous vamp and wisely played for laughs, getting her first grudging reviews – but not in Britain. The film was banned because it was 'so tough' ('Film Pictorial'). *Red Dust* followed and it did as much for her as she did for it – as the wise-cracking, predatory blonde who wanders into Gable's masculine little world and disrupts it. She was

superb. 'Time' magazine spoke of the film's 'brazen moral values' and for a long time it was regarded as the epitome of sexual daring.

She was duoed with Gable again in *Hold Your Man* (33), a comedy, and was a movie sexpot who wanted to be a wife and mother in *Bombshell*, one of the funniest satires ever on Hollywood life. At the end of the year, she was reckoned one of the top 10 draws in pictures. Appropriately enough then, she was among the distinguished company invited for *Dinner at Eight* and she practically stole the film from all of them as the cheap, indolent wife, goading tycoon Wallace Beery and amusing herself on the side with Edmund Lowe. She got some good notices with another comedy, *The Girl From Missouri* (34) – who goes millionaire-hunting but falls for the son of one, Franchot Tone; but in the musical opening of *Reckless* (35), her dancing was not up to much and her singing voice reputedly dubbed. The film was based loosely on the Libby Holman case (Holman, a Broadway star, had been suspected of murdering her husband) and had been intended till the last minute for Joan Crawford; but William

Wallace Beery and Harlow arriving for Dinner at Eight (33), *nouveau-riche in a* haut-monde *world. As the film ends Harlow is making small talk with Marie Dressler: 'Do you know that the guy said machinery is going to take the place of every profession?' Dressler: 'Oh my dear, that's something you need never worry about.'*

China Seas (35) *was a rip-roaring melodrama which borrowed at least one plot strand from* Red Dust, *in that Clark Gable (as the captain) spends most of the time thinking he's in love with a lady when all the time he has a yen for a fast and loose broad, played again by Jean Harlow. Rosalind Russell was the patrician British widow and it's Sir C. Aubrey Smith looking on. Like* Bombshell *it was part-written by Jules Furthman, who gave Harlow's (black) maid a marvellous exit line, 'Goodbye Miss Dolly, you sure were good to me even if they does hang you.'*

Powell was the co-star and MGM wished to capitalize on his offscreen romance with Harlow (they eloped in 1936 but did not marry).

China Seas was a variation of the *Red Dust* theme, with Harlow as a tropical trollop called China Doll; Gable co-starred again, and Beery – and the three of them were box-office dynamite. She went into *Riff Raff*, a hard-boiled thriller with Tracy; *Wife vs Secretary* (36), a brittle Faith Baldwin story with Gable and Myrna Loy; and *Suzy*, a silly spy story with Cary Grant. MGM were tentatively trying to broaden her range, to let her play some scenes straight, but *Libeled Lady* was pure comedy and with her, Tracy, Powell and Loy pure joy. Which cannot be said about *Personal Property* (37), much frivolity and no plot at all, though she and Robert Taylor take it to feature-length by sheer star power. She is supposed to be a penniless widow marrying his brother (Reginald Owen) for money, but of course with a heart of gold. The tightening of the Production Code in 1934 meant that the sluttish character she had once played was now *verboten*: and, of course, it would not do for a big MGM star. The 'good dame' qualities which her co-star admired in her glow on the screen and as Bosley Crowther said of this role, it is 'the indignant lady of a Peter Arno drawing'.

During the making of *Saratoga* she became seriously ill and she died (reportedly of uraemic poisoning) before it was completed (37). The piece, a horse-racing comedy-drama, again with Gable, has its moments, but it is difficult to guess what it might have been like. Some later sequences are clearly curtailed and the double used is laughably obvious (she is either hiding her eyes or has her back to the camera). Certainly there is nothing in it to suggest why it should have been the biggest film hit of 1937, with a colossal take of $2 million – unless the public were either anxious or morbidly curious to see Harlow for the last time.

In 1964 a scurrilous biography of her was published, dealing mainly with her second marriage to MGM executive Paul Bern, who committed suicide (1932) in mysterious circumstances. (His suicide note spoke of impotency and the subsequent newspaper headlines threatened to ruin Harlow and the forthcoming *Red Dust*: they did not.) The book became a bestseller and was filmed with Carroll Baker. A rival film with Carol Lynley was made simultaneously by a process called Electrovision (which meant that it was filmed, for speed, like a TV play): both were rushed to the market to meet with complete public apathy. Neither book, nor the films, seemed to have anything to do with that jolly girl who traded insults with Clark Gable and Spencer Tracy.

WILL HAY

The number of British comics who have made it in the international market can be numbered on the fingers of one hand and Will Hay, fondly remembered in Britain, is not one of them. His films were not exportable when made and Americans chancing on them on British TV find them slow, laboured and crude. The dialogue does not go snap snap snap as with the American comics, following a vaudeville tradition that was altogether more swiftly paced than the British music hall style. The British have laughed at the major US comedians while their own laughter-makers thudded overseas. The films of Will Hay *are* slow, laboured and crude. But they are also genuinely funny: a Will Hay Festival at London's National Film Theatre in the 50s

was as well received as later seasons of the Marxes and W.C. Fields.

Hay was like Fields in that he perfected a certain character that was at its best in situation comedy. The laughs depended on the reaction of that character to what was happening around him, on the follies and foibles of that character. Some comics – as disparate as Bob Hope and Buster Keaton – worked subjectively, through instinct rather than intellect. Chaplin worked both ways and Jack Benny, for instance, had it both ways: he was not a character comedian, but he got a hundred laughs out of his meanness. Interestingly, Benny once cited Hay as one of the two artists from whom, technically, he had learnt most (the other was Alastair Sim).

Will Hay was not instinctively funny, but he constructed a character that was. He was invariably in a position of authority for which he was totally unfitted. He looked seedy and disreputable and indeed was. He had so far advanced through the world by bluffing, bragging and cheating, and the shiftiness of his eyes suggested that it would not be long before he was caught up with. That being so, one more lie, one more dishonesty, would not come amiss. His eye was to the main chance where cash or booze were concerned – he seldom began to consider his chances with women; nor was he often seen intoxicated, a state which might suggest that he had abandoned his normal wary stance. His successes were minor and non-lasting and were due mainly to luck – an odd flash of cunning that went undetected. He never went soft, was never pitiable.

In parentheses, a later comedian, Tony Hancock, owed something to both Hay and W.C. Fields. The character carefully created for him by his scriptwriters, Galton and Simpson, had elements of both: he was also a braggart without conviction, a little man who dreamt of glory, of routing his enemies. His first starring picture, *The Rebel* (60), met a hostile reception in the US and Dwight Macdonald (who was living in Britain at the time and might therefore have been sympathetic) observed drily for the readers of 'Esquire' that he was much admired over there 'for inscrutable reasons'. Yet informed British comment on Hancock at his best, both before and since his death, insists that he was a great clown.

Just as Hancock was at his best with Sid James, so Hay was at his best with his two sidekicks, both of them cynical about his abilities and otherwise downright contemptuous: Graham Moffat (Albert), the fat boy, insolent, lazy and sarcastic, and Moore Marriott (Harbottle), the senile gap-toothed old codger, ever-hopeful and suspicious. Like

An atmosphere of mutual distrust: Will Hay (centre), Graham Moffat and Moore Marriott in Ask a Policeman *(33),* with, at left, Herbert Lomas. One of the film's funniest scenes.

Hancock and James, these three matched each other in duplicity. The profound comic invention of their best scenes (Val Guest contributed to most of Hay's best scripts) – Hay arriving at 'his' station in *Oh Mr Porter!*, the business with the station poor-box in *Ask a Policeman* – is as funny as anything on celluloid. But British indulgence over the matter of timing may always restrict revivals to indigenous audiences.

Hay was born in Aberdeen in 1888. The family moved to Manchester, where he was apprenticed to an engineer; reputedly he was fired with ambition to go on the stage when he saw W.C. Fields do his juggling act. He entertained at charity shows till an offer was made to him to turn professional. He made his début on the Halls in 1909, writing his own sketches, based often on his sister's experience as a schoolteacher. Gradually – after World War I – there evolved 'The Fourth Form at St Michael's' which was to be the prototype for all his future work: the idea of course was that the boys were brighter than he. During the 20s he toured in the US and the then British Empire, and successfully adapted his technique to radio; he also obtained a considerable reputation as a leading amateur astronomer.

He entered films in a short, *Know Your Apples* (33), followed by *Those Were the Days* (34), which was Pinero's farce 'The Magistrate' with music hall sequences easily slotted

in; he was the unfortunate magistrate. He was the DG of BH (head of the BBC) in *Radio Parade of 1935*, imitating Hollywood models, and was involved in another adaptation of Pinero, *Dandy Dick* (35). These were made for BIP, but he signed a contract with Gainsborough, starting with *Boys Will Be Boys*, which, though the credits claimed it was based on Beachcomber's Narkover College, was in fact an extension of his best-known music hall sketch. He was then an incompetent private eye in *Where There's a Will* (36) and an incompetent skipper in *Windbag the Sailor*, his first teaming with both Marriott and Moffat.

There was another school story, *Good Morning Boys* (37), and then *Oh Mr Porter!*, the funniest British film of that era. Hay was the station-master of a derelict and probably haunted country station, Buggleskelly, and Moffat and Marriott were his helpmates. In *Convict 99* (38) he became a prison governor via the usual first-reel misunderstanding and had Moffat as a warder and Marriott as the oldest lag in the business. Basil Wright wrote that Hay 'makes a success of the job partly by mistake and partly by that shady but genteel ability to tell lies and conduct swindles which he invests with so much genuine charm'. He was, alas, bereft of his cohorts in *Hey Hey USA*, perhaps his weakest film, a satire on gangsters. *Old Bones of the River* was a take-off of Edgar Wallace's 'Sanders' stories and the three of them were again at their best in *Ask a Policeman* (39) and *Where's That Fire?*. Moffat and Marriott continued to be of inestimable advantage but Hay disliked being dependent on them and quarrelled with Gainsborough over it; as a result he left and moved over to Ealing.

His first film there, *The Ghost of St Michaels* (41), was in the old mould, but distressingly near a boy's comic-book strip in style and content. Thereafter he tried less familiar situations: two war stories, *The Black Sheep of Whitehall* and *The Goose Stepped Out*, are uneven in quality, though they have sequences of moment (similar difficulties were confronting the Marxes in Hollywood). On the former Dilys Powell compared him to other British comics: 'Will Hay with his evasions, chases, absurd disguises, and the inevitable débâcle seems to me streets ahead of the rest.' Hay then did a straight character part in a semi-documentary, *The Big Blockade* (42), one of a large number of stars. His last film, *My Learned Friend* (43), had savage moments, a *cómedie noire* with very few let-ups and an irreverence worthy of his best work at Gainsborough (Hay knew he was to be the sixth victim of a homicidal maniac). Ill-health caused a semi-retirement, alas for the laughter of Britain (from 1937 to 1942 he was one of the best draws at the box-office, of British stars trailing only Gracie Fields and George Formby). He did an occasional music hall booking and had a popular radio pro-gramme until he died in 1949.

HELEN HAYES

It is a distinguished name in the theatre: Helen Hayes, an actress of great resource and impeccable technique, an actress who has spent her life in the business and has been acclaimed (as have several others) 'The First Lady of the American Theatre'. For a brief while she was one of the first ladies of films.

She was born in 1900 in Washington DC, where she made her first stage appearance only five years later in 'The Royal Family', as Prince Charles. She had a fairly prolific career as a child actress and made her Broadway début in 1909 in 'Old Dutch'; the following year she appeared in a Vitagraph two-reeler, *Jean and the Calico Doll* (Jean was a dog); in 1912 she was touring in a play for the Shuberts, 'The Never Homes' (and the Boston authorities banned her because she was under age); from 1913 to 1916 she was in stock in Washington and in 1917–18 toured as 'Pollyanna', also making a film at this time, *Weavers of Life* (17), for F.B. Warren; but

In an Italian garden: Gary Cooper and Helen Hayes in the best of the two screen versions of A Farewell to Arms *(32), directed by Frank Borzage.*

thereafter was seldom away for long from the Broadway scene. Among her successes were 'Dear Brutus' (18), 'Clarence' by Booth Tark-ington (19), 'To the Ladies' (22), 'Caesar and Cleopatra' (26), 'What Every Woman Knows' (26), 'Coquette' (27); and on tour thereafter: when she left the cast to have a baby the management sued. Hayes won, amidst head-lines, and had what was known as the Act of God baby. 'Petticoat Influence' (30) was her last play before accepting an MGM contract.

Hayes did not really want to go to Holly-wood and did not want to be in films, but her husband Charles MacArthur, the dramatist, had had lucrative writing offers. He wrote her first film, not entirely seriously, an incredibly maudlin tale of mother-love – from innocent girlhood to decrepit old whore – *The Son of Madelon Claudet* (31). Neither of them liked it but it did bring her a Best Actress Oscar. The next two were nothing to be ashamed of, however – both from good novels: *Arrow-smith* at Goldwyn, an imposing performance as Ronald Colman's wife, and *A Farewell to Arms* (32) at Paramount, an exquisite one as Catherine, with Gary Cooper. Had all her pictures been as good, she might not have left Hollywood (she did return to New York briefly in 1931 for 'The Good Fairy'). But the next two were not an improvement on *Made-lon Claudet*. In *The Son-Daughter* she and Ramon Novarro were Chinese soulfully in love, with her sacrificing herself to Warner

Oland whom she finally strangles with his own pigtail; and *The White Sister* (33), the remake of a Lillian Gish film, was another 'impossible' love story – about a girl who thinks her lover (Clark Gable) has been killed (in war) but meets him again after she has become a nun. Somewhat better were *Another Language*, a dullish version of Rose Franken's play about a dominating mother (Louise Closser Hale) and the one daughter-in-law who opposes her; and *Night Flight*, again with Gable, a version of the novel by Antoine de Saint-Exupéry.

She rushed back to New York to appear in Maxwell Anderson's 'Mary of Scotland' and stayed in 'Scotland' for *What Every Woman Knows* (34) with Brian Aherne, a vehicle which MGM chose hoping that it would please her; then she toured as Mary. She had told MGM that she had no wish to continue her film career and made an announcement, part of which ran: 'I am leaving the screen because I don't think I am very good in the pictures and I have a beautiful dream that I'm elegant on the stage.' Long before it appeared, *Vanessa Her Love Story* (35) was publicized as her last film. It was an adaptation of a novel by Hugh Walpole (who much approved of her) and co-starred Robert Montgomery.

At the end of 1935 Hayes scored perhaps her biggest stage success: in the title-role of Laurence Housman's 'Victoria Regina'. Here is a partial list of subsequent stage work: in Chicago, 'The Merchant of Venice' (38); in New York, 'Twelfth Night' (40) as Viola; 'Harriet' (Beecher Stowe) (43–45); 'Alice-Sit-by-the-Fire' on tour (46); 'The Glass Menagerie' (as Amanda) in London (48); 'The Wistaria Trees' (50); 'Mrs McThing' (52); 'Time Remembered' (57); and 'A Touch of the Poet' (58) in the New York theatre named after her. There were also numerous revivals of 'What Every Woman Knows'. In 1955 she starred on TV in 'Arsenic and Old Lace' with Billie Burke, Peter Lorre and Boris Karloff. In 1961 she toured Europe in 'The Skin of Our Teeth' (as Mrs Antrobus) and 'The Glass Menagerie' for the State Department; there were a few other appearances: a Shakespeare recital with Maurice Evans and a chronicle play about the wives of the presidents, 'The White House' (64).

She appeared as herself, briefly, in *Stage Door Canteen* (43), but remained away from movies till *My Son John* (52), frankly looking her age and trailing clouds of prestige: the performance, though never hammy, is clearly designed to knock you between the eyes – but few were willing to submit to the test for this anti-red drama made by Leo McCarey. Hayes was also in: *Main Street to Broadway* (53), again as herself; and *Anastasia* (56), as the

Grand Duchess. In 1960 she agreed to do *A Pocketful of Miracles*, but when its schedule was delayed she was on tour (Bette Davis played the part). Ten years later she did *Airport* (70), billed as 'Miss Helen Hayes' and playing her cute-old-lady part with the accumulated mannerisms of a lifetime – and thus winning a Best Supporting Oscar (the first player to win in both Best and Best Supporting categories). She had done much live television and returned to the medium in *Do Not Fold Spindle or Mutilate* (71), with Myrna Loy, Mildred Natwick and Sylvia Sidney, as four ladies threatened by a psychopath after inventing a fictional woman. NBC liked the teaming with Natwick and made them *The Snoop Sisters* (72); they liked that, too, for they had them play these spinster detectives for a while on a rotating series of 'NBC Tuesday Mystery Movie'. She found herself forced to give up the theatre, adding, 'I have known very few artists in my time. Laurette Taylor was one. Olivier is another. Me, I'm proud of my craft.' The resumption of her film career has, however, been restricted to playing little old ladies in Disney films: *Herbie Rides Again* (74); *One of Our Dinosaurs is Missing* (75); and *Candleshoe* (78). She did do some more television: *The Moneychangers* (76), a mini-series, and *Victory at Entebbe*; *The Family Upside Down* (78) with Fred Astaire; *Murder is Easy* (82); *A Caribbean Mystery* (83); and *Murder With Mirrors* (85). As admirers of Mrs Christie's detective stories will know, these last three tele-movies are based on them; in the last two Miss Hayes went sleuthing again, as Miss Marple. Her son, James MacArthur, had an indifferent movie career, after a brilliant start in Frankenheimer's fine *The Young Stranger* (56).

RITA HAYWORTH

The appellation 'The Love Goddess' has been used about a dozen stars, but mostly about Rita Hayworth. Whatever other girls had – and sexy, desirable girls were never in short supply in films – Rita had more of. She was ravishing in black and white, and breathtaking when (very sensibly) they put her into Technicolor: auburn-haired, brown-eyed and with the proverbial peaches-and-cream complexion. It was not just physical allure. Naturally it is preferable when the woman on the seducing end is attractive – provocation was an early Hayworth speciality – but she did have that special star lustre. One fan magazine writer in 1963 considered her 'an interesting interval – if not an especially dynamic one – between Jean Harlow and Marilyn Monroe', but her sex appeal was really somewhat more subtle than either. She was once described as 'the intellectual's glamour girl', presumably implying that a lot of people liked her who were not expected to. Later in the career the lustre dimmed (in fact quite quickly) and she became a very dull player; but the face, still beautiful, suggested an interesting past.

She was born in New York in 1918, the daughter of Eduardo Cansino, a Latin-American dancer (and because an uncle married an aunt of Ginger Rogers, somewhat related to that lady). She followed in her father's steps – under her real name Margarita Cansino – and got a job dancing at the Agua Caliente in Tijuana, then popular with film folk. As she hoped, she was noticed – by Winfield Sheehan, who signed her to a Fox contract at $200 a week. She appeared in *Under the Pampas Moon* (35) and in some other films, mostly dancing in the background; but had small parts in *Charlie Chan in Egypt*, *Dante's Inferno*, *Paddy O'Day*, which starred Jane Withers, and *Human Cargo* (36), with Claire Trevor. Hayworth played a Mexican dancer and Allan Dwan, who directed, later observed that she was 'very nervous – she'd cry – very worried at working around others who seemed more pro'. Fox decided she was star material and planned *Ramona* for her and Gilbert Roland; but when 20th combined with that company and the new management took over, they were replaced by Loretta Young and Don Ameche. Her small role in *A Message to Garcia* was deleted and she was dropped. She got some leading parts in B pictures: *Meet Nero Wolfe* at Columbia, with Edward Arnold as Wolfe, Rex Stout's detective; *Rebellion* and *Old Louisana* (37), both with Tom Keene, made for a company called Crescent; *Hit the Saddle*, a Three Mesquiteers Western; and *Trouble in Texas*, with Tex Ritter.

In 1937 she married a businessman, Ed Judson, and he decided to take a hand: on the strength of that one role at Columbia he talked that studio into giving her a contract (for seven years, starting at $250 weekly and going to $1,750). Her first name had already been reduced to Rita and now she got a new surname, Hayworth. Columbia considered her strictly B-picture stuff: *Girls Can Play*; *The Game That Kills*; *Criminals of the Air*; *The Shadow*; and *Convicted* (38), all with Charles Quigley; *Paid to Dance* (37) with Don Terry; *Who Killed Gail Preston?* (38) with Robert Paige; *Juvenile Court* with Paul Kelly and *Homicide Bureau* (39) with Bruce Cabot. She supported Joan Blondell and Melvyn Douglas in *There's Always a Woman* (38) and Cukor tested her for the role of Hepburn's sister in *Holiday* without success; she played

Gene Kelly and Rita Hayworth in Charles Vidor's Cover Girl (44), *the backstage musical that broke the conventions of backstage musicals, and broke box-office records.*

opposite Warren William in *The Lone Wolf Spy Hunt* (39) which was not quite a B; and was loaned to RKO for *Renegade Raider* with George O'Brien.

Judson had also transformed Rita's appearance by having the low hair-line removed by electrolysis and changing the hair colour to auburn, and with a dress costing $500 she was at a neighbouring table at the Trocadero when Harry Cohn and Howard Hawks were discussing the casting of *Only Angels Have Wings*: and thus she had her first unequivocally good role, the second lead, as Richard Barthelmess's philandering wife. Then it was back to Bs: *Special Inspector*, *Music in My Heart* (40) with Tony Martin and *Blondie on a Budget*. But Cukor recalled the test and at MGM borrowed her for a good part in *Susan and God*. This, and the response to the plethora of pin-up pictures that Columbia had issued, suggested to the studio that she might play the part Jean Arthur had turned down in Ben Hecht's uncertain fable, *Angels Over Broadway*; Douglas Fairbanks Jr and Thomas Mitchell co-starred and it flopped. However, they then decided to star her in *The Lady in Question*, a remake of the French *Gribouille*, for which Luise Rainer had been considered. In it, Hayworth was on trial for murder and Brian Aherne co-starred.

On the evidence of both films it seemed that Hayworth was decorative but unlikely to go very far: thus the studio were not averse to loaning her to WB when Ann Sheridan walked out of *Strawberry Blonde* (41). As the other woman, James Cagney's recurrent crush, she was assured and sparkling. WB sagely kept her to add some spice to *Affectionately Yours*, a comedy with Merle Oberon and Dennis Morgan. The word was out: Hollywood had a new star (at last) and 20th jumped in with an offer (and five times her normal salary) to play another temptress in *Blood and Sand*, a part originally destined for Carole Landis and for which they had tested Gene Tierney and Dorothy Lamour. It was in colour and Hayworth was superb.

The reception accorded these three loan-outs, plus enthusiastic reaction to a spread in 'Life Magazine', caused Columbia to build a vehicle for Hayworth. They hired two classy talents, Cole Porter and Fred Astaire, to help her through a medium musical about an amorous producer (Robert Benchley), a stage star conscripted into the army (Astaire) and the Colonel's daughter (Hayworth): *You'll Never Get Rich*. She did not sing a note, but she danced well with Astaire. She did another musical, at 20th, when Alice Faye became pregnant (and Betty Grable was halfway through *Song of the Islands*), *My Gal Sal* (42), with Victor Mature, in Technicolor. Her singing was dubbed. 20th kept her to appear in the Charles Boyer episode in *Tales of Manhattan*, while Columbia prepared another musical with Astaire, *You Were Never Lovelier*, with Jerome Kern songs. Again the story was farcical but not very funny – frigid daughter of wealthy South American is wooed by stage-star Astaire; and Hayworth's assets were mainly physical. She came on looking so terrific that you expected things to happen: but after a while you realized she was not too fascinating.

Her marriage was over and Judson demanded $30,000 in payment, and although Hayworth admitted that 'running my career was his only concern . . . and his efforts paid off', she refused. She said that he had never let her make a decision, a complaint which would recur in her marriages, though she would probably not accuse any of the later husbands of robbing 'everything of excitement'. The bill was, incidentally, paid by Cohn.

Jerome Kern provided the score for the next Hayworth musical and Gene Kelly co-starred: *Cover Girl* (44), which was lush, inventive and way ahead of most musicals of the period. Business was great, but *Tonight and Every Night* (45), supposedly a follow-up (based on London's Windmill 'We Never Closed' Theatre), did not have Kelly – or Astaire – and was feeble in every way.

It was followed by *Gilda* (46): 'There Never Was a Woman Like Gilda!' said the ads. Hayworth was the postwar epitome of screen eroticism, a somewhat déclassé adventuress who descends on Glenn Ford and George Macready and splits their (surprisingly explicit) liaison. The first hour is keen with mystery, but as C.A. Lejeune observed, there are hints 'subsequently confirmed, that nothing is going to happen except Miss Hayworth'. However, in a clinging black satin dress, in elbow-length gloves, she sang 'Put the Blame on Mame'. After that, *Down to Earth* (47) was all too aptly named; she was Terpsichore, posing as a mortal for a Broadway show. Her own status as a goddess had certainly not been hurt by marriage to Tinseltown's genius, Orson Welles, who owed Cohn $25,000, which he had lost in a Broadway venture. He proposed paying it off by making a film for Columbia, with Hayworth, from whom he was already separated. Cohn agreed, believing that the reunion would make excellent publicity. He did not expect to like the result, but Welles had promised that it would confirm her status as a sex symbol. Cohn did not like *The Lady From Shanghai* (48), nor the fact that Hayworth's trademarked flame-coloured tresses had been swopped for a blonde bob; she did play a treacherous lady, but the public found her an all too colourless one. Columbia tried to retrieve the situation with *The Loves of Carmen*, again with Ford (as Don José), but she just was not fiery enough.

At this point she eloped to Europe with Prince Aly Khan, a match that occasioned screaming headlines. The marriage of playboy and movie star did not conflict with the Hayworth image, but Columbia wanted her back – she was, after all, by far the most popular of their contract players. She did so as the marriage died: and something within her had also died. The old vivacity had gone, even if Columbia were now paying her $242,000 a year. *Affair in Trinidad* (52), with Ford, resumed her career, but she and the film were monotonous together and business was only fair. It was followed by a couple of classic vamps, *Salome* (53) and *Miss Sadie Thompson* – Maugham butchered to make a Hayworth holiday. Both films were ludicrous, but it is unlikely that, in kinder circumstances, Hayworth could have measured up to the parts. Married now to Dick Haymes and

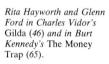

Rita Hayworth and Glenn Ford in Charles Vidor's Gilda (46) *and in Burt Kennedy's* The Money Trap (65).

uncertain of public interest, Hayworth stayed away for three years – though in 1954 she had signed a new contract with Columbia. In 1955 she was involved in one of Harry Cohn's pet projects, *Joseph and His Brethren*. The film was started, with Frank Capra directing, but was abandoned when Cohn died. Hayworth received half of her $150,000 salary and sued: the case was settled out of court. As a result, she was required to do three more films for Columbia, including *Fire Down Below* (57) and *Pal Joey*. The former was an actioner with Robert Mitchum and she was very subdued. From time to time she was her old self in *Pal Joey* and appeared to some advantage as the ageing beauty in *Separate Tables* (58), among whose producers was her new husband, James Hill (they were divorced in 1961). Her fee was $200,000.

Few of her subsequent films caused a squeak at the box-office, but it was not her fault. Most of them were terrible. The best of them was perhaps *They Came to Cordura* (59), an adventure yarn with Gary Cooper in which she was, personally, excellent; and the most expensive was *Circus World* (64) with John Wayne. Said Henry Hathaway, who directed: 'Then we ran into a bad thing with Rita Hayworth in that picture because she was drinking a lot through it.' The others: *The Story on Page One* (59) was Anthony Franciosa; *The Happy Thieves* (61), a so-called comedy with Rex Harrison; *The Money Trap* (65), a reunion with Ford which played the lower half of bills; *The Poppy Is Also a Flower*, UNESCO's anti-drug thriller, shown on TV in the US and in cinemas abroad; and *L'Avventurio/The Rover* (67) with Anthony Quinn, a version of Conrad directed by Terence Young, which only had a couple of bookings.

In 1969 she told a reporter that she considered she had a new career, a modest one – and quite different from the earlier one. To prove her point she was seen in *I Gatti/Sons of Satan* (69), an Italian programmer, as a drunken actress – a role Joan Crawford declined at the last minute to do; *Sur la Route de Salina/Road to Salina* (70), an absurd puzzle picture; and *The Wrath of God* (72), with Robert Mitchum, as a South-of-the-Border dowager. She made an independent film in Florida in 1970 which has never been shown (possibly called *The Human Zoo*) and in 1973 began a British film, *Tales that Witness Madness*, but walked out – to be replaced by Kim Novak – and was sued. Plans of other films came to naught and when signed to replace Lauren Bacall in 'Applause', the management had to annul the contract. In 1977 she was reported 'gravely disabled by mental disorder' and a court in Santa Ana,

California, was told she was 'unable or unwilling to accept responsibility for her treatment and is a chronic alcoholic'. In fact, poor lady, she was ill with Alzheimer's disease. In 1981 she was committed to the care of her daughter and she died in 1987.

SONJA HENIE

A Sonja Henie, like an Esther Williams, can, one assumes, only happen once to the film business. They were speciality performers and today TV would probably display their talents to audiences who craved such thrills. Sonja skated. She was undoubtedly a great skater. Beyond that, it was dimples and a mile of kitsch.

She was born in Oslo in 1913; at four she learned dancing and at eight began ice-skating. At 11, she won the Figure Skating Championship of Norway and two years later was placed second in the World Championships. The following year she gained the World title and held on to it for 10 consecutive years. Meanwhile, she began to study ballet under Karsavina. In the Olympic Games of 1928, 1932 and 1936 she broke records and gained Gold Medals; it was after the 1936 Games that she decided to turn professional.

Henie desperately wanted to be in movies and indeed had already appeared in one at home, *Syv Dager for Elisabeth* (27). She underwent extensive beauty treatment and Hollywood was certainly interested – but not at her asking price, $75,000 per film. So she hired a rink in Los Angeles so that producers could gauge her appeal; as ever, she was an SRO success. Darryl Zanuck decided to gamble and cast her in *One in a Million* (36), backed by Adolphe Menjou, Don Ameche and the Ritz Brothers. Although she had learnt her dialogue phonetically, it was so successful that she was hurried into *Thin Ice* (37) with Tyrone Power and at the end of the year she had zipped into the top 10 money-makers. After *Happy Landing* (38), with Ameche, 20th negotiated a new contract for three films, at $125,000 each, but as that film did continued fine business and edged into the year's top hits, Henie – noted for her keen business sense – demanded revised terms. The contract was amended: five years, three pictures a year at $160,000 per picture – which, working out at $16,000 a week for 10 weeks per film, made her the highest paid of stars.

The films were all much of a muchness. Most of them were set in winter sports resorts, with stories devised to keep audiences as mindless as possible between the Henie bouts on skates. They were gay and glamorous, with

a war refugee: hooray for a new formula) in *Sun Valley Serenade* (41) nary a spark flew, but the Glenn Miller Orchestra and two hit songs caused it to more than smoulder at the box-office. However, *Iceland* (42) with Payne and *Wintertime* (43) with Cornel Wilde and Jack Oakie did not do well and 20th quietly did not renew her contract. She signed with International for two films, the first of which was *It's a Pleasure* (45), with Michael O'Shea, but whatever the addition of colour did to the skating scenes, it was ineffective at the box-office. (It was released by RKO, who had earlier had their own Henie-rival, Irene Dare; but the only other skater who made it in films – in a very mild way – was Belita.)

International Pictures had amalgamated with Universal and they released the skating remake of an old Universal property, *The Countess of Monte Cristo* (48). It was a flop and, as Henie insisted on her films being built round her, there were no more takers in Hollywood. But she had always found 'in-person' shows lucrative and most of her subsequent fortune came from them. She had played Madison Square Garden annually for years and did so until 1952 when there was a row with the management. She 'was considered temperamental' said 'Variety'. She transferred her show to the Knightsbridge Armory in the Bronx, but ticket sales were meagre. She then gave up. She had appeared also in Europe and was a very wealthy lady indeed. But even if she needed films as little as they needed her, in 1958 she turned up in Britain to make something called *Hello London*, in which she played herself and Michael Wilding, as himself, tried to get her to do a show for charity against her agent's wishes. London did not say hello in return and after a couple of provincial bookings it disappeared until 1968 when it appeared among some afternoon TV schedules. That same year Henie made news when it was announced that she and her wealthy (third) husband were going to donate most of their fine modern art collection together with a new gallery to the city of Oslo. She died in 1969, of leukaemia, while on a plane journey to that city.

Sonja Henie in One in a Million: *it was 20th Century-Fox's Christmas present to cinemagoers in 1936.*

excellent supporting casts, and as beautifully crafted star vehicles as the Deanna Durbins at Universal; she was invariably found irresistible by the most handsome louts on the 20th lot – like Richard Greene (department store heir who chases her to college) in *My Lucky Star*. None of these gentlemen was a great talent, but they made the lady twinkle a bit and with the aid of such things as the Irving Berlin score for *Second Fiddle* (39) the films were amiable entertainment. Power and Rudy Vallee were also in that, but it was not the expected hit. Ray Milland and Robert Cummings were in *Everything Happens at Night* and they were journalists involved with the Gestapo – but not too seriously (yet). There was no Henie film in 1940 and her contract was revised again: only one film a year. The novelty had worn off; the trouble was that when she was not skating, unassuming and sweet as she was (on screen: off it, she was hell on wheels, which was part of her undoing), she was as interesting as a cold potato. Confronted with John Payne (she was

KATHARINE HEPBURN

The longevity of Katharine Hepburn's career must have confounded her early detractors: both in and out of Hollywood she evoked strong feelings for and against and sometimes only the praise of reviewers saved her from the wrath of producers and exhibitors. The fan magazines watched from the wings, half-admiring, half-aghast: 'Is Hepburn Killing

Her Own Career?' asked 'Photoplay' in 1935, detailing the new exploits of this *enfant terrible* and the bumpy road of her latest movie at the box-office. George Cukor described her: 'a person whose rare charm and strength is her uncompromising individuality. . . . From the beginning, Miss Hepburn chose a direct line and stuck to it. It can frankly be said that Hepburn has not grown up to Hollywood. Hollywood has grown up to her.' She herself has said: 'I suppose when I was a very young actress I was very unsure of myself, and I thought you had to be nice to everybody, so I was. Then I got to be a big star rather quickly, and it occurred to me that you didn't, then I was difficult with the press and everybody. Then after a while, things didn't go so well, so I decided it was time to be sweet again. And by that time, the press and I had got to be rather old and sweet together. You know, when someone has been around as long as I have, people get fond of you, like some old building.'

'Fond' is hardly an adequate word to describe the attitude to Hepburn: when, in 1967–9 she returned to films and decided to give a series of interviews, journalists searched in dictionaries for new superlatives and critics did not so much review her performances as send her love-letters. The fact is that towards the end of her career she became a Very Big Star Indeed, after years of a strictly limited popularity (for instance, since the 30s she has seldom attained top billing).

She was a star from the word go. She had a whacking part in her first film and the world knew there had arrived a star to be reckoned with, perhaps challenging the supremacy of Garbo (which resulted in a silly fan magazine rivalry). But it is in the Garbo stratosphere that she belongs (Kenneth Tynan once termed her 'the Garbo of the Great Outdoors'), though clearly stronger in personality than in versatility.

Hepburn was born in Hartford, Connecticut, in 1909, into a wealthy family. She acted at college and made her pro début in Baltimore in 1928 in 'The Czarina'; she acted for four years without success ('Death Takes a Holiday', 'Art and Mrs Bottle') and was also married (1928–34) with similar results. She was often fired (hence the insecurity) and was at one point dropped from the lead in an updating of 'Lysistrata' – 'The Warrior's Husband' (32); but taken on again, she became a Broadway star. Paramount had already offered a test, but Hepburn had preferred to wait: now she went on her own terms, on a one-picture deal at RKO at $1,500 a week. The studio hesitated, however, till Laurence Olivier took his wife Jill Esmond back to England and they needed a replace-ment for *A Bill of Divorcement* (32), but he said that that was because he had seen Hepburn's contract, which would pay her twice as much as Esmond. George Cukor ran a test that Hepburn had done and requested that she be cast as John Barrymore's daughter, fearing she might inherit his mental derangement. RKO took up their option for four more pictures.

Said the 'Daily Telegraph' (London): 'Miss Hepburn has many limitations. She is not at all beautiful and her voice is uncommonly harsh, though, thank heaven, not shrill. But give her 10 minutes to work her spell and you forget these things. You realize that here is something new and different – a very young actress with the power of a well-trained tragedienne, a strange, dynamic and moving young person in a profession full of character-less, synthetic blondes.' Such notices brought some reaction by the time *Christopher Strong* (33) was shown. But in the 'New York Herald Tribune' Richard Watts Jr declared defiantly that she remained 'just as good an actress and just a distinctive a personage'. She played, with the same burning conviction, a celebrated British aviatrix, the sort of resolute part she was to play so often. Co-star Colin Clive told an interviewer: 'There is nobody quite like her in Hollywood – or anywhere else for that matter. . . . She is not just a face, but a terrific personality. I said just now that she is not beautiful and that is true, though she understands the art of acting so amazingly that she can convey the illusion of beauty if the part demands it!' And Paul Muni said, after her third film: 'There's no one to touch her among the younger actresses – the only one approaching her is Margaret Sullavan, but she's soft, charming, lovely. She hasn't Hepburn's drive.'

The third film was *Morning Glory* and Hepburn was *very* determined as a struggling actress, until Adolphe Menjou said, 'You don't belong to any man now – you belong to Broadway.' Said A.J. Harman of this performance in the London 'Evening News': 'The most remarkable acting I have ever seen.' In Hollywood she won the Best Actress Oscar. Cukor directed her again in (his favourite among his own films) *Little Women*. She was perfectly cast as Jo, again got great notices and the film was a huge grosser. *Spitfire* (34) – as a wild girl of the mountains – did not do so well and did not deserve to. She received, per her contract, $6,000 for four weeks' work, but was able to claim another $10,000 for overtime, since a Broadway venture, 'The Lake', had to be rescheduled. The play served her with a rebuff which might have sunk a lesser person and it provided her with a famous line: 'The calla lilies are in bloom

again'. It also provoked two more deathless lines: Dorothy Parker's comment on her performance, 'She ran the gamut of emotions from A to B' and George S. Kaufman's (on hearing that she had had sheets put up in the wings), 'She's afraid she might catch acting'.

She limped back to Hollywood, initially on a new six-picture contract. Technicolor tests exist from around this time of her as Shaw's Saint Joan, but the film was not made. RKO offered little solace from her Broadway failure with J.M. Barrie's synthetic and cloying *The Little Minister* (34) – she was Babbie, the gypsy girl – and the weak *Break of Hearts* (35), desperately loving Charles Boyer after a Cinderella romance. Of *Minister* she confessed (in an interview in 'Sight and Sound') years later: 'I didn't really want to play it until I heard another actress was desperate for the role. Then of course it became the most important thing in the world for me that I should get it. Several of my parts in those days I fought for just to take them from someone who needed them.' (*Minister* had at one time been bought by Universal for Margaret Sullavan and at least two Hepburn roles – *Christopher Strong* and *A Woman Rebels* – had been intended for Ann Harding.) It was announced that she would play George Sand and Elizabeth I; instead she played *Alice Adams*, based on Booth Tarkington's novel about an affected small town girl. The film still looks good today, due as much to the direction of George Stevens, a new man

whom Hepburn insisted on having.

Cukor directed her again, in the transcription of a novel by Compton Mackenzie, *Sylvia Scarlet* – 'Father, I'm going to cut my hair off! I'm going to be a boy!'; and John Ford helmed the film of Maxwell Anderson's *Mary of Scotland* (36), a lush and silly picture with memorable solecisms. Hepburn despised *Mary* and was better cast in two more costume dramas: *A Woman Rebels*, a saga of a woman's emancipation in Victorian England with Van Heflin as her lover and Herbert Marshall as the man who stands by her; and better Barrie, *Quality Street* (37), beautifully directed by Stevens with Fay Bainter equally fine as the older sister. Quality was the keynote again with *Stage Door*, directed by Gregory La Cava, with Ginger Rogers and a fine cast in this excellent adaptation of the Ferber-Kaufman stage hit about aspiring actresses; and with *Bringing up Baby* (38), directed by Howard Hawks, with Cary Grant and Hepburn displaying a dazzling aptitude for screwball comedy.

Despite great reviews for most of this batch, they did increasingly badly (*A Woman Rebels* achieved the no mean feat of losing even more money than *Mary of Scotland*) and since three well-received comedies had done nothing to reverse the decline, RKO had to face the fact that she was no longer a prize property. At this juncture their pessimism was confirmed when a group of exhibitors labelled her box-office poison (for some reason the label stuck to Hepburn longer than to the others on the list). RKO then proposed a property they had had hanging around for some time, *Mother Carey's Chickens*, and rather than submit, she bought up her contract. She cast around for a job and had a yen to do *Holiday*, a play she had understudied; it so happened that Columbia owned this, among a batch of old Pathé properties acquired from RKO. She negotiated with Columbia to do it there, with Cukor directing and herself getting a fee of $175,000, which was $25,000 more than RKO had paid her. Cukor and she did their usual accomplished work, but the film was too talky for general acceptance. There were no further film offers, though there was an outside chance that Selznick would cast her as Scarlett O'Hara; he had produced some of her early films and Cukor was set to direct *Gone With the Wind*. Eventually she was offered Scarlett, one of the three actresses who were, but she sensed that Selznick had only approached her out of desperation and accepted provisionally: it was widely accepted that she had not the requisite sex appeal and it was known that Clark Gable did not want her. She was not surprised when Selznick discovered Vivien Leigh at the last minute and preferred her.

Katharine Hepburn in her second film, Christopher Strong (*33*). *She's got up like this for a fancy-dress party, but the pose and the costume – artificial, absurd and disdainful – indicate why the young Hepburn had difficulty imposing herself on the public at large. The fan magazines ensured that the public knew that she was like this in life, as they predicted a speedy end to her career.*

The next offer was from MGM and involved a mere $10,000; true, it was a Lubitsch film, but she did not like the script. She decided that she needed an exceptional film if she was to continue. She approached Philip Barry, the author of 'Holiday', and asked him to write a play for her. He came up with 'The Philadelphia Story', a comedy about a girl on the eve of her second marriage – and Hepburn also quietly purchased the movie rights. As the spoilt, aristocratic, emotionally indecisive Tracy Lord, she avenged herself with a vengeance for the flop of 'The Lake'. It was the hit of the Broadway season and Hollywood began bidding for the movie rights. Hepburn's price included herself and Goldwyn offered Gary Cooper and director William Wyler, but MGM promised even better box-office insurance in the form of Cary Grant (Clark Gable was at first mooted) and James Stewart. With Cukor directing, the film (40) did as well as on the screen as it had on stage and Hepburn was the New York critics' Best Actress of the Year because of it.

If on the screen she was intrinsically the same (mannered, extravagant, but now with her technique polished needle-sharp), in private she was more cooperative, less patronizing. She badly wanted an MGM contract and when MGM were not forthcoming, she offered them another property she had acquired as a co-starring vehicle for Spencer Tracy and herself. MGM bought it and paid her in addition a salary of $100,000. When producer Joseph L. Mankiewicz introduced them, she said: 'I'm afraid I'm too tall for you, Mr Tracy.' Mankiewicz observed, 'Don't worry, he'll soon cut you down to size': it was the beginning of an offscreen friendship which was to last until Tracy's death and an on-screen partnership which may well be the most rewarding in film history. There were 10 films all told. This first one set the pattern: *Woman of the Year* (42), directed by Stevens. They were journalists of opposing interests on the brink of divorce. She was eager, 'intellectual', idealistic; he down-to-earth, mocking, 'tolerant' – presumably reflections of real-life characteristics. They were urbane and completely captivating as a team; and the success of the film caused Metro finally to offer her a long-term contract. It is doubtful whether the studio ever cared much for her: the films she made without Tracy were poor and the subsequent films they made together were initiated by themselves rather than by the studio.

For the moment they turned to drama: Cukor's version of I.A.R. Wylie's *Keeper of the Flame*, a novel about a widow and the reporter who makes her admit that her husband was a fascist. Without Tracy she did *Stage Door Canteen* (43) at UA, as herself –

one of Hollywood's love-songs to show business, and my, was she gracious, coming in at the end after a long parade of stars; and *Dragon Seed* (44), a melodramatic Oriental charade after Pearl S. Buck in which she, of all people, was a patriotic Chinese peasant in Peck and Peckish pyjamas. She and Tracy did *Without Love* (45), a comedy that she had done on stage without him in 1942; then Robert Taylor tried to murder her in a psychological melodrama directed by Vincente Minnelli, *Undercurrent* (46). She was in period costume for *The Sea of Grass* (47), directed by Elia Kazan, with Tracy, and in *Song of Love*, where she and Paul Henried were the Schumanns and Robert Walker a boyish Brahms: her mighty efforts to get Clara's fingering right must be one of the cinema's lost causes. Then there were two excellent comedies with Tracy: *State of the Union* (48), a witty political piece directed by Frank Capra – his best postwar film; and *Adam's Rib* (49), directed by Cukor, written by Ruth Gordon and Garson Kanin, about husband-and-wife lawyers who find themselves on opposing sides in a serio-comic attempted murder case. Their lines were good and they batted them back and forth like Wimbledon champions: their mutual admiration remains a pleasure to see. There was much speculation about their offscreen relationship and she, asked once by a reporter whether she loved Tracy, replied: 'Everyone loves Mr Tracy.'

In 1950 she returned to Broadway in 'As You Like It', and there were several further forays into Shakespeare over the next few years: Portia, Isabella and Katharina ('The Shrew') on an Australian tour for the Old Vic in 1955 and, later, Portia again, Beatrice, Viola and Cleopatra at the Shakespeare Festival in Connecticut.

She was off the screen for two years and returned with a bang: as the prissy spinster who found love ('Dear – what's your first name?') on a tramp steamer chugging through the African jungle, *The African Queen* (51). C.A. Lejeune said: 'We always knew that Miss Hepburn was a dab hand with the timing of a comic line, but it is a long while since she gave so much heart and tenderness to a role. To sustain such a long and complex part without a fault is something of a *tour de force*.' Humphrey Bogart was the unshaven and unlikely object of her affections and John Huston directed from a novel by C.S. Forester: raves all round, her greatest box-office hit to that time – and a constant winner in newspaper polls of readers' favourite film of all time (Los Angeles 1967; London 1972). *Pat and Mike* (52) was below-par for the *Adam's Rib* team, with Tracy as her trainer

The beginning of a great screen partnership: Tracy and Hepburn in Woman of the Year (42). *He was a sports columnist and she a commentator on international affairs: her citation as Woman of the Year almost broke up their marriage.*

and she as an all-round athlete, 'at her most enchanting' said Dilys Powell, 'spirited, gay, the voice with its curiously attractive flat tones modulating into triumph, the harassed rectangular look melting into affection': it was her last for MGM. Prior to that, she had acted in 'The Millionairess' in London and New York, whose author – Shaw – had once described her as 'the born decider, dominator, organizer, tactician, mesmiriser', but he was not prophetic, for she had set her heart on a film of that play, with Preston Sturges directing, but could not get backing.

After a further absence, she played a spinster schoolteacher having her first – and probably last – affair, with a Venetian Lothario, in the Anglo-US *Summer Madness/Summertime* (55), directed by David Lean from Arthur Laurents's 'The Times of the Cuckoo'. It was a captivating performance, poised on the right side of laughing-through-tears, but if the combination of Hepburn and the Serenissima was irresistible to aficionados the film was not popular at the time. It was ambrosia beside the British *The Iron Petticoat* (56), a pseudo-*Ninotchka* comedy: whoever

advised her and Bob Hope to cross the Atlantic did them a profound disservice. *The Rainmaker* was popular, because Burt Lancaster was in it, the object of the plain jane's last-gasp love-affair; but when she was not doing a useful transformation job, it was pure sludge. At 20th, she and Tracy did *The Desk Set* (57), a ponderous CinemaScope comedy that was simply a reminder of better days; and she was offscreen till she played the bereaved but voracious mother in *Suddenly Last Summer* (59) – in fact only a supporting role, but wiping the floor with the other players. *Long Day's Journey into Night* (62) was another filmed play – O'Neill's, directed by Sidney Lumet, and as the drug-addicted mother she 'emerges as a superb *tragedienne*', said Dwight Macdonald. She and her fellow-players – Ralph Richardson (Tracy had refused the role, despite her pleas, because this was not a major studio production), Jason Robards and Dean Stockwell – won an ensemble acting award at Cannes, but the film, though critically admired, was of limited appeal (which was why the cast accepted $20,000 each, plus varying percentages).

A brief encounter in Venice: Hepburn and Rossano Brazzi in Summer Madness *(55). 'She plays every scene with characteristic attack and insight . . . but she is often simply too fascinating' – Gavin Lambert in 'Sight and Sound'.*

Then she stayed away for five years, neglected, one felt, though notes in the press suggested that she was devoting her time to the increasingly ill Tracy (she certainly turned down *Rosie*, which Universal had bought for her); it was further suggested that she only accepted the uninteresting role of the mother in *Guess Who's Coming to Dinner* (67) to be

close to him. (Her fee was $200,000; he got $300,000.) It was their last film together and a triumph no one could have foreseen: critics who disliked the material talked of the 'alchemy' of this 'legendary' team and crowds flocked to see them. Aided by the box-office potency of Sidney Poitier, the film made a fantastic $20 million-plus. Hepburn received an Oscar and if general reaction was that for this performance it was hardly deserved, no one would deny her a second – 35 years after the first.

In the wake of Tracy's demise, she embarked on *The Lion in Winter* (68), as Eleanor of Aquitaine to Peter O'Toole's Henry II, and the cinema equivalent of book club history – but highly thought of in some quarters. Critics predicted an Oscar for Hepburn and with an almost unparalleled 11 nominations she became the first actress to win a third (in a tie with Barbra Streisand). The film itself, however, looked good beside *The Madwoman of Chaillot* (69), directed by Bryan Forbes after John Huston left: Giraudoux's play was unlikely screen material – as this film amply proved.

Hepburn found herself, because of *Lion*, at ninth among box-office stars, which, after so long a career, delighted her: at which point she returned to the stage, in 'Coco', at a record salary for a performer in a regular Broadway show: but poor notices for every aspect of this musical, except her, limited the run and caused Paramount to cancel plans to film it. In fact, she left to make a third dreadful film in a row, *The Trojan Women* (71), directed by Michael Cacoyannis, as Hecuba, almost rising above the incompetence around her. MGM signed her to do the film of Greene's *Travels with My Aunt* under Cukor's direction, but as she continued to doubt the script prepared and approved, she was fired – fortuitously, as it turned out. Still stretching her talent, she did *A Delicate Balance* (73), Edward Albee's play filmed for limited showings in cinemas; and for TV there were *The Glass Menagerie*, over-querulous as Amanda, and *Love Among the Ruins* (75), a jig about a litigious fiancée (Hepburn) and her lawyer, once an old flame (Laurence Olivier) – which was all right if you did not expect more from this team and their director, Cukor. *Rooster Cogburn* found her out West with John Wayne, a geriatrics' treat but not for general audiences; and after that she was on Broadway, and touring, in 'A Matter of Gravity'. There was another film, an independent venture, *Olly Olly Oxen Free* (78), a dire kiddies' tale, playing a sort of bag-lady who reminisces to the skies while in a hot-air balloon with two toddlers. Much better was Cukor's TV version of *The Corn is Green*, photographed on location in Wales, but she did not eclipse memories of Bette Davis in the same role. She worried about husband Henry Fonda's health and his daughter Jane's love-life in *On Golden Pond* (81), which was a great success and brought her a fourth Oscar: but apart from the Fondas' acting there was little merit in it. Ernest Thompson wrote the screenplay from his own play and concurrently he provided Hepburn with a Broadway vehicle, 'The West Side Waltz'.

On Golden Pond proved, after several years of movie failures, that she was everyone's favourite aged actress. Thus she persuaded Cannon to back *The Ultimate Solution of Grace Quigley* (84), which she had been hawking round Hollywood for a decade. She even put her own money into it. It exists in several versions – one entitled simply *Grace Quigley* – but has been little seen, except by critics, who gave ample reasons why no one should go to a comedy-drama about an old lady so keen on euthanasia that she hires a hit man (Nick Nolte). She narrated a television documentary on Tracy, tactfully acknowledging their offscreen relationship, which anyway is public knowledge (after a book about it by Garson Kanin, which infuriated her), and has done two other films, for television, including *Mrs Delafield Wants to Marry* (86) – a Jewish doctor, Harold Gould. On paper, it sounds terrible, but it was freshly written and handled, providing her with her most acceptable performance in years. George Schaeffer, who directed, guided her again through *Penthouse Paradise* (89), as a novelist who stirs up trouble when she writes a book by that title. She then planned to do an autobiographical

The Lion in Winter (68), *a historical charade enlivened by some good performances: Hepburn's brought her her third Best Actress Oscar.*

opus with her secretary, *Phyllis and Me*. In 1969 she said 'I only want to go on being a star. It's all I know how to be': neither age nor material has impeded that wish.

WENDY HILLER

Wendy Hiller's screen appearances have been few, presumably because 'she has very strong views on the feminine problem of Home versus a Career. It is her opinion that it is impossible to make a success of both all the time' ('Picture Show', 1957). Equally, she has limited her theatre work; and this would seem to be one actress genuinely committed to domesticity (she married dramatist Ronald Gow in 1937). She was born in Bramhall, Cheshire, in 1912 and went straight from school into the theatre, studying at Manchester rep – ASM, understudies and small parts. In 1934 she was given the lead in 'Love on the Dole' (by Gow) and took it from the provinces to London and thence to New York in 1936. It established her quite firmly as one of Britain's leading young actresses and brought her her first film part – another North Country dialect role – *Lancashire Luck* (37). Already

she had played the part – Eliza Doolittle – which was to bring her world fame: in 1936 she had done that and Saint Joan at the Malvern Festival, to the delight of Shaw himself, who recommended her for the film version of *Pygmalion* (38). Her Eliza was very touching and was an admirable foil for Leslie Howard. Gabriel Pascal produced and put Hiller under contract. The film's success in the US brought Hollywood offers, which she or Pascal refused.

She did a second Shaw film for Pascal, *Major Barbara* (40), and was again memorable, playing with a steely determination, a wit and a blazing sincerity which have made this part difficult for other actresses. Her particular qualities were utilized nicely by Powell and Pressburger in their Scottish love story, *I Know Where I'm Going* (45) with Roger Livesey and Pamela Brown. She went to the Bristol Old Vic in 1946 to play in her husband's adaptation of 'Tess of the d'Urbervilles', which she later did in London. Other stage appearances at this time included 'The Heiress' in New York (47) and in London (50), taking over from Peggy Ashcroft. She returned to the screen as Mrs Almayer, the drab, resigned wife, in *An Outcast of the Islands* (52); somewhat less notable were the

Leslie Howard as Higgins and Wendy Hiller as Eliza in Pygmalion (*38*).

20th-backed *Singlehanded* (53) from a novel by C.S. Forester, where she was the mother of Jeffrey Hunter, and a duo in 1957, the American *Something of Value* and a British comedy, *How to Murder a Rich Uncle*. She went to Hollywood to play the stern, embittered hotelier of *Separate Tables* (58) and won the Best Supporting Actress Oscar. Other stage appearances of the 50s included an Old Vic season (55–56) and New York visits for 'A Moon for the Misbegotten' and 'Flowering Cherry' (the latter she also did in London for a while). In 1963 she appeared in 'The Wings of the Dove'.

She was once again memorable as the sad mother in *Sons and Lovers* (60) – this time Dean Stockwell was the unlikely son; and she was good in Hollywood's *Toys in the Attic* (63), which as a play she had done in the West End, though in a different part. As Thomas More's impatient nagging wife, however, in *A Man for All Seasons* (66), she entirely misjudged her effects. But she was excellent as Mrs Micawber in *David Copperfield* (70).

Among stage and TV appearances, she makes occasional films: *Murder on the Orient Express* (74), her stock *grande dame* performance as a countess; *Voyage of the Damned* (76), decorating a second film heavy with names and little else; and *The Cat and the Canary* (79), an exceptionally ill-advised remake, with some more 'names'. Most of these were American-backed, as was *The Elephant Man* (80), in which she was the head nurse. And she returned to the US to play an aunt in *Making Love* (82), the tale of a married man (Michael Ontkean) discovering his homosexuality. Shortly after she was in two plays filmed for TV, *The Kingfisher*, opposite Ralph Richardson, and *Witness for the Prosecution*, supporting Rex Harrison. *The Last Viceroy* (86) and *Attracta* (87) were made for that medium, the former in the US and the latter – in which she starred, playing a teacher – in Eire. She returned to cinemas in a supporting role in *The Lonely Passion of Judith Hearn* (88). She was created a Dame of the British Empire in 1975.

VALERIE HOBSON

Valerie Hobson was – to her disadvantage – ineffably ladylike. The British film industry of the 30s and 40s was a man's world and the female stars got short shrift. Those British girls who did go to Hollywood were criticized back home for submitting to that town's despised 'glamour treatment'. But whether or not they emerged with their individuality gone – and some did – they were invariably better to look upon.

Hobson's time in Hollywood was not at all worthwhile and she might have made no stronger mark in the British industry had not she managed to assert her distinctive personality from time to time. It was not until the 60s that British girls got less of a raw deal from their own studios: as the British industry became internationalized, the girls – many of them clearly less talented than Hobson – became more attractive and more sexy. It was not, of course, part of Hobson's function to be sexy, but through three dozen films, she represented British womanhood and it was, overall, a prospect unlikely to stir the blood in Dallas and Delhi, or even, come to that, in Droitwich.

She was born in Larne, Northern Ireland, in 1917, of English parents (father was a naval officer); she studied at RADA and found stage success early when she appeared in 'Ball at the Savoy', starring Maurice Evans at Drury Lane. Around the same time she landed the female lead in a B picture, *Eyes of Fate* (33), which used the same idea as Clair's later *It Happened Tomorrow*; and there were further leading roles in *Two Hearts in Waltz-time* (34), which starred Carl Brisson; *The Path to Glory*, whose cast included Maurice Evans and Henry Daniell, a satire on war that she had done as a radio play; and *Badger's Green*, a cricketing comedy that had been a success on the stage. Then Hollywood – Universal – offered a contract; that studio planned a version of *Great Expectations* and thought Hobson would be ideal as Estella. But they changed their mind; the part went to Jane Wyatt and Hobson, briefly a platinum blonde, was given a featured part in a domestic comedy with Roger Pryor, *Strange Wives* (35). She was sent to Britain for another B picture, *Oh What a Night*, a comedy about amnesia, and returned to Hollywood for another, *Rendezvous at Midnight*. Her standing marginally improved: *The Mystery of Edwin Drood*, with Claude Rains, as Helena Landless; *The Bride of Frankenstein*, as the protective wife of the Baron (Colin Clive); and *The Werewolf of London*, as the wife of same (Henry Hull), a scientist by day. She was the heroine of *Chinatown Squad*, with Lyle Talbot, and of *The Great Impersonation*, with Edmund Lowe as the wastrel peer in this version of the oft-filmed Oppenheim novel. Neither the films nor she were impressive (she had little to do but look afraid and scream) and she was dropped by Universal when it was reorganized. She lingered hopefully in Hollywood to make two Bs, *August Weekend* (36), at Chesterfield and *Tugboat Princess* at Columbia, supporting Edith Fellows.

In Britain she prepared to start again at zero, but was offered a star part in *Secret of Stamboul* with James Mason, a preposterous little picture based on a novel by Dennis Wheatley; then she got leads in *No Escape*, an air drama with Leslie Perrins, and (as an adventuress) in *Jump for Glory* (37), which Raoul Walsh crossed the Atlantic to direct. It was the first time she had come into her own on the screen. Korda liked her and cast her as the Colonel's wife in *The Drum* (38), a tale of tension on the NW Frontier: she did it as if to the manner born (she was) and was delightful as well. Korda used her again, as a reporter, in *Q Planes* (39); and before that she had been a reporter's wife – Barry K. Barnes's – in a thriller, *This Man Is News* (38). It was a modest success and a sequel was made, *This Man in Paris* (39). The producer was Anthony Havelock-Allen and he and Hobson were married in 1939. Until they were divorced in 1952, she certainly enjoyed a privileged position in the British film world.

She made *A Spy in Black* with Conrad Veidt and *The Silent Battle*, with Michael Redgrave, and she was with Veidt again in *Contraband* (40); after which she was decorative while clever Redgrave forded the ocean with the *Atlantic Ferry* (41), just in case, one

day, as the film put it, 'Britain and the United States should be united against a common enemy'. She made *Unpublished Story* (42) with Richard Greene and *The Adventures of Tartu* (43) starring Robert Donat, as a Resistance worker posing as the girlfriend of a prominent Nazi. In 1942 it was announced that she had signed a Hollywood contract, but she did not go to Hollywood; and she did not film again till she played a woman MP in Daphne du Maurier's *The Years Between* (46) with Redgrave. Her husband, meanwhile, had become Exec-Producer of Cineguild, which released through Rank, using the talents of director David Lean and producer Ronald Neame – which could be why Hobson at last played Estella in *Great Expectations*, a highly praised version of Dickens, with John Mills as the grown-up Pip. The whole cast was memorable, with Hobson the ideal Estella. She had not achieved the popularity of actresses like Margaret Lockwood or Phyllis Calvert, but at last she was in the forefront of British stars. She was not too happy in Cineguild's *Blanche Fury* (47) with Stewart Granger, a period melodrama purportedly done in an effort to show rival British studios how. It didn't. Havelock-Allen left Cineguild, and Hobson went with him, to make *The Small Voice* (48),

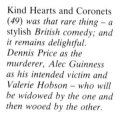

Kind Hearts and Coronets (49) was that rare thing – a stylish British comedy; and it remains delightful. Dennis Price as the murderer, Alec Guinness as his intended victim and Valerie Hobson – who will be widowed by the one and then wooed by the other.

with James Donald and Howard Keel, about the household held to ransom by escaped convicts (an old theme liable to at least three more goings-over during the next few years).

Ealing gave her a couple of rare chances to play elegant comedy: felicitiously in *Kind Hearts and Coronets* (49), unhappily in *Train of Events*, an episoder where she was fighting with husband-conductor John Clements. *The Interrupted Journey* was also, more direly, about trains, with Richard Todd, and she was his solicitous wife; *The Rocking Horse Winner*, with Mills, was a version of a D.H. Lawrence story and she was the little boy's worried mother. She brought her own special glitter to three comedies – *The Card* (51), as a Duchess with Alec Guinness, and a couple where she was well matched by Nigel Patrick, the unpretentious *Who Goes There?* (52), which was otherwise spoiled by Peggy Cummins in the leading role, and *Meet Me Tonight*, which completely wrecked three of Noël Coward's 'Tonight at 8.30' playlets: weak direction handicapped the stars (who included also Stanley Holloway and Kay Walsh). There were two minor dramas, *The Voice of Merrill* and *Background* (53), and then Hobson's last chance to demonstrate how she could flower under a good director: René Clement's fine *Monsieur Ripois/Knave of Hearts* (54) with Gérard Philipe.

Hobson had already announced her retirement. In 1953 she had been chosen to play the Gertrude Lawrence role in the British production of 'The King and I' (and did, beautifully) and she said that she did not think her career could top this and she would not try. She had married an MP, John Profumo, and proposed to devote her life to being his wife. Whereupon, when 'King' ended, she passed from the headlines – until the scandal of 1963, involving Profumo, by then a prominent Minister of the Crown. Hobson stood by him during his difficulties.

BOB HOPE

Bob Hope's film work now seems but an interval in his long career. Although he made films for over 30 years, only those of the first decade are good – it was these which firmly established him as a popular favourite and it is for these, with their hugely confident and unpretentious scripts, that he will be remembered. We might think of him less as a film star than (with George Burns) the last survivor of the golden age of radio, perhaps marginally more popular and slightly less esteemed than his peers, Jack Benny and Fred Allen. Since for over 30 years his TV appear-

ances have drawn huge ratings – even today, though he is in his 80s – we shall certainly think of him as a star of that medium. We remember him entertaining the troops, emceeing the Oscar ceremony, cracking jokes at the White House or a charity 'roast'; we read of him still planing off for a charity golf match, a première, a TV show in Britain or Australia. He is, in the words of 'Time Magazine' a 'workaholic'. As early as 1949, John Steinbeck observed that he could only conjecture what goes on inside the man: 'He is cut off from rest and even admitting weariness. Having become a symbol he must lead a symbol life.'

His team of scriptwriters is legendary and there are those who grant him little beyond a status as a stand-up comedian, mechanically firing off high-speed patter. One of the joys of that, though, is in his professionalism, his control of his audience; he clearly gets a kick out of doing it. Certainly he is adept at ad-libs and seems – which is important in his line of comedy – underneath it all a regular guy. His screen counterpart is much less trustworthy. He saunters on in the same way as the stage Hope, primly smug, boyishly audacious, a smart-Aleck supremely in command: but at the first sign of danger his eyes go big and his knees go weak. He is mean and avaricious, but above all he is cowardly. He will certainly ditch Crosby and he has been known to ditch Lamour. He fancies himself as a sexpot and is not sexy. At his best, he is midway between a great comic like W.C. Fields and a fine light comedian like Jack Lemmon; what spoils him is that he is too knowing, especially when he shares it with the audience.

He was born in Eltham in south-east London in 1903, the fifth of seven sons. His father, a stonemason, took the family to Cleveland when Hope was four. Before trying vaudeville, he had done various jobs – soda-jerk, boxer and newsboy. He had won some Charlie Chaplin impersonation contests and started out professionally, advertising himself as a master of 'Songs, Patter and Eccentric Dancing'. But he gradually worked humour into his act. 'Variety' reviewed him under 'New Acts' in 1929 – favourably. He played a vaude performer in his first Broadway show, 'Ballyhoo', but did not make his mark till cast in 'Roberta' (33). In 1934 he married night-club singer Dolores Reade – one of the proverbially happy marriages of show business. He was featured in the 1936 'Ziegfeld Follies' with Fanny Brice and in 'Red Hot and Blue' with Merman and Durante. He made several shorts for Educational and other companies, e.g. *Going Spanish*, but said he had no interest in movies; he became a radio draw and it was because of that that Para-

Martha Raye and Bob Hope in College Swing *(38). The cast list read: Burns & Allen, Martha Raye, Bob Hope, Edward Everett Horton, Ben Blue, Betty Grable, Jackie Coogan, Florence George, John Payne, Robert Cummings, Skinnay Ennis – in that order.*

mount signed him for *The Big Broadcast of 1938* (38) with a host of names, including W.C. Fields. Hope was more or less the juvenile lead, with some funny moments and a great duet with Shirley Ross, 'Thanks For the Memory'. He was partnered with Martha Raye in *College Swing*, one of the coed musicals popular at the time; and *Give Me a Sailor* was a starring vehicle for the two of them. He got $20,000 for each of them and then was dropped – till Damon Runyon wrote an article about him. The studio recalled him. Throughout Hope's career he was to reprise themes and leading ladies and Paramount now shared him with Ross and Raye: *Thanks for the Memory* with Ross, a remake of 1931's *Up Pops the Devil*; *Never Say Die* (39) with Raye, as a rich hypochrondriac; and *Some Like It Hot* with Ross, a remake of *Shoot the Works* (which had Jack Oakie); then Paramount thought he might be right for the remake of the creepie-funny *The Cat and the Canary* with Paulette Goddard: he made the hero a real scaredy-cat. Its box-office success was such that the studio signed him to the standard seven-year contract. They would not regret it.

Hope found his first great popularity, however, with *Road to Singapore* (40) with Crosby and Lamour. Though Crosby was one of the studio's top stars, great things were not expected, but the film grossed the sort of money usually taken only by big prestige pictures. Follow-ups were called for: *The Ghost Breakers*, in a haunted house with Goddard, and *Road to Zanzibar* (41). Now the fun was zany and sometimes witty, and the gross was again around $1½ million. Later films in the series – after seat prices had risen – took $4½ million, less than some of Crosby's Hope-less films but still huge. The 40s would not have been quite the same without the *Road* films, but they revive variably. The more conventional Hope material has dated, though when his lines are good he is extremely funny. The Crosby-Hope teaming, however, works immaculately with, at their best, a combined sympathy/timing that is unequalled by any other screen partnership.

There were two more hits: *Caught in the Draft*, an army comedy with Lamour, and *Nothing But the Truth*, the old farce remade with Goddard; and at the end of 1941 Hope was among the top 10 money-makers. He stayed there till 1953, usually a place or two behind Crosby. And the next few were popular: *Louisiana Purchase*, in Technicolor, a stagey and bowdlerized version of Irving Berlin's Broadway show about corruption in

Road to Morocco (*42*),
*perhaps the best of the
'Road' pictures: Hope has
just double-crossed Crosby
in an attempt to get to
grips with Lamour on the
couch.*

politics; *Road to Morocco* (42); *My Favorite Blonde*, a spy comedy with Madeleine Carroll; *Star Spangled Rhythm* in a guest spot; *They Got Me Covered* (43), another spy story, with Lamour, out on loan to Goldwyn at a fee of $100,000 (Hope had asked him for this sum in 1940, when he was only getting $50,000 per film. Now Goldwyn was only too happy to meet the figure, though the deal included him getting the writing team of Brackett and Wilder, and his promise to let Paramount have Gary Cooper for *For Whom the Bell Tolls*); *Let's Face It*, another army comedy, with Betty Hutton; *The Princess and the Pirate* (44), a spoof swashbuckler – and one of the best of its kind – again for Goldwyn (who this time paid Paramount $133,50 for Hope, for 12 weeks' work); and *Road to Utopia* (45).

In 1945 he signed a new seven-year contract with Paramount and after a guest spot in *Duffy's Tavern* played Valentino's old part in *Monsieur Beaucaire* (46), a splendid comic swashbuckler. Its success was such that Hope went on strike for a year, wanting to make pictures that he could own: so the next dozen belong to him. *My Favorite Brunette* (47) was yet another follow-up, with Lamour in a clinic of homicidal doctors, and *Where There's Life* was a return to the formula of the wartime spy

comedies, with Hope in this case the unknowing heir to a European kingdom being stalked through New York by a motley gang of crooks, agents of his political rivals. There was more guesting, in *Variety Girl*, and then *Road to Rio*; and *The Paleface* (48) – out West and as cowardly as ever, his biggest hit sans Crosby. On the strength of that he overtook Crosby and everyone else and was voted 1949's biggest draw. In 1948 he was getting $150,000 per film. *Sorrowful Jones* (49) with Lucille Ball was a remake of *Little Miss Marker* and Hope fitted Damon Runyon's world so well that *The Lemon Drop Kid* was redone with him in 1951 (it was first done by Lee Tracy in 1935). Before it came *The Great Lover* (49), a shipboard frolic, the mélange as before – a killer (Roland Young) and a mysterious redhead (Rhonda Fleming); and *Fancy Pants* (50), with Ball again, and out West again, as a butler based more than somewhat on *Ruggles of Red Gap*.

More follow-ups: *My Favorite Spy* (51) with Hedy Lamarr, *Son of Paleface* (52), with Jane Russell again and not up to the original, and *Road to Bali*. Then, an army comedy again, *Off-Limits* (53), with which the scripts became considerably weaker: *Here Come the Girls* (54) with Rosemary Clooney and *Casanova's*

The Paleface (48): Jane Russell as Calamity Jane and Hope as dentist Painless Potter – who, much to his horror, is mistaken for Wild Bill Hickok.

Big Night, a period romp with Joan Fontaine. It was the last of his Paramount contract. Still at Paramount, he tried a more serious piece, *The Seven Little Foys* (55), a biopic of vaudevillian Eddie Foy, but it was so cliché-ridden that fewer fans than usual cared. Katharine Hepburn asked him to co-star in a British film she was making, *The Iron Petticoat* (56): Alas. Cary Grant had wisely turned it down. *That Certain Feeling* raised the standard, but it was not vintage Hope. *Beau James* (57) was another biopic and Hope might have made a convincing Mayor Walker had the writers not seemed uncertain whether to let the loved American comedian play the all-American heel; also it neglected to suggest that Walker might have been guilty and at no point was astringent enough. Paramount made it and Hope's fee was $200,000 plus 50 per cent of the profits. It was not very successful and Paramount decided he was too expensive. Much to-do was made about *Paris Holiday* (58), at UA, as co-star with Fernandel, made at Hope's own request, but their styles did not jell. He returned to Paramount, for the last time, for *Alias Jesse James* (59), a movie in *Paleface*-vein and almost of *Paleface* standard.

Most of his succeeding films were produced by his own company for UA. He was more serious again in *The Facts of Life* (60), in which he and Lucille Ball leave their respective spouses in an attempt to commit adultery: delicately handled, delightful together and, if the fun was gentle, it was at least there. Which is more than can be said for: *Bachelor in Paradise* (61) at MGM; *The Road to Hong Kong*; *Critic's Choice* (62) at Warners, with Ball, from a play by Ira Levin; *Call Me Bwana* (63) with Anita Ekberg; *A Global Affair* (64); *I'll Take Sweden* (65); *Boy Did I Get a Wrong Number* (66); and *Eight on a Lam* (67) with Phyllis Diller. The latter did well in the US (TV plugs?), but in Britain the press clobbered it and it went out as a second feature. Something similar happened to *The Private Navy of Sgt O'Farrell* (68), *How To Commit Marriage* (69) with Jackie Gleason and Jane Wyman, and *Cancel My Reservation* (72). Indeed, the low quality of Hope's movies became a byword: the reviews were sorrowful rather than peeved and one wondered why he bothered. Certainly he said: 'You do a movie and you have to wait to find out if it's any good. But personal appearance tours, that's instant satisfaction.'

An article in 'Show Magazine' in 1972 estimated Hope the wealthiest man in show business, with assets of between $400 million and $700 million – mostly because of shrewd investment in real estate. Since 1954, it said, he had never earned less than $1 million a year – and he has turned down $250,000 a week from Las Vegas. He was then getting $100,000 from each of his nine TV specials a year and around $500,000 each for his movies, with at least $25,000 for one nightclub or concert date. The article also disclosed that he paid his seven scriptwriters $500,000 a year (and noted that he is remarkably loyal to his employees). After him, 'Show' said, Bing Crosby was the wealthiest of show business people – with assets of $200 million to $400 million.

At the same time, the changing state of life in the US eroded Hope's once impregnable popularity. His TV specials remained popular, but the press began to attack him. 'Life Magazine', in particular, did a devastating piece on him in 1972, claiming, among other things, that he had been booed at a football match and that he had squashed GI criticism of his shows for the troops in Vietnam. He returned to the screen guesting in *The Muppet Movie* (79) and after many hold-outs agreed to do a tele-movie, *A Masterpiece of Murder* (86) with Don Ameche.

MIRIAM HOPKINS

In an odd book published in the mid-30s, 'The American Cinema', William H. Rideout claims: 'On all counts, Miss Hopkins is easily the finest actress on the screen today' – a curious judgment, even though, at the time, there were executives in Hollywood who shared it. Hopkins was supposedly versatile – an actress capable of moving from floozies to *grandes dames*: but unlike Ruth Chatterton or Barbara Stanwyck in such roles, she lacked warmth, over-compensating with expression and gesture in a way that is positively screen-hogging – and quite diverting when late in her screen career she was playing against better actresses in better roles, as in *Old Acquaintance* and *The Heiress*. Her hostessy graciousness and cracked-ice delivery seldom varied, as audiences patently told the front office – for she had the distinction of being dropped at least twice from major contracts. Nor was she a cooperative worker: Edward G. Robinson in his memoir called her 'puerile and silly and snobbish, complaining about every line, [using] every trick to upstage me'. It is a sad thing to have reached the top of your profession and leave no golden opinions from either side of the footlights.

She was born in 1902 in Savannah, Georgia. Although her publicity claimed that she was university-educated and studied ballet, the truth is different: she won a prize for public speaking (in Barre, Vermont, where her mother lived after leaving her father) and, via an uncle with Broadway connections, became a chorus girl in Irving Berlin's 'Music Box Revue' (21). She turned legit, successfully, in 'Little Jesse James' (23) and was thereafter seldom out of work: 'Puppets' (25), after replacing Claudette Colbert out-of-town; 'An American Tragedy' (26), 'Excess Baggage' (27), 'The Bachelor Father' (29) in London and 'Ritzy'. Her modest Broadway reputation caused Paramount to offer a seven-year contract starting at $1,000 a week and while appearing in 'Lysistrata' she was filming by day in the Long Island studio – starring in *Fast and Loose* (31), with Carole Lombard, as the offspring of indulgent parents, with too much money and too little to do. Though adapted by Preston Sturges from Avery Hopwood's play 'The Best People', the film, too, did little – and she was generally considered poor in it. She returned to the boards in 'Anatol' and Paramount gave her a second chance – in Lubitsch's *The Smiling Lieutenant* as the Queen-bride of the unwilling Chevalier; then she was a cabaret girl who got murdered in the Clive Brook-Kay Francis *24 Hours* – which put her in line for Ivy the barmaid in *Dr Jekyll and Mr Hyde* (32). She had her

sights on the ingénue part but director Mamoulian convinced her that she was the only actress on the Paramount lot capable of playing the drab.

Her stock went soaring, as Mamoulian had promised, though already in the can were three weak programmers: *Two Kinds of Women* with Phillips Holmes; *Dancers in the Dark* with Jack Oakie; and *The World and the Flesh* with George Bancroft, a story of Russian aristocrats fleeing the Revolution of 1917. She had the lead in Lubitsch's delightful *Trouble in Paradise* with Kay Francis and Herbert Marshall, and the success of that reinforced her position on the lot; she got another important part as the kidnapped heiress who takes to life in a brothel, in *The Story of Temple Drake* (33), a bowdlerized version of Faulkner's 'Sanctuary'; and then was loaned to MGM for a pointless rural drama, *The Stranger's Return*. Lubitsch directed her again in *Design for Living*, but unnoticeably: not only did it seem unlikely that she could enslave either Gary Cooper or Fredric March, but they all lacked the style for the Coward dialogue. She had another good role, a dramatic one, in *All of Me* (34), afraid that marriage would ruin her love for March, but before it was finished Paramount had decided to drop her. She was pushed into the farcical *She Loves Me Not*, as Bing Crosby's leading lady, but before either film came out she had returned to Broadway in 'Jezebel' (replacing a sick Tallulah Bankhead before the première; Bette Davis later filmed it).

Fredric March, Miriam Hopkins and Gary Cooper in Lubitsch's film version of Noël Coward's Design for Living *(33). Coward's dislike of the picture was not alleviated by a remark of its scriptwriter Ben Hecht: 'There's only one line of Coward's left in the picture – see if you can find it.' Needless to say, the film was not an improvement on the play.*

Goldwyn signed her and while preparing the right vehicle, loaned her to RKO for both *The Richest Girl in the World*, in which she was a thinly disguised Barbara Hutton, and *Becky Sharp* (35). This was in fact an RKO release of a Pioneer film, the first feature-length film completely in three-colour Technicolor: the system was not entirely new to cinemagoers and the film was not a great success (unlike the first Talkie, the first in CinemaScope, the first feature in 3-D, etc.). It curtails the original novel and achieves the feat of making what little is left considerably dull, including the machinations of Becky, played by Hopkins in a wildly conventional way. Of her, Cedric Hardwicke, also in the cast, wrote later: 'I fancy that she was little different, except perhaps in enjoying a degree more talent, from the other women stars of the era, most of whom behaved like a combination of Florence Nightingale and Catherine the Great.'

She made only four films for Goldwyn. She was a mercenary lady redeemed by love in *Barbary Coast*, moving in the process from Edward G. Robinson to Joel McCrea; and in *Splendor* (a title that does *not* convey the film's quality) she was a nice Southern girl marrying into a family of broke Manhattanites. In *These Three* (36), directed by William Wyler, she was a schoolteacher caught up in a web of scandal – but not one involving lesbianism, as in Lillian Hellman's

original play, 'The Children's Hour': the Hays Office would not let Goldwyn use either title or subject, but Hellman cleverly adapted her own work into a strong conventional triangle story, with Joel McCrea and Merle Oberon. Hopkins was loaned to Korda to play a journalist (with a plethora of close-ups to make the trip worth while) in a silly British drama, *Men Are Not Gods* (37), where Gertrude Lawrence, as a bitch, was somewhat more sympathetic than she was; and then to RKO for *The Woman I Love*, overacting again with Paul Muni. The director was Anatole Litvak and it was a remake of his French film, *L'Equipage*; when it was finished he became the third of her four husbands: Brandon Peters 1926–31; Austin Parker 1931–32; Litvak 1937–39; Raymond Brock 1945–51. Her last for Goldwyn was a screwball comedy, *Woman Chases Man*, with her chasing McCrea, she as an architect and he as the practical son of her crazy employer, Charles Winninger. She was an heiress chasing Greenwich Village painter Ray Milland in *Wise Girl*, a B picture for RKO: since the marvellous notices for *These Three* had not improved her standing, Goldwyn lost interest and in this ignominious way ended the contract.

She returned again to the stage, in 'Wine of Chance', but it did not get beyond Chicago. She was off the screen for a year, while her agent negotiated a contract at Warners, with script approval; but her time there was no

The Old Maid (39) *was directed by Edmund Goulding from a play by Zoë Akins based on a novel by Edith Wharton. Bette Davis had the title role – here being comforted by Miriam Hopkins after being jilted on her wedding day (and it was Miriam who was responsible for the groom's defection). Bette's bastard – brought up by Miriam – much preferred Bette's mothering.*

happier. Great plans were announced, but after some months she co-starred with Bette Davis in *The Old Maid* (39), in a part which was secondary in interest and tertiary or worse in terms of audience sympathy. And her part in *Virginia City* (40), as a saloon-cutie again, was subsidiary to Errol Flynn's. He had not wanted her in the film and there was trouble on the set. 'Picturegoer' commented: 'Miss Hopkins seems to be singularly unfortunate. Most of her pictures have been stormy affairs.' She had a good part in *The Lady With Red Hair* with Claude Rains, as Mrs Leslie Carter, but James Agate wrote: 'I don't feel she is a sufficiently good actress to impersonate one who was, in Mr Shaw's words, "a melodramatic actress of no mean powers".' Further, director Curtis Bernhardt said that Hopkins was 'terribly difficult to work with'. Also in 1940 the 'Harvard Lampoon' cited her 'the least desirable companion on a desert island'.

In 1941 she announced that she had bought a property about Nellie Bly and hoped to find a producer; she turned down *Badlands of Dakota* as unsuitable and instead appeared in a trite sentimental drama at UA, *A Gentleman After Dark* (42), as Brian Donlevy's ruthless wife. She returned to Warners for *Old Acquaintance* (43), with Davis again as the put-upon heroine and she the spoilt rival who causes most of the trouble. According to Davis this was a pattern repeated on the set: 'I don't think there was ever a more difficult female in the world' but she added that Hopkins was not happy with bitchy parts. She could have been no happier with the notices, which Davis stole again. Said Edgar Anstey in the 'Spectator': 'Miss Davis has never been better. Miss Hopkins tends to overact.'

A memo, nestling today in the Warner archive, advises that she should be run out of Hollywood, because of her behaviour while filming, which may be why she returned to Broadway, taking over Tallulah Bankhead's part in 'The Skin of Our Teeth', which she continued to play in New York and in summer theatres over the next few years. Wyler recalled her to Hollywood for a supporting role, the aunt in *The Heiress* (49), with Olivia de Havilland in the title-role – a part which Hopkins herself played, on tour, before the film came out. She tested, at Warners, for the role of the mother in *The Glass Menagerie* and when she did not get it, reconciled herself to being a supporting actress in films, playing Gene Tierney's snobbish mother in *The Mating Season* (51) and a whore in *The Outcasts of Poker Flat* (52); and then Wyler used her again in *Carrie*, as the selfish nagging wife who drives Olivier into the arms of Jennifer Jones. There was a certain drink problem, but it was not that which kept her from the public eye till 1958, when she took over from Jo Van Fleet in the Broadway production of 'Look Homeward Angel'; at that time she told an interviewer that if she was starting her career over again she would do everything differently. In 1959 she was supposed to do *Ma Barker and her Killer Brood*, but changed her mind and the film was cancelled. Thus a decade had passed before film audiences saw her again, when Wyler signed her for the new version of *The Children's Hour* (62), now with the original title and subject intact: instead of playing Martha, she was Martha's aunt. Similarly the years had withered either Wyler's talent or the effectiveness of the piece.

A couple of years later Hopkins accepted the star role – that of a madam – in a tinny German-filmed version of *Fanny Hill* (64), which, when it was not banned, was turned down by exhibitors on more aesthetic grounds. She was Robert Redford's mother in *The Chase* (66) and in 1969 played an ageing movie star in an independent production, *The Comeback*, with two other revenants, Minta Durfee Arbuckle and Gale Sondergaard: but the film had not been shown publicly by the time of her death, of a massive heart attack, in October 1972. Retitled *Hollywood Horror Home* it surfaced in 1976.

LESLIE HOWARD

Leslie Howard was the ideal Englishman – to Americans at least. Hollywood in the 30s was a haven for aristocratic-seeming English actors and although Howard was a gentleman all right, he was much more approachable than most of his compatriots. He could not have played the squire, like Nigel Bruce and C. Aubrey Smith, or the military commander, like Sir Guy Standing and Clive Brook, or the double-breasted cad, like Lionel Atwill and Herbert Marshall. In fact, Howard could only really play himself, tweedy, idealistic, vague and dreamy, kindly and upright; he seemed to have nostrils as sensitive as a thoroughbred's (offscreen, he only *seemed* to be like the roles he played – for instance, the idealistic and romantic poet-wanderer in *The Petrified Forest*: he could be a very practical ladies' man). He tried a wider range and was seldom unconvincing simply because he was a relaxed and relaxing actor: in his time he was held in more or less unparalleled esteem. His sure touch in comedy remains a pleasure.

Curiously, he was only half-English. His father was a Hungarian Jew who had not long been in Britain when Howard was born in 1893, in London. He studied at Dulwich

College and went to work in a bank. In 1917 he was invalided home from the Western Front suffering from shell-shock: to help him recuperate his mother – who was involved in local dramatics – suggested that he try acting. Theatre companies at that time were taking young men with even a modicum of talent and Howard had little difficulty in getting into a (professional) tour of 'Peg o' My Heart'. He got a brief film job, in *The Happy Warrior* (17), and had a bigger role in *The Lackey and the Lady* (19); and he had the lead in two short comedies directed by Adrian Brunel and written by A.A. Milne, *Five Pounds Reward* (20) and *Bookworms*. On the stage he established himself rapidly and after a good part in Milne's 'My Pym Passes By' (22) he was offered a leading role in the New York production of 'Just Suppose' by A.E. Thomas. It was there that he achieved real fame, in a sequence of hit plays: 'Aren't We All?', 'Outward Bound', 'The Green Hat' (25) with Katharine Cornell, 'Her Cardboard Lover' and Galsworthy's 'Escape'. In 1926 he returned to the West End for 'The Way You Look at It' with Edna Best and in 1928 he crossed the Atlantic again for 'Her Cardboard Lover', appearing in it with Tallulah Bankhead (also that year he produced a play he had written, 'Tell Me the Truth'). He stayed on in London for a revival of 'Berkeley Square' and while there received overtures from WB, who were planning a film of *Outward Bound* (30).

A long introduction now reminds us how important contemporaries thought this, with its new concepts of 'life, death and the hereafter' – as some passengers on a liner begin to realize that they are dead. Howard ceded his old role to Douglas Fairbanks Jr and for $5,000 a week (and again under the direction of Robert Milton) took on Alfred Lunt's old role of the drunk, whose muddled life turns out to have been of more worth than some of the wealthier travellers. It was again a success, at least with those audiences who wanted more than mere talk (though the British censor banned it). It proved that Howard was as effective on screen as he had been in the flesh and with offers from most of the studios he chose to go to MGM, with the right to approve his material (which was rare at the time): *A Free Soul* (31), as Norma Shearer's ineffectual fiancé, losing her to Clark Gable; *Never the Twain Shall Meet*, being told by C. Aubrey Smith, 'This girl's of a different race, of a different world, you've got your friends, your position'; and *Five and Ten*, as a young architect in love with pampered department-store heiress Marion Davies. Robert Milton, who was directing, invited him to play a married lawyer in *Devotion*, falling in love with governess Ann

Harding, and according to some sources it was the first of a new deal with RKO. According to others he was on loan from MGM, and probably both are true, for Howard ran his career with acumen, taking advantage of the fact that he was in great demand and could write his own ticket. It was at this time that he told a reporter: 'The movie studios are sweat shops killing the best in actors' and described his movies as 'drivel'. He also thought his salary sheer lunacy: 'No actor is worth that much money.'

Perhaps he would feel differently in Britain: when Herbert Marshall was not free Korda made him an offer to star in the first film of his new set-up (while still with Paramount – before founding London Films), *Service for Ladies* (32), at £500 a week, said to be the highest salary in British films till that time. He scored again in this remake, in Adolphe Menjou's old role as a Paris king of waiters who falls for an American heiress. He returned to New York for Philip Barry's 'The Animal Kingdom' and then to Hollywood for a new version of the lachrymose *Smilin' Through*, billed under the title and after Fredric March, and spending most of the film in aged make-up: still he was Norma Shearer's true love. At RKO he did *The Animal Kingdom*, marrying Myrna Loy and wishing he had not because of Ann Harding. Then *Secrets* (33) took him and Mary Pickford from elopement and infidelity (his, not hers) to doddery old age; and he was *Captured!* at WB, an incredible war drama with Douglas Fairbanks Jr; at Fox he did the successful film version of *Berkeley Square*, of which he was personally fond, as a modern young man who transplants himself to 1784; and was in *The Lady Is Willing* (34) with Binnie Barnes, the first picture that Columbia ever made in Britain – a farce which deservedly flopped. He also turned down the role of Garbo's lover in *Queen Christina* because he thought he would not be noticed. The last under his RKO contract was John Cromwell's *Of Human Bondate*, as the club-footed young doctor obsessed with a cockney Bette Davis – a concise version of the Maugham novel which the public did not much care for.

Due rather to prevarication than ill-will Howard was not an easy man to please and he now signed a contract with Warners which was to give him and them several headaches. He was supposed to make three films yearly over a three-year period, but it became extended as he refused most of what they offered him. The association began with him as a *British Agent* in St Petersburg – a thinly disguised Bruce-Lockhart, who, Warners were relieved to find, did not sue over misrepresentation of himself or his memoir of the Revolution. For

Leslie Howard and Merle Oberon as Sir Percy and Lady Blakeney in The Scarlet Pimpernel (34), *based on Baroness Orczy's popular novel, first published in 1905. There had been an earlier film version, in 1917, and Korda was to make another Pimpernel film in the late 40s.*

Korda in Britain he did a period version of a similar tale, *The Scarlet Pimpernel*, as the foppish, laconic Sir Percy who whisked out the aristos from under the eyes of the Terror. The film cost £81,000 and grossed a nice £420,000 – and Howard's performance brought him the 1935 'Picturegoer' Gold Medal. Sir Percy had been a role to which his style was admirably suited and he was even better cast in *The Petrified Forest* (36), which he had done on the stage, adrift in the Arizona desert and encouraging Miss Davis in her yearning for France and literature. It gave a lift to both careers (and Humphrey Bogart's) and reinforced MGM's choice of Howard to play Romeo after Fredric March had turned it down. Howard was wary and almost certainly would not have done it had not WB refused to loan him. Thus he partnered Shearer in *Romeo and Juliet*. He was too old and violently unsuitable by modern standards, but he spoke the verse beautifully and was much liked at the time. Later that year he played Hamlet on Broadway, which did not detract from his prestige, although he

was considered less good than John Gielgud, also in New York in that role.

He had become ambitious in all directions. He negotiated with Warners to form his own company in Britain (where he lived throughout the decade, with – not *quite* openly – a Frenchwoman), releasing through UA. Two pictures were announced, *Riviera* and *Bonnie Prince Charlie*, in Technicolor; but, instead, in Hollywood, he made a couple of likeable comedies: *It's Love I'm After* (37) with Davis as his wife, a couple of squabbling thespians; and *Stand-In*, as a bewildered accountant taking over a film studio: the teaming with the brash Joan Blondell was particularly felicitous. In 1938 his own company did produce a movie, Shaw's *Pygmalion*, one of the few movies of the time that Britain was proud of and able to export with profit. His Higgins was a perfect performance and at least until music was added the definitive one; he co-directed with Anthony Asquith for the temperamental producer Gabriel Pascal, who announced plans for Howard to play both Nelson and Lawrence of Arabia. While Pascal

Leslie Howard, with David Niven, in his last picture, The First of the Few (42): it was one of a fine group of wartime films that seemed to herald a renaissance of the British Cinema. The 'Few' were the Battle of Britain pilots – in the US the film was retitled Spitfire.

prepared them, Howard returned to Hollywood looking for work. According to his daughter's biography, there were no offers, apart from *Gone with the Wind* (39), which was not due to start yet anyway. Jack L. Warner has said that he made Selznick kowtow to him in order to borrow Howard, which was little consolation to Howard, who did not want to do it really. He boasted that he had not read the book and had no intention of doing so; and there was some strife with Vivien Leigh because he would not learn his lines. It is, for all that, a conscientious performance, the least highly regarded of the four star performances; his dialogue is stilted and priggish (so maybe he was right after all). He was paid a princely $7,500 a week for doing it, to go to $10,000 a week for *Intermezzo: a Love Story*, because he was also Associate Producer, his consolation for doing *Gone With the Wind*, though the agreement stated that the director must be William Wyler, whom Selznick fired: but even under Gregory Ratoff the piece was a love story of superb vintage, with Howard in fine form as the married violinist who falls in love with his accompanist, Ingrid Bergman (in the 40s in Britain it had a record three circuit bookings).

Howard returned to the UK to make *The Man Who Lost Himself*, but the outbreak of war cancelled that project (nor were Pascal's projects more advanced). Howard, however, found himself a leading figure in a British film industry gradually revitalizing itself. As he grew older, he realized that his roots were in London and not in Los Angeles, and he set to work with a will: *Pimpernel Smith* (41), producing and directing, and playing an absent-minded professor whose alter ego is a spy in Germany; *49th Parallel*, one of a starry cast, as an idealist and art lover who clashes with a Nazi (Eric Portman); and *The First of the Few* (42), also directing, as R.J. Mitchell, inventor of the Spitfire. His co-star, David Niven, remembered him as 'not what he seemed. He had the kind of distraught air that would make people want to mother him. Actually, he was about as naïve as General Motors. Busy little brain, always going.' His last movie-work found him behind the cameras: *The Gentle Sex* (43), co-directing this tribute to the ATS, and *The Lamp Still Burns*, producing, a like paean to nurses.

The 'British Film Yearbook 1945', summing up the local industry during the war, observed that Howard's 'presence in England as a producer, director and actor, constituted in itself one of the most valuable facets of British propaganda'. Early in 1943 the British used him for something less overt: afraid that Spain and Portugal might enter the war on the Axis side, Howard was sent there, ostensibly to lecture on the Theatre. His plane was shot down not long after it left Lisbon on the return journey. It was the day that Churchill returned from a conference in Algiers and the Germans believed that he was on the same plane as Howard. A son, Ronald Howard, was a mild success in British films later in the 40s, persuaded into the profession by a strong resemblance to his father.

WALTER HUSTON

Walter Huston was one of the great actors of the first half-century. James Agee wrote of his work in *The Treasure of Sierra Madre*: 'I doubt we shall ever see . . . better acting than Walter Huston's beautiful performance', which was more or less the culmination of a professional lifetime of praise. Stanislavsky was among his greatest admirers. Since he did not come into films till he was in his mid-40s, he played fathers and other figures of authority: he was never a top-ranking star, but he did such roles for a decade before allowing himself to be relegated to being a supporting actor. He could be, on occasion, an effective villain, but he is best remembered as a man of exceptional probity – direct and as understanding of human folly as he was amused by it. His rule, he once told Gregory Peck, was 'Son, always give 'em a good show and travel first class'.

He was born in 1884 in Toronto. He studied engineering and at the same time attended drama classes; he was 18 when he had a chance to appear with a stock company in his native city. He gave up engineering and went touring. In 1905 he reached New York in a melodrama called 'In Convict Stripes' and appeared in vaudeville also that year, but he gave it all up when he married. When his son John was born in 1906 he was working in water and electricity plants in Missouri, but in 1909 (he was 25) he returned to the stage, doing a song-and-dance act with Bayonne Whipple. She became his second wife in 1914. He stayed in vaudeville until 1924, writing his own acts, but in that year was offered the lead in 'Mr Pitt' in New York. The critics liked him and (after a Shubert Road Show) he was starred in 'Desire Under the Elms', as the old man. He was made for life. He starred on Broadway until 1928 when a flop play, 'The Commodore Marries', caused him to think

about Talkies. He signed a contract with Paramount and made *Gentlemen of the Press* (29), as one of them – a dedicated journalist who goes downhill after succumbing to Katharine (Kay) Francis – and *The Lady Lies*, a sophisticated comedy about a man whose kids interfere in his romance with a shopgirl (Claudette Colbert). He had two Broadway successes, 'The Barker' and 'Elmer the Great' (and made three shorts around this time: *The Bishop's Candlesticks*, *The Carnival Man*, *Two Americans*); then headed for Paramount's West Coast studio to play the villain, Trampas, in a classic Western, *The Virginian*, with Gary Cooper. He played *Abraham Lincoln* (30) with integrity and authority for D.W. Griffith in his otherwise undistinguished study (and penultimate film), but was less convincing in another Western, *The Bad Man*, as a dashing Mexican bandit. *The Virtuous Sin* was a penny-dreadful: 'Torrid love in frigid Russia', said 'Photoplay', adding that Huston and Kay Francis were 'simply grand'.

After playing the prison governor in *The Criminal Code* (31) for Columbia he did three for Warners: *The Star Witness*, as the father of a family caught up with gangsters; *The Ruling Voice*, where he was required to be shady and noble at the same time: *A Woman of Monte Carlo*, the first Hollywood vehicle for Lil Dagover (only it was a hearse and she returned to Germany); and a couple at Universal, both written by son John, a budding scriptwriter (and described in Dad's studio biography as one of his hobbies). *A House Divided* (32) may have started as a rehash of 'Desire Under the Elms', but as directed by William Wyler and acted by Huston, at his best, it is impressive: he plays a crusty old seadog, unlikeable but eventually pitiable, who is crippled in an accident after discovering that his young mail-order bride (Helen Chandler) prefers his son (Kent Douglass); in *Law and Order* he was a fictionalized Wyatt Earp with Harry Carey as his Doc Holliday. He signed with MGM and made six more pictures that year, starting with *The Beast of the City*, and scoring a sensational success with his portrait of an over-zealous cop. He was put among the Prohibition problems of Upton Sinclair's *The Wet Parade*, but the chief problem was how to stay in the cinema when his drunken, run-down hotel proprietor was not on the screen. He was a judge in *Night Court* (and 'magnificent' – 'Photoplay') and a humanitarian banker in Columbia's *American Madness*, Capra's fine Depression movie – after which he moved temporarily away from contemporary social problems. At UA he was the Reverend Davidson in *Rain* with Joan Crawford – only

Wyler's Dodsworth (*36*). *Like the novel on which it was based, the film was basically an account of New World puritanism and plain-speaking* vis-à-vis *European sophistication. Walter Huston represented the former, and Mary Astor was the fellow-countrywoman who comforted him when his wife left him for the latter.*

he was not a reverend, but demoted to amateur status to conciliate religious groups. In *Kongo* he was the bitter, bestial Deadlegs Flint, a part he had originated on Broadway; it had already been filmed with Lon Chaney as *West of Zanzibar* and there was some discussion as to which was the sillier of the two versions.

Gregory La Cava's *Gabriel Over the White House* (33) was a brave film – and an unlikely one to come from MGM (Louis B. Mayer loathed it, partly because he thought it an attack on ex-President Hoover), but if well-timed not a big success: Huston played a crooked President who becomes an idealist after an accident, solving the problems of the Depression. He was a brutal submarine commander in *Hell Below*; the husband who sacrifices himself for the lover (Nils Asther) of his wife (Kay Francis) in *Storm at Daybreak*, which started with the assassination at Sarajevo but drops that event for more exciting matters; in *Ann Vickers* at RKO, based on the novel by Sinclair Lewis, as Irene Dunne's unhappily married lover, a judge who goes to gaol for corruption; and in *The Prizefighter and the Lady*, as Max Baer's slick trainer, billed not only after him and Myrna Loy but

Primo Carnera and Jack Dempsey, playing themselves. It was clearly time to leave MGM, but RKO offered little better: the footling *Keep 'Em Rolling* (34), playing a soldier who loves horses. He returned to the stage in a dramatization of Lewis's 'Dodsworth', to great acclaim, but despite that the only interesting film offer he got was from Britain. While waiting for it to start he was a 'courtesy player' with one scene, in *The Tunnel* (35), the remake of a German thriller, as the American President. The other film was *Rhodes of Africa* (36), playing the title-role in such a way as to support the film's thesis that he was not an entirely admirable hero; Oscar Homolka was Kruger.

In Hollywood, Goldwyn's film of *Dodsworth* was waiting for him. There is unlikely to be unanimity on Goldwyn's contribution to the screen, but for this one he must be admired. None of the principals was box-office, but much money and care was spent on it. Wyler directed and Huston was magnificent as Sam, impulsive, bewildered, firm and childlike, the manufacturer from the mid-West who in Europe finds himself drifting away from his wife (Ruth Chatterton) and towards a widow (Mary Astor). The New

Devil is a really brilliant performance. This clever actor makes the fellow at once likeable and loathsome – a droll combination of pure logic and stark unreason' – James Agate). Another asset was the success of son John, now a director, with films like *The Maltese Falcon* and *In This Our Life* (42), in both of which Dad did friendly walk-ons. He got top billing for a small part as the father in Renoir's *Swamp Water* (41) and was in Von Sternberg's silly *The Shanghai Gesture*, as the enigmatic Englishman. He played fathers again in *Always in My Heart* (42), a soap opera with Kay Francis, and *Yankee Doodle Dandy*, George M. Cohan's.

In 1941 he was in Howard Hughes's *The Outlaw*, not released until after the war, as Doc Holliday to Thomas Mitchell's Pat Garrett, and was warbound himself with *Edge of Darkness* (43) starring Errol Flynn, as a Norwegian doctor who does not want to get caught up in the Resistance; *Mission to Moscow*, as US Ambassador Joseph E. Davies, who in the preface endorsed this well-meaning account of US-Soviet relations in the 30s; *The North Star*, again as the town doctor, in Russia this time, but leading the Resistance; and MGM's shameless *Dragon Seed* (44), 'a kind of slant-eyed *North Star*' ('Time Magazine'), 'unimaginably bad' (James Agee), in Chinese drag as a peasant resisting the Japanese (but one of the film's few believable performances).

In 1946 he did his last Broadway play, 'The Apple of His Eye', and there were three supporting stints, none of them among his better work: *And Then There Were None* (45), René Clair's filming of Agatha Christie's 'Ten Little Niggers', as the judge; *Dragonwyck* (46), as Gene Tierney's father; and *Duel in the Sun*, as a fiery evangelist – still the film's best performance. He gave a slight, charming performance as the father in *Summer Holiday* (47) and then showed the others How again, in his son's *The Treasure of Sierra Madre* (48): he was really the only choice for the Best Supporting Actor at the Oscar ceremonies. His fee around this time was $40,000 and he got it only twice more, for *The Great Sinner* (49), as Ava Gardner's gambling father, and *The Furies* (50), as the fond and proud dad of scheming Barbara Stanwyck – the first of the Freudian Westerns. He was about to begin *Mr 880* – Edmund Gwenn played the role – when he died in 1950.

Walter Huston in The Treasure of Sierra Madre (48). *Said José Ferrer once: 'Certainly Walter is one of the greatest actors who ever lived. . . . Just because every time I saw him do anything he just hit me sort of deeper in the pit of the stomach than most actors ever did.'*

York critics voted him the year's Best Actor. The film, much praised, just realized its cost, but by dint of revival finally earned a profit. Huston himself set much store by its success, but no studio rushed to employ him; so he went to Broadway and played Othello, but after notices complaining that he did not let himself go sufficiently, it closed after three weeks. There was only one film offer, from MGM, *Of Human Hearts* (38), to play the village priest in Ohio just before the Civil War, with an actress of his quality, Beulah Bondi, as his wife (the last time they had been so cast was in the different circumstances of *Rain*). He returned again to New York and played in Kurt Weill's 'Knickerbocker Holiday', singing 'September Song'. He reminded reporters that he had once been in vaudeville and twice turned down the lead in 'Life With Father', which became the longest-running play in Broadway history.

He had a supporting role in *The Light That Failed* (39), as Ronald Colman's loyal friend, and also in 1940 did two plays. He then found himself consistently in demand in the film city. One thing that helped was *All That Money Can Buy* (41), when his performance met with resounding success ('Mr Walter Huston's

BETTY HUTTON

The pyrotechnic talent of Betty Hutton was not to everyone's taste, but during her 10 years of stardom she was a valuable asset to Paramount and all the time she kept improving herself. She first appeared in films as the US entered the war when, in musicals, the jitterbug was replacing the aria. Hutton was as brash and volatile as any weary GI demanded: not for nothing was she known as The Blonde Bombshell (and The Huttentot, The Blonde Blitz and Bounding Betty). Her eagerness was appealing then but in her early films the exuberance is now merely alienating. She is like a grown-up Shirley Temple. Says Dorothy Lamour in one film, playing her sister: 'I don't like leaving Bobbie alone with all those men.' 'Don't worry,' replies another sister, 'they can probably take care of themselves.' One wonders. Later Hutton simmered down and displayed an unexpected sweetness of disposition and real dramatic ability.

She was born in Battle Creek, Michigan, in 1921; her father died when she was a child. She became a band-singer while still in her teens and originated her bombshell act during her first important engagement, singing with Vincent Lopez. She graduated thence to vaudeville and appeared in some shorts: *Vincent Lopez and his Orchestra* (39), *One for the Book*, *Public Jitterbug Number One* and *Three Kings and a Queen*. She moved to Broadway, notably in 'Panama Hattie' (40); June Allyson was her understudy. One of the show's writers, Buddy de Sylva, was appointed production chief at Paramount and he decided that she would be an asset to that company. Others had doubts about her, till she was cast as second lead/comedy relief in *The Fleet's In* (42), teamed with sad-sack sailor Eddie Bracken. The contrast between him and high-spirited her was appealing to both the public and the studio, so in *Happy Go Lucky* (43) she was again uninhibited and man-mad, but mainly for him. They were partnered again in the plot sections of *Star Spangled Rhythm*, in which she again showed no indication of relaxing. She was mad for only Bob Hope in a service comedy, *Let's Face It*, but was much less selective in *The Miracle of Morgan's Creek* (44), written and directed by the studio's leading light, Preston Sturges, who hoped to get away with murder because he had de Sylva's backing in promoting Paramount's newest, brightest star. So in an era when the Hays Office looked askance at any impropriety, Hutton was a small-town girl who got drunk and was impregnated for an eventual sixtuplets, the same night, by a GI whose name she could not even recall (one line had them married betweenwhiles). Bracken was the faithful swain and James Agee found it 'funnier, more adventurous, more abundant, more intelligent and more encouraging' than any Hollywood film in years.

Agee liked Hutton. Reviewing *And the Angels Sing* he found her 'almost beyond good and evil, as far as I am concerned'. The film was somewhat between the two and quite tasteless, with sisters Hutton and Lamour getting drunk in pursuit of band-leader Fred MacMurray and the money he had conned from them. However, *Here Come the Waves* was agreeable despite its patriotic finale: Bing Crosby was in it and Hutton was twins – one of them grave and subdued. She did make it seem like two different actresses. She made a strong bid in the drama stakes as Texas Guinan, nightclub queen and *Incendiary Blonde* (45) – though the title referred to Hutton rather than Guinan, who had never been known as that. After one song, guesting, in *Duffy's Tavern*, she was in two programmers, *The Stork Club*, as its hat-check girl, saving Barry Fitzgerald from drowning, and *Cross My Heart* (46), a remake of *True Confession* with Sonny Tufts. In fact, her popularity had rather caught the studio off its guard, but they looked at the grosses of *Incendiary Blonde* and put together the same tears-and-laughter formula, *The Perils of Pauline* (47), a biopic of serial queen Pearl White. This did even better business and Paramount announced similar films for her on Clare Bow, Theda Bara and Sophie Tucker.

Her limitations were clearly exposed by *Dream Girl* (48), based on Elmer Rice's satire/whimsy, which his wife, Betty Field, had done on Broadway: as the wealthy, idealistic bookseller who refuses to stock 'Always Opal', Hutton hangs on to her last syllables like Field and opts, between monotony, for all-out emotions. Mitchell Leisen, who directed, says that she was convinced that she would win an Oscar and was 'devastated' when she was not even nominated: her fans, he went on, 'were disappointed when she didn't go around screaming "Murder He Says" and the rest of the public who couldn't stand her didn't go either'. He had only taken on the job after being assured that she was of great importance to Paramount's shareholders. In Dorothy Lamour's autobiography she mentions that he had remade one of his best films, *Midnight*, to avoid being assigned to work with a certain temperamental blonde star. Hutton once asked Lamour why she was popular at the studio and she was not, to which Lamour replied that she liked her co-workers, adding that Hutton would not always have Buddy de Sylva around to protect her.

The noisy *Red Hot and Blue* (49), with Victor Mature, confirmed that picturegoers were about to side with the Paramount crews, but Judy Garland got sick and thus handed her a dream part. MGM borrowed her for *Annie Get Your Gun* (50) and George Sidney,

It may not be quite fair to say that Annie Get Your Gun *(50) is the only one of Betty Hutton's films which is watchable today, but it is an occasion when her high spirits are not positively alienating. It was the best, biggest and most showy role for a musical star in years, and originally cast was the greatest there has ever been, Judy Garland. MGM did not want to do Paramount a favour by borrowing Hutton, but no other star on their own contract list was quite so suitable – except Betty Garrett, whose agent asked for what Metro considered was too much money for the plum role of the decade. Garrett might have been better than either; like Hutton here, she would have had the inestimable advantage of Howard Keel as co-star.*

directing, pitched it to her own style, over-emphatic, over-exuberant, a blaze of colour and song (Irving Berlin's). Garland's troubles had sent it hugely over budget before Hutton took over, but MGM were more than compensated at the box-office. Co-star Howard Keel later recalled Hutton as 'difficult . . . alienating everyone by upstaging them' but said she was 'insecure' because she wanted to give of her best. MGM had paid $150,000 for her services and reputedly tried to buy her contract: 'Picturegoer' reported that Metro had signed her for both the pictures she was allowed to do outside it. Paramount put her into *Let's Dance* with Fred Astaire and gave her the leading role in De Mille's *The Greatest Show on Earth* (52), a multi-star, multi-cliché circus picture that quickly went to second on 'Variety' list of all-time grossers. It also won a Best Picture Oscar.

Hutton then did another biopic (Blossom Seely), *Somebody Loves Me*. She married her dance director on this, Charles O'Curran, and insisted that he direct her next film. Paramount refused and Hutton walked out on her contract: the row was over a movie called *Topsy and Eva* and she abandoned it as it was about to go into production. Paramount announced that Rosemary Clooney would play in all the projected Hutton vehicles. That

did not happen – nor did any of the independent productions which Hutton announced. In 1953, Universal announced a *Red Hot Mama* for her, a life of Sophie Tucker, but that fell through when Miss Tucker insisted on playing her aged self. In 1954 she did a 90-minute TV show, at a reputed fee of $50,000. In 1955 she turned down the role of Ado Annie in *Oklahoma!* because the part was not big enough. At the time of the break with Paramount it had been predicted that she would never appear before the cameras again: when she did, it was in an unimportant little picture for UA, *Spring Reunion* (57). She gave an excellent account of a spinster scared of marriage, but no more film parts were forthcoming, straight or musical.

For a decade she worked in nightclubs and stock, if never again coming near to repeating her personal triumphs at the London Palladium in 1948, when she was held over for a third week, and 1952. That engagements dwindled may be due to headline-making feuds with managers – such as her impulsive defence of Judy Garland when that lady had her own backstage trouble. In 1960 she married a trumpet-player, Pete Candoli, and the following year she appeared in cabaret in London. In 1962 her mother was burnt to death in her apartment. In 1965 she failed to make an impact in New York, when she substituted for the ailing Carol Burnett in 'Fade In Fade Out' – the receipts fell away to nothing – and in 1966 she failed to do a film which would have reunited her with Howard Keel: but it was a B, *Red Tomahawk*, and it was said she could not work quickly enough for a low-budget movie.

In 1967 she filed a petition for bankruptcy – and later said that she had made and spent $9½ million in her life. In 1971 she was divorced from Candoli, her fourth husband. In 1972 she said that years of unhappiness were finishing, because she had discovered the Bible and knew that people wanted her to make a come-back. The following year she was in a revival of 'Anything Goes' in stock and later in the year was hospitalized with a severe nervous breakdown. There were reports of a similar illness two years later, but she claimed to be content working as maid to a priest; in 1976 there was a nightclub engagement in Chicago. She does occasional TV commercials and has said to numerous magazine interviewers that she wanted to make a come-back – but a three-week holiday stint in Broadway's 'Annie' (80) does not seem to have led to further offers.

EMIL JANNINGS

During the time of his American career and for a long while afterwards Emil Jannings was accepted without question as the screen's greatest actor. In 1941 James Agate repeated his view that he was 'one of the world's great actors . . . is there any film actor living today who is possessed of the sheer power of Jannings, who always in his massivity reminded me of Richter's handling of Wagner?' He had weight, he had authority, he was good at disguises and he played tragic parts. More significantly, he was directed by some of the finest talents in Silent pictures. When he died, Richard Winnington, with his customary lucidity, wrote that Jannings 'learned the differing tricks of film acting, but only in the narrowest sense. His ritual, for all the temporary disguises, almost invariably expressed the same figure of pomp, respectability or power, brought low and destroyed by weakness or fate – a routine that fitted like a glove into the German neurosis and incidentally got him spotted at once by Hollywood. Because of his one-track technique he was not and never could have been a great film actor, and many of his films were pathetic, even ludicrous imitations of the *Vaudeville* and *Waxworks* Jannings.'

He was born in Rorschach, Switzerland, in 1884 of German parents, who shortly afterwards went to live in New York but returned to Germany during his childhood. He was educated in Zürich and Gorlitz, and at Gorlitz he joined a stock company, playing boys' parts and doing odd jobs. He was restless and the life of a touring actor suited him; he played with companies in Bremen, Leipzig and Mainz, until Werner Krauss, a mutual friend, got him an invitation to participate in the Darmstadt Royal Theatre in Berlin, studying under Max Reinhardt. He was attracted to films because they paid better than the theatre and began to do bit parts; then the actor-director Schmidt-Hässler gave him a role in *Im Banne der Leidenschaft* (14), which was followed by *Passionels Tagebuch* (15), directed by Louis Ralph; *Arme Eva*, directed by Robert Weine, from a story by Daudet; *Nächt des Grauens*, directed by Arthur Robison; and *Die Ehe der Luise Rohrbach* (16), with Henny Porten, who became one of his most frequent partners. After *Klingendes Leben* (17), *Lulu*, *Das Leven ein Traum* and *Seeschlacht*, directed by Richard Oswald, he was directed by Ernst Lubitsch, a fellow-actor, and the two of them would make international reputations together. Their first film was a comedy, *Wenn Vier Dasselbe Machen*, which they followed with *Ein Fideles Gefängnis*, a version of 'Die Fledermaus'. In the former he had an affair which paralleled that of his daughter (Ossi Oswalda); in the latter he was the gaoler, mugging away like mad, which impressed contemporaries. He was now in leading roles: *Der Mann der Tat* (18), directed by Victor Janson; *Rose Bernd*, from Hauptmann's peasant drama, with Porten in the title-role; *Führmann Henschel*, another Hauptmann story, in the title-role, a coachman driven to suicide by his wife; and *Die Augen der Mumie Mâ*, as an Arab religious fanatic, pursuing Pola Negri to Europe. Lubitsch directed and he cast Jannings as M. Dubarry in *Madame Dubarry* (19) with Pola Negri – but Jannings persuaded him to let him play the King instead.

With that film, the great age of the German cinema was dawning and Jannings knew it. He left the theatre permanently and though his publicists insisted that he despised the cinema, that was because publicists liked to imply that major actors were honouring films by deigning to appear in them: *Kölhiesels Töchter* (20) and *Anna Boleyn*, both with Porten and made by Lubitsch, in the former as an ox-like farmhand taming a Bavarian shrew and in the latter as another monarch Teutonized. The Dubarry film was shown abroad as *Passion* and Boleyn as *Deception* and, as the world began to applaud German historical films, the

Emil Jannings in (left to right top to bottom) Anne Boleyn *(20),* Othello *(22),* Der Letzte Mann *(25) and in Hollywood, in* The Way of All Flesh *(27). Joseph von Sternberg wrote: 'his position in the history of the motion picture is secure, not only as a superlative performer but also as a source of inspiration for the writers and directors of the time. This, in my opinion, is the highest compliment within the scope of an actor to earn.'*

German studios immersed themselves in history – and Jannings played the title-role in *Danton*, directed by Dimitri Buchowetsky, with Werner Krauss as Robespierre. This was to be a frequent teaming and the two actors were joined in Carl Froelich's *Die Brüder Karamasoff* by Fritz Kortner: the work of Krauss and Kortner, both great actors, now stands up better than most of that of Jannings. He was in two films with Hanna Ralph, *Algol* and *Der Stier von Olivera* (which seems not to have been generally shown), and in *Die Ratten* (21), directed by Hans Kobe; and *Vendetta* with Negri. He was directed by Lubitsch for the last time during his German period in the spectacular *Das Weib des Pharao*, as the Pharaoh – a companion to his other tyrant-monarchs, i.e. with a spark of decency. Paramount, due to American interest in Lubitsch, etc., had an interest, but Jannings thought the film a total flop and for years cited it as the reason for refusing Hollywood offers.

He played *Othello* (22), but was overshadowed by Krauss's Iago: Buchowetsky directed and after *August der Stark* and *Die Gräfin von Paris* (23) they were reunited for another gloomy prestige subject, *Peter der Grosse*. They collaborated on the direction of *Alles für Geld*, in which Jannings was a profiteer who causes his son's death. He was in Joe May's four-part *Tragödie der Liebe* (24), in *Nju*, married to Elisabeth Bergner – who leaves him for Conrad Veidt, and then in some of his most famous films. Paul Leni's *Das Wachsfigurenkabinett* is another episode film, a fantasy, with Jannings in a rare comic portrayal of Haroun al Raschid and Krauss as Jack the Ripper; *Quo Vadis?* is the third film version of that tale, an Italian-German co-production, with Jannings inevitably Nero. Said 'Picturegoer': 'Pompous and cruel, vain and false, repulsive in his utter bestiality he dominates the canvas until one gets heartily sick of what is undisputedly a remarkable and wonderful piece of work!' But the praise which Jannings had been receiving was as nothing to the chorus that greeted *Der Letzte Mann*, directed by F.W. Murnau, playing a proud hotel doorman reduced to lavatory attendant: the performance, however, is now monotonous – along with the film. After playing a supporting role in *Liebe Macht Blind* (25), a Parisian comedy with Lil Dagover, he was in E.A. Dupont's *Variete*, also greatly admired in its day, a triangle story of trapeze artists, with new boss (Warwick Ward) stealing Jannings's wife (Lya de Putti) and being murdered because of it. He played the title-role in Murnau's *Tartuff*, to the marvellous Orgon of Krauss, and Mephisto to the *Faust* (26) of Gosta Ekman – a super-production by Murnau which remains wondrous for at least half its length. Murnau went to Hollywood and Jannings himself joined the exodus of German artists by signing a three-year contract with Paramount, at a reported $10,000 a week.

The studio proceeded to construct 'Emil Jannings vehicles' – as much as possible like his German successes, stories of 'tragic old men broken by fate . . . a series of pictures in which tragedy struck in retribution for the old man's sexual peccadilloes. . . . Jannings was made to feel every sling and arrow of outrageous fortune that the Paramount script department could devise,' said Arthur Knight, adding that 'his suffering was arbitrarily conceived, his retribution so mechanical that not even the great Jannings could conceal the basic falseness of both the stories and their characters.' All the same, his directors were distinguished: Victor Fleming directed him when, as a bank clerk, he went *The Way of All Flesh* (27) and von Sternberg when he gave *The Last Command* (28), a drama of a Hollywood extra who had once been a Russian general. For both performances – it was done differently then – he was voted Best Actor of the Year by the Academy (it was the first given, before it was called Oscar). Mauritz Stiller directed *The Street of Sin*, in which he was a street bully reformed by a Salvation Army girl (Fay Wray), and Lubitsch *The Patriot*, with Jannings playing the mad Tsar Paul I. In Ludwig Berger's *The Sins of the Fathers* (29) he was a bootlegger deserted by wife Ruth Chatterton and cronies at the end. Like all his Hollywood films it was a big success – but the next was a disaster: *The Betrayal* (29), a triangle story in which he was a Swiss mayor and Gary Cooper a visiting painter. Lewis Milestone directed and he found Jannings 'very difficult to work with. You had to know how to handle him. Like most Germans, he could understand a shout, bark or command, but if you tried to be a gentleman with him he would mistake it for weakness.' It had been predicted when he had got his Oscar that he would not be able to do American Talkies and Paramount did not, in fact, like the tests they made. But it was the loss of such actors which caused so many commentators to be bitter about the coming of Talkies. For, as Lionel Collier wrote in 'Picturegoer', in 1929: 'Nine people out of 10 if asked to say who is the greatest actor on the screen . . . would unhesitatingly reply Emil Jannings.' But he returned to Germany, planning to play Rasputin, but instead did *Der Blaue Engel/The Blue Angel* (30) in both German and English, with the latter being generally considered the inferior. Resoundingly, he played a professor brought low after a glimpse of Marlene Dietrich's begartered thighs, as who wouldn't? Paramount took her up, but the film confirmed Jannings's incomprehensible English and he was not re-signed. She always referred to his performance as 'hammy', but he would not have agreed, for at this time he pronounced, 'The future belongs to the Talking films and Germans, who are the best actors in the world, will and must take the leadership in this respect.'

Certainly, the German film industry was at a peak and it welcomed Jannings for *Leibling der Gotter* (in French as well) and *Stürme der Leidenschaft* (31), the latter an underworld story with Anna Sten in a part too much like that of Dietrich in *The Blue Angel*. In 1932 he made a weird Austrian-French effort, *König Pausole/Les Aventures du Roi Pausole*, a Pierre Louys tale about a king with 365 wives. It was heavily cut by censors and on its first night in London in an English version, *The Merry Monarch*, was greeted with jeers and catcalls; it was withdrawn the following day and has hardly been heard of since. The reviews said that Jannings himself was bad. It was then announced that he had retired, but in fact when the Nazis came to power he was appointed the head of the second largest German film company, Tobis. He made some German films – some of which were shown abroad: *Der Schwarze Walfisch* (34), a version of Pagnol's *Marius*, with Jannings in the Raimu part; *Der Alte und der Junge König* (35), a hymn to military glory, as Friedrich Wilhelm, the father of Frederick the Great; *Traumulus*, as the dreamy director of a boys' school in the Prussia of the 1890s; *Der Herrscher* (37), as an industry boss with family trouble; *Der Zerbrochene Krug*, a literal version of Kleist's comedy, as the pompous magistrate whose drunken evening and subsequent loss of memory causes all the havoc; and *Robert Koch der Beckämpfer des Todes* (39), with Werner Krauss, a bleak study of the medical scientist Koch. Like most of Jannings's movies at this time, it was blatant Nazi propaganda. Unlike them, it was good and was indeed one of the regime's notable films.

In 1940 the Nazis appointed him head of UFA and that year he played the Boer leader, *Ohm Kruger*, in an anti-British film, He made *Die Entlassing* (42), with Krauss, as Bismarck ungratefully dropped by the Kaiser, and *Altes Herz Wird Wieder Jung* and was in the process of making *Wo Ist Herr Belling?* (45) when the Allies advanced to Berlin. It was not finished. For his work in conjunction with Geobbels's Ministry of Propaganda he was blacklisted by the Allies and he retired to Austria, where he died in 1950, mourned by few other than his fifth wife, the former Mrs Conrad Veidt.

AL JOLSON

Jolson is one of the legendary figures of American show business. As a vaudeville artist, many considered him the best there was or would ever be: Jack Benny once said that in the business he was commonly regarded as such (adding that Judy Garland could have been greater, 'had she wanted to be'); and he has a niche in film history because he was the first person to talk on the screen. Opinions vary as to his gifts. Chaplin, for instance, thought him 'a great instinctive artist with magic and vitality. . . . He personified the poetry of Broadway, its vitality and vulgarity, its aims and dreams.' He added that only a shadow of the real Jolson appeared in films, but Don Herold, reviewing *Go Into Your Dance*, clearly disagreed: 'Al Jolson, like so many members of his race and several other races, has unbelievable vitality rather than any singing or dancing ability, but his vitality eventually interests me to some extent. It is all no doubt a business with Al, if he were manufacturing pants he would be at it just as hard.'

Jolson was overpowering. He did not sing songs, he sold them. He seized the limelight, strutting, nimble and magnetic. He believed that egotism and vanity were virtues. He exuded self-confidence and he dared – dared moments of outrageous sentiment, of effeminacy, of a ham delivery of his songs. Between them his personality often seemed unctuous and arrogant at the same time. He was a Jewish performer from the top of his head to the soles of his feet and in his big black Jewish eyes was a deep sensitivity. One might respond or not to his singing, but on the screen when given the chance, he really could act: you have only to watch his eyes to realize that.

He was born in what was then St Petersburg in 1888 and brought to the US as a child. It was intended that he should become a cantor, but instead he ran away from home and joined a circus as a ballyhoo man, graduating to cafés and then vaudeville. His vaudeville act evolved with the years: he first wore blackface in 1906, as one of the minstrel show. He appeared solo at the Fifth Avenue Theater, New York, in 1909 and was in 'La Belle Paree' and 'Vera Violetta', a Gaby Deslys vehicle. Mae West was also in it. From that time on he was a star and he began his famous Sunday night stands at the Winter Garden. In 1913 the Shubert brothers signed him to a seven-year contract (some reports say five): 'The Honeymoon Express' with Gaby Deslys in 1913, 'Robinson Crusoe Jr' in 1916, 'Sinbad' (in which he first sang 'Swanee') in 1918 and 'Bombo' in 1921. He was idolized through the US, partly through his records – the first big pop star there was.

In 1923 D.W. Griffith decided that he would try to capture some of Jolson's personality on film and they started *Mammy's Boy*, but Jolson disliked the rushes so much that he refused to finish it, leaving Griffith with a loss of $100,000. Griffith sued for $500,000, but there was no signed contract and he settled in 1926 for $2,627. Two years later, however, Jolson was happy to make a short – because he could sing, as the short had Sound. The inventor of the system, Dr Lee de Forest, sold the system to Warners, who sent for Jolson again: he sang three songs in *April Showers*.

Warners decided to risk all on a Talkie feature and they selected *The Jazz Singer* with George Jessel repeating his Broadway success. It was a mild tale – about a Jewish boy who does not want to be a cantor and becomes a big success in vaudeville. WB were to pay Jessel $30,000. When Jack L. Warner informed Jessel by phone that songs and some dialogue were to be part of the set-up, Jessel asked for another $10,000 and insisted on the offer in writing. It was therefore offered to Eddie Cantor, who turned it down on the grounds that it was impossible to follow Jessel in the part. It was then offered to Jolson, who asked – and got – $75,000 for his services.

The Jazz Singer opened in New York in October 1927. It was mostly background music; after 10 minutes, the actor playing Jolson as a boy sings, then it is back to music

'Climb upon my knee Sonny Boy', one of the more maudlin moments from The Singing Fool *(28): Al Jolson and Davey Lee.*

till, 20 minutes later, Jolson appears and after a song says 'You ain't heard nothin' yet.' The film caused a sensation and racked up the then considerable gross of $3½ million. Jolson went on to make another for Warners, of similarly shopsoiled sentiment, *The Singing Fool* (28), about a singing waiter who becomes a star and goes to pieces when his wife walks out on him. It was only part-Talkie, but the Silent sequences were few and he sang 'Sonny Boy' to Davey Lee (and to the audience after he died; perhaps the worst ending on record). It was, by the time it was shown, only one of several part-Talkies, but its success was astounding – it made $5½ million, a record unbroken for 10 years (*Gone With the Wind* overtook it in 1939).

One result was that Warners signed just about every stage personality of note – Fanny Brice, Texas Guinan, Marilyn Miller, Ted Lewis – most of whom were soon going back whence they came. Another was that with Jolson they followed the same formula to such an extent that audiences fell away with rapidity, which was particularly dangerous if – as reputed – Jolson was getting $½ million per film. In *Say it With Songs* he is a radio singer sent to gaol for killing the man who made overtures to his wife and Davey 'Little Pal' Lee is run over. In *Mammy* (30) he is a mammy singer framed for murder, which gives him a chance to sing 'I'll Still Be a King to My Mammy'; he also sings 'Let Me Sing and I'm Happy' three times, which is twice too many. His vivacious personality was being swamped by the lachrymose intentions of the studio – or that is one way of putting it; another is that his high spirits are alienating in such arch, tedious material – as in *Big Boy*, in which he is in blackface throughout, as the groom on an English stud farm. Clearly a change of formula, based on a stage show he had done, it did not improve things much. He returned to Broadway in 'Wonder Bar' (31) but it was only a qualified success. He signed a long-term contract with UA, but only one film emerged: *Hallelujah I'm a Bum* (33), directed by Milestone, with Rodgers and Hart rhyming couplets. Jolson played a hobo and it was not a success. He did not need the money: in vaudeville he could demand $15,000 a week and in 1932 was getting $17,500, the highest salary yet known to show business. The following year he signed a radio contract worth $5,000 a week. Then he was involved with a Theater Guild plan to play the title-role in a Jerome Kern musical based on Dubose Hayward's novel, 'Porgy', but someone had second thoughts and the project was taken over by the Gershwins. Jolson returned to WB for *Wonder Bar* (34) – as a cabaret owner; and it was announced that he had signed a

Wonder Bar (*34*): *Dolores del Rio with four of her leading men: Dick Powell, Ricardo Cortez, Jolson and Robert Barrat. Del Rio and Cortez were a dance team – till she stabbed him. Powell was the man she fell for in the end, and Jolson ran the club – the Wonder Bar.*

new contract for one film a year with certain executive powers. But Jolson was both touchy and loathed – he was known at the studio as 'Cruel' Jolson – and there were only two films (though a third, *Bowery to Broadway*, was announced): *Go Into Your Dance* (35), about a big-headed singer down on his luck and saved by Ruby Keeler (his real-life wife), and *The Singing Kid* (36), with Beverly Roberts, the maudlin tale of a big star who loses his voice and goes into the country to recuperate. It started with Jolson singing a medley of his old songs – something with which the public was now over-familiar.

That did not prevent 20th from letting him do it all over again throughout *Rose of Washington Square* (39), in a characterization clearly based on himself, Alice Faye's old vaudeville buddy. It was not much of a characterization and it was not much of a part, but Jolson was solid gold. He played E.P. Christy (of the 'Minstrels') in the Stephen Foster biopic, *Swanee River* (40). No more film offers were forthcoming, so he returned to Broadway for the first time in 10 years, in 'Hold on to Your Hats' with Martha Raye and Ruby Keeler. It was a qualified success. In 1944 he played himself in the film about George Gershwin, *Rhapsody in Blue*, and the following year he married for the fourth time.

Jolson was a wealthy man, but career-wise he had been on his uppers for some years

(though as one of the biggest egos in the business, he probably did not recognize it). To general surprise, he regained popularity singing to the troops during the war. As a result, Sidney Skolsky planned to produce *The Jolson Story* (46). Warners turned down the project, but after Harry Cohn had seen him at a Hollywood concert, Columbia took it – and the huge gross netted Jolson $5 million as his percentage – a compensation for not being allowed to play himself, which peeved him. But he dubbed Larry Parks who did. The film was a monumental assembly of backstage clichés, but a new generation was discovering the Jolson voice and the Jolson songs, and it was a huge money-maker; further, it opened up a new career for Jolson on radio and records – there, once again, he was a hot property. Columbia felt called upon to make a sequel to *The Jolson Story*, all about how Jolson made a come-back because of *The Jolson Story*. It was called *Jolson Sings Again* and had a scene where Parks as Jolson meets Parks playing Parks. Marginally more entertaining than the earlier film, it was one of the top box-office films of 1949. In 1950 it was announced that he was trying to buy the rights of 'Porgy and Bess' as a star-vehicle for himself. Then RKO announced *Stars and Stripes Forever*, which would co-star Dinah Shore. But it was cancelled when he died (1950). He left $4 million. 'This great personality,' said Eddie Cantor, 'never learnt to live. The moment the curtain came down he died.'

BORIS KARLOFF

He was, said London's 'Evening Standard' when he died, 'the acknowledged king of Hollywood horror films'. Boris Karloff was/is one of Hollywood's most famous names, but he was not a great star. He found his niche and he stayed in it. He was a master of make-up; his monsters and villains were varied but they almost all had a touch of pathos: in life he was a gentle, courteous, thoughtful man and these qualities were always somewhat present in the grotesques he played (he liked gardening and poetry and was a devotee of cricket). His fame obscured the fact that the films in which he starred were invariably unimportant, B pictures and programme-fillers, and that in better films he was merely one of the supporting cast. Almost certainly he could not have widened his range, could not have sustained a real star part. He was one of those actors whom everyone likes while having no illusions about the talent. He is revered by fans of horror pictures, to the extent that more books have been published on him than on any comparable figure in the second echelon of movie names – but then, the most curious standards obtain among the followers of such films. It is a tiresome genre, mainly because its practitioners do not try hard enough – as exemplified by the British horror films of the 50s and 60s. Karloff belongs to what has been called 'the golden age' of horror films – an odd appellation for what amounts to about three and a half fairish entertainments. Of the almost 200 films he made only a handful of them are good; his professionalism is therefore all the more cherishable.

He was born in Dulwich, South London, in 1887, the youngest of nine children (a brother, Sir John Pratt, had a distinguished diplomatic career; their father was in the Indian Civil Service). Educated at Merchant Taylors' School and at London University, he was destined for the consular service but in 1909 emigrated to Canada, where in Ontario he worked on a farm. One of his brothers had been an actor – and the theatre was his main interest. An advert in a newspaper gave him a chance to join a touring company and it was then he adopted the name of Boris Karloff. His first role was an old man in Molnar's 'The Devil'. For 10 years he played the sticks in melodramas, often a different one every night, sometimes doubling as stage manager; he worked for several troupes, perhaps the

most distinguished of which was the one which took 'The Virginian' to the West. He was out of work in 1919 in Los Angeles and thinking about turning to vaudeville, but instead he became a film extra, in a crowd scene directed by Frank Borzage at Universal. He returned to San Francisco for three months and then in Hollywood was employed to play a soldier in *His Majesty the American* (19).

His work in Silent pictures was not notable. Occasionally he had a fair-sized part – often type-cast as a trapper – but his roles were small and often, to pay the rent, he returned to labouring. The titles were: *The Prince and Betty*; *The Deadlier Sex* (20), starring Blanche Sweet, his first sizeable part, as a fur-trapper; *The Courage of Marge O'Doone*, again as a trapper; *The Last of the Mohicans*; *Without Benefit of Clergy* (21), as the Oriental villain; *The Hope Diamond Mystery*, a serial, as the villainous high priest; *Cheated Hearts*, as a bandit; *Cave Girl* (22), as a half-breed kid-napper; *The Man From Downing Street*, as a maharajah; *The Infidel*, as a native chieftain; *The Altar Stairs*; *Omar the Tentmaker*, the first picture in which he was not evil; *A Woman Conquers* (23); *The Prisoner*; *Dynamite Dan* (24); *Parisian Nights* (25), in a good part as one of Lou Tellegen's apache gang; *Forbidden Cargo*, being mean to Evelyn Brent; *Prairie Wife*, as a Mexican half-breed; *Lady Robin Hood*; *Never the Twain Shall Meet* with Anita Stewart; *The Greater Glory* (26), with Anna Q. Nilsson and Conway Tearle, from a stage play about the effects of the war on the Viennese; *Her Honor the Governor*; *Flames*; *The Golden Web: Flaming Fury*; *The Bells*, with Lionel Barrymore in Henry Irving's old part and Karloff as the mesmerist; *Eagle of the Sea*, a pirate story with Florence Vidor and Ricardo Cortez; *Old Ironsides*; *Man in the Saddle*, starring Hoot Gibson; *Tarzan and the Golden Lion* (27) with James Pierce as Tarzan; *Let It Rain*; *The Princess from Hoboken*; *The Meddlin' Stranger*; *The Phantom Buster*; *Soft Cushions*, a comedy at Paramount with Sue Carol and Douglas McLean; *Two Arabian Knights*, as a sheik; *The Love Mart* (28) with Billie Dove; *Vultures of the Sea*, a Mascot serial; *Little Wild Girl* (29); *The Devil's Chaplain*; *Phantoms of the North*; *Two Sisters*; *Burning the Wind*; and *The Fatal Warning*, a serial.

His first Sound picture was *The Unholy Night*, a melodrama set in London in which he was a Hindu servant. He did another serial for Mascot, *King of the Kongo*, and the following: *Behind That Curtain*, as a murder suspect; *The Bad One* (30), as a prison guard; *The Sea Bat*, notable as Nils Asther's first audible Talkie role; *The Utah Kid*, for Tiffany, as the villain; and *Mother's Cry*, notable for the performance of Dorothy Peterson as the mother. That he had so far achieved no sort of fame in films is made apparent by the fact that 'Picturegoer' thought the next, *The Criminal Code* (31), was his first picture. Some months earlier an offer had come out of the blue to play a small part in the original play, in its Los Angeles production, and that had led to Columbia offering Karloff the same role in the film, as the trusted convict who turns killer. He scored a small success and was immediately much in demand in films: *Cracked Nuts* with Wheeler and Woolsey, as a revolutionary; *Young Donovan's Kid*; *Smart Money*, as a gambler; *The Public Defender*; *I Like Your Nerve*, as a butler; *Five Star Final* as the aide of ruthless editor Edward G. Robinson for whom, literally, he will stop at nothing; *The Mad Genius*, as the hero's vicious father; *The Yellow Ticket*, as an orderly who tries to rape the heroine; *The Guilty Generation*, as Robert Young's father, a prohibition racketeer; and a serial in which he was the star, *King of the Wild*.

Universal, meanwhile, had had a big success with *Dracula*, starring an actor of Hungarian origin, Bela Lugosi. A follow-up was planned, *Frankenstein*, from Mary Shelley's old novel, and Lugosi was set for the lead. Lugosi, however, demurred because he planned a picture called *Quasimodo* (it was never made) – and he was, in any case, a difficult man. Karloff was on the Universal lot playing a murderer in *Graft*, starring Regis Toomey and Sue Carol. Director James Whale tested him in the make-up of Frankenstein's monster, a huge automated creature, blind-eyed and somehow pathetic. Colin Clive had the title-role and Mae Clarke was the girl. The film was a huge success and Universal signed Karloff to a seven-year contract. Like Lugosi before him, he was boosted as the successor to Lon Chaney.

Meanwhile, Karloff had several commitments to other studios: *Tonight or Never*, in a funny scene as a waiter; *Business and Pleasure* (32), as a sheik whom Will Rogers meets on a trip to the East; *Scarface*, as a rival mobster; *The Miracle Man* with Sylvia Sidney, as a man running a fake mission; and *Behind the Mask* with Jack Holt, one of the year's best chillers, as a dope pedlar. In the first film of his new contract he played himself in one sequence, *The Cohens and Kellys in Hollywood*. He was the nightclub owner, a sympathetic part, in *Night World*, but soon reverted to type: the title-role in *The Mummy*, returning to life after 3,700 years in an Egyptian tomb to claim the girl he considers a reincarnation of his dead love, with David Manners and Zita Johann; and *The Old Dark House*, a ferocious performance as the deaf-mute butler/killer. MGM borrowed him to play Fu in *The Mask of Fu Manchu*, the hated enemy of Lewis Stone, Karen Morley *et al*.

Karloff was occasionally billed merely as

Karloff made up for Frankenstein's monster.

Goings-on in The Old Dark House (*32*). *Karloff as the butler, with Eva Moore – who for plot purposes was married to Ernest Thesiger.*

The Mask of Fu Manchu (32): Karloff as Fu Manchu, Myrna Loy as his equally wicked daughter and Charles Starrett as their victim.

'Karloff', but all was not well with him and Universal. He wanted more salary, but they refused and dropped him. He took a holiday and returned to Britain, where he made the inferior *The Ghoul* (33), with Ernest Thesiger and Cedric Hardwicke. 'Photoplay' found 'audiences are apt to be amused when action is intended to be most terrifying'. Karloff returned to Hollywood to two good films: John Ford's *The Lost Patrol* (34) with Victor McLaglen, about British soldiers stuck in the desert, with himself at his most outrageously hammy as the one with religious mania; and *The House of Rothschild* with George Arliss, as an anti-Semitic baron. He made it up with Universal, who put him at the head of a devil-worshipping cult in *The Black Cat*, with Lugosi enjoyably his deadly enemy: 'Photoplay' found 'no great suspense . . . all too unconvincing'. He did a guest appearance in that company's *Gift of Gab*, starring Edmund Lowe; went to Monogram to play a kindly detective – the title character – in *The Mysterious Mr Wong* (35); and returned to Universal for a good sequel, *The Bride of Frankenstein* – Elsa Lanchester in that part, and also *The Raven*, half paralysed, with Lugosi, based loosely on Poe and described by 'Photoplay' as an 'absurd mélange'. At Columbia he had a dual role in *The Black Room* with Katharine De Mille, then went back to Universal for another with Lugosi, *The Invisible Ray* (36).

There followed *The Walking Dead* at Warners, as a man who, returned from the dead, seeks out his killers, and *The Man Who Changed His Mind*, in Britain with Anna Lee, directed by her husband Robert Stevenson, as a mad scientist. After that Karloff was in Bs: *Charlie Chan at the Opera* with Warner Oland as Chan; *Night Key* (37), as an inventor whose burglar alarm device is stolen from him and whose subsequent neutralizer is wanted by crooks; *Juggernaut*, as a devil doctor; *West of Shanghai*, as a Chinese general; *The Invisible Menace* (38); *Mr Wong Detective*; *Son of Frankenstein* (39) with Lugosi and Basil Rathbone; *The Mystery of Mr Wong*; *Mr Wong in Chinatown*; *The Man They Could Not Hang*, again scaring people after being resurrected from the dead; and *The Tower of London*, with Rathbone as Richard III and Karloff as Mord, the limping headsman. He did: *The Fatal Hour* (40); *British Intelligence*, a remake of *Three Faces East*; *Black Friday* with Lugosi; *The Man With Nine Lives*, once again as a scientist-zombie; *Devil's Island*; *Doomed to Die* as Mr Wong; *Before I Hang*, as a scientist seeking a clue to eternal youth; *The Ape*; *You'll Find Out*, sharing the villain role with Peter Lorre and Lugosi in this Kay Kyser musical; *The Devil Commands* (41); and *The Boogie Man Will Get You*. Most of these were

poverty row efforts – several were at Monogram. Whether or not he was depressed by the quality of these is not known, though he considered it more important to work than to worry about artistic principles; but at that point he accepted a stage offer, 'Arsenic and Old Lace', playing the old ladies' mad and equally homicidal nephew. One of his lines went: 'I killed him because he said I looked like Boris Karloff.'

This *comédie noire* ran for three years and Karloff returned to Hollywood with renewed prestige. His come-back was in an A, in colour, *The Climax* (44), billed after Susannah Foster and Turhan Bey: it was designed as a follow-up to *The Phantom of the Opera*, which had been a big hit for Foster and Universal some months earlier, and had to do with hypnotism at the opera. Karloff then returned to B pictures. *The House of Frankenstein* (45) was only notable because Karloff played the mad scientist and Glenn Strange took on his old role as the monster. RKO decided that he would be an asset to Val Lewton's famed 'horror' unit and put him into three pictures, the first directed by Robert Wise and the others by Mark Robson. Each followed Lewton's dictum that terror can be aroused more by implication than by indication: *The Body Snatcher(s)* – the *s*, rightly, was added for Britain, from Robert Louis Stevenson's story based on the case of Burke and Hare – with Lugosi, and Henry Daniell as the anatomist

In the 40s Karloff often dispensed with heavy makeup: in The Climax *(44) he looked like his off-screen self. The lady in distress is Susanna Foster.*

who bought the corpses they collect; *Isle of the Dead*, with Karloff as its overlord; and *Bedlam* (46), ditto.

After that Karloff was sometimes in A pictures, in support: *Lured* (47) with Lucille Ball; *The Secret Life of Walter Mitty*, rather funny as a would-be writer with an infallible way of killing; *Unconquered*, as an Indian chief, with Gary Cooper; *Dick Tracy Meets Gruesome* with Ralph Byrd as Tracy and Karloff as the other title character; *Tap Roots* (48), again as an Indian; and *Abbott and Costello Meet the Killer* (Boris Karloff) (49) – with his name used as part of the title in some bookings. In 1948 he returned to Broadway in J.B. Priestley's 'The Linden Tree' – one of his rare 'straight' performances – but the play was not a success. His subsequent films were not distinguished: *The Strange Door* (51) starring Charles Laughton, as an obsessed gaoler; *The Black Castle* (52) with Richard Greene; *The Hindu*, a weird (in the wrong sense) international effort; *Abbott and Costello Meet Dr Jekyll and Mr Hyde* (53); and *Il Mostro dell'Isola* (54). He began to work frequently in TV and had his own series, 1956-58, 'Colonel March of Scotland Yard'. He returned to films: *Voodoo Island* (57); *Frankenstein 1970* (58) – 'the whole inept effort is a slight on the horrific name of Frankenstein', said the 'MFB'; and *The Grip of the Strangler*, with Jean Kent in a dual role. The last-named was made in Britain, whither Karloff had returned to live, deep in the countryside; there was a companion picture, equally good, *Corridors of Blood*, made around the same time but not shown until four years later. By that time Karloff had acceded to the demand of Roger Corman, then making a series of pictures for AIP: *The Raven* (63), a spoof of the films based on Poe tales, with Vincent Price and Peter Lorre; *The Terror*; *A Comedy of Terrors* (64) with Lorre and Price again, plus Basil Rathbone; and *I Tre Volti della Paura*, a three-part film directed by Mario Bava, with Karloff as a grandfather vampire in an episode based on a Tolstoy story. There were three more for AIP: *Bikini Beach*, in a walk-on as himself; *Monster of Terror/Die Monster Die* (65), made in Britain, once again as a mad scientist; and *The Ghost in the Invisible Bikini*; after which he did his first major studio picture in 15 years, *The Venetian Affair* (67), with Robert Vaughan, playing an important international figure – which reflects more aptly than his other roles his private status at the time, modest but aware of his legend. He was up to no good again in the British *The Sorcerers*, directed by Michael Reeves, as a hypnotist; in *El Coleccionista de Cadaveres/Blind Man's Buff* (68), as a blind hypnotist; and the British *Curse of the Crim-*

son Altar, as a witch reincarnated as a man.

He was also in *Targets*, made in fuzzy colour by Peter Bogdanovich, a dual story of an ageing star of horror movies (a tired Karloff virtually playing himself) and a clean-cut American youth who takes to sniping at cars on the freeway because he loves guns. Cruel and gripping, it was more intelligent and more terrifying than anything Karloff had done and with its gentle self-portrait was an unusual swan-song. At least, he made four more films, in Spain, apparently called *Isle of the Snake People*, *The Incredible Invasion*, *The Fear Chamber* and *The Hour of Evil*, but they appear never to have been shown. During 1960-62 he worked again in TV ('Starring Boris Karloff') and at one time told bedroom stories to children over the radio. In interviews he never knocked the type of films he made, but did speak wistfully of more 'serious' material: he scored a great success as Mr Darling and Captain Hook to Jean Arthur's 'Peter Pan' (50-51) and later played Cauchon in 'The Lark' to Julie Harris's Joan of Arc. He married twice and died in 1969.

BUSTER KEATON

Buster Keaton was not born in a trunk, but it was a near thing. His parents were on tour in Kansas – with a troupe that included Houdini – when Buster was born in 1895. By the time he was three, the child had, at his own insistence, joined the act. Later, 'The Three Keatons' were one of the best-known vaudeville acts and Buster, following in his father's steps, became a remarkable athlete, adept at pratfalls, handsprings and marksmanship: the star of the act and, before he reached his teens, a celebrity in his own right.

There was a movie offer in 1913 when it was proposed that they should appear in a series based upon the strip cartoon 'Bringing Up Father', but this Father disapproved of movies. Thereafter things went badly: the famous quarrel between the vaudeville artists and their employers, the owners of the circuits, put the Keatons out of the big time; and Father's drinking threatened the safety of his wife and Buster during the stage acrobatics. In self-defence they ditched the old man and Buster went to New York where he was offered a turn in 'The Passing Show of 1917'. Instead, he went into movies, via a chance street meeting with a vaudeville chum. He was invited to watch Roscoe 'Fatty' Arbuckle filming one of his two-reelers, *The Butcher Boy* (17), and was asked to participate – without rehearsal. During that one day he fell in love with the whole paraphernalia of

filming and he joined Arbuckle at $40 a week – instead of the $250 he would have been paid on Broadway. His salary with Arbuckle was to climb until it reached that figure, but in the meantime he was soon regarded as the second chief member of the company and he and Arbuckle became friends. He made 14 shorts with Arbuckle – in one of which, *Fatty at Coney Island*, can be glimpsed his only on-screen laugh. Other titles were: *His Wedding Night*, *Goodnight Nurse*, *Moonshine*. After *The Cook* (18) he left for military service and when he returned he received two offers, at $1,000 a week, from Jack Warner and William Fox. He chose to stay with Arbuckle, but Arbuckle was about to leave the company to go to Zukor; their producer, Joseph M. Schenck, proposed to Keaton that he take it over – at $1,000 a week plus 25 per cent of the profits. Metro were to release.

First, however, Metro wanted Keaton for a feature, *The Saphead* (20). It was adapted from 'The New Henrietta' that Douglas Fairbanks had done as play and film, and it was he who suggested Keaton for the lead. The script was reworked to make Keaton the central character, a foppish man-about-town who, *almost* by chance and much to their surprise, saves the family from ruin. Little of it is typical of his work to come, but he scored a hit and some critics said that Chaplin would have to look to his laurels. The first two-reeler starring Keaton in his own right, *The High Sign*, was already in the can, but release was delayed because he was not satisfied with it; thus the first one released was *One Week*, described by Keaton himself as 'a mild parody of Elinor Glyn's "Three Weeks" – only one-third as shocking . . . built around my efforts to put together the portable home I'd bought for our love-nest'. Keaton himself said it was this film which made his reputation. There followed *Convict 13*, *The Scarecrow*, *Neighbors*, *The Haunted House* (21), *Hard Luck*, Keaton's own favourite among his shorts, and *The Goat*, all made within the space of a year. Each marked an advance both visual (e.g. the incredible escape leap through the transom window in *The Goat*) and thematic. Keaton had never been a banana-peel/custard-pie comic, but he was beginning to express himself in almost surrealistic terms, with two predominant conceits – Buster caught in the toils of machinery and Buster dogged by misfortune and misunderstanding.

Then came four consecutive masterpieces: *The Playhouse*, with its theatreful of Busters, done by photographic sorcery still not adequately explained; *The Boat* – which pulls down the garage in which it was built and then the house and which, when launched, promptly sinks; *The Paleface* – Buster, chasing butterflies and pursued by Indians; and *Cops* (22), a whole city police force after a Buster who had inadvertently crossed them. The level of visual wit is Everest-high, but *The Boat* and *Cops* suggest a blacker vision, a fatalism, inexorable and absurd.

My Wife's Relations and *The Blacksmith* were, in the words of Keaton's biographer, Rudi Blesh, 'like early Keystones, little more than good slapstick', but *The Frozen North* – intended as a parody of William S. Hart – was wild fantasy. The mechanism of *The Electric House*, naturally, collapses disastrously. *Daydreams* is a bitter piece, juxtaposing the fancies in the letters to the girl back home with the harsh truth. *Balloonatics* again was fantasy with, at fade-out, Buster and his girl paddling their canoe in the sky. There followed *The Love Nest*, after which Schenck informed Keaton that he could make features under a new deal with Metro, who had released the first half of this batch of shorts (First National had handled the rest).

Keaton was by now world-famous. Though neither he nor Lloyd nor – more debatably – Chaplin had the prestige of the dramatic stars, they were hugely popular: they were merely funny men, albeit in what has been called 'the high summer of comedy'. It was to be a long time before Keaton was considered a genius. His behind-the-camera contribution to his own films, as writer, innovator and director, was around 90 per cent – though he shared credit wherever he could (in *The Playhouse* he had ridiculed those Hollywood directors – specifically Thomas H. Ince – who accepted half a dozen credits on each movie). As his biographer Tom Dardis remarks (in fact, in his book on Harold Lloyd), even a casual viewing of Keaton's films shows 'film-making of an extraordinarily complex nature, in which all the details have been worked out with a fine precision that perhaps has never had its equal in American film'.

The Keaton the public saw was a dignified, impressively grave young man, 'the great stone face'. Deadpan, but not inscrutable: 'He was very handsome and generally silent. Most of the emotional work was done by a pair of remarkable eyes and a brave, schooled body. He had his own fashions for expressing feelings' (John Coleman). A slight blink meant bewilderment, a slight frown meant determination, as he struggled against the perversities of his opponents. A long gaze meant ardour, passion for his heroine – usually more a handicap than a help – but his aloofness was really shyness imposed on a sense of his own inadequacies. He needed to have patience and infinite resource, as well, of course, as his body: he was incredibly lithe and strong '. . . he brought pure physical comedy to its greatest heights. Beneath his lack of emotion he was always uninsistently sardonic; deep below that, giving a disturbing tension and grandeur to the foolishness of those who sensed it, there was in his comedy a freezing whisper not of pathos but of melancholia. With the humour, the craftsmanship and the action there was often, besides, a fine, still and dreamlike beauty' (James Agee).

Economically, it made sense to go into features: the Keaton shorts were often the biggest attraction on the bill, but they took much less in rentals than the features. His salary went to $2,000 per week (later to go to $2,500) plus his percentage bonus. The features themselves were to cost between $200,000 and $220,000 – about 25 per cent more than most dramatic films, but the cost was justified by much bigger profits. Keaton's features each grossed between $1½ and 2 million, a little less, he estimated, than Harold Lloyd's.

The first of them was *The Three Ages* (23), a burlesque on *Intolerance* and basically three two-reelers, with a boy-meets-girl, loses, wins, common to each; the ages were the Stone Age, Ancient Rome and the present day. The same year came *Our Hospitality* – an ironic title: he became involved in a family feud in the Deep South. The film contains some of his most outrageous physical feats, including the rescue from the waterfall. *Sherlock Junior* (24) was Buster – in his alter ego: the rest of the time he is a cinema projectionist, roaming, like the film, between dreams and reality; at one time he walks straight into the screen, but that is not half as magical as the chase sequence, with a motorcycle ride which is pure poetry.

The Navigator has Keaton and his girlfriend on a deserted liner, he, with daffy ingenuity, mastering its mechanics. It was the biggest money-maker of all his films and one of the two most highly regarded (the other is *The General*: they were Keaton's own favourites). He did not care for *Seven Chances* (25) which he unwillingly constructed from a play that Schenck had bought for him: to inherit a fortune, he advertises for a bride; 500 turn up at the church – and give chase – perhaps the best he did, bedevilled by falling boulders. He himself did not care for the chase in *Go West* and for the first time since leaving Arbuckle the effect is less than sublime. Buster is besotted with a cow and although the idea is good, the laughter is sparse. *Battling Butler* (26) also has weaknesses, but it causes something nearer the normal laughter quotient, especially the sojourn in the wild with attendant valet; and there is a fine example of Keaton originality – the serious boxing match at the end.

The General (27) came next, a unique contribution to Civil War mythology and Keaton's most inspired and hilarious chase; and then *College*, a Keatonish variation on Lloyd's *The Freshman*. *Steamboat Bill Jr* is basically just Buster in a cyclone, 'the most fantastic dithyrambs of disaster ever committed to film' (Blesh). It was previewed with Buster smiling at the end, but the audience would not take it.

Then in 1928, 'I made the worst mistake of my career. Against my better judgement I let Joe Schenck talk me into giving up my own studio to make pictures at the booming MGM lot in Culver City' ('My Wonderful World of Slapstick', 1960). Both Chaplin and Lloyd advised against it. Keaton thought Schenck acted in his best interests, but he did approach Paramount to take on the distribution of his films, retaining autonomy on production, but they had just undertaken to release Lloyd's product and did not want two comics. Keaton understood that there was an underground conspiracy to get him to MGM, whose boss, Nicholas Schenck, was Joe's brother. His pictures had become expensive and according

Most Keaton admirers would find it difficult to choose the most brilliant of the masterpieces he made between 1923 and 1928. Contenders would certainly be Sherlock Junior *(24), in which he played a cinema projectionist.*

Keaton, the greatest of the Silent clowns, in what may be his funniest film, Seven Chances *(25). He has asked all of these ladies to marry him.*

Keaton had two ambitions in The Cameraman *(28) – to get a newsreel scoop and make his name, and of course to win the girl. For a moment he is diverted from the latter by an unknown buxom beauty he meets on the beach: he appears to be clutching her hand, but she was really the pursuer, and a very determined one.*

to Dardis the last to make a profit was *Battling Butler*. He was at least, to be paid $3,000 a week – for 50 weeks a year for two years, or an annual salary of $150,000 for two films a year for two years, plus an additional $50,000 if a further film was made. The first was *The Cameraman* (28), a fable about a tin-type photographer who wants to make newsreels to impress his girlfriend. He had to fight to make it his way and was not allowed to use his own team or develop his ideas. And since it made a mint, that only proved to MGM how well they could make a Keaton comedy: so the battles with executives intensified on *Spite Marriage* (29), which concerned a pants-presser so infatuated with an actress that he spends his evenings watching her in a Southern melodrama, till he gets a chance to be her leading man. It broke records.

A synchronized version was made of *Marriage* and Buster made a French version (with Françoise Rosay); and he did a Salome dance in *Hollywood Revue of 1929*; but his first Talkie is reckoned to be *Free and Easy* (30), in which he is trying to make a Hollywood star of Anita Page. It was hardly a good Keaton film (he sang 'Conchita!'), but it was successful and Louis B. Mayer renewed his contract for another two years, offering a further $12,500 for foreign language versions, plus an immediate bonus of $10,000 and three months

holiday. In fact, the public were turning up to see anything that talked, however muffled, and were no longer interested in the visual comedies of the silent screen. Keaton's popularity, however, had continued to grow and was now at its peak, surpassing that of Lloyd. The descent was to come a couple of films later and be rapid and sudden. Blesh says that *Doughboys* is 86 per cent Keaton (he provided its original story), but Dilys Powell has recalled 'a snigger of amusement, the rest was disaster'. Contemporary critics were commenting favourably, but *Parlour Bedroom and Bath* (31) really marked a decline. Reginald Mortimer wrote in 'Picturegoer': 'When you consider the brilliant comedies Keaton has given us . . . there is something rather pathetic in his efforts to retain his following in Talkies that frequently remind one of a burnt-out squib.' It was not entirely his fault: he said of *The Sidewalks of New York*, which came next, that the directors 'alternated in telling me how to walk, how to talk, how to stand, and how to fall – where and when, how fast or slow, how loud or soft. . . . It came out such a complete stinker, such an unbelievable bomb.' As grosses tumbled, MGM dickered with the idea of a 'straight' Buster and he tested for the role Lionel Barrymore played in *Grand Hotel*. Instead, they announced that his new contract called for split-billing – a sure

sign that he was on the skids. Jimmy Durante teamed with him in *The Passionate Plumber* (32), a version of *Her Cardboard Lover*, and though the notices were terrible MGM, undeterred, teamed them again: *Speak Easily*, as an absent-minded professor, involved with a theatrical troupe, and *What No Beer* (33), a comedy about bootlegging. Filming proceeded badly, with Keaton missing days. His contract had been renewed again in 1932, on the original terms – but the second of these penalized him for 'alcoholic absences'.

That his drinking – he was an alcoholic by this time – was a contributory factor to the decline of his career cannot be doubted. The Hollywood of the 20s was a heavy-drinking place, but Keaton was not hooked until his marriage to Natalie (youngest of the Talmadge sisters) as well as his career went to pieces. Unlike Lloyd and Chaplin, he was not a businessman. He was only an artist, a gentle man, never pushing himself forward, always trusting, an innocent in the film jungle that had grown up round him in the last decade. He had only one obsession: to make people laugh. His waking hours were spent devising new ways to create laughter, even in the agony of these days: booze could provide the dreams he needed, for he dreamt of laughter.

When *What No Beer* demonstrated another marked decrease in public interest, MGM decided that they wanted no further truck with their 'difficult' star and after a quarrel (Mayer wanted Keaton to be on the set to greet visitors one Saturday when Keaton wanted to be at a baseball game) he was told that his services were no longer required. Thalberg asked him to go back some months later ('Aside from Norma Shearer, his wife, I think I was his favourite MGM star') to discuss a spoof version Keaton had planned of *Grand Hotel*, but Keaton was too proud. Instead, broke – the divorce had left him penniless – he went to Florida to make an independent film, but was so appalled by the set-up that he persuaded the backers to abandon the project. It had been widely publicized 'so what I got from it was a couple of weeks' work and another failure on my record'. No Hollywood studio would touch him, so he accepted an offer for a French film, *Le Roi des Champs Elysées* (34), at $15,000, and then one in Britain, for Sam Spiegel, *The Invader* (35). The first had a reasonable budget, some excellent gags and an engaging plot about a bit-actor who is dead ringer for a notorious gangster (also played by Buster). An American title was ready, *The Champ of the Champs Elysées*, but it does not seem to have been imported, while the other, a horrible skinflint effort, did turn up as *An Old Spanish Custom*. Buster plays an American

millionaire who, docking in a Spanish port, becomes embroiled in the affairs of some squabbling lovers. The only resemblance to his great days is that the dialogue is kept to a minimum, so that what gags there are are silent.

Back in Hollywood and cured of alcoholism (he did not drink again until 1940 and after that had occasional outbursts; though on doctor's orders he did not drink during the last years of his life) he approached Educational to let him make comedy shorts. They agreed to pay him $2,500 per short, the things to be shot in three days each. He made 18 for Educational over a three-year period (35-37) and the quality is generally low. In 1939-41 he had a similar arrangement with Columbia for six a year. He begged Columbia to let him make a feature, but there was no interest. However, he did begin to get feature work again in 1939, starting with a four-week stint at 20th on *Hollywood Cavalcade*, where, ironically, he was called upon to heave a custard pie, almost his first. He was in, and worked on the scripts of, two of 20th's Jones family series (*The Jones Family in Hollywood* and *The Jones Family and Quick Millions*), but most of his work was for a day's duration: *The Villain Still Pursued Her* (40) and *Li'l Abner*. Sick of the 'cheaters' at Columbia, he approached MGM for a job and was assigned to be comic relief in the MacDonald-Eddy *New Moon*, but the role was eliminated during filming. The studio kept him on, however, as a gag man, at $100 a week (and later, $300), and although he failed to find any accord with either the Marx Brothers or Abbott and Costello, many of the routines of his great Silents turned up in the vehicles for Red Skelton. He also began to do stock, touring in 'The Gorilla'.

Dilys Powell says in her introduction to his memoirs: 'He was in fact missed rather than forgotten. Few film-stars have been missed so much and so long. It was with a shock of delight that, one day in the war, one recognized in a film called *San Diego I Love You* (44), the long, sad, glacier face of Buster Keaton.' He was also in *Forever and a Day* (43), *That's the Spirit* (45), *That Night With You* and *God's Country* (46). Then he made a film in Mexico, *El Moderno Barba Azul* (45), and one in France with Bourvil, *Un Duel à Mort* (48); and in 1947 commenced the first of several successful sorties into the Cirque Medrano in Paris, billed as 'L'homme qui rit jamais'. He had featured roles in *You're My Everything* (49), *The Lovable Cheat* and MGM's *In the Good Old Summertime*, as a shop assistant, nephew of the boss, the dire S.Z. Sakall, who has a better role and bigger billing: but Buster's one pratfall can still bring

the house down. He made a wan, if effective appearance in *Sunset Boulevard* (50), as one of Gloria Swanson's bridge-playing cronies, and another in *Limelight* (52), in a comic stage routine with Chaplin – though that was cut to nothing when Chaplin discovered that Keaton was getting more laughs than himself.

It was then that the resurrection began: he had a successful TV show on the West Coast 1950-51 and film societies began to show his films; James Agee's famous 'Life' magazine piece on the great Silent comedians had appeared in 1949. In 1952 his fee in Paris at the circus was $3,500 and afterwards he toured the British provinces with his wife (his third, last and enduring – since 1940 – marriage). He was honoured by Eastman House, in their Festival of the Arts, as one of the 10 who had contributed most to the art of the movies (the others were Pickford, Lillian Gish, Mae Marsh, Lloyd, Barthelmess, Norma Talmadge, Swanson, Ronald Colman, Chaplin). He made a film in Italy, *L'Incantevole Nemica* (54), starring Silvana Pampanini and Robert Lamoureaux, a comedy about factory life – and the family who owns the factory – and he was in *Around the World in Eighty Days* (56), where he, the forgotten star, the one who did not want to be loved, drew more audience response than any of the other guest stars. In 1957 came *The Buster Keaton Story*, with Donald O'Connor as Keaton – an inept biopic, but one which made Keaton a fairly wealthy man for the rest of his life. In 1959 he was awarded a special Oscar for his contribution to the art of the cinema.

But the real acclaim was to still come. In 1954 Keaton had approached Raymond Rohauer, managing the Society of Cinema Arts in Los Angeles, with an offer of several decomposing reels of his great films. Soon after that a cache was found in James Mason's

home (which had once been Keaton's). Rohauer set out to restore to Keaton not only his films but the glory and by the time that Keaton died he had managed to purchase for him – sometimes saving from destruction – all his best work. The films began to be shown: there was a retrospective at the Venice Film Festival in 1963 and in 1965 Keaton was at the Festival to experience a 20-minute standing ovation which reduced him to tears, perhaps the most moving and most justified tribute in the whole history of movies. In Germany in 1962-63 *The General* broke records in most cities and a revival in Paris was also mobbed (the best London could do was to put it in support of a re-run of *The Ipcress File* for two weeks).

Also, there was work: supporting roles in *The Adventures of Huckleberry Finn* (60), the Canadian *Ten Girls Ago* (62), *It's a Mad Mad Mad Mad World* (63) and *The Triumph of Lester Snapwill*; in 1965 Buster appeared in no less than seven films, either in guest spots or in shorts; two of them were made in Canada, *The Railrodder* and *Keaton Rides Again*, a survey of his career. There were Samuel Beckett's *Film* (half an hour of the back of Keaton's head!); *Pajama Party*, *Beach Blanket Bingo*, *How to Stuff a Wild Bikini*; there was the Italian *Due Marines e un General*; and there was Lester's *A Funny Thing Happened on the Way to the Forum*. His last films were *The Scribe*, made in Canada, and *Sergeant Deadhead*, which starred Frankie Avalon. He died in 1966.

'But that game, ridiculous little figure in its flat hat, stumping about on stiff short legs, with arms that are inclined to start into sudden motion like a windmill and, at the centre of all the activity, a still face of absurd solemnity and astounding *beauty*, cannot die. Undefeated, he continues to match his ingenious little devices against the Goliaths; and passes into the universal folk heritage, as the supreme clown-poet' (David Robinson in 1968). He left behind a bunch of films, all Silent, to most of which the word 'masterpiece' easily fits. His greatness as clown and creative film-maker is more available now than it was through most of his lifetime – and, to judge from the laughter to be heard at successive showings, is more appreciated than that of Chaplin, who overshadowed him for so long. Posterity had reversed their reputations – as, indeed, it had to.

Keaton in his short, sad, guest appearance in Sunset Boulevard *(50). He said later that he never saw the film.*

RUBY KEELER

In 1965 the New York Gallery of Modern Art arranged there and elsewhere showings of the

Ruby Keeler came all the way to New York to break into show business – but all she managed was to get a job on showman James Cagney's backstage staff. Until one day . . . Footlight Parade (*33*). *Watching her are Cagney and his adoring secretary, played by Joan Blondell.*

Dick Powell and Ruby Keeler in Frank Borzage's Flirtation Walk (*34*). *Though they liked working together they both fought against being teamed because they thought that limited them.*

films of Busby Berkeley, who specialized in mammoth girlie routines: girls geometric, girls floral, girls as harps, girls as waterfalls, hundreds of girls playing hundreds of grand pianos. In the midst of this amusing but Freudian old tat can be glimpsed a couple singing, an aggressively grinning juvenile, Dick Powell, and a dark little girl with more than a passing resemblance to a bush baby, Ruby Keeler. She danced, too, a spirited but unexpressive tap, a suitable counterpoint to her cracked nasal soprano. At these Cinematheque showings, Berkeley appeared and reminisced about these antique movies, accompanied by Keeler, a slim and attractive middle-aged woman. She disarmed audiences by confessing: 'It's amazing. I couldn't act. I had that terrible singing voice, and now I can see I wasn't the greatest tap dancer in the world either.'

Keeler was born in Halifax, Nova Scotia, in 1909; her family moved to New York when she was three and in New York at 13 she began her career as a buck-dancer with Patsy Kelly. She was also in the chorus of Broadway shows for four years, starting with 'The Rise of Rosy O'Reilly', till she got a part in 'Bye Bye Bonnie', followed by 'The Sidewalks of New York' (24) and 'Whoopee!'. In 1928 she married Al Jolson, whom she had met while she was hoofing in Texas Guinan's club. Ziegfeld then starred her in 'Show Girl' – remembered now because Jolson sometimes wandered into the theatre when his own show was over and sang 'Liza' to her walking

through the stalls. He was already a Warners star but it was not until three years later that that studio placed Keeler under contract. Fox tested her and issued a short to demonstrate how effectively her tap-dancing sounded in their Movietone sound process.

42nd Street (32), directed by Lloyd Bacon (Berkeley did the musical numbers), cast her as the girl picked from the chorus line to replace the ailing, temperamental star (Bebe Daniels): 'You've got to go on and give and give' exhorts Warner Baxter, '. . . and Sawyer, you're going on a youngster, but you've got to come back a star!' Most of her subsequent films seemed to have the same plot, or at least she was always naive (indeed, downright imperceptive), swimming to success in the hard-boiled, soft-hearted showbiz pool. But *42nd Street* was different, hard and fierce and almost melancholy, quick-moving and tuneful: the prototype of the 'new' musical, more realistic than those hitherto. It grossed over $2¼ million, an enormous sum. Hardly less good was *Gold Diggers of 1933* (33), paired again with Dick Powell, a couple of innocents in a world composed of the likes of Aline McMahon, Joan Blondell, Guy Kibbee, Warren William, Ginger Rogers, Una Merkel and Ned Sparks. And *Footlight Parade*, aided by Cagney's energetic performance, is as enjoyable now as it was then. Powell was in it and he and Keeler continued their romance through *Dames* (34), *Flirtation Walk*, *Shipmates Forever* (36) and *Colleen*. She eventually made a film with Jolson, *Go*

Into Your Dance (35), as a dancer teamed with him in an attempt to steady him up and restore him to favour.

In 1937 she was getting $4,000 a week. In an interview that year with W.H. Mooring, she said that she did not think she was good enough to carry a film and that she was sick of backstage romances. She added: 'This film business isn't my whole life.' Her last film for Warners was a 'musical extravaganza', *Ready Willing and Able* (37), with Ross Alexander (just before he shot himself during a drinking bout).

About the time it finished shooting, Jolson quarrelled with Warners and walked out, angrily taking Keeler with him. She had two films to go under her contract, which was quietly settled. She signed a new one for two films a year at $40,000 each with RKO, who finally dumped her into *Mother Carey's Chickens* (38), already turned down by Ginger Rogers, Katharine Hepburn and Joan Bennett among others. It was an old-fashioned piece – and not a musical – about a widow, Fay Bainter, who keeps a boarding house; Keeler and Anne Shirley played her daughters and because Keeler was billed under Shirley she terminated her contract. She appeared in a play with Jolson and Martha Raye, 'Hold on To Your Hats', but left it in Chicago because of ad-libbed references to their marital difficulties. They were divorced in 1940 and she has never publicly discussed the marriage, except to say, 'It was a mistake – a long mistake.' She played a wise-cracking showgirl in a B at Columbia, *Sweetheart of the Campus* (41), and that year married a Californian land developer; they have four children. She refused to let her name be used in *The Jolson Story*. During the next two decades she made a few appearances on television and she did 'Bell Book and Candle' (68) in stock. Her husband died in 1969 and she accepted a film role, a guest appearance in *The Phynx* (70), and starred in a very successful Broadway musical, 'No, No, Nanette' (71).

ALAN LADD

In the hierarchy of tough-guy stars, Alan Ladd holds an honoured name: through 50 or so formula pictures he strolled, stone-faced, in roles which fitted him as snugly as the iron strapped to his side. No one ever pretended that he could act. He got to the top, therefore, by a combination of determination and luck.

He was born in Hot Springs, Arkansas, in 1913. His father died when he was three and with his mother and stepfather he went to California. At high school he was noted for his athletic prowess and was later a diving champion. He was further noted, if anything, for the variety of jobs he had, including gas-station attendant and life-guard. He was taken on by Universal in 1932 as one of a group of college boys to be groomed for stardom, but apart from a bit in *Once in a Lifetime* (32) they did not use him, an experience which left a vivid impression. He managed to get a job as a grip at Warners and also worked on a newspaper and owned a hot-dog stand. He did not despair. Finally he got some local stage and radio work and a few 'extra' jobs in films – he can be glimpsed in *Pigskin Parade* (36), *The Last Train from Madrid* (37), *Souls at Sea*, *Hold 'em Navy*, *The Goldwyn Follies* (38), *Born to the West*, with billing, and *Come on Leathernecks*.

In 1938 he met Sue Carol, a former star who had turned agent, purportedly after hearing him on the air. Despite his small stature she could sense star potential in his cool, blond looks and she took him under her wing, pushing him with determination and devotion. She got him a small part in *Rules of the Sea* (39) and the juvenile lead in a minor piece at PRC, known both as *Beasts of Berlin* and *The Goose Step*; he was second lead in a Universal serial, *The Green Hornet* (40), but no one was impressed and he spent the next two years in either unbilled bits or with some ignominious credits such as *Light of Western Stars*, billed 12th, and *Those Were the Days*, billed 26th as Alan Laird. He is also said to be in these: *In Old Missouri*, *Gang of Chicago*, *Captain Caution*, *Wildcat Bus*, *Meet the Missus*, *Her First Romance*, *Petticoat Politics* (41), *Citizen Kane*, as a reporter, *The Black Cat*, *They Met in Bombay*, as Clark Gable's CO, Disney's *The Reluctant Dragon* in the live-action sequence, *Great Guns* and *Cadet Girls*. A number of these were made at Republic and other places where most people were too discriminating to work; but Carol's best contacts were at Paramount and RKO, and these paid off. At RKO he had about 20 lines at the climax of *Joan of Paris* (42), in which Michèle Morgan helped shot-down airmen, including him, to escape the Nazis.

As a result, RKO offered a contract starting at $450 a week, but she had already got him one at Paramount for $300 per week and the promise of fourth billing on *This Gun for Hire*, Graham Greene's 'A Gun for Sale' transferred to an American setting. Of the four leading roles his was the best, as Carol recognized when she saw the script, and he was excellent as the hired gun who gets caught in a trap like a rat. 'Picturegoer' readers voted him their annual Gold Medal for Best Actor and the studio raised his salary to $750 a week. Miss Carol's persistence had paid off in

Neither Alan Ladd nor Veronica Lake were quite so effective without the other: her sulky looks and little-girl-lost voice were ideally complemented by his unsmiling countenance and discourteous manner. Here in This Gun for Hire *(42), the film that made him a star.*

another way, too, for Ladd divorced his (first) wife and married her, her fourth husband. Paramount quickly put him into another thick-ear thriller, the remake of Dashiell Hammett's *The Glass Key*, and again the contrast between the taciturn, unsmiling Ladd and the silky, provocative Veronica Lake worked potently at the box-office. They had become one of the most celebrated teams of the era, though apart from guest appearances they worked together again only twice – which was not, in any case, an experience he enjoyed.

Paramount of course were delighted. The majority of stars were earmarked as such when they appeared on the horizon – from Broadway or from wherever they came; if it seemed unlikely that public acceptance would come with one film they were trained and built up: the incubation period was usually between two and five years. As far as Ladd was concerned, he was a small-part actor given a fat part *faute de mieux* and after his second film for them he had not merely hit the leading-men category, but had gone beyond it to films which were constructed round his personality. In *Lucky Jordan* he was a gangster reformed by the love of a Good Woman (Helen Walker) and a stint in the army. He guested in *Star Spangled Rhythm* and in *China* (43) was a tough oil man redeemed by Loretta Young and the suffering around him. Bosley Crowther wrote: 'Mr Ladd consumes countless cigarettes and gets into some ludicrous postures in pretending to be a tough dead-panned guy.' Ladd then did his own hitch in the USAAF, until invalided out some months later – it was said at the behest of himself and Paramount, which did not help his image within the industry. He was with Young again in *And Now Tomorrow* (44), but it was more her vehicle than his – a soap opera about a spoilt woman going deaf and her harsh-seeming doctor. They ended in a clinch. It was a pitch to sell Ladd to women filmgoers, though he had not changed one iota and he did not have a noticeable romantic aura. But Paramount hoped that women might feel that beneath the rock-like expression there smouldered fires of passion, or something like. His black-lashed eyes, however, gave nothing away: it was 'take me as I am' or 'I'm the boss around here'. He never flirted nor even seemed interested (which was one of the reasons he and Lake were so effective together).

He was *Salty O'Rourke* (45), a drama about what the ads called 'The Sport of Kings', with Gail Russell, and he guested again in *Duffy's Tavern*, spoofing his image. When 'Modern Screen' polled its readers for their new favourites, he was the only Paramount star on the list, at No 4 (the others, in order, Van Johnson, Frank Sinatra, June Allyson, Peter Lawford and Robert Walker, were all at MGM). He refused to work until a more favourable contract was drawn up, returning after a suspension, at $75,000 per film (but without story approval or the right to do outside films, as he had wanted): *The Blue Dahlia* (46) with Lake and a clever Raymond Chandler script, as a war veteran who returns to find his wife first unfaithful and then dead – one of the classic thrillers of the period; *OSS* with a new type of leading lady, cool and ladylike, Geraldine Fitzgerald; and *Two Years Before the Mast*, a vigorous adaptation of Richard Henry Dana's autobiographical novel, with William Bendix and Barry Fitzgerald, two scene-stealers who lost in this case to Howard Da Silva in a masterly interpretation of the vile captain. This had in fact been made after *Salty O'Rourke*, but release had been delayed while he did two war-related items, for the public might find them no longer topical.

Now – 1946/7 – he was one of the 10 most popular stars in Britain and in the US he was No 10 in 1947. This was despite a mouldy couple of pictures that year, *Calcutta* with Gail Russell and *Wild Harvest* with Lamour, though just prior to this the two of them had duetted on Frank Loesser's prime 'Talahassee', guesting, in *Variety Girl*. Nor were the 1948 trio much better: *Saigon*, the last with Lake; *Beyond Glory* with Donna Reed, as a West Point officer accused of illtreating a cadet; and *Whispering Smith*, his first Western

since his 'extra' days.

Physically, he was perfect as *The Great Gatsby* (49) and his emotional immobility might have worked better in a better film. Critics disliked the picture – though Scott Fitzgerald had not then been rediscovered – and the public did not go because it was not what they expected of a Ladd movie. More popular was a thriller, *Chicago Deadline*, again with Donna Reed, and assorted similar vehicles: *Captain Carey USA* (50), with Wanda Hendrix; *Branded*, another Western, with Mona Freeman; *Appointment with Danger* (51), with Phyllis Calvert as a nun; and *Red Mountain*, with Lizabeth Scott. Meanwhile, he and Paramount were fighting: they had bought for filming a Broadway play, 'Detective Story', which he wanted to do – so when they preferred Kirk Douglas he was determined to get out of his agreement. It had two years to run: he was offered 14 films over a five-year period at $100,000 a film, plus 75 per cent of all the earnings from four further films. He refused and his contract was amended to only two further pictures, at $100,000 each, with the right to do outside films. He immediately signed with Warners for six films over a six-year period, at $150,000 each plus 10 per cent of the profits – starting with *The Iron Mistress* (52), a title referring to the Bowie knife he invented and not co-star Virginia Mayo.

There were, however, three further Paramount films. *Thunder in the East*, with Deborah Kerr, had been made before the contract negotiations and release was delayed almost two years, till 1953 – and so was *Botany Bay*, which turned up at the end of the year (both had been seen abroad much earlier). Thus did Paramount hope to extend their earnings from Ladd; but *Shane* (53) went into release quickly in an attempt – a successful one – to recover its huge cost. George Stevens had taken one of the oldest Western clichés for his ambitious drama of pioneer homesteaders: the gunman who rides into town and out only when order has been restored. In that role Ladd's monolithic presence was well present, but Karel Reisz in the 'MFB' found the performance 'empty . . . the only box-office concession in an otherwise single-minded film'. It remains the film with which he is chiefly associated, grossing a huge $9 million and restoring him to the box-office 10 in 1953 and 1954.

Ladd had also made other deals, with Universal for two films and with Warwick in Britain, releasing through Columbia, for three, on a percentage deal in both cases, though for the first Warwick film he would get only a flat fee, a hefty $200,000 plus $50,000 living expenses, while the second Universal

Ladd in 1945.

George Stevens's Shane *(53): among other things, there was a touching depiction of hero-worship from Ladd and Brandon de Wilde (as the son of pioneers Van Heflin and Jean Arthur).*

film would be made wholly on location in Canada, thus keeping Ladd out of the country for 18 months to qualify for tax concessions. Universal's *Desert Legion*, with Richard Conte and Arlene Dahl, and Warwick's *The Red Beret/Paratrooper* were mediocre pictures; so were the former's *Saskatchewan* (54), in which he was a Mountie. The other British ones were *Hell Below Zero*, faced with Jill Bennett in this version of a Hammond Innes novel, and *The Black Knight*, particularly ludicrous as a medieval warrior. British critics scoffed, but exhibitors found him the Britons' favourite star.

The films he made for Warners, some produced by his own company, Jaguar, are of as little interest except to action buffs: *Drum Beat*, a Western, as a Government agent; *The McConnell Story* (55) with June Allyson, as a jet pilot; *Hell on Frisco Bay* with Edward G. Robinson, as an ex-con seeking the men who

had framed him; *Santiago* (56) with Rosanna Podesta, a story of gun-runners; and *The Big Land* (57), a post-Civil War Western. He was an archaeologist involved with Sophia Loren and sunken treasure in *Boy on a Dolphin*, in Greece for 20th; and there were more watery matters in *The Deep Six* (58), a naval drama in which he was a Quaker.

He refused the role that James Dean played in *Giant* and was in turn turned down when he asked for the one which Rock Hudson played. He did, however, get into another good one, *The Proud Rebel*, a gentle drama about a drifter and his mute son (played by his own son David). His own performance is his best work, sincere and likeable (due perhaps to an odd resemblance in long shot to Buster Keaton), but the film did not have the success it deserved: Ladd's own fans missed the bang-bang and Olivia de Havilland's fans were not persuaded that any film she did with Ladd could be that good. He was considered for *The Angry Hills*, but the producers preferred Robert Mitchum, who explained that they had met Ladd after 'he'd just crawled out of his swimming pool and was all shrunken up like a dishwasher's hand'. After that, it was usually the bottom half of double-bill programmers: *The Badlanders*, with Ernest Borgnine, a rehash of *The Asphalt Jungle* which was given a quick saturation release; *The Man in the Net* (59), as a man suspected of murdering his wife; *Guns of the Timberland* (60), with Jeanne Crain; *All the Young Men*, serving in the Korean War with Sydney Poitier; and *One Foot in Hell*, as an embittered sheriff. He became one of the many less-than-glorious names who hit the Italian trail, for *Orazi e Curiazi* (61), as Horatio, with Franco Fabrizi as Curazio. He was distinctly ill at ease as a Roman officer. Originally offered at two hours, its makers cut it to 93 minutes and then 71, before finding an American distributor, who in 1964 got it a few showings as *Duel of Champions*. His career seemed over with *13 West Street* (62), a thriller he produced at Columbia, playing an atomic engineer who seeks revenge after being attacked by some well-dressed hoodlums.

In 1962 he was found at his home with gunshot wounds, said to be accidental. He had been drinking heavily for years and when he died in 1964 cause of death was said to be the result of sedatives on top of a high level of alcohol. There was one more picture to come – a sort of come-back – in a key role in *The Carpetbaggers* (64), a razzamatazz tale of sex and skulduggery in old Hollywood. The novel had been a bestseller, and the film raked up giant grosses. Ladd played a cowboy star of the Silent era, but he was only one of several names in the cast and went more or less unnoticed.

VERONICA LAKE

When Veronica Lake was tub-thumping for her autobiography ('Veronica', 1968) some suggestion was advanced that she had been the queen of Hollywood in the 40s. Not so, by any means, though at least in cinemas for some time she held a certain sway. She came in with the decade, and was gone by the end of it. She had been called 'the apogee of 40s glamour' and she was certainly an effective vamp, slinking on to the screen with hooded shoulders and a blonde mane which, if (as rarely) thrown back, revealed an expression as rewardingly blank as the voice which preceded it: neither offered more than a little-girl petulance, but there was something

aggressive about it, entirely appropriate to the silks and satins draped on her tiny frame.

She was born in Brooklyn, New York, in 1919. Paramount publicity had her father alternatively as a college professor and a commercial artist, but in a 1955 interview (and in her book) she said that he had been a German-Danish seaman. The official version also has her studying at McGill University for a while, before moving to California (because of the health of her stepfather who *was* a commercial artist), but she appears rather to have been entering beauty contests in Florida. In Los Angeles she joined the dramatic class of the Bliss-Hayden theatre and appeared in some plays. She was interviewed by RKO and under the name of Constance Keane (she was born Constance Ockelman) appeared in *Sorority House* (39), followed by equally small roles in *All Women Have Secrets* at Paramount and *Forty Little Mothers* (40) at MGM,

Veronica Lake was one of the most pinned-up girls of the Second World War, and as far as movies were concerned this contemptuous, 'see-if-you-dare' expression had hardly been seen since Theda Bara. But it went when the peek-a-boo bang had to go (see text), and it turned out that there wasn't much else on offer.

as one of the schoolgirls, with one close-up. Her agent got her a test there, but that studio was not impressed. He showed it to Paramount, who thought her perfect for *I Wanted Wings* (41), the same old service story as ever as, with one good girl (Constance Moore) and one bad girl (Lake) to get involved with the boys. As the scheming band singer, Lake has a tinny quality and not one-tenth of the talent of Moore, but she had what Moore had not, individuality, which Paramount recognized at once and which made her a much bigger star. She was seventh on the cast list and was signed to a seven-year contract, starting at $75 a week.

She might have languished had Preston Sturges not chosen her for *Sullivan's Travels*, to play the companion of a film director, Joel McCrea, while he posed as a bum. It was a notable comedy and she brought sulk and spirit to the role of The Girl, as the credits called her. She added a sneer when confronted with Alan Ladd in *This Gun for Hire* (42), a partnership which made such happy box-office that they were speedily reunited in *The Glass Key*. That – the partnership – plus the peek-a-boo bang and her insolence suited this genre, the *film noir*, as no other and these qualities, as it turned out, were all she had going for her: Bogart and Bacall were better, but Ladd and Lake came first. After the Sturges film her salary had been raised to $350 a week and it was now rising dramatically. She was also admirable as the witch in Clair's *I Married a Witch*, released by UA, but inept doing a song ('A Sweater, a Sarong and a Peek-a-Boo Bang') with Paulette Goddard and Dorothy Lamour in the all-star *Star Spangled Rhythm* (43). It promptly went. The hair, that is. So many girls had emulated Lake's locks that there were many accidents in munitions factories when hair got caught in machines. The US Government made an official request to Paramount to change her style; thus she appeared with it rigidly knotted in *So Proudly We Hail* (43), playing a nurse. She was remarkably less engaging without the hair.

The Hour Before the Dawn (44) had been a novel by Somerset Maugham written for the US market (he never allowed it to be published in Britain): Lake played a Nazi spy posing as a refugee in Britain. The film was too slow to be good propaganda and it also marked the end of the Lake vogue. Further, she was difficult to handle: Paramount threw her into three little pictures with the also fading Eddie Bracken: *Bring on the Girls* (45) – in her own words, 'an inane musical'; *Out of This World*, a take-off on the Swoonatra business, with Bracken playing the crooner (dubbed by Bing Crosby); and *Hold that Blonde* – 'It was another in Paramount's formula of the moment – put a comic and a popular sexy type together and the folks will come see.' She then did *Miss Susie Slagle's*, a 1900s boarding house, with Sonny Tufts; a guest spot in *Duffy's Tavern*; and appeared again with Alan Ladd in an excellent melodrama, *The Blue Dahlia* (46). The short-lived Enterprise Co. borrowed her for a Joel McCrea Western, *Ramrod* (47), and her Paramount contract petered out with a guest spot in *Variety Girl* and three duallers: *The Sainted Sisters* (48), *Saigon* with Ladd and *Isn't It Romantic* (49). She was in a picture at 20th, *Slattery's Hurricane*, and then, she says, there were no offers; in 1950 there was talk of a British film, directed by her then husband, André de Toth, called *Before I Wake* (a film of that title was made in the UK five years later by Mona Freeman).

In Mexico she made *Stronghold* (52) with Zachary Scott, a tale of the Mexican Revolution, and not long afterwards the de Toths filed voluntary bankruptcy petitions. She toured or appeared in stock for some years: 'The Voice of the Turtle', 'The Little Hut', etc. and then disappeared from view. In 1962 the 'New York Post' discovered her, working in a Manhattan cocktail lounge, and she hit the headlines again a couple of times when convicted of drunkenness. Also in that year she married for the fourth time. But she was offered work again: TV hostess in Baltimore; in the 1964 off-Broadway revival of 'Best Foot Forward'; in stock in Florida in 1965-66, and in a Z-budget movie made in Montreal in 1967, *Footsteps in the Snow*. Her memoirs also focused some attention on her. As a result she toured in Britain in a flop play, 'Madam Chairman', and played 'A Streetcar Named Desire' in a suburban theatre with Ty Hardin. In 1969 she began an independent film in Florida – called either *Flesh Feast* or *Time is Terror* – but it was never finished. In 1972 she married her fifth husband, an English naval captain, but a divorce was pending at the time of her death from acute hepatitis, in 1973.

HEDY LAMARR

In her autobiography ('Ecstasy and Me: My Life As a Woman', 1966) Hedy Lamarr pauses in an account of some love-making to quote the critics on her first American film performance (in *Algiers*): 'The reviews spoke of "definite artistry", "beauty that enthralls", "a new star shining bright", "alluring like a night horizon of jewels", "a surprising and vital performance for a newcomer" and

"Hedy Lamarr is glorious".' Neither the artistry nor vitality were much in evidence afterwards, but – as she points out in every chapter – she was considered the most beautiful woman in films at the time.

She was born in Vienna in 1914. According to her account she was still at school studying design when she gatecrashed one of the studios in Vienna and was selected by director Alexis Granowsky for a bit part in a Silent picture, *Sturme im Wasserglas*. In fact, she seems to have made her début in *Geld auf der Strasse* (30), a Talkie directed by Georg Jacoby at Sascha-Films. Jacoby also directed *Sturme im Wasserglas* – better known as *Die Blumenfrau von Lindenau* – which was remade in Britain some years later as *Storm in a Teacup*. Lamarr was in that under her own name, Hedwig or Hedy Kiesler (it was MGM who changed it). Sascha-Films then gave her a leading role (she was fifth on the cast list) in *Man Braucht Kein Geld* (31), the heroine opposite Heinz Rühmann. She says that at this point she went to Berlin to study and via Max Reinhardt got parts in two plays, 'The Weaker Sex' and 'Private Lives'. In Berlin she met up with Granowsky again and he gave her a role in *Die Koffer des Herrn O.F.*, a comedy about a small town which gets into a tizzy when it thinks a fictitious famous man is staying at its large hotel. As the mayor's daughter Lamarr is podgy, shrill and pretty, but nothing like the ethereal creature she would become – or indeed like the slimmed-down version to be seen in the leading role of a Czech-Austrian movie, directed by Gustav Machaty, *Symphonie der Liebe/Extase* (33). The plot concerned an impotent old man, his young bride and the young man who spies her swimming in the old water-hole. The technique was as naïve as the plot, but the point is that young Hedwig was swimming nude, and that and the subsequent run through the wood – still starkers – guaranteed the film a notoriety that has lasted to this day. (In Germany it was banned because Lamarr was Jewish: but the loss of the German receipts was compensated by the interest elsewhere.) Soon after completion, its star married an Austrian millionaire, Fritz Mandl, who tried to buy up all copies of the film. He did not succeed; the film was shown in the US in 1937, the year the couple were divorced.

Kiesler/Lamarr went to London, where her agent introduced her to Louis B. Mayer, who was not certain whether – because of *Extase* – she was respectable enough to fit into the MGM family. But when he sailed for the US on the 'Normandie' he found her on board and by the end of the voyage had capitulated, offering her a seven-year contract starting at $500 a week. After some delay, uncertain what to do with her, MGM loaned her to Wanger for *Algiers* (38), at a 200 per cent mark-up on her salary. It was a sensational role (as the society beauty for one last glimpse of whom Charles Boyer leaves the Casbah) and when it was shown her name became synonymous with glamour. A delighted Mayer decided he would make her the greatest motion picture star there ever had been – greater than Garbo (who was troublesome anyway). Dietrich's old director, Josef von Sternberg – thought to be the ultimate in packaging European glamour – was brought in and Spencer Tracy was assigned to co-star as an East Side doctor who marries a society beauty, with Subsequent Problems. But Mayer interfered; von Sternberg was fired; *I Take This Woman* stopped and started so often and so much was scrapped (including Walter Pidgeon's part) that studio wags called it 'I Re-take This Woman'. Woody Van Dyke, the third director to work on it and the one credited, said the result as the funniest thing in Hollywood since Jean Harlow's funeral. During one lull, when Tracy was otherwise engaged and in case she was forgotten, Lamarr was rushed into *Lady of the Tropics* (39) as a half-caste, with Robert Taylor as a millionaire. Said the ads: 'You too will be "Hedy" with delight and your verdict will be "Lamarrvellous",' but 'Picturegoer's was not: 'Hedy Lamarr shows that Sex with a capital S is rather dull.' Such reviews convinced Meyer she could never be a great star and when

Clarke Gable and Hedy Lamarr in Comrade X *(40), directed by King Vidor. Gable was an American newspaperman in Moscow and she was a streetcar driver.*

Woman too flopped he lost interest. In fact, in that film she gave a performance which shows some emotion. You could say she was good; but you could not say she was interesting. Looking the way she does, you always hope she will rally and give a performance.

Her own response was to stop battling with the studio for the first time since *Algiers*. She needed a hit and *Boom Town* (40) provided it, when she lured Clark Gable away from Claudette Colbert – but with her advent halfway through, the film fell apart; just as in *Comrade X*, again with Gable, her performance in a *Ninotchka*-like part was as unlike Garbo's as possible. Her sole comic skill was to open her eyes wide. Nor was she any more animated in a comedy with James Stewart, *Come Live With Me* (41), or a musical, *Ziegfeld Girl*, though her work in *HM Pulham Esq*, from John P. Marquand's novel, was a distinct improvement: she played an old flame of Robert Young. She worked in a canning factory and married John Garfield in *Tortilla Flat* (42), also with Tracy, was married to William Powell in *Crossroads* and tempted Walter Pidgeon in *White Cargo*. The remake of this old war-horse found her as Tondelayo, 'a half-caste jungle temptress'; 'I thought with some interesting make-up, a sarong and some hip-swinging I would be a memorable nym-

phomaniac.' She was not, which was maybe why she took a sabbatical. In fact, she was difficult about her material: she turned down *Casablanca*, *Gaslight* and *Saratoga Trunk* (all of which, coincidentally, were big ones for Ingrid Bergman). MGM tried again, making her the neglected wife of astronomer Powell in *The Heavenly Body* (44), but she was 'no substitute for Myrna Loy' ('Picturegoer'). They found again that she was not the draw her fame implied, so were happy to loan her out, to Warners for one of their many imitations of *Casablanca*, *The Conspirators*, and to RKO for *Experiment Perilous*, which was *Gaslight* with a twist and Paul Lucas as the sinister husband. It is her own favourite among her films because the 'innocent, unworldly' heroine is closest to her real self. Her MGM contract finished with a comedy with Robert Walker, *Her Highness and the Bellboy* (45). She was then getting $7,500 a week.

Lamarr says she asked for release from her contract – which had a short time to run – and was granted it on condition that she made three pictures for MGM over the next five years (in fact, only one was made). She formed her own producing company and did two for UA, *Strange Woman* (46) with George Sanders and *Dishonoured Lady* (47) with her

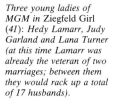

Three young ladies of MGM in Ziegfeld Girl *(41): Hedy Lamarr, Judy Garland and Lana Turner (at this time Lamarr was already the veteran of two marriages; between them they would rack up a total of 17 husbands).*

then husband, John Loder. In both she was a *femme fatale*; of the second one she says in her memoirs: 'Again there were critics who pointed out that I had played a dissolute woman, while my nature in real life was different.' (Another remark worth noting in the book: 'I think if I were to compare my style to some actresses, I would say I am a cross between Judy Garland and Greta Garbo.') Neither film did smash business; and her next was a flop, *Let's Live a Little* (48), a comedy for Eagle-Lion with Robert Cummings. Lamarr says that her judgment of scripts brought this decline: 'At MCA, the biggest talent agency in the world, I had the reputation of being hard to handle. . . . I was the highest-priced and most important star in Hollywood, but I was "difficult".'

In fact, she was very much a back-number when Paramount cast her as Delilah in *Samson and Delilah* (49), but by general agreement her box-office risk was compensated for by a beauty that was ideal for the role: audiences might not to see Lamarr in a comedy, but they would be tempted to see her as the world's most famous temptress. And they did – in huge numbers. It turned out that Lamarr, Victor Mature as Samson and the directional touch of De Mille were ideally suited: critical put-downs did not prevent it from being the top box-office film of the year. MGM's interest was revived and she was offered a tropical melodrama with John Hodiak, *Lady Without a Passport* (50), for which she was paid $90,000: it is doubtful whether it took more than that at the box-office. Because she had refused to do a PA tour Paramount were not anxious to employ her again, but a Western with Ray Milland, *Copper Canyon*, was already scheduled and at Bob Hope's insistence she co-starred with him, conspicuously out of place, in *My Favorite Spy* (51); she refused to do PAs for that, too, and did not work in Hollywood again for some years.

In 1953 it was announced that she would make her come-back picture in Britain, *Queen Esther and the King of Egypt*, a script she had bought for $25,000, but nothing came of it. Later in Italy she began *Femmina* – to be called in English *The Loves of Three Women* – Helen of Troy, the Empress Josephine and Genevieve de Brabant. It was abandoned, but the Helen footage was retrieved and some material added to it: *L'Amante di Paride* (54), which got a few Stateside bookings, dubbed and christened *The Face That Launched a Thousand Ships*. In 1957 her interest in playing the famous women of history may have got her the part of Joan of Arc in an episode of *The Story of Mankind*, but the result was generally judged ludicrous. That

year Hollywood gave her another chance: at Universal she was *The Female Animal*, as an ageing film star in love with the same man as daughter Jane Powell: it was a silly picture not helped by the Lamarr histrionics.

Since *Delilah*, Lamarr's name was in the press less as an actress than as one of those movie stars always getting divorced – her sixth was in 1965; the same year she was on a shoplifting charge that brought headlines round the world, and was found not guilty. She admitted to journalists that she was broke and lost a part ($10,000-worth) in a B called *Picture Mommy Dead* due, it was said to the adverse publicity – Zsa Zsa Gabor played it. The following year she published the autobiography and though in some quarters it was rated 'sizzling' the press was repelled and the industry shocked: at its end Lamarr intimated that she was taking up her career again, but Hollywood is prudish and there were no offers. In 1966 she unsuccessfully sought an injunction against the publication of the book and three years later she sued her collaborators for $21 million damages for misrepresentation.

DOROTHY LAMOUR

Dorothy Lamour loathed the sarong she was famous for wearing. She begged her studio to let her play more considerable parts and, ironically, her request was granted as a result of a successful comic picture in which she wore it, *Road to Singapore*. She played it fairly straight, in her dumbly pretty way, but in the enormously successful sequels, with Hope and Crosby in full cry, she developed into a rather pleasing comedienne and a box-office star. If, as a dramatic actress, she was only as good as the director, her work in those *Road* pictures is fondly remembered. She was at her best with Bob Hope: the hint of asperity in her voice always suggested that she knew exactly how to deal with him.

She was born in 1914 in New Orleans. In 1931 she was elected 'Miss New Orleans', but, ungratefully, went to Chicago and worked as an elevator operator at Marshall Field. She wanted to be a singer, however, and after several auditions Herbie Kay took her on to sing with his band and married her. In New York she sang at the Stork Club, which led to a contract with NBC and her own radio show in LA, 'The Dreamer of Songs'. She was singing in the Clover Club when Paramount discovered that she looked as good as she sounded, if not better, and after a screen test she was signed to the standard seven-year contract, starting at $200 a week for 20 weeks'

John Ford's The Hurricane (*37*): *Jon Hall as the young man unjustly convicted and Dorothy Lamour as the new bride he keeps escaping for. None of it was very interesting till the climactic hurricane which destroyed the island and most of the characters.*

The studio otherwise did not think she was experienced enough to carry a film, so she lured Fred MacMurray from Carole Lombard in *Swing High Swing Low*; headed the cast of a programmer about the Spanish Civil War, *The Last Train from Madrid*, but had very little footage as an unhappy senorita; and was Alan Hale's unhappy mistress in *High Wide and Handsome* starring Irene Dunne. Her second big break came when Goldwyn borrowed her (in exchange for Joel McCrea) to play with Jon Hall as the decorative foreground to *The Hurricane*: she had no dialogue that was not monosyllabic and no acting apart from moulding the sarong, but the film's success made her well known. Back home she had nothing to do in *Thrill of a Lifetime* except pop in to sing the title song, and little more in *The Big Broadcast of 1938* (38) than transfer her affections from Bob Hope to Leif Erickson. The studio decided it was time she donned a sarong again, so they swished around the ingredients of *The Jungle Princess*, added Technicolor and called them *Her Jungle Love*. He was Ray Milland and it was on a *Tropic Holiday* that he met up with her again, a Mexican beauty. She gave a spirited and vigorous performance as the saloon owner in *Spawn of the North* with Henry Fonda, replacing the originally cast Lombard, then kidded her sarong image in *St Louis Blues* (39), playing a film star fleeing from it and finding love in the arms of Lloyd Nolan. After a stint as Jack Benny's romantic interest in *Man About Town* she found a glum one, *Disputed Passage*, based on the novel by Lloyd C. Douglas, in which professor Akim Tamiroff thinks John Howard should put science before marriage – to her, despite the fact that she is a brilliant doctor/aviatrix, if half-Chinese. Her performance was a little heavy, though you could not blame her.

After playing foil to Hope and Crosby in *Road to Singapore* (40) she showed her mettle on loan to 20th in *Johnny Apollo*, as the moll who transfers her affections from Lloyd Noland to Tyrone Power: she was cheaper, more brittle than she ever was at Paramount, and most effective. As the *Road* figures came in, the studio decided that the public could not get enough of Lamour in a sarong, so she climbed into it and up the trees in both *Typhoon* and *Moon Over Burma*, both with Robert Preston, with whom she was photographed in nightclubs. She had been divorced from Kay in 1939 and would wed William Howard in 1943, one of the Hollywood's most enduring and devoted marriages. Loaned to 20th again she looked lovely in Technicolor but had little to do in *Chad Hanna*, as the bare-back rider on whom Henry Fonda gets a crush. But her career really began to zing

work, and to be paid at the standard rate if they wanted her during the rest of the year. It was soon clear that they had a major star, so that the schedule was extended to 40 weeks. Because her looks were fairly exotic, she was cast as *The Jungle Princess* (36) with Ray Milland. It was a nothing programmer, but the reception at previews persuaded Paramount to release it as an A picture, and it did well. Said 'Picturegoer': 'The main asset of the picture is the naturalness and unsophisticated charm of Dorothy Lamour who makes the main character as credible as it is possible for it to be.'

Dorothy Lamour at the time when Bing Crosby and Bob Hope were double-crossing each other for her favours: singing 'Personality' in Road to Utopia (45).

when she hit the *Road to Zanzibar* (41), which really kidded jungle epics. Crosby and Hope double-crossed each other for love of her and she was hardly less perfidious than they. She was with Hope again when he was *Caught in the Draft* and then was *Aloma of the South Seas*, immortalized thus by C.A. Lejeune: 'Extensive tour/Of D. Lamour,/Nearly all/Of Jon Hall./Sudden panic,/Cause volcanic,/And a torso/Or so.' She was more pleased with a hit musical, *The Fleet's In* (42), and might have been more so if she had been given the hit song, 'Tangerine', or had a solo on 'I'll Remember You', which became a standard

years later. She played a nightclub singer known as Countess because she is so formidable, which is why William Holden's buddies wager that he will not kiss her. Looking stylish, she made chilliness amusing and they team so well that Eddie Bracken and Betty Hutton only irritate when they keep us from them – today, anyway, and it is now that Lamour refers to those 'silly, but wonderful jungle pictures', of which *Beyond the Blue Horizon*, with justice, is her 'least favourite', with bad back projection and worse process work; the particularly idiotic story has her leading an expedition up the jungle to prove that she did grow up with swimming tigers. She was almost suspended for refusing to do it and its reception proved that Paramount had insulted the public's intelligence once too often.

So she spent the next year mainly as foil to Hope or/and Crosby: *Road to Morocco*; *Star Spangled Rhythm*, guying her image in one song with Veronica Lake and Paulette Goddard; *They Got Me Covered* (43) with Hope at Goldwyn; and *Dixie* with Crosby and Billy de Wolfe in the sidekick-rival role – rivals for Lamour, the landlord's daughter, a part she plays in sassy fashion, but it is another that wastes her. There were three musicals: *Riding High* with Dick Powell; *And the Angels Sing* (44), with Fred MacMurray; and *Rainbow Island*, a particularly juvenile tale with Eddie Bracken and the end of Paramount's fetish about sarongs – an item of attire she had donned again in the interest of wartime morale.

At this point she was probably the most popular of Paramount's actresses (at the studio as well as in cinemas), so *A Medal for Benny* (45) might have been made because she wanted to do a dramatic role again, but more likely because the studio wished to team her with their new Mexican heart-throb, Arturo de Cordova, who was not too easy to cast. As the missing Benny's father, J. Carroll Naish stole this version of Steinbeck's novel from the two of them, playing Benny's best pal and his girlfriend. Then: *Duffy's Tavern*, guesting; *Masquerade in Mexico* with de Cordova, Mitchell Leisen's medium remake of his own sparkling *Midnight*; *Road to Utopia*; *My Favorite Brunette* (47) – Hope's; *Variety Girl*, one duet with Alan Ladd; *Wild Harvest*, also with Ladd; and *Road to Rio*.

She had often asked Paramount whether she could work during her vacation and they finally allowed her to do *On Our Merry Way* (48) aka *A Miracle Can Happen*, kidding the sarong in one song. She was one of the few participants not to quarrel with its producer, Benedict Bogeaus, so she followed him to Columbia to do *Lulu Belle*, a corny melodrama, and to UA for *The Girl From Manhattan*, a small-town comedy. Howard Hughes, noting that she was doing outside movies, offered $400,000 for four pictures over several years, with story and director approval: but neither Paramount nor RKO had anything ready, so she signed to do *The Lucky Stiff* (49), on the basis of Jack Benny producing and Leo McCarey thinking of directing (he did not). The film, a mystery with Brian Donlevy, was made on a low budget for a new company, so to help it Lamour deferred her salary of $125,000 – which she never saw, since it failed. All of these films had devalued her box-office standing, a trend not reversed by *Slightly French* with Don Ameche or *Manhandled* with Dan Duyrea, another tired mystery and a belated, unceremonious return to Paramount.

In 1950 she played the London Palladium and the following year a Las Vegas nightclub. Apart from a guest spot, singing, in *Here Comes the Groom* (51), Hollywood showed little interest, so De Mille had a role specially written into *The Greatest Show on Earth* (52), though it gave her little to do; later in the year Paramount reunited her with the boys in *Road to Bali*. As on the last trip, it was owned by them and the studio in a three-way split; no one had asked her whether she would have liked a four-way split and when she was asked to cut the album of the *Bali* songs she merely observed that that did not seem fair when they were getting a bigger cut than she. When she next heard of the matter, the recording had gone ahead with Peggy Lee and, as she says in her memoir, 'It would have been nice if I had been informed.' She spent some time on the straw hat circuit in 'Roger the Fifth' and in 1953 announced her retirement, to bring up her two sons, but she did occasional cabaret work throughout the decade.

Various returns to the *Road* were announced in the late 50s, without her name ever being attached to them. As *The Road to Hong Kong* (61) became a certainty she told Hope and Crosby that she understood that they wanted a bigger name, but that she had no intention of accepting a bit part. She was therefore annoyed to receive a script indicating one song and two lines of dialogue, but after refusing it the two stars became remarkably and cheerfully insistent, offering to build her role: only when she arrived in Britain for shooting did she learn that her name was an essential part of the project as presented to the backers. The press reported that she was snappy on the question of age and did not like close-ups, but that was what was expected of an ageing actress when confronted with a younger rival, Joan Collins. On screen she looked relatively stunning and the final result might have been more bearable if they had jettisoned Collins and given her the lead. When neither Hope nor Crosby invited her on their TV shows plugging the film she offered her services, which Hope accepted; Crosby said that there was not time to write her in, but when she watched she found that she was very much 'in', by virtue of liberal use of her name and photographs.

She had little to do as the town madam, a feature role in a lesser John Ford piece, *Donovan's Reef* (63), but she does get Lee Marvin at the end. She did another guest spot in an innocuous teenage film, *Pajama Party*

(65). For a while she enjoyed a big success as the star of one of the numerous touring versions of 'Hello Dolly!' and said that she would not film again unless the offers were more interesting than those she had been getting. With other names, she did brief appearances in both *The Phynx* (70) and *Won Ton Ton the Dog Who Saved Hollywood* (76). She was in a tele-movie, *Death at Love House*, and after returning to nightclubs (81) was in a house show in Pittsburgh, 'Great Ladies of the Silver Screen', with Kathryn Grayson, Mamie Van Doren, Patty Andrews and Vivian Blaine. There as another brief return to movies, in one segment of *Creepshow II* (87) with George Kennedy.

ELISSA LANDI

Elissa Landi was beautiful, capable and charming. She moved lightly and gracefully, somewhat like a gazelle. She was ladylike and intelligent, but there was nothing bluestocking about her, nothing formidable, nothing glacial. But she seemed to be acting behind gauze. Her quality never came through the screen. She was not remote, but she was intangible without being quite magical enough: so in the end she was one of Hollywood's most publicized failures.

She was aristocratic by birth and 'claimed to be' (as her publicity carefully put it) descended from Franz Joseph of Austria via an illegitimate daughter whom he never recognized; her stepfather was an Italian count. She was born in Venice in 1904, was educated in England and studied to be a dancer. While still in her teens she published a novel, 'Neilson', and then wanted to write a play so joined Oxford rep for experience: she made her stage début in the Playhouse Theatre in that city in 'Dandy Dick' (23). This determined her on an acting career and she made her first prominent London appearance in 'Storm' at the Ambassadors in 1924. Later she was a successful Desdemona and also played in 'The Painted Swan', 'Lavender Ladies' (25) and 'The Constant Nymph' (26), among others. She published two more novels and in 1928 married a barrister.

She made her film début for Herbert Wilcox in *London* (26), as Dorothy Gish's Mayfair benefactress, but stardom came at British Instructional: *Bolibar* (28), based on Leo Perutz's novel, as an artist's daughter involved with some German officers during the Peninsular War; and *Underground*, directed by Anthony Asquith, as the shopgirl loved by subway worker Brian Aherne. They also sent her to Sweden for a co-production based on Strindberg in which the Germans also participated, *Synd*, released in Britain literally translated as *Sin*: she played the drudge of a wife of playwright Lars Hanson, who, once he is successful, forgets her for one night of love with its leading lady, Gina Manes. According to 'Picturegoer' 'she was much in demand abroad', which meant also France, for a mountaineering drama, *Le Leurre sur la Cime*. Her role in *Bolibar* led to another exotic one in *The Inseparables* (29), as a gypsy torn between the man who has saved her from the sea and the one she loves. She returned to France to make her Talkie début, in the English version of a bilingual vehicle for Adolphe Menjou, *The Parisian* (30) – which was preceded to New York by the French version, *Mon Gosse de Père*. In Britain, she made two films written and directed by Elinor Glyn, who since her return from Hollywood had established her own company: *Knowing Men*, as atrocious as it was ambitious, and *The Price of Things*, unfortunately in production when the critics got at the first. In that, Landi is a convent girl constantly in danger of violation, especially by Carl Brisson, while in her aunt's château. 'The New York Times', noting British derision, nevertheless reported that those at the US trade show thought it the first movie to show the British [sic] aristocracy in its true light: but United Artists which had the American rights, opened neither film, perhaps because of dialogue like 'Frank Bamber, if you do not learn to follow my moods I shall not come to your fancy dress ball next Tuesday'. *Knowing Men*, made in colour, was shown in Britain in black and white; the other film was hardly shown at all. Landi was hardly better served by *Children of Chance*, made for BIP, with John Stuart and Mabel Poulton (a big British Silent star whose Cockney accent was at this time killing her Talkie career).

Landi went to New York to appear in 'A Farewell to Arms' and Fox, who had earlier offered a contract, renewed their blandishments. She signed a long-term contract and co-starred with one of their biggest stars, Charles Farrell, in *Body and Soul* (31), a melodrama about American flyers in Britain during the war and memorable mainly because the supporting cast was headed by Humphrey Bogart and Myrna Loy – playing a spy who tries to throw the blame on Landi. Then she did *Always Goodbye*, in which she played a movie star; *Wicked*, a specious mother-love drama with Victor McLaglen; and *The Yellow Ticket* with Laurence Olivier and Lionel Barrymore, a melodrama which she considered her best film. A year later she was to describe herself as 'the miraculous survivor of seven pictures', in defence of the

silly tag that Fox had stuck on her, 'The Empress of Emotion'. Fox were seriously worried about her: they had boosted her to the skies and her four films so far had not been box-office smashes. Indeed, the last one had failed and so did the next two: *The Devil's Lottery* (32) with McLaglen again, which went through the old 'money doesn't bring happiness' routine (they won the Calcutta Sweepstakes), and *The Woman in Room 13*, a dreadful picture in which Landi was a concert singer and all the marriage vs career clichés were dragged in. Ralph Bellamy co-starred and Loy was again in the cast. Fox did not blame themselves for the failure: they announced that Landi would be loaned to other studios or play featured roles until her contract expired. Meanwhile, she was making *A Passport to Hell*, a triangle drama with Paul Lukas, but the critical and the box-office receipts did nothing to retrieve the situation.

Rescue came in the form of Cecil B. De Mille, who borrowed her to play the Christian heroine in *The Sign of the Cross* (33), who enslaves Roman centurion Fredric March (she was billed second to him, above Claudette Colbert). Then 20th-UA borrowed her for the lead opposite Ronald Colman in *The Masquerader*. Fox hoped that two such important films might at last establish Landi and starred

her again, in *The Warrior's Husband*, a modern telling of the Lysistrata story, from a play that Katharine Hepburn had done on Broadway, and in *I Loved You Wednesday*, from another play, as a ballerina, with Warner Baxter. Tired of poor films, she refused to do *I Am a Widow* and Fox took the opportunity to annul the contract.

She was offered a plum part in another filmed play at Universal, *By Candlelight* (34), playing a ladies' maid who masquerades as her mistress and dines with butler Lukas, masquerading as his master: it did something to revive her fortunes, but she was still suffering from Fox's publicity campaign, which had seriously overestimated her appeal and ability. Her next film co-starred another artist who was also to suffer from over-exploitation, Francis Lederer, direct from a Broadway success, *Man of Two Worlds* at RKO: he was an Eskimo and she the explorer's daughter with whom he falls in love. She moved on to Columbia for *Sisters Under the Skin*, in which Frank Morgan made himself her guardian. Once again she showed a flair for sophisticated dialogue and she did well in the sentimental *The Great Flirtation* at Paramount, as a girl who becomes a star at the same time as husband Adolphe Menjou loses popularity. At UA she was the heroine of *The Count of*

Before disaster strikes: Robert Donat and Elissa Landi at the ball celebrating their betrothal. The Count of Monte Cristo (34), *the most popular of several film versions.*

Monte Cristo opposite Robert Donat and 'Photoplay' thought her 'perfect'.

As a freelance so far she had been notably successful. Other studios considered that Fox had misused her, but they still could not find her public. Paramount gave her a two-picture deal, *Enter Madame* (35), with Cary Grant, in which she was a prima donna, and *Without Regret*, a marital drama with Paul Cavanagh, but were not encouraged to endeavour further. And her shaky position was threatened by Madeleine Carroll, also from Britain, and somewhat more regal and beautiful. Landi went to France to make *Koenigsmark* (36), in English and French, not a story of Hanover but of Ruritania, from a novel by Pierre Benoît, with Pierre Fresnay and John Lodge; and then in Britain she co-starred with Douglas Fairbanks Jr in *The Amateur Gentleman*. Said 'Picturegoer': '. . . as the heroine, Elissa Landi is somewhat colourless.' She returned to Hollywood, to MGM, where Myrna Loy had recommended her for a supporting role in *After the Thin Man*, though first she starred in a programmer there with Edmund Lowe and Zazu Pitts, *Mad Holiday*. She then did a B thriller there with Dame May Whitty and Madge Evans, *The Thirteenth Chair* (37), behaving suspiciously; but she was a lost cause.

She was divorced in 1936. In 1939 she was lecturing in American colleges and in 1943 she married again. She also appeared in an independent production, *Corregidor* (43), opposite Otto Kruger. It was a silly film and occasioned no further offers. She made news in 1944 when she gave birth to a daughter; in 1948 she died of cancer in New York.

HARRY LANGDON

'Harry was called the baby-face comedian,' said Harold Lloyd. 'It was an apt description, for his actions were like that of a little boy. He'd start to do something, then he'd change. Indecision was an integral part of his character. Also innocence.' James Agee had said: 'There was also a sinister flicker of depravity about the Langdon character, all the more disturbing because babies are premoral. He had an instinct for bringing his actual adulthood and figurative babyishness into frictions as crawley as a fingernail on a slate blackboard, and he wandered into areas of strangeness which were beyond the other comedians.' Agee's famous 1949 essay ('Comedy's Greatest Era') re-established Langdon by bracketing him with Chaplin, Keaton and Lloyd; noting that they used much physical comedy, he said 'Langdon showed how little

of that one might use and still be a great silent-film comedian . . . [he] had one queerly toned, unique little reed. But out of it he got incredible melodies.' From that point on Langdon became accepted by some observers as the fourth Big Silent film comic, though it is difficult now to be as enthusiastic about his work: perhaps his whey-faced, dolly humour is much too cute for modern taste and his 'strangeness' still too far ahead of it.

Langdon was born in Council Bluffs, Iowa, in 1884. His parents worked for the Salvation Army and at an early age he learned to fend for himself. After doing an amateur night in nearby Omaha, he joined a travelling medicine show and spent the next 20 years in minstrel shows, circuses, burlesque and vaudeville. Early on his baby-faced little man evolved and it was this physical aspect which so pleased Frank Capra when he first saw him. At that time Capra was working for Mack Sennett; Langdon had just come to Sennett's attention and been signed as a lead comic. Altogether Langdon made some 25 two- and three-reelers for Sennett, starting with *Picking Peaches* (24) and ending with *Soldier Man* (26). A few of the titles in between were: *Shanghaied Lovers*, *The Luck of the Foolish*, *Feet of Mud*, *The Sea Squawk*, *Boobs in the Wood*, *His Marriage Wow*, *There He Goes* and *Fiddlesticks*. There was also a feature, *His First Flame*, released in 1927, after Langdon had left Sennett.

He had become nationally popular and other companies sought to steal him from Sennett. Capra, in his memoirs, says Langdon went to First National for three films, with an option for three more – a million-dollar contract. Sennett in his autobiography gives more precise details: $6,000 a week plus 25 per cent of the net, provided he could make the six films in two years, at $150,000 each. Sennett is caustic about this deal; noting that Langdon had managed to spend the production cost of the first film before it started, he writes: 'Harry suddenly forgot that all his value lay in being that baby-witted boy on the screen and he decided he was also a business man. His cunning as a business man was about that of a backward kindergarten student and he complicated this with marital adventures, in which he was about as inept as he was on the screen.' Langdon took with him his usual director, Harry Edwards, and his gag man, Capra. Their first film there, *Tramp Tramp Tramp* (26), was 'a beautiful thing in which Harry wins a cross-country walking race, despite imprisonment, a cyclone and infatuation for Joan Crawford' (David Robinson). Capra directed the next two and they were again well received, full of gags and admirably paced: *The Strong Man* and *Long Pants* (27).

Harry Langdon made only three successful features, of which The Strong Man *(26) was the second and perhaps best: an episodic comedy about the adventures of a weightlifter's meek assistant in cleaning up – unwittingly – a modern Sodom.*

faults of both and died at the box-office. First National did not renew the contract; and Langdon had acquired a reputation for being difficult and autocratic – something which took years to live down. He had made important enemies. After an 18-month absence from the screen, Hal Roach (at MGM) announced that Langdon was returning to the shorts which had made him famous: Roach produced him in eight (Talkies) but the arrangement lasted only a year. Also that year Universal teamed him with Slim Summerville in *See America Thirst* (30) and Warners finally released *A Soldier's Plaything* (31), which they made to see whether Langdon had a potential in Talkies: it concerned the antics of Langdon and Ben Lyon, and despite or because of much off-colour humour, rare then, was totally unfunny. The studio had delayed release on the assumption that there would be a renewal of enthusiasm for army farces, but this was not the film to do it. Langdon returned to vaudeville and in 1931 filed a petition for bankruptcy.

In 1933 he began to make shorts for Educational and he subsequently made a few for Paramount; in 1934 he began a similar operation at Columbia and except for the period 1935-38, when he made no films, that continued to his death in 1944, at an average of two a year (some of the later ones were directed by Edwards). He had only a few substantial roles in the features he made. He supported Al Jolson in *Hallelujah I'm a Bum* (33), but it did nothing to revive either ailing career, and he played a cupid in *My Weakness* with Lew Ayres and Lilian Harvey. He had

Langdon then, egotistically, decided that he did not need either Edwards or Capra, and decided to direct himself. The results were disastrous: *Three's a Crowd* was overtly sentimental and although Langdon took note of that and returned more to gags for *The Chaser* (28), most of them concerning a chap in skirts, because a divorce judge has decreed that he change places with his dragon of a wife, but the few that were not hackneyed were not funny either. *Heart Trouble* combined the

After his career nose-dived, Langdon was offered three or four come-back chances, of which the best-remembered is Hallelujah I'm a Bum *(33), with Al Jolson.*

comic parts in *Atlantic Adventure* (35), supporting Lloyd Nolan as his photographer pal; in Britain, in *Stardust* (37), a comedy about films with Lupe Velez and Ben Lyon; and *There Goes My Heart* (38), as a minister. By the kindness of Stan Laurel he was taken on by Roach as a gag man, which led to two film roles: *Zenobia* (39), a charming but unfunny comedy about a rogue elephant (he was its owner), notable mainly for the teaming of Oliver Hardy and Billie Burke as a country doctor and his wife; and *All-American Co-ed* (41) starring Frances Langford. He also had roles in some products released by Monogram and its kin: *Misbehaving Husbands* (40), *Double Trouble* (41), as a Cockney evacuee in the US, *House of Errors* (42), *Spotlight Scandals* (43), *Hot Rhythm* (44), *Block Busters* (the East Side Kids) and *Swingin' on a Rainbow* (45). He died of a cerebral haemorrhage in December 1944. He was broke and left as widow his third wife, whom he had married in 1935.

CHARLES LAUGHTON

Charles Laughton was a total actor. His range was wide. He was only in mid-career when James Shelley Hamilton wrote in the National Board of Review magazine: 'Laughton has made an astonishing gallery of screen portrayals. The pitiful little Cockney murderer in *Payment Deferred*, Nero, Henry VIII, Ruggles, Javert, Captain Bligh – no screen actor has come anywhere near so large a compass of characterizations, each one vivid and individual.' One always imagined Laughton seizing these parts with relish, his eyes glinting as he read the scripts, already selecting from his bag of tricks. In performance, you could see him savouring his own artifice. He was a big, brazen, show-off actor. He went overboard sometimes and, in some of the poor films he made, he got near to chewing the scenery; but as well as the bold, daring gesture – the hallmark of the great actor – he could perform with infinite delicacy. His enjoyment – his mastery – of his art was infectious though, paradoxically, he was violently uncertain of his talent. He was one of the few film stars able to overcome an unprepossessing personal appearance (fat, blubbery) and go on to receive wide audience acceptance. He was reliable box-office for at least half of his 30-year screen career; later, his films faltered, but he was among the screen's finest artists.

Born in Scarborough, Yorkshire, in 1899 into a family of hoteliers, it was confidently expected that Laughton would go into the family business. But from early childhood he wanted to act; after his war service, he joined a company of amateurs. He does not appear to have been exceptional, but he finally broke down family opposition and was permitted to study at RADA. His mentor there was Komisarjevsky, who gave him a small part in his production of 'Three Sisters' in 1925 and then the more considerable part of Lepihodoff in 'The Cherry Orchard'; and it was in Komisarjevsky's production of 'Liliom' that Laughton made his first definite impression. He went on to success in the West End – in 'The Greater Love', 'The Happy Husband', 'Paul the First', 'The Man With Red Hair', 'Mr Pickwick' (as Pickwick) and others. In one play, Arnold Bennett's 'Mr Prohack', he met a young actress, Elsa Lanchester, who was appearing in a series of comic two-reelers devised (they were Silent) by H.G. Wells. Laughton made his screen début in one of these (uncredited) – probably *Bluebottles* (28). He was a burglar in that; in *Daydreams* he was an Eastern potentate. He and Miss Lanchester were married (though he was homosexual) in 1929, the year in which he made his 'official' screen bow, a cameo of a piggish diner in E.A. Dupont's *Piccadilly*. He also appeared in: *Comets*, a 'talkie-review', and later bought the US rights to prevent its being shown there; Wilcox's *Wolves* (30), not shown in the US – despite ads in the American trade press describing Laughton as 'England's greatest character actor' – till 1936, much cut and retitled *Wanted Men*: it was an Arctic melodrama and Laughton was a self-sacrificing hero; and *Down River* (31), as the Eurasian skipper of a tramp steamer. Meanwhile, on stage, he had a big success as Tony Perelli in Edgar Wallace's 'On the Spot' and a mild one with C.S. Forester's 'Payment Deferred'. Gilbert Miller took the latter to New York, with Laughton and Lanchester, and when the run finished Laughton revived 'Alibi', playing Hercule Poirot, which he had done in London. Acclaim meant that film offers were inevitable and he signed with Paramount, who thought he might take the place vacated by Emil Jannings. He signed on his own terms, for three years, two films per annum.

Neither husband nor wife was certain how they would make out in Hollywood and she, petite and birdlike, had to wait a couple of years before having any success (as a character actress). Laughton had always been neurotic about his deficiency in those physical qualities expected of a star; by now he had relaxed, but he felt insecure when watching Gary Cooper act with him in *The Devil and the Deep* (32). He liked Cooper and learned from him but stole the notices: '. . . but Mr

Laughton's forceful and resilient portrait is the outstanding histrionic contribution', said 'The New York Times'. It was his second American film, for he had been loaned to Universal to play the crass North Country business man who turns heroic in *The Old Dark House*, one of that studio's tall tales, constructed from J.B. Priestley's 'Benighted' – but on the proviso that it be released after his début for Paramount. He was also loaned to MGM to repeat his stage role of the petit bourgeois murderer in *Payment Deferred*, but Lanchester's part as his daughter was taken by Maureen O'Sullivan. The film was not a success. De Mille then cast him as Nero in *The Sign of the Cross*, which he played for laughs (to De Mille's initial annoyance), with more than a sidelong glance at Mussolini: during the rest of that dictator-prone decade he often looked to Europe for the several species of oligarchs he played (and when playing the Emperor Claudius, he got the key from the abdication speech of Edward VIII). He had the briefest episode in *If I Had a Million*, as the suddenly wealthy clerk who mounts to the executive suite to blow a raspberry at the boss; and, finally, was the sinister Dr Moreau in an H.G. Wells story, *Island of Lost Souls* (33), a scientist who turned men into animals. Despite a nationwide publicity campaign to find a girl to play the Panther Woman, the film was a box-office dud and the British censor banned it outright. Today, when the goings-on are not preposterous, they are unpleasant; and Laughton looked back on it with unease.

In London, Korda was preparing *The Private Life of Henry VIII*, an irreverent chronicle of the king's marriages; Lanchester played Anne of Cleves for the film's funniest sequence. It was a totally unexpected success, the first British film to find wide acceptance internationally: for Laughton it meant an Oscar, numerous imitators and – partly due to his resemblance to Holbein portraits – a common conception that he was more like Henry than Henry (today, his lusty portrayal shines in a generally anaemic movie). Recognizing that he had the role of a lifetime and that Korda was in financial difficulties – as he had begun, so he would continue, despite the money this brought in – Laughton accepted a mere £1,000 for his participation (the total budget was £50,000), so he was glad to return to Hollywood and $2,500 a week to play a cockney king of the river ill-treating wife Carole Lombard in a rubbishy jungle adventure, *White Woman*; and then he elected to go to the Old Vic to play Shakespeare's idea of bluff King Hal, as well as Prospero, Angelo in 'Measure for Measure', Macbeth (there were reservations about his handling of the verse)

and Wilde's Canon Chasuble.

He increased his fame as the tyrannical Victorian father in *The Barretts of Wimpole Street* (34), a performance long considered the prototype; and he stayed at MGM for *David Copperfield*, to play Micawber (Lanchester was the Micawbers' maid) – but he became increasingly convinced that the only actor who could play the role was W.C. Fields and after three days' shooting persuaded the company to replace him. At Paramount he led a superb team of farceurs (Ruggles, Boland, Roland Young, Zazu Pitts) in a classic comedy about an English butler in the Wild West, *Ruggles of Red Gap* (35); and then played Javert against Fredric March's Valjean in *Les Misérables*, which Lanchester considered one of his best performances. But everything he did at this time was outstanding and when he played Bligh in *Mutiny on the Bounty*, Mark van Doren remarked that this performance 'fixes him in my mind at any rate as by far the best of living actors'. The New York critics, in the first of their annual awards, cited him for his Bligh and his Ruggles. *Mutiny* was judged by the Hollywood Academy as the year's best film and it was the year's number one moneymaker; *Misérables* was a runner-up.

Laughton was at a pinnacle: no character actor since Jannings had had so much prestige – and he was far more popular than Jannings had been. He was now under personal contract to Irving Thalberg, who intended to take him with him when he left MGM to start up his own company, but Thalberg died.

Laughton decided to turn his back on Hollywood, which he found artistically stifling: it did not allow him sufficient latitude – he wanted more sympathetic parts. He and Lanchester had kept a home in Britain despite paying double taxes and he planned a future with Korda in that country: Korda directed him in *Rembrandt* (36), a remarkably sober account of the artist's life – too sober perhaps,

because the public did not take to it. Laughton's performance, however, held to his standard: he tried hard not to appear to act and 'The New York Times' gratifyingly noted: 'Mr Laughton becomes Rembrandt as nobody else in the world could – of this we are firmly and unmistakably convinced.' Thirteen years later, when the film was revived in London, the 'Daily Telegraph' (Campbell Dixon) said: 'Laughton never again did anything so good.' Still with Korda, he began *I Claudius*, from Robert Graves's novel, under the direction of Joseph von Sternberg. After several weeks' work, shooting was stopped when Merle Oberon was injured in a car crash and after she was better it was not resumed. The reasons remain mysterious. Elsa Lanchester in her book 'Charles Laughton and I' merely remarks that she did not listen to the gossip; and a BBC documentary made in 1965, 'The Epic That Never Was', hardly clarified the matter, though it interviewed the surviving principals, including Merle Oberon and von Sternberg himself. It seems likely that the project was stymied by von Sternberg's callous disregard for costs, and Laughton's temperament – especially directed towards the director. But von Sternberg, speaking of the film in his memoirs, said: 'The well from which a man draws his talents is deep, but Laughton's well had no bottom.' (Two other Laughton projects abandoned by Korda were a *Cyrano de Bergerac* with Vivien Leigh as Roxanne and a life of Diaghilev with Anton Dolin as Nijinsky.)

Laughton joined Erich Pommer (formerly

Charles Laughton in two of his most famous roles. Left, in Korda's The Private Life of Henry VIII *(33) which broke the existing records of New York's Radio City Music Hall (it had been open nine months): it was the only British film of the decade to find wide acceptance in the US. (Robert Donat in foreground.) Right, as* Ruggles of Red Gap *(35), a part played by Edward Everett Horton in the 1923 silent version.*

There have been at least six film versions of Victor Hugo's 'Les Misérables' – of which the best is generally considered to be the 1935 film version directed by Richard Boleslawski: with Fredric March, Charles Laughton and John Carradine.

with Ufa) to form a company called May-flower to make films starring Laughton. The first was *Vessel of Wrath* (38), from a Maugham story about a beachcomber and a prissy missionary – Lanchester in a touching and funny performance. There followed *St Martin's Lane*, an odd little film about buskers in a London that looked suspiciously like the Berlin of Pommer's Ufa films, and the character that Laughton played was like those played by Emil Jannings (Pommer had produced *Varieté*). However, Basil Wright said in the 'Spectator': '. . . Laughton gives quite the finest performance of his career, and it is by sheer acting technique, not to say the electric discharge of his personality, that he forces us . . . to examine our own hearts, not his.' Neither of the two movies was a success, despite the fact that *St Martin's Lane* had Vivien Leigh in it and it opened in the US not long after *Gone with the Wind*. An attempt to resurrect the fortunes of Mayflower with a Hitchcock thriller was no more successful: there was a good movie to be made out of Daphne du Maurier's *Jamaica Inn* (39), but this – distorted version – was not it. A fourth project – *The Admirable Crichton* (with Lanchester as the tweenie) – was shelved (the rights were sold back to Paramount, but the film was never made) when two things happened simultaneously: war broke out and RKO offered a contract for five films, to begin with the role of Quasimodo in *The Hunchback of Notre Dame* (40). He liked the RKO offer, which was amended to include the settling of the debts incurred by his British ventures – and he had had, in any case, enough of playing an impresario (especially an unsuccessful one). His Quasimodo was a marvellous, pitiful creation, regardless of make-up.

He was uneasily cast as the Italian immigrant with a mail-order bride (Lombard) in *They Knew What They Wanted*; but in *It Started With Eve* (41), as an old man fascinated by his son's fiancée, Deanna Durbin, he was delightful – though the role was less substantial than usual. Other films or roles were negligible – *The Tuttles of Tahiti* (42), a family comedy and just one step up from a B picture; an episode in the all-star *Tales of Manhattan* as a saloon pianist who gets a chance at Carnegie Hall; *Stand-by for Action* as an admiral; *Forever and a Day* (43), another all-star effort, as a tippling butler; and *The Man From Down Under*, in the title-role. But the latter was preceded by *This Land is Mine*, a piece about the French Resistance in which he was a meek schoolteacher. Despite Jean Renoir's clearly deeply felt direction it is a superficial picture: Laughton's performance, with its impassioned plea for freedom at the end, was not liked at the time, but is today

Laughton's make-up for Rembrandt *(36) was remarkable: and so was his performance – still the best film about a painter.*

one of the few effective aspects of the film.

His salary throughout this period was $100,000 per film, but there began criticisms of the roles he accepted and sometimes of how he played them. He turned his energies towards entertaining the troops (readings, recitals, lectures – work he continued after the war). The next two films proved that he was a better actor than ever: inventive and witty as *The Canterville Ghost* (44), the Wilde story updated for Margaret O'Brien: and *The Suspect*, an Edwardian murder story which was unconvincing except for his own gentle performance as a man driven to kill his nagging wife (Rosalind Ivan).

But he might well have reflected on the euphoria of a decade earlier as he played *Captain Kidd* (45), a cardboard children's epic which would have been the low point of anyone's career, or as he rejoined Deanna Durbin in what was a weak one for both of them, *Because of Him* (46), which wasted his study of a ham Broadway actor. He returned to the stage, in Brecht's 'Galileo' (47), managing to fit in a cameo in Hitchcock's dreadful *The Paradine Case* (48), billed below the title for the first time since arriving in Hollywood, but with such prestigious names as Ethel Barrymore: and he was the most enjoyable, as a snob-ridden judge. He replaced Michael Chekhov, who was ill, as the Gestapo chief in *Arch of Triumph* and although the role was built up for him it was still brief; he then seized his best chance in years in a good thriller, *The Big Clock*, as a megalomaniac

It Started With Eve (*41*): *Charles Laughton is supposedly dying, and Robert Cummings can't find the fiancée he wants to meet – so he 'borrows' Deanna Durbin. And that's as good a premise as any comedy ever had.*

publisher, 'both ludicrous and magnificently repulsive' said Peter Ericson in 'Sequence'. His $100,000 fee included the services of Lanchester, in a cameo role. He had had a role in the episode film, *On Our Merry Way*, which was cut, and for the same producer he played a bishop in *The Girl From Manhattan* with Dorothy Lamour. He had a fine old time in *The Bribe* (49), as the unshaven, unsavoury and fawning drunk who offers it, to Robert Taylor, but the heart seemed to have left him when he came to play Maigret in *The Man on the Eiffel Tower*, made in France by Burgess Meredith, who co-starred; he forgets about the accent after a while and is 'soporific to the point of catatonia . . . one of the few performances in his output which has almost nothing to recommend it' (Simon Callow in his book, 'Charles Laughton: a Difficult Actor'). Disheartened, he remained offscreen till *The Blue Veil* (51) and though his fee had gone down to $65,000 it was an episode film: but he gave a touching portrayal as the elderly widower who offers his hand to Jane Wyman. Conversely, *The Strange Door* is an unabashed B, but is one of the few rotten films Laughton made where he is not hammy – as a rascally squire. And his sketch as the tramp in the *Clarion Call* episode of O. Henry's *Full House* (52) further heartened fans – but a stint in *Abbott and Costello Meet Captain Kidd* shocked and saddened them. His salary was now down to $25,000 per film. He then played Herod in *Salome* (53), an appalling film and a performance which clearly indicates his dilemma as a fine actor offered only poor material: he seems uncertain whether to play the part straight, whether to send it up or just not bother at all. He was more his old self again in another bash at Henry VIII in *Young Bess*, with Jean Simmons, and made one good film, David Lean's *Hobson's Choice* (54), in Britain, but his own performance as the tyrannical, selfish patriarch was over-exuberant, throwing the film off balance.

His thoughts increasingly turned away from films: in the early 50s he toured extensively in Shaw's 'Don Juan in Hell' (with Cedric Hardwicke, Agnes Moorehead and Charles Boyer) and directed another 'reading', Stephen Vincent Benét's 'John Brown's Body' (with Tyrone Power, Raymond Massey and Judith Anderson). Solo readings included Dickens, the Bible, Thurber, etc., and Laughton made recordings and appeared on TV and radio. His producer on these occasions was Paul Gregory, who now guided Laughton's career, ensuring that he made more money than he could have done in films. He also had Laughton direct 'The Caine Mutiny Court Martial' on tour and in New York, and he decided that would also direct a film, *The Night of the Hunter* (55), which despite its flaws suggests that Laughton might have been a great film-maker. Although its status is now unassailable, it was then an abject failure, so much so that Laughton had doubts about directing Norman Mailer's *The Naked and the Dead*, which Gregory had purchased for him.

Laughton's film work of the 40s and 50s contains only isolated fine performances: but his last film, Advise and Consent *(62), found him again at his most showily brilliant. With Don Murray.*

He wrote a script of which the author approved, but it was long and, director George Sidney told Gregory, would cost $20 million to shoot. Gregory sold the project (after $500,000 had been spent) and Laughton dissolved the partnership after learning from his current boyfriend that Gregory had boasted that he could get anything out of him that he wanted. A while later he did another good film, Wilder's *Witness for the Prosecution* (57), as the QC: both he and Lanchester received Oscar nominations.

He now felt ready to tackle Shakespeare again and at Stratford-upon-Avon appeared – with qualified success – as King Lear and Bottom (the latter production included the then unknown Albert Finney, Vanessa Redgrave and Ian Holm). He and Lanchester then gave, in their different styles, dazzling performances in a dim play, 'The Party', in London.

In order to show Rome to a new lover, he chose to do *Under Ten Flags/Sotto Dieci Bandiere* (60), playing an admiral again, in this daft war film with a conscience, with Van Heflin. His fee had gone back to $100,000 for this occasion and then, for just over $41,000 for 13 days' work, he was a Roman senator in *Spartacus*, with Olivier and Ustinov providing the most satisfactory elements of an above-average spectacle. His last film was *Advise and Consent* (62) as the wily Southern senator, Seab Cooley. He died from cancer before it was shown and Hollywood did not bother even to nominate him posthumously for an Oscar. But it was far and away the most subtle, the most engaging and most convincing performance of the year, as he intended.

LAUREL AND HARDY

The question of what is funny is so notoriously difficult that it is best left alone. Laurel and Hardy were left alone by critics for most of their careers and the merit in rehabilitating them is indeed debatable – though the fault there lies less in the action than in the claims made for them: 'They are the most universal of comics, in range as in appeal,' said Charles Barr in 'Laurel and Hardy', his monograph on them, 1968. There were and are people who find them unfunny; it was and is possible to find on one day an audience laughing its head off at Laurel and Hardy and the next day to find another stony-silent – in both cases, in both commercial houses and film societies. The truth is that their work is extremely variable, even in the stuff which their admirers take to be their peak; plus the fact that in order to relish them some prior acquaintance is desirable. David Robinson, writing in 'Sight and Sound' in 1954, commented on their recurring jokes: 'the pleasures of *recognition* which have always been exploited in the music hall – in the use of catchphrases, of dialogue which becomes comic by its very familarity. . . . Stan's cry, or the frequent sight of Oliver, prostrated and turning up his face in speechless appeal, may seem unfunny at first acquaintance, but gradually grow upon one until they are hilarious, irresistible, looked-for and cherished.'

Non-adherents find the trade-marked gags obvious, resistible and laboured, the bag of tricks almost empty, the two comics merely like great babies; Hardy's timing invariably seems off, his look of despair (straight into the camera) or his waggling of his tie repeated merely because no other material was available to them. But in fact Laurel and Hardy never aspired to be anything but simple funny men. Their work is more primitive than that of the great screen clowns, but it never pretended to be otherwise. They never went in for subtlety. They were pals, the rotund, grand, slow-moving Hardy ('Ollie'), with his pretensions to elegance, omniscience and lady-killing; and the wiry, bumbling, crushed, comparatively minuscule Laurel ('Stan'), whose good intentions were the bane of Ollie's life – though he bumbled too. There was seldom any justification for his impatience with Stan. The mistakes they made they made together, each compounding the felony. On occasions their building a gag could be glorious, like their antics delivering a piano in *The Music Box*; but they were even better at sustaining quite simple ideas, like their incompetence as waiters in *From Soup to Nuts* or the foiled attempts to change trousers in *Liberty*. They seldom eschewed a healthy vulgarity – the trouser-tearing sequence in *You're Darn Tootin'*, the hen-pecking wives and cheap broads of their domestic films; but most glorious of all are the mystic orgies of chaos that, united now, they would heap upon the common enemy – the destruction of James Finlayson's villa in *Big Business*, the pie-throwing sequences in *The Hoosegow* and *The Battle of the Century*. At times like these they can stand up and be counted among the screen's great comics.

Stan Laurel was the creative one of the two. He was British, being born in Ulverston, Lancashire, in 1890, the son of an actor and theatre manager, and grammar-school educated – for a while. In 1903 he joined 'The Juvenile Pantomime Company' and thereafter played music halls. Later he joined Fred Karno's Company and went with it to the US in 1910 and again in 1913; sometimes he understudied Chaplin, who was also with Karno. He played in vaudeville in the US at one point, imitating Chaplin. Adolph Ramish, who managed a Los Angeles theatre where he played, liked him enough to put him in a two-reeler, *Nuts in May* (18); Universal bought it and signed Laurel for a year to play a character called 'Hickory Hiram', but after three or four shorts he was sacked. He returned to vaudeville but in 1919 did a short for Bronco Billy Anderson, now a producer: *Lucky Dog*. Metro bought it and Anderson signed Laurel to make a series of spoofs – *Mud and Sand*, *When Knights Were Cold*; and Hal Roach signed him to continue the series at his studio. He moved over to Universal for his own series, 'The Stan Laurel Series', but it was not till he signed with Roach again in 1926 that he began to be well known. He had made over 50 shorts when the partnership with Hardy started the following year.

Oliver Hardy was born in Atlanta, Georgia, in 1892; he wanted to be an attorney but instead ran a cinema – from which he went into films, as early as 1913. He was an extra, a bit-player (he was in *Lucky Dog*) and had some success as a heavy in Billy West comedies; he worked in various capacities for several companies, but did not really come into prominence until he appeared in and co-directed some Larry Semon comedies in the early 20s, by which time he was generally known as 'Babe' Hardy. Later Hal Roach signed him to join his Comedy All-Stars team.

The partnership began this way: Laurel was directing *Get 'em Young*, in which Hardy had a small part as a butler; but Hardy could not do it because of illness and Laurel played it. They acted together in the next one, *Slipping Wives*, and played as part of the company in 10 two-reelers before Roach decided to pair them permanently; coincidentally, the lead in

most of these films was Finlayson, who was often to support them later. Their first short was *Putting Pants on Philip* (27), a mild prank as a team with Philip (Laurel) as a Scotsman in a kilt, embarrassing his American relative (Hardy); it is not typical of their work, but they were to find their feet very quickly. Over the next three years they turned out almost one short a month (most of them directed by Leo McCarey, who went on to bigger things). The other 1927 titles (generally considered to be 'Laurel and Hardy' rather than the 'All-Stars'): *The Second 100 Years*, *Hats Off* and *The Battle of the Century*. The 1928 ones: *Leave 'em Laughing* (which added Edgar Kennedy, so often their policeman foe), *The Finishing Touch*, *From Soup to Nuts*, *You're Darn Tootin'*, *Their Purple Moment*, *Should Married Men Go Home?*, *Early to Bed*, *Two Tars* (they cause a great traffic jam), *Habeas Corpus* and *We Faw Down*.

These shorts were often divided into two or more sections; thus *Liberty* (29) starts with Ollie and Stan as escaped convicts, has the gag where they are wearing the wrong pants and concludes with some precarious antics (almost as good as Lloyd's) on some scaffolding at the top of a skyscraper. There followed: *Wrong Again*, *That's My Wife*, *Big Business*, *Double Whoopee*, *Berth Marks*, *Bacon Grabbers*,

The Battle of the Century (27) – *one of their earliest shorts and one of their most anarchic: it ended with a giant custard-pie battle involving every extra on the lot.*

Angora Love (their first 100 per cent Talkie), *Men of War*, *The Perfect Day*, *They Go Boom* and *The Hoosegow*. It was an astonishingly creative period – hardly disturbed by the coming of Sound; sensibly, Laurel and Hardy virtually ignored it – and later, when they depended more upon it, their dialogue exchanges were seldom memorable. For many years they made versions of their films in French, German, Spanish and Italian after the English one was completed – though they spoke these languages only phonetically. They were also in *Hollywood Revue of 1929*. In 1930: *Night Owls*, *Blotto*, *Be Big*, *Brats*, *The Laurel and Hardy Murder Case*, *Below Zero*, *Hog Wild*, *Another Fine Mess* and *The Rogue Song*, made originally as a starring vehicle for Lawrence Tibbett – then MGM decided that they needed comic relief to boost foreign sales, so constructed a sub-plot which was cut in later. It was made in colour. In 1931: *Laughing Gravy* (which is a masterpiece), *Our Wife*, *Come Clean*, *One Good Turn*, *Beau Hunks* and *Helpmates*. But something happened that year: the sets for *Pardon Us* became too expensive for a short subject and it became a feature: it was little more than a series of gags, but the public, accustomed to

finding Laurel and Hardy thrown into the programme for good measure, still turned up to see it. 'Picturegoer', however, though it liked the shorts, thought 'three-quarters of an hour of this comedy team is too much'; nor were contemporary critics kind to their subsequent features.

In 1932 they tried another one, *Pack Up Your Troubles*, and did the following shorts: *Any Old Port*, *The Chimp*, *County Hospital*, *Scram*, *Their First Mistake* and *The Music Box*, which won an Oscar in a category established that year: Short Subjects (Live Action) – Comedy. But although they had always reprised their best routines – often improving upon them – there was now beginning to show a remarkable fluctuation in quality. There were only six shorts in 1933: *Towed in a Hole*, *Twice Two* (they both had dual roles – as the other's wife), *Me and My Pal*, *The Midnight Patrol*, *Busy Bodies* and *Dirty Work*. The two features were *Fra Diavolo*, a pokey version of Auber's old operetta, with Dennis King and Thelma Todd, and our heroes as fumbling bandits, and *Sons of the Desert*, free of their wives at a convention. The former was successful enough to bring forth two similar ventures,

Babes in Toyland (34), from the Victor Herbert musical, and The Bohemian Girl (36), from the one by Michael W. Balfe (and in 1934 they did a turn in a revue, Hollywood Party, notable only for a sequence provided by Walt Disney).

They did only a few more shorts: The Private Life of Oliver VIII, Going Bye Bye, Them Thar Hills and The Live Ghost in 1934; and Tit for Tat, The Fixer Uppers and Thicker than Water (which concluded with each impersonating the other) in 1935. Laurel no longer wished to do two-reelers and Roach announced a separation, with Hardy to appear in a family series called The Hardys. Instead, they did do a feature, Bonnie Scotland (35), notable for one of their funny and astonishingly beautiful dance duets, moving ever more ecstatically into their private world: and it was successful, as for a few years were their other features; in Britain for a couple of years (36 and 37) they were among the top 10 box-office draws. Laurel was allowed to produce a feature, Our Relations (36), but he remained unhappy and though their quarrel had been considered patched up he issued a statement in 1936 about an intended vacation, considered by the industry to be a challenge

to Roach and Hardy. Laurel produced Way Out West at the end of the year, but in 1937 the break was considered irremediable and Hardy was announced for a project, Road House, with Patsy Kelly and Buster Keaton. They did both appear as themselves in a Patsy Kelly vehicle, Pick a Star (37): as an aspiring actress she watches them making a film – and they also had a sequence of their own. It was not till late that year that things went smoothly again. Swiss Miss (38) was one of their frowsty 'musicals' and Blockheads one of their traditional features – the situations that result after a 20-year separation and Hardy's marriage. They separated in life: Laurel's contract with Roach was up and at the same time Roach's 11-year distribution agreement with MGM ended. To use up Hardy's contract Roach put him in a comedy about a sick elephant, Zenobia (39) – but he also wanted to see whether the public would accept him with a new partner, Harry Langdon. Laurel and Hardy then solved the problem of their future by making Flying Deuces for an independent releasing through RKO, but were then prevailed upon to do a pair for Roach at UA, A Chump at Oxford (40) and Saps at Sea – of which 'Picturegoer' said: 'Just a series of gags, which is more likely to please juveniles than anyone else.' But Laurel's differences with Roach had not been patched up and since he and Hardy were always the best of friends, they formed their own company – but since no backers were forthcoming, they were forced into employment with the big studios: six pictures for 20th and two significantly for MGM, who had made a lot of money out of them over the years.

In 1940-41 they toured in 'The Laurel and Hardy Revue' with some success, but they were ageing and their recent film work had been seldom inventive or even funny. In their remaining eight films they were allowed no creative control and, predictably and justly, these played the lower half of double bills: Great Guns (41), A Haunting We Will Go (42), Air Raid Wardens (43) at MGM, Jitterbugs, Dancing Masters, The Big Noise (44), Nothing but Trouble at MGM and The Bullfighters (45). Laurel loathed these films and until he died was bitter at the 20th management for giving them so little freedom. In 1947 they went to Britain for a music-hall tour and planned a film there that came to nothing. They did make in France Atoll K/Robinson Crusoeland (51), but they lost heart as the 12-week schedule stretched out to a year, and it showed: there were only spotty bookings.

They continued to work in music halls when possible: neither were wealthy men. When Hal Roach sold their movies to TV in 1951, he got $750,000 for them. It was reported that

The Laurel and Hardy Murder Case (30), one of their most popular films – though probably because of its title rather than any intrinsic merit.

Laurel and Hardy received nothing of this. Hardy did two solo supporting roles: in *Fighting Kentuckian* (49), starring John Wayne, and *Riding High* (50) with Bing Crosby. He died in 1957 after a heart attack. He had been married twice. Laurel married four times, twice to the same woman. He died in 1965, in poverty, but he had lived long enough to see the team's work restored from semi-oblivion and given its due (or more than its due). He received a special Oscar in 1960 'for his creative pioneering in the field of cinema comedy'. There as much applause when Laurel and Hardy excerpts were included in films like *When Comedy Was King* and there were later three anthologies devoted to them: *Laurel and Hardy's Laughing Twenties* (65), *The Crazy World of Laurel and Hardy* (66) and *The Further Perils of Laurel and Hardy* (67).

VIVIEN LEIGH

Even if she had not played Scarlett O'Hara, the most coveted role in movie history, it is probable that Vivien Leigh's striking Dresden Shepherdess beauty would have won her a place among the great stars. She was recognized, even by unbelievers, as one of the beauties of her era: what with that and Scarlett, and being for much of her life Lady Olivier, fame and acclaim rather obscured her actual ability. On a couple of occasions she was breathtakingly good, but much of her screen and stage work was no better than that of any other decent, hard-working and abnormally ambitious actress. James Agate wrote in 1946: 'She's heavenly to look at, and is an exquisite, charming, delightful, witty, entrancing little actress. She is, indeed, everything except what I should call a good actress, and can be played off the screen any time by any number of actresses with one-tenth of her looks, exquisiteness, charm, delightfulness, etc.'

Her parents were living in India when she was born in 1913, in Darjeeling. She was educated in Britain, Germany, France and Italy; and was planning to go to RADA when she met her first husband, a barrister. She did study at RADA for a short while after her marriage and made her professional début in a film, *Things Are Looking Up* (34), as one of the schoolgirls; she was also in a couple of quickies, *The Village Squire* (35) and *Gentlemen's Agreement* (top-billed), and in *Look Up and Laugh*, starring Gracie Fields, with only a few sentences to speak. Her stage début was in the London suburbs, at the Q Theatre, in 'The Green Sash' (35); four months later, in

May, she appeared in the West End in Ashley Duke's comedy, 'The Mask of Virtue', and became famous overnight. Every British studio offered a contract, but she signed with Korda for five years, for two films a year, starting at £1,300 the first year and going to £18,000 – and thus publicized as the £50,000 contract. She did not, however, make a film for over a year; she continued on the stage until cast as a lady-in-waiting, the heroine of *Fire Over England* (37), an Elizabethan adventure with Olivier. Then she was Conrad Veidt's dangerous love interest in a complicated spy story, *Dark Journey*, and the very ingénue lead of a slight comedy, *Storm in a Teacup*; she and Olivier were re-teamed in *21 Days*, a clodhopping melodrama which was not released in Britain until 1939 and the US a year later. MGM-British borrowed her for the lead opposite Robert Taylor in *A Yank at Oxford* (38), but due to Louis B. Mayer's intervention she was replaced by Maureen O'Sullivan and relegated to the part of a don's minxish wife who liked to philander with the students. She was considerably effective, as she was in *St Martin's Lane*, as a self-centred little busker who, helped by Charles Laughton, becomes the toast of Shaftesbury Avenue. At the same time she continued to enhance her stage reputation: among other parts she played were Titania and Ophelia to Olivier's Hamlet, in Elsinore. When he was offered Heathcliff in *Wuthering Heights* she asked for Cathy and was offered Isabella Linton, with William Wyler's assurance that she would not get a better role for her Hollywood début. It was always said that she rejected Isabella, but one biography of Goldwyn says that he would not meet her fee.

She was about to start *The Thief of Bagdad* when on a whim she flew to see Olivier in Hollywood, late in 1938. *Gone with the Wind* (39) had started without a Scarlett after two years' search; according to the usual version, Olivier, Leigh and Selznick's agent brother Myron were watching the burning of Atlanta and Myron (who was also Olivier's agent) turned to David and said 'I want you to meet Scarlett.' She had set her sights on the role after reading the novel and later said that this famous story was apocryphal, that she had already been tested and signed. She was paid $25,000 for it and Selznick negotiated a new contract with Korda, who was in Hollywood (to be with Merle Oberon); for seven years, starting with one film for each of them, thereafter to be divided so that she spent six months in Hollywood and six months in Britain. One source says that she was to make two films for Selznick and two for Korda annually, but it is unlikely that a star of this magnitude (as she was expected to become) would be exposed to the public so often: it seems more than likely that the six months in Britain were to be spent on the stage, where she and Olivier believed they belonged. Olivier, in any case, was against the terms of the contract and only withdrew his objections when Selznick pointed out that he had blighted the career of his first wife (when they were both under contract at RKO) by insisting that she return to Britain with him. Although they were publicly seen together and were living openly together, this latter fact was kept from the press by Selznick, for it would certainly damage the film. As it was, there was some furore over the choice of an English girl, particularly among the partisans of the other aspirants. She told the 'Observer' in later years that her performance only satisfied her in a couple of places and: 'I never liked Scarlett. I knew it was a marvellous part, but I never cared for her. I couldn't find anything of myself in her, except for one line . . . it was the only thing in the character I could take hold of. It's in the scene after Frank's funeral, when she gets drunk and tells Rhett how glad she is her mother's dead and can't see her. "She brought me up to be kind and thoughtful and ladylike, just like her, and I've been such a disappointment." I liked her then, and perhaps at the end.' It is difficult to find an endearing trait in Scarlett beyond her determination and, whether Leigh realized it or not, she was basically an unsympathetic actress: this was a perfect mating of artist and character. Fascinating certainly, if far from flawless: but any other Scarlett is inconceivable. John Coleman reviewing the 1968 revival thought her contribution the 'paramount'

Vivien Leigh was one of the most beautiful women of the century, and Laurence Olivier its greatest actor: so, as they both had resplendent careers, their marriage was one of the most famous of its time. We know now that it was traumatic, at least as far as he was concerned, though they acted together memorably on stage on several occasions. They made, however, only three films together, including, above, Fire Over England (37), just after they met, and That Hamilton Woman (41), left, not long after they wed. Both movies, curiously, were similar in theme, for they concerned the gallant efforts of the British against the might of would-be conquerors, respectively Philip II of Spain and Napoleon.

one. She won the Best Actress Oscar and the New York critics' award.

She was under contract to Selznick and the hottest property in Hollywood. Of this period Wolfe Kaufman wrote years later in 'Variety': '. . . she made life hell for everybody near her, unless they did everything she wished, as she wished, and when she wished. Despite which she was surrounded by people who worshipped her and were ready to carry out her whims.' She did not, however, get her way over Olivier as co-star: she had tested unsuccessfully for *Rebecca* and now she wanted to be with him in *Pride and Prejudice* or have him with her in *Waterloo Bridge* (40). Instead, Robert Taylor was cast in this World War I saga (considerably inferior to the 1931 version) about an aristocrat and a ballerina; they marry and while he is away fighting, she becomes a tart (to survive); he recovers her, never learning of her fate, but she abandons him for the sake of the regiment, as personified by C. Aubrey Smith. There was, apparently, a large audience for such things in 1940. Said the 'Evening News' (London): 'Vivien Leigh gives a performance of beauty, inspiration and sensitivity which I do not expect to see surpassed this year.' In New York she and Olivier were 'Romeo and Juliet' to a distinctly unappreciative public; and they were married. Prestige was regained with *That Hamilton Woman/Lady Hamilton* (41), made by Korda in Hollywood quickly and cheaply, but it was effective both as romance and propaganda. Leigh's Emma was visually right and she did not shrink from the less attractive qualities in the lady's character: like most of her screen portraits this one was not withal a one-man woman.

She and Olivier returned to Britain, but apart from a stage appearance as Jennifer Dubedat, illness prevented her from working; a further barrier was Selznick, who refused to let her play the French princess in her husband's *Henry V* because the part was too small. It was believed, however, that he acted in retaliation for her refusal to leave either Britain or husband. He did loan her to Rank for *Caesar and Cleopatra* (45), Gabriel Pascal's version of the Shaw play and at £1¼ million or $5 million the most expensive movie yet made anywhere in the world. Critics were caustic about the cost and generally liked only Claude Rains and her (she was appropriately kittenish and wily) in the title-roles. In Britain it did good business, but in the US the reviews dampened any curiosity to see Leigh after a four-year absence. In 1945 the Selznick contract was declared invalid by a British court when he tried to stop her doing 'The Skin of Our Teeth' on the stage; she continued to turn down Hollywood offers, but after recovering

from TB she agreed to be Korda's *Anna Karenina* (48) under Julien Duvivier's direction: an unsatisfactory film, hindered more than somewhat by an inadequate Vronsky (Kieron Moore). She invited comparison with Garbo and few critics were kind enough not to make it. Said James Agee: 'Vivien Leigh is lashed about by the tremendous role of Anna like a pussy-cat with a tigress by the tail.' Nor did the public like it.

Meanwhile, with Olivier she was touring Australasia with the Old Vic company; in London in 1949 she played Lady Teazle, Lady Anne in 'Richard III' and Anouilh's 'Antigone'; in 1951, in London and New York, still opposite Olivier, she played Shaw's and Shakespeare's Cleopatras: all to generous appreciation. Also, in 1949 in London she played Blanche in Tennessee Williams's 'A Streetcar Named Desire'; and when Olivia de Havilland declined the film version (51) she was invited to do it, opposite Marlon Brando, and got her best film reviews since Scarlett. Milton Shulman thought: 'She just misses pathos. But this is, nevertheless, a performance such as the screen rarely sees.' C.A. Lejeune: 'One would have to be blind not to appreciate the brilliance of Vivien Leigh's performance. It is possible not to be touched by her, inconceivable not to be impressed and dazzled. Her Blanche is a woman shimmering in a sheath of gold, never very clearly seen, by taking glint and radiance from every facet.' For the second time both the Academy and the New York critics discerned her the Year's Best Actress and the British Film Academy voted her the Year's Best British Actress. In Venice her performance won her the Grand Prix. One of the most touching tributes ever paid to an actress was made by the author, Tennessee Williams, who later told 'Life' magazine that she had brought everything to the part he had intended and much that he had never dreamed of. Olivier later observed 'Poor darling Vivien was very much haunted. [It] didn't do her any good at all.'

In 1953, much to the industry's surprise, and at a fee of $255,000, Leigh began work with Peter Finch in what was clearly a prorammer, *Elephant Walk*; after locations in India and some studio work in Hollywood she had a nervous breakdown and was replaced. Olivier flew out to bring her home, which killed, temporarily, speculations about the break-up of the famous marriage. As is now known, she had an affair with her co-star, Peter Finch, which may even have begun when he met the Oliviers on their Australian tour; he was only one of several men during her life with Olivier. She was inclined to bouts of manic depression, a condition not helped by a feeling, endorsed by the critics, that her

Marlon Brando and Vivien Leigh in Elia Kazan's film of A Streetcar Named Desire *(51): one of the most potent clashes in screen dramaturgy – from Tennessee Williams's play.*

own talent was not of the level of her husband's. She recovered from her illness to appear with him on stage in Rattigan's 'The Sleeping Prince' (54); a year later they were at Stratford where her Lady Macbeth and Viola cruelly exposed her limitations as a 'classical' actress. She returned to films with *The Deep Blue Sea* (56), Korda's version of the Rattigan play about a middle-aged woman trying to hang on to her lover, a garish, soupy film, directed by Anatole Litvak; Leigh's austere, carefully modulated performance was outclassed by Kenneth More as the lover. (He later revealed that they had not got on, partly because he objected to her insistence on her character's physical beauty.) Business was not lucrative.

Stage appearances included 'Duel of Angels' (London and New York), 'Look After Lulu' (a Coward adaptation of Feydeau) and, after the divorce (1960), a musical 'Tovarich' in New York and 'The Lady of the Camellias', touring in Australasia and South America. Both her last films included an undue proportion of lines which could be construed as masochistic: in both she was a fading beauty with a lot of past but no future. In *The Roman Spring of Mrs Stone* (61) she was a retired actress (who had been bad in Shakespeare) involved with an Italian gigolo and in *Ship of Fools* (65) an embittered divorcée who drank too much. The former was a competent version of Tennessee Williams's only novel; the second transformed Katharine Ann Por-

Vivien Leigh in 1951. Since this picture was issued by Warner Bros it can only have been taken while she was under contract to that studio to make A Streetcar Named Desire.

ter's ambitious bestseller into a pretentious pot-boiler: neither was over-successful.

'La Contessa' (65), based on a novel by Maurice Druon, folded on tour; her last stage appearance was in 'Ivanov' with John Gielgud, in New York the following years. She did not know that she was ill when she told Radie Harris, 'I would rather have lived a short life with Larry than face a long one without him.' A recurrence of TB killed her in 1967. The public, who had increasingly regarded her as a remote deity, were nevertheless shocked and saddened; and it seemed improbable that this most genuinely glamorous of creatures should have had her funeral in a London crematorium rather than in some special Nirvana.

Harold Lloyd

Harold Lloyd completes the great triumvirate of the Silent clowns. After Keaton and Chaplin there is no other whose reputation is quite so secure and at the time he as probably the most popular of the three: certainly he was the best bet at the box-office during the 20s. Lloyd's humour sprang more from plot and situation than the others: he was a very ordinary, indeed conventional young man. Keaton was a loner and Chaplin thumbed his nose at society, but Lloyd was the eager young American, Alger-indoctrinated, dressed in duds which were the 20s equivalent of the grey flannel suit – plus the ubiquitous straw hat and the glasses, betokening anxiousness and shyness. To what extent he was satirizing the all-American boy is debatable, but the public did respond enormously to the character; James

Harold Lloyd and Bebe Daniels in a short made not long after he began what he called his 'glass' character. The man with the droopy moustache behind is Stan Laurel.

Agee is one critic who did find Lloyd 'funny from inside'. After acknowledging what Lloyd had described as his 'unusually large comic vocabulary' he went on: 'more particularly he had an expertly expressive body and even more expressive teeth, and out of his thesaurus of smiles he could at a moment's notice blend prissiness, breeziness and asininity, and still remain tremendously likeable.' In 'Harold Lloyd's World of Comedy' (64) William Cahn went on from there: 'It was Harold's aim to develop a character the public could believe in. His antics and adventures were stretched, but never beyond the post of possibility. . . . An extrovert to the core, Harold was the young man who would not take no for an answer. Evidently, nobody ever told him that anything was impossible. Therefore, he proceeded to do what could not be done.' Tackling the impossible for Lloyd often meant some incredible, perilous feat of daring or athletics, like scaling the skyscraper in *Safety Last* – the supreme example of its kind. Less imaginative, in the end, than Keaton, he could sustain a gag longer, like his attempts to help the girl in the convertible, in the rain, in *Movie Crazy*.

Lloyd was born in Burchard, Nebraska, in 1893, into a fairly poor family. His first stage job was to cry 'Help' in 'Macbeth' (he was Fleance) with a local touring company; he had further acting experience at school and with another stock company. When he was 17 the family moved to San Diego and there, in 1912, came the Edison Co. to do locations: Lloyd volunteered and was paid $3 to play a near-naked Red Indian extra. He was movie-besotted – the original, almost, of *Merton of the Movies*. He continued to get intermittent extra work until a fellow-extra, Hal Roach, inherited a few thousand dollars and invited Lloyd to join him in his own company. They experimented with a character called Willie Work, played by Lloyd, but none of the shorts they made found a buyer. One short they did, *Just Nuts* (15), was, however, liked enough by Pathé for that studio to approach Roach: but at this point Lloyd left because he discovered that Roach was paying Roy Stewart (the dramatic star of the little company) $10 a day while he was getting $5. He went to Essanay and did a few small parts, but returned to Roach and Pathé some weeks later when offered $50 a week. They worked out a character called Lonesome Luke. Chaplin was their inspiration (for one thing, distributors preferred other comedians to ape him), only where his clothes were too roomy, Luke's were too tight. Lloyd himself loathed the character, but the films, one- and two-reelers, became very popular: starting in January 1916 he made over 100 of them. Sometimes he was making several simultaneously. Lloyd said: 'The picture always ended with 200 feet of chase. I was pursued by dogs, sheriffs, angry housewives, circus tigers, motor-cars, baby carriages, wild bulls, trolley cars, locomotives, and, of course, legions of cops.'

Within a short while Lloyd had worked out a successor to Lonesome Luke. He had the idea of playing a college boy and on to that was grafted the mild manner (and spectacles) of a screen hero whom he had recently seen, a person who was not so mild when roused. To his surprise Pathé gave their permission to try out the new character, which Lloyd did, in early 1917, in *Over the Fence*, a one-reeler. He continued making the Lonesome Luke shorts till the end of that year and then Pathé let him drop them. He stuck to one reel only for his glass character, as he called him: with Roach's cooperation, and sometimes writing and directing himself, he did around half a dozen alongside Luke; but once that character was out of the way, he did not stop – around 60 were released in 1918 and another 30 in 1919. Almost all of them included two stalwarts from the Lonesome Luke period, Bebe Daniels and Snub Pollard. In 1919 Pathé suggested that Lloyd become more ambitious and do two-reelers. The first was *Bumping into Broadway*, followed by *Captain Kidd's Kids*, after which Bebe Daniels defected and Lloyd found a new heroine, Mildred Davis: she was featured in all his films until *Safety Last*, when her contract expired. Lloyd married her and she retired. Meanwhile, she made her début in *From Hand to Mouth* and after the next, *His Royal Slyness*, the formula changed slightly – when Pollard left. More seriously, during the making of *Haunted Spooks* (20), Lloyd was posing for a publicity photograph with what was thought to be a papier mâché prop bomb – only it was not; seriously injured, he was hospitalized for six months and handicapped thereafter by the loss of his right thumb and forefinger and a stiffness in that hand. Apparently Douglas Fairbanks believed that the accident rendered Lloyd's contract with Roach null and void, so he made overtures to him to join United Artists: Lloyd knew that once there he would always be in Chaplin's shadow, but he used the offer to make Roach increase his salary for the second time that year: he had already had a $100 weekly increase, and it now went from $400 to $500 a week, plus 50 per cent of the profits, but this remained nothing compared to what Chaplin and even Arbuckle were making.

The film was finally completed and Lloyd did *An Eastern Westerner* and then *High and Dizzy*, the first time he attempted sky-scraping on a grand scale; following were *Get*

Out and Get Under and *Number Please*, the last one Roach directed. Lloyd moved on to three-reelers: *Now or Never* (21), *Among Those Present*, *I Do* (though that was cut to two reels after previewing) and *Never Weaken*, another successful excursion into the high and dizzy. And then four-reelers: *A Sailor-Made Man* – which proved that the public would accept him as a feature attraction. *Grandma's Boy* (22) was a five-reeler and those that followed were six or more: the new Pathé contract signed in 1921 stipulated six features and Lloyd welcomed the change. His profit participation had already gone to 75 per cent and was now to go to 80 per cent, with the 20 per cent to Roach being now regarded as the use of his studio facilities. Already he had managed to give his character a variety of professions and now he was able to develop stronger plot lines. The first premeditated feature was *Dr Jack* (22), in the title-role, but it was little more than a series

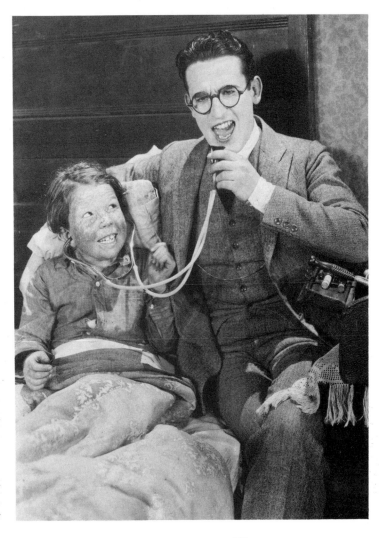

Harold Lloyd as Doctor Jack *(22). Lloyd's ceaseless efforts to give his work variety miscast him, in this case, as a useful member of society: but he fortunately turns out to have the most unorthodox ways of attending his patients.*

In the Twenties audiences gasped at, were thrilled by, and laughed at Harold Lloyd's antics on the sides and tops of skyscrapers: here, in the most memorable of his high-climbing feats, in Safety Last *(23). It's a sure bet that a hundred years from now audiences will be reacting similarly.*

of gags; but half of *Safety Last* (23) consists of the famous vertical climb (as a store employee he replaces a professional climber in a publicity stunt). Audiences were, in fact, thrilled more than amused – to the tune of making the picture one of the year's top five money-makers. Sam Taylor joined Fred Newmeyer – who had directed the previous features – as co-director and they worked together on all Lloyd's subsequent pictures. Lloyd also broke with Roach, reporting directly to Pathé, and the Harold Lloyd Corporation paid him $1,000 per week; he was still to enjoy his large profit participation: 70 per cent of the gross up to $250,000, then 50 per cent up to $500,000 and 65 per cent of any monies taken in excess of that.

The new leading lady was Jobyna Ralston: she first appeared in *Why Worry?* in which they were involved in a South American revolution. *Girl Shy* (24) was one of the year's top five money-makers, due possibly to the climactic ride on top of a runaway streetcar. The *Hot Water* he was in was caused by troublesome in-laws and his new 'used' car; then he was *The Freshman* (25) – the shy college boy who scores the winning goal. This

took over $2½ million at the box-office, one of the most successful of all Silent pictures.

His contract with Pathé was up and he asked for one that was more flexible. Paramount offered terms which after negotiation were the most attractive ever put to an artist: the company would pay for the Corporation's sales and advertising, which it would still control – while Lloyd was offered 77½ per cent of the domestic gross and 90 per cent of the foreign, unless he should want an advance to a ceiling of $500,000 for production, in which case the first figure was amended to 75 per cent. As before, he had complete artistic control and the ownership of the negative. The first under this agreement were: *For Heaven's Sake* (26), as a wealthy do-gooder; *The Kid Brother* (27), who helped the sheriff recover the gold, and *Speedy* (28), as a cab-driver with an obsession for baseball. Lloyd had tried never to repeat himself. He knew he could never top the climax of *Safety Last*, but he opted for variety and these three films respectively feature a beautifully managed chase, almost as magical as any of Keaton's, a fight-to-the-death with a huge brute and a street battle. About this time he published an autobiography, 'An American Comedy'. With the advent of the Talkies came *Welcome Stranger* (29), venturing into Chinatown, shot as a Silent and completely refilmed before the première. He did not care for the restrictions imposed by early Sound, but it was a success. However, his first real Talkie, *Feet First* (30), was so disappointing at the box-office, despite another high building antic, that Paramount considered cancelling the distribution agreement. Lloyd decided that he should have a co-star of some rank to help the box-office and brought in Constance Cummings for *Movie Crazy* (32), a variation on the plot of *Merton of the Movies*: it opened to warm notices but did only fair business. He blamed Paramount's distribution arm, who swiftly replied that they were in the midst of a Depression, that his profits were low because his costs were high – of the level Paramount marked only for a Cooper or a Dietrich picture.

Joseph Schenck offered him $350,000 for a film, presumably to be distributed by United Artists, but Lloyd preferred to go to Fox, now headed by Sidney Kent, who had brought him to Paramount. Fox, however, was in receivership and could not advance costs, so Lloyd borrowed $250,000 from a bank. He decided to leave the go-getter character he had played since donning specs, to subordinate gags to plot and to use a popular novel as his source, Clarence Budington Kelland's *The Cat's Paw* (34), the story of an innocent conned into running for mayor by gangsters. It did not do well and exhibitors were resentful that they had had to book it on the same terms as the very successful Will Rogers vehicles. As Lloyd's biographer Tom Dardis says, 'The talking Lloyd lost thousands of his old fans every time he released a new film . . . He lacked that special magic of personality required to compete against the [new] performers in the best comedy films.' He himself was aware that less than a handful of Silent stars had survived and when Schenck declined to advance him any money for his next venture he returned to Paramount, as a salaried performer (for the first time since 1923). The studio, in any case, had just bought a property ideally suited, *The Milky Way* (36), about a timid milkman who becomes a prize-fighter; they were willing to pay him $125,000, to offer the Lloyd Corporation 50 per cent of the net profits and that the director be Leo McCarey, considered Hollywood's best in the comedy business. It did even less well than *The Cat's Paw*, but on the strength of the notices Lloyd had put forward a cooperative deal which Paramount almost would not have signed had they seen the returns. He would get no salary, but would receive a 15 per cent of the net receipts up to

$1 million; and any costs above $600,000 would be borne by him: these were considerable, since he was a perfectionist, and as with its predecessor it was a long time shooting: but *Professor Beware* (38) looked less like a high-budget comedy than an assembly of gags and chases from the Silent days, as an Egyptologist is plagued by a daffy girl who believes in reincarnation. It would be 25 years, after the advent of films on television, before either he or Paramount would see a return on their investments. In 1940 he did contemplate another film, but said: 'I had come to the conclusion nobody had any particular use for me as a comedian any more.' He decided that his comedy expertise could be valuable and he produced *A Guy a Girl and a Gob* (41) with Lucille Ball and *My Favorite Spy* (42) with Kay Kyser, but these were clinkers for RKO.

He did not return to the studios till Preston Sturges, at the start of his sad decline and with the connivance of Howard Hughes, decided to examine the fate of *The Freshman* in middle age (failure as a clerk, followed by misjudged slapstick), for a fee of $150,000, which included footage from that film: *The Sin of Harold Diddlebock* (47). Lloyd did not like the material and most scenes were filmed his way and Sturges's: the critics and the public agreed with Lloyd and hastily retitled *Mad Wednesday* it did no better. Hughes reissued it in 1951 after he took over control of RKO, but again to general apathy. Lloyd sued Hughes for the loss of his reputation 'as an outstanding motion picture star and personality' and accepted $30,000 in damages. He turned down further offers. An extremely wealthy man, he did not need the money. In 1952 a special Oscar was awarded him, 'Harold Lloyd, master comedian and good citizen'. In 1962 he put together a compilation of his best old stuff, *Harold Lloyd's World of Comedy*, and it was so popular that he did another one a couple of years later, *Harold Lloyd's Funny Side of Life*. He died in California in 1971.

Lloyd in The Freshman (25): *he lost his coat instead of his pants, too easy a way to get a laugh. But when audiences didn't laugh at previews, he re-shot – losing both.*

MARGARET LOCKWOOD

Margaret Lockwood was not by any means a great screen actress, but she was spirited and likeable: the British pubic queued to see her until blatant mishandling ruined her career. Possibly (age apart) she might not have retained her popularity: there was something about her South-London-bred personality which suited the 40s and by the mid-50s she and her fellows (Phyllis Calvert, Patricia Roc, Jean Kent) were passée as far as the cinema was concerned. One can only speculate as to what they might have been like had they ever had good scripts or first-rate directors during their heydays, though the critic Milton Shulman, in the 'Evening Standard' in 1946, had little doubt; in an open letter to Mr Rank he claimed that he could find five girls as pretty and talented as this bunch by watching the secretaries get off the escalators in Leicester Square station.

Maggie Lockwood was born in Karachi in 1916. She studied for the stage at the Italia Conti School and made her first stage appearance as a fairy in 'A Midsummer Night's Dream' in 1928 at the Holborn Empire. She later walked-on in 'Cavalcade'; and studied at RADA. Her first success was in 'Family Affairs' (34), which led to a small part in *Lorna Doone* (34). Victoria Hopper was Lorna and Dorothy Hyson had the second lead: when the latter fell ill Lockwood took over and British Lion offered a long-term contract. She was a starlet of some promise through *The Case of Gabriel Perry* (35), *Some Day* and *Honours Easy*, a 'revenge' drama. Her first leading role was in *Midshipman Easy* and her biggest early breaks came when she was cast with Douglas Fairbanks Jr in *Man of the Moment*, poor though it was, and then leading lady to Maurice Chevalier in the English version of *The Beloved Vagabond* (a French one was made simultaneously with Betty Stockfeld). 'Variety' said she 'had a pleasing personality and a voice that is less British than the average. Her wistfulness reminds me of Janet Gaynor.' She was the fresh young heroine in another half-dozen films: *Jury's Evidence*, *The Amateur Gentleman* (Fairbanks again), *Irish for Luck* (36), *The Street Singer* (Arthur Tracy), *Who's Your Lady Friend?* (37), with Vic Oliver and Frances Day, and *Melody and Romance*, as the ingénue in this vehicle for boy-star Hughie Green 'and his gang'. Gainsborough borrowed her for *Dr Syn* with George Arliss, and after a few days negotiated to buy her contract. She was in *Owd Bob* and in Carol Reed's *Bank Holiday* (38), an affectionate look at a British institution and her role as a nurse bent on a 'dirty weekend' (she has second thoughts) established her as the white hope of British films. She made another for Reed, *A Girl Must Live*, a comedy about showgirls involved with the aristocracy, and Hitchcock's superb thriller, *The Lady Vanishes*. She was not really up to the demands of either role and when she and Michael Redgrave swop insults on Hitchcock's transcontinental express you feel that they would have been happier at a suburban tennis club. She was now earning £6,000 a year.

Gainsborough wanted to send her to Hollywood under a lend-lease scheme operated with 20th Century-Fox (and perhaps with Paramount, since she moved on there: neither studio sent anyone in return, but both would have wanted to be on good terms, because of Gainsborough's financial links with the circuit which showed their films in Britain). She was Randolph Scott's romantic interest in *Susannah of the Mountains*, with Shirley Temple, and Fairbanks Jr's again in *Rulers of the Sea* (39). She had little more to do than smile in sickly fashion and the experience was not a happy one. When she returned to Britain she found herself much in demand: *The Stars Look Down*, doing her first villainess, the flibbertigibbet who marries teacher Michael Redgrave and abandons him for Emlyn Williams, and *Night Train to Munich* (40), as the daughter of a refugee, involved with the Nazis and Rex Harrison. Carol Reed directed both and for him she was *The Girl in the News*, wrongfully accused of murder. With Michael Wilding she had a supposedly *Quiet Wedding* (41), a stagey but agreeable light comedy and that year she ceded her role in Reed's *The Young Mr Pitt* to Phyllis Calvert when she found that she was pregnant. After a poor performance in *Alibi* (42), a remake of *L'Alibi* with Raymond Lovell in the von Stroheim part, she played in *The Man in Grey* (43) and that made her a super-star – in Britain, at any rate. Audiences loved her as Hesther, who steals her best friend's husband and later murders her, only to find that he spurns her. She cornered the British market in feminine deviousness and that lasted her for several years (just as the same film established James Mason as her male equivalent). There were other films – *Dear Octopus*, *Give Us the Moon* (44) and most notably the riotous *Love*

Hugh Williams and Margaret Lockwood en route for the sea in Bank Holiday *(38), an enjoyable study of the way some of the British take their pleasures.*

Felix Aylmer, Margaret Lockwood and Patricia Roc in The Wicked Lady *(45). Aylmer is dying and there are no prizes for guessing who put the poison in his porridge.*

Story in which she, a pianist with a fatal disease, fought with Pat Roc over Stewart Granger, an RAF pilot who was going blind. She never did take any of this stuff seriously, but begged for better parts. She was a frightened heroine in *A Place of One's Own* (45) susceptible to ectoplasm, and an Edwardian music-hall star in *I'll Be Your Sweetheart*, her singing voice dubbed. The same year came her apotheosis as *The Wicked Lady*, with Mason and Roc, as a calculating husband-pinching murderous bitch who, to further amuse herself, takes to playing highwaywoman at night. Audiences then lapped it up and today the film remains great, if doubtful, fun. She was the bad *Bedelia* (46), poisonous and worse, as dictated by Vera Caspary's novel; and was patient and afflicted in a version of Daphne du Maurier's *Hungry Hill*, ageing to matriarchy. She signed a new seven-year contract with Rank, who controlled Gainsborough and who made her repeat this pattern of sinning and suffering: *Jassy* (47), as a gypsy marrying into a Technicolored aristocracy and being accused of murder; and *The White Unicorn*, being misunderstood because of a baby. She was, she told Rank, sick of sinning.

Her popularity was astonishing. In 1946 she replaced Greer Garson as Britain's favourite female star and twice again she was in the list of top money-makers in Britain. During the same three years she was overwhelmingly voted Britain's Best Actress by the readers of the 'Daily Mail'. She was in the Britons-only list consistently from 1943 to 1949. Hollywood dangled contracts – she was offered *Forever Amber* – but she was not tempted. However, she finally began to quarrel with Rank about her parts and films. She refused to do the role Jean Kent eventually played in *The Magic Bow* and was later suspended for refusing an innocuous little comedy, *Once Upon a Dream* (which Googie Withers did); but, as was observed at the time, one could feel little sympathy because she promptly accepted an even worse one, *Look Before You Love* (48). Indeed, that bore a strong claim to being the worst film of the year – until *Madness of the Heart* came along to squash all competition, with Lockwood as a blind girl whose husband's ex-fiancée keeps trying to murder her. Rank had got the message and did not show it to the critics. She played Nell Gwynn in *Cardboard Cavalier*, a period comedy which vainly tried to capture the considerable talent of comic Sid Field. She had pleaded for the part, but the best that could be said for her comedy technique was that she was hearty and well-meaning. Rank then promised her a good film. She turned down several subjects which might have been ideal (*The Browning Version* and *The Reluctant Widow*: Jean Kent played both) and several films were announced which never materialized (*Elisabeth of Austria* and *Ann Veronica*). In the end, she made a modest thriller, *Highly Dangerous* (50): a Hollywood leading man (Dane Clark) was imported and for the first time in 10 years she was given a director who was better than mediocre (Roy Baker). Eric Ambler wrote the script and the result was reasonably, if not highly, entertaining.

Her Rank contract was dissolved and she

Cast a Dark Shadow (55):
*Margaret Lockwood gave
a good character study of a
wealthy widow who
marries Dirk Bogarde.
Here's a wedding-day toast
from Philip Stainton.*

signed a two-year contract with Herbert Wilcox, who had been churning out a series of very successful vehicles for his wife, Anna Neagle. Neagle had supplanted Lockwood as Britain's No 1 female star and thus much was made of this move. Doubtless Lockwood felt that what Wilcox had done for his wife, he could do for her. She could not have been more wrong. The first was a dull version of a classic mystery tale, *Trent's Last Case* (52), and the second an inadequate version of a Conrad story, *Laughing Anne* (53), in which she was a gay lady out East. Of *Trouble in the Glen* (54), a so-called Scottish comedy, 'Picturegoer' wrote: 'But what actress could stand the dreadful dressing, dreary photography – not to mention the unspeakable script?' With that, the Lockwood-Wilcox association came quietly to an end. She accepted a character role in an independent film, *Cast a Dark Shadow* (55): as the blowsy ex-barmaid who marries Dirk Bogarde she got her best notices in years and might, in a different set-up, have continued her film career as a character actress. But the British film industry seemed no longer interested.

She accepted the decline in her film fortunes with high good humour and returned to the stage. Already, in 1949, she had toured in 'Private Lives' and in 1950 had played Peter Pan. The plays she elected to do were invariably undistinguished, apart from – perhaps – 'An Ideal Husband' (65) when she was most accomplished as Mrs Cheveley. The same year she had a successful TV series, 'The Flying Swan', and in 1970 she played in Somerset Maugham's 'Lady Frederick'. She

had the misfortune to return to the screen in a dopey version of 'Cinderella', *The Slipper and the Rose* (76) – though looking radiant as the wicked stepmother. Her daughter Juliet acted in films and on the stage for a while; nowadays she fends off would-be biographers by explaining that her mother is a recluse.

CAROLE LOMBARD

Very early on, movie stars became confused with gods and goddesses. As the cinema grew up the concept went completely out of fashion, but there is a strong case to be made for the divinity of Carole Lombard. One is certain that, at Olympian banquets, she is right up there next to Zeus. If she is not (invited), she is probably throwing things. Lombard's tantrums were a staple of 30s screwball comedy, though these were the least of her. Catherine da la Roche wrote ('Sight and Sound', 1953) that she was 'the most delicate satirical comedienne the screen has ever had'. Here are two colleagues' views: Barbara Stanwyck (explaining why Lombard was Hollywood's most interesting person in 1936): '. . . because she is so alive, modern, frank, and natural that she stands out like a beacon on a lightship in this odd place called Hollywood', and Bing Crosby: 'She had a delicious sense of humour; she was one of the screen's greatest comediennes and, in addition, she was very beautiful. The electricians, carpenters and prop men all adored her because she was so regular; so devoid of temperament and showboating. . . . The fact that she could make us think of her as being a good guy rather than a sexy mamma is one of those unbelievable manifestations impossible to explain.'

She was born Jane Peters in 1908 in Fort Wayne, Indiana. Her parents were divorced while she was young and she moved with her mother and brothers to Los Angeles. Her movie début came when she was spotted in a neighbour's yard by Allan Dwan, who was visiting that family; he was then directing for Fox and needed just such a high-spirited girl to play Monte Blue's daughter in *A Perfect Crime* (21). She continued at high school, went to a drama school and kept hoping for another movie chance: she was tested for the lead in *The Gold Rush*, but another test, at Fox, did get her the female lead opposite Edmund Lowe in *Marriage in Transit* (25), at $75 per week. Fox changed her name to Carole Lombard (though the 'e' on Carol disappeared for a while, returning for good in 1930) and signed her to a five-year contract. However, after *Hearts and Spurs*, a Buck Jones Western, she was involved in an automobile accident and it was annulled because her face was scarred. When she recovered she got a job with Mack Sennett, appearing in two-reelers, including *The Girl From Everywhere* (27), *His Unlucky Night* and *The Swim Princess* (28). During this time she rose from $50 a week to $400 and learnt the timing which was the basis of her comedy technique.

She left Sennett and got small parts in *The Perfect Crime* at FBO with Clive Brook and in Raoul Walsh's *Me Gangster* at Fox: the me was Don Terry. Then Pathé gave her a year's contract. The films were not much: *Power*, starring William Boyd, as a flapper; *Show Folks*, starring Eddie Quillan; *Ned McCobb's Daughter*, a version of Sydney Howard's play, with Irene Rich; *High Voltage*, her first all-Talkie, with Boyd and Owen Moore; Gregory La Cava's *Big News*, as the wife of reporter Robert Armstrong; and *The Racketeer*, again with Armstrong. At Fox she vamped *The Arizona Kid* (30) – Warner Baxter, who fell for her only to discover she was a crook (Mona Maris consoled him); then Paramount cast her as one of the reasons for Charles Buddy Rogers's creed, *Safety in Numbers*. (Rogers knew her socially and earlier had tried to pressure Mary Pickford to give her a small role in *My Best Girl*.) Paramount were delighted with her work and signed her to a seven-year contract, starting at $350 a week.

She had good parts in two comedies, *Fast and Loose* with Miriam Hopkins and *It Pays to Advertise* (31) – soap, with Norman Foster. The *Man of the World* and *Ladies Man* were both with William Powell and they were married not long after meeting on the set. She achieved star status without being thought of as anything extraordinary – effervescent and competent as a super-sophisticated but basically nice girl, noted more for her slinky blonde looks, good legs and daring gowns than for anything else: *Up Pops the Devil*, a marital comedy with Stuart Erwin, Lilyan Tashman and Foster; *I Take This Woman*, pursued by cow-hand Gary Cooper; *No One Man* (32) as a pleasure-mad divorcée, with Ricardo Cortez; and *Sinners in the Sun* with Chester Morris, which was little but fashion parades. She was cast in *One Hour With You*, but replaced by Genevieve Tobin and instead loaned to Columbia for a couple: *Virtue* (she had none, as Pat O'Brien's wife, a lady with a Past) and *No More Orchids* (she did not want any; in love with Lyle Talbot, she rejected money for love). As a small-town librarian she had *No Man of Her Own* (33) when gambler Clark Gable walked into her life: he pursued and married her (the comic half) and reformed for her (the dramatic half). She put up a fine showing, but her comic abilities continued to be wasted. Still, she maintained a light touch when she could get away with it: *From Hell to Heaven*, a 'Grand Hotel' imitation with Jack Oakie, as a bookmaker's daughter; *Supernatural*, a silly attempt at a horror picture with Randolph Scott; *The Eagle and the Hawk*, where she had one brief sequence, consoling doughboy Fredric March; *Brief Moment*, as a nightclub singer who marries playboy Gene Raymond to reform him, a poor version of S.N. Behrman's play, at Columbia; and a steamy melodrama, *White Woman*, betraying Charles Laughton with Kent Taylor. And there were fights with the studio when she refused to do *The Way to Love* and refused to be loaned to WB for *Hard to Handle*.

Her roles in *Bolero* (34), where she danced, and *We're Not Dressing*, when she listened, were subsidiary to those of George Raft and Crosby respectively, but it was more than ever clear that here was a witty, sinewy, leading lady; she got a beautiful chance and took it beautifully, as the temperamental actress courted – for professional reasons – by John Barrymore, on a trip in the *Twentieth Century*. Howard Hawks directed for Columbia and it shot Lombard into the forefront of Hollywood stars. Said Barrymore: 'She is perhaps the greatest actress I ever worked with.' It was hardly to be expected that she would be happy playing second fiddle to Shirley Temple in *Now and Forever* and her battling with Paramount intensified. However, two outside pictures did not help: *Lady by Choice* at Columbia was really a vehicle for May Robson, who had recently

Carole Lombard in the days when she was more noteworthy as a beauty than as an actress.

Gary Cooper and Carole Lombard in Henry Hathaway's Now and Forever *(34). Shirley Temple is not in this still but she was much in evidence in the film.*

had a hit in *Lady for a Day*: 'Men Who Loved Her Grew Sadder – but Wiser' said the ads, ambiguously. And *The Gay Bride* at MGM cast her as a mercenary showgirl who marries bootlegger Chester Morris. Said Richard Watts Jr in the 'New York Herald Tribune': 'Miss Lombard achieves the feat of being almost as bad as her picture, and plays her part with neither humour nor conviction.' She did not care much for *Rumba* (35) with Raft (an attempt to cash in on the success of *Bolero*) but liked *Hands Across the Table*, as directed by Mitchell Leisen a film of divine facetiousness: she was again a gold-digger, but as like met like in the person of Fred MacMurray, true love got the better of greed.

Very spoilt and very rich, she did two comedies at Universal: *Love Before Breakfast*, dedicated to the proposition that a man chases a girl until she catches him – and the man was Preston Foster; and *My Man Godfrey*, with ex-husband Powell as a Depression-bum taken on as butler by a family consisting of Lombard, Gail Patrick, Eugene Pallatte, Alice Brady and Mischa Auer: they were all wonderful. There were three in a row with MacMurray, two of them almost as good as that: *The Princess Comes Across* – she was a bogus princess and it was the Atlantic she was crossing; *Swing High Swing Low* (37), one of the several screen versions of 'Burlesque'; and *True Confession*, as a congenital liar in a farce about a murder trial. In *Nothing Sacred* she was a bogus invalid exploited by Fredric March to boost circulation. Said William Whitebait: 'The acting is superb . . . Carole Lombard has a touch of comic genius.' And William Wellman, who directed, said years later, that she was 'the greatest star in the

world . . . the greatest actress . . . she could do anything' (he was not noted for his diplomacy in handling stars; the only female stars he ever liked were Lombard and Barbara Stanwyck).

She was the highest paid star for 1937, at $465,000. Her contract with Paramount had expired in 1936, when she was getting $3,500 per week. They had signed a new deal, worth $2 million, three films a year, beginning at $150,000 per film, and she was permitted to freelance: *Nothing Sacred* was the first of three contracted with Selznick at $175,000 per film. She did not in fact ever make another film for Paramount, because she had script approval and resented the fact that they had tried to turn her and MacMurray into a regular team. At the end of 1937 in 'Film Weekly' Freda Bruce Lockhart wrote: '. . . there is one very significant indication of a star's ranking – Hollywood's own opinion. Every visiting Hollywood producer or director I have spoken to this year has mentioned Carole's name with that mysterious professional enthusiasm whose authenticity cannot be mistaken. And they all declare that she is as fine an emotional actress as a comedienne.'

Fools for Scandal (38) ws a weak comedy at WB with Fernand Gravet. She said: 'I knew it wasn't a sensation when my friends confined their comments to how beautifully I had been photographed.' Its failure caused her to go serious, first with Selznick and then with RKO, with whom her agent got her a deal – in compensation for not getting Scarlett O'Hara – four pictures in two years, at $150,000 plus a percentage of the profits: *Made for Each Other* (39), a comedy of newly-weds that went from comedy to tragedy; *In*

They didn't, alas, make them like this any more. Left, Gregory La Cava's My Man Godfrey *(36): William Powell in the title role and Carole Lombard as the daughter of the house who pursued him – to put it mildly. Right, William A. Wellman's* Nothing Sacred *(37): Lombard, as the heroine of the hour, participates in a fire-rescue operation. With her, Fredric March and John Qualen.*

Name Only, in love with Cary Grant to the chagrin of his wife, Kay Francis; *Vigil in the Night* (40), from A.J. Cronin's novel, beautifully directed by George Stevens, but too virginally perfect as a dedicated nurse who falls for Dr Brian Aherne; and *They Knew What They Wanted*, as the mail-order bride, with Charles Laughton as the immigrant. This is her best straight performance, cleverly scouting the aspects of a woman motivated by money and having to learn the hard way that love is not merely a matter of physical attraction. She returned to comedy with *Mr and Mrs Smith* (41), again for RKO: there are complications when she and Robert Montgomery discover they are not married – an ordinary comedy and Hitchcock's only US film that had nothing to do with murder (he only did it to please Lombard; he 'adored' her, he said). He could have learnt from Lubitsch, whose *To Be or Not To Be* brilliantly uses the unlikely setting of Poland at the onset of the Nazi invasion: Lombard and Jack Benny – two temperamental Shakespearian thespians – lead their troupe in outwitting the Germans (he having jettisoned Miriam Hopkins when he heard that she wanted to do a film). A revival in Paris in 1960–61 ran for more than a year.

She was killed in an air crash in early 1942, when the plane in which she was travelling flew into a mountain near Las Vegas. She had just sold over $2 million worth of war bonds in Indianapolis, near her home town. She left heart-broken widower Clark Gable (they were married in 1939 after a courtship which probably deserved all the affectionate publicity it got). President Roosevelt cabled him: 'She brought joy to all who knew her, and to millions who knew her only as a great artist. . . . She is and always will be a star, one we shall never forget, nor cease to be grateful to.'

MYRNA LOY

It is widely known that Myrna Loy was an Oriental vamp before becoming the perfect screen wife, but it is less generally realized that she made over 60 films before becoming a star; she served a long apprenticeship in Silents – from leads to walk-ons and back again – without ever quite making it. By the time stardom came, she was an excellent all-round actress, but her forte was comedy. She was an adroit and irresistible comedienne, with a dry-martini voice, calm and measured in the two-piece suits and hats that Adrian designed for her – silly hats like saucers cocked over one eye. She was seldom in the kitchen or even by the fireside: perfect wife she may have been, but more for exchanging barbed comments in the Oak Room at the Plaza. Certainly she *cared* – like all the good actresses of that era she had great warmth – but presumably her appeal lay in the fact that she was more chic and more sophisticated than any real wife could be. Both men and women adored her: somewhere around her 80th film she was the most popular female star in Hollywood. And her expertise was much admired – only two or three of today's girls approach it.

She was born in Helena, Montana, in 1905. Her father died when she was 10 and in 1919 the family moved to Los Angeles where for a while she taught dancing; she moved on to the chorus of Grauman's Chinese Theater, dancing in prologues. A photographer, Harry Waxman, noticed her and through him she was tested by Valentino for a part in *Cobra*. She did not get it, but he recommended her to his wife who gave her a brief role in *What Price Beauty* (25, released in 28). Bitten now by the film-bug, Loy was pleased to be tested for the role of the Virgin in *Ben Hur*, but she settled for the briefest of roles as a courtesan; also at MGM she was a chorine in *Pretty Ladies* (25), starring Zazu Pitts.

She haunted the casting offices and then through Waxman she met Lowell Sherman, who thought she might be useful at Warners: they gave her a five-year contract, but in the first film, *Cave Man* (26) starring Matt Moore, she ended in the chorus again. She made five more films that year: *The Gilded Highway*; *Why Girls Go Back Home*, starring Patsy Ruth Miller; *So This is Paris*, directed by Lubitsch, in an unbilled bit as a maid; *Don Juan*, as a spy of the Borgias; and *Across the Pacific*, as a native girl in this tale of the Spanish-American war. Thereafter, till she became a star, she averaged eight films a year. 1927: *Ham and Eggs at the Front*, a Negro army comedy – only the Negroes were 'blackface', including Loy, playing a spy; *The Climbers*, starring Irene Rich; *Bitter Apples*, her first lead, as a girl who marries Monte Blue from revenge and learns to love him; *Simple Sis*, starring Louise Fazenda; *The Jazz Singer*, where she was glimpsed but briefly, as a showgirl; and *The Girl From Chicago*,

Roy del Ruth's Across the Pacific *(26) was a melodrama set in the Philippines starring Monte Blue, who dallied with Myrna Loy between battles.*

second-billed, after Conrad Nagel, in this Underworlder. 1928: *If I Were Single*, supporting Mae McAvoy; *Beware of Married Men*, starring Irene Rich; *Turn Back the Hours*, on loan-out, as a Spanish Beauty; *Crimson City*, which was Shanghai, second-billed again in her first Oriental role; *Heart of Maryland*, starring Dolores Costello; *Pay As You Enter*, supporting Louise Fazenda; *State Street Sadie*, as Slinky, a cop's daughter, in this melodrama with Sound sequences; and *The Midnight Taxi*, as gangster Antonio Moreno's moll. 1929: the spectacular *Noah's Ark*, starring Dolores Costello and George O'Brien, as a dancer in the modern part and a slave girl in the Biblical sequences; *Fancy Baggage*; *The Desert Song*, all-Sound with colour sequences, starring John Boles and Carlotta King, with Loy as Azuri and generally considered to be the best thing in the film; *The Squall*, in a small part as a gypsy adventuress; *The Black Watch*, as an Indian mystery woman at Fox; *Evidence*, as a native girl; *Hard-boiled Rose*, as a Southern belle; and *The Show of Shows*, in two dance sequences. Like many 'Silent' players, Loy was worried by the competition offered by newcomers from the stage and decided to get as much exposure as she could: when Warners did not need her she worked elsewhere. Nine Loy pictures were released in 1930: the third film version of *Cameo Kirby*, starring J. Harold Murray; *The Great Divide*, as a Mexican, starring Dorothy Mackaill and Ian Keith; *Isle of Escape*, as a native belle; *Under a Texan Moon*, getting the guy (Frank Fay) in spite of four exotic contenders – the others were Raquel Torres, Armida and Betty Boyd; *Cock o' the Walk*, a real chance as a potential suicide who is married and then insured by gigolo Joseph Schildkraut – but a pretentious piece, made by an independent producer; *Bride of the Regiment*, back in support, as a camp follower; *The Last of the Duanes*, Zane Grey's Western starring George O'Brien; *The Jazz Cinderella*: 'Myrna Loy and Jason Robards do as well as they can, which isn't much' ('Photoplay'); and *The Truth About Youth*, as Kara, the firefly, a grasping cabaret artist.

Early in 1931, after *Naughty Flirt*, starring Alice White, Warners dropped Loy, but she was established as one of the most reliable leading women in Hollywood and had no difficulty getting work. Most of the year she spent at Fox, starting with *Renegades*, as one of Bela Lugosi's harem, but betraying him for love of hero Warner Baxter. She sang and danced in a minor Western, *Rogue of the Rio Grande*, returning to Fox for: *Body and Soul* starring Elissa Landi and Charles Farrell; *A Connecticut Yankee*, as Morgan Le Faye;

Hush Money; *Transatlantic*, a liner drama, and down to sixth on the cast-list, as a long-suffering wife; and *Skyline*, as builder Thomas Meighan's girlfriend. At RKO she was the Other Woman in both *Rebound* (Ina Claire and Robert Ames), directed by Edward H. Griffith, and *Consolation Marriage* (Irene Dunne and Pat O'Brien). But her best opportunities were in a similar role in two Ronald Colman vehicles, one earlier in the year and the other at its end: the blonde first in *The Devil to Pay* and the sympathetic Joyce in *Arrowsmith*.

Critics were asking when Loy was going to be raised to official stardom, but in Hollywood there was only one producer who could see that she had that extra something – Irving Thalberg. He liked her so much in *Skyline* that he signed her to an MGM contract. She was just treading water at first – indeed, her parts got smaller: *Emma* (32) as Marie Dressler's daughter; *The Wet Parade*; *Vanity Fair*, as Becky in an almost unrecognizable modern version, made by an independent producer and hardly shown; *New Morals for Old*; *The Woman in Room 13*, starring Elissa Landi (Fox); *Love Me Tonight*, as a wise-cracking man-hunter ('Do you ever think about anything but men?' someone asks her, and the reply comes, 'Yes, schoolboys'); *Thirteen Women*, as a (half-caste) homicidal maniac; and, back at MGM, *The Mask of Fu Manchu*, as Manchu's sadistic daughter, a role she considered virtually unplayable. But there were to be no more Oriental parts and as with many another player, it was a loan-out – at the insistence of the director, Edward H. Griffith – which was to show her own studio what she could do, as Leslie Howard's vicious wife in *The Animal Kingdom*: she herself considered this her first real break in pictures. RKO liked her so much they kept her to play the tycoon's kind-hearted mistress in *Topaze* (33) and Dwight Macdonald observed that she was 'the most attractive, intelligent, and charming of present-day movie actresses'.

MGM decided to build Loy and for the first time officially listed her as one of their stars, but *The Barbarian* was a dopey start, as the British socialite who is the object of Ramon Novarro's passion: she is kidnapped and after bathing with rose petals are her off-screen screams because she is being both whipped and raped? She loves him in the end, anyway. Since we now know her as the perfect wife it is nice today to see her up to her neck in fantasy. She looked chic and MGM put her into the sort of smart roles RKO had proved she could play: *The Prizefighter and the Lady*, a vehicle for boxer Max Baer and rechristened *Every Woman's Man* for Britain – Loy was his wife; *When Ladies Meet*, as the young writer;

and *Penthouse*, as a heart-of-gold callgirl used by Warner Baxter to get an underworld confession (demonstrating, said 'Picturegoer', what strides she had made in her acting ability). *Night Flight* was the first of several movies with Clark Gable and the first of Loy's Perfect Wives (only here she was William Gargan's). In *Men in White* (34) Gable was a doctor and she a flighty society dame and in *Manhattan Melodrama* he was a gangster and she a nice girl who deserts him for politician William Powell. (The film gained notoriety – and a quite undeserved popularity – by virtue of the fact that Dillinger the gangster was trapped while watching it and shot while emerging from the cinema.)

The director was W.S. Van Dyke, who became convinced that Loy and Powell could be profitably teamed in comedy; MGM saw them both primarily as heavies, but gave the go-ahead for a film version of Dashiell Hammett's light-hearted murder mystery, *The Thin Man*. The result swept the world. It was something quite new: Nick and Norah Charles, affluent private eye and wife, bantering, and affectionately bitching each other; their chief interest seemed to be alcohol and neither could be said not to have a philandering nature. she: 'Go ahead, see if I care. But I think it's a dirty trick to bring me all the way to New York just to make a widow of me.' He: 'You wouldn't be a widow long.' She: 'You bet I wouldn't.' He: 'Not with all your money.' There was a spontaneous gaiety which had much to do with the understated incisiveness of the stars' playing. Their styles matched perfectly and it is obvious (as Loy has confirmed) that they loved acting together. The team became one of the keystones of MGM in the 30s.

Now a big star, she was wasted in one of the manifold screen versions of the 'Fraulein Doktor' tale, *Stamboul Quest* with George Brent, but was Powell's wife again in *Evelyn Prentice*, on trial for murdering a blackmailer, with him defending her. She was loaned to Columbia to play a high-spirited rich girl in Capra's delightful version of Damon Runyon's horse-racing tale, *Broadway Bill*, with Baxter; and to Paramount for *Wings in the Dark* (35) with Cary Grant, playing a stunt flyer. As she emerged into the limelight, Loy was seen to be one of the least typical of movie actresses: a shy, quiet girl, living with her mother, working hard without any great ambition to be Queen of the Lot. She considered that she had been working *too* hard and her salary, at $1,500 a week, was only half of Powell's. Starting *Escapade* with him, clearly miscast (it was Paula Wessely's role in *Maskerade*, bought by Metro) and learning that Luise Rainer was being tested,

Most of the Myrna Loy – William Powell pictures were smart comedies with sophisticated dialogue, but Love Crazy (*41*), *being mainly slapstick, was a new departure. It was still very funny. They were married at the start of the film – and at the very end – and in-between-whiles dickered with divorce.*

she forced the studio to give her a release and left for Europe. After a number of legal threats MGM gave her a revised contract and $100,000 for signing it. She returned for *Whipsaw*, but Powell was not ready and Spencer Tracy replaced him. She was a jewel thief and he her pursuer. Said 'Time': '. . . but Myrna Loy's charm and Tracy's skilful underplaying are assets that no picture can have and be bad.'

Wife vs Secretary (36) had Jean Harlow as the latter and Gable as the husband; *Petticoat Fever* was a farce with Robert Montgomery; Loy was Billie Burke, the wife of *The Great Ziegfeld* (Powell); and at 20th gave one of her best performances opposite Warner Baxter in a tale of marital discord, *To Mary With Love* ('They say the movies should be more like life – I think life should be more like the movies'). After *Libelled Lady* (Powell, Tracy, Harlow) and *After the Thin Man* (it was up to the original), she accepted the part that Joan Crawford turned down in *Parnell* (37) – Katie O'Shea. Its commercial and critical failure harmed neither her nor Gable and in Ed Sullivan's poll they were voted King and Queen of Hollywood. Loy also entered the exhibitors' top 10 list, trailing Shirley Temple and Sonja Henie as the nation's biggest female draw (in 1937 and 1938). She was happily back wth Powell in the screwball *Double Wedding*, but less happy as the spoilt ingénue in *Manproof* (38) with Franchot Tone, an insufferably dull drama. She was

admirable as a country girl who marries *Test Pilot* Gable and as his romantic interest in *Too Hot to Handle*; but neither she nor Robert Taylor found *Lucky Night* (39) very lucky. 'Here's a galloping case of whimsy,' said 'Photoplay'.

In a deliberate attempt to get away from type-casting Loy asked 20th whether she could play the silly socialite who found redemption when *The Rains Came*. Then she did a run with Powell: *Another Thin Man*, *I Love You Again* (40), the deft *Third Finger Left Hand* (partnered instead by Melvyn Douglas), *Love Crazy* (41), some fun on the old divorce game – mad, vulgar, logical and witty, and *Shadow of the Thin Man*. There were rumours of retirement: she had been upset over two broken marriages (she married twice again, first to writer-producer Gene Markey, who had been married to Joan Bennett and Hedy Lamarr); she asked MGM for leave-of-absence and spent the war years working full-time for the Red Cross. MGM announced that Irene Dunne would replace her in the next Thin Man movie, but in fact Loy did it, her only wartime picture, *The Thin Man Goes Home* (44). Then, with one year to go, she asked for release from her contract. She had watched the other great MGM female stars of the 30s leave unmourned; she had seen Dunne, Colbert and Hepburn arrive to play her sort of roles; she was being offered nothing interesting – yet the studio refused to let her to go to Broadway for 'State of the

Union' (which was written for her) or to London to play Elvira in *Blithe Spirit*. The last straw came when Hepburn was cast in *Sea of Grass*, bought for Loy and Tracy (who, ironically, had chased Loy – unsuccessfully – till Hepburn came into his life). She promised she would return if ever they wanted her to do another comedy with Powell. She did *Song of the Thin Man* (47), but like the 1944 one it was, in her own words, 'very bad indeed'.

In 1946 she attended the initial meetings of the United Nations; went to Paris as an observer with the American delegation and in 1949 was with UNESCO. Hence she filmed thereafter only occasionally, as a freelance. She sought to change her image but hardly did: she was soon playing perfect mothers. There was a period comedy at Universal with Don Ameche, *So Goes My Love* (46): said Richard Winnington, 'Myrna Loy is much too lovely and clever for such nonsense'; and then came the apotheosis of her screen wife portrayal, *The Best Years of Our Lives*. The part was built up for her because Goldwyn and Wyler were determined to have her and she considered it too small; Fredric March was the husband and Teresa Wright her daughter. The film was a huge success. RKO released and

Loy had a three-year contract at that studio, but did only two more films there – *The Bachelor and the Bobby Soxer* (47) with Cary Grant and the amusing *Mr Blandings Builds His Dream House* (48), with – after The *Thin Man* film – Grant and Melvyn Douglas as her leading men. At Republic, under Lewis Milestone's direction, she was the mother in John Steinbeck's *The Red Pony* (49), but, like some other Milestone films, it did not turn out as well as expected.

She signed a one-picture deal with Korda in Britain and it was announced as being *Love in Idleness* (which, coincidentally, RKO bought for her, but never filmed) with Ralph Richardson; instead she did a perfectly dreadful sudser about a woman's affair with her stepdaughter's boyfriend (Richard Greene) while her husband goes blind: *That Dangerous Age*. For 20th she played the mother of a large brood in *Cheaper by the Dozen* (50) and its success led to a sequel, *Belles on Their Toes* (52). She accepted an assignment to be one of the US representatives with UNESCO in Paris and while there took a poor part (but with star billing) in a poor comedy, *The Ambassador's Daughter* (56). Back in Hollywood, she played an alcoholic wife (Robert

Myrna Loy and Jack Lemmon on the set of The April Fools (69): *Lemmon also produced and it was he who persuaded Loy back before the cameras after a nine-year absence. She and Charles Boyer played a middle-aged couple who encouraged Lemmon and Catherine Deneuve to run off together.*

Ryan's) in *Lonelyhearts* (58) and an alcoholic mother (Paul Newman's) in *From the Terrace* (60). For this and for *Midnight Lace* – Doris Day's aunt, the best thing in the film – she accepted below-title billing.

The failure of her fourth marriage, to a Washington bigwig, was one reason for this renewed activity. Tempted by the stage and spurning many offers, she eventually accepted the challenge, beginning in stock with 'Marriage-Go-Round'. She toured in 'There Must Be a Pony!', which did not reach New York, and in the national tour of 'Barefoot in the Park'. She would like to film again, she said in 1967, but did not want to play the sort of 'psychotic, disintegrated old bags' which were being offered to the older actresses; other offers 'that have come up have, frankly, not been exciting enough' (they include the Chinese Empress in *55 Days to Peking*, the mother of Lana Turner in *Madame X* which Kay Francis also turned down, the Norah Charles role in *Murder by Death* and a role in *Voyage of the Damned*). She did elect to do *The April Fools* (69), married to Charles Boyer and befriending Jack Lemmon, after which she was in a clutch of tele-movies: *Death Takes a Holiday* (71), reunited with Melvyn Douglas; *Do Not Fold Spindle or Mutilate* with Helen Hayes; *The Couple Takes a Wife* (72) with Paula Prentiss, as her mother; *Indict or Convict* (74) with George Grizzard, as a judge; and *The Elevator* with James Farentino. During this period she made her Broadway début as the mother in a revival of 'The Women' and after the Farentino piece she returned to the big screen in *Airport 1975*, as a tippling passenger. After another tele-film, *It Happened at Lakewood Manor* (77), she played Burt Reynolds's mother in *The End* (78), reunited with a co-star of 1931, Pat O'Brien. Reynolds said that he had been trying to find a role for her in one of his films for a long time and so did director Sidney Lumet, who made her Alan King's devoted secretary in *Just Tell Me What You Want* (80). Her last credit to date is another TV movie, *Summer Solstice* (81), opposite Henry Fonda. Her autobiography, 'Seeing and Believing' (87), is one of the best books ever written on show business, having charm, perception, honesty and – which is not quite the same thing – a sense of realism. It reflects, in fact, those qualities we have always admired in her acting.

PAUL LUKAS

At the outset of his career, in the Silent days, Paul Lukas was cast as the suave Middle-

European seducer. As he aged, his thoughts turned otherwise than to women, but he remained villainous – the epitome of that experienced Continental elegance that was always such a bogyman for Hollywood script-writers. He did it very well: smooth, sharply shod, upright, moustached and with sleek hair that was always slightly greying. To that extent he did what was required of him. He realized very early on that if he wanted a Hollywood career he was going to be type-cast and he simply played his specious lines as professionally as he knew how. He always regretted that his accent limited him. He did, now and then, get to play sympathetic parts and for one of these he won his Oscar.

He was born on a train in Budapest in 1895 and received his stage training at the Actors' Academy of Hungary; he made his début in the title-role of Molnar's 'Liliom' in his native city in 1916 and for the next nine years played, says one source, 'every conceivable character in the works of Shakespeare, Chekhov, George Bernard Shaw, Oscar Wilde and Galsworthy'. He was also making films: *Sphynx* (17), *Udvari Levego, Sárga Árnyék* (20), *Little Fox*, *Névtelen Vár* (the first one to be shown outside Hungary, as *Castle Nameless*), *Masomód, Olavi, Szinészno, New York Exprez Kábel* (21) and *Hétszázéves Szerelem*. Max Reinhardt saw him on the Budapest stage and negotiated for him to act in Berlin and Vienna. In Vienna, he was engaged by a fellow Hungarian, Alexander Korda, to appear in *Eine Versunkene Welt* (22), a story of sea and politics, as one of the crew, and he was engaged by him again for *Samson und Delila*.

He returned to Budapest and *A Szürkeruhás Hölgy, Lady Violette, Diadalmas Élet* (23) and *Egy Fiunak a Fele*; and was appearing on the stage there in 'Antonia' when he was seen by the head of Paramount, Adolph Zukor, there on a visit to what was his native land also. Zukor offered a Paramount contract and Lukas left for Hollywood. He made his bow in a Pola Negri picture, *Three Sinners* (28), and was then loaned out for the Colman-Banky *Two Lovers*. He made *Hot News* with Bebe Daniels; *The Night Watch* at First National, as Billie Dove's husband, a naval melodrama; *The Loves of an Actress* and *The Woman From Moscow*, both with Negri; and *Manhattan Cocktail* with Nancy Carroll and Richard Arlen. He was then cast opposite Carroll in *The Shopworn Angel* (29): she had the title-role, as the 'kept woman' who falls for the younger Gary Cooper. This was part-Talkie and so, originally, was the *The Wolf of Wall Street*, but during production the studio liked it so much that the Silent sequences were redone: Lukas's part was painstakingly dubbed by Lawford Davidson. His role, anyway, was already brief because of his accent: the stars were Carroll and George Bancroft (in the title-role).

Lukas's future in the US was now in the balance. He had not reached the front rank of stars and therefore it would not harm his prestige to retire to smaller roles, which was what he did after some months of inactivity, in another Carroll vehicle, *Illusion*. He stayed with Paramount: *Halfway to Heaven* with Charles Buddy Rogers; *Behind the Makeup* (30), in a role that was little more than a bit; *Slightly Scarlet* (30) starring Evelyn Brent and Clive Brook; *The Benson Murder Case* starring William Powell; *Young Eagles*, William A. Wellman's follow-up to his own *Wings*, again with Charles Buddy Rogers; *The Devil's Holiday* with Phillips Holmes and Carroll (replacing Jeanne Eagles, who had just died); *Grumpy*, who was British actor Cyril Maude reprising his famous stage role in his screen début; and *Anybody's Woman*, as Ruth Chatterton's lover before she returned to husband Clive Brook. Lukas's accent had diminished enough to allow him to be Chatterton's leading man in her next two: it was him she had *The Right to Love* (31) and him with whom she was *Unfaithful*. Paramount thought their 'worldliness' well matched. In *City Streets* he was the vicious gang boss with whom Gary Cooper got involved and in *The Vice Squad* an embassy attaché-turned-informer loved by Kay Francis. There followed: *Women Love Once*; *Beloved Bachelor*, starring, in the title-role, as a man who adopts an orphan (Dorothy Jordan) and later falls in love with her; *Strictly Dishonorable*, the film of Preston Sturges's play at Universal, as the lecherous opera singer intent on seducing the innocent and impressed Sidney Fox; *Working Girls*, as a lecherous archaeologist, with Judith Wood and Dorothy Hall in the title-roles; *Tomorrow and Tomorrow* (32) as a Viennese psychiatrist, with Chatterton; *No One Man*, one of the idle rich, opposite Carole Lombard; and *Thunder Below* with Tallulah Bankhead.

At this point Lukas left Paramount and began to freelance. Nevertheless his next picture, *A Passport to Hell*, was like his last – only this time it was Elissa Landi who was the bone of contention in the lonely outpost. He then supported John Gilbert, as the butler who is cuckolded by him, in *Downstairs* and Constance Bennett in *Rockabye* (33). He co-starred with Loretta Young in *Grand Slam* and then had a good part in James Whale's fine *A Kiss Before the Mirror* as the husband who murders his faithless wife, almost prompting Frank Morgan to follow suit with his, Nancy Carroll. Universal produced and

signed Lukas to a loose two-year contract. He did *Sing Sinner Sing* at Majestic, with Leila Hyams, based on the Libby Holman case; *Captured!* at Warners as a German officer; *The Secret of the Blue Room*, having to spend a night in it in order to qualify for the hand of Gloria Stuart; and *Little Women* (34), as the shy and gentle Professor Bhaer, virtually his first chance in Hollywood to exploit his versatility. With one exception, his next seven pictures were all for Universal: *By Candlelight* with Landi, as the perfect valet trying to emulate his philandering master, Nils Asther – and as so often in comedy, much too coy: *The Countess of Monte Cristo* with Fay Wray in the title-role, a film extra posing as a countess and unmasking crook Lukas; *Glamour*, an Edna Ferber story with Constance Cummings as the showgirl who becomes a star and Lukas as her composer husband; *I Give My Love*, a mother-love story with Wynne Gibson, who had been his mistress in *City Streets*; *Affairs of a Gentleman*, a murder mystery, as a thriller-writer; *The Fountain* at RKO, as Ann Harding's German officer husband; and *The Gift of Gab*, a guest appearance in a 'radio' musical whose cast included Ruth Etting, Ethel Waters and Gene Austin.

Universal had done very well by Lukas but had not succeeded in turning him into a top star. Freelancing again, he was in Bs: Paramount's *Father Brown Detective* (35), G.K. Chesterton's character played by Walter Con-

Thunder Below *(32) was one of Paul Lukas's best early performances, but it is impossible to believe that he and Charles Bickford could so easily ignore such a vibrant personality as Tallulah.*

nolly and Lukas miscast as his prey; *The Casino Murder Case*, as Philo Vance detective, with Alison Skipworth; and *The Age of Indiscretion*, a divorce story with Madge Evans. He then received an invitation from RKO to play Athos in *The Three Musketeers*, originally planned in colour with a starry cast, but now much less glamorous with Walter Abel (fresh from Broadway) as D'Artagnan, Onslow Stevens and Moroni Olsen: still, it was good if not very popular. At Warners he supported Kay Francis and Ian Hunter in *I Found Stella Parish* and his next two parts were small, if telling. In *Dodsworth* (36) he was the Continental charmer with whom Chatterton dallies – he played it beautifully – and in *Ladies in Love* he was Constance Bennett's 'protector'. His only other work at that time was supporting Madge Evans and Edmund Lowe in *Espionage* (37); he then departed for Britain where he stayed long enough to suggest that he was starting a new career.

The British studios were surprised to find that Lukas's offscreen personality was lighthearted and friendly, in contrast to his screen image; nevertheless, they conspired to represent the sinister Lukas: *Brief Ecstasy*, a silly melodrama directed by Edmond T. Greville, and *Mutiny on the Elsinore. Dinner at the Ritz*, with Annabella, had moments of gaiety, but then came *The Lady Vanishes* (38), where he did for Hitchcock his Continental menace act. He did it again, back in

Hollywood, in *Confessions of a Nazi Spy*, with Edward G. Robinson, and still in Hollywood was in *Captain Fury*, in a small part. He returned to Britain for a supporting role in *A Window in London*, as the stage magician whom Michael Redgrave thinks is murdering Sally Gray, when he looks through it. But he remained to be top-billed as another heavy, Matheson Lang's old role in *The Chinese Bungalow* (40), as the Chinese merchant who murders his English wife's lover. Back in the States he remained nasty but his parts were small: *Strange Cargo* as a fascist, starring Clark Gable, and *The Ghost Breakers*, being sinister to Bob Hope. After supporting parts in *The Monster and the Girl* (41) and *They Dare Not Love*, a trite anti-Nazi film with George Brent and Martha Scott, he accepted the offer of a play in New York.

This was Lillian Hellman's 'Watch on the Rhine' and he played an undercover agent arrived in Washington, a man whose life was dedicated to fighting the Nazi cause: the character was something of a cipher, but Lukas gave him dimensions that encompassed both his past and future (or lack of it). He got great reviews and there was seldom any doubt that he would repeat in the film version: Warners made it in 1943 with Bette Davis as his wife and Lucille Watson also repeating as his mother-in-law, and Lukas won both the New York critics' award and the Best Actor Oscar. Star parts were offered him again, even if the next three were all anti-Nazi

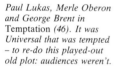

Paul Lukas, Merle Oberon and George Brent in Temptation *(46). It was Universal that was tempted – to re-do this played-out old plot: audiences weren't.*

dramas: *Hostages* with Luise Rainer, as a Gestapo chieftain; *Uncertain Glory* (44), another fine performance as the detective in this Errol Flynn drama; and *Address Unknown*, one of Columbia's better war films, as an American Jew living in Germany, who is hounded to his death.

His good fortune did not hold, perhaps because he had a reputation for being difficult. All he was offered were the sorts of melodramas he had done at the start of his career: *Experiment Perilous* (45), very villainous, with Hedy Lamarr; *Deadline at Dawn* (46) with Susan Hayward, as a philosophizing taxi-driver; *Temptation* with Merle Oberon; *Whispering City* (47) made in Quebec, as a barrister; and *Berlin Express* (48) with Oberon, as a famous statesman. After a two-year absence he headed the supporting cast of *Kim* (50), as a lama. Then he returned to the stage: 'Call Me Madam' (51) and 'Flight into Egypt' (52). He had his last good film role in Disney's *20,000 Leagues Under the Sea* (54), as the professor, though the 'MFB' thought him 'colourless'. He had bits in *The Roots of Heaven* (58); *Scent of Mystery* (60), a film produced by Mike Todd Jr that was supposed to bring the 'smellies' to cinemagoing via a device under the seats – but the thing that stank was the film; *The Four Horsemen of the Apocalypse* (61), a bigger part as one of the invading Germans; *Tender Is the Night*, excellent as a psychiatrist, Dick Diver's boss – and without his hairpiece for the first time on screen; *55 Days at Peking* (63), as a doctor tending the wounded; *Fun in Acapulco*, starring Elvis Presley; *Lord Jim* (65), as the shipowner who starts him on his adventures; and *Sol Madrid* (67), a thriller starring David McCallum. His final credit was a telefilm, *The Challenge* (70).

Lukas was married twice. He was widowed in 1962 and married again the following year. He died in 1971.

IDA LUPINO

Ida Lupino was a strong, challenging actress who for a brief period looked like a rival for the Bette Davis crown at Warners. Indeed, she was sedulously built up by that studio as a successor: but the public never responded in enough numbers and she retreated behind the camera where her solid professionalism surprised no one. However, of her blonde cutie period at the beginning, there is very little to be said that is complimentary.

She was born in London in 1918, into a British vaudeville family of Italian origin. Her father was Stanley Lupino, who had left the acrobatic troupe to become a star comedian in revue, pantomime and films. Ida was trained at RADA while still very young; and she had experience at this time in tours and as an extra. Her film chance came when Allan Dwan, filming in Britain, wanted a young girl who seemed a likely trap for a much older, married author: *Her First Affair* (33). She was much less 'trampy' in some of *Money for Speed*, starring John Loder, and when Paramount saw these sequences they thought she might be ideal for their *Alice in Wonderland*. Meanwhile, she was making a lot of films: *High Finance* starring Gibb McLaughlin; *Prince of Arcadia*; *The Ghost Camera* with Henry Kendall; and Ivor Novello's *I Lived With You*. Paramount signed her, but she was decidedly too sexy for Alice, so they starred her in *The Search for Beauty* (34) with Larry 'Buster' Crabbe. Then she did two with Richard Arlen, *Come on Marines* (she had little to do) and *Ready for Love*, a small-town tale; next she was the ingénue in *Paris in Spring* (35) which was the first of the vehicles intended to make native-born Mary Ellis a star after her successes on the London stage.

The studio were as disenchanted with Lupino: through *Smart Girl*, *Peter Ibbetson* and *Anything Goes* (36) her parts got successively smaller, until (fortunately) in the last of these, she is hardly there at all. But she had a good chance in *One Rainy Afternoon* at United Artists, a satirical comedy with Robert Young and Francis Lederer; and then Paramount put her into *Yours for the Asking* starring George Raft. The same UA producers borrowed her again for *The Gay Desperado*, a musical starring Nino Martini, which got good notices and did well. Paramount loaned out Lupino again: for *Sea Devils* (37) with Victor McLaglen at RKO, where she had little to do; and a B, *Let's Get Married*, with Ralph Bellamy at Columbia. On her home lot, she had an uninteresting part in Jack Benny's *Artists and Models*: so, on the basis of her success on loan, she asked to be released from her contract. Paramount complied; but after a job in RKO's *Fight For Your Lady*, a comedy with John Boles and Jack Oakie, she did not appear in a picture for over a year and 'Picturegoer' later reported that she had tried unsuccessfully to get work in Britain. In 1938 she married British-born Louis Hayward.

Finally she got parts in two Bs at Columbia: *The Lone Wolf Spy Hunt* (39), in which 'Variety' found her 'at times ridiculous'; and *The Lady and the Mob*, with Fay Bainter. Her English accent helped her get a part in 20th's *The Adventures of Sherlock Holmes*, but her performance as a lady in distress was sulky and not sufficiently aristocratic. Desperate for a good part, she bearded William Wellman in his den at Paramount and insisted on reading for the part of the floozie, Bessie, in *The Light That Failed*. Wellman's subsequent championing of her led to discord with Ronald Colman (who wanted Vivien Leigh). Paramount supported Wellman, but did not sign her to a contract. Warners did, after seeing the rushes of *They Drive by Night* (40), in which she was Alan Hale's trampy wife. Since it was for seven years, guaranteeing stardom, she decided at the start to be difficult. According to Jack L. Warner's memoir, she stayed away during filming because an astrologer had told her the film would be bad luck: $½ million had been spent and the crew were put on another picture before she returned. He implied that she was not a very easy star to handle, but she got another fine part, opposite Humphrey Bogart and top-billed, in *High Sierra* (41). Said William Whitebait: 'Ida Lupino gives us the best moll I have ever seen.' She had meaty roles in *The Sea Wolf*, as an ex-convict and the only woman on board, and *Out of the Fog*, as a Brooklyn girl with too much class for the place, or so John Garfield tells her. She then went to Columbia with husband Hayward for *Ladies in Retirement*, as the steely housekeeper who murders her employer, a vulgar ex-actress, rather than see her two mental sisters put away. (It is her favourite role.) She refused to do *Manpower* because she did not want to work with Bogart again, so was replaced by Dietrich (and then Edward G. Robinson did the Bogart role) and she turned down the Betty Field part in *King's Row* because she would be billed below Ann Sheridan. having nothing more for her, Warners let her do two more on loan-out, at 20th. *Moontide* (42) with Jean Gabin, turned out to be a rehash of *Quai des Brumes* set in California. Lupino had the Michèle Morgan role of the tramp-waif; there was trouble during production and Gabin's Hollywood career was blunted at the start. *Life Begins at 8.30* was a theatrical tale and she was Monty Woolley's crippled daughter.

She returned to Warners to do it *The Hard Way* (43), an ambitious girl who does not care how she makes it to the top, in fact pushing her sister (Joan Leslie) to Broadway stardom – a 'Lady Macbeth of the slums' as 'Picturegoer' put it, though there are clues in the film that the role was based on Ginger Rogers's mother. But at last people took her seriously as an actress: the New York critics voted her the Year's Best. She was in three starry efforts: RKO's *Forever and a Day*, as a maid; *Thank Your Lucky Stars*, jitterbugging with Olivia de Havilland; and *Hollywood Canteen* (44); then more suitably, in *In Our Time*, as an Englishwoman in love with Polish aristo-

Ida Lupino and John Garfield in The Sea Wolf *(41), the fifth of the seven movies based on Jack London's novel of that name.*

crat Paul Henried at the time of the Nazi invasion. *Pillow to Post* (45) was a minor comedy and *Devotion* an idiotic biopic on the Brontës (she was Emily). She got better chances in *The Man I Love* (46) – he was Robert Alda and she was a torch singer; *Deep Valley* (47), as a backwoods girl with a speech impediment; and *Escape Me Never*, in Elisabeth Bergner's old part as a European peasant girl weeping over the heel she loves (Errol Flynn). It was her last film for Warners: she had acted conscientiously for them in a series of inferior soap operas, but she ranked after the other three Warner ladies who were making similar films – Davis, Joan Crawford and Ann Sheridan. Of them, only Davis was consistently able to rise above her material and, having done so often enough, she was in a position (during the time that Lupino was at Warners) to demand the best that was going.

Lupino played another torch singer in an enjoyable mish-mash, *Road House* (48), and that year married a Columbia executive, Collier Young. She appeared in a Columbia Western, *Lust for Gold* (49), and went into

she also scripted; *Women's Prison* (55), as its sadistic boss; *The Big Knife* – the only poor performance in a well-acted film, as the wife of film star Jack Palance; Lang's *While the City Sleeps* (56), as a newspaper sob-sister; and *Strange Intruder*, with Edmund Purdom. It was clearly time to desert the cinema and she and Duff did a TV series, playing film stars, 'Mr Adams and Eve'.

She returned to films with *The Trouble with Angels* (66), directing only, and could be seen in *Backtrack* (69) with James Drury and Doug McClure, which was composed of two episodes of two TV series, 'The Virginian' and 'Laredo'. She made her television dramatic début in *Women in Chains* (72), virtually reprising her role in *Women's Prison*. She returned to the big screen in *Junior Bonner*, as Steve McQueen's maw, and then worked for a while in TV: *The Strangers in 7A*, as Andy Griffith's wife, held hostages by some hoods; *Female Artillery* (73) with Dennis Weaver, as a pioneer woman; *I Love a Mystery*, based on a radio show and in fact made six years earlier; and *The Letters*, in one of its episodes. Still in there pitching, she did two horror films, *The Devil's Rain* (75) and *The Food of the Gods* (76), the latter from a story by H.G. Wells. There were 'artistic differences' on *The Thoroughbreds* and she was replaced by Vera Miles; but she stayed on *My Boys are Good Boys* (79) with Ralph Meeker, directed by his wife, on a budget of $50,000. That did not make it to cinemas – but *Deadhead Miles* (82) did. Just. Made 10 years earlier and shelved by Paramount, it starred Alan Arkin, with Lupino and George Raft in guest roles based on their stint many years before in *They Drive By Night*.

From the publicity desk: 'She paints; is simply out of her mind about lampshades . . . enthusiastic over $16.75 dresses' ('Photoplay').

TV, writing and producing. Out of this came a film about a pregnancy, *Not Wanted*, which she produced and directed, when the credited director became ill; it starred Sally Forrest and Keefe Brazelle. She was the *Woman in Hiding* (50) at Universal, co-starring with Howard Duff, whom she later married, but she also managed to put together another low-budget film, *Never Fear* – directing this time. The (modest) critical success of her two productions brought her a deal at RKO. She directed and scripted *Outrage* and directed *Hard Fast and Beautiful* (51); at the same studio she played a blind girl in *On Dangerous Ground* with Robert Ryan and a woman menaced by a killer (Ryan again) in *Beware My Lovely* (52) from Mel Dinelli's play 'The Man'; and she directed *The Hitchhiker*. In 1952 she was in Britain reputedly discussing plans to produce and act, with both Rank and Korda: but nothing came of this. In 1953 she appeared in *Jennifer* and directed *The Bigamist*, which starred her and Joan Fontaine (now married to Lupino's ex-husband Young). She was in *Private Hell 36* (54) with Duff, which

JEANETTE MACDONALD

Jeanette MacDonald said that if she ever published her memoirs she would call the book 'The Iron Butterfly': that, she knew, was what some people called her. Like most operetta ladies, she was a butt for comics and an object of derision to some of those more concerned with the higher reaches of cinema art – which was really getting her all wrong. She was a superb comedienne and even in that age of great comedy players she could run rings round most of her rivals: as the daffy heroine of Lubitsch's boudoir comedies, she established a standard which others sought to reach. She was a critics' pet – vivacious, excessively pretty – at the time when she first carried her brand of self-parody to Nelson Eddy. There are indications that after a while she began to take the conventions of operetta seriously and in her later films it is hard to defend her from charges of coyness and artificiality.

She was born in Philadelphia in either 1907 or 1901 – the latter date seems more likely as she made her New York début in 1920, in the chorus of 'The Demi-Tasse Revue'. She had been schooled in singing and dancing and followed her sister Blossom into the chorus. By 1923 she had progressed to leading roles and had her first success with 'The Magic Ring'. The Shuberts signed her to a contract and gave her the ingénue role in the Gershwins' 'Tip Toes' (25). Among other shows, she starred in 'Bubbling Over' (26) and was in 'Angela'(28) when Richard Dix saw her and wanted her for his leading lady in *Nothing But the Truth*. Paramount tested her, but nixed her as his or anybody else's leading lady. Lubitsch, however, saw the test and was impressed enough to take the train to Chicago to see her in 'Boom Boom', whereupon he knew that she was just the thing for *The Love Parade* (29), as the Queen who would marry rakish attaché Maurice Chevalier.

The reception of both film and MacDonald was cordial and Paramount co-starred her with Dennis King in a coloured (two-tone) version of *The Vagabond King* (30). 'Picturegoer', one of the dissenters over her first film performance, now said: 'she seems absolutely lost and incapable of rising to the opportunities the part offers'. But Lubitsch still liked her and put her into *Monte Carlo* with Jack Buchanan, singing 'Beyond the Blue Horizon' in a railway train in a slip and furs. She was then in a Jack Oakie comedy about castaways, *Let's Go Native*, which was nonsense but enjoyable. Paramount then dropped her. At UA she did a pretentious musical, *The Lottery Bride*, arriving at Nome on a ship and belting out a Friml song with gusto; and then did three comedies for Fox: the piquant *Oh for a Man!*; *Don't Bet on Women* (31), starring Edmund Lowe and Roland Young; and *Annabelle's Affairs* with Young and Victor McLaglen, the remake of an old Billie Burke picture.

After a concert tour of Europe, which confirmed her aspirations to grand opera, Lubitsch persuaded Paramount that she was the best possible partner for Maurice Chevalier, so she replaced Kay Francis as his wife in *One Hour With You* (32), with such merry results that they kept her on to play a frigid widow melted by Chevalier in *Love Me Tonight*. In both she was billed below the title and both were pieces of immortal facetiousness, but musicals at this point were 10 a penny and even goodies like these failed to attract. She was out of work again and she accepted a British offer from Herbert Wilcox to make *The Queen's Affair* with Herbert

Marshall, with the possibility of *Bitter Sweet* to follow. The first was in rehearsal when the stars left: no explanation was ever given. Anna Neagle took her parts in both films and she was certainly soon at work again. Musicals were back in vogue, because of the success of *42nd Street*, and MGM signed her for two pictures, the first of which was to be *I Married an Angel*, a spicy farce with Rodgers and Hart songs: but those responsible for the new Production Code turned down the script (and the composers departed with their songs, to make a Broadway hit out of them). The studio offered two alternatives, the film of Jerome Kern's *The Cat and the Fiddle* and/or *Naughty Marietta*. She loathed the idea of both of them, but agreed finally to do the Kern film (34), with Ramon Novarro. *Marietta* was postponed because they could not find a suitable leading man, though MGM were considering teaming MacDonald with a new star, singer Nelson Eddy, in a (straight) remake of *The Prisoner of Zenda*.

Meanwhile, Chevalier and Lubitsch had moved to MGM to make a new version of *The Merry Widow* with Grace Moore; there was a dispute about billing and MacDonald stepped in. 'The picture was so expensive that only a box-office miracle could have made it profitable. [It] did not occur' (Deems Taylor) – but the film itself is miraculous. MGM signed her to a five-year contract and decided to put Eddy with her in *Naughty Marietta* (35). Then, when Grace Moore could not make the schedule for *Rose Marie* (36), they were teamed again. Directed with humour by W.S. Van Dyke, it stands today as their best movie: MacDonald's performance as a petulant prima donna has asperity and style, at least until she succumbs to Eddy and the Indian Love Call. She was also rather terrific in *San Francisco*, a property that she had sold to the studio on the proviso that Gable co-star: he and Jack Holt fought over her – at least until the Earthquake. It was a big hit and brought MacDonald into the top 10 draws of 1936 (she never made the list thereafter; but in Britain she was one of the top 10 from 1937 to 1942 inclusive).

MGM dusted off another hoary old property, *Maytime* (37), and the Eddy and MacDonald voices again blended in harmony. It was her own favourite film (she liked working under Robert Z. Leonard's direction) and a wow at the time, a banal piece about a singer who marries her impresario (John Barrymore) rather than the student (Eddy) she loves; it ends with an aged MacDonald watching the young spirits of herself and Eddy warbling among the cherry blossoms. As a change of pace, she was given Allan Jones (somewhat less wooden an actor than Eddy) for *The*

Jeanette MacDonald sings for her supper in The Firefly (*37*). *The gentleman – glimpsed only this briefly in the film – was Ralph Byrd. Her leading man was not Nelson Eddy but Allan Jones.*

Firefly: improbably, they were both master-spies ('You're a clever woman, señorita, but not clever enough'), but the film was good of its own crumby kind and a big success.

However, fans were clamouring for Eddy and MacDonald. It was not until now that MGM came to consider them as a permanent team and they were together in *The Girl of the Golden West* (38), the old Belasco play with a new, non-Puccini score, and in *Sweethearts*,

the studio's first all-colour film and one of the top money-makers of 1938. She had a new (non-singing) co-star, Lew Ayres, for *Broadway Serenade* (39), but was back with Eddy again in the risible *New Moon* (40) and a lavish chocolate-box version of *Bitter Sweet*, which its author/composer Noël Coward hated. MGM bought from other studios both *The Vagabond King* and *Show Boat* for the team, among other properties, including *The Chocolate Soldier*: but she ceded her role in that to opera star Risë Stevens in order to prove that she was a box-office star in her own right. Instead she did a new version of *Smilin' Through* (41) with Brian Aherne and her husband Gene Raymond; then she and Eddy did something much less saccharine, *I Married an Angel* (42) returned with thanks from Broadway; but the public liked not the change. And *Cairo*, a send-up of spy films with Robert Young, was none too successful. MacDonald's contract had been extended by a couple of years in 1940, but now it was not. She had once been Louis B. Mayer's favourite star, but at the time of *The Firefly* she had gone over his head to the New York office about the dubbing of her own voice in the foreign editions of her films; the quarrel was never patched up and she herself believed that that was why she was dropped.

Certainly there had been only slight indications that her popularity was waning, even if the changing taste of the war years favoured the younger girls like Lana Turner. Mac-Donald took the chance of this hiatus to go into grand opera – with Ezio Pinza she sang

Nelson Eddy and Jeanette MacDonald in the last picture they made together, I Married an Angel (*42*). *MGM had announced the split before it went into production, but the public did not rush to see them together for the last time – perhaps because this was not a typical vehicle for them.*

'Romeo and Juliet' in Montreal and 'Faust' in Chicago, but the notices were not overwhelmingly favourable. She did a guest spot (singing two songs) in *Follow the Boys* (44) and, at the behest of Joe Pasternak, returned to MGM for two mature roles: reconciling *Three Daring Daughters* (48) to her marriage with José Iturbi and being reconciled to widowhood by the charms of Lassie and Claude Jarman Jr in *The Sun Comes Up* (49). Both were prime examples of the genre MGM-Has-No-Shame, which the public had learned finally to avoid: it stayed away and MacDonald settled into semi-retirement, realizing that her type of movie was outmoded – though she might well have continued in the sort of parts that Ina Claire had once done. But the less sentimental aspect of MacDonald's screen character was virtually forgotten. She did some concerts from time to time, appeared in cabaret and in stock in musicals like 'The King and I'. In 1951 she declined the opportunity to play Doris Day's mother and an offer of a British picture; and toured in 'The Guardsman' with her husband. She died in 1965.

Her fans stayed remarkably faithful and when MGM took to reviving her films with Eddy in the 50s, they found they could pack cinemas for limited bookings. In fact, MacDonald's fame well outlasted her career and should survive as long as there is a market for Palm Court romance.

Five Star Final (*31*): *Aline MacMahon, the perfect secretary, gets a shock from a telephone caller about her boss, newspaper editor Edward G. Robinson.*

ALINE MACMAHON

Aline MacMahon did not want to be a star, or so went the publicity: 'Of course I did, dear,' she said, on reading an earlier edition of this book. But according to Warners she was offered stardom after her third picture and turned it down to remain a leading character actress. She was, perhaps, not really suitable star material. She was too tall, a little ungainly; her features – her mouth, her eyes – were too big for classical beauty. She had a lovely presence and sharp common sense, which made her ideal for the secretary roles she played several times. In her first film, *Five Star Final*, she was secretary to Edward G. Robinson and she had every detail right; unlike most film typists she did not merely tap on her machine: it seemed to be part of her. In a couple of sentences she conveyed much of her life outside the office – or what there was of it, for she doted on Edward G. more than somewhat, though her yen was masked under a string of barbed, unfazed comments on his behaviour. She was later publicized as 'the perfect screen secretary', a description which just as effectively concealed her very

real abilities. She was one of the screen's few perfect actresses.

She was born in McKeesport, Pennsylvania, in 1899, the daughter of an Irish telegraph operator who wrote stories and articles on the side and later took up journalism as a profession. She was educated at Erasmus Hall and then Barnard College, where she enjoyed acting so much that she decided to take it up professionally. After graduating, she joined a stock company in Yorkville and later got a small Broadway part in 'The Mirage' (21). She joined the Neighborhood Playhouse, where she made a hit in one of their 'Grand Street Follies' with a take-off of Gertrude Lawrence. This led to a contract with the Shuberts and a role in the 1925 edition of 'Artists and Models'. She scored a great success in a revival of O'Neill's 'Beyond the Horizon' (26) and later appeared in 'Spread Eagle', 'Her First Affair', 'Maya' (28) and 'Winter Bound' (29). She was then engaged by Moss Hart to do a play he had written with George S. Kaufman about the coming of Talkies to Hollywood, 'Once in a Lifetime', specifically to play the passée vaudeville star who teaches Speech to the Silent stars: but the New York management preferred Jean Dixon and MacMahon was offered instead the West Coast company. On the night after the Los Angeles opening, she was approached by Warners for the role in *Five Star Final* (31). This brought her rave notices and meanwhile she did do 'Once in a Lifetime' on Broadway. Warners were waiting with a contract, which she signed

MRS. L

Fred Zinnemann's The Search *(48) was one of the best pictures of the 40s, and Aline MacMahon was superb as a voluntary officer looking after displaced persons.*

on condition that filming was restricted to certain periods so that she could live in New York where her architect husband practised (Clarence S. Stein; they were married in 1928).

Her contract with Warners called for four films a year: *The Heart of New York* (32) with Jewish comedians Dale and Smith, as the tenement janitress; *The Mouthpiece*, as secretary to Warren William, who was carrying on with fellow worker Sidney Fox; *Weekend Marriage*, as Loretta Young's sister; *One Way Passage*, as the bogus countess; *Life Begins*, as a nurse; and Universal's film version of *Once in a Lifetime*. Richard Watts Jr wrote in the 'New York Herald Tribune': 'She provides the best acting of the picture – a customary occurrence, in the films in which Miss MacMahon appears.' She certainly gave a beautiful performance in *Silver Dollar*, as the wife who Understands when Edward G. Robinson dallies with Bebe Daniels. She was with Loretta Young again in *The Life of Jimmy Dolan* (33) and was the most practical of the *Gold Diggers of 1933* – she landed millionaire Guy Kibbee. She was a soup-kitchen worker in Wellman's *Heroes for Sale*, comforting Richard Barthelmess when wife Young is killed; and was Paul Muni's mother in *The World Changes*, ageing throughout the picture. *Heat Lightning* (34) was a melodrama based on a play by Leon Abrams and George Abbot, with MacMahon (top-billed) and sister Ann Dvorak running a gas station at a tourist spot suddenly invaded by Reno divor-cees and robbers, including Ruth Donnelly, Glenda Farrell, Preston Foster and Lyle Talbot. Dvorak longed for excitement and got it. In *Side Streets* Dvorak was the threat to her marriage; said 'Photoplay': 'Aline Mac-Mahon's characterization of the love-starved woman who marries a jobless sailor (Paul Kelly) is superb.'

The Merry Frinks was a modest comedy in which MacMahon was married to Hugh Herbert and Kibbee was his wealthy uncle who thinks she is too good for him. Warners liked the combination of Kibbee and MacMahon so much that they co-starred them together in four more consecutive films: *Big Hearted Herbert*, with Kibbee as the grouchy husband whom she finally decides to reform; in *Babbitt* as his wife in this competent version of Sinclair Lewis's bestseller; *While the Patient Slept* (35), a murder mystery; and *Mary Jane's Pa*, in which they are married again, separate and come together again. MacMahon liked acting with Kibbee and did not mind that because he was 13 years older than she, Warners moved her into an older age group; but she did not like the sameness of the parts. She asked to be released from her contract and after some hesitation Warners agreed.

MGM immediately put her into three pictures: *I Live My Life*, supporting Joan Crawford; *Ah Wilderness!*, as the spinster aunt in love with Wallace Beery; and *Kind Lady*, based on a Hugh Walpole story, in the title-role, terrorized by Basil Rathbone. MGM also tested her for the lead in *The Good Earth*

– and when she did not get it, she visited China. She was off the screen for more than a year, then returned as Grace Moore's secretary in *When You're in Love* (37). She did 'Candida' in stock and made occasional stage appearances over the next few years. Her film appearances became rare: *Back Door to Heaven* (39), as a schoolteacher in this Paramount programmer; *Out of the Fog* (41), as Ida Lupino's shrewish mother; and *The Lady is Willing* (42), as stage star Marlene Dietrich's secretary. In *Tish* she and Marjorie Main and Zasu Pitts were three middle-aged ladies constantly getting into hot water. She was in *Stage Door Canteen* (43), was Walter Huston's wife in *Dragon Seed* (444) and had more featured roles in *Guest in the House*, as an aunt, and *The Mighty McGurk* (46), opposite Wallace Beery as his sceptical but ever-lovin' fiancée.

Her best film part in years was in Zinnemann's *The Search* (48), of which Albert Johnson wrote a while later (in 'Sight and Sound', 1955): 'Here is Aline MacMahon as Mrs Mallory, the careworn directress of this outpost of destitute youngsters. Her uniform somehow enhances a warm, matriarchal sympathy, and although she is a secondary figure, one is curious to know more about her. This is MacMahon's forte, to make everything she does stick in the memory. She brings a nobility to the part, a kind of native sagacity that lingered in my childhood impressions of her as one of the sharp-tongued, brittle *Gold Diggers of 1933*. . . .' After that her film appearances were disappointingly few and most of them were unworthy: *Roseanna McCoy* (49), a silly Goldwyn melodrama with Farley Granger and Joan Evans; *The Flame and the Arrow* (50), as a crone: *The Eddie Cantor Story* (53), as his grandmother; *The Man From Laramie* (55), as a lonely rancher; *Cimarron* (60), well down the cast-list as the newspaper proprietor; *The Young Doctors* (61), as a kindly doctor; and *Diamond Head* (62), as a Hawaiian woman.

She did another lovely job in the small role of Judy Garland's dresser-companion in *I Could Go on Singing* (63): anyone who had coped with Edward G. Robinson, Grace Moore and Dietrich could handle Garland and MacMahon's attitude of scepticism and affection was entirely right, and unforgettable. She was also fine in *All the Way Home* with Jean Simmons and Robert Preston, as aunt Hannah, a part that she had played on the stage. Other stage appearances over the 40s to 60s were: 'The Eve of St Mark' (42), 'The Confidential Clerk' (54) and 'A Day by the Sea' (55), all in New York; the Nurse in 'Romeo and Juliet', and the Countess in 'All's Well That Ends Well' (59) and Volumnia in

'Coriolanus' (65) in Stratford, Connecticut; and 'The Madwoman of Chaillot' (51) in Los Angeles. She has also done TV.

FRED MACMURRAY

Fred MacMurray's forte was playing the all-American go-getter, genial and deceptively lazy – nice, but determined. It is not a characterization that offers much after a couple of viewings, but it was available on average twice a year for almost 40 years; now and then he abandoned it to play a heel – and it is perhaps significant that by far his most memorable performances (and good acting by any standards) are as such in *Double Indemnity* and *The Apartment*.

His pre-Hollywood career is not unlike the stories in which he used to appear. He was born in Kankakee, Illinois, in 1908, the son of a concert violinist. He was educated at a military academy, among other establishments, and studied for a time at the Chicago Art Institute – but while playing in school bands he decided to become a full-time saxophonist. His peregrinations took him to Hollywood and he worked as an extra – in *Girls Gone Wild* (28) among others; between films he worked with orchestras – sometimes as a vocalist – and recorded with Gus Arnheim. He joined the Californian Collegians and with them played Broadway in a revue, 'Three's a Crowd' (30): Libby Holman sang 'Something to Remember You By' to him. In two further shows he doubled as saxophonist and featured player: 'The Third Little Show' and 'Roberta' (33).

Then – there were two studio versions – either a Paramount talent scout saw him in 'Roberta' or he went to Hollywood and signed on with Central Casting. But certainly he was under contract to Paramount in 1934: he had been loaned out to RKO for *Grand Old Girl* (35) with May Robson when Claudette Colbert was looking for a leading man for *The Gilded Lady*. She saw his screen test and this became the first of several co-starring comedies – and a big success.

Paramount put him into *Car 99* and *Men Without Names*, a gangster film with Madge Evans in which he was an ambitious young G-man: both were programmers, but his success in the Colbert film made him the hottest tip in town. Katharine Hepburn at RKO asked for him for *Alice Adams*; Carole Lombard okayed him as a replacement for George Raft in *Hands Across the Table*, as the poor man she gives up dreams of wealth for – the first and funniest of their teamings; and Colbert wanted him again for *The Bride Comes Home*:

Carole Lombard was one of the most adroit and subtle of comediennes, with an effervescence which Paramount considered to be complemented by the affable manner of Fred MacMurray – as here, in their first film together, Hands Across the Table *(35). Off-screen, she called him 'Uncle Fred', sufficient comment on her feeling for him, though she liked him; but she did eventually revolt against Paramount's frequent teaming of them.*

it was his seventh film within a year and by the time it was shown he was established. He did *The Trail of the Lonesome Pine* (36) with Henry Fonda and Sylvia Sidney; *Thirteen Hours by Air*, a comedy with Joan Bennett; *The Princess* (Lombard) *Comes Across*; and *The Texas Rangers* with Jean Parker, a good Western directed by King Vidor and originally meant for Gary Cooper. His salary had been raised from $200 a week to $350 after his first six months, but no one at Paramount thought it should go higher till he took Lombard's advice and absented himself at Palm Springs for a couple of months.

Apart from that last one, MacMurray's abilities had so far not been stretched; but he was entirely misplaced as a swashbuckling parson in a historical piece with Colbert, *Maid of Salem* (37); however, he was at ease again in the contemporary settings of *Champagne Waltz*, the third attempt by Paramount to make prima donna Gladys Swarthout into a movie star – a film the studio reputedly liked so much that they added bits to it to the tune of $40,000 after it was finished. MacMurray played a band-leader whom Swarthout falls for after he has taught her to chew gum. Then he did *Swing High Swing Low* with Lombard; *Exclusive* with Frances Farmer, as a news-paper editor battling against big-time rack-eteer Lloyd Nolan; *True Confession*, as the husband for whom Lombard lies; and *Cocoanut Grove* (38), where he crooned a bit, with Harriet Hilliard. He and Ray Milland were the *Men with Wings*, a Technicolored history of aviation told in soap-opera terms; William A. Wellman's direction almost makes it work (he was a specialist in aeroplane pictures) and the characterless playing of the two men is somewhat offset by Louise Camp-bell as the girl they both (naturally) love. In *Sing You Sinners* Bing Crosby did most of the singing and MacMurray was his no-good brother. He then did the first of several with Madeleine Carroll, *Café Society* (39). *Invita-tion to Happiness* with Irene Dunne took a prize for the year's most deceitful title, but *Honeymoon in Bali* with Carroll made up for it.

In 1940 he renewed his pact with Para-mount for another five years, two films a year plus the right to make one outside one. He was not, after all, the big star that had been predicted when he started, but he was a dependable leading man and this was prob-ably his most popular period. Comedy remained his mainstay, but he did crop up in certain serious situations, such as *Remember*

the Night (40), a good sentimental drama about an assistant DA who falls for the shoplifter (Barbara Stanwyck) he has to look after. He was loaned to 20th Century-Fox for *Little Old New York* with Alice Faye and then to Columbia for *Too Many Husbands*: it was Jean Arthur who had them. There was a feeble Western with Paramount's new bid for the stellar stakes, Patricia Morison, *Rangers of Fortune*, and then two poor ones with Carroll, *Virginia* (41), a historical story, and *One Night in Lisbon*, which was a wartime tale set in Britain (Lisbon at that time was the leading neutral European city). MacMurray went to *New York Town* with Mary Martin and then to Warners for *Dive Bomber* with Errol Flynn. At Columbia he tamed Dietrich in *The Lady Is Willing* (42); then was dictated to by Rosalind Russell: *Take a Letter Darling*. *The Forest Rangers* was a singularly unattractive adventure story, in colour, with Paulette Goddard, not improved by the obtuseness of the character that MacMurray played, nor by

a jingly song, 'We've got spurs that jingle jangle jingle'. He guested in *Star Spangled Rhythm* and then he and Russell took a *Flight for Freedom* (43); he and Joan Crawford were *Above Suspicion* at MGM, much heavier histrionics; he and Colbert had *No Time for Love*; and there was *Standing Room Only* (44) in wartime Washington for him and Goddard. He stayed on the lighter side in *And the Angels Sing* with Betty Hutton and Dorothy Lamour.

According to director Billy Wilder, neither he nor Barbara Stanwyck wanted to do *Double Indemnity*: 'He in particular was afraid of what it would do to his image' – which was curious, because the shifty insurance agent/murderer of this was hardly less admirable than the lecherous band-leader of *And the Angels Sing*; 11 other actors had turned it down and it brought MacMurray the best notices of his career. And naturally it boosted it: the trade now talked of him as an *actor*. But after a mild comedy with Claudette

Colbert, *Practically Yours*, he and Paramount came to an impasse. He had one film to go on his contract and Paramount had nothing for him. Director George Marshall put together a crazy comedy, *Murder He Says* (45), with Helen Walker, in which he was a public opinion surveyor billeted with a family of murderous hicks: his comedic touch was seldom more beneficially displayed, but you may still wish they had saved the material for Bob Hope.

MacMurray then, to Hollywood's surprise, accepted a bid from 20th and signed a new long-term contract that gave him approval over his films. He was announced for *A Tree Grows in Brooklyn* (for the part that won James Dunn a Best Supporting Oscar) and *Nob Hill*, but he presumably turned them down – certainly he did not do them. What he did do was *Where Do We Go From Here?*, a historical/musical romp, and *Captain Eddie*, a routine biopic (Captain Richenbacker) with Lynn Bari. His co-star in the first of these was June Haver, who in later years gave up her career and went into a convent – which she left after MacMurray's wife died in 1953; they were married in 1954.

At Columbia he produced and starred in *Pardon My Past* (46) – a venture behind the camera that did not encourage further efforts – and then did *Smoky* (46), a horsey picture with Anne Baxter. It was his last for 20th. It was announced that he was unhappy there and returning to Paramount on long-term contract. In fact, he did one more film with 20th, *Suddenly It's Spring* (47), with Paulette Goddard, and then started to freelance. As an independent, he started off with a big hit, Universal's *The Egg and I* with Claudette Colbert, but thereafter settled into those programmers – mostly comedies – which were churned out in the late 40s and early 50s and which not only helped to kill the cinemagoing habit, but murdered most of the stars as well. MacMurray just survived. The names and co-stars will suffice: *Singapore* with Ava Gardner; *The Miracle of the Bells* (48) with Frank Sinatra and Alida Valli; *On Our Merry Way* in the sequence with William Demarest; *Don't Trust Your Husband* with Madeleine Carroll; *Family Honeymoon* with Colbert; *Father Was a Fullback* (49) with Maureen O'Hara; *Borderline* (50) with Claire Trevor; *Never a Dull Moment* with Irene Dunne – and for their second film together, another dishonest title; and *A Millionaire for Christy* (51) with Eleanor Parker. *Callaway Went Thataway* with Dorothy McGuire was a minute improvement, but that his star had definitely waned was evident from his acceptance of a junk vehicle at Republic, *Fair Wind to Java* (52), opposite the lovely Vera Hruba Ralston. *The Moonlighter* (53) with Stanwyck got lost somewhere.

He had turned down the role of the writer in *Sunset Boulevard*, after Montgomery Clift had decided not to do it and despite his success in an unsympathetic role under Billy Wilder's direction. But there were now many fewer offers and he took something similar in *The Caine Mutiny* (54), fourth-billed as the smarty-pants officer who is the captain's first critic. He was excellent in it, as he was again in *Pushover* as a cop staking out Kim Novak and turning bent because of her. Then he was in a couple of those 20th Century-Fox pictures which CinemaScoped half a dozen names into one movie: *A Woman's World* and *The Rains of Ranchipur* (55) in the latter in George Brent's old role (in *The Rains Came*). Between the two he did the unimportant *The Far Horizons* (55) supporting Charlton Heston. He now emulated Randolph Scott and Joel McCrea and kept his career going with budget-price actioners, mostly Westerns: *At Gunpoint, There's Always Tomorrow* (56), a soap opera, with Stanwyck, *Gun for a Coward* (57), *Quantez, Day of the Badman* (58), *Good Day for a Hanging, Face of a Fugitive* (59) and *The Oregon Trail*. But in 1958 Walt Disney had cast MacMurray in one of his early excursions into domestic comedy, *The Shaggy Dog*. Undistinguished in every way, the film – presumably due to the magic of the Disney name – drew huge audiences and was one of the year's top money-makers. (MacMurray also invested in Disney stock; that and other investments made him one of the wealthiest figures in show business, along with Hope, Crosby, Gene Autrey, Lucille Ball, Joel McCrea, Roy Rogers, Randolph Scott, Frank Sinatra and Stuart Whitman.) Then in 1960 Billy Wilder asked for MacMurray again, for *The Apartment*, when Paul Douglas died a week before filming: it was only a featured role, but effective, as Shirley MacLaine's boss/seducer.

In the early 60s MacMurray began a highly successful TV series, 'My Three Sons', but it was undoubtedly Disney who prolonged his film career. He had as much faith in MacMurray as MacMurray in him: *The Absent-Minded Professor* (61), in the title-role; *Bon Voyage* (62), a 'family' comedy with Jane Wyman; and *Son of Flubber* (63), as that professor again. *Kisses for My President* (64) at Warners, as the spouse of the President (Polly Bergen), died the death of all bad films and a comedy about scouting, *Follow Me Boys* (66), was one of the rare flops of the Disney Organization. *The Happiest Millionaire* (67) was another, leading to a hiatus – and a resumption of the Disney MacMurray films, *Charley and the Angel* (73), passed unnoticed.

He made two tele-movies, *The Chadwick Family* (74), somewhat of a return to the formula of his TV series, and *Beyond the Bermuda Triangle* (75), as a retired business-man investigating that mystery. He returned to films in *The Swarm* (78).

FREDRIC MARCH

'I'm just a ham,' said Fredric March once, discussing acting, a modest, deprecatory remark, but accurate on more than one occasion. Still, he was normally quietly excel-lent, seldom memorable and less affection-ately regarded than two other actors who twice won Best Actor Oscars, Spencer Tracy and Gary Cooper. He did go through a spell of being a Very Romantic Leading Man, but for most of his career he was a dedicated no-nonsense actor, authoritative and reliable; if you look at publicity stills of March you will find them more direct, less affected, than those of any other leading star: he did not pose. He was direct. And he managed to be in an above-average number of good movies.

He was born in 1897 in Racine, Wisconsin, and studied at the state's university. He was destined for banking, but during a spell in hospital determined to become an actor; he went to New York and made the rounds of the agents. His appearance – handsome, healthy, middle-class – got him some model-ling work and 'extra' jobs in movies, including *Pay the Piper* with Dorothy Dickson and *The Great Adventure* starring Lionel Barrymore. His first stage appearance was a two-line bit in Granville-Barker's adaptation of Sacha Guitry's 'Deburau' (20) and he progressed until he had a role in 'The Devil in the Cheese' (27), which netted him good notices from the New York press. He described himself at this period as a 'general-utility' actor and in that capacity the Theater Guild sent him on tour ('Arms and the Man', 'The Guardsman', etc.); he was in the West Coast production of 'The Royal Family' as the member of that family based on John Barrymore (Barrymore adored his parody). That led to a Paramount offer of a five-year contract.

March was virtually the first new star of the Talkies and certainly of the new intake he was the only one who endured. He was in *The Dummy* (29), opposite Ruth Chatterton, a modest version of a stage melodrama, and in *The Wild Party* as the professor enticed by student Clara Bow. Few people noticed him, but he was an oasis of sobriety and integrity in an unbelievable, corny film. He made more impression as a philandering movie star in *The Studio Murder Mystery* (his wife, Florence

Dr Jekyll into Mr Hyde: Fredric March in Rouben Mamoulian's film version (31).

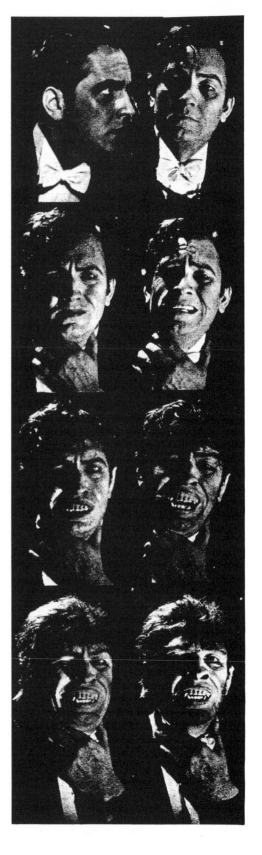

Eldridge, made her film début in it), but it was on loan-out for *Paris Bound* with Ann Harding that he first got his film career off the ground. Jeanne Eagels asked for him for *Jealousy*: the film had been finished, with Anthony Bushell, when she demanded it be reshot with March. She was seriously ill, and dead before it was released, to indifferent notices and business. Another big star, Colleen Moore, asked for him to be her stage-door johnny in *Footlights and Fools*. He played with Mary Brian in *The Marriage Playground*; with Ruth Chatterton in *Sarah and Son* (30), as her lawyer lover; with most of the Paramount roster in *Paramount on Parade*; Mary Astor in *Ladies Love Brutes*; Clara Bow in *True to the Navy*, as a brash gob; and Claudette Colbert in *Manslaughter*, George Abbott's remake of some old De Mille hokum.

He liked doing *Laughter*, as the amorous composer yearning for married Nancy Carroll, and the film is a superb study of the jazz era; after which he moved out of the co-star status when he redid his Barrymore impersonation in the film version, retitled *The Royal Family of Broadway*, all high spirits and zip: today it seems a very awkward performance. He was a Wall Street broker and Colbert was his secretary in *Honor Among Lovers* (31) – he lost her and won her back – and Carroll was *The Night Angel* (a part intended for Dietrich, which did much to kill off Carroll's career – the film was a giant flop). March was in a second failure, *My Sin*, playing a degenerate lawyer opposite Tallulah Bankhead, but he came back in force when Mamoulian selected him to play *Dr Jekyll and Mr Hyde*, over the studio's choice, Irving Pichel. In the transformation scenes wonders were accomplished with make-up and trick photography, but March's two impersonations were gripping and won a well-deserved Oscar.

Naturally, his parts got better: in a dual role (twins, good and bad) in *Strangers in Love* (32) with Kay Francis; in *Merrily We Go to Hell*, as a hard-drinking journalist; on loan to MGM for *Smilin' Through*; guesting, as himself in *Make Me a Star*; in *The Sign of the Cross*, as the Roman centurion; in *Tonight is Ours* (33), as the commoner who marries princess Claudette in this poor version of Noël Coward's 'The Queen Was in the Parlour'; in *The Eagle and the Hawk*, as an aviator; and in *Design for Living*, as one of the unholy trio – Gary Cooper and Miriam Hopkins were the others. March liked none of these, nor *All of Me* (34) with Hopkins, but he did like *Death Takes a Holiday* (which he considered one of his four best films, with *Dr Jekyll*, *A Star Is Born* and *The Best Years of Our Lives*). 'As Death, who mingles with guests at a house

Sylvia Sidney and Fredric March – socialite wife and ne'er-do-well reporter husband – in Merrily We Go to Hell (32), *directed by Dorothy Arzner, virtually the only successful woman director.*

party, and finds love with Evelyn Venable, Fredric March is superb' ('Photoplay'). Thus, after *Good Dame*, a silly programmer thrown together because he and Sylvia Sidney were available when the film of *R.U.R.* was cancelled, he refused to re-sign with Paramount (also, he had not liked the studio publicity which insisted that he was a successor to John Gilbert: he wanted to be a character actor).

He signed a contract with 20th, with the proviso that he had control over his material and could do outside parts. Years later, Hume Cronyn was to refer to him as a total actor, because he could play anything. But not quite yet. Hollywood was at that point embarking on costume epics galore and March was one of the few native actors who was not incongruous: but he was not *always* at home in the parts that followed. He might well have been good in the Damon Runyon story that 20th announced for him, but he was only fair in *The Affairs of Cellini*, which he did instead, bearded. And James Agate said his Robert Browning in *The Barretts of Wimpole Street* 'is just a joke in so far as he must be supposed to resemble the poet. He is a good, straightforward, manly lover, though we feel the intricacies of "Mary had a Little Lamb" would be beyond him.'

We Live Again was a new Goldwyn version of Tolstoy's 'Resurrection' and March received the then large sum of $100,000 for the indignity of being billed after Anna Sten. It was his 'honesty' said 'Photoplay', as the Prince 'who loses his ideals in the debauchery of life among Russian officers, betrays first love (Anna Sten), and lives to atone . . . that makes this a thing of beauty'. He was also an excellent Valjean in *Les Misérables* (35) at 20th, but returning to the Russian army under protest he was a callow and unconvincing Vronsky to Garbo's *Anna Karenina*. He did not want to be type-cast as a costume actor and chose a modern subject, *The Dark Angel*, a lachrymose Goldwyn remake, with Merle Oberon. He turned down, among others, *The Count of Monte Cristo*, *The Prisoner of Zenda* and a *Two Years Before the Mast* which Republic were contemplating, which makes his choice of *Mary of Scotland* (36) very odd: he was a spirited if unlikely Bothwell; and his wife was Elizabeth I (even less likely). In *The Road to Glory* this French lieutenant's woman was June Lang and captain Warner Baxter was also in love with her; March was good, but he was stilted on Warner's big-budgeted and long-winded version of Hervey Allen's bestseller, *Anthony Adverse*, which, though enjoyable, often seemed as though Runyon had written the dialogue.

He signed for two contemporary subjects with Selznick (at $125,000 each – now the fifth-highest paid actor in Hollywood). William A. Wellman steered both, helping to rescue the faltering March reputation. *A Star Is Born* (37) cast him as a falling movie star – a beautiful performance (quite the equal of James Mason's in the remake) and in *Nothing Sacred* he was a newspaper editor, flummoxed by the lies of Carole Lombard: it was her film, but he more than held his own. He then returned to Paramount for *The Buccaneer* (38), with an acceptable French accent: a De Mille spectacular and another big success for

March. But he and his wife had decided to return to Broadway and they did a play about Richard Steele of the 'Spectator', 'Yr Obedient Husband': it opened to dire notices and closed after a week. They returned to Hollywood.

But Hollywood is a funny place and yesterday's hero is today's redundancy: the only offers March got were from two independents, at half his usual salary (but plus a share of the profits). For Hal Roach he did a comedy, *There Goes My Heart*, as a reporter, with Virginia Bruce as an heiress, and for Wanger a poor adventure tale, *Trade Winds* (39). Hollywood's fickleness did not distress the Marches and they worked thereafter in that city and New York alternately. They liked working together, but Eldridge was unable to command the attention in Hollywood that she could on Broadway; she was clearly less obvious film material than her husband. Despite her poor Elizabeth I, in their Broadway appearances and in the three films they made together in the 40s she was, in talent, his equal. In 1939 they appeared in New York in the Hart-Kaufman pageant of Americana, 'The American Way'; in 1941 in 'Hope for a Harvest'; in 1942 in the successful 'The Skin of Our Teeth'; and in 1946 in 'Years Ago' (Ruth Gordon's play that became *The Actress* for films). March was on his own in 'A Bell for Adano' in 1944.

After their second absence on Broadway (1939), March astonished the trade by getting

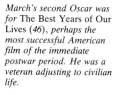

March's second Oscar was for The Best Years of Our Lives *(46), perhaps the most successful American film of the immediate postwar period. He was a veteran adjusting to civilian life.*

$100,000 each for his two return movies: *Susan and God* (40), being driven to drink by his wife Joan Crawford, and *Victory*, as the recluse who shelters frightened Betty Field – Conrad with a happy ending. Then: *So Ends Our Night* (41) with Margaret Sullavan, as a political agitator in Nazi Germany; *One Foot in Heaven*, a meandering but much-liked study of a Methodist minister, with Martha Scott; *Bedtime Story* – famous playwright battling with actress-wife Loretta Young, and vainly, for laughs; René Clair's gay *I Married a Witch* (42), from a Thorne Smith story, as a gubernatorial campaigner who marries her (Veronica Lake); *The Adventures of Mark Twain* (44) with Alexis Smith, and with the make-up men literally making up for the deficiencies of the scriptwriters; and *Tomorrow the World* with Betty Field, about an American family who discover their adopted son is a Nazi.

After a two-year absence March returned to the screen as the senior of the three returning war veterans in Wyler's *The Best Years of Our Lives* (46): the press reception was rapturous and helped to make this by far the biggest money-making film in which March had appeared. It also won seven Oscars, including a second Best Actor for March; but it did not lead to anything big, partly because in the flood of postwar leading men he was considered a veteran. At Universal he did two films with his wife, *Another Part of the Forest* (48), a cheap-jack version of Lillian Hellman's

sequel to 'The Little Foxes', and *Act of Murder*, a drama about euthanasia; but good acting did not bring either to box-office respectability. The next was his first major mistake since he had started freelancing: a trip to Britain for Rank's *Christopher Columbus* (49), an effort, more determined than usual, to capture a share of the American market; with a risible script the Marches (she was Isabella) floundered, until the direction scuttled them.

There were three stage appearances in 1950–51 (including 'An Enemy of the People') and a spot in the all-star, patriotic *It's a Big Country* (51); then March got the much-coveted part of Willy Loman in the film of Arthur Miller's *Death of a Salesman* (52). His performance was prized at the Venice Film Festival, but was unfavourably compared – as being over-hysterical – with those given by Lee J. Cobb in New York and Paul Muni in London. It brought March a fifth Oscar nomination and was a box-office failure. So was Kazan's *Man on a Tightrope* (53), an odd – but exciting – Iron Curtain/circus melodrama, proving again that March's name alone could not carry a film. However, helped by good reviews and some other big names, he was in three successes: *Executive Suite* (54) with Barbara Stanwyck, William Holden, etc.; *The Bridges at Toko-Ri* with Holden and Grace Kelly, as an admiral; and *The Desperate Hours* (55), splendid as the householder menaced by escaped thug Humphrey Bogart and agonizingly thinking in circles. In 1954 he did 'The Royal Family' on television with Claudette Colbert and Helen Hayes. He had supporting roles (but star billing) in the so-so *The Man in the Grey Flannel Suit* (56) and the flop *Alexander the Great*, unrecognizable – fortunately – as Philip of Macedonia.

After those, he returned to New York with his wife for O'Neill's 'Long Day's Journey into Night' and the general opinion was that this was the most distinguished work of their stage careers (he won the critics' Best Actor award); its run kept him off the screen until 1958, when he played a middle-aged man prepared to sacrifice everything for Kim Novak in Paddy Chayevsky's *The Middle of the Night*. Said 'Time' magazine: 'What most strikingly meets the eye is the profound performance of Fredric March. Seldom have youth and crabbed age lived together in one face with so much suffering and meaning'. The film failed pitiably – and sadly, because his next performance was knots below, in *Inherit the Wind* (60), with Spencer Tracy. 'Newsweek', having commented on Tracy's almost motionless performance, kindly said that March 'by contrast achieves a magnificence of over-acting'. He was more his old self

Fredric March, Diane Cilento and Paul Newman in Hombre *(67). Newman was a white man reared by Apaches and returning to the white man's world.*

in *The Young Doctors* (61); and in the weird international production of Sartre's play, *The Condemned of Altona* (63), as the patriarch, again indicated the comprehension and authority of which he was capable. His other roles were not big: *Seven Days in May* (64), as the President of the US; *Hombre* (67), as an Indian agent; and *Tick Tick Tick* (70), as a Southern mayor adjusting to the town's new black sheriff. On starting the latter he confirmed that he had retired, 'however, not as definitely as Jimmy Cagney'; and later appeared in a filmed-play film, *The Iceman Cometh* (73) with Lee Marvin. He died of cancer in 1975.

HERBERT MARSHALL

Herbert Marshall's co-stars included Garbo, Hepburn and Bette Davis, not to mention Claudette Colbert, Margaret Sullavan, Deanna Durbin, Dietrich, Joan Fontaine, Jean Arthur, Joan Crawford, Barbara Stanwyck, Constance Bennett, Kay Francis, Shirley Temple, Mary Astor, Ruth Chatterton, Miriam Hopkins and Norma Shearer: which suggests that he was a somewhat self-effacing actor. Norma Shearer once explained: 'The first time I saw Mr Marshall on the screen was in a picture with Claudette Colbert. I thought I had never seen a lady so thoroughly and convincingly loved. He is both manly and wistful. He wins the sympathy of women because his face expresses tenderness and silent suffering.' Actually he was urbane, soft-spoken and somewhat distant, but he let the ladies act rings round him – except perhaps in comedy, where his skill added much to the sophistication of some of the screen's best pieces; at the same time he was seldom outmatched and his performances – both as cuckolded husbands – in *The Painted Veil* with Garbo and *The Letter* with Bette Davis give much weight to both films.

He was born in London in 1890, into a theatrical family, was educated at a school in Essex and afterwards articled to a firm of chartered accountants. He became business manager for impresario Robert Courtneidge, from which it was a short step to acting, making his début in a rep at Brighton in 'The Adventures of Lady Ursula' (11). Two years later he appeared in London in 'Brewster's Millions' and then toured the US with the Cyril Maude Company in 'Grumpy'. He served with the BEF during the war and was severely wounded: his right leg was amputated (but apart from a slightly stiff walk this was never apparent to audiences and did not affect his career). He returned to the stage

and soon became a West End favourite; he appeared on Broadway in 'These Charming People' (25); in London in Noël Coward's 'The Queen Was in the Parlour' (26) and in New York again in 'The High Road' (28) with Edna Best. They married and became one of the most popular teams of the time. They both preferred Britain (Miss Best came from Hove), but certainly where films were concerned the opportunities were not there: Marshall appeared in two Silents, *Mumsie* (27) starring Pauline Frederick and *Dawn* (Sybil Thorndike as Edith Cavell; it was at first banned for political reasons), but his film career really began with Somerset Maugham's *The Letter* (29), as the lover, playing opposite Jeanne Eagels: Paramount produced and Marshall was offered a short-term contract.

Prior stage commitments took the Marshalls to Britain, however, and while he was there appearing in 'The Swan' he made *Murder* (30), a brilliant performance as an actor-knight, directed by Hitchcock from Clemence Dane's story, 'Enter Sir John'. He and Best co-starred in two British pictures: *The Calendar* (31), a racing story by Edgar Wallace, and *Michael and Mary*, from their stage hit about a smug, middle-aged couple disturbed by a blackmailer; then he returned to Hollywood for *Secrets of a Secretary* with Claudette Colbert. The Marshalls went home again, to make *The Faithful Heart* (32), in which he was a cocky First Mate and she both wife and daughter; then they crossed the Atlantic again to do 'There's Always Juliet' on Broadway. Meanwhile audience reaction to Marshall in the Colbert film was very strong, especially among the women, and Paramount could not wait to have him back. They bought him out of his Broadway play and hurried him into *Blonde Venus*, as Dietrich's husband, and *Trouble in Paradise*, a Lubitsch soufflé in which he and Kay Francis tried to cheat Miriam Hopkins out of her fortune. This film established him as a romantic, mature leading man and he was given a similar part, as an impoverished European nobleman offering *Evenings for Sale* to Sari Maritza and other ladies. Paramount saw him as the next 'great lover' and were disappointed when he insisted on returning to Britain to honour three commitments: *Clear All Wires* (33), *The Solitaire Man* and *I Was a Spy* with Madeleine Carroll.

After that, however, he fretted less in Hollywood – and, indeed, films there occupied him exclusively over the next score of years. The break-up of his marriage lessened his interest in the stage and in Britain; and shortly his name would be romantically linked with Gloria Swanson (a brawl over her in a Hollywood night spot brought headlines).

Richard Boleslawski's The Painted Veil (*34*) *reduced Maugham's study of the Colonial mentality to a mere regeneration theme. Here's Garbo as the unfaithful wife at the time she's redeeming herself for husband Herbert Marshall, a doctor curing an epic outbreak of cholera.*

Marshall did not, however, become the great star that Paramount had envisaged: he had another five years as a star actor, but his reserve and age limited him. He was one of the *Four Frightened People* (34) stranded in the Malay jungle for De Mille, from which he went to MGM for three, reputedly at the request of the ladies concerned: *Riptide* with Norma Shearer, as the jealous husband whose suspicions force her into the arms of Robert Montgomery; *Outcast Lady* with Constance Bennett; and *The Painted Veil* with Garbo. M.D. Phillips, in 'Picturegoer', wrote of his performance in the Bennett picture: 'Marshall is becoming too mannerized and is inclined to walk through his part with too obvious an air of nonchalance.' He was scheduled for a fourth with another big Metro star, *Three Weeks* with Swanson, but it was never made. He was: the attractive older man who wins Margaret Sullavan at the end of *The Good Fairy* (35); the sober industrious older man who waits by while Ann Harding dallies with dipsomaniac Louis Hayward in *The Flame Within*; the attractive older man who is won by secretary Sylvia Sidney in *Accent on Youth*;

and the noble older man who waits while Merle Oberon loves Fredric March in *The Dark Angel*.

In two comedies he got out of the rut somewhat: with Ann Harding in *The Lady Consents* (36), as a philanderer, and with Jean Arthur in *If You Could Only Cook*, blueblood in a gangster's pantry. There were two with Gertrude Michael, *Till We Meet Again* (spies, ex-lovers meeting again) and the remake of *Forgotten Faces*, in Clive Brook's old role, described thus by 'Photoplay': 'Herbert Marshall is superb as the cultured murderer trying to keep his daughter clear of his wife's clutches.' Then it was back to type-casting: the headmaster on whom Simone Simon has a crush in *Girls' Dormitory* and Katharine Hepburn's Old Faithful in *A Woman Rebels*. He made the minor *Make Way for a Lady* with Anne Shirley; and was then Dietrich's husband again and cuckolded again in *Angel* (37). He and Barbara Stanwyck had a comic *Breakfast for Two*; and he was a famous actor adopted by Deanna Durbin as a father to impress her schoolmates in *Mad About Music* (38). He was less congenially trapped in three

399

The Foreign Correspondent *(40) was Joel McCrea, in Europe on the eve of war. Among those he becomes involved with is his girlfriend's father, Herbert Marshall, whose peace propaganda campaign is a front for pro-Nazi activities.*

sudsers: *Always Goodbye* with Stanwyck; *Woman Against Woman* – Mary Astor and Virginia Bruce and divorce and remarriage; and *Zaza* (39), as the wealthy patron who loves and leaves Claudette Colbert.

In the remake of *The Letter* (40) he was this time the husband; in the remake of *A Bill of Divorcement* he was the man mother Fay Bainter wants to marry; and in Hitchcock's marvellous *Foreign Correspondent*, with Joel McCrea and Laraine Day, her father, sympathetic and the surprise villain. After a tame political drama, *Adventure in Washington* (41), with Virginia Bruce, he was again Bette Davis's suffering husband in another Wyler-directed film, *The Little Foxes* – a strong portrayal of a weak man; he did *When Ladies Meet* with Joan Crawford and Greer Garson, and *Kathleen* as Shirley Temple's widowed father; and then, memorably, *The Moon and Sixpence* (42), playing the narrator (Somerset Maugham) *vis-à-vis* the 'Gauguin' of George Sanders. It was more or less his last leading role and the beginning of a period of decreased activity.

In 1943 he did *Flight for Freedom* with Rosalind Russell, teaching her to fly; *Forever and a Day* as a London parson; *Young Ideas* with Astor; and in 1944 only *Andy Hardy's Blonde Trouble*; he was the understanding blind friend of the lovers in *The Enchanted Cottage* (45) – for the first time appearing on the screen with stick and limp; and was in *The Unseen* as the family friend – and the villain.

He repeated his discreet Maugham impersonation in *The Razor's Edge* (46); was in the Pat O'Brien *Crack-Up* and then did another of the gloomy roles in which he was being increasingly cast, as the proud father of

Jennifer Jones, killed off early in *Duel in the Sun*. Predictably, he was ensnared and cuckolded by the poisonous *Ivy* (47) – Joan Fontaine, but it was not a big role; he had good ones in *High Wall* (48), as the educational publisher whose schemes get Robert Taylor caught up in a murder hunt, and in *The Secret Garden* (49), as the child's unfeeling guardian.

The Underworld Story (50), starring Dan Duryea, was almost the first time in his career that Marshall had done an unabashed B product and not all of his later films were more distinguished: the US-Spanish *Black Jack*; *Anne of the Indies* (51), a pirate drama with Jean Peters and Louis Jourdan, as Anne's humanitarian 'doc'; and *Angel Face* (52), as Jean Simmons's father, accidentally murdered by her. In 1952 he did a TV series, 'The Unexpected'. In a couple of low-budget sci-fiers produced by Ivan Tors for United Artists, *Riders to the Stars* (54) and *Gog*, he had conventional 'doctor' roles and did them impeccably; even reduced to the rubbishy cardboard castles of a Hollywood Merrie England in *The Black Shield of Falworth*, with Tony Curtis, he could not help being good. But his name was well down the cast-list and it was again in *The Virgin Queen* (55), as an ageing Leicester to Davis's Elizabeth. He returned to Britain for a couple of Bs, *Wicked As They Come* (56), which referred to Arlene Dahl, pronounced dull, and *The Weapon* (57) with Steve Cochran and Lizabeth Scott: despite the US names, neither got many bookings Stateside.

Stage Struck (58) with Henry Fonda, in which he was an ageing actor, was more the quality he had been used to, but neither *The Fly* (58) nor *College Confidential* (60) was – though Vincent Price, who co-starred in the former, has recalled that Marshall treated the whole thing as a great joke. Maybe he was as light-hearted about his last pictures: *Midnight Lace*, as business partner to Rex Harrison; *A Fever in the Blood* (61), as unconcerned uncle to a man on trial; *Five Weeks in a Balloon* (62), as the prime minister; *The List of Adrian Messenger* (63), as a Scotland Yard man; *The Caretakers*, as a doctor, and *The Third Day* (65), as a paralysed tycoon. He died of a heart attack in 1966. He had married five times; he and Edna Best divorced in 1940. Their daughter, Sarah Marshall, has had roles in a few films (*The Long Hot Summer*) and seems to have inherited more than a share of their talents.

MARY MARTIN

Mary Martin is regarded as one of Hollywood's lost causes. At the time of her Broadway peak ('South Pacific', 49) some publicity was made from her failure in Hollywood some years earlier. It is a failure hard to fathom: she could sing, she was a delightful comedienne, she was pretty – in fact, she comes out high in any assessment of the Musical Ladies of that time. Her voice was her best asset: speaking, it was melodic and nicely Texas-accented; and singing, she could range within her warm soprano from 'Il Bacio' to 'Wait till the Sun Shines Nellie'. Maybe she was just too talented and too individual to fit into the wartime mould.

She was born in Waterford, Texas, in 1913 and educated in Nashville, Tennessee, but returned to her home town and taught dancing. She took her troupe (the Martinettes) to Fort Worth for the Centennial Celebrations, but Billy Rose, who was staging it, advised her to return home (some of the Martinettes got engagements, however). Instead, Martin tried Hollywood. She made the rounds and even got screen-tested (by five studios) plus a bit part as Danielle Darrieux's dancing teacher in *Rage of Paris* (38); she eked out a living by singing in clubs – and was caught one night at the Trocadero by Broadway producer Lawrence Schwab. She went to New York, but the show Schwab was planning fell through and he loaned her to another producer, Vinton Freedley, for a Cole Porter musical, 'Leave it to Me'. It was a minor role, but it included 'My Heart Belongs to Daddy' to a simulated strip-tease and overnight Martin became the toast of Broadway.

She returned triumphantly to Hollywood with a Paramount contract in her pocket. Her first film was *The Great Victor Herbert* (39), which used tunes from his operettas – and him as a subsidiary character (Walter Connolly) – for an utterly conventional story of a showbiz marriage; Martin, second-billed, made a favourable impression as Allan Jones's long-suffering wife, and she sang a lot. The film was popular; and she went on to play opposite Bing Crosby in *Rhythm on the River* (40) and Jack Benny in *Love Thy Neighbor*, refereeing in the fights with Fred Allen (whose niece she played). *Kiss the Boys Goodbye* (41) gave her a fine chance as a would-be Scarlett O'Hara, a funny musi-comedy which spoofed the search for the screen Scarlett, and she was again captivating as Crosby's *vis-à-vis* in *The Birth of the Blues*. *New York Town* – without music – effectively cast her as a hard-working city girl, a sort of lower-case Jean Arthur, but it was not good. She duetted with Dick Powell on 'Hit the Road to Dreamland' in *Star Spangled Rhythm* and starred with him in another musical, *Happy Go Lucky* (43), but that, though Technicolored, was again very ordinary. Nor was *True to Life* much improvement. W.H. Mooring in 'Picturegoer' suggested that the trouble was that Martin only got offered the pictures that Claudette Colbert turned down. She left Hollywood, dissatisfied, and no Paramount executive cried over her departure.

She herself really preferred a live audience. She hated the waiting about on film-sets. There were two simultaneous stage offers: 'Oklahoma!' and 'Dancing in the Streets'. She chose the latter: it failed to reach New York. In late 1943 she did have another Broadway musical smash, 'One Touch of Venus', which kept her busy for 18 months. She scored such

Mary Martin in two wartime musicals. Left, with Bing Crosby in Birth of the Blues *(41); it wasn't really about the blues, but it was good anyway. Right, with Dick Powell in* Happy Go Lucky *(43): not a bad title for a musical about a stenographer who spends her life savings on a cruise in an effort to entrap a wealthy husband. It's no surprise when she lands Powell instead.*

a hit that UA (Mary Pickford) wanted her to repeat for the film version and borrowed her from Paramount, to whom she still owed three films. However, for some reason it was not made (director Gregory La Cava sued UA for his salary). Martin returned to New York and 'Lute Song', and Paramount announced she would do *Alice-Sit-by-the-Fire* – but her only film work was singing 'My Heart Belongs to Daddy' in WB's Cole Porter biopic, *Night and Day* (46). As on Broadway, she stole the notices with this number and Hollywood renewed its interest – particularly Warners, who had no musical lady to match the appeal of the Garlands and Huttons and Grables at other studios. In 1948 Martin was to have made *Romance on the High Seas*, but as with her first screen tests, she was thought unphotogenic. And she herself, once-bitten, was wary. Meanwhile, in London she had done 'Pacific 1860' by Noël Coward; she turned down the London lead in 'Annie Get Your Gun', but agreed to tour the US in it. In 1949 came 'South Pacific', an undreamt-of success, which placed her (alongside Ethel Merman) as the first lady of the American musical stage. In 1952 she played herself in *Main Street to Broadway*: despite its roster of stars, it got few bookings. She continued to have great successes on the stage: 'Kind Sir' (53), 'Peter Pan' (54), 'The Sound of Music' (59), 'Hello Dolly' (65) on tour and in London; and on TV, in some of the most successful specials in the history of the medium – including 'Peter Pan' (55), 'Born Yesterday' (56) and 'Annie Get Your Gun' (57). But, incredibly, she was passed over for the film of *South Pacific*. Joshua Logan, who directed – as he had on stage – said: 'Outside of my own family, I love Mary more than anyone in the world, but I felt I couldn't subject her to the endless adjustments she would have to make in putting her superb performance on film.' The film was inescapably, infinitely, poorer for that decision.

She was eventually coaxed back before the cameras – now perhaps famous as the mother of J.R. (Larry Hagman) – for a telefilm, *Valentine* (79) co-starring with Jack Albertson in a tale of a couple in their 70s falling in love.

THE MARX BROTHERS

It should have been an occasion for rejoicing when the Marx Brothers began to enter the realms of mythology. Is there a figure of this century more wholly admirable than Harpo? or Groucho? or even Chico? The reverence accorded them these days is hardly in accordance with their own anarchic attitude to everything, but it does mean that they are often with us and it is possible to keep in touch with them at repertory cinemas; and apart from their myth-status their clowning still makes them immortal. Some of their gags have dated, but they remain on the whole funnier than ever – funnier and more modern than any other comic team (or, indeed, any other comic) which came afterwards. As Allen Eyles says in his excellent study of them (1966) they 'are the heroes of everyone who has suffered from other people's hypocrisy, pomposity, pedantism, and patronage. They settle for none of it. The Marxes assume that we join them on their comic crusade.' Not that the world that the Marxes inhabit is sane to begin with – it is not only the amorous, deluded and indestructible Margaret Dumont who takes them seriously: the connivers and cheats whom they are trying to outwit accept them – with exasperation, perhaps – as rational beings. It really was a world turned upside down into which the Marx Brothers tore with antic delight, tipping it further askew with a wild defiance of logic.

Groucho is generally accepted as the best of them – perhaps because he got most of the (often audacious) wisecracks. He was the one with fake moustache and cigar, with the sardonic asides to the audience, the one who was one-step-up, an aspiring bureaucrat, a parvenu chasing after the ever-ready Mrs Rittenhouse, Mrs Claypool or Mrs Emily Upjohn (whose trains and feathers Dumont inhabited so majestically). Groucho had no illusions though – he was modest enough to accept the others in uneasy alliance whenever he was about to be found out, or before that, if he was in a gullible mood.

Harpo was the one with the hair like Bubbles, the dumb one, the one with the recalcitrant leg and the propensity for collecting things like bicycle horns. To state categorically that Groucho was Harpo's superior (plot exigencies aside) takes into account the softening of the Harpo character in the later films, where he can be found aiding the lovers or entertaining children. The early Harpo was much too bent on lechery and larceny – and between times causing as much chaos as possible ('unregenerate destruction' in Dilys Powell's words) – for such slop: indeed, he pursued his entirely selfish aims as ferociously as a demon. Chico aided and abetted them both, usually with a bias towards Harpo who, after all, was more destructive and less pretentious than Groucho – indeed, Chico himself had no pretensions; he knew his place. Despite his Italian–American punning (or perhaps because of it), he is not as funny as the others, but his readiness to obstruct is quite endearing.

They were a New York family, of German–Jewish descent. Chico was born in 1891, Harpo in 1893, Groucho in 1895 and Zeppo – the straight man in the early films – in 1901. (Another brother, Gummo, never appeared in films with them.) Their mother – whose brother was Al Sheean, the vaudeville star – pushed them into show business quite early, singly or as a troupe, and Sheean was sometimes called in to help polish the act. With mother and an aunt they started as 'The Six Musical Mascots'. In 1912 they did an act called 'Mister Green's Reception', supported by a cast of 19. As the Four Marks Brothers they appeared in 'The Duke of Bull Durham', a tab-show (i.e. an abbreviated musical comedy which toured vaudeville theatres). In 1914 they had an act called 'Home Again' and billed themselves as 'The Greatest Comedy Act in Show Business: barring none'. Bit by bit they evolved the characters that they were to bring to the screen. Their first break came when they left the halls and appeared in a 'book' show, 'I'll Say She Is'; after two years flogging this around the country, they took it to Broadway and became cult figures overnight. It had a smash run (during which Harpo had a small role in a Richard Dix comedy, *Too Many Kisses*) and was followed by 'The Cocoanuts' in 1925 and by 'Animal Crackers' at the end of 1928.

During the run of 'Cocoanuts' they had made a film privately – for $6,000 – but it was never released; now, while they were in 'Animal Crackers', Paramount and Fox offered them contracts. They signed with Paramount for three films, at $75,000 per film, and made a movie version of *The Cocoanuts* (29) in New York, with stage routines and painted settings, no more than a filmed record of the stage show – and with too much plot not involving them. The filmization of *Animal Crackrs* (30), which followed, was more cinematic; the plot centres on a fake African explorer – Groucho as Captain Spaulding – and a fake Old Master.

The next one was made in Hollywood, *Monkey Business* (31), and they were stowaways on a liner, adventitiously involved with gangsters, who include Thelma Todd, a more glamorous but less exacting foil than Dumont. Dumont is not in the next one, either, *Horse Feathers* (32), but otherwise it has some bright ideas, such as casting Groucho as a college dean and the others as students. Said C.A. Lejeune: 'There is nothing persuasive about the Marx Brothers. They coolly turn their backs on their audience and get on with their business. They never solicit applause and they go out of their way to reject sympathy. Their clowning is an emetic for emotion. They play to one another and criticize one another;

Chico and Harpo in Horse Feathers *(32) which, as far as can be ascertained, concerned a college football match. Groucho was certainly the new head of the college. Harpo was a dog-catcher and Chico had something to do with a speakeasy.*

Marx is occupied with Marx to the exclusion of the public, the orchestra, the plot and the rest of the cast.' S.J. Perelman worked on the screenplay of both these films and later recorded his impression of the Marxes: 'As far as temperaments and their personalities were concerned, they were capricious, tricky beyond endurance, altogether unreliable, and treacherous to a degree that would make Machiavelli absolutely kneel at their feet. They were also megalomaniac to a degree which is impossible to describe, despite the fact that they were not yet what they were to become after these pictures.

'I did two films with them, which in its way is perhaps my greatest distinction in life, because anybody who ever worked on any picture for the Marx Brothers said he would rather be chained to a galley oar and lashed at ten-minute intervals until the blood spurted from his frame than ever work for these sons of bitches again.' *Duck Soup* (33) had even

Groucho Marx, Margaret Dumont, Louis Calhern and Raquel Torres in Duck Soup *(33), the most delirious of the Marx Brothers comedies. Said Cecelia Ager of Miss Dumont: 'There ought to be a statue erected, or a Congressional Medal awarded, or a national holiday proclaimed, to honour that great woman, Margaret Dumont . . . a lady of epic ability to take it, a lady whose mighty love for Groucho is a saga of devotion, a lady who asks but little and gets it . . . once again her fortitude is nothing human. It's godlike.'*

brighter ideas than *Horse Feathers*, like Groucho as President (of a banana republic), Rufus T. Firefly. His stunning ineptitude, blindly supported by the wealthiest widow in the land (Dumont), leads to friction with a neighbouring state – whose idea of secret agents is Harpo and Chico (not that they stay on one side for very long). In no sense a political satire, though heavily involved with dictators and revolution, it was banned by Mussolini. Eyles says: '*Duck Soup* is the most highly regarded of the Marxes' pictures. Groucho himself thinks it is the craziest' – but at the time it fared badly at the box-office.

At Paramount the success of the Marx Brothers was – according to a biographer, Kyle Crichton – 'solid but not sensational': following the flop of *Duck Soup* and a change of management the studio was not interested in renewing the contract. But Irving Thalberg at MGM was keen to have the Marxes and the contract that Chico and he worked out gave them a salary plus 15 per cent of the gross (which meant, for instance, that the team earned $30,000 from a reissue of *A Night at the Opera* in 1949). Thalberg in other ways was shrewd – he let the Marxes take the key sequences out on a road-tour to test them before audiences (an idea they welcomed) and he insisted on a love interest (not involving them): the result, *A Night at the Opera* (35), drew big crowds, made more money than any

of their other films and remains the most famous. The second one at MGM is only a whit less enjoyable, *A Day at the Races* (37), except for an insipid romance and bang in the middle of the film a lavish production number; what was more worrying was that a softening of their characters was becoming apparent.

They then moved over briefly to RKO, who had bought – for $225,000, then a record sum – a Broadway hit, with the idea of letting the Marxes loose on it: the result, *Room Service* (38), has them bothering a mite more with plot than usual, but it does not diminish them. Back at MGM, *At the Circus* (39) does: Thalberg was dead and no one now at the studio cared. Groucho's son, Arthur, wrote (in 'Groucho', 1954) that he 'didn't like MGM without Thalberg and apparently MGM was beginning to feel the same way about the Marx Brothers.' The film on the whole was preferable to *Go West* (40), which, after a typically Marxian opening, degenerates into gags which any team could have done.

Groucho himself wrote that the team was unhappy with the material MGM forced on them and they found the atmosphere uncongenial – but they themselves were ageing and less interested. They agreed to go their separate ways but did one more first: *The Big Store* (41), which was funnier than the last two put together. They changed their minds about

Two scenes from A Night at the Opera *(35). Left, the Ocean crossing – in the Marx's cabin. Right, after the 'opera' with Margaret Dumont, who for love of Groucho will bail them out as usual.*

Norman Krasna he wrote a screenplay, *The King and the Chorus Girl* (filmed in 1937 with Joan Blondell), and a play, 'Time for Elizabeth'; he wrote several books – mostly memoirs – and had considerable success on TV, notably with his own quiz show, 'You Bet Your Life'. In 1960 he played Koko in *The Mikado* on TV. And he made several films without the others: *Copacabana* (47) with Carmen Miranda; *Mr Music* (50), as guest star; *Double Dynamite* (51) with Sinatra and Jane Russell; *A Girl in Every Port* (52) with William Bendix; and, after a long interval, Preminger's flop *Skidoo* (69). He died in 1977.

JAMES MASON

There was a considerable outcry when James Mason quit British films for Hollywood not long after the end of the war. It had always irked the British – their journalists if not their filmgoers – that most home-made actors yielded sooner or later to the blandishments of the wealthier and more glamorous American industry. It was beside the point that until the war most British films were tombs for talent: at that point the only British stars of international note were those who had worked for Hollywood or/and Alexander Korda. During the war, however, British films suddenly – and temporarily, as it turned out – improved and at the same time threw up a whole new crop of stars. Not all these new stellar attractions were in the good films, but for the first time there was more than a handful of Britishers competing with the Americans for the box-office cash. None of them was bigger than James Mason, who from 1944 to 1947 inclusive was easily the top British box-office draw: in 1946 he drew more patrons into cinemas than anyone else, including Bing Crosby. His retreat or escape to Hollywood lost him his special place in Britain, yet almost alone of those wartime stars he survived. So did Deborah Kerr, who came along a while later, and she also deserted the gloomy skies of Bucks for sunnier climes; but in both cases the reason has less to do with Hollywood than with talent.

Mason was born in Huddersfield in 1909 and was educated at Marlborough and Cambridge. He studied architecture, but the Drama claimed him and he made his first appearance in 'The Rascal' (31) in Aldershot. Two years later he scored a London hit in 'Gallows Glorious', after which he played secondary roles at the Old Vic. Korda saw him as Jeremy in 'Love for Love' and signed him for a part in *The Private Life of Don Juan*:

retiring when they were offered a percentage of the profits on an independent venture, *A Night in Casablanca* (46): to a postwar world agog for laughter, it was a gas, but their devotees knew that it was not up to much. Another comeback, *Love Happy* (49), was greeted sadly and did poor business: the Marxes could not give impetus any longer to feeble scripting – not that it was really a Marx Brothers picture, being mainly Harpo, some Chico and about 10 minutes of Groucho. Chico and Harpo semi-retired, but did TV and miscellaneous stage work. The three of them appeared, but not together, in a weirdie of a film *The Story of Mankind* (57): Chico was a monk who advised Columbus, Groucho, who later said they had only done it because Harpo needed the money, was Peter Minuit and Harpo Sir Isaac Newton. Chico died in 1961 and Harpo in 1964.

Their work separately throughout their career was often varied – e.g. Harpo once played in 'The Man Who Came to Dinner' and Chico once had his own band. But Groucho's work is the most interesting: with but after a few days decided he was miscast and let him go. For the next three years (1934–37) Mason was with the Gate Company in Dublin, but he commuted to Britain, tentatively beginning his film career as the star of quota quickies: *Late Extra* (36), co-starring with Virginia Cherrill, as a reporter; *Twice Branded*, as the son of a man wrongly convicted; *Troubled Waters*, as a detective; *Prison Breaker*, as a Secret Service agent; *Blind Man's Buff*, supporting Basil Sydney in this triangle drama; and *Secret of Stamboul* (37) opposite Valerie Hobson. He was Tom Tulliver to Geraldine Fitzgerald's Maggie in a fair screen transcription of *The Mill on the Floss* and he had a good role supporting Lionel Atwill in Thorold Dickinson's *The High Command*, as a young officer involved in an adulterous affair. During this time he was under contract to Fox, hoping to be sent to Hollywood; but instead they dropped him.

Korda gave him a small role, without billing, in *Fire Over England*, as the traitor who, after he has drowned himself, Laurence Olivier impersonates at the Spanish court: but that producer still could not see his potential. On stage he was Hannibal in Sherwood's 'The Road to Rome' and that cut down his movie activity: *Catch As Catch Can*, as a Customs officer in this ocean-liner crime drama; and *The Return of the Scarlet Pimpernel* (38) – who returned not as Leslie Howard but as Barry K. Barnes. Mason was a young aristo threatened with the guillotine.

With two friends, Roy and Pamela Kellino, Mason set up *I Met a Murderer* (39), co-scripting as well as starring. It had a brief critical success; and when the friends later divorced, Mason married her (the marriage lasted till 1964). In 1941 he was on the stage again in 'Jupiter Laughs', but it was his last London appearance because films began to claim all his attention (he disliked acting in the theatre): *This Man is Dangerous* (41), as a brash private eye; *Hatter's Castle*, from A.J. Cronin's novel, as the young doctor who saves the heroine from the wrath of her power-crazy father, Robert Newton; *The Night Has Eyes* (42), as a Spanish Civil War veteran framed for murder; *Alibi*, as a detective, the role played by Louis Jouvet in an earlier version; *Secret Mission*, as a Free Frenchman; *Thunder Rock*, as an old chum of Michael Redgrave; and *The Bells Go Down* (43), as the disciplinarian boss of a Fire Service station. Not always starred, he was invariably better than the stars, with looks, authority and, when needed, charm.

Then came the one that made the difference: *The Man in Grey*. Eric Portman had turned it down and Mason took it reluctantly (he recalled later, with glee, Agate's descrip-tion, 'bosh and tosh'): a preposterous Regency novel, wherein he was terribly mean to Phyllis Calvert while carrying on with her supposed friend, Margaret Lockwood – till she murdered Calvert and he took a horse-whip to her. For this 'Picturegoer' readers voted him Actor of the Year; and when the film arrived in the US 'Time' magazine observed: 'Swaggering through the title role, sneering like Laughton, barking like Gable and frowning like Laurence Olivier on a dark night, he is likely to pick up many a feminine fan.' Gainsborough/Rank, who produced, signed him to a contract, for six films over a four-year period.

There were some ordinary chores to be got out of the way: *They Met in the Dark*, *Candlelight in Algeria* and *Hotel Reserve* (44): then he returned to villainy in *Fanny By Gaslight*, from Michael Sadleir's novel – and the only one of these films to have much merit. Audiences gloated while he was mean again to Phyllis Calvert, taking it all much more seriously than he did. As a change, he insisted on doing a character part, as a bluff elderly Yorkshireman in the film of Osbert Sitwell's ghost story, *A Place of One's Own* (45). But as World War II ended British audiences were queueing to see Mason up to his neck in dirty work, driving Dulcie Gray to drink and death in *They Were Sisters*. Michael Powell asked him to appear in *I Know Where I'm Going* and he agreed to take billing below Wendy Hiller in the US, where she was a

Margaret Lockwood and James Mason in The Man in Grey (*43*), which leap-frogged them to the fore of all other British stars.

bigger name, but not in Britain, though Mason himself in his memoir says that negotiations foundered because they would have to live in tents during the extensive location work and Powell refused to let him and his wife stay in a hotel 30 miles away. He was to prove grateful because he was able to accept *The Seventh Veil*, which made him world famous. The role had been intended for the portly Francis L. Sullivan, who specialized in villains, so in the course of the piece Mason, as her guardian, brought his stick on Ann Todd's hands as she played the piano: only she loved him at the end. This well-received farrago of nonsense was a big success in the States: 'That Mason,' said D.W. Griffith to Ezra Goodman, 'is the greatest actor.' 'The Times' (London) had earlier commented that Mason had made the character 'attractive in spite of his aberrations and [he] suggests a passion for art that is strong and selfless.'

After the series of Gainsborough romances Mason finally made a film the critics liked: Odd Man Out (46). *With him is Fay Compton.*

After lusting after Lockwood in *The Wicked Lady* he had his first big critical success: Carol Reed's version of a novel by F.L. Green, *Odd Man Out* (46), a sad and almost surrealistic tale of a wounded gunman on the run in Belfast; but *The Upturned Glass* (47) was a psychological thriller of no discernible merit, admittedly done in desperation since he had planned to make a film about Bramwell Brontë, with that title, when Hollywood sent over its own, *Devotion*, with Arthur Kennedy in that role. Mason himself produced, but this concession on the part of his employers did not mollify him; as he, wife and cats embarked for the USA he patiently explained that he did not care for the production set-up in Britain and that he had no confidence in an industry dominated by J. Arthur Rank. Further, there were fantastic offers from Hollywood. There were, however, still commitments in Britain (including a two-picture deal with Korda, one of which was to have been *The King's General*, though that was postponed and then cancelled) and once in the US Mason found himself in the midst of litigation and injunctions preventing him from filming. He appeared in a Broadway play that flopped, 'Bathsheba' (47), and appeared on TV where he made a few chance criticisms of Hollywood, so that when he eventually arrived there he was a very much cooler property.

Later he agreed that he had bungled this move and he considered that he permanently ruined his chances of top Hollywood stardom by playing mainly negative roles – losers, nice guys, weaklings – the sort of parts which attracted him as a change from villainy. Certainly he started badly: trapped in Max Ophüls's *Caught* (49), as the nice doctor keen on Barbara Bel Geddes – but it marked no

advance in his career, done largely because there were few other offers. MGM offered the role of Boulanger in *Madame Bovary*, but he did not feel he could play it (Louis Jourdan did) – and asked for the role of Flaubert in the curious prologue tacked on to the story. Then he returned to Ophüls to play the white-hearted blackmailer in *The Reckless Moment* with Joan Bennett; after which he was Barbara Stanwyck's playboy husband in *East Side West Side*; and the disgraced doctor involved with crooks in *One Way Street* (50) with Marta Toren. He returned to Britain to play a ghost in love with Ava Gardner in the beautiful but muddled *Pandora and the Flying Dutchman* (51).

His fee was a round $100,000 per film. He refused all long-term contracts, but had a one film a year contract with 20th – who now provided him with two films which gave his career renewed interest: *The Desert Fox*, a fine portrayal of Rommel in this good biopic, and Mankiewicz's gripping *Five Fingers* (52), based on 'Operation Cicero', a true account of the valet/spy (Mason) at the British Embassy in Ankara during the war. But as Mason once commented wryly, each time he did what he and the critics considered a good job, there was seldom a follow-up; and there was now a long hiatus – though his position was weakened by *The Lady Possessed*, produced by himself at Republic with his wife and June Havoc. He was fine, again, as Rupert of Hentzau in *The Prisoner of Zenda*, though the

John Gielgud as Cassius and James Mason as Brutus, 'the noblest Roman of them all', in Julius Caesar (53). The film's director, Joseph L. Mankiewicz, was in Britain when it was due to open, but fled because he feared the wrath of the country's critics. However, as he said later, reading their reviews was one of the most satisfying experiences of his career.

role was much smaller than that of Stewart Granger, his erstwhile second lead in a couple of British films. For producer Huntingdon Hartford he played one of Conrad's sea captains in *Face to Face*, a two-part film which got few bookings. He remained at the helm in *Botany Bay*, ill-treating Alan Ladd, and was forced to do some more repeats: *The Story of Three Loves* (53), doing his *Seventh Veil* bit in Episode One, with Moira Shearer as his ward/victim; and *The Desert Rats*, a brief appearance as Rommel. But at that point where he looked like becoming a meanie in second-rate movies he was offered Brutus by Mankiewicz in his excellent *Julius Caesar* – 'Greater than Ivanhoe' as the ads put it – and of the distinguished cast many thought his the best performance.

His row with Korda settled (he had sued Mason for $50,000 and settled out of court for $40,000), he returned to Britain for *The Man Between*, produced by him and directed by Carol Reed – his attempt to do for Berlin what *The Third Man* had done for Vienna, with Mason as the mysterious figure, a mere shadow of Harry Lime. It was not even a half-success when Mason needed a big one, but pity was not in order in view of *Charade*, released in Britain only, three stories he and his wife had made for American TV, directed by Roy Kellino, and 'an almost embarrassingly amateurish failure' ('MFB'). Mankiewicz offered him the role of the impotent Italian count in *The Barefoot Contessa*, but he

decided that he had played too many losers and that in any case his role was subsidiary to Humphrey Bogart. Instead, he went to 20th to be top-billed as the villain opposing Robert Wagner, the *Prince Valiant* (54), based on a comic strip, but producers were not exactly lining up at his door. Warners had wanted Olivier originally for *A Star is Born* and Cary Grant changed his mind at the last minute; others afraid of being swamped by the talent of Judy Garland and the memory of Fredric March were Gary Cooper, Bogart, Marlon Brando and Montgomery Clift (Richard Burton, also asked, was unavailable). For $12,000 a week Mason responded to Garland, his fading movie star portrayal offering some of the best emotional acting seen on the screen. Said the director, George Cukor: 'He is a complete actor. He is a man who has the greatest discretion . . . rather reserved by nature, a mysterious creature. To see that man break down was very moving. But all the credit for that goes to James.' He had another personal success in another popular film, Disney's *20,000 Leagues Under the Sea*, as Captain Nemo. In 1954 at Stratford, Ontario, he played Angelo in 'Measure for Measure' and 'Oedipus Rex'.

For some years he plodded on without great éclat: in big parts in mainly poor films and subsidiary roles in some goodish films. He never lost star billing, but once or twice it was a close thing. After two big movies, there were simply no offers, so 'in desperation' he agreed to play an angel in a thudding Lucille Ball comedy, *Forever Darling* (56), a film he tried to forget, and he was a drug addict – a superb performance – in *Bigger Than Life*; but this was otherwise a disastrous venture, as produced by himself and directed by Nicholas Ray – and it resulted in 20th annulling their agreement with him. But he stayed at that studio to be let down by Robert Rossen on his film of Alec Waugh's bestseller, *Island in the Sun*, which turned out to be a tour of the dreariest couples on the island. There were good parts in two modest thrillers made by Andrew and Virginia Stone, *Cry Terror* (58) and *The Decks Ran Red*, sympathetic in both – and modest was the way MGM pushed them. He stayed at that studio for Hitchcock's *North by Northwest* (59) and in his small part was so suavely villainous that he outshone Cary Grant; and in Jules Verne's *Journey to the Center of the Earth* he played with a tongue-in-cheek that set new standards for this sort of thing. But in the British *A Touch of Larceny* (60) and the American *The Marriage-Go-Round* (61) he demonstrated, as the press told him, that he could not play comedy – at least, not under these directors. In between came *The Trials of Oscar Wilde* (60) with Peter Finch and some observers informed him that his interpretation of advocate Sir Edward Carson was inferior to Ralph Richardson's in the rival film: a strange verdict.

Perhaps disheartened, Mason took a guest spot (on the cast list but unbilled) in *Escape From Zahrain* (62), with Yul Brynner. But he then got his best change in years, when Noël Coward turned down Stanley Kubrick's film of Nabokov's virtually unfilmable *Lolita*; but as the hapless middle-aged victim of nymphet Sue Lyon his performance divided the press. Dwight Macdonald found it as 'earthbound' as expected from this actor, but 'Sight and Sound' in Britain found him 'so much better than American reviews had hinted at as to suggest some sea-change in mid-Atlantic', adding, 'James Mason has been quietly good, or merely quiet, for so long, in so many films, that it is easy to under-estimate his achievement here.' But the most impressive accolade was Sidney Lumet's, who said that he had read the script and considered that without Mason to pull it together the film would have been a mess. (Mason himself thought it his best film, with *Odd Man Out* next.)

What is certain is that, despite the critical and popular success of *Lolita*, Mason's career resumed its oscillating pattern and he went on to this trio: *Hero's Island*, an adventure story which he co-produced; the Rank *Tiara Tahiti* with John Mills; and *Finchè dura la Tempesta/ Torpedo Bay* (64), an Italian war film with

English dialogue. The Rank one was shown on the Rank circuit in Britain, but the three of them were for strictly lowercase bookings, if that. However, he then began to accept supporting roles and in film after film stole the notices: *The Fall of the Roman Empire* ('only James Mason's Timonides emerges with honour and authority undiminished' – Peter John Dyer in the 'MFB'); *The Pumpkin Eater* with Anne Bancroft, as the lecherous and malicious family friend; *Lord Jim* (65) with Peter O'Toole, as Gentleman Brown; and *Genghis Khan*, an 'international' effort with Omar Sharif and Stephen Boyd. The 'MFB' said that Mason 'once again shows up the dreary wastes of acting round him'. But *Les Pianos Mécaniques*, made in Spain by J.A. Bardem with Melina Mercouri and Hardy Kruger, was so badly received in some countries that it surfaced only briefly in the US and not at all in Britain.

Mason then had three hits: *The Blue Max* (66), a World War I aviation story with George Peppard; *Georgy Girl* with Lynn Redgrave; and *The Deadly Affair* with Simone Signoret, a most undeadly thriller, directed by Lumet from John Le Carré's novel. Then three failures: *Stranger in the House* (67), a British remake of Raimu's *Les Inconnus dans la Maison*; *Duffy*, a 'swinging' film with James Coburn; and *Mayerling* (68), another cosmopolitan effort with Omar Sharif as Rudolph and himself as the Emperor Franz Joseph, but that, for some reason, did well in Britain. Mason's was virtually the only reputation salvaged from poor reviews and when he played Trigorin for Lumet in his film of Chekhov's *The Seagull*, 'Variety' said: 'And for those who have long admired Mason, even in latter-day roles played, figuratively, with one arm tied behind his back and both eyes closed, this will be rewarding evidence that the original fire still burns brightly, when permitted.'

In 1967, on the occasion of the Montreal Exposition, he was named 'Cinema Actor of the Century', perhaps a consolation for no Oscars and only one nomination (for *A Star is Born*). With so many choices, we might wonder how the judges came to this one: but it is not unjust. He may also have found it consolation, in this career full of riddles, for finally abandoning his dream project of *Jane Eyre* – offered to the studios for years, with himself (of course) as Rochester, it was on the point of becoming viable when another company announced their production. Meanwhile, in conjunction with Michael Powell, who directed, he produced *Age of Consent* (69) in Australia, playing an artist seeking peace on the Great Barrier Reef; and was a Yorkshire paterfamilias in *Spring and Port*

dimension. . . . By creating characters that command attention, he gives the other characters in the films importance they do not deserve under the circumstances. For some time I'd been thinking that Mason was becoming a better, more interesting actor with the passage of time. Having recently reseen *Lolita*, *North by Northwest* and *Georgy Girl* it now occurs to me that he has always been superb. He is, in fact, one of the few film actors worth taking the trouble to see, even when the film that encases him is so much cement.'

But actors must eat and *11 Harrowhouse* (74) must have looked promising – a caper film with a cast including Trevor Howard and John Gielgud, and so perhaps did *The Marseille Contract* with Anthony Quinn and Michael Caine: Mason was crooked in both, as English clerk in the one and French crime czar in the other. He played Magwitch in *Great Expectations* for American TV and had a big Hollywood star role in *Mandingo* (75), as a tyrannical overlord of the old plantations, but the film was trounced. Michael Powell failed to get backing for a film of *The Tempest*, with Mason as Prospero, and the actor supported Telly Savalas in the Anglo–German *Inside Out*, as an ex-Nazi in this caper film. He was the friend and interviewer in James Ivory's *Autobiography of a Princess*, a film of Indian memories, but not one of much importance. So he went to Italy for three thrillers: *La Città Sconvoluta/Kidnap Syndicate*, as an industrialist married to Valentina Cortese; *Gente di Rispetto/The Flower in His Mouth* (76) with Jennifer O'Neill and Franco Nero; and *La Polizia Interviene: Ordine di Uccidere!/The Left Hand of the Law*. None of them went to cinemas in the US or Britain. Then there were two 'name' occasions, *Voyage of the Damned*, as a Cuban Minister of State debating over a boatload of Jewish refugees, and the mini-series, *Jesus of Nazareth/Gesu di Nazaret* (77), at one point sharing a scene with Olivier and Ian Holm, and it is not often that either he or the medium are matched with actors of this quality. In *Cross of Iron* he was a German officer again and then he returned to Hollywood to play Claude Rains's old role in *Heaven Can Wait* (78), Warren Beatty's remake of *Here Comes Mr Jordan*; in Britain he was a Yorkshireman in *The Water Babies*; both *The Boys from Brazil*, with Olivier, and *The Passage* (79), with Quinn, were filmed in Europe and both concerned Nazis – *now* and *then*, respectively; after which he was an outstanding Watson to the feeble Holmes of Christopher Plummer in *Murder by Decree*. The film itself was poor, but *Sidney Sheldon's Bloodline* was an even lower point in a career

James Mason in Sidney Lumet's film of The Seagull *(68), the first successful filming in English of a play by Anton Chekhov.*

Wine (70), based on Bill Naughton's play. Neither was well-received and when Mason remarried in 1971 (actress Clarissa Kaye) his career was in the doldrums. He made a film in Hong Kong, directed by and also starring Burgess Meredith, and never shown – though still being advertised in the trade press, as late as 1976, as *The Third Eye*. He accepted a role supporting Alain Delon, but the film was abandoned: in compensation he was offered a role in *De la Part des Copains/L'Uomo dalle Due Ombre/Cold Sweat*, but as directed by Terence Young it diminished him (as a crook from the Deep South), Charles Bronson and Liv Ullman. Doubtless the proximity of his home in Switzerland persuaded him to accept two more European efforts, *E Continuano a Fregarsi il Milione di Dollari/Bad Man's River* (71), a Western with Lee Van Cleef and Gina Lollobrigida, and the French *Kill*, a melodrama about drugs with Curt Jurgens and Stephen Boyd, in both as an agent – government and Interpol respectively.

It was gratifying to find him back in Hollywood in a leading role, as the paranoid school teacher opposed by Robert Preston in *Child's Play* (72), but the film was not a success. For American television he was Dr Polidori in *Frankenstein: the True Story*, a mini-series edited down for cinemas abroad. For cinemas two more did not do well: *The Last of Sheila* (73), a 'joke' film with a name cast, as a veteran film director, and *The Mackintosh Man* with Paul Newman, as a platitudinous Tory MP. Reviewing both films together in 'The New York Times', Vincent Canby found 'he gives them unexpected too full of low points at this stage, even if the role – another Tory MP – had been turned down by Olivier and colleagues in the film included Audrey Hepburn. Matters improved slightly with *North Sea Hijack* (80) which starred Roger Moore, as an admiral, and a TV mini-series based on a Stephen King novel, *Salem's Lot*, starring David Soul, as a sinister antique dealer.

It was clearly time to return to the stage, but 'A Partridge in a Pear Tree' with his wife, in Washington, was his second failure in half a dozen years (the earlier one had been on Broadway). But at least his four next movies included three worth doing and one which was actually good – though in the first of them, an all-star Agatha Christie thriller, *Evil Under the Sun* (82), Mason seemed embarrassed. He was Isaac of York in an *Ivanhoe* made for TV and a Lloyds' investigator Down Under in a daft Oz thriller, *A Dangerous Summer*, with Tom Skerritt. Mason did not seem to have minded taking second-billing to lesser talents, but it was Paul Newman in *The Verdict*, the good film of the batch, with Mason in superb form – he was Oscar nominated – as the wily, successful lawyer opposing him. He indignantly turned down roles in both the US telefilms recreating the Charles and Diana royal romance and was rewarded for his patriotism (or taste) by a wretched British pirate spoof, *Yellowbeard* (83), part-written by two of its stars, Graham Chapman and Peter Cook; Mason was a tyrannical captain and again seemed embarrassed. He was a British general in an American mini-series, *George Washington*, and he replaced Paul Scofield when the latter had an accident during the making of *The Shooting Party* (84): it was at least a class piece, with co-stars of the calibre of Dorothy Tutin and Gielgud – but it was also a weak rehash of *La Règle du Jeu*. *Dr Fischer of Geneva* was hardly better – for which blame the short story this tele-movie was based on. That was by Graham Greene, whose tribute to Mason warmed all of those who believed him to be an exceptional talent among movie actors. For he had died of a heart attack a few weeks earlier, at his home in Switzerland. The two pieces seen subsequently were not of a quality to occasion further tributes: *A.D.* (85), an all-star Biblical mini-series made two years earlier, as Tiberius, and *The Assisi Underground* with Maximilian Schell, a war movie which did so poorly in the US that Cannon did not open it in many territories.

JESSIE MATTHEWS

'When you've got a little springtime in your heart' warbled Jessie Matthews in *Evergreen* and it should have been her signature tune; she was Springtime when the movies were young and she stayed in people's hearts. She was slight, cool and, when she danced, as light as thistledown. They advertised her as 'The Dancing Divinity'. Not that she did not have her detractors: some people found her over-cute and others liked neither the trill in her singing voice nor the ersatz Mayfair accent. Today, almost everything about her early screen performances has dated – in a way that those of, say, Ginger Rogers have not. But more than any other British artist, Matthews benefits from nostalgia for the period. With that accent, the giggle, the teeth and those silly high kicks, she fits only into the 30s; you cannot begin to imagine her in Technicolor, for instance. For all that, her films do not survive as mere historical relics: many of them have a genuine gaiety – a rare quality in British films – and the impish charm of the star does not fade.

She was born in poverty – one of 11 children – in 1907 in Soho, where she used to dance in the streets for passers-by, or so runs the fable. Certainly as a child she was so interested in dancing that she was sent to study it, though her theatrical ambitions began when she won third prize in an elocution contest. In 1917 she made her first stage appearance at the Metropolitan, Edgware Road, in 'Bluebell in Fairyland'. In 1923 she was in the chorus of 'The Music Box Revue'. She made her film début also that year in *This England*, as one of the Princes in the Tower, followed by bit parts in *The Beloved Vagabond* and *Straws in the Wind* (24). One night she went on for the star. . . . Success came with 'The Charlot Revue of 1926' and stardom with 'One Dam Thing After Another' (27). There were other Cochran shows: 'This Year of Grace' (28) with Sonnie Hale, 'Wake Up and Dream' (29), in London and New York, and 'Ever Green' (30).

She was the toast of London. No one, however, believed that she was film material, until she was signed to play the heroine in *Out of the Blue* (31), starring a popular song-and-dance man of the period, Gene Gerrard. She returned to the stage for 'Hold My Hand' and was then offered the lead in a much-liked comedy with Owen Nares, *There Goes the Bride* (32). A few days into filming, Michael Balcon signed her to a Gaumont-British contract, for two years, at £7,800 for the first of them and £9,000 the second; when it expired, she signed for three more years, two films a year with a guaranteed £10,000 for

each and script and director approval. After a stage flop, 'Sally Who?', she took up that contract, which forbade her to do stage or radio work. *The Midshipmaid* was part farce/part musical and crude, but *The Man From Toronto* (33) was a pleasant comedy about a young widow who will inherit a fortune if she marries a Canadian she has never met. And Victor Saville's *The Good Companions* was a beautiful piece of work. It caught exactly J.B. Priestley's bestselling, picaresque novel and had fine lead performances by John Gielgud, Edmund Gwenn and Matthews (as Susie). For her, the 'Observer' thought it 'a tremendous personal triumph'.

It was now a question to find vehicles for her. After *Friday the Thirteenth*, an all-star thriller, she did *Waltzes in Vienna* (34), though 'Picturegoer' thought her 'out of her depth as a romantic ingénue'. Hitchcock directed, making much of little, and Gwenn and Esmond Knight were the two Strausses. The next one was aptly titled *Evergreen*, an enchanting fable about an Edwardian music-hall star blackmailed into retirement and the daughter who impersonates her to win success for herself. Matthews played both parts and it was her biggest success. Wrote André Sennwald in 'The New York Times': 'A joyous and captivating nymph, she is the feminine counterpart of Fred Astaire.' Then came *First a Girl* (35), an attempt to do a transvestism theme with charm.

Mystery surrounds the next step. She left for Hollywood to make a musical with Robert Montgomery at MGM, *This Time It's Love*: it was not made and 'Picturegoer' merely noted laconically that the scripts that MGM had prepared for Matthews were retailored for Eleanor Powell. It seems that MGM had second thoughts about her box-office value and decided to showcase her with four other stars: that was why Balcon turned it down (and it became *Born to Dance*, with Powell). He (among others) testifies to the Hollywood interest during this period, but says that she turned down all offers because she wanted to stay near her family; he also says 'her taut nerves, combined with her passionate involvement with her work, kept her at a dangerous point of strain'. She did have a breakdown in 1937.

MGM sent Robert Young over to appear with her in *It's Love Again* (36), but had no other connection with it. Also in the cast, as usual, was Sonnie Hale, now her husband. (He had earlier been married to Evelyn Laye and there had been much publicity when he left one lady for the other.) An unprepossessing appearance prevented him from co-starring and as comic relief he was wearing. As if he knew it, he went behind the cameras for the next three, as director. He had appeared in the British editions of some of the Lillian Harvey vehicles and these looked back to those in an attempt to break with British film musical conventions: *Head Over Heels* (37), in which Matthews is a Paris cabaret star loved by two friends (Robert Flemyng, Louis Borell), one of whom is stolen by a Hollywood star; *Gangway*, in which she is caught up with jewel thieves and gangsters both on an ocean liner and in New York; and *Sailing Along* (38), in which she is a barge girl discovered by impresario Roland Young, who wants to put her in a show with the American dancer Jack Whiting (who had been in London starring in 'On Your Toes'). All have songs in the American style, but except when the star is dancing she is increasingly embarrassing. The films are atrociously made and 'Picturegoer' suggested 'a director of wider experience . . . would be better able to give her the important pictures her talent and popularity warrant'. These had devalued her American standing and one-picture deals with RKO and 20th came to nothing, since she insisted that Hale was part of them; he was to have been Associate Producer on *Lovelies From America*, which MGM announced and never made. His contract was due to expire and the studio kept finding reasons for delaying the start of *Climbing High*; five musical numbers were scrapped and after waiting around six weeks co-star Kent Taylor returned to the US. As the rich boy who pretends to be in the same line of business as her, modelling, Michael Redgrave took over and the direction was given to another prize

John Mills and Jessie Matthews in The Midshipmaid *(32), the adventures of a soubrette on one of His Majesty's ships.*

Jessie Matthews in It's Love Again *(36).*

property of the studio, Carol Reed. It was now owned by J. Arthur Rank, who was ordered off the set by Matthews. She did not film for Gaumont-British again.

If Hollywood was still panting for her, she was in no haste to go. Alas! For there began the years in the wilderness. In 1939 she and Hale toured in 'I Can Take It', but because of the world situation it did not reach London: she lost £10,000 of her own money and her marriage began to come apart. She did marry a third time, unsuccessfully, and believed that her new husband had done so only for money. The daughter she and Hale had adopted believed that they had done so only for publicity and is another witness to the star's temperament and unhappy personal life.

With the war, the British cinema stopped making musicals and she was dropped, in her own words, 'completely and utterly'; she tested unsuccessfully for *Love on the Dole*. In 1940 she had a short run in 'Come Out to Play' and in 1941 there was a Broadway offer and Matthews started a tour of 'The Lady Comes Across', but she had a breakdown and the show was cancelled. In the meantime, its producers refused to permit her to go to Hollywood for an RKO musical with Fred Astaire; she did spend some time at RKO and while there was asked by Columbia to make a film with him, but that also came to nought. She later did make a film at RKO, to please Victor Saville who was involved in the project: *Forever and a Day* (43), an all-star episode made for war charities; she was in the episode with Charles Laughton and because of it she was offered a cheap little B by British National, *Candles at Nine* (44), playing an heiress in a creepy old house frightened by some grotesques including Beatrix Lehmann, whose friend Christopher Isherwood thought it was 'worst and funniest' film ever made. Looking puffy-faced and appearing in a dream sequence in a chic hat, a fox fur and cami-knickers, the star gives an unnattractive performance, to confirm those who considered that she had no future in films. To prove otherwise she appeared in two shorts, *Life Is Nothing Without Music* (47) and *Making the Grade*, which contained footage from *There Goes the Bride*: they were no better than any others made by Inspiration, who cobbled them and others together to fulfil quota requirements.

Matthews's only stage work in a while was in a London revival of 'Wild Rose', though two years later she left another, 'The Quaker Girl', just before it opened. She reappeared, glory considerably dimmed, in 1948 in 'Maid to Measure' and did another revue, 'Sauce Tartare', the following year: these were her last West End appearances. In her case, the public was fickle. To an austerity Britain she represented pre-war luxury; apart from a brief moment in 1936 when she was the sixth biggest box-office attraction in Britain, she had never been popular with all classes and she lacked the common touch which enabled Gracie Fields also to come back after years of eclipse. There was work to be had on tour and in the provinces – in plays like 'The Browning Version' and 'Private Lives'. In 1952 she went to Australia with 'Larger Than Life' and she toured with this play in South Africa in 1955. She visited Australia again the following year and in 1958 she made a welcome return to the screen in *Tom Thumb* (as Tom's mum). She then spent two years visiting her daughter in Australia, working in TV there as well as on the stage, and she opened a Drama School in Melbourne. She returned to Britain and toured as the mother in 'Five Finger Exercise'; she was plump now and cosy – no longer the sylph of memory. But, like a groundswell, the public began to make amends for the neglect and in club and theatre engagements they cheered the stout lady, doubtless happy to find her charm undimmed. In London and New York there were retrospectives of her films. Matthews herself, though flattered, did not care too much to go on singing 'Dancing on the Ceiling' and 'Over my Shoulder'. She wanted to be a character actress and spent six years playing the mother in a radio soap opera ('The Dales', 1963–69). Then she returned to the stage. Her third marriage had ended many years earlier and she lived with a sister. Finally returning to films, she did a small supporting role in a poor and pointless new version of *The Hound of the Baskervilles* (78), starring Peter Cook and Dudley Moore. She died in 1981.

JOEL McCREA

Joel McCrea was one of the leading Leading Men of the 30s, a tall, good-looking, reliable actor without any great pretensions. Physically he was not unlike Gary Cooper and they generally played the same sort of roles. Curiously, he was in as many good films as Cooper was, and was hardly less competent, but he did not have the same allure; there was something just a little forced about his playing. He reached his peak in the early 40s and thereafter quickly reversed and buried himself in programmer Westerns where he stayed, comfortably, for almost another 20 years. He had no illusions about his ability: 'Acting? I never attempt it. A placid sort of fellow, that's me. . . . So when I face the cameras I just stay placid . . .' (to the 'Evening Standard', London).

Chance at Heaven (*33*):
*Ginger Rogers, right, lost
Joel McCrea to Marion
Nixon in reel one, but after
several reels of unhappy
marriages he returned to
her in time for the fade-
out.*

His talent carried him so far; but just as some – a very few – people became great stars simply because they wanted to be, McCrea did not reach the heights because he did not really want to.

He was born in South Pasadena, California, in 1905. He graduated from Pomona University, where he had taken part in dramatics, and for the next two years he acted in community theatre plays, often in leading parts. He wanted to be in films and worked during that time as an extra. One day he was picked out when a goodish part in *The Jazz Age* (29) remained uncast; whence he moved over to MGM on contract and was given small parts in *The Single Standard* (with Garbo) and *So This Is College*. Cecil B. De Mille took over his contract and made him the juvenile lead in *Dynamite* and after some months of inactivity he moved on again to RKO to play the hero in *The Silver Horde* (30): this led to two good parts at Fox, *Lightnin'* with Will Rogers and *Once a Sinner* (31) with Dorothy Mackaill, in the former as a friend who has been swindled out of some land, and in the latter as a nice country boy who cannot prevent his wife returning to her old ways. This was the sort of dilemma he was to face in most of his serious films.

It was at RKO that he finally settled. That studio had liked the McCrea–Mackaill teaming and reunited them in *Kept Husbands*, where they had similar parts, but he found his most consistent partner when Constance Bennett decided that she was *Born to Love* him:

he was an aviator. In *The Common Law* he was an American painter in Paris and she his high-living model. He was loaned to Paramount for *Girls About Town*, as a small-town boy who bewitches one of them (Kay Francis), and to Fox for *Business and Pleasure* (32). There followed *The Lost Squadron*, as a flyer again, with Richard Dix; *Bird of Paradise*, on a desert island with Dolores del Rio; *The Most Dangerous Game*, on an island again, this time with Fay Wray, both as the human prey of mad Leslie Banks and his hounds; *Rockabye* with Bennett; *The Sport Parade*, as a wrestler; *The Silver Cord* (33) at MGM with Irene Dunne and Frances Dee (whom he married that year; they were long considered one of Hollywood's happiest couples but temporarily separated in the late 60s); *Bed of Roses*, as a riverboat captain redeeming Bennett; *One Man's Journey* – Lionel Barrymore's, from obscurity to fame as a country doctor; and *Chance at Heaven*, as an uppercrust boy torn between wealthy Marion Nixon and poor Ginger Rogers. He had a similar part in *Gambling Lady* (34) – Barbara Stanwyck – but a second loan-out, for *Half a Sinner*, found him merely as the juvenile: the star was Berton Churchill, repeating his 'Alias the Deacon' performance. In *The Richest Girl in the World* he was tested by Miriam Hopkins's friends to see whether he was a fortune hunter.

Hopkins was under contract to Goldwyn and he liked McCrea's work in this enough to sign him to a contract some months later. In the meantime McCrea left RKO and got parts in *Private Worlds* (35), *Our Little Girl* – Shirley Temple – and *Woman Wanted*, an MGM mystery with Maureen O'Sullivan. Goldwyn put him into three pictures in a row: *Barbary Coast*; *Splendor* with Hopkins, where their earlier positions were reversed and he was now the society boy and she the poor girl – though they were married; and *These Three* (36), replacing Leslie Howard, Goldwyn's first choice for the role. The other two of the triangle were Hopkins again and Merle Oberon. He and Joan Bennett were the *Two in a Crowd*, a horse story; he had an *Adventure in Manhattan*; and then Goldwyn gave him perhaps his strongest role to date, in *Come and Get It*, as a lumberjack, but both his playing and the writing were conventional. He was with Stanwyck again in *Banjo on My Knee* at 20th and *Internes Can't Take Money* (37) at Paramount, in the latter playing a Dr Kildare; and with Hopkins again in *Woman Chases Man*. His next for Goldwyn should have been *The Hurricane*, but he did not want to do it and was put into *Dead End* instead – the lead role, though no longer crippled and misanthropic, as in the original play. The film was stolen from him by Bogart, Claire Trevor, Marjorie Main, Sylvia Sidney and others. He was loaned again to Paramount for *Wells Fargo*, his first Western and one of the year's top money-makers.

He was borrowed by 20th for *Three Blind Mice* (38) opposite Loretta Young and he did *Youth Takes a Fling* at Universal, playing a Kansas hired man who yearns for the sea, with Andrea Leeds. Goldwyn did not use him: he had taken Gary Cooper under contract – it was reported that McCrea often got roles that he or Cary Grant had turned down. McCrea later expressed his surprise that a number of directors – La Cava, Stevens, Hitchcock – preferred him to the bigger names that their producers wanted; and he was to become the ideal leading man for the comic genius of Preston Sturges. He did not mind taking second place to Cooper, whom he adored, but when he heard that he was unavailable to make *Union Pacific* (39) he asked for the role. He was upset that Goldwyn was getting a 600 per cent mark-up for his services and Goldwyn told him that if he broke his contract he would ensure that he would never work in Hollywood again; but McCrea knew that an important picture with De Mille was proof against any harm Goldwyn might try. De Mille was pleased with his performance, as a trouble-shooter – and he was again with Stanwyck (with Jean Arthur, his favourite leading lady). The film was a big one. He did his last for Goldwyn, *They Shall Have Music*, a sort of musical *Dead End* with guest appearance by Jascha Heifetz. McCrea was reported in 'Picturegoer' as saying: 'I've never had star rating because I disliked the responsibility. . . . A picture hangs on a star. When a

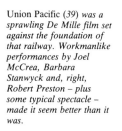

Union Pacific (39) was a sprawling De Mille film set against the foundation of that railway. Workmanlike performances by Joel McCrea, Barbara Stanwyck and, right, Robert Preston – plus some typical spectacle – made it seem better than it was.

picture is bad, the star is washed up. A leading man, such as I am, hangs on to a picture.'

He freelanced: *Espionage Agent* at WB; *He Married His Wife* (40) at 20th; *The Primrose Path* with Ginger Rogers; and Hitchcock's *Foreign Correspondent*, his best role in some time. Then he signed a deal with Paramount: William A. Wellman's *Reaching for the Sun* (41), a sentimental comedy with Ellen Drew; Preston Sturges's funny *Sullivan's Travels* – another good part, as a movie director with a conscience – with Veronica Lake; Wellman's *The Great Man's Lady* (42), an insufferable pioneering drama with Stanwyck; Sturges's *The Palm Beach Story*, married to Claudette Colbert; and George Stevens's *The More the Merrier* (43), sharing a Washington apartment with Jean Arthur. In most of these he played second fiddle to the ladies, but he was the focal point of both Wellman's *Buffalo Bill* (44) at Fox, in the title-role, and Sturges's *The Great Moment* with Betty Field, a serious picture about the first dentist to use ether; and *The Unseen* (45), a follow-up to *The Uninvited* with Gail Russell. He turned down *The Southerner*; and his last picture for Paramount was a remake of *The Virginian* (46), in Gary Cooper's old role.

That was a Western and so, with two or three exceptions were all of McCrea's subsequent films: *Ramrod* (47) with Veronica Lake and *Four Faces West* (48) with his wife, both at Enterprise; *South of St Louis* (49) with Alexis Smith; *Colorado Territory* with Virginia Mayo; and *Stars in My Crown* (50), as a militant parson who tamed a small Southern town first with guns and then with preaching: it was the last of his films to be well-noticed. The rest were duallers: *The Outriders*; *Saddle Tramp*; *Frenchie* with Shelley Winters, a remake of *Destry Rides Again*; *Cattle Drive* (51); *The San Francisco Story* (52) with Yvonne de Carlo, a tale of the honky tonk days; and *Rough Shoot* with Evelyn Keyes, a poor thriller made in Britain. McCrea continued to be among the surest Western draws. He made: *Lone Hand* (53), *Border River* (54), *Black Horse Canyon*, *Stranger on Horseback* (55), *Wichita* (he also did a TV series under this title), *The First Texan* (56), *The Oklahoman* (57), *Trooper Hook* with Stanwyck, *Gunsight Ridge*, *The Tall Stranger*, *Cattle Empire* (58), *Fort Massacre* and *The Gunfight at Dodge City* (59).

Most of these were poor films and in the words of a reviewer in the 'MFB' McCrea played with 'stolid competence'. He said around this time that he had never been in a film which had lost money – even the two he had made for Enterprise had made a little. He resolutely refused to return to TV Westerns. But he came out of retirement to give a good performance in one of the best Westerns of the 60s, Sam Peckinpah's *Ride the High Country* (62), teamed with Randolph Scott: they were two old-timers taken on to escort gold dust from the mine to the bank. MGM treated it as just another McCrea (or Scott) Western, but it established Peckinpah's reputation and for McCrea was a fine curtain. His earlier retirement had been due to the fact that TV had taken the audience for medium-budget Westerns; he retired now because the parts offered required him to change his image – play a villain – and he refused to do that. He did play an ageing pioneer in a low-budget movie starring his son Jody, *Cry Blood, Apache* (70); but was more notably seen in *Mustang Country* (76).

VICTOR McLAGLEN

The Beloved Brute was the name of Victor McLaglen's first American film and it was thus, afterwards, that publicity usually described him. He was a big, grinning man, type-cast throughout a long career as a tough NCO with a heart of gold, a Wallace Beery without the cunning. he won an Oscar for playing a slight variation of this part, in a rather good picture, but was not, overall, an actor of great subtlety.

He was born in Tunbridge Wells, Kent, in 1886, the eldest of eight brothers (Cyril, Leopold, Clifford, Arthur and Kenneth also worked in films later, with considerably less success). Father was a clergyman. In 1900 Victor joined the Life Guards (lying about his age), hoping to be able to fight in the Boer War: his father later bought him out. He went to Canada where he worked on farms and did casual labour, became a professional prize-fighter (he once went six rounds with Jack Johnson, world heavyweight champion) and graduated from that to exhibition boxing with Wild West shows and circuses, which led in turn to vaudeville. He toured in the US and in Australia, where he took part in the Kalgoorlie Gold Rush, and was in South Africa (where Father was now Bishop of Claremont) on the outbreak of war in 1914. He returned to Britain, joined the Irish Fusiliers and served in the Middle East: he was Provost-Marshal of Baghdad and was demobbed with the rank of captain. After the war he took up boxing again and was in the National Sporting Club in London when a producer, I.B. Davidson, saw him and offered him the lead in *The Call of the Road* (20). He accepted in a non-serious mood, but this costume romance was good, the best British picture of the year, and he found himself somewhat in demand.

He played a baron in *Carnival* (21), a British perennial about a jealous actor (Matheson Lang) who tries to strangle his wife during a performance of 'Othello'; and had the lead again in *Corinthian Jack*, as a Regency boxer. He continued to establish a masculine image in an Australian tale, *Prey of the Dragon*, and in *The Sport of Kings*; then J. Stuart Blackton engaged him to play the ruffian who abducts Lady Diana Manners in a Jacobean drama, 'The Glorious Adventure' (22). They repeated on the screen – in colour (it was the first British colour film) and designed mainly to exploit the beauty of Lady Diana; but McLaglen's was the most important male role and it reinforced his position as one of Britain's leading male stars. There followed: *A Romance of Old Baghdad*, supporting Lang again; *Little Brother of God*, a Canadian tale; *A Sailor Tramp*, in the title-role; a version of Edgar Wallace's *The Crimson Circle* with a 'name'-cast that included Flora le Breton; *The Romany* (23), as a gypsy chief; *Heartstrings*, as a sailor returned from the dead; *M'Lord of the White Road*, another highwayman story; *In the Blood*, another period boxing melodrama; *Women and Diamonds* (24), a South African story with Madge Stuart and Florence Turner; *The Gay Corinthian*, made for Butchers, as another Regency boxer; and *The Passionate Adventure* starring Clive Brook. McLaglen had only a supporting role in the latter and times were bad for British films generally: there was a slump in 1924 (the release of these last three pictures was delayed over a year).

He was therefore delighted to get a Hollywood offer; indeed he was so broke that his fare had to be cabled to him. His rescuer was the same J. Stuart Blackton who had employed him earlier (Blackton was an Englishman who worked mainly in the US). He wanted him for *The Beloved Brute*, a Vitagraph feature, to star along with William Russell and Marguerite de la Motte, as a tough ex-con, the brother of the pious Russell. McLaglen did not lack for further offers. At Fox he was in *The Hunter Woman*, who was Seena Owen; at Pathé in *Percy*, who was Charles Ray; and at MGM one of *The Unholy Three*, along with Lon Chaney and Harry Earl. He went to First National for Frank Lloyd's *The Winds of Chance* starring Anna Q. Nilsson and his work in that brought him a contract there. He returned to Fox for a supporting part in *The Fighting Heart*, which had George O'Brien as a boxer who gives up fame for the love of Billie Dove. John Ford directed and he was to use McLaglen in numerous pictures over the years.

McLaglen's next were *The Isle of Retribution* (26) and *Men of Steel* with Milton Sills; then he was loaned to Paramount for a supporting role in *Beau Geste*. It was another loan-out which made him a big Hollywood star: *What Price Glory?* This had been a fine anti-war play by Maxwell Anderson and Laurence Stallings done on Broadway some years earlier with Louis Wolheim and William Boyd, but which had aroused no interest in Hollywood. The success of *The Big Parade*, however, had changed that and Fox had bought it and assigned Raoul Walsh to direct. Edmund Lowe was cast as Sergeant Quirt and McLaglen was borrowed to play Captain Flagg. In the transition to the screen, their amorous exploits somehow took precedence over the bitterness expressed in the title, but the film was a big hit with critics and public (it took over $2 million at the box-office) and before shooting was finished Fox had negotiated to buy McLaglen's contract.

However, Fox did not yet see him as real star stuff and his next two parts were only featured ones: in Ford's *Mother Machree* and *The Loves of Carmen* (27) with Dolores del Rio. The Ford film was in fact not released until early 1928, while some sequences were tinted (later a music track was added). It starred Belle Bennett, in a reprise of her *Stella Dallas* performance, only in Irish immigrant circumstances, and was excessively sentimental. McLaglen followed with another big hit, Howard Hawks's *A Girl in Every Port* (28), top-billed with Louise Brooks; then Ford's *Hangman's House*, an Irish melodrama; *River Pirate*; *Captain Lash* (29) with Claire Windsor; and Ford's *Strong Boy*, in the title-role, a conventional tale about a baggage porter who outwits a gang of train robbers. The last two were released with music tracks; McLaglen's first Talkie was *The Black Watch*, directed by Ford, a British army story set in India with McLaglen as an officer thought to be a coward but in fact on a secret mission. It did well, but not as well as Walsh's *The Cock-Eyed World*, a Flagg and Quirt reunion (with Lily Damita) whose gross exceeded all of Fox's wildest hopes: it was third among the year's money-makers.

McLaglen was now one of the two or three sure draws at Fox and pictures were devised for him which were increasingly decried as McLaglen-formula stuff: *Hot for Paris* and Fifi D'Orsay, with El Brendel as his sidekick thickhead this time; *Happy Days* (30), the studio's all-star revue; *On the Level* with William Harrigan; and *A Devil With Women*, as a mercenary in a banana republic with Mona Maris, who at the end prefers Humphrey Bogart to him. His role (turned down by Gary Cooper) in Paramount's *Dishonoured* (31) got him somewhat out of the rut, as the bluff but kindly Russian officer who falls in love with, and is betrayed by, Marlene Dietrich. Then he and Lew Cody were *Not Exactly Gentlemen* with Fay Wray; and he was demoted to sergeant to make him the same rank as Quirt in *Women of All Nations*, only they were in the Marines this time and it was not as good. He had another change when he became involved in *Annabelle's Affairs*, as a strong and silent Westerner who marries Jeanette MacDonald as a favour and is later wooed by her when they meet again, after he has become a gentleman. He: was *Wicked* with Elissa Landi; *The Gay Caballero* (32), with George O'Brien now in support of him; won *The Devil's Lottery*; and was with Helen Mack *While Paris Sleeps*, as an escaped convict. Paramount borrowed him and Lowe for *Guilty as Hell*, a murder mystery, but it was not up to their earlier teamings; McLaglen was *Rackety Rax* in a college football tale; then Fox teamed him and Lowe for the last time in *Hot Pepper* (33). The girl this time was Lupe Velez and it was some sort of nadir; 'Picturegoer' observed that the series had been growing ever more pointless and licentious.

McLaglen's career was indeed in trouble. He left Fox at that point and there were no Hollywood offers beyond one from Mascot, *Laughing at Life*. So he accepted an offer from a British company to do the sort of film he had done at the start of his career, *Dick Turpin*. It was not a success. It was Ford who rescued him, by casting him as the sergeant, the one survivor of *The Lost Patrol* (34), one of his best films. This helped rid McLaglen of the Flagg image and established him as a reliable supporting player again: *No More Women* at Paramount with Lowe and Sally Blane; *Wharf Angel* with the piquant Dorothy Dell in the title-role and Preston Foster; *Murder at the Vanities* with Carl Brisson and Kitty Carlisle and *The Captain Hates the Sea* (35) with John Gilbert, in both as a detective; and at Fox, a couple of programmers with Lowe, *Under Pressure*, in which they were tunnellers, and *The Great Hotel Murder*, in which McLaglen was the dumb house-dick and Lowe a suave thriller-writer.

It was as though Ford was McLaglen's guardian angel: he chose him against RKO's opposition to play Gypo Nolan, *The Informer*, who ratted on a pal because he wanted the £20 reward to buy a steamship ticket to the States. It was set in Dublin in 1922, at the height of the Troubles, and was based on a novel by Liam O'Flaherty; RKO disliked it, but it won a New York critics' award at year's end for Ford and then five Oscars, including a Best Actor one for McLaglen. RKO then began patting themselves on the back. Conversely, today it seems like one of Ford's weakest

efforts and McLaglen's work is not exceptional. He began getting top parts again: *Professional Soldier* (36), in the title-role, opposite Freddie Bartholomew; *Klondike Annie*, as the bruiser who falls for, but is not fooled by, Mae West; *Under Two Flags* with Ronald Colman; *The Magnificent Brute*, in the title-role, with Binnie Barnes; *Sea Devils* (37), a drama of the Coast Guard patrol with Preston Foster; and *Nancy Steele Is Missing!* – because he has kidnapped her; he brings her up as his daughter, adores her, but will the Hays Office let him have a happy ending? The momentum had not been maintained. He had a supporting role in *This Is My Affair* as the saloon owner nuts about his singer, Barbara Stanwyck. His role in *Wee Willie Winkie* – Ford directing Shirley Temple – was good, but the next two were programmers: *The Battle of Broadway* (38) with Louise Hovick – who was Gypsy Rose Lee at a time when Hollywood was chary of using her 'striptease' name; and *The Devil's Party*, the one about the boys who grow up to be priest (Paul Kelly) and night-club boss (McLaglen), but nowhere as bad as he is painted.

20th sent him to Britain to play opposite

McLaglen in another Ford picture, Wee Willie Winkie *(37), the adventures of a meddling brat (Shirley Temple) with her grandfather's regiment in India. McLaglen was the tough sergeant who first tolerates her and then befriends her – until he is killed.*

Gracie Fields in *We're Going To Be Rich*, then he took another trip, as the chief engineer, on a *Pacific Liner* (39), hampering doctor Chester Morris in his efforts to cure an outbreak of cholera. He was the menace to Nelson Eddy in *Let Freedom Ring*, then returned to India for *Gunga Din* with Cary Grant and to Australia for a second rip-roaring thriller, *Captain Fury*, where he and Brian Aherne were ex-cons. He was the *Ex-Champ*, now a doorman, teaching his old craft to Tom Brown, and then a murderer on his deathbed making a *Full Confession* to a priest – before recovering. There were more uninteresting films for Universal: *Rio* with Basil Rathbone; *The Big Guy* (40), as a prison warder, with Jackie Cooper; *South of Pago Pago*, heading the pearl hunters invading Jon Hall's island paradise; and *Diamond Hunter*, as a dealer who is framed. *Broadway Limited* (41) was a comedy set on a long-distance train, with Dennis O'Keefe, and was McLaglen's only film in a year; but he had no intention of retiring and *Call Out the Marines* (42) actually teamed him with Lowe again, this time rounding up spies, though it is really one of those jolly recruiting films turned out as the US prepared to enter the war. He was the recalcitrant foreman of a munitions plant in *Powder Town* and then somewhat more devious in *China Girl* with Gene Tierney.

After a guest spot in *Forever and a Day* (43) he was villainous again in *Tampico* (44), starring Edward G. Robinson, and in *The Princess and the Pirate*, as a pirate, starring Bob Hope. Inbetweenwhiles, he was with old co-stars Preston Foster (in the title-role) in a B at 20th, *Roger Tuohy Gangster*, and then with Chester Morris in *Rough Tough and Ready* (45) at Republic. Still at that studio he was with some other faded glories – Virginia Bruce, Nils Asther and Edward Ashley (in real life the Earl of Warwick) – in *Love Honor and Goodbye*. He did: *Whistle Stop* (46) with George Raft; *Calendar Girl* (47) starring Jane Frazee; *The Michigan Kid*, supporting Jon Hall in this his first Western, a B and a poor one at that; and *The Foxes of Harrow*, supporting Rex Harrison. Ford came to the rescue again and cast him as a sergeant in the three films that make up a trilogy about the US Cavalry, *Fort Apache* (48), *She Wore a Yellow Ribbon* (49) and *Rio Grande* (50) – in the latter two as Sgt Quincannon, a character played in the first one by Dick Foran. Then he was in Ford's *The Quiet Man* (52), followed by *Fair Wind to Java* (53), a Republic adventure in Trucolor; *Prince Valiant* (54) as a faithful retainer of that gentleman (Robert Wagner); the British *Trouble in the Glen*; *Many Rivers to Cross* (55), a Robert Taylor Western; *City of Shadows*, a Republic B in

which he starred; *Lady Godiva* (Maureen O'Hara); *Bengazi*, as the owner of an underworld café, with Richard Conte; and *The Abductors* (57), a B directed by his son, Andrew V. McLaglen, in which he was once again an ex-con.

His last picture was made in Britain, Rank's *Sea Fury* (58), with Stanley Baker, and he played a belligerent and hard-drinking captain who at the end realizes that he is too old for his job. McLaglen's colleagues felt similarly about him: he had difficulty remembering his lines and it was believed that he would not film again. He died of a heart attack in 1959. He was married three times; son Andrew was by his first wife, who died in 1942. McLaglen then married his secretary, but that marriage ended in divorce in 1948.

RAY MILLAND

One of the staples of the old days was the featured leading man – the actor who was never quite starred: he was the hero's brother, the hero's rival or the Other Man, and sometimes – in comedies – the hero's friend. There were dozens of them: John Carroll, John Loder, John Sutton, often Ralph Bellamy. Ray Milland spent a good 10 years in such parts before making his mark as a light comedian, cheery and good-natured; and he went on from there to be a highly competent actor. He made some costume films and Westerns, but was most at home in a double-breasted pin-stripe suit. Real life rarely breathed into any of the films that he was given to do and it is therefore somewhat difficult to assess him as a serious actor.

He was born in Neath, Glamorganshire, in 1905 and educated at King's College, London. He served for a while as a royal guardsman and all accounts of his early career suggest a dilettante existence, but at one point he toured Europe, under his own name, Reginald Truscott-Jones, as one half of a dance team: the other was the equally unknown Anna Neagle. He toured in 'The Woman in Room 13' and had some walk-ons in films. According to early publicity, he was friendly with Estelle Brody and while visiting her on the set was offered a small role in *The Plaything* (29), in which she starred. However, earlier in the year he had had biggish roles, as Raymond Milland, in two films for the same studio, BIP, in *The Flying Scotsman* and *The Lady from the Sea*, both directed by Castleton Knight with Moore Marriot, in the latter as his son, a Goodwin Sands lifeboatman. C.B. Cochran offered a contract, but Milland had heard that Anita

Loos had recommended him to MGM, who signed him up in Britain. In his memoir he says that he was first given a bit role in *Son of India* (31), but that was released several months after *The Bachelor Father*, in which he had a good role as Marion Davies's brother, both children of the gentleman of the title. He supported William Haines, pretending to be *Just a Gigolo* to avoid marrying, and was then mostly loaned out: to WB for *Bought* (where he did wrong to Constance Bennett); to Fox for Will Rogers's *Ambassador Bill*; and to Warners again for *Blonde Crazy*, as the rich boy Joan Blondell plans to marry, and *The Man Who Played God* (32), as a potential suicide helped by George Arliss. He had an insignificant part in *Polly of the Circus* and a reasonably good one in *Payment Deferred*, as the Australian nephew murdered by Charles Laughton. Both of these were at his home studio, which promptly dropped him. He returned to Britain and got parts in an old army farce, *Orders is Orders* (33), and *This Is the Life* starring Gordon Harker; and then decided to try his luck again in Hollywood.

By chance he bumped into Joe Egli, Paramount's casting director, who had heard he was back in town; the actor cast in *Bolero* (34) had just been stabbed by his boyfriend, so they urgently needed a 'British officer' type to play Carole Lombard's fiancé. They kept him to play Bing Crosby's supercilious rival in *We're Not Dressing*, offered him a long-term contract and cast him as the romantic lead in a very funny Burns and Allen vehicle, *Many Happy Returns*. He was threatened in *Charlie Chan in London* (at Fox) and featured in *Menace* with Gertrude Michael and *One Hour Late* (35) with Helen Twelvetrees. His parts were getting bigger and his best chance came as Fred MacMurray's rival for Claudette Colbert in *The Gilded Lily*. He was Miss Michael's caddish lover in *Four Hours to Kill*; was fourth on the cast list of the George Raft *The Glass Key*, despite being murdered in reel one; and had the lead in a Universal B, *Alias Mary Dow*. That studio liked him enough to keep him on as James Stewart's rival for Margaret Sullavan in *Next Time We Love* (36). He then did *The Return of Sophie Lang*, one of a series that starred Gertrude Michael; *The Big Broadcast of 1937*; and *The Jungle Princess*, as a writer discovering Dorothy Lamour in Malaya. He says in his memoirs he was cast in this because of his reviews for the next one, which cannot be possible, but this would be the point to mention Lamour's opinion of him as 'a genuinely unselfish actor – a rarity in the film business'. Certainly he was well-noticed in *Three Smart Girls* (37) at Universal, in a small role originally meant for Louis Hayward. He was already committed to

playing the eponymous hero of *Bulldog Drummond Escapes*, but was replaced by John Howard for the others in this B series, for his star was rising rapidly – especially when Universal asked for him again, to co-star with Wendy Barrie as her airman husband in *Wings Over Honolulu*. Milland was now of sufficient standing for his agent to renegotiate his contract to send him to Universal as a star. So Paramount gave him his first lead in an A picture, *Easy Living*, and were rewarded: he made his first real impact as the millionaire's son trying to make his own way – until Jean Arthur brings the automat crashing down around them; and he ended up with the girl for once.

Frances Farmer was the girl in *Ebb Tide* and she and Oscar Homolka were billed above him in this Technicolor version of a Robert Louis Stevenson story; and Miriam Hopkins was the *Wise Girl* at RKO. He was recognized as a fully fledged leading man, but again in the next two the biggest attraction was considered to be the Technicolor: *Her Jungle Love* (38) – Dorothy Lamour's; and *Men With Wings* – Fred MacMurray was the other one. He was with Lamour again on a *Tropic Holiday* and then he did another B, *Say It in French* with Olympe Bradna. He was with another doomed import, Isa Miranda, in the remake of *Hotel Imperial* (39), and after playing one of *Beau Geste*'s brothers was with a third broken-accented lady, Sonja Henie, in *Everything Happens at Night*, at 20th. Paramount then gave him his biggest chance, as

The second of the three film versions of Beau Geste *(39), a story about three brothers who join the Foreign Legion when one of them – Beau – is falsely suspected of robbery. In this early scene Ray Milland is contemplating disgrace, watched by the girl all three brothers love (Susan Hayward).*

the only 'name' in the cast of their British-made version of the Terence Rattigan stage hit, *French Without Tears* (40): his skill with the bright lines was one of the best things about a disappointing film. They announced that Milland was being groomed to be one of the biggest stars on the lot.

He starred in *Irene* at RKO, an Anna Neagle musical which badly needed his elegance; in *The Doctor Takes a Wife*, a slight marital comedy with Loretta Young; and in *Untamed*, a title which referred both to Patricia Morison and the Frozen North (it was a remake of *Mantrap*). Nonchalant, smiling (often, over-smugly), well-tailored, he breezed his way through mechanical pieces: *Arise My Love* and *Skylark* (41), both with Claudette Colbert and intended originally for Joel McCrea and Melvyn Douglas respectively. Earlier in the year he was in one of those films which were Hollywood's way of letting the world know that the USA was not unprepared for war, *I Wanted Wings*; and then he and Paulette Goddard were gallant Americans in wartime Lisbon in *The Lady Has Plans* (42). Goddard was with him again in De Mille's *Reap the Wild Wind*, a big box-office hit and notable for his battle with a giant squid. He gave his opinion of the film to a reporter years later: 'I thought it was horrible.' There were four comedies: *Are Husbands Necessary?* with Betty Field was pleasant; Billy Wilder's *The Major and the Minor* with Ginger Rogers was somewhat better, though less good than its reputation allows; a sketch in *Star Spangled Rhythm*; and *The Crystal Ball* (43) with Goddard again.

There was more serious stuff in *Forever and a Day*, about a big house in London; and in *The Uninvited* (44), about a big house on the Cornish cliffs which is haunted, with Gail Russell. But *Lady in the Dark* with Rogers was his last escapist entertainment for some time. *Till We Meet Again* was a war story with Barbara Britton and *The Ministry of Fear* was a thriller set in London during the blitz, Fritz Lang's enjoyable but unsatisfactory version of Graham Greene's 'entertainment'. Marjorie Reynolds co-starred. *The Lost Weekend* (45) had originally been a novel about an alcoholic by Charles Jackson and Wilder's surprising choice of Milland for that part was due to his satisfaction with his work in *The Major and the Minor*. It was a sympathetic and convincing performance – undoubtedly his best screen work – and it won him a Best Actor Oscar and the New York critics' award. Wilder directed with perception – the film has dated less than almost any other 40s drama – and it won a Best Picture Oscar and did well at the box-office.

Few of Milland's next films were worthy of

his new status: *Kitty*, a period drama in which he had little to do but shoot supercilious lines at Paulette Goddard; *The Well-Groomed Bride* (46), a weak comedy with Olivia de Havilland; *California*, a Western with Barbara Stanwyck; and *The Imperfect Lady* (47) and *The Trouble With Women*, a couple of programmers with Teresa Wright, period thriller and marital farce respectively. Indeed, Milland could not hold his box-office status either and after the next two they played double bills. *Golden Earrings* was some nonsense in which, as an escaping British officer, he was disguised as a gypsy with the aid of Marlene Dietrich; but *The Big Clock* (48) was a first-rate thriller directed by John Farrow with Farrow's wife, Maureen O'Sullivan, and Charles Laughton. Milland made *So Evil My Love* in Britain with Ann Todd, another period melodrama. Then: *Sealed Verdict*, a silly romantic drama; *Alias Nick Beale* (49) with Thomas Mitchell, an interesting crime melodrama with a Faust theme; *It Happens Every Spring* at 20th with Jean Peters; *A Woman of Distinction* (50) at Columbia with Rosalind Russell; and *Copper Canyon*, a conventional Western. 'Copper Canyon I loathed,' he said later in an interview. 'I hated working with Hedy Lamarr.'

It was almost his last film for Paramount and he began to freelance successfully: *A Life of Her Own* with Lana Turner; *Circle of Danger* (51), which he produced in Britain, a muddy little drama with Patricia Roc; *Night Into Morning* with John Hodiak, battling with the Bottle again; *Rhubarb*, some whimsy about a cat; *Close to My Heart* with Gene Tierney; and *Something To Live For* (52), another study in alcoholism but this time Joan Fontaine was a bigger drunk than he. His box-office after this lot was decidedly shaky, but it perked up with a Western, *Bugles in the Afternoon*, and there was considerable interest in *The Thief*, which had the novelty or gimmick of having almost no dialogue. His final film for Paramount came up: *Jamaica Run* (53), a pathetic farewell gift to one of the old reliables.

However, it cannot be said that his work was very distinguished: in *Let's Do It Again* with Jane Wyman he seemed to have congealed; and he looked rather bored throughout his participation in both Hitchcock's *Dial M for Murder* (54) with Grace Kelly and in *The Girl in the Red Velvet Swing* (55), as Stanford White in this account of a famous turn-of-the-century *crime passionel*. In 1953/4 he had a TV series, 'Meet Mr McNulty', playing a college professor.

This trio was virtually the end of his First Feature days, but he turned to directing himself: *A Man Alone* (56) was greeted by audience laughter, but he was not a natural man of the West; and *Lisbon*, which he also produced, was a routine melodrama. After two programmers at 20th, *Three Brave Men* (57) with Ernest Borgnine, as a lawyer, and *The River's Edge* with Anthony Quinn, as a fugitive bank robber, he went to Britain to play the CO in a mundane film about the RAF, *High Flight* – experiences which convinced him that he preferred to direct himself, which he did again in *The Safe-Cracker* (58).

He busied himself with TV, acting and directing, notably with a series of gothic horror stories: 'Markham', returning to films in a similar tale, under the aegis of Roger Corman, *Premature Burial* (62); which was followed by two sci-fi horrors, *Panic in Year Zero*, which he also directed, and *X: The Man with the X-Ray Eyes* (63). In 1965 he and Ginger Rogers made a film in Jamaica, which as *Quick Let's Get Married* had a few fugitive showings many years later. *Daughter of the Mind* (69) was a tele-movie with Don Murray and Milland, second-billed, played a professor. *Hostile Witness* (70) was little luckier than the Rogers film: he directed this British film of a play he had recently done in New York and in Australia, but it went out as a B.

He played Ryan O'Neal's father in *Love Story*, a supporting role in this phenomenally successful load of schmaltz – and was bald, 'the first time since 1948 without a toupee' he said. The film gave his career new impetus, if not exactly interesting projects: *River of Gold* (71); *Company of Killers* with Van Johnson;

and *Black Noon*, an occult Western, all for television. He returned to cinemas with: *Embassy*, a thriller with Richard Roundtree, as the American ambassador; *Frogs*, a horror film in which reptiles up and attack humans, as an aged patriarch; and *The Thing with Two Heads* (73). *The House in Nightmare Park* co-starred the British comic, Frankie Howerd, and the murky, low-budget bent continued with *Terror in the Wax Museum*, in the role done previously by Lionel Atwill and Vincent Price. Respite was at hand with *Gold* (74) and Disney's *Escape to Witch Mountain* (75), in both as a very wealthy fellow indeed – but poverty was more in order when it came to entertainment value. His activity over the next few years was considerable: *The Dead Don't Die*, a tele-movie with George Hamilton; *Ellery Queen: Too Many Suspects*, also in that medium, with Kim Hunter as his wife and Jim Hutton as Queen; and *Rich Man Poor Man* (76), a mini-series. He did a guest appearance in *The Swiss Conspiracy* and then was in *Aces High*, an unnecessary British re-doing of *Journey's End* (as a high-ranking army officer); *Look What's Happened to Rosemary's Baby* and *Mayday at 40,000 Feet*, both for television; *The Last Tycoon*, an uninspired version of Scott Fitzgerald's novel, as a lawyer; *Seventh Avenue* (77), a 'name' mini-series and *Testimony of Two Men*, also for TV. He played an Arab in *Slavers* for a German company, along with several other names; he was with some others in the Italian *Oil*; and a doctor in *Mayday at 40,000 Feet*, which starred David Janssen. He was a publisher encouraging Peter Cushing in the three stories which comprise *The Uncanny*, after which he was supposed to make *I Gabbiani Volano Bassi*, but the role was played by Mel Ferrer. He did make another Italian film, *La Ragazza in Pigiamo Giallo* (78), in Australia, playing a retired police inspector. *Cruise into Terror* for TV and *Blackout*, made in Canada, continue the list of dreary credits, after which he repeated an earlier role in an unpopular sequel, *Oliver's Story*, with O'Neal.

These were a notch or two, if only just, above some of the stuff which Milland had been doing: *The Attic* (79), as Carrie Snodgress's father, tyrant and invalid; *The Darker Side of Terror* for TV, as a professor; *Battlestar Galactica*; *Games for Vultures*, as a London financier, associate of hero Richard Harris; and *Survival Run* (80), one of the villains in pursuit of the youngsters – who were doing just that. He was one of several veterans (Howard Duff, José Ferrer, Fernando Lamas) supporting Morgan Fairchild in an absurd TV mini-series, *The Dream Merchants*, and he supported Alberto Sordi, who also directed, in *Moi et Catherine*. Matters did not improve with four tele-movies: *Our Family Business* (81), well down the cast-list but with an imposing role as a sick Mafia boss; *The Royal Romance of Charles and Diana* (82), as a palace factotum; *Starflight: the Plane That Couldn't Land* (83), as a greedy tycoon; and *Cave-In*, an Irwin Allen disaster, again as a professor. He looked dyspeptic throughout the lot and who could blame him? – especially when he lost *Trading Places* because of illness. He died of cancer in 1986. One film surfaced (just) posthumously, *The Sea Serpent* (86), made in Spain and starring Timothy Bottoms.

He had married in 1932 and the marriage endured happily.

Carmen Miranda

Carmen Miranda was known as The Brazilian Bombshell. Her specialty was Latin–American songs-and-dances, particularly the faster numbers, rumbas and sambas. She came on flamboyantly decorated; her head-dresses towered, often with half an orchard and a couple of baskets of fruit; the platforms of her shoes were three inches high (which did nothing to impair her dancing). She was great fun. In between songs there was little that scriptwriters could find for her to do: she was usually the heroine's friend – or rival – and she was loyal, fast-talking, with a very low tolerance point. She showed occasional skill with a comedy line and, in other circumstances, might have had a longer career.

She was born in Marco Canavezes, Portugal, in 1909 and taken to Brazil as a child. Later she established a reputation as a nightclub entertainer, with her own band and her own radio show, and she made four films: *Alo Alo Brasil* (34), *Estudantes*, *Alo Alo Carnaval* and *Banana da Terra* (38). She was known throughout South America when Marc Connelly brought her to the attention of the Shuberts, who gave her a featured part in a Broadway show, 'Streets of Paris' (39). In it she sang 'South American Way' and 20th asked her to repeat it for a Betty Grable musical, *Down Argentine Way* (40): she filmed her songs in New York for interpolation into the film, possibly at the intervention of Nelson Rockefeller, Co-Ordinator of Inter-American Affairs, a government organization which did in fact give the studio $40,000 to reshoot sequences likely to offend Argentinians. Not only was it Washington policy to foster friendship with the countries south of the border, but Hollywood wanted to improve trade there now that the European market was cut off. So there were smiles all round –

not least on the face of the lady herself, because she wanted desperately to be a Hollywood star – when on the strength of the rushes she was offered a long-term contract.

Her success was instantaneous; she was imitated everywhere, both seriously and in parody. She made two more lush musicals, designed partly to encourage America's Good Neighbour Policy: *That Night in Rio* (41) and *Weekend in Havana*. 20th reluctantly let her do an Olsen and Johnson revue, 'Sons o' Fun', but she returned to the west and moved north for *Springtime in the Rockies* (42). By the time of *The Gang's All Here* (43) her limitations were all too painfully obvious.

All the same, after guesting in *Four Jills and a Jeep* (44) she was top-starred over Don Ameche in *Greenwich Village* and was, said the 'Sunday Chronicle' (London), 'dazzlingly dynamic'. The 'Evening Standard' was 'invigorated' by her 'bounding vitality'. She was not, of course, the romantic lead – that was Vivian Blaine, whom 20th hoped would replace the decamping Alice Faye. Miranda and Blaine were starred again in *Something*

It could be a scene from any Carmen Miranda *film, but it is in fact from* That Night in Rio *(41). The leads were Alice Faye and Don Ameche, but she stole the film.*

for the Boys (45), a good Broadway musical which 20th standardized with their usual skill; and in both *Doll Face* and *If I'm Lucky* (46), but these two were in black and white, a fair indication that the combined box-office worth of the two ladies could not encompass Technicolor. And Miranda in monochrome was much less impressive. 20th had no further plans for her and she signed a long-term deal with Universal; but she made no films for them and instead turned up at UA opposite Groucho Marx in *Copacabana* (47), a mild little comedy. She herself was fine and MGM took her up for featured parts in *A Date With Judy* (48) and *Nancy Goes to Rio*: neither studio publicity nor box-office returns indicated that this was a new lease of life for her. She turned to nightclubs and personal appearances, including the London Palladium in 1949, and got one last break with featured billing: *Scared Stiff* (53), fighting flab in this Martin and Lewis remake of *The Ghost Breakers*. Since it takes them to Havana, they see her do two numbers, one on shipboard and the other in a nightclub. She has just two

lines of dialogue. She died that same year, it was said of a broken heart (really peritonitis). She had been married in 1947 to David Sebastian.

MARIA MONTEZ

The name of Maria Montez brings joy to the hearts of some fanciers of 1940s nostalgia. (Not for nothing is her name sacred to one of 'The Boys in the Band'.) Queen of some wartime dustbin epics, her reign was brief: if talent will out, then so will the lack of it.

Born in 1920 in Barahona, in the Dominican Republic, to the Spanish consul there, she was, needless to say, convent-educated. That over with, she journeyed to Europe where she joined a theatrical troupe; in Belfast (when she was 17) she married an officer in the British army. After the divorce she went to New York and became a model. Her striking Latin beauty led to a screen test with Universal, who signed her at $150 a week. Her first

One of the most curious aspects of wartime entertainment was the proliferation of comic-strip Oriental 'extravaganzas' all starring Maria Montez. The best of them was probably the first, Arabian Nights *(42), produced by Walter Wanger. The gentleman in charge in this picture is Sabu.*

Montez in one of her costumes for Cobra Woman *(43), in which she played sisters, one a slave-girl and one a pagan ruler. Robert Siodmak, who directed, observed that she couldn't act, but that he got results from her if he treated her off-set as either a slave or a queen, whichever she was playing that day.*

work consisted of bits in *The Invisible Woman* (41) and *Lucky Devils*, and her first real part was opposite Johnny Mack Brown in *Boss of Bullion City*, a B Western; then she was loaned to 20th Century-Fox for a small role in *That Night in Rio*. Her demands for better parts got her the leads in the likes of *Raiders of the Desert*, *South of Tahiti* starring Brian Donlevy, *Bombay Clipper* (42) and *The Mystery of Marie Roget*, freely adapted from Poe, with Marie Ouspenskaya well cast as her grandmother; while some interest accrued to her because she was almost the only artist on the contract list considered dishy enough to compete on barrack-room walls with the Grables and Hayworths of other studios. It occurred to Universal that she might be showcased (as they were) in some lavish escapist entertainment. As she could not sing or dance, the solution was *Arabian Nights*. She played Scheherazade (and did dance – of sorts) and Jon Hall was Haroun al Raschid. Its success spawned a sequel, *White Savage* (43) – which had been the British title for *South of Tahiti*, so for audiences there this was retitled *White Captive*. And more . . . all of them remarkable for their Technicolor and dozens of girls with bare midriffs, plus some less ingratiating ingredients – cheap painted sets, grade-school dialogue and acting which would not have disgraced a cigar-store Indian. As twin sisters in *Cobra Woman* Montez's performance (the plural would be inappropriate) has to be seen to be believed. C.A. Lejeune observed of the film that it 'certainly dragged its slow length along'. The others were: *Ali Baba and the 40 Thieves* (44), *Gypsy Wildcat* and *Sudan* (45). Hall and usually Turhan Bey supported Montez. That year the 'Harvard Lampoon' named her the year's worst actress. As public interest waned, the studio tried her in a period musical, *From Bowery to Broadway*, but although top-billed, she does not appear for the first hour and has only about 15 minutes' screen time before being obviously doubled in her one dance number. She also proved less alluring in black and white, as was demonstrated again in a modern drama, *Tangier* (46), playing a Spanish dancer seeking revenge on the Nazis. She had only a small role in *The Exile* (47), as a French countess who was an old friend of Douglas Fairbanks Jr, but Universal tried once more, putting her back into Technicolor for *Pirates of Monterey* with Rod Cameron. Unsurprisingly, when her contract ran out, it was not renewed.

With her husband, Jean-Pierre Aumont, she did an independent, black-and-white throw-back to her heyday, *Siren of Atlantis* (48): she got $100,000, but the film did not get its money back. She and Aumont went to

Europe, where she made a motley group of French and Franco-Italian pictures. The titles: *Hans le Marin* (48); *Portrait d'un Assassin* (49), as a circus proprietor; *The Thief of Venice/Il Ladro di Venezia* (50), made in English; *Amore e Sangue/Schatten über Neapel*, an Italian-German co-production; and *La Vendetta del Corso* (51). She had begun to have weight problems and tried to counter them by taking hot saline baths. She died in one, of a heart attack, in 1951. Her daughter Tina married actor Christian Marquand and has acted in French pictures.

ROBERT MONTGOMERY

Robert Montgomery is probably remembered less for what he did in his own right than for squiring on-screen the famous ladies of MGM – Garbo, Shearer, Crawford. He was MGM's all-purpose actor, but he was best in light comedy, a *jeune premier* of the Park Avenue set, immaculate, boyish and smooth.

Whether or not he came from the requisite background is not known. MGM publicity insisted that he was born into a wealthy family (in Beacon, New York, in 1904) who became penniless when Montgomery's father died. He became a mechanic's mate and a deck-hand on an oil-tanker. Said a studio blurb: 'He used to write sea stories, having had adventures in a tanker.' Montgomery was still in his teens and trying to make a living as a writer when he was offered five different walk-ons in a nearby Greenwich Village theatre, in 'The Mask and the Face' (21). He was later in rep in Rochester, New York, in over 70 plays in 18 months; and his Broadway appearances included 'Dawn', 'Arlene O'Dare', 'One of the Family' and 'Possession' (28). He was well-noticed in the latter and Goldwyn announced that he would head the supporting cast of Vilma Banky's *So This Is Heaven*; but after testing him changed his mind. MGM executives in New York saw the test, however, and signed him to a contract at $350 a week. The Hollywood end of the company were dismayed when they saw him – 'too skinny and fragile and unprepossessing.' Eventually he was cast in *So This Is College?* (29) and director Sam Wood had him padded to play a full-back.

Somewhat less desperately he was loaned to UA for a remake of *Three Live Ghosts*, the story of three soldiers returned to London on Armistice Day. But whatever he may have been like in the flesh he photographed well and was cast opposite jungle-flower Joan Crawford in *Untamed* and then as one of the

children, with Leila Hyams, in *Father's Day*: Louis Mann was father.

His big lift came when cast opposite Norma Shearer in *Their Own Desire* (30), after which he was not too happy at being the love interest in *Free and Easy*, pinching from Buster Keaton his adored protégée, Anita Page. He was back with Shearer, seducing her, in *The Divorcée* and back with the cast of *Father's Day* in a sequel known variously as *The Richest Man in the World* and *Sins of the Children*. His rating advanced again as the yellow welcher in the hit prison drama, *Big House*, with Wallace Beery and Chester Morris, and, less spectacularly, with *Our Blushing Brides* with Crawford and *Love in the Rough*, a remake of a 1927 William Haines vehicle, *Spring Fever*. He was also the leading character in *War Nurse*, supported by Robert Ames, June Walker, Anita Page and Marie Prevost, a tribute that 'Photoplay' found 'by turns gruesome and silly'. After that it was back to the Great Ladies: Garbo in *Inspiration* (31) – he was poor as the country boy who loves her; Constance Bennett in *The Easiest Way*, deserting her on hearing of her past; and

Our Blushing Brides *(30).
'You must see Joan Crawford in those lace step-ins,' said 'Photoplay'. Robert Montgomery, however, wasn't impressed.*

Shearer in *Strangers May Kiss*. It was Dorothy Jordan in *Shipmates*; then he was *The Man in Possession*, an ex-con turned broker's man in the house of wealthy widow Irene Purcell, from a successful play. *Private Lives* had also been lived out on the stage first and its author, Noël Coward, thought Montgomery and Shearer played 'charmingly' though on the whole he did not care for it. Montgomery's performance is perhaps too knowing. The *Lovers Courageous* (32) were he and Madge Evans: 'On her wedding night she ran to the arms of her lover' said the ads, suggesting (erroneously) that the film might be either salacious or dramatic. He did *But the Flesh Is Weak*, an adaptation of Ivor Novello's play 'The Truth Game'; *Letty Lynton* with Crawford again; *Blondie of the Follies* with Marion Davies; and *Faithless* with Tallulah Bankhead.

Hell Below (33) was a submarine drama with Jimmy Durante, Walter Huston and Madge Evans; the girl he *Made on Broadway* was Sally Eilers, a weak satire on publicity methods; he was present *When Ladies Meet*; married Helen Hayes and introduced her to his family, who spoke *Another Language*; and took a *Night Flight* with her, Clark Gable and two of the Barrymores. He and Madge Evans were lovers again, not courageous this time, but *Fugitive Lovers*: this made a run of poor parts, but Metro signed him to a new contract and he was seen to advantage in *Riptide* (34) with Shearer, as the charming, playboy Other Man; *The Mystery of Mr X*, with Lewis Stone and Elizabeth Allen, as the slick playboy thief; and *Hide-Out* with Maureen O'Sullivan, as the smooth-tongued playboy racketeer. He was with Crawford and Gable, *Forsaking All Others*; with Helen Hayes in *Vanessa Her Love Story* (35) – inadequate as Benjie; with Ann Harding in *Biography of a Bachelor Girl*; with Crawford again in a fair version of a hit stage comedy, *No More Ladies*; with Myrna Loy in *Petticoat Fever* (36), as the wireless operator for whom she leaves stuffy fiancé Reginald Owen; and with Rosalind Russell in *Trouble for Two*, from – a long way from – Robert Louis Stevenson's 'The Suicide Club', as a Crown Prince with a moustache and curls above his ears. *Piccadilly Jim*, from a P.G. Wodehouse story, was one of his best pictures and the fact that he was not, for once, supporting one of MGM's queens (though it had the underrated Madge Evans) gave him fine chances: he was more or less evenly matched with Crawford in *The Last of Mrs Cheyney* (37). His employers, however, were not very happy with him; he had done sterling work on behalf of the newly formed Screen Actors Guild and when he asked to play the homicidal maniac in *Night Must Fall* the

studio readily bought it for him, thinking it would destroy his popularity. It had been a very successful stage thriller and Montgomery was only too convincing as the maniacal Danny, outwardly sane, with the head in the hat-box: it increased his stature, in fact. The studio, unmollified by his success, loaned him out for the first time since 1929, to Warners for *Ever Since Eve* with Marion Davies; they then threw him into *Live Love and Learn*, a comedy with his *Night Must Fall* co-star Rosalind Russell – though rumours enanated from the studio that they did not get on – and then into a couple of programmers with Virginia Bruce, *The First Hundred Years* (38) and *Yellowjack*, in which he is an Irish sergeant who volunteers to be a guinea pig when doctors search for a cure for that disease.

Montgomery had in any case never had the first choice of the MGM farceur roles (they had gone to William Powell), but was considered the leading young light comedian in films; a situation eroded by Cary Grant, who had come to the fore as *the* leading purveyor of this sort of comedy. MGM lost all interest in Montgomery as an asset: he was virtually in support of Janet Gaynor in *Three Loves Has Nancy* and he took over a role just vacated by Melvyn Douglas, sleuth Joel Sloan, in *Fast and Loose* (39) with Russell as his wife (the Douglas film had been *Fast Company* with Florence Rice and the characters would be played in the next one, *Fast and Furious*, by Ann Sothern and Franchot Tone). Montgomery was back on a better track with *The Earl of Chicago* (40), an enjoyable comedy about a bootlegger who becomes a member of the British aristocracy; and he remained ennobled, as Lord Peter Wimsey, in *Busman's Honeymoon* with Constance Cummings – and that was actually filmed in Britain. Shooting was stopped on the outbreak of war and resumed early in 1940: in the interim, as a gesture of friendship, Montgomery visited the BEF in France.

At RKO he was half of the mere *Mr and Mrs Smith* (41) with Carole Lombard as the other half; then he was a paranoiac again in *Rage in Heaven*, trying to murder wife Ingrid Bergman and best friend George Sanders because – as far as could be discerned – he had a subliminal crush on Sanders. He did not want to do the film and to annoy MGM walked through the part – thus was somewhat disconcerted to be praised for his performance. It was Columbia who proudly announced *Here Comes Mr Jordan*, with Claude Rains as Mr Jordan, helping (dead) boxer Montgomery to find himself a new body – one of the few acceptable film whimsies and one of the few Montgomery films where he

There was something a little smug about Robert Montgomery's screen persona which qualified him best for playing playboys. That was all right, for it meant that he could decorate the sort of luxurious apartments that the studios saw as the perfect setting for their big female stars. The film above is Riptide *(34), the lady is Norma Shearer and, oh yes, he had been to a fancy-dress party. At left is* Unfinished Business *(41), the lady is Irene Dunne, and the valet watching their failing marriage is the invaluable Eugene Pallette.*

assumed an accent – in this case an effortless Bronx. He was loaned out again to Universal for a comedy with Irene Dunne, *Unfinished Business*, after which he joined the US navy, ending up as a lieutenant-commander.

He had a beautiful *rentrée*, Ford's *They Were Expendable* (45) with John Wayne, one of the most lyrical of war films, but MGM had already lined up *Desire Me*: Montgomery in his old role as chief courtier, in this case to Queen Greer. But there was trouble during the shooting and he was replaced by new-comer Richard Hart (the film later went out without director credit). *Lady in the Lake* (46) was much talked about. From one of Raymond Chandler's novels, it told the film in first person: Montgomery was Marlowe, seen only in an occasional mirror – but he directed, which put him very much in front. The studio, however, had never forgiven him for his pre-war complaints and dealings; so at this point he left them.

He went to Universal to direct and star in *Ride the Pink Horse* (47) – and did both almost brilliantly; but the confused plot (hoodlum on the revenge trail) and a poor title killed it at the box-office. His career wilted again with *The Saxon Charm* (48), a melodrama at Universal with Susan Hayward and John Payne, in which he played a self-centred, ruthless and nasty theatre producer, but revived with *June Bride*, opposite Bette Davis (who disclosed in her memoirs that she loathed working with him). He directed as well as starred in *Once More My Darling* (49), a comedy about a playboy and a débutante (Ann Blyth); and had the same functions on *Your Witness*, made for Warners in Britain. With that, as he said later, he got out while the going was good: he had had a long and successful career and did not feel disposed to continue in the sort of weak films he had had since he left MGM.

He turned to TV, first in the 'Lucky Strike Theatre' and then in 'Robert Montgomery Presents', a dramatic series in which he sometimes starred and which he often directed; he also appeared in some TV specials, including 'The Great Gatsby' and 'The Lost Weekend'; and for most of the 50s he was consultant to President Eisenhower on all things televisual, including the presentation of said President. He became executive producer of Cagney-Montgomery Productions, but the film in which he directed long-time friend Cagney (and which took three years to set up), *The Gallant Hours*, did poor business. In the 60s his daughter Elizabeth demonstrated that she had inherited much of his comedic skill in a TV series, 'Bewitched'. He died in 1981.

GRACE MOORE

It almost beggars belief that Grace Moore was once a popular film star, but at the time she was considered an attractive as well as an accomplished artist. True, she was skinny at a time when prima donnas were expected to be obese. Unfortunately, as well as her opera-trained voice, she brought to films too many prima donna characteristics (including tantrums on the set). She was always inappropriate: her face though not uncomely bore an unhappy resemblance to that of comedienne Joan Davis, disqualifying her for the dainty heroines she ventured to play; too often she frisked about the screen, like a horse thinking it was a kitten. But here is a contemporary opinion: 'She is one of the few singers who is easy to look at even when tackling a high C; she acts pleasantly, moves engagingly, has obvious wit and character' (C.A. Lejeune on *One Night of Love*).

She was born in Del Rio, Tennessee, in 1903 and educated at Nashville, where her remarkable voice was first trained; while still a student she sang in a Martinelli concert at the National Theater, Washington. She went into operetta and had her first important role in 'Up in the Clouds'. She also appeared in some of the Music Box Revues (in the 1924 edition she introduced 'What'll I Do?') and was in one of the later 'Hitchy Koo' shows. She continued to study voice – with Maraflot – but really turned her attention to higher things when she was befriended by millionaire music patron Otto Kahn: under his auspices she studied in Europe and began to give concerts. She made her Metropolitan début in 1928 as Mimi in 'La Bohème'.

MGM signed her to a contract and put her into two films, *A Lady's Morals* (30), an inept concoction based on the life of Jenny Lind, and *New Moon*, with Lawrence Tibbett, which kept the songs but threw away the story of the stage version. Both were resounding failures and Moore returned to opera and concerts. In 1933, she starred on Broadway in 'The Dubarry' and her success caused Hollywood to look at her again. She desperately wanted to return to MGM, who had dropped her ignominiously three years earlier, and when she heard that they wanted her for *The Merry Widow* she was prepared to waive her fee. But neither she nor Chevalier would accept second billing and when MGM backed Chevalier, she dropped out and Jeanette MacDonald played the part. She was consoled by a contract from Columbia at $25,000 per film. But the studio had second thoughts and wanted out. She threatened to sue, so they went ahead with *One Night of Love* (34), in which she mixed ballads with bits of grand

opera. To everyone's surprise, the public lapped it up (and even more surprising, the star was nominated for an Oscar). Thalberg at MGM now wanted Moore more than ever and MGM announced that she would appear for them in both *Rose Marie* and then *Maytime*; but she missed the schedule on the first and again MacDonald played both parts; with the death of Thalberg, interest in Moore at MGM ceased.

Columbia, however, had Grace Moore vehicles lined up: *Love Me Forever* (35); and more frou-frou, *The King Steps Out* (36), which had suitable music by Fritz Kreisler. Franchot Tone was an incognito Franz Joseph II enraptured by publican's daughter Moore. Von Sternberg directed and Moore made it clear that she thought he did not know what he was doing. It did not do as well as the earlier two and grosses dropped on the next couple, *When You're in Love* (37) and *I'll Take Romance*, despite the presence of leading men Cary Grant and Melvyn Douglas respectively – and the fact that in the first of these Moore essayed a much-publicized 'Minnie the Moocher'. Her temperament was a Hollywood byword and when no further offers were forthcoming, she accepted the lead in Charpentier's *Louise* (39), made in France. Abel Gance directed and it was a monumental bore. She never filmed again, but in 1953 – six years after she was killed in an air crash on a Copenhagen runway – WB made a biopic, *So This Is Love*, with Kathryn Grayson as Moore.

'Princess or pauper, I love you': Emperor-in-disguise Franchot Tone thinks Grace Moore is an innkeeper's daughter, but she's incognito too and really Elisabeth of Bavaria. The King Steps Out (36).

By this time, chunks of opera were accepted screen fare. In 1935 Grace Moore had been a pioneer. The Society of Arts and Sciences had given her a gold medal for 'distinctive service in the arts, especially for conspicuous achievement in raising the standard of cinema entertainment'.

FRANK MORGAN

There was a time when no MGM film seemed complete without Frank Morgan, a stocky middle-aged man with an air of perpetual surprise: his neigh of astonishment is one of the soundtrack's enduring memories. He dithered, he was just short of being eccentric, he was the beloved family fool: the characteristics had been worked out early in his stage career and MGM at least were not going to let him lose them. His actual range was much wider, though perhaps it does not matter: whatever he did Morgan was one of the most satisfying and endearing performers ever to make movies. He was an artist with a talent for gauging the tones of co-players and script and acting up or down accordingly.

He was born in New York City in 1890 into a family of importers (Angostura bitters; later, during his film career, he was Vice-President) and was educated for a time at Cornell University. He sold space for a Boston newspaper, but quit that and went West where he worked as a cowboy. His brother Ralph had taken up acting and Frank decided to follow him and worked up a vaudeville sketch: like his brother, he changed his surname from Wuppermann to Morgan. He was doing his sketch in vaudeville when he was offered the juvenile lead in 'Mr Wu' (14), starring Walter Whiteside. At least, that was the way Studio Biographies had it; but 'Who's Who In the Theatre' (33) says he studied at the AADA and made his New York début in 'A Woman Killed with Kindness' and, later, was in stock, playing leads, in Northampton, Massachusetts. Not long afterwards Vitagraph signed him to a contract and when Anita Stewart lost her normal leading man, Earle Williams, Morgan was appointed in his place. His early films: *The Suspect* (16), *The Daring of Diana*, *Light in Darkness* (17), *A Modern Cinderella* with June Caprice, *That Girl Philippa* with Stewart, *Who's Your Neighbor?*, *A Child of the Wild*, *Baby Mine* at Goldwyn starring Madge Kennedy, *Raffles the Amateur Cracksman* starring John Barrymore, *The Knife* (18), *At the Mercy of Men*, *Gray Towers of Mystery* (19) and *The Golden Shower*.

It could not be said that he was conspicuously successful and his stage work continued

to give him more fame and satisfaction. Among his stage appearances were: 'Seventh Heaven' (22), 'Lullaby' (23), 'The Firebrand', 'Gentlemen Prefer Blondes' (26) and 'Topaze' (30) in the title-role. He had mostly small roles in his other Silents: Gloria Swanson's *Manhandled* (24); *Born Rich* (25) starring Doris Kenyon; *The Man Who Found Himself* starring Thomas Meighan (also in the cast were brother Ralph and Lynn Fontanne); *The Crowded Hour*; *The Scarlet Saint* with Mary Astor; and *Love's Greatest Mistake* (27). He was in 'Rosalie' (28) on Broadway, as the fluttery King. Two years later Paramount starred him in a short, *Belle of the Night*, and as a result signed him to a long-term contract: *Queen High* (30), a musical strung around him and Charles Ruggles as partners in a garter business, gambling on who should buttle for the other for a while; *Dangerous Nan McGrew*, which was a vehicle for Helen Kane; *Laughter*, where he was Nancy Carroll's elderly millionaire husband; and *Fast and Loose* as Miriam Hopkins's wealthy father, virtually the film's only professional performance.

The contract ended abruptly when he was offered a part in 'The Band Wagon' with the Astaires and he was off the screen for almost two years. He returned with a Fox contract, but mainly freelanced and seven Morgan pictures were released within six months: *Secrets of the French Police* (32) co-starring with Gwili Andre; *The Half-Naked Truth*, as a producer to whom Lee Tracy wants to promote a fake princess, Lupe Velez; *The Billion Dollar Scandal* (33) with Robert Armstrong, as a big time con-man; *Hallelujah I'm a Bum* starring Al Jolson, as the mayor of New York; *Luxury Liner* at Paramount from a bestseller by Gina Kaus; *Sailor's Luck*, a Sally Eilers-Jimmy Dunn programmer; and *A Kiss Before the Mirror*, in which he was Nancy Carroll's cuckolded husband. At that point MGM signed Morgan to a contract and he appeared in a further six films that year: *Reunion in Vienna*, as Diana Wynyard's elderly husband; *The Nuisance* – who was Lee Tracy, with Morgan as a drink-sodden medicine man; *When Ladies Meet* with Ann Harding, his best Hollywood part so far; *Best of Enemies* at Fox; *Broadway to Hollywood* starring with Alice Brady in a beautifully made and acted story of two vaudeville hoofers; and *Bombshell* as Jean Harlow's sponging father.

Morgan's skill was recognized by Metro, who gave him good parts even if they failed to consider him one of their top stars; and he was doing very well in a town where most actors of his age were considered past their prime. After he had played a professorial philanderer in *The Cat and the Fiddle* (34) MGM acceded to demand and loaned him to virtually every other studio: *Success at Any Price*, as the magazine boss betrayed by an ambitious Douglas Fairbanks Jr, and *Sisters Under the Skin* at Columbia; *Affairs of Cellini* at 20th-UA as the Duke, the role he had played in the stage version ('The Firebrand') 10 years earlier; *A Lost Lady* at Warners; *There's Always Tomorrow* at Universal, as a father tired of being taken for granted, with Binnie Barnes; and *By Your Leave* at RKO with Genevieve Tobin. 'Photoplay' said there was 'a gilt-edged guarantee of abundant chuckles. As the husband in his 40s, seeking by a week of wild-oat sowing to re-charge his ego, Frank Morgan gives the most completely inspired portrait yet of that pathetic creature – a man who wants to be naughty, but who has forgotten how.' At Universal he did *The Good Fairy* (35), ogling Margaret Sullavan, and at RKO *The Enchanted April*. Then MGM kept him busy: *Naughty Marietta*, as the amorous governor; *Escapade*; *I Live My Life*; *The Perfect Gentlemen* – 'as Major Hugo Charteris, the shabby aristocrat, the confused alcoholic and the genial humbug' – 'The New York Times' (André Sennwald) found him 'completely delightful': it was set in an English village; and *The Great Ziegfeld* (36) as Ziegfeld's showman rival.

Pioneer-RKO borrowed him for *The Dancing Pirate*, which was the third all-Technicolor feature: Charles Collins had the title-role and Steffi Duna was the girl, but Morgan was the star by both billing and right, as the befuddled mayor of the village that is invaded by the pirates. He was in *Trouble for Two*, as aide to a Crown Prince (Robert Montgomery); *Piccadilly Jim*, as Montgomery's disreputable father; *Dimples* at 20th, as an old vaudevillian; *The Last of Mrs Cheyney* (37) as a rather asinine suitor of that lady; *The Emperor's Candlesticks*, as aide to a Grand Duke (Robert Young); *Saratoga* as Una Merkel's fond and foolish sugar-daddy of a husband; and *Rosalie* in the part he had done on the stage (only there was a new Cole Porter score). Before that he had one of his few star roles in a good while in *Beg Borrow or Steal*, with Florence Rice, a pleasant comedy set on the Riviera. Normally MGM found him more useful to head their supporting casts – which were usually the strongest of all the companies.

He and Rice were co-starred again in *Paradise for Three* (38); there followed *Port of Seven Seas*, MGM's version of the *Fanny* trilogy, in the Panisse part, happy with Maureen O'Sullivan till the father (John Beal) of the baby tries to break it up; *The Crowd Roars*, as a dipsomaniac father; *Sweethearts*,

According to The Great Ziegfeld *(36) Ziegfeld started his career running a sideshow in a carnival. Frank Morgan played his chief rival for the public's attention.*

as an impresario; *Broadway Serenade* (39) as an impresario; *The Wizard of Oz* in the title-role; *Balalaika* (40), as the head of the opera house, not blowing Nelson Eddy's cover; and *Henry Goes to Arizona*, in which he played an ex-vaudevillian inheriting his brother's farm and, along with Virginia Weidler, getting involved with outlaws. It was the first of several Bs in which MGM were to star Morgan over the next few years and was not improved by changing directors, many re-writes and the deletion of George Murphy after several weeks' filming. Murphy, in fact, superseded Morgan – again as an impresario – at the head of the supporting cast of *Broadway Melody of 1940*, which came along just after *The Shop Around the Corner*, in which Morgan was the irascible but kindly store-owner. He was a professor in *The Mortal Storm*; then co-starred with Billie Burke in *Hullabaloo*, as a middle-aged hoofer trying to get into radio, and *The Ghost Comes Home*; and was the buddy/rival of Gable and Tracy in *Boom Town*. He made *Keeping Company* (41) with Ann Rutherford;

Rouben Mamoulian's Summer Holiday *(48): the spinster aunt is wooed by the bachelor uncle on the other side – Frank Morgan and Agnes Moorehead.*

Washington Melodrama as a kindly do-gooder; *The Wild Man of Borneo*, playing a sponger, with Mary Howard; *Honky Tonk*, as Lana Turner's father and killed off in reel one; and *The Vanishing Virginian* with Kathryn Grayson.

Then, just as cinemagoers were forgetting what a fine serious actor he could be, he was cast in a straight role in *Tortilla Flat* (42) and won a deserved (second) Oscar nomination, for despite Spencer Tracy, he was the only bearable aspect of it, as a black-bearded hobo thought to have a cache of money. He followed with parts in: *White Cargo* as that stock figure of tropical movies, the drunken doctor; *Night Monster*, with Bela Lugosi, as a helpless cripple: *The Human Comedy* (43) as a newspaper man, and as so often the best performance in the film; *A Stranger in Town*, starring again, as a Supreme Court judge; *Thousands Cheer*; *The White Cliffs of Dover* (44), as Irene Dunne's father, sceptical of the English; and one on loan-out, *Casanova Brown*, as Gary Cooper's confidante and prospective father-in-law. He gave a rich making-bricks-without-straw performance in *Yolanda and the Thief* (45), as a con-man, and then did sterling service in the third Lassie picture, *Courage of Lassie* (46). He was in *Lady Luck* at RKO; *The Cockeyed Miracle* as Keenan Wynn's son (they were both ghosts);

Green Dolphin Street (47); *Summer Holiday* (48) as the tippling uncle, the part done by Wallace Beery in the earlier version, *Ah Wilderness!*; *The Three Musketeers* as the King; *The Stratton Story* (49) as an old baseball hand; *Any Number Can Play* and *The Great Sinner*, in both as an inveterate gambler; and *Key to the City*, as Gable's firechief pal. He was working on *Annie Get Your Gun*, playing Buffalo Bill, when he died in his sleep (1949): the film was reshot with Louis Calhern in the part. He left a widow, whom he had married in 1914. His brother also had a long career in films, but without the same success.

PAUL MUNI

Paul Muni was the 30s idea of a Great Actor: he never looked the same twice. 'King of the Character Actors' says 'The Picture Show Annual for 1939', showing him in 11 of his roles – moustached or bearded (three beards of different shape), hair combed forward or in a mop. centre-parted and slicked down or just curled. He took meticulous care with his make-up. Bette Davis, who acted with him in *Juarez*, said in her autobiography: 'Mr Muni seemed intent on submerging himself so completely that he disappeared. There is no question that his technique as an actor was superb. But, for me, beneath the exquisite petit point of details, the loss of his own sovereignty worked conversely to rob some of his characterization of blood.' He was over-conscientious: in 1937 W.H. Mooring observed admiringly in 'Film Weekly' that Muni was never content to 'walk through' a part. In retrospect, it is a pity: he was an actor of great integrity – but much of his work has dated.

He was born in Lemberg, (then) Austria, in 1895, into a family of strolling players; they emigrated to the US when he was a child and in 1918 he joined the Yiddish Theater stock company in New York, moving on to the Jewish Art Theater (inbetweenwhiles being educated in New York and Cleveland). He acted in London in 1924, but it was not until 1926 that he made his first appearance in an English-speaking part, taking over from Edward G. Robinson, in 'We Americans' (it was filmed, but Muni was considered unsuitable and was replaced by George Sidney). The following year 'Four Walls' really established him and when Talkies came in he was immediately considered likely film material. Fox signed him to a long-term contract (and announced him in their early publicity as a new discovery from Russia), but he made only two pictures for them, both failures. The first,

The Valiant (29), was almost abandoned, because he was considered, after all, to have limited appeal; but it brought him an Oscar nomination – playing a murderer hiding his true identity from his mother. The second, *Seven Faces*, cast him as a concierge in a waxworks (allowing him for some reason to portray seven different characters). Fearing that Fox wanted to make a second Lon Chaney out of him, he took himself back to New York and scored a huge success in Elmer Rice's 'Counsellor-at-Law' (31). Hollywood decided to try again, in the person of Howard Hawks, and cast him in the title-role of his searing gangster picture, *Scarface* (32). Then Warners gave him a whirl with *I Am a Fugitive From a Chain Gang*. The success of both films, critically and with the public, established Muni and WB offered him a long-term contract. It was a unique contract. He had the right to approve his material. If he refused three projects in a row, Warners were bound to do a fourth – which would be his choice entirely: this led, needless to say, to constant battles.

He supplanted George Arliss and for eight years was that studio's most important actor. Cagney and Robinson and, later, Dick Powell, might be more popular, but Muni had Class. He had the pick of parts, although at the same time WB realized that he was too powerful an actor for ordinary roles. *The World Changes* (33), cast him as an immigrant farmer who rises to meat-packing king, with Mary Astor; in *Hi Nellie!* (34) he was a tough newspaperman reduced to doing the sob-sister column; in *Bordertown* (35) he was a failed Mexican lawyer making it big as a café boss – a studied and ebullient performance; in *Black Fury* a miner rebelling against injustice – he called it 'Coal Diggers of 1935'; and in *Doctor Socrates* a small-town doctor who gets caught up with gangsters – perhaps his most likeable performance. When it was suggested to him – not by the Warners management – that he play Louis Pasteur, the great French scientist, he opposed the idea. But when it was pointed out that he would be playing one of the saviours of mankind, he agreed. He had turned down three Warner scripts, so they were bound to do this one – and the bitterness of his fights with them reached a new peak, so whole-heartedly did they loathe the project. The completed film brought them more prestige than anything yet in the history of the studio: *The Story of Louis Pasteur* (36), a painstaking and sincere portrait which brought Muni a Best Actor Oscar.

Muni went to MGM to play a Chinese peasant in *The Good Earth* (37), based on Pearl S. Buck's bestselling epic novel and the most eagerly awaited of the year's big pic-

tures. It lived up to expectations and this was a triumphant year for Muni even if he did elect to go to RKO for a poor picture about the Lafayette Esquadrille, *The Woman I Love*: the woman was Miriam Hopkins, the I was Louis Hayward and his new CO, the bearded, moody Muni, is, you have guessed it, her husband. But when his third film that year, like his first, mopped up at the box-office (both took over $1½ million) and he was again extravagantly praised he was in an unprecedented position in Hollywood. He played another famed Frenchman in *The Life of Emile Zola*. Said the very dignified ads: 'Warner Brothers takes pride in presenting Mr Paul Muni . . . in one of the few great pictures of all time. . . .' *Zola* won a best picture Oscar and for Muni the Best Actor Award from the New York critics. It concentrated mainly on Zola's involvement with

Two sides of a triangle: Paul Muni and Bette Davis in Bordertown *(35). The third was Eugene Pallette – his employee and her husband – soon to be killed by her.*

Muni as Juarez *(39). Graham Greene found his make-up 'extraordinarily impressive'.*

Muni in his last film, The Last Angry Man *(59), directed by Daniel Mann.*

a gangster again, in *High Sierra*, but he thought otherwise and proposed a life of Beethoven. Although they had recently drawn up a new contract, they decided that they could no longer afford him – he had at no point been the most docile of contract players – and they settled his contract.

Muni returned to New York and made a great success there in 'Key Largo' by Maxwell Anderson. He went back to Hollywood under contract to 20th, but made only one film: *Hudson's Bay* (40), a pointless historical film not improved by his own tiresome performance as a French fur-trapper. He starred again on Broadway as a has-been actor in 'Yesterday's Magic' (Emlyn Williams's 'The Light of Heart' retitled) and in Hollywood for Columbia *The Commandos Strike at Dawn* (42), a syrupy tribute to Norwegian resistance fighters. After playing himself in *Stage Door Canteen*, he returned to Columbia for *Counter-Attack* (45): '. . . excellent in his quieter moments he is too often an over-generalized stagey embodiment of Russia' (James Agee). Released a few months earlier was *A Song to Remember* which had been held up because the studio feared that classical music was not box-office. This life of Chopin had at one time been a cherished project of Frank Capra (a screenplay prepared for him was eventually used). When Columbia finally took the plunge, Chopin became top of the pops for a while. The film was, however, 'appallingly silly' (Richard Winnington). Cornel Wilde was Chopin and Muni, though top-

Dreyfus in terms which today seem plodding and cliché-ridden (as indeed is Muni's interpretation of his role); but to many at the time this series of Warner biographies – all directed by William Dieterle – seemed to grapple nobly with Important Issues. By far the best is *Juarez* (39), which does attempt to explain in real terms the reasons for, and the consequences of, Napoleon III's Mexican adventure; Muni was fine in the title-role, the great native patriot, but it might have been better had he not bolstered his own part at the expense of the original conception. All the same, Graham Greene thought 'a quite impressive film has emerged'. Warners had agreed to do *Juarez* against their better judgment and it did not do well; nor did *We Are Not Alone*, from James Hilton's novel, and that was also much praised. He played a doctor in a small English village who befriends an Austrian girl as World War I breaks out. He had gone to great trouble to get his English accent right, but few people went to see it. Warners thought he could be restored to public favour if he played

billed, had only a featured role as his professor, 'so buried beneath whiskers and senile whimsy that I had a shock when I read his name on the programme afterwards' (Winnington).

It was virtually the end of his film career. There was an odd fantasy with Claude Rains, *Angel on My Shoulder* (46), which did poorly. He played a gangster sent back to earth in the person of a very sober judge. In 1948 he was reported as preparing a film life of Alfred Nobel. In 1949 he went to London to appear there in 'Death of a Salesman' and later he went to Italy for a movie with Joan Loring, *Imbarco a Mezzanotte* (52), playing a down-and-out who commits a murder. Though credited to one Andrea Forzano, it was in fact directed by Joseph Losey. In Britain and the US, it was eventually released under the title *Stranger on the Prowl*: it did nothing to resurrect his career, but in 1955 he had another Broadway hit, 'Inherit the Wind'. This reawakened the interest of Hollywood and Columbia signed him for *The Last Angry Man* (59), from a bestselling saga about a GP in the Brooklyn slums; Muni did very well as the doctor, cranky, cantankerous, kindly – but proved an unsaleable commodity at the box-office. In Britain it was a Royal Performance selection and was agreed to be dull but (just about) worthy. Prior to its making he had toured in the US as Kringelein in 'At the Grand', a musical version of 'Grand Hotel', and he had appeared on TV in a 'Playhouse 90' production, *Last Clear Chance* – that, at least, was a last success for him. He died in 1967 and it was disclosed that he had been virtually blind for the past several years. His wife was Bella Finkle, who married him before his Hollywood days and was always thought to be the guiding light behind his career.

ANNA NEAGLE

'As a box-office star-maker, my masterpiece was, of course, Anna Neagle,' wrote Herbert Wilcox in his autobiography. 'His unquestioning adoration of Anna shines through every page,' wrote Noël Coward. 'You would think, from reading it, that dear Anna is the greatest actress, singer and dancer and glamorous star who ever graced the stage and screen. The fact that this is not strictly accurate never for a split second occurs to him.' Still, as Wilcox pointed out, she was Britain's biggest female draw for seven years, which – even taking into account the paucity of such species – remains a record. And five times she won the 'Picturegoer' Gold Medal award, twice alongside Laurence Olivier. The story of Anna Neagle is

not unlike the plots of some of her films – she was created a Dame of the British Empire in 1969. Born in 1904, in a working-class district of London (Forest Gate), she decided at an early age that she wanted to be a dancer and went in for ballroom championships. At 20 she set out to make her fame and fortune on the stage. She danced in the chorus of a Charlot revue and later became a Cochran 'Young Lady'. Cochran made her Jessie Matthews's understudy for 'Wake Up and Dream' and though there is no record of the star falling sick and Anna going on in her place, the big break was not long in coming: Jack Buchanan selected her as his leading lady for 'Stand Up and Sing' (31) at the London Hippodrome. Enter Wilcox, then a leading producer-director. He happened to drop by the theatre one night to discuss a film he was to make with Jack. Chili Bouchier, whom Wilcox was directing in *Carnival*, says that he presented her, Bouchier, with a script and a glass of champagne, imploring her to be Trilby to his Svengali. She refused, but Neagle, seen backstage with Buchanan, accepted. According to Bouchier she was not like her 'gracious public image' but 'a cold and calculating schemer'.

She was not without film experience – pictures had already appeared in the fan magazines of 'Ann Eagle' and she had had a small part in an old farce, *Should a Doctor Tell?* (30), and another in the remake of *The Chinese Bungalow* (31) with Matheson Lang as an evil Chinese, less a film than a series of stills of him in fancy dress. Neagle's flower girl in the Buchanan film, *Goodnight Vienna* (32), so impressed Wilcox that he placed her under long-term contract and during the rest of her career she was only twice directed by other people. The first time was in her next picture, *The Flag Lieutenant* (33) with Henry Edwards. Wilcox directed her again in *The Little Damozel* and her performance as a sexy cabaret singer was, said 'Picturegoer', only 'fair'. However, he thought she had world potential and began to build her into a big star. The first attempt, a version of Coward's musical *Bitter Sweet*, was a commercial failure and 'Picturegoer' thought her 'disappointing'. When Jeanette MacDonald left the cast Wilcox made Neagle the New York shopgirl in *The Queen's Affair* (34), but the film which established her was *Nell Gwynn*. It flopped in the US for whom – to please the Hays Office – Wilcox had added a scene showing Charles (Cedric Hardwicke) and Nell marrying, but the British lined up for miles to see Anna's Cockney sparrow act. A sort of sequel was arranged, with Hardwicke again, but Anna was Irish this time: *Peg of Old Drury* (35) as Peg Woffington.

It was then decided that she should dance again and Wilcox shoved her into three ratty musicals: *Limelight* (36), *The Three Maxims* and *London Melody* (37), the last two with Tullio Carminati, a failed Hollywood 'name'. But to compensate for these he had one of the best ideas of his career, a life of Queen Victoria – just in time for Coronation year. The ban on representations of the Queen on stage and screen had just been lifted, so Anna became *Victoria the Great*, surrounded by a fine cast. RKO released and Neagle and Wilcox sank their last penny into the project. It is a very good film in its dignified Land-of-Hope-and-Glory way, marvellously authentic in appearance and never historically inaccurate, except for the portrait of the Queen, realized here as coy and kittenish, and en-un-ci-at-ing carefully. James Agate called her 'Victoria the Little', but its success all over the world was such that plans were scrapped for Neagle to play 'Nell Gwynn' on Broadway and a Lyons *Nippy* on film, and Wilcox promptly remade it, in Technicolor and using some different incidents, as *Sixty Glorious Years* (38). During the war years the first half of the first one and the second half of the second one were spliced together and patriotically reissued under the title *Queen Victoria*. The public apparently could not get enough of the Saxe-Coburg-Gotha saga, but Wilcox set Anna to play Marie Lloyd, the Queen of the Halls. However, he could not get a suitable leading man and instead she played another, and more inspiring, British heroine, *Nurse Edith Cavell* (39).

Graham Greene chastised Wilcox: 'We get from his films everything except life, character, truth. Instead we have flags, anthems, leading articles, a tombstone reticence. It would be unfair to call his Way of a Neagle vulgar showmanship . . . for there is seldom anything vital enough to be called vulgar in the successive patriotic appearances of this rather inexpressive actress. Miss Neagle looked nice as Queen Victoria, she looks just as nice as Nurse Cavell: she moves rigidly on to the set, as if wheels were concealed under the stately skirt; she says her piece with flat dignity and trolleys out again – rather like a mechanical marvel from the World's Fair.'

This was made in Hollywood for RKO, who had made a deal with the Wilcox-Neagle team after the success of the *Victoria* films; they stayed on in Hollywood and Anna danced again, in three old musicals updated, *Irene* (40), *No No Nanette* and *Sunny* (41). Of the first of these, Bosley Crowther observed in 'The New York Times' that the star performed 'with all the city charm and grace of a self-conscious musical comedy actress trying to be a Dresden china Pollyanna doll.' The

other two films were already announced and Crowther observed that the concept of Neagle in further American musicals was 'very depressing indeed'. *Irene* did well, but the success of the other two was not (to put it mildly) sufficient to hold the team in Hollywood and after doing their sequences in an Anglo-American effort, *Forever and a Day* (released in 1943), they returned to a blitzed London to make *They Flew Alone* (42), the inspiring story of Amy Johnson with Robert Newton. Then they made their last under their agreement with RKO, *The Yellow Canary* (43), a melodrama with Richard Greene in which everyone thinks she is a German spy (!); and got married.

During 1944 Neagle toured with ENSA and did a stage version of Jane Austen's 'Emma' under Robert Donat's management. When she returned to the screen it was for another attempt to better Anglo-American relations: *I Live in Grosvenor Square* (45) and she loved both Dean Jagger and Rex Harrison. The success of this, though relative, led to another contemporary story with a London setting, this time with a comparative newcomer, Michael Wilding. *Piccadilly Incident* (46) told how they met in the blackout, fell in love and married; how war separated them and how he, believing her dead – she was cast away on a desert island – married again; how she came back and, after meeting his wife, disappeared – to entertain the troops; and how he found her again, just before she was killed by a bomb. This load of old codswallop (which was based on a story outline by the star herself) certainly hit the public fancy and clearly called for a follow-up; so Britishers queued again to see both stars in *The Courtneys of Curzon Street* (47), a tenth-rate if flattering imitation of Coward's 'Cavalcade'. They were thereupon paired a third time, this time in a comedy, *Spring in Park Lane* (48); the critics liked it and the public adored it, so Wilcox thereupon remade it, in colour, with a few plot changes and called it *Maytime in Mayfair* (49). It did well, but less well, and the same might be said for one that Neagle did earlier that year without Wilding, *Elizabeth of Ladymead*, an inspiring episode film detailing the effects on four wives of their husbands returning from the Crimea, the Boer and the two World Wars. Apart from the one where the star was, ludicrously, a 20s flapper, it was paralysingly boring.

Nor was Wilding in *Odette* (50), the inspiring story of a war heroine, which Anna agreed to do for her husband only after Michèle Morgan and Ingrid Bergman had turned it down. It was well received and big box-office. Wilding was back with Anna for *The Lady With the Lamp* (51) – Florence Nightingale,

Anna Neagle and Michael Wilding, with Josephine Fitzgerald, in Spring in Park Lane *(48). She was a wealthy young lady and he a milord masquerading as a footman. 'Miss Neagle is in the true tradition of screen starriness in that she doesn't act or do anything much. . . . Her chief weapon is the coy, knowing, self-protective smile' (Richard Winnington).*

who else? – and for *Derby Day* (52), of which Richard Winnington wrote: '. . . the principal jokes consist of gibes at the dire state of the British film industry. Gibes that have an insolent ring in a film that falls well short of accepted Wilcox mediocrity.' In 1953 she returned to the stage in 'The Glorious Days', recapping some of her famous roles (Victoria, Nell Gwynn, etc.). It was, as Tynan said, 'Anna Neagle anthologized', but it did not run too long because she had 'film commitments'. The film committed was the screen version of this, retitled *Lilacs in the Spring* (54). It had the unlikely assistance of Errol Flynn and so did *King's Rhapsody* (55), a stagey, stultifying film of an Ivor Novello musical: 'Here, beneath these bastions of rock we lay our story . . .' said the foreword. The Neagle-Novello combination might once have been potent, but it was too late. Wilcox, later, commenting on the failure of both films, said that Anna's public was not Errol's public. He then put her into an 'up-to-date' story, *My Teenage Daughter* (56), cruelly referred to as 'My Stone-Age Mother', and – in another attempt to re-interest the public – loaned her to ABPC to play a hospital matron in *No Time for Tears* (57). But it was: *The Man Who Wouldn't Talk* (58) played just a week in a small West End cinema and did not make the circuits; and many cinemas showing her last film, *The Lady Is a Square* (59), omitted her name. It was a harsh verdict on someone who had coined a lot of money for the same

houses. At the same time this tired old stuff – all about a gracious lady converted to pop by her butler, an undiscovered pop singer – indicated that Wilcox no longer had his finger on the public pulse.

The butler was played by a pop singer, Frankie Vaughan, who was under personal contract to Neagle, but the three films she produced with him were failures. Early in the 60s Wilcox was in the bankruptcy courts. She sold her jewels and went to work with a will. She starred in a critically panned but much patronized musical, 'Charlie Girl', on the stage. Its long run confirmed her very special place in British show business; although her abilities as actress, singer or dancer were rather like painting with numbers, her genteel charm was considerable enough to have endeared her to great sections of the public.

After Wilcox died in 1977 she made it known that she would work till she dropped, and she did – in revivals of 'No, No Nanette' and 'My Fair Lady', in 'Relative Values' at Worthing, in pantomime (as the Fairy Godmother) both in the suburbs and at the London Palladium. Some friends claimed that she was bored if she was not busy, but others said that she was still trying to pay off her husband's debts. She died in 1986.

POLA NEGRI

Pola Negri was the first of Hollywood's European imports. She was extravagantly admired in her German films and every American studio was prepared to meet her price; but despite great fame and publicity, she never really caught on among Anglo-Saxons – which is why, perhaps, she is remembered today less as an actress than as an exotic, a hot-house flower that bloomed briefly in the Hollywood garden. That was the sort of simile that was used about her: 'she has eyes like dark lagoons' went another, 'wherein men drown'. A later reporter dismissed her as 'all slink and mink' and most film histories pass her by, with a frivolous footnote on her titled husbands and the other, similar, publicity. But she was a vivid and, on occasion, convincing film actress. Lotte Eisner has described her as 'the Magnani of the Silent Screen' and she was much admired by contemporary critics. The most fulsome modern assessment is by Theodore Huff, writing on *Madame Dubarry* in 'The Films of Ernst Lubitsch': 'Miss Negri gave a colourful performance almost never equalled for vitality and emotional depth. Never before had a screen star burst on the public in such full bloom. With grace, verve and vivid radiance, she created a living character who was simple, vivacious, a capricious child one minute and the next a restless and passionate woman, carried away by her love of luxury. In spite of the character of Dubarry, Miss Negri made her a fascinating and disturbingly sympathetic figure who was actually pathetic towards the end – a "toy of erratic destiny" in the grip of events beyond her simple and extremely feminine nature.'

It was part of Negri's own extremely feminine nature to live the life of a film star up to the hilt and, depending on her caprice, she altered the facts of her pre-US career to provide more drama for reporters. 'Fled from Russian Revolution', says one account, while another, not taken in, 'was a shopgirl in Berlin'. The following, most likely, facts are therefore offered cautiously: she was born in Yanowa, near Lipna, Poland, in 1894; her father died (or disappeared) when she was six and she was brought up by relatives in Warsaw. She seems to have begun her stage career with the Russian Imperial Theatre in St Petersburg as a dancer, but left there, apparently to go into cabaret – probably playing the violin; in 1913 she made her legit début in Warsaw in Hauptmann's 'Hannele' and the following year was starring in her first film, financed and written by herself, *Niewolnica Zmyslów/Love and Passion* (14). The director was Aleksander Hertz, who was responsible for all her Polish films: *Bestia* (15), *Czarna Ksiazka* or *Zólty Passport*, *Pókoj Nr 13* or *Tajemnica Hotelu*, *Arabella* (16), *Jego Ostatni Czyn*, *Studenci* and *Zona*. On the stage she was appearing in an Oriental spectacle, 'Sumurun', when Max Reinhardt saw her and persuaded her to go with him to Berlin (he also changed her name from Apolonia Chalupec – but as Poland's leading film star, that name was retained for her there right through her Hollywood days).

She did 'Sumurun' in Berlin and commenced another successful film career: *Nicht Lange Tauschte mich das Glück* (17), *Die Toten Augen*, *Rosen die der Sturm Entblättert*, *Wenn das Herz in Hass Erglüht* (18), *Küsse die Man Stiehlt in Dunkeln*, *Manja* and *Die Augen der Mumie Mâ/The Eyes of the Mummy* – as a temple dancer, which enabled her to reprise her dances from 'Sumurun'. The director had been an actor in that spectacle, Ernst Lubitsch, just embarked on his brilliant career. After *Der Gelbe Schein*, she was directed again by Lubitsch in *Carmen/Gypsy Blood* and its success put him at the head of his profession in Europe. She made *Karussell des Lebens* (19) and *Kreuziget Sie*, and after these Lubitsch directed her again in *Madame Dubarry*, with a Louis XV played by Emil Jannings. It was a sensation in Europe, but there were no takers for a while for the US. Finally First National bought it for $40,000 and opened it cautiously – advertised as 'A European Spectacle' because of anti-German feeling – and retitled *Passion*: it caused a furore in the States, as it had done in Europe. Meanwhile, Negri was filming *Comtesse Doddy* and *Vendetta* (the dates of both are uncertain but are believed to belong to the Lubitsch period); *Die Marchesa D'Arminiani* (20); *Sumurun/One Arabian Night* with Lubitsch directing; *Das Martyrium*; *Die Geschlossene Kette*; *Arme Violetta/The Red Peacock* – 'Camille' taken from Verdi rather than Dumas; Lubitsch's crazy *Die Bergkatze/The Mountain Cat* (21), in the title-role – a robber's temperamental daughter who gets mixed up with an army garrison – a satire on militarism which was a complete failure; *Sappho/Mad Love* (21); and Lubitsch's *Die Flamme/Montmartre* (23).

Due to the success of *Passion* most of these were shown very profitably in the US, though at least two of them, said 'Photoplay', were 'frightfully shoddy' and could only injure her career. The public could not get enough of Negri or of Lubitsch and emissaries from Hollywood waited on the lady offering contracts; she accepted one from Paramount (Lasky) and sailed for Hollywood. Her first film there was *Bella Donna* – after many script revisions on which she insisted. But nothing

could change the basic story – that of an adventuress who, finally forsaken by both her lovers and her deceived husband, walks out into the sands of Egypt and is eaten by a panther. The second one was not much better: *The Cheat*, already filmed in 1915 with Fannie Ward: she cheated on her Oriental potentate lover (Charles de Roche), who had her branded in retaliation. It was considered absurd by the critics and the public stayed away in droves – though partly because her German films were playing off still and the public was satiated with Negri (few fans realized that these films were European in origin).

The next was *The Spanish Dancer*, a part meant for Valentino but rewritten for her; curiously, it was from the same play that gave birth to Mary Pickford's *Rosita*, filmed the same year by Lubitsch, who had also crossed the Atlantic. The dancer in question was befriended by Wallace Beery (as Philip IV) and loved by Antonio Moreno. It did somewhat better at the box-office, but Paramount's hoped-for repeat of the success of *Passion* was not repeated. They tried: *Shadows of Paris* (24), as queen of the Apaches, with Adolphe Menjou; *Men*, with Robert Frazer and a ludicrous ending ('The woman who pays and makes men pay', said the posters); *Lily of the Dust*, as a girl in a German garrison town, with Ben Lyon, which failed, 'Photoplay' thought, because 'Pola Negri isn't particularly interesting as the Lily'; Lubitsch's *Forbidden Paradise*, 'his most brilliant film' (Paul Rotha), a story of Catherine the Great, with Rod la Rocque and Menjou; *East of Suez* (25), as a half-caste, with Edmund Lowe, from Somerset Maugham's play, with a happy ending and Raoul Walsh directing; *The Charmer*; *Flower of Night*; *A Woman of the World*, directed by Mal St Clair, an attempt to make her more palatable to Middle America, by casting her in a comedy about a vamp let loose in a small country town; *The Crown of Lies* (26), as a boarding-house slavey declared queen of a mythical kingdom; and *Good and Naughty*, a farce with Tom Moore. 'The better she was photographed,' wrote Griffith and Mayer, 'the more lavishly she was coiffed and gowned and sleeked and groomed, the more standardized she became, until in the studied attitudes of stylized acting in her last films nothing was discernible of the highly individual heroine of *Passion* and *Gypsy Blood*.' An exception was the Lubitsch film in the middle of this batch and it was regarded as a come-back: but generally the tigerish Negri had been metamorphosised into a pussycat – at least, on screen. 'Picturegoer' complained that she did too many peasant roles, observing 'the electric energy of a

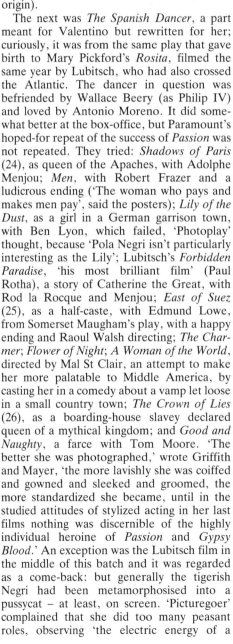

Pola Negri as A Woman of the World *(25), married to a playboy husband and considerably worse than he is – until reformed by social worker Holmes Herbert. Here's the reform in action.*

magnetic Pole is usually undisputed'. Offscreen, her battles for better parts gave her a reputation for temperament. 'Everyone knows,' said 'Picturegoer' later, 'how narrowly she escaped artistic annihilation under the Lasky banner.'

But what was basically wrong was that the brooding, remote Negri was out of key with the times; her so-called feud with the other queen of the Paramount lot, Gloria Swanson, might have been fodder for the fan magazines, but it deprived her of dignity – while robbing Swanson, the all-American girl, of little. Her ostentatious mourning for Valentino provoked giggles instead of sympathy; and worse, she hardly tried to hide her contempt for her films and the cultural level of Los Angeles as compared with Berlin. As with several other Europeans, it was acknowledged that she was in Hollywood for the money and, once she had got a lot, would return to make the sort of films she wanted to make. However, she did have a big hit in *Hotel Imperial* (27) as a hotel maid who lets an Austrian hussar (James Hall) pose as a valet in order to shield him. Erich Pommer (formerly with Ufa) produced, as he did the next, *Barbed Wire*, a moving story of a French girl in love with a German prisoner (Clive Brook): but these were respites in a public apathy which was soon to cause exhibitors to leave the Negri name off the bills. Films like *The Woman on Trial*, though directed by Mauritz Stiller, did not help much either. Next came *Three Sinners* (28), an artificial story about a drab wife who becomes a woman of the world, with Paul Lukas, Warner Baxter and Tullio Carminati; *The Secret Hour* with Jean Hersholt, a version of

'They Knew What They Wanted' which did so badly that it could be remade as a Talkie two years later – ironically as a vehicle for Vilma Banky (but it did not save her career either, which was also killed by her accent); *Loves of an Actress*, a biopic of the French trage- dienne, Rachel, with Nils Asther; and finally, *The Woman From Moscow*, based on Sar- dou's play 'Fedora', with Paul Lukas. Negri pocketed her last salary cheque ($8,000 a week) and left the set. Her dressing-room was made over for Clara Bow.

There were no Hollywood offers. And she, in Europe, said she would never return. She began a film in France, *Le Collier de la Reine*, but walked out after some weeks and was replaced by Marcelle Chantal. She petitioned Shaw for the rights to 'Caesar and Cleopatra', but he refused to part with them. She did make a British film, *The Woman He Scorned* (29). Paul Czinner directed for Imperial, as a Silent, and it was partially dubbed – but not by its stars. One of the cast, Warwick Ward, sought an injunction because he was dubbed by another artist and the film was withdrawn in Britain; but in the US, WB gave it a limited release. During her stay, she also appeared in a sketch at the London Coliseum, 'Farewell to Love'. But in 1932 RKO, encouraged by the success of Dietrich in US movies, decided to give Negri another fling: *A Woman Com- mands* was based on the romantic story of Queen Marie Draga of Serbia and it co- starred Basil Rathbone and Roland Young. Negri had a song, 'Paradise', which she sang beautifully, but her speaking voice was deep and too heavily accented to be acceptable. Besides, it was a rotten film and its failure

killed her Hollywood hopes. She toured in 'A Trip to Pressburg', which closed in Pittsburgh, returned to Europe and went to France to make *Fanatisme* (34) with Pierre-Richard Wilm. The following year she was in Austria making *Mazurka* (35) for director Willi Forst, playing a woman who prevents her seducer from also 'ruining' her daughter. There was some move by MGM to star her in *The Good Earth*, but when this came to nothing, she returned to Germany. Goebbels did not like her and called her 'the Polish Jewess'; but Hitler did and had her Aryan origins proved. She returned his admiration and when asked whether he was responsible for her return to German films, replied: 'Why not; after all, there have been many important men in my life – Valentino for example.' She signed a three-year contract with Ufa and audiences in Germany eagerly awaited her come-back film, *Moskau-Shanghai* (36), a 'transcontinental express' melodrama. It was quite exciting, but audiences found Negri's style of acting old- fashioned. For Terra Film, she played *Madame Bovary* (37) and, according to David Stewart Hull ('Film in the Third Reich'), she was laughed off the screen all over Germany. It is curious, for in fact she underplays; seen today, both she and the film lack passion (and are too Germanic to be convincing). *Tango Notturno* was considered her best German film and was more favourably received, but this stage of her career faded out with two pictures directed by Nunzio Malasomma, *Die Fromme Lüge* (38) and *Die Nacht der Entscheidung*, in the part which Olga Tche- kowa had played in the 1931 version.

At the outbreak of war she was on the Côte d'Azur; she joined the Red Cross, but returned to the US only in 1943 after much haggling with the immigration authorities. Hollywood welcomed her and offered her a comedy with her one-time co-star, Adolphe Menjou, *Hi Diddle Diddle* (43). It led to no further offers. She later retired to San Anto- nio with a friend, a Texas heiress (she made headlines some years later when the woman married and she threatened to sue – but she did not; soon after, the heiress divorced and the ladies were reunited). She took an interest in real estate and in writing her memoirs (planned over many years and announced in 1957, they finally appeared in the spring of 1970). In 1964 Disney, after reading a piece about her in a San Antonio newspaper, signed her to play the enigmatic jewellery expert in *The Moonspinners*. Accompanied by a cheetah and outrageously gowned, she gave a small lift to the climax of the film. She was still hoping for offers when she died in 1987. A memorable portrait was painted by Rodney Ackland in his memoir, 'The Celluloid Mis-

When Pola Negri's American career ended, she made half a dozen films in Germany, but returned to the US during the war. She has filmed only twice since, the first time in 1943: Hi Diddle Diddle, *a farce with Martha Scott.*

tress' (1947): 'She had a blind and uncritical admiration of her own genius in the blaze of which her sense of humour evaporated like a dew-drop on a million-watt arc lamp.' She told him that one sequence she had done in *Mazurka* was 'the greatest piece of acting that has ever been seen on the screen'.

RAMON NOVARRO

Ramon Novarro was one of the 'Latin' actors thrown up in the wake of Valentino's success (others: Ricardo Cortez, Antonio Moreno) and he possessed a similar facility for the same sort of romantic costume parts – though with little of Valentino's peculiar intensity. De Witt Bodeen says 'he was too audacious, too droll, too impudent to be the "Great Lover" or "The Sheik". Romantically, he never took himself seriously either on screen or off.' However, as the vogue for their type of exotica waned, so did Novarro's career. His studio tried him as an All-American boy, as a comedian. In *Huddle* he was the hero of a Yale football game, in *The Flying Fleet*, a hapless serviceman in his shirt-tails searching endlessly for his stolen trousers and smiling all the while. He did survive the advent of Sound and made over a dozen Talkies, but it is as a Silent star that he is remembered.

He was born in Durango, Mexico, in 1899, the son of a dentist. The family fled the country at the time of the Huerta Revolution in 1914 and settled in Los Angeles. When the father died Ramon became the chief breadwinner: he worked as a waiter and also sang in restaurants, did some vaudeville and – more suitable to his ambitions – became a film extra. Among the films he is known to have appeared in are *The Hostage* (17, Wallace Reid), *The Little American* (Mary Pickford), *Joan the Woman* (Geraldine Farrar) and *The Goat* (18). Several name actors (including Moreno) interested themselves in him and he was tested by D.W. Griffith and Sam Goldwyn among others, but it was not until 1921 that vaudeville dance director Marion Morgan (he had danced with her troupe since 1919) helped him to surface above his fellow-extras. She suggested him for the novelty dance in a full-length Sennett comedy with Ben Turpin and Phyllis Haver, *A Small Town Idol*, in turban and loincloth with Derelys Perdue. He had a featured part in Goldwyn's *Mr Barnes of New York* (22) starring Tom Moore; and the same year was chosen to play the lead in a small independent production, *The Rubaiyat of Omar Khayyam*, directed by Ferdinand Binney Earle. One of Earle's associates was Mary O'Hara, who had written the scenario

for Metro's *The Prisoner of Zenda*, and through her its director Rex Ingram got to see *Omar Khayyam* (though no one else did; it was not released till three years later, under the title *A Lover's Oath*). Ingram chose Novarro – still under his own name of Ramon Samaniegos – to play Rupert of Hentzau, complete with beard, monocle and long cigarette holder; Lewis Stone was Rudolph and Alice Terry and Barbara La Marr the women.

Ingram had directed *The Four Horsemen of the Apocalypse* and he saw in Ramon some of the qualities which had made the world's females swoon over Valentino; so he signed him to a personal contract (at $125 per week), changed his name and gave him a part as the tragic hero of *Trifling Women*, again with La Marr and Stone. Then, also for Metro, he put him into the three pictures which made him a star (all co-starring Alice Terry, Ingram's wife). *Where the Rainbow Ends* (23) cast him as a native boy in love with the missionary's daughter: in the original he drowned at the end, but exhibitors found audience resentment at the cruel fate awaiting the new screen idol and Ingram shot an alternative ending in which the boy discovers he's a sun-burnt Caucasian and can thus marry the girl. *Scaramouche* was a highly successful version of Rafael Sabatini's swashbuckler and *The Arab* (24) an enthusiastic reprise of the racial romance theme. It made no bones about being also inspired by Valentino's *The Sheik* – only it was actually filmed in North Africa. The Ingrams elected to remain (he made the 1927 *Garden of Allah* there and later became a Muslim) and sent Novarro back to Hollywood, where his $500 a week Ingram contract became, after protracted negotiations, $10,000 a week with Metro-Goldwyn.

He did three pictures before the one for which he is best remembered – *Thy Name Is Woman* with La Marr, *The Red Lily* with Enid Bennett and *The Midshipman* (25), made at Annapolis with Navy co-operation. *Ben-Hur* (26) had been an old pseudo-religious novel by Lew Wallis that had seen sturdy service in stage adaptations: the film was begun in Italy with Charles Brabin directing George Walsh as Ben-Hur. Things had gone badly and at the moment that Mayer was added to Metro-Goldwyn, Mayer's right-hand-man, Thalberg, elected to start again, replacing director and star by Fred Niblo and Novarro respectively. It cost $4 million, the most expensive film made up to that time: fortunately for the studio it was a box-office triumph, taking $9 million worldwide. A version with synchronized sound materialized in 1931 – and that was still around in the 1950s, at least in Paris, not long before the 1959 remake opened. And, restored in all its glory (with the colour

The l
on Ra

■ 'FOR once I'm not being cast for my looks,'
said Danish ham Brigitte Nielsen at Cannes
last week, promoting her role as a sadistic
prison warder in something called Chained Heat 2.
Not being cast for her looks? As a sadistic
prison warder? Look at her — this is the blonde, beefy
stuff that Everyman's dominatrix dreams are
made of!
Is the laugh on Miss Nielsen here — or on us?

RADIO One is pr
paring to celebra
its 25th birthda
with an orgy of sel
congratulation.

That means live co
certs and the usual ca
of brain-dead jocks sla
ping themselves on th
back.

Yes, Radio One, twent
five years but going o
seventy-one!

It sees itself as a 'cu
tural patron', doing fo
pop music what Radi
Three does for classica
music — according t
its controller, Johnn
Beerling.

This inflated notio
of Radio One's role i
the nation's cultural lif
would be risible if i
weren't so sad.

When it comes to po
music the BBC ha
always lagged behin
and resisted change. I
1956, the year of Heart
break Hotel, not on
rock 'n' roll record wa
featured in the new
annual review of popu
lar songs.

Only after the success

right to publish Burke's Peerage and is not involved in the updating of Burke's Peerage or in the preparation for publication.'

In other words, Mr Brooks-Baker *is* the publishing director of the Burke's Peerage company but the archives of the book itself are not owned by that company. To further cloud the issue the printing plates actually belong to the Earl of Errol.

Harmless

Brooks-Baker has a company called Brooks Marketing which is involved in the harmless, but not nationally important, pursuit of genealogical research, verifying feudal baronies.

Nevertheless as we have seen in the past week Mr Brooks-Baker supplies a ready stream of opinion to a receptive Press, television and radio. Why?

Quite simply he provides useable quotes to journalists without having the degree of royal or highly-placed contacts his self-confidence could imply.

While Buckingham Palace Press office, which was once moved to denounce Brooks-Baker ('He is speaking with no knowledge or authority'), is all too quick with a 'no comment', Brooks-Baker is like any number of standard rent-a-quote MPs. He can be relied upon to pontificate on any given subject just so long as the hacks spell his name right.

And while he hardly knows a member of the House of Windsor, only having met them in line-ups and has only a slight acquaintance with the aristocracy, he does have an abiding, touchingly-absurd interest in etiquette and the upper class.

So when next you see a reaction from 'Brookie' on the television or in the papers, remember that though he is an Anglophile and snob, it might just as well have come from Terry Venables or Jeremy Beadle.

sequences), it is considerably superior). Novarro's popularity went to new heights, even if some critics thought that his portrayal was not sufficiently masculine.

He returned to less epic fare: *Lovers?* (27) with Alice Terry, a tale set in Spain, of how gossip united Novarro and his best friend's wife, making the rumours a reality; *The Road to Romance* with Marceline Day, an adaptation of 'Romance' by Conrad and Ford Madox Ford; and *The Student Prince*, which Lubitsch directed. Said 'Picturegoer': 'Ramon Novarro and Norma Shearer give of their flawless acting and radiant charm'; but 'Film Daily' was unhappy with his performance in *Across to Singapore* (28), thinking him 'miscast as a tough sea dog'. Joan Crawford was the girl and it was the second of the three screen versions of Ben Ames Williams's 'All the Brothers Were Valiant'. The next two cast Renée Adorée as his leading lady: *A Certain Young Man* (which had been started two years earlier and abandoned for some time) and *Forbidden Hours*, a Ruritanian romance between a king on a clandestine night out and his premier's daughter. MGM were at a loss to understand why Novarro was not more popular: his pictures did well, but strictly with the distaff side. *The Midshipman* had been notably successful and another attempt was made to 'sell' him as a normal young American: in *The Flying Fleet* (29), as one of six guys training for the Navy Air Corps. This was the one in which he spent most of the footage exposing his garters and it was uncertain

whether MGM wanted him to look attractive to the ladies or merely ridiculous. It had a soundtrack added and there was a music score with *The Pagan*, where Novarro retreated to a more primitive existence and only opened his mouth to sing 'Pagan Love Song' to Renée Adorée. A Napoleonic romance, *Devil May Care*, was all-Talkie and had four songs and some Technicolor sequences; Novarro was with Dorothy Jordan and also sang – playing a Spanish troubadour both times – in *In Gay Madrid* (30) and *Call of the Flesh*, the latter a retitling after it looked like flopping as *The Singer of Seville* (Adorée was also in it, in a supporting role – her last film; Novarro also directed and co-directed the Spanish and French versions respectively).

'Frankly,' said 'Picturegoer', 'Ramon is one of the disappointments of the Talkies.' He was a disappointment to MGM too and there were rumours that he would retire or take up opera singing. He continued, however, with *Daybreak* (31), as a moustached and monocled ne'er-do-well who meets an innocent (Helen Chandler) at a brothel and who becomes a kept woman because he has deflowered her; the source was a novel by Schnitzler. *Son of India* was another inter-racial romance, with Madge Evans. Jacques Feyder directed both and both were fine: and unpopular. Novarro got a boost by being cast with Garbo in *Mata Hari* (32) – except that her art cruelly exposed the immaturity of his acting style. The end was in sight. Surprisingly, therefore, MGM announced that he had been signed to a new

Garbo as Mata Hari *(32), and Novarro as the Russian officer. Playing opposite Garbo helped prop up Novarro's ailing career.*

Novarro's last major role in a major film was The Night Is Young *(35), a Ruritanian musical with Evelyn Laye as his leading lady. Here he is with second lead Rosalind Russell.*

seven-year contract, to act and direct (but such announcements were not uncommon and were a reiteration of faith rather than the truth). The studio tried Yale – *Huddle*; then another Oriental prince, with the prestigious Helen Hayes, in *The Son-Daughter*; then a remake of *The Arab* called *The Barbarian* (33) – only this time the barbarian's white passion (Myrna Loy) had to have an Egyptian mother before the censor would pass it. None of them worked and indeed *The Barbarian* became *A Night in Cairo* for British audiences in the hope of making it more attractive. But the studio persevered and believed that *The Cat and the Fiddle* (34) opposite Jeanette Mac-Donald would bring back his own public. It didn't. Nor, more understandably, did the next two. The publicity line on *Laughing Boy* was that it had taken a two-year search to find the right actor (no wonder he was laughing): Novarro is a Red Indian brave in love with Slim Girl (Lupe Velez), whom he accidentally kills after she has taken to the Oldest Profession. It was from the Pulitzer-prize-winning novel by Oliver LaFarge. At least it was very different from *The Night Is Young* (35), the result of Hollywood's second flirtation with British stage star Evelyn Laye: they made the most arch screen couple on record and plans to reteam them in another musical (*Love While You May*) were scrapped.

So was the rest of Novarro's contract. He turned to other fields: he appeared in London at the Palladium and in a flop musical, 'A

Royal Exchange', and was bitter about Hollywood when he spoke to reporters. In Hollywood he wrote, produced and directed (but did not star in) a Spanish feature, *Contra la Corriente* (36), and then was signed by Republic for a come-back, *The Sheik Steps Out* (37), which tried to kid the old image. The studio liked it enough to sign him for four more, but *A Desperate Adventure* (38) with Marian Marsh, set in Paris, was desperate indeed and he asked to be released. In 1940 in Rome he began a French movie, *La Comédie de Bonheur*, with Micheline Presle, Michel Simon and the young Louis Jourdan: it was unfinished when Italy entered the war and abandoned – later the director, Marcel l'Herbier, managed to complete it, but some of the negative had been burnt, two of the cast were dead: the result as shown was very unsatisfactory. It was popular in Europe but does not appear to have hit the Anglo-Saxon market, possibly due to the war. In Mexico he made *La Virgen que Forjo Una Patria* (42) and towards the end of the decade made an effort to become accepted as a character actor: *We Were Strangers* (49), with just two scenes as a rebel leader; *The Big Steal*, as a wily Mexican police chief; *The Outriders*, as a grinning gunman; and *Crisis*, again as a chief of police. He was effective in each, so it is surprising that he was not seen again till Cukor's *Heller in Pink Tights* (60), impressive in his small role as the chief villain.

He did not want for money. He never

married; and there were rumours throughout his career that he would retire into a monastery. He did, however, show a most unmonk-like propensity for alcohol and on numerous occasions was arrested by the Los Angeles police for drunken driving. In 1968 his nude corpse was found, after what appeared to have been a tremendous struggle; his apartment had been ransacked. Later two teenage hustlers were arrested and convicted of the murder.

MERLE OBERON

Merle Oberon was a brown-eyed, dark-haired beauty whose work when young singularly lacked interest. She retained her looks throughout a long career and at some point late in it displayed an authority which is the hallmark of all stars.

Studio biographies maintained that she was born in Tasmania and educated in India; in fact she was born in Bombay – in 1911 – to an Indian mother (whom she later used to pass off as her maid). With a girlfriend (claimed the same source) she used to give recitals in the Railway Institute at Lahore. She arrived in the mother country at the age of 17 and under her own name of Queenie O'Brien began to seek theatrical work. She became a dance hostess at the Café de Paris; and got work as a film extra. It is said that her asking price at this time was £100 a night. Alexander Korda noticed her on the set of one of his films (his biographer, Paul Tabori, notes that Oberon's 'extra' file-card read 'A.K. interested'), tested her and signed her for five years. Briefly she was Estelle Thompson before getting the name by which we know her. Her early screen credits are uncertain, as she invented some of them in an effort to seem more important ('. . . I'd not only never been in but never even seen' she admitted in 1969), but she was in *Alf's Button* (30), as a harem girl, *Never Trouble Trouble* (31), *Fascination, Service for Ladies* (32), *Ebb Tide* and *Aren't We All?* Korda had signed her to a five-year contract, at £20 a week, along with three other girls, to be 'new faces'; and when Ann Todd had an accident she replaced her as the 'plain' girl who ensnares Roland Young in the dire *Wedding Rehearsal*, followed by a lead (the Other Woman) in *Men of Tomorrow*; then the small but telling part of Anne Boleyn in *The Private Life of Henry VIII* (33), after which she was considered a star – big enough to be sought for a leading part in the English-language version of a Charles Boyer vehicle, *The Battle* (34): she was a Japanese. When she returned from filming this in France, Korda loaned her out for *The Broken Melody*, made her one of Douglas Fairbanks's entourage in *The Private Life of Don Juan* and Lady Blakeney in *The Scarlet Pimpernel* (35) with Leslie Howard.

But Hollywood, impressed by Mistress Boleyn, was offering better things: Oberon became a vamp and one of Maurice Chevalier's leading ladies, in *Folies Bergère*, and though she was poor in it Goldwyn was offering a contract. He needed a new star more than somewhat and hesitated for a while between her and Madeleine Carroll; but Oberon was having an affair with Leslie Howard and since she had persuaded him to accompany her to Hollywood – to make *The Petrified Forest* – Goldwyn thought he might be tempted to co-star with her in *The Dark Angel*, the remake of a Silent weepie about two friends in love with the same woman, one of whom marries her after the other has gone off to war. Korda, who was in love with her, saw only the advantages of a Hollywood career and agreed to share her, so a contract was worked out for three pictures a year between them (both released through United Artists) starting at $60,000 per film and going to $100,000 for each in the final year. Howard, however, went back to his wife and Oberon's co-stars were Fredric March and Herbert Marshall. Goldwyn put her into two more dramas in the hope of transforming her from a cheap exotic to an international name: *The Dark Angel*, a remake of a Silent weepie, with Fredric March; *These Three* (36) with Miriam Hopkins, a triangle tangle which is perhaps her best early performance; and *Beloved Enemy*, a tale of the Irish troubles with Brian Aherne. She returned to Britain to play opposite Charles Laughton in *I Claudius* and it was her near-fatal car crash which was the pretext for abandoning that film. When she recovered, Korda put her into two Technicolor comedies with two of his brightest leading men: the sluggish *Over the Moon* (37, release delayed till 40) with Rex Harrison and the trivial *The Divorce of Lady X* (38) with Laurence Olivier. She was then cast in something else that did not get made: *Graustark*, with Gary Cooper and Sigrid Gurie. Huge sets had been erected on the Goldwyn lot, but the day before shooting was due to commence he called the whole thing off and Oberon and Cooper instead did a comedy, *The Cowboy and the Lady*. It was cynically constructed for them by Leo McCarey, since she was not going down with the American public and Goldwyn was desperate to get her into a film with Cooper. Olivier was her co-star again in *Wuthering Heights* (39), which Goldwyn envisaged as primarily a vehicle for her, an artistic error of major proportions. She did

Merle Oberon's best-remembered film, ironically, contains one of her worst performances: Goldwyn's production of Emily Brontë's Wuthering Heights *(39), directed by William Wyler. Here she is as the dying Cathy, being supported literally by her Heathcliff – Laurence Olivier.*

A Song to Remember *(44): Merle Oberon and Cornel Wilde as George Sand and Chopin. Said Richard Winnington: 'William Bendix being Chopin would have been no less incongruous than Merle Oberon being George Sand in a smart sort of Vesta Tilley outfit.'*

not hit it off with her co-star, who said in 1989, 'I think she may have thought that because I was a stage actor of considerable experience by that time, I looked upon her as a pick-up by Alexander Korda, which she was.' Goldwyn, however, looked at the returns of her films and dropped her.

In 1939 she was married to Korda (earlier, she had broken off an engagement to Joseph M. Schenck, one-time chairman of UA and head of 20th, on the ground that her career was more important to her): he starred her in *The Lion Has Wings*, a piece of propaganda turned out quickly in the autumn of 1939 and honoured by the King and Queen with a Royal première – a rare event in those days. It was her last British picture for more than a decade. With the coming of the war the Kordas went to Hollywood where she had fortuitously signed a short-term contract with Warners: *Till We meet Again* (40), with George Brent, a remake of *One-Way Passage* that was even more lachrymose; and *Affectionately Yours* (41), a comedy with Dennis Morgan. Both parts had been destined originally for Bette Davis and WB were seriously considering Oberon as her successor. Between the two she did the Lubitsch *That Uncertain Feeling* with Melvyn Douglas, and

that was all: this was Lubitsch's remake of his 1925 *Kiss Me Again* and much less amusing. Then came *Lydia*, in which an ageing lady recalled her four lost loves – as inspired by Duvivier's *Un Carnet de Bal* – and he again directed. Korda produced: it was the end of his professional relationship with Oberon; he returned to Britain the following year and they were divorced in 1945.

In 1943 she made brief appearances in *Forever and a Day* and *Stage Door Canteen*, and was a Norwegian patriot in the idiotic *First Comes Courage* with Brian Aherne; then she almost became one of the victims of Jack the Ripper (Laird Cregar) in *The Lodger* (44). Said 'Picturegoer': 'Merle Oberon is rather colourless as Kitty; she performs two can-can dances.' – 'Might one call it the can't-can't?' suggested C.A. Lejeune. She was also threatened in *Dark Waters*, a dim variation of the one about the heroine being driven insane. 1945 was a bad year; only ridicule greeted both her George Sand in the Chopin biopic *A Song to Remember* and a tear-jerker called *This Love of Ours* (with Charles Korvin), a very distant adaptation of Pirandello. That was the first of three for Universal: Wanger's *A Night in Paradise* (46) with Turhan Bey, an Arabian Nights extravaganza that made Purgatory seem attractive; and *Temptation* with George Brent and Paul Lukas, a curious attempt to film – for the sixth time – an Edwardian bestseller, 'Bella Donna'. After which, not surprisingly, Oberon went to the lower half of double bills: *Night Song* (47) with Dana Andrews; *Berlin Express* (48) with Korvin and Lucas, as the latter's French secretary. They had not been meant for B dates, so they hardly made an auspicious start to Oberon's new six-film deal at RKO. Then she went to France for *Pardon My French* (51) with Paul Henried, filmed in English and bought by UA for US distribution.

The British cinema offered a chance back to the top: *24 Hours of a Woman's Life* (52) with Leo Genn and Richard Todd – one of the many filmizations of Stefan Zweig's novel and probably the worst. Earlier that year, in March, it was reported that she drew $500,000 for not making the four films signed for at RKO. A year later RKO was reported to have paid her another $300,000 to settle the contract. In 1954 she appeared on TV in *The Man Who Came to Dinner*, with Joan Bennett, Monty Woolley and Buster Keaton. Then she made a Spanish film with Francisco Rabal, *Todo es Possible en Granada* (54), and rather unexpectedly got prime parts in two major Hollywood films: *Desirée*, as the Empress Josephine to Brando's Napoleon; and *Deep in My Heart*, as Sigmund Romberg's lyric writer, Dorothy Donnelly. Both demonstrated conspicuously her major asset as an actress: style. But a stupid melodrama, *The Price of Fear* (56) with Lex Barker, put paid to further ambitions for the time being. After several years she played a nympho who goes bonkers because *Of Love and Desire* (63): its bookings were severely limited. But her work in the next two was widely seen (and admirable), both adaptations of meretricious bestsellers. Stephen Boyd was the actor-heel, a most unlikely candidate for *The Oscar* (65), and Oberon a fading screen star with a couple of minutes' screen time; in *Hotel* (66) she was a duchess who had her jewels stolen.

In life she was renowned for same. A very wealthy woman, she lived with her fourth husband in four homes – one in California, three in Mexico. In 1969 it was announced that she would leave them to make a British film, *The Private War of Mrs Darling*, but nothing came of it. She did film again, in the incredible *Interval* (73), written by Gavin Lambert and made in Mexico, playing an ageing woman who falls in love with a much younger man: she personally financed it and married the actor concerned, Robert Wolders. It was not a success. She died in 1979 and her jewellery when auctioned netted £1 million for cinema charities.

MARGARET O'BRIEN

American children – or at least Hollywood children – are an acquired taste. Non-American audiences have remained immune through the likes of Bobby Breen, Gigi Perreau, the Corcoran sisters and Cora Sue Collins, that child in *Queen Christina* who, incredibly, grew up to be Garbo. An exception was Margaret O'Brien, a one-time goldmine for MGM and one of the top 10 ranking box-office stars in 1945 and 1946.

She was born in 1937 in Los Angeles (some months after her father's death). MGM chose her for a one-minute shot in a sequence involving would-be child actresses in *Babes on Broadway* (41) and later put her into a well-meaning film about the blitz, with Laraine Day and Robert Young, *Journey for Margaret* (42). Her success caused MGM to change her name from Maxine O'Brien to Margaret and put her under contract. She appeared in *Dr Gillespie's Criminal Case* (43) and *Thousands Cheer*; was starred in *Lost Angel*, a comedy about a group of scientists involved with a child genius, and had a bit in *Madame Curie*, given birth to by that lady. She was loaned to 20th to play Adèle in *Jane Eyre* (44), where she was fairly dreadful (Peggy Ann Garner, playing the young Jane, was also an exception among child stars). She co-starred with Laughton in *The Canterville Ghost*, which caused James Agee to remark: 'She is an exceptionally talented child, and it is infuriating to see her handled, and gradually being ruined by oafs.' However, in *Meet Me in St Louis*, part of a well-nigh flawless cast, Agee this time approved, adding, 'many of her possibilities and glints of her achievement hypnotize me as thoroughly as anything since Garbo.' The director, Minnelli, did not compare her to Garbo: 'her speciality was crying hysterically. She had been taken in hand by a dramatic coach whom she imitated; so much that she wasn't like a child – or a human being, even. She was just like Sarah Bernhardt; every gesture was enormous. . . . The problem was to have her act like a child again, and to get her to do so was incredibly difficult.' In 1944 she won a special Oscar.

Of the next, *Music for Millions*, C.A. Lejeune wrote: 'This grave little girl, who can give the screen a morning glow by simply stumping into camera range . . . is something out of the ordinary in performing children. She belongs more with the Menuhins and Mozarts than with the Shirley Temples. . . . The child is as formal and old-fashioned as your grandmother's bonnet, but she has something of the same decorum and authority.' Lejeune also considered her the year's best actress for *Our Vines Have Tender Grapes*

Margaret O'Brien can be considered the most successful child actress after Shirley Temple, and the most talented of all the children who attained stardom. Our Vines Have Tender Grapes (45) contains one of her most delicate performances: a tale of a Norwegian farming community in Wisconsin, with Edward G. Robinson.

(45), a folksy tale with Edward G. Robinson as her father and Jackie 'Butch' Jenkins as her playmate.

MGM were now in the position that 20th had been with Temple, of finding suitable star vehicles. They did not succeed. The child's work continued to be impeccable, with only a hint of artifice, but each film did less business until the company did not bother to exploit them properly: critical thumbs-down for the films themselves did not help. She was cast with Wallace Beery in a Western, *Bad Bascomb* (46), melting his heart; with Lewis Stone, Frank Morgan, Lionel Barrymore and Edward Arnold in the remake of *Three Wise Fools*, melting their hearts; and then in a series of weepies: *The Unfinished Dance* (47), a glammed-up remake of *La Mort du Cygne*; *Tenth Avenue Angel* (48); and *The Big City*, where she was an orphan adopted jointly by Jew, Catholic and Protestant. After a gap she was in two children's classics, Louisa May Alcott's *Little Women* (49) and Frances Hodgson Burnett's *The Secret Garden*. O'Brien was Beth in the former and was very touching – the best of the four March girls. The film was a big one for MGM; the other was not, though

it is a rare and unexpected treat. MGM were not pleased when the child refused to go to Disney for *Alice in Wonderland*, then intended to be part live-action. They suspended her.

It was coldly announced that she was leaving MGM for Columbia; there she received her first screen kiss in *Her First Romance* (51): the film was conventional adolescent stuff and passed unnoticed. She went into summer stock at a reported $3,500 a week and toured in a play by Clare Booth Luce which did not reach town: her own notices were good. She should have been in the Gene Kelly-Danny Kaye *Huckleberry Finn*, which MGM cancelled in 1952. Instead, she was in Japan making *Futari No Hitoni/Two Persons Eyes* (52), as a girl who visits her father: it was a failure. In Italy she made *Agente S3S Operazione Uranio* (54), with Peter Carsten, and an attempt at a dewy young heroine in *Glory* (56) at RKO – it was about a horse of that name – was doomed by the film's own ineptness. She had a small character part, as an unwilling ingénue in a stock company, in *Heller in Pink Tights* (60), but there were no more screen offers. She did try TV, including *Split Second to an Epitaph* (68), an Ironside movie with Raymond Burr. She has also appeared in stock, in 'Barefoot in the Park', 'Under the Yum Yum Tree' and 'A Thousand Clowns' etc. She has been married and divorced. There were reported supporting roles in two minor independent movies, *Annabelle Lee* (72) and *Diabolic Wedding*, which seem never to have been seen. In 1977 the money she earned as a child came to her (at the age of nine she was earning $2,500 a week). A while later, she might have been seen on TV as a post-bellum belle in *Testimony of Two Men* (78). She was sixth on the cast-list of a Disney film starring Jenny Agutter, *Amy* (81).

LAURENCE OLIVIER

Laurence Olivier bestrode his profession in this century as Shakespeare bestrides the art of the drama. 'I consider him, in common with my colleagues,' said Charlton Heston, 'the greatest actor alive'; and Spencer Tracy referred to him as 'the greatest of them all'. Yet for one so much admired within and without the industry it had not been a smooth career: his screen work was recognized by eight Oscar nominations (surpassed by one by Tracy), but for years he was not considered box-office. Neither Oscars nor box-offices were important in the context of his career – moving resplendently from overenthusiastic *jeune premier* to character player of always astonishing versatility: but we cherish him most for his romantic Hollywood heroes and the three Shakespeare films – still the best screen Bard – of his middle years. He was endowed with the actor's blessed gift of looks, magnetism and intelligence, these qualities balanced to a better degree than in his contemporaries; but he had a quality few actors have, and that was his willingness to take risks. As actor-manager, stage director, film director and film star he always *dared*: it is a marvellous experience to have seen him in action on the stage, but his film performances leave a partial record.

The son of a clergyman, he was born in Dorking, Surrey, in 1907, into, his own words, 'an atmosphere of genteel poverty . . . probably the most fertile ground for ambition there can be'. While at school he played Katharine in 'The Taming of the Shrew' and was encouraged to take up a stage career. He studied at the Central School, had his first professional experience as an ASM at Letchworth and made his début at the Brighton Hippodrome in a curtain-raiser. He joined a company which did Shakespeare in the London suburbs, in places like Camberwell Baths, and was with Sybil Thorndike's troupe for a while. He was with Birmingham Rep 1926–28 and with that company in a London season, which brought an offer to take over a lead in 'Bird in the Hand'. He did a number of West End plays and made his New York bow in 'Murder on the Second Floor', which flopped. His film début was in Germany, in a short called *Hocus Pocus* (30), and also in that country he made a feature, in the English version of a murder mystery with Lilian Harvey, *The Temporary Widow* at Ufa, in the part Willy Fritsch did in the original. He did four days' work on a quickie, *Too Many Crooks*, and was in *Potiphar's Wife* as the chauffeur heart-throb of the lady of the house. This was the sort of part for which he was physically ideal, with his marcelled hair and dandy's moustache – but his ambition at that time was only to be a matinée idol. It was recognized that he had talent – Cedric Hardwicke recalled that he was noisy and lacked subtlety, 'but I knew instinctively he'd be a great actor'. Olivier credits Noël Coward, who cast him as Victor in 'Private Lives' (30), for persuading him to move onward as well as upward. However, the route was to be circuitous and during the New York run of the Coward play his sights were on Hollywood. Several companies tested him and he accepted a dazzling offer from RKO, who thought his bounding energy might be harnessed in roles of a likeable bounder/cad (his screen personality, he said, was constructed from John

Barrymore, Ronald Colman and Douglas Fairbanks). The films were not dazzling: *Friends and Lovers* (31), in which he and Adolphe Menjou scrapped over Lily Damita; *The Yellow Ticket*, on loan to Fox, as a British journalist in love with Elissa Landi; and *Westward Passage* (32) as a hot-tempered writer bickering with Ann Harding in this light-hearted tale of an on-off-on again marriage. RKO tested him for the lead opposite Pola Negri in *A Woman Commands*, but did not use him. 'Picturegoer' reported that the US authorities had refused to renew his work permit, but he had also had a British offer, from Gloria Swanson, filming *Perfect Understanding* (33) in London: the result Olivier considered the worst film he ever made. With Gertrude Lawrence he did a farce, *No Funny Business*, about male and female divorce co-respondents – and *that* has to be the worst film he ever made.

Then MGM, having failed to interest Leslie Howard or to contact Ronald Colman, offered him the male lead in Garbo's *Queen Christina*, but he was replaced after some days by John Gilbert: 'I couldn't hold a candle to her,' he said later. MGM consoled him with a contract offer worth $1,500 a week, but he refused and went to New York to do 'The Green Bay Tree'. In London he appeared in 'Biography' and other plays, and accepted a Korda contract. He played Lunardi the balloonist in one sequence of *Conquest of the Air*, a semi-documentary directed by John Monk Saunders and written by H.G. Wells – but the film was abandoned when costs mounted (some of it was used in later Korda films and the rest released, under the same title, in 1941). Thus his first Korda film was *Moscow Nights* (35), playing an impetuous young officer in hock to Harry Baur for gambling debts (the concurrent French version starred Pierre-Richard Wilm in Olivier's part). His stock had risen when he and John Gielgud had alternated Romeo and Mercutio on the stage – which earned him the part of Orlando opposite Elisabeth Bergner in *As You Like It* (36). 'Picturegoer' chastised him for announcing that he preferred plays to films, but the stage did not claim him entirely: he was romantic again, with Vivien Leigh, and swashbuckling vigorously in *Fire Over England* (37); and romancing Merle Oberon in a comedy, *The Divorce of Lady X* (38). Also in 1937 he and Leigh made *21 Days* (script by Graham Greene from a Galsworthy story), but it was not released until 1939 after they had both become very famous – and if they had not, it would not ever have been, in his opinion. They were both unbelievably bad.

He had tired of the West End and had asked to be taken on at the Old Vic: in 1937–

Olivier at the time of his RKO contract.

(Top left) Olivier and Vivien Leigh in a publicity shot for 21 Days *(39), a film for which neither is remembered. (Right) Olivier and Renée Asherson in the wooing scene in* Henry V *(44) – conversely, one of his biggest achievements. (Below) Ley On and Olivier in* 49th Parallel *(41), a fervid piece of wartime propaganda designed, via some international names, to bring the US in on 'our' side.*

38 he played Henry V, Hamlet, Macbeth, Sir Toby Belch, Iago and Coriolanus, and on screen he and Old Vic colleague Ralph Richardson brought style and attack to an adventure story, *Q Planes* (39); then with some reluctance he returned to Hollywood for Goldwyn's expensive *Wuthering Heights*. He was no happier making it than expected, but William Wyler gradually changed his aloof attitude to films. Richard Griffith wrote later: 'Olivier's Heathcliff, a figure of earth, belongs to the great screen performances.' It was marred only by being too well-spoken. The picture was much admired, but did not start to make a profit until it was reshown.

In New York he played 'No Time for Comedy', then returned to Hollywood for Selznick's *Rebecca* (40), directed by Hitchcock from a novel by Daphne du Maurier; as the moody aristocratic Maxim he gave another superb performance. And he was also fine as Mr Darcy in MGM's *Pride and Prejudice*, the only one of the cast whom Jane Austen might have acknowledged. Also in 1940 he and Leigh (now his wife; his marriage to Jill Esmond had been dissolved) did 'Romeo and Juliet' in New York, partly financed by himself from the salary that Warners had paid him for a projected remake of *Disraeli* (it was cancelled and revived a year later in Britain, with Gielgud). The 'Romeo' was critically roasted and he lost his money. In Hollywood Korda co-starred the two of them in *That Hamilton Woman/Lady Hamilton* (41), a jingoistic piece designed to sway Americans to the British side in the European war. Olivier's Nelson brought him a second 'Picturegoer' Gold Medal – the first was for *Rebecca* – and the film rounded out a remarkable Hollywood quartet. All four films have been endlessly revived: in 1942 a poll of New York cinemagoers voted *Rebecca* and *Wuthering Heights* among their 10 favourite films and in Los Angeles in 1967 both were voted in the top 10 films people most wanted to see again.

What distinguished Olivier from his peers was his refusal to look and act the same way twice in his films. Such had been the prerogative of character actors like Charles Laughton, till Paul Muni and then Bette Davis also insisted on interpretation before personality and performance. In Hollywood Olivier might now have had everything on his own terms (Zanuck offered to delay *How Green Was My Valley* until he was ready), but he did not, he said later, want to be a mere film star 'like dear Cary'; he admitted that he had been snobbish towards films and, though later happy to be remembered for them, had been persuaded towards the theatre by two factors – a desire to be his own boss and a love of being entrepreneur. However, he returned to

Britain because of the war, to serve in the Fleet Air Arm, from which he was released to play in two films of propaganda intent: *49th Parallel* (41), as a French-Canadian fur trapper, and *The Demi-Paradise* (43), as a Russian visiting Britain – his accents both demonstrating Gielgud's point that he was a great 'observer'.

His biggest propaganda effort was however, Shakespeare's *Henry V* (44). It was an idea he had considered, but the project became reality under the auspices of Filippo del Giudice, who ran Two Cities Films. Olivier approached Wyler to direct, but he could not take it on, nor could Terence Young or Carol Reed, so he took the plunge himself. When the film came out, his undeniably imaginative work as director/producer as well as star caused the word 'genius' to be bandied about – not unfairly, if one considers the other films directed by Britain's other theatre figures. It was a milestone; great chunks of it have been frequently copied and for the first time screen Shakespeare seemed not only feasible but desirable. But neither Olivier's name nor great reviews helped the box-office at first. It built into a success; in the US it did very well (in New York it ran almost a year) and brought Olivier the New York critics' award (Best Actor) and a special Oscar. He referred later to it: '. . . a rather sweet film. I like it. I feel proud of it.'

Back at the Old Vic he did the series of performances which established him as the first actor of his time – Hotspur, Astrov, Lear, Oedipus, Richard III. Films beckoned vainly, but as he and Leigh were on the point of signing for a Hollywood *Cyrano de Bergerac*, del Giudice proposed a film *Hamlet* (48). It was somewhat less ecstatically received than *Henry V* (and is decried today mainly because of a too-restless camera), but Olivier's own prestige soared even higher. He won a Best Picture and a Best Actor Oscar, and indeed the prizes copped worldwide for both films were considerable, as Rank (who financed) used to announce in special ads. Financially, *Hamlet* was a palpable hit, especially in the US, and 'made a great deal of money at the moment when the British film industry particularly needed it' (Felix Barker, 'The Oliviers', 1953). Olivier was knighted while it was in production.

His chief functioning ground, however, remained the stage; he went into management and presented, *inter alia*, the Shaw and Shakespeare Cleopatra plays, with himself and Leigh. He was one of many stars in cameo parts in *The Magic Box* (51), but as a Cockney policeman stole the notices. That year Leigh was offered a Hollywood film she wanted to do and Olivier let it be known that he was

'All for Love' was always one of the cinema's pet themes, and it was never more heart-breakingly rendered than by Laurence Olivier in Wyler's Carrie *(52) – perhaps his finest screen acting. These three pictures give only some idea of his disintegration: in stills one and two with Jennifer Jones – the cause. The source was a novel by Theodore Dreiser.*

open to offers. The one he accepted, Wyler's version of Theodore Dreiser's (Sister) *Carrie*, contained 'the finest acting of his career' said Richard Winnington, noting 'the refinement with which this actor compels the raptures, miseries and final suicidal despair of an obsessive passion' (for Jennifer Jones). He was not, however, Oscar-nominated, presumably because the film failed at the box-office. His next picture fared worse and according to Herbert Wilcox, who produced, it was taken off the circuits after one night and compensation paid; the title, *The Beggar's Opera* (53), contained not one but two off-putting words (Olivier himself refused to agree to a post-première change to *Macheath the Highwayman*). Further, it opened in London during Coronation week and got a grudging press reception.

The trouble was that as a film artist Olivier was associated with so-called 'high-brow' stuff and it was no longer the star of *Rebecca* who sought to immortalize his stage portrayal of *Richard III* (55). Said Gavin Lambert: 'Olivier's performance was brilliant on the stage; here it is even more impressive, the irony sharpened, the arrogance made more breathtaking by the camera's intimacy.' Half-wolf, half-vulture, Olivier dominated this hand-some interpretation of one of the less compulsive plays, perhaps the best of his three Shakespeare films. In an attempt to get its cost back quickly, it was premièred on TV in the US – where 'The New York Times' gave it front page treatment – and otherwise did satisfactory business. Korda, who presented it, died and Olivier failed to get backing for his next Shakespeare venture. Rank was not interested, nor were the American majors; he went cap in hand till the last minute, with all preparations made for location – shooting in Scotland two days later. It was to have been *Macbeth*, a part that he had played a year earlier (1956) at Stratford and regarded by all who saw it as his greatest stage performance.

Amidst great publicity, however, the next embarked on was *The Prince and the Showgirl* (58), directing and co-starring with Marilyn Monroe (in that part that Leigh had played with him on the stage); and the result was, inevitably, an anticlimax, though his own performance as a mittel-European princeling was impeccably done. He took on the title-role in *John Gabriel Borkman* for his postwar TV début, unlike most players coasting into that medium choosing both a difficult role and a massive but not popular play; and he was similarly bold when working in American TV,

'I can add colours to the chameleon . . .' Olivier as Richard III (55).

The screen teaming that made headline news: Olivier and Marilyn Monroe in The Prince and the Showgirl *(58). Olivier directed, and it was a soufflé that failed to rise.*

in two adaptations of novels, *The Moon and Sixpence* and *The Power and the Glory*. Earlier, he and Leigh had signed to do a Hollywood version of *Separate Tables*, but according to its author, Terence Rattigan, they left the cast when Burt Lancaster advised him on interpretation. He fulfilled his obligation to Lancaster's company by doing a featured role in *The Devil's Disciple* (59), with him and Kirk Douglas: it was brave of them rather than him; his stylish general Burgoyne almost saved the day, causing the 'Evening Standard', uncharacteristically, to blazon their review on their front page, headed 'The Greatest Actor in the World'. But prestige he did not need and the film of John Osborne's *The Entertainer* (60) did little to raise his box-office. On the stage he had played Archie

Rice, a run-down music-hall comic, and on screen he was even more mesmerizing, *being* rather than acting. But some critics did not like Tony Richardson's direction and the popular press was then waging war on Osborne: few films have been so ridiculously treated. (Olivier's film daughter was played by Joan Plowright, who became his third wife in 1961.)

'Show Magazine' in 1962, in an article on salaries, said that Olivier was no crowd-drawer, but was worth millions in prestige; he certainly pocketed a huge fee for *Spartacus* (61) in Hollywood and confessed he only did it for money, with Peter Ustinov and Charles Laughton backing such unlikely Romans as Kirk Douglas and Tony Curtis. This was Olivier the sly one, the senator who calmly

Olivier in The Entertainer *(60): 'And the movie, if it gave us nothing but Olivier's interpretation of this character, would be a rare and important experience' (Pauline Kael). With Joan Plowright (his third wife), a magnificent stage actress in one of her rare film performances.*

awaits his eventual triumph. He played a schoolteacher in the bleak *Term of Trial* (62), whose 'only interest,' said Dwight Macdonald, was 'in confirming, once more, one's opinion that Laurence Olivier is the best actor now going . . . but what a waste of talent'.

His commanding lead in prestige and achievement made him the logical choice to head Britain's National Theatre Company which started up in 1963: very quickly it became one of the world's best companies; his own work there included two definitive productions of English-Chekov, some deliberately chosen supporting parts and two more acting triumphs, in 'Othello' and 'The Dance of Death'. The 'New Statesman' said that a film should be made of his Othello for posterity, but the film that was made (65) – a sort of TV version, in colour and Scope, not directed by him – gave little idea of what it had been like as a theatre experience and bewildered people who had only read about it.

Bunny Lake Is Missing called for no special abilities, an amiable performance as a Scotland Yard inspector and almost the only one in his later screen career where he looked like his offscreen self. He returned to blackface as the Mahdi in *Khartoum* (66), a performance not much liked, and did not film again till: *The Shoes of the Fisherman* (68) as the Soviet premier; *The Dance of Death* (69), filmed in a similar way to the *Othello* and ruined by a miscast Geraldine McEwan, as his wife; and cameo parts as high-ranking officers in two world wars: Sir John French in *Oh! What a Lovely War* and Lord Dowding in *The Battle of Britain. David Copperfield* (70) was made for US TV and cinemas elsewhere, with its distinguished cast on a percentage – likely to be minute, since it was not of a quality to justify revival; Olivier's Mr Creakle offered its only Dickensian and indeed enjoyable minutes. He directed *The Three Sisters*, from his own stage production, and played the small role of the doctor, but this was another case of a National play taking uneasily to film. In all his cameo roles, he was singled out by reviewers for special praise, as happened again in two more starry ventures, *Nicholas and Alexandra* (71) and *Lady Caroline Lamb* (72), examples respectively of good historical and bad: his vigorous portrayals enhanced both, but in both cases he had taken on the most interesting characters on display – the Russian prime minister, Witte, and the Duke of Wellington.

In 1970 he was created a peer, the first actor to be so honoured; and during these years he played Shylock and the father in 'Long Day's Journey into Night', the last of his National triumphs. His tenure as Director was terminated in 1972, but with reason the largest of the National's three new auditoriums was named the Olivier. He had said that he no longer enjoyed acting – 'Perhaps the responsibility is too great' – but the extraordinary energies he had displayed in running the National and acting there were able to deploy themselves in full-scale roles in films and indeed after a series of illnesses he announced that he had acted for the last time on stage. The films he chose, however, are more likely to find themselves consigned to oblivion with *David Copperfield* than revived with *Rebecca: Sleuth* (72), from a long-running stage play, as a foxy, military-like writer, in a cat and mouse game with Michael Caine; *The Rehearsal* (74), seen (only) reading a poem in a film by Jules Dassin not apparently shown outside Greece; *Love Among the Ruins* (75), as a lawyer, with Katharine Hepburn, for TV; *The Marathon Man* (76), a bald, vicious Nazi, being sadistic to Dustin Hoffman in modern-day New York; *The Seven Per Cent Solution*, an ill-advised attempt at Sherlock Holmes (Nicol Williamson) pastiche, as Moriarty; *Jesus of Nazareth/ Gesu di Nazaret* (77), Zeffirelli's long, noble and star-studded attempt to tell the Bible story for TV, as Nicodemus; and *A Bridge Too Far*, a soporific all-star attempt to turn the Battle of Arnhem into 'Mother Courage', as a Dutch doctor. A venture into TV, as producer, acting in most and directing one, is also of doubtful benefit to posterity – at its best with his performances in *The Collection* and *Daphne Laureola*, and at its worst with the performances (including Natalie Wood and Robert Wagner) in *Cat on a Hot Tin Roof*.

Harold Robbins saw the latter and wrote *The Betsy* (78) for him. Wrote Jack Kroll in 'Newsweek': 'God bless Laurence Olivier. And God only knows what the incomparable actor of the Western world is doing in a piece of hilarious idocy like *The Betsy*. Taking away a zillion dollars, one hopes. This is no cameo role; the great septuagenarian is playing the lead. And lead he does, in the greatest put-on performance you've ever seen. Having plumbed the depths of Shakespeare and Chekov, Olivier has little trouble probing the nooks and crannies of Harold Robbins (the thinking man's Sidney Sheldon) from whose best seller this farrago was farragoed. Only the great Hamlet could create the great Loren Hardeman Sr., mighty Detroit automobile tycoon and founder of the silliest industrial dynasty in junk-novel history.' Michael Caine takes credit for assuring Olivier that his reputation was inviolable and that he should take the money and run; other friends claimed that he believed that as long as he was working he could not die.

Certainly these are a mixed bag of credits, though it was often rewarding to see him still meeting the challenge of difficult roles: *The Boys From Brazil*, as an elderly Jewish Nazi-hunter; *Dracula* (79), as the savant Van Helsing; *A Little Romance*, as a lovable old (French) buffer, who helps the teenage lovers run away to Venice; *The Jazz Singer* (80), as Paul Anka's cantor father; *Clash of the Titans* (81), as Zeus; and *Oh Inchon*, as General MacArthur. The last-named, funded by the head of the 'Moonies' religious cult, was one of the most expensive films ever made, but the name cast could not help it in the US – while MGM/UA, who bought it, never opened it in Britain. The director, Terence Young, was no luckier with *The Jigsaw Man* (82), despite the presence of Sir Laurence and Michael Caine; money ran out during filming and after being eventually completed it went direct to videocassette. The great man concentrated on television: the much acclaimed series 'Brideshead Revisited' (81), as Lord Marchmain; John Mortimer's autobiographical 'A Voyage Round My Father' (82), as a blind lawyer, with Alan Bates as his son; 'King Lear' (83), alas, too studio-bound but with a glittering supporting cast and almost to be set with his finest achievements; the execrable 'Wagner', in a very brief role as the Bavarian Chief of Police (a long, long movie, this, available in several lengths); and 'Halperin and Mr Johnson', a two-hander with Jackie Gleason. For cinemas he was a sea-lord, frail now, in the prologue and epilogue examining the voyage of *The Bounty* (84); and, for TV, he played a patrician in 'The Last Days of Pompeii'. He spent his own last days in major roles – for TV: with Angela Lansbury in a weak thriller, 'A Talent for Murder', and 'The Ebony Tower', more worthy of him, a study of a monstrous aged artist, based on a story by John Fowles. Olivier himself seemed to have based his interpretation on his friend Ralph Richardson, now dead. He played Rudolf Hess in an action movie, *Wild Geese II* (85), an inauspicious finale to his often bewildering but still exceptional film career; and he played an old seedy music-hall star in the first episodes of a mini-series, *Lost Empires* (86), once again enjoying the admiration of the critics.

None of these pieces dented his reputation – which brought him, incidentally, a second honorary Oscar in 1978. In 1987, on the occasion of his 80th birthday, he announced that he would only be able to do radio in future. The era he dominated was over, but he did make a frail three-minute appearance as an old soldier in the prologue to a subsequently unwatchable opus set to Benjamin Britten's *War Requiem* (88). He died in 1989, and there was hardly an obituary the world over which did not refer to him as 'the actor of the century'. He was one of the few of the century's celebrities to have his ashes buried in the national shrine, Westminster Abbey.

LILLI PALMER

Lilli Palmer was the most cosmopolitan of stars. She worked in Britain, the United States, France, Germany, Austria and Italy – and apart from Italy (only twice) several times in each country. She projected exactly what you might expect: the elegant, sophisticated, much-travelled and much-experienced *dame d'une certaine âge*. Late in her career she observed that she was no longer interested in acting, which might account for a later mechanical streak in the still potent charm; but she remained effective whenever a good role came her way.

She was born in Posen, Germany, in 1914, the daughter of a surgeon, and after studying acting in Berlin was taken on by the State Theatre in Darmstadt, playing the leads in musicals. When the Nazis took over in Germany, she decided to join her sister in Paris and after a number of false starts the only work they could get was singing in cabaret. Curtis Mellnitz, the head of the local office of United Artists, thought she had movie potential and introduced her to Douglas Fairbanks, who showed no interest in her; but he also invited her to meet Alexander Korda, who told her to look him up if she was ever in London. Not apparently too interested, he could not get her a work permit, but the cameraman who tested her, Hal Rossen, sent her to an agent, who knew of a B production whose leading lady had just been taken ill: *Crime Unlimited* (35) was seen by executives at Gaumont-British, who signed her to a seven-year contract – and invariably cast her as a Continental mantrap: *First Offence* (36) starring John Mills, a remake of *Mauvaise Graine*; *Wolf's Clothing*, a spy story set in Paris with Claude Hulbert and Gordon Harker; Hitchcock's *Secret Agent*, in a small supporting part; *Good Morning Boys* (37) starring Will Hay; *The Great Barrier*, as a camp follower in this epic of Canada starring Richard Arlen; and on loan for *Sunset in Vienna* starring Tullio Carminati, which was the first time the critics noticed her favourably. As a result she was given leads in *Command Performance*, as a gypsy loved by 'The Street Singer' Arthur Tracy, and in *Crackerjack* (38), starring Tom Walls, as a baroness. GB dropped her, but asked her back to play a tough Hungarian chorus girl in *A Girl Must Live* (39), which was followed by *Blind Folly*, a B comedy with Clifford Mollison, and *The Door with Seven Locks* (40), a thriller with Leslie Banks. But if this was hardly a glittering screen career, she was carving a small niche in the theatre in, among others, 'Road to Gandahar', 'Little Ladyship' and 'Ladies in Action' (40), as Felicity Van der Loo.

The first time she made any considerable impression was as the Other Woman in 'No Time for Comedy' at the Haymarket in 1941; and in marked contrast to that glittering performance she played a sad-eyed little ghost in *Thunder Rock* (42). She was now accepted as a serious dramatic actress. She appeared in Leslie Howard's tribute to the ATS, *The Gentle Sex* (43), and in Rattigan's comedy, *English Without Tears* (44) as a Norwegian translator. She was with her husband, Rex Harrison, in *The Rake's Progress* (45), as a Jewess who is married by the Rake in order to get her out of Austria. She then did an inferior version of Stefan Zweig's *Beware of Pity* (45), as the crippled heroine deceived into believing that a handsome lieutenant (Albert Lieven) is in love with her. This might have been one of the screen's great romantic stories with any other director but Maurice Elvey, but because of him both stars gave ludicrous performances.

Harrison had a Hollywood contract and Palmer accompanied him, with a rather less good one at Warner Bros: *Cloak and Dagger* (46), as an Italian partisan who helps Gary Cooper; *Body and Soul* (47), as the fiancée of boxer John Garfield, on loan; the underrated *My Girl Tisa*, with Sam Wanamaker, about turn-of-the-century immigrants; and *No Minor Vices* again on loan to Enterprise, a marital comedy with Dana Andrews. She looked lovely and acted with her usual sensitivity, but none of the films was oversuccessful. When Harrison bought up his contract after a Hollywood scandal, she went with him to New York and appeared in Jean-Pierre Aumont's 'My Name is Aquilon' and as Shaw's Cleopatra; as a favour to Aumont she went to Paris to co-star with his wife, Maria Montez, in *Hans le Marin*. She and Harrison reappeared in Britain in a damp thriller, *The Long Dark Hall* (51), and their careers picked up with a Broadway play, 'Bell Book and Candle' – which led to another Hollywood chance, *The Four-poster* (52), a witless two-character study of a marriage. She made two more Broadway appearances, in 'Venus Observed' and 'The Loves of Four Colonels', and, as herself, appeared with Harrison in *Main Street to Broadway* (53). When a film offer came from Germany she

The Gentle Sex *(43) at war: Lilli Palmer as a refugee girl who joined the women's branch of the army. With (right) Rosamund John.*

accepted the challenge – because 'bridges must be built'; the film was *Feuerwerk* (54), a musical.

On the British run of 'Bell Book and Candle' the Harrison marriage fell apart and her role was taken by Joan Greenwood. She returned to Germany to make *Teufel im Seide* (56), a high society drama with Curt Jurgens, and when her performance was prized at Berlin she decided to accept more German offers: *Anastasia die Letze Zarentochter* with Ivan Desny, which clashed with the 20th-Ingrid Bergman film on the same subject; *Zwischen Zeit und Ewigkeit*, women's magazine stuff, with Carlos Thompson, the Argentinian actor whom she married in 1957; *Wie ein Sturmwind* (57); *Der Gläserne Turm* with Peter Van Eyck, a study of backstage jealousies; *Montparnasse 19*, in France, in a small role as a patroness of the painter, with Gérard Philipe as Modigliani; *Ein Frau Die Weiss Was Sie Will* (58); and the remake of *Mädchen in Uniform*. In France she appeared with Jean Marais in an all-star episode made as a posthumous tribute to Sacha Guitry, *La Vie à Deux*.

Out of the blue Hollywood recalled Palmer to play opposite Gable, as his ex-wife, in *But Not for Me* (59): mocking and glamorous, she created a firm impression. In Britain she made a revoltingly sentimental nun-film, *Conspiracy of Hearts* (60), and in Germany a version of a Shaw play, *Frau Warren's Gewerbe* – Mrs

W.'s Profession, which was of course, prostitution; but the combination of Shaw and sex
got it no more bookings outside Germany
than Palmer's earlier German films. World
audiences had chances of seeing her in two
more films for Paramount: *The Pleasure of
His Company* (61) with Fred Astaire and *The
Counterfeit Traitor* with William Holden. This
was the beginning of a period of intense
activity – the suitcases hardly had time to get
unpacked: *Leviathan* from Julien Green's
novel in France, with Louis Jourdan; with her
husband, *Frau Cheney's Ende*, MGM's old
warhorse, taken on by the Germans; and in
France, Roger Leenhardt's beautiful *Le Rendezvous de Minuit*, in a triple role – as a
suicidal woman, as an actress in a film and,
for one brief moment, as herself. She played
an actress again in the Franco-Austrian *Adorable Juila/Juila, du Bist Zauberhaft* (62), a
cheap and badly made version of Somerset
Maugham's 'Theatre', and there was more
Maugham, with *Finden Sie das Constance sich
Richtig Verhält?* – 'The Constant Wife'. She
was wasted as Robert Taylor's wife in Disney's filmed-in-Vienna *The Miracle of the
White Stallions* (63), but delightful in her
episode, married to Bernhard Whicki, of the
Italian-German *L'Amore Difficile*; and then
wasted again, along with James Mason, in the
Italian-British *Finchè Dura la Tempesta/
Torpedo Bay* (64), a war film in which she
played the doctor. She was an actress again in
Das Grosse Liebesspiel, a poor rehash of that
German subject we know best as *La Ronde*,
after which she did: *Le Grain de Sable/Il
Triangolo Circolare* (65) with Pierre Brasseur;
Operation Crossbow with Sophia Loren and a
number of British actors, as a Dutch partisan;
and *The Amorous Adventures of Moll Flanders*, disheartened – as who wouldn't be? – as
a madam.

After playing Jean Gabin's wife in *Le
Tonnerre de Dieu* she was Princess Metternich
to the Czar of Jurgens in *Der Kongress
Amusiert Sich* (66) – which was not a remake
of the old movie, but had the same setting.
Her former compatriots wasted her yet again
in the Anglo-German *Jack of Diamonds*, a
heist movie with George Hamilton, in which
she played herself, but the French co-starred
her with another of their most popular players, Fernandel, in *Le Voyage du Père*. In
Germany she made *Paarungen* (67) with Paul
Verhoeven, a version of Strindberg's 'The
Dance of Death' which failed horribly; and
there were three more rewarding roles when
Noël Coward wanted her to appear with him
in London in his 'Suite in Three Keys', but the
best the British cinema could offer were dull
supporting roles in two mediocre thrillers,
Sebastian (68), with Dirk Bogarde, and

Nobody Runs Forever, with Rod Taylor –
though it is clear that Palmer hoped more
from her roles, in themselves promising, as
respectively a German-Jewess de-coder in the
British Secret Service and the wife, revealed
as a murderess, of the Australian High Commissioner.

Unsuitably cast as Jocasta to Christopher
Plummer's *Oedipus the King* (69), there was
concurrently in London an exhibition of her
paintings; she said that she and her husband
intended to spend more time at their home in
Switzerland, and it is a pity she did not stay
there instead of participating in *Hard Contract*
(69), with James Coburn, and the US-German
De Sade, with Kier Dullea, as respectively,
this time, international jet-setter and Madame
de Montreuil. She did *Night Hair Child*; *La
Residencia* (70), but despite good notices and
the genre – horror – it was seen little abroad;
a tele-movie based on a story by Curt Siodmak, *Hauser's Memory*; and *Le Peau de
Torpedo*, with Stephane Audren, in which she
was head of a spy ring. Despite Jason Robards
in the lead – she was his mother-in-law – this
Murders in the Rue Morgue (71) must be the
least of the several versions. For German TV
she did *Eine Frau ist Eine Frau* (74) and in
East Germany she made *Lotte in Weimar*
(75), from the novel by Thomas Mann;
because she was pleased with the project, she

said it would be her last film – but she could not resist a film with Laurence Olivier, *The Boys from Brazil* (78).

In 1980 she appeared in Washington in a one-woman show, 'Sarah in America', based on material the writer Ruth Wolff had not managed to get into *The Incredible Sarah* (Bernhardt). It did not go on to New York, as planned, but it was televised. There were a few last credits: *Feine Gesellschaft – beschränkte Haftung* (82), as Elisabeth Bergner's affluent younger sister; *Imaginary Friends*, an Anglo-German telefilm with Peter Ustinov; *The Holcroft Covenant* (85), as Michael Caine's anti-Nazi mother; and the mini-series *Peter the Great* (86). She died in 1986.

MARY PICKFORD

If popularity were the sole criterion of stardom, then Mary Pickford is without doubt the greatest star there has ever been. For most of the 24 years she was on the screen she was the biggest draw of them all – bigger, even, than Chaplin. In the US she was called 'America's Sweetheart' and outside it, less chauvinistically, 'The World's Sweetheart'. Pollsters for 14 years found she was the world's most popular woman. She started before players in films were named on the credits or adverts, at that moment when movie-making was becoming big business, and rode to success on the crest of this new industry. In less than 10 years she was, said Benjamin B. Hampton in 'A History of the Movies' (1931), 'the industry's most valuable asset. Woman's place in business has grown enormously in importance in the last three decades, but Mary Pickford is the only member of her sex who ever became the focal point of an entire industry. Her position is unique; probably no man or woman will ever again win so extensive a following.'

Her very success may have contributed to her popularity – an inspiration to the 20th-century woman seeking emancipation; at the same time the Pickford character – 'Little Mary' of the titles – belonged firmly to the world of Victorian melodrama and was probably a great consolation to those people who did not care for the changing modern woman. Her public was mainly rural; for millions of people who had never been to a theatre it was an entirely new experience to see a 'star', someone to identify with, to love from a remote distance; it must often have seemed like the incarnation of the heroine from the printed page – more clearly defined, but infinitely more mysterious. She represented purity, innocence and determination, and it is possible that her major appeal to audiences was a realization that the latter quality, sitting not too well with the other two, reflected the real Pickford – the lady out there in Hollywood. Audience preference was increasingly clear: they only wanted to see her play a child, preferably an underprivileged one, going to adulthood and sudden riches in the last reel. Her films are too remote from our own experience in environment or truth – and in industry terms their technical qualities are antediluvian – but we can recognize in the completely manufactured Mary character more gumption, vigour and 'cheek' than in her rivals. Contemporary critics never put her in a class with Lillian Gish, but then she was never required to display the range. In the best of her late films, *My Best Girl*, playing Cinderella as a teenager, she is a delightful comedienne, if a little too roguish and cute, but with a tendency to overact in the serious scenes. Aware of her limitations, she chose her Talkies carefully, but with her range extended by voice she became simply another actress and one of no extraordinary skill or magic.

She was born in Toronto in 1893; her mother was widowed when Mary was four, but the family income was saved when the child was taken on by a local stock company for such melodramas as 'Uncle Tom's Cabin' and 'The Little Red Schoolhouse'. At nine she was starring in 'The Fatal Wedding', billed as 'Baby Gladys Smith' (her real name). She toured extensively and at age 13 decided that unless she made Broadway soon she would give up the theatre for good; so she cornered producer David Belasco, who gave her a part in 'The Warrens of Virginia'. Tours of this and the New York run kept her busy 1907–8, but in 1909 family fortunes (now they all acted – mother, brother, sister) were low and Mary decided to try films. She went to Biograph where D.W. Griffith interviewed her, made her up and ushered her on to the set of *Pippa Passes*. At the end of the day he asked her to return the following day, offering her $5 per day. She asked for $10 and got it.

The next day they were filming *Her First Biscuits* (often given as her first film; another contender is *The Lonely Villa*) – its stars were Florence Lawrence and William Courtright, both of whom Pickford was to feature in her *My Best Girl*, almost 20 years later. She had a big part as 'one of those who suffered from a bride's first baking' (remembered Adolph Zukor in 'The Public Is Never Wrong'). Her first star part was *The Violin Maker of Cremona* with Owen Moore (to whom she was married, till drink killed it); after that Griffith offered her a contract with a guarantee of $40 for five days' work weekly. She played in *In*

.The end of Rebecca's circus career.

MARY PICKFORD
IN
**REBECCA OF
SUNNYBROOK FARM**
FROM THE PLAY BY KATE DOUGLAS WIGGIN ᴀɴᴅ CHARLOTTE THOMPSON
SCENARIO BY FRANCIS MARION ... DIRECTED BY MARSHALL NEILAN
PRESENTED BY
ARTCRAFT PICTURES CORPORATION

*'The Girl With the Curls':
Mary Pickford when she
was the world's sweetheart.*

paid her $175 a week; a year later Majestic offered $275 and the first picture Pickford and Moore made for that company was called *The Courting of Mary* (11). But soon they returned to Biograph and Griffith, then at the peak as film-makers.

Some titles: *The Italian Barber, The Way of a Man, The One She Loved, Wilful Peggy, White Hills* and *In a Sultan's Garden* (IMP). Pickford contributed the scenarios for some of them – *May to December, Lena and the Geese* (12). Of *Friends* – with Lionel Barrymore – she said in her memoirs ('Sunshine and Shadow', 1956) that she thought it was the first film ever to feature a close-up. Her biggest Biograph success was *The New York Hat*, but she had already decided to leave that company, enraged that a newcomer without stage-training – Mae Marsh – was being given the leads in *Man's Genesis* (which she had turned down, because it meant appearing in a grass skirt) and *The Sands of Dee*. She went back to Belasco and told him she wanted to return to the stage; he cast her as a blind girl, the childhood sweetheart the hero eventually realizes he loves, in 'A Good Little Devil'. When New York learned that this starred 'The Girl with the Curls' the theatre was mobbed. It was the first time in history that film fans had seen an idol in person. At the same time the industry felt honoured that a film player had made it in legit.

The play was filmed (13) and some publicity accrued from the fact that Belasco himself appeared in the prologue – a rare honour for a mere film; and also from the fact that 'Little Mary' was returning to the screen. It was, however, 'a monumental failure' (her memoirs). Famous Players produced and Zukor, its boss, a few months later offered her a contract to play in his 'B' products at $500 per week; but their success – *Caprice* with Moore, *In a Bishop's Carriage*, where she was a thief, and *Hearts Adrift* especially (in that she was shipwrecked) – was such that early in 1914 it went up to $1,000 a week. Zukor's 'A' pictures ('Famous Players in Famous Plays') were not doing too well, but the 'B' films were doing fine. She had a resounding hit with *Tess of the Storm Country* and lesser ones with *Such a Little Queen, The Eagle's Mate* with James Kirkwood, *Behind the Scenes, Fanchon the Cricket, Cinderella* (14) with Moore, *Mistress Nell* (as Nell Gwyn) and *A Dawn of Tomorrow* (15). Meanwhile, her salary had gone to $2,000 per week – and when an offer came from the American Film Co. to do a serial, *The Diamond in the Sky* at $4,000 a week, Zukor had to match it or lose her (so potent was the Pickford name that her sister, Lotte, was engaged instead). She soon went on to $10,000 a week. Details of her contracts

Old Kentucky, The Hessian Renegades, To Save Her Soul (09) and others, often cast as a dusky maiden (*Song of the Wild Wood Flute, Ramona*), but it was as herself that she had her first big hit, *The Little Teacher* (10); the intertitles on that identified her as 'Little Mary' and thus audiences began to refer to her. Exhibitors advertised her as 'Goldilocks' and 'The Girl with the Curls' or – in succession to Florence Lawrence – 'The Biograph Girl'. The film's title was immaterial: 'What Happened to Mary Twice Nightly' was all that was needed when a Pickford pic played in Haddington, Scotland. She had achieved such fame that when she left Biograph for the Indepedent Motion Picture Co. (IMP), her first film for them (with Moore), *Their First Misunderstanding* (10), was advertised thus: 'Little Mary is an Imp now'. IMP were published and they are covered in Terry Ramsaye's 'A Million and One Nights', 1926. He says at one point: 'The fame of all the other famous players was nothing unless it was supported by Mary Pickford. She was the one player really famous to the motion picture exhibitors and their public.'

According to her memoirs, her resolve to get every penny she could from Zukor was due to the fantastic offers from the other companies; plus the fact that one evening she had noticed enormous queues for her *Rags* and none at all for another Famous Players film down the road. Later it became a cause with her that whenever Chaplin's wage got a hike, she got a bigger one. Zukor says in his memoirs: 'There is no doubt about her tremendous drive for success and the cash register nature of a segment of her brain.' *Little Pal*, *The Girl from Yesterday*, *Poor Little Peppina* (16), *Madam Butterfly* (with Marshall Neilan as Pinkerton), *The Foundling*, *The Eternal Grind* and *Hulda from Holland* were the others that kept the public queueing. Eventually, in the summer of 1916 Zukor announced the formation of two new companies, The Mary Pickford Studio and Artcraft (to release its product); for some months she had been flirting with other companies, including Mutual (whose salary to Chaplin grieved her somewhat). The two new companies were both a ruse to keep her and a front to discourage poachers, but she was to get a guarantee of $1,040,000 for two years, plus bonuses, privileges and power.

At the same time Zukor merged Famous Players with Lasky (later to become Paramount); Pickford soon found that her new bosses wanted to interfere. She let them have their way with *Less Than the Dust*, which was awful, but quarrelled over the next one, *Pride of the Clan* (17). But it was, she says, 'an even more disastrous failure'. So she claimed autonomy when making *A Poor Little Rich Girl* – but no one at the studio liked it; so she buckled under De Mille for a couple: *Romance of the Redwoods*, as an orphan sent out West to live with an uncle, only he (Elliott Dexter) is not really an uncle but a handsome young imposter who makes her unwelcome (at first); and *The Little American*, a propaganda piece about the sinking of the 'Lusitania', with our heroine threatened with rape at one point. But then *A Poor Little Rich Girl* became a big success; and so was *Rebecca of Sunnybrook Farm*, which followed the two De Milles; and so was *The Little Princess*, which followed that – so she was able to work with little interference; but these three juvenile parts had typed her. She was irrevocably stuck with 'Little Mary'. In *Stella Maris* (18) she had a dual role, enabling her to play both the angelic crippled title character and the older maid who dotes on her – thus one of the characters could end unhappily but the film still have the required happy ending. She was more conventional in *Amarilly of Clothes Line Alley* and in *M'liss*, a version of a Bret Harte novel, as a 'fearless trusted friend of forest creatures'. (The last five were all directed by Marshall Neilan and written by Frances Marion, who wrote some dozen Pickford vehicles.) Then came the less popular *How Could You Jean?* and *Captain Kidd Junior* (19). Her last picture for Zukor was a short, *Johanna Enlists*.

She had spent much of this period with Chaplin and Douglas Fairbanks encouraging people to buy war bonds. Now she wanted some money for herself. First National offered $250,000 each for three pictures, plus $50,000 to her mother. Zukor could not, or would not, meet the price. To prevent her from going to a competitor he offered her $1,000 a week for five years for doing nothing – claiming that she was tired; but she was not about to agree to that. Her years with Zukor, she said, were the happiest of her life, implying that, having 'saved' him at the time of *Tess of the Storm Country*, he might have been more generous. First National were generous – once again her salary was no longer second to Chaplin's and eventually she got an extra $100,000 each for the three pictures she made there – plus complete independence. They were, however, big money-makers for the company: *Daddy Long Legs*, a semi-classic about an 'orphan' adopted by a wealthy benefactor; *The Hoodlum*; and *Heart o' the Hills*.

UA was formed by Pickford, Griffith, Chaplin and Fairbanks (to whom she was married that year): it was partly a defensive action against rumours that the moguls were going to put a ceiling on star salaries. For UA, as part-owner and producer, Pickford did very well. *Pollyanna* (20) – the 'glad girl' – was their first film and the first ever sold on a percentage basis (initially exhibitors boycotted the new company, but public opinion forced them to give in). The film put UA on a sound financial basis, though she herself hated it. There followed several like products – *Suds*, as a plain little skivvy; *The Love Light* (21), as an Italian lighthouse keeper betrayed by a German spy; *Through the Back Door*, as a Belgian refugee; *Little Lord Fauntleroy*, in a dual role – awful in drag as the noble lord but good as Dearest, his mother; and a remake of *Tess of the Storm Country* (22). But she yearned to play adult roles.

On the strength of the German *Dubarry*, Pickford brought Ernst Lubitsch to Hollywood to direct her in her 'first' adult role,

Dorothy Vernon of Haddon Hall; but he did not like the script and instead directed her in a lavish period melodrama, *Rosita* (23), where she was a fiery señorita – 'the worst picture, bar none, that I ever made' (Pickford). It was a financial failure of large proportions – but, if it is not typical of Lubitsch's work, it compares very favourably to her other available films. She then tried *Dorothy Vernon* (24), a drama set in Elizabethan England – 'Mary Pickford as an 18-year-old spitfire' said the ads – but it was little more successful. She felt it was a punishment for ignoring the public's expressed wish – via a contest in 'Photoplay' – that she continue to play parts like Pollyanna and Cinderella. Her popularity had begun to diminish a little; in the 1923 'National Star Popularity Contest' she trailed both the Talmadge sisters. There were those who thought that had she been less interested in money she might have persevered and eventually won over the public to a grown-up Mary, but instead she plunged back into the

Mary Pickford in two of her best-remembered films, in Little Lord Fauntleroy *(21), left, as the American boy heir to an earldom (she also played his mother), and in* Sparrows *(26), right, as the eldest of several deprived orphans, and 'mother' to them. Both movies have strong stories, which is why they revive well, but they also have, in common with all the Pickford movies, that contentment and peace of mind provide a surer way to happiness than riches.*

pathos of *Little Annie Rooney* (25) and *Sparrows* (26), her defiantly bobbed hair hidden under a wig of golden curls (she looked older than the other kids but audiences accepted her). One fan magazine observed that she had drunk deep from the elixir of youth. She did at least play a 17-year-old in *My Best Girl* (27) – a gentle and funny comedy centred on a young girl's romance with the boss's son. Her co-star was Charles 'Buddy' Rogers whom she married after the famous marriage to Fairbanks ended in 1935.

With the coming of Sound, she hesitated, but wisely chose *Coquette* (29), which had been a success on stage for Helen Hayes, as a flapper whose night of love with a bounder (John Mack Brown) leads to murder; sex is okay if you are in love, but if you are found out Society will exact its price. Pickford's voice is all right, if a little soft. She has much emoting to do, but it is all stagey, exterior. She was a subtle actress on the Silent screen because she understood its language. Forced into adopting a different technique after years of being away from the stage, she is just another actress. Her performance did bring an Oscar, which was what persuaded her into doing *The Taming of the Shrew* against her better judgment. For years fans had been clamouring for Doug and Mary, the King and Queen of Hollywood – their palace was called 'Pickfair' – to make a film together; their selection of *The Shrew* betokens perhaps a consciousness of their exalted status, plus a desire to do away with the old era now that Talkies were here. But it was an odd choice in view of both the fans' preference for 'Little Mary' and a complete lack of Shakespearian experience. 'I have no qualms about admitting that Katharine was one of my worst performances' – you can say that again – 'instead of being a forceful tiger-cat, I was a spitting little kitten.' Few people were curious enough to turn up to see it and for years it was remembered only because of a credit: 'Additional dialogue by Sam Taylor'; less generally known is that a Silent version was prepared, in case Talkies were a passing fad. It was the first Talkie to be shown in London with separate performances.

Undeterred, Pickford then decided to get in on the all-talking, all-singing, all-dancing craze, and did all three in *Kiki* (31), playing a Parisian soubrette. She had left it too late to escape from type. Said E. Rossiter Shepherd in 'Picturegoer': 'It will take another picture to efface from my mind the vision of an over-rouged, under-dressed vamp and replace it with the curly demureness of the real Mary.' She then went back to *Secrets* (33), which she had abandoned before *Kiki* at a loss of $300,000 ($50,000 less than her salary for

Mary Pickford made only four Talkies, including Kiki (31), but the public refused to accept her in her new persona as a mature woman. Also, Sound revealed that she really wasn't much of an actress.

Kiki). Based on a sentimental play which traced a marriage from the teens to old age, it had been a great hit for Norma Talmadge in 1924. But the public did not want to see Pickford (and Leslie Howard) in it. Having made what she herself called three 'costly and disheartening moving-picture failures' in a row, she retired from the screen. In 1933 she made a vaudeville appearance in New York. In 1934 she published a book entitled 'Why Not Try God' and in 1935 a novel and something called 'My Rendezvous With Life'; and she broadcast frequently for NBC. In 1936 she transferred her talents to CBS; that year she became the first vice-president of UA and co-produced *One Rainy Afternoon* and produced *The Gay Desperado*. Long after the deaths of Fairbanks and Griffith (who, anyway, had been bought out) Chaplin and Pickford co-owned UA. They finally sold out in 1953. In 1937 was formed the Mary Pickford Cosmetic Co. There were rumours of a come-back in Britain in 1939 and in 1947 she tested for *Life With Father* (she would probably have got it if Irene Dunne had not agreed to do it). In the early 50s she was definitely set for *Storm Center* – but she changed her mind after a day's rehearsal when she learnt it was not to be made in colour (Bette Davis played the role). At least she did not need the money. She died in 1979.

WALTER PIDGEON

Walter Pidgeon: 'that handsome piece of screen furniture', as James Agate termed him, but less, surely, because he was wooden than because he seemed to be around in almost every film. He was not an exciting actor, but was successful at projecting a good masculine dependability – capable, intelligent, honourable. He and Greer Garson together embodied a multitude of the domestic virtues of their time.

He was born in East St John, New Brunswick, Canada, in 1897 and studied at the University of New Brunswick for a year before being commissioned in the Artillery. He was invalided out after an accident and was sent to Boston for his health. There he became a bank runner and married his childhood sweetheart, who died two years later in childbirth; he also studied singing and made his stage bow in a local production of 'You Never Can Tell'. Fred Astaire heard him sing at a party and recommended him to friends in New York, but they turned him down after auditioning him. Pidgeon was encouraged to approach Elsie Janis, whom he had met while she was doing troop concerts. She took him as her singing partner and he made his professional début in 'At Home' with her; they toured with this, in Britain as well as the US, and did vaudeville. He was on Broadway in 'The Puzzles of 1925'. He also had a contract with Victor and was the first artist to record Irving Berlin's 'What'll I Do?' and 'Remember'. Joseph M. Schenck wanted him for a film with Constance Talmadge and procured his release from his stage contract; but when Pidgeon arrived in Hollywood Schenck had changed his mind and arranged for him to go to Paramount for a supporting role in *Mannequin* (26), which starred Alice Joyce and Dolores Costello.

Pidgeon stayed on and freelanced: *The Outsider* at Fox; *Miss Nobody*, who was Anna Q. Nilsson in drag; *Old Lives for New*, as the bounder who pinches Lewis Stone's wife, from E.M. Hull's novel 'The Desert Healer' (its British title); *Marriage License*, from a British play, 'The Pelican', with Alma Rubens, again as the Other Man; *The Heart of Salome* (27) again with Rubens, but this time he was the hero; *The Girl From Rio*, as

a visiting businessman involved with Carmen Myers; *The Gorilla*, from the old stage comedy-thriller; *Woman Wise* with June Collyer; and *The Thirteenth Juror*, with Anna Q. Nilsson and Francis X. Bushman – Pidgeon on trial for a murder that defending counsel Bushman committed. He had reached the position of leading actor without being a real star, conveying the same qualities as later in his career: nor did he look either different or much younger, except that he was usually moustached. Fox, for whom he had worked on several occasions, made him the male lead in *The Gateway of the Moon* (28), which got him the star role in an independent venture, *Turn Back the Hours*, stuck with Myrna Loy on a desert island; for Tiffany he made *Clothes Make the Woman*, a poor Hollywood tale; and for Universal, *Melody of Love*, which had Sound sequences – he was a pianist who loses the use of his hands until redeemed by the love of a Good Woman.

The coming of Talkies gave a lift to Pidgeon's career: as an experienced stage artist he was in demand and of the several offers he accepted one with Warner Bros. Both his first pictures there were made in Silent and Talkie versions: *Her Private Life* (29) – Billie Dove's; and *A Most Immortal Lady* – Leatrice Joy. But Warners wanted Pidgeon for something more spectacular than supporting fading stars in heavy melodramas – for something which could not have been done in Silents. They were embarking on a series of Technicolor (two-toned) operettas (the first two had already appeared: *Song of the West* with Vivienne Segal and John Boles; and *Song of the Flame* with Bernice Claire and Noah Berry). Pidgeon and Segal starred in the next: *Bride of the Regiment* (30), adapted from Sigmund Romberg's 'The Lady in Ermine'. Several Pidgeon pictures were released in the fall: *Sweet Kitty Bellairs*, from Belasco's old play about Olde England, with newcomer Claudia Dell; a remake of *The Gorilla*, in the same part he had before; and *Going Wild*, in support of Joe E. Brown, a remake of *Going Up?* which had starred Douglas MacLean. He had a small part in *Renegades* – and it seemed that no month was complete without a Pidgeon picture: in November also *Viennese Nights* was released, 'written specially' for the screen by Romberg and Oscar Hammerstein II. The ads showed Pidgeon kissing Segal, but their names were not mentioned: a good indication of their standing. In the next one he kissed Bernice Claire and it was called *Kiss Me Again* (31) after its most popular song: it was from 'Mlle Modiste' and was called in Britain *Toast of the Legion*: American reference books have it under all three titles, a good indication of its

standing. Indeed, after the first two or three the series was a box-office dud and *The Hot Heiress* (in support of Ona Munson and Ben Lyon) ended Pidgeon's Hollywood career for the time being.

In fact, illness kept him off the screen. During this period he married for the second time. He returned in a supporting part at RKO, in *Rockabye* (32), starring Constance Bennett; was in James Whale's *The Kiss Before the Mirror* (33), as Nancy Carroll's lover; and *Journal of a Crime* (34), starring Ruth Chatterton. Jobs were not plentiful, though Pidgeon was offered musicals; he wanted to establish himself as a serious actor and went to New York to appear on the stage: 'No More Ladies', taking over from Melvyn Douglas, 'Something Gay' (35) with Tallulah Bankhead, 'The Night of January 16th' and 'There's Wisdom in Women'.

He turned down the lead in Universal's *Show Boat* because he did not want to be a singer, but returned to Hollywood, under contract to Wanger: he had a supporting part in *Big Brown Eyes* (36) starring Joan Bennett and co-starred with Mary Ellis in *Fatal Lady*, a confused mixture of backstage drama and murder mystery with Ellis as a prima donna. This film was supposed to make her a star. The film flopped and Wanger dropped Pidgeon. He moved over to Universal: *She's Dangerous* (37) – Tala Birell was; *Girl Overboard* – Gloria Stuart was; *As Good As Married* – John Boles and Doris Nolan were;

and *A Girl With Ideas* – Wendy Barrie was. These were not important parts or pictures and when MGM offered a General Utility contract Pidgeon accepted: to play the hero's friend, the Other Man, etc. He had such parts in *Saratoga*; *My Dear Miss Aldrich* with Edna May Oliver and Maureen O'Sullivan; *Manproof* (38); *The Girl of the Golden West*, as the cold (moustached again) sheriff who loves Jeanette MacDonald until he realizes how much more she loves bandit Nelson Eddy; *The Shopworn Angel*, losing Margaret Sullavan to James Stewart; and *Too Hot to Handle*, Gable's rival in love (Myrna Loy) and business (newsreels). In *Listen Darling* he was the handsome stranger Judy Garland contrives to get married to mother Mary Astor. He was upped to star billing in four programmers: *Society Lawyer* (39), a remake of *Penthouse*, with Virginia Bruce; *6,000 Enemies*, as a DA, with Rita Johnson; *Stronger Than Desire*, a domestic drama with Bruce; and *Nick Carter Master Detective* with Johnson. Around this time ads were issued for Hedy Lamarr's *I Take This Woman* with Pidgeon leading the supporting cast; but he was not in the film as finally released.

He was loaned to Universal for a similar part to the one in *Listen Darling* – in *It's a Date* (40) he was involved with Deanna Durbin's mother, Kay Francis: at last he was carving a niche as a nice, pipe-smoking, mature, leading man. He was so easy, so comfortable, so solid (in the best sense) that his way to real stardom was finally going to be short and simple. He was in demand: Republic borrowed him for *Dark Command* with John Wayne and United Artists for *The House Across the Bay*. MGM put him into two Bs, *Phantom Raiders*, another Nick Carter mystery, and *Sky Murder*, and then into one of those films with which Hollywood prepared for war, *Flight Command* with Robert Taylor. 20th borrowed him for his first lead in years in an A product, *Man Hunt* (41), in which the Nazis are out to get him for once trying to assassinate Hitler: one of Fritz Lang's weakest films. His own studio co-starred him with Greer Garson, in her first flush of success, in *Blossoms in the Dust* and there was a strong positive reaction; he had been so convincing as an Englishman in *Man Hunt* that 20th asked for him again for *How Green Was My Valley*, as the priest in the Welsh village that was built on the back lot – Richard Llewellyn's 'trouble at the mine' novel, transformed by John Ford's cheering gift for finding the world in an oyster: a highly popular film and an Oscar winner.

He made a comedy with Rosalind Russell, *Design for Scandal*, and then was with Greer Garson in *Mrs Miniver* (42): and no matter what one thinks of the film or the Minivers he was beautifully cast as Mr. The film put him in the front rank of MGM male stars. *White Cargo* and Hedy Lamarr almost yanked him out again, but two with Garson consolidated the position: *Madame Curie* (43), as Mon-

sieur, and *Mrs Parkington* (44), as Mr. *Weekend at the Waldorf* (45) found him in the arms of Ginger Rogers and in *Holiday in Mexico* (46) Jane Powell was the daughter trying to match him with Ilona Massey. *The Secret Heart* with Claudette Colbert and *If Winter Comes* (47) with Deborah Kerr were the sort of films in which women were supposed to like Pidgeon, but *Command Decision* (48), with Gable, was a strong man's film and one of his best performances. Before it, *Julia Misbehaves* was a misguided attempt to lighten his and Greer's image. *The Red Danube* (49) was anti-Commie drivel; *That Forsyte Woman* and *The Miniver Story* (50) were two more English subjects with Garson.

He was a Britisher again in *Soldiers Three* (51), as their C.O., and *Calling Bulldog Drummond*, in the latter as Drummond: business was poor, so it was not the first of a new series. He eased back into Bs again: *The Unknown Man* with Ann Harding and *The Sellout* with Audrey Totter, but MGM were remarkably loyal as they eased him into supporting roles: *Million Dollar Mermaid* (52), as Esther Williams's musician father, and *The Bad and the Beautiful*, as the studio boss. The sentimental *Scandal at Scourie* was an ignominious end to his partnership with Garson. He began to specialize in elderly businessmen or serving officers, hiding a heart of gold behind a testy if understanding exterior: *Dream Wife*; *Executive Suite* (54), as one of its occupants; *Men of the Fighting Lady* (54); *The Last Time I Saw Paris*, as Elizabeth Taylor's father; *Deep in My Heart*, as J.J. Shubert to José Ferrer's Sigmund Romberg; *Hit the Deck* (55), as Jane Powell's admiral father; *Forbidden Planet* (56), as a mad scientist, with Anne Francis; *The Rack*, as Paul Newman's father; and *These Wilder Years* with James Cagney and Barbara Stanwyck, billed below them and indeed below the title. It was the last film of his MGM contract: 19 years ('They were the best,' said Pidgeon later. 'I'd like to have them all back again. Favourite pictures? Any of the ones with Greer Garson').

He returned to Broadway as 'The Happiest Millionaire' (56). In 1959 he did a musical, 'Take Me Along'. He came back to films, top-billed, as Admiral Nelson, a world-famous scientist, making a *Voyage to the Bottom of the Sea* (61), and was top-billed again in Disney's pleasant boy-and-dog picture, *Big Red* (62). His last good part in a good film was as a senator in *Advise and Consent*. He went to Italy to make *I Due Colonelli/The Two Colonels* with Toto and then was not seen on the big screen for five years. Two TV films he had made were shown in British cinemas as features (but not in the US) in 1967: *Deadly*

There was an inevitability about the teaming of urbane Walter Pidgeon and dignified Greer Garson. They made an ideal married couple, devoted and ever-so-understanding, so that when Mrs Miniver sent them into stratospheric popularity MGM found it hard to tear them apart. As their box-office value tumbled, together and separately, MGM tried The Miniver Story, *to little avail. The studio tried again three years later with* Scandal at Scourie *(53), in which they played a high profile Protestant couple (the Church, politics) thought to have base motives when they adopt a Catholic child. Awash with sentiment, whimsy and noble feelings, it stands as one of the last examples of that important sub-genre, MGM-had-no-shame.*

Roulette with Robert Wagner, which got good notices, and *Cosa Nostra An Arch Enemy of the FBI* with Efrem Zimbalist Jr. Also for television he was in *How I Spent My Summer Vacation* (67). He was one of several old-time names (Lillian Gish, Keenan Wynn, Joan Collins, Eleanor Parker) supporting David Jansen in *Warning Shot* and was seen briefly as Ziegfeld in *Funny Girl* (68). He returned to Italy to make *A Qualsiasi Prezzo*, with Klaus Kinsky, and spent the next few years – when he worked at all – in television: *House on Greenapple Road* (70), as the mayor in this small-town murder mystery; *The Mask of Sheba*, a jungle tale, as a doctor; and *The Screaming Woman* (72). He returned to the big screen in *Skyjacked* (72), supporting Charlton Heston, as a US senator; and then did a second disaster tale, playing a scientist, in his native Canada, *The Neptune Factor: an Undersea Odyssey* (73), with Ben Gazzara. That was followed by *Harry in Your Pocket*, with James Coburn, as king of the pickpockets. Television again: 'Live Again Die Again' (74), as the husband Donna Mills finds aged after being frozen; 'The Girl on the Late Late Show'; 'You Lie So Deep My Love' (75); 'Murder on Flight 502'; and 'The Lindbergh Kidnapping Case' (76), as the judge. He was announced for other films, including *Twilight's Last Gleaming*, but in the end only did guest appearances in *Won Ton Ton the Dog Who Saved Hollywood* and Mae West's *Sextette* (78). He died in 1984.

DICK POWELL

Dick Powell was one the roundest all-rounders in the history of Hollywood. He was crooner, film star, director and producer, TV executive. His most successful manifestation seems to have been as TV executive. It is difficult now to fathom wherein lay his appeal as an actor – but in the 30s he was very popular indeed, as the leading man of innumerable Warner Bros. musicals. Cherubically smiling, he chased Ruby Keeler or Priscilla Lane and was serious only when crossed by the producer who was always putting on the show featuring the songs which Powell was always writing. It was all so predictable; and though many WB musicals had admirable things in them, Powell's performances were not any of them. He knew it. He fought for years to escape from the inane parts written for him and finally emerged as a tough guy in the Bogart tradition. But, it must be said, only just.

He was born in 1904 in Mountain View, Arkansas, where he sang in the church choir;

and was educated at Little Rock College. He worked for a telephone company for a while but was more interested in bands – he could play most instruments. He got a job with a band and then toured with several different ones, as instrumentalist and vocalist; he finally became emcee at the Stanley and Enright Theaters in Pittsburgh. Here he was spotted by a WB talent scout, who knew the studio was looking for a man to play the title-role in *The Crooner*. David Manners got the part but WB cast Powell as another crooner, rather wet – and a small part – in *Blessed Event* (32). Powell indicated qualities beyond mere wetness and was signed to a long-term contract. He was loaned to Fox for *Too Busy to Work* with Will Rogers; back at WB he was in *The King's Vacation* (33), starring George Arliss, and then *42nd Street*: he and Ruby Keeler were the young lovers, fighting and making-up backstage, with Powell emerging now and then to front a lavish and improbable musical number (danced to by her). His warbling was not unpleasant, nor was his personality – willing, teasing, amorous; it was neither strong nor individual enough to work against the other elements. It became a staple of Warner musicals and comedies.

He made *Gold Diggers of 1933*; *Footlight Parade*; *College Coach*; *Convention City*; *Wonder Bar* (34) – reputedly the only one of its stars who did not fight during the making; *Twenty Million Sweethearts* ('I'll string along with you,' he sang to Ginger Rogers); *Dames* ('I only have eyes for you,' he sang endlessly to Keeler); and *Happiness Ahead* (in reality a vehicle for newcomer Josephine E. Hutchinson). There were more of same: *Flirtation Walk* with Keeler, *Gold Diggers of 1935* (35) with Gloria Stuart, *Page Miss Glory* with Marion Davies, as a bumptious aviator, *Broadway Gondolier* with Joan Blondell and *Shipmates Forever* with Keeler, the one about the crooner who enters Annapolis because his dad's an admiral (Lewis Stone) – and is unpopular until he proves himself a hero. At 20th, *Thanks a Million* was a comedy about a crooner who runs for governor – with the aid of Fred Allen, Ann Dvorak, Paul Whiteman, etc. The part had been written for Bing Crosby, but Paramount refused to loan him. Warners did not mind loaning Powell – and the film was a big success for him; the title tune also gave him one of several hit records. Meanwhile, he was making the box-office top 10 list: he was seventh in 1935, sixth in 1936 – a fact which may have influenced his casting in *A Midsummer Night's Dream* to boost it. No other explanation seems probable in the light of his performance (as Lysander), though he was currently fighting with WB over his parts. He returned at once to more typical fare: *Colleen* (36) the last of the seven with Keeler; *Hearts Divided*, a period piece with Marion Davies as a southern belle, Betsy Patterson and himself as Jerome Bonaparte; and *Stage Struck*, which also starred Joan Blondell, in life now his wife, but not here his romantic interest. (Her autobiographical novel, 'Center Door Fancy', contains an unflattering portrait of a big movie crooner – pompous, priggish, penny-pinching and humourless.)

After *Gold Diggers of 1937*, he was loaned to 20th again, to woo Madeleine Carroll *On the Avenue* (37); back at WB, who else could have been *The Singing Marine*? He put on a *Varsity Show* with the Lane sisters, stayed at the *Hollywood Hotel* with Frances Langford and Lola Lane (as a temperamental movie queen) and was *The Cowboy From Brooklyn* (38), as a boosted cowboy crooner afraid of cows. And it was he, not Olivia de Havilland, who was *Hard to Get*, a routine comedy about an heiress being tamed by a gas station attendant. But he refused point-blank to do *Garden of the Moon* and was replaced by John Payne, then just starting. *Going Places*, with

Anita Louise did not go anywhere, but a song from it did ('Jeepers Creepers'); then Powell sang for the last time on the screen (he hoped) to Ann Sheridan in *Naughty But Nice* (39).

His contract was up and he had no intention of renewing it. He had loathed playing the same singing ninny and he signed with Paramount on the understanding that that company would give him more meaty roles. His first there was better than anything he had done at his old studio, *Christmas in July* (40), a Preston Sturges comedy about a guy who mistakenly thinks he has won a contest and begins to buy out the shops of New York on tick; but *I Want a Divorce* with Blondell was stark enough. He was *In the Navy* (41) with Abbott and Costello and his *Model Wife* was Blondell, a romantic comedy about a couple working for the same firm, both at Universal, and routine; and back at Paramount he was put to singing again, to Mary Martin in *Star Spangled Rhythm* and in *Happy Go Lucky* (43); and then he did a comedy with her, *True to Life*. But *Riding High* with Dorothy Lamour was the last straw: it was precisely the sort of film Powell did not want to make. He

Hearts Divided *(36) was a lavish historical romance directed by Frank Borzage from a play called 'Glorious Betsy'. Marion Davies was effective in that part, but whoever cast Powell as one of the Bonaparte boys deserved a prize for imagination. Claude Rains was Napoleon.*

The 'new' 'tough' Powell: As Philip Marlowe in Murder My Sweet *(45), directed by Edward Dmytryk from Chandler's 'Farewell My Lovely' – to which title it reverted for British audiences (the book had already served as the basis of one of the Falcon movies).*

left Paramount, did an interim musical at MGM with Lucille Ball, *Meet the People* (44), and jumped at René Clair's offer of the lead in *It Happened Tomorrow* with Linda Darnell, a comedy/fantasy about a reporter who gets tomorrow's paper a day early – until one day it carries his own obituary. The critics liked it, but public reception was so-so.

Powell eventually persuaded RKO to cast him as a tough guy: Chandler's private eye Marlowe. There were two concurrent Marlowes: Bogart in *The Big Sleep* and George Montgomery in *The High Window* (from 'The Brasher Doubloon'). Powell's *Murder My Sweet* (45) was from 'Farewell My Lovely' and it was a new Powell on display, and vastly different from the old one – but his still cheery face was not Marlowe's, if otherwise the film had a good feel of Chandler. Similarly unshaved, hard-bitten and gun-toting, he appeared in *Cornered* and there followed several melodramas poised precariously between first- and second-feature level: *Johnny O'Clock* (47)

with Evelyn Keyes; *To the Ends of the Earth* (48) with Signe Hasso; *Station West* with Jane Greer; *Pitfall* with Jane Wyatt and Lizabeth Scott; and *Rogue's Regiment* with Marta Toren. There was a sentimental piece with Evelyn Keyes, *Mrs Mike* (49), about a Mountie marriage in the frozen North; and then a couple of minor pieces with his now-wife, June Allyson, *The Reformer and the Redhead* (50) and *Right Cross*. In 1951: *The Tall Target*, *Cry Danger* and *You Never Can Tell*. It was clearly time to quit movies.

Few other washed-up actors ever revitalized their careers as astutely as Powell. As far as TV was concerned the time was ripe. In 1952, with David Niven and Charles Boyer, he inaugurated 'Four Star Playhouse' wherein the three of them rotated with a guest star for a TV public mostly starved for big film names. This paved the way for Four Star Television, with numerous series, including 'The Dick Powell Show', a tough-guy drama. Powell became regarded as one of the leaders of TV.

Also in 1952 he went into directing, starting with the modestly budgeted *Split Second*, a tense little melodrama. And he got into a good film, Minnelli's *The Bad and the Beautiful* (52), playing a novelist who goes to Hollywood to be a disillusioned scriptwriter. He appeared in only one more film, *Susan Slept Here* (54), a May–September romantic comedy with Debbie Reynolds; and was 'smug and harassed by turns' ('MFB'). RKO was the studio and there were current rumours that he was taking over there as production chief.

But as director or producer/director he was increasingly in demand – though none of the pictures he directed could be said to have met with a warm critical or public reception: *The Conqueror*, *You Can't Run Away From It*, *The Enemy Below*, *The Hunters*, etc.

He died of cancer in 1963, leaving more than a million dollars.

ELEANOR POWELL

Eleanor Powell came to the screen as 'The World's Greatest Tap Dancer', a citation from the Dancing Masters of America. She was born in Springfield, Massachusetts, in 1912 and got her professional start dancing in Atlantic City clubs during the summer months. When she was 16, Gus Edwards saw her there and signed her for his revue at the Ritz Grill in New York. In New York she took dancing lessons from Jack Donahue and got a small role in 'The Opportunists' at the Casino de Paris (28). The following year she was starred in 'Follow Through'; other Broadway shows included 'Fine and Dandy', 'Hot Cha' and 'George White's Scandals'. When Fox made a film called *George White's Scandals* (35) she had a guest spot. She was not considered film material.

But an MGM producer, Sam Katz, had seen her on Broadway and wanted her for *Broadway Melody of 1936*. According to Roger Edens, who worked on that and other MGM musicals for 20 years, the studio was unenthusiastic, thinking she lacked femininity. Their beauticians were turned loose on her. Edens said: 'Still, she had a certain unusual quality that was very fresh and appealing and she certainly could dance.' According to contemporary publicity she was signed for a small role in the *Broadway Melody*, but after some days filming it was given to Una Merkel and a new, big part was made for her. She was a howling success and MGM signed her to a seven-year contract. After a brief return to Broadway for 'At Home Abroad' (with Beatrice Lillie) Powell

Fred Astaire and Eleanor Powell in Broadway Melody of 1940: 'The World's Greatest Dancers in the World's Greatest Musical Show!' said MGM with accustomed modesty.

settled in at Metro as their dancing equivalent to Jeanette MacDonald. She tapped her way through Cole Porter's *Born to Dance* (36), which had the most grandiose musical finale yet done in Hollywood; through *Broadway Melody of 1938* (37) with Robert Taylor and *Rosalie* with Nelson Eddy, which were equally lavish. She was off the screen for a while, not a good sign, and neither the budget of *Honolulu* (39) nor its leading man, Robert Young, were the best MGM could do; Burns and Allen brightly supported. The studio made a bid to co-star her with Fred Astaire because she 'has never quite reached the heights expected of her' ('Picturegoer'): though at a fee of $150,000 a film. Thus she became his first dancing partner after leaving Ginger Rogers and RKO, in *Broadway Melody of 1940* (40), but unfortunately their styles did not quite jell. *Lady Be Good* (41) found her, despite top-billing, very much in support of Ann Sothern, as her best friend. MGM tried once more, in *Ship Ahoy* (42), which mixed her tapping with Nazi agents and Red Skelton. They were reteamed in *I Dood It* (43), which introduced more spies into what was otherwise a straightforward remake of *Spite Marriage*: the hero may adore a stage star from the stalls, but once they meet she is little more than foil to him. To make matters worse, Powell had only three numbers, one extracted from *Honolulu* and another from *Born to Dance*, which her fans would have noticed if no one else did. She was rehearsing *For Me and My Gal* with Dan Dailey when she learnt that they had been replaced by Judy Garland and Gene Kelly; and was filming *Broadway Melody of 1943* with Kelly when it was scrapped. Some of the numbers turned up in *Thousands Cheer*, in which she did a guest stint: she left Metro, claiming that she wanted to retire – especially now that she had married Glenn Ford.

She decided to make a come-back at UA in *Sensations of 1945* (44) with Dennis O'Keefe, but at the box-office it was not one. In the late 40s she was one of the American stars imported by the London Palladium. She danced. She had a guest spot in an Esther Williams vehicle, *The Duchess of Idaho* (50), and in the late 50s a TV series called 'Faith of Our Children', a religious affair. Her marriage broke up in 1959 and in 1961 she made world headlines by starting a nightclub act: she danced for an hour nightly in Las Vegas and then New York. It was extraordinarily successful, but it did not last long. Powell's trouble was, as Gene Kelly once remarked, that she could only do one thing – tap-dance: and that had gone way out of fashion. The other dances she did in her films – like waltzing with high kicks – look ludicrous when seen today. There was little else – a certain charm. William Whitebait once said of Cyd Charisse that when she was acting, he had to keep reminding himself what a good dancer she was: it was equally true of Powell. She died in 1982.

WILLIAM POWELL

The suave, moustached appearance of Mr William Powell did not work entirely in his favour. Graham Greene wrote in 1936: 'Mr Powell is a little too immaculate, his wit is too well-turned just as his clothes are too well-made, he drinks hard but only at the best bars; he is rather like an advertisement of a man-about-town in "Esquire", he shares some of the irritating day-dream quality of Lord Peter Wimsey.' He was considering Powell's portrait of that sophisticated detective, Nick Charles, pursuer of the 'Thin Man', and he

was right about the clothes, except that in some films Powell seemed to alternate only between silk robe and pyjamas and white tie and tails. When he was not playing Nick it would be someone similar, a soul-brother, perhaps another detective. Or he had a nice line in shady lawyers, a hangover from his early days of screen skulduggery. His skill and charm disguised somewhat the fact that his screen character was basically unpleasant – that his attitude to most people and especially women was a refined superiority: it was a character perfected by Noël Coward in 'Private Lives' (what one would not give to have seen Powell play Elyot!).

Later in his career he was able to branch out somewhat and portray genial and ageing businessmen and somewhat away from type he gave a clever performance in *Life With Father*. By this time he was a matchless light comedian, possibly the most polished of all. It was not unusual for his contemporaries to coast along on personality and mannerisms, letting audiences' familiarity with them do the work. Relaxed though he was, Powell never did. His acting, like his clothes, was impeccable.

He was born in Pittsburgh in 1892, the son of a public accountant. The family moved to Kansas City and Powell was educated at the University there briefly; he withdrew and worked as a clerk in a telephone office, and from there went to New York to study at the AADA for a season. His first stage work was with one-night stands and fit-up companies, but in 1912 he made his New York début in 'The Ne'er Do Well'; the following year he played an important part in 'Within the Law'. He toured two years with that and then in other plays and he worked in stock. He had his first Broadway success, with 'Spanish Love' (20), and that led to a film offer, that of the villain in John Barrymore's *Sherlock Holmes* (22). It was not a big part, but he never looked back. He was cast as François I in Marion Davies's *When Knighthood Was in Flower*; in *Outcast*; in *The Bright Shawl* (23), as a Spanish officer in oppressed old Cuba, duelling with American adventurer Richard Barthlemess – and stealing the film from him; and in doublet and hose again as the Duke of Orleans in *Under the Red Robe*, starring Robert Mantell and Alma Rubens.

His screen villainy began in earnest in *Romola* (24) as a conniving Italian count, when he wronged both Gish sisters; then he was nasty to Bebe Daniels in *Dangerous Money* at Paramount. Richard Dix at that studio asked for him for *Too Many Kisses* (25), as the Police Chief who ran a gang of bandits on the side, and because of his work in that, Paramount gave him a contract. There followed *Faint Perfume*; *My Lady's Lips*; *The Beautiful City*, on loan to Inspiration; *White Mice* (26), out on loan and sympathetic for once; *Sea Horses* – he was the blackguard who deserts Florence Vidor to go beachcombing; *Desert Gold*, a Western; *The Runaway* and *Aloma of the South Seas*, in both of which he tried to do the dirty on Warner Baxter. He was memorable as the cringing Italian thief in Ronald Colman's *Beau Geste*, after which he did *Tin Gods*, a triangle drama with Thomas Meighan and Aileen Pringle. He was wicked again in a small role in *The Great Gatsby* and had a good run as the baddie: *New York* (27); *Love's Greatest Mistake* – he blackmailed Evelyn Brent; *Special Delivery* with Eddie Cantor; *Senorita*; *Time to Love* starring Raymond Griffith; *Paid to Love*, as a prince, trying to wrest Virginia Valli from Crown Prince George O'Brien; *Nevada*, as a trusted hand unmasked as the rustlers' leader by Gary Cooper; and two in the desert, *She's a Sheik* – Bebe Daniels was, and he was an Arab brigand, and *Beau Sabreur* (28) – who was Cooper, and he was a treacherous rebel legionnaire.

Whether bent on rape or mere mayhem, he was often more enjoyable than the leads, a fact recognized by Paramount when they gave him a substantial role – though still pretty nasty – as the film director in von Sternberg's *The Last Command*, after which he was Bebe's *bête noire* again in *Feel My Pulse*, a bootlegger. He supported in *Partners in Crime*, one of the Beery-Hatton comedies, and was directed by the 'von' again in *The Drag Net*, playing a slimy czar of crime. For a change, he was a loyal pal, Clive Brook's, in *Forgotten Faces*, but after *The Vanishing Pioneer* Brook had good cause to resent him in *Interference*, a subtly degenerate performance in Paramount's first all-Talkie. Paramount were pleased with how well Powell's voice recorded: in the shuffle brought about by Sound, they decided to try him in something else and cast him as A.A. Dine's sleuth Philo Vance in *The Canary Murder Case* (29). The next was Silent, with sound effects only, *The Four Feathers*, from A.E.W. Mason's rousing adventure story set in British Africa during the war. Brook and Richard Arlen starred and Powell was again on the side of the law. He was the Other Man with Brook and Ruth Chatterton in *Charming Sinners*, demonstrating his ability to play high comedy. Then he was Philo Vance again in *The Greene Murder Case*.

Particularly in the Vance films his stock had risen: he was a surprise asset to his studio, who now put him in his first 'official' star vehicle, *Pointed Heels*, as a theatrical producer, with Fay Wray. He supported Hal

Skelly in *Behind the Make-Up* (30), as the unscrupulous vaudeville performer who steals his act. Kay Francis had a small role and Paramount began to see them as a team, starting with *Street of Chance*. She was his wife, he was a stockbroker by day and a gambler by night – saving his brother from the same fate. Then he made his last two appearances at Paramount as Vance: *The Benson Murder Case* and a sketch in *Paramount on Parade*. After *Shadow of the Law* he was with Francis again, in *For the Defence*, as a hard-drinking attorney who goes to gaol for love of her. Said 'Picturegoer': 'What an amazingly good actor Powell is! His silent screen villains were clever studies in a serio-comic vein, but his talkie appearances are even better.' Then he did two films with Carole Lombard, who became his wife: *Man of the World* (31), in which he was a blackmailer, and *Ladies' Man*, in which he was a gigolo.

Francis was also in the latter and she and Powell (and Chatterton) were involved in the deal whereby it was considered that WB filched the three of them from Paramount. Powell, however, felt that he had too many set parts and was delighted when Warners gave him story approval. That company regarded him as one of their top three male stars (Arless and Barthelmess were the others, with Edward G. Robinson just behind) – not that they did much with him: *The Road to Singapore* with Doris Kenyon; *High Pressure* (32) with Evelyn Brent in which he was a get-rich-quick promoter; and a couple romancing Francis, in both of which he was the most suave and elegant of crooks, the fake-Lubitsch *Jewel Robbery* (she was a society wife) and a magnificent weepie, *One-Way Passage* – the latter by far his most successful Warner film. He was an East Side *Lawyer Man* with Joan Blondell; in *Double Harness* (33), with Ann Harding, a drawing-room comedy at RKO; *Private Detective 62*; and Vance again in *The Kennel Murder Case*. There followed *Fashions of 1934* (34) with Bette Davis and *The Key*, a triangle drama with Edna Best and Colin Clive set against the Irish troubles.

Powell, with Chatterton, was now the highest salaried actor on the lot (it had been $6,000 weekly, but was cut to $4,000 during the Depression economy drive) and WB decided he was not worth it. It was announced that he was leaving because he wanted to freelance, but later it was tacitly agreed that his salary demands were too high. After a short spell Columbia signed him to a four-picture deal and Universal announced that he would play Florenz Ziegfeld for them in a film they were preparing. At Selznick's urging he did a picture at MGM, *Manhattan Melo-*

Libelled Lady *(36)*. *'Bill Powell, Myrna Loy, Spencer Tracy and Jean Harlow topping their own previous vivid performances in a highly original farce built around Bill's efforts to compromise Myrna who has sued Spencer's paper for libel. A wow.'* – *'Photoplay'*.

drama, teamed with Myrna Loy, and its director, W.S. Van Dyke, liked them together enough to try them again in the low-budgeted *The Thin Man*, from Dashiell Hammett's detective story; as a result Powell became a bigger star than ever: MGM secured his release from the Columbia deal and took over the Ziegfeld project.

The Thin Man was a roaring copper-bottomed success all round: MGM teamed Loy and Powell again in *Evelyn Prentice* and the two of them became the studio's stock pairing, an adult, worldly, brittle couple, clearly in love, but wise to the other's – manifold – failings. Of the films Powell made at MGM over the next half dozen years only a couple of them were not originally intended for them as a team – although circumstances in the end saw to it that they were not over-exposed. And although Powell was regarded at once by MGM as a major asset, he at first negotiated for two or three films at a time. However, until he left Metro 13 years later in 1947, he only made four films for other studios. The first of these was the vastly entertaining *Star of Midnight* (35) at RKO, in his stock role of sophisticated detective, with Ginger Rogers. Back at MGM he was in *Reckless*, which co-starred his fiancée, Jean

Harlow, as the old standby who gets her in the last reel.

He was in *Escapade* and *Rendezvous*, both intended for Loy, but played by Luise Rainer and Rosalind Russell respectively. Loy did play Mrs Ziegfeld No. 2 in *The Great Ziegfeld* (36), though the project as envisaged by Universal had had the lady as herself (Billie Burke). *Ziegfeld* was a lucky acquisition for the studio, justifying its length and lavishness at the box-office; it won that year's Best Picture Oscar and was a big hit especially in Britain (N.B. Powell never quite made the US top 10 stars list, but he was ranked in Britain in 1937 and 1938), and acquired a legendary status among MGM product. He played Ziegfeld in his familiar urbane manner, mocking slightly his own vanity: and with imperiousness added to his asperity. He went to other studios to play with two more delightful comediennes: Jean Arthur in *The Ex-Mrs Bradford* and Lombard (now the ex-Mrs Powell) in *My Man Godfrey*, in the title-role and perfect as the perfect butler. He did another outstanding comedy, *Libelled Lady* with Loy, Harlow and Spencer Tracy ('just about as perfect a comedy foursome as you will encounter anywhere' – Frank S. Nugent in 'The New York Times'); and *After the Thin*

Life With Father *(47) had
been a Broadway hit and
both in Britain and the US
the movie version was one
of the year's top five
money-makers. Powell was
Father, Irene Dunne was
Mother, and most of the
fun centred on her efforts
to get him baptized.*

Man which delighted fans by being only a half-strike less than the original one. This completed 1936, making it Powell's *annus mirabilis*.

The following year could only be less happy and it was: the remake of *The Last of Mrs Cheyney* (37) with Joan Crawford and *The Emperor's Candlesticks*, with him and Rainer as spies on opposing sides (Russian, Austrian) pursued over half of Europe just prior to World War I. However, *Double Wedding*, a farce with Loy, enhanced, and was enhanced by them, though mismatched this time, he as a Bohemian artist and she as a starchy dress designer with a sense of her own importance but no humour. It was now that Powell and MGM came to terms: a seven-year contract *without options* at $155,000 a film. Ill-health intervened. At 20th (unwillingly on loan-out) he and Annabella were *The Baroness and the Butler* (38); he was too ill to play with Garbo in *Ninotchka* and in the light of his decreased activity, MGM sagely cast him with Loy: *Another Thin Man* (39), *I Love You Again* (40), *Love Crazy* (41) and *Shadow of the Thin Man* (which title avoids the ambiguity of the two earlier sequels – the 'Thin Man' himself having been killed off in the original film). Hedy Lamarr was his wife in both *Crossroads* (42), a remake of *Carrefour* in which he was

an upright industrialist exposed to blackmail, and a dull comedy, *The Heavenly Body* (44), after which he reprised Nick Charles in *The Thin Man Goes Home* and Ziegfeld in the prologue to the *Ziegfeld Follies* (46).

The title-role in *The Hoodlum Saint*, with Esther Williams, was not his finest hour at Metro, but he did beautifully as the irascible father in *Life With Father* (47), loaned to Warners for $200,000 and Errol Flynn for their version of one of the longest-running plays in Broadway history, based on Clarence Day's memoirs: this was, said Howard Barnes, 'the greatest performance of a distinguished career' and while audiences were enjoying Powell, MGM rushed to them the last and least of the famous series, *Song of the Thin Man*. The New York critics voted Powell the year's Best Actor, citing also his performance as an irretrievably stupid senator in *The Senator Was Indiscreet*. Like *Mr Peabody and the Mermaid* (48), a less successful satire, it was produced independently and released by Universal; for that company itself Powell found himself suspected of murder in *Take One False Step* (49). He was better served at 20th in *Dancing in the Dark*, as a Hollywood has-been who discovers Betsy Drake in Technicolor, but none of these films found audiences stampeding.

When he returned to films he was white-haired, settling – with the good humour expected – for character roles, in MGM's all-star episode film, *It's a Big Country* (51), as a professor, and a Universal version of a story by Robert Louis Stevenson, *Treasure of Lost Canyon* (52), as an old prospector. He had one film to go under his MGM contract and it was to finish with another loan-out to 20th; but he changed his mind and remained at MGM for a remake of *A Free Soul* called *The Girl Who Had Everything* (53) – Elizabeth Taylor did, including him as her father. In his last two films he had featured roles, but the second restored him to star-billing: *How to Marry a Millionaire*, as one of the millionaires who gets away, and *Mister Roberts* (55), as Doc, his genial and cynical presence an asset – as ever – above the other popular ingredients. He retired to Palm Springs with his third wife, Diana Lewis, a former MGM starlet – a retirement so complete that he refused to see the press. Miss Loy once said: 'Bill's doing fine. He's over eighty now, and he's getting rather deaf, but other than that, he's in wonderful shape . . . he's always been very happy with his wife, so more power to him.' (The marriage, in 1940, had not been expected to last because the bride was twenty-seven years younger than he.) He died in 1983.

TYRONE POWER

Darryl F. Zanuck once told 'Variety': '. . . I think perhaps the greatest contribution I have made to this industry was the discovery of genuine talent. To have been involved in giving the world personalities like Betty Grable, Gene Tierney, Alice Faye, Linda Darnell, Tyrone Power, Marilyn Monroe and Gregory Peck has given me perhaps my deepest satisfaction.' In fact, as a discoverer of talent, 20th had a lower average than any other major studio and right back to the Fox days it was a notorious launcher of non-talent. Mr Zanuck is not strictly correct, either, in roping in Peck or Monroe, but the company can certainly claim Tyrone Power as its own.

Whether Power was a 'genuine talent' is debatable. As a young man he was so scrumptious-looking that it hardly seemed to matter, but as he grew older he was simply rather vacant. He was always likeable and certainly as a young man projected a quality of 'natural modesty' in the same way that James Stewart and Franchot Tone did. He wanted to be a better actor than he was and would perhaps like to be remembered most for his stage work, which he did to get out of the rut. He did not care much for most of his films; when his 20th contract expired he said, 'I've done an awful lot of stuff that's a monument to public patience.'

He came from a theatrical family; his father was a matinée idol who had acted with Irving and Tree. The junior Power was born in Cincinatti in 1913 and was always intended to follow in Father's footsteps; in his teens he was put with a Shakespearian company in Chicago and made his début in 'The Merchant of Venice' (31); and he did some radio work with Don Ameche. He accompanied his father to Hollywood later that year; Father died (while filming) but Power stayed on and got small roles in *Tom Brown of Culver* (32) and *Flirtation Walk* (34). Discouraged, he tried Broadway and after a small role in 'Romance' was engaged by Guthrie McClintic to understudy Burgess Meredith in 'The Flowers of the Forest', which starred Katharine Cornell. He stayed with the Cornell company and was playing a small role with them, in 'St Joan', when a 20th talent scout saw him and offered a test for a part in *Sing Baby Sing*. He did not get it, but 20th took him under contract and gave him small parts in *Girls' Dormitory* (36) as Simone Simon's cousin and *Ladies in Love* as Loretta Young's romantic interest.

He had a stronger part in *Lloyds of London*, a period piece, and it made him famous. The studio met the demand by rushing him into four films in 1937, three of them with Loretta Young: *Love Is News*; *Café Metropole*, as a playboy posing as a Russian prince; *Thin Ice*, opposite Sonja Henie, as a European prince travelling incognito and giving a good semblance of a playboy; and *Second Honeymoon*. His 1938 films were more sturdy fare. The first two were directed by Henry King, who was responsible for more than a dozen of his films. In *Old Chicago* he was one of Mrs O'Leary's boys, a politician corrupt till the fire when her cow started; and in *Alexander's Ragtime Band* he was *the* Alexander, competing with Ameche for Alice Faye. In life, in 1939, Ameche was best man when he married Annabella, the first of his three wives, who later observed of the revelations of homosexuality in several biographies that Power was no more capable of same than she of singing in grand opera.

He went to MGM (in exchange for Spencer Tracy – curiously, the role Tracy finally did for 20th had first been planned for Power – Stanley in *Stanley and Livingstone*) to play Count Fersen in *Marie Antoinette*, but in that overloaded spectacle got swamped: so much so that 20th refused to loan him out again (thus he later lost *King's Row*). His next was

In Old Chicago (38): Alice Faye was a dancehall singer, and Tyrone Power and Don Ameche were both contenders for her favours. Power, as usual, got her in the end (Ameche was conveniently killed). The film's climax was a spectacular re-creation of the great Chicago fire.

20th's own bid in the historical stakes, *Suez* with Annabella, a $2 million effort concerned over-muchly with the love affair between de Lesseps (Power) and the Empress Eugenie (Young), a fiction which hardly endeared the film to critics.

The first two of this quartet were big box-office and Power was 10th among the stars. In 1939 he had overtaken Gable and Tracy and was runner-up only to Mickey Rooney. He was also voted King of Hollywood (Jeanette MacDonald was Queen); and most of his next films were huge grossers, especially *Jesse James* (39), a Technicolor Western with the facts distorted to make him (Power) sympathetic; and *The Rains Came*, from Louis Bromfield's novel about India. There was a lot of spectacle when the rains finally came and Power was a smiling but improbable Indian prince. Between the two he was merely leading man: to Faye in *Rose of Washington Square* – a gambler/gangster, but decent withal – and, as a press agent, to Henie in *Second Fiddle*. In any case, beyond the rigging of the script, Power was never able to simulate any sort of villainy: he merely looked perplexed. Lloyd Nolan gave a strong performance as a pretty racketeer in Henry Hathaway's *Johnny Apollo* (40), one of the first 'black' 40s films, but Power, said C.A. Lejeune, 'fre-

quently unlikely on the screen, seems less likely than ever as a "varsity man who puts his soul in hock" to get his father out of prison'. The one before this, *Day-Time Wife* (39), and the one after, *Brigham Young, Frontiersman* (Dean Jagger had the title-role), gave him few opportunities, but Power did some of his best work in Mamoulian's remake of *The Mark of Zorro* – fop by day and bandit by night – even if his bravado was not in the Fairbanks class. At the end of the year he was still up there in the ratings.

He was in another Mamoulian remake, *Blood and Sand* (41), as a bullfighter (the rise and fall of). It was a part he was ideal for, provided that you accepted him as a Spaniard: he gave of his best and the film was a success, aided in no little way by its elegant use of colour. He wanted to return to the stage, but the studio would only spare him for a few weeks in stock (in 'Liliom' with his wife) – nor were they anxious to have him fail on Broadway. He returned to the same old parts in the same old (very different) films: *A Yank in the RAF*, and a popular one, with Betty Grable; *Son of Fury* (42), a Southseaser, as a wronged British aristocrat; *This Above All*, another wartime romance, from Eric Knight's novel, again as a Britisher, a left-wing anti-war one, till wealthy WAAF Joan Fontaine reforms him; *The Black Swan*, from Rafael Sabatini's novel, embodying all the clichés of the pirate film, and quite beautifully; and *Crash Dive* (43), a war film. Then 20th had to spare him for somewhat longer as he joined the US Marines for the duration of the war.

His come-back was the much-touted version of Maugham's *The Razor's Edge* (46): Cukor refused to direct because he did not like the script and it was, inevitably, not a very good film. Power was as much like a very nice bank clerk as ever (though he smiled less), but as an effective return it was blunted because his part was impossible. Still, the public turned up in large numbers to see him or the film or both. They stayed away, however, from *Nightmare Alley* (47), received indifferently for being an emasculation of the original novel. Power got the best notices of his career; he had begged to play the part, that of a braggart who climbs to the top of the carny business only to end up alcoholic and an exhibit in the freak house. The studio, worried that his star was on the wane, put him into an expensive swashbuckler, *Captain From Castile*, and that, dull as it was, did good business. Then they hurried him into two comedies, *The Luck of the Irish* (48) with Anne Baxter and *That Wonderful Urge* (a remake of *Love Is News*) with Gene Tierney, but neither did much to reassure the company that he still had a following. Two more costume films followed: *Prince of Foxes* (49) – in black and white, a sure sign of faltering confidence – about the Borgias, and the more lavish *The Black Rose* (50), a medieval drama from a novel by Thomas B. Costain. Both

were tiresome and the latter was not improved by dialogue like 'Tris! You can't die on me!'

It was made in Britain and Power stayed in London to play the lead in 'Mister Roberts'; he remained up to his neck in war, as *An American Guerilla in the Philippines* (Fritz Lang made it because, he said, a director has to eat). A Western followed, *Rawhide* (51), with Susan Hayward, and then a romantic drama, *I'll Never Forget You*, with Ann Blyth, a remake of *Berkeley Square*. 'Variety' found Power's performance in the latter 'monotonous' and all these films were indifferently received; Power found, for the first time since 1938, that the top roles at 20th were going to another actor, Gregory Peck. He signed a new non-exclusive pact with the studio, however, for two films a year, to begin with *The Robe*. It was postponed and Power was promptly suspended for refusing *Lydia Bailey*. They made it up and he took the title-role in both *Diplomatic Courier* (52), set against the Cold War, and *Pony Soldier*, set amongst the Mounties: both were medium-budget action films and only in such material did 20th think the career of their bland actor could be prolonged. He himself agreed to a similar venture at Universal, *The Mississippi Gambler* (53), working on a participation basis – and although the film was a limited success he was reckoned to have made $1 million. He returned to 20th for more of same: *King of the Khyber Rifles* (54), a remake of Ford's *The Black Watch*. He planned his own production of *Lorenzo the Magnificent*, but there was script trouble (for the rest of the decade Power hoped to do it, among several indepen-

The Razor's Edge *(46), directed by Edmund Goulding: Gene Tierney was Isabel and Tyrone Power was Larry in this box-office version of Somerset Maugham's last major novel.*

dent projects of his own). Instead, at 20th, he did *Untamed* (55), a 'Western' with Hayward set in South Africa. For Ford himself he did *The Long Grey Line*, described by the 'Spectator' critic as 'the longest and greyest film' she had ever seen. At Columbia he did *The Eddie Duchin Story* (56), a rather pleasant biopic about a pianist and one of the year's top 10 money-takers.

In 1953 he had joined Charles Laughton in a Broadway reading of 'John Brown's Body'; once free of contracts, Power again turned his thoughts to the stage. In London he did 'The Devil's Disciple' (56), but as in his earlier appearance there, was only partially successful; he was much better in a TV 'Miss Julie' with Mai Zetterling, suggesting, virtually for the first time, reserves of talent. In Britain he produced *Seven Waves Away* (57) with Zetterling, a relentlessly grim drama of survivors in a lifeboat; then returned to 20th for the dim film version of Hemingway's *The Sun Also Rises* (58). Billy Wilder cast him as the suspect in *Witness for the Prosecution*, from a play by Agatha Christie, and it seemed he might again push his way to the forefront of Hollywood actors. He then toured the US with Faye Emerson in an abridged version of 'Back to Methuselah'. Towards the end of 1958 he went to Madrid for *Solomon and Sheba* and died there, of a heart attack, after filming a fight with George Sanders. King Vidor, who directed, said that Power and he himself felt that it was his best part and his best film. He felt that with Power it would have been 'a simply marvellous picture', but without him it turned out to be 'an unimportant, nothing sort of picture'.

GEORGE RAFT

George Raft was at his most appealing in his early days, be-gloved and be-spatted, a fedora pulled down over his eyes. He was sleek and tough and menaceful (especially when flipping that coin in *Scarface*) – and suitably punished: he reckoned that he met a violent death in over 80 of his films (i.e. a good 75 per cent of them). Not coincidentally he knew the background of the shady and sinister character he usually played on the screen.

He was born in New York City in 1903 and brought up in that area known as Hell's Kitchen. By his own confession (his memoirs in the 'Saturday Evening Post', 1957) he was a layabout, though he did some boxing, graduating from gymnasium to the prize-ring. It was said that he lost only seven of his 22 bouts. He also danced, and earned a living at

one time as a dance-hall gigolo – again, moving upwards to clubs in London and New York, and thence to the Broadway stage, where he partnered Elsie Pilcer. He danced in such shows as 'The City Chap', 'Gay Paree', 'Palm Beach Nights' and 'No Foolin'; but at the same time his cronies were not always on the right side of the law. One was racketeer Owney Maddon who, according to Raft, supported him until he made it big in the movies: 'If I had any ambition it was to be a big shot in my pal Owney Maddon's liquor mob' and 'I had a gun in my pocket and I was cocky because I was working for the gang boss of New York.' It was Maddon who sent him as one of the protection crew to Texas Guinan's nightclub and it was Miss Guinan who suggested that he take a small role in her movie, *Queen of the Night Clubs* (29). This took him to LA and according to his own report he was sitting in the Brown Derby when director Rowland Brown saw him and told him to report for another bit part in *Quick Millions* (31). He said that he was nervous, though as merely one of the gang the part should not have been difficult. He had similar parts at other studios: *Hush Money*, *Palmy Days*, *Taxi* (32) as a ball-room contestant, *Scarface*, *Dancers in the Dark* (very nasty as a murderer), *Night World* and *Love is a Racket*. *Scarface* was the biggest and best of these parts and it brought the offer of contracts.

He signed with Paramount who put him in support of *Madame Racketeer* Alison Skipworth; then they starred him in the film which defined his image, *Night After Night*, as the snappily suited nightclub boss, tough but softhearted, knowing his place but wanting class – in the person of Constance Cummings; then he had the weakest episode in *If I Had a Million*. He crossed to the other side of the law to be *The Undercover Man* (33) with Nancy Carroll. Gee, but he was tough, even if he did not rival Cagney or Robinson in public favour. He was tough with Paramount, too, and was suspended for refusing *The Story of Temple Drake*. He was taken back for *Pick-Up* with Sylvia Sidney, as an ex-gaol bird: he was a taxi-driver and they shacked up together till melodrama intervened. He was a detective out to get Clive Brook in *Midnight Club*; Wallace Beery's rival in *The Bowery* at the newly formed 20th-UA; and an ex-con out to destroy Miriam Hopkins's love for Fredric March in *All of Me* (34). Paramount kept insisting that he was a second Valentino, but the public refused to accept him except as a gangster or something similar; however, he was successful as a hoofer stomping his way to the top in *Bolero* with Carole Lombard. It was popular enough for a follow-up a year later –

Rumba (35) – after Raft had been a bullfighter in *The Trumpet Blows* and slit-eyed in *Limehouse Blues* with (of course) Anna May Wong.

Stolen Harmony (35) was a gangster-angled musical with Grace Bradley; and *The Glass Key* with Claire Dodd, a version of Dashiell Hammett's novel, and a weak one. He did a musical with Alice Faye, *Every Night at Eight*, which was about a radio programme – and the film, alas, looked like one. Columbia borrowed him for *She Couldn't Take It* – Joan Bennett couldn't – and 20th for *It Had to Happen* (36) – to Rosalind Russell. Back on his home lot he walked out of a reunion with Lombard because he disliked her choice of cameraman and was replaced by Fred Mac-Murray (*The Princess Comes Across*). Around this time he said, 'I'm not a good enough actor to trust myself to any but the best director, best cameraman, best story.' Paramount to appease him raised his salary to $4,000 a week – even though his box-office was shaky. 'Photoplay' reported that in Texas 'they just don't bother to put Raft's name on the marquee'. His only other film that year was *Yours for the Asking* with Dolores Costello.

Next he objected to his role in *Souls at Sea* (37) with Gary Cooper and went on suspension until it was more sympathetically written. His salary was raised by another $200. He and Sylvia Sidney were ex-cons in Fritz Lang's *You and Me* (38); after which he did an adventure yarn, *Spawn of the North* with Henry Fonda and Dorothy Lamour. Then Paramount and he rowed again when he

refused *St Louis Blues*: Lloyd Nolan replaced him and Paramount were glad to see him go after playing a gambler in *The Lady's From Kentucky* (39) – Ellen Drew.

Warners made a bid for his services: tough-guy films had been a staple of that studio for almost a decade and they were anxious to add him to their stable of such actors – none of whom were docile, though they might become more amenable with another rival on the home lot. They put him with Cagney in a prison melodrama, *Each Dawn I Die*, and with Bogart in *Invisible Stripes* (40); in between which he committed crime at Universal, *I Stole a Million* (39), as a cab-driver, with Claire Trevor. At Wanger-UA he was a con, furious when wife Joan Bennett falls for nice Walter Pidgeon, in *The House Across the Bay* (40). Then he was expected to do either or both *The World We Make* and a remake of *A Free Soul* at MGM with Norma Shearer (with whom he was frequently seen socially), but nothing came of either project. His first walk-out at Warners was over *South of Suez* and George Brent did it; but he was seen, to advantage, in *They Drive By Night* with Bogart. There was dissension between him and Edward G. Robinson on the set of *Manpower* (41), but Agate said 'their performances have that kind of compulsion which makes you think you're seeing them for the first time'. Warners were much less happy. Raft went to Universal again for *Broadway* (42), supposedly playing himself in this 20s gangster piece, but in fact in the part taken by Glenn Tyron in the 1929 version. He then turned down *Casablanca*. Back in 1937 he had

Raoul Walsh's They Drive by Night *(40): Humphrey Bogart and George Raft were truck-driving brothers, and Ann Sheridan was the girl they pick up at a roadside hash-house.*

turned down *Dead End* and at WB he had already refused both *The Maltese Falcon* and (because he did not want to die at the end) *High Sierra*: all four pictures became mighty important ones for Bogart and now that Bogart was a top draw WB had really no need of Raft. (Raft also turned down the Garfield role in *The Sea Wolf.*) After the totally undistinguished *Background to Danger* (43), one of the studio's many *Casablanca* imitations, his contract was annulled. According to Jack Warner's memoirs the company were prepared to pay him $10,000 in settlement, but due to a misunderstanding on Raft's part he paid that to them: he was equally anxious to be free.

However, having cast himself adrift, Raft found things difficult. After a guest spot in *Stage Door Canteen* he was in another such, *Follow the Boys* (44), though in the story surrounding the revue acts, teamed with the equally somnolent Vera Zorina. He went to 20th to play a Frisco saloon-keeper in *Nob Hill* (45), with Joan Bennett and Vivian Blaine, and then went from one minor melodrama to another, mostly at UA or RKO: *Johnny Angel*, *Whistle Stop* (46), *Mr Ace* and *Nocturne*. Said Richard Winnington: 'Detective George Raft's approach to recalcitrant citizens, innocent or guilty, is to wreck their rooms, throw hot coffee in their faces, or just plain beat them up, always without a flicker of expression or removing his hat.' After the sentimental *Christmas Eve* (47) with Ann Harding, he held on via lower-case melodra-

mas: *Intrigue* (48), with June Havoc, set in Shanghai; *Race Street*, with William Bendix, set on the turf; *Outpost in Morocco* (49), with Marie Windsor, as a legionnaire; *Johnny Allegro*, with Nina Foch, as an undercover agent; *Red Light*, with Virginia Mayo, once again in gaol; and *A Dangerous Profession*, with Ella Raines and Pat O'Brien, an underworld tale. Each of them reduced his boxoffice and at this time it was consequently at zero; so he went to France for *Nous Irons à Paris*, with Ray Ventura. The next offer was from Britain, though filmed in Italy: *I'll Get You For This* (51), as a gambler who turns detective when framed for a murder he did not commit. In the US, *Loan Shark* (52) was a B for an independent and he was a con; *Escape Route* was a B in Britain with Sally Gray and he was an FBI man. The US-Italian *The Man from Cairo/Avventura ad Algeri* (53) marked another low. An American TV series brought a revival of interest: *Black Widow* (54) with Ginger Rogers, as a detective; *Rogue Cop*, with Robert Taylor in the titlerole, in the pay of crime boss Raft; and *A Bullet for Joey* (55), pitted again against Edward G. Robinson, who is investigating a spy ring involving gangster Raft.

After being one of the many names in *Around the World in 80 Days* (56) he hit a bad patch in Britain: there to make a B, *Morning Call*, he did not like the script and the Government refused a work permit for him to do instead *Women of the Night*. He told a reporter (Logan Gourlay in the 'Sunday

Express'): 'This is a cruel business if you're sensitive. And Hollywood's a cruel place. The moment you start slipping nobody wants to know you.' But Billy Wilder did want to know and Raft did a guest stint in *Some Like It Hot* (59), as a gang boss. The *Jet Over the Atlantic* had, as well as Guy Madison and Miss Mayo, a bomb aboard; and Raft's own career continued to bomb: *Ocean's 11* (60), in a cameo role; Jerry Lewis's *The Ladies' Man* (61), guesting; the British *Two Guys Abroad*, which has never been publicly shown; *For Those Who Think Young* (64) with James Darren, and Lewis's *The Patsy*, again in bit roles described euphemistically as 'guesting'. When the US Government came after him for back taxes, he managed to get a co-starring role with Jean Gabin in *Du Rififi à Paname* (65). In Britain he did guest appearances in the disastrous *Casino Royale* (67), with several actors playing James Bond and as many directors, and in a B starring Robert Cummings, *Five Golden Dragons*; and he worked in that country as host of a gambling club, but was refused re-entry after a trip to the US by British immigration authorities because of alleged 'associations'. And his bad luck held firm: Preminger's *Skidoo* failed miserably with press and public; *Hammersmith Was Out* (72) was so bad that all copies were reputedly bought up by one of its stars, Richard Burton; *Deadhead Miles* was put on the shelf for 10 years, receiving some isolated showings in 1982; and Mae West's *Sextette* (78) went equally unseen. There were few bookings for a spoof, ironically titled *The Man With Bogart's Face* (80). Raft's part in these ventures had been minimal and he could not be blamed for *The George Raft Story* – made in 1961 with Ray Danton playing him – which must be one of the worst-ever biopics. It was as though the gods were paying him back for having had one decade of success on a minute talent. He died penniless in 1980.

LUISE RAINER

Once, to his intense shame and annoyance Raymond Chandler found himself keyed up at the prospect of winning an Oscar. His wife tried to persuade him that the whole thing was merely a lark: 'After all,' she reminded him, 'Luise Rainer won it twice.' She might have added that the second of Rainer's Oscars was won over Garbo's performance in *Camille*. . . . But then, Hollywood at that time considered Rainer to be of the same stature as Garbo. She arrived in the movie capital in 1935, picked up her two awards in consecutive years, 1936 and 1937, and swiftly departed.

By that time her potential was probably exhausted. She was not without charm or ability, but most of the parts she played required her to be fey, kittenish and long-suffering – a deadly combination, as other middle-European actresses have proved (notably Maria Schell, again briefly, in the 1950s). Failing further evidence, one must assume that MGM did not underestimate Rainer's range (Myrna Loy, looking back on that time, has observed that Louis B. Mayer, for all his faults, really did know what was best for his stars).

She was born in Vienna in 1912 and made her stage début, after auditioning in Düsseldorf, when she was 16. She trained with Max Reinhardt and acted in Vienna, Paris and London in, among other plays, 'An American Tragedy', 'Measure for Measure' and 'Six Characters in Search of an Author'; she also had two film engagements, in *Sehnsucht 202* (32), with Magda Schneider, and *Heut' Kommt's Drauf an* (33), a musical with Hans Albers about a jazz contest. An MGM talent scout sought her out because he had heard she might be a successor to Garbo. In Hollywood, the studio kept her under wraps, not quite knowing what to do with her. Then she replaced Myrna Loy in *Escapade* (35) with Willian Powell: it was a remake of the Austrian *Maskerade* and thus seemed a suitable début vehicle for Rainer, in the Paula Wessely part. Both film and Rainer's performance were carbon copies of the original and were generally considered inferior.

But it was apparent to the studio after a few days' rushes that Rainer gave off a glow to the camera, that she had that quality of which great stars are made; she was cast with Powell again in *The Great Ziegfeld* (36), as the first Mrs Z., Anna Held, a (temperamental) star who loved her impresario husband very much, but would not countenance his infidelities. The 'telephone scene' at the end of the film has been considered a classic example of great acting – or it is the classic smiling-through-tears bit: at all events this portrayal brought Rainer Oscar No. 1 and the New York critics' Best Actress Award.

Her second Oscar was for *The Good Earth* (37), as O-Lan, in the prestigious screen version of the Pearl S. Buck bestseller. James Agate thought she gave 'an exquisite rendering of what my clever Austrian actress imagines a Chinese peasant woman to be like', but 'Picturegoer', among others, was scornful of the Oscar and spoke on different occasions of 'stolid immobility' and 'bovine vacuity'. Max Breen wrote: 'Can it be that the Academy has been dazzled by her stage fame, or is there really something in her two very limited performances, not perhaps apparent to ordin-

The Big City (37): Spencer Tracy was an independent cab-driver involved with a big combine who used gang-warfare to try to destroy him. Luise Rainer as his wife offered encouragement.

ary mortals, which has transcended anything done in those two years by the great Garbo herself?' The film itself, however, drew no adverse reviews and was one of the year's top hits. With Powell she then did a romantic comedy, *The Emperor's Candlesticks*, about spies on different sides who fall in love; and then started battling for more salary. Next, she was the immigrant wife of taxi-driver Spencer Tracy in *The Big City* and he acted her right off the screen: she soffered, and soffered and soffered, and smiled through her tears without a sniffle.

For some months there were rumours of temperament and impending retirement; then there turned up *The Toy Wife* (38) with Melvyn Douglas and Robert Young, some melodramatic junk in which she was an unlikely Southern belle; and *The Great Waltz* in which she was on more familiar ground, as the mousy (or kittenish) Mrs Strauss, willing to sacrifice Johannes (Fernand Gravet, with a smirk and a song) to glamorous diva Miliza Korjus. A foreword noted that this was a fiction based on 'the spirit' of Strauss's music and the ads proclaimed proudly, and more accurately: 'Only MGM could make such a picture.' It was a great success, notably in Russia, where audiences were perhaps impressed by the five-minute revolution in the middle of the plot.

Of *Dramatic School* C.A. Lejeune's sole critical comment was that it was 'designed to accommodate, accentuate, and perpetuate the dewy charms of Luise Rainer': it was by no means a success. Rainer was then given six months leave to visit her husband, Clifford Odets, reputedly to patch up their quickly failed marriage. MGM did not contradict new rumours of retirement and she was quietly dropped from their contract list. W.H. Mooring wrote later she had made too many enemies 'living up to Hollywood stardom', but considered, too, that her nerves had been unable to take the stress of studio life plus the break-up of her marriage.

In 1939 she turned up in London in 'Behold the Bride'; and was in a dud Broadway revival of 'A Kiss for Cinderella'; she returned to Hollywood determined to try again. She was genuinely embarrassed by her two Oscars and the run of poor films. But 'Picturegoer' reported that no studio was interested. Eventually Paramount signed her for *Hostages* (43) with William Bendix and Arturo de Cordova, just another version of the European underground. Lejeune again: 'Her idea of playing a collaborationist's daughter is to open the eyes very wide, fixing the startled subject with a gaze that would do credit to a passionate

Alderney.' There had been talk of two more films at Paramount, but nothing came of it. And at RKO Renoir's *The Temptress* was cancelled when co-star Jean Gabin preferred Dietrich to her.

Since, she has done occasional stage work in Austria. She lived in London till her husband, a publisher, retired, but she made only two professional appearances in Britain, on TV in 1950, when it was unusual for big stars to appear on TV. She starred in 'By Candelight' and 'The Seagull': no one who saw her Nina in the latter is likely to ever forget it. She turned up in Boston in 1981 reading her own adaptation of 'Enoch Arden'.

CLAUDE RAINS

Claude Rains must be reckoned among the finest actors who ever played in films; he managed to get himself into a score or so of the most enjoyable movies of the 30s and 40s, and they, and weaker efforts, all benefited from his presence. He had a fine speaking voice, like honey with some gravel in it, and that neatly typed him as the most suave and sarcastic of villains, very neat and polished, with a scornful right eyebrow. He encompassed almost every sort of worldly wickedness, though he tended to the artistic rather than the executive; and he could go the sympathetic line with ease and authority. His effectiveness depended on his response to his material; he could ham when he felt like it, but he was never lazy and never uninteresting. He was not physically shaped to be a Hollywood leading man, but producers recognized his worth to the extent that he did get star parts throughout his career, and star-billing; and when he did not, he led the supporting cast.

He was born in 1889 in South London and made his first appearance on the London stage at the age of 10, when his choir master was asked to provide some boys for a crowd scene in 'Nell of Old Drury' at the Haymarket. It was an experience which convinced him that he was going to be an actor and he became a call-boy at His Majesty's and subsequently ASM: an engagement that lasted seven years. Finally, in 1911, he got a small part in 'The Gods of the Mountain' by Lord Dunsany at the Haymarket and later in the year began an Australian tour of 'The Blue Bird', as stage manager, and in Melbourne and Sydney played some small parts; in 1914–15 there he was Granville-Barker's general manager, again playing occasional parts. He returned to Britain to join the army and served until 1919, when he appeared in 'Uncle Ned' at the Lyceum, Sheffield, in Henry

Ainley's company, also supporting that actor in a film, *Build Thy House* (20). Then he began to make a name for himself in London: he did an admired 'Government Inspector' and appeared notably at the Everyman in Shaw: Dubedat in 'The Doctor's Dilemma', Napoleon in 'The Man of Destiny', Dick in 'The Devil's Disciple'. He was seldom out of work and by day taught at RADA (John Gielgud speaks warmly of him as a teacher in his memoir, 'Early Stages'). In 1926 he accompanied his wife, Beatrix Thomson, to New York where she was to star in 'The Constant Nymph': he took a small role, but later played the male lead on a US tour. (He married seven times altogether; his first wife was British stage actress Isabel Jeans.)

He settled in the US and was soon a respected Broadway name: 'And So to Bed' (28) as Samuel Pepys, 'Volpone' in the title-role, 'Marco's Millions' (on tour), 'The Apple Cart' (30) as Proteus, 'The Man in the Yellow River' (32). 'The Man Who Reclaimed His Head' and 'The Good Earth', among others. He was screen-tested for the role John Barrymore played in *A Bill of Divorcement* but was considered unlikely film material. James Whale, however, saw the test and thought him suitable for his version of H.G. Wells's *The Invisible Man* (33) – where only his voice mattered. The film's success made Rains a film name and after one more Broadway venture ('They Shall Not Die') he was in demand in Hollywood. The publicity angle on *Crime Without Passion* (34) was that it was his

Crime Without Passion *(34), the film that established Claude Rains. He was a criminal lawyer who tried to frame an unwanted mistress – and found himself on a murder charge. Esther Dale was his secretary.*

film début, as he was *seen*: otherwise it was a much admired but pretentious (Hecht and MacArthur) drama about a lawyer (Rains) who, despite the title, becomes unhinged through love. He did his stage role in *The Man Who Reclaimed His Head* (35), going insane again in this anti-war propaganda; and then returned to Britain to play *The Clairvoyant* – a fake music-hall seer who finds he really can. In Hollywood he was mad again as John Jasper in Dickens's *The Mystery of Edwin Drood* and 'The New York Times' found him 'brilliantly repellent'. Since neither of these latter two were 'class' features, he must have been glad to go to Paramount's idea of British Africa in *The Last Outpost*.

Then he signed a five-year contract with Warner Bros., beginning an association which seems to have been happier than that of other top-flight Warner talent. He was mostly the heavy, but in a widely contrasting range of pictures: *Anthony Adverse* (36), as the domineering stepfather; *Hearts Divided*, as Napoleon: *Stolen Holiday*, as a crooked French financier based on Stavisky, co-starring with Kay Francis; and *The Prince and the Pauper* (37) – a piece of historical twee by Mark Twain – as the villain. He was then in *They Won't Forget*, a film much admired for its integrity; and though luridly melodramatic, it did attempt to state some of the differences between North and South and did ask its audiences to consider its issues. But Rains,

the film's sole star, as the DA whose kindness comes second to his ambition, was majestically bad (though at the time he was much admired – C.A. Lejeune thought he had 'never done anything quite as good').

He was better as a rancher, Olivia de Havilland's father, in *Gold Is Where You Find It* (38) and superbly right as the wily Prince (later King) John in *The Adventures of Robin Hood*. Then he was in *White Banners*, as a small-town chemistry professor married to the lovely, underrated Kay Johnson, both of them beautifully matched by Fay Bainter, as their 'maid', in this Lloyd C. Douglas 'inspirational' drama; the popular *Four Daughters* (the Lane sisters, etc), as their feckless father; *They Made Me a Criminal* (39) as a relentless detective out to get John Garfield; *Juarez*, hamming as that pocket Caesar, Napoleon III; and *Daughters Courageous*, as their feckless father. He got one of his Best Supporting Oscar nominations for his performance as the most corrupt of the senators in Columbia's *Mr Smith Goes to Washington*. (He was nominated again for *Casablanca*, *Mr Skeffington* and *Notorious* but never won. Contrast Walter Brennan; four nominations, three wins, one performance.)

He was kept busy on his home lot by *Four Wives*; *Saturday's Children* (40), as a kindly New York pop; *The Sea Hawk*, as a Spanish grandee, as suavely villainous as ever; *The Lady With Red Hair*, as David Belasco; and

Claude Rains and Ingrid Bergman in Casablanca *(42), a film notable for the harmony of its many elements, and not least among these is its deployment of the Warner Bros stock company. Of these players, however, Peter Lorre was not yet under contract and Rains had left after several years of sterling work for the company, which would continue to employ him regularly for the next five years. His role on this occasion was comparatively small and he was paid $22,000 for 5½ weeks' work – as opposed to Bergman and Conrad Veidt, borrowed from other studios for $25,000 each for the 7 weeks' shoot.*

Four Mothers (41). He went outside for a couple – *Here Comes Mr Jordan*, an amiable and deeply unlikeable performance as a messenger from the Devil, and *The Wolf Man*, as the father of that unfortunate creature, Lon Chaney Jr; and returned to Warner Bros. for *King's Row*, back yet again on the maniacal path, as the grim doctor who wants to keep his daughter (Betty Field) from the town's eyes. Twentieth Century-Fox then borrowed him to play the intellectual bum in *Moontide* (42), after which he was Bette Davis's kindly psychiatrist in *Now Voyager* and the French police chief with a sinister line in epigrams in *Casablanca*. He was in an episode of *Forever and a Day* (43); then was *The Phantom of the Opera* – in a performance verging towards the pathetic, but hugely enjoyable in its obsessions. *Passage to Marseilles* (44) and *Mr Skeffington* gave him sympathetic parts, the former as a Free French Commander and the latter as Davis's understanding husband.

He was apparently chosen by Shaw himself to play Caesar in *Caesar and Cleopatra* (45) and was notably good in trying circumstances (it was filmed in London during the flying bomb period and he loathed Gabriel Pascal, who produced and directed). On his return to the US he and Arch Obeler purchased *Strange Holiday*, which they had made for General Motors in 1940, an inept venture in which Rains played a man who returns to his country to find it occupied by a foreign power. MGM bought it in 1942, but never released it. It was finally shown as the Shaw film flopped in the US, perhaps the reason why Rains did five in a row: *This Love of Ours* at Universal, a real character part (as an old man); Hitchcock's *Notorious* (46) as a wealthy sophisticate whom Ingrid Bergman marries for the sake of patriotism; a *Mr Jordan*-type fantasy, *Angel on My Shoulder*, with Paul Muni; and his last two for Warner Bros., *Deception*, as an egomaniac conductor reluctant to let Davis get away – the sort of performance to give 'ham' a good name, and *The Unsuspected* (47), as the villain of the piece again, an egomaniac radio crime reporter. His other films were less distinguished, starting with a British film, David Lean's weak-kneed version of H.G. Wells's *The Passionate Friends* (49), as Ann Todd's cold and malevolent husband. He followed with *Rope of Sand*, supporting Burt Lancaster as the wily, urbane boss of villain Paul Henreid; *Song of Surrender*, married to Wanda Hendrix in a pointless period melodrama; *The White Tower* (50), as an alcoholic; *Where Danger Lives* with Faith Domergue; and *Sealed Cargo* (51), as a German officer. In 1950 he returned to the stage and scored a New York hit with Sidney Kingsley's adaptation of Koestler's 'Darkness

Twilight of Honor (63): Rains's penultimate. He was an elderly lawyer befriending a young one.

at Noon' and in 1952 did 'Jezebel's Husband' in stock.

He returned to films, at his worst, in an unworthy British adaptation of Simenon, *The Man Who Watched Trains Go By* (53), playing a mild Dutch shipping clerk corrupted by money. He did T.S. Eliot's 'The Confidential Clerk' in New York in 1954; and another indifferent film, *Lisbon* (56), where he appeared as a suave international crook. Ageing, and now white-haired, he was the patriarch in *This Earth is Mine* (59), with Rock Hudson, and the professor in a new version of *The Lost World* (60). A journey to Italy brought *Il Pianeta degli Uomini Spenti/ Battle of the Worlds* (61), which played the US in minor situations; after which he brought distinction to small parts in *Lawrence of Arabia* (62) as a diplomat, *Twilight of Honor* (63) and *The Greatest Story Ever Told* (65), as Herod. His last acting appearance was at the Westport Country Playhouse in 'So Much of Earth, So Much of Heaven' in 1965. He died in May 1967.

Basil Rathbone

Basil Rathbone was, said William K. Everson, 'the best all-round villain the movies ever had . . . adept at any kind of role, including romantic drama and comedy, [he] was at his best in villainy (including modern wife-killers and Nazis) and was absolutely unmatched at playing swaggering scoundrels of other days, where his rich delivery of full-blooded dialogue, while attired in doublets or court finery, made him truly a sight to behold – and to listen to' ('The Bad Guys'). Other commentators occasionally thought that Rathbone, lean and saturnine, was *too* villainous, but he seldom overweighted his material; he is remembered, too, as a fine Sherlock Holmes.

He was born in 1892 in Johannesburg, South Africa. He was sent to England to be educated (Repton College), after which he went into an insurance office. But he wanted to be an actor and in 1911 got a job with Sir Frank Benson's No. 2 company; he made his début at Ipswich in 'The Taming of the Shrew' as Hortensio. In 1913 he travelled to the US with Benson's company, still doing small parts. His London début was in 'The Sin of David' (14) and the same year he played the Dauphin in 'Henry V'. He was called up in 1916, into the Liverpool Scottish Regiment, and was later commissioned and awarded the MC. He returned to the stage at Stratford-upon-Avon, starring as Romeo, Cassius and other parts; in London he played the title-role in 'Peter Ibbetson' (20), subsequently playing Hal in 'Henry IV Pt 2' and Iago; he made his film début in Maurice Elvey's *Innocent* (21), in the lead, as an artist who betrays an orphan (Madge Stuart), followed by the same director's *The Fruitful Vine*, as the Italian Don who provides the wherewithal for a young British bride of an old husband: Marie Corelli and Robert Hitchens respectively provided the plots.

In 1922 he made his New York bow in 'The Czarina', returning to London for 'East of Suez', 'RUR' and the role of Joseph Surface in *The School for Scandal* (23). He was in New York again for 'The Swan', but his film career in that country got off to an inauspicious start with a programmer for PDC, *Trouping with Ellen* (24), a theatrical story with Helen Chadwick; he was more gainfully employed at Metro in *The Masked Bride* (25), supporting Mae Murray, and at First National being suave to Aileen Pringle in *The Great Deception* (26). He acted in San Francisco, London and New York, but mainly in the latter city – in 'Love Is Like That', 'Julius Caesar' (as Cassius) and 'The Command to Love'. A play of which he was part-author, 'Judas', failed, leaving him free to accept an offer from MGM, who wanted a well-speaking British actor to do *The Last of Mrs Cheyney* (29), as the milord who falls for jewel thief Norma Shearer – and his work in this Lonsdale piece

The Masked Bride *(25): Basil Rathbone as a jewel thief and Mae Murray as one of his gang. He sent her to vamp Francis X. Bushman so that they could rob him but – surprise surprise – she fell in love with him. Christy Cabanne directed.*

resulted in an MGM contract. He was loaned to Universal for *Barnum Was Right* and was then Philo Vance – MGM's rival to William Powell – in *The Bishop Murder Case* (30). He was loaned to Warners for *A Notorious Affair* with Billie Dove and then flirted with Ruth Chatterton, the *Lady of Scandal*, an actress engaged to his cousin: and this was more Lonsdale, being 'The High Road', to which title it reverted overseas. After playing a French spy in a foolish war story, *This Mad World*, MGM dropped him, but he had offers to do comedies at other studios: *The Flirting Widow* with Dorothy MacKaill, from a story by A.E.W. Mason; *A Lady Surrenders* with Genevieve Tobin; and *Sin Takes a Holiday*, this time philandering with Constance Bennett. He returned to Broadway for three plays and went back to Hollywood for *A Woman Commands* (32) with Pola Negri; then he was on Broadway again in 'The Devil Passes'.

He was about to start *Reunion in Vienna* for MGM when he got a more attractive offer from Britain. Hollywood, he said, 'is a cruel place – relentless, stern and unforgiving – as I suppose all great industrial centres must be'. The British pictures hardly enhanced his prestige: *After the Ball*, a comedy with Esther Ralston, a bored wife wooing him; *One*

Precious Year (33), as a cad wooing a wife (Anne Grey) with one year to live; and *Loyalties*, from Galsworthy's play, overplaying as the wealthy Jew who accuses a British officer of stealing. Said 'Photoplay': 'An all-British cast, the accent is practically unintelligible for American audiences.' He did 'Tonight or Never' and 'Diplomacy', and was invited by Katharine Cornell to appear opposite her, as Romeo, in 'The Barretts of Wimpole Street' and 'Candida', which kept him occupied in various places over the next year. MGM recalled him to play Mr Murdstone in *David Copperfield* (35) and he was, in that, more loathsome than he ever was to be again. But in terms of success, this meant that he was unable to return to the stage for more than 10 years. He was offered more irresistible heavies by a Hollywood that saw everything, metaphorically, in black and white. He was typed. In the autumn of 1935 he was to be seen in six films and he was villainous in five of them: *Anna Karenina*, again at MGM, suave as the hard-done-by Karenin; *The Last Days of Pompeii* at RKO, as Pontius Pilate; *A Feather in Her Hat* at Columbia, vaguely sympathetic towards Pauline Lord; *A Tale of Two Cities*, briefly seen as the Marquis St Evremonde; *Captain Blood*, unconvincing as a French pirate captain, but in the first of two memorable sword fights with Errol Flynn; and *Kind Lady*, terrorizing wealthy recluse Aline MacMahon in this fine version of Hugh Walpole's story.

In *Private Number* (36) he was mean to Loretta Young and Robert Taylor; and in *Romeo and Juliet* he was Tybalt. There was a fairly sympathetic role as a suspicious sheik in *The Garden of Allah*, but he was trying to murder Ann Harding in the British *Love From a Stranger* (37), one of his few poor villains, for even she must have known his intentions as soon as she set eyes on him. After that his chore in Warner Bros.' *Confession* was comparatively light, seducing Kay Francis and later trying same on her daughter. For the same company he was sneering and suspicious in *Tovarich*, as the Russian commissar enemy of Boyer and Claudette Colbert: but what could one make of the one in between, *Make a Wish*, where he was distinctly sympathetic towards child singing star Bobby Breen? He turned down the Raymond Massey role in *The Hurricane* because he was tired of playing heavies, but he was then dastardly towards Gary Cooper in *The Adventures of Marco Polo* (38), as the would-be usurper of the throne of Cathay, and Flynn again in *The Adventures of Robin Hood* (as Sir Guy). Then he was in a character role as the sly, hunch-backed Louis XI in *If I Were King* (38), the first of a very loose contract with Paramount, and he was with Flynn again in *The Dawn Patrol*, as the sour martinet commander.

Son of Frankenstein (39) was him, involved with both Boris Karloff and Bela Lugosi: all the same, thought Howard Barnes in the 'New York Herald Tribune', 'this latest variation of the original horror tale commits the ultimate sin. It is singularly unfrightening'. In a small role is Gustav von Seyffertitz, in the Silent era

Rouben Mamoulian's The Mark of Zorro *(40) with Basil Rathbone in his familiar role of hero's enemy and pursuer. In this case it's Tyrone Power he's out to kill.*

a villain beside whom even Rathbone pales. He then had a complete change and played Sherlock Holmes twice for 20th Century-Fox, *The Hound of the Baskervilles* and *The (unexciting) Adventures of Sherlock Holmes*. Nigel Bruce was his Watson and both pictures were well received. At Universal he played the brother of Douglas Fairbanks Jr in *The Sun Never Sets*; starred with Sigrid Gurie in *Rio*, as a crooked financier sweating it out in a jungle prison; and did a good Richard III in *The Tower of London*, which, *sans élan*, followed the plot line of Shakespeare's play. There was another change when he played an egotistical songwriter ghosted by budding musician Bing Crosby in *Rhythm on the River* (40). He was swashbuckling again in *The Mark of Zorro* – the sworn foe of Tyrone Power – almost his last full-scale excursion into villainy – though he was a wife-murderer and master hypnotist again in *The Mad Doctor* with Ellen Drew. Then, *The Black Cat*, about the reading of a will, with Hugh Herbert; *Paris Calling* with Randolph Scott and Elisabeth Bergner; *International Lady* with George Brent and Ilona Massey, as a Scotland Yard man; and *Fingers at the Window* (42) as a Jack-the-ripper-type doctor, with Lew Ayres: these were duallers. Only half a notch up was *Crossroads* with William Powell, as a suave blackmailer.

Universal contracted with Rathbone and Bruce to make a Sherlock Holmes series: these were Bs of uncertain, and deteriorating, quality. The titles: *SH and the Voice of Terror, SH and the Secret Weapon, SH in Washington* (43), *SH Faces Death, SH and the Spider Woman* (44), *The Scarlet Claw, Pearl of Death, The House of Fear* (45), *Pursuit to Algiers, The Woman in Green, Terror by Night* (46) and *Dressed to Kill*. They were modernized and bore little resemblance to Conan Doyle. Rathbone during this period also did *Above Suspicion* (43) with Joan Crawford, as a Gestapo chief; *Frenchman's Creek* (44), leching after Joan Fontaine who rejects him: 'You have more conceit of your kisses, m'lord, and less reason for it, than any scoundrel in England' – later she hurls a suit of armour at him; *Bathing Beauty* with Red Skelton, as a Broadway impresario; and *Heartbeat* (46), as a modern Fagin, with Ginger Rogers. Then, sick of Sherlock, he returned to the stage: on tour and in New York in 1946 he did 'Obsession'; in 1947 he was Dr Sloper in 'The Heiress', in which, at the end of its New York run, he toured. In 1950 he did 'The Winslow Boy' in summer stock and later 'The Gioconda Smile' in New York; he played Sherlock Holmes in a play of that name in 1953, but it did not run.

Apart from the commentary over the 'Mr

Toad' sequence of Disney's *The Adventures of Ichabod and Mr Toad* (49), he had done no film work until he appeared in Bob Hope's *Casanova's Big Night* (54). Times had changed: he was sinister, but in two more comedies, *We're No Angels* (55) and *The Court Jester* (56). He did *The Black Sleep* with Akim Tamiroff; in 1957 he played in 'Hide and Seek'; in *The Last Hurrah* (58) with Spencer Tracy, nasty again, as a banker, and one of his best performances; and in 1959 as 'JB'. In 1960 – his last stage work – he toured Australia in 'The Marriage-go-Round'; he also did TV ('Criminal at Large'; 'The Lark' and 'Victoria Regina', both with Julie Harris).

Rathbone's films of the 60s are a sorry bunch and he gave them no more than they were worth. He traded in his reputation and collected his pay packet: the Italian *Ponzio Pilato* (61), as the high priest of the temple, *The Magic Sword* (62), Roger Corman's *Tales of Terror, The Comedy of Terrors* (63), Curtis Harrington's *Queen of Blood* (66) – a good cut above the others, *Dr Rock and Mr Roll* (67), *The Ghost in the Invisible Bikini* and *Hillbillies in a Haunted House* (68). Most of them were not shown abroad.

Rathbone died in 1967. He had been married twice, the second time to novelist Ouida Bergere: they were noted Hollywood hosts and party-givers.

MICHAEL REDGRAVE

Michael Redgrave had an eminent position in the British theatre, but his work in the cinema was relatively less interesting. As a young romantic screen actor he was never quite dashing or fiery enough. He was always too cerebral. This was a mixed blessing during his career as a whole: at times too much care and thought compelled him to give a misconceived or dull interpretation, but at others – particularly in less stereotyped roles – he turned this characteristic to good advantage and managed to be wholly original. Certainly his major performances in both mediums were men of thought rather than of action.

He was born in Bristol in 1908, of theatrical parents, and educated at Cambridge; after an attempt at journalism, he went into teaching (Modern Languages). But his experience of acting at Cambridge and producing at school warmed him towards a stage career: after three years he changed course again and got a job with Liverpool Rep. His first appearance was in 'Counsellor-at-Law' (34) and his first London engagement was with the Old Vic Company in the 1936–37 season, in leads – including Ferdinand in 'Love's Labours Lost', Mr Horner in 'The Country Wife' and Orlando to Edith Evans's Rosalind. By the time war broke out, he was an established West End actor, having, among other activities, played in the famous Gielgud season of 1937–38 (as Bolingbroke, Charles Surface and Tusenbach) and in 'The Family Reunion' (39) as Harry, Lord Monchensey.

He was with the Gielgud company when he was offered a long-term film contract by Gainsborough (later part of the Rank Organization) which allowed six months a year for stage work: he accepted reluctantly and was then starred in Hitchcock's *The Lady Vanishes* (38) as the cocky but colourless hero. He was, he recalled later, rather snooty with the film people because he was acting with such a distinguished company during the evening, but Hitchcock brought him down to earth. Hitchcock told the press, 'He'll be a second Donat, he can't miss.' It was, of course, a good start. Redgrave described it as 'quintessential Hitchcock' and mentioned that the director taught him much about screen acting. Success seemed assured when he was assigned two more plum roles before being seen by the film public: Jessie Matthews's love interest in *Climbing High* and Elisabeth Bergner's, a mountaineer, in *A Stolen Life* (39). He was less well cast in *A Window in London*, married to Patricia Roc and smitten with Sally Gray: it would seem Frenchified even if you did not know it was a remake of *Metropolitain*, in which Albert Préjean was far more convincing as a son of the people. Redgrave did not have the common touch, nor would he ever acquire it, but he got by in Carol Reed's *The Stars Look Down* because he is a miner yearning to be a teacher.

He was better in the title-role of *Kipps* (41), perhaps because he treated it as a character role, but he is still more convincing after Kipps has become a gentleman. Reed directed this enjoyable version of H.G. Wells's novel and Redgrave was beautifully partnered by Diana Wynyard and Phyllis Calvert as the two women from different social spheres. He co-starred with Valerie Hobson in *Atlantic Ferry* and then took Eric Portman's stage role in *Jeannie*, as the blunt Yorkshireman who brings back to earth the little Scots girl who had come into an inheritance: Barbara Mullen was in the title-role, as on the stage, and it was a pleasant, sentimental film. He then did a part that he had done on the stage, Robert Ardrey's *Thunder Rock* (42), a notably sincere performance as the misanthropic lighthouse-keeper who had fled society because he had failed to convince Britain of the Nazi menace (ghosts come to persuade him that it is futile to desert causes). And he was a Russian in *The Big Blockade*. By the time both of these were shown he was in the Navy, but he was invalided out in 1942, taking advantage of his contract to do stage work. He returned to films in *The Way to the Stars* (45), Terence Rattigan's painstaking account of life, love and death on an RAF station – a fantastic success in Britain, voted overwhelm-

Kipps *(41): Michael Redgrave in the title role, the haberdasher's assistant who inherits a fortune and is taken up by Society, with Diana Wynyard as that member of Society who is most taken with him. But in the end he chooses scullery maid Phyllis Calvert.*

ingly by 'Daily Mail' readers their favourite movie of the war years; in the same poll his co-star, John Mills, emerged as the second most popular actor in the country, but Redgrave was not among the leaders. He was a little too remote, too cold, he was automatically 'officer-material': it was no surprise to find him as an MP/army officer in the silly *The Years Between* (46) and as one of the higher-ranking prisoners in *The Captive Heart* (even if he was only a Czech impersonating one). This contrived and slushy POW tale was a great success in Britain at the time; it has one of the rare major screen parts played by his wife, Rachel Kempson (mother of Vanessa, Lynn and Corin).

Earlier, he had had one of his favourite parts, that of the ventriloquist obsessed and then possessed by his dummy in the episodic *Dead of Night* (45), an uneven collection of ghost stories: his was generally considered to be the best. He played a cold-blooded tyrant in a dreary piece about smugglers from Graham Greene's old, first novel, *The Man Within* (47); and the 'hero' of *Fame Is the Spur*, an unsuccessful Boulting Brothers movie based on a Howard Spring novel based in turn on the life and times of Ramsay Macdonald. He was type-cast as this practical idealist; the film was stodgy and predictable, with pretensions to 'art' and 'meaning'. He accepted a Hollywood offer for two pictures, neither of which turned out well. One was *Mourning Becomes Electra*, in which he was

Orin. It was finally sneaked into Britain where the critics thought him, and not out of chauvinism, the best thing about it. In the other, *Secret Beyond the Door* (48), wife Joan Bennett suspects him of murdering her predecessor; he described this as 'a very bad film', though – unlike Henry Fonda, Sylvia Sidney and many others – he liked working with Fritz Lang. He did not like Hollywood: 'I couldn't take the publicity, the status symbols, and all that foolishness.'

He returned to Britain to play Macbeth and in 1948 did it in New York. He joined the Old Vic again for the 1949–50 season and, among other parts, played Hamlet. He should have appeared in the film version of Coward's *The Astonished Heart*, but, wisely, after a couple of days' work he stepped out and Coward stepped in. He did instead another filmed play, Terence Rattigan's *The Browning Version* (51), dangerously inviting comparison with Eric Portman's superb stage performance as the ageing, failed schoolteacher. It was, however, the high point of his film career. Dilys Powell thought him 'beyond praise. In this intimate view of a man who is made to reveal in an hour or so the gradual petrification of a lifetime it is the actor who really counts; at so close a distance the story must be unfolded not simply in actions and words but in tell-tale movements of the eyes, the tightening of the muscles in lips and cheeks. Redgrave puts an infinity of variation into gestures which are involuntary in the driven

The Browning Version (51), Anthony Asquith's film of what is probably Terence Rattigan's best play: Michael Redgrave as Crocker-Harris, the failed schoolteacher, and Jean Kent as his contemptuous wife – about to leave him for one of the junior masters.

human being; and when at a touch of kindness control suddenly gives way the contrast with the hardness and tightness of the earlier scenes is heart-breaking. Screen playing is often a matter less of acting than of being; here for once the player both becomes the character and acts it.'

There is, however, little to be said for his heavy interpretation of John Worthing in *The Importance of Being Earnest* (52), but Anthony Asquith's insistence on a theatrical style could hardly have helped. Redgrave was now letting the theatre take precedence: during two Stratford seasons (51 and 53) he played some of the titanic parts – Hotspur, Richard II, Prospero, Lear, Shylock and Antony; in the West End he did 'Winter Journey' (52) and in New York 'The Sleeping Prince' (56); in both cities 'Tiger at the Gates' (55). On screen, during this period, he played (not well) an ageing, unsuccessful and long-bearded French lawyer in *The Green Scarf* (54), with Ann Todd and Leo Genn; and an Air Commodore in *The Sea Shall Not Have Them*, a war film floated on clichés (not the worst of which was the moment when the 'chaps' found out he had risen from the ranks and was really 'one of us'). He played an Air Commodore again in *The Night My Number Came Up* (55), a neat idea lumberingly done, and was still involved with the RAF in *The Dam Busters*, but as scientist Barnes Wallis, another of his favourite parts. Like most British war films, it was violently overpraised in its country of origin and, briefly, queues reappeared outside British cinemas; it was more competent than most. Also, Orson Welles's *Confidential Report* turned up, with Redgrave as a pussy-loving, antique-dealing old queen, a cameo that was much liked; but he was embarrassing as an ooh-la-la Frenchman, in *Oh Rosalinda!!*, which was 'Die Fledermaus' modernized by Powell and Pressburger and turned into a morgue.

Following a highly successful TV adaptation of Orwell's '1984', it was hastily filmed (56) with Jan Sterling and Edmund O'Brien: Redgrave was again judged the best thing, as the major representative of Big Brother. Losey's *Time Without Pity* (57) – he was an alcoholic – was more or less ignored at the time and, along with a minor comedy, *Law and Disorder* (58), and a silly melodrama, *Behind the Mask*, suggests either an indifference on Redgrave's part towards scripts or lack of better offers. Hollywood, however, came up with a good one – Mankiewicz's remarkable version of Graham Greene's bestselling *The Quiet American* (58): Redgrave, as well as Audie Murphy in the title-role, was excellent; the film was literate and faithful to the novel until the last reel, when it brazenly upended

Greene's (anti-American) thesis. The resulting brouhaha hurt the box-office.

In 1958 he played Hamlet at Stratford again, as well as Benedick; in 1959 he appeared in his own adaptation of Henry James's 'The Aspern Papers' (he had also written plays and published two volumes on acting and a novel). Also in 1959 he was knighted, but the elevation did nothing for his film career. After a decade of mainly depressing pictures it was hardly surprising that he accepted supporting roles in two that looked okay, both American: *Shake Hands With the Devil* (59) with James Cagney, as an IRA general; and *The Wreck of the Mary Deare* with Gary Cooper, as a lawyer hostile to him. He did an elephantine British comedy, *No My Darling Daughter* (61), only the daughter was not one of his own, but one of John Mills's, Juliet; and a brief cameo as the Master of the Household who engages the governess in *The Innocents*. Subsequently, his attitude towards the cinema was rather that of an elder statesman. He was: the prison governor in *The Loneliness of the Long Distance Runner* (63); W.B. Yeats, the 'senior' playwright, in *Young Cassidy* (64); the drunken medical officer in *The Hill* (65); and an uncle in *The Heroes of Telemark*. In *Vingt-Cinquième Heure/The 25th Hour* (67) he defended Romanian peasant Anthony Quinn at the Nuremberg trials. He appeared, but fleetingly, in a silly programmer with Stephen Boyd, *Assignment K* (68), and remarked to an interviewer during its making that the pay was good and the work easy. Unsurprisingly, he played senior officers again in *Oh! What a Lovely War* (69) and *The Battle of Britain*, and was the headmaster in the remake of *Goodbye Mr Chips*, scripted by Rattigan. He was dreadful as Peggotty in *David Copperfield* (70); then was with Bette Davis in *Connecting Rooms*, playing an old man who is a janitor in the school in which he once taught – a film so bad that it was not released till 1972. The next was so bad that it would have been better if it had never been released: *Goodbye Gemini*, a story of retarded twins (Judy Geeson and Martin Potter) who get mixed up in Chelsea orgies. Redgrave played a 'progressive' MP they meet at one. Stage performances during these years included: Claudius in the National Theatre's 'Hamlet', Uncle Vanya, and Solness in 'The Master Builder', also at the National (63–64), and Ratkin in 'A Month in the Country' (65) with Ingrid Bergman.

He was in *The Go-Between* (71), playing the boy (Dominic Guard) as an old man, in that silly flash-forward device; and in *Nicholas and Alexandra*, as Sazonov. He returned to the theatre in 'The Old Boys' (71) and took over from Alec Guinness in 'Voyage Round My

Schoolmastering on: Redgrave as the headmaster in the remake of Goodbye Mr Chips *(69), with Peter O'Toole as* Chips.

Father', which he subsequently did in Australia. After supporting Kirk Douglas in a TV *Dr Jekyll and Mr Hyde* (75) he went into semi-retirement – which became permanent, due to the debilitating illness which finally killed him in 1985. His wife later published a memoir movingly revealing how she coped with his bisexuality.

RALPH RICHARDSON

Like the little girl with the curl, there was no happy medium with Sir Ralph: when he was good, he was very, very good, and when he was bad he was horrid. It was a curious talent. Younger cinemagoers (and theatregoers) were sometimes puzzled that he should be considered one of Britain's leading actors; they found him mannered and inflexible, too often the elderly clubman he was in life. But dotted throughout his career were performances of excellence; he was particularly good at projecting the intellectual 'ordinary' man and the aristocrat 'sickled o'er with the pale cast of thought' – but he was not willowy or aesthetic; he probably would not have been a convincing Hamlet. He was nimble, blunt, trusting, but there was an intelligence which overrode every other quality.

He was born in Cheltenham, Gloucester, in 1902; on leaving school he became an office boy with an insurance company at Brighton, where he lived, but was then left a small legacy. After a few weeks studying art he decided to be an actor and joined a semi-amateur company in Brighton, moving on to a professional company a few months later. This was a group which toured and he stayed with them for three years. In 1926 he joined the Birmingham Rep, with whom he did a two-week London season in 'The Farmer's Wife', which led eventually to a small part in another play by Eden Phillpotts, 'Yellow Sands' (28), with Cedric Hardwicke. He joined the Old Vic in 1930, playing Caliban, Prince Hal and Bolingbroke; in 1931 there he did Petruchio, Bottom and Henry V, and in 1932 Iago, Brutus and Sir Toby. (He returned to the Vic in 1937 and 1938; and was one of its mainstays during its great days, 1944–47 – probably the peak of his career.)

The Vic in the early 30s had not attained the exalted status it was to know later, but Richardson had appeared also in the West End and had achieved a small reputation. It was Hardwicke who recommended him to the makers of *The Ghoul* (33), in a small but telling part as a seemingly kind vicar; and he then played Jessie Matthews's fiancé in *Friday the Thirteenth*, a good 'cross-section' movie

(what has happened before the leading characters are involved in a bus crash). He returned a star in *The Return of Bulldog Drummond*, a poor thing compared with the Ronald Colman Drummond film which turned up a month later: he outwitted a gang planning world domination. He was one of a 19th-century shipbuilding family in *Java Head* and on Hardwicke's recommendation was featured with him in *The King of Paris*; and he was the fuzzy-haired maniac/villain of *Bulldog Jack* (35) – Hulbert.

Korda then offered him a contract, with the idea of starring him in *Sanders of the River*, but stage commitments prevented that and the part went to Leslie Banks; in October 1935 Richardson made his American bow as Mercutio in Katharine Cornell's company, touring and later in New York. He was to remain with Korda 21 years (until Korda's death in 1956). During that time he made only a dozen or so films for him and as many more for other companies – but, as he said in later years, his heart was always in the theatre: 'I don't think films give an actor much satisfaction, when he's making them; but if they go well and they're successful, well, then he's very happy and lucky.' Beyond that, Richardson did not have the matinée idol looks of his friend and colleague, Olivier, and was cast mainly in supporting roles, usually in parts requiring integrity: *Things to Come* (36), H.G. Wells's story, written specially for the screen, where he was unbelievably hammy; *The Man Who Could Work Miracles*, Wells again, as a peppery old colonel; *Thunder in the City* (37) for Atlantic, with Edward. G. Robinson; and *South Riding* (38), as the squire in Victor Saville's version of Winifred Holtby's Yorkshire novel – perhaps his best part and played with exact, realistic detail. Stage plays of the period: 'Bees on the Boat Deck' (36), 'The Amazing Dr Clitterhouse', 'Othello' (38), in the title-role and 'Johnson Over Jordan'.

His parts in *The Divorce of Lady X* and MGM's *The Citadel* were small compared to those of Olivier and Robert Donat respectively, but he was effective, especially in the latter, as a hearty and boozy colleague. He did much better the following year alongside Olivier in *Q Planes* (39), as a devil-may-care SS man, and with John Clements in *The Four Feathers*, from A.E.W. Mason's novel, as the officer who is blinded by the desert sun. He also starred with Merle Oberon in Korda's patriotic *The Lion Has Wings* and before war broke out did *On the Night of the Fire*, with Diana Wynyard. He joined the Fleet Air Arm and was released temporarily for some pictures all about the war: *The Day Will Dawn* (42); *The Silver Fleet*; and *The Volunteer* (43), a documentary extolling the Fleet Air Arm, in

The Fallen Idol (48) remains the best screen version of a Graham Greene work, and it has Ralph Richardson's best screen performance, as Baines, the – married – Embassy butler in love with French typist Michèle Morgan.

which he played himself. His first wife died and he married Meriel Forbes. Then he was released permanently to help run the Old Vic; and played there Blunschli, Peer Gynt, Uncle Vanya, Falstaff, Cyrano de Bergerac, etc.

His stage work prevented him from accepting a good Hollywood bid – to play the King in *Anna and the King of Siam*, but he returned to films in *School for Secrets* (46), a muddled and vapid picture about boffins; and the following year was knighted. He made his first film for Korda in almost 10 years: *Anna Karenina* (48), where his Karenin – to Vivien Leigh's Anna – is one of its few satisfactory ingredients. Later that year he was in Carol Reed's film of Graham Greene's *The Fallen Idol*, as the pivotal character, the butler whom the boy thinks betrays him: it is an admirable performance (in one of the best films of that era) and Greene himself thinks it is the best screen delineation of any of his characters. He went to Hollywood to play Dr Sloper in *The Heiress* (50), a part he had played on the London stage, and another domestic tyrant: but it was as different from his Karenin as it was as good. From whence there was a considerable drop to his hammy sea captain in *An Outcast of the Islands* (51) and his drear little clerk in *Home at Seven* (which he had also done on the stage and which he directed: wisely, he never repeated the experiment). But as an aircraft manufacturer in Lean's meretricious *The Sound Barrier* (52) he was at his best and the New York critics voted him the Best Actor of the year. So did the BFA (Best British Actor).

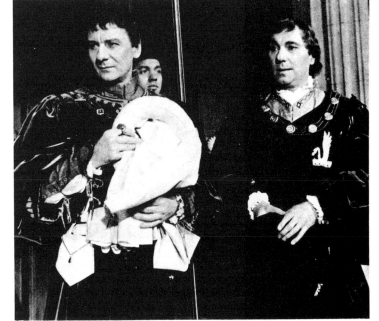

Sir John Gielgud as Clarence and Sir Ralph Richardson in Richard III *(55), produced and directed by Sir Laurence Olivier. A theatrical knighthood is given rather for service than for achievement, but Gielgud and Richardson qualify on both counts.*

He continued to see-saw: as the elderly parson in *The Holly and the Ivy* he was dull, but his Buckingham in Olivier's *Richard III* (55) was a brilliant one. Like all his work, the quality has to be explained by direction or casting, because his performances, once conceived, are consistent. No one could have done much with *The Passionate Stranger* (56), a little novelette that seemed to have been run up on a wet afternoon; but in the better

Smiley earlier the same year, a sentimental Australian 'boy' story, he was better. Stage work during the 50s: 'Three Sisters' (51) as Vershinin; 'A Day by the Sea' (53); 'Separate Tables' and 'The Sleeping Prince' (55), both on tour in Australia; 'The Waltz of the Toreadors' (57), in New York; 'Flowering Cherry' (57); and 'The Complaisant Lover' (59) by Grahame Greene, who this time did not like his interpretation.

After that, most of his film roles returned to the supporting category: *Our Man in Havana* (59), as a high-ranking bureaucrat; *Oscar Wilde* (60) as Sir Edward Carson; and Hollywood's *Exodus* and *Long Day's Journey into Night* (62). His role in the latter would seem to be cruel type-casting – the bombastic, ageing, dreamy and vague actor, but Richardson got way under the surface for a memorable portrayal. What he was doing, however, in 20th's silly Greek thing, *The 300 Spartans*, is anybody's guess. It was increasingly clear that he needed careful casting: a disaster in both *Woman of Straw* (64), as Gina Lollobrigida's nasty elderly husband, and *Doctor Zhivago* (65), he got fine notices for his doddery old uncle in *The Wrong Box* (66) and was exactly right for his brief stint as Gladstone in *Khartoum*. Stage work included at this time 'The School for Scandal' in London and New York, 'Six Characters in Search of an Author' and 'What the Butler Saw'.

After an absence from films, he elected to do as odd a bunch as anyone ever chose: *Oh! What a Lovely War* (69), in the prologue as Sir Edward Grey; *The Battle of Britain*, as Our Man in Switzerland; *The Looking Glass War*, from a novel by John Le Carré, as the head of the secret service; and *The Midas Run/A Run on Gold*, still there, but not so prominently. After a sad excursion as Mr Micawber in *David Copperfield* (70), for US TV, he played the title-role (!) in Richard Lester's *The Bed Sitting Room*. Audiences in New York applauded him and Gielgud in their London success, 'Home', but no one, apparently, saw *Eagle in a Cage* (71), in which they were British officials on St Helena with Napoleon (Kenneth Haigh). It had been made much earlier, as had *Upon This Rock*, a semi-documentary about the Vatican, which finally premièred on US TV in 1973. In the meantime, Richardson did two medium-budget horror films, *Whoever Slew Auntie Roo* (72), which lost the '*ever*' for the US and had him as a supposed medium, with two kids murdering Shelley Winters; and *Tales from the Crypt*, as the link-man, the crypt-keeper. He was the caterpillar in *Alice's Adventures in Wonderland* and an odd choice for George IV in *Lady Caroline Lamb*: as both films might also be called horrors – by the few who saw them –

we might suppose an improvement with *O Lucky Man* (73), Lindsay Anderson's over-long study of a salesman (Malcolm McDowell), in a double role as a shady lodger and a millionaire financier. He was Dr Rank in the Claire Bloom version of *A Doll's House*, no match for Trevor Howard in the rival version. In *Frankenstein the True Story* (74), made for US TV and cinemas elsewhere, he was a blind hermit and between roles at Britain's National Theatre he was a computer librarian in *Rollerball* (75). He was in two TV ventures, Zeffirelli's *Jesus of Nazareth/Gesu di Nazaret* (77), as a prophet, and *The Man in the Iron Mask*, which predictably starred Richard Chamberlain. After playing John Gabriel Borkmann for the National and in 'The Kingfisher' he took respite in two violent fantasies aimed uncertainly at teenagers: *Dragonslayer* (81), as a sorceror, and *Time Bandits*, as the Supreme Being. *Witness for the Prosecution* (82) was a television remake and, thought 'Variety', 'Laughton's performance was a model of restraint by comparison'. Richardson behaved similarly – one would not call it acting – in *Wagner* (83), but then he had only a few minutes' screen time in this nine-hour saga. He died in October 1983, leaving two films to be released posthumously. The first was *Greystoke – the Legend of Tarzan, Lord of Apes* (84), in which he was Tarzan's eccentric grandfather. The producers insisted on keeping all of Richardson's footage – against the wishes of the director, Hugh Hudson. This did not improve the film – and it is doubtful whether the public cared, for they stayed well away from Paul McCartney's vanity production, *Give My Regards to Broad Street*, in which Sir Ralph was an elderly publican dispensing wisdom to the hero, 'Paul'.

A third film, made before these two, seems to have disappeared after horrendous reviews in the trade press, *Invitation to the Wedding*, a daft celebration of the British aristocracy. It was the last throw of a surprisingly durable double act, Sir Ralph, playing a bishop, and Sir John. It is also a sour end to an often brilliant career – but an overrated one, as can be testified by those who in 1958 saw his Timon of Athens literally empty the Old Vic. It cannot be seen again, but his best screen performances will always be savoured and studied.

PAUL ROBESON

Paul Robeson was a moment in time: the wrong moment, perhaps. He was one of the century's great artists, but his skin was the wrong colour. Had he come earlier, few might ever have heard of him. Had he come later he might have been welcomed with the same eagerness as Sidney Poitier and other popular black artists. He was successful, but he found the going tough. He had intelligence and fame; was in demand as a concert and recording artist, worked in films and on the stage; but remained always a loner in show business. Even those who admired him often thought it better so. As a great singer, he was clearly qualified to be a solo artist, but his very greatness calls into question the neglect of Robeson by Hollywood. Hollywood, the eternal whipping boy ... but this same Hollywood did try to make stars out of singers like Lawrence Tibbett. The point is that no singer before or since ever caught the public imagination as Robeson did. To most people the fact that he was black was immaterial; no singer before had seemed so real, so unencumbered by artifice, so warm, so sincere: his rich bass-baritone, whether he sang aria or spiritual, 'spoke' to millions. Today we are accustomed to the singer who 'acts' his lyric: Robeson was virtually the first modern singer, in that the emotion conveyed was as true as the voice.

He acted in the same way: powerful, direct, entirely natural. His few film performances were delightful. Most of them were in British films, but even in the British studios there was always conflict between him and the recessionists over whether he should play parts as a human being or as Amos 'n' Andy's second cousin. Marie Seton's biography (1958) movingly portrays his struggles. A note at the front by Alexander Woollcott speaks of his 'greatness as a person ... his unassailable dignity, and his serene, incorruptible simplicity' and Arthur Bryant in his foreword says that 'no one who has seen him act or heard that wonderful voice is ever likely to forget the experience'. His films were mainly poor and they were *not* important in the Civil Rights movement, which, inevitably, he espoused – nor important in any way except for his presence in them.

He was a remarkable man – indeed, an improbably brilliant one. Born in Princeton, New Jersey, in 1898, the son of a minister of the Church, he graduated from Rutgers University, New Brunswick, NJ, with the highest scholastic average in the history of that institution, then studied Law at Columbia University (he was actually admitted to the Bar in New York). He was excellent at athletics and during his college years was an All-American football player. As an entertainer, he had merely sung as an amateur at parties, but in 1920 he was persuaded to act in 'Simon the Cyrenian' which was being revived by the Harlem YWCA. This was one of the few plays to break away from the Negro stereotype and Robeson indignantly turned down a consequent offer to play in Eugene O'Neill's 'The Emperor Jones', because that, he felt, did not. He also did not want a career in professional football; to earn money while studying he sang at the Cotton Club and appeared in a play called 'Taboo', making his British début in this, in 1922, in Blackpool. After graduating, he was offered O'Neill's 'All God's Chillun Got Wings' and he also did 'The Emperor Jones' after all, because he needed the money. These established him as a force in the New York theatre; and in the latter play he made his London début in 1925. In 1926 he was in 'Black Boy' and in 1928 took over the role of Crown in 'Porgy'. Later that year he went to London again, to appear in 'Show Boat' and Britain became his adopted home for 13 years: there he did 'Othello' (30) and 'The Hairy Ape' (31), as Yank. He became renowned, internationally, on the concert platform; in 1932 he returned to New York to appear in a revival of 'Show Boat'.

At this point a movie of *The Emperor Jones* (32) was proposed by an independent group: it was made in New York and distributed by United Artists, for whom it did good business – though nominally an 'art film'. Robeson and others, however, considered it a vulgarization of the play (some scenes were added after he had signed the contract, to bring it more in line with the conventional concept of Negro behaviour – cf. King Vidor's *Hallelujah*). The next film offer came from Korda in London: *Sanders of the River* (35), from Edgar Wallace's novel. Robeson was attracted to the idea of playing an African chief as a human being and by the promise that the film would include much documentary material; but the film was reworked to make it a hymn to British imperialism in the person of white administrator Sanders: 'Sandy the strong/Sandy the wise/ Righter of Wrongs/Hater of Lies' sang Robeson, not insincerely. He loathed the film and walked out of the London première when asked to make a speech. A British TV company resurrected it in 1959 and there were protests by the representatives of African governments because of the film's prehistoric attitudes. Robeson's cheery performance was its sole, shining, virtue.

There was less disillusionment with the next, Hollywood's *Show Boat* (36), where his brief was to do little more than sing 'Ol' Man River'. He continued to turn down offers, said director Harry Watt, 'because he felt they did not show the Negro in a sympathetic light', but at the same time felt the onus of taking inferior parts in an attempt to improve the Cinema's usual conception of Negroes. After

Robeson at the time of Show Boat *(36).*

The only one of Paul Robeson's films to be at all worthy of him was Ealing's The Proud Valley *(40), about an American Negro who becomes a miner in Wales. It was directed by Pen Tennyson, of whom great things were expected (he was killed during the war). With Robeson here are Simon Lack, Jack Jones and Charles Williams, all trapped below in a pit disaster.*

his experience on *Sanders*, he had a clause in his contract giving him the right to approve the final cut of *Song of Freedom* (36), a melodramatic but not dishonest tale about a London-born Negro – a concert artist – who returns to his African heritage. Robeson himself was fairly enthusiastic (and so was the press), but his attempt to do something with the cardboard character of the chieftain in *King Solomon's Mines* (37) was hardly noticeable. *Jericho* (38) with Henry Wilcoxon, was another melodrama, this time about an American Negro who flees from justice and becomes chief of an Arab tribe: some play was made of friendship between black and white and this, Robeson thought, justified its naïvety and the improbabilities of the plot. The same year he did *Big Fella*, a melodrama with songs, set in Marseilles; and *The Proud Valley* (40), the story of an American Negro who adopts and is adopted by a Welsh mining village and who becomes a hero during a mine disaster. Of course. But at the time this was a significant film and the only one of which he was proud.

In September 1939 he returned to New York and three months later starred in 'John Henry' on Broadway. In 1943 he began his record-breaking revival of 'Othello' and toured in it: in 1959 he returned to Britain and played the part at Stratford-upon-Avon. In 1947 it was reported that Jean Renoir was preparing a film for him called *Freedom Road*, but nothing came of this. Between these years he had gradually decreased his activity, due in some measure to the poor press he was receiving in the US because of his Communist affiliations. (In 1949, in Paris, he made a speech which was interpreted as suggesting the American Negro should not fight for Uncle Sam against Communism. Because of this, a later concert in the US was cancelled; another one was the scene of right-wing-inspired riots.) The State Department indeed had withdrawn his passport so that he was unable to travel to the USSR in 1952 to receive the Stalin Peace Prize. When at last he was able to travel he settled again in Britain, but in 1963, in ill-health, he returned to New York, where he lived in seclusion, enduring a series of nervous breakdowns and attempting suicide at least once. Towards the end of his life there were amends made: a tribute at Carnegie Hall and an award from Actors Equity for exemplifying 'the ideals of true brotherhood of all mankind and the dignity of the individual'. He died in 1976.

He made one film after *The Proud Valley*, the final episode of 20th's *Tales of Manhattan* (42) with Ethel Waters: folksy and patronizing, it was a negation of everything both artists stood for and was cut by the more discerning of exhibitors.

EDWARD G. ROBINSON

'Why did we last?' reiterated Edward G. Robinson in 1963 to an interviewer who asked about the great generation of stars: 'Well, they were people before they were stars. You can have someone new, with a few tricks and a new face and the people will go along with him for a while and then they see through you. To last you need to be real. Integrity as a person. And you have to work. I still work as hard, probably harder, at each role I get as I did at the beginning. To my mind, the actor has this great responsibility of playing another human being. It's a great responsibility, you know, it's like taking on another person's life and you have to do as sincerely and honestly as you can.'

He was the least film-starrish of stars. Small, robust, not handsome, he seldom made the fan magazines. There was never a Robinson cult nor was he *nominated* for an Oscar – which comes, perhaps, of being consistently good and versatile. His standard of playing was as good as anyone's, but the reason he lasted so long at the top (his physique might have fitted him better to supporting parts) was not simply because he was a fine actor – he was an exciting one. For much of his career he had to snarl and rant, but he could be very quiet, very placid. He always seemed to have an understanding of human frailties – and he said that he never visualized himself as a gangster. But, as Raymond Chandler said when discussing him and Bogart, he 'only has to enter a room to dominate it'.

Robinson was born in Bucharest, Romania, in 1893. The family emigrated to New York when he was nine. After a short spell at Columbia University he moved over to the AADA and it was there he changed his name from Emmanuel Goldenberg (the G in the middle stands for nothing – 'God only knows or gangsters,' he said once). His first stage appearance was in Binghampton, New York, in 'Paid in Full' (13); he toured Canada in 'Kismet' and made his Broadway bow in two small parts in 'Under Fire'. After the war (he was in the Navy) he began to make a reputation, notably in 'Banco' (22), which resulted in a film part, as an elderly revolutionary in *The Bright Shawl* (23). Among the plays over the next few years: 'A Royal Fandango' (23), 'Androcles and the Lion' (25), as Caesar, 'The Goat Song', 'Juarez and Maximilian' (as Diaz), 'The Brothers Karamazov' (26) and 'The Racket' (27), his first star role, as a gangster. He was in 'The Man With Red Hair' and in 'Kibitzer', which he wrote with Jo Swerling; then he was asked by Paramount to co-star with Claudette Colbert in *The Hole in the Wall* (29), the two of them

as part of a gang using a clairvoyant's parlour as a front: a creaky old melodrama. He played another gangster in *Night Ride* (30) and then was the Italian immigrant in *A Lady to Love*, with Vilma Banky as the mail-order bride in this second of the four film versions of 'They Knew What They Wanted'; he also appeared in the German version (he spoke eight languages). He was a gangster again in Tod Browning's remake of his own *Outside the Law*, an Oriental in *East Is West* with Lupe Velez and again a gangster in *The Widow from Chicago*.

'Mr Samuel' was his last play for over 20 years; when it folded he went to Hollywood to play *Little Caesar* (30) and his performance as the vicious, bragging, Al Capone-like killer made him a star: power and style and personality. The film itself, a pungent account of his rise and fall ('Is this the end of Little Rico?'), was one the year's top money-makers and Robinson became at once one of Warners' most important stars. *Smart Money* (31) with James Cagney was more conventional – he was a small-time gambler who works his way to the top of the systems – but it was some years before Warners lost the impetus of these early gangster films, 'torn from today's headlines'. *Five Star Final* still has an impact, the story of a ruthless tabloid editor who finally succumbs to humanity. It was one of the top money-makers.

Edward G. Robinson – in spats and grey derby – with his henchmen in Little Caesar *(30), a gangster film that is hardly less exciting today than it was then. It was directed by Mervyn Le Roy, a good director in those days.*

Robinson continued to play bigwigs and bosses, most of them crooked and all of them wily; he was an Oriental one in *The Hatchet Man*, Wong Low Get. 'There is nothing of the usual theatrical Chinaman,' said 'Picturegoer'. 'Robinson's performance is a brilliant one.' The film was not up to much, though. He was a pathetic working man driven to kill his slatternly wife in *Two Seconds* (32), looking back on his career in the electric chair – though the performance itself is a virtual self-parody; and he had a similar role in *Tiger Shark*, a variation on *A Lady to Love* with Zita Johann as the unfaithful wife and Richard Arlen as the lover; Robinson was a one-handed Mexican fisherman. He was a senator in *Silver Dollar* and 'Picturegoer' said: 'Once again . . . an outstanding characterization and one which is quite unlike any he has done to date.' It was an impressive film and so was *Little Giant* (33), a gentle tale about a retired gangster; and he had a third good one in *I Loved a Woman*. The woman was opera singer Kay Francis and the wife Genevieve Tobin; and it was based on a real-life tycoon, in this case Chicago meat-packer Samuel Insull – though unlike *Citizen Kane* the film showed the fall as well as the rise. *Dark Hazard* (34) – the title referred to a greyhound – was more conventional, as was *The Man With Two Faces*, playing an actor who uses stage make-up to rid his sister (Mary Astor) of her vile husband (Louis Calhern); but John Ford's Capraesque *The Whole Town's Talking* at Columbia is one of his best films. Cast because of his authority as a gang leader, he was touching in the other half of the dual role, the mild bank clerk mistaken for same. He was back in the big time in *Barbary Coast* at Goldwyn, running – not honestly – his own saloon and his mistress (Miriam Hopkins).

William Keighley's fine *Bullets and Ballots* (36) found him for the first time on the Right Side of the Law – Bogart was the quarry. *Thunder in the City* (37) in Britain was poor, but back on the Warner lot *Kid Galahad* was well up to standard, with Bette Davis, Bogart, Wayne Morris in the title-role and Robinson as his unscrupulous but soft-hearted Italian manager. He went over to MGM to be *The Last Gangster*, then returned to Warners for the last under his contract, *A Slight Case of Murder* (38), another comedy about a retired gangster, but this time rather a black farce in the unmistakable tones of Damon Runyon. A splendid supporting case included Ruth Donnelly, as his wife, and Allen Jenkins. Graham Greene in his review observed that the funniest film of 1937, *True Confession*, had one corpse and that 'this has four and is four times as funny'. Robinson re-signed with Warners,

but the first picture was no cause to celebrate, *The Amazing Dr Clitterhouse* – in the title-role, a psychologist who joins the rackets to study crime.

At Columbia *I Am the Law* indicated a desire to stay Good, for he was the I, a prosecuting attorney, and he was an FBI man rounding up a spy ring in *Confessions of a Nazi Spy* (39), a hard-hitting semi-documentary and a courageous film to make, the first anti-Nazi film and not mealy mouthed – granted that MGM was the only company still releasing in Germany. Robinson had asked the Warners, who were also Jewish, to let him do the film 'for my people'. At MGM he was wronged and blackmailed in *Blackmail* – and also fighting fires and on the chain gang; and then he played a scientist in *Dr Ehrlich's Magic Bullet* (40), which also contrived to be anti-Nazi without much difficulty. Ehrlich was a German Jew whose discoveries benefited mankind and at the film's climax he prophesied that one day Man would fight diseases of the mind more dangerous than those of the body. . . . The film was timid, however, about Ehrlich's discovery of a cure for syphilis: the word was mentioned fearlessly, but the film managed to suggest that it was some form of TB. In the 'Spectator' Basil Wright paid tribute to Robinson's acting: 'To say that Otto Kruger is almost unrecognizable is an extreme compliment; but to say that Edward G. Robinson is almost unrecognizable is really

For most of its length Lloyd Bacon's Brother Orchid *(40) was a good crime comedy, and both Robinson and Ann Sothern, as his moll, were at their best.*

500

unbelievable; yet it is true. The star of *Two Seconds* . . . here subordinates himself so completely to the story, and to his make-up, that it is Ehrlich, and Ehrlich only, that we see.'

After which it was quite a descent to *Brother Orchid*, as a crook turned monk, his astringency offset by a painfully holy performance from Donald Crisp. He did another biographical film, *A Dispatch from Reuters*, again directed by William Dieterle, about the founding of the news agency, and then *The Sea Wolf* (41), beautifully judging the captain's grim humour, his paranoid viciousness and the pathos of his attacks of blindness. *Manpower* was a remake of *Slim*, with Robinson in his old familiar part as the nice little man who loses his wife (Dietrich) to his buddy (George Raft). He was a newspaper editor again in *Unholy Partners* (the partner was crook Edward Arnold) and an ex-con in *Larceny Inc.* (42), a pleasant comedy and his last film for Warners under his contract. In 1942, in a gesture of friendship, he toured British service installations, which left him time otherwise for only an episode of *Tales of Manhattan*, by sheer, beautiful acting making his the best in the film: the Bowery drunk who dresses up for a college reunion. After a poor war picture, *Destroyer*, as its blinkered martinet commander, he was in Duvivier's other all-star episode, *Flesh and Fantasy* (43), in a loose adaptation of 'Lord Arthur Savile's Crime'. *Tampico* (44) was wartime melodrama, with Lynn Bari and Victor McLaglen; then he did *Double Indemnity*, as the claims investigator, a role subsidiary to those of Barbara Stanwyck and Fred MacMurray and less showy, but he invested it with great humanity – it was as if he was inspired by his material. He played the elderly soldier in the folksy *Mr Winkle Goes to War* with almost no interest: 'In the Great *Mr Deeds* Tradition' said Columbia's adverts, hopefully. He was first-rate again as a professor whose involvement with *The Woman in the Window*, Joan Bennett, leads to crime: Fritz Lang directed and it was a success for all of them.

He returned to Britain and broadcast to the European Underground movement, and appeared as a flying instructor in an RAF propaganda film, *Journey Together*, for which he took no salary. Then he toured France. Back in Hollywood he played Margaret O'Brien's father in the over-sweet *Our Vines Have Tender Grapes* (45) and then got together with Lang for a follow-up to *The Woman in the Window*, *Scarlet Street*, as a hen-pecked husband smitten with Bennett – a remake of Renoir's *La Chienne*. The next half dozen alternated between good and bad: *The Stranger* (46), as the representative of the war crimes commission hunting down Nazi Orson Welles in a small New England town; *The Red House* (47), an incredible melodrama that he produced himself as a one-legged farmer with

It was obvious to even the youngest cinemagoer that his marriage was doomed: Robinson and Marlene Dietrich in Manpower *(41), with George Raft as Best Man and Joyce Compton as Maid of Honour. Raoul Walsh directed this drama of dime-novel dilemmas.*

a guilty secret; *All My Sons* (48), a good performance as the paterfamilias in this mediocre version of Arthur Miller's play; Huston's superb *Key Largo*, recreating with affection a gang boss with galloping paranoia; *The Night Has a Thousand Eyes*, a silly thriller about a clairvoyant; and *House of Strangers* (49), a good solid melodrama directed by Joseph L. Mankiewicz, as a Napoleon of East Side finance. Easily the worst was *My Daughter Joy* (50), as a possessive father again (Peggy Cummins's): he made it in Britain, coincidental with his being called before the Un-American Activities Committee to explain Communist affiliations. He was cleared, but his film work thereafter was for a while confined to programmers or even Bs: *Actors and Sin* (52), a two-part film by Ben Hecht that had no success at all; *Vice Squad* (53) with Paulette Goddard; *The Big Leaguer*, a baseball story with Vera-Ellen; *The Glass Web*, again as a murderer, this time for a TV show; *Black Tuesday* (54), as a gangster; *The Violent Men* (55), a Western – a species he loathed – with Stanwyck, as a power-hungry cattle-king; *Tight Spot* as a DA with Ginger Rogers; *A Bullet for Joey* with Raft; *Illegal*, as a crooked lawyer; *Hell on Frisco Bay* with Alan Ladd; and *Nightmare* (56). It looked as though either he or producers or both were capitalizing on his reputation, re-hatching the great parts of his early career, but in fact some of these modest pictures were better than the As of the time and look excellent now on TV. *Illegal* is particularly good. De Mille's *The Ten Commandments*, at least critically, was not worth one of these films: he was a Hebrew leader and he regarded the film as removing him from the black list.

In 1952 he had played in Koestler's 'Darkness at Noon'; now he spent two years, in New York and on tour, in Chayefsky's 'The Middle of the Night'. He returned to films with a stint as Frank Sinatra's 'managing' brother in Capra's *A Hole in the Head* (59) and then did a good film about a heist, *Seven Thieves* (60). David Robinson took the occasion to observe that he was 'one of the most perfected actors the cinema has produced'. In mainly supporting roles, he played various executives and men of authority: *Pepe*, one of many guest stars, and *My Geisha* (61), in both as a film producer; *Two Weeks in Another Town* (62), ditto; *Sammy Going South* (63), a British film made in Africa and his last lead, as a warmhearted diamond smuggler involved with a small boy; *The Prize* (64), along with Paul Newman a Nobel prize-winner, and also – another dual role – his evil brother; *Good Neighbor Sam*, as a puritanical client of Jack Lemmon's agency; *Robin and the Seven Hoods*, in a guest role as a gang leader – it

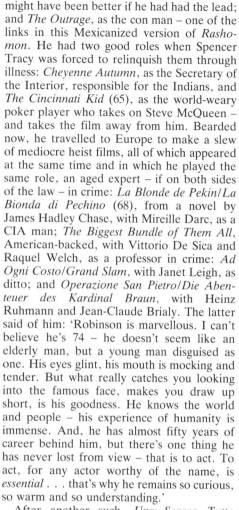

might have been better if he had had the lead; and *The Outrage*, as the con man – one of the links in this Mexicanized version of *Rashomon*. He had two good roles when Spencer Tracy was forced to relinquish them through illness: *Cheyenne Autumn*, as the Secretary of the Interior, responsible for the Indians, and *The Cincinnati Kid* (65), as the world-weary poker player who takes on Steve McQueen – and takes the film away from him. Bearded now, he travelled to Europe to make a slew of mediocre heist films, all of which appeared at the same time and in which he played the same role, an aged expert – if on both sides of the law – in crime: *La Blonde de Pekin/La Bionda di Pechino* (68), from a novel by James Hadley Chase, with Mireille Darc, as a CIA man; *The Biggest Bundle of Them All*, American-backed, with Vittorio De Sica and Raquel Welch, as a professor in crime: *Ad Ogni Costo/Grand Slam*, with Janet Leigh, as ditto; and *Operazione San Pietro/Die Abenteuer des Kardinal Braun*, with Heinz Ruhmann and Jean-Claude Brialy. The latter said of him: 'Robinson is marvellous. I can't believe he's 74 – he doesn't seem like an elderly man, but a young man disguised as one. His eyes glint, his mouth is mocking and tender. But what really catches you looking into the famous face, makes you draw up short, is his goodness. He knows the world and people – his experience of humanity is immense. And, he has almost fifty years of career behind him, but there's one thing he has never lost from view – that is to act. To act, for any actor worthy of the name, is *essential* . . . that's why he remains so curious, so warm and so understanding.'

After another such, *Uno Scacco Tutto Matto*, with Terry-Thomas, he returned to Hollywood for a Disney adventure in the same vein, *Never a Dull Moment*, with Dick Van Dyke, playing (as he was in life) an art expert. Eschewing Europe, with reason, he managed to do an inept starry Western, *Mackenna's Gold* (69), and *Song of Norway* (70), a biopic on Greig, as a piano dealer. Among several TV appearances was *The Man Who Cried Wolf*, as a man convinced his best friend had been murdered, and fans were heartened to hear that he had landed a big role in *The Angel Levine* – but the brokers would not insure him for such a strenuous role. In Israel he made *Neither by Day or by Night* (72), as an American father whose blinded son is adjusting in hospital, and then *Soylent Green* (73), supporting Charlton Heston, in this sci-fi tale, as an old man who had seen it all. He died just a few days before it came out – and just a few days before he was awarded a special Oscar for his contributions to cinema.

Cheyenne Autumn *(64) is one of John Ford's less interesting works. The best thing about it was Edward G. Robinson's cameo as Secretary of the Interior Carl Schurz.*

FLORA ROBSON

All great stars have a quality which cannot be exactly pinned down. You can say that Flora Robson had a beautiful speaking voice, but how do you define that stillness, that urgent inner momentum, the flick of humour, the smile that could light up a room – the combination of all four? Perhaps the clue to her art is in the stillness, always an indication of confidence, of an artist having mastered her art. It would have been her wish rather, it is known, to have been beautiful, but she was much more interesting than most of her contemporaries. She played a wider spectrum of parts than most actresses but was, in the end, better in sympathetic parts.

She was born in South Shields, Durham, in 1902, but went to school in London; she studied at RADA and was a bronze medallist – which netted her the part of Queen Margaret (one of the 'shadows') in Clemence Dane's 'Will Shakespeare' (21); for the next three years she did rep with Ben Greet and at Oxford, and returned to London in 'Fata Morgana' (24). But she left the stage suddenly and worked as a welfare officer in a factory for four years. In 1929 she wanted to act again and was in rep in Cambridge for a year (with Robert Donat); in 1931 she did two plays at London's Gate Theatre, including 'Desire Under the Elms' (as Abbie). As a result of these she was offered a small role in *A Gentleman of Paris* (31), as a middle-aged French woman; but she had bigger roles in *Dance Pretty Lady* (32), Anthony Asquith's version of Compton Mackenzie's 'Carnival', as the heroine's mother – the only good thing in the film; and *One Precious Year* (33), with Basil Rathbone and Owen Nares, as the heroine's best friend. At the same time her theatrical career was blooming: among others, 'The Anatomist' (her first London hit), 'Six Characters in Search of an Author', 'Dangerous Corner', 'All God's Chillun' and an Old Vic season with Charles Laughton – Varya ('The Cherry Orchard'), Isabella ('Measure for Measure'), Gwendolen ('The Importance of Being Earnest'), Katherine ('Henry VIII'), Lady Macbeth, etc.

It was Laughton who helped put her on the screen map, when he recommended her to Alexander Korda for the Dowager Czarina in *Catherine the Great* (34): apart from the fact that she was too clean, she was the only one of the cast who might have been like the original. She said later that Korda was very good to her: he financed James Bridie's 'Mary Read: Dragoon and Pirate', which she and Robert Donat did, and then sent her on holiday. In 1935 she played 'Mary Tudor' and then Korda had her play Mary's sister Eliza-beth in *Fire Over England* (37) with a script that included the Tilbury speech (she looked more like the portraits than Bette Davis did later, but lacked some of the fire). She did a few weeks as another such, the Empress in the aborted *I Claudius*; and that year also played in a moving World War I story, *Farewell Again*, with Leslie Banks. She played the CO's (fatally ill) wife, but Korda dropped her (she was getting £30 a week, as opposed to Vivien Leigh's approximate £5,000 per annum) because he considered her only suitable for playing queens. Stage appearances included 'Anna Christie' and 'Autumn'.

She went to Hollywood to play Mrs Read in *Wuthering Heights* (39), returning to Britain for *Poison Pen* (as a spinster, she of course writes the offending letters and 'dominates the picture with a performance full of subtle changes' – 'Photoplay'). She refused the part of Mrs Danvers in *Rebecca*, but returned to Hollywood on a two-picture contract for Warner Bros.: *We Are Not Alone* (39) as the domineering wife of English doctor Paul Muni, and *Invisible Stripes* (40), as George Raft's mother. Warners also asked her to do a supporting part – as Elizabeth I again – in Errol Flynn's *The Sea Hawk* (41) and two years later, before leaving for Britain, she was for them Ingrid Bergman's maid in *Saratoga Trunk*, in a peculiar dusky make-up. She was also in Paramount's *Bahama Passage*

Flora Robson as the ageing Queen Elizabeth I – she was in her 30s when she played the part – in Fire Over England *(37), from A.E.W. Mason's novel. The lady-in-waiting – and the film's heroine – was Vivien Leigh.*

(42), as Sterling Hayden's mother. During this American period she did two plays in New York, 'Ladies in Retirement' (40) and 'The Damask Cheek' (42); toured in 'Elizabeth the Queen' in summer theatres (42) and did a season of Grand Guignol in Los Angeles (43).

She returned to the London stage as Thérèse Raquin in a play after Zola; and to British films in Gainsborough's *2000 Women* (44), a few of whom were Phyllis Calvert, Patricia Roc and Jean Kent, all in an internment camp for English women in France. Robson played the understanding, motherly spinster – a role in which she was to be frequently cast in films, particularly in her Rank contract days, just beginning: *The Years Between* (45); *Great Day,* a cosy tale about the preparations in an English village for a visit by Mrs Eleanor Roosevelt; and *Caesar and Cleopatra*, as Cleopatra's sinister maid Ftatateetah. She followed with solid supporting chores in three successful ones, but star-billed: *Black Narcissus* (47), as a nun; *Frieda*, as a spinster MP claiming good guys among the Germans, but less sure in real life; and *Holiday Camp*, as a spinster relaxing after looking after her mother. She played another, succumbing to a handsome Italian in a stage version of Francis Brett Young's 'A Man About the House', and had a change of pace in *Good Time Girl* (48) with Jean Kent in the title-role, as the head of a reform school in this topical story of postwar youth; and again in *Saraband for Dead Lovers*, painted and scheming as the mistress of both the Elector and Koenigsmark.

In 1948 she returned to New York to play Lady Macbeth opposite Michael Redgrave and she stayed away from films for four years ('Black Chiffon' in London and New York, 'The Winter's Tale', 'The Innocents' – later filmed with Deborah Kerr – and others). She might have stayed away longer: *The Tall Headlines* (52) had no other distinction than her performance. She was an embittered Maltese in *The Malta Story* (53), the Nurse in Castellani's *Romeo and Juliet* (54); then again she concentrated on the stage, returning in another unworthy pair, *High Tide at Noon* (57) and *No Time for Tears* (Anna Neagle), down to eighth on the cast-list. Her 'great actress' portrait was almost the only lively feature of *The Gypsy and the Gentleman*, but she just about sank under *Innocent Sinners* (58), a heavy adaptation of Rumer Godden's 'An Episode of Sparrows'. On the stage she had two more big successes – 'Ghosts' and Redgrave's adaptation of 'The Aspern Papers'; she toured South Africa in the latter and in 'Time and Yellow Roses' in 1960 and 1962 respectively, and in 'Time . . .' appeared in the theatre in Newcastle named after her.

Times, otherwise, were not very exciting. Two stage ventures were disappointing and

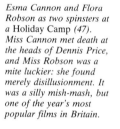

Esma Cannon and Flora Robson as two spinsters at a Holiday Camp *(47). Miss Cannon met death at the heads of Dennis Price, and Miss Robson was a mite luckier: she found merely disillusionment. It was a silly mish-mash, but one of the year's most popular films in Britain.*

she had only dull roles in *55 Days at Peking* (62), as the Chinese Empress; *Murder at the Gallop*, as the dead woman's frightened companion, as investigated by Margaret Rutherford; *Guns at Batasi* (64), as a Socialist MP touring Africa; *Young Cassidy*, as his mother; and it was sad to see her in a one-line part – as a nun – amid the frantic goings-on of *Those Magnificent Men in Their Flying Machines* (65). She was, however, seen to great effect in John Ford's *Seven Women*, made in the United States, but she was not well served by either the Gig Young-Carol Lynley *The Shuttered Room* (66), as an old crone, or by the Greek-British *Cry in the Wind*, or again by *Eye of the Devil* (67). After a play, 'Justice is a Woman' (66), she retired – because she thought the cast disliked her. However, in 1968 she played Miss Prism in a West End revival of 'The Importance of Being Earnest' and got rave notices. She told an interviewer that she had lost all interest in her craft, but the notices for her Prism had revived it; later, a slated revival of 'Ring Round the Moon' might have damaged her; but in 1969 another revival, the Rodney Ackland-Hugh Walpole 'The Old Ladies', was another success for her. In films, she was murdered at the beginning of *Fragment of Fear* (70) and was hardly more fortunate with *The Beast in the Cellar* (71), despite co-star billing with Beryl Reid. In Cyprus she supported Raquel Welch in *The Beloved* (72) and then played the White Queen in *Alice's Adventures in Wonderland*: if few people saw that, no one in her own country imported the film with Welch, or that made on a subsequent trip to the Mediterranean, *La Grande Scrofa Nera* (74), with Mark Frechette (star of *Zabriskie Point*, and later bank-robber and murder victim). For the next few years she did occasional TV and then *Dominique* (79), with Jean Simmons. She was memorable as a palsied spinster in the TV 'Eustace and Hilda' and was then in *A Man Called Intrepid* for TV in the US and cinemas elsewhere.

She made two American telefilms, *Gauguin the Savage* (80), playing a nun, and *A Tale of Two Cities*, as Miss Pross; and received star billing for her last movie, *Clash of the Titans* (81) – but had only a brief stint as one of the three eyeless witches. It was strange to see her interviewed on TV in her last years in an obvious, hideous black wig, for plainness, ordinariness, had been one of her great virtues. She died in 1984.

GINGER ROGERS

When Ginger Rogers went to London to play 'Mame' (69) the ads were in no doubt: 'The legendary Ginger Rogers.' The claim is best justified by her having been one half of a dancing team – Fred Astaire's most popular and durable partner – than by her later work without him. Not that her own work was undistinguished: she was seldom less than competent and always professional and likeable. Out of her dancing shoes, her flair was for not very high comedy. 'Time' magazine once put her among her peers: 'Less eccentric than Carole Lombard, less worldly-wise than Myrna Loy, less impudent than Joan Blondell, Ginger Rogers had a careless self-sufficiency they lack.' One thinks of her as cheerful, calculating and spunky; attractive in both youth and middle age.

The driving force, the power behind the throne, was her mother (till past middle age, as she admits in interviews). Mother gave birth to her in 1911 in Independence, Missouri; there was a divorce and the two girls went to Hollywood, where Mother wrote scripts. Ginger was offered a contract at the age of six, but Mother turned it down. Later Mother was a reporter and theatre critic in Fort Worth and it was here that Ginger started appearing in local plays and concerts. She substituted as a dancer when Eddie Foy's vaudeville act played the neighbourhood and after she had won a Charleston contest Mother decided it was time she went into vaudeville. She toured Texas and Oklahoma as 'Ginger and her Redheads'; and later, with her first husband, Jack Pepper, had an act called 'Ginger and Pepper'. She was on the stage in St Louis in 1928, then went to New York as a singer with Paul Ash's Orchestra. She appeared in a Rudy Vallee short, *Campus Sweethearts*, and got a part in a Broadway musical, 'Top Speed' (29). The critics noticed her and so did Paramount, who put her into *Young Man of Manhattan* (30), as Charles Ruggles's dumb-bell girlfriend. She had a song, 'I've got IT but IT don't do me no good', and became typed as a wise-cracking flapper. She was on Broadway with Ethel Merman in the Gershwins' 'Girl Crazy', but was not yet a major star. Paramount gave her a contract and between performances sent her to their Astoria studio for some featured roles: *The Sap from Syracuse*, as Jack Oakie's love interest; *Queen High*, starring Ruggles and Frank Morgan; *Follow the Leader* with Ed Wynn and Merman, a film also known as *Manhattan Mary*, the title it had had when he had done it on Broadway; and *Honor Among Lovers* (31), comedy relief with Ruggles. But she asked to be released from her contract,

For the first three years of her film career Ginger Rogers was just another wise-cracking blonde. Here she is as one of the Gold Diggers of 1933, *obviously digging it with Warren William.*

claiming that filming and stage work were too much for her. In reality she had had a better offer from RKO Pathé and when her show closed she went to Hollywood. She starred in *The Tip Off* with Robert Armstrong and was also the girl left behind by him, William Boyd and James Gleason – selling candy on Coney Island in *The Suicide Fleet*, an incredible war story. She sang on the *Carnival Boat* (32), but the results were less than sensational and Pathé dropped her. She worked around: *The Tenderfoot* with Joe E. Brown, based on George S. Kaufman's 'The Butter and Egg Man'; *The Thirteenth Guest* with Lyle Talbot, a thriller at Monogram; *Hat Check Girl* starring Ben Lyon and Sally Eilers; and *You Said a Mouthful* with Brown. She said later: 'I started playing second leads in comedy, then leading women, then second leads in musical comedy – things like . . . *42nd Street*' (33). In that, as Anytime Annie, the chorine with society ambitions and monocled – 'The only time she ever said no she didn't hear the question' – she scored a hit and after *Broadway Bad* at Fox (as Joan Blondell's pal) Warners put her into another of their musicals, *Gold Diggers of 1933*.

But her best chance came when returning to RKO, to play the *Professional Sweetheart*, the Purity Girl of the Air, who deliberately set out to shock a shy suitor, Norman Foster. It was not much of a film, but RKO now liked her and signed her to a long-term contract. Meanwhile she did *A Shriek in the Night* with Talbot, *Don't Bet on Love* with Lew Ayres and *Sitting Pretty*, as a waitress who helps songwriters Jack Oakie and Jack Haley. Then RKO cast her as the second lead, typically brash, in a musical, *Flying Down to Rio*. She was fourth-billed, after Dolores del Rio, Gene Raymond and Raul Roulien, but it was she and partner Fred Astaire, a newcomer from Broadway, who stole the notices. She was a small-town girl in a triangle drama with Joel McCrea, *Chance at Heaven*, and then with Foster again in the unpretentious and enjoyable *Rafter Romance* (34). She went to *Finishing School* with Frances Dee and Billie Burke, which qualified her for three loan-outs, *Change of Heart* at Fox and two at Warners, *Twenty Million Sweethearts,* opposite Dick Powell, and *Upper World*, where Warren William dallied with her when wife Mary Astor neglected him; she played a chorus girl, at which, by this time, she was more than adept, and got killed.

Her first marriage had lasted 10 months. In 1934 she married one of her co-stars, Lew Ayres; they separated in 1935 and were divorced in 1941. She was married again 1943–49 to Jack Briggs, 1953–57 Jacques Bergerac and 1961–71 to William Marshall (who had

been married to Michèle Morgan and Micheline Presle).

RKO paired Rogers and Astaire again in *The Gay Divorcée* and they were an even greater success. Rogers did a pointless drama with Francis Lederer, *Romance in Manhattan*, and then another with Astaire (and Irene Dunne), *Roberta* (35). She had not wanted to be a musical star and saw herself becoming successful as such with misgiving. But she said later: 'I loved Fred so, and I mean that in the nicest, warmest way: I had such affection for him *artistically*. I think that experience with Fred was a divine blessing. It blessed me, I know, and I don't think blessings are one-sided.' It is doubtful whether her mother, still guiding her career, felt the same way: until stopped by Astaire's protests, she insisted on elaborate costumes for Rogers because she feared that no one would look at her when dancing with him. Financially, RKO were blessed: most of the Astaire-Rogers films were big money-makers and the team went into the top 10.

As often as she could, Rogers did 'straight' films: *Star of Midnight*, an enjoyable, polished and typical William Powell vehicle; and after *Top Hat* with Astaire, *In Person*, as a jaded movie star bullied and wooed by George Brent. She danced in *Follow the Fleet* (36), *Swing Time* and *Shall We Dance?* (37) and as a reward begged to play Elizabeth in *Mary of Scotland*. The studio said no, but did put her to play with Hepburn in *Stage Door*, as the young hopeful whose wise-cracks mask her own uncertainty and determination: it was a return to her early screen persona – in her films with Astaire she had become somewhat refined and ladylike. Further, it was a good film and proved that she could be effective without Astaire. She was now getting $3,000 a week. There were two comedies: *Having Wonderful Time* (38), a weak one about a holiday camp with Douglas Fairbanks Jr, and *Vivacious Lady*, a good one about professor James Stewart bringing his cabaret singer wife to meet his country-club friends.

The break-up of the public's favourite screen team was on the cards for some time. *Carefree* and *The Story of Irene and Vernon Castle* (39) were the last. The official reason was that Rogers wanted to go dramatic and fans soon accepted the split as inevitable. However, drama waited on two excellent comedies, *Bachelor Mother*, with David Niven, as a salesgirl landed with an abandoned baby; and *Fifth Avenue Girl*, as an out-of-work girl landed with a wealthy man (Walter Connolly). She was as good as her films, but carefully cast as a working girl there would be times when she only compromised a bit with her film-starriness – including the one which won her an Oscar. She did one such, *The Primrose Path* (40), from a hit play about a girl trying to escape from the wrong side of the tracks by marrying respectability in the person of Joel McCrea: Marjorie Rambeau and Queenie Vasser were a marvellously funny Mother and Grandmother. And *Lucky Partners* was a dim version of Sacha Guitry's 'Bonne Chance', notable only for her smooth teaming with Ronald Colman, though reputedly there was dissension on the set when she found that his part was bigger than hers.

Then came *Kitty Foyle*, from Christopher Morley's bestseller about a salesgirl who married money (Dennis Morgan) but yearned for a man from her own stratum. 'The result of pounding on the doors of executives was *Stage Door, Primrose Path, Kitty Foyle*. Those last two are my favourites.' Rogers won an Oscar against stiff competition (Davis in *The Letter*, Fontaine in *Rebecca*, Hepburn in *The Philadelphia Story* and Martha Scott in *Our Town*). She was certainly fine in Garson Kanin's *Tom Dick and Harry* (41), a comedy about a girl with too many suitors, though the film lost its way. Under the terms of her new contract she was allowed to freelance, but RKO were making much of her as a Great Actress: they announced dozens of appropriate projects, including *Rain* and *Sister Carrie*. She did a variety of parts, but her performances were less versatile than her hair-dos – successively a bubble cut, shoulder-length, brunette page-boy, pig-tails of indeterminate colour and page-boy again in her usual blonde. The bubbles were for the gum-chewing *Roxie Hart* (42), who takes the rap for a murder her husband committed (a remake of *Chicago*, in which Phyllis Haver had starred, and intermittently amusing), and the page-boy for her episode with Henry Fonda in *Tales of Manhattan*, also at 20th. Warners offered *King's Row* – the role that the studio's own Ann Sheridan played so beautifully.

She signed a three-picture deal with Paramount, on the proviso that the second one be *Lady in the Dark* – the rights then purchased from Alexander Korda (who owned them) for the hefty sum of $285,000. The first of the arrangement was *The Major and the Minor* with Ray Milland, a comedy about a girl who poses as a child to travel half-fare: the co-scripter, Billy Wilder, turned director on this, on Roger's okay, and he remembered her as 'an absolute delight' to work with. She was posing again in *Once Upon a Honeymoon*, a Brooklyn beauty queen pretending to be a blueblood, chased over most of Nazi-torn Europe by Cary Grant – an idiotic 'comedy' directed by Leo McCarey. *Tender Comrade* (43) was some sentimentality about war wives

Ginger Rogers's appearances these days are confined to television, so it's good to be reminded how pretty and how down-to-earth she used to be, as in Follow the Fleet *(36), her fifth film with Fred Astaire, above, and* Kitty Foyle *(40), left, which brought her an Oscar. Maybe she was a bit dreamy in this one, but she's still good to look at – and it's a reminder that she was successful at impersonating children on several occasions.*

– of whom Rogers in life was one, after meeting a marine – Briggs – while touring for USO. Disappearing to get married during the making of *Lady in the Dark* (44; like her previous film, its release delayed) was 'the last straw' said co-star Milland; making it, said Mitchell Leisen, 'took ten years off my life', but as the dialogue coach, Phyllis Loughton, explained, Ginger 'was a star with a capital S' at that time. 'Picturegoer' had another word on its making: 'Phyllis Brooks almost stole the show. So Ginger got a great deal of it cut out of the film and insisted that Phyllis be given little or no publicity.' As the inhibited magazine editor, Rogers tried for an impersonation of Gertrude Lawrence's original performance. The critics were kind to neither her nor film, but according to the 'Motion Picture Herald' it grossed nearly $4½ million.

Her next films were concoctions of little distinction: *I'll Be Seeing You*, in love with soldier/mental patient Joseph Cotten; *Weekend at the Waldorf* (45) with Walter Pidgeon, absurdly over-graceful as a sad little great big movie star – but getting over $292,000 for it, making her one of the best-paid women in the US; *Heartbeat*, a remake of Danielle Darrieux's *Battement de Coeur*, about a pickpocket who falls for victim Jean-Pierre Aumont; *Magnificent Doll* (46), a dull version of the Dolly Madison story; and *It Had to Be You* (47), a much-too-late attempt to revive screwball comedy, which in any case co-star Cornel Wilde could not play.

She signed a two-picture deal with Enterprise, the first attempt at a major production company since 20th Century, which had also started by offering big names short contracts. In this case they offered – to Rogers, at least – script approval and she turned down *Caught*, which Barbara Bel Geddes did before the studio went under. So she had been off the screen for a while, till MGM needed a replacement for Judy Garland in *The Barkleys of Broadway* (49), which may account for the speed with which she grabbed her dancing shoes: this reunion with Astaire was the first in colour and got a great reception everywhere. It also revived her career: two at WB, *Perfect Strangers* (50) with Dennis Morgan, falling in love in the jurors room, and *Storm Warning*, a dramatic piece with Doris Day about the KKK; and *The Groom Wore Spurs* (51) – he was Jack Carson and she was his wife and his attorney. Then there were three comedies at 20th: *We're Not Married* (52), the best episode, with Fred Allen, about a radio couple whose real marital life is one of mutual aggression; *Monkey Business* with Cary Grant, embarrassingly got up as juveniles for

The latter screen work of Ginger Rogers was variable, but she always gave the others lessons in how to be glamorous and soignée. Forever Female (53), a comedy with William Holden.

the sake of the plot; and *Dreamboat* with Clifton Webb, about two Silent stars caught up in the world of TV. She signed another three-movie deal at Paramount, the first of which was to be *Topsy & Eva*, co-starring with Betty Hutton, but that was cancelled when Hutton left the studio. The second was *Forever Female* (53), in which she was delicious as an actress who will not face the fact that she is ageing. The third was not made. She also played an actress (atrociously) in a mild murder mystery, *Black Widow* (54), at 20th.

Like several American stars in the 1950s, she made the mistake of thinking a British film might revitalize her career and brought in tow director David Miller and a brand-new husband, Bergerac: *Beautiful Stranger*. Better was a programmer at Columbia, *Tight Spot* (55), considerably enlivened by her performance as a gangster's moll and Edward G. Robinson's as the DA. The next three made little impression, but *The First Travelling Saleslady* (56) gave her a delightful sidekick in Carol Channing. *Teenage Rebel*, with Michael Rennie, gave her a teenage daughter; and *Oh Men Oh Women*, a heavy-handed farce, gave her little to do.

In 1951 she had been in a Broadway dud, 'Love and Let Love', in which she had invested $23,000 of her own money, and she tried again some years later, with 'The Pink Jungle', but it did not get even as far as Broadway. Paul Gregory, who produced, said: 'She's one of the reasons I left show business . . . We'd give her a new scene, and she couldn't remember the lines. She couldn't sing and, surprisingly, she couldn't do the dances. And all through the horror of it all she was smiling and grinning and unreal. There's no denying her appeal to the public. That's what makes her so dangerous. She almost smiled me into bankruptcy.' He added that although she was a Christian Scientist he saw little of the Christian side of her nature. In stock she appeared in, among others, 'Bell Book and Candle', 'The Unsinkable Molly Brown' and 'Annie Get Your Gun' (the film of which she had hoped to do: 'I wanted that role so badly . . . I'd have done it for one dollar'). Her TV début was in 'Three by Coward' (54) and in Britain she did a musical for the BBC, 'Carissima' (59). She came into her own again in the 60s, first in a TV spectacular in which she sang and danced, and later when she took over from Channing in 'Hello Dolly'. When she and Astaire danced on to the stage to make a presentation at the 1968 Oscar ceremony, they received an ovation such as Hollywood has seldom seen. Her contract for 'Mame' guaranteed her in excess of £250,000, the highest sum yet paid to an artist in London's West End.

In 1965 with husband Marshall she entered into an agreement with the Jamaican government to make films there – a new series of Rogers vehicles: in the first, with Milland, she played the madame of a brothel. Filming was a débâcle and ended in dissension: years later the film received an occasional booking as *Quick Let's Get Married*. The same year she replaced Judy Garland as Mama Jean in the Electrovision *Harlow*, never shown outside the US – where the critics thought she was the best thing about it. Of other films she has said: 'All the roles I refused were unnecessarily vulgar'; and of the past: 'I'm most grateful to have had that joyous time in motion pictures . . . Pictures were talking, they were singing, they were colouring. It was beginning to blossom out: bud and blossom were both present.' And of the future: 'The most important thing in anyone's life is to be giving something. The quality I can give is fun and joy and happiness. This is my gift . . . I would not like a talent to go to waste.' With this in mind she put together a nightclub act in 1976 and in 1978 played the London Palladium. In 1980 she starred in a stage show at Radio City Music Hall (which had had to give up its role as a cinema) and later in the year was in a tour of 'Anything Goes' which collapsed prematurely.

WILL ROGERS

Even in his lifetime it was common to refer to Will Rogers as an American folk hero; after his untimely death the description was bandied around so often that he dwarfed everyone else in the category. But for many years his pictures were not revived and he is merely a name to most people under 50.

He was born in Oolagah, Indian Territory (now Oklahoma), in 1879 of ancestry said to be part Irish, part Cherokee Indian. He was educated in Neosho, Missouri, and at a military academy at Booneville in that state. As a boy he became proficient at riding and lariat throwing and during his time as a ranch hand and later cow-puncher established a battery of tricks. At one point he worked on a ship that plied between Buenos Aires and South Africa, supplying mules to the British engaged in the Boer War, and it was in Johannesburg that he joined his first Wild West Show, billed as 'The Cherokee Kid'. Back in the US he joined another show and twirled ropes at the St Louis World's Fair of 1904; part of that outfit was engaged to appear at Madison Square Garden the following year during the Annual Horse Fair. He then got on the vaudeville bill at Keiths, Union Square, sitting on a pony, chewing gum and twirling a lasso; he was soon appearing in Hammerstein's Roof Garden and becoming known. He never spoke – until one day one of his tricks went wrong and an ad lib comment brought a laugh. Gradually, as he toured in vaudeville in the US and overseas (he was booked into Berlin's Winter Garden for a year, 1906–7), he added dialogue: first he commented on the act that had preceded him; later he was to comment on public figures and the political affairs of the day. He longed to go into a musical comedy and got a part in 'The Wall Street Girl' (12). Later he did 'Hands Up' (15), 'The Passing Show of 1917' and the Ziegfeld 'Midnight Frolic' supper show, which led to appearances in the Follies of 1917 and 1918. His home-spun philosophy and cracker-barrel wit made a surprising hit with New Yorkers: he spoke with seeming sincerity and without malice. He was Mr Everyman – it was soon realized that he spoke for Mr Joe Public. He sauntered shyly on to the stage, pushed back his cowlick and slowly began.

Goldwyn at that time had invested in a unit called Eminent Authors Inc, whose job was to provide films with better scenarios. The boss-man of the outfit was Rex Beach, the most eminent of the eight eminent authors, and when he sold his *Laughing Bill Hyde* (18) to Goldwyn he recommended Rogers as the lead. Rogers, he said, did not need to play the character: he *was* the character. It was not a huge success but Rogers did a cross-country tour which proved him to be a national favourite. So Goldwyn signed him to a contract worth $2,250 a week, with an option for a second year at $3,000 per week, and prepared a series of vehicles which would convert him into a big movie star: *Almost a Husband* (19) with Peggy Wood; *Jubilo,* a popular 'Saturday Evening Post' story about a carefree hobo that was perhaps the best of this bunch; *Water Water Everywhere* (20); *Jes' Call Me Jim* with Irene Rich; *The Strange Board*; *Cupid the Cowpuncher*; *Honest Hutch*; *Guile of Women* (21); *Boys Will Be Boys*; *An Unwilling Hero*; and *Doubling for Romeo,* as a cowhand who falls asleep while reading Shakespeare and dreams he is a movie star. That one was made in an attempt to kid the Rogers image, which was noticeably cold-shouldered by female audiences. After *A Poor Relation* (22) Goldwyn did not renew the contract. The comedies were slowed down by Rogers's offscreen 'pithy epigrams' which were increasingly incorporated into the intertitles.

Paramount used him in a vehicle originally prepared for Fatty Arbuckle, *One Glorious Day* – when a spirit takes over his meek professorial body to best a bunch of crooked politicians: but it did no better. An independent, Hodkinson, tried him in a version of Washington Irving's story, *The Headless Horseman*. Also, Rogers tried being his own impresario – and writer and director; but his two-reelers, *The Ropin' Fool, Fruits of Faith* and *One Day in 365,* were disastrous and he lost all his money. He returned to the Follies in 1922 and 1924, during which time Hal Roach approached him with an offer to make some two-reel comedies. This was not necessarily a come-down after features, as Roach, who specialized in shorts, was at that time ambitious. Rogers made 12 for him, of which the most successful was *Two Wagons Both Covered,* but he was essentially a dialogue comedian and with slapstick no match for Keaton or Lloyd; Roach wisely had him parody his more serious confreres – Tom Mix, Valentino, etc. – in *Big Moments From Little Pictures, Uncensored Movies* and others. He was offered a lecture tour – and in 1925 on a concert tour was earning $10,000 to $12,000 per week. He also began to write humorous pieces for the newspapers: he had already published 'Rogerisms – The Cowboy Philosopher on the Peace Conference' and a similar book on Prohibition. He was sent by the 'Saturday Evening Post' to observe Europe for them and while there appeared at the London Pavilion and accepted an offer from Herbert Wilcox to co-star with Dorothy Gish in *Tip Toes* (27), a story about three broke American vaudevillians in Britain. Paramount released in the US.

In Hollywood First National was anxious to give Rogers another film fling and selected *A Texas Steer,* about a rancher who is elected to Congress and generally straightens things out, including cynicism and corruption in high places, but the film was not a success (unlike *Mr Smith Goes to Washington* later; not a remake but the same idea). In 1928 he returned to Broadway in 'Three Cheers' and he was one of the stage performers whom Hollywood re-examined when Talkies came in. Fox proposed a new version of *The County Chairman,* already successful as a play and a Silent; Rogers was wary but submitted, though the film they actually made was *They Had to See Paris* (29) with wife Irene Rich and daughter Marguerite Churchill, leaving Oklahoma for culture. It gave him a fine opportunity to show his American-ness, his tolerance of things foreign and contempt for the others who fell for all the pomp frivolity. Frank Borzage, who directed, commented on Rogers's ability 'to portray the simple, human emotions that touch the very soul of mankind. The sincerity and conviction with which he did

The films Will Rogers made for Fox were of a good standard, like A Connecticut Yankee (31), with Myrna Loy as Morgan La Faye. One of his virtues was his ability to extemporize much of his own dialogue (indeed, few scriptwriters could write for him): he knew how to play himself superbly, and within those limits was an impressive actor.

them is what is expected of a great comedian. Audiences forget Rogers the wisecracker.' Now, with Speech, cinema audiences fell for him. He had got $50,000 for it and Fox offered $60,000 for another picture. First he played himself in their review, *Happy Days* (30), which was photographed in 'Grandeur', or 'wide film'; then he did *So This Is London*, an old George M. Cohan farce that was much like his first Talkie: Rich was again his wife, but Maureen O'Sullivan the daughter.

Fox put him under contract and starred him in *Lightnin'* (31), which had been, years earlier (1918), the longest-running play on Broadway. 'Photoplay' said: 'Here's willrogersing at its best. . . . As the shiftless, whimsical, truth-embroidering Bill Jones, he's a nine-reel scream.' Henry King directed and Louise Dresser was Rogers's wife. He then was Mark Twain's *A Connecticut Yankee* (transported in time to King Arthur's Court) and it was his biggest film hit to date. There followed: *Young As You Feel* with Fifi D'Orsay; *Ambassador Bill*; *Business and Pleasure* (32) with Jetta Goudal, a version of Booth Tarkington's 'The Plutocrat', and *Down to Earth*, which was specially written by Homer Croy, the author of *They Had to See Paris*, and was a sequel, set in the US with Rogers giving good advice on coping with the Depression. *Too Busy To Work* was a remake of *Jubilo* and his most serious film to date.

On radio and in the press he was a political figure of some influence. 1932 was the year of the presidential elections and Rogers was considered instrumental in Roosevelt being elected – he seemed to be, at least, the people's spokesman. He now started appearing in film popularity polls and at the end of the year he was ninth at the box-office. The following year he trailed Marie Dressler and in 1934 supplanted her – due in part to some above-average films: *State Fair* (33), about a family's visit to that institution, beautifully directed by King from Phil Stong's novel, with Dresser again as his wife; and *Doctor Bull*, as a country doctor. Its director, John Ford, called it a downbeat story, 'but Bill managed to get a lot of humour into it – and it became a hell of a good picture. It was one of Bill's favourites . . . it was always a lot of fun to work for Bill.' Rogers, he went on, extemporized, taking only what he wanted from his scripts and getting the sense in his own inimitable way. *Mr Skitch* concerned a family escaping the Depression, with Zazu Pitts and the British Florence Desmond doing her impressions; and *David Harum* (34) was about a small-town banker horse-trading on the side – already a succesful novel and Silent, and now equally welcomed. It did not matter that most of these were formula pictures: audiences revelled in the situations of *Handy Andy*, in which he was the lackadaisical

Rogers's – and Janet Gaynor's – best-remembered film is the charming State Fair *(33), directed by Henry King. The two (musical) remakes were both inferior.*

husband of social climber Peggy Wood. Said 'Photoplay', 'Sophisticated or softie, sixteen or sixty, you'll love this.' Thus he was the ideal interpreter for what are taken to be among Ford's most personal works, like *Judge Priest*, set in a Kentucky town where Civil War passions still run high.

At the beginning of 1933 he was the highest paid star, at $15,000 a week (Garbo and John Gilbert followed, at $13,000 each, and then, in descending order, Chevalier, Ruth Chatterton, Ann Harding, Richard Barthelmess, Mae West, Constance Bennett and Ronald Colman), which was revised to $110,000 per film, revised again at this time to $125,000 per film, plus 50 per cent of the profits. At last he did *The County Chairman* (35); then *Life Begins at Forty*, as a small-town editor, and *Doubting Thomas* with Billie Burke. Fearing he was slipping at the box-office, he asked for *Steamboat 'Round the Bend* to be released before *In Old Kentucky*. The former was certainly the better; it was John Ford's, with Rogers this time as a medicine man running a steamboat. But before either was released he was killed in an aircrash (1935), in Alaska, with Wiley Post, the aviator.

He had always had a fondness for flying. The United States was grief-stricken: apart from films his daily press pieces were still widely read. At the end of the year he was still Box-Office King – after Shirley Temple. Fox, now 20th, made a couple of films in 1936 with

Irvin S. Cobb, who was also a newspaperman and an actor – he had appeared in two of Rogers's films – but after Rogers, he was strictly minor league. In 1952 Warners produced *The Will Rogers Story* with Will Rogers Jr and Jane Wyman as his loving and guiding wife.

If he was far more than a regional figure, few of his comments can be read today with ease and some are positively thought-stunting, like this to a 'Picturegoer' interviewer in 1926: 'Oh yes, I write. I have done for a long time now. I don't write *good* but I write a lot. My stuff's only for ordinary yappin' rubes. I don't know nothin' about these new movements. You know – the intelligentsia, or whatever they call themselves. Some of them came to see me the other day.' Added the interviewer: 'His look spoke volumes.'

But on the screen he had a genuine charm and was amusing even if he could not be considered an actor of any range. In life he was friendly and, like Gracie Fields, completely unconcerned with and unspoilt by success. Homer Croy, his biographer – 'Our Will Rogers' (53) – speaks eloquently of Rogers's real meaning to his contemporaries: 'He was the most influential private citizen in the world. He was always hopping off on some air trip; when he arrived in any country in the world (except Russia) he was given an ovation. If there was an earthquake or a disaster of any kind, he would fly to the place; the people would receive him with touching acclaim. He could help them. He was their friend. He was America.'

MICKEY ROONEY

Like most child stars, Mickey Rooney's misfortune was that he had to grow up – though he was well into his 20s when the decline hit (which made it harder): his small stature had kept him a teenager longer than most teenagers. He says in his autobiography (1967): 'In the year 1938 I had starred in eight pictures. In the years '48 and '49 together, I starred in three. . . . The American public was not clamouring for my work.' Yet for a while he had been the biggest drawing card of them all.

He was born in Brooklyn in 1920, the son of a vaudeville couple: at the age of two he joined their act and three years later he was touring with Sid Gold's dance act. An appearance in a tear-jerker called 'Mr Iron Claw' led him to be cast as a midget in *Not to Be Trusted* (26), followed by a Colleen Moore vehicle, *Orchids and Ermine* (27). He trouped as Joe Yule Jr, his real name, but was now rechristened Mickey McGuire by Radio, who hired him to play in a series of shorts featuring a strip cartoon character of that name, from 1927 onwards: *Mickey's Midnight Frolic, Mickey's Mixup, Mickey the Romeo,* etc. He made over 40 before the series was dropped in 1933, but in the meantime he was prevented from using Mickey McGuire as a professional name for other work and someone at Universal suggested Mickey Rooney. He was there to make *My Pal the King* (32) starring Tom Mix. As Rooney he got a featured part in *Fast Companions* and was 'the big surprise' ('Photoplay'). But fame was a long way off. He had small parts at various studios: *Sin's Pay Day*; *The Beast of the City*; *High Speed*; *The Big Cage* (33), a Clyde Beatty feature; *The Life of Jimmy Dolan*; and *The Big Chance*. At MGM he played Eddie Quillan as a boy in *Broadway to Hollywood*, which starred Alice Brady and was an expensive item as most of it was scrapped and filmed again. Still at Metro, Rooney was in *The Chief* and then he moved over to Universal for three: *Beloved* (34); *I Like It That Way* and *The Love Birds*, supporting Zazu Pitts and Slim Somerville. He was also in a serial with Beatty, *The Lost Jungle*.

At MGM Selznick had noticed him and thought his cockiness made him ideal to play Clark Gable as a boy in *Manhattan Melodrama*. They signed him on a week-to-week basis, because they already had one boy star under contract, Jackie Cooper, who had only achieved a mild popularity. He was loaned to Universal for *Half a Sinner* with Joel McCrea and to Columbia for *Blind Date*, and then, after *Chained* and *Hide-Out*, MGM put him under long-term contract at a starting salary of $150,000 a week. That would go to $200 if the option was picked up after six months and then to $300 a week, to go to $1,000 a week in the last and seventh year, 1941, with a guaranteed 40 weeks' work and the right to loan him out, which they did for three of the next four: *The County Chairman* (35) at Fox; *The Healer* at Monogram with Ralph Bellamy; *Reckless*, in a bit as a newsboy; and his much-liked Puck in Warners' *A Midsummer Night's Dream*, which he had just done on the stage for Reinhardt; he then played the kid brother in *Ah Wilderness!*, the first version of Eugene O'Neill's 'happy' family play and a beautiful film. He supported Jean Harlow in *Riff Raff* and Freddie Bartholomew in Selznick's *Little Lord Fauntleroy* (36); and the contrast of the young English gentleman and the American toughie was so winning that Metro teamed them again, with a young Cooper this time, in *The Devil Is a Sissy*. He starred for the first time in a B at Warners, *Down the Stretch*, as a jockey, with Patricia

Mickey Rooney as Puck in A Midsummer Night's Dream *(35).*

Ellis, and gave a beautiful performance as the cabin boy who befriends Bartholomew in *Captains Courageous* (37).

In March 1937 MGM released *A Family Affair*, a very modest version of a minor Broadway play called 'Skidding', about Judge Hardy (Lionel Barrymore), his wife (Spring Byington), their son Andy (Rooney) and their life in the small town of Carvel. It hit the public nerve, which startled MGM, for B pictures seldom did: a sequel was ordered, more from curiosity than anything else. Meanwhile, he did *Slave Ship*, again at sea, with Wallace Beery at 20th, *The Hoosier Schoolboy* at Monogram, *Live Love and Learn, Thoroughbreds Don't Cry*, as a jockey – his first film with Judy Garland, and *Love Is a Headache* (38). *You're Only Young Once* reunited the Hardy family, with Lewis Stone replacing Lionel Barrymore as the father, partly because he thought his reputation would suffer if he did a B series and MGM were not about to recompense him for the indignity; but he also agreed with his colleagues that Rooney was the biggest scene-stealer on the lot and was less happy than some of the others to suffer because of it. Fay Holden came in as Mrs Hardy and Ann Rutherford as Andy's crush: good wholesome family entertainment, and exhibitors asked a beaming Louis B. Mayer for another one. . . . *Judge Hardy's Children*: more money was spent, lifting it from B product to programmer level. Rooney's agent pointed out that $400 a week was too little for an actor of growing popularity and MGM added a further $250 per week as a bonus.

He was featured in *Hold That Kiss* starring Maureen O'Sullivan and Dennis O'Keefe, whom MGM at that point considered would be their next big star, and then opposite Bartholomew in another formula film, *Lord Jeff*; while Garland was added to that other formula, *Love Finds Andy Hardy*. 'The best of it is that love not only finds Andy Hardy but finds him being played by Mickey Rooney . . . he's the perfect composite of everybody's kid brother' (Frank S. Nugent); '. . . an exuberant performance' (Howard Barnes). He gave another good performance, touching if conventional, as the young punk reformed at *Boy's Town*: in this instance he did not steal the picture, but he took *Stablemates* from Wallace Beery. In this respect he was a threat to all the big stars at MGM and then, suddenly, after *Out West With the Hardys*, he was a star in his own right: he turned up at third in the top 10; and was awarded a special Oscar. His agent now pointed out that he was only making $5,000 per picture and towards the end of the following year negotiated a new three-year contract, starting at $1,000 a week, to rise in two stages to $1,500 in the last year with a bonus of $25,000 per film and a guarantee of at least two of these each year. The studio had an option for four more years, with Rooney to start at $1,750, which would reach $3,000 in the fourth.

The studio had already put him into *The Adventures of Huckleberry Finn* (39); he was rushed into *The Hardys Ride High* and *Andy Hardy Gets Spring Fever*; then he and Garland were the *Babes in Arms*, a pleasant musical about a second generation of vaudevillians. It betrayed the Rodgers and Hart original, as James Agate pointed out, adding, 'I am a great admirer of this young gentleman who, when he likes, has more power and pathos than almost anybody else on the screen today.' 'Mickey Rooney can act the legs off a centipede' said the 'Sunday Times' (London). The public agreed: at the end of 1939 Rooney was the biggest attraction in the US and second in Britain; he was top in both countries in 1940 and 1941. But after *Judge Hardy and Son* he had his first flop as a star, *Young Tom Edison* (40), a quiet, old-fashioned rural drama; though *Andy Hardy Meets Débutante* soon made up for it. Garland was in the latter and the two of them continued their calf-love in *Strike Up the Band*. They were a good team, he brash and she wistful, both brimming with vitality and keenness, and they played beautifully together. He did *Andy Hardy's Private Secretary* (41) and *Men of Boy's*

Town; then the two of them were reunited for *Life Begins for Andy Hardy* and *Babes on Broadway*.

Of that one, Dilys Powell wrote: 'It may be argued Mr Rooney, with his extraordinary (though to me not pleasing) talents, has for some years now had nothing to learn except, perhaps, reticence', and 'The New York Times' cavilled: 'Mickey doesn't leave much room for anybody else.' He was, indeed, increasingly like a male, adult Shirley Temple: singing, dancing, clowning . . . imitations, always a Big Scene where he cried or made others cry; and it was all increasingly mechanical. Still, in Britain in 1942, the readers of 'Picturegoer' voted him their favourite star (followed by Spencer Tracy, Deanna Durbin, Gary Cooper, Clark Gable and Bette Davis). That year he was in *The Courtship of Andy Hardy*, *A Yank at Eton* (with Bartholomew now supporting him) and *Andy Hardy's Double Life*; then in Clarence Brown's good film of William Saroyan's hokey *The Human Comedy* (43) as the son of the central family coping with life on the home front, becoming a telegraph boy after leaving school; out West with Garland in *Girl Crazy*; and he compèred the all-star show which made *Thousands Cheer* as well as doing his imitations of Gable and Tracy. It was only a couple of years since he had been a bigger box-office draw than either; he had moved down the list in 1942 to No. 4 and in 1943 to No. 9. Fearing overexposure – and noting the critics' barbs – his activity was reduced: *Andy Hardy's Blonde Trouble* (44) and *National Velvet*, as the exjockey who trains her, conceivably his first adult role and subsidiary in interest to that of Elizabeth Taylor, who owns her. During this period he had also married Ava Gardner (1942–43), the first of many.

He joined the Army, which promoted him to sergeant. During his absence a new agent negotiated a new contract for seven years, with an immediate bonus of $140,000 and $5,000 a week during the 40 weeks he was working; he was also permitted to do radio work (an important concession since radio was anathema to Mayer) to the extent of 39 weeks a year plus four guest appearances, to be restricted to 26 weeks if MGM considered radio was impairing his screen value. It was announced that *Love Laughs at Andy Hardy* (46) would be Andy's farewell, but that did not bring in the public, nor did *Killer McCoy* (47), with which the studio tried to give Rooney a new image: he played a boxer in this remake of the Robert Taylor *The Crowd Roars*. The old one was only too boringly back in *Summer Holiday* (48), but then it had been made 18 months earlier and shelved: he now played the elder brother in this musical

Strike Up the Band *(40)*.
*Said 'The New York
Times': 'Roll out the red
carpet, folks, and stand by.
That boy is here again, the
Pied Piper of the box-
office, the eighth or ninth
wonder of the world, the
kid himself – in short,
Mickey Rooney. With a
capable assist by Judy
Garland. . . .'*

remake of *Ah Wilderness!*, which confirmed MGM's doubts by performing disastrously. Another musical, *Words and Music*, did better, with its strong line-up of guest stars, including Garland, for a last duet: but in this biography of Rodgers and Hart they were 'played with fantastic incompetence by Tom Drake and Mickey Rooney' ('The New York Times'). And 'Time': '. . . Mickey Rooney runs his own narrow gamut between the brash and the maudlin, tottering finally to a ludicrous death on the rain-pelted sidewalk.' At this point Rooney crossed Mayer and they even came to blows when the actor asked for the rights to do the Hardy series on radio: although MGM had announced there would not be another Hardy film, Mayer reserved the right to change his mind – in which case, said Rooney, he would refuse to play him. Believing that he would do better if he accepted outside offers, his contract was amended again, in complicated terms but amounting to $2,500 per week per year for 20 weeks' work, for five pictures. Two at United

Artists, *The Big Wheel* (49), a racing drama, and *Quicksand* (50), a thriller about a car mechanic whose troubles start when he falls for a blonde, proved that he no longer had box-office value and when he complained to MGM at not being cast in their big and expensive *Battleground* his contract was settled. A third UA project, *Francis the Talking Mule*, was cancelled and sold to Universal, where it became a big success for Donald O'Connor.

By his own admission, Rooney was bumptious and big-headed at this time. He appeared at the London Palladium and in nightclubs over the next few years; and again got mixed notices. Part of the trouble was that the qualities which had sat well on him as a youngster now began to look like aggressiveness; and he was the same offscreen as on, which meant that he made enemies.

He set about rebuilding his career with the expected energy, but the independent company he formed (with backing from an ex-exhibitor) made only a series of duds: *The*

Fireball with Pat O'Brien, *He's a Cockeyed Wonder* with Terry Moore and *My Outlaw Brother* (51), a Western with Robert Preston in which Rooney was 'woefully miscast' ('Variety'). Under his contractual break with MGM they still had a call on his services and they exercised it on *The Strip*, a B in which he was a bandsman accused of murdering a racketeer. At Columbia Harry Cohn still had faith in him and was prepared to pay him $75,000 each for three films over the next three years, starting with an army comedy, *Sound Off* (52), directed by Richard Quine, who had been a close chum of Rooney since they had acted together at MGM a decade earlier. Quine's *All Ashore* (53), a naval farce with Dick Haymes, was the second of the Columbia deal. Rooney stayed in uniform for *Off Limits*, co-starring with Bob Hope for a fee of $75,000 – but only because Alan Young was suffering from overwork and Paramount needed a replacement. Rooney's performance as an eager prize-fighter – Hope was his manager, who also joins up – was his most attractive in years and he might have returned permanently to A features if MGM had not suddenly discovered that he owed them another film under the settlement – a B with Eddie Bracken, *A Slight Case of Larceny*, for which they again paid him $25,000. He was a car mechanic again in *Drive a Crooked Road* (54), the film which first drew attention to Quine, though it was again a B, as was *The Atomic Kid*, a daft spy story in which Rooney became radioactive. He was also in a TV series at this time, 'Hey Mulligan' (53–54); in 1954 he sued for $30,000 for not being used in *45 Minutes to Broadway* – it was never made – and the case was settled out of court. He was fourth-billed in a big one, *The Bridges of Toko-Ri* (55), as a helicopter pilot supplying lower-decks humour and saving William Holden's life; was in the maudlin *The Twinkle in God's Eye* as a parson; got good notices for a war picture, *The Bold and the Brave* (56), where he had a very funny crap-playing scene; ironically took over Donald O'Connor's role with the talking mule, *Francis in the Haunted House*; and co-starred with Jack Carson in an old-hat melodrama about oil-drillers, *Magnificent Roughnecks*.

Rooney continued to announce plans with himself as producer, star, writer, director or any combination of these, but few materialized. Those that did arrived without *éclat* (like *My True Story*, which he directed in 1950). He continued to do his Mickey Rooney act and had a great success on television in 'The Comedian', in the title-role, a heel of the first order. That resulted in a CBS contract and while it was clear that he would do almost anything to recover his former glory, at the

Rooney in one of the several fine, judicious performances he has given since he became a character actor: The Last Mile *(59), a prison drama.*

same time he began to acquire a reputation as a character actor: as the bullet-headed sergeant in *Operation Madball* (57) and as gangster *Baby Face Nelson*, Don Siegel's exciting thriller. He talked the new management at MGM into *Andy Hardy Comes Home* (58) and for doing so was paid $35,000, but it was a B, unhelped by the performance of Patricia Breslin as Andy's wife, forced into the film because she was the girlfriend of a studio executive. There was, anyway, little welcome for this homecoming, but work continued to be plentiful: *A Nice Little Bank That Should Be Robbed* with Tom Ewell; *The Last Mile* (59), an unsuccessful remake of the old prison drama that Preston Foster had once done; *The Big Operator*, in the title-role; *Platinum High School* and *The Private Lives of Adam and Eve* (60), both Albert Zugsmith junk, the latter co-directed by the two of them; *King of the Roaring Twenties* – Arnold Rothstein, played by David Janssen; *Breakfast at Tiffany's* (61), unconvincing as a Japanese; and *Requiem for a Heavyweight* (62), in a superb performance as Anthony Quinn's buddy. If he had been as good in *Its a Mad Mad Mad Mad World* (63) it might have been that much more bearable: he was paid $125,000, far more than its producer thought him worth, but that was what the other comics were paid. Rooney was fine as an Irish Resistance leader helping to liberate an Italian general in Yugoslavia during the war, in *The Secret Invasion* (64), but there was little to be done with *How to Stuff a Wild Bikini* (65) and little more with the British *24 Hours to Kill*, or *Ambush Bay* (66). In 1966 his fifth wife, Barbara Ann, was shot dead by an actor, Milos Milosevic, who then committed suicide. At the time she and Rooney were on the verge of divorce. He went to Italy to make *Il Diavolo Innamorato/The Devil in Love* with Vittorio Gassmann; and returned to the US for *The Extraordinary Seaman* (68), *Skidoo* (69), *The Comic*, *80 Steps to Terror*, as a drunk, and *The Cockeyed Cowboys of Calico County* (70), eighth-billed in this whimsy starring TV favourite Dan Blocker.

After a role for television in *Evil Roy Slade* (72), he had his best chance in years, in the British *Pulp*, as an ageing gangster who employs Michael Caine to write his memoirs. That year he appeared in stock, in 'See How They Run', and then he made two films overseas, *Rachel's Man* (75) in Israel, with Rita Tushingham, and *Bons Baisers de Hong Kong*, with an unspeakable French comic troupe, Les Charlots. He was one of the obligatory old names in *Won Ton Ton the Dog Who Saved Hollywood* (76) and in a supporting role in the Canadian *Find the Lady*, after which he had good roles on his old stamping ground, Hollywood, in *The Domino Principle* (77), which starred Gene Hackman, and a Disney fantasy, *Pete's Dragon*, as a lighthouse-keeper, father of the heroine, Helen Reddy. He also appeared in *The Magic of Lassie* (78) and *The Black Stallion* (79), in both playing trainers – of, respectively, wrestlers and racehorses. He was the Guardian of the Rose in a British-made fantasy, *Arabian Adventure*.

'Sugar Babies', a recreation of an old burlesque show, co-starring Ann Miller, brought him wonderful notices and re-established him as a box-office name. One of its most striking features was the professionalism of the two stars: they did not get on well and Rooney's role in particular gave him endless opportunities for mugging and treading on other people's material, none of which he took. During the five years he was with it, touring and on Broadway, he managed to fit in other work, usually for television: *My Kidnapper My Love*, as a small time crook who persuades his brother, James Stacy (who starred), into a kidnapping; and two telefilms based on fact: *Leave 'em Laughing* (81), directed by his former co-star Jackie Cooper, as a Chicago clown who looks after homeless children while fatally ill, and *Bill*, playing a mentally retarded man trying to cope after spending most of his life in an institution. He won an Emmy for this and in 1983 was awarded an honorary Oscar. He also appeared in a TV series, 'One of the Boys', and commuted to Montreal to star in a children's film, *La Traversée de la Pacific/Odyssey of the Pacific* (83), again caring for unwanted kids, this time as an eccentric former railway engineer who calls himself the Emperor of Peru. There was another tele-movie, a sequel, *Bill: On His Own*. Somewhere within him remained the young Mick, a junior Wallace Beery, always mugging – tough, bragging, cocky, but soft-hearted underneath. Yet he is 'The Ultimate Performer' as an ad in 'Variety' put it, celebrating the end of his time in 'Sugar Babies'. The ad also listed many, many projects. So what else is new? For TV he starred in *It Came Upon a Midnight Clear* (84), as an angel, an ex-cop, showing his grandson a Manhattan Christmas, and had a cameo as a movie agent in *The Return of Mickey Spillane's Mike Hammer* (86), which starred Stacy Keach. For cinemas Rooney appeared in *Lightning – the Wild Stallion*, a typically cheapjack Harry Alan Towers production which Cannon bought – to little avail. Telecast later that year on the same night were Disney's *Little Spies*, in which he plays a recluse who teaches some children how to get their puppy back, and *There Must Be a Pony* with Elizabeth Taylor, in which he does a walk-on as himself. In 1987 he toured in a revival of 'A Funny Thing Happened on the Way to the Forum' and in 1988 'Sugar Babies' was revived in London but did not run. While in Britain he made a film, *The Saga of Erik the Viking* (89).

His personal life has been as chequered as his professional one. When he filed a bankruptcy petition in 1962 it was disclosed that he had earned over $12 million – and much of the money he had been paid as a child had been in trust funds; but he had also been married eight times. When MGM were in difficulty in 1970, according to 'Variety', he offered to take over the reins, promising to make 20 films for $20 million. The offer was refused.

ROSALIND RUSSELL

In the musical 'Wonderful Town', in an awkward moment, trying to make conversation, Rosalind Russell said, 'I was re-reading "Moby Dick" the other night. . . .' Still no response. 'It's worth picking up again.' Still no response. Desperately: 'It's about this *whale*.' To anyone who read 'Moby Dick' the moment was unforgettable; and Russell's delivery as preserved on the Original Cast album is a source of never-ending delight. But then, Russell had an enviable record of stylish and poised light comedy playing, as well as some neat, serious performances. Unfortunately – too often in her last years – she seemed to be trying to kill her reputation.

She was born in Waterbury, Connecticut, in

Rosalind Russell as Craig's Wife *(36).*

1912 and studied at the AADA in New York. According to some sources she appeared in the 'Garrick Gaieties' of 1926, but her first considerable professional experience was in stock at Saranac Lake in 1930, playing 26 parts in 13 weeks. In 1932 she got a Broadway chance in 'Talent' and that led to an engagement with the Theater Guild, acting in and around New York. She was in a Broadway revival of 'The Second Man' when Hollywood became interested. Universal paid her fare out to Hollywood, but by the time they got around to deciding what to do with her, MGM had tested her and signed her: not that that studio was very interested until she had scored a hit in LA in 'No More Ladies', put on by the Metro drama coach. She was given a small part as the Other Woman in the Myrna Loy–William Powell *Evelyn Prentice* (34), followed by hardly more important roles in *The President Vanishes* at Paramount with Edward Arnold, as a political hostess; *Forsaking All Others,* as one of Joan Crawford's set; *The Night Is Young* (35); and *West Point of the Air.*

A B picture with Paul Lukas as Philo Vance, *The Casino Murder Case,* gave her her first chance, even if she thought 'It was so bad and I was so bad in it that it gave my maid Hazel ammunition for seasons to come.' It led, anyway, to the role of Franchot Tone's starchy fiancée in *Reckless* and that caused her to be cast in a similar role as the woman Clark Gable thinks he prefers to Jean Harlow in *China Seas.* She later observed that Harlow was the only one of the other female stars she felt close to and that Gable was 'the only man who made a love scene comfortable'. Then, when Loy refused to do *Rendezvous* with Powell, Russell replaced her. 'Picturegoer' thought that Loy 'has perhaps more natural charm, but Rosalind Russell is a distinct competitor'. Russell herself said years later: 'I was always the threat, you see, to all the great women stars at Metro and they certainly were legion.' She was loaned to 20th for *It Had to Happen* (36), as a wealthy wife attracted to immigrant George Raft, and *Under Two Flags* as Claudette Colbert's rival, the upright British society dame; she was a mysterious lady in *Trouble for Two,* neither she nor Robert Montgomery happily cast in this version of Robert Louis Stevenson's 'The Suicide Club'; and loaned to Columbia for *Craig's Wife,* too young but credible as the house-proud Harriet Craig in this adaptation of George Kelly's play.

It moved her career on further and she was teamed with Montgomery again in *Night Must Fall* (37), a thriller, and *Live Love and Learn,* a comedy; in both she was type-cast – as a Britisher and as a wealthy socialite (married to a penniless painter) – but the latter proved her light touch. There was a recession with *Manproof* (38), as Loy's rival, but a loan-out for a Warners comedy, *Four's a Crowd,* found her for the first time in a role she would make spectacularly her own – the snazzy ace reporter (and she got Errol Flynn at the end). She was sent to Britain to play Robert Donat's wife in *The Citadel,* an agreeable performance, correctly accented – and the film's success did not hurt her either. She was with Montgomery again in *Fast and Loose* (39), yet another detective tale (MGM were never ones to let up when they had had a success); then fought the studio to play the catty gossip, Sylvia, in *The Women.* To some observers she stole the film and she credits its director, George Cukor, with the skills that would soon make her reputation as a comedienne, which is curious, for he makes her overplay in exaggerated manner, though she is still very funny. Thereafter she played comedy with great subtlety; it was when she acted in drama that she often went overboard.

Most people would agree that she was both a less charming and less subtle comedienne than Irene Dunne, Claudette Colbert, Carole Lombard and Jean Arthur, all of whom turned down *His Girl Friday* (40), on the grounds that this updating of *The Front Page* could not survive a sex-change – made on the whim of Howard Hawks who, after a reading of the script with a woman friend, realized that the reporter bullied by the editor into getting one last scoop could be played by a female. Columbia decided to gamble on Russell and borrowed her from MGM, though there was dissension between her and Cary Grant when her role was beefed up to be the size of his. The result was hilarious and Russell's performance was superb, a lesson to all aspiring actresses and one to stand with the best of her peers. If every artist has a right to one great performance, this is hers. Not surprisingly, it led to her being cast in a series of comedies, most of them above average and all much of a muchness. As she said herself (in two different interviews): 'I played – I think it was 23 – career women. I've been every kind of executive and I've owned everything – factories and advertising agencies and pharmaceutical houses. . . . Except for different leading men and a switch in title and pompadour, they were all stamped out of the same Alice in Careerland. The script always called for a leading lady somewhere in the 30s, tall, brittle, not too sexy. My wardrobe had a set pattern: a tan suit, a grey suit, a beige suit, and then a negligee for the seventh reel, near the end, when I would admit to my best friend on the telephone that what I really wanted was to become a dear little housewife.'

His Girl Friday *(40):* Cary
Grant as the editor and
Rosalind Russell as his star
reporter and ex-wife. She is
now on the point of re-
marrying Ralph Bellamy,
in the centre of the picture.

Joan Crawford, Rosalind
Russell, Norma Shearer
and Joan Fontaine in The
Women *(39),* MGM's
campy comedy about
divorce. Crawford has
stolen Shearer's husband,
and is advised by her
about a certain dress
because 'Stephen doesn't
like anything too obvious'.
'If Stephen doesn't like
what I'm wearing,'
Crawford replies, 'I take it
off.' Russell wasn't around
to hear that particular
exchange, even though she
didn't think an ear at the
keyhole beneath her: for
she was the chief gossip
and trouble-maker.

The titles: *Hired Wife* with Brian Aherne at Universal; *No Time for Comedy* with James Stewart at WB, a rich and warm performance – as an actress – though the film itself had third-act willies; *This Thing Called Love* (41) at Columbia with Melvyn Douglas; and the last three under her contract: *They Met in Bombay* with Gable (only the first half was intentionally funny), *The Feminine Touch* with Don Ameche and *Design for Scandal* with Walter Pidgeon. At Paramount, she did *Take a Letter Darling* (42) – which Katharine Hepburn had turned down – with Fred Mac-Murray as her secretary; and then she signed a five-year non-exclusive pact with Columbia. She had left MGM because she felt she was swamped by the other ladies, but she was irrevocably typed; and her career went gently downhill. Not, however, with the agreeable *My Sister Eileen* with Aherne and Janet Blair, from a hit Broadway play. *Flight for Freedom* (43) was not much, though, a fiction based on the loss of aviatrix Amelia Earhart in the Pacific. *What a Woman!* with Aherne was very ordinary and she was off the screen after that for more than a year.

She returned with something more serious: *Roughly Speaking* (45) with Jack Carson, a saga of 'an independent woman' (for WB at a fee of $200,000); and *Sister Kenny* (46), a sanctimonious peek at a great figure, played by her in the most obvious way (dewy-eyed and invincible while young, crusty and imperious when old). In between, *She Wouldn't Say Yes* (45) to Lee Bowman, then she was a mixed-up war-widow in *The Guilt of Janet Ames* (47). And then, *Mourning Becomes Electra*, O'Neill's retelling of Sophocles, reverently filmed by Dudley Nichols with Katina Paxinou, Raymond Massey *et al.* It flopped as a road show handled by the Theater Guild and much cut, at ordinary prices; it sneaked into Britain five years later when a few showings did nothing to offset losses of over $2 million. Russell was nominated for an Oscar, perhaps due to her courage, for a worse performance would be hard to imagine. She remained at RKO for a joint venture with her own short-lived production company, *The Velvet Touch* (48), which begins with her, a Broadway actress in a chic hat, murdering her producer and ex-lover Leon Ames for laughing at her because she wants to play Hedda Gabler – which she does later, to prove how right he was. It did not do well and she took another sabbatical, until *Tell It to the Judge* (49): 'Variety' said she flavoured 'the pic with a sophistication that ranges between brashness and sweetness', but her career was really in the doldrums and two more unfunny films did not help: *A Woman of Distinction* (50), as a college dean pursued by Ray Milland, and

Never Wave at a Wac (52), as a high-ranking officer married to Paul Douglas. She could play this stuff blindfolded.

Hollywood had written her off. In 1951 she toured in 'Bell Book and Candle' with Dennis Price and in 1953 was invited to do a Broadway musical of *My Sister Eileen*, 'Wonderful Town'. It made her the toast of the Great White Way; she got a 'Time' cover and innumerable awards – and Hollywood wanted her back. Now that she was a *musical* star Paramount constructed *The Girl Rush* (55) for her, but it was a poor film and few went to see it. The other Hollywood bash was her first character part, the spinster aunt in *Picnic*: it was not the sort of performance likely to elicit further offers, so she went back to New York for a play wrought from Patrick Dennis's funny 'Auntie Mame'. Many actresses subsequently played the part, but she was the only choice for the film version (58): it was a huge money-maker in the US, but was not much liked elsewhere.

Most of the films that followed were not liked anywhere and Russell's overplaying, in mostly character parts, netted her as poor a set of notices as anyone ever reaped: *A Majority of One* (61), as a Jewish matron; *Five Finger Exercise*, Peter Shaffer's play ruined and – 'Rosalind Russell has never been more campy, a large statement' (Dwight Macdonald); *Gypsy* (62); and *Oh Dad Poor Dad Mama's Hung You in the Closet and I'm Feeling So Sad* (66). Most of these properties were owned by her husband, Frederick Brisson, the theatrical producer. *Gypsy* was not and indeed Russell was not bad in it; but it was one of the weakest box-office musicals in years (because audiences resented Ethel Merman not being in her original part?). *Oh Dad Poor Dad* was so bad that it did not get more than a dozen bookings. She played an understanding Mother Superior in *The Trouble with Angels*, which was successful enough, in a modest way, to give vent to a sequel, *Where Angels Go Trouble Follows* (68). That had no success, nor did her last two films, *Rosie*, a murky mixing of 'King Lear' (she the unwanted mother) and *Mr Deeds Goes to Town*; and *Mrs Pollifax Spy* (71). There was one last tele-movie which also marked her dramatic début in that medium, *The Crooked Hearts* (72) with Douglas Fairbanks Jr. Since she spent her last years battling with cancer it is a shame that she could not look back on any recent successes. She died in 1976. A memoir, 'Life is a Banquet', was published posthumously.

GEORGE SANDERS

For over 35 years George Sanders did a roaring trade in what Stephen Potter called Oneupmanship. On screen, George seldom stopped sneering. Claude Rains was more dapper, Basil Rathbone more villainous, Clifton Webb more supercilious, Vincent Price more arrogant; but, for an elegant assumption of superiority over the other cast members, George won hands down. He made an extraordinarily successful career out of it, moreover, which was not easy for even a top supporting actor if you have only one string to your bow. Suave he may always have been, but he managed a variety of parts, including a fair run of romantic leads.

He was born in St Petersburg in 1906; his father was a rope manufacturer, his mother a British horticulturist. The family fled to Britain during the Revolution and Sanders was educated at Brighton College, specializing in textiles. He was in the textile business for a while, then became involved in a tobacco venture in South America. This did not turn out at all well and on his return to Britain there seemed nothing for it but the stage. He had his voice coached and was heard at a party which landed him a small role in 'Ballyhoo'; followed by parts in 'Further Horizon' with Edna Best, 'The Command Performance' with Dennis King and Noël Coward's 'Conversation Piece' (34). He finally got a small film part, in *Find the Lady* (36), followed by the lead in *Strange Cargo* – gun-running; he had a brief flash as a Greek god in *The Man Who Could Work Miracles*; and then another good part, moustached, as Eugene Pallette's assistant in *Dishonour Bright*, which starred Tom Walls. He was also *The Outsider*, Harold Huth's old role of the foreign quack who effects a miraculous cure: but it was not released until 1939.

The producers of *Strange Cargo*, British and Dominions, had signed him to a long-term contract, but when their studio burned down they let him go and he went to Hollywood to try his luck there. He was tested by 20th for the role of Madeleine Carroll's unscrupulous foppish husband in *Lloyds of London* (37). It was a small role, but he impressed and was signed to a long-term contract. There were three feature parts: *Love Is News*, again as a fop; *Slave Ship*; and *The Lady Escapes*, as a French writer, a B starring Gloria Stuart. He was then starred opposite Dolores del Rio: *Lancer Spy* and *International Settlement* (38). Both are war stories, in both he is masquerading as something he is not and in both she falls in love with him unwillingly. He did *Four Men and a Prayer* and *Mr Moto's Last Warning*, one of

the series which starred Peter Lorre as a Japanese detective. RKO had their eye on Sanders for their own B series, based on Leslie Charteris's 'The Saint' and they negotiated with 20th to share Sanders on a 'featured' basis. 'The Saint' was a smooth adventurer and Sanders played him well: *The Saint Strikes Back* (39) and *The Saint in London*. The latter was made in London and there for 20th Sanders appeared in a remake of Will Rogers's *So This Is London*, never shown in the US.

In Hollywood he was hunted down, along with Francis Lederer, by Edward G. Robinson, in *Confessions of a Nazi Spy*; already in *Lancer Spy* he had pretended to be a Hun, with Prussian crew-cut and monocle, and until the end of the war this was an impersonation he was to repeat a couple of times a year. He did it again in *Nurse Edith Cavell*. He was in *Allegheny Uprising* supporting Douglas Fairbanks Jr; *The Saint's Double Trouble*; *Rebecca*, as that lady's caddish cousin, a small but satisfying part; *The House of Seven Gables*, again at Universal, co-starring with Margaret Lindsay in a cheap version of Nathaniel Hawthorne's novel; *The Saint Takes Over*; *Foreign Correspondent*, as a nice young Englishman, a part that Rex Harrison had turned down; and *Bitter Sweet*, as the Hun-headed Viennese officer who tried to ravish Jeanette MacDonald on the dance floor. He was the baddie again in *Son of Monte Cristo* at UA, with Louis Hayward, and it was Hayward who was to take over 'The Saint' after Sanders's last fling, *The Saint at Palm Springs* (41) – and *he* relinquished the part in turn to Hugh Sinclair.

Before that one, Sanders was in the arms of Ingrid Bergman in *Rage in Heaven* (41), but

George Sanders in an unaccustomed role – as romantic hero: in Rage of Heaven *(41) with the young, radiant Ingrid Bergman.*

being nice did not last and he was a nasty Nazi again in *Manhunt*, tracking Walter Pidgeon. RKO then gave him a new series, 'The Falcon', which was heavily indebted to 'The Saint'; *The Gay Falcon* and *A Date With the Falcon*, both with Wendy Barrie. He was one of the loyal British tackling the Nazis attempting to take over Africa in *Sundown*, with Gene Tierney, but was evil again in *Son of Fury* (42) – who was Tyrone Power. After *The Falcon Takes Over*, Sanders was more gainfully employed, trying to get Norma Shearer from Robert Taylor in *Her Cardboard Lover* and snobbishly needling Edward G. Robinson in an episode of *Tales of Manhattan*. His first real star part in a real A was in *The Moon and Sixpence*, a good shot at Maugham's novel by director Albert Lewin, with Sanders effective as Strickland-Gauguin.

This put him among Hollywood's more important actors and RKO reluctantly agreed to release him from 'The Falcon', with *The Falcon's Brother*: his own brother, Tom Conway, was in it and Sanders got killed during the action . . . so that Conway could take over the series. Sanders supported Tyrone Power again in *The Black Swan*, as a villainous privateer with a thick ginger beard; then starred with Gail Patrick in a B, *Quiet Please Murder*. He was a Nazi again in Renoir's *This Land Is Mine* (43), from which it was a comedown to *They Came to Blow Up America* with Anna Sten; *Appointment with Berlin*, as an undercover agent; *Paris After Dark* with Brenda Marshall, helping the French underground; and *Acting in Arabia* (44), with Virginia Bruce. Just before the last of these low-budget actioners on behalf of the war effort he was the nice detective in *The Lodger* (44) with Laird Cregar and he was now to eschew the B field for some years: it could not be said, however, that the features in which he was top- or second-billed were among the best of their time. He seemed to have a compulsive desire to make films; or as he told a reporter years later: 'I am not one of those people who would rather act than eat. Quite the reverse. Larry Olivier was born with the desire to act. I was not. My own desire as a boy was to retire. That ambition has never changed.'

The war was ending and for a change he made three period pieces: *Summer Storm* from a Chekhov story, as the caddish local judge who seduces Linda Darnell, the bored wife of Hugo Haas, and murders her; *The Picture of Dorian Gray* (45), from Wilde's novel, as Lord Henry Wooton – the first of his later world-weary, cynical portrayals – in a film about which opinion seems equally divided between terrible and fair; and *Hangover Square*, with Cregar and Darnell at

20th, his last under his contract. *The Strange Affair of Uncle Harry* was almost his only out-and-out sympathetic part, as a mild man driven to murder when his sisters try to break up his romance. *A Scandal in Paris* (46) and *The Strange Woman* were two more (undistinguished) period pieces and so was *The Private Affairs of Bel Ami* (47), from Guy de Maupassant, with Sanders as Bel Ami, a performance which almost sinks the enterprise, since he plays him as merely another bored cad, without charm and energy; and since the censor permitted no amorous antics we have merely a long-winded movie about a rake. However, he did well under a good director, Joseph L. Mankiewicz, in *The Ghost and Mrs Muir*, as the writer of children's books who falls in love with her, Gene Tierney, without knowing that she loves a ghost. He did *Lured* with Lucille Ball and was the obvious choice to play Charles II in *Forever Amber*, the film's only decent performance. After an absence he was in an inferior version of a play by Oscar Wilde, *The Fan* (49), as Lord Darlington; and De Mille's *Samson and Delilah*, as the heavy, and a rather jaded one at that. A European trip brought one of the early, misguided 'international' films: *Black Jack* (50), with Herbert Marshall and Patricia Roc, made in Spain by France's Julien Duvivier. He signed to replace Ezio Pinza in 'South Pacific' but a psychosomatic illness prevented him from doing it.

Fortunately, a new phase in his career opened with *All About Eve*, in which he played 'that venomous fish-wife Addison de Witt', as Hugh Marlowe put it, the cynical drama critic: the dialogue had bite and he did beautifully, winning a Best Supporting Oscar. He was immediately given two similar roles, in *I Can Get It for You Wholesale* (51) opposite Susan Hayward, as a leading couturier hoping to lure her to his firm, and *The Light Touch* with Stewart Granger, as a crooked art dealer (of the cast Sanders alone had it, but this dialogue defeated even him). Another European trip dissipated what his career had gained through *Eve*: *Ivanhoe* (52), made in Britain, as Robert Taylor's Norman rival, de Bois Guilbert; and a couple more hybrids, *Assignment Paris* with Marta Toren and, even more so, Rossellini's *Viaggio in Italia/The Strangers/Voyage to Italy* (53) with Ingrid Bergman, which Sanders thought a muddle and hated making. However, in Hollywood he landed a plum role, the lead opposite Ethel Merman in *Call Me Madam*, one of the year's big musicals and almost his last important role.

After trying to kill Barbara Stanwyck in *Witness for Murder* (54), he was in a bevy of historical pieces: *King Richard and the Cru-*

Call Me Madam *(53), with Ethel Merman repeating her Broadway success as a Washington hostess appointed ambassadress to a mythological European kingdom (it was based on the real-life Perle Mesta). George Sanders was the country's foreign minister, at whom she set her cap.*

saders, as that monarch: *Jupiter's Darling*, a musical with Howard Keel, as Fabius Maximus, ruler of Rome; *Moonfleet* (55), as a villainous milord; *The Scarlet Coat*, as a doctor; and *The King's Thief*, again as Charles II. Then: *Never Say Goodbye* (56), in Claude Rains's old role (in *This Love of Ours*, as it was then), making Rock Hudson jealous over Cornell Borchers; *While the City Sleeps*, as a conniving newspaper executive; *That Certain Feeling*, with Bob Hope, as a monomaniacal strip-cartoonist; and *Death of a Scoundrel*, the odyssey of a master crook, cheating his way from Czechoslovakia to death in New York as produced, written and directed by one Charles Martin, an ambitious effort which played B dates. His wife, Zsa Zsa Gabor, was in it; he later married Ronald Colman's widow, Benita Hume, and was widowed by her after nine years; in 1970 he married Zsa Zsa's sister, Magda. In 1960 he published his 'Memoirs of a Professional Cad' and in the late 50s he did a TV series, 'The George Sanders Mystery Theater'.

After *The Seventh Sin* (57), a dreary remake of *The Painted Veil* with Eleanor Parker, as a wily trader, he went to Britain to do a thriller with Stewart Granger, *The Whole Truth* (58), as the villain; and after a Jules Verne tale, *From the Earth to the Moon*, he stayed in Hollywood to play Sophia Loren's millionaire lover in *That Kind of Woman* (59); and after doing the villain in *Solomon and Sheba* and being the captain on *The Last Voyage* (60), he stayed in Britain: *A Touch of Larceny*, as James Mason's rival for Vera Miles (no comment); *Bluebeard's Ten Honeymoons*, as Landru, murdering – to no public approval – a number of passé names, Patricia Roc, Greta Gynt and Jean Kent; *Cone of Silence*, as the prosecuting attorney in this air drama with Michael Craig; and *Village of the Damned*, from John Wyndham's novel, as the physicist who tries to destroy the sci-fi children. He seemed intent on choosing films meant to downgrade the cinema, but *The Rebel* (61) at least had Tony Hancock – if below his TV best – as an artist, with Sanders as an art dealer. He supported: Ernie Kovacs in the Anglo-Italian *Five Golden Hours/ Cinque Ore in Contanti*, a supposed comedy; Annie Girardot in *Le Rendezvous*, a French policier; Terry-Thomas in *Operation Snatch* (62), as an intelligence officer; a host of Disneyites in *In Search of the Castaways*; Richard Johnson in the Anglo-American remake of *The Asphalt Jungle*, *Cairo* (63), as the criminal mastermind – Sam Jaffe's old part; another British comic, the unfunny Charlie Drake, in *The Cracksman*, as a master crook; Rossana Pedesta and Jacques Sernas in *Una Moneta Spezzata FBI Operazione Baalbeck* (64); and Shirley Jones, Rossana Brazzi and Micheline Presle in *Dark Purpose/L'Intrigo*. That Hollywood had not quite forgotten him was proved by *A Shot in the Dark*, as the employer of murder suspect Elke Sommer, and *The Golden Head*, a flop Cinerama adventure made in Hungary, as an international crook posing as an art dealer; and he was in two equally hopeful efforts, *The Amorous Adventurers of Moll Flanders* (65), as one of Kim Novak's husbands, and *The Quiller Memorandum* (66), in a guest appearance as a callous British spy-master. More: *Trunk to Cairo*, an Israeli–German co-production, with Audie Murphy; *Warning Shot* (67), starring David Janssen, as a broker; *Good Times*, with an egregious 'pop' team, Sonny and Cher; and *Rey de Africa/One Step to Hell*, an Italian–Spanish melodrama, as a police commissioner.

That Broadway had not forgotten him was witnessed by 'Sherry', playing the title-role in this musical version of *The Man Who Came to Dinner*, but Broadway's patrons did not want to know; so he was back in a dud trio: *The Candy Man* (69), filmed in Mexico City, as a British drug pedlar – the star role; *The Body Stealers*, with Maurice Evans, as an English general; and *The Best House in London*, as a bored British aristocrat in this equally tired collection of Victoriana jokes. His career seemed on the upgrade with a role in Huston's *The Kremlin Letter* (70), though playing a homosexual spy with a penchant for drag – and he seemed disinterested. His career finished on three cheap horror films: *Doomwatch* (72), as an admiral; *Endless Night* – though by Agatha Christie; and *Psychomania* (73), as the butler of medium Beryl Reid – but at least he was top-billed. He died just after the second of these came out, from an overdose in a Costa Brava hotel. The note he left said 'Dear World, I am leaving you because I am bored' – which had been apparent from his later films and his work in them.

RANDOLPH SCOTT

'I've always thought that if he had only ever worked in our films, he could have been a great star of the Western', said Budd Boetticher, who directed the Ranown cycle Randolph Scott made towards the end of his career. The remark is not entirely clear, but presumably means that Scott may be considered one of the great Western stars on those films alone: or if it does not, it should do. Randy, as his friends and fans called him, guaranteed a treat to those fond of the genre. 'Customers come to see him knowing exactly what to expect,' said Nat Holt, his co-producer on the Ranown films. 'They are never disappointed. It was the same with Bill Hart.'

Like William S. Hart, Scott was a tall man, but better-looking, with a particularly sunny smile. He was born in Orange County, Virginia, in 1903, son of an administrative engineer and the only boy in a family of five children. He lied about his age in order to serve in World War I, after which he completed his education at the University of North Carolina, where a back injury prevented him from becoming an All-American tackle. He studied textile management, but decided to try the movies after being given a letter of introduction to Howard Hughes. He was an extra in some films for Fox, *Sharpshooters* (28), *The Black Watch* (29) and *The Far Call*; was recommended to De Mille for the juvenile lead in *Dynamite*, but the test was disappointing and the role went to Joel McCrea, whose career would resemble Scott's in many ways. De Mille suggested to Scott that he should get some acting experience, so he joined the Pasadena Community Playhouse. During this period *Headline* gave him a small role in *The Women Men Marry* (31), but he did not get another crack at the movies till someone at Paramount saw him in 'The Broken Wing' at the Playhouse with Leo Carillo. He was signed to a long-term contract and given a role in a Richard Arlen vehicle, *The Sky Bride* (32). He was just another handsome hulk, but Warners borrowed him to play one of the juveniles clustering round George Arliss in *A Successful Calamity*.

Paramount decided that he was ready for leading roles and billed him third on *Hot Saturday*, after Cary Grant and Nancy Carroll, all under the title, to prove that her star was very much on the wane. They were rivals for her, Grant the wealthy playboy and Scott an honest hard-working geologist, and in this pre-Code era it is suggested that she 'gives' herself to both. Scott, however, wins her in the end; and in life he and Grant began their long friendship. He first sat in the saddle for the cameras in the remake of a Zane Grey Western, *Wild Horse Mesa* (33), in the chief role, and after playing the juvenile in *Hello Everybody*, which failed to signal a movie career for radio's singing star, Kate Smith, he did another such, *Heritage of the Desert*, Henry Hathaway's first film as a fully fledged director. The reaction to Scott so far was mild, so he was dumped into two of the studio's contributions to the horror cycle, *Murders in the Zoo*, discovering how Lionel Atwill is bumping off his wife's lovers, the two actors merely stooges to Charles Ruggles's drunken reporter, and the silly *Supernatural*, standing around to watch Carole Lombard come out of her trances. He was loaned to Columbia for *Cocktail Hour* and then settled into a series of Westerns, most of them remakes, most of them based on Zane Grey originals and most directed by Hathaway: *Man of the Forest*, *Sunset Pass*, *To the Last Man*, *Broken Dreams* (not of the series, but released at this time, by Monogram), *The Lone Cowboy* (34), *The Thundering Herd*, *The Last Round-up*, *Wagon Wheels*, *Home on the Range* (35) and *Rocky Mountain Mystery*.

By this time Hathaway had moved on to bigger things and it was clear that Scott must do the same, or be for ever just another B movie cowboy. The plum parts at Paramount for his sort of actor went to Gary Cooper and then McCrea – or even Cary Grant, who encouraged him to cast around for a change of pace: so he went to RKO to play Irene Dunne's romantic interest in *Roberta*, with the bonus of hearing her sing 'Smoke Gets In Your Eyes'. The studio kept him on to do *Village Tale*, from Phil Stong's rural novel, quarrelling with Arthur Hohl over Hohl's wife, Kay Johnson, and *She*, from Rider Haggard's adventure tale, as the courageous explorer to whom She (Helen Gahagan) offers eternal life, or nearly. Paramount took notice and made Scott the good ol' standby admirer of Southern coquette Margaret Sullavan in *So Red the Rose*: 'So red the ink' went the joke at Paramount, when the film confirmed the fear that no Civil War movie had yet been popular. RKO borrowed him again to play Fred Astaire's buddy and suitor for Ginger Rogers's mousy sister in *Follow the Fleet* (36).

Just after it came out Scott married Marion duPont Summerville, a divorcee and a member of the wealthy Delaware duPonts. 'As the fan magazines quickly pointed out,' says Warren G. Harris, one of Grant's biographers, 'she was older than Scott, homely and rather mannish-looking, hardly the kind of wife that a Hollywood dream prince would be expected to choose for himself.' Scott and Grant had shared a house since 1932, except for the period of one of Grant's brief marriages. Carole Lombard, who stayed with them, remarked: 'Cary opened the bills, Randy wrote the checks and if Cary could talk someone out of a stamp, he mailed them.' Paramount's publicity happily sent out photographs of their domestic bliss, even of the two of them in pinafores, but someone had second thoughts about a co-starring vehicle, *Spawn of the North*, and it was made with George Raft and Henry Fonda. Jules Furthman's dialogue retains a number of homosexual innuendoes, which may make us in this more knowing era question the innocence of some of those involved; and certainly today several of Grant's biographers have no doubts about the nature of the relationship. Grant married again several times and Scott only once again, in 1944 to Marie Patricia Stillman, who survived him.

Meanwhile, Paramount put Scott into a B, *And Sudden Death*, as a cop who reforms speed-crazy Frances Drake, and he was then loaned to UA to play Hawkeye, the frontier scout in James Fenimore Cooper's story of the Indian wars, *The Last of the Mohicans*. Paramount upped him to being Mae West's romantic interest in *Go West Young Man* – in fact, the fiancé of the daughter of the family with whom she is staying and who is tempted by her – and promoted him again for one of their big two-a-day ones, the Kern-Hammerstein musical *High Wide and Handsome* (37), as a Philadelphia farmer, Irene Dunne's husband. He did not join her above the title and in fact gives a fairly dull showing in his non-musical role. Nothing came of this, since he was off the screen for a while, till loaned to 20th to play one of the radio men who discovers Shirley Temple, the *Rebecca of Sunnybrook Farm* (38). His last film under his contract was *The Texans*, a drama about their problems just after the Civil War, with Joan Bennett.

Freelancing, he started with top-billing at Universal with *The Road to Divorce* – but then his opposite number, playing his estranged wife, was the faded Hope Hampton. He went to 20th for three in a row, the first for several at that studio over the next three years: *Jesse James* (39), as the marshal friendly to that gentleman (Tyrone Power); *Susannah of the Mounties*, with young Temple, moustached as a redcoat; and *Frontier Marshall* as Wyatt Earp, with Cesar Romero as Doc Holliday. There were two medium action pictures, *Coast Guard* at Columbia with Ralph Bellamy and *20,000 Men a Year* at 20th, and then a bigger one, *Virginia City* (40), as a Confederate officer helping his old rival Errol Flynn to retrieve the gold to finance the Southern cause. Michael Curtiz, who directed, said: 'Randy Scott is a complete anachronism. He's a gentleman. And so far he's the only one I've met in this business of self-promoting sons-of-bitches.' At RKO Scott did the second and last comedy (discounting the musicals and the Temple films) of his career, playing Irene Dunne's second husband in *My Favorite Wife*, with Grant as the first, believed dead. He was back in the saddle in *When the Daltons Drove*, as the lawyer of those bad boys at Universal, Fritz Lang's *Western Union* (41) with Robert Young, as a gunman on the run who reforms, and *Belle Starr*, who was Gene Tierney, both at 20th.

Too old for war service, he toured army bases with a stand-up comic act and saw fictional war service as a downed pilot being helped by Elisabeth Bergner in *Paris Calling* (42) and again in *To the Shores of Tripoli*, as the tough but golden-hearted drill sergeant who persuades John Payne that Uncle Sam needed him. Though billed over John Wayne in both *The Spoilers* and *Pittsburgh* (43), he loses to him both their epic fist-fight and the girl in the first of these, Marlene Dietrich; she married him in the second, but continues to pine for Wayne. A Western, *The Desperadoes*, and a war film, *Bombardier*, were routine, but *Corvette K-225* is one of the most authentic accounts the cinema has in the matter of World War II, seriously underestimated by 'The New York Times' as lacking

Randolph Scott, late in his career when audiences only saw him in double-bill Westerns. With the money he made invested wisely, he was by this time a billionaire several times over.

'the scope and compassion of *In Which We Serve*'. As written by a retired officer in the Royal Canadian Naval Reserve and directed by the otherwise unnotable Richard Rosson, it presents a vivid picture of life aboard one of the ships escorting a convoy across the North Atlantic; Scott is its commander, all the better for once for non-dimpling. He was in another of the better war films, *Gung Ho* (44), built around the attempt to retake Makin Island, and one of the worst, *Follow the Boys*, which showed how Universal's stars and some other odd bodies entertained the troops: he did little more than appear, but the studio's top star, Deanna Durbin, sensible puss, did not even do that.

He stretched himself for once in *Belle of the Yukon* (45), by playing a smooth-talking, smiling, trouble-making con-man, with Gypsy Rose Lee, and he had a hand in the production; RKO distributed and for that studio he was a doctor under a *China Sky* with Ruth Warrick, adapted from a novel by Pearl Buck. *Captain Kidd* was Charles Laughton and Scott was the young crewman who unmasks him; *Abilene Town* (46) and *Badman's Territory* were Westerns, wth Scott as the sheriff in both. He was a detective in *Home Sweet Homicide*, helping some children, including Peggy Ann Garner and Dean Stockwell, to solve a murder, and he was Bat Masterson in *Trail Street* (47), produced for RKO by Nat Holt, who would be responsible for many of Scott's Westerns over the next few years, at various studios. *Gunfighters* needs no gloss, other than to remark that it returned Scott to Zane Grey, but *Christmas Eve* does, since it was the last of his starring vehicles which was not a Western. George Brent, George Raft and he played the sons of Ann Harding, with their troubles shown in flashback: he was a has-been rodeo rider caught up in a blackmarket baby racket.

The Westerns were formula stuff in which he played the retired gunfighter, the reluctant sheriff, the peaceable stranger forced into clearing out the bad men: *Albuquerque* (48), *Coroner Creek*, *Return of the Badmen*, *The Walking Hills* (49), *The Doolins of Oklahoma*, *Fighting Man of the Planes*, *The Nevadan* (50), *Colt 45* and *The Cariboo Trail*. It may be that other offers dried up, but Scott was an astute businessman and he had noted that twice in the mid-40s Roy Rogers had shown up among the acknowledged top money-making stars, at No. 10. He reasoned that if Rogers could do that well in low-budget items which played only B dates, he might achieve something similar with medium-budget double-bill fodder. So it proved and in 1950 he was at No. 10 (going to 7 in 1951, 10 again in 1952, and thereafter not far out of the golden list): accordingly, he signed agreements with Warner Bros. and Columbia, and with one exception filmed almost alternately for one or the other till he retired: *Sugarfoot* (51), *Santa Fe, Fort Worth, Man in the Saddle, Starlift* (guesting, as himself in this Warner Bros. Korean War version of *Follow the Boys*), *Carson City* (52), *The Man Behind the Gun, Hangman's Knot, The Stranger Wore a Gun* (53), *Thunder Over the Plains, Riding Shotgun* (54), *The Bounty Hunter, Ten Wanted Men* (55), *Rage at Dawn* (for RKO), *Tall Man Riding* and *A Lawless Street* with Angela Lansbury.

At this point he teamed up with Harry Joe Brown to co-produce a series of oaters, most of which would be written by Burt Kennedy and/or directed by Budd Boetticher, often pitted against some up-and-coming heavies, and many of them of bleak aspect. Some of the following, however, are not of the Ranown cycle, since he continued to be merely a paid employee of Warners or Columbia: *Seven Men From Now* (56) with Lee Marvin, eliminating the men who killed his wife in a stage hold-up; *7th Cavalry*, fighting an accusation of cowardice after the Battle of Little Big Horn; *The Tall T* (57), rescuing Maureen O'Sullivan from the clutches of Richard Boone; *Shoot-Out at Medicine Bend*, masquerading as a Quaker; *Decision at Sundown*, on the trail of the man who caused his wife's suicide; *Buchanan Rides Again*, the lightest of this bunch, which foreshadows some of Kennedy's own; *Ride Lonesome* (59), battling James Coburn and Lee Van Cleef; *Westbound* with Virginia Mayo, perhaps the weakest of his last films, trying to ensure that the gold gets through; and *Comanche Station* (60), searching for his wife, kidnapped by Indians.

But by this time the proliferation of TV Westerns had rendered Scott's type of film redundant. He had invested in real estate and was a very wealthy man: so he retired. But someone at MGM had an excellent script requiring two ageing gunfighters to transport gold from a mining colony to a nearby town. It was offered to Scott and Joel McCrea, who had also retired, and they flipped a coin to determine which of the two would be the villain, i.e. the one who would betray the other by succumbing to greed. Sam Peckinpah, called in to rework the script, directed and the result, *Ride the High Country* (62), was a triumph for the three of them. It would have been a much bigger one if the studio, under a change of management, had not decided to throw it away as the lower half of a double bill. Both actors, however, knew it was a good one to go out on and neither faced the camera again. Scott, an intensely private man, gave a last interview: 'Frankly, I don't like publicity. I always remember something David Belasco said and incorporated into the contracts of his stars. His theory was, "Never let yourself be seen in public unless they pay for it." To me that makes sense.' He died in 1987, with claim to being the last cowboy in a noble line which stretched back to William S. Hart.

NORMA SHEARER

Acting ability is incidental to screen stardom. Says Kirk Douglas playing a film director to star Lana Turner in *The Bad and the Beautiful*: 'You acted badly, you moved clumsily, but the point is however bad you were, every eye in the audience was on you.' It is debatable whether this is true of Turner, but it is supremely true of Norma Shearer, one of her predecessors at MGM ('The Studio of Stars' and 'More stars than there are in Heaven'). Take a film like *Escape*: within minutes of her appearance, you can see it. It is a wet film and her part is ridiculous, but there it is – the poise, the authority, the extra-something of the real star. She was not beautiful but, to take a line from Noël Coward, she made millions believe she was. Robert Morley recalled in his memoir: 'Shearer reminded me of Marie Tempest. . . . Both were small women possessed of immense determination and few illusions about themselves. Both were stars because they had decided that that was what they wanted to be. Shearer had many more obstacles to overcome than Mary [*sic*]. Her voice wasn't particularly pleasing and she was by no means a good actress but her determination was, if anything, the greater. She could leaf through a hundred photographs of herself in a couple of minutes and know exactly which should be passed. . . . Her knowledge of lighting was as great as the cameraman's, and she could tell from a dozen lights bearing down on her which was likely to cast the wrong shadow.'

This is an assessment considerably at odds with the contemporary image of Shearer: the epitome of glamour, of femininity, of beauty. Fans claimed she was a great actress. She was certainly popular. From 1930 through 1934 she featured prominently in all box-office polls and only lost her place because of diminished activity. In Britain in 1932, 1934 and 1937 she was voted the top woman star in the Bernstein Questionnaire and, incredibly, on the last occasion had had only one not-too-popular film released since the last poll. The fans were not wrong: her command of the medium was very sure. She could be maternal and girlish, loyal and frivolous – the one desired by men and emulated by women: the epitome of film starriness.

She was born in Montreal in 1904 and trained as a pianist: she began in show business by playing the piano in a music-shop and later in a nickelodeon. When her father's business failed, her mother took her and her sister to New York to try to get them into films. It was a hard grind, but when the girls faltered, Mother was there pushing them. They worked as extras – *The Flapper* (20), *The Restless Sex* and *Way Down East* – before Shearer met a talent agent, Edward Small (later a producer), who got her a role in a two-reeler, *Torchy's Millions* (21), and that led to a role as the minister hero's daughter in the Robertson–Cole *The Stealers*, which led to some small roles in the Universal–Jewel series, *The Leather Pushers*, which starred Reginald Denny. The first picture in which she played the female lead was *The Man Who Paid* (22), as the wife of Wilfred Lytell in this melodrama set in Canada. It was followed by: *The Bootleggers*, operating mainly at sea and wronging her for FBO; *Channing of the Northwest*, with Eugene O'Brien as a Mountie; *A Clouded Name* (23), with Gladden James sharing her – undeserved – disgrace; *Man and Wife*, finding her husband (Maurice Costello) has married her sister, believing her dead; *The Devil's Partner*, another story of

the Great Northwest. Her work had individually impressed both Louis B. Mayer and Irving Thalberg, about to join forces, and she arrived in Hollywood with a five-year contract worth $150 a week. Her first film for Metro was *Pleasure Mad*, 'A Story of Today and the Mad Lust for Pleasure among the Bright Lights and Gilded Cafés', and she was a flaming deb.

Some dissension with Thalberg over roles led to 18 months of loan-outs: *The Wanters*, as the sister of the guy who falls in love with the maid, Marie Prevost – for whom it was a vehicle; *Lucretia Lombard*, who was Irene Rich, with Shearer as her rival for the affections of Monte Blue; *The Trail of the Law* (24), leading lady to Lytell again, masquerading as a boy; *The Wolf Man*, out West with John Gilbert, he as a wronged milord and she as an heiress; and *Blue Water*, apparently made in New Brunswick two years earlier. Her director on Warners' *Broadway After Dark* was the accomplished Monta Bell and her home studio was impressed by her performance as a maid introduced into society by playboy Adolphe Menjou. Also, the fan magazines were full of pictures of her, in *très chic* clothes and bobbed hair – just what Metro wanted for *Broken Barriers*, as a sympathetic flapper who attracts unhappily married James Kirkwood; and after a guest appearance as herself in *Married Flirts*, she was a flapper for Paramount in *Empty Hands*, marooned on a desert island with Jack Holt.

Bell's *The Snob* found her as an heiress pretending to be a teacher, Conrad Nagel as her true love and Gilbert, in the title-role, ill-treating her. She and Gilbert were teamed as a result of *He Who Gets Slapped*, in fact the first MGM film after the amalgamation and whose release was delayed because of the value of its star, Lon Chaney, and its director, the great Victor Sjöström. As Consuelo, the bareback rider, she was overlookable, but MGM decided that she was ready for star treatment: *Excuse Me* (25), with Nagel, a farce about honeymoon predicaments on a train and *Lady of the Night*, in a dual role as a gentle socialite and as a reform school girl who gets all dolled up and goes to speakeasies but is still a good joe at heart. The contrast between the two was meant to impress fans and few stars of note shirked from playing dual roles at this time. Thalberg was now in love with Shearer and wanted her to become the biggest star on the lot.

So she did: *Waking Up the Town* at UA, a small-town tale with Jack Pickford as co-star and director; *A Slave of Fashion* with Lew Cody, as a girl who impersonates another in order to wear glamorous clothes; and *Pretty Ladies*, a story of the Follies mainly about its star comedienne (Zazu Pitts), in a guest appearance. Sjöström directed *The Tower of Lies*, with Chaney as a crazed Swedish peasant and Shearer as the daughter, turned hooker in town; and after *His Secretary* (26), as a plain girl who becomes a raving beauty,

she was directed by another Scandinavian, Benjamin Christiansen (his first American film) – *The Devil's Circus*, going from poverty to the high wire and back. Then: *The Waning Sex*, a comedy about a modern Portia, with Nagel; Bell's *Upstage*, as a vaudeville dancer who when fame comes deserts the partner who has worked so hard for her; *The Devil's Bride* (27), a French farce in the Lubitsch fashion, as Cody's sophisticated wife; and *After Midnight*, yet another show business tale of Bell's, as a hard-working cigarette girl tempted by the high life till her good-time sister is killed. Shearer was now a good second-grade star, at $1,000 a week: she asked for a revised contract, starting at this figure and rising to $5,000 over a five-year period. Mayer agreed, intending to drop her before then; but early in 1927, after a brief romance, she and Thalberg were married.

Thalberg was the boy wonder of Hollywood, the producer of some of its most ambitious pictures: his talent for selecting people and properties has become one of Hollywood's enduring legends. He was an inveterate believer in the star system and there was no star he believed in so deeply as his wife. His handling of her career was a triumph.

His plan was to wean Shearer from the ultra-sophisticated parts she had been playing, so she became the gay heroine of Lubitsch's version of *The Student Prince* with Ramon Novarro. Next, she yearned (as of old) for

Those of Norma Shearer's performances most often seen today – her Elizabeth Barrett Browning, her Juliet and her Marie Antoinette – represent her as a demure and suffering heroine, but for most of her screen career she played a sophisticated woman of the world, as in A Lady of Chance *(29), left, with Johnny Mack Brown, and* A Free Soul *(31), right, with Lionel Barrymore. Her ability to switch personalities was presumably what led contemporary audiences into believing she was a great actress*

The Latest From Paris (28), but was a simple girl again as *The Actress*, Pinero's 'Trelawney of the Wells', following a Broadway revival; then again she was a demi-mondaine, *A Lady of Chance* (29), a part-Talkie. But with the coming of sound, the sweet, gentle Shearer was put in abeyance. After some months of uncertainty, Thalberg cast her as a brassy showgirl, the Mary of *The Trial of Mary Dugan* (29): it was a smart move – her voice was *supposed* to be like that. The cast rehearsed beforehand as for a play and it was photographed like one: Shearer came through with flying colours. She was then the light-fingered Mrs C. in Frederick Lonsdale's *The Last of Mrs Cheyney*, an intelligent performance, and Juliet, to John Gilbert's Romeo, in the balcony scene included in *The Hollywood Revue of 1929* (*not* an intelligent performance).

Her success in her first Talkies launched her into a series of even more ultra-sophisticated parts. For the next couple of years she specialized in restless, over-wealthy, over-sexed (by contemporary standards) women-of-the-world. In the dramas she suffered, in the comedies She Learned the Meaning of True Happiness. The titles tell everything: *Their Own Desire* (30) and *The Divorcee*, both with Robert Montgomery. The latter was strong meat and it was said that Shearer begged to be allowed to do it: it brought her a Best Actress Oscar. In *Let Us Be Gay* (made and released before *The Divorcee*) she was again a frump who becomes a beauty and in *Strangers May Kiss* (31) a free-loving woman who fails to realize, as Montgomery put it in the film, that 'a man will mix anything else, but takes his women straight'. This was the first under a new contract, at $6,000 a week, one of the highest fees in Hollywood.

The box-office bonanza continued with *A Free Soul*, partly because audiences wanted to see Clark Gable knock her around, after which she and Montgomery knocked each other around, in *Private Lives*, taking on the Coward–Lawrence parts without too heavy a loss – she succeeded in looking entirely wrong and sounding exactly right. She attained screen respectability again in the diluted screen transcription of *Strange Interlude* (32) – even if the role did call for her to have a bastard by lover Gable – and sainthood almost in *Smilin' Through*, an unnecessary but well-done (and popular) version of the lachrymose old warhorse, with Fredric March and Leslie Howard. She was billed unequivocally 'The First Lady of the Screen', a tag the MGM publicity mill hung on her for years to come.

In *Riptide* (34) she leaves what was then termed the gay life for marriage – to British aristocrat Herbert Marshall who, finding her with American playboy Robert Montgomery, thinks her unfaithful because, as he says, 'In New York you weren't the sort of girl to stop at a kiss': so she decides she might as well be. Direction, story and script were by Edmund Goulding, remembering the plays of Pinero. He also provided Shearer with a swansong to the 'new woman' roles which had been her speciality, for with the strengthening of the Production Code new women would not be permitted. That was not why her appearances became rarer, but part of a policy to put her on a standing with Garbo, whose films the studio treated as events in themselves. *The Barretts of Wimpole Street* was a drama which had been a success in London and New York and was a hit for MGM ('Oh papa, let us get this over and forget it – I can't forgive myself for having made the whole house miserable over a tankard of porter'). Charles Laughton was papa, March was Robert Browning and Shearer a virginal Elizabeth: her performance – all shining eyes and elegant hand gestures – now makes the film watchable, if you are in the mood.

Since that balcony scene with Gilbert, she had had a hankering to make a film of *Romeo and Juliet* (36). Her husband indulged her. Howard co-starred and $2 million were spent on it. It did not make a nickelsworth of profit, but was good enough (Cukor directed) to do MGM some good (i.e. prestige) and it did not do Shearer any harm. There had been scoffers before the event, but apart from being too old for it, her performance was OK, netting her a fifth Oscar nomination. At this point Thalberg died and it was thought that she would retire; but she signed a new three-year contract with MGM at $150,000 per picture. It was not until 1938, however, that *Marie Antoinette* appeared and Thalberg had worked on it already for some years before he died. It was reasonably accurate, but the facts were so telescoped as to make it appear that the Revolution was caused by the disputed purchase of a diamond necklace. Shearer was charming and sympathetic, at home among MGM's marble halls, but in the wrong film.

Robert Morley, who played Louis XVI, says that rumours were rife that the Front Office wanted to do Shearer in: that this film was to be sabotaged in an attempt to persuade Shearer to sell her large stock in Loew's Inc. (left to her by Thalberg): at the last minute her chosen director, Sidney Franklin, was replaced by W.S. Van Dyke, known as a fast worker. He was allegedly getting a large sum for every day he was under schedule. Thalberg and Mayer had not been friendly for some while before the former's death and tentative plans had been made for Thalberg to go independent, taking half the stars with

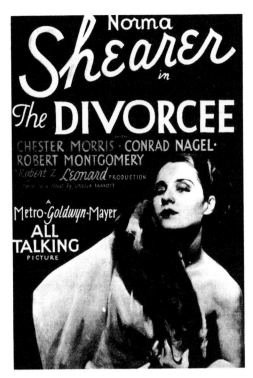

Norma Shearer's popularity was so great and her later appearances so rare that each film was considered a major filmgoing event – and none was more major than Marie Antoinette *(38), made, lavishly, after a two-year absence. She wasn't much like the Queen, but only pedants minded.*

him. Whether Shearer knew there was a plan to oust her is not known, but Bosley Crowther ('The Lion's Roar') says that she realized that her regal position was threatened – and was uncertain whether she wanted to continue without Thalberg's aid.

However, she did owe the company five films and when offered two that had been big Broadway hits, she jumped at them – both comedies: *Idiot's Delight* (39) in a blonde

page-boy wig, with Gable, and Clare Boothe Luce's fable about divorcées at Reno, *The Women*. Both were among the year's brightest movies. These followed: *Escape* (40) with Robert Taylor and two synthetic comedies, *We Were Dancing* (42) from Coward's playlet (she was poor as the Countess), with Melvyn Douglas, and *Her Cardboard Lover* with Taylor. Both flopped. She told Crowther: 'On those two, nobody but myself was trying to do

If Shearer aspired to be the Lynn Fontanne of movies she was encouraged by MGM, who even made her up to look as Fontanne had looked in the original production of Idiot's Delight *(39): but it was still a triumph for her – and Gable. The others are Peter Willes and Pat Paterson.*

me in.' She also admitted that, whatever unhappiness there was at the studio, those two films – plus her rejection of two others – were fatal. The two she turned down were *Mrs Miniver* and *Gone With the Wind* (she had accepted Scarlett provisionally in 1938, but changed her mind when her fan clubs disapproved).

So she did retire; and married again (a skiing instructor). Offers were made (Bette Davis wanted her for *Old Acquaintance*) and in 1946 the ill-fated Enterprise Studio announced that she had signed with them for two films – which were not made. She was blind for several years before she died (of bronchial pneumonia) in 1983 – forgotten by all except buffs, who continue to cherish her work and remember the lofty place she once occupied in Hollywood.

Sheridan after Warners discovered she had 'oomph'.

ANN SHERIDAN

One of the great screen teams was James Cagney and Ann Sheridan. It was not written up at the time and, as far as is known, legions of fans did not write in to ask Warners to reunite them. Indeed, they were only really *teamed* together twice, in two not very notable films, *City for Conquest* and *Torrid Zone*. They complemented each other perfectly, he all bombast and bounce, she more knowing, sharp and disillusioned. The second of these two films provides almost total enjoyment, even if it is partly a rehash of *Only Angels Have Wings*. As with Jean Arthur before her, it is soon clear that she carries a torch, but he is too busy, too modest and too male to notice. They admire and warm to each other from their first meeting, but circumstances keep them sparring till the fade-out.

She was a good all-rounder but was at her most direct as a Brooklynesque hash-slinger, quick with the wise-cracks, slamming back at Cagney (or George Raft or Pat O'Brien). It was not a type that was appreciated too much, when great acting was confused with Greer Garson or Norma Shearer; nor was Sheridan in the same league as Betty Grable as a pin-up. Warner Bros. christened her 'The Oomph Girl' and the name stuck, but she really was too warm, too lush and too genuinely glamorous to compete with the other tinny girls. Her singing voice, for instance, a warm contralto, is much more in tune with today's taste. At all events, she never received her due.

She was born in Denton, Texas, in 1915 and was completing her studies at the North Texas Teachers' College when, unbeknownst to her (so her studio biographers insisted), her family entered her in a 'Search For Beauty' contest. She won the regional prize, which was a trip to Hollywood and a Paramount test: which resulted in a contract and a small part in a film called, unsurprisingly, *Search for Beauty* (34). She appeared in publicity under her own name, Clara Lou Sheridan, a 'Paramount Star of the Future'. She was photographed for thousands of cheesecake pictures and a few motion pictures. Some old sources list as many as 20 credits during her Paramount period, but when that studio decided to star her they issued a list of 12, in most of which she was an extra (*Bolero, It's a Gift*, etc.). She had bit parts in only *Come on Marines, Murder at the Vanities* (that was left on the cutting-room floor) and *Home on the Range* (35), at which point it was decided to build her and 'Clara Lou' became 'Ann': she was given a featured part (seventh on the cast-list, a big leap) in *Behold My Wife*, followed by co-starring assignments in a couple of unimportant movies, *Car 99* with Fred Mac-

Murray and *Rocky Mountain Mystery* with Randolph Scott. She headed down the cast-list again with *Mississippi, The Glass Key*, as a nurse, and *The Crusades*. Then Paramount dropped her.

She managed to get a lead in a Grade Z Western, *Red Blood of Courage* with Kermit Maynard, and in a B at Universal, *The Fighting Youth*. She had been out of work a long time and was contemplating returning to Denton when the WB casting director sent for her. He had seen her in something and thought she had possibilities. She signed with Warners. The association began gloomily with *Sing Me a Love Song* (36) starring James Melton and Patricia Ellis, but then she had neat roles in *The Black Legion* (that was the Ku Klux Klan) as a weepy girl; *The Great O'Malley* (37) as star Pat O'Brien's school-teacher girlfriend; and *San Quentin* as a gangster's moll. She had passed the test and was starred in a series of Bs: *Wine Women and Horses* with Barton MacLane; *The Footloose Heiress; Alcatraz Island* (38) with John Litel; *She Loved a Fireman* with Dick Foran; and *Little Miss Thoroughbred*. She had a featured part in Dick Powell's *A Cowboy From Brooklyn*, then returned to Bs: *The Patient in Room 18* with Patric Knowles, *Mystery House* and *Broadway Musketeers*.

But just before that last one two other films had changed things. She had been loaned to Universal for *A Letter of Introduction* and Universal had discovered she had glamour; and she had done a good gutsy job in Cagney's *Angels With Dirty Faces* (the Angels were the Dead End Kids). Till then WB had seen her as a nice healthy outdoor girl; now they cast her as the girl who started John Garfield on the path to crime in *They Made Me a Criminal* (39) and she was convincing. So she was cast as the saloon floozie in Errol Flynn's *Dodge City* and opposite Dick Powell in a modest musical, *Naughty But Nice*, converting him, a professor, to swing. The prof in *Winter Carnival* was Richard Carlson, she was a divorcée in love with him and they were on loan to Wanger; she cheered on another sporting event in *Indianapolis Speedway*, with O'Brien. She had a stock Warners role in *Angels Wash Their Faces*, as the elder sister of a young punk going crooked, and another in *Castle on the Hudson* (40), as the girl who waits when her guy (Garfield) goes to the pen. She might have played Belle Watling in *Gone With the Wind*, but Warners insisted she be the fifth-billed star and Selznick would not agree.

Her biggest chance came when she was top-starred in *It All Came True*, a pleasant comedy-drama written by Louis Bromfield, with Bogart in support. At the same time the 'oomph' publicity stunt went into action when the publicity department announced that she

James Cagney, always a critics' favourite, scored a triumph in Angels With Dirty Faces *(38). It didn't hurt Ann Sheridan either, playing his sweetheart, but she wasn't at that time a big star. Later, co-starred with him and the other Warner tough guys, she showed a knowing, sassy style to prove that she was, if not their equal, a match for them.*

had been chosen America's 'Oomph' girl by a panel of 25, including Lucius Beebe, Bob Hope and Earl Carroll. With the label went a new five-year contract. She was publicized up-hill and down-dale. At the end of the year observers were saying that she had a helluva lot to live up to. (Sheridan herself did not care for the 'oomph' tag, but she had been in Hollywood too long to fight it.) Then she co-starred with Cagney in *Torrid Zone* and (top-billed) with Raft and Bogart in *They Drive By Night*. Here was her waitress, discovered by Raft in a truck-drivers' café and complaining of the boss's hands, 'all ten of 'em'. It was an appealing performance: a young girl, basically innocent, who had been around too many men to care much, but who would drop the hard-boiled surface if the smile was the right

Ann Sheridan as musical comedy star Norah Bayes in Shine On Harvest Moon, *the only time she carried a musical. A pity that, for she had a rich, warm singing voice and when it went into Technicolor for the last reel she looked stunning.*

one. She was equally good, if not very different, in *City for Conquest*, as an ambitious dancer with whom boxer Cagney tries to keep up: disillusionment for them both and you could see it in the first reel.

Honeymoon for Three (41) co-starred her with George Brent and in life they had one without a third party – a long one, on Brent's yacht, while waiting for WB to capitulate over Sheridan's salary demands (she was getting only $600 a week despite the 'oomph' publicity and wanted $2,000). They did not. Sheridan went back to work anyway, after six months, and did *Navy Blues*, vamping Jack Oakie, and *The Man Who Came to Dinner*, in the part of the actress. Made and shown simultaneously was *King's Row*, one of the year's big successes: Sam Wood's emotional small-town drama and considered a classic by many (with Ronald Reagan, Robert Cummings, Betty Field and Claude Rains). Now her salary did begin to rise. *Juke Girl* (42) was a dreary piece set among the migratory workers in Florida and *Wings for the Eagle* was set in California's giant Lockheed aircraft factory (with Dennis Morgan and Jack Carson); more cheerful was *George Washington Slept Here* with Jack Benny, about a couple settling in a derelict cottage. She did not have much to do in an Errol Flynn actioner, *Edge of Darkness* (43), as a Norwegian resistance worker, and in the all-star *Thank Your Lucky Stars* she had only one song ('Love Isn't Born It's Made') but was pretty sensational doing it.

Her biggest bid for the big time was a musical, *Shine On Harvest Moon* (44), based on the life of Norah Bayes; at last Sheridan was getting the sort of stuff that Grable and Hayworth were getting at their studios – only her musical was not in colour except for the finale. It was popular, due perhaps to more plot (too much, in fact) than was usual in backstage musicals, and because Sheridan suggested that old-time magic more convincingly than Grable or Hayworth. She followed with a couple of comedies, *The Doughgirls* from a Broadway success, and *One More Tomorrow* (46), a rehash of *The Animal Kingdom* with topical references (wartime profiteering). Warners were at that time having great success with their women's fictions (Davis, Crawford) and they passed a couple on to Sheridan, *Nora Prentiss* (47) and *The Unfaithful*, both superior examples of their kind as directed by Vincent Sherman: Nora was a nightclub singer falling in love with a meek and unhappily married doctor (Kent Smith) and the unfaithful lady was a wartime wife in this rehash of *The Letter*. She looked bored throughout *Silver River* (48) – and who could blame her? – an Errol Flynn Western, and it completed her contract.

Sex: the likes of June Allyson and Joan Collins were not in her class, but the film was a mess and did nothing for her career. She made only one other film, a useless Kenyan safari triangle, *Woman and the Hunter* (57) – in which she was trampled to death at the end: mercifully, it got few bookings.

She turned to the stage and appeared with Franchot Tone and Dan Dailey in the special presentation of 'The Time of Your Life' which played in Brussels during the 1958 Exposition. When it was televised in Britain colleagues recalled that alcohol was getting the better of her. She did stock in the US, including a tour of 'Kind Sir' with Scott McKay, who became her third husband. On TV she had two series, an NBC daytime soap opera, 'Another World', and the much more successful (but equally dire) 'Pistols and Petticoats', which was current when she died early in 1967. In London 'The Times' obituary said: 'Without ever quite achieving the mythic status of a super-star, she was always a pleasure to watch, and, as with all true stars, was never quite like anyone else.'

Ann Sheridan up to her neck in trouble in The Unfaithful *(47): she's just killed – in self-defence – the man with whom she committed one small wartime indiscretion. Now's the time to Confess All to husband Zachary Scott.*

She started freelancing from a position of strength and netted co-starring roles opposite Gary Cooper in *Good Sam* (48) – a humorous and compelling performance – and Cary Grant in *I Was a Male War Bride* (49), where she was even better. She said: 'There have been three phases in my career – and the present one, playing comedy and to hell with the oomph, is by far the most satisfying.' Her subsequent films were not, however, prepossessing and they certainly do not indicate that she had free choice of material. In 1950 she sued RKO for breach of contract, claiming that the lead in *My Forbidden Past* should have gone to her and not Ava Gardner: she won her action and got $55,000. She had moved to Mexico in 1948 and journeyed to Hollywood for a batch of routine films: *Stella* (50) at 20th, a comedy with Victor Mature; *Woman on the Run* at Universal with Dennis O'Keefe; *Steel Town* (52) with John Lund and Howard Duff; *Just Across the Street*, a mild romantic comedy with Lund; and a musical, *Take Me to Town* (53), with Sterling Hayden, yet again at Universal. She suffered, along with the other waning stars at Universal, from the fact that their films played double bills.

Somewhat forgotten, she made a B, *Appointment in Honduras*, and another 'little' picture, *Come Next Spring* (56), a bucolic tale which received some attention (her 'mother' performance stood out like a beacon). Later that year she walked away with *The Opposite*

SYLVIA SIDNEY

There were five female stars ruling the roost at Paramount in the early 30s: Dietrich, Miriam Hopkins, Carole Lombard, Claudette Colbert and Sylvia Sidney. Sidney was dark, petite, moist-eyed and an exceptional emotional actress. Unlike the others, she hardly survived leaving the studio and this would be more understandable had her offscreen personality been anything like the characters she played, which were vulnerable to the hundred-and-one buffetings that the plots had them heir to. She revolted against these parts by being glamorously groomed in her publicity stills, but even then she hardly conformed to the ideal beauty of the time. She was not a star from the same mould as the other ladies.

She was born in New York City in 1910 of a Romanian father and Russian mother; she studied elocution and dancing as a child and at the age of 15 entered the Theater Guild School. Her stage début was in Washington in 'The Challenge of Youth' (26) and the following year she took over a lead in 'The Squall' in New York. There were stock engagements in Denver and more parts in New York (she was once in a play called 'Crime' with the also unknown Kay Francis, Chester Morris and Robert Montgomery); and an unbilled bit as a chorus girl in *Broadway Lights* (27). She first attracted major attention in 'Gods of the Lightning' (28) and Fox proposed a featured

Sylvia Sidney as the centre of attraction in Mamoulian's City Streets (31). On the left are boyfriend Gary Cooper and gang boss Paul Lukas; on the right, Stanley Fields, Wynne Gibson and Guy Kibbee.

role in a court-roomer, *Through Different Eyes* (29): an outstanding performance as a murderess, but there were no other offers and she went into stock in Rochester, NY.

She scored in New York in 'Bad Girl' and Paramount offered the lead in *An American Tragedy* which Eisenstein was to direct from Theodore Dreiser's novel; it was postponed and she was offered the role intended first for Clara Bow and then Nancy Carroll in *City Streets* (31), a nice young girl whose nice boyfriend (Gary Cooper) gets caught up in New York racketeering. B.P. Schulberg, the head of the studio, fell in love with her and offered a contract, seeing her as Bow's successor (for which she was clearly unsuited). She became an unmarried mother in *Confessions of a Co-Ed* and in a similar plight (pregnant) in *An American Tragedy*, reactivated under Josef von Sternberg. The author, in common with critics and audiences, disliked the picture (he sued Paramount for infidelity and lost), but it stands up today – better than the 1951 remake, *A Place in the Sun*, which in parts is a carbon copy; and just as that was notable for Shelley Winters as the slum girl victim, so is this for Sidney's performance in that part. Phillips Holmes was the boy and Frances Dee the socialite.

A flop the film may have been, but it doomed Sidney thereafter to a series of waifs in overalls, put-upon girls in back streets. Goldwyn borrowed her for such a role after negotiating with Paramount for Miss Carroll, who became unavailable. Sidney was suggested instead because *Street Scene* was expected to be an important movie – which was why director King Vidor merely restaged Elmer Rice's play, thus killing it at the box-office. Back at Paramount she was one of the

Ladies of the Big House (32) and in the remake of *The Miracle Man* (Hobart Bosworth had the Chaney part); then she suffered in more elegant surroundings in *Merrily We Go to Hell*, flirting broken-heartedly with Cary Grant while husband Fredric March loses himself in booze and other women. After playing herself in *Make Me a Star*, she had to cope in the non-operatic *Madame Butterfly* with dialogue like 'Honor-able Lieutenant, the most best nice man in all the world' (needless to say, it was a terrible film). Then it was back to rags (she was an ex-con) in *Pick-Up* (33). *Jennie Gerhardt* was a poor version of another Dreiser novel, but the author thought hers 'a beautiful interpreta-tion'. She was promised a film of his 'Sister Carrie' but instead was put into *The Way to Love* with Chevalier – then, because she was ill, had to be replaced by Ann Dvorak (there was some controversy as to whether she was really sick or not). She returned to be a *Good Dame* (34) with a lecherous March, so good indeed that although they bum around after leaving the carnival she will not give in till they are married, and the *30 Day Princess*, a welcome (and accomplished) stab at comedy in a dual role, with Cary Grant. After a silly drama in which she was a squaw – *Behold My Wife* (35), proclaimed Gene Raymond – she did another comedy, *Accent on Youth*, from Samson Raphaelson's play about the boss (Herbert Marshall) with a crush on his secretary.

Since this situation continued to be paralle-led in real life Sidney tried to ease the situation by leaving Paramount, but she did so only technically, for she signed an exclusive contract with Walter Wanger, who released through that company. She made as classy a

clutch of movies as any artist was ever landed with, but only in what she considered to be constricting parts, invariably suffering: *Mary Burns Fugitive* with Melvyn Douglas and the Technicolored *The Trail of the Lonesome Pine* (36), as a backwoods girl being scrapped over by Henry Fonda and Fred MacMurray. She worried her way through: Fritz Lang's *Fury* at MGM as Spencer Tracy's fiancée; Hitchcock's *Sabotage* in Britain as Oscar Homolka's wife; and Lang's *You Only Live Once* (37) as Fonda's wife. 'What chance have they got against all this?' asked Joel McCrea of the *Dead End Kids*, one of whom was her brother: she was on the picket lines, and William Wyler directed. *You and Me* (38) was summed-up (or put down) thus by 'Photoplay': 'You have seen Sylvia Sidney and George Raft hounded by the law too many times to find any freshness in this story of two paroled convicts who marry each other. George backslides to his old gang, is brought up short by the little woman.'

Wanger then cast her in *Algiers* with Boyer, but she refused to play another weepy, underprivileged heroine and the part went to Sigrid Gurie. The film as such did not matter to her, because she considered herself an actress and not a star. For some while she had told reporters that she disliked being a property, an investment, and that she disliked Hollywood. She bought up her contract, leaving as unfortunate legacy Merle Oberon's Cathy in *Wuthering Heights*. Wanger had once announced an *Ivanhoe* for her (as Rebecca) and Gary Cooper; a script for the Brontë film existed by Hecht and MacArthur, which Wyler read and wanted to do at Warners with Bette Davis. Wanger, who planned to cast Charles Boyer as Heathcliff, sold it in pique

to Goldwyn, who wanted it for Oberon. So there was no chance of Sidney playing the role on which she had set her heart.

She went to New York to re-establish herself as an actress (she said later that more than anything else Wyler had killed her self-confidence as same). She appeared on the stage with Franchot Tone in 'The Gentle People' and in . . . *One Third of a Nation* (39), an independent film dealing with slum problems – the sort of subject she was supposedly running away from and certainly an inferior film by any standards. It got few bookings. She returned to Hollywood to re-establish herself there, but did very few films. She played opposite Humphrey Bogart in *The Wagons Roll at Night* (41), as a fortune-teller in a circus, and with James Cagney in *Blood on the Sun* (45), dressed to the nines as a Eurasian vamp: it looked like a new career for Sidney. For Paramount she starred in the film version of Lillian Hellman's horribly superficial play about a crusading journalist examining the advances of European dictators in the 30s, *The Searching Wind* (46), but at least it was meant to be an important production, which could not be said of *Mr Ace* with Raft and the remake of *Love From a Stranger* (47), as the would-be murder victim of husband John Hodiak. After a break she did three more films: *Les Misérables* (52) as Fantine and also for 20th, *Violent Saturday* (55); and a B for Universal, *Behind the High Wall* (56), co-starring with Tom Tully.

But she became one of the most hard-working of stage actresses. At the height of her film career she returned to New York to play in 'To Quito and Back' (37) by Ben Hecht; 'Pygmalion' and 'Tonight at 8.30' in stock (38). Subsequently, in stock and on tour (and in new York) she played in some of the best roles in modern and classical drama, from Auntie Mame to Lady Bracknell. A few of the many titles: 'The Four Poster', 'Enter Laughing', 'Angel Street' ('Gaslight'), 'Joan of Lorraine', 'Anne of a Thousand Days', 'Black Chiffon', 'The Madwoman of Chaillot' and 'The Rivals'; she also had good parts on TV, in dramas and guesting in series; and published a book on needlepoint. She married three times: the first and second husbands were Bennett Cerf and Luther Adler.

She finally accepted a role on television, in *Do Not Fold Spindle or Mutilate* (71), with three other ageing actresses, Myrna Loy, Helen Hayes and Mildrid Natwick, and made an equally impressive return to the cinema in Paul Newman's *Summer Wishes Winter Dreams* (72) as Joanne Woodward's mother. After a short gap, she was seen frequently, usually in supporting roles: *The Secret Night Caller* (75), *Winner Take All* and *Death at*

Fritz Lang's *Fury (36): Sylvia Sidney as the worried girlfriend of Spencer Tracy, arrested – wrongly – on a kidnapping charge, and starting off a wave of mob violence – the 'fury' of the title.*

Love House (76), all for television; *God Told Me To* starring Tony Lo Bianco; *Raid on Entebbe* (77) for TV, in the role played in the better, rival version by Miss Hayes; *Snowbeast*, replacing Gloria Swanson just before shooting, and *Siege* (78), also for television. After two more for cinemas, *Demon!* with Sandy Dennis, and *Damien: the Omen II*, as a dowager aunt, she returned to telefilms: *The Gossip Columnist* (80); *FDR: the Last Year*, as one of his cousins; *The Shadow Box*, directed by Newman, as one of the patients in the clinic; *A Small Killing* (81), a title which referred to her, playing a skid row crone; *Finnegan Begin Again* (82) as Robert Preston's senile wife; and *Come Along With Me*, directed by Woodward with Estelle Parsons. *Hammett* had a troubled production history as produced by Coppola's Zoetrope Studio and directed by Wim Wenders: the result was a laughable transcription of the cod Hammett parody it was based on – let alone of those films based on the real thing. Sidney must have been glad her role was small. After playing Dyan Cannon's mother in another telefilm, *Having It All*, she was in an Italian movie filmed in English in New York with Harvey Keitel, best known as *Corrupt* (83). She was in a superior tele-movie, *An Early Frost* (85), more tolerant than some on learning that her grandson is gay and has AIDS, and was in another, *Pals* (87). Then she was in cinemas again in *Beetlejuice* (88), as a chain-smoking bureaucrat welcoming the dead to the next world.

ANN SOTHERN

The title is disputatious, but Ann Sothern had the best claim to the crown of Queen of the Bs. Perhaps she did not (quite) make the most, but she was easily the best and most popular of the many ladies who toiled in those particular vineyards. The industry thought so well of her that she was given, belatedly, some 'A' chances, recognition long overdue for a star who was warm and direct and versatile. Most of her stills show her as a glycerine-eyelidded siren, but in her films she was really a friendly, jolly girl.

She was born in 1909 in Valley City, North Dakota, and educated in Minneapolis and at the University of Washington. Her mother was a soprano and singing coach, and it was she, Sothern insisted, who pushed her into show business. She had an unbilled bit in *Broadway Nights* (27), made in New York, and later joined her mother in Hollywood – where the latter's services were in demand as a result of the coming of Talkies. That connection enabled her to get a bit in *Hearts in Exile* (29) and, with her sister, a brief appearance in *The Show of Shows*, in a song and dance item about sisters; at the same studio she did a brief role in *Hold Everything* (30) and was briefly a Goldwyn Girl in *Whoopee*; then MGM tested her and signed her. The fan magazines of the period carry pictures of her, brunette, under her own name of Harriet Lake, but Metro used her in only one film, *Doughboys* (30), and then dropped her. She went to Broadway, got a small part in 'Smiles' (30) and then the lead in 'America's Sweetheart' (31), the Rodgers and Hart satire on Hollywood; she was in 'Everybody's Welcome' and toured in Gershwin's 'Of Thee I Sing'. She returned to Hollywood to try again and considering that she had acquired a small reputation, rather surprisingly changed her name to Ann Sothern: as such she appeared briefly in *Broadway Through the Keyhole* (33), which starred Russ Colombo, Texas Guinan and Blossom Seeley. Lucille Ball – whose early career was similar to Sothern's – was also in it.

Then Columbia signed her to a contract, and starred her opposite Edmund Lowe in *Let's Fall in Love* (34), as a side-show girl promoted to stardom for devious reasons. Sothern, however, was not quite up to her material. She was loaned to Paramount for the Ruggles-Boland *Melody in Spring*, as the daughter of tycoon Ruggles, wooed by radio singer Lanny Ross, and then flung into the following Bs: *The Party's Over* with Stuart Erwin; *The Hell-Cat*, a newspaper story with Robert Armstrong; and *Blind Date*, Cinderella-stuff with Neil Hamilton and Paul Kelly. Goldwyn gave her a chance of sorts when he cast her and George Murphy as the juvenile leads in Eddie Cantor's *Kid Millions*: she had little to do except sing, but she scored; as she did in another musical, 20th's *Folies Bergere* (35), as Maurice Chevalier's tempestuous chorine girlfriend.

Columbia put her into *Eight Bells* with Ralph Bellamy and then into two musicals: *Hooray for Love* at RKO, a poor imitation of *42nd Street*, with Gene Raymond, and notable mainly for a Harlem sequence with Bill Robinson and Fats Waller; and their own *The Girl Friend* with Roger Pryor, which was not the Rodgers and Hart show of that title, but a burlesque on amateur actors, with a Napoleon skit. Sothern and Pryor were married in 1936. She then returned to Bs: *Grand Exit* with Lowe; *You May Be Next* (36) with Lloyd Nolan; *Hell-ship Morgan* with George Bancroft; and *Don't Gamble With Love* with Bruce Cabot. She was dropped – in one of Columbia's periodic economy drives – and she could not, in view of her films, have been sorry. At Paramount she was *My American Wife* to European Count Francis Lederer and an heiress, in this sharp satire on snobbery. RKO signed her to an exclusive seven-year contract and promptly reunited her with Raymond, in *Walking on Air* and *The Smartest Girl in Town*. She went to MGM for *Dangerous Number* (37), opposite Robert Young, and to 20th for *Fifty Roads to Town*, where she and Don Ameche played 'with captivating lightness' ('Picturegoer'). After *There Goes My Girl* with Raymond and *Super Sleuth* with Jack Oakie, 20th borrowed her again, to replace Simone Simon, who was unable to play comedy. The film was *Danger Love at Work* and she was the daughter of a crazy, improvident family (the cast included Mary Boland, Edward Everett Horton, Jack Haley and Walter Catlett). After *There Goes the Groom* with Burgess Meredith there was yet another with Raymond, *She's Got Everything* (38). In reality, they did not get on at all, at all; and she disliked intensely the colourless films they made together. She felt she was being overexposed and in poor pictures and sought a loophole in her contract.

As a consequence, she was unemployed when Wanger cast her in *Trade Winds* (38), second lead to Joan Bennett, as Fredric March's ever-loving wise-cracking secretary. She stole the picture and MGM signed her for a property they had once bought for Jean Harlow and since had been unable to cast, *Maisie* (39): Sothern played a resourceful if scatterbrained blonde always getting in and out of scrapes. Already it was planned as the first of a series, although as a film it was saved only by her performance. MGM signed her to a seven-year exclusive contract. As a B-picture star, it could not be expected that she would rank with their top-rank ladies, but neither was she palmed off with low-budgeters. Later MGM did give her top vehicles, but most of her early films for them were halfway efforts, able to top the bill at smaller situations or play second feature at bigger houses. There were manifold reasons why she could not be catapulted into A pictures at once, for all the respect that filmgoers and critics had for her: other interested parties – exhibitors, leading men, studio executives, etc. – had to be wooed into accepting her as an A-budget talent. 20th cut her role in *Hotel for Women*, due, it was said, to her having accepted the MGM offer rather than theirs – for this film had had a checkered career, being known at one point as *Elsa Maxwell's Hotel for Women*. Settling into Metro, Sothern was with Franchot Tone in the inaptly named *Fast and Furious*, a Thin Man imitation, and with William Gargan visiting Lewis Stone in Damon Runyon's hilarious *Joe and Ethel Turp Call on the President*; and then was *Congo Maisie* (40), a loose-working-over of *Red Dust*. She was to have played Vivien Leigh's colleague in *Waterloo Bridge*, but had appendicitis and was replaced by Virginia Field.

At Warners she had a good part as a wise-cracking moll in *Brother Orchid*, replacing Lee Patrick, already cast, at Mark Hellinger's insistence, and was then *Gold Rush Maisie*. She was also *Dulcy*, a programmer from a Broadway play by George S. Kaufman and Marc Connelly, about a daffy girl trying to get Roland Young to buy one of Ian Hunter's inventions; then *Maisie Was a Lady* (41). She was *Ringside Maisie* with George Murphy, called *Cash and Carry* in Britain: all the subsequent films in the series lost the name Maisie in that country, suggesting that there was not a huge popularity for them. They were now Bs: but Sothern got the lead in a big musical, *Lady Be Good*, alongside Eleanor Powell – and it was Sothern's film all the way. There were *Maisie Gets Her Man* (42), and then the coveted lead in another musical, Cole Porter's *Panama Hattie*, with Red Skelton;

Ann Sothern spent years in B pictures before MGM gave her some good chances, as in Panama Hattie *(42), playing a brassy nightclub singer. Ethel Merman had done it on Broadway.*

but none of the quality of the Broadway original survived and it was merely a succession of turns. Maybe if it had gone better, she would have been given more important roles. Instead she returned to programmers: *Three Hearts for Julia* (43) with Melvyn Douglas; and *Swing Shift Maisie*. In *Thousands Cheer* she did a sketch with Lucille Ball and Frank Morgan; in *Cry Havoc*, along with Margaret Sullavan and Joan Blondell, she gave a remarkable performance as one of the nurses, an ex-waitress. Afterwards, *Maisie goes to Reno* (44). . . .

Her marriage had ended in divorce in 1942 and in 1943 she had married another B picture star, Robert Sterling; she was away from the screen while daughter Trisha was born and worked only intermittently thereafter: *Up Goes Maisie* (46) with Murphy and *Undercover Maisie* (47) with Barry Nelson, the last of the series. She did a pleasant Warner musical with Jack Carson, *April Showers* (48), about the tribulations of a vaudeville couple, and yet again her work suggests that if this had been a better film it might have opened up a new career. She looked lovely in colour in MGM's *Words and Music*, guesting and sing-

ing – an all too brief appearance. She had then the best film of her career, Mankiewicz's *A Letter to Three Wives*, along with Linda Darnell and Jeanne Crain, as a radio serial writer whose schoolteacher husband (Kirk Douglas) is contemptuous of both those and her crass boss (Florence Bates); but *The Judge Steps Out* (49) at RKO, a romantic drama with Alexander Knox, set her back a good 10 years (it had been seen in Britain one year earlier, as *Indian Summer*). MGM put her into *Shadow on the Wall* (50), as a murderess, with Zachary Scott, and, pleased with the response to her participation in *Words and Music*, cast her as Jane Powell's mother in *Nancy Goes to Rio* – a fair indication that she was never going to make it, though, in terms of appeal, in that film she left her 'daughter' at the starting-post. She was seriously ill in 1950; recovered, she went to Broadway in 'Faithfully Yours', with Robert Cummings, but it did not run; she went into TV and nightclubs, and when the best she could get in films was Ann Baxter's wise-cracking roommate in *The Blue Gardenia* (53) she quit Hollywood.

Gratifyingly, she did nicely in TV – in a

Miss Sothern disappeared from the screen for over ten years; returned, with charm, personality and professionalism undimmed, in films such as Sylvia *(65), which starred Carroll Baker.*

special, 'Lady in the Dark', and in her own series, 'Private Secretary', 1954–57. There was another, 'The Ann Sothern Show', playing an employee in a resort hotel. It was co-owned by her own company and that of Lucille Ball, causing Sothern to remark, 'Lucy used to complain that she got all the parts I turned down. Now I produce the show and she owns the studio. I guess that settles that.' There was more work in TV and stock, including 'The Glass Menagerie', 'The Solid Gold Cadillac' and 'Gypsy', keeping her away from cinemas till *The Best Man* (64), as a political committee woman, clearly an amalgam of several party harpies with more power than is good for them. Stoutish, she was deliberately blowsy as the vicious bitch indifferent to the fate of Olivia de Havilland, the *Lady in a Cage*, and as part-time whore and lush in a neat minor thriller, *Sylvia* (65) – and the best thing in that film. When she played a madame in *Chubasco* (68), with Richard Egan, it looked as though films had found a first-rate character woman – if liable to type-casting – but she returned to television: *The Outsider* (67), a pilot for Darren McGavin, playing a private eye, which became a series for him; *Congratulations It's a Boy!* (71), as Bill Bixby's mother; *A Death of Innocence* with Shelley Winters and her daughter, who suggested her as a replacement when Kim Hunter hurt her foot; *The Weekend Nun* (72), as a Mother Superior; and *The Great Man's Whiskers* (73). Sadly, her cinema films were low-budget shockers: *The Killing Kind*, directed by Curtis Harrington; *Golden Needles* (74), made in Hong Kong; *Crazy Mama* (75); and *The Manitou* (78), with Tony Curtis. There was also a mini-series, *Captains and the Kings* (76). She was a hick mama in a kiddie tale for cinemas, *The Little Dragons* (80), and then was the mother in what had been the Linda Darnell episode in a tele-version of *A Letter to Three Wives* (85) – which was of such quality that she apologized to Joe Mankiewicz. But she was, after these several years, in a 'quality' cinemovie, *The Whales of August* (87), as friendly neighbour to Bette Davis and Lillian Gish, for which she was nominated Best Supporting Actress in the Oscar Derby.

BARBARA STANWYCK

Barbara Stanwyck was never one of the great box-office attractions, but in 1944 she was listed by the US Treasury Dept as the highest paid woman in the country (at over $400,000 – Bette Davis was second). At that time she had been in movies over 15 years and the eminence she had reached was rather the result of slogging than by anything showy in the way of performance or publicity. She was to the public exactly what she was to the film companies – reliable. Right from the start she was a thoroughly professional actress, De Mille's favourite, for example: 'I have never worked with an actress who was more co-operative, less temperamental, and a better workman, to use my term of highest compliment.' Fritz Lang said that 'working with Barbara Stanwyck was one of the greatest pleasures of my career'. Frank Capra: 'Barbara Stanwyck, is destined to be beloved by all directors, actors, crews and extras. In a Hollywood popularity contest she would win first prize hands down.'

Such, in fact, were the qualities she projected on screen: accomplished, down-to-earth and self-assured. She was immediately at home in any milieu and in any costume, though dry and perhaps somewhat cynical. With Bette Davis and Joan Crawford, she makes a Hollywood triumvirate of 'strong' women. Like them, in a couple of films she was menaced, the frightened heroine, but it was unlikely casting. She was in her element running the show, directing the traffic. She was an incomparably better actress than Crawford and if she hardly measures up to Davis at her best, she was never as bad as Davis at her worst. In fact, she never gave a bad performance (something, one feels, she would like as an epitaph).

She was born in Brooklyn in 1907, of Scots-Irish parentage, the youngest of five. They were orphaned while she was young and she was partly brought up by one of the older sisters, who was a showgirl. Stanwyck went to work at 13, wrapping parcels, and did a variety of menial jobs before trying the stage: she wanted to be a dancer and by sheer grind she made it. At 15, she started in speak-easies, moving on to Broadway and tours, and finally landed a straight part – as a dancer – in 'The Noose' (26). The part was enlarged *en route* for Broadway, so that when it reached there she was a 'star'. She became a real star in the next one, 'Burlesque', the classic story of a showbiz marriage on the rocks – she goes up as he, drinking, goes down (a situation she would soon in real life find herself in: but at this time she had just married – comic Frank Fay). MGM offered a screen test, but she refused; however, she agreed to support Lois Wilson and Sam Hardy in a very similar vaudeville tale, *Broadway Nights* (27), at First National, and when her 'Burlesque' run was through she did another film in New York, *The Locked Door* (30), a strong sex drama where she got fourth billing.

'That film was so bad, it nearly locked the

Barbara Stanwyck in her first major film role, The Locked Door *(30), with Harry Mestayer, Harry Stubbs and Clarence Burton. They think she's just murdered her husband: she hasn't, but in typical Stanwyck fashion, she sure looks guilty.*

door of my screen future,' she said later. She accompanied Fay to Hollywood, where he persuaded WB to test her – without result. He went to Columbia (Harry Cohn), offering to pay Stanwyck's salary secretly and the cost of dressing her if they would give her a break: Columbia refused, but did give her a chance in the low-budget *Mexicali Rose*. Fay continued to fight for her and eventually talked Frank Capra into using her as one of Columbia's *Ladies of Leisure*, a jazz-baby who repents after finding True Love. This time the studio liked her and signed her to a contract. Warners borrowed her for *Illicit*, a drama about a girl who refuses to marry her lover (James Rennie). 'Photoplay' found it as 'daring as youth' and 'another big triumph for that perfectly grand actress' Stanwyck; but 'Picturegoer' thought her accent 'unattractive and her acting stilted'. She was a taxi-dancer in the enjoyable *Ten Cents a Dance*, marrying a poor wrong-'un (Monroe Owsley) instead of the moneybags (Ricardo Cortez) who loves her. She learns the hard way, to unanimously good reviews: critics found her interpretation refreshing after the 'innocent' way such parts

were usually played. With three hits to her credit Stanwyck sued Columbia for more salary and the matter was settled by sharing her contract with Warners, who wanted her. She divided her time between the two: *Miracle Woman*, a satire on an Aimee Semple MacPherson type evangelist, directed by Frank Capra; William A. Wellman's *Night Nurse*, who was no better than she should be; and *Forbidden* (32), as a small-town librarian, who swops pince-nez and a bun for glamour, which ensnares a married rich man (Adolphe Menjou) while she is vacationing in Havana: she has his baby while falling in love with a nice guy (Ralph Bellamy). 'Picturegoer' had changed its mind: 'Barbara Stanwyck is, literally, great. We hear a lot about la Garbo, la Dietrich, la this and la that; but I doubt if any of these publicity-haunted stars could have put so much natural feeling into a part which requires the most sensitive handling and the soul of a true artist.' The film really put Stanwyck on top; when the same magazine listed the top six women stars (Garbo, Constance Bennett, Dietrich, Chatterton, Shearer and Crawford) Menjou himself told the editor that in Hollywood Stanwyck was rated above the last two.

She was then *Shopworn*; and was in a remake of Edna Ferber's *So Big* and in *The Purchase Price*, a marital drama with George Brent: she was a cabaret girl. In *The Bitter Tea of General Yen* (33), which Capra directed, she was an Occidental harboured by lascivious Chinese warlord Nils Asther – and she beautifully conveyed an intrigued sexual repulsion. (It was a theme which got the film banned in Britain and the Commonwealth.) She was less resistant in *Ladies They Talk About*, as a hard-boiled gun moll, with Preston Foster; and certainly not at all in *Baby Face*, moving from the stockroom to the executive penthouse. Her image was established: a working girl in recognizable surroundings, but considerably more pushy than the working girls you met in the street. She was much more jaded; she was amoral; and she was not, if the crunch came, averse to murder. The censors saw to it that she suffered at the end, if only by losing her man. The following were mostly melodramas: *Ever in My Heart*, a war drama, as a woman who marries a German immigrant (Otto Kruger) – and becomes a nurse in France after he has returned there; *Gambling Lady* (her, with Joel McCrea); a remake of Willa Cather's *A Lost Lady* (34), in a marriage of convenience to Frank Morgan but falling for Ricardo Cortez; *The Secret Bride* (35) with Warren William; and *The Woman in Red*, about the girl from the other side of the tracks married into society. During this period she also starred in a stage musical with Fay, 'Tattle Tales' (33), but it did not save the marriage.

Her two contracts were up and she made *Red Salute*, as a college girl attracted – temporarily – by Communism. RKO now promised her better things and she was *Annie Oakley* for them, under George Stevens's direction. The film is negative, as if waiting for Irving Berlin's score, but the 'Sunday Times' (London) thought the original Annie 'had not the personal fascination Barbara Stanwyck brings to the part'. The RKO contract was non-exclusive – Stanwyck never in her career tied herself to any one studio – but at this time it was a (typically) bold move. She protected herself with multi-pic deals: *A Message to Garcia* (36) at 20th with Wallace Beery, a silly distortion of history, taken from a famous (1898) bestseller as the daughter of a Cuban patriot; *The Bride Walks Out* at RKO with Gene Raymond; and *His Brother's Wife* at MGM with Robert Taylor: on the last day of shooting, the crew presented Stanwyck with a scroll describing her 'Number One Actress and Swell Person'. *Banjo on My Knee* at 20th was a very serious piece, though set on

a Mississippi riverboat and containing some slapstick. John Ford's version of Sean O'Casey's *The Plough and the Stars* was a mess, not helped by a happy ending tagged on: he did not want a star and Stanwyck appeased him by playing the gentle Nora without make-up; publicity maintained that he got the Abbey Players in exchange for her presence. She was a desperate mother in *Internes Can't Take Money* (37) at Paramount, with Joel McCrea as a helpful doctor, and she was a saloon singer at 20th, replacing a sick Alice Faye, in *This Is My Affair*; Taylor (soon to be her second husband) was an undercover man.

Her eclecticism did not impress Goldwyn, who thought her not sexy enough to play *Stella Dallas* in the remake. He asked her to test and she declined till McCrea insisted on paying for the test because he thought she would be perfect. 'Photoplay' agreed, finding her 'superbly suited' to the role, for 'enormous vitality must justify crude vulgarity and leave the character sympathetic'. After that, her fans were pleased to see her with a Lombard-like wardrobe in a hopefully screwball comedy, *Breakfast for Two*, heiress to Herbert Marshall's playboy. Refusing to be typed, she went from another sombre piece, the remake of *Always Goodbye* (38), a mother-love drama with Marshall, to a madcap murder mystery, *The Mad Miss Manton*, as an irresponsible socialite to the editor of Henry Fonda.

And she did a Western, De Mille's *Union Pacific* (39), with McCrea and Robert Preston, who later said, 'A lot of people feel like I do about Barbara Stanwyck – or Missy, as we all called her. Bill Holden was one newcomer she helped a great deal, and she helped me. She was the first big star with whom I worked, and later, when I got involved with others who were selfish or put on the big star act, I didn't get bugged because Missy had shown me that all stars aren't like that. It's true that nobody else was quite like her. For 20 years I haven't stepped on a stage, or in front of a camera, without wearing the St Genesius medal she gave me. If he was the patron saint of actors, she, in my opinion, is the patroness.' The film on which she helped Holden was *Golden Boy*. After that she played a shop-lifter, one of her best performances, in *Remember the Night* (40); and she was splendid in *The Lady Eve* (41), again up to no good as a cardsharp cheating Henry Fonda; this was Preston Sturges's funny comedy with, at one point, Stanwyck doing a breathtaking parody of a British socialite. Capra's *Meet John Doe*, with Gary Cooper, and *You Belong to Me*, again with Fonda, were weak ones; but then she was in a good one with Cooper, Howard Hawks's *Ball of*

Stanwyck was one of the few serious actresses who consented to do leggy pin-up pictures for GIs during the war: coincidentally she displayed those legs in a couple of films, playing hard-bitten showgirls. This one was Lady of Burlesque *(43), and her performance was fine too.*

Fire (41), in the title-role as a gum-chewing, hip-swinging, slangy showgirl who uses and then falls for meek professor Cooper. She did a similar role equally well a couple of years later, William A. Wellman's *Lady of Burlesque* from Gypsy Rose Lee's 'The G-String Murders': they were not allowed to use that title. Inbetweenwhiles, Wellman's *The Great Man's Lady* (42), with McCrea again, was one of her drearier films, though it gave her a chance to age; and *The Gay Sisters* (Nancy Coleman and Geraldine Fitzgerald were the others) was not much better. Then, after the Gypsy Rose Lee film, she co-starred with Charles Boyer in an episode of *Flesh and Fantasy* (43).

Double Indemnity (44) was probably the peak of Stanwyck's career; Billy Wilder directed, Raymond Chandler scripted from a novel by James M. Cain, about a blonde tramp (Stanwyck) in cahoots with an insurance man (Fred MacMurray) to murder her husband and share the loot: perhaps the best of the 40s black dramas. Her insolent, self-possessed wife is one of the screen's definitive studies of villainy – and should have won (it

was thought, then and since) an Oscar over Ingrid Bergman's performance in *Gaslight*.

After that, she was mostly nice, but in several of poor quality – mainly for Warners and Hal Wallis, who had her under joint contract (Warners were paying her $225,000 per film). *Christmas in Connecticut* (45) with Dennis Morgan and *My Reputation* (46) with George Brent were romantic trifles; and *The Bride Wore Boots*, a comedy with Robert Cummings, was completely unworthy of her. She did play a rich bitch in *The Strange Love of Martha Ivers*, a heavy melodrama and probably her best vehicle of the late 40s (to which period it belongs absolutely); she had a conventional sturdy part in a coloured Western, *California*; did an Erich Maria Remarque sudser with David Niven, *The Other Love* (47), and was frightened by Humphrey Bogart in *The Two Mrs Carrolls*. 'Time' magazine said: 'Miss Stanwyck, who does well enough with a tough, worldly kind of part, is baffled by the sleight of hand required for this one.' It's a pity that this was the only time they were teamed. Warners bought *The Fountainhead* for the two of them, but King Vidor, scheduled to direct, was another who did not think her 'sexy' enough. So she wanted out of her contract and settled it by being frightened again – by Errol Flynn – in *Cry Wolf*.

At MGM she replaced Katharine Hepburn in John P. Marquand's story, *B.F.'s Daughter* (48), as a stinking rich gal who marries a Socialist (Van Heflin) and cannot understand why he does not like the palace she has bought in his absence; and she was frightened again, by Burt Lancaster at Paramount, in *Sorry Wrong Number*, dubiously extended from a classic short radio thriller: the additions included establishing the Stanwyck character as a typical Stanwyck character – self-willed, wealthy, obstinate and selfish (so who cared if she did get murdered at the end?). This brought her her fourth Oscar nomination.

The next few, as ever, varied: *The Lady Gambles* (49) – compulsively, with Robert Preston as her husband; *The File of Thelma Jordan*, as a classy lady who lets herself be picked up by D.A. Wendell Corey – 'Maybe I'm just a dame and didn't know it' she says, which is our Barbara all over; *East Side West Side* at MGM, offering a thoughtful performance in a hackneyed part – the long-suffering wife; *No Man of Her Own* (50) with John Lund; and *The Furies*, at her most determined, squabbling with father Walter Huston – whose playing showed up hers as being wildly conventional. That was her last for Wallis and she went to MGM for two: *To Please a Lady*, as a tough columnist who succumbs to the charms of one of her 'victims', Clark Gable; and *The Man With a Cloak* (51) as a period Mrs Danvers. In Fritz Lang's *Clash By Night* (52) she was a tramp again, and a weary one – with one of Clifford Odets's more memorable lines: 'Home is where you come to when you've run out of places.' Marilyn Monroe was in it and co-star Paul Douglas resented the fuss made over her. 'It's this way, Paul,' said Stanwyck, 'she's younger and more beautiful than any of us.' *Jeopardy* (53) was a programmer, but a neat one – about a trapped man and a rising tide; *Titanic* was a lavish recreation of a Certain Event and she was Clifton Webb's American wife, bringing the children away from corrupt old Europe. She was another sad mother in *All I Desire*, a gratuitous weepie, and again self-possessed out West in *The Moonlighter*, with MacMurray. She was evil in the oilfields in *Blowing Wild*, with wildcatter Cooper, but the public was losing interest in teamings of ageing stars. The men withstood the years better and her last good picture was *Executive Suite* (54) when of the all-star boardroom (Holden, Douglas, Fredric March, Walter Pidgeon, Shelley Winters, Nina Foch) hers was the outstanding performance.

She was, as she implied to Douglas, ageing. She had let her hair go grey and perhaps that was the trouble. Maybe she should have stopped working until a good offer came along, or maybe she was realistic enough to realize that with the onset of the 50s good parts for actresses of her generation were hard to come by: but she went on, bossy and managing as ever, in a series of programmers of little consequence except for her presence: *Witness to Murder* with Gary Merrill; *Cattle Queen of Montana* with Ronald Reagan; *The Violent Men* (55), as a ranchhouse Regina Giddens carrying on with Brian Keith and killing husband Edward G. Robinson in a fire by withholding his crutches; and a particularly nasty cheapie, *Escape to Burma* with Robert Ryan. *There's Always Tomorrow* found her as an old flame of MacMurray, a neglected

A posed still for Jeopardy *(53), but that's our Barbara all right, looking anguished. It isn't one of her major credits, but it's an excellent minor thriller in which she is menaced by some thugs, including Keith Andes, while her husband is caught in the tide.*

Miss Stanwyck is virtually the only major Hollywood talent that Elvis Presley has played with during his film career: Roustabout *(64). The film wasn't worthy of her but she brought style and authority to her role as the carnival boss.*

husband whom she comforts; *The Maverick Queen* (56) is a Republic Western and she is queen of the gambling saloon, claiming 'I did what I had to do to get to the top'; and *These Wilder Years* at least saw her pitted against James Cagney. He played a wealthy industrialist who comes to see her, the head of an orphanage, about a child he has not seen in years. Both are as compulsively watchable as ever, but the thing never amounts to much, which may be why it played B bookings. *Crime of Passion* (57) with Sterling Hayden, *Trooper Hook* with McCrea and *Forty Guns* were all, to say the most, duallers.

After a five-year absence she returned as the lesbian madame in the film of Nelson Algren's *A Walk on the Wild Side* (62); Laurence Harvey played the lead and it flopped. After an interval she had some footage as the carnival boss who employs Elvis Presley in *Roustabout* (64), but she was not in her element, while *The Night Walker* (65), a 'fright' thriller with ex-husband Taylor and borrowings from *Sorry Wrong Number*, hardly made a ripple. And thus did one of Hollywood's most accomplished talents disappear from the big screen. She turned down the role Mary Astor played in *Hush Hush Sweet Charlotte*.

In an interview some years ago, she said: 'It isn't that I don't want to work. The trouble is nobody asks me. Some actresses and actors in my position say they can't find the right roles, but I can't fool myself so easily. . . . I don't let it get me down. I'm not made that way. I'm not giving up. . . . Maybe everything hasn't worked out exactly the way I hoped it would, but I've had more than my share of good times.' Hedda Hopper reported that she advised Stanwyck to try Europe, but that she preferred to stay in her Hollywood home, where she lives with a companion.

Ironically, TV brought her a popularity she had not dreamt of. She did much TV over the next decades, including the short-lived 'The Barbara Stanwyck Theatre' in 1960. But in 1965 she was starred in her own Western hour-long series, 'The Big Valley', which ran four seasons and won her a cluster of awards.

She starred in three tele-movies, *The House That Would Not Die* (70), *A Taste of Evil* (71), both directed by John Llewellyn Moxey, and *The Letters* (73), after which she turned down all offers – including Lincoln Center's prestigious Life Achievement Award 10 years later, which she was, however, prevailed upon to accept. In New York for the occasion, she was apparently astonished to find herself the recipient of a standing ovation on a visit to the theatre. This was due to television – not to

'The Big Valley' but to showings of her old movies, reminding viewers that hers was a very superior talent. When the Academy awarded her an honorary Oscar, in 1982, many considered it long overdue. She was wooed by TV again, to play a rancher in a 10-mini-series, *The Thornbirds* (82), but she died after the first three, and to play a matriarch in another series, 'The Colbys', a sequel to 'Dynasty', opposite Charlton Heston. She considered it 'the biggest load of junk' she had ever done and did not stay long.

ANNA STEN

Anna Sten must take her unfortunate place in any anthology of the stars as the prime example of those who never made it. She was unlucky, because she was as comely and as talented as many who did. There had been manufactured stars before and there would be as long as the studio system lasted: many of them cued as little response from the public as she did. Unfortunately, her mentor Sam Goldwyn produced few films and could not hive her off into supporting roles or second features. He brought her to Hollywood in 1932 as his own candidate to oust Garbo and dropped her after three films. She became known as 'Goldwyn's Folly' and was referred to years later as 'The Edsel of the Movie Industry'.

She was born in 1910 in Kiev, Russia. Her father died when she was 12 and, according to Goldwyn publicity, she 'worked as a slavey in a restaurant'. She appeared in an amateur production of Hauptmann's 'Hanneles Himmelfahrt' when she was 15: Stanislavsky saw her and arranged for her to enter the Russian Film Academy; later she joined his company. As far as can be traced, she started in films as a star: Boris Barnet's delightful *Devushka s Korobkio/Girl with the Hatbox* (27), in the title-role, a country girl who marries in name only and finds her student husband refuses to exploit her when she wins a lottery; *Moi Sin/My Son* (28); *Provokator/The Provocateur*; and *Zemlya v Plenu/The Yellow Ticket*, directed by Ozep. The original title translates as *Earth in Captivity*, so we may suppose the heroine's lot to be typical of the Russian peasant: poverty causes her to leave her husband to become a wet-nurse in Moscow, where she is sacked after rejecting the advances of her employer, and since she cannot get another job or afford the fare home she sinks into prostitution. She followed with *Byelyi Orel/The White Eagle* (29), based on Andreyev's story, 'The Governor' – and his moral dilemmas; and *Zolotoi Klyuv/The Gol-*

den Beak. Some of her films were seen abroad and *The Yellow Ticket* was particularly admired in Germany, where Ozep was already working; he found backing for a version of Dostoevsky with Fritz Kortner and invited her to contribute. While waiting for it to start, she did a Silent, *Lohnbuchhalter Kremke* (30), with Hermann Vallentin, directed by Marie Harder; and there also appeared before the Dostoevsky, *Bomben auf Monte Carlo* (31), directed by Hanns Schwarz for Ufa, in which she was the queen of a Ruritanian country who becomes involved with an Englishman (Hans Albers) who has joined her navy after some gambling losses. She was undoubtedly impressive in *Der Mörder Dimitri Karamasoff*, lithe, lovely and keen, a Grushenka whose coquetry is in no sense posey or conventional (we may see her as part Nancy Carroll and part Marilyn Monroe) – if inevitably overshadowed by Kortner. She went on to do *Salto Mortale*, which was another of E.A. Dupont's triangle dramas with a show business background, with Anton Walbrook; and *Stürme der Leidenschaft*, betraying her lover, Emil Jannings. In this, 'The New York Times' found her 'a sad disappointment' – which should have been a warning to Goldwyn.

He saw a picture of her and as a result asked to see the Dostoevsky film, which so impressed him that he decided to remake it in English. He signed Sten to a five-year contract and she left for Hollywood with her new husband, Eugene Frenke. 'Here was an accomplished actress and a genuinely individual personality quite unlike the imitation Garbos and Dietrichs who were the characteristic imports of the period' (Richard Griffith). Every studio had to have one sooner or later: Lil Dagover at WB, Gwili Andre at RKO, Tala Birell at Universal, Lilian Harvey at Fox. . . . Goldwyn took no chances. His first task was to have Sten taught English. During two years reams of publicity emanated from the Goldwyn studio – as well as some uncomfortable rumours. It was confidently announced that Sten's American bow would be in *Karamazov* opposite Ronald Colman. In the end it turned out to be a lavish production based on Zola's *Nana* (34) to be directed by Josef von Sternberg who had done so much for Dietrich; but it was eventually directed by George Fitzmaurice. Goldwyn scrapped this version – at a cost of over $400,000 – and signed the reliable Dorothy Arzner to direct a new one. He was so pleased with it that he arranged an unprecedented deal of a two-week run at Radio City Music Hall with himself taking 75 per cent of the profits: but the film opened to unrestrained critical jeers, partly because the original novel had been

The film that Goldwyn chose to launch Anna Sten in was Nana *(34), the story of a nice girl who becomes a tart after her lover goes to war – only to lose him* Forever *when he discovers the Truth in the last reel. It was a plot that Hollywood filmed endlessly and one could speculate endlessly on why. The wealthy admirer here is Lawrence Grant successfully coercing her into forgetting the said lover.*

tailored (i.e. emasculated) for American audiences. In the end, they stayed away and the film was hopefully retitled *Lady of the Boulevards* for British audiences. Those that did go laughed at Sten's mangling of English and her coquettish performance. Today both she and the film are silly together, but there was a little something to suggest that if Goldwyn could do anything about her English she might pull through.

He tried again with *We Live Again*, a version of Tolstoy's 'Resurrection', with Fredric March as the prince who returns to coldly seduce and desert her, only to make amends when he realizes the depths to which she has sunk. As directed by Rouben Mamoulian, it was a much better film, but it did no better business – perhaps because cinemagoers had sampled the tale just three years earlier (with John Boles and Lupe Velez) and before that in 1927 (with Rod la Rocque and Dolores del Rio). Goldwyn's headache was increased because she was feuding with him over publicity – but she became more co-operative when her role in *Barbary Coast* was assigned to Miriam Hopkins. He persisted: he offered Eugene O'Neill any amount to write anything he wanted for Sten; then a friend, Edwin Knopf, was commissioned to write something which would win audiences over, 'with due respect for her special liabilities and limitations' (Griffith). The result, *The Wedding Night* (35), was directed by King Vidor, but it never amounted to much as it detailed the forbidden affair between a city-soured married writer (Gary Cooper) and a peasant girl living in Connecticut who is forced to marry a

fellow Pole. The critics liked it, but it proved for the third time that Miss Sten, effective in Russian and German, was merely doll-like. Her voice lacks the individuality of Garbo or Dietrich and her acting the seeming spontaneity of Ann Harding or Claudette Colbert. It was a major mistake to cast Helen Vinson as her rival, for this actress's warmth and her quick dispatch of her dialogue only emphasize Sten's shortcomings. She does not perform badly, but she fails to interest. Even Cooper was no help at the box-office and the contract was dissolved by mutual consent; she was then getting $2,500 a week. Two years later Goldwyn signed Sigrid Gurie. . . .

It was unlikely that a major studio would pick up such a well-publicized failure and it was a British company which did, anxious to break into the American market. With reason, her husband wanted to see her (re)establish herself and he directed from a story by Ozep – a romance of a Russian peasant girl with an army official (Henry Wilcoxon): *A Woman Alone* (36). When Gaumont British stole that title for the US release of *Sabotage* it was rechristened *Two Who Dared* as it crossed the Atlantic, but was hardly heard of under either title. She was signed to a contract by Grand National, but made only one picture for that company, a B, *Exile Express* (39). Then she had supporting parts in *The Man I Married* (40) and *So Ends Our Night* (41), as a local party worker who 'comforts' political agitator Fredric March. She was in a Resistance drama (Yugoslav guerillas) with Philip Dorn, *Chetniks* (43), and in a B spy thriller with George Sanders, *They Came to Blow Up America*. *Three Russian Girls*, directed by Ozep, was a remake of the Russian *The Girl From Leningrad*, now telling of the love between a nurse and a grounded American flyer (Kent Smith): it did much less for Soviet-American relations than its makers intended. She worked very occasionally subsequently: in *Let's Live a Little* (48) and *Soldier of Fortune* (55), in minor parts, but she had star roles in two silly Bs, *Runaway Daughters* (56) and *The Nun and the Sergeant* (62).

JAMES STEWART

As a young man, James Stewart's gangling figure and modest demeanour qualified him at once for the real all-American boy – the grocer's clerk, the telegraph boy, even the junior college professor; he was 'so unusually usual' said director W.S. Van Dyke in 1939. As he matured he endeared himself to audiences: comfortable, cool-headed, trustworthy, he was (in the 50s, his best period) the ideal Hitchcock hero. He first made the box-office top 10 in 1950 (in Britain as well as the US) and was in the American list from 1952 to 1959 inclusive – in number one position in 1955 (thanks to Hitchcock); and he popped up again in 1965, though by now he was making strictly formula films – and the quality of performance had deteriorated. He had always been variable. His prized performance in *Mr Smith Goes to Washington* now seems overstuffed with mannerisms – the drawl, the quirky look of astonishment, the shy smile – but if insufferably idealistic, he remains likeable. The more human the character he plays, the better his acting.

He was born in 1908 in the town of Indiana, Pennsylvania, studied civil engineering and then architecture in Princeton, where he met Joshua Logan, then working with a summer stock company. Logan gave him small parts and after graduation he joined Logan's University Players, whose members included Henry Fonda and Margaret Sullavan. With Fonda he went to New York in 1932 and began getting small parts in plays ('Carrie Nation', 'Yellow Jack', 'Page Miss Glory',

etc.). MGM screen-tested him after a recommendation by Hedda Hopper and signed him to a long-term contract. He started with a bit as a reporter, colleague to Spencer Tracy in *The Murder Man* (35), followed by another in *Rose Marie* (36), as the man got at the end by Mountie Nelson Eddy. Better for him was *Next Time We Love* at Universal with Margaret Sullavan, who had requested him for the part of her husband. He was second lead to Ray Milland and he had similar assignments in *Wife vs Secretary* to Clark Gable and *Small Town Girl* to Robert Taylor. His first lead was a B, *Speed*, and he was one of the men who considered Joan Crawford *The Gorgeous Hussy*. His real break came as Eleanor Powell's leading man in *Born to Dance*, a gob who introduced to the world Cole Porter's 'Easy to Love'. 'There is James Stewart,' wrote Alistair Cooke, 'trying to be ingenuous and charming like Gary Cooper but many tricks and light years behind!' He was the baddie in *After the Thin Man* and then got loaned to 20th for the remake of *Seventh Heaven* (37), wildly implausible as a Paris sewer rat, coping with dialogue like 'Don't

MGM made the most spectacular musicals of the 30s, often with Eleanor Powell. Her leading man in Born to Dance *(36) was James Stewart, who croaked his way through 'Easy to Love'.*

ever leave me or like a candle I'll go out.'

The Last Gangster with Edward G. Robinson and *Navy Blue and Gold* with Robert Young kept him a bit off-centre, but the next three gave him fine chances: Clarence Brown's *Of Human Hearts* (38), as the poor parson's son who puts himself through medical school; George Stevens's funny *Vivacious Lady*, as a professor having problems because he has married a showgirl (Ginger Rogers); and *The Shopworn Angel*, in Gary Cooper's old part of the doughboy who falls in love with a kept woman (Sullavan). So did Capra's fine *You Can't Take It With You* at Columbia, as the tycoon's son who falls for the daughter (Jean Arthur) of the crazy family Dad is trying to dispossess; and the Selznick *Made For Each Other*, as the just-married junior exec husband of Carole Lombard. His big breaks so far had been away from MGM, who now offered him only *Ice Follies of 1939*, as an ice carnival impresario. Said 'Picturegoer' 'James Stewart is becoming rather stereotyped, he needs to watch out that his engaging naturalness which first singled him out does not develop into forced artificiality.'

But then he came up with as fine a run of pictures as any actor ever had, starting with *It's a Wonderful World*, as a private eye, a crazy comedy with Claudette Colbert. Capra

borrowed him again for *Mr Smith Goes to Washington* which, like his earlier *Mr Deeds*, was a modern morality tale, with innocence (i.e. good) triumphing over cynicism (i.e. evil). This also co-starred Jean Arthur and it made Stewart almost as big a star as Cooper; it was one of the year's big hits and won Stewart the New York critics Best Actor award. Also much prized, metaphorically, was his portrait in *Destry Rides Again* of the untypically quiet and gun-shy sheriff who proves to Dietrich and the other townsfolk that words speak louder than actions: Universal made it, it was a remake of Tom Mix's first Talkie and, like so many of Stewart's roles at this time, had been turned down by Gary Cooper. At last MGM gave him superior material: two good ones with Sullavan – Lubitsch's *The Shop Around the Corner* (40), a comedy mainly concerned with a secret penpal romance carried on by a couple of shop employees who loathe each other till they learn the truth; and Frank Borzage's *The Mortal Storm*, a very stark tale of the impact of Nazism on a small Bavarian town. It could even be claimed that he took the first of these from her, and, since she was at her most captivating, this was no mean achievement. The weak one in this batch was Warners' too-well-named *No Time for Comedy*, as a hick-

Lubitsch's The Shop Around the Corner *(40): the scene in the café where James Stewart realizes that fellow-employee Margaret Sullavan is also his penpal.*

town dramatist who falls for the actress (Rosalind Russell) playing the lead in his first Broadway play; but *The Philadelphia Story* was a peak for most of the people involved and especially Stewart, who got a Best Actor Oscar – though he was second lead (as a reporter) to Cary Grant, who got the girl. His luck suddenly ran out: *Come Live With Me* (41) with Hedy Lamarr, *Pot o' Gold* with Paulette Goddard and *Ziegfeld Girl*, loving and losing Lana Turner.

His war service was distinguished – he remains one of the highest-ranking officers in the US Auxiliary Air Force. He returned to Hollywood, but it was not to MGM, much to their surprise and annoyance. Instead, he joined Liberty Films, the independent company started by Capra and Stevens. Like most of the postwar independent groups, it did not last long and Stewart only made one film for them, *It's a Wonderful Life* (46), about a small-town bank manager on the brink of ruin who is taught that life is still worth living by guardian angel Henry Travers; but the war years had taken toll of Capra's rosy view of the scheme of things. Richard Winnington found it 'only really momentous because it brings back to the screen that charmingly gauche actor, James Stewart'. A Capraesque piece directed by William A. Wellman, *Magic Town* (47), did little better. Most of the Hollywood talent who had served during the war returned anxious to make better and more honest films, and there was nothing wrong with the sentiments expressed in either of these – but postwar audiences did not want sentiment. Stewart's next film, fortunately, was exactly what they did want: *Call Northside 777* (48), a hard-hitting thriller in the 'new' semi-documentary style, though that simply meant location-shooting and other trappings of verisimilitude – factors which audiences now found not only desirable but essential (often under this same director, Henry Hathaway). He played a reporter. He and Henry Fonda were musicians in the most amusing episode of *On Our Merry Way* and then he was involved in another technical 'innovation', the 10-minute take devised by Hitchcock for *Rope*. The director made much publicity out of it, but it was basically the technique then used in TV and after another film he dropped it. It certainly did not improve *Rope*, a version of Patrick Hamilton's play about the Leopold-and-Loeb-like students who murder a friend and give a tea-party in the same room as the corpse. Stewart was the professor who suspected – taking a $300,000 fee out of the $1½ million budget.

You Gotta Stay Happy was a minor comedy with Joan Fontaine; *The Stratton Story* (49) a sentimental baseball biopic which did great business in the US but not elsewhere; and *Malaya* an adventure story that wasted his talents and Spencer Tracy's. Next he did a couple of Westerns, *Winchester 73* (50) for Universal, directed by Anthony Mann, and *Broken Arrow* for 20th, directed by Delmer Daves; and the financial success of both films was to have a far-reaching effect on Stewart's career: for over a decade he was to eschew comedy – in which he had made his name – for movies of like genre. His partnerships with Mann and/or Universal were to be very profitable. His last two comedies were *The Jackpot* with Barbara Hale, which flopped, and *Harvey*, the one about the drunk and his invisible rabbit friend (he had already done this on Broadway for a while). He went to Britain for 20th's *No Highway* (51), from a Nevil Shute novel, and returned to play the whole of *The Greatest Show on Earth* under clown make-up. He married in 1949.

There are many claimants to the title of first successful freelance star and the first to have his or her own production company; but almost every permutation of star-studio relationship had already been tried out in the early Silent days. Nor was Stewart's 1952 agreement to work with Universal on a percentage basis the first such deal, as has been claimed, but it *was* the first modern step in a direction which was soon to be stampeded by almost every star in the business. Roughly for 10 years (the 50s) Universal was an assembly line studio, run by accountants, churning out cut-price formula products. Although the studio manufactured stars, Stewart was the first *big* established star to work there during this period. His pictures had a larger budget than most Universal products and he worked for less than his usual salary, plus a percentage of the profits. The first, a Western, *Bend of the River* (52), turned up second on the 'Motion Picture Herald' list of the year's top money-makers: he played a former bad man – now helping the homesteaders.

He then did two for MGM on normal salary conditions, *Carbine Williams* and the Mann-directed *The Naked Spur* (53). Mann directed all but one of the next six films as well: *Thunder Bay*, *The Glenn Miller Story* (54), *The Far Country* (55), *Strategic Air Command* and *The Man From Laramie*. The last two were made for Paramount and Columbia respectively (now that the percentage principle had become generally accepted). They were all successful, but in particular *The Glenn Miller Story*, giving Stewart a great 1954 – he was asking and getting 50 per cent of the profits, and he thus made more than $1 million from this particular film; his non-Mann film, Hitchcock's *Rear Window*, was

James Stewart in one of the many Westerns he made for Anthony Mann, The Far Country *(55).*

Hitchcock's The Man Who Knew Too Much *(56), with Doris Day and James Stewart. Hitchcock preferred to work with actors like Stewart and Cary Grant, with whom audiences could identify.*

also a big hit later that year. He was back with Hitchcock for more revenue in 1956, that director's remake of his own *The Man Who Knew Too Much*, polished, expensive and altogether more laboured than the 1934 version. Then he was determined to get the part of Lindbergh in *The Spirit of St Louis* (57) and did, after initial opposition from the studio because he was too old. But the public would not touch it: Jack L. Warner described it as 'the most disastrous failure we ever had'. It did not take enough in a week in Lindbergh's birthplace to cover the staff's wages. It was, nevertheless, a gripping account of the Lindbergh transatlantic flight, directed by Billy Wilder, with a dedicated performance by Stewart and virtually his last interesting film.

Night Passage was another routine Universal actioner; Hitchcock's *Vertigo* (58) and Quine's *Bell Book and Candle* were both good subjects not improved by Kim Novak's involvement in them; and *Anatomy of a Murder* (59) was an endless court-roomer whose box-office profited from the reputation of the original bestseller and some 'dirty' words. Stewart's performance as the defence attorney brought him another New York critics' citation. He then had three flops in a row: *The FBI Story*, *The Mountain Road* (60) and Ford's *Two Rode Together* (61), but a second consecutive one with Ford, *The Man Who Shot Liberty Valance* (62), did respectably. Stewart, greying and paunchy, seemed as old and tired as the film, but as a father in a comedy, *Mr Hobbs Takes a Vacation*, there was wide public acceptance. Knowing his limitations, he thus prolonged his career, alternating the two roles: *How the West was Won* (63), as a Westerner; *Take Her She's Mine*, as a father; *Cheyenne Autumn* (64), out West; *Dear Brigitte* (65), as a father; and

Shenandoah, directed by Andrew McLaglen. When the last father-film failed, he did an adventure story, *The Flight of the Phoenix* (66), and when that was only mildly received, he did three Westerns in a row, *The Rare Breed*, *Firecreek* (67) with Fonda and *Bandolero*, the first and last directed by McLaglen. After *The Cheyenne Social Club* (70) did badly – a comic Western with Fonda – he returned to 'Harvey', in New York, and in London five years later. He played an ex-convict in a melodrama, *Fools' Parade* (71), at his normal fee of $250,000 plus 10 per cent of the gross, but when that also failed he went into TV, first in 'The Jimmy Stewart Show' (71–72) and then in 'Hawkins' (73–74). *Hawkins on Murder* (73) is the tele-film pilot for the series.

As far as movies were concerned, he said that he was in semi-retirement, which he left for some welcome guest appearances: in *The Shootist* (76), as John Wayne's doctor; as the millionaire owner of the cutlery at the centre of *Airport 77* (77); and as the old Colonel in the unnecessary remake of *The Big Sleep* (78), aptly christened 'The Big Yawn' by 'Newsweek'. And it is hard to say whether *The Magic of Lassie* was a welcome renaissance. He was, oh dear, Gramps. But the next two credits are odd for a star of his magnitude: *Afurika Monogatari/A Tale of Africa* (81), a Japanese venture filmed in Kenya, living there with his granddaughter in isolation till Philip Sayer crashes nearby; and *Dr Krueger's Secret*, made for the Mormons and village halls rather than cinemas. He did a considered job married to Bette Davis in a TV movie, *Right of Way* (83), and for that medium did a mini-series, *North and South Bk II* (86).

MARGARET SULLAVAN

Margaret Sullavan's Hollywood career was not very lucrative but she made some good films – which, if there was any justice, would be as readily available as those of Garbo. She was, quite simply, an enchantress, always offering a very real woman in the patient and suffering heroines she was most often given. She was warm and winning, honest and independent, always playing with an underlying sense of humour; she could add malice, as in her portrait of the film star in *The Moon's Our Home*, or harshness, as in her small-time chorine in *The Shopworn Angel*, and thus no other actress managed so well the suggestion of smiling through tears. Her eyes, in fact, were ever on the brink of laughter or sadness and she spoke lightly and quickly in a husky voice that seldom dared risk a definite inflexion. Her mastery of both comedy and drama was complete. Yet in life she suffered from a lack of self-confidence and a dislike of show business (there is a touching portrait in the memoir by her daughter, Brooke Hayward, 'Haywire') and was consequently considered temperamental. She certainly did not care for filming, which did not help matters.

She was born in 1911 in Norfolk, Virginia. She acted with the Baltimore University Players, studied dancing in Boston and then acting. Through a friend she joined the University Players at Cape Cod and made her pro début with them, in 'The Devil in the Cheese'. She stayed a couple of seasons and then got a job in a tour of 'Strictly Dishonorable', after which she was offered a Broadway chance in 'A Modern Virgin' (31). It did not run, but the Shuberts saw her and offered a contract, which took her through several mediocre ventures. Then she took over the ingénue in 'Dinner at Eight' and was seen in that by director John M. Stahl, who offered her a role that Claudette Colbert and Irene Dunne had turned down: inevitably it was a weepie, *Only Yesterday* (33). She sacrificed *Everything for an Hour of Love* with John Boles – as Joan Fontaine would do later, in the remake, *Letter from an Unknown Woman*.

After a few days' rushes, Universal knew that they had a radiant new star and she knew it too. When they offered her a contract, it was on her terms: three-year, non-exclusive, starting at $1,200 a week plus approval rights, a privilege seldom given to an unknown. Nor was she likely to make things easy for Universal, a studio already in (financial) difficulties. On arrival, she had announced: 'Perhaps I'll get used to the bizarre, elaborate theatricalism called Hollywood, but I cannot guarantee it.' Her second film was again excellent and awash with sentiment, Frank Borzage's Depression drama, *Little Man What Now?* (34) with Douglass Montgomery; and her third was also sentimental, though it was a comedy: *The Good Fairy* (35), in the title-role, from Molnar's comedy about the girl from the orphanage who invents a husband, Herbert Marshall. William Wyler directed, and married her (in succession to Henry Fonda, from whom she had been divorced for some time).

At Paramount (loaned for Carole Lombard) she was a spirited belle in a crushingly soppy Civil War drama, *So Red the Rose*, with its phoney portrait of the Old South; then was in *Next Time We Love* (36), an imitation of one of Fannie Hurst's soggier works: James Stewart and Ray Milland helped her form a triangle. Back at Paramount there was a welcome change with *The Moon's Our Home*, even if the title tried to disguise the fact. It degenerates at the end, but for most of its length is a slanging match between a temperamental movie queen and a bestselling author, played by Fonda. Still at Paramount she did a few days' shooting on *I Loved a Soldier/Hotel Imperial* before breaking her arm; the film was abandoned. She returned to the stage, scoring a great success in 'Stage Door', playing, not too ironically, a dedicated actress who scorns films. Motherhood (twice) did keep her away from Hollywood for a while; she was married now to agent Leland Hayward.

Hayward arranged a deal for her at MGM for six films; none of these was destined to

One of the lighter moments of Next Time We Love *(36): Margaret Sullavan was a singer who gave up her career to follow reporter-husband James Stewart on a foreign assignment.*

They met, fell in love and were parted by chance; they met again, fell in love again, but he was married now: so she spent the rest of her life as his Back Street *(41) mistress. Margaret Sullavan and Charles Boyer.*

depart much from the Maggie-Sullavan-suffers-so-prettily routine, but they were generally more weighty than what had gone before and allowed her to extend her range; her touching performance as Robert Taylor's tubercular wife in *Three Comrades* (38) brought her the New York critics Best Actress award and the 'Picturegoer' Gold Medal. Frank Borzage directed from Erich Maria Remarque's novel about postwar Germany. The same year she was *The Shopworn Angel*, the kept woman who falls for another man, a remake of a Nancy Carroll picture intended originally for Joan Crawford. She and Crawford were together in *The Shining Hour* and did not, despite all predictions, fight. Except on the screen: this is a quadrangle drama – they are sisters-in-law and Robert Young and Melvyn Douglas are their husbands; and then Joan falls for Robert. . . . Next she was in Lubitsch's enchanting comedy *The Shop Around the Corner* (40) – a performance of impish and infinite delicacy – and, again with Stewart, faced *The Mortal Storm* – in Germany again, and anti-Nazi, the story of a family destroyed by Hitler. She tested for *Rebecca* and although her vulnerability was right for the role, two of Selznick's advisors, George Cukor and John Cromwell, agreed that she was still not the sort to be frightened by Mrs Danvers.

She was once more greatly in demand and, though not very interested, flirted: every studio was announcing movies to star Margaret Sullavan. Meanwhile she would not play ball with Universal, to whom she owed one film, and the battle that had begun when she had signed that contract now culminated in an injunction to prevent her working elsewhere until she had made *The Invisible Woman* for

them. They were not entirely joking, and she knew it, so she came to terms. Universal let her go to UA for *So Ends Our Night* (41) – Remarque again and anti-Nazi again, with Fredric March – until they prepared a suitable vehicle, *Back Street*, quite the equal of the earlier version. As (again) a kept woman, she gave a beautiful performance and Charles Boyer was as good; she stayed on at Universal to do another film with him, a comedy, *Appointment With Love*.

She made her last film for MGM, a terrific performance as an overworked staff nurse at the battle front in an above-average war movie, *Cry Havoc* (43). It was reported that her terms were too high for any studio to meet. She packed her bags and departed for New York and 'The Voice of the Turtle' by John Van Druten. After a considerable run she went with it to London (47), but it failed to repeat its US success. Seeing the film version is a doubly depressing experience, for Eleanor Parker's imitation of Sullavan's performance not only reminds us of Sullavan's superiority over most actresses, but how much we lost because she and Hollywood could not come to terms. *No Sad Songs for Me* (50) also provides a woeful experience, both because it is her last film and because it concerns a relatively young woman dying (of cancer). Wendell Corey played her husband, Columbia made it and as rarely with actresses of her generation she looks her age; she also saves it, said 'Variety', 'from falling into a maudlin bog . . . by a standout performance that accents intelligence and underplays the agony of her predicament'. But if her reviews might have tempted her to stay on, the film's performance did not. Her stage work continued to emphasize Hollywood's loss: 'The Deep Blue Sea' (52), 'Sabrina Fair' (53) and 'Janus' (55). In 1956 she walked out of a TV play ('The Pilot') after rehearsing for weeks; and went into a sanatorium.

She was married to a businessman now and was bringing up her children. In 1959 she decided to return to the stage, in 'Sweet Love Remember'd'; on the tour, on New Year's Day 1960, she died from an overdose of barbiturates. It was disclosed that she was worried by increasing deafness: her doctors said that as long ago as 1948 she was 40 per cent deaf and that by the time she died, she could only act by lip-reading. Three weeks earlier she had told 'Theater Arts': 'I have something of a reputation of not wanting to go to work. . . . I have never been what you call "a dedicated actress". . . .'

GLORIA SWANSON

Alongside Pickford and Gish, Gloria Swanson is the only female Silent star whose name still means anything. She made only one major film, *Sunset Boulevard*, during the last half century, but she had only to enter a TV studio or appear on the stage at some charity matinée for audiences to applaud wildly – and apart from that film, few of the younger generation can ever have seen her on the screen. Audiences warm to longevity but the fact is that Swanson remained very much a star. She would answer the questions of even the most doltish TV interviewer with good humour and a dash or two of wisdom, looking chic and still very glamorous. Perhaps one was merely pleased that she appeared to be the reverse of the character she played in *Sunset Boulevard*, displaying a candour unexpected of stars of her generation; or perhaps she is revered because even those who have never seen her are aware that she was one of the best actresses of Silent pictures and one of the major personalities of that time.

Philip Hope-Wallace in 'Sight and Sound' (1950) was not so certain about the talent: 'Gloria Swanson never struck me as being a particularly good actress: not for example in the same class as Pola Negri. True, she had a face (as she says in *Sunset Boulevard*) and could give most speaking looks which would be effective even in the total silence which sometimes descended if the pianist took time off to rub her chilblains. But they never seemed to me to be subtle speaking looks, seldom in fact imbued with the art of concealing art; in fine, generally self-conscious.'

On the evidence of those of her pictures available today, it is difficult to agree, though she was not very good at the outset: she was early on considered the classic example of the actress who 'grew' with her career. She was forbidding (though in life quite a tiny woman) with no great gift for distinguishing between the many different sorts of women she played; but she had a considerable gift for comedy – *then*, her looks could be very subtle. Compared with her contemporaries she underplayed: she had a refreshing gaiety and spirit at a time when audiences were accustomed to their heroines being fey and frolicsome. She comes over today better than any other Silent actress except Gish and Garbo.

She was born in Chicago, probably in 1898 ('Time' in 1950 reported that the date on the birth certificate had been obliterated), and was brought up on a succession of army camps, both in the US and the Philippines (her father was a civilian employee with the army). She was living in Chicago working as a notions-counter clerk and studying singing when an aunt took her to visit the Essanay Studio – and it all started. She worked as an extra that day and continued to work for Essanay, both as an extra and in bit parts. She was an exceptionally timid child with no ambition towards films and appears simply to have been flattered that Essanay thought her photogenic. She was tested by Chaplin at this time for his leading lady in *His New Job*, but was unco-operative because she had decided that, if she was going to stay in films, she would be a dramatic actress. The first film on which she had billing appears to have been *The Fable of Elvira and Farina and the Meal Ticket* (15). She also had small parts in *Sweedie goes to College*, *The Broken Pledge* and *A Dash of Courage* (16), all of which featured Wallace Beery. Swanson married him in 1916 – they were divorced three years later – and they went to Hollywood, where she signed with Mack Sennett: she played in 10 two-reelers, including *Hearts and Sparks*, *Love on Skates*, *Teddy at the Throttle*, *Dangers of a Bride* and *The Sultan's Wife*, as Bobby Vernon's leading lady. At one point she went to Universal when Sennett would not raise her salary, but after one short, *Baseball Madness*, she returned to Sennett. She said once: 'I did my comedies like Duse might have done them. . . . I was funny because I didn't try to be funny. The more serious I got, the funnier the scene became.' However, pursued by Mack Swain and Chester Conklin, as *The Pullman Bride*, she decided to leave Sennett: 'He wanted to make me a second Mabel Normand. I told him I didn't want to be a second anybody, so he tore my contract up.'

She followed Bobby Vernon to Triangle, but did not play comedy – and was at last a star and the heroine of eight Triangle dramas, all released in one year: *Society for Sale* (18), as a mannequin trying to crash London society; *Her Decision*, as a secretary who marries her boss for money but falls in love with him; *You Can't Believe Everything*, as a society vamp who discovers her true self after saving a man from drowning; *Every Woman's Husband*, as a woman whose husband leaves her because her mother is always interfering; *Shifting Sands*, as a wife whose life is disturbed when an old friend tries to blackmail her into spying for Germany; *Station Content*, as a spouse who runs away to go on the stage; *Secret Code*, as a censor's wife suspected of being a spy; and *Wife or Country*, actually spying for Germany and taking poison at the end, so that her husband can marry the girl he truly loves.

Cecil B. De Mille had already made overtures which Triangle had rejected: when that company went bankrupt she contacted Para-

exhibitors confused 'Admirable' with 'Admiral', but the new title certainly indicated the slant that De Mille gave to it, including a flashback with Swanson and Thomas Meighan (Crichton) to Babylonian times. In *Why Change Your Wife?* she is neglected for the more saucy Bebe Daniels, but wins her husband back by competing on equally glamorous terms. *Something to Think About* (20) was more sober, a thoroughgoing melodrama in which she suffered through widowhood, her father's loathing and an unhappy marriage to a cripple. She did one without De Mille, *The Great Moment*, with her name above the title for the first time. Elinor Glyn wrote the story, the adventures of an English socialite out West before settling down with Milton Sills, who had saved her life in an earlier reel. Her last for De Mille was *The Affairs of Anatol* (21) from the Schitzler play. Wallace Reid was the unfaithful Anatol and she the understanding wife who welcomes him back. This group of films – and especially *Male and Female* – not only put Swanson on the world map, but influenced other film-makers who felt they might be as frank about the pleasures of sex as De Mille.

Sam Wood, who had directed *The Great Moment*, did so again on her nine next films: *Under the Lash*, as a drab wife suspected of infidelity by her South African farmer husband; *Don't Tell Everything* with Wallace Reid, an expanded version of some footage left over from *Anatol*; *Her Husband's Trademark* (22) – he throws her into the company of an ex-lover; *Beyond the Rocks* with Valentino; *Her Gilded Cage*, about a publicity stunt that links an actress with a prince until she falls for an American; *The Impossible Mrs Bellew*, as a mother who loses her good name but is compensated by true love with Conrad Nagel; *My American Wife* (23), in the title-role, with Antonio Moreno; *Prodigal Daughters* – she was one of them; and *Bluebeard's Eighth Wife* with Huntley Gordon – in the roles to be taken in the Talkie version by Cooper and Colbert.

She was at this time supposedly feuding with Pola Negri, the studio's new continental star, but it was an invention of the publicity office and seized upon by gossip columnists. She really had no rival on the Paramount lot. She had said: 'I have decided that when I am a star, I will be every inch and every moment the star! Everybody from the studio gateman to the highest executive will know it.' The highest executives did: Zukor described her as 'temperamental', but she was also the first film player to be fully aware of the full value of publicity; fans marvelled at a report that she never wore the same dress twice. When a new contract was drawn up in 1923 – four

mount, who released De Mille's pictures, and by the time she left the company in 1926 she was its highest-paid star. The six films which she made for De Mille gave her career a powerful impetus, as the décor and costumes he chose for her began to influence fashion: she was always gowned in styles meant to suggest intrigue and sophistication, and was seen to exist in impeccable luxury. And usually wronged. She was a living demonstration that riches do not bring happiness – until the last reel. De Mille was, of course, incurably moral: it did not matter what you gave audiences in the way of sex and sin provided that good triumphed in the end. *Don't Change Your Husband* (19) had Swanson doing just that, only to find that the neglect by hubby number one was preferable to the womanizing of hubby number two. *For Better For Worse* found her denouncing her sweetheart as a coward only to discover his true worth later.

Male and Female was an adaptation of Barrie's 'The Admirable Crichton', with Swanson as Lady Mary, chief suitor on the island for Crichton's affections. The title-change was made, apparently, because some pictures a year for three years – her demands were considerable and included the right to film in Paramount's New York studio as well as a say in the selection of her material – official publicity gave her chief hobby as looking for vehicles for herself. She insisted on playing *Zaza*, which had already seen sterling service with Mrs Leslie Carter (stage) and Pauline Frederick (film): it was to be the first of a series in which she would undergo chameleon changes in order continually to surprise her fans. A star's career in those days was very short and she detected a slight but dangerous public indifference; she believed that she saved her career by ringing the changes. In *The Humming Bird* (24) she was a French gamine during wartime; in *A Society Scandal* a wronged wife; and in *Manhandled* a shop-girl who is taken up by society. *Her Love Story* was a Ruritanian romance – in which she wore a bridal outfit reputedly costing $100,000 – and *Wages of Virtue* saw her demoted from queen to pride of the Foreign Legion, with Ben Lyon. She actually went to France to make *Madame Sans-Gêne* (25), from the Sardou play about Napoleon's laundress, and directed by Léonce Perret, whom she considered the best director she ever worked with; and she reappeared in the US with the Légion d'Honneur and a brand-new husband, the Marquis de la Falaise de la Coudraye. Earlier, her popularity had suffered when it was announced that she had become a mother – an unwelcome reminder to the public that stars were human after all. Now, with the Marquis, she fulfilled every fan's dream of glamour.

De Witt Bodeen has detailed some items of her homecoming with husband and completed film: her 'billing was the largest ever seen on Times Square up to that time. Her name in electric lights occupied the whole front of the Rivoli Theatre, with the stars and stripes and tricolour flying above.' In Hollywood a brass band met them and they drove in a motorcade like royalty. At the film's West Coast première the audience rose and sang 'Home Sweet Home'. She made only four more films for Paramount, none of them very interesting: *The Coast of Folly*, a tale of dormant mother-love, in which she played three roles, including mother and daughter; *Stage Struck*, probably the best of the quartet, a comedy in which she was just that; *Untamed Lady* (26) – a spoiled beauty who meets her match in Lawrence Gray, Fannie Hurst's version of Shakespeare's 'Shrew'; and *Fine Manners*. Paramount offered to renew her contract at the sensational $18,000 per week, but she refused; nor was she interested in even bigger money. United Artists had made overtures, on the principle that she was one of the few

Gloria Swanson as Maugham's Sadie Thompson *(28), the trollop who converted a minister – despite his attempts at vice-versa. It was directed by Raoul Walsh, who doubled up by playing Sergeant O'Hara.*

stars big enough to be one of them, and capable of producing her own pictures. She thought Paramount had exploited her and the new agreement allowed her to make only one film a year if she desired; she was to receive $100,000 in shares and profits from all UA projects if they made any; the actual money she would receive on her own would depend on whether the company was to provide financing. So when the exhibitor 'Roxy' Rothafel asked her whether one of his cinemas could have the world première of her first UA vehicle, she borrowed its $200,000 cost from him.

For her first vehicle she chose *The Loves of Sunya* (27) which as *The Eyes of Youth* had once seen service for Clara Kimball Young. She appeared in several guises, most of them exotic, but it was not a great success. *Sadie Thompson* (28), in the first year of the Oscars, won for her the first of three nominations. It was, of course, the notorious 'Rain' – the Hays Office would not let the original title be used – and is the most satisfactory of the three attempts to film it: her Sadie, at least, seemed to have stepped straight from the pages of Maugham's story, as she leaves whoring for religion, till the minister converting her proves just as human as her soldier clients. A large number of industry bigwigs implored her not to make it, because of its notoriety, but she believed most of them to be hypocrites. Among them was Joseph P. Kennedy, an East Coast distributor and banker (and later ambassador to Britain): she went to ask him for financing for her next film, which he

Swanson became her own producer in order to prolong her career but was dogged by ill-luck, like Queen Kelly (28). This scene is from the uncompleted second half, though it appears today in the restored prints, and shows her as an innocent who has been taken to Africa to become the mistress of a bordello. Here two of its inmates are preparing her for her future life.

provided. He also became her lover.

In *Queen Kelly* she is a convent schoolgirl noticed by the putative Prince Consort when she loses her knickers and thereafter an object of wrath to his beastly regal fiancée, Seena Owen. It was directed by Erich von Stroheim who, said Lotte Eisner, found in Swanson, 'recognized star though she was, malleable material, ready to submit to his direction. She makes an adorable Kelly, roguish and innocent without any affectations.' Von Stroheim, however, was at his most extravagant and Swanson fired him with the film unfinished and $600,000 down the drain. Her backers would contribute no more money and the film was heavily in debt. She spent $200,000 of her own money on a salvage operation, bringing in as director Edmund Goulding, but it was not, she said, until 1950 when she made *Sunset Boulevard*, that all its debts were paid off. A version of it was shown in Europe and South America, but it was never shown commercially in the US.

She did get back many of her losses with *The Trespasser* (29), a soap opera about a marriage split by her father-in-law. It was her first Talkie and she sang – 'Love, Your Magic Spell Is Everywhere' – as well as she spoke. She was one of the very few stars without stage training who made an easy transition to Talkies, but it was soon apparent that, accomplished though she was, the public was no longer interested: the great influx of new favourites left room for very few of the old ones. There is too much of Norma Desmond in her early Talkie persona. Charming she may be, but she is also imperious, over-made-up, over-vivacious and rather hard. Audiences did not find her sympathetic, as they did Garbo and Ronald Colman, the only two Silent stars who remained stars (Chaplin excepted), and they tended to think back to the old Swanson; and it was not in her favour during the Depression that she was associated with much exotic nonsense. After *What a Widow!* (30), some slapstick in Paris with Lew Cody, United Artists drew up a new contract and under the aegis of Joseph Schenck she made *Indiscreet* (31), a tiresome tale about a socialite who compromises her engagement to a novelist (Ben Lyon) by exposing her sister's fiancé as a lecherous bounder. Goldwyn was responsible for the next and the auguries were not good, for because of his role in the company he had disputed some of the films she wanted to make. *Tonight or Never* makes her a prima donna whose voice improves after deserting teacher and fiancé Ferdinand Gottshalk for a gigolo, Melvyn Douglas (only he isn't): it did nothing to restore her popularity. *Perfect Understanding* (33) was made in Britain and the title referred to affairs outside marriage for a modern young bride and groom (Laurence Olivier). Swanson's own new husband, Michael Farmer, proved inadequate in a supporting role; the director, Rowland V. Lee, was replaced by the man who had come to cut it and *he* went to pieces when his parents died, as predicted by a fortune-teller. The cost rose from $75,000 to $275,000 – the extra provided by United Artists to finish this folly by purchasing Swanson's stock, thereby forcing her out of the company, which was what they wanted. A further $100,000 came from British sources and then the film grossed only $170,00.

Understandably she decided to give up producing and accept the offers she was getting. Other companies announced *The Divine Sarah* and *Twentieth Century*, but she did neither. Thalberg at MGM signed her for a remake of *Three Weeks* with Clark Gable and several other projects (including a life of Lola Montez), but when she flouted his professional advice she felt a chill there and elsewhere. She was loaned to Fox for one film, the screen version of the Kern-Hammerstein operetta, *Music in the Air* (34),

and finally dropped. There was also some interest later at Columbia whose president Harry Cohn was always pleased to employ cut-rate talent: first it was announced that she would star in *Maisie Kenyon*; and Swanson brought him a story, *The Second Mrs Draper*, to star herself, but work was abandoned when Cohn disagreed with the screenwriter (it later became *Dark Victory*).

Then it was to be the remake of *Holiday*; while Columbia vacillated, Swanson began certain business enterprises and then undertook some theatre work, beginning with a tour of 'Reflected Glory' by George Kelly. In 1938, after Columbia dropped her, she signed with Republic – but nothing came of this. Eventually, she made a film for RKO, the first of her two screen come-backs and quickly forgotten: *Father Takes a Wife* (41), a comedy with Adolphe Menjou. She was paid $35,000 for it. Her second come-back was really something: in the part of Norma Desmond (which Norma Shearer had reputedly turned down) in the Wilder-Brackett *Sunset Boulevard* (50), a bizarre black comedy about an ageing Hollywood queen living in the past ('I am big – it's the pictures that got smaller'). 'Miss Swanson, required to play a hundred per cent grotesque, plays it not just to the hilt, but right up to the armpits, by which I mean

Billy Wilder's Sunset Boulevard *(50), a glittering, bitter study of a Hollywood Miss Havisham who dreams of a come-back and sees in William Holden – a scriptwriter fleeing from the bailiffs – a means of attaining it. She paid for his white tie and tails, which is why he isn't quite sure what to do next. Her great reviews were some compensation for the misapprehension that she was like the role she played.*

magnificently' (James Agee). 'In a truly out-standing performance she shows us a woman to whom playing a part has become second nature, and an actress to whom acting is life: here is the star of the days when a face had to speak without words' (Dilys Powell). No critic disagreed: Swanson's performance was – and remains – a revelation; but despite the film's brilliance and subsequent fame it was too downbeat for 1950 audiences (now, on TV, it is highly popular).

On the last day of shooting at Paramount the crew gave Swanson a plaque inscribed 'To the Greatest Star of Them All'; Paramount disagreed – or at least had not read the eulogies for her performance as Norma; there was some question of putting her in *Darling How Could You!* but they asked her to test, a request which she thought impertinent (Joan Fontaine played the part). Hedda Hopper, however, records that she suggested to Swanson a certain novel as a follow-up to *Boulevard*; Swanson replied, 'I couldn't possibly play the mother of an 18-year-old daughter.' Hopper comments that she was already a grandmother.

In 1951 she was announced for *Another Man's Poison* in Britain, but Bette Davis played it. Then she was supposed to make a film called *Crosstown* at a fee of $80,000 – but it was cancelled. WB offered her a B-budget comedy, *Three for Bedroom C* (52), about a movie star travelling to Hollywood, and it was sad to see her trying to cope with such dastardly lines and situations. She referred to it and the next one – *Mio Figlio Nerone/Nero's Weekend* – as mistakes. The latter was a satire on costume epics, made in Italy in 1956; Alberto Sordi, Brigitte Bardot and De Sica were in the cast and she played Agrippina. A mistake perhaps; terrible certainly.

There were offers to play parts like Norma Desmond, but Swanson declined them all. She said often, however, that she would like to film again, should the right part come along. If she felt bitter at the neglect by producers, the warmth of her public reception should have dispelled it. In 1970/1 she toured in 'Butterflies Are Free' and subsequently played the same role in the New York production. She was scheduled to take over from Katharine Hepburn in 'Coco' but that did not work out. She did make two tele-films, *Who Is Jennifer?* (66) and *The Killer Bees* (74), in the latter playing a matriarch with a mysterious power over the creatures of the title; she also appeared in *Airport 75* as herself (though they had hoped for Garbo). In 1976 she was married – for the sixth time and briefly – to a man who shared with her an enthusiasm for health foods. She died in 1983.

ROBERT TAYLOR

The assets of Robert Taylor hardly went beyond a good physique and a handsome face, so that with age he encountered the career decline inevitable to a matinée idol. He summed up his career adequately in 1967 (quoted in 'Films in Review'): 'I've never been terribly ambitious – simply wanted to do a good job at whatever I did. The reviews usually said I gave an adequate or good performance. I never got raves, but neither did I get pans. I've never had an Oscar and probably never will. I'm content to try to do as well as I can.' He went on: 'My metabolism doesn't lend itself to the Davis-Cagney brand of high-pressure careering. I stayed with one studio for 20 years, took what they gave me to do, did my work. While I wasn't happy with everything, I scored pretty well.'

He was born Spangler Arlington Brough (probably the best remembered 'real name' in show business) in Filley, Nebraska, in 1911, the son of a doctor. There was a plan to follow in Father's footsteps, but instead at college he studied the cello and turned from that to acting after enjoying himself on the amateur stage. He was studying at a Los Angeles (Pomona) drama school when a talent scout saw him in a production of 'Journey's End'. He was screen-tested by Goldwyn without result, but was signed by MGM to a seven-year contract, starting at $35 per week. MGM loaned him to Fox for a Will Rogers vehicle, *Handy Andy* (34), and then to Universal for a programmer, *There's Always Tomorrow*. He did one film, *Wicked Woman*, on his home lot before getting the part which really started him, in the first of the MGM shorts-series *Crime Does Not Pay*, called *Buried Loot*. Some minor roles followed – *Society Doctor* (35), *West Point of the Air* – and leads in a couple of Bs – *Times Square Lady* and *Murder in the Fleet* – before being cast as a theatrical producer in *Broadway Melody of 1936* with Eleanor Powell. 1936 was in fact to make some very sweet music: four Taylor films were released and at the end of it exhibitors voted him No. 4 box-office attraction. MGM were overjoyed – it was the sort of rise of which studio executives dream – but the film which did it was *Magnificent Obsession*, made on loan-out to Universal, a popular soap opera with Irene Dunne, although audiences fell about (then and now) when he boasts of being a Nobel prize-winner. All the ladies wanted him – Janet Gaynor for *Small Town Girl* (36), Loretta Young for *Private Number*, Barbara Stanwyck for *His Brother's Wife*, Joan Crawford for *The Gorgeous Hussy* – and Garbo. It is more likely, in the case of Garbo, that Taylor was foisted on her and *Camille* (37), from that point of view, is one of the great mis-matings of the cinema. As James Agate pointed out, he and Lionel Barrymore made a grotesque pair as the Duvals, but Taylor's campus-bred Armand becomes, after several viewings, almost inoffensive; and it should be stressed that as far as MGM were concerned his appeal was much more commercial than hers (he was No. 3 in 1937, No. 6 in 1938).

He was quite pleasing in a Jean Harlow comedy, *Personal Property* (37), the remake of *The Man in Possession*, beginning to find his feet, as notably in 20th's *This Is My Affair* with offscreen friend Barbara Stanwyck. Said the ads, unashamed: '*Thrillingly* these real-life sweethearts achieve their true greatness in the most important story either one has ever had . . .', adding, 'the picture the whole world is talking about'. There could be much speculation as to what the world could have found to say about this routine romance; but Stanwyck and Taylor were eventually married (in 1939; it lasted till 1952). At least Taylor as a Secret Service agent had a better chance than in a revamp of an old part, in *Broadway Melody of 1938*, again with Powell. His performance as the breezy, cocky *A Yank at Oxford* (38) is quite enjoyable and did much to kill the prevalent image of him as a ladies' man. The filming of it was accompanied by unprecedented publicity for a British film (MGM produced). He was one of the popular *Three Comrades* – the one who got Margaret Sullavan; and he did his image another good turn by playing a boxer in the rip-roaring *The Crowd Roars* and by doing a Western, *Stand Up and Fight* (39), with Wallace Beery. No one was done any good by *Lucky Night* – he was a poet rescued from a park bench by heiress Myrna Loy – or by *Lady of the Tropics* – he was in love with dusky Hedy Lamarr; and after the gloom of them *Remember?* with Greer Garson must have been immensely cheering. It was followed by *Waterloo Bridge* (40), with Vivien Leigh, his own favourite film and the first in which he wore the moustache he was to shave off and grow again with monotonous regularity through the years. He had an impossible role in *Escape* as an American trying to get his mother (Nazimova) out of a Nazi-occupied country, and was a naval airman in *Flight Command*, made to reassure the US about its own forces.

For Warners Errol Flynn had been Robin Hood and other folk-heroes, including some of the Old West; for 20th Tyrone Power was Jesse James. Now, for MGM, Taylor was *Billy the Kid* (41) – again, considerably romanticized – rather Billy the Kitten. The early Technicolor locations were breathtaking, inevitably dwarfing a good script and Taylor's Kid. He played with panache the

fought-over lover in *When Ladies Meet*, but could do little with the role of the 'decent' gang boss in *Johnny Eager*. Her *Cardboard Lover* (42), with Norma Shearer, was a weak comedy and *Stand By for Action* and *Bataan* (43) were war films – navy/fair and army/fine respectively. His last picture before joining up was *Song of Russia*, a piece of pop (Tchaikowsky) propaganda about an American orchestra conductor visiting the USSR (not the least funny aspect was its being exhumed and labelled pernicious by the Un-American Activities Committee some years later). Taylor was in the Navy for the last two war years.

There is little to be said about (or for) Taylor's immediate postwar films. *Undercurrent* (46) cast him as a homicidal maniac opposite Katharine Hepburn and he was trampled to death at the end by a horse – for which action it deserved honorary membership of the Critics Circle; in *High Wall* (47) he

Looks and a mild charm played a greater part in Robert Taylor's success than acting ability, but since he was in the right place at the right time he acted opposite all of MGM's great women stars. Although Margaret Sullavan was under contract to the studio she was not as prolific as the others, but she was perhaps the most enchanting. Together in Three Comrades *(38).*

was a neurotic war veteran. *The Bribe* (49) and *Conspirator* (made in Britain) were thrillers; *Ambush* and *The Devil's Doorway* (50) were Westerns: each did less well than the one before – Taylor was not to blame – but his standing was rescued when the studio failed to interest Gregory Peck in *Quo Vadis?* (51) and gave the lead to Taylor. MGM, often looking for another *Gone With the Wind*, i.e., a film with powerhouse reissue potential, remembered that a Silent *Ben-Hur* had been a huge success and the same was hoped for this: it was filmed in Italy with no expense spared and reaped a gigantic $11 million, at that time the fourth biggest grosser in movie history. Taylor and Deborah Kerr as the Roman centurion and his Christian girlfriend were competent, to say the most, but then talent was less in evidence than money (MGM were inspired perhaps by a line spoken in the film by Petronius: 'History will not say the burning of Rome is good but they must say it is colossal'). After a Western, *Westward the Women*, he did a film for which Stewart Granger was too busy, an enjoyable spectacle, *Ivanhoe* (52), from Scott's novel: it was one of the big ones of the year. *Above and Beyond* dealt cursorily with the dropping of the A-bomb; then came another Western, *Ride Vaquero!* (53) and a whaling adventure, *All the Brothers Were Valiant*. *Knights of the Round Table* was an attempt to repeat the success of *Ivanhoe*, but was too much like a children's cut-out book: cut-out figures in front of a cut-out castle.

MGM were very good to Taylor. His box-office star had waned, but they consistently put him into top-budget films – mostly adventure films which would not stretch his resources: *Valley of the Kings* (54), a thriller filmed on location in Egypt; *Rogue Cop*, in the title-role; *Many Rivers to Cross* (55), a backwoods 'Taming of the Shrew', with Eleanor Parker as the bride and Taylor the retiring groom; and *Quentin Durward*, marginally better than *Ivanhoe* and more faithful to Scott – though Taylor in the title-role was conspicuously out of place. After *The Last Hunt* (56), after buffaloes with Granger, he did his first outside film in 19 years, *D-Day the Sixth of June*, at 20th: it was not worth the journey. There followed: *The Power and the Prize*, as a ruthless tycoon who decides It's Not Worth It; *Tip on a Dead Jockey* (57), as a pilot involved with smugglers, and two Westerns, *Saddle the Wind* (58) and *The Law and Jake Wade*. There was a decreasing trickle to the box-office and it is doubtful whether anyone would have heard much of *Party Girl*, an ersatz gangster thriller, were it not for that weird cult for its director, Nicholas Ray. With that, MGM settled his contract, which had two years to run: 'Picturegoer' had commented that had it gone its full term it would have been a record; as it was, he equalled Gable's record with one company – 24 years. He found himself at sea both professionally and privately – not knowing, for instance, how to order an airline ticket.

After a programmer at Paramount, *The Hangman* (59), he returned to MGM for another minor thriller, *The House of the Seven Hawks*, directed in Britain by an old MGM contract man, Richard Thorpe; they stayed across the Atlantic for *Killers of Kilimanjaro* (60), one of the deadly programmers turned out by Warwick for Columbia, and Taylor was in Vienna for a Disney item, *The Flight of the White Stallions* (63), about the flight of the Lippizaner horses during the War. In the interim he had a TV series, 'The Detectives'. He returned to MGM for a Western that got lost, *Cattle King*, and did a guest role as the backer of Polly Adler's cathouse, in *A House is Not a Home* (64).

The Night Walker (65) was a reunion with Stanwyck, put together for the curious by the opportunistic William Castle, who worked on medium budgets, but not a bad credit for the stars, she suspected of adultery by her blind husband and he as the lawyer with whom she says she commits it: the result proves her to be as professional and committed as ever, while he looks as if he still did not know which chalk-line to stand on. For such an actor, he had had a Class career and he hoped to keep it that way; but after a weak Western at

Taylor endured long enough to co-star with a new generation of leading ladies, including Elizabeth Taylor, as in Conspirator *(49). Though this still would seem to belie the fact, the plot has her worrying for ten reels as to whether he, her husband, is a Communist – a species of which the film distinctly disapproved. It was MGM's way of atoning, at the time of McCarthyism, for its wartime pro-Soviet* Song of Russia, *which also starred Taylor (R).*

Universal, *Johnny Tiger* (66), he decided to take the money and run: *Pampa Salvajo/ Savage Pampas*, a remake in Spain of a famous Argentine film: *Hondo and the Apaches*; *Return of the Gunfighter* (67), a TV feature; *La Sfinge di Vetro/The Glass Sphinx*, replacing Dana Andrews (who was too busy) at the last minute in this Spanish-Italian Western, with Anita Ekberg; *Where Angels Go Trouble Follows* (68), in a brief guest appearance; *La Rouble à Deux Faces/The Day the Hot Line got Hot*, scampering around Paris and Barcelona with opposing secret agent Charles Boyer; and *Rublo de Dos Caros*.

He died in 1969 after a long battle with cancer. Ronald Reagan, then the Governor of California, said at his funeral: 'He was more than a pretty boy, an image that embarrassed him because he was a man who respected his profession and was a master of it.'

SHIRLEY TEMPLE

In the 1937 edition of 'Who's Who in America' there were 19 lines devoted to Shirley Temple, only two less than to Mrs Roosevelt and eight more than to Garbo, her Hollywood runner-up. Normal J. Zierold mentions this in his study, 'The Child Stars', and among a host of other extraordinary facts, he says that Shirley, on her eighth birthday, received 135,000 gifts from all over the world. Well, she was officially the biggest-drawing star in the world and had she not already won a special Oscar for bringing 'more happiness to millions of children and millions of grown-ups than any other child of her years in the history of the world'?

She was the infant 'It' girl. It was impossible to escape from her. Apart from films and records, there were Shirley Temple dolls, books and games of all kinds, clothes, items of nursery furniture, etc., and the little girl, smiling broadly, endorsed household goods of which her mother and her studio approved. There was a tremendous upsurge in the popularity of dancing classes for kids and probably no child within the orbit of Hollywood films was immune from her. Ringlets became popular; children were told to behave 'like Shirley' – and if they did not, as a punishment they were not taken to see her. Meanwhile, this dainty object of the world's love sat at home in Hollywood, playing with her dolls and receiving her distinguished visitors. Everyone attested to how completely unspoilt she was (and certainly her mother was an epoch-making watch-dog).

There were two discordant notes: one was

the realization that the child had to grow up and the other (less disturbing in view of their minority) was the sour tone affected by some sections of the press. They were baffled by the phenomenon. Shirley went through the whole bag of tricks in every film, but they remained unimpressed by her many-faceted talent: they found her singing coarse and flat, her dancing merely jigging up and down, her acting nauseatingly cute and her mimicry in a ken with Dr Johnson's lady preacher. They refused to appreciate the technique that others praised, they remained unpersuaded. Only the pessimists would have prophesied that today she would still be famous. She is known to people who have never seen a Shirley Temple film, her name carried forward, living on in the parodies of a hundred music-hall comics. She was not, in fact, anywhere near as bad as these imitations would pretend: she had the authentic star's glitter – perhaps in her beaming self-confidence. But, alas, the mockers were right: by any standards prevailing to child performers, talented she was not – which makes the whole saga so odd.

It began in Santa Monica in 1928, where Mr and Mrs Temple became the parents of a new baby. He was a bank manager; she, Gertrude Temple, soon perceived in the child the qualities of stardom and she began hawking her round the studios. At Educational, which specialised in shorts, Shirley was engaged to play in a series called *Baby Burlesks* which were take-offs on movies. She played in *The Incomparable More Legs Sweetrick* (as Dietrich), *The Pie-Covered Wagon*, *Polly-Tix in Washington*. At the same time she began getting small parts in feature movies: *Red-Haired Alibi* (32), *Out All Night*, *To the Last Man* (33), starring Randolph Scott, billed in the credits as Shirley Jane Temple, and *Mandalay* (34). Mrs Temple failed to get Shirley signed on as one of 'Our Gang' and some slight interest by Paramount led to nothing (yet). The child did another series for Educational, *Frolics of Youth*, and was seen in some of these by songwriter Jay Gorney, who was working at Fox on *Stand Up and Cheer*: a tot was needed to sing 'Baby Take a Bow' at the film's climax and Gorney advised Mrs Temple to have Shirley auditioned. She was chosen and signed at $150 a week. Fox first gave her a bit in *Carolina*, followed by small parts in *Now I'll Tell* and *Change of Heart*. Meanwhile, her song in *Stand Up and Cheer* was receiving much attention, to be followed a couple of weeks later by her performance in *Little Miss Marker*, as the orphan who reforms bookie Adolphe Menjou in Damon Runyon's story. This was made at Paramount, under a two-film deal Mrs Tem-

having won the heart of the regiment; *Our Little Girl*; *Curly Top*, a remake of *Daddy Long Legs* which splits the heroine's chores between her and an older sister, Rochelle Hudson; and *The Little Rebel*, which repeated the formula of the first film this year, Civil War melodramatics and a dance with Bill 'Bojangles' Robinson. 'You're almost nice enough to be a Confederate,' she tells Abraham Lincoln in this equally glutinous drama which, seen today, is enough to make even the strong throw up, but this clutch of movies must have had a meaning to audiences who had overcome their own adversity – the Depression – as she invariably did. At all events, she had become America's top box-office draw, a position she was to hold steadily over the next three years, in Britain as well. In 1936 she was estimated (by 'Variety') the most popular US entertainer in foreign cinemas (followed by, in this order, Gary Cooper, Gable, Astaire and Rogers, Chaplin, Garbo, Dietrich, Grace Moore, Laurel and Hardy and Robert Taylor). There were four more in 1936: *Captain January* ('Cap! Cap! I don't want to go, I don't want to!' she pleads to Guy Kibbee), the remake of a Baby Peggy vehicle; *Poor Little Rich Girl* with Alice Faye; *Dimples* with Frank Morgan, a weepie with a blackface minstrel finale which even pro-Shirley critics found hard to take; and *Stowaway* with Faye, impersonating Jolson, Crosby and Cantor. Kipling's hero, *Wee Willie Winkie* (37), changed sex to accommodate Shirley, with Victor McLaglen under John Ford's direction; and Graham Greene's review in the magazine 'Night and Day' brought a libel suit from Fox (now 20th). The review was taken to imply that Shirley was an adult masquerading as a child (Greene spoke of coquetry). The magazine settled out of court (and although the amounts involved were not great, a further libel suit brought bankruptcy).

There was only one other film that year – possibly her best – *Heidi*: 'Dear God' said the child, 'please make every little boy and girl in the world as happy as I am', and it was seriously considered that the ending of this picture might influence world affairs. The world trembled when, for the new version of *Rebecca of Sunnybrook Farm* (38), 20th cut off her ringlets; but she danced with Bojangles and did her impersonations again. The result was a hit; and so were *Little Miss Broadway* with George Murphy and *Just Around the Corner* with Bojangles and Joan Davis. Said 'Film Weekly': 'Shirley Temple has her now unvaried role of good fairy to a lot of bewildered grown-ups. . . .' She was now getting $100,000 per film and was the biggest Hollywood earner after Louis B. Mayer. Her

ple had made earlier in the year: and now it was all happening at once. In September Fox released *Baby Take a Bow* (Shirley as the daughter of ex-con going straight James Dunn) and in October Paramount presented *Now and Forever* (Shirley reuniting estranged couple Gary Cooper and Carole Lombard). After her first Paramount film Mr Temple had got Shirley's salary raised to $1,250 weekly and now he started negotiations for a further increase, as Fox released *Bright Eyes*: she sang 'On the Good Ship Lollipop' and was no longer an adjunct to the plot. Now films were to be built round her. At the end of 1934 she was the eighth draw in the US.

There were four Shirley films the following year: *The Little Colonel* (35), who is her, public remained faithful through the lavish, Technicolored *The Little Princess* (39), 'orphaned' in London; but began to fall away with *Susannah and the Mounties*, another classic tale in which the original heroine is split between Shirley and an ingénue, Margaret Lockwood. 20th had refused to loan the tot to MGM for *The Wizard of Oz* and as that became the summer's big film, the studio rushed her into their own fantasy, *The Blue Bird*, Maeterlinck adapted and in colour. Put into some cities as a Christmas attraction it did so badly that it was replaced within days by a Sonja Henie vehicle, *Everything Happens at Night*; generally released in 1940, it did no better. It is true that this Happiness-is-in-the-backyard tale is not to all tastes, but it has tremendous production values. The heroine, however, fatally lacks the wistfulness of Garland.

The writing was on the wall. Temple had slipped in all the 1939 box-office polls and clearly the mileage that 20th could get out of her as a child star was circumscribed. Besides, her fee was now $300,000 a picture. She had earned, it was estimated, $3 million (not counting the trust fund the studio had set up for her), a good round sum. Moreover, the never-too-good relationship between the studio and the mother had deteriorated; and when, after *Young People*, co-starring Charlotte Greenwood and Jack Oakie, the Temples offered to buy up the rest of the contract, the studio did not demur. In her memoir Temple says her parents were upset that Zanuck had dithered for months between that title and two others, *Lady Jane* and *Schoolmates*; she implies that they were annoyed that Zanuck could think of little but remaking Mary Pickford's old vehicles. There was bitterness, for he announced at once that the child intended to retire.

She was 11 (though studio publicity, having from the start taken a year off her age, still insisted she was 10) and Mrs Temple announced that it was time Shirley had some schooling like an ordinary child. She was sent away for an ostensible 18 months, which was an adequate period in which to negotiate a favourable contract at another studio. There was much speculation on the choice (for it was widely believed that the public would want to watch Shirley grow up) and it was expected to be Universal, where Joe Pasternak was managing Deanna Durbin's career with such success; however, it turned out to be MGM, with its own noted stable of teenage stars. MGM proudly announced that Temple would team with two of them, Mickey Rooney and Judy Garland, in *Babes on Broadway*, but Temple in her book says her mother frowned on that. She was supposed to be supported by

In the good old days before they entered politics: George Murphy and Shirley Temple in Little Miss Broadway *(38): it was all about an orphan taken up by some vaudevillians and the threat that she might be sent back to the orphanage.*

Wallace Beery in *Lazy Bones*; they bought *Panama Hattie* (originally written as a Broadway co-starring venture for her and Ethel Merman) and *National Velvet* to co-star Spencer Tracy. In the end, all they came up with, after more than 18 months, was a programmer, *Kathleen* (41), about a teenager matchmaking for her father (Herbert Marshall). In her book Temple implies that her mother was unhappy with MGM's treatment and took her away; but she also said that Roger Edens, who coached Garland, observed that she would need strenuous singing and dancing lessons to be worthy of the studio. Temple's fall was precipitous and did not coincide with the emergence of Deanna Durbin, but it happened as Garland became a second major musical star while still in her teens. Ironically, Temple did a remake of a Pickford film at that lady's suggestion, at UA, *Miss Annie Rooney* (42), being 'overwhelmed by jitterbugs mixed with saccharine' ('Picturegoer'). There had been an attempt to drum up interest in Temple's first screen kiss (it had worked for Durbin) but the public no longer had time for such frivolities and war audiences would almost certainly not have wanted to watch an adolescent Temple in the sort of films that Durbin had made. Changing taste partly accounted for the flop of both these films, for, more than Durbin or Garland, Temple belonged firmly to a former era.

She had been away long enough for interest

Shirley Temple with Claudette Colbert in Since You Went Away *(44). Her enormous popularity had almost disappeared overnight, and this was one of the attempted come-backs.*

in a come-back to be engendered when Selznick signed her to a seven-year-contract, convinced that he could succeed where others had failed. He put her into *Since You Went Away* (44), a definite third in interest after Claudette Colbert and Jennifer Jones. She was a typical teenager and that was the trouble: she was just another Hollywood youngster. Selznick in her only other film for him put her in support of Ginger Rogers and Joseph Cotten in *I'll Be Seeing You* and then she had a real star part again, in *Kiss and Tell* (46), a distasteful Broadway comedy (she was suspected of being pregnant). It did not make the circuits. That she did have a following was demonstrated by her much-publicized nuptials to an army sergeant, John Agar; and she got herself into the excellent company of Myrna Loy and Cary Grant in the successful *The Bachelor and the Bobby Soxer* (47). But *Honeymoon* with Guy Madison and *That Hagen Girl* with Ronald Reagan were not good ideas and her part in Ford's *Fort Apache* (48) was small. Her husband, beginning a career as an actor, was in this; but they were divorced in 1949 with the former child star alleging mental cruelty and habitual drunkenness. Selznick loaned her to 20th – at a fee of $100,000 – to play the ingénue in a Clifton Webb vehicle, *Mr Belvedere Goes to College* (49), and her career petered out ignominiously with *Adventure in Baltimore*, as a turn-of-the-century daughter with modern

ideas – a minister's (Robert Young); *A Kiss for Corliss*, a sniggering follow-up to *Kiss and Tell*, with David Niven; and a horsey picture, *The Story of Seabiscuit*. With that her Selznick contract expired.

In 1950 she was married again, happily, to a non-professional and declared that she was no longer interested in making movies; however, on TV in the US in 1957 she began a series called 'Shirley Temple's Storybook', as narrator and occasional actress, and three years later had a similar series. She made headlines again when she became involved in politics and ran on the Republican party ticket for Congress (unsuccessfully) and when she protested at the San Francisco Film Festival about a Swedish movie she considered immoral. In 1969 President Nixon appointed her representative to the United Nations and she became Ambassador to Ghana in 1974. She said: 'I class myself with Rin-Tin-Tin. At the end of the Depression people were perhaps looking for something to cheer themselves up. They fell in love with a dog and a little girl. It won't happen again.'

FRANCHOT TONE

The Cinema had known only two sorts of heroes: the successful and, sometimes, the failures. Apart from some of the characters

Bogart played in the 40s there has been no room for the plodders. In the 30s nine out of 10 heroes had stepped straight from the Social Register. The only failures permissible were those hit by the Depression, so heroes were successful: successful lawyers, playwrights, industrialists, detectives, bankers, advertising executives. The male stars of the period were good at playing these confident, worldly people. Franchot Tone's screen character was basically that of the bar-fly, the lounge-lizard; like his confrères he was seldom to be seen actually working, but because he was successful he was never despicable. And of course he had charm and a certain amount of modesty. The war virtually killed the type and Tone was not a good enough actor to survive; his quietly-spoken well-bred assurance went out of fashion. One cannot regret it, but there are few actors today as sympathetic, or who can play comedy with such ease.

He was born at Niagara Falls in 1906, the son of the president of the Carborundum Co. of America. He was educated privately before going to Cornell University and planned to teach languages, but became an actor instead: his first appearance on the stage was in stock in Buffalo in 1927 and later the same year he made his début in New York City, in 'The Belt'. He worked successively for the New Playwrights Company, the Theater Guild and the Group Theater, and established himself notably in 'The Age of Innocence' (28) starring Katharine Cornell and 'Green Grow the Lilacs' (31), as Curly. He made his film début for Paramount in *The Wiser Sex* (32) with Claudette Colbert and Lilyan Tashman, while appearing on the stage at nights, but it was not until some months later, while playing the lead in 'Success Story', that a studio made a good offer. MGM signed him to a five-year contract.

His first two films for them appeared almost simultaneously: *Gabriel Over the White House* (33), in which he was Walter Huston's secretary, and *Today We Live*, in which he was Joan Crawford's brother (two years later he and Crawford became man and wife). He did normal leading man assignments: opposite Loretta Young in *Midnight Mary*, Miriam Hopkins in King Vidor's *The Stranger's Return*, Maureen O'Sullivan in *Stage Mother* (who was Alice Brady), Jean Harlow in *Bombshell* and Crawford again in *Dancing Lady* (34), in both as a Social Register type enamoured of them. His status improved when he was loaned to 20th-UA to co-star with Constance Bennett in *Moulin Rouge*; then again he was just one of several flies around honeypot Crawford in *Sadie McKee*, in fact the lover who deserts her on her wedding day, turning up to be cynical when

she, from revenge, marries wealthy Edward Arnold. He was loaned to Fox for *The World Moves On* with Madeleine Carroll, to play a dual role, the son of a New Orleans cotton magnate and his descendant, a French soldier, and had top billing for the first time in *Straight As the Way*, a remake of *Four Walls*, with Gladys George, trying to go like that after a stretch, despite the old mob led by Jack La Rue. He co-starred with Harlow again, as the Park Avenue swell she finds she prefers to his wealthy father in *The Girl From Missouri* and got one of the better parts he wanted in Warners' *Gentlemen Are Born*, a topical tale about four college chums trying to get jobs in these difficult times. 'It has reality', said 'Photoplay'. He was in two of the year's big masculine adventures: *The Lives of a Bengal Lancer* (35), one of his best performances, at Paramount with Gary Cooper, and *Mutiny on the Bounty* in the part that Robert Montgomery turned down, with Gable. Between them he starred in *One New York Night* with Una Merkel and did routine chores in *Reckless* with Harlow, as an admirer wealthy enough to buy up the theatre to watch her perform, and *No More Ladies* with Crawford and Montgomery.

Tone was a successful architect who picks up Bette Davis while slumming in *Dangerous*, but his next films were routine: *Exclusive Story* (36) as a newspaperman, with Madge Evans; *The Unguarded Hour* as a barrister, with Loretta Young; *The King Steps Out* as the young Emperor Franz Joseph, with Grace Moore; and *Suzy* as a dashing flyer, with Harlow and Cary Grant, a war film that was set in 1914 but did not acknowledge it in the costumes. There followed two with Crawford: *The Gorgeous Hussy* and *Love on the Run*. They had been married a year earlier and during their much publicized romance fan magazines had noted that in the films they had made together it was some other guy with her in the final clinch. He did get her in *Hussy*, but it was a minute role; and Gable got her in the other one. Of *Hussy* Crawford says in her memoir that Tone took the part for her sake, that 'it was the breaking point in his career and the breaking point in our marriage'. She speaks tenderly of him while complaining that his late appearance on the set was 'unprofessional and intolerable': perhaps for this reason 'Variety' later described the marriage as 'tempestuous'. Whether or not Tone, like other actors before and after him, found it difficult to be married to a lady who was a bigger star than he was, he did object strenuously to the 'stuffed shirt' parts in which MGM cast him. It was no good reviewers saying he stole *Love on the Run* from Crawford and Gable, as the unsuccessful candidate

The Lives of a Bengal Lancer (35) was a popular adventure story glorifying one of the regiments which supported the British Raj. Gary Cooper and Franchot Tone were brother officers, and Tone's devil-may-care performance brought him his best notices to date.

for her favours: these were not the sort of parts he wanted to play.

He had a chance to play period comedy in *Quality Street* (37), excellent as an officer of the Regency opposite Katharine Hepburn, and to do stark drama in *They Gave Him a Gun*, as a vicious racketeer and killer, Spencer Tracy's old wartime chum: a good subject that descended to melodrama at the end. He enjoyed both, but then it was back in the old routine: he was a successful surgeon caught *Between Two Women* (Virginia Bruce and Maureen O'Sullivan), a story and screenplay by von Stroheim, and was with Crawford again in *The Bride Wore Red*, as a mere (Austrian) postman: at the end, of course she prefers him to rich Robert Young. In 1937 he appeared among the top 10 male stars in the Bernstein questionnaire, at seventh, beaten only by Gary Cooper, Clark Gable, Charles Laughton, Robert Taylor, Ronald Colman and William Powell. Then he was a playboy in *Manproof* (38) with Myrna Loy. He did *Love Is a Headache* with Gladys George, *Three Comrades* with Margaret Sullavan, Robert Taylor and Robert Young, *Three Loves Has Nancy* with Janet Gaynor and

Montgomery, *The Girl Downstairs* (39) with Franciska Gaal, *Thunder Afloat* with Wallace Beery and *Fast and Furious* with Ann Sothern. That concluded his contract and the parting between him and MGM was not amicable. That year, too, he and Crawford were divorced. He returned to New York and the Group Theater and appeared in 'The Gentle People' with Sylvia Sidney – and although it did not impair his work he was by this time drinking heavily.

He returned to Hollywood and signed deals with Universal, Columbia and Paramount: *Trail of the Vigilantes* (40), a good comedy Western; *Nice Girl?* (41) as the older man who captivates Deanna Durbin; *She Knew All the Answers; This Woman Is Mine*, a period story with Carol Bruce and John Carroll; and *The Wife Takes a Flyer* (42). He returned to MGM for *Pilot No. 5* and then appeared in *Star Spangled Rhythm*, in the sketch 'If Men Played Cards As Women Do', with MacMurray, Ray Milland and Lynne Overman. Still at Paramount he did one of his best jobs, the British officer disguised as the waiter in *Five Graves to Cairo* (43), and he stayed there to rival Dick Powell for Mary Martin in *True to*

Life, which it notably was not. He was a Broadway composer in *His Butler's Sister*, a title incorporating both Durbin and Pat O'Brien, and at Paramount again was a Britisher discovering that his wife (Veronica Lake) is a spy, in *The Hour Before the Dawn* (44). He followed with two more thrillers, Robert Siodmak's overrated *Phantom Lady*, as the murderer (which is giving nothing away) who lets his best friend be convicted, and the shallow *Dark Waters*, as the doctor ready at hand to help frightened Merle Oberon.

That Night With You (45) was a conventional musical about waitress Susannah Foster becoming a star; and it indicated that it was time Tone returned to the theatre: 'Hope for the Best' in New York, a title which might well describe his attitude to his film career. Those films he made were mainly poor: *Because of Him* (46) with Durbin again, as a successful dramatist; *Lost Honeymoon* (47), a tasteless comedy, uncertain whether or not he is the father of twins; *Honeymoon*, playing third fiddle to Shirley Temple and Guy Madison; *Her Husband's Affairs* with Lucille Ball; *I Love Trouble* (48) with Janet Blair; and *Every Girl Should Be Married*, supporting Cary Grant and Betsy Drake, as her philandering boss, whom she uses to snare Grant. That year he was reported as planning an Italian film with Linda Christian. He was in *Jigsaw* (49), a cheap little thriller made by the Danziger Brothers for UA, with Jean Wallace, Tone's wife of seven years – which was as long as the marriage lasted. He got custody of the sons and she later married Cornel Wilde. The third of his four wives was starlet Barbara Payton, over whom he came to blows with actor Tom Neal in a nightclub, which made headlines. She left him after a month for Neal (and later became a hooker and an alcoholic).

The genuine charm of his early days had long gone and with no real thespian ability to replace it, it was inevitable that his film career should go the way of that marriage, if not so quickly: *The Man on the Eiffel Tower*, made in Europe; *Without Honor* (50), a silly, verbose melodrama with Laraine Day; and *Here Comes the Groom* (51) billed under the title, as the man Jane Wyman does not prefer to Bing Crosby. He returned to the stage, where he was sometimes able to appear in stuff of the quality he craved: 'The Second Man' in summer stock in 1950 and 1952; 'Oh Men Oh Women' (53) in New York; a revival of 'The Time of Your Life' (55) at the City Center; 'Uncle Vanya' (56) off-Broadway; and Eugene O'Neill's 'A Moon for the Misbegotten' (57) at the Bijou, New York. He produced and starred in a film of the *Uncle Vanya* (58), but it was a wretched thing and despite a personal visit by him was unable to get a single public showing in Britain. He sat enthralled through the screenings, but was an alcoholic mess on either side. His fourth marriage ended in divorce in 1959.

In the 60s he continued his occasional stage appearances in New York, notably in a revival of 'Strange Interlude' (63). There were also occasional film parts, of which the most impressive was his ageing and physically sick President in *Advise and Consent* (62). But his wan apparition in one sequence of the Franco-Italian *La Bonne Soupe* (63), with Marie Bell and Annie Girardot sharing the title-role, was merely pathetic. He also had small parts in *In Harm's Way* (65) and Arthur Penn's *Mickey One*; and in Britain, as an ambassador in *Nobody Runs Forever* (68). At the time of his death, of cancer, in 1969, he was trying to set up a film of Jean Renoir's biography, 'Renoir My Father', with himself in the title-role; some months earlier he had relinquished his interest in an off-Broadway theatre that he had hoped to use for experimental work.

SPENCER TRACY

During the latter part of his career it became customary for both press and his peers to instance Spencer Tracy as one of the greatest – if not *the* greatest – of screen actors. Katharine Hepburn has said so on several occasions ('. . . he never gussied it up. He just did it, he let it ride along on its enormous simplicity. That's what was absolutely thrilling about Spencer's acting'), but if we dismiss her as partial, there are others. Humphrey Bogart: 'What is a good actor? Spencer Tracy is a good actor, almost the best. Because you don't see the mechanism working, the wheels turning.' Richard Widmark: 'He's the greatest movie actor there ever was. If he had wanted to go the classical route, he could have been as great in that field as Laurence Olivier. I've learned more about acting from watching Tracy than in any other way. He has great truth in everything he does.' Fredric March: 'One of the finest actors of our time. . . . I'm nuts about Spencer.' As this sort of adulation (or appreciation) increased and Tracy was asked about acting, he would reply gruffly: 'Just know your lines and don't bump into the furniture.' (There is another story that Lee Marvin was having some difficulty with his character and asked Tracy what *his* motivation was. Tracy replied: 'Look, I'm too old, too tired and too goddam rich for all this bull. Let's just get on with the scene.') In fact, Tracy studied his scripts, locked away for days, though the result was – Widmark again – 'so honest and seems so effortless'. And the public liked him: Tracy was one of the few actors whose career went only in an upward curve. Not all his films were hits, but his career had few reversals and he went from being a solid, reliable young actor to Grand Old Man of the movies.

He was born in Milwaukee, Wisconsin, in 1900, of Irish-Midwest stock, was educated at Rippon College, where he discovered that he enjoyed debating – which caused him to consider an acting career and he went to study at the AADA. His first job was as a robot in 'R.U.R.' at $10 a week and his first real Broadway part was in a comedy starring Ethel Barrymore, 'A Royal Fandango' (23). Later he worked under George M. Cohan in three plays and by 1929 was well enough known to go from one to the next when they failed: but a fifth was a success, 'The Last Mile', and as an imprisoned killer he became a Broadway name. During its run, he made two shorts for Vitaphone (*The Hard Guy* and *Taxi Talks*) and was tested by MGM, Universal, Fox and WB, all of whom considered him unsuitable for films. John Ford, however, saw him in the play and insisted on having him for the lead in *Up the River* (30), another prison story. As he finished it, Fox signed him to a five-year contract starting at $800 dollars a week.

His second film was the genial *Quick Millions* (31), as a truck driver who becomes a ruthless racketeer. It was not a success, but he was thereupon typed as a gangster, though

by fighting Fox he managed to get other parts – but mostly as a big-headed tough guy who learns humility in the last reel. He cut his teeth on both comedy and drama, in a series of mainly poor films (most Fox products of this period were clinkers); *Six-Cylinder Love*, a domestic drama with Sidney Fox as his wife; *Goldie* with Warren Hymer, a Flagg and Quirt type comedy, also with Jean Harlow; the poor *Sky Devils* (32) at UA; *She Wanted a Millionaire*, as Joan Bennett's faithful swain; *Disorderly Conduct*, as a demoted cop who goes wrong but reforms; *Young America*, a sentimental domestic piece directed by Frank Borzage; *Society Girl* and *Painted Woman*, both of whom were Peggy Shannon (in the latter as a dance-hall girl reformed by pearl-trader Tracy); and *Me and My Gal*, with Bennett – and Tracy playing a wise-cracking cop.

The film that established him was *20,000 Years in Sing Sing* (33). He was borrowed by WB to replace James Cagney who was feuding with that studio; and his position was consolidated by two other fine movies that year. *The Face in the Sky* with Marion Nixon was not one of them, but *The Power and the Glory* was, an epic drama written by Preston Sturges, with a much-publicized 'revolutionary' way of story-telling called 'narratage' – it turned out to be Tracy's voice over the images. Of his performance William Troy wrote in the 'Nation': 'Spencer Tracy's railroad president is one of the fullest characterizations ever achieved on the screen.' There

Colleen Moore – one of her last films – and Spencer Tracy in The Power and the Glory *(33). When the New Yorker Cinema revived it in 1970 the ads said: 'Famous as the film which influenced the style and content of* Citizen Kane'.

was *Shanghai Madness*, a poor melodrama in which he was a naval officer cashiered after firing on Chinese communists, and *The Mad Game*, as a bootlegger; and then the other good one, Borzage's *Man's Castle*, a romance with Loretta Young against a realistic Depression backdrop, with Tracy's acting again the best thing in a beautiful film. Fox extended his contract to 1937, four films a year, though he was decidedly not the studio's most popular guy as far as the Front Office were concerned. He was loaned to UA for *Looking for Trouble* (34), teamed with Jack Oakie, as telephone linesmen in a successful comedy, and to MGM to play the title-role in *The Show-Off*, George Kelly's play, which was hailed as a triumph for him. He and MGM got on well together.

He played a fast-talking promoter in a musical, *Bottoms Up*, and a gambler in *Now I'll Tell*, after which he refused to start *Helldorado* and was replaced by Richard Arlen; then he refused to start *Marie Galante* and was replaced by Edmund Lowe – but he changed his mind after a few days and paid out of his own pocket to have the film restarted with himself. He was right the first time; in any case, it was mainly a showcase for Fox's new discovery, Ketti Gallian. Then there was a small-town comedy, *It's a Small World* (35); at the end of shooting, in Yuma, Arizona, Tracy was arrested for drunkenness and kindred matters (resisting arrest, etc.). This was a studio ploy to discipline him and now another was tried: he was cast in a supporting role (the heavy) in *The Farmer Takes a Wife*. He refused to do it and was fired, though he did do one last film for Fox, a remake of the 1924 *Dante's Inferno*, where he was a dishonest fairground entrepreneur. He was already negotiating with MGM. Mayer did not want him because they already had one noted roisterer and trouble-maker (Wallace Beery), but Thalberg was enthusiastic.

To be fair to Fox, they had recognized his talent, but had not known how to handle it. Also, they had doubted whether he had sex-appeal – and so did MGM. This was somewhat paradoxical because it was hoped that the threat of being supplanted by Tracy would tame Clark Gable, who was playing up. MGM continued to worry about Tracy's lack of appeal to female audiences, even after he had won two Oscars, and for some years they were to give him roles subsidiary to Gable. On the whole, however, the studio did as well by him as he did by them – not that the association began auspiciously; he was featured in *Riff Raff*, as a fisherman. Harlow starred; there was a delay and MGM hurried him into a quickie, *The Murder Man*, as a reporter, and

then rushed through *Whipsaw* (36), in which he was a detective, because Myrna Loy had been off the screen for some time.

The next four, however, pushed him to the forefront of Hollywood stars. He was disappointed when MGM refused to loan him to John Ford for *The Plough and the Stars* (they thought it would flop), but they did put him in Fritz Lang's noble *Fury*, as an innocent man facing a lynching (though his own performance shifted uneasily from the gentle to the maniacal), and then into their huge-budgeted *San Francisco*, which was shown simultaneously. As the battling (mostly against Gable) priest he received the first of his nine Oscar nominations (a record for a male star). He was one of a quartet of big stars (Loy, Powell, Harlow), playing a newspaperman in the screwball *Libeled Lady* and then the Portuguese fisherman in Victor Fleming's version of Rudyard Kipling's *Captains Courageous* (37), uneasy with the accent – or so he claimed: the performance is still the best Hollywood attempt at that stock-figure – the earthy, elemental son of the sea/soil (it is Hepburn's favourite Tracy performance). He won an Oscar for it.

After these peaks, he was back at sea level (at least) with *They Gave Him a Gun* (the 'him' was Franchot Tone); *Big City*, as a taxi-driver; *Mannequin*, as Joan Crawford's love interest – but MGM raised his salary by $1,000 a week; and *Test Pilot* (38), merely as Gable's sidekick – but 'Time' magazine commented that Tracy was 'currently cinema's No. 1

Even great actors lose their pants: Spencer Tracy in Libelled Lady *(37).*

Captains Courageous (37) detailed the adventures of a spoilt child (Freddie Bartholomew) on a Cape Cod fishing smack and specifically with old sea-dog Spencer Tracy: a surprising performance even from this actor. It was fine enough to win him an Oscar.

actor's actor'. *Boy's Town* gave him a good part as the crusading Father Flanagan, a performance that was 'perfection itself and the most eloquent tribute to the Nebraska priest' (Frank S. Nugent in 'The New York Times'): this brought him an Oscar for the second year running and though the movie was often little more than cops-and-robbers with social overtones, it was much praised and a hit (so was *Test Pilot*).

He continued crusading, on loan to his old studio (now called 20th), as the front half of *Stanley and Livingstone* (39), another good one; and, back home, took Hedy Lamarr in *I Take This Woman (40)*. He was adventuring again in *Northwest Passage*, 'as impressive as ever' (William Whitebait) in an overlong version of Kenneth Roberts's bestseller – or, rather, the first part of it: MGM abandoned plans to film the rest, either as part of this film or as a sequel, as costs and length of shooting rose. There was disagreement between Tracy and producer Hunt Stromberg on how this version should end – and MGM sided with Tracy, reputedly because his contract was up for renewal. Then, again, he went biographical, in the good *Edison the Man*; buddied and fought Gable again in *Boom Town*; and did another reprise job with *Men of Boy's Town* (41). He essayed *Dr Jekyll and Mr Hyde*: Somerset Maugham visited the set and asked, 'Which one is he supposed to be now?' Both performance and film were considered – wrongly – inferior to Fredric March's version, but Tracy agreed with Maugham and had only played it after several battles with the studio.

He had now overtaken Gable at the box-office. He made his first appearance in the top 10 in 1940 and was to appear again six more times through 1951 – and when he was out of it, he was just out of it. These were peak years. He began filming *The Yearling* with Anne Revere, under King Vidor's direction, but difficult locations resulted in postponement (four years later Gregory Peck took over the part). Instead, Katharine Hepburn entered his life as the *Woman of the Year* (42), as the prissy political columnist whom he, a down-to-earth sports writer, marries. It was downhill then to the schmaltzy *Tortilla Flat*, playing a decent but roguish Californian-Spanish man-of-the-soil, one of the few Tracy films which he cannot make watchable, though it is challenged by *Keeper of the Flame* – Hepburn, a widow refusing to admit to him, a journalist, or indeed anybody, that her husband was a Fascist. There were three war films: *A Guy Named Joe* (43), a disgraceful enterprise in which he returns from the h(e)aven of dead pilots to encourage Irene Dunne and Van Johnson; *The Seventh Cross* (44), as an anti-Nazi German; and *30 Seconds Over Tokyo*, in a 'special' appearance as Lt Colonel Doolittle. *The Seventh Cross* was infinitely the best but did not achieve the outstanding success of the other two. There had been too many anti-Nazi chase dramas: this one was set in pre-war Germany and was directed by Fred Zinnemann. Said Tracy's biographer, Larry Swindell: 'The performance illustrated Tracy's sure footing on what Garson Kanin called his plateau beyond greatness, when "the audience is made aware of what a character is saying or thinking no matter what he is doing".' Co-star Signe Hasso said, 'I have seldom worked with an actor so engrossed in his role'. While filming, she found him 'intense and withdrawn', and MGM's copywriters were now saying 'The perfect actor'.

After another comedy with Hepburn, *Without Love* (45), Tracy returned to the New York stage, in 'The Rugged Path' by Robert E. Sherwood: its notices were bad, but his were not. Apart from two with Hepburn his next films were unworthy of him: *The Sea of Grass* (47), as a wheat baron whose wife (Hepburn) has another man's child; Sinclair Lewis's *Cass Timberlane*, unevenly married to Lana Turner; Capra's *State of the Union* (48), running for President with Hepburn as his wife and corruption all round – a film that seems fresher than ever since Watergate; Cukor's uncertain version of a West End success, *Edward My Son* (49) with Deborah Kerr, about an overdose of paternal pride (filmed in Britain); *Adam's Rib* with Hepburn; and *Malaya* with James Stewart, a particularly dull adventure melodrama. The new decade kicked off with the Minnelli-directed *Father of the Bride* (50), which was a very popular comedy: 'But amidst so much excellence, Spencer Tracy is still outstanding; this is his best playing for years,' said Dilys Powell. There was a sequel, *Father's Little Dividend* (51), and then the poor *The People Against O'Hara*, in which Tracy was a lawyer who loses a case through drink. In real-life Tracy was drinking again: he was depressed by these two films and by Hepburn's absence filming in Africa. On her return he made two good films with Cukor directing, *Pat and Mike* (52) (with Hepburn), written by Garson Kanin and Ruth Gordon, and *The Actress* (53), written by Gordon, in which Tracy was Jean Simmons's pa and disapproving of her aspirations. It was a critical but not box-office success. In neither category was the one between them, *Plymouth Adventure* (52), a drama of the 'Mayflower', described by more than one critic as a 'Thanksgiving Turkey'. It was 'Sight and Sound' who called Tracy 'a Lear of the Plains', in 20th's heavy Western, *Broken Lance* (54), and it was Gable who said

this (to Hedda Hopper): 'Spence *is* the part.
The old rancher is mean, unreasonable, and
vain. All he has to do is show up and be
photographed.'

Tracy got $165,000 plus a percentage for it,
his first movie outside MGM in years. For
MGM he made a much-praised modern Western, *Bad Day at Black Rock* (55), and he was
scheduled to do *The Desperate Hours* with
Bogart, but neither would give way on top-
billing (though, privately, they were friends).
Another Western, *Tribute to a Bad Man*, was
started, but after some weeks on location
director Robert Wise fired Tracy, with
MGM's concurrence. The actor never made
known publicly his side of the dispute, but the
unit's point of view was disclosed in an article
in 'Look' in 1962, from which it is clear that
Tracy's conduct was unreasonable. In his later
years he was cantankerous and virtually
undirectable. The 'Look' piece also made him
out to be embittered and sourly conscious of
death, which by then had taken Bogart and
Gable, among many other friends. Tracy was
certainly not happy at MGM during the 50s –
it had changed too much. It has been acknowledged that few people could handle him
during these last years: one was director
Stanley Kramer, another was Hepburn, his
constant companion. (Tracy had married an
actress, Louise Treadwell, in 1923; the mar-

riage endured, though in later years they lived
separately.)

MGM and Tracy came to the parting of the
ways, 'by mutual agreement', and he moved
over to Paramount for *The Mountain* (56) and
then to 20th for *The Desk Set* (57), with
Hepburn. He was then embroiled in WB's
film of Hemingway's *The Old Man and the Sea*
(58), but it was hardly worth the considerable
effort: he found the location work under
Zinnemann arduous – and it was redone in the
studio tank, with John Sturges now directing;
the public stayed away. Tracy took the failure
very hard. Said 'Time' magazine on Tracy as
the old Mexican fisherman: 'In most roles
Tracy plays himself, but usually, out of defer-
ence to the part, he plays himself with a
difference. This time he plays himself with
indifference.' But the same critic thought him
Oscar-worthy for his job in John Ford's
entertaining *The Last Hurrah*, from Edwin
O'Connor's novel, about a wily politician on
his last campaign, surrounded by a host of old-
time character actors; and also at Columbia,
three years later, he did *The Devil at Four
O'Clock* (61), playing an alcoholic priest.
Both did poorly, the latter deservedly.

Meanwhile, he had started to work with
Kramer, who produced and directed his last
films (though he should also have been in
Cheyenne Autumn and *The Cincinnati Kid*:

Spencer Tracy's last four films were made for producer-director Stanley Kramer: perhaps the best of them was Judgment at Nuremberg *(61) with Marlene Dietrich.*

when at the last moment ill-health caused him to withdraw from them, Edward G. Robinson replaced him in both). Kramer adored Tracy and Tracy was amenable with him, but the films are a poor reflection of such cordiality, being mainly viewable for Tracy's participation. *Inherit the Wind* (60) was a dreary evocation of the famous 'monkey-trial', with the Tracy character based on Clarence Darrow (the film was taken from a Broadway play): Tracy was pitted against Fredric March. He was at law again, as a judge, in *Judgment at Nuremberg* (61), a specious enactment of the century's most important trial. Neither film did well, though *Nuremberg* had a certain cachet in the US. The last two were giant box-office, however. In *It's a Mad Mad Mad Mad World* (63), he was surrounded by a bevy of some of America's least funny comics, a sledgehammer comedy on the subject of greed. He was the police chief who (also) finally succumbed. (In 1965 he was approached to play the lead in *Walk Don't Run*, but the producers changed their minds

and signed Cary Grant instead.)

After four years his health improved enough to permit him to do *Guess Who's Coming to Dinner* (67) – even if no insurance company would touch him. Courageously, Kramer went ahead and put Tracy into this facile comedy about a mixed marriage, with Hepburn as his wife and Sidney Poitier as the prospective son-in-law. He died shortly after shooting was concluded and was awarded a year later the BFA Best Actor Award (the first time a major film prize was given posthumously). Said Penelope Mortimer in her downbeat review in the 'Observer': 'Which brings me, thank goodness, to Tracy and Hepburn, and while either of them are on screen the most savage criticism is replaced by gratitude. It is odd, looking back at the film reviews of 20 years ago, to find that Spencer Tracy was not always considered the giant that he appears today. There were more giants, it's true. To me, at any rate, that craggy face and burly build, the exploding humour, extraordinary gentleness and toughness of old leather, have always represented the ideal man – and that is real film-fan talk. I found it very moving to see him in this, his last picture, talent, presence and personality all unimpaired.'

CLAIRE TREVOR

There were certain male stars – George Brent, Herbert Marshall – who made their careers primarily in women's pictures: and there were ladies who specialized in masculine adventures. Every Western had its saloon floozie, every gangster picture its moll – or several. These were the broads, the beaten-up dames (sometimes literally), hand on hip, cigarette dangling from their lips, usually blonde, cynical, warm-hearted and tough. No one was more sure-footed in her portrayal of these ladies than Claire Trevor, who started as an ingénue and got side-tracked into such parts. She was a man's star. She had not good enough curves and was too careful an actress to be raised to top stardom by her audiences and she later considered that she had not played the Hollywood game strenuously enough; but most of her work is glowing. It is not gaudy or bright, but has the dark satisfying polish of a piece of amber. Audiences may have taken her for granted, but buffs cherish her.

She was born in New York City in 1909 or 1912 and educated at schools in Larchmont; she took an art course at Columbia and later enrolled with the AADA. Her professional experience began at the Festival Theater in Ann Arbor, Michigan, after which a Warner talent scout saw her and recommended her for some of the Vitaphone shorts then being made at that company's Flatbush studio. She also played with a stock company that Warners had established at St Louis as a training ground for talent. She was in stock again at Southampton, Long Island, when she was offered a star role in 'Whistling in the Dark' (32), opposite Edward Arnold. The following year she was in 'The Party's Over' and during its run signed a five-year contract with Fox.

Her first film was a Western starring George O'Brien, *Life in the Raw* (33), and she performed a similarly innocuous function in another picture with him, *The Last Trail*. She had a good part, as a reporter, in *The Mad Game* with Spencer Tracy, but her chance came when Sally Eilers walked out of *Jimmy and Sally*, one of several slight pictures Eilers had been doing with James Dunn: Trevor replaced her and Fox teamed her with Dunn again in *Hold That Girl* (34), again as a tabloid newsgal, sharp and full of wise-cracks.

She was Shirley Temple's mother in *Baby Take a Bow* and a cabaret singer in *Wild Gold*, a poor drama of the ghost towns, with John Boles as a drunken engineer. The pattern was already established. Fox were impressed by the verve of so young a girl and put her into *Elinor Norton* (35), based on a Mary Roberts Rinehart story about a girl who marries a neurotic (Hugh Williams). 'Photoplay' described it as 'unbelievably dull' and 'completely boring', a verdict echoed by the public, and Trevor's chances of becoming a star at this stage receded.

It was, in any case, a B picture and Trevor now found herself firmly established as a B picture actress: *Spring Tonic* with Lew Ayres; *Black Sheep* with Edmund Lowe, a shipboard comedy with jewel thieves and others; *Dante's Inferno*, an A with Spencer Tracy, watching him climb to the top of the carnival business; *Navy Wife* in the title-role, with Ralph Bellamy; *My Marriage* (36) and *Song and Dance Man*, both with Paul Kelly – the latter based on an old musical by George M. Cohan; *Human Cargo* with Brian Donlevy, the two of them reporters uncovering a smuggling ring; *To Mary With Love*, supporting Myrna Loy, and tempting her husband, Warner Baxter, when they quarrel; *Star for a Night*, a mother-love drama; *15 Maiden Lane* with Cesar Romero, again as a reporter; and *Career Woman* and *Time Out for Romance* (37), both with Michael Whalen. Paramount borrowed her to play a nightclub singer in a programmer, *King of Gamblers*, starring Akim Tamiroff and Lloyd Nolan, and then Fox – now 20th – made her a reporter again in *One Mile From Heaven*, a timid attempt at a radical drama – about a coloured woman who claims parentage of a white child: its melodramatics were redeemed by Bill Robinson's dancing.

Goldwyn borrowed her for *Dead End*, where she had one showy scene: she was Humphrey Bogart's ex-girlfriend who had taken to street-walking. This was a big picture, much praised, and she hoped it would do for her what *Of Human Bondage* had done for Bette Davis; it did bring her an Oscar nomination in the Supporting category, but not better parts. She said later that if Darryl F. Zanuck 'hadn't confidence in a player, said player might just as well up and leave at the outset'. She completed her contract with *Second Honeymoon*, as confidante to Loretta Young; *Big Town Girl* with Donald Woods; and *Walking Down Broadway* (38), a tale of six showgirls that had nothing to do with von Stroheim's earlier film.

She went to Warners to make a film with Edward G. Robinson (with whom she was doing a radio programme), *The Amazing Dr Clitterhouse*: she was Bogart's moll who in the

John Ford's Stagecoach
*(39) marked his return to
his first love, the Western,
after ten years of (mainly)
dramas that varied from*
The Lost Patrol *to* Mary
of Scotland. *It was equally
significant for some of its
performers, including
Claire Trevor and John
Wayne.*

last reel betrays him. She stayed at Warners for the Technicolor *Valley of the Giants*, as the saloon girl with a past reformed in the last reel by Wayne Morris. Some slight prestige accrued from these two performances, despite the stereotyped parts, but that was dissipated when Trevor unaccountably returned to 20th to play yet another reporter in *Five of a Kind* (39), whose sole purpose was to exploit the Dionne quintuplets. However, *Stagecoach* was on its way, Ford's Western with John Wayne, and she expectedly cast as an American *boule de suif*: her reputation and everyone else's rose as a result of the film's success.

At Universal she was George Raft's anxious wife in *I Stole a Million*; then she co-starred with Wayne again, sparring with him, in *Allegheny Uprising* and *The Dark Command* (40); she stayed out west for *Honky Tonk* (41), supporting Clark Gable and Lana Turner (but alas, most of Trevor's scenes were cut), and *Texas*, starring with William Holden and Glenn Ford. She starred with Ford again in *The Adventures of Martin Eden* (42), but at MGM again was in support, in *Crossroads*. Then she returned to Bs and programmers: *Street of Chance* with Burgess Meredith; *The Desperadoes* (43) with Randolph Scott and

Ford; *Good Luck Mr Yates*; and *The Woman of the Town* with Albert Dekker. She was off the screen for a while, becoming a mother (by her second husband; she married for the third, and last, time in 1948), and returned in a series of thick-ear melodramas, starting with *Murder My Sweet* (44), adapted from Raymond Chandler, as a dangerous lady – perhaps less memorable than Mary Astor in *The Maltese Falcon* or Barbara Stanwyck in *Double Indemnity*, but that is good company to be in. RKO understandably liked her and kept her on for *Johnny Angel* (45) with George Raft and *Crack-Up* (46), as Pat O'Brien's fiancée. As a change of pace she moved to UA to be a hard-boiled shopgirl in *The Bachelor's Daughters* and was then back at RKO for *Born to Kill* (47) with Lawrence Tierney, as a mercenary divorcee. She was with Dennis Keefe in *Raw Deal* (48) at Eagle Lion and although these last two were directed respectively by Robert Wise and Anthony Mann, it was before they hit the big time and they were programmers at best. Depressed by these outings Trevor returned to the stage, including a New York appearance in 1947 in 'The Big Two', which soon folded, though she got nice notices. She said later that this experience finally rid her of the ambition to be a Broadway star and that she would try to be a movie star instead – at last.

It was too late. Within a year she gave two of her best performances, demonstrated her versatility and won an Oscar; but she did not thereafter get better parts in better pictures. In *Key Largo* she supported Bogart, Bacall, etc., in a flashy part as Edward G. Robinson's drink-sodden mistress or moll, so desperate for a drink she would croak her way through 'Moanin' Low' to please him: it was a great performance and brought her a Best Supporting Oscar. Then she had one of her rare 'normal' parts in *The Babe Ruth Story*, as Mrs R opposite William Bendix as the baseball player, and was splendid again as a Broadway actress in *The Velvet Touch*, supporting Rosalind Russell. And she gave a lively comedy performance in *The Lucky Stiff* (49), but it was not a good picture. Nor were these: *Borderline* (50) with Fred MacMurray, *Best of the Badmen* (51) with Robert Ryan, *Hard Fast and Beautiful*, as the ruthless mother of Sally Forrest, *Hoodlum Empire* (52) with Brian Donlevy and *My Man and I* with Shelley Winters and Wendell Corey.

Stop You're Killing Me (53) was a musical remake of *A Slight Case of Murder*, with Broderick Crawford in the Edward G. Robinson role and Trevor as his wife, played before by Ruth Donnelly. Trevor was inferior, but then, so was the film. *The Stranger Wore a Gun* was a typical Randolph Scott Western, originally made in 3-D, with Trevor 'easy and graceful as the hard, good girl' ('MFB'). She could play such parts blindfold: she gave her usual loose-lady performance in *The High and the Mighty* (54), but in a reasonably good film it could stun – and this one brought her third Oscar nomination. *Man Without a Star* (55) was a Western with Trevor propped up against the saloon bar as usual – Jeanne Crain was her rival for Kirk Douglas and the sweet Crain, of course, got him. She had small parts in *Lucy Gallant*, as the woman who sells her bar to Jane Wyman, and *The Mountain* (56), as the woman waiting to marry Spencer Tracy; and another good chance in *Marjorie Morningstar* (58), as Natalie Wood's mother. On TV she won an Emmy for her performance as Fran in 'Dodsworth' (56), with Fredric March, and she appeared regularly if not frequently in that medium.

Three of her last four films gave her good parts. In *Two Weeks in Another Town* (62) she was Edward G. Robinson's scornful harpy of a wife and in *The Stripper* (63) – a role turned down by Jean Arthur – she was Richard Beymer's mother, a widow whose generous kindness to old friend Joanne Woodward turns somewhat sour. In *How To*

Claire Trevor hasn't had all the luck she deserved in films and she has only made four films in the last decade: but her part in The Stripper (63) was a good one. With Joanne Woodward as the old friend who seduces her son.

Murder Your Wife (65) she was another man-hating harridan, married to Eddie Mayehoff and anxious that Virna Lisi should start to treat Jack Lemmon in the same way. Her last pictures have been *The Cape Town Affair* (67), an amateurish South African thriller, where she had a brave stab at playing an old pedlar who is also a police informer; and *Kiss Me Goodbye* (82), in which she gave a stylish performance as Sally Field's mother.

LANA TURNER

Lana Turner was a film star for 40 years. She has no other identity than that of film star – and that in its most obvious sense: a glamour girl from a mould, a fabulous creature who moves, on-screen, among beautiful furnishings and who, offscreen, is primarily noted for a series of love-affairs and marriages. She has been married seven times and her name has been linked by the fan magazines with a score of other men. It is presumably due to this that she owes the longevity of her career, which has consistently triumphed over appalling personal notices. Even her admirers would admit that she could not act her way out of a paper bag.

Her beginnings seem to be on a par for those of a Hollywood glamour queen. She was born in Wallace, Idaho, in 1921. Her parents moved to California, where they separated; the child was partly brought up by cruel foster-parents. Her father was a victim of murder for robbery. When the young Turner was reunited with her mother they often lived in poverty – until she was 15, when, having cut typing class, she was seen by Billy Wilkerson of the 'Hollywood Reporter' in a Los Angeles drugstore, an event which passed into Hollywood folklore. Struck by her nubile figure, he took her to the Zeppo Marx Agency, whose Henry Willson got her a job as an extra in *A Star is Born* (37); turned down by RKO, 20th, etc., her agent got her a small role in *They Won't Forget* – sipping soda at a drugstore fountain. Its director, Mervyn LeRoy, gave her a personal contract starting at $50 a week and Wilkerson gave her a rave in his journal: that led only to bits in *The Great Garrick*, at Goldwyn as a Eurasian dancer in *The Adventures of Marco Polo* (38) and in *Four's a Crowd*. When LeRoy moved from Warners to MGM there was some question of her remaining, but Jack Warner said she would never amount to anything: LeRoy managed to sell her contract to MGM.

They made her one of Mickey Rooney's love interests in *Love Finds Andy Hardy*, followed by some programmers: *Rich Man Poor Girl* with Robert Young; *Dramatic School*, produced by LeRoy, and *Calling Doctor Kildare* (39). She starred in two Bs, *These Glamour Girls*, a campus comedy in which she revenged herself on the socialite likes of Jane Bryan and Anita Louise, and *Dancing Coed*, which featured Artie Shaw, the bandleader. After *Two Girls on Broadway* (40), a remake of the first *Broadway Melody*, billed over Joan Blondell, she married Shaw and did a tinny drama, *We Who Are Young*. It could not be said that public response to Turner was enthusiastic, but the 'Hollywood Reporter' was; and she got publicity by moving from the studio schoolroom to nightclubs and by moving to New York to be with Shaw. She was not the new Jean Harlow, for whom MGM hoped, but could best be sold as a sex symbol: labelled 'The Sweater Girl', stills began to be in demand – and she would come thus into greater prominence when the US entered the war. It was simply to be hoped that her inability to emote would not be too noticeable and thus she was put alongside Judy Garland and Hedy Lamarr in *Ziegfeld Girl* (41), as the one whose preference for luxury led to tragedy and death; in *Dr Jekyll and Mr Hyde* she was ludicrously cast as an English deb.

MGM saw her as a successor to Joan Crawford: a remake of *Our Dancing Daughters* was contemplated, but instead she was given the accolade of starring opposite Clark Gable in *Honky Tonk*, playing a prim young miss who is wooed by him and converted into something more carnal; the other MGM biggie, Robert Taylor, changed her from sociology student to gangster's moll in *Johnny Eager* – but the public had preferred the teaming with Gable and they became war correspondents in *Somewhere I'll Find You*. A poor comedy, *Slightly Dangerous*, was released at the time she married Stephen Crane: a remarriage was required when his divorce proved invalid and Louis B. Mayer's fury and her pregnancy kept her off the screen for a year. She returned in *Marriage is a Private Affair* (44), one of the myriad films about hasty wartime marriages and totally undistinguished; but she carried it to a certain success – co-star John Hodiak meant little at the box-office. Equally topical was *Keep Your Powder Dry*, in which she joins the WACs – spoilt, selfish and uncooperative, until vouchsafed a vision of what Serving her Country Really Means. *Weekend at the Waldorf* (45) had several other stars – Van Johnson, Ginger Rogers – and was a big success; and *The Postman Always Rings Twice* (46) was the third cinematization of James M. Cain's masterly thriller (already filmed in France in 1939 and Italy in 1942). She was a *femme fatale* who inveigles John Garfield into murdering her elderly husband, probably her most effective performance.

Now entrenched as one of the top ladies on the MGM lot, she had a couple of box-office hits: *Green Dolphin Street* (47) with Van Heflin, a period melodrama from a novel by Elizabeth Goudge, set in New Zealand. Said 'The New York Times': 'Lana Turner . . . changes her costume more than the expressions on her face.' And *Cass Timberlane*, where she was a girl from the other side of the tracks married to judge Spencer Tracy. At first there was trouble between them because she did not know her lines, but later he sort-of respected her. A re-teaming with Gable proved them a star-team no longer with crackle, as he 'found' her, a nurse, all over war-torn Europe, in *Homecoming* (48); and she was unremittingly modern as Milady de Winter in the otherwise enjoyable *The Three Musketeers*. She was off the screen again for a year before doing *A Life of Her Own* (50) and was wiped off the screen by Ann Dvorak in a supporting role: this study of a model's life is probably the least of George Cukor's films.

MGM were in a quandary: Turner's box-office was falling rapidly and she was not worth keeping as a prestige item. The solution was to put her into musicals, where acting ability did not matter. She could not sing, but that did not matter either – she could be (and was) dubbed. *Mr Imperium* (51) co-starred Ezio Pinza, in an attempt to launch him into screen stardom after his success in 'South

Pacific'; it was a box-office disaster. Her second musical was altogether in a bigger league – *The Merry Widow* (52) – and it was in every way but one entirely worthy of the Lehar score, curtailed though it was. But that one was crucial – Turner herself. Critic after critic cracked that she was the unmerriest widow you ever saw. Her salary was now $300,000 a year, for only 20 weeks' work (which would normally consist of two films a year). Then she was still out of her depth as the (alcoholic) movie star in the much-liked *The Bad and the Beautiful* (53), though Richard Winnington thought casting her as 'a star of the genus Lana Turner could be a master stroke!'

In *Latin Lovers* she and Ricardo Montalban were more or less incidental to a camera tour of Brazil. It was a flop and so was *The Flame and the Flesh* (54), a curious remake of a 1937 French melodrama (*Naples au Baiser du Feu*). The 'MFB' thought some pleasure could be derived from the playing, described as 'intriguingly inept', and added that Turner gave 'a rich display of familiar mannerisms'. Once more she was hopefully teamed with Gable in *Betrayed* – but to no avail; and her own performance, as a Dutch double agent helping the Resistance, was notably useless – though the dialogue did not help. Not even Garbo could have made much of her role as a high priestess in *The Prodigal* (55), a Biblical effort with Edmund Purdom, but she was competent

in *The Sea Chase* with John Wayne – her first outside MGM in over 15 years. Her contract wound up with *Diane* in which, again, she was inappropriate – as Diane de Poitiers. Christopher Isherwood worked on the script. The film was a failure and Turner's contract was not renewed (but anyway MGM were shuffling off all their contract stars). 'Picturegoer' at this time described her as 'a difficult actress on set'.

20th signed her to play Myrna Loy's old role in the remake of *The Rains Came*, *The Rains of Ranchipur*. It was another flop. She stayed away again until the modestly budgeted *The Lady Takes a Flyer* (57), with Jeff Chandler, at Universal, and then played a frigid widow in *Peyton Place*, neurotically concerned about her bastard daughter's virginity. The original novel had been one of the most successful ever published and 'Peyton Place' had become a synonym for any small town with an underground sex-life of bizarre complexity. There was nothing to prevent the film from becoming a giant grosser – nothing, not even script, direction and acting of soporific dullness; and the box-office got a boost from the scandal involving Turner in 1958.

Her daughter (by her second husband) stabbed to death a small-time gangster-gigolo, Johnny Stompanato, who was her lover. The subsequent headlines raked up such items as the letters Turner had written to Stompanato and her not insubstantial love-life. The verdict was justifiable homicide and Turner emerged from the case as a rather pitiable figure and, despite *Peyton Place*, a dubious bet to continue in films. The British film she had made just before the scandal, *Another Time Another Place* (58), died at the box-office, but more probably of press maulings. However, she was engaged by Ross Hunter of Universal to appear in *Imitation of Life* (59) and that copped some of the year's biggest money. It was a remake of the Fannie Hurst novel that Claudette Colbert had done earlier, centring on an actress's troubles with her daughter. Dated and vulgar, it bore out Hunter's allegation that in the right vehicle, the public (especially the female part of it) would turn out to see the old stars. He thereupon put Turner into a follow-up, *Portrait in Black* (60), and another remake of an old soap opera, *Madame X* (66), but the grosses – particularly of the second one, indicated that Turner was one old star the public did not want to see. (Said one critic: 'She's not Madame X, she's Brand X; she's not an actress, she's a commodity.') Also, a dim film version of James Gould Cozzens's novel, *By Love Possessed* (60), did poorly; so did *Bachelor in Paradise* (61) and *Who's Got the Action?* (62), where Turner was little more

Nubile young wife, old husband, and convenient handyman (John Garfield): James M. Cain's The Postman Always Rings Twice *brought some exciting twists to an old situation, and the film version (46) provided Lana Turner with one of her best chances.*

Madame X had been a famous tearjerker for Dorothy Donnelly (16), Pauline Frederick (20), Ruth Chatterton (29) and Gladys George (37): it was silly of Lana Turner (66) to invite comparison (but sillier still of Universal to re-do it at all). With Ricardo Montalban.

than a foil to Bob Hope and Dean Martin respectively. Her only films were duallers, *Love Has Many Faces* (64) and *The Big Cube* (70) made in Mexico. In 1969 she married for the seventh time and began a TV series with George Hamilton, 'The Survivors', based on an idea by Harold Robbins. It did not run long. In 1971 she toured in 'Forty Carats' and was divorced; she did a British horror film, *Persecution* (74), of which she said 'It's a bomb. I hope they burn it' – and it might have been, as far as audiences cared. In 1975 she performed in a Chicago suburb with Louis Jourdan in 'The Pleasure of His Company' and she returned to films in another no-no, *Bittersweet Love* (76), a tale of incest with Robert Alda and Celeste Holm.

More recently she has toured in 'Bell, Book and Candle' and played in 'Murder Among Friends' in Providence, Rhode Island. She also guested in *Falcon's Crest* (82). *Witches' Brew* (85), in fact filmed in 1978, found her as a witch helping Richard Benjamin and Terri Garr to further his (academic) career.

RUDOLPH VALENTINO

He was born in Castellaneto, in southern Italy, in 1895 and christened Rudolpho Alfonzo Raffaelo Pierre Filibert Guglielmi di Valentina d'Antonguolla, a bizarre start to a life which, like the name, was really too grandiose for him: witnesses speak of his intelligence and sensitivity (as if surprised to find he had these qualities), but he seems to have been an uninteresting man. Certainly today, as an actor, his much-vaunted magnet-

ism is barely discernible – little more than a flashing of the eyes and a flaring of the nostrils. In ardour, he looks most like a vampire about to bite, but he does have a certain panther-like grace in movement. No personality comes through, as – to take a couple of names at random from the same period – it does with William Haines or Antonio Moreno; but if he appears to us today a ridiculous figure, snarling at some heroine while rigged up as if for a camp carnival ball, so indeed did he at the time to large sections of the public – particularly the masculine half, who despised him for his foppishness and resented him for such accoutrements as the slave bracelet he flaunted.

It is unlikely that he would have been a star at any other time – in the unlikely event of his happening at any other time: his life bore a pleasing resemblance to the films and novels of the day, rags-to-riches and fierce, unrequited passions. 'In my country men are the masters – and I believe that women are happier that way' was his creed, but in life he was completely subject to the whims of his second wife, Natacha Rambova (born Winifred Shaunessy in Salt Lake City), even to the extent of allowing her almost to sabotage his film career. Efforts were made to persuade the public that he was a regular two-fisted guy, but it was generally conceded, even among his admirers, that he had been a gigolo of no particular discrimination as to sex – rather than starve, of course. However, such things were not admitted at the time and some accounts of Valentino's youth are entirely fictitious.

In his birthplace he was regarded as a failure. His father, an army vet, died when he was young. The boy was sent to a military academy at Taranto and later joined the navy, but was unacceptable as officer-material in either service; he did have some success when, as a bleak alternative, he studied agriculture. However, he preferred to squander the family money and at 18 was packed off to New York. His friends were other Italian immigrants until, according to Adela Rogers St John, he was befriended by three wealthy Frenchmen. When they dropped him, he became a gardener on a Long Island estate; but the occupation he found most congenial was dancing: after a while as a 10¢-a-dancer, he began exhibition dancing with a regular partner, in dance-halls and then in clubs. Then he met Bonnie Glass, one of Manhattan's favourites and he replaced Clifton Webb as her partner; he later danced with Joan Sawyer . . . but to the police department he was known as a petty thief and blackmailer. He left New York in the cast of a musical, 'The Masked Model'; it failed in Ogden and he made his way to San Francisco, where he danced in 'Nobody Home' until it folded. But he made friends easily and managed to cadge money: one friend recommended him to try the movies and he moved to Los Angeles.

He had two great advantages, Mae Murray and Norman Kerry, stars whom he had known in New York. Kerry introduced him around and director Emmett Flynn gave him a job dancing in a ballroom scene in *Alimony* (18), at the standard 'extra' fee of $5 a day. Its writer, Hayden Talbot, offered to write him into a film and while waiting Valentino danced in a nightclub: in the film he had a good role as a villainous Italian count, but as an independent production it ran into difficulties and was not released till two years later, as *A Married Virgin*. He accepted another extra job from Flynn, playing a tough Bowery Italian in *The Blackmailer*, and returned to dancing till Universal took him on to play leading man to Carmel Myers, who was *A Society Sensation* – and he was the society scion who treated her oh! so romantically. He was paid $125 a week and remained to romance Miss Myers *All Night*; at the same studio Murray asked for him as she played *A Delicious Little Devil* (19), as the nice guy who waits while she flirts with an underworld Duke. But producers simply did not see him as a leading man and he was reduced to playing an Apache dancer at Vitagraph, in *A Rogue's Romance* starring Earle Williams, then nearing the end of his reign as one of the screen's first heart-throbs. Thomas Ince gave Valentino a role in *The Home-breaker*, with Dorothy Dalton and Douglas McLean, but it mostly ended on the cutting-room floor. Kerry got him a job in *Virtuous Sinners*, in

which he starred, and Murray asked for him again when she played *The Big Little Person*, but disliked his attempt at an Irishman; and Dorothy Gish asked him to play the villain in a comedy, *Out of Luck*. He applied for and got one of the leads in *The Eyes of Youth*, starring Clara Kimball Young, as a 'society parasite' romancing her and finally revealed to be a professional co-respondent employed by her husband.

Once again, the best he could do afterwards was a bit part in *An Adventuress* (20), which starred female impersonator Julian Eltinge: It was reissued, after Valentino's success, as *The Isle of Love*. He also had parts, mostly as the villain and usually moustached, in *The Cheater* at Metro; *Passion's Playground*, worked into it by Kerry, as his brother; *Once to Every Woman*, a starring vehicle for Dorothy Phillips directed by her husband, Allan J. Holubar, as an Italian count; and *Stolen Moments*, a starring vehicle for diva Marguerite Namara, as the heavy. He was married at this time to Jean Acker, who left him on the wedding night. He had slept with both sexes to get ahead, he knew many of the right people and seemed doomed to shunt from studio to studio as an oily villain; he accepted a Selznick film in New York, at $350 a week, *The Wonderful Chance* starring Eugene O'Brien – and he was merely an underworld boss, if, as ever, impeccably dressed.

One of the powers behind Metro's throne was June Mathis, a plump and aggressive spinster who picked most of the studio's properties, and she insisted on doing *The Four Horsemen of the Apocalypse* (21), a bestseller by Vicente Blasco-Ibañez. She produced and wrote the scenario and was resolved to have Valentino for one of the leads when she saw him in *The Eyes of Youth*. He was a success from the first day of shooting and his part was built up – that of a South American ne'er-do-well in France during World War I who becomes a hero. The première in New York was a sensation: this was another step that made moviegoing respectable and it made $4½ million (only three other films of the 20s figure on the 'Variety' list of top grossers). Valentino had only featured billing, but all prints were soon recalled and the credits altered to make him the star.

His massive new public could see him a month later in *Uncharted Seas*, an Alaska gold-rush adventure directed by Wesley Ruggles, with Alice Lake in the lead; but his real follow-up was his Armand to Nazimova's modernized *Camille* – absurdly over-designed by Rambova, 'the Ice Maiden', who was the art-director. Mathis reunited him with his director and co-star from *The Four Horsemen*, for *The Conquering Power*, a heavy version of

Stunned by his success in The Sheik *and in other exotic roles, Valentino and his cronies forced upon Paramount a vehicle called* The Young Rajah *(22), ostensibly a tale about a princeling trying to win back his throne, but in reality little but an excuse to present Valentino thus. Public ridicule proved Paramount right – but female fans still queued.*

Balzac's 'Eugénie Grandet'. During its making, Mathis demanded a salary hike for him, from $350 a week to $450, but the studio offered only $400. So, when the film was completed, they moved together in some dudgeon to Paramount, where he got $500 a week, to increase to $1,000 or more over a three-year period.

Paramount's announcement of their coup was ecstatic and they had just the property for their new star: *The Sheik*, a rubbishy but bestselling desert charade by E.M. Hull. Valentino, of course, had the title-role, the kidnapper of a high-born English girl (Agnes Ayres, who was top-billed). The action, in the words of Griffith and Mayer, consisted of little but 'a menacing Valentino staring at a pleading Agnes Ayres while they warily circled each other for a clinch that was a long time in coming'. Clearly this was as appealing as had been Miss Hull's prose, for within two years it had earned $2 million – Valentino's second most successful film (reissued in 1938 with a music-track and some success). Susceptible females fainted and went Sheik-mad; an Arabian influence became noticeable in interior decoration; and a hit song emerged, 'The Sheik of Araby'. Already, Valentino's salary had risen to $1,250. The next was unspectacular, *Moran of the Lady Letty* (22), from a story by Frank Norris about a society sprig shanghaied aboard a yacht and falling for the captain's daughter (Dorothy Dalton). Critics found him unconvincing as a normal young man, so the next one, a modern triangle story, *Beyond the Rocks*, included lots of flashbacks to more romantic eras with him and Gloria Swanson as all the lovers; it was specially concocted for them by Elinor Glyn.

He was delighted with the next, *Blood and Sand*, from Ibañez's bull-fighting story, co-starring Nita Naldi and directed by Fred Niblo. 'The New York Times' decreed that Valentino was acting again, after just 'slicking his hair and posing' in recent films, and it was a big one at the wickets: but it had been difficult to make, with Valentino, spurred on by Rambova and Mathis, becoming more finicky. Now he demanded choice of properties and complete control of his career; his films, he told a reporter, 'do not live up to my artistic ambitions'. Paramount unwillingly let him make *The Young Rajah*, written by Mathis, directed by Philip Rosen, but the result – Rudy in little but a jewelled jock-strap and a turban and some pearls – was a fiasco. The studio reasserted their contractual rights and had to take out an injunction to prevent him working elsewhere (his second legal difficulty at that time; earlier, a tangle had caused him to be indicted for bigamy). They

offered him new terms, including $7,000 a week provided they had artistic control, but at Rambova's bidding, he refused – despite the fact that they were penniless. To make some money they embarked on a nationwide dancing tour and he published a book of 'poems' called 'Day Dreams'.

They holidayed in Europe and at the end of 1923 a compromise was reached: Valentino would make films for an independent, J.D. Williams, and Paramount would distribute. The first was to have been *The Moor* and stills were issued of him bearded; but instead he did a version of Booth Tarkington's *Monsieur Beaucaire* (24) – French aristocrat disguised as a barber at the court of the Spanish king – which was eagerly awaited by fans and restored him generally to favour: 'Gorgeous is a word we invariably avoid,' said 'The New York Times', 'but this pictorial effort is thoroughly deserving of such an adjective, as never have such wondrous settings or beautiful costumes been seen in such a photoplay.' James R. Quirk in 'Photoplay', however, thought it a pity that Valentino was trying to be an actor at the expense of the personality that made him a sensation. In the end, however, the public did not respond as hoped and the effeminacy of Valentino's costumes was blamed. He was given a more masculine image in *A Sainted Devil*, an Argentinian tale

After the débâcle of The Young Rajah *and many highly publicized private misfortunes, Valentino needed a good film, and he got it in* Monsieur Beaucaire *(24), the story of a barber who masquerades as a nobleman. The lady whose honour he's defending is Doris Kenyon.*

Valentino in The Son of the Sheik *(26): most of his acting was like that.*

from E.M. Hull's new bestseller; Banky was the girl again and there was a special guest appearance by Agnes Ayres as the hero's mother. Said 'The Times' (London): 'It is impossible to ignore him. He is a personality on the screen, not merely a handsome presence.' Both films did smash business, which went some way towards consoling Valentino for the dreadful publicity he was now getting, culminating in the Chicago newspaper attack headed: 'The Pink Powder Puff' (a men's restroom had installed a slot-machine with face-powder, supposedly to please him).

In August 1926 he went into a New York hospital with a perforated ulcer . . . the world (the female part of it) held its breath, and much of it gathered outside the hospital. He died $200,000 in debt; he had earned over $5 million. The lying-in-state and the funeral were both major Happenings, with thousands of women lining the streets and several riots. This was the start of an entirely new form of necrology and there are today, still, Valentino fan clubs. Three years after he died, June Mathis died and was buried beside him. Among the several memoirs published was Rambova's, which included conversations with Valentino from the Beyond. Interest in him hardly abated; in 1938 UA reissued both its films, with surprisingly successful results. Film producers continually announced plans for a life of Valentino (20th planned one with Tyrone Power) and in 1951 one finally materialized from Columbia called *Valentino*, with Eleanor Parker and Anthony Dexter. It was a flop, as was one in 1977 with Rudolf Nureyev. In 1967 Marcello Mastroianni appeared in an Italian stage musical based on Valentino: doubtless the last has not been heard of him.

by Rex Beach ('Rope's End') – entangled with two women and getting drunk. And in *Cobra* (25), also with Nita Naldi he was a womanizer but a good joe at heart. Both films were laughed off screen – something which Valentino, of all stars, could least surmount.

Rambova was blamed for the downbeat response: willy-nilly, she had had the say-so on all three Williams pictures – designing the costumes on *Beaucaire*, interfering with the scripts of the other two (both, finally, were a mess). Now, Williams refused to back a tale that she had constructed for her husband, *The Hooded Falcon*, and the association was dissolved. But Rambova was out: Valentino was sought by other companies only on that condition – UA offered him the moon ($10,000 per week, plus a percentage) provided that Rambova was kept off it. To console her, he financed *What Price Beauty?* in which, producing and directing, she indulged her taste for outré décor and what looked like lesbian fantasies; when finally released, by Pathé, it was another fiasco. Not long afterwards she left him.

His first film for UA was *The Eagle*, from Pushkin's 'Dubrovsky', a Russian Robin Hood during the days of Catherine the Great (Louise Dresser). Vilma Banky co-starred and Clarence Brown directed: it was favourably received and so was *The Son of the Sheik*,

CONRAD VEIDT

Robert Morley was, in his early days, Dialogue Director on one of Conrad Veidt's pictures. Veidt, said Morley, 'was a master at delivering lines and had been delivering them in the same way for years. He always spoke them very slowly when everyone else spoke rather fast, and softly when everyone else spoke loudly. On the screen this seemed most effective.' In other words, Veidt was a highly accomplished technician, but not an actor likely to capture the imagination – even if doting fan magazines spoke of his 'intriguing moodiness and reserve'. His tall, gaunt figure, the broken accent, the command and the haughty face, expressing often an aloofness and a possibility of cruelty: these qualified him to play with great skill a certain type of person – usually, of course, a German person.

He was born in Berlin in 1893 and educated there at the Hohenzollern Gymnasium; enchanted by the theatre, he made the acquaintance of Max Reinhardt and acted under his management till the war; released to act for the soldiery, he made his way back to the Berlin theatre and made what is probably his first film, *Der Spion* (17). He did *Der Weg des Todes* and *Furcht*, and had his first leading film role in *Das Ratsel von Bangalor*; while appearing in 'Korallen' by George Kaiser he was approached by Richard Oswald to appear in *Tagebuch einer Verlorenen* (18), as the doctor caught in the toils of a coquette. Oswald was associated with a number of films dealing with morality and sexuality, which, if not explicit, were encouraged officially in the hope of curbing VD, and Veidt, with his moody, haunted face, was the ideal interpreter of a life ruined by debauchery. For Oswald he did the similar *Dida Ibsens Geschichte* and *Das Dreimaderlhaus*, a story about Schubert; after *Columba* he played a doctor again for Oswald in *Jettchen Geberts Geschichte*, a Jewish family drama, and its sequel *Henriette Jacoby*. He did: Oswald's *Sundige Mutter*, on abortion; *Opfer der Gesellschaft*, as a flamboyant city prosecutor; *Nocturno der Liebe*, as Chopin; Dupont's *Die Japanerin*; *Opium*; *Die Reise um die Erde in 80 Tagen*, as Phileas Fogg; a two-part *Peer Gynt*, for Oswald, as the button-maker; and Oswald's *Anders als die Andern*, as a homosexual musician whose life goes to pieces after a liaison with a student. The film, because it was sympathetic, caused an uproar; in life, Veidt's friends regarded him as heterosexual when sober, homosexual when drunk. The next of Oswald's moralities, *Die Prostitution*, was so successful that there was a sequel, *Die Prostitution II Die Sich Verkaufen*, around which time Veidt was also in *Die Mexikanerin*, as a seducer, and *Die Okarina*. Then: Paul Leni's *Prinz Kuckuck*, in the title-role, a parvenu so rich that he is able to destroy all about him; Oswald's *Unheimliche Geschichten*, a group of grisly stories, in several roles, including Death; *Wahnsinn*, a romance which he directed himself; Oswald's *Nachtgestalten*, as an actor; and Murnau's episode film *Satanas*, again in a multiple role. At this time for Reinhardt he played the title-role in 'Faust', inspiration of many of these films, with their brooding, troubled spirits and elements of the macabre. Cinematically, *Das Kabinett des Dr Caligari* (20) was thought to have taken such elements to the extreme, but as entertainment today it is inferior to many of these films (those which survive); Veidt's interpretation of the zombie-like maniac made him an international name.

Oswald's *Der Reigen* was a free version of Schnitzler's play, with Veidt as one of the reasons for Asta Nielsen's downfall; and after *Patience* came Murnau's *Der Januskopf*, a free adaptation of 'Dr Jekyll and Mr Hyde', with Veidt in those roles. He had another *doppelrolle* in *Die Nacht auf Goldenhall*, directing himself – surprisingly, in view of the slew of acting jobs to be had: *Liebestaumel*, as a gypsy; *Die Augen der Welt*; Oswald's *Kurfurstendamm*, with Nielsen, as the Devil; *Moriturus*; Murnau's *Abend-Nacht-Morgen*; Oswald's *Manolescus Memoiren*, as the great confidence trickster; *Kunstlerlaunen*; Murnau's *Sehnsucht*, as the student; Murnau's *Der Gang in die Nacht*, as a blind artist; the two-part *Christian Wahnschaffe*, in the title-role; *Der Graf von Cagliostro*, made in Austria; *Das Geheimnis von Bombay*; *Menschen in Rausch*; Oswald's *Die Liebschaften des Hektor Dalmore* (21), as Dalmore; *Der Leidensweg der Inge Krafft*; and *Landstrasse und Grosstadt*. He was Nelson in Oswald's *Lady Hamilton*, the first of several historical roles; after playing a fanatical Hindu in the two-part *Das Indische Grabmal* he was Cesare Borgia in Oswald's *Lucrezia Borgia* (22), *Paganini* (23), for his own company, and *Wilhelm Tell* – and after doing *Glanz gegen Gluck* he was Don Carlos in Oswald's free adaptation

Asta Nielsen and Conrad Veidt in Der Reigen *(20), he as a sinister blackmailer and she as a girl singularly unlucky in her choice of men. This tale of a waif forced into prostitution has the same source as Max Ophüls's* La Ronde; *and is mainly notable for the work of Miss Nielsen, a great Danish actress who was the cinema's first international star.*

Conrad Veidt and the hands of Orlac: Orlacs Hände *(24) is the first of several versions of this gruesome tale, in which a pianist suspects that his new hands (grafted on after an accident) belonged to a murderer.*

of Schiller, *Carlos und Elisabeth* (24), also briefly playing his grandfather.

He was a fantasy Ivan the Terrible in one episode of Leni's *Das Wachsfigurenkabinett* and the afflicted pianist in another evocation of the supernatural, *Orlacs Hände*, made in Austria by Robert Wiene; and after *Nju* and *Schicksal* he went to France to play the title-role in *Le Conte Kostia* (25) and to Sweden to do Molander's version of part of Selma Lagerlof's 'Jerusalem', *Ingmarsarvet/Ingmar's Inheritance*, as a wandering priest whose hold over the villagers is considered malign by the hero (Lars Hanson). He played this with his usual wild-eyed intensity on the theory that that was what he had done in *Caligari*, bringing him international recognition. He was to allow more variety over the next few years: *Liebe Macht Blind*, a marital comedy with Lil Dagover; *Der Geiger von Florenz* (26), in a small role as Elisabeth Bergner's father, pursuing her to Italy whither he has gone, disguised as a boy; *Die Brüder Schellenberg*, as both brothers – as financier-playboy he ruins Liane Haid, but as bearded philanthropist he saves her; *Durfen Wir Schweigen?*, Oswald's return to the sex-film genre; *Kreuzzug des Weibes*, which was similar, as the Prosecutor; and *Der Student von Prag*, given unlimited wealth in return for his soul – a film which first made him famous outside Germany and which was to overshadow all his later work. In Italy he did a co-production with Austria, *Die Lebende Maske/Enrico IV*, a version of Pirandello's play directed by Amleto Palmeri and called in Germany *Die Flucht in die Nacht*.

Veidt's association with 'demoniacal' roles led to an offer from Universal, still smarting

from having let Lon Chaney get away: they signed him for four films and promptly loaned him to UA to play Louis XI to John Barrymore's Villon, *The Beloved Rogue* (27), before starring him in three melodramas: *A Man's Past*; *The Man Who Laughs* (28), in the title-role, a man whose face is permanently scarred, directed by Paul Leni from Hugo's historical romp; and *The Last Performance* (29), directed by Paul Fejos, as Erik the Great (its British title), a stage magician with a devilish murder plan. None of them was very successful and Veidt's accent, at this stage, precluded a Hollywood career. He returned to Germany to make his first Talkie, *Das Land Ohne Freuen*, a 19th-century adventure set in Australia; and he played a Prussian officer in a relentlessly grim anti-war fable (the war was one of Napoleon's), *Die Letzte Kompanie* (30), and in the English version, *The Last Company* (GB)/*Thirteen Men and a Girl*. He played himself, with other stars, in a musical set in a film studio, *Die Grosse Sehnsucht*; and in Britain starred in Dupont's *Menschen im Kafig* (31), the German version of *Cape Forlorn*, in Ian Hunter's role – the shipwrecked thief who steals the lighthouse-keeper's wife. In Germany he made: *Der Mann der den Mord Beging*, in the title-role, as a French attaché in Istanbul who murders the vile husband of his British mistress; *Die Nacht der Entscheidung* for Paramount, a version of *The Virtuous Sin*; *Der Kongress Tanzt/Congress Dances*, a hugely successful musical for Ufa in all three versions (the other was French), as Metternich, stealing the film from his co-stars, Willy Fritsch (the Czar) and Lilian Harvey (a shop-girl); *Die Andere Seite*, as Stanhope in this version of 'Journey's End'; *Rasputin*, in the title-role; and *Die Schwarze Husar* (32), another romance of Napoleonic times. Also for Ufa he was in *F.P.I.*, the English version of a science-fiction thriller, in Hans Albers's role of a self-sacrificing reprobate, and in a musical with Harvey, *Ich und die Kaiserin*, as a Marquis (played in the English version by Charles Boyer).

The anarchic – not to say decadent – nature of many of these roles did not endear Veidt to the Nazi Government and he accepted an offer from Gaumont British to play a master-crook in *Rome Express*, with Esther Ralston, considered by both 'Picturegoer' and 'Variety' the best British film made till that time; and he remained in Britain to play *The Wandering Jew*, homeless through 2,000 years, a wheezy old melodrama that Matheson Lang had done to death in innumerable tours; and then he was – prophetically – a German commandant, being mean to Madeleine Carroll in *I Was a Spy* (33). He went to Germany to be even meaner to *Wilhelm Tell* (34) and the Nazis held him because his next film was announced as *Jew Süss*, under a new contract wth GB (signed partly because his new, third, wife was half-Jewish); they claimed that he was too ill to travel, but after GB had sent over their doctors, let him go rather than cause an international incident. The film was an expensive version of Feuchtwanger's novel about Jews in 18th-century Germany and specifically of the one (Veidt) who achieves renown by his financial genius. Veidt, brilliantly miscast – as ever, an outsider – is no match for Ferdinand Marion in the later Nazi distortion of the same tale and the film is in no way distinguished; nor was there any kind reaction to another venerable property, *Bella Donna*, one of several versions and probably the worst, with Mary Ellis as the fatal lady, or to *The Passing of the Third Floor Back* (35), from Jerome K. Jerome's popular stage thriller; he was, of course, the mystical stranger who is probably Christ. He was the *King of the Damned* (36), a rebel convict, with Hollywood's Helen Vinson; and was stylish but unlikeable in one of his few purely heroic roles as the emissary of Richelieu (Raymond Massey) in *Under the*

Conrad Veidt was probably the most likeable German actor who worked extensively outside his own country, even if some of his performances weren't: but his Metternich in Congress Dances *(31) was in every way admirable.*

International intrigue in Casablanca *(42): Veidt as a German officer and Claude Rains, warily, a Free Frenchman.*

Red Robe (37), directed by Sjöstrom from Stanley J. Weyman's swashbuckling novel. He was not, in fact, a popular star – colleagues adored him, for he was not afflicted with the egotism common to most German actors, but he had trouble with Korda, who had picked up his contract after GB had dropped him. For his role as the mysterious aristocrat in *Dark Journey* he had billed him under Vivien Leigh. Veidt's contractual agreement caused him to demand the change, but reputedly he never spoke to Korda again. He did work for him again, for Korda appreciated that Veidt was an international name, as he proved by accepting two star offers in France: *Tempête sur l'Asie* (38), directed from the Russian classic by his old guiding hand, Oswald; and *Le Joueur d'Echecs*, another remake, as another outsider, the Austrian maker of life-size puppets at the court of Catherine the Great (Françoise Rosay). Back in Britain, he did two spy-plotty movies directed by Michael Powell with Valerie Hobson, *The Spy in Black* (39), as a German captain in the Hebrides, and *Contraband* (40), on the other side, as a Danish captain thwarting Nazi spies in London.

With the outbreak of war he had announced that he would remain in Britain, but it was a British producer, Alexander Korda, who demanded his presence in Hollywood, for, because of the war, *The Thief of Bagdad* had been abandoned: started again in the US, Veidt was needed to complete his role as the wicked Grand Vizier – and thank goodness, for the film is one of the most magical of all movies. There were special negotiations with the British Government because travel was restricted: Veidt – who had become a British citizen in 1939 – gratefully gave much of his subsequent fees to British war relief (more, according to W.H. Mooring in 'Picturegoer', than most British stars there) – all of his salary for *Escape* went to that source. In that, he was Countess Norma Shearer's menacing Nazi lover and under contract to MGM but losing his star status, there were similar roles to be had: as Joan Crawford's protector in *A Woman's Face* (41), directed by Cukor, who found him 'absolutely charming to work with . . . really gay and funny'; as a gang leader trying to kill off Red Skelton in *Whistling in the Dark*; as Loretta Young's dancing master in *The Men in Her Life* – an artificial performance; as a Nazi agent in New York foiled by Humphrey Bogart in *All Through the Night* (42); as the *Nazi Agent* and his twin brother, a meek bookseller, starring in this phoney B; and as a Gestapo man in both *Casablanca* and back at MGM *Above Suspicion* (43). Warners paid MGM $25,000 (the same fee as Ingrid Bergman) for Veidt's

services in what must now be his most famous film. He died of a heart attack after completing the second film, in 1943.

ERICH VON STROHEIM

'The Man You Love to Hate.' Erich von Stroheim's tag is remembered and his appearance, through countless stills, must be familiar even to those who have not seen him: bull-headed, close-cropped, dark eyes gleaming, sometimes monocled, in a pudgy face; immaculately uniformed in the panoply of a Prussian hussar or a Viennese musical comedy star – helmets, caps, epaulettes, with silk gloves, boots or gaiters, gleamingly polished; brandishing the ultra-long cigarettes or cigarette-holder, the cane or riding whip – an insistence on detail with a consistency which suggests fetishism. He was an adventurer, a tyrant, a parvenu: as with his clothes, there was an element of personal predilection in the parts he played. He was a strong actor, a superb villain – he seldom played anything else – a bizarre and fascinating figure. His work as a director has been much chronicled and the Silent pictures he made are accepted classics, rich, entirely personal and engrossing. Like Orson Welles he failed to meet Hollywood on its own terms: a great directorial talent went to waste and he enlivened a series of mainly poor pictures with his acting.

He was born in Vienna in 1885, the son of a Prussian dealer in felt, feathers and straw, and a Czech mother, both Jewish. His official Hollywood biographies insisted that he was of Austrian aristocratic origins with a distinguished military record – and such he led people to believe not long after emigrating to the US in 1906; he also claimed to have had a play produced – he had certainly written one. He married, in San Francisco in 1912, but his drinking and his rages soon ended that. Some of his early life in his adopted home remains mysterious. He wrapped packages, waited on table and was a tourist guide and horse handler at Lake Tahoe when he decided that his expertise with these animals might be employed in the new medium, films.

His first screen work appears to have been a bit part in *Captain McLean* (14), which starred Lillian Gish, and he had further bits in *Ghosts* (15), in which Henry B. Walthall played the dual role of Captain Alving and Oswald, and *The Failure*, which starred John Emerson. These brought him into the orbit of D.W. Griffith and von Stroheim attached himself to his company, though in less important status than he later claimed. He had his first real part as the villain in a short, *Farewell to Thee*, and may have appeared in Griffith's *The Birth of a Nation* in a minute role. When Emerson directed *Old Heidelberg* (from the play on which 'The Student Prince' is based), von Stroheim claimed to have studied at the university in that city and was appointed technical advisor; he also played the Prince's valet, in a costume doubtless of his own devising. He married for the second time and under Emerson's direction had small roles in *His Picture in the Papers* (16) with Douglas Fairbanks, as a member of a gang, *The Social Secretary*, as a reporter, and *The Flying Torpedo*. He assisted Emerson on the production of *Macbeth*, starring Sir Herbert Beerbohm Tree and Constance Collier, and was one of the assistant directors on *Intolerance*, with a brief appearance as a pharisee, billed as Count von Stroheim. He returned to Emerson for a Mary Pickford vehicle, *Less Than the Dust*, and when Emerson was between pictures played a Russian officer in *Panthea* (17) with Norma Talmadge. Moving to Fairbanks' new company with Emerson, he had small roles in *In Again Out Again, Wild and Woolly* and *Reaching for the Moon*, but was dropped because of his Germanic name.

That proved to be a blessing as other studios wanted him to play horrible huns in their war stories, in more extended roles than he had done till now: *For France* with Betty Howe, *Sylvia of the Secret Service* with Irene Castle, *Draft 258* (18), *The Unbeliever, Hearts of the World* and *The Hun Within* with Dorothy Gish. He had expected one of the leading roles in *Hearts of the World* when Griffith had sent for him, but he had to wait till Universal approached him for a 'superproduction', *The Heart of Humanity* (19), which was, however, little more than an imitation. In one scene he is trying to rape a nurse, ripping off her clothes with his teeth; a crying baby disturbs him, so he throws it out of the window. This made him famous, but an entry in the 'Motion Picture Almanac' noted, 'when war was over he was inactive for nine months due to dearth of war pictures'. But he had an entrée at Universal and a script, possibly based on his experiences at Lake Tahoe; he offered his services as director and star, promising that the film could be done for the lowly sum of $25,000 – which was attractive to this studio, which after some early successes did little but churn out programme pictures. *Blind Husbands* was set in the Tyrol and there were three main characters: an austere surgeon and his bored young wife and an army lieutenant, ostentatiously well-groomed. It is the habit of the officer to seduce whatever serving maid happens to be handy, but he turns his attention to the wife – until foiled by a mountain guide and later punished by the

husband. The climax in particular is preposterous, but its realism was much admired. Universal were delighted with the results, both critical and commercial, and von Stroheim made for them a similar story, *The Devil's Passkey* (20), in which he did not appear.

He had a new wife and a new contract, paying him $800 per week as a director and a further $400 as an actor, to be augmented at six-monthly intervals. He directed and wrote *Foolish Wives* (21), as well as playing its central character, a bogus (uniformed) Count. Again there is an American couple who are to be sundered by his old-world morals – the Ambassador to Monaco and his wife: just as the film is both a condemnation and glorification of frivolous Riviera society, so it remains ambiguous as to the effect of these 'morals' on those encountering them. In the film many people do: almost every woman who crosses the screen is seduced and one poor soul who proves unwilling gets summarily raped. There is also a snide hint that his female accomplices, 'cousins' and 'maid', are not carnally unknown to him. Von Stroheim brought to the part, said Lotte Eisner, 'a ferocious irony, a kind of sub-conscious love-hate'. The film was originally very long because von Stroheim wanted to eliminate any supporting programme; but Universal disagreed and cut it by one-third. Its budget had been much publicized and Universal, now regarding itself as a major studio, because of von Stroheim, demanded increased rentals. There was some controversy over the film's morality, a little over its merits, but one thing was clear: it would not return its negative cost.

The battles of von Stroheim vs studio chiefs had begun and at Universal Irving Thalberg hoped to curb his extravagance by refusing to let him play the lead in *Merry-Go-Round*: as doubts about the budget and story mounted von Stroheim was replaced with only one-third of the film shot. He moved to the Goldwyn Company and made *Greed* (23), directing only, and again its great length was reduced despite his appeals. This same Goldwyn Co. became part of MGM and Thalberg joined it as producer. It was therefore somewhat surprising when von Stroheim was invited to direct *The Merry Widow* (25) at that studio: he worked with his own crew and it was a von Stroheim picture rather than the intended vehicle for John Gilbert and Mae Murray, or even a transcription of the stage success. Again there were erotic scenes which could not be used and although he completed the filming his contract was cancelled five weeks later.

The film's enthusiastic reception meant that he would not be workless yet and Pat Powers, producer of poverty row Westerns, agreed to back *The Wedding March* (28) after a social encounter. Von Stroheim was to play the lead, Prince Nicki, an officer torn between the girl he loves (Fay Wray) and the cripple he is forced by parental decree to marry (Zazu Pitts). His screen character was now softened and humanized; it could not be called sympathetic, but the rapes, if not the seductions, were left to others. The obligatory orgy sequence went to the fathers of the bride and groom, getting drunker and drunker on the floor of a brothel. Again von Stroheim filmed lengthily while Powers watched cautiously, but he had to bring in Paramount to share the financial burden. It had become a two-part film which the company, in any case, did not want. With one sequence left to shoot the film was closed down. Part One was released, cut, simply as *The Wedding March*; Part Two was released, mutilated, as *The Honeymoon*, but only in Europe: before he died von Stroheim re-cut both parts – the copies possessed by the Cinematheque Français, but Part Two was subsequently destroyed in a fire. No other copy exists (nor, it seems, does any archive have a copy of *The Devil's Passkey*).

Powers had von Stroheim under contract for another picture, which he had no intention of making. Von Stroheim worked, uncredited, on the script of *The Tempest*, in which John Barrymore is a military man much in the von Stroheim manner. Gloria Swanson decided at this point that she wanted him to be her next director and negotiated with Powers to take over the contract but *Queen Kelly* too was closed down in mid-production

Von Stroheim as The Great Gabbo *(29). Even as a ventriloquist he got into uniform.*

and with it went his last chance, for the moment, of directing. He was only to find employment as an actor.

A deep, sonorous, sad voice could have made him an asset in Talkies, especially as the public remembered him as the man they loved to hate: but *The Great Gabbo* (29) was a mistake. It gave von Stroheim a memorable role as a ventriloquist who goes mad after being rejected by his former assistant (because she had married) and it was directed by James Cruze, who said: 'He never enters a room; he makes an entrance.' But Cruze had also been one of the most acclaimed directors and the industry noted that the film was technically crude and made for poverty row's Sono Art. Von Stroheim was, however, offered a leading role at Warners, as a butler in the second of three film versions of *Three Faces East* (30), until unmasked by Constance Bennett as a German spy. Universal, in a change of policy, decided to make some large-budget films and von Stroheim was engaged to remake *Merry-Go-Round* and then, in a change of plan, *Blind Husbands*: but when that too was cancelled he returned to acting. He took Lily Damita from Adolphe Menjou and Laurence Olivier in *Friends and Lovers* (31) at RKO, who kept him on to play a fanatical film director in *The Lost Squadron* (32), a man who knowingly sent men to their deaths for the shots he needed for his 'flying' film. Von Stroheim played it with no apparent sense of self-parody, but from all accounts the character was not unlike him, in its mirthless sarcasm, its rages and its senseless extravagance (e.g. all the soldiers in *The Merry Widow* had been dressed in silk underwear that was never seen). In *As You Desire Me* he was Garbo's protector, exerting a hypnotic influence over her.

He had already been given another chance to direct, by Fox: *Walking Down Broadway*. It was done on a reasonable budget, but was never released, and indeed was largely re-shot by Alfred Werker. Seen today, the reworked version, *Hello Sister!*, has much *echt* von Stroheim, especially in the sleazy, cheap erotic sequences, making one speculate on what was eliminated. It has been claimed that the fate of the film was decided by a studio feud at executive level, but the débâcle spelt finis to von Stroheim's career as a director. He acted again, in a couple of cheap independent films: *Crimson Romance* (34) with Ben Lyon, and *Fugitive Road* with Leslie Fenton. On both he was military adviser and he advised at MGM on *Anna Karenina*. He acted in Republic's *The Crime of Dr Crespi* (35), based on Poe's 'The Premature Burial', and worked at MGM on stories and screenplays. He reputedly cabled Eisenstein for a job in 1935 and although there was a possibility that MGM might have let him direct again, again entirely on their terms, a series of chances opened up an acting career in Europe.

There was an invitation from France to play a crack Prussian officer, implacable opponent of Edwige Feuillère as *Marthe Richard Au Service de la France* (37), and he was invited by Renoir to play one of two similar roles in *La Grande Illusion*: he suggested combining the two and thus the friendly German officer later turns up as prison camp commandant, sympathizing with fellow aristocrat Pierre Fresnay. Dita Parlo was in the cast and she recommended him for a leading role in *Mademoiselle Docteur*: she had just done this espionage story in French and its success encouraged its producer, Max Schach, to remake it in English. Von Stroheim had the role done by Louis Jouvet in Pabst's French version: this much inferior one was directed by Edmond T. Greville.

Jouvet and von Stroheim were matched in Pierre Chenal's *L'Alibi*, the former as a detective and von Stroheim as his prey, an illusionist in a cabaret. He worked almost non-stop, often with top-billing: Christian-Jacque's *Les Pirates de Rail*, as a Chinaman in this drama set in China; Chenal's *L'Affaire Lafarge*, based on a famous poisoning case, as the partner of the dead man (Pierre Renoir), making trouble for the widow who so justifiably killed him; and Christian-Jaque's good thriller with a school setting, *Les Disparus de St Agil*. In that, as a kindly modern languages professor he helped to solve the mystery of the secret tunnel behind the sliding blackboard. In June 1938 it was announced that he would direct and star in *La Couronne de Feu*, but nothing came of this. He did instead two espionage dramas, *Ultimatum*, directed by Robert Weine, with Parlo, as a Serbian general, announcing the 1914 declaration of war with sadness; and *Gibraltar*, with Viviane Romance, as the boss of a beauty parlour. Neither was distinguished. Nor were: *Derrière la Façade* (39), as a mysterious stranger, one of an apartment building being investigated by the police after a murder; *Macao Enfer de Jeu*, as an arms trafficker during the Sino-Japanese war; *Rappel Immédiat*, as an American diplomat trying to make peace in Europe while his film star wife has an affair in Paris; and *Le Monde Tremblera*, with Claude Dauphin and Madeleine Sologne. According to Thomas Quinn Curtiss, his salary was $1,000 a day – doubtless paid with the daily whisky bottle also called for contractually and needed to get through the day. Charles Spaak once observed that that was why French producers refused to trust him with direction.

His comparatively huge fee usually meant that producers tried to economize elsewhere, so that von Stroheim's huge popularity after his arrival was being eroded by cheap films. His fee for *Coups de Feu* was to be $10,000 – presumably for 10 days' work – with an advance of $3,000 and the right to 'modify' the scenario. The producers considered his changes too radical and refused them. He refused to do the film and sued. They countersued for their advance and von Stroheim lost. (The film was made with Aimé Clairiond in his role.)

He was in a good film, *Pièges*, a thriller with Maurice Chevalier, as a genial megalomaniac couturier; and then in *Tempête sur Paris* (40), as a master swindler blackmailed by Arletty; *Menaces*, a study of life in a small Paris hotel between September 1938 and September 1939, as a pitiable professor, hiding his scars behind a mask; and *Paris–New York*, a tale set (and filmed) aboard the 'Normandie', with Gaby Morlay, Michel Simon and others. Also in the cast was Denise Vernac, a journalist; he persuaded her to give up journalism for acting. She became his collaborator, mistress and, later, wife. War had broken out. One casualty was *La Dame Blanche*, which he was to have co-directed with Renoir, a return to his opulent Ruritanian dramas of the 20s, with roles for himself and Jouvet.

Filming in Europe had become difficult and he was surprised and delighted to be offered a role in Hollywood, the elegant impostor-villain in *I Was an Adventuress* (40), 20th's remake of a French film similarly titled, with Vera Zorina inadequate in the part played by Feuillère; and *So Ends Our Night* (41), expectedly, as the Hun pursuing the Jewish refugees. For the next year or so he was occupied with the part of Jonathan Brewster in a tour of 'Arsenic and Old Lace', but he returned to films with a good one, Wilder's *Five Graves to Cairo* (43): he played Rommel and though he was like him neither physically nor in any other way, was so powerful that it hardly seemed to matter and within the limitations of his acting style, it was an excellent performance. He was in Goldwyn's *The North Star*, as a Nazi medical officer using Ukrainian peasants for his scientific experiments, but his subsequent American films were another matter. He did a quartet at Republic to pay his medical bills after a serious illness: *The Lady and the Monster* (44), adapted from Curt Siodmak's 'Donovan's Brain'; *Storm Over Lisbon*, about a nightclub bursting with spies, again with Richard Arlen; *The Great Flammarion* (45), as a vaudeville sharpshooter who murders his wanton assistant Mary Beth Hughes; and *Scotland Yard Investigator* with C. Aubrey Smith. He did Lew Landers's *The Mask of*

Peter Van Eyck, Anne Baxter and von Stroheim, as Rommel, in Billy Wilder's Five Graves to Cairo *(43). Wilder has recalled that when he told von Stroheim that his films were ten years before their time, von Stroheim confidently corrected him: 'Twenty'.*

Dijon (46) with Vernac, then wisely returned to France.

But again, it was mostly formula stuff: Chenal's *La Foire aux Chimères*, as a scarred man in love with Madeleine Sologne, who was blind; *On ne Meurt pas Comme Ca!* with Vernac, again as a film director; *La Danse de Mort* (47), Strindberg's bitter play which he helped adapt and script, with Vernac as the wife and himself as an Austrian officer, made in Rome; *Le Signal Rouge* (48) made in Vienna, as a mad country doctor who at night tries to derail the train which killed his wife; and *Portrait d'un Assassin* (49). It was Wilder who recalled him to Hollywood for *Sunset Boulevard* (50), his best film by far since his last Wilder film; he was Gloria Swanson's valet-butler. He was full of suggestions for typical von Stroheim touches, some of which Wilder used. The rest of his films were made in Europe: the remake of *Alraune* (52) with Hildegarde Neff, in Germany, in the part played in the earlier versions by Paul Wegener and Albert Basserman; *Minuit Quai de Bercy* (53) with Madeleine Robinson, as a self-styled evangelist; *L'Envers du Paradis* (54) with Vernac, as an alcoholic sea-captain; *Alerte au Sud* with Jean-Claude Pascal, as a half-mad German general who has refused to acknowledge that the war is over; Sacha Guitry's all-star *Napoléon* as Beethoven; *Série Noire* (55) with Robert Hossein; and *La Madone des Sleepings* (55) with Gisele Pascal. He was

awarded the Légion d'Honneur not long before he died in 1957.

ANTON WALBROOK

Anton Walbrook was an actor of authority, style and persuasive Continental charm and, in life, an overweening egotism; after a successful career in Germany playing the Viennese equivalent of a *boulevardier* he settled in Britain – and those certain faults in his character prevented his later career from being more prolific. He was born in Vienna in 1900, into a circus family – they had been clowns for 300 years. He preferred the legitimate stage and won a scholarship to the Max Reinhardt school in Berlin. He went on the stage at 20 and acted in Vienna, Dresden and Munich – in Ibsen, Molnar, Capek, Shakespeare, etc. He appeared in a small role in *Der Fluch der Bösen Tat* (25) and it was after establishing himself as a matinee idol that E.A. Dupont chose him to play the lead opposite Anna Sten in *Salto Mortale* (31), which, coincidentally, was about circus life; *Der Stolz der Drei Kompanie* was a comedy about army life (which the Nazis later banned), and Heinz Rühmann was his fellow soldier. He, Fritz Kampers and Paul Kemp were the *Drei von der Stempelstelle* (32), one of the many imitative – of *Drei von der*

Tankstelle – comedies on coping with the Depression; he was the hero of *Die Fünf Verfluchten Gentlemen*, an adventure in Morocco with Camilla Horn, directed by Julien Duvivier (simultaneously with *Les Cinq Gentlemen Maudits*); but had only a supporting role in a Richard Tauber musical, *Melodie der Liebe. Baby* was also made in French and German, and Walbrook was in the latter version only: it was a farce about a young actress, Anny Ondra, and one of the many films in which she was directed by her husband, Carl Lamac. Things did not go too well, for Walbrook was only one of several men hovering around Renate Müller in two musicals: Ludwig Berger's *Walzerkrieg* (33), a highly popular film about the rivalry between Lanner (Paul Hörbiger) and Strauss (Walbrook), with Willy Fritsch as his best friend; and *Viktor und Viktoria*, as the English gentleman who falls for the girl who is impersonating the female impersonator – a role he also played in the French version, *Georges et Georgette* (there was a later British version, with Jessie Matthews, *First a Girl*).

He was leading man to Liane Haid in *Keine Angst vor Liebe*, his third consecutive musical, and to Ondra in *Die Vertauschte Braut* (34), a crazy comedy; but then, in his native Vienna, he did *Maskerade*, which put him in the forefront of German stars and made him known throughout the world. It was the usual tale of intrigue in the ballrooms and opera houses, specifically about an artist who compromises a girl to hide another's indiscretion (posing in the nude), and what made it memorable were Walbrook and Paula Wessely – especially he as the roué, haughty as an amorist and then touchingly human as the man in love. And he had perfected that elegance of manner and appearance which he thereafter seemed unwilling to throw off – and which could be seen again almost immediately in three stories vying for the same romanticism: *Die Englische Heirat*, a comedy with Müller; *Eine Frau die Weiss Was Sie Will*, a musical with Lil Dagover as an actress and he as her daughter's suitor; and Erich Waschneck's beautiful *Regine* (35), with Luise Ullrich. He played the title-role in *Zigeunerbaron/Le Baron Tzigane*, an exiled heir living with the gypsies, and for a change did a crime story, *Ich War Jack Mortimer*, and the title-role in *Der Student von Prag*, directed by Arthur Robinson, a student somewhat less tortured than Paul Wegener and Conrad

When in the 30s, the world fell in love with a film from Europe, it was usually romantic and very, very sad: Anton Walbrook and Paula Wessely in Maskerade *(34) – which Hollywood remade as* Escapade.

Veidt in earlier versions. He was *Michel Strogoff/Der Kurier des Zaren* (36), Jules Verne's tale of Tartar times, before rejoining Müller and Willi Forst in his director's hat for a comedy, *Allotria*: but Forst was a rotten director, his work on *Maskerade* a one-time-thing. In Czechoslovakia Walbrook was a Russian in love with Japanese Danielle Darrieux in the French-German *Port-Arthur* (which is in China); and he was thinking of settling in Britain.

Like many of his colleagues he disliked working under the Nazis and negotiated a contract with Gaumont British: but that was sold to RKO, who had also purchased some of the spectacular footage from *Strogoff* for their own version. They decided that that should kick off Walbrook's American career – after rechristening him, from Adolf Wöhlbruck – with a remake, now called *The Soldier and the Lady* (37), the lady being Fay Bainter as his mother. This time he merely walked through his part, but 'Photoplay' called him 'magnificent'. The compliment was not reciprocated: Walbrook loathed Hollywood and returned to Britain, where Herbert Wilcox was looking for a Prince Albert to marry *Victoria the Great* – a miscast Anna Neagle. His interpretation, said Agate, of gentleman as well as Prince, indicated that on meeting the lady he might well have returned to Germany muttering the German equivalent of 'baggage'. However, Wilcox was happy and

put him into a remake of Ivor Novello's Silent vehicle, *The Rat*, as a Paris apache involved with ritzy Ruth Chatterton, and then Albertized him again for *Sixty Glorious Years* (38) – where he again evinced disinterest in doing remakes.

Charming to his friends, but professionally reserved, his career faltered by his refusal to compromise; the British film industry in return tended to be reserved towards Continental actors. He was regarded as 'difficult', but his integrity refused to allow him to play the roles offered of Nazi officers (and much later he refused an offer to star in Germany because he regarded the proposed leading lady as a friend of Goebbels). He made his British stage début in 1939 in the first presentation there of 'Design for Living', with Rex Harrison and Diana Wynyard, and with that lady he made *Gaslight* (40), Thorold Dickinson's much-praised version of the stage melodrama, as an Edwardian husband who tries to drive his wife mad in order to pick up her fortune (the film was not seen for a while after MGM bought the remake rights). His next was his biggest success: *Dangerous Moonlight* (41), which introduced the 'Warsaw Concerto'. That was the reason: there was little else to be recommended in this tale of a Polish pianist-cum-fighter pilot. Walbrook's lion-like but soulful presence was admirable, as he was as the leader of the religious community in *49th Parallel*, made by Powell

The Courtship of Queen Victoria: Anton Walbrook as Albert and Anna Neagle as Victoria the Great *(37). Walbrook's performance suggested that Albert married beneath him.*

and Pressburger – who used him again as Roger Livesey's German friend in *The Life and Death of Colonel Blimp* (43). He played a Czech resistance leader in *The Man from Morocco* (45), but its reception proved that he was hardly a name to conjure with at the box-office.

He became a British citizen in 1947 and was used by Powell and Pressburger as the dominating impresario of *The Red Shoes* (48), an expensive project dedicated to The Dance. Rank financed, but when the makers overstepped the budget there was a tentative move to sell the thing to Korda. The film went on to be a huge money-maker and took more money than any other foreign film in the US until then. It was the first intelligent attempt to portray the world of the ballet and it had assets in Sadler's Wells dancer Moira Shearer and names such as Massine and Helpmann: but as a film it was pretty poor stuff. Walbrook followed it with the less successful *The Queen of Spades* (49), as the guardsman seeking to wrest the secret of the cards from the old Countess (Edith Evans); and then was off the screen till Max Ophüls's *La Ronde* (50), playing the elegant master of ceremonies. This gave his career a new lease of life in Britain, but meanwhile in Austria he starred in *Wien Tanzt* (51), a musical about the Strauss family, as Johann the Elder; returning to the London stage in 1952 in 'Call Me Madam'. A while later he was in another, lesser, musical, 'Wedding in Paris'; and in a French picture with Madeleine Robinson, *L'Affaire Maurizius* (54), directed by Julien Duvivier, as the Svengali-like friend of Daniel Gelin.

He made two more films, one execrable and one of quality. The bad one was *Oh Rosalinda!!* (55) made by Powell and Pressburger. After *Red Shoes* they had attempted the even more ambitious *Tales of Hoffman*, again with Shearer – but it was a box-office failure; they attempted to renew faith in their 'class' musicals by this modernized version of 'Die Fledermaus' – Walbrook had that part and was the only good thing in it, but, warned by the press, the public stayed away in millions. The good one was Max Ophüls's *Lola Montés* (Martine Carol), a typical dramatic action based loosely on that loose lady's life: the unusual narrative form caused difficulties with both distributors and public when it came out, but its status as a 'classic' grew and it was accepted as such on a highly successful New York showing in 1969. It was made in Munich, in French, German and English versions; in Austria, Walbrook played in *Köning für eine Nacht* (56), and in Britain he was Cauchon in *Saint Joan* (57), making him a fair man with the instincts of a fox, or vice-versa, and

Esterhazy in *I Accuse* (58), easily taking the latter from Emlyn Williams (Zola) and José Ferrer (Dreyfus). He did a couple more plays in London, but increasingly found it easier to get work on the Continent and was virtually forgotten by his adopted country when he died in Munich in 1967. His friend of some years standing killed himself shortly after his death.

JOHN WAYNE

Future historians of the art of the film will probably pause at the name of John Wayne only because he appeared in some of John Ford's best Westerns; but it is a name which gives pause to everyone interested in the industry. 'Time' in 1967 said he was 'the greatest moneymaker in movie history: the gross comes to nearly $400 million'; he probably earned more than any other movie actor during a long and always rising career. His popularity was consistent: during the 23-year period 1949–72 there was only one year (58) when he was not one of the USA's 10 top draws; there were five occasions (50, 51, 54, 69, 71) when he was No. 1 and another three when he was No. 2 (56, 57, 63). 1971 was his 22nd year in the 'Motion Picture Herald' list (the runners-up were Gary Cooper – 18 times, Clark Gable 16 times). The British rated him less highly, but as late as 1968 he headed the list of top box-office stars in that country. In 1968, too, a poll was taken among US TV viewers to find out the most popular artists on TV, including stars in films: Wayne headed the list (followed by some more film stars: (2) Bob Hope, (3) Spencer Tracy, (4) Clark Gable and at No. 8 Gary Cooper and Sydney Poitier tying with some TV performers).

It is true that actors in action pictures hold their public easily. Wayne's audiences are generally less discriminating than Brando's (there was even an audience for a poor Wayne vehicle, whereas a poor Brando picture would sink without trace). It is significant that the one year he was not in the top 10 was the year he had only one film, and it was a 'straight' one – and a disaster. Yet he offers much more than a 'ride 'em cowboy' image. To justify himself in 1951 he commented: 'Success in films has little to do with acting', and 10 years later he was saying: 'Sometimes I wonder about my career. I don't do much really, I suppose. Just sell sincerity. And I've been selling the hell out of it ever since I got going.' In fact, his hallmark is integrity rather than sincerity. He is never mean and dirty (like Bogart) or possessed of doubts (like Cooper): he is the idealized American, representing, as one writer had it, 'the indomitable spirit which

making ends meet. Wayne entered the University of Southern California on a football scholarship and a USC coach through an old friend (Tom Mix) got him a job in the property department at Fox. He decorated the sets of Ford's *Mother Machree* (28) and thus began a life-long association with the director. Ford gave him a bit as a goose-herder in that and made him a racetrack spectator in *Hangman's House*; then used him and another USC football player, Ward Bond, in a football game in *Salute* (29). He had a bit in Ford's *Men Without Women* (30) and another in *Rough Romance*; then Ford recommended him to Raoul Walsh for *The Big Trail*, which had a big budget – it eventually reached a huge $4 million – that did not encompass a star name. Thus Wayne was the leader of the wagons-west, wise, experienced, a loner, friend of the Cheyenne, the sort of role which would be his indelibly. But not yet. The film had been shot in both wide- and standard-screen, and Wayne himself felt that Fox's temerity in pushing the wide-screen version was the reason for its failure. In fact, apart from one sequence of lowering the wagon train down a precipice it is a dull thing. After *Girls Demand Excitement* (31), a college comedy, and *Three Girls Lost* opposite Loretta Young, Fox dropped him.

Columbia signed him to a five-year contract, starting at $350 a week, and put him into *Men Are Like That*, in which Laura La Plante takes revenge on a lover. He lost co-starring status and believed that he was relegated to supporting roles for making a pass at one of Harry Cohn's girlfriends. 'You're a money actor, Duke,' Cohn told him, but 'keep your fly buttoned up', and he proceeded to humiliate him by putting him in support of Buck Jones in *Range Feud* and Jack Holt in *Maker of Men*, in the latter as a dishonest football player. Wayne never forgave him and when he regained stardom never worked for Columbia. Almost 20 years later Cohn bought *The Gunfighter*, a script that he knew Wayne liked, but Wayne refused to do it (20th made it with Gregory Peck). Hollywood noted that the much-promoted star of *The Big Trail* had been demoted, but knew that he could be effective in the saddle, so he became the lead in cheap, factory-line Westerns. For the next 10 years he was sovereign of the sagebrush at Saturday matinées, along with Hoot Gibson, Tim McCoy, Johnny Mack Brown, Tom Mix, Buck Jones, Gene Autrey, Bob Steele and others. There were so many that Wayne himself was unsure whether he made 200 or 400. Most of the lists differ, but here is one, with some other events. 1931: *Range Feud*, *Maker of Men*. 1932: *Hurricane Express* and *Shadow of the Eagle*, both serials for Mascot;

sent our forefathers Westward'. He is leathery, weather-beaten, tough and masculine: hard-drinking, impatient of men, polite towards women. The Galahad image was not harmed by the divorce allegations – cruelty, drunkenness – of his first wife, nor by his rabid right-wing politics. His frequently expressed admiration for Senator McCarthy indicated a stubborn and not uncommon mentality, but even his opponents granted him the courage of his convictions. Louis B. Mayer once summed him up: 'John Wayne has an endless face and he can go on forever.'

Wayne was born Marion Morrison in Winterset, Iowa, in 1907, the son of a druggist. For health reasons the family moved to California, where they had difficulties in

Lady and Gent, Two-Fisted Law. Columbia dropped him and he went to Warners. *Ride Him Cowboy, The Big Stampede*. 1933: *Haunted Gold, The Telegraph Trail, His Private Secretary, Central Airport* with Richard Barthelmess, *The Life of Jimmy Dolan* with Douglas Fairbanks Jr, *Baby Face* with Barbara Stanwyck, *The Man From Monterey, College Coach*. Wayne had made no impact in his small roles in the A pictures and he moved on to Monogram. *Riders of Destiny* as 'Singin' Sandy', though his song was dubbed. In this era of crooning cowboys he would sing in three more movies, in each case dubbed. *The Three Musketeers*, a Mascot serial, as a French legionnaire. 1934: *The Lucky Texan, West of the Divide, Texas Terror, Blue Steel, The Man From Utah, Randy Rides Alone, The Star Packer, The Trail Beyond* which was a cut above the others, *The Lawless Frontier, 'Neath the Arizona Skies*. 1935: *Rainbow Valley, Paradise Canyon, The Dawn Rider*. He left Monogram for Republic. *Westward Ho!, The New Frontier, Lawless Range*. 1936: *The Lawless Nineties, King of the Pecos, The Oregon Trail, Winds of the Wasteland, I Cover Chinatown, Sea Spoilers*, which is the first of six non-Western Bs contracted by Universal over the next year, *The Lonely Trail, Conflict*. 1937: *California Straight Ahead, Idol of the Crowds, Adventure's End*. 1938: *Born to the West* for Paramount. He returned to Republic for 'The Three Mesquiteers' series. *Overland Stage Raiders, Pals of the Saddle, Santa Fe Stampede, Red River Range*. 1939: *The Night Raiders, Wyoming Outlaw, Three Texas Steers, New Frontier*.

But his first film released that year was *Stagecoach*. Dudley Nichols's screenplay had been lying around Hollywood for a couple of years, partly because the concept of a high-budget Western had died in the Silent era; but Paramount had made some tentative steps to revive it. Walter Wanger produced this for United Artists with John Ford directing, his first Western for 13 years. When Gary Cooper turned down the lead he borrowed Wayne from Republic to join a cast of reliable but not star players: the role required little more of him than he usually did and, wisely, he did not have too much dialogue. Few people expected the opus to be the success it was and his name began to be known to more than the patrons of his Z Westerns. His teaming with Claire Trevor appealed to RKO, who reunited them to play spatting sweethearts in *Allegheny Uprising*, set during the last days of British rule: it was no *Stagecoach*, but its budget was bigger than Wayne had been wont to have.

Republic suddenly had a valuable property under contract. Since its foundation in 1935

that studio had had no aspirations above Bs (most of which turned out to be Ds and Es): now it stood to make a lot by loaning Wayne to other companies: he had signed a new five-year contract just before *Stagecoach* and was getting $200 a week; he was loaned to Paramount a year later for $1,500 weekly. And so as not to devalue him, his pictures for them had to be better: so *Dark Command* (40) was infused with a big budget (by Republic standards) and the borrowed talents of Trevor, Walter Pidgeon and director Walsh (Roy Rogers had a small role). It was a Civil War story; and was followed by *Three Faces West*, a heavy trek from the dustbowl country, with Charles Coburn and Sigrid Gurie joining Wayne as European refugees. Ford borrowed him again to play a seaman in *The Long Voyage Home*, a beautiful series of vignettes about the merchant marine taken from some plays by Eugene O'Neill, supporting Wilfred Lawson, Thomas Mitchell and Ward Bond. Universal borrowed him to play the nonchalant naval officer whom Dietrich falls for in *Seven Sinners* and he proved that in this particular sort of part – tough and humorous – he was unbeatable. In life they were reputed to be having an affair, but in her memoir almost 50 years later she described American actors as 'unpleasant people', citing Wayne in particular. With *A Man Betrayed* (41) co-starring Frances Dee and the period-piece *The Lady From Louisiana* (who was Ona Munson), Republic settled Wayne into a series of double-feature actioners.

The star of True Grit *meets the star of* Pandora's Box: *John Wayne (left) and Louise Brooks in* Overland Stage Raiders *(38). It was one of the 'Three Mesquiteers' pictures: Ray Corrigan (right) and Max Terhune (front) were the other two.*

After Stagecoach *Wayne became one of the most sought-after actors in Hollywood, and Universal borrowed him three times to co-star with Marlene Dietrich – for whose favours his rival in two of these films was Randolph Scott (left). This one is* The Spoilers *(42).*

Outside he did better. At Paramount Henry Hathaway teamed him with Betty Field in *The Shepherd of the Hills*, a tale of feuding in the Ozarks and considerably better than Republic's *Lady for a Night* (42), who was Joan Blondell. In *Reap the Wild Wind* he and Ray Milland scrapped over Paulette Goddard and in *The Spoilers* he and Randolph Scott fought over Dietrich; the first was in Technicolor and he got eaten by a squid. His agent renegotiated his Republic contract to reflect the demand from other studios, bringing him $100,000 per annum, including loan-outs. At Republic itself *In Old California* and *Flying Tigers* (in war-torn China) spewed out all the cliches of their respective genres, making Wayne eager to get back to Universal and *Pittsburgh* (43), the saga of two buddies with a friendship so great that only an exceptional vamp could break it up: Dietrich, with Scott again. The MGM accolade arrived in the form of a *Reunion in France* with Joan Crawford; he was an escaped flyer whom she hides from the Gestapo. At RKO he romanced Jean Arthur in *A Lady Takes a Chance*, while the best Republic could do was *In Old Oklahoma* with Martha Scott. Still, they were the first to get him into World War II, whose battles he was to continue to fight throughout his career. The film was *The Fighting Seabees* (44), with Susan Hayward frequently diverting him from duty. He was *Tall in the Saddle* for RKO, a programme Western, and Ann Dvorak was *The Flame of the Barbary Coast* (45); he was a Montana cattleman and with an effort they jerked it above the usual Republic level.

Hollywood noted that he even drew audiences to Republic pictures and now that he was free of that contract RKO signed him for one picture a year for six years, starting with *Back to Bataan*. He originally turned down *Dakota*, not wishing to co-star with the lovely Vera Hruba Ralston, the wife of Republic's president, Herbert Yates, till Yates promised a big-budget picture. Wayne had been around Hollywood too long to want a complete break and was still not certain of his status, though that was boosted by co-starring stints at MGM with Robert Montgomery and RKO with Claudette Colbert, respectively in Ford's fine war picture, *They Were Expendable*, and *Without Reservations* (46), a peripatetic comedy about a novelist who sees in him, a marine, the ideal hero for a film of her bestseller. Yates conceded Wayne producer status on *The Angel and the Badman* (47), a Western with Gail Russell that was not much liked. After *Tycoon* with Laraine Day, as a determined railroad builder, he was in three notable Westerns, Ford's *Fort Apache* (48) with Henry Fonda, a Civil War tale; Howard Hawks's *Red River*, Wayne's biggest commercial success to date; and Ford's *Three Godfathers*, the remake of an old fable about three escaping outlaws lumbered with a baby. It was for Ford enthusiasts only and did not do well.

Meanwhile, Yates did not care for the idea of paying Wayne his $150,000 salary on top of a million-dollar budget for the long-promised big film, so he offered Wayne a cut of profits in lieu of same – and from *The Wake of the Red Witch*, a sea story, again with Russell,

Wayne earned $750,000. Again, it was not much liked; but his six films with Ford at this period comprise his best work, proof of a sympathetic professional relationship but not (see below) a friendship. Ford's *She Wore a Yellow Ribbon* (49) was a Technicolor tribute to the US Cavalry and an exceptional film, his own favourite among his Westerns and Wayne's favourite role. *The Fighting Kentuckian* did not do well, despite the presence again of Vera Hruba Ralston, but her two films with Wayne were the only two she made to show up in black ink on the Republic ledgers. *Sands of Iwo Jima*, however, was a tremendous hit, though in fact a very ordinary war film. As the tough Sergeant Stryker, Wayne got his first Oscar nomination. There followed Ford's *Rio Grande* (50) and *Operation Pacific* (51), the first of a non-exclusive pact with WB; Wayne was about to finish with both RKO and Republic. *The Flying Leathernecks* and *Jet Pilot* were the last two for RKO. The latter was made in 1950, produced by Howard Hughes and directed by Joseph von Sternberg – one of Hollywood's *films maudits*: after many trade rumours about cutting and mutilating, it did not surface until 1957. Wayne, looking uninterested despite the patriotic stance, is an American colonel who falls in love with a Russian aviatrix (Janet Leigh) amidst *Ninotchka*-like cavortings: 'without doubt one of the most childish, tedious and futile spy dramas yet concocted' wrote John Gillett. Wayne left Republic with a bang: that company would fold in the mid-50s and he and Ford now gave it the biggest box-office hit of its life: *The Quiet Man* (52), which wove together a great number of tattered Irish strands – rumbustious humour, sentiment – into an enormously attractive fabric.

Few of the Warner films that he made were as distinguished: *Big Jim McLain*, in which he was the scourge of the subversive left; *Trouble Along the Way* (53), as a football coach (very sticky); *Island in the Sky*; *Hondo*; *The High and the Mighty* (54), an aviation drama; *The Sea Chase* (55) as a German officer; and *Blood Alley*, a dislikeable mixture of synthetic heroics and Commie-baiting. The last four were particularly strong at the wickets, but *Hondo* was the only one with any real merit. His earnings for 1954 were said to be $500,000. He turned down a fee of $400,000 for *The Indian Fighter*, which he did not want to do, and returned to RKO for *The Conqueror* (56), which Dick Powell produced and directed. An expensive epic about the young Genghis Khan, it was little more than a Western with Wayne dolled up in droopy moustache and slit eyes – and struggling with lines like 'I feel this Tartar woman is for me'. The critics pulled it and him apart, but it did

quite well. In 1956 he signed for four films at 20th for $500,000 each – with them paying his agent's fee; he was the highest-paid actor in the world, at $666,666.66.

He was back on familiar ground in *The Searchers*, not merely Monument Valley or even riding shotgun in the saddle, for this epic adventure is a special film, perhaps the most rewarding Ford ever made. Wayne is a man searching for his niece, kidnapped by Indians, and since he is not given to wooing or fighting you think of him less as man than Hollywood monument – except at that moment when Jeffrey Hunter says 'I hope you'll die' and he replies laconically, 'That'll be the day'. It was also potent at the box-office, but when they were reunited for *The Wings of Eagles* (57) the magic eluded them. Wayne was Spig Wead, a dedicated flyer who had later written screenplays for Ford. *Legend of the Lost* did no better, a protracted adventure story set in the Sahara with Sophia Loren, which Wayne produced. He had made no films for 20th under his agreement, having rejected the proffered scripts, so it was readjusted, for three pictures a year over a two-year period for a total of $2 million. Only two of them were made, perhaps because the first, *The Barbarian and the Geisha* (58), proved a humiliating experience when on whim director John Huston insisted on take after take. The loathing was mutual and Wayne disliked the result as well, a pretty, plodding account of Townsend Harris's diplomatic descent on the Japanese in 1856. Said the 'MFB': 'Wayne, now corpulent and ageing, can only achieve a weary monotone sincerity.'

Rio Bravo (59) found another old Hollywood hand below his best, Hawks, borrowing themes from his old movies and the plot from *High Noon* (which Wayne had disliked); the sheriff he played had some not-too-helpful colleagues, so it was not a lone vigil. Even more tired was Ford, with *The Horse Soldiers*, a handsome, mechanical Civil War Western with Wayne as the commander and William Holden as his (in)subordinate.

The Alamo (60) was his own folly, a grandiose flag-waving epic about the struggle of Texas to secede from Mexico which he had dreamed about for years. Wayne had wanted Republic to distribute and finance, but neither they nor any Hollywood company would let him produce unless it was directed by a.n. other, preferably someone experienced in Westerns. Eventually UA agreed to put up $2½ million if Wayne played the lead instead of the intended cameo and if his own company put up a like amount; a group of wealthy Texans contributed another $3 million, but the budget then rose to $12 million, with Wayne himself directing, because no one

John Wayne in Rio Grande *(50).*

599

These days movies, television and video nestle together as one industry, but throughout the 50s and most of the 60s Hollywood battled against the small screen in the corner of the living room: there were wide screens, all-enveloping screens and 3-D. There was also the all-star movie, with dozens of names turning up for a couple of minutes – including The Longest Day *(62), concerning the D-Day landings in Normandy in 1944, perhaps the most crucial operation of the War. No, said John Wayne, he didn't want to be in it, but since 20th Century-Fox felt that that particular war couldn't be won without his cooperation, they eventually met his hefty fee.*

would take the job on. James Edward Grant, a reformed drunk whom Wayne often brought in to improve scripts which he only half-liked, was solely responsible for the screenplay, and had Wayne, playing Davy Crockett, lecturing us on liberty, freedom and God. Given his position it is understandable that he should want us to share his values, but the effect is patronizing. It took less than $8 million at the domestic box-office and in the year of *The Apartment*, went Oscarless, though Wayne thought it was hurt by Chill Wills's energetic campaign to get himself a Best Supporting Oscar.

Henceforward, he contented himself in the big budget affairs of others: *North to Alaska* with Stewart Granger; *The Comancheros!* (61), a sprawling Western in which he is out to trap those supplying arms to the Indians; Ford's predictable, often-cute *The Man Who Shot Liberty Valance*, teaching young (!) lawyer James Stewart the ways of the West;

and Hawks's genial African lark *Hatari!* (62), which was particularly – if unaccountably – successful. The 40 or so names in *The Longest Day* were paid $25,000 for two or three days work, but Wayne, after turning down the role – a lieutenant-colonel – several times, got the $250,000 he asked for; in another all-star film, *How the West Was Won*, he popped in as General Sherman. Ford's free-wheeling South Seas romp, *Donovan's Reef*, was their last together, which neither could have been sorry about. Their professed friendship was not real, said Jim Henaghan, who was on Wayne's staff for years: each respected the professionalism of the other and their records, but Ford's contempt for Wayne irritated him, causing him to think of Ford as an embittered and bad-tempered son-of-a-bitch. In *McLintock!* (63) he was a debauched cattle baron, and a nepotist to boot, since the cast included four of his family. Either as *Circus World* (64) in GB or *The Magnificent Showman* in the US, it finished the career of one of America's greatest directors, Frank Capra. Wayne brought in his writer friend Grant, who considered that Capra was trying to turn the Wayne role into one of his 'little' people: it would not have worked that way, Wayne considered, forgetting that Capra had been associated with more fine movies than Grant. Hathaway replaced him before shooting began, for a big, hollow epic. Wayne had 10 seconds in *The Greatest Story Ever Told* (65), in long-shot as a Roman centurion, intoning 'This truly is the Sahn of Gahd'. He followed with *In Harm's Way*, a war movie, and a Western, *The Sons of Katie Elder*, his most enjoyable film since *The Searchers*.

About this time he successfully underwent an operation for cancer. It could not be said that he returned to the screen with renewed vigour: for some time now he had been giving a tired parody of his old self. The effect worked in Hawks's *El Dorado* (67), but not in such tiresome pieces as *Cast a Giant Shadow* (66) and *The War Wagon* (67). He was involved in a simple-minded defence of the Vietnam war, *The Green Berets* (68), which aroused the wrath of anti-war demonstrators all over the world. Despite that (and its notices) it achieved a huge domestic gross of over $8 million. The Wayne-plus-war formula still worked, but *The Hellfighters* fought fire – and to the action fans that was nowhere near as alluring. *The Undefeated* (69) with Rock Hudson was a so-so Western, but *True Grit* was a touching one, about the relationship of an old gunfighter and a determined teenager (Kim Darby). It did good business, made Wayne again the No. 1 box-office star and brought him a Best Actor Oscar and the best notices of his career. Dilys Powell wrote this tribute: 'It is thirty years since in *Stagecoach* as the romantic and touching Ringo Kid he first made a notable appearance. The physical image has changed since then – the figure thickened, the face lined (though still truculently handsome); and the character which fits the actor, that too has changed. The gallant cowboy who addressed every woman as ma'am has given way in *True Grit* to a drunken tough who wants his price. Nevertheless with a director such as Henry Hathaway – another of the old-style spellbinders – he can still re-create for us the golden mythology of the West.'

Despite the film's success, it was unlikely that Wayne's career could be prolonged unless he restricted himself to Westerns: so *Chisum* (70) was a wise choice, a tale of rival land barons, though you knew Forrest Tucker was mad to take him on. Hawks's swan-song, *Rio Lobo* was underrated, perhaps because it was a revamp of *Rio Bravo*, with Wayne again routing the bad men with unlikely help. The cast included Bill Williams and Jim Davis, who had been stars briefly in the 40s: they were now old and grey, while Wayne in a brown wig was acting half his age. *Big Jake* (71) was another reprise, with Wayne scrapping again with Maureen O'Hara. The director of *The Cowboys* (72), Mark Rydell, had this to say: 'I came prepared to fight with him, to "handle" him, and I find him one of the most incredible professionals I have ever met. He is always ready, always listens to reason, our political differences have never interfered with our work, and this is the fourth week of shooting and we are well ahead of schedule; it's very unusual to be charmed by such a figure. But then, I thought, why should I think this? There must be a good reason why for 41 years this man has captured the world. There are very few stars of his magnitude. All you need is a week with him to realize that his qualities are quite remarkable.' However, there is something repellent about the morals of the film – boys being taught to kill: and the same may be said of *Cahill US Marshal* (73). Both marked a considerable falling-off in Wayne's box-office. He had turned down Don Siegel's *Dirty Harry* and claimed that had he done it he would still be Number One. He did two films similar to it, as a law-enforcer at loose in the violence of big cities, in the latter case in London, '*McQ*' (74) and *Brannigan* (75), and their moralities were again questionable: both were inferior to their prototype and did poorly. Wayne struggled with a bout of cancer and returned as his *True Grit* character, *Rooster Cogburn* (75), a concoction which mismatched him with fiery spinster Katharine Hepburn. Dire reviews did not help it, but good ones could not help *The Shootist* – an

old gunfighter with cancer, a role turned down by Paul Newman and George C. Scott. His cinema reign clearly over – who needed that paunchy, bewigged old gunfighter? – he signed some lucrative deals with TV for specials, e.g. 'John Wayne's America'. He died in 1979.

JOHNNY WEISSMULLER

Of all the screen Tarzans, Johnny Weissmuller remains most identified with the role and it with him. He was neither the first nor last, but he lasted the longest. With the possible exception of the first Tarzan, Elmo Lincoln with his shoulder-length hair, Weissmuller was the most physically right. He was brawny and big-boned, with features that were not entirely unsimian. His face expressed a sort of brooding gentleness which was about all that was required in the way of acting; he seldom looked harried as he swung from branch to branch or outdistanced the crocodiles but, again, a look of contentment in his prowess was not inappropriate. Later in the series when they made him talk – after a fashion – he was no worse or no better than the other Tarzans.

Tarzan was the creation of an American hack-writer called Edgar Rice Burroughs (1875–1950): in the original novel, 'Tarzan of the Apes', published in 1914, Tarzan was an orphaned English milord lost in the African jungle and reared by apes; he eventually learns of his inheritance, outwits the baddies, but returns to the jungle – which, profitably, permitted Burroughs to write a number of sequels. National Pictures filmed the first novel with Lincoln in 1918 and its success spawned an immediate sequel, *The Romance of Tarzan*. Three years later Lincoln did a serial, *The Adventures of Tarzan*. Other Silent Tarzans: Gene Polar in *The Return of Tarzan* (20), P. Dempsey Tabler in *Son of Tarzan* (20, a serial) with Kamuela C. Searle in the title-role, James Pierce in *Tarzan and the Golden Lion* (27), and Frank Merrill in *Tarzan the Mighty* (28) and *Tarzan the Tiger* (30). In 1932 MGM revived the character with Weissmuller.

Weissmuller was born in Chicago in 1907 and educated in that city's university. Under the auspices of the Illinois Athletic Club he became renowned as a swimmer long before MGM became interested: in 1924 at the Olympic Games in Paris he broke three swimming records. He was also at the 1928 Games in Amsterdam and when he turned professional in 1929 was unchallenged as the world's finest swimmer. He had made some

Maureen O'Sullivan, Cheetah the Chimp and Johnny Weissmuller in the first of the very successful Tarzan films in which they appeared, Tarzan the Ape Man *(32).*

sport shorts and was on holiday in California when MGM approached him to test for Tarzan after the actor they had signed became ill – and signed him at $250 a week: the film, *Tarzan the Ape Man* (32), was strictly back-projection stuff and studio jungle, but the schedule could not wait: under W.S. Van Dyke's direction Weissmuller played the part. The enterprise is dull till he appears and then it becomes magical – because he is lithe, handsome, mostly silent, fantastically coura-geous and genuinely strange. Jane, the heroine, was played by Maureen O'Sullivan, an attractive actress whom MGM usually restricted to second leads and wishy-washy parts. Her affection, after her initial fears, seems genuine and it is quite clear she has gone sexually ape about this apeman. Together they were *Tarzan and His Mate* (34), which is a jot less effective. Weissmul-ler's thespian limitations were increasingly evident as the series wound on, itself becom-ing increasingly conventional: *Tarzan Escapes* (36), *Tarzan Finds a Son* (39), *Tarzan's Secret Treasure* (41) and *Tarzan's New York Adven-ture* (42). The son was, literally, found – the survivor of a plane crash – and when relatives came to claim him he too preferred the jungle way of life.

Meanwhile, there were other Tarzans, but most cinemagoers considered them impostors. Sol Lesser at Principal produced *Tarzan the Fearless* (33) with Buster Crabbe and then at 20th *Tarzan's Revenge* (38) with Glen Morris; while Burroughs himself was involved in a serial with Herman Brix, *New Adventures of Tarzan* (35), later released as two features, one of that title and one called *Tarzan and the*

Green Goddess. None of these approached the standard of the MGM pictures, but MGM during the war lost interest and Lesser, now producing at RKO, took over Weissmuller and son, Johnny Sheffield.

After a guest spot in *Stage Door Canteen* (43), Weissmuller did *Tarzan Triumphs* and *Tarzan's Desert Mystery*, in both of which he was Jane-less. He got a new mate, Brenda Joyce, in *Tarzan and the Amazons* (45) and she stayed with him as long as he was with the series: *Tarzan and the Leopard Woman* (46), *Tarzan and the Huntress* (47) and *Tarzan and the Mermaids* (48). Before the last two, he did his only 'straight' film, a Paramount B, *Swamp Fire* (46). He, or Tarzan, was no longer potent box-office and Lesser replaced him by the younger Lex Barker, who made five Tarzan pictures between 1948 and 1952. Later Tarzans include Gordon Scott and, again at MGM, Denny Miller (in a remake of *Tarzan the Ape Man*, 60) and Jock Mahoney.

Weissmuller moved over to Columbia where Sam Katzmann produced him in a series of low-budget actioners featuring one who might have been Tarzan's less sophisti-cated cousin, Jungle Jim, and including a chimpanzee to replace Tarzan's famous Cheetah. His fee was $175,000 per film, as opposed to the Tarzan pictures, where he was paid $100,000 each for what was normally three weeks' work. By the look of them the Jungle Jims were made in three days. The titles: *Jungle Jim* (48), *The Lost Tribe* (49), *Captive Girl* (50), *Mark of the Gorilla, Pygmy Island, Fury of the Congo Land* (51), *Jungle Manhunt, Jungle Jim and the Forbidden Land* (52), *Voodoo Tiger, Savage Mutiny* (53), *Jungle Man-Eaters* (54) and *Cannibal Attack*. These were strictly for the lower half of double bills at less discriminating situations. The 'MFB' waxed indignant over the next one: 'This is a preposterous and in some respects rather distasteful film, which insults the intelligence of the most tolerant specta-tor.' This was *Jungle Moon Men* and like Weissmuller's last, *The Devil Goddess* (55), the leading character was called 'Johnny Weissmuller': again he was Tarzan's cousin. 'Jungle Jim' became a TV series in 1958. Weissmuller was the Vice-President of a swimming pool company named after him. He lived in Florida. After a long absence from the screen he appeared in *The Sphynx* (70) and *Won Ton Ton the Dog Who Saved Hollywood* (76). He died in 1979.

He was married and divorced five times. His third wife (1933–38) was Lupe Velez, a Silent screen star who faded with the coming of Talkies but kept going in a B series based apparently on her own personality and called 'The Mexican Spitfire'.

ORSON WELLES

Orson Welles's actual acting achievements (if such they can be called) have been heavily overshadowed by his prowess as a director and that, in turn, has been usually overrated – due perhaps to one of the best possible reasons: that he did make, at the outset of his career, at least one-and-a-half masterpieces. Not that he was negligible as an actor, far from it: his ebullience and generous authority have given focus to more dull films than seems humanly possible.

As a young man he was known as 'the boy wonder' or the *enfant terrible*: 'There but for the grace of God, goes God' was a famous quip. He came to the cinema with an already strong reputation for the *étonne-moi* bit, and a large ego. He started young. He was born in Kenosha, Wisconsin, in 1915 and educated in Woodstock, Illinois; for a very short while he was an artist and journalist. While on a walking and sketching tour of Ireland in 1931 (he was 16) he bluffed his way into a part at the Gate Theatre, Dublin (as the Duke of Württemberg in 'Jew Süss'). He appeared subsequently in the Abbey as guest star. In 1934, back in the US, he was managing and organizing the Woodstock (Illinois) Theater Festival; through Alexander Woollcott he met Katharine Cornell and toured with her as Mercutio and Marchbanks. His first New York appearance was with her as Chorus and Tybalt. In 1936 he became director of the Negro People's Theater and directed a coloured 'Macbeth'; in 1937 he was appointed a director of the Federal Theater Project, New York, for whom he produced 'Horse Eats Hat' (a version of Labiche's 'An Italian Straw Hat'), 'Doctor Faustus' (he played Faustus) and 'The Cradle Will Rock'. The same year, with John Houseman, he founded the Mercury Theater, starting with a modern-dress Fascist-orientated 'Julius Caesar', in which he played Brutus; the Mercury's subsequent fame was based on that and only three other productions, the last of which, 'Danton's Death', closed the project. Most commentators find it difficult to assess how original or influential the Mercury was. At the same time he was broadcasting regularly and in 1938 was responsible for the radio production, 'The War of the Worlds', which is remembered for the panic it caused among those of its listeners who did not realize it was a play.

RKO, under one of its ever-recurring new managements, was hiring new talent and the contract Welles negotiated was unprecedented: $100,000 per film, one a year, to be produced, written, directed and performed by himself, with a subject of his own choosing and no interference. He began work on a film

of Conrad's 'The Heart of Darkness', but the studio deemed it too expensive; he wrote *The Smiler With the Knife* for Carole Lombard, who refused it. It was writer Herman J. Mankiewicz who had the idea for a thinly disguised study of the career of William Randolph Hearst; and with a nucleus of Mercury talent and with a budget of $750,000 Welles made *Citizen Kane* (41). The reaction of the Hearst press was only one reason why it was disastrous at the box-office, though the most important: the hammering by Hearst certainly negated the huge critical acclaim. Welles intended it as sociology, but despite its comment and its technique it is most successful as a study of human relationships. He played the tycoon with panache, both as Young Turk and ageing megalomaniac, and the screenplay by Herman J. Mankiewicz (for which Welles took co-credit) has pungency, but the plotting is taken from two then-forgotten films of the 30s, *The Power and the Glory* and *The Woman I Loved*. The techniques are taken from the German films of Pabst, Lang and Dupont, though reused with vigour. It is one of the mysteries of Anglo-American movie history that you could filch so much from European classics (though other major film-makers have done it, John Ford with *The Informer*, Carol Reed on *Odd Man*

Orson Welles in Citizen Kane *(41): his achievements behind the camera on this film have tended to overshadow the fact that his performance in it was one of the most dynamic in the history of films.*

As Harry Lime in The Third Man *(49).*

In his own production of Othello *(52).*

As the lawyer in Compulsion *(59).*

I Tartari *(60), one of the mediocre films of the latter days of his career.*

Out) and end up with 'the greatest film of all time'. Over the years it turned into a neat pension for RKO; but then, Welles's contract was amended to deprive him of the final cut.

He was already at work on a remake of *The Magnificent Ambersons* (41), from the novel by Booth Tarkington (filmed in 1925 as *Pampered Youth*), as producer/director/writer only. The result is perhaps Welles's most accomplished achievement, sharp, lucid and graceful. It was cut and laughably added to after he left and released in the US in a double bill with *Mexican Spitfire Sees a Ghost*. In Britain no West End cinema would take it, and few others, but those that did played to packed audiences, who applauded at the end. In view of the fact that at his death he left, reputedly, over 20 uncompleted films, it is tempting to suggest that his enthusiasm for any given project soon waned, but that does not seem to be the case at this stage of his career. He was working in Brazil on a film to enhance Pan-American relations, *It's All True*, when it was cancelled by a change of management at RKO, who were happier with a thriller based on Eric Ambler's *Journey Into Fear* (43), which Welles supervised, co-wrote with the star, Joseph Cotten, and acted in, in the supporting role as a Turkish colonel of police. He signed a contract with Korda to co-produce, direct and play the lead in *War and Peace* (with Merle Oberon as Natasha) but, like many Korda projects, it came to nothing. That left him free to play Mr Rochester to Joan Fontaine's *Jane Eyre* (44), a curious performance, for though he moved and looked the part, darkly romantic, it was hard to believe that he was not as insane as his wife.

During the war he entertained the troops and in *Follow the Boys* he did a variation of his act – sawing Marlene Dietrich in half. He did a soap opera, *Tomorrow Is Forever* (46), with Claudette Colbert, incredibly hammy as an Enoch Arden figure, and in quick succession directed and acted in *The Stranger*, an artificially heightened drama about an ex-Nazi (Welles) settled in a small American town. He then became involved in a stage project with Mike Todd, 'Around the World in 80 Days'. They ran into money difficulties – and he conned Harry Cohn at Columbia into agreeing to *The Lady From Shanghai* (48) to be made for $300,000. Welles directed, wrote it and co-starred – with, at Cohn's suggestion, the wife from whom he was separated, Rita Hayworth: the final cost (reputedly $2 million) and confusion virtually brought about the end of his work as a director in Hollywood. His own performance was weird; the film neither poor nor accomplished but incomprehensible.

He did persuade Republic to let him film –

in 21 days – *Macbeth*, which he described as 'a kind of violently sketched charcoal drawing of a great play': it *looked* more like a disused coal-mine serving as a pantomime set and Welles's own headgear was entertaining. At this point, perhaps wisely, he left Hollywood and, except briefly, did not work there again. 'I came to Europe because there was not the slightest chance for me (or for anybody, at that) to obtain freedom of action.' His European career began brilliantly with *The Third Man* (49): his Harry Lime, the suave, mocking blackmarketeer sought by Joseph Cotten in Vienna, was his best performance since *Kane* and one of the cinema's most memorable creations – which could not be said of his Cagliostro in *Black Magic*. By nature endowed to be a screen villain, he essayed another two, more happily budgeted, both historical, both for 20th with Tyrone Power: *Prince of Foxes*, as Cesare Borgia, and *The Black Rose* (50), as a sort of Genghis Khan, in this dull swashbuckler with pretensions; its director, Henry Hathaway, said he and the crew disliked working with Welles. He was preoccupied with his film of *Othello* (52). He played the role first on the London stage and the film finally appeared only after many vicissitudes, including the sinking of his own money into it. He did not think, he said later, that he was 'particularly good' in the role. The support was worse; and though, like the *Macbeth*, the film has its adherents, there is little to choose between them.

When he needed work Herbert Wilcox offered the role of the dead tycoon, Manderson, in the flash-backs of *Trent's Last Case*. He went over-the-top, as he invariably did thereafter, perhaps to compensate for an increasingly dispiriting career. He was Benjamin Frank in Guitry's *Si Versailles m'était Conté* (53), in a sequence with Charles Vanel, who wiped the floor with him by being both more subtle and more showy; he was in *L'Uomo, La Bestia e La Virtu*, a version of a Pirandello play, as a sea-captain, with Viviane Romance as his neglected wife, and Toto; and the French *Napoléon* (54), as Sir Hudson Lowe, the governor of St Helena. None of these had wide showings outside their countries of origin. As much may be said of two British efforts, the Trucolored *Trouble in the Glen*, a mishmash in which he was a Latin-American laird, directed by Wilcox, and *Three Cases of Murder*, as Somerset Maugham's Lord Mountdrago in the sequence based on that story. Personally more upsetting was the failure of *Confidential Report* (55) aka *Mr Arkadin*, a European Citizen Kane and a grotesque self-parody as acted, written and directed by him.

Another flirtation with Hollywood proved

more fruitful. He was paid $20,000 for one day's work on *Moby Dick* (56) – he played Father Mapple; he did a thriller, *Man in the Shadow* (57), Texan despot to Jeff Chandler's sheriff; and was then engaged to direct another, *Touch of Evil* (58), apparently at the insistence of the star, Charlton Heston, who would not believe that Welles was only to co-star. Welles was paid only to act in it – a bizarre performance as the villain, a corrupt cop – and wrote and directed for nothing. Once again, the gremlins got to work after he left the studio, though the changes this time were slight. At least it emerged as recognizably Welles and, while not perfect, as entertainment it left most of the year's films standing. For 20th he made three: the serviceable version of Faulkner, *The Long Hot Summer*; *The Roots of Heaven* in Africa; and *Compulsion* (59). *Compulsion* jettisoned most of the atmosphere and strength of Meyer Levin's novel based on the Leopold/Loeb murder trial, but Welles's own performance in the Clarence Darrow role moved Dilys Powell to say: 'And it scores – to come down to brass tacks – in having Orson Welles. Mr Welles is among the great solo performers of the screen; more than once his noble organ-voice with its capacity for irony or persuasion, throwaway or thunder, has brought a few remarkable minutes into some unremarkable film.'

Then again, all was dross, starting with the Rank Organization's *n*th attempt to interest the world market, *Ferry to Hong Kong* (his co-stars were Curt Jurgens and Sylvia Syms); a Zanuck-produced-in-Paris *Crack in the Mirror* (60), and a bunch of European 'spectaculars': *David e Golia*, as King Saul; Abel Gance's *Austerlitz*; *I Tartari* and *La Fayette*. He was perhaps trying to get money to finance the completion of his *Don Quixote*, begun in Spain in 1957 and unfinished at his death. He did get backing for his own version of Kafka's *The Trial* (62), filmed in English and French in Paris. The French reviews were good; the British and American ones were not. A small part (smiling benignly as a film director) in the Pasolini sketch of an unspeakable four-part film, *Rogopag*, was followed by *The VIPs* (63) – again a film director, but foreign, volatile and gross. His figure had become mountainous by this time. And it seemed inevitable that he should be in such 'all-star' efforts as *La Fabuleuse Aventure de Marco Polo* (64), a French-Italian-Yugoslav-Egyptian-Afghanistan co-production with Horst Buchholz as Marco (it had started out three years earlier with a different star, director and title), and *Paris Brûle-t'il?/Is Paris Burning?* (66). His performance as the Swedish ambassador in the latter was one of the few

satisfying things about it and he brought the same distinction to his Cardinal Wolsey in a fine film, *A Man for All Seasons*. Simultaneously appeared another venture into Shakespeare, *Chimes at Midnight/Campanadas a Medianoche/Falstaff*, from a stage adaptation he had made of the Falstaff scenes of 'Henry IV', Parts One and Two. His own Falstaff was bemused and melancholy, and the film had taken on the character of that part of Spain in which it was filmed: dark, chilled, harsh. But more than anything since *Ambersons* it made one regret the wastage of his talent.

With it out of the way, Welles was able to take on more assignments to pay for his next directing venture – and once more seemed to pick some of the worst films ever made (how on earth did he miss out on *Candy*?): the all-star 'false' James Bond, *Casino Royale* (67), as a big boss; *A Sailor from Gibraltar* with Jeanne Moreau, in a fez as Louis from Mozambique; *I'll Never Forget Whatsisname*, as an advertising tycoon; *Oedipus the King*, as Tiresias; and *House of Cards* (68), as an arch-villain facing George Peppard. For French TV he made *Histoire Immortelle*, with Moreau, shown in cinemas abroad as *The Immortal Story*, but neither his direction nor performance (as an old man who hires a sailor to make love to his wife) confirm any wastage of talent. After *Una su 13* (69) and *Tepepa*, both in Italy (the latter a tale of Mexican revolt), he was in a Jules Verne tale in Africa, *The Southern Star/L'Etoile du Sud*, as one of the obstacles confronting George Segal – a large, lethargic and petulant ex-police chief. He did a stint in the Yugoslav *Bitka na Neretvi/The Battle of Neretva*, with Yul Brynner, Curt Jurgens, Sergei Bondarchuk and Sylva Koscina, and was with a similarly cosmopolitan cast in John Huston's *The Kremlin Letter* (70), as a conniving Russian official. Not the best work of either of them, it was his best film in a while: and after playing Louis XVIII in a similar venture, an Italian-Russian *Waterloo*, directed by Bondarchuk with Rod Steiger as Napoleon, he had one of his periodic reunions with Hollywood. He was the narrator, a part tacked on after the film was finished, in *Start the Revolution Without Me*, and a high-ranking officer in *Catch-22*; in 1971 he was awarded a special Oscar.

The industry's attitude to Welles was schizophrenic: its younger members genuinely admired him and others paid lip-service to the man who made the movie many Americans now believe is 'the greatest American film of all time', but there were too many tales of waste, extravagance and self-indulgence – the latter a besetting sin since his earlier days, as pointed out in 'Run Through' by his old

Mercury partner, John Houseman. And he bewildered: at such times of *rapprochement*, were the offers so poor or did he pick from the worst available scripts? – *A Safe Place* (71), 'an involved, non-linear study of time and memory' explained 'Sight & Sound', 'in which everything is seen through the mind of a girl played by Tuesday Weld' (he was a magician), and, trapped in self-parody again as a grandiloquent patriarch, *La Décade Prodigieuse/Ten Days' Wonder*: of which he said that he made so many rotten films that he felt like a *putain de luxe* to be in a good one for a change – seemingly unaware that the director (Chabrol), while good, feels compelled to make a real stinker from time to time, as he did in this instance. Unbelievably, apart from a Franco-Belgian horror film, *Malpertius* (72), things got worse: *Get to Know Your Rabbit*, a barely released comedy starring Tom Smothers, during the making of which Welles insisted on using cue cards on the grounds that that was how Brando worked; *Necromancy*, a low-budget occult tale; a British-French-West German-Spanish *Treasure Island* which dropped out of sight in all those countries and the US, as a stagey Long John Silver – and with a script contribution by him under the pseudonym O.W. Jeeves; an unfunny attempt at the title-role of a critically roasted TV 'The Man Who Came to Dinner'; and *Upon This Rock* (73), as Michelangelo in this tale of the Vatican which gave up an attempt to get into cinemas and went to TV.

In 1974 a film in Greece was abandoned, *Rider*, with Oliver Reed – which should surprise no one acquainted with the work of its director, Andrew Sinclair; and in 1975, when Welles was presented with the American Film Institute's Life Achievement Award, the TV coverage included chunks of a film of Welles's own – which was then apparently almost finished (perhaps only he himself knew exactly how many there were of these). His *F for Fake* (75) was a semi-documentary based on someone else's, containing the unsurprising view that Welles identified with charlatans. There was a cameo in an all-star film, *Voyage of the Damned* (76), gross and bearded as a Cuban industrialist supposedly interested in the passengers, and a large television role in *It Happened One Christmas* (77), which was *It's a Wonderful Life* with a sex-change to accommodate Marlo Thomas in James Stewart's old role and Welles in that of Lionel Barrymore, the greedy tycoon. Around the same time the voice that once told us he wrote, produced and directed *Citizen Kane* could often be heard in many a home over the TV commercials. He was one of the guests in *The Muppet Movie* (79), as Lew Lord.

No more impressive were *Butterfly* (81) starring Stacey Keach and Pia Zadora, with Welles as a corrupt judge, or *Where is Parsifal?* (84), in a cameo as a gypsy tycoon. He also appeared towards the end of Henry Jaglom's personal statement, *Someone to Love* (87) – posthumously, for he died in 1985. To add to his own unfinished films there would seem to be three others, presumably completed, for they have been advertised in the trade press: *The Secret of Tesla*, made in Yugoslavia in 1979; *A Step Away*, from around the same time; and *Hot Money* aka *Never Trust an Honest Thief*, ditto, made in Canada.

MAE WEST

Mae West's first appearance in films is perhaps the most famous first appearance of them all. She sidled on to the screen in bejewelled splendour and the hat-check girl said 'Goodness, what beautiful diamonds!' 'Goodness had nothing to do with it, dearie,' said Mae. She wrote the exchange herself and she also wrote the following: 'The man I don't like doesn't exist', 'It's better to be looked over than overlooked', 'Opportunity knocks for every man, but gives a woman a ring', 'I always say, keep a diary and one day it will keep you', 'I used to be Snow White but I drifted', 'There are no withholding taxes on the wages of sin', 'It's not the men in my life that count, it's the life in my men', 'A man in the house is worth two in the street', 'Beulah, peel me a grape' and 'A man has more character in his face at 30 than 20 – he has suffered longer'. There are hundreds more, though one, 'Come up and see me sometime' makes most dictionaries of quotations. However, the RAF named their inflatable life-saving device 'Mae West', to which her response was: 'I've been in "Who's Who", and I know what's what, but it's the first time I've been in a dictionary.'

Her witticisms may seem limp if you have never seen her, but they are irresistibly funny to anyone who has once been exposed to her. Big, blowsy, blonde and bosomy, she sways on to the screen with all the aplomb of a good female impersonator. Frank Marcus wrote once: 'A good drag act should express the assumption that a man makes a better woman than a woman. There are two ways in which this can be achieved: by a display of extravagant glamour, or by caricaturing female characteristics, making them appear ridiculous or even faintly disgusting.' It is as good a description of West as there is, even to the 'disgusting': Mae West caused many tempera-

It is still refreshing to experience Mae's unbridled and luxurious enjoyment of men, sin and diamonds. We may take her for granted, but with an effort you can imagine why she once seemed so shocking: there were men in her past, there would be men in her future and undoubtedly the present found her pursuing one without a single inhibition.

tures to rise in her time, not least that of William Randolph Hearst, who thought that Congress should do something about her. One critic, Don Herold, opined, 'I think I would rather let my daughters see Mae West's films regularly than see Hearst newspapers regularly. . . . Mae West burlesques sex, kids it, and I prefer that as moral fare for young American junior misses to the over-serious consideration of sex suggested by Garbo, Dietrich, Joan Crawford and others.' But as a tribute it is a trifle serious for an artist who never took herself seriously, a great clown who could put more innuendo in the flicker of an eyelash than seemed possible.

Rather surprisingly, she admitted to a birthdate in her memoirs: 1893 in Brooklyn. Her father was a prominent heavyweight boxer and encouraged her bent for showing off – at five, she was doing public imitations of Eva Tanquay and a year later she was with Hal Clarendon's stock company at the Gotham Theater in Bushwick, Brooklyn, playing all the famous kid-parts: Little Eva, Little Willie, Little Lord Fauntleroy. She studied dancing and went into burlesque as The Baby Vamp. 'Variety' found her act unusual as early as 1912. In 1914 she billed herself as 'The Original Brinkley Girl'. In 1916 she did a double-act with her sister. Although others claimed to be, she *was* the originator of the shimmy dance; she also did imitations of George M. Cohan and Eddie Foy. In 1919 she went legit, in a show called 'Sometime' with Ed Wynn. In 1921 Pathé offered her a big part in *Daredevil Jack* (Dempsey), but at the last minute she changed her mind, to star on the Pantage's vaudeville circuit (her pianist was Harry Richman, later to be famous in his own right).

She wrote her own material; in 1926 she returned to legit in a show she wrote, produced and directed: 'Sex'. It caused a furore: half of New York – those that had seen it – were at her feet; the other half were after her blood and finally they got her: she was fined and sent to gaol for 10 days for obscenity. She was more careful with 'The Drag', in which most of the characters were fags (she was not in it), a novel idea then: it played Paterson, New Jersey, but she was persuaded not to bring it into town. One called 'The Wicked Age' did not run long, but 'Diamond Lil' in 1928 was a smash. In 'The Pleasure Man' most of the leading characters were female impersonators: the police closed the show and West was hauled into court again. She won her case, but instead of reviving it, she went on tour with 'Lil'. Her last play was 'The Constant Sinner', adapted from a novel she had written. Then she accepted a Hollywood offer. (She had already been tested by Charles

Walsh, who had tried to 'sell' her to Fox, where he worked, and to WB, but neither studio was interested.)

George Raft had requested her for *Night After Night* (32) and because of her eminence (or notoriety) Paramount offered her $5,000 weekly for 10 weeks' work, a staggering sum for a part which was not the biggest in the film (she was fourth-billed) – but she wanted out when she saw the script. Such was the interest engendered that Paramount could not let her go and finally she agreed to stay provided that she could write her own lines. Raft said later: 'In this picture, Mae West stole everything but the cameras.' It was hardly a performance. West did not act, she postured – but whatever it was, it was mighty effective. Paramount begged her to stay – at a salary of $8,500 a week – and she agreed on condition the next film was *Diamond Lil*; but because of its notoriety the studio insisted on its being called *She Done Him Wrong* (33). Like many of her subsequent films, it gave her a chance to sashay about in the feathers and sequins of the gay 90s, devouring every man in sight. She never vamped them – nothing so common: she simply let men know she liked them (though she liked diamonds better). Cary Grant was one of the enslaved, as he was in *I'm No Angel*: she was a lady lion-tamer – 'a girl who lost her reputation but never missed it'. The film sprawled somewhat and grossed $3 mil-

lion. Producer William Le Baron made this statement to exhibitors: 'In the middle of the Depression the Mae West pictures . . . broke box-office records all over the country and attendance records all over the world. In fact, *She Done Him Wrong* must be credited with having saved Paramount at a time when that studio was considered selling out to MGM, and when Paramount theatres – 1,700 of them – thought of closing their doors and converting into office buildings. Mae West is a lifesaver to the motion picture industry.' She was voted the eighth biggest draw of 1933. This success saved her too: blue-noses all over the country were up in arms and their counterparts in Hollywood were out to get her. The Hays Office brought in a new production code in 1934 to combat the more insidious code of the West; and throughout her career there were influential Hollywood figures waiting for her to fail. Even less biased people considered her a nine days' wonder.

Her next vehicle started out as *It Ain't No Sin*, but the Hays Office decreed a title change and it became *Belle of the Nineties* (34). The censor objected, again, to certain scenes and dialogue, but the expurgated version was 'a triumph of Mae over matter' as 'Photoplay' said – and got her elected the fifth biggest money-maker for 1934 (the only girl to beat her, Janet Gaynor, had several films to her one). Despite the censor, Paramount signed Mae to a new two-year contract for two films at $300,000, including $100,000 for the original story and screenplay, and in 1935 she was the highest-paid woman in the US. Her film that year was *Goin' to Town* and she was a thoroughly bad lot (a cattle-rustler's widow) who schemed her way into marriage and high society: at her best giving better than she had got from the socialites who insulted her, and as Delilah in an opera. Her script clearly scouted the provisions of the Hays Code – and probably contains more quips than any of her films. She was down to 11th on the list of money-making stars but that was still impressive, with only one film released. There was more censor trouble when, as *Klondike Annie* (36), for plot reasons, she impersonated a Salvation Army-type sister. The Hearst press rose to new heights of virulence, though Hollywood gossip claimed that this time this was due to some unflattering remark that she had made about Marion Davies. However, the posters claimed: 'She made the Frozen North . . . Red Hot!' and only prudes were worried. (Another slogan used for Mae was: 'Nothing else matters – here's Mae West/ When she's good she's very good/When she's bad she's better.') A former Paramount chief, Emmanuel Cohen, made her next two pictures – but Paramount still released. *Go West*

I'm No Angel (33): that fact was clear from the opening number, when Mae sauntered into view and sang 'They Call Me Sister Honky Tonk'. It isn't quite clear what she does in the carnival and what plot there is has to do with her tiring of one group of suitors and finding a new set. 'Find 'em, fool 'em, forget 'em' is her motto, and one found and fondled is Cary Grant. 'We both need a rest,' he tells her, 'let me take you away somewhere.' 'That's no rest,' she replies.

Young Man (37) was adapted from a Gladys George stage success, 'Personal Appearance', and she was a movie star staying in a small town boarding house, one of the rare occasions when she was not in the fashions of the 90s. She was also doing radio-work. After one broadcast the Manhattan College magazine launched a broadside: West was 'the very personification of sex in its lowest connotation' polluting 'the sacred precincts of homes with shady stories, foul obscenity, smutty suggestions and horrible blasphemy'. In 1938 *Every Day's a Holiday* and Mae was Peaches O'Day, a con girl who takes refuge in a black wig and disguise as Mlle Fifi. She was allowed no double entendres or salty dialogue and the film was dull in the extreme.

Paramount then turned down her request to play Catherine the Great (Dietrich's version had flopped). It was also clear from the receipts of the last two films that her popularity had nose-dived: either the novelty had worn off or Puritanism had triumphed. At that point Universal approached Mae to co-star with W.C. Fields in *My Little Chickadee* (39), a film more notable for promise than achievement. She wrote her own script, and he wrote his, and it was he of course who refused to compromise: the result is messy and unworthy of either of them. Universal made her another offer but they could not agree on a script; and there were similar difficulties with some propositions from Columbia. No studio was interested in her Catherine project. Instead, she let Gregory Ratoff talk her into an independent venture, *The Heat's On* (43), which Columbia released, on the strength of the plot-line which found her as a famous stage-star involved with William Gaxton and Victor Moore – in a faint reprise of their stage teamings. She was filming the musical numbers when she saw the script, which would put her on screen for only 25% of its length. Ratoff claimed that he risked bankruptcy if she defected, and with Hollywood now little interested in her she did not want to get a reputation for temperament. She is the best thing about the film, but its reception proved that she was a name rather than a box-office star.

She returned to Broadway with a revue made from her Catherine material, 'Catherine Was Great', and in 1947–48 was in London and the British provinces, chalking up more cheers for 'Diamond Lil'. She toured in it in the US for four years after that, including New York, and then turned to TV and nightclubs, in an act with a group of musclemen. For over a decade her only public appearance was in an edition of a vapid TV series, 'Mr Ed', in 1964, although she occasionally attended film society showings of her

After the revised Production Code of 1934 really began to bite, Miss West's humour, without its doubles entendres, was to become rather thin. She could still be witty, as was proved by Klondike Annie two years later. She was unfortunate with two of her last films in the 30s – and misguided when she returned to films thirty years later. So here is a memory of happier times, when visited by Noël Coward and Cary Grant at the time of Go West Young Man.

films. Interviews suggested that she was clinging to a former glory and photographs indicated a reluctance to look her age. But then,
she was Mae West and the interviewers had
got it wrong, because she was as famous as she
ever was. She was often reported buying
properties to suit herself, such as *The Male
Harem* in 1952, but she was not neglected:
among the many projects she rejected were
Belle of the Yukon, *The First Travelling
Saleslady* and *The Belle of New York* (the role
eventually played by Marjorie Main); she was
the first actress approached by Billy Wilder
for *Sunset Boulevard* and was 'insulted' –
though she agreed to do *Pal Joey* for him, with
Brando, till Harry Cohn decided that that had
to be a Rita Hayworth vehicle. She did agree
to take a smallish part, a madam, in *The Art
of Love* in 1964, on condition that she wrote
her own lines: her offer was rejected and
Ethel Merman played the part.

Finally she appeared as a Hollywood agent
in Gore Vidal's sex-change comedy, foully
filmed, *Myra Breckinridge* (70). Raquel
Welch played the boy/girl title-role and both
castings were a publicity man's dream. 'Variety' commented that West's $350,000 for 10
days' work (plus writing her own dialogue)
was worth every cent in publicity to the
studio. Her reasons for returning were not
disclosed, but were probably not financial.
But then her film career is curious: perhaps,
like Buster Keaton's, it was a progression
from vaudeville rather than an end in itself.
When she found that conditions were not
ideal, she preferred to go back to the stage,
to hear audiences rather than technicians
laugh. But it is she who had the last laugh –
over the snide interviewers – because she was
Mae West. She was unique, a legend, part of
American folk-lore – a status hurt badly by
her decision to star in a version of one of her
old plays, *Sextette* (78), as a bride trying to
consummate her sixth marriage – to a much
younger man (Timothy Dalton), as, inevitably, he had to be. Looking like a wax-work,
apparently moved about the set mechanically,
and miked, she and the film were grotesque,
or in 'Variety''s word, 'embarrassing'. Paramount dropped their interest during production and the film did not even have a freak
success even when revived after her death in
1980.

DIANA WYNYARD

Had she wanted it, Diana Wynyard might
have had a screen career as long and distinguished as that of Davis or Hepburn. As a
stage actress she was excellent but seldom

outstanding; nor was her later screen work
likely to make anybody's eyes pop out. But
her early film work is quite, quite stunning.
Quiet, cool, gracious, ladylike, she was warmer and more believable than those adjectives
imply: either her acting has not dated an iota
or it was years before its time. In *Rasputin and
the Empress* the Barrymores are acting away
like mad and about as convincing as a tree-full
of parrots, but Wynyard simply exists, in the
same naturalistic way that someone like
Spencer Tracy existed. In *One More River* the
cast are, expectedly, more subdued; the film
is still Galsworthy junk: but when Wynyard is
on the screen, at any point you might be
watching a film made yesterday.

She was born in 1906 in London; was
educated in Croydon at a school where she
studied dramatics; made her London début
walking-on in 'The Grand Duchess (25). She
went into rep and laid the foundations of her
career with William Armstrong's company in
Liverpool, 1927–29. London fame came with
'Sorry You've Been Troubled' by Walter
Hackett in 1929; Wynyard's biggest success
after that was probably in Congreve's 'The
Old Bachelor' with Nigel Playfair's company.
In 1932 she went to New York to appear in
'The Devil Passes' with Basil Rathbone – and
took the place by storm. MGM offered a
contract and cast her as a character based on
the Princess Youssoupoff in *Rasputin and the
Empress* (32).

Fox borrowed her for *Cavalcade* (33),
opposite Clive Brook, Noël Coward's jingoistic account of 30 eventful years in the life of
a British family. The stage production was
filmed, as a guide, and claims were made for
the final result – the best 'British' film ever
made. It was certainly exquisitely directed (by
Frank Lloyd) and authentic (an all-British
cast) by the standards of the time; there were
rave notices and, surprisingly, in a
Depression-torn US it turned out to be the
year's biggest grosser – at $3½ million.
Coward said he found Wynyard's performance 'entirely entrancing. . . . To her I am
immensely grateful. . . . I again repeat, I find
her performance magnificent.'

Back at MGM she played in *Men Must
Fight*, an interesting mother-love drama with
Lewis Stone and Phillips Holmes – instilling
pacifist ideas into the latter; the film concluded with an air raid on New York in 1940. It
was not a success and, worse, like *Cavalcade*,
gave audiences the impression that she was a
middle-aged woman. Next she was with John
Barrymore again in *Reunion in Vienna*, from
Robert E. Sherwood's play about old
romance in old ditto. She was loaned to RKO
for a couple with Clive Brook, *Where Sinners
Meet* (34), from A.A. Milne's comedy, 'The

(39), about a couple who commit a minor theft and find themselves wading gradually deeper into tragedy. Interest quickened and she began to accept offers: *Gaslight* (40), with Anton Walbrook, in a touching performance as his frightened wife; *Freedom Radio* (41), as an actress in charge of a branch of Nazi propaganda, whose husband (Clive Brook) is a member of the underground; and Warners' remake of an old George Arliss film, originally planned as one of their biographical series in Hollywood, *The Prime Minister*, as Mrs Disraeli to John Gielgud's unsemitic Dizzy. She was the wealthy betrothed of *Kipps*, Michael Redgrave, for Carol Reed, whom she married (the second of three husbands). She returned to the stage in 'Watch on the Rhine' (42) and was not seen again on screen until she played Lady Chiltern in *An Ideal Husband* (47).

She did a cameo, Tom's mother, in *Tom Brown's Schooldays* (51), with Robert Newton as Dr Arnold; and managed to make touching the harsh matron in a weak nurse drama starring Belinda Lee, *The Feminine Touch* (56); she was James Mason's mother in the American *Island in the Sun* (57). Her work on the London stage was often memorable. It included: 'Captain Carvallo', 'Much Ado About Nothing' (a perfect Beatrice to Gielgud's Benedick), 'The Seagull' (as Arkadina) and 'Hamlet' (as Gertrude). She was with Britain's National Theatre as its inception, playing Gertrude again; she was in 'Andorra' and was rehearsing a revival of 'Hay Fever' when she died, in 1964.

LORETTA YOUNG

As a young woman, Loretta Young was very pretty, with big eyes and apple cheeks, and as she aged she remained lovely to look upon. Her screen presence was crisp and glamorous in the best tradition and these factors presumably determined her success. She slipped with ease from comedy to drama – especially if her roles required her to dress elegantly. She was known as 'Hollywood's beautiful hack'. She also seems to have been one of those masterly lady stars who knows all about lighting and costumes, and keep a mirror beside them on the set. Her first husband, Grant Withers, described her after their separation as 'a steel butterfly', though at this time (the early Talkies), on screen, she was anything but. Later, perhaps, but her early acting can stand with the best: a radiant young woman doing with sensitivity a series of mainly working-class and put-upon heroines.

She was born in 1912 in Salt Lake City. Her parents separated when she was four and

Cynics scoffed when the Fox Film Co. poured a small fortune into Noël Coward's very British Cavalcade *(33) – why, it hadn't even been done on Broadway! – but it was a big hit in the US and Britain; Clive Brook and Diana Wynyard.*

Dover Road', and *Let's Try Again*, a marital drama. Of the former 'Photoplay' said 'much, much too talkie' and of the next 'a trifle ponderous' – *One More River* at Universal. It was yet another British subject and again authentic, though with clichés (C. Aubrey Smith as the squire) to match those of the book (it is one of the later volumes of 'The Forsyte Saga'). Wynyard was the unhappy wife whose husband tries to frame her with a man she likes (Frank Lawton).

She had had a London offer to play Charlotte Brontë in 'Wild Decembers' (35) and she did not return to Hollywood. Neither MGM nor she ever made any public announcement of the break and observers later concluded that she was homesick and longing to return to the stage. She did say that she did not care for filming and that she was unhappy in Holywood. But then she was a failure in Hollywood, by Hollywood's standards: all the films she made after *Cavalcade* did poorly (in Britain as well), and she was not prepared to fight the front office for any of the parts earmarked for Crawford or Shearer. In Britain she certainly refused film offers for some years, while having several big stage hits: 'Lean Harvest', 'Sweet Aloes', 'Candida' revived, 'Design for Living' (39) and 'No Time for Comedy'. Producer Joseph Somlo finally talked her into doing a picture with Ralph Richardson, *On the Night of the Fire*

Loretta Young – epitome of 30s glamour – in The Devil To Pay *(30).*

Mother moved to Los Angeles where she opened a boarding-house and hired out her four small daughters as film extras whenever possible: *The Only Way* (26), as a screaming child, and *Son of the Sheik*, with her sisters. For a while Loretta attended a convent; her real film career began by accident, when director Mervyn LeRoy telephoned the household asking for Polly Ann Young to appear in a Colleen Moore vehicle, *Naughty But Nice* (27): she was away, so sister Loretta went instead. After that she had bits in *Her Wild Oat* (28) and *Whip Woman*, starring Antonio Moreno and Estelle Taylor, and was selected from 50 candidates to play in *Laugh Clown Laugh* as the high-wire performer adored by Lon Chaney and loved by Nils Asther. She was in Paramount's *The Magnificent Flirt* starring the magnificent Florence Vidor; then Warners signed her. There were featured roles in *The Head Man* and a Richard Barthelmess starrer, *Scarlet Seas*; then the lead in *The Squall* (29), her first all-Talkie, as a Hungarian girl upset by the advent of gypsy Myrna Loy; plus a fine chance in the minor *The Girl in the Glass Cage* – i.e. box-office. *The Careless Age* and *The Fast Life* were grim melodramas with Douglas Fairbanks Jr and WB liked them together so much that, after she had put in an appearance in *The Show of Shows* (part of the sister-act number, with Sally Blane), they were teamed together again in the more cheerful *The Forward Pass* and *Loose Ankles* (30), where she was an heiress and he a gigolo who answers her marriage ad. In real life she married Withers, after they had been involved together in *The Second Floor Mystery*. She was the governess in love with John Barrymore in *The Man from Blankleys*; twin sisters in *Road to Paradise*, one a crook trying to heist the other's jewellery; the daughter of Otis Skinner in *Kismet*; and a young girl married to the ageing Conway Tearle in *Road to Paradise*.

Goldwyn borrowed her to replace Constance Cummings during the shooting of *The Devil to Pay*, opposite Ronald Colman, but she was less lucky on loan to RKO for a Foreign Legion tale starring Ralph Forbes, *Beau Ideal* (31) – hers was not much of a part. She was married to an older man again, Conrad Nagel – while he was suffering from amnesia – in *The Right of Way* and the film certainly lost its way before the end. Young was loaned to Fox for *Three Girls Lost* and was then back on the same old theme again, *Too Young to Marry* – Grant Withers. It may have been a successful Broadway comedy ('Broken Dishes') but bore an uncanny relevance to real life, with Mother objecting to her marrying an older man – except in life there was no happy ending as they were divorced not long after the film was released. Then Young was the *Big Business Girl* with Ricardo Cortez. She said *I Like Your Nerve* to Fairbanks; was a reporter and Jean Harlow's rival in *Platinum Blonde* and Walter Huston's daughter in a gangland story, *The Ruling Voice*. Possibly her best work was as James Cagney's wife in the fast-moving *Taxi* (32).

Warners were at last beginning to consider her one of their major assets, but as a divorcee not yet 20 she had to be very carefully cast not to offend cinemagoers. She was too virginal-looking to be anything but an innocent – but her circumstances were usually unfortunate. In William A. Wellman's *The Hatchet Man* she married fellow-Oriental Edward G. Robinson, who had killed her father. 'Picture-goer' thought she had 'never appeared to better advantage . . . she is almost unbelievably different from her normal screen self'. She did a couple of career-vs-marriage stories, *Play Girl*, as an ambitious working girl married to gambler Norman Foster, and, also with Foster, *Weekend Marriage* – called *Working Wives* in Britain. *Life Begins* was never shown in that country, being banned by the censor (Young was a convicted murderess dying in childbirth); while *They Call It Sin* there became *The Way of Life* – neither of which suggests the mild little triangle drama it was. George Brent co-starred. She was a shopgirl in *Employees Entrance* (33), tempted by boss Warren William to be unfaithful to husband Wallace Ford, not once but twice, while drunk; and then partnered by Paul Lukas in a double sense in *Grand Slam*, a satiric comedy about bridge players. In Fox's *Zoo at Budapest* she was a refugee from an orphanage, loved by zoo-keeper Gene Raymond, and in *The Life of Jimmy Dolan* with Fairbanks she ran one. She, Cortez and Wellman went over to MGM for *Midnight Mary* – she was a murderess again – with Franchot Tone; then Wellman directed her as a working-girl, in love with Richard Barthelmess, one of the *Heroes for Sale*. There was a change from maudlin melodrama with *The Devil's in Love*, but it was just another Foreign Legion story (with Victor Jory, at Fox). There were more tears in her last for Warners, *She Had to Say Yes*; nor was she exactly happy in *A Man's Castle* being saved from prostitution (or worse) by Spencer Tracy, but it was by far her best film of the period.

Warner's Darryl F. Zanuck believed in her: when he left to found 20th Century Pictures, he saw her as a likely replacement to succeed Janet Gaynor as the screen's favourite waif and was prepared to pay her over $700 more than she had been getting at Warners, which was $1,000 a week. They started well with

As a young woman Loretta Young had a spiritual quality and a sensitivity that were but hinted at in her later performances. She was at her early best in Frank Borzage's A Man's Castle *(33), with Spencer Tracy, left, and Walter Connolly. And Marjorie Rambeau.*

House of Rothschild (34), which turned out to be a big hit. Young was George Arliss's daughter and a good cast included Helen Westley, C. Aubrey Smith, Robert Young, Boris Karloff and Reginald Owen. She was simply Colman's leading lady in *Bulldog Drummond Strikes Back*. *Born To Be Bad* was not her but her son – though she reformed at the end when Cary Grant made her realize that she was responsible for his delinquency. She was loaned to Fox for *Caravan* (a Countess marrying gypsy Charles Boyer) and for *The White Parade* (nurses and John Boles); and was back with Colman, as his wife, in *Clive of India* (35) and with Gable in *Call of the Wild*, a terrible performance, as she later admitted. She was absent for a while (for various reasons which are explained in 'Ginger, Loretta and Irene Who?' by George Eels), moving on to Paramount for two: Wanger's *Shanghai* with Boyer again and De Mille's *The Crusades*, as Berengaria, married to Coeur-de-Lion (Henry Wilcoxon) by proxy: a film memorable for a comforting soldier saying 'It's kinda rough for you, my lady'. She was hardly less incongruous, but the film was a great grosser. At MGM she was wife to a prosecuting attorney, Franchot Tone, in a twisty mystery directed by Sam Wood, *The Unguarded Hour* (36).

In the meantime 20th Century had 'amalgamated' with Fox and Young's contract was redrawn on an exclusive basis, on the understanding that she got the company's plum roles. Already with 20th she had acquired prestige, had left her suffering days way behind. Whether the films were better is doubtful (they were certainly bigger): she seldom was. She did suffer just twice more, in *Private Number* – a remake of *Common Clay* – with Robert Taylor, and as the brave *Ramona*: 'Film Weekly' thought 'too much weeping blurs her portrayal'. However, *Ladies in Love* was very funny: in the cast was Janet Gaynor (whose place at the studio Young was taking) plus Tyrone Power – this was the first of several co-starring vehicles. Their *Love Is News* (37) was also delightful and their *Café Metropole* a passable romance. Over to Don Ameche and *Love Under Fire* as a jewel thief; to Warner Baxter in a weak triangle drama, *Wife Doctor and Nurse* with Virginia Bruce; then back to Power for a *Second Honeymoon*.

John Ford directed *Four Men and a Prayer* (38): the prayer was to clear their father, cashiered Colonel C. Aubrey Smith, and to win Loretta. Richard Greene did. She was one of the *Three Blind Mice* (girls after wealthy husbands – a plot 20th were to utilize again at least six times), and the Empress Eugenie in *Suez*, darn-sure that Tyrone Power must build *that* canal. *Kentucky* was an ordinary (if popular) horsey picture, with

Greene; and *The Story of Alexander Graham Bell* (39) merely a chore, although the cast included her sisters (one of them, Sally Blane, had some slight Hollywood success). She loathed all these parts and *Suez* had been the last straw – but it was *Alexander Graham Bell* that broke the camel's back: she had wanted to play Mrs Bell as the deaf-mute she was and had to compromise by being deaf only. After *Wife Husband and Friend* (a comedy with Warner Baxter) she quit the studio. Some sources suggest this Zanuck-Young dispute was over money, that 20th withheld a raise, due to differences with her agent.

At all events, after a dull marital comedy for Wanger-UA, *Eternally Yours*, she was, according to Bob Thomas in 'King Cohn', black-listed. After months without an offer, Harry Cohn of Columbia agreed to take her at $50,000 each for three films – reported at the time as $75,000, which was half her normal fee. She was only too pleased to accept. *The Doctor Takes a Wife* (40) and *He Stayed for Breakfast* were both comedies; then she went to Universal for *The Lady From Cheyenne* (41), hokum directed by the once esteemed Frank Lloyd. At Columbia she was the 'Ballerina' of Lady Eleanor Smith's novel, adapted as *The Men in Her Life*, and she stayed on for two more: *Bedtime Story* (42), a comedy in which she was an actress scrapping with her playwright husband, Fredric March,

and *A Night to Remember*, a thriller in which she and hubby Brian Aherne are up to their necks in mayhem. Paramount sent her to *China* (43) with Alan Ladd and she was one of Universal's *Ladies Courageous* (44), one of the worst of the women-at-war dramas; and she was a deaf socialite falling in love with Dr Ladd in *And Now Tomorrow*, from Rachel Field's novel. Her performance, said 'The New York Times', 'may best be compared to a Fanny Brice imitation of a glamorous movie queen. Whatever it was that this actress never had, she still hasn't got it.' She didn't have it either as a pioneer woman in *Along Came Jones* (45), who was Gary Cooper, after which along came *The Stranger* (46), who was Edward G. Robinson, on the track of her Nazi husband, Orson Welles. *The Perfect Marriage* was one of the flavourless marital comedies (in this case with David Niven) that she had already done several times too often.

Her career was in the doldrums, but Dore Schary at RKO believed that a script Selznick had developed for Ingrid Bergman might restore her to favour: so she presumably reached the peak of her career with *The Farmer's Daughter* (47), a comedy with Joseph Cotten. It was not a performance that the press had remarked, except for a good Swedish accent and her blonded hair, but it won a Best Actress Oscar (the competition: Joan Crawford in *Possessed*, Susan Hayward

The Farmer's Daughter (47) was a comedy about a Minnesota Swedish farm girl (Loretta Young) who wins both the heart of her employer (Joseph Cotten) and a seat in Congress. With them is Charles Bickford. She later played variations of this character on television.

in *Smash-Up*, Dorothy McGuire in *Gentleman's Agreement* and Young's friend Rosalind Russell in *Mourning Becomes Electra*). Oscar did little for her and she was only offered *The Bishop's Wife*, some whimsy about a top cleric (David Niven) and an angel called Dudley (Cary Grant), because Teresa Wright became pregnant. She did have an excellent role as a bondswoman married and neglected by William Holden but wooed by a wandering Robert Mitchum, *Rachel and the Stranger* (48), and though good in it she did not convince anyone that she had ever been near a kitchen. Few of her later films were memorable: *The Accused* (49), a so-called psychological thriller with Wendell Corey and Robert Cummings; *Mother Is a Freshman*, a comedy at 20th with Van Johnson; and a nice nun film at same, *Come to the Stable*. *Key to the City* (50) cast her agreeably as a lady mayor having a fling with fellow-mayor Gable; and, also at MGM, *Cause for Alarm* (51) was a neat thriller in *Sorry Wrong Number* mould produced and co-written by second husband Ted Lewis. She gave a fine performance, but it played as a B. So did the last four, more or less: *Half Angel* with Joseph Cotten; *Paula* (52), a melodrama with Kent Smith; *Because of You*, a sudser with Jeff Chandler; and *It Happens Every Thursday* (53) with John Forsythe.

In 1953 she went into TV with 'The Loretta Young Show', a drama series more notable for the *haute couture* of the introduction than for drama. Nevertheless it was highly popular, and won several Emmys over the years – to everyone's surprise it ran until 1961. In that year was settled out of court her (estranged) husband's suit alleging malpractice over the dissolution of their TV company; and she published a book, 'The Thing I Had to Learn'. In 1962 she tried 'The New Loretta Young Show', but the only new thing about it was that it was one continuing sudser instead of many different ones. It lasted only one season. She finally divorced her husband in 1969.

When honoured at Filmex in 1981 she said that she could only be lured back to movies for the female equivalent of a *Beckett* or *A Man for All Seasons*; and that, anyway, she preferred TV because there was no waiting around. There were rumours of movies for cinemas and television over the next few years, till in 1985 she began a mini-series, *Dark Mansions*, but left due to 'creative differences'. When she finally did appear in a tele-film, *Christmas Eve* (86), she won a Golden Globe for Best Actress.

ROBERT YOUNG

Robert Young was the all-purpose leading man. For over 20 years his fortunes hardly varied: A pictures and B pictures; comedy and drama; lead roles and second leads; co-starring with big stars and little ones; at this studio and that – but mostly MGM, to whom he was under contract during the greater part of this period. Naturally, he was dependable, but he had two qualities, often overlooked: he was amiable and as a romantic hero he hardly ever aged.

He was born in Chicago in 1907 and educated in Seattle and Los Angeles; he worked as a bank teller, reporter and salesman, learning a certain amount of his craft at a small theatre in Carmel. He started in films as an extra, got his chance when he was chosen to assist another artist in a screen test and impressed the director in charge of the test. MGM signed him and loaned him to Fox for a role in *The Black Camel* (31), a Charlie Chan feature with Warner Oland. He played the son of Helen Hayes in *The Sin of Madelon Claudet* and was loaned to Columbia where he (moustached) and Constance Cummings were members of *The Guilty Generation*; and back at MGM he was an ardent prohibitionist in *The Wet Parade* (32) because Dad killed Mommy in a drunken frenzy. His first star role was in *New Morals for Old* opposite Margaret Perry in this version of John Van Druten's 'After All' and he had another good part in *Unashamed*, as a murderer: he shot the lover of sister Helen Twelvetrees to avenge the family honour – though she had deliberately kept the lover with her all night in order to force the family's consent to her marriage. It made an interesting court-roomer. Less noticeable were his stints in *Strange Interlude* and *The Kid From Spain*, as Eddie Cantor's chum, a volatile (moustached) Mexican.

He learned why *Men Must Fight* (33) – a lesson useful in both *Today We Live*, when he lost Joan Crawford to Gary Cooper, and in *Hell Below*, a submarine drama with Walter Huston. He was Marie Dressler's captain son in *Tugboat Annie* and a disillusioned football hero in *Saturday's Millions* at Universal, the first of a string of loan-outs. He was Ann Harding's bounder-husband in *The Right to Romance*, Janet Gaynor's romantic interest in *Carolina*, Katharine Hepburn's in *Spitfire* (34) and Loretta Young's (as one of Wellington's officers) in *House of Rothschild*. On his home lot he was a prodigal son in a Southern drama with Jean Parker, *Lazy River*, and in a *Paris Interlude* he hero-worshipped a shoddy adventurer, Otto Kruger. These were Bs and Young stayed in Bs for a while: *Whom the Gods Destroy* at Columbia with Walter Connolly:

Death on the Diamond, a mystery with a baseball setting, with Paul Kelly and Madge Evans; and *The Band Plays On*, collegiate stuff with Betty Furness. He was Wallace Beery's son – and superior officer – in *West Point of the Air* (35) and Evelyn Venable's in Hal Roach's *Vagabond Lady*: 'really coming into his own as the captivating scapegrace son of a too, too dignified family' ('Photoplay').

He was an adman in *Calm Yourself* with Madge Evans; a soldier seduced from his duty by Commie Barbara Stanwyck in the funny *Red Salute*, made by Reliance; and was involved in Universal's *Remember Last Night?*, an irresponsible comedy thriller directed by James Whale with Edward Arnold and Constance Cummings. At Paramount he competed with Fred MacMurray for Claudette Colbert in *The Bride Comes Home*. Also in 1935, billed as Joe Young and moustached, he appeared in a Buster Keaton-Educational short, *The Gold Ghost*: and is clearly recognizable. MGM, ever prodigal with his services, then loaned him to Gaumont-British for a couple – neither of them very important roles: Hitchcock's *Secret Agent* (36) and *It's Love Again*, as Jessie Matthews's leading man. He returned to a B, *Three Wise Guys*, and was with Stanwyck again, at RKO, in *The Bride Walks Out*; there were two more Bs, both with Florence Rice, *Sworn Enemy* and *The Longest Night*; then he was loaned to 20th to support Shirley Temple and Alice Faye in *Stowaway*. He and Ann Sothern did *Dangerous Number* (37) at MGM and then he was loaned to Paramount again to compete for Claudette Colbert again, this time with Melvyn Douglas: *I Met Him in Paris*. He and Florence Rice were *Married Before Breakfast*; he had a rare historical role in *The Emperor's Candlesticks* as a Grand Duke; he was Franchot Tone's rival for Joan Crawford in *The Bride Wore Red*; but *Navy Blue and Gold* was one of the few A films in which he was top-billed (over James Stewart and Lionel Barrymore). He was top-billed again in a programmer, *Paradise for Three* (38), with Frank Morgan and old sidekick Rice, but he was the second, or other, man in three pictures released in June that year: 20th's *Josette* with Don Ameche and Simone Simon; *The Toy Wife* with Melvyn Douglas and Luise Rainer; and *Three Comrades* with Robert Taylor, Margaret Sullavan and Tone: he was the one who got killed. *Rich Man Poor Girl* was a funny little picture with Young and Ruth Hussey in the title-roles and Lew Ayres and Lana Turner in support; *The Shining Hour* was another Crawford opus, with other familiars – Sullavan and Melvyn Douglas; and *Honolulu* (39) was an Eleanor Powell vehicle, with Young in a dual role as a film star who changes places with an ordinary man. He was a playboy who jilts Virginia Field at the altar and then falls for alpine maid Annabella in *Bridal Suite*; and a misogynist rancher who gets wrongly accused of murder in the goings-on caused by *Maisie* (Ann Sothern). *Miracles for Sale* was a mystery involving magicians, with Rice, and Young as the man who solves it; and *Florian* (40) was a horse, from Felix Salten's novel, with Helen

Robert Young was less a star in his own right than a good leading man: this is one of several appearances opposite Joan Crawford – The Bride Wore Red *(37), directed by Dorothy Arzner.*

Gilbert, and Young's best chance in a long time. He supported Spencer Tracy in *Northwest Passage*, in a role that Robert Taylor turned down; had the minor role, as Margaret Sullavan's fiancé (till he turned Nazi), in *The Mortal Storm*; was in the minor *Sporting Blood*; was wrongly diagnosed by Lew Ayres in *Dr Kildare's Crisis*; and was loaned to 20th to play a city dude vying for the girl with Randolph Scott in *Western Union* (41).

He co-starred with Laraine Day in the remake of *The Trial of Mary Dugan*; coped with Powell and Sothern in *Lady Be Good*, as one half of a songwriting team (Sothern was the other); and was a *Married Bachelor* with Ruth Hussey. Then MGM out of the blue gave him the title-role in one of their most important productions, *H.M. Pulham Esq.*, from John P. Marquand's novel. Young seized his chance, encouraging all the people who had been rooting for him for years, gave a fine performance as the Bostonian scion and got superb notices. MGM put him into another B, *Joe Smith American* (42), from a story by Paul Gallico, but after that his position was no longer equivocal: he starred opposite Jeanette MacDonald in *Cairo* and was top-billed in an important weepie, *Journey for Margaret* (O'Brien), playing an American war correspondent in Britain; he then co-starred with Lana Turner in *Slightly Dangerous* (43).

20th borrowed him for another top role, that of the husband in *Claudia*, opposite Dorothy McGuire, and kept him on to co-star with Betty Grable in *Sweet Rosie O'Grady*, but in that musical he was somewhat out of place. He played a Yank in Britain – 'with naturalness and humour' (Forsyth Hardy) – in *The Canterville Ghost* (44) with young O'Brien and Charles Laughton; his last at MGM after 14 years. Freelancing, he started strong, but as with others in that position, could not maintain the impetus: at RKO he appeared with McGuire in *The Enchanted Cottage* (45) and with Laraine Day in a soft-centred romance, *Those Endearing Young Charms*; he went to Paramount for *The Searching Wind* (46), with Sylvia Sidney, and to 20th for *Claudia and David* with McGuire. At RKO he did a minor comedy, *Lady Luck*, with Barbara Hale; *They Won't Believe Me* (47) with Susan Hayward; and *Crossfire*, as a detective, with Roberts Mitchum and Ryan, a much-praised murder-tale with an anti-semitism twist.

After almost a year's absence he turned up in a Western, *Relentless* (48), at Columbia, not a distinguished picture, though he was quite convincing as a wandering cowboy; then he had a successful comedy, *Sitting Pretty*, with Clifton Webb and Maureen O'Hara. After that his career gently declined: *Adventure in Baltimore* (49) with Shirley Temple;

Bride for Sale with Claudette Colbert; *That Forsyte Woman* at MGM, as Philip Bossiney; *And Baby Makes Three* (50) with Hale; *Goodbye My Fancy* (51) with Joan Crawford; *The Second Woman* with Betsy Drake (this was announced in 1949 and when it was for a while cancelled, Young sued for his salary – $75,000 plus 15 per cent of the profits); *The Half-Breed* (52), a poor Western; and, in a supporting role, an archaeologist discovering the *Secret of the Incas* (54) with Charlton Heston.

In 1947 he had begun a radio series, 'Father Knows Best', and in 1954 Screen Gems persuaded him to take it to television – where it ran for six years. By this time he was, according to 'Ciné-Revue', a self-confessed alcoholic: but he gave up drinking. He toured for a while, as an alcoholic in 'A Generation', and starred on television as *Marcus Welby MD* (69), a pilot for a series which ran until 1976. During that time he also appeared in that medium in *Vanished* (71) with Richard Widmark, as a senator; *All My Darling Daughters* (72), as a judge with four daughters, and a sequel, *My Darling Daughters' Anniversary* (73). Also on TV he was in *Little Women* (78), a four-hour pilot for a series which did not materialize, as grandpa; *The Return of Marcus Welby MD* (84); *Mercy or Murder?* (87), which concerned euthanasia (he killed his sick wife); and *Conspiracy of Love* as Grampa Joe, a Chicago barber in this sentimental drama. He married in 1933 and has four daughters. He said in 1972: 'I've never hit the heights, but then I've never plumbed the depths – just nice and steady.'

ROLAND YOUNG

Roland Young was a short, elderly English-born character actor with two or three expressions. He was somewhat bemused, vaguely quizzical and never surprised at the madness of others. He usually appeared in comedy, where he underplayed with skill and charm. Said Phil Lonergan years ago in 'Picturegoer': 'Roland Young is very popular with the ladies. His wit and sparkle are more interesting to the fair sex than Adonis figures and clear-cut noses.' One lady he was popular with was Catherine Deneuve, who said in an interview with the 'Sunday Times' in 1968: 'I think the best film performance I've ever seen was given by Roland Young as the Earl in an old Leo McCarey film called *Ruggles of Red Gap*. I love that quiet, easy comedy – that's how I would like to act.' James Agee wrote in 1944 that he 'is able to make anything he appears in seem much more intelligent,

human and amusing than it has any intrinsic right to'.

Young was born in London in 1887, the son of an architect. He was educated at Sherborne School, Dorset, and at London University; and then studied at RADA. He made his London début in 'Find the Woman' in 1908 and in 1912 went to New York to appear in 'Hindle Wakes'. Most of his subsequent career was in the US and in World War I he served in the US army. By that time he was an established stage name, most notably in three comedies written for him by Clare Kummer: 'Good Gracious Annabelle!' (16), 'A Successful Calamity' (17) and 'Rollo's Wild Oat' (20). He later married Miss Kummer's daughter, Frances (1921–40). Among other stage appearances: 'Luck in Pawn' (19), 'The Devil's Disciple' (23), as General Burgoyne, in London 'Beggar on Horseback' (24) and 'The Last of Mrs Cheyney' (26). He made two Silent pictures: *Sherlock Holmes* (22) with John Barrymore and *Moriarty* the same year: in both he was Dr Watson.

With the coming of Talkies MGM signed him to a contract and he made his Talkie début in *The Unholy Night* (29), a thriller directed by Lionel Barrymore, followed by *Her Private Life* – Billie Dove's, at Warners; *The Bishop Murder Case*, prime suspect as a science professor; *Wise Girls* (30); De Mille's *Madam Satan* starring Kay Johnson and Reginald Denny, as his reprobate friend; and *New Moon* with Lawrence Tibbett. Fox borrowed him for two farces: *Don't Bet on Women* (31), in which he is the over-trusting husband of Jeanette MacDonald and bets Edmund Lowe he will not be able to kiss her; and *Annabelle's Affairs*, the new film version of 'Good Gracious Annabelle!', between which he was in *The Prodigal* co-starring with Tibbett, as a renegade doctor who turns hobo. He was in De Mille's *The Squaw Man* and in *The Guardsman*, as an impresario, supporting Lyn Fontanne and Alfred Lunt in the only film they made together, a version of the play by Molnar. At Columbia he was a drunken doctor in *The Pagan Lady*, starring Evelyn Brent and Conrad Nagel. At RKO he was featured in Pola Negri's *A Woman Commands* (32), as a no-nonsense king who gets assassinated, and he then supported Rogert Montgomery in *Lovers Courageous*, written specially for the screen by Frederick Lonsdale: it was Young's last for MGM and as he began to freelance he found himself enormously in demand. At Paramount he did three which benefited greatly from his presence: *One Hour With You*, dallying with Jeanette MacDonald while his wife Genevieve Tobin is courted by her husband, Chevalier; *This Is the Night*, a musical, starring as a philanderer, with Charlie Ruggles and Lily Damita; and *Street of Women* with Kay Francis. 'Roland Young's sprightly acting saves this story from gloom' said 'Photoplay'.

He was now, if not a big crowd-puller, an audience favourite and officially a star. It was considered a great coup when Korda persuaded him to return to Britain to star in *Wedding Rehearsal*, as a Guards officer. Back in Hollywood he aided and abetted butler Slim Summerville and maid Zasu Pitts in *They Just Had To Get Married* (33) – only they were trying to make up their minds about a divorce; and co-starred with Alison Skipworth in *A Lady's Profession*, about two British aristocrats unwittingly running a speakeasy. He did: *Pleasure Cruise* at Fox with Genevieve Tobin, a tale of a jealous husband and his pretty wife; *Blind Adventure*, a murder mystery with Robert Armstrong; and *His Double Life*, excellent as the shy artist who impersonates his valet and marries the latter's mail-order bride Lillian Gish, when he himself is supposed to be dead. He went to Broadway to appear in 'His Master's Voice' and returned

to Hollywood for a supporting role in Bing Crosby's *Here Is My Heart* (34) and to be a memorable Uriah Heep in *David Copperfield* (35). While there he also did his engaging job in *Ruggles of Red Gap*. There were two more Broadway plays, including one as Dr Crippen, then some unrewarding supporting stints in films: *The Unguarded Hour* (36) starring Loretta Young; *One Rainy Afternoon* starring Francis Lederer; and *Give Me Your Heart*, as the novelist who acts as a *deus ex machina* to the problems of Kay Francis.

He went to Britain to be *The Man Who Could Work Miracles* and stayed on to co-star with Chili Bouchier in *Gypsy* (37); in Hollywood he did *Call It a Day*, then was back in Britain for *King Solomon's Mines*. In Hollywood he was Thorne Smith's *Topper*, the mild little man who finds that he is beset by a couple of squabbling ghosts (Constance Bennett and Cary Grant). It is for this series he is best remembered; Billie Burke was Mrs Topper and in her memoir she said that he was 'always dry and fun to work with'. They made several more films together. In Eddie Can-

The Philadelphia Story *(40) was designed primarily as a showcase for Katharine Hepburn, but another reason it was so good was the supporting cast – like Virginia Weidler and Roland Young, respectively her cynical sister and indulgent uncle.*

tor's *Ali Baba Goes to Town* he was an Arab potentate (of sorts); then he crossed the Atlantic once more to play an art-lover who makes Jessie Matthews a star in *Sailing Along* (38). He was married to Billie Burke again in *The Young in Heart* and *Topper Takes a Trip* (39); then to Fay Bainter in an adequate version of a funny Broadway comedy, *Yes My Darling Daughter* – Priscilla Lane was the daughter. He returned to supporting parts in three weak programmers, *The Night of Nights* with Pat O'Brien and Olympe Bradna; *Here I Am a Stranger* with Richard Dix; and *He Married His wife* (40) with Joel McCrea and Nancy Kelly, a divorce comedy whose title gave away the dénouement, as if anyone cared.

Indeed, Young's parts were now often smaller: *Irene*; *Star Dust*, as a talent scout; *Private Affairs*; *Dulcy*, with Ann Sothern; *The Philadelphia Story*, as Katharine Hepburn's whimsical uncle; and *No No Nanette*. His last star part was in *Topper Returns* (41) with Burke and Joan Blondell, but he brought his genial presence to *The Flame of New Orleans* with Dietrich, as her elderly and rather devious admirer: *Two-Faced Woman* with Garbo; *The Lady Has Plans* (42); and *They All Kissed the Bride* with Joan Crawford. He had small parts in two all-star episoders, *Tales of Manhattan* and *Forever and a Day* (43), and 'stole' the latter, according to 'Picturegoer' – appearing with Gladys Cooper, in a sequence where they receive news of their son's death during a party. In 1945 he began a radio series and he later appeared regularly on TV, but his film work diminished: *Standing Room Only* (44) with Paulette Goddard; *And Then There Were None* (46) with Walter Huston, Barry Fitzgerald and Louis Hayward; *Bond Street* (48), a poor British four-part film, with Jean Kent as the inevitable streetwalker; and *You Gotta Stay Happy* with Joan Fontaine. He was a mass murderer in Bob Hope's *The Great Lover* (49) and then he supported Fred Astaire in *Let's Dance* (50); but the last two were hardly worthy of his participation, *St Benny the Dip* (51) with Dick Haymes and Nina Foch, and *The Man From Tangier* (53) with Nils Asther and Nancy Coleman.

He died in 1953. In 1948 he had married for the second time.

ACKNOWLEDGEMENT OF SOURCES

Grateful acknowledgement is made to the many critics, authors and journalists who are quoted in this book – also to their publishers. The newspapers and magazines that have been helpful are The Times, The Daily Telegraph, The Daily Mail, Daily Mirror, Daily Express, The Guardian, Financial Times, Evening News, The Evening Standard, Daily Herald, The Observer, The Sunday Times, The Sunday Telegraph, Sunday Express, The New York Times, News Chronicle, New York Daily News, New York Herald-Tribune, New York World-Telegram, New York Mirror, The New York American, The Spectator, The New Statesman, New York Magazine, The Nation, The New Republic, The New Yorker, Life, Time, Esquire, Newsweek, Look, Playboy, Vanity Fair, Films in Review, Films and Filming, Cinémonde, The Australian Film Guide, L'Ecran Français, Film Weekly, The National Board of Review Magazine, The Hollywood Reporter, Kine Weekly, The Bioscope, Picturegoer, Photoplay, Picture Show, Motion Picture Herald, Punch, Sequence, Show Magazine, Theatre Arts Magazine, Variety, The Silent Cinema, Sight and Sound and the Monthly Film Bulletin. The Bernstein Questionnaire and the programmes of the National Film Theatre were also most useful.

TITLE CHANGES

As the titles listed in the text are the original titles, this index is arranged alphabetically according to the changed or alternative titles – with the original title, country and date appearing on the right. We have not taken into account those cases where films are re-titled for television.

Abandon Ship, US — *Seven Waves Away*, GB (57)
Abbott and Costello Meet the Ghosts, GB — *Abbott and Costello Meet Frankenstein*, US (48)
Adios, GB — *The Lash*, US (31)
Advance to the Rear (alternative title) — *Company of Cowards?*, US (64)
Adventure for Two, US — *The Demi-Paradise*, GB (42)
Affair in Monte Carlo, US — *Twenty-four Hours in a Woman's Life*, GB (53)
Affairs in Versailles, US — *Si Versailles m'était Conté*, F (54)
The Affairs of Sally, GB — *The Fuller Brush Girl*, US (50)
After Midnight, GB — *Captain Carey*, US (50)
Alias Bulldog Drummond, US — *The Return of Bulldog Drummond*, GB (33)
All That Money Can Buy, GB — *The Devil and Daniel Webster*, US (41)
All This and Money, Too, GB — *Love Is a Ball*, US (63)
Along Came Sally, US — *Aunt Sally*, GB (34)
Always in My Heart, GB — *Mr Imperium*, US (51)
Angel Street, US — *Gaslight*, GB (40)
Arms and the Girl, GB — *Red Salute*, US (35)
Arms and the Woman, GB — *Mr Winkle Goes to War*, US (44)
Arouse and Beware, GB — *The Man from Dakota*, US (40)
The Avengers, US — *The Day Will Dawn*, GB (42)

Bachelor Bait, GB — *Adventure in Baltimore*, US (49)
Bachelor Girls, GB — *The Bachelor's Daughters*, US (46)
Bachelor Knight, GB — *The Bachelor and the Bobby-Soxer*, US (47)
Bachelor's Folly, US — *The Calendar*, GB (31)
Bad Sister, US — *The White Unicorn*, GB (47)
The Badge of Courage, GB — *Turn Back the Hours*, US (28)
The Bank Detective, GB — *The Bank Dick*, US (40)
The Battle of Austerlitz, US — *Austerlitz*, F (60)
The Battle of the Worlds, US — *Il Pianeta degli Uomini*, It (60)
The Beachcomber, US — *Vessel of Wrath*, GB (38)
Beau Chumps, GB — *Beau Hunks*, US (31)
The Beautiful Cheat, GB — *What a Woman!*, US (43)
The Beautiful Rebel, GB — *Janice Meredith*, US (24)
Behold We Live, GB — *If I Were Free*, US (33)
The Big Bankroll, GB — *King of the Roaring Twenties*, US (61)
Big Deal at Dodge City, GB — *A Big Hand for the Little Lady*, US (66)
Birds of Prey, GB — *The Ace of Aces*, US (38)
Blackout, US — *Contraband*, GB (40)
Blood Money, GB — *Requiem for a Heavyweight*, US (62)
Blood on my Hands, GB — *Kiss the Blood off My Hands*, US (48)
Bonaventure, GB — *Thunder on the Hill*, US (51)
Borderlines, GB — *The Caretaker*, US (68)
The Boy from Barnardo's, GB — *Lord Jeff*, US (38)
A Boy Is Ten Feet Tall, US — *Sammy Going South*, GB (62)
Breaking the Sound Barrier, US — *The Sound Barrier*, GB (52)
Broadway Singer, GB — *Torch Singer*, US (33)
By Hook or by Crook, GB — *I Dood It*, US (43)

Cadets on Parade, GB — *Junior Army*, US (42)
Café of Seven Sinners, GB — *Seven Sinners*, US (40)
Call Me Genius, US — *The Rebel*, GB (61)
Cardigan's Last Case, GB — *States' Attorney*, US (32)
Cargo of Innocents, GB — *Stand by for Action*, US (42)
Caribbean Gold, GB — *Caribbean*, US (52)
Carnival Nights, GB — *Carnival*, US (35)
The Case of Mrs Pembroke, GB — *Two Against the World*, US (36)
Cash and Carry, GB — *Ringside Maisie*, US (41)
Casino de Paree, GB — *Go Into Your Dance*, US (35)
Caught by Television, GB — *Trapped by Television*, US (36)
Chamber of Horrors, US — *The Door With Seven Locks*, GB (40)
Charley's American Aunt, GB — *Charley's Aunt*, US (41)
Chinese Den, US — *The Chinese Bungalow*, GB (40)
Choose Your Partner, GB — *Two Girls on Broadway*, US (40)
The City Jungle, GB — *The Young Philadelphians*, US (59)
Clouds over Europe, US — *Q Planes*, GB (39)
College Days, GB — *The Freshman*, US (25)
Colonel Blimp, US — *The Life and Death of Colonel Blimp*, GB (43)
Compromised, GB — *The Sophomore*, US (29)
Concealment, GB — *The Secret Bride*, US (35)
The Contact Man, GB — *Alias Nick Beal*, US (49)
Continental Express, US — *Silent Battle*, GB (39)
Courageous, US — *A Lost Lady*, US (34)
The Courteney Affair, US — *The Courteneys of Curzon Street*, GB (47)
Crooks in Clover, GB — *Penthouse*, US (33)

Czarina, GB — *A Royal Scandal*, US (45)

Dark Sands, US — *Jericho*, GB (37)
A Date With Destiny, GB — *The Mad Doctor*, US (41)
Daughter of Luxury, GB — *Five and Ten*, US (31)
Daughters of Destiny, US — *Destinées*, F (53)
Dead Image, GB — *Dead Ringer*, US (64)
Deadline, GB — *Deadline USA*, US (52)
Devil on Wheels, GB — *Indianapolis Speedway*, US (39)
The Devil Takes the Count, GB — *The Devil Is a Sissy*, US (36)
The Diamond Earrings, US — *Madame de . . .*, F (53)
Die! Die! My Darling, US — *Fanatic*, GB (65)
The Dover Road, GB — *Where Sinners Meet*, US (34)
Drums, US — *The Drum*, GB (38)

East of the Rising Sun, GB — *Malaya*, US (50)
Edge of Divorce, US — *Background*, GB (53)
Elephants Never Forget, GB — *Zenobia*, US (39)
Ellen, GB — *The Second Woman*, US (49)
Embassy Girl, GB — *Hat Check Girl*, US (32)
End of the Rainbow, GB — *Northwest Outpost*, US (47)
Enemies of the Public, GB — *Public Enemy*, US (31)
Escape From Yesterday, GB — *Ride a Crooked Mile*, US (38)
Escape If You Can, GB — *St Benny the Dip*, US (51)
Escape to Happiness, GB — *Intermezzo – A Love Story*, US (39)
Eternal Youth, GB — *West Point*, US (28)
Every Other Inch a Lady, GB — *Dancing Co-ed*, US (39)
Every Woman's Man, GB — *The Prizefighter and the Lady*, US (33)
Eye Witness, US — *Your Witness*, GB (49)

The False Idol, GB — *The False Madonna*, US (32)
Farewell My Lovely, GB — *Murder My Sweet*, US (44)
The Faun, GB — *Bought and Paid For*, US (16)
Female Co-respondent, GB — *Adventure in Washington*, US (41)
The Fifth Chair, GB — *It's in the Bag*, US (45)
Fine and Dandy, GB — *The West Point Story*, US (50)
The Flight of the White Stallions, GB — *The Miracle of the White Stallions*, US (62)
The Flood, GB — *The Johnstown Flood*, US (26)
For Love or Money, US — *Cash*, GB (33)
For You Alone, GB — *When You're in Love*, US (37)
The Forsyte Saga, GB — *That Forsyte Woman*, US (49)
Forward March, GB — *The Dough Boys*, US (30)
Four Against Fate, US — *Derby Day*, GB (52)
Fraternally Yours, US — *Sons of the Desert*, US (34)
Free to Live, GB — *Holiday* (38)
The French They Are a Funny Race, US — *Les Carnets de Major Thompson*, F (55)
The Frightened Bride, US — *The Tall Headlines*, GB (52)
Frou Frou, GB — *Toy Wife*, US (38)
The Fugitive, US — *On the Night of the Fire*, GB (39)

The Gay Divorce, GB — *The Gay Divorcée*, US (34)
The Gay Nineties, GB — *The Floradora Girl*, US (30)
The Gay Mrs Trexel, GB — *Susan and God*, US (40)
A Genius in the Family, GB — *So Goes My Love*, US (46)
Gentleman for a Day, GB — *Union Depot*, US (32)
The Girl from Mexico, GB — *Mexicali Rose*, US (29)
The Girl I Made, GB — *Made on Broadway*, US (33)
The Girl in Overalls, GB — *Swing Shift Maisie*, US (43)
Girl in Pawn, GB — *Little Miss Marker*, US (34)
The Girl in Room 17, GB — *Vice Squad*, US (53)
Girl in the Streets, US — *London Melody*, GB (37)
The Girls He Left Behind, GB — *The Gang's All Here*, US (43)
Girls Never Tell, GB — *Her First Romance*, US (51)
The Golden Hour, GB — *Pot o' Gold*, US (41)
Golden Virgin, US — *The Story of Esther Costello*, GB (57)
Golden Youth, GB — *Just Suppose*, US (26)
Good Girl, GB — *Good Dame*, US (34)
Good Morning Doctor, GB — *You Belong to Me*, US (42)
The Grace Moore Story, GB — *So This Is Love*, US (53)
The Green-eyed Woman, GB — *Take a Letter Darling*, US (42)
Guilty As Charged, GB — *Guilty As Hell*, US (32)
Guns in the Afternoon, GB — *Ride the High Country*, US (62)

Hallelujah I'm a Tramp, GB — *Hallelujah I'm a Bum*, US (33)
Harmony Parade, US — *Pigskin Parade*, US (36)
Haunted Honeymoon, US — *Busman's Honeymoon*, GB (40)
Head Over Heels in Love, US — *Head Over Heels*, GB (36)
Her Dilemma, GB — *Confessions of a Co-ed*, US (31)
Her Reputation, GB — *Broadway Bad*, US (33)

Her Sacrifice, GB
The Hideout, US
High Fury, US
The High Road, GB
His Affair, GB
His Lady, GB
His Other Woman, GB
His Temporary Affair, GB
Hit Me Again, GB
Hold That Girl, GB
Hollow Triumph (alternative title)
The Honourable Mr Wong, GB
Hot Spot, GB
Hounded, GB
The Hounds of Zaroff, GB
The Hours Between, GB
The House in the Square, GB
Husbands and Lovers, GB

I Accuse, GB
I Am a Fugitive, GB

I Shall Return, GB

If You Feel Like Singing, GB
If This Be Sin, US
I'll Get You, US
Imaginary Sweetheart, GB
Immortal Battalion, US
Impetuous Love, GB
The Impossible Lover, GB
Indiscretion, GB
Innocence is Bliss, GB
Into the Night, GB
The Invaders, US
The Iron Road, GB

Jailbirds, GB
The Jealous Six, GB
John Doe – Dynamite, GB
Johnny in the Clouds, US
Johnny Vagabond, GB
Justice for Sale, GB

Katy's Love Affair, US

The Kid's Last Fight, GB
Killer on a Horse, GB
King of the Khyber Rifles, GB

The Lady From Boston, GB
Lady Hamilton, GB
Lady in Distress, US
Lady of Deceit, GB
Lady of the Boulevards, GB
A Lady Surrenders, US
Lady Windermere's Fan, GB
Larceny Inc., US
Larceny Lane, GB
Let's Make Up, US
The Light of Heart, GB
Little Old New York, GB
Live Today for Tomorrow (alternative title)
Looking for Trouble, GB
Love Never Dies, GB
The Love Test, GB
Lovely to Look At, GB
Lovers Happy Lovers, US

Loves of the Mighty, GB
Lucky Nick Cain, US
The Lullaby (alternative title)

Macdonald of the Canadian Mounties, GB
Mad About Money, GB
Mlle France, GB
The Magic Bullet, GB

Magic Night, US
The Man From the Folies Bergère, GB
The Man Maker, GB
The Man of 100 Faces, US
Man of Affairs, US
Man of Evil, US
Man of the Hour, GB
The Man Who Came Back, GB

Blind Date, US (34)
The Small Voice, GB (48)
White Cradle Inn, GB (46)
The Lady of Scandal, US (30)
This Is My Affair, US (37)
When a Man Loves, US (20)
The Desk Set, US (57)
Ex-bad Boy, US (31)
Smarty, US (34)
Hold That Co-ed, US (38)
The Scar, US (48)
The Hatchet Man, US (32)
I Wake Up Screaming, US (41)
Johnny Allegro, US (49)
The Most Dangerous Game, US (32)
Twenty-four Hours, US (31)
I'll Never Forget You, US (51)
Honeymoon in Bali, US (39)

Life of Emile Zola, US (37)
I Am a Fugitive From a Chain Gang, US (32)
An American Guerilla in the Philippines, US (50)
Summer Stock, US (50)
That Dangerous Age, GB (49)
Escape Route, GB (52)
Professional Sweetheart, US (33)
The Way Ahead, GB (44)
Die Geiger von Florenz, G (24)
Huddle, US (32)
Christmas in Connecticut, US (45)
Miss Grant Takes Richmond, US (49)
The Wise Guy, US (26)
The 49th Parallel, GB (41)
Buckskin Frontier, US (43)

Pardon Us, US (31)
Her Market Value, US (25)
Meet John Doe, US (41)
The Way to the Stars, GB (45)
Johnny Come Lately, US (43)
Night Court, US (32)

The Courteneys of Curzon Street, GB (47)
The Life of Jimmy Dolan, US (33)
Welcome to Hard Times, US (67)
The Black Watch, US (29)

Pardon My French, US (51)
That Hamilton Woman, US (41)
A Widow in London, GB (39)
Born to Kill, US (47)
Nana, US (34)
Love Story, GB (44)
The Fan, US (49)
Smash and Grab, GB (37)
Blonde Crazy, US (31)
Lilacs in the Spring, GB (54)
Life Begins at 8.30, US (42)
Lights of Old Broadway, US (25)
Act of Murder, US (48)

The Tip-off, US (31)
Lilac Time, US (28)
Two Can Play, US (26)
Thin Ice, US (37)
Knave of Hearts/Monsieur Ripois, GB/F (54)
Danton, G (20)
I'll Get You For This, GB (51)
The Sin of Madelon Claudet, US (31)

Pony Soldier, US (52)

He Loved an Actress, US (38)
Reunion (in France), US (42)
(The Story of) Dr Ehrlich's Magic Bullet, US (40)
Goodnight Vienna, GB (32)
Folies Bergère, US (35)
Twenty Dollars a Week, US (35)
Crackerjack, GB (38)
His Lordship, GB (36)
Fanny by Gaslight, GB (44)
Colonel Effingham's Raid, US (45)
Swamp Water, US (41)

The Man With 30 Sons, GB
Manhattan Madness, GB
Marie Walewska, GB
The Marines Have Landed, GB

The Marriage Symphony, GB
Married But Single, GB
Married in Haste, GB
Marrying Mary, GB
The Mask of Comedy, GB
Medals, GB
Melody Inn, GB
The Melody of Life, GB

Memory Expert, GB
Men on Her Mind, GB
Merrily We Go to –, GB
The Merry Wives of Gotham, GB
Mightier Than the Sword, GB
Military Policeman, GB
Millionaire for a Day, GB
Mimi, US
Mr Ashton Was Indiscreet, GB

Mr Griggs Returns, GB
Mr Hobo, US
Mr V, US
Mrs Loring's Secret, GB
A Modern Miracle, GB

Money for Jam, GB
More Than a Kiss, GB
Mother Knows Best, GB
The Murder in Thornton Square, GB
Murder Inc., GB
Murder on Monday, US
Murder Will Out, US
My Son Alone, GB
My Two Husbands, GB

The New Adventures of Don Juan, GB
Next Time We Live, GB
Night and Day, US
A Night in Cairo, GB
A Night in Havana, GB
The Night Is Ending, GB
Nine Days a Queen, US
Notorious Gentleman, US

Oh For a Man!, GB

Old Great Heart, GB
On the Carpet, GB
Once a Hero, GB
Once There Was a Princess, GB
Once to Every Man, GB
One Against Seven, GB
One Hundred Per Cent Pure, GB
One Man Mutiny, GB

One Woman's Story, US
Operation X, US
O'Rourke of the Royal Mounted, GB
Outpost in Malaya, US
Over the River, GB

Panic on the Air, GB
The Paratrooper, US
Paris Does Strange Things, US
The Paris Express, US

Paris Love Song, GB
The Passionate Sentry, US
Passport to Fame, GB
The Patient Vanishes (alternative title)
Pay the Devil, GB
A Perfect Week-end, GB
Personal Column, GB
Pier 13, GB
The Player Pianos, US
Pluck of the Irish, GB
The Politic Flapper, GB
Polly Fulton, GB
Power, US
Present Arms, GB
The Private Wore Skirts, GB
The Promoter, US

The Queen's Husband, GB

The Magnificent Yankee, US (50)
Adventure in Manhattan, US (36)
Conquest, US (37)
The Leathernecks Have Landed, US (36)
Let's Try Again, US (34)
This Thing Called Love, US (41)
Consolation Marriage, US (31)
Getting Mary Married, US (19)
Upstage, US (26)
Seven Days Leave, US (30)
Riding High, US (43)
Symphony of Six Million, US (32)
The Man on the Flying Trapeze, US (35)
The Girl From Tenth Avenue, US (35)
Merrily We Go to Hell, US (32)
Janice Meredith, US (24)
A Girl With Ideas, US (37)
Off Limits, US (53)
Let's Be Ritzy, US (34)
La Bohème, GB (35)
The Senator Was Indiscreet, US (47)

The Cockeyed Miracle, US (46)
The Guv'nor, GB (35)
Pimpernel Smith, GB (41)
The Imperfect Lady, US (47)
The Story of Alexander Graham Bell, US (39)
It Ain't Hay, US (43)
Don't Bet on Women, US (31)
Mother Is a Freshman, US (49)
Gaslight, US (44)
The Enforcer, US (51)
Home at Seven, GB (51)
The Voice of Merill, GB (52)
American Empire, US (42)
Too Many Husbands, US (40)

The Adventures of Don Juan, US (48)
Next Time We Love, US (36)
Jack's the Boy, GB (32)
The Barbarian, US (33)
The Big Boodle, US (57)
Paris After Dark, US (43)
Tudor Rose, GB (36)
The Rake's Progress, GB (45)

Will Success Spoil Rock Hunter?, US (57)
Way Back Home, US (32)
Little Giant, US (46)
It Happened in Hollywood, US (37)
Misbehaving Ladies, US (31)
The Fighting Heart, US (34)
Counter Attack, US (45)
The Girl From Missouri, US (34)
The Court Martial of Billy Mitchell, US (55)
The Passionate Friends, GB (49)
My Daughter Joy, GB (50)
Saskatchewan, US (54)
The Planter's Wife, GB (52)
One More River, US (34)

You May Be Next, US (36)
The Red Beret, US (53)
Elena et les Hommes, F (56)
The Man Who Watched the Trains Go By, GB (53)
Paris in Spring, US (35)
Who Goes There?, GB (52)
The Whole Town's Talking, US (26)
This Man is Dangerous, GB (41)
Man in the Shadow, US (57)
Saint Louis Kid, US (34)
Lured, US (47)
Me and My Gal, US (32)
Les Pianos Mécaniques, Fr/Sp (65)
Great Guy, US (36)
The Patsy, US (28)
B.F.'s Daughter, US (48)
Jew Süss, GB (34)
Leathernecking, US (30)
Never Wave at a WAC, US (52)
The Card, GB (52)

The Royal Bed, US (31)

Racing Luck, GB
The Randolph Family, US
Rendezvous, GB
Reserved for Ladies, US
The Rich Full Life, GB
Ring Up the Curtain, GB
The Rise of Helga, GB

Rivets, GB
Road Show, GB
Romance and Rhythm, GB
Romance for Three, GB
The Romantic Age, GB
A Romeo in Pyjamas, GB
Rommel The Desert Fox, GB
Rookies, GB
Rosalie, GB
Rough Company, GB

Sabrina Fair, GB
Salomy Jane, GB
The Sap Abroad, GB
Saraband for Dead Lovers, GB
Sealed Lips, GB
Secret Flight, US
Secret Interlude, GB
The Shame of a Nation, GB
Sherlock Holmes and the Secret Code, GB
She's Got That Swing, GB
Shoot First, US
Should a Woman Tell, GB
Sidewalks of London, US
Silent Barrier, US
The Silent Voice, GB
The Silent Voice, GB
The Singer of Seville, GB
Smiling Along, US
A Soldier's Pay, GB
Sons of the Sea, GB
Spitfire, US
Spy in the Pantry, US
Spy 13, GB
Stampede, GB
The Star Said No, GB
The Steel Highway (alternative title)
Step Down to Terror, GB
Stranded in Paris, GB
The Strange Conspiracy, GB
Strange Incident, GB
Strange Interval, GB
The Strangers, US
Strictly Confidential, GB
Striptease Lady, GB
Suicide Battalion, US
Suicide Squadron, US
Summertime, US
Swing Teacher Swing, GB

The Taxi Dancer, GB
Teenage Bad Girl, US
Ten Little Niggers, GB
That Navy Spirit, GB
This Is My Affair, GB

This Man Reuter, GB
Thunder of the Gods, GB

Red Hot Tires, US (25)
Dear Octopus, GB (43)
Darling How Could You, US (51)
Service for Ladies, GB (32)
Cynthia, US (47)
Broadway to Hollywood, US (33)
Susan Lenox: Her Fall and Rise, US (31)
Fast Workers, US (24)
Chasing Rainbows, US (30)
Cowboy From Brooklyn, US (38)
Paradise for Three, US (38)
Sisters Under the Skin, US (34)
Parlor, Bedroom and Bath, US (31)
The Desert Fox, US (51)
Buck Private, US (41)
Not So Dumb, US (30)
The Violent Men, US (55)

Sabrina, US (54)
Wild Girl, US (33)
The Sap from Syracuse, US (30)
Saraband, US (48)
After Tonight, US (33)
School for Secrets, GB (46)
Private Number, US (37)
Scarface, US (32)
Dressed to Kill, US (46)

She's Got Everything, US (38)
Rough Shoot, GB (52)
Wandering Fires, US (25)
St Martin's Lane, GB (38)
The Great Barrier, GB (37)
The Man Who Played God, US (32)
Paula, US (52)
The Call of the Flesh, US (30)
Keep Smiling, GB (38)
A Soldier's Plaything, US (31)
Old Ironsides, US (26)
The First of the Few, GB (42)
Ten Days in Paris, US (39)
Operator 13, US (34)
The Big Land, US (57)
Callaway Went Thataway, US (51)
Other Men's Women, US (30)
The Silent Stranger, US (24)
Artists and Models Abroad, US (37)
The President Vanishes, US (34)
The Ox-Bow Incident, US (43)
Strange Interlude, US (32)
Viaggio in Italia, It (53)
Broadway Bill, US (34)
Lady of Burlesque, US (43)
Sunset in Vienna, GB (38)
Dangerous Moonlight, GB (41)
Summer Madness, GB (38)
College Living, US (38)

The Taxi Driver, US (27)
My Teenage Daughter, GB (56)
And Then There Were None, US (45)
Hold'em Navy, US (37)
I Can Get It for You Wholesale, US (51)
A Dispatch from Reuters, US (40)
Son of the Gods, US (30)

Tiger in the Sky, GB
The Time of Indifference, US
Toast of the Legion, GB
To the Victor, GB
Too Dangerous to Love, GB
Transatlantic Tunnel, US
Trapped by the Wireless, GB
Treason, GB
Tree of Liberty, GB
Trelawney of the Wells, GB
Troopship, US
Tropicana, GB
Trouble in the Sky, US
The Trumpet Call, GB
The Trumpet Calls, GB
Twenty-one Days Together, US
Twist of Fate, US
Two-gun Cupid, US
Two Men and a Girl, GB
Two Smart Boys, GB

U-Boat 29, US
Under the Clock, GB
Undercover Girl, GB
Unfit to Print, GB
The Unholy Four, US

Vacation From Marriage, US
The Varsity Girl, GB
The Voice in the Night, US

The Warriors, US
The Way of Life, US
We Humans, GB
Wedding Bells, GB
Wedding Breakfast, GB
Week-end Madness, GB
What a Man!, GB

What Wives Don't Want, GB
When the Crash Came, GB
When New York Sleeps, GB
When Thief Meets Thief, US
Where the River Bends, GB
White Captive, GB
The White Man, GB
White Savage, GB
Will Tomorrow Ever Come, GB
Winning Through, GB
A Woman Alone, US
The Woman Between, GB
The Woman in Command, US
The Woman in His House, GB
Woman of the World, GB
Woman Tamer, GB
Working Wives, GB
The World and His Wife, GB

A Yank in Dutch, GB
A Yank in London, US
Years Without Days, GB
The Yellow Passport, GB
The Yokel, GB
You Belong to My Heart, GB
You Can't Sleep Here, GB
You Can't Take Money, GB
You Never Know, GB

The McConnell Story, US (55)
Gli Indifferenti, It (64)
Kiss Me Again, US (31)
Owd Bob, GB (37)
Perfect Strangers, US (50)
The Tunnel, GB (35)
Panic on the Air, US (36)
Rebellion, US (36)
The Howards of Virginia, US (40)
The Actress, US (28)
Goodbye Again, GB (37)
The Heat's On, US (43)
Cone of Silence, GB (60)
Rough Riders, US (27)
The Trumpet Blows, US (34)
Twenty-one Days, GB (39)
The Intimate Stranger, GB (56)
The Bad Man, US (41)
Honeymoon, US (47)
The Spirit of Culver, US (39)

The Spy in Black, GB (39)
The Clock, US (45)
Undercover Maisie, US (47)
Off the Record, US (39)
The Stranger Came Home, GB (54)

Perfect Stranger, GB (45)
The Fair Co-ed, US (27)
Freedom Radio, GB (40)

The Dark Avenger, GB (55)
They Call It Sin, US (32)
Young America, US (42)
Royal Wedding, US (51)
The Catered Affair, US (56)
August Week-end, US (36)
Never Give a Sucker an Even Break, US (41)
The Virtuous Husband, US (31)
Alimony, US (24)
Now I'll Tell, US (34)
Jump for Glory, GB (37)
Bend of the River, US (52)
White Savage, US (53)
The Squaw Man, US (31)
South of Tahiti, US (41)
That's My Man, US (47)
Classmates, US (24)
Sabotage, GB (36)
The Woman I Love, US (37)
Soldiers of the King, GB (33)
The Animal Kingdom, US (32)
Outcast Lady, US (34)
She Couldn't Take It, US (35)
Weekend Marriage, US (32)
State of the Union, US (48)

The Lady and the Flyer, US (42)
I Live in Grosvenor Square, GB (45)
Castle on the Hudson, US (40)
The Yellow Ticket, US (31)
The Boob, US (26)
Mr Imperium, US (51)
I Was a Male War Bride, US (49)
Internes Can't Take Money, US (37)
You Never Can Tell, US (51)